VOICES & VIEWS

A HISTORY OF THE HOLOCAUST

EDITED, WITH INTRODUCTIONS, BY DEBÓRAH DWORK
THE JEWISH FOUNDATION FOR THE RIGHTEOUS
NEW YORK

This book is a publication of
The Jewish Foundation for the Righteous
305 Seventh Avenue, 19th Floor
New York, New York 10001-6008
www.jfr.org

Telephone orders: 888-421-1221
Fax orders: 212-727-9956
Orders by e-mail: jfr@jfr.org

Library of Congress Control Number: 2002104707

ISBN 0-9700602-0-3 (cloth : alk. paper)
ISBN 0-9700602-1-1 (pbk. : alk. paper)

Printed in the United States of America.

The paper in this book meets the guidelines for permanence and durability of the
Committee on Production Guidelines and Book Longevity of the Council on
Library Resources.

Contents

Contents

Contents

Maps and Charts

Preface

THE JEWISH FOUNDATION FOR THE RIGHTEOUS is pleased and honored to sponsor the publication of *Voices and Views*. Our foundation was established to fulfill the traditional Jewish commitment to *hakarat hatov*, the searching out and recognition of goodness. We fulfill this mission primarily by providing financial assistance to those non-Jews, known as the Righteous, who risked their lives and those of their families to rescue Jews during the Holocaust. Many of the Righteous are aged and needy, and the support the Foundation provides has made a critical difference in their lives.

But if we fulfill our mission of honoring the Righteous first by providing them with the essentials of life, we fulfill it also by honoring their names, and assuring that the world is made aware of their courage. To this end the Foundation sees Holocaust education as a fundamental part of its mission. The Righteous are ordinary people who performed extraordinary acts under pressure that is almost unimaginable to us today, and we want their stories to be understood as a part of the tragic history of the Holocaust. The Jewish Foundation for the Righteous seeks not only to help the surviving Righteous live comfortable and dignified lives, but also to assure that all of the Righteous are remembered and honored by future generations. It was with this in mind that *Voices and Views* was created.

PAUL GOLDBERGER
President
The Jewish Foundation for the Righteous

Dedication

SOCIETY TODAY IS BOMBARDED BY REPORTS OF HATRED, VIOLENCE AND BETRAYAL that lay a heavy stone of despair on our hearts. The media gravitate toward the sensational and sadistic. In the post-Holocaust era, evil is credible and goodness is suspect.

Those we teach were not yet born when the sinister cloud of the Holocaust descended to blot out the sun. What can we teach them about the Holocaust that can strengthen their morale, morals and wisdom and thus provide tools to live in a scarred universe? What sparks of light can be sifted from the ashes of the crematoria?

From the behavior of thousands of non-Jews who risked their lives and those of their families to rescue Jews from the Nazi predators, we learn that goodness existed even in the face of indescribable evil, that passive complicity was not the only alternative to totalitarian oppression and murder. Without denying the devastation of the Holocaust, the empirical evidence afforded by the ordinary men and women who, during civilization's darkest hours, sought to protect Jews by turning their own lives into "hiding places from the wind, and shelter from the tempest," serves to correct the deeply cynical portrayal of human nature propagated in contemporary popular culture.

People from all walks of life and from all countries in which the Nazis carried out their genocidal enterprise refused to turn a blind eye to the plight of Jewish victims, and imperiled their own lives, and often those of their loved ones, in order to rescue Jews. The rescuers transcended the barriers of their own religion, class, and national and ethnic affiliations to recognize in the victim the common humanity that they shared.

People need moral heroes in their lives; not celebrities, but men and women of flesh and blood like their own. Learning about real heroes whose moral courage saved real people will allow individuals to discover their own humanity. When the Italian author Primo Levi wrote of his experience in Auschwitz, he recalled Lorenzo, a non-Jewish Italian worker in the camp who, at great personal risk, brought Levi a piece of bread and the remnant of his ration every day for six months. "I believe," Levi wrote, "that it was due to Lorenzo that I am alive today. Not so much because of his material aid as for his natural and plain manner of being good. Thanks to Lorenzo, I managed not to forget that I myself was a man."

Levi's recognition of his shared humanity with Lorenzo is the conjoint of the rescuers' recognition of their shared humanity with those they saved. By their example, the rescuers help those who are alive today and those who represent our future to live in the world with greater lucidity and firmer resolve to make the world hospitable to all its people.

The conduct of the rescuers thus both elucidates and implements the Talmudic prescription, "Whoever saves a single life is as if one saves the entire world." It is therefore to The Righteous Among Nations, those non-Jews who risked their lives to save Jews during the Holocaust, that *Voices and Views* is dedicated.

RABBI HAROLD M. SCHULWEIS
Founding Chairman
The Jewish Foundation for the Righteous

Acknowledgements

ONE OF THE PLEASURES OF FINISHING A BOOK is that it provides the opportunity to thank the people who helped make the project a product. *Voices and Views* was written for – and with – The Jewish Foundation for the Righteous (JFR), and therefore these acknowledgements are from both Debórah Dwork and Stanlee Stahl.

Bob Goldman was Chair of the JFR Education Committee and a strong advocate of the education mandate of the Foundation until his sudden death in August 1998. We miss his wisdom and his warmth, and we are grateful he was our friend and advisor. Hannah Waldman succeeded Bob as Chair and her acuity and insight served us – and this book – very well. She engaged with the intellectual issues, and was committed to a cutting-edge educational mandate. Generous with her time as well as her keen insight, Hannah was our true colleague.

Harvey Schulweis, Chairman of the JFR Board and, in Debórah's words, a King of New York and a Prince of the Bronx, took the recommendation of the Education Committee and gave the project wings to fly. In this, he was supported by the entire Board, and we thank each trustee. Paul Goldberger, now President of the JFR, gave us the gift of good suggestions; Rabbi Schulweis, Founding Chairman, inspiration; and Mark Goldsmith, Secretary/Treasurer and Attorney, farsighted advice.

A project such as *Voices and Views* depends on the help, interest, and energy of many people. We thank Ed Barber, Vice Chairman of W. W. Norton and Debórah's editor, for his practical counsel and for not complaining too much that Debórah's work on this book diverted her attention from the book she is writing for him. And if Ed Barber grumbled only a little, Robert Weil, a philanthropist who defrayed Debórah's research costs for a project she bumped for this one, did not say a word. We are tremendously grateful to both for taking the long view.

We thank Andrew Marasia, also of W. W. Norton, for his help; Barry Werbin, the head of the intellectual property practice group at Herrick Feinstein for his astute counsel; Barbara Grenquist for her painstaking copy editing; Jacques Chazaud for his eye to map detail; and Leslie Singer and Liza Aelion of Singer AllBrand, and Stephanie Pine and Jamie Lyman for the talent and creativity they brought to this project.

The staff of the JFR has been staunchly committed to the education program. Patrycja Warda Castillo, Executive Assistant, brought her special talents to the project. We thank David Weinstein, Ilana Kuschuk and Katie Senior, former JFR education staff, for their dedication. Ann Millin, Sharon Muller, Judith Cohen and Christopher Sims, enthusiastic and helpful, are a great credit to the United States Holocaust Memorial Museum. They brought photographic material to our attention that we would not have found ourselves.

Dr. William Shulman, Professor Emeritus of History at City University of New York and President of the Association of Holocaust Organizations, has played a vital role in linking the JFR's national education program with the people it seeks to serve. With his encyclopedic knowledge of Holocaust education programs and of the organizations devoted to Holocaust education and commemoration, Bill was uniquely able to identify the strengths of our vision and, ultimately, our program. His generous praise was both comforting and energizing.

Robert Jan van Pelt, Professor of Cultural History at the University of Waterloo, was our unofficial academic advisor. Unstinting with his time and advice, Robert Jan served as intellectual critic and map and photo consultant. It is our good fortune that he is so very knowledgeable in so many areas, and that he is also so very good natured. We thank him for his willing engagement and his grace.

Voices and Views was piloted by the Social Studies Team of Worcester Public School teachers at the Jacob Hiatt Center for Urban Education at Clark University. Furthermore, when the JFR launched its national education program at the Center for Holocaust and Genocide Studies, Clark University, with a one-week residential Seminar, the participants reviewed *Voices and Views*. We are grateful for these educators' enthusiasm and their suggestions.

We thank the American Jewish Joint Distribution Committee for its ongoing help and support in all of the JFR's endeavors and especially for opening its photo archives for *Voices and Views*.

Finally, Stanlee Stahl thanks her husband George Ackerman and their son David. Debórah Dwork thanks her husband Ken Marek and their daughters Hannah and Miriam. Neither of our families read a word, offered advice, or was particularly patient, but they love us and they honor our commitment to Holocaust education. We are fiercely grateful to them.

DEBÓRAH DWORK
New Haven, CT

STANLEE J. STAHL
New York, NY

Introduction

Introduction

THE SKYLINES OF WASHINGTON, NEW YORK, BOSTON, AND LOS ANGELES have been changed in recent years by the establishment of a major museum, monument, or memorial to commemorate the Holocaust. No other historical event has been accorded this attention or this respect. No other historical event has been set so visibly in the center of our civic domain.

Despite the extraordinary importance of the Holocaust, many professionals who deal with the history of this event as part of their job have had little or no classroom education on the subject because colleges and universities have only recently begun to offer courses in this area. Reporters, teachers, lawyers, and business people, to name but a few, may be intrigued by continuing news stories and fascinated by the museums and memorials, yet they may lack a context to help them understand the articles they read and the exhibits they see. For the same reason, many such professionals also may not have the broad and deep context they might need to do their work in as informed a manner as they would wish. They may not know what the central issues are that should be covered and how those issues have been understood and explained by leading scholars in the field.

Teaching the Holocaust: History, Perspectives, and Choices is an educational resource about the Holocaust, and it is designed for people across a spectrum of professions who wish to know more than they do now about the history of the Holocaust. Simply put, this is the course most people did not have the opportunity to take when they were in college, and its purpose is to enrich knowledge. *Voices and Views: A History of the Holocaust*, the first volume of the resource, introduces key historical events and central issues as explained and understood by eminent scholars. Readers of *Voices and Views* will become familiar with the works of many different minds, each with her or his own perspective and voice. Readers of this volume also will examine diary entries, speeches, and propaganda from the Third Reich era (1933-45), and excerpts of oral histories of people who lived through that time. Some of this material will be more directly applicable to one teaching situation than another, but each piece was selected because it is especially informative.

The history of the Holocaust is a multifaceted story. It encompasses moral and ethical dilemmas, in addition to social, cultural, and political history. It spans all of Europe and goes back to the years before the Second World War as well as forward to our time. Above all, it is a story about people, individual people. A great number were perpetrators and collaborators, far too many were victims, most were bystanders, and a few were rescuers.

Voices and Views focuses on the rescuers, the Righteous, to a greater degree than was their proportional impact during the war because of their disproportionate moral significance. During the Holocaust there were thousands of non-Jews, as well as many Jews (persecuted themselves), who refused to be passive in the face of the evil they witnessed. At great personal risk and often endangering their loved ones, they took it upon themselves to rescue Jews they knew and Jews they had never met before. Their activities and efforts were moments of grace in an abyss of atrocities. These heroic women and men are role models for teachers and students alike, for their lives illustrate that, in the hell that was the Holocaust, each human being had the capacity to act humanely.

It is important to emphasize, however, that rescue must be analyzed and understood within the context of the Holocaust. *Voices and Views* is divided into ten chapters reflecting important aspects of that history. Chapter 1, "Jews, Gentiles, and Germans," addresses the problematic issue of the position of the Jews in modern European society: Who are the Jews? What was the basis for anti-Judaism, and how did it evolve into antisemitism? In particular, how was German antisemitism expressed?

From there *Voices and Views* moves directly to World War I and the postwar (now seen as interwar) period, which is the focus of Chapter 2, "World War I and the Interwar Period." The Great War wreaked havoc in Europe. The carnage of millions of young men put France on a militantly pacifist path; the one thing the French did <u>not</u> want to do was go to war again – which was hardly a constructive or appropriate frame of mind to deal with her militantly aggressive neighbor, Germany. Italians, by contrast, turned to Mussolini, who extolled the virtues of war and created a public education system to politicize and militarize Italian youngsters. Germans, frustrated by military defeat and civilian unrest, flocked to "back to the land" movements, searching for what they believed to be the true relationship between a people and its land. While their neighbors to the east, the Poles, did not use the phrase "blood and soil," they certainly agreed with the principle of the nation-state: one people, with one language and culture, and a shared history, is entitled to a state of its own. The re-creation of Poland after the First World War expressed that ideology, but one-third of Poland's population was not Polish. Would Poland become a multicultural state, or a nation-state? Each country's political agenda was different, but they all had fundamental social problems in common: poverty, unemployment, instability, and hopelessness.

Millions of Germans looked to Hitler and his National Socialist Party for prosperity, employment, stability, and hope. Chapter 3, "The National Socialist Regime," examines what the Nazis offered the German people and how they structured the state bureaucracy to implement their plans. German Jews, of course, were offered nothing except the opportunity to leave, but few countries were willing to admit them. International indifference (and especially the indifference of the United States and Great Britain) to the desperate plight of Jews seeking asylum is the subject of Chapter 4, "Refugee Policy."

Few Jews made it onto the admission quota lists and through the endless bureaucratic red tape of exit, transit, and entry visas in time. After the Germans invaded Poland on September 1, 1939, the rescue of Jews became much more complicated and infinitely more dangerous. As Germany occupied one country after another, "rescue" became an illegal operation. What used to be called "emigration" became an intricate web of clandestine flight. What used to be called "living" became, for Jews, an outlawed activity, carried on in secret by hiding, or seemingly openly by passing as a gentile. No one could do any of this alone. Every Jewish person who survived the war in hiding, or by passing, or through escape to a safe haven, was helped by non-Jews. And, as we shall see in Chapter 5, "Gentile Life under German Occupation," the conditions of life under German rule or German occupation made it practically difficult and personally perilous for gentiles to offer that help.

Harsh as were the living conditions for the gentile population in most of Nazi-occupied Europe, to live at all became nearly impossible for the Jews. What Jews did every day in ghettos and in hiding – their hopes, fears, observations, and thoughts – is the focus of Chapter 6, "Jewish Life under German Occupation." People went on living, and to the best of their ability, went on with their lives until the moment of death – or liberation.

For millions of Jews, the former came first, and the subject of Chapter 7 is "The Machinery of Death and the Murderers." The "Final Solution" to what the Germans saw as the "Jewish Problem" was death – death through the hot violence of mass massacre and death through the cold violence of the organized, systematized, bureaucratized murder installations at Treblinka, Sobibor, Belzec, Majdanek, and Auschwitz. Who were the men who personally participated in the face-to-face slaughter of unarmed civilians? And who were the men who transformed the once-innocent town of Auschwitz into the central killing field of the Holocaust? None of them was born to be a mass murderer; step by step, they inched their way to iniquity.

Rescue networks to save Jews from the murderers and the machinery of death were organized here and there throughout Europe, in villages, towns, and cities. As we shall see in Chapter 8, "Rescue," some of these were run by gentiles, and others were operated by Jews. Not every effort was successful, and far too often powerful people who could have helped a great deal did not.

The heroic few who chose to act are the focus of Chapter 9, "The Rescuers." These women and men, from many different countries, of all social classes, religions, and occupations, teenaged to elderly, resisted the Germans and their orders. They confronted and combated what they knew to be not simply wrong, but heinous. The rescuers realized that they were living in a world in which exceptional evil had become an unexceptional occurrence, and common courtesy to their Jewish compatriots had become an uncommon kindness. They held fast to a moral code of good and evil that valued life and forbade murder. They refused to give in, found – or were faced with – an opportunity to help, and they did. In so doing, they left us a legacy of action and hope. It is both our privilege and our task to transmit this inheritance to our students: to show them that they have options as to how to act in, or respond to, difficult situations; to make it clear that choices are theirs to make, and to give them models of behavior they may choose to emulate.

The moral actions of these rare people – who were not born to be saints but inched their way to heroism step by step – help us penetrate the madness of the Holocaust. One of the greatest atrocities that western civilization both permitted and endured, the Holocaust looms large on the horizon of modern history, but it has not yet been fully integrated and assimilated into our understanding of history. What is the place of the Holocaust in history? Was it a unique genocide? How did people after the war absorb (or ignore) the events they had experienced and witnessed? More than half a century has passed since the war ended in 1945, and the immediate postwar avoidance of the Holocaust has been followed by efforts to analyze this willfully wrought disaster within the context of the national history of the perpetrators (Germany) and the national history of an occupied country (like the Netherlands). These are the issues with which Chapter 10, "After the Holocaust," wrestles. And these are the issues with which all of us continue to wrestle. It is precisely because they loom large that *Voices and Views* was written.

ABBÉ RENÉ DE NAUROIS

MARSEILLES, FRANCE... SUMMER 1942 – Having studied in Germany during the 1930's, Abbé René de Naurois was an outspoken critic of Hitler. Even after the fall of France to Germany, he continued to speak out against Hitler.

In 1941, he joined the resistance and was actively involved in smuggling Jews across the border into Spain. He provided false papers and refuge to those needing assistance. He hid Jews with families in the mountains and in Catholic institutions.

Wanted by the Gestapo, the Abbé fled France in 1942 and joined the Free French. He returned to France with General de Gaulle during the Allied invasion at Normandy. Abbé René de Naurois was decorated by General de Gaulle and received the *Croix de Guerre*.

(JFR Photo Archives)

CHAPTER 1 **Jews, Gentiles, and Germans**

The question often is asked how the Holocaust could have happened in such a civilized country as Germany was in the 1930s.

Deбórah Dwork **Introduction**

For nearly two thousand years, European Jews and European Christians lived side by side. In many communities, Jews and Christians coexisted peaceably for generations. But anti-Judaism (opposition to the Jewish religion), followed by antisemitism (opposition to Jews), was a staple of Christian theology, practice, and tradition. Antisemitism, in other words, was not Hitler's invention. And while the Holocaust was not entirely due to antisemitism, Christian antisemitism was an essential factor. The purpose of this unit is to explore how gentiles (non-Jews) in general, and German gentiles in particular, viewed and understood Jews. It is a story as old as Christianity itself.

Historians of the early Christian Church, such as William Nicholls, have explained that Christians initially did not think of themselves as separate from the Jewish people. Jesus was a Jew, and the first Christians considered themselves to be Jews too. By the year 100 C.E., however, church and synagogue separated. At that time, Jews were not ruling Christians, nor were Christians ruling Jews: both were ruled by the Roman Empire.

The Roman Empire has a fascinating history of conquest, division, development, and disintegration. The Empire gave rise to many institutions, customs, and traditions that have become an integral part of western civilization. And with the deathbed conversion of the Emperor Constantine (in 337 C.E.), the Empire embraced Christianity, which is perhaps its most important legacy. Within a hundred years, most of the cities in the Roman Empire had adopted Christianity, and the Church and the Empire fused into a single entity. Jews found themselves in a Christian world for the first time.

The Jews' rights and privileges began to erode immediately. Discriminatory tax laws were followed by discriminatory occupation laws. Finally, according to laws passed during the reign of the Emperor Justinian in the sixth century, known as the Code of Justinian, the Jewish religion lost the status it had held under Roman law as a legitimate national religion, and Jews lost the citizenship the Roman Empire had previously granted them.

From the Christian point of view, the Jews were guilty of two grave transgressions: First, they did not convert to Christianity. More ominously, however, according to common belief, Jews were not simply nonbelievers; they were Christ killers. Contrary to historical fact, Christians (and Christianity itself) saw Jews as the enemy who had conspired to kill Jesus.

Jews, in other words, were not Europeans like the other Christian Europeans. They were different. Throughout the following centuries, old

> The Holocaust was not entirely due to antisemitism, but Christian antisemitism was an essential factor.

13

problems, issues, and questions flared sporadically into terrible and bloody conflicts. In the middle of the twentieth century, they came to a catastrophic head. "The Holocaust cannot be comprehended without taking into account the way the people of Europe had been taught about Jews from their childhood up by their own religious traditions,"[1] William Nicholls has explained. The Holocaust also cannot be comprehended without taking into account why Germans in particular took on the task of annihilating this "enemy."

How did the Germans become so self-absorbed and xenophobic that they ultimately tried to annihilate not only the culture but even the existence of another people?

The question often is asked how the Holocaust could have happened in such a civilized country as Germany was in the 1930s. In much earlier periods of their history, German people had been interested in and sympathetic to other peoples and cultures. How did they become so self-absorbed and xenophobic that they ultimately tried to annihilate not only the culture but even the existence of another people?

One event of singular importance in effecting this ghastly self-transformation was the French occupation of Berlin during the Napoleonic Wars in the early nineteenth century. To bolster resistance against the French "cosmopolitan empire," as the Germans called it, the Germans adopted the Biblical rhetoric of God's Chosen People – and they were the Chosen. They, the Germans, were the people chosen by God to fulfill His mission; it was their task to protect the "Germanic" from the "non-Germanic." The main spokesman for this new patriotism forged in defeat and despair was the eminent Prussian philosopher Johann Gottlieb Fichte.

During the French occupation of Berlin, Fichte mounted a series of fourteen weekly lectures, which he called *Addresses to the German Nation*. Exhorting his audience to rediscover their German identity, he argued that they, the Germans, unlike other nations, had remained true to themselves. Fichte called on the nation to accept its unique vocation: Germany was to be the re-generator and re-creator of the world. "You, of all modern peoples, are the one in whom the seed of perfection most unmistakably lies, and to whom the lead in its development is committed," he declared. "If you perish in this your essential nature, then there perishes together with you every hope of the whole human race for salvation from the depth of its misery."[2]

His audiences believed him. His readers believed him. From Fichte on, generations of Germans saw themselves as the saviors of the world. It was, according to the English historian of Germany E. M. Butler, "the real beginning of German megalomania."[3]

Fichte's words delineated a philosophical, if not religious, vocation for Germany. As the nineteenth century progressed, his appeal was transformed into an obsession about Germany's calling. Somehow a world mission had been imposed on Germany and had become Germany's task. Fichte's ideas, which had been a rallying cry for defeated Germans in 1807, became a fantasy unrelated to any concrete current event. His notion of patriotism became a shell to be filled with whatever content came along.

To make matters worse, the distinction and division between

"Germanic" and "non-Germanic" was solidified by the demise of the idea of one, unified humanity and the development of a concept of race that separated "Man" into superior and inferior peoples. Grounded in the English biologist Charles Darwin's ideas about natural selection and survival of the fittest, and crudely applied to human beings, this new idea of "Man" held that the strong were destined to command and the weak to obey. Social Darwinism, as these theories are called (and which Darwin himself repudiated), was a pan-European phenomenon. The Germans did not have a corner on the racism market.

Europeans took these ideas about race with them as they carved out empires abroad, and they maintained them at home. The rapid economic and social modernization of Europe in the nineteenth century and the concomitant revolutionary democratic rhetoric made many conservatives uneasy. They identified these developments with the specter of Jewish ascendance. The old anti-Judaism, which had oppressed Jews for religious reasons, was reconfigured into a condemnation of Jews as the champions of political radicalism and economic change. Jews, in short, were to blame for the dissolution of the foundations of society. The identification of capitalism with Jews and the definition of capitalist society as "Jewish" established Judaism as a metaphor for the evils of modern life. A new kind of sociological antisemitism became a staple of the language of both reactionaries and revolutionaries united in their abhorrence of capitalist society. An excerpt from William Nicholls's *Christian Antisemitism*, and an excerpt from Robert Wistrich's *Antisemitism: The Longest Hatred*, analyze the evolution of modern antisemitism from traditional anti-Judaism from two different perspectives.

Richard Wagner was one of the main proponents in Germany of the corrupting influence of Jews, and he focused on the issue of culture. According to Wagner, the Jew "rules, and will rule, as long as Money remains the power before which all our doings and dealings lose their force."[4] The great political economist Karl Marx (on whose ideas modern Marxism is based) had said as much already in his criticism of capitalist society. What Wagner added was his insistence on the importance of commercialization of the art world as a measure of Jewish power. Claiming that the Jews had transformed the suffering of artists for their art into financial profit, Wagner maintained that it had become impossible to create at all. In "Judaism and Music," he argued further that Jews could not be part of the European community or participate in its culture because they were unable to speak properly the language of their adopted countries, and language was the soul of the nation. Wilhelm Marr, a follower of Wagner, drew the logical conclusion: The Jew could never become German because he would never be able to speak German. Their

The composer Richard Wagner (1813–1883) was one of the main proponents in late-nineteenth century Germany of the corrupting influence of Jews on German culture. Wagner's son-in-law, the English-born Houston Stewart Chamberlain, brought the theories of Wagner and other late-nineteenth century German antisemites together in his *Foundations of the Nineteenth Century* in which he claimed that Jews were engaged in a sinister conspiracy to dominate the world. Wagner was Hitler's favorite composer and his music was performed at many Nazi party functions. (Süddeutscher Verlag-Bilderdienst)

original tongue was a Semitic language; therefore those who opposed Jews because they defiled and usurped German culture should identify themselves proudly as anti-Semites.

"What is German?" Wagner asked. Culture, not economy, was at the core of German identity, he answered, and the Jew's manipulation of language and art was infinitely more pernicious than his control over money ever had been. The Jew had bought the German soul with his trade in works of culture. Jewish management reduced German *Kultur* (culture) to a sham, a mere image; it destroyed "one of the finest natural dispositions in all the human race."[5] Wagner and his followers transformed the many-centuries-old religious opposition between Christians and Jews into a hostile, secular, cultural conflict between the idealist German and the scheming Jew. Very quickly, this hostility came to signify the incongruities and discordance of modern society: rural and urban, culture and civilization, creativity and imitation, interior vitality and superficial sophistication, authority and democracy, morality and intellect, idealism and materialism, tradition and innovation, loyalty and opportunism, clarity and confusion, health and disease, purity and degeneration.

Wagner's son-in-law, the English-born Houston Stewart Chamberlain, brought all of this together in his *Foundations of the Nineteenth Century*. In his grandiose theory of history, Chamberlain claimed that the industrial and scientific revolutions, liberalism, and internationalism had swept away the traditional structures that had given people a sense of their own individual place in the world. European Jews, however, according to Chamberlain, did not suffer from this self-alienation because they had preserved the idea of Zion and the hope of rebuilding their Temple. They alone had preserved a sense of purpose and destiny, and this had made them a dangerous force. Chamberlain believed that the realization of the Jewish dream depended on their acquisition of power over the gentiles. A core group of biologically pure Jews would rule the biologically degenerate gentile masses. Jews, in short, were engaged in a sinister conspiracy to dominate the world. In his own time, Chamberlain was a marginal figure. Under National Socialism, however, his doctrine became official and institutionalized, informing political actions as well as daily practices in schools, propaganda, and popular education.

German paranoia in the late nineteenth century about a "Jewish threat" was also fed by the rising migration of Jews after 1868 from the east to the west. Fleeing poverty and pogroms (sporadic violent attacks against individual Jewish communities), and in search of a better life, some three million Russian, Austro-Hungarian, and Rumanian Jews left their homelands between 1868 and 1914. Moving west, primarily en route to America, hundreds of thousands passed through Germany, and many Germans feared they might stay. In the popular imagination, this potential inundation by hordes of eastern Jews spelled disease, economic corruption, and political radicalism. Germany, the famous German historian Heinrich von Treitschke believed, had a "Jewish Problem," and it was the Jews pouring over the border. "Their children and grandchildren

> German paranoia in the late nineteenth century about a "Jewish threat" was fed by the rising migration of Jews after 1868 from east to west.

will dominate in the future Germany's stock exchanges and newspapers." Convinced that the Jews were responsible for national degeneration wherever they settled, he wondered whether the downfall of German culture could be averted by the violent ejection of the Jews. Deploring the crude character of the antisemitism that had arisen so quickly in Germany, Treitschke nevertheless believed that "the instinct of the masses had, in fact, recognized a very serious damage to the life of the new Germany."[6] It was left to him to lament publicly and respectably in the *Prussian Annals* of November 1879, "The Jews are our misfortune."

"The Jews are our misfortune."
— Heinrich von Treitschke

Notes

1. William Nicholls, *Christian Antisemitism,* (N.J.: Jason Aronson, Inc., 1995), xvii.
2. Johann Gottlieb Fichte, *Addresses to the German Nation,* ed. George A. Kelly, trans. R.F. Jones and G. H. Turnbull (New York and Evanston: Harper and Row, 1968), 228.
3. E. M. Butler, "Romantic 'Germanentum,'" in G.P. Gooch et al. *The German Mind and Outlook* (London: Chapman and Hall, 1945), 100.
4. Richard Wagner, "Judaism in Music," *Prose Works,* trans. William Ashton Ellis, 8 vols. (London: Kegan Paul, Trench, Trübner & Co., 1894), vol. 3, 82.
5. From: Richard Wagner, "What Is German?" *Prose Works,* trans. William Ashton Ellis, 8 vols. (London: Kegan Paul, Trench, Trübner & Co., 1894), vol. 4, 158.
6. Heinrich von Treitschke, "Unsere Aussichten," *Preussische Jahrbücher,* vol. 44 (1879), 572f.

WILLIAM NICHOLLS # Christian Antisemitism and Secular Antisemitism

INTRODUCTION

THE HOLOCAUST of six million Jews in Nazi-ruled Europe was the greatest outpouring of evil in the history of the planet. No matter how much we learn about the Holocaust, there is always more to defeat the mind's capacity for comprehension and shock the soul. Taking its full measure may be impossible. Its near absolute evil calls in question all hopes for human civilization and threatens faith in divine rule over history. To retain hope in humanity, let alone in God, we must somehow come to terms with it and learn its lesson so that any repetition may be made impossible.

A number of writers have said outright that we cannot comprehend the Holocaust. The very attempt trivializes it, they insist, and removes its uniqueness, assimilating it to other catastrophes, other massacres, atrocious in themselves, but lacking what renders the Holocaust itself without parallel. Many historians, on the other hand, do attempt to account for the Holocaust within categories of explanation they have learned to use in investigating other historical events. They warn us that mystifying the Holocaust by removing it from the historical process may blind us to the early warning signs of a possible repetition.

What defies explanation in the Holocaust is the magnitude of hatred that overflowed upon the Jews. At this point in world history, evil jumped off any scale of computation. Such annihilating hatred cannot be understood as the effect of causes historians normally analyze. When every social, economic, and political factor has been taken into account, the question still remains: why?

Writing about the Holocaust requires us to deal with passions that have nothing to do with reason and calculation. There is no science of the radically irrational. Nevertheless, it makes sense to look at factors often underrated by modern historians just because they are irrational.

The history of the twentieth century ought to have shown us that religion remains a powerful motor of human action. The Holocaust cannot be comprehended without taking into account the way the people of Europe had been taught about the Jews from their childhood up by their own religious traditions.

To say that the Holocaust was the ultimate outcome of antisemitism[1] is illuminating, but only to a point. Many volumes have been written on antisemitism, without satisfactorily accounting for the degree of hatred Jews attracted from their neighbors. Antisemites account for their hatred by accusing Jews of unpleasant racial characteristics and undesirable activities; however, it does not take much investigation to convince anyone of normal goodwill that Jews as a group do not possess these characteristics or take part in these activities. Without exception, the charges that have been leveled at Jews by antisemites are baseless. The origins of antisemitism are not to be sought in Jews but in antisemites.

Antisemitism is causeless hatred. The reasons given for it are always rationalizations of a hate already present in the mind of the antisemite. The antisemite needs such rationalizations to tolerate the inner pressure of a passion that might threaten his or her mental stability if recognized as causeless. We should never be trapped into taking these justifications seriously, trying to see if there was anything in Jewish behavior that might have provided a basis for them.

When Jews do so, they internalize antisemitism and indulge in self-hatred. When non-Jews do so, they collude with antisemitism. There can be no way to understanding along this route. When we attempt to describe the historical development of antisemitism, we do not explain or justify it. We can only show how it grew up and how it was explained by the antisemites themselves.

Nevertheless, although we cannot explain the intensity of antisemitic hate, we do know how to ex-

WILLIAM NICHOLLS, CHRISTIAN ANTISEMITISM: A HISTORY OF HATE, XVII–XX, 313–21, 441–42, 468–69. COPYRIGHT © 1993 BY WILLIAM NICHOLLS. REPRINTED BY PERMISSION OF THE PUBLISHER, JASON ARONSON INC., NORTHVALE, NJ © 1993.

plain the choice of the Jews as its victims. The explanation is not new, but it has understandably been resisted. Many Jewish writers have said, quite simply, that the Nazis chose the Jews as the target of their hate because two thousand years of Christian teaching had accustomed the world to do so. Few Christian historians and theologians have been sufficiently open to a painful truth to accept this explanation without considerable qualification. Nevertheless, it is correct, though perhaps needing fuller substantiation.

Modern antisemitism, though not identical with the historic Christian hostility toward Jews, clearly sprang from it. The links are there to be traced. Secular antisemites had learned from the Christian past that Jews were bad. When they abandoned the religion of their upbringing, they retained its prejudices.

Jews had experienced hostility from their neighbors well before Christianity came upon the scene. Pagan hostility toward the Jewish people was aroused, above all, by the refusal of the Jews to join the ecumenical consensus of paganism, whereby the gods of one people could be satisfactorily equated with those of another. Olympian Zeus was the same as Jupiter Capitolinus, and so on. Jews obstinately refused to admit that the One they worshiped, YHWH,[2] could be identified with these or any other god known to man. Eventually, the Romans at least gave in, and recognized Judaism as a lawful national religion; from 212 C.E. the Jews were Roman citizens.

Pagan calumnies against the Jews seem to be outgrowths of this central rejection. If the Jews would not worship the gods, their religious customs must have been inhuman and barbaric. They were strange and incomprehensible and anything could be believed of them. Thus, pagan anti-Jewishness can be regarded as a specific form of xenophobia, the fear and dislike of the stranger simply because he or she is seen as strange.

Nevertheless, pagan hostility lacked the peculiar intensity of hatred that came to mark Christian anti-Judaism and its secularized child, antisemitism. Sometimes it could even turn into admiration for the purity of Jewish monotheism and Jewish ethics. Not all pagans were antisemites, and some became Jews by conversion. Many more would have done so if it had not been for the barrier of circumcision.

Christian hostility toward Jews possessed a uniquely powerful feature. Christians believed that the Jews had killed Christ, their divine Savior. The myth of the Jews as the Christ-killers has powered anti-Judaism and antisemitism all through the Christian centuries. It is present even in the New Testament, and it has not yet died under the impact of modern critical history.

Like all religions, Christianity is powered by a myth, its charter story that tells believers who they are and where they fit into the divine plan. It is important to this particular myth that it be based in real history. In it, the Jews are cast as the enemies of Christ and God: the Jews that are meant are actual historical people, not just mythic abstractions.

We know from modern scholarship that many features of the myth are historically untrue and are therefore myths in the popular sense as well. Nevertheless, until modern times the myth that tells the Christian story has been firmly believed, and most Christians still do believe it to be literally and historically true.

According to this story, because the Jews rejected and killed Christ, they in turn have been rejected as God's chosen people. The Jews have broken their ancient covenant with God, and he has made a new covenant, sealed in the blood of Christ, gathering to himself a new people, drawn from the Gentiles. This new people has now superseded the old Israel.

The Jews have lost their status as the covenant people, and the new Israel is now the true Israel. As a punishment for this cosmic crime, the Jews have lost their Temple and been exiled from their land. Until the return of Christ they will remain homeless wanderers upon the earth. What theologians are beginning to call the theology of supersession joins hands with the myth of the deicide,[3] Christ-killing people, to make the Jews a permanent target for Christian hostility and contempt.

In the Christian state of the Constantinian era theological hostility led to social and legal measures, discriminating against Jews and relegating them to a subordinate status in a Christian world. Raul Hilberg has shown in a famous comparative table[4] how many of the Nazi measures against the Jews, short of the Final Solution itself, were not novelties, but reenactments of older measures of the Christian world, laws of state and church that kept the Jews in their place.

Nevertheless, the Christian world did stop short of a final solution. Christian legislation was governed by a principle apparently first formulated by Augustine in the fifth century: The Jews should be preserved, but in misery. They are to remain in the world as a permanent witness to their own crimes, bearing the mark of Cain, but like Cain, not to be killed by others.

Misery is not extermination. There could be no Holocaust while Christian restriction on genocide remained binding. There could be calumnies of all sorts, even massacres and expulsions of whole communities from countries where they had lived for centuries, but no one could claim Christian sanction for total extermination of the Jews. Loss of Christian authority in a secularized world removed that ultimate restraint, setting Hitler free to act out the last consequences of the ancient hatred.

In the Middle Ages, the myth had already begun to generate popular paranoia. The Christian people had been taught for centuries about the misdeeds of the Jews, how they had rejected and killed their own clearly prophesied Messiah, and how even this was but the culmination of a "trail of crimes"⁵ extending from the beginning of Jewish history. About such a people, much could be believed.

The popular Christian mind now began to spin novel and destructive fantasies about the Jews. These are the famous calumnies, from financial greed to ritual murder, the armory of later antisemitism. Unfortunately, they did not die with the Middle Ages. They are still alive in the imagination of large numbers of antisemites, and they are being revived in full strength by the enemies of Israel. It is possible to show that every one of these fantasies can be accounted for by the pathological mechanism of paranoia, and I shall attempt to do so in a later chapter.

If Christian anti-Judaism was now assuming a paranoid form in the mass mind, we are out of the realm of rational justification. Paranoia is transmissible from mind to mind, but it does not go by the route of reason. It can therefore change its rationalization while remaining essentially the same.

This may be the often missing explanation of how the secularized children of Christian parents in the modern world retained their anti-Jewish prejudices even after abandoning the Christian dogma that alone gave them a semblance of plausibility. Detached from its theological justification, hate could live on, unrestrained by Christian limits. . . .

SECULAR ANTISEMITISM

EMANCIPATION LED TO ANTISEMITISM. When Jews began to move with relative freedom in European society, sharing citizenship and civil rights with their neighbors, the latter found new justifications for hating them. But they were still hated above all because they were Jews. What did that now mean? Previously, their Christian neighbors had thought of Jews as members of an alien and false religion, adherents to a broken covenant. Now secularized antisemites would hate them as members of an alien and inferior race, unassimilable by those among whom they lived, a dangerous source of pollution for the cultural and racial purity of their neighbors.

Substantial numbers of Christians would also borrow racist ideas from the new secular antisemitism and incorporate them into new forms of their old theological rejection. In the latter part of the nineteenth century, Christian antisemitism also becomes racist, and (with rare exceptions) directed against all who are Jewish by descent, whatever their religious adherence.

Most of the non-Jewish world now took it for granted that all Jews, whether observant, secular, or Christianized, together constituted a unique group in society, whom it might still be appropriate to hate. The new reasons were not after all absolutely new. They owed something to the old ones, and we shall find clear lines connecting the old and the new forms of anti-Judaic hostility to one another.

By far, the most important line of continuity between the old and the new was not intellectual at all. This was the paranoia inherited from the Middle Ages and transmitted from mind to mind at a nonrational level, often below the level of conscious thought. Paranoid hatred for Jews is picked up in early childhood from the attitudes of parents and teachers. No intellectual indoctrination is needed to make an antisemite. Looks and tones of voice are sufficient for the sensitive mind of a child. Loyalty to parents will make the impression permanent. Only a strong and independent conscience can shake off such powerful early conditioning.

Causeless hatred for Jews came first, and conscious reasons for the hatred were always rationalizations. Whatever people thought and said against Jews was only a way to account for a hatred already in their minds and passions; the semiconscious aim of antisemitic ideas was to assist the antisemite to feel comfortable with his or her own hatred, by furnishing it with spurious justification.

Christian parents could therefore transmit their own dislike of Jews to their offspring without its essential character changing even when the latter subsequently became secularized. The definition of a Jew could change, and the reasons for thinking ill of a Jew could be modernized. What did not change was the constant assumption of others that there was something uniquely bad about Jewish character and Jewish behavior that justified hostility and discrimination. The rationalizations would differ. The hate did not.

Throughout the centuries during which the Church had been teaching people what to think, Christians had marked out Jews as their one constant target for hate, even though they sometimes hated others too. Loss of Christian influence on society did not change that. Understanding the spurious reasons by which the new antisemites explained their hatred is much less important. If Jews continued to be hated in the modern secular world, while some now hated them even more than before, it was because the Church had successfully taught the world (even if not in so many words) that the Jews were the right people to hate. The effects of the teaching lasted even after the teacher had lost much of her ancient authority.

The reasons for hating Jews, whether theological or secular, have always been bad reasons, that will not stand up to critical investigation, as we have found throughout the present inquiry. Nevertheless, they still need to be exposed, so that the irrationality and baselessness of all forms of antisemitism can be confronted head-on and dealt with by the conscience at the proper level. There is also an intellectual line of descent from older Christian anti-Judaism to the new secular antisemitism, at least in some of its forms, and it remains important to trace it.

So far, I have attempted to be consistent in reserving the term *antisemitism* for hostility toward the Jews based on supposed racial grounds, while using *anti-Judaism* and its variants for the traditional, religiously based hostility. The dividing line was the possibility of effective conversion: on the older, Christian view, a Jew ceased to be a Jew upon baptism. Now the assimilated Jew was still a Jew, even after baptism or abandonment of any form of religion. From the Enlightenment onward, it is no longer possible to draw clear lines of distinction between religious and racial forms of hostility toward Jews.

Once Jews have been emancipated and secular thinking makes its appearance, without leaving behind the old Christian hostility toward Jews, the new term *antisemitism* becomes almost unavoidable, even before explicitly racist doctrines appear. Emancipated Jews had often abandoned their religion for Christianity, or for no religion at all. They could no longer be identified by their religion. However much they tried to join their neighbors, their neighbors refused to assimilate them. Jews remained aliens. They were still considered a distinct group, whether as individuals they remained Jewish, converted to Christianity, or became altogether secularized. In the eyes of their neighbors, all were still Jews. This is a new way of defining Jews, unknown to traditional Christianity and not easily conceivable before emancipation.

The secular antisemite can no longer object to Jews for religious reasons. He may object to their religion, since he objects to all forms of religion, but he must deny to Jews an authentic religious identity. If he wishes to distinguish Jews from their neighbors at all, which on his own secular assumptions he should not, he must regard them as a social group defined only by their descent. Indeed, once they abandoned the Torah, that is what assimilated Jews had effectively become.

It is only a small step from hostility toward Jews as a social group with a unique descent to full-blown racist antisemitism, and historically also it did not take long for this step to be taken. I shall therefore now begin to use the more familiar term *antisemitism* to denote all the new secular forms of hostility toward Jews, while acknowledging that the full racist doctrine emerged only later in the nineteenth century.

The Left-Wing Hegelians

Hegel, the great Berlin idealist, was the dominant figure in philosophy in the nineteenth century. In spite of the popularity in the twentieth century, especially in the English-speaking world, of empiricist thinkers, whose ideas are more consonant with the scientific outlook, Hegel's shadow still extends over a vast area of modern thought. His most remarkable disciple and critic, Karl Marx, still dominates the outlook of a considerable portion of world, but Hegel's influence is by no means confined to the Marxist current of thought. Hegel's indirect legacy is also apparent in the prevalence of social criticism, Marxist and otherwise, in intellectual circles, and indeed wherever the form of critical thinking called dialectical is practiced. By general consent, Hegel is acknowledged to be one of the hardest of philosophers to understand, though some of his interpreters write much more clearly than he usually did.

Hegel is also a principal link between the older theological and the modern, secular thinking. He is one of the few modern philosophers whose work explicitly reflects Christian themes. In fact, he intended his system to be a rational explication of Christian faith in a modern or enlightened form. It was not without substantial justification that his left-wing critics accused him of being theological, instead of basing his philosophy on reason alone.

Fewer have noticed (perhaps because the idea was until recently taken so much for granted) that his system also incorporates the ancient theology of supersession, according to which Christianity has replaced Judaism, while incorporating in itself all that was true in its predecessor.

Hegel's thought traces the movement of the absolute Spirit through history, as it continuously acquires self-knowledge through objectification of modes in its own being. The historical development of the movement of thought, as each new philosophy negates its predecessor and at the same time takes it up into itself in transfigured form, successively presents in time

that which is eternally present in the being of the Absolute. What is true of philosophy is also true of religion. Religions also negate and subsume their historical predecessors.

For Hegel, Christianity is the final religion: it embodies the unity of God and man, of which the Incarnation of God in Christ is the historical expression. In negating its immediate predecessor, Judaism, Christianity also takes up into itself in a higher form what was true in Judaism, as well as the truth in all its other predecessors from the beginnings of religion.

Hegel writes of Judaism with respect, a respect rare in Christian thinkers. But this does not mean that for him the Jewish faith has a continuing historical destiny alongside Christianity. For Hegel, no less than for the church fathers, Christianity comes to bring Judaism to an end. From the point of view of Hegel's system, this is not an ultimate loss, since Judaism is not simply negated. Since it is taken up into Christianity in transfigured form, it is therefore in a sense still present in it. Once Christianity appears on the scene, however, Judaism has no further historical role or destiny.

Hegel attempted to rationalize Christianity completely, thus converting theology altogether into philosophy, but there is no doubt that theology is at the root of his system. One might even guess that the very idea of *Aufhebung*, the subsuming of a past phase in the history of thought into its successor, is simply a philosophical version of the old Christian idea of the supersession of Judaism in its fulfilment by Christianity. Even in this enlightened way of thinking, Christianity is still understood as replacing Judaism at the same time as it fulfills it.

A number of Hegel's most important followers, known as the Left Hegelians, among whom Feuerbach and Bruno Bauer were prominent, were critical of elements in Hegel's system that they thought inconsistent or insufficiently critical. They accepted his dialectical method and his historical orientation, but they disagreed with him on the application of the method to the historical material before them.

Just as Hegel believed Christianity to be the final form of religion, he also believed the Prussian constitutional monarchy, somewhat idealized, to be the final form of the state. In various ways, the Left

Hegelians criticized both these assumptions. They argued that Christianity might indeed be the final form of religion so far; however, thought could still move on to the negation of Christianity, and if Christianity was the final religion, its negation could only mean the negation of religion as such. Similarly, the Prussian monarchy could also be negated by further historical change, and in particular to democracy, in which every individual would embody the principle of sovereignty, so far confined to the person of the monarch. Thus in various ways they looked forward to a further historical epoch in which religion would no longer be supported by the state: it would become a private matter, or perhaps even cease to exist in any form, while in the state itself, democracy would prevail.

Karl Marx and Antisemitism

The argument between Karl Marx and Bruno Bauer, on what was coming to be known as the Jewish question, or the Jewish problem, illustrates ways in which the Left Hegelians continued Hegel's scheme of thought and pushed it further, while disagreeing with him and with one another on important matters of content.[6] The same argument also reveals something of great importance for the present inquiry: certain traditional Christian assumptions about Jews and Judaism were being transmitted to the modern secular world through Hegel and his intellectual descendants. While there can perhaps be debate about whether Bauer or Marx were antisemites in the strict sense of the term, they were certainly among those who laid the foundations for the left-wing version of antisemitism, later to become so prominent in the Soviet Union and in much of the rest of the world.

People often wonder how Marxism in its Soviet Communist form could have turned out to be so antisemitic, since they regard Marx himself as a Jew. Moreover, his theory had apparently left no place for racial distinctions. Doubtless the main reason is simply paranoia transmitted from the Christian past, still powerfully influencing the minds of the masses in the Communist states, as well as those of the Marxist intellectuals themselves.

However, we cannot absolve Marx himself of responsibility for providing ideas to justify the inherited paranoia. Marx was not in fact a Jew, except by descent. If anything, he was a Christian. Unless we share nineteenth-century assumptions about the all-importance of race and breeding, we should not think of him as a Jew in any sense that throws intellectual light on what he thought about Jews or anything else.[7]

Karl Marx's father, Herschel Levi, early embraced the diffuse and free-thinking religion of the Enlightenment. After the setbacks to emancipation following on the Congress of Vienna, he found it necessary for career reasons to adopt Lutheranism, a year before the birth of his son Karl. Herschel was hardly more than a conventional Christian, before or after joining the Church, but given his Enlightenment views, "conversion" was not an important issue for him. He changed his last name to Marx, from one of his father's given names, and he took the Christian name of Heinrich. Karl Marx's mother was a Philips, of the same family as the founders of the present Dutch electronics giant.[8]

Karl was the descendant of learned rabbis on both sides of his family, but he received no Jewish education and apparently not much of a Christian one, though some of his high school essays did deal with Christian topics. He was baptized in the Lutheran church at the age of five and brought up in the family as a Christian in the liberal tradition of the Enlightenment. His father would read to him from the works of Voltaire and [Jean] Racine. As we have seen, Voltaire was no friend of the Jews; his writings are full of unfavorable references to Jews.

When we turn to Marx's own writings, we cannot help being struck by their extremely hostile tone when they do refer to Judaism or to individual Jews. Jewish thinkers sympathetic to his ideas attempt to defend Karl Marx from the charge of being an antisemite, in spite of the evidence to the contrary.[9] For a hundred years Jewish Socialists refrained from translating Marx's writings on the Jewish question into Yiddish or Hebrew.[10]

As Sydney Hook acknowledges, however, Marx certainly used the epithet Jew in a highly opprobrious sense.[11] In the famous theses on Feuerbach, he uses the expression "dirty Jewish" as a characterization of a form of economic activity. In private correspondence, among many other such references, he characterized Lasalle, a prominent socialist who had not converted to Christianity, as a "Jewish nigger," and spoke of detecting a "Jewish whine" in his utterances.

Marx described the Jewish refugees from Poland as "this filthiest of all races, [who] only perhaps by its passion for greedy gain could be related to [the Jewish capitalists of] Frankfort."[12] In the 1850s, he sneered at those who fought for the seating of Lord Rothschild in the House of Commons. "It is doubtful whether the British people will be very much pleased by extending electoral rights to a Jewish usurer."[13]

More important still, in the discussion with Bauer, now to be examined, dealing explicitly with the Jewish question, Marx firmly identifies Jews and their practical religion with "hucksterism," or "haggling," that is, with commerce having a crass profit motive. What else is this but the old medieval identification of the Jews with usury and greed, as in the comment on Lord Rothschild just cited?

He did not derive this identification from any objective study of contemporary Jewish activities, a study that his family connections would doubtless have made possible. He must have learned it from the Christian mythology surviving among those with whom he was brought up and spent his formative years and from the attitude of the Germans of his own intellectual milieu to emancipated Jews.

Marx, who was critical of so much, failed to be critical of anti-Jewish ideas widely held in the circles in which he moved. One might also speculate that the knowledge of his own Jewish descent, which he desired to repudiate, may have made him especially hostile toward others who did not repudiate it as he did. If this is not antisemitism – and I think it is – it certainly served to perpetuate and encourage antisemitic ideas among those who would later treat his writings as holy writ. Marx takes his place among a long line of former Jews who did not scruple to slander their own people in the Gentile world.[14]

Bruno Bauer had written a substantial essay on the Jewish question, *Die Judenfrage,* published in Brunswick in 1843. He also wrote a smaller discussion of the question, entitled *Die Fähigkeit der heuti-*

gen Juden und Christen frei zu werden (The capacity of present day Jews and Christians to become free), in a work called *Einundzwanzig Bogen aus der Schweiz* (Twenty-one Sheets from Switzerland). The following year, Marx replied critically to each of these essays in separate articles of his own.[15]

Together, Marx's two articles constitute his final views on the Jewish question, to which he did not explicitly return. Although they did not circulate widely in his own time, they are the basis of modern Communist theory about the Jews. They also have substantially influenced the thinking of many left-wing, non-Zionist Jews about Jewish identity and destiny, and hence (directly and indirectly) about Israel, though of course Marx did not refer to Israel.

Erich Fromm calls the articles brilliant, and in a special sense perhaps they are, provided the reader is able to ignore the anti-Jewish prejudice and post-Christian triumphalism that lie at the basis of the argument and vitiate it. In contrast, Isaiah Berlin calls the reply to Bauer "a dull and shallow composition."[16]

Marx and Bauer were in very sharp theoretical disagreement, and it is therefore particularly instructive to observe the assumptions they shared. These are presumably at least the legacy of Hegel, and in all probability the common view of the society they both belonged to. Both assume almost without argument that in order for the Jews to be emancipated they must cease to be Jews. Both also believe that Jews, although not yet emancipated, already exercise disproportionate power in society through the control of financial institutions.

These are very familiar ideas in the outlook of the traditional antisemite, and neither of the two has learned to criticize them, empirically or theoretically. For Marx, the Jew is the essential capitalist. His religion is money. The abolition of capitalism and the abolition of Judaism are essentially identical.

The two differ, however, mostly because Marx is the more radical thinker of the two, carrying ideas Bauer begins to formulate to their logical conclusion. Bauer believes that Jews are incapable of emancipation while they remain Jews, and that likewise Christians are incapable of giving emancipation to them while they remain Christians. Jews lag behind the development of history, and in order to be emancipated they must first become Christians, though the Christianity that they should embrace is one already in process of dissolution. Like the new post-Hegelian theologians, of whom Bauer himself was one, they should study historical criticism and take part in the radical criticism of Christianity.

Both Jew and Christian must come to see religion as simply an outmoded stage of development in the human mind, a snakeskin to be sloughed off. Ultimately, the political emancipation of both the Jew and the Christian will come about through the abolition of religion, which will be effectuated when the connection between the state and religion is thoroughly broken and religion becomes a purely private matter.

Marx, however, considers it essential to ask, not only who should emancipate and who should be emancipated, but what is emancipation. His own answer is that political emancipation, as considered by Bauer, is not real emancipation. Real emancipation is human emancipation, the identification of man with himself as a social being, what Marx, following Feuerbach, called *species-being*. "The political emancipation of the Jew or the Christian – of the religious man in general – is the *emancipation* of the state from Judaism, Christianity, and *religion* in general."[17] But from this purely political point of view Christians have no right to ask Jews to renounce their religion, as Bauer claims.

This is still a theological controversy. "The theological doubt about whether the Jew or the Christian has the better chance of attaining salvation is reproduced here in the more enlightened form: which of the two is *more capable of emancipation*? It is indeed no longer asked: which makes free–Judaism or Christianity? On the contrary, it is now asked: which makes free – the negation of Judaism or the negation of Christianity?"[18]

Political emancipation leaves religion still in existence, while withdrawing privileges from a particular religion. "The emancipation of the state from religion is not the emancipation of the real man from religion. We do not say to the Jews, therefore, as does Bauer: you cannot be emancipated politically without emancipating yourselves completely from Judaism. We say

rather: it is because you can be emancipated politically, without renouncing Judaism completely and absolutely, that *political* emancipation itself is not *human* emancipation."[19] Marx argues that Jews cannot be emancipated as human beings without cutting themselves off completely from the faith of their people and ceasing to be Jews.

Establishing the rights of man is no solution, since such rights are based on egoism, not on the transcendence of egoism by identification with the social being of man. (Here Marx, remarkably, argues like many a conservative, who considers duties, not rights, to be fundamental to society.) In the French and American movements for human rights, man was not yet liberated *from* religion or property, he was only liberated *for* them.

In the second reply to Bauer, Marx's specific views on the Jews come out much more clearly and polemically. Now Marx disengages himself from Bauer's theological formulation of the question, and he asks, what specific *social* element is it necessary to overcome in order to abolish Judaism?

> Let us consider the real Jew: not the *Sabbath Jew,* whom Bauer considers, but the *everyday Jew.* Let us not seek the secret of the Jew in his religion, but let us seek the secret of the religion in the real Jew.
>
> What is the profane basis of Judaism? *Practical* need, *self-interest.* What is the worldly cult of the Jew? *Huckstering.*[20] What is his worldly god? *Money.*
>
> Very well: then in emancipating itself from *huckstering* and *money*, and thus from real and practical Judaism, our age would emancipate itself.[21]

Marx sees in Judaism a universal antisocial element of the present time, whose "historical development, *zealously aided in its harmful aspects by the Jews,* has now attained its culminating point" (emphasis mine, here only). "In the final analysis, the *emancipation of* the Jews is the emancipation of mankind from *Judaism*."[22]

Marx considers that Judaism, thus understood, has in fact taken over the Christian world, so that it now shares completely in Jewish egoism and commercialism. "The Jew, who occupies a distinctive place in civil society, only manifests in a distinctive way the Judaism of civil society."[23] Practical need or egoism is the basis of civil society. "The god of *practical need and self-interest* is *money*."[24]

> Money is the jealous god of Israel, beside which no other god may exist. Money abases all the gods of mankind and changes them into commodities. Money is the universal and self-sufficient *value* of all things.
>
> It has, therefore, deprived the whole world, both the human work and nature, of their own proper value. Money is the alienated essence of man's work and existence; this essence dominates him and he worships it.
>
> The god of the Jews has been secularized and has become the god of this world. The bill of exchange is the real god of the Jew. His god is only an illusory bill of exchange.[25]

These passages display with extraordinary clarity both the spiritual insight of which Marx was capable and its no less remarkable vitiation by anti-Jewish prejudice. Unfortunately, however, his thinking is so closely integrated that the two are inseparable. In these passages, at least, you cannot have the one without the other. A Marx without antisemitism would no longer be Marx.

He goes on to explain how Judaism as he understands it has taken over Christianity.

> Christianity is the sublime thought of Judaism; Judaism is the vulgar practical application of Christianity. But this practical application could only become universal when Christianity as perfected religion had accomplished, in a *theoretical* fashion, the alienation of man from himself and nature.
>
> It was only then that Judaism could attain universal domination and could turn alienated man and alienated nature into *alienable*, saleable objects, in thrall to egoistic need and huckstering.[26]

Marx concludes:

> As soon as society succeeds in abolishing the *empirical* essence of Judaism – huckstering and its conditions – the Jew becomes *impossible*, because his consciousness no longer has an object . . . The *social* emancipation of the Jew is the *emancipation of society from Judaism*.[27]

Even if we attempt to minimize the antisemitic elements in this thinking, by emphasizing the emancipatory and ethical context in which they appear in Marx's own writings, we cannot fail to see that for his later followers, the actual communists of the twentieth century, including the men in power in the communist states, such ideas would inevitably encourage the perpetuation of ancient hates and foster them where they had been weak or nonexistent.

Notes

1. The word *antisemitism*, coined in nineteenth-century Germany (German, *Antisemitismus*) was originally a disguised way of expressing the writer's real meaning. Hatred was cloaked in pseudoscientific language by the reference to "Semitism," a concept corresponding to nothing in the real world. Antisemites are hostile to *Jews*, not to "Semitism." Over the years, different interpretations of the word have led to different spellings in English, of which the most widely used is probably "anti-Semitism." The pioneering author James Parkes always believed that it should be spelled "antisemitism" in English, without a hyphen, as in German. (The German initial capital is simply the result of the practice of capitalizing all nouns in written German.) He thought that the word should be used to designate the hating attitude of antisemitics, and should not be dignified with a capital, while further currency should not be given to the phony concept of Semitism by separating it from the rest of the word by means of a hyphen, and giving it a capital letter. Some careful writers follow him in this spelling. I believe it would be the best solution, if sufficient agreement could be obtained.
2. YHWH is a conventional transliteration of the four Hebrew consonants of the name of God, not to be pronounced by Jews, and usually represented in the English versions by "the LORD," corresponding to the Hebrew Adonai, which is actually read where these consonants are found in the text. (In Hebrew Bibles, the vowels of Adonai are placed under the four letters of the original divine name. When a late medieval Christian writer, ignorant of this practice, encountered such texts, he thought the divine name was Jehovah, which is approximately how the resulting word, as it seemed to him to be, would have sounded. Of course, the biblical writers never called God Jehovah.) Though in early times it

must have been pronounced more freely, and forms of it seem to enter into personal names, by Jesus' time it was pronounced only once a year on the Day of Atonement, within the Most Holy place. The custom now growing up among Christian writers of spelling out a vocalized form of the consonantal name (which is by no means certainly correct) is offensive to observant Jews and should be avoided.

3. The term *deicide* has been used for much of Christian history as a description of the Jews. Literally, it means God-killing. Of course, God cannot be killed. However, since it was believed that the Jews killed Christ and that Christ was God incarnate, it was thought suitable to magnify the supposed crime by the use of this term. Few would now defend it.

4. The table is reproduced in Chapter 6, 204ff.

5. I am here quoting Rosemary Ruether. In her important book *Faith and Fratricide*, (San Francisco: Seabury Press, 1974), she uses the phrase to characterize the Christian view of the behavior of the Jewish people throughout their history, of which the killing of Christ was thought to be the paradigm. In Chapter 6, I will consider her findings at length.

6. On Bauer, Marx, and the twentieth century New Left, see (from a slightly different point of view) the excellent analysis of Shlomo Avineri, "Radical theology, the New Left, and Israel," in *Auschwitz: Beginning of a New Era?*, ed. Eva Fleischner (New York: Ktav, 1977, 241–54; also Milton Himmelfarb, "Response to Shlomo Avineri," in Fleischner, *Auschwitz*, 267–72.

7. Since he was born of a Jewish mother, if she had not yet converted to Christianity by the time he was born Marx would be considered a Jew halachically. However, his own baptism and membership in a Christian church would in any case have constituted him an apostate, a condition from which he could have returned by repentance, without reconversion. But in Orthodox Jewish eyes, he was only in this minimal sense Jewish. As a Jewish apostate, his descent made him potentially, not actually, Jewish.

8. Isaiah Berlin, *Karl Marx: His Life and Environment* (New York: OUP Galaxy Books, 1963), 26ff.

9. E.g., Erich Fromm, foreword to T. B. Bottomore, ed. and trans., *Karl Marx; Early Writings* (New York: McGraw-Hill, 1963), iv–v.

10. Dennis Prager and Joseph Telushkin, *Why the Jews?* (New York: Simon and Schuster, Touchstone Books, 1985), 138.

11. Sidney Hook, *From Hegel to Marx: Studies in the Intellectual Development of Karl Marx* (London: Victor Gollancz, 1936), 278n.

12. Cited by Prager and Telushkin, *Why the Jews?*, 139.

13. Ibid.

14. Prager and Telushkin call them "non-Jewish Jews," following Isaac Deutscher, who uses the term in a positive sense about himself and people like him. They devote a chapter to them. From medieval converts to Christianity to current Jewish apologists for the Arab enemies of Israel, converts from Judaism have been among the most dangerous enemies of the Jewish people.

15. English translations are to be found in Bottomore, *Karl Marx; Early Writings,* 1–40.

16. Berlin, *Karl Marx: His Life and Environment,* 99.

17. *Bruno Bauer on the Jewish Question,* Bottomore, 10.

18. *Bauer on the Capacity of the present-day Jews and Christians to become free,* Bottomore, 32.

19. *The Jewish Question,* Bottomore, 21.

20. Other translators have "haggling," which may convey the idea better.

21. *Capacity*, Bottomore, 34.

22. Ibid.

23. Ibid., 36.

24. Ibid., 37.

25. Ibid.

26. Ibid., 39.

27. Ibid., 40.

An engraving of a priest during the reign of Philip V of France (1316–1322) condemning Jews to be burned at the stake. During the Middle Ages, European Jews were often the victims of expulsion, forced conversion, or execution. (Getty Images)

Cover of a popular French edition of the *Protocols of the Elders of Zion,* entitled "Le Péril Juif." The *Protocols of the Elders of Zion* was a nineteenth century antisemitic forgery purporting to be a report of a Jewish plot to take over the world. 1934. (Institute of Contemporary History and Wiener Library Limited, courtesy of the USHMM Photo Archives)

Antisemitic political cartoon entitled "Rothschild" by the French caricaturist, C. Leandre. The Rothschilds were a wealthy European Jewish family which was viewed by antisemites as part of an international Jewish conspiracy to control the world economy. 1898. (Courtesy of the USHMM Photo Archives)

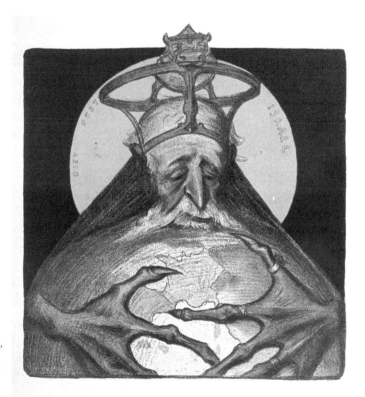

Rothschild

Französische Karikatur von C. Léandre. 1898

This drawing from the late nineteenth century depicts Captain Alfred Dreyfus, a French Jew, standing before his regiment as he is stripped of his sword by an officer. Dreyfus was falsely accused and convicted of passing on French secrets to the Germans in 1894 and sentenced to life imprisonment on Devil's Island. The incident led to widespread antisemitic rioting in France and pogroms in French-ruled Algeria. Dreyfus was exonerated and restored to rank in 1906. On Septermber 7, 1995, the French army officially declared Dreyfus innocent. (AP/Wide World Photos)

In this medieval illustration, reprinted in the Nazi Julius Streicher's antisemitic newspaper, *Der Stürmer* ("The Attacker") the ritual murder of a Christian child by Jews is depicted. Originating in the twelfth century, this antisemitic myth held Jews responsible for the ritual murder of Christian children and the use of their blood during the Passover holiday. This false charge, called a "blood libel," was a pretext for murderous rampages against Jews throughout Europe.

The bottom of the page reads "The Jews are our misfortune," quoting the nineteenth century German historian, Heinrich von Treitschke. This page from *Der Stürmer* was submitted as evidence at the Nuremburg trials of Nazi war criminals. The tribunal sentenced Julius Streicher, who founded *Der Stürmer* in 1923, to death. He was hanged on October 16, 1946. May 1939. (National Archives, courtesy of USHMM Photo Archives)

Robert S. Wistrich **Antisemitism**

INTRODUCTION

"ANTISEMITISM" IS A PROBLEMATIC TERM, first invented in the 1870s by the German journalist Wilhelm Marr to describe the "non-confessional" hatred of Jews and Judaism which he and others like him advocated. The movement which began at that time in Germany and soon spread to neighbouring Austria, Hungary, France and Russia was a self-conscious reaction to the emancipation of the Jews and their entry into non-Jewish society. In that sense it appeared to be a novel phenomenon, since, as the early antisemites were at pains to stress, they were not opposed to Jews on *religious* grounds but claimed to be motivated by social, economic, political or "racial" considerations.

Religious hostility in late nineteenth-century Europe was regarded by many intellectuals as something medieval, obscurantist and backward. There was clearly a need to establish a new paradigm for anti-Jewishness which sounded more neutral, objective, "scientific" and in keeping with the liberal, enlightened *Zeitgeist*. After all, Jews by virtue of their emancipation had become *equal* citizens before the law in European societies which, formally at least, had abandoned discrimination based on religious differences. Antisemitism which grounded itself in racial and ethnic feelings provided a way around this problem. By focusing attention on allegedly permanent, unchanging characteristics of the Jews as a social and national group (which depicted them as being fundamentally 'alien' to their fellow citizens) the antisemites hoped to delegitimise Jewish equality. They sought to restore the social boundaries which had begun to disappear in Europe and they ultimately expected to return the Jews to their earlier pre-emancipated status.

"Antisemitism" – a term which came into general use as part of this politically motivated anti-Jewish campaign of the 1880s – was never directed against "Semites" as such. The term "Semitics" derived from the Biblical Shem, one of Noah's three sons, and des-ignated a group of cognate languages including Hebrew, Arabic, Aramaic, Babylonian, Assyrian and Ethiopic, rather than an ethnic or racial group. Similarly, the contrasting term "Aryan" or "Indo-European," which became popular at this time, referred originally to the Indian branch of the Indo-European languages. Strictly speaking, "Aryans" were people speaking Sanskrit and related languages who had invaded India in pre-historic times and subjugated its indigenous inhabitants. Indians and Iranians were "Aryans" but Germans and North Europeans certainly were *not*, any more than European Jews, who no longer spoke Hebrew, could be meaningfully described as "Semites."

Nevertheless, in the late nineteenth century this pseudo-scientific nonsense became eminently respectable even among the European intellectual élites, so that the distinction between "Aryan" and "Semite" was easily grafted on to the much older distinction between Christian and Jew. As a result, for the last hundred years, the illogical term "antisemitism," which never really meant hatred of "Semites" (for example, Arabs) at all, but rather hatred of Jews, has come to be accepted in general usage as denoting *all* forms of hostility towards Jews and Judaism throughout history.

There is clearly a danger in using antisemitism in this overly generalised way, extending it to all times and places regardless of specific circumstances, differences between historical epochs and cultures, or other factors that might give the term more specificity and critical sharpness. Antisemitism is *not* a natural, meta-historical or a metaphysical phenomenon whose essence has remained unchanged throughout all its manifestations over the centuries. Nor is it an intrinsic part of the psychic structure of Gentiles, a kind of microbe or virus which invariably attacks non-Jews, provoking the "eternal hatred" for the "eternal people." Such a theory, which has some roots in the

Jewish tradition "Esau hates Jacob," the legacy of Amalek, etc.) and was adopted by early Zionists in Eastern Europe such as [Leo] Pinsker, [M.] Lilienblum and [Nachum] Sokolow, is quite unhistorical.

It ignores the fact that Jews have often been welcomed by the surrounding society; that their equality of status and integration was accepted as a binding legal and social principle in many countries during the modern period; and it crucially forgets that Jewish participation in cultural, scientific, economic and political life since the Western Enlightenment has in many respects been a remarkable success story. If antisemitism had really been a "hereditary disease of the Gentiles," or been based on an instinctive racial aversion to Jews (as antisemites sometimes claim), such a development would have been impossible. Admittedly, there has also been a backlash to Jewish integration, influence or success at some points in time – whether in first-century Alexandria and Rome, in medieval Muslim or Christian Spain, in fin-de-siècle Paris and Vienna or in Weimar Germany – but this pattern has definite historical causes and has nothing to do with any theory of innate Gentile antisemitism.

Any empirically valid discussion of antisemitism or hatred of Jews must, in my opinion, first of all come to terms with the problem of its historical continuity and development. This necessarily leads us back to the Hellenistic era, when a widespread Jewish Diaspora first emerged which was quite distinctive in the ancient world. Not only were the Jews the only monotheistic minority in this pagan world, bearers of a doctrine of election which claimed that Judaism was the sole truth, the supreme ethical teaching; not only did they persist in their historic existence as a separate social and religious group; not only did they refuse even to intermingle with the Gentiles because of their own dietary laws, Sabbath observance and prohibition on intermarriage; above all, this unique Diasporic nation which had set itself apart asserted spiritual supremacy over the polytheistic majority.

There is nothing surprising in the fact that such special characteristics and claims could provoke the hostility or resentment which one finds in Greek and Latin literature. To some extent this pre-Christian antisemitism looks like the normal, xenophobic prej-

udice which has prevailed between ethno-religious groups during virtually every period of history. But such a plausible conclusion ignores the *unique* character of the Jewish Diaspora, its unusual social cohesion, compactness and religiously sanctioned exclusiveness. This does not mean that the cause of antisemitism lay in the Jews themselves, but it can help us to understand how the peculiar brand of social hostility which we call by this name first arose as *one* possible response (there were of course others, ranging from admiration to indifference) to the reality of Jewish exclusiveness.

Pagan anti-Jewishness is important because it provided fertile soil for its Christian heirs, and it also reminds us that there was a significant form of hostility to Jews in Antiquity which *preceded* the birth of Christianity. Not a few early Christians had, for example, absorbed this Jew-hatred as a consequence of their pagan upbringing. Nevertheless, it is undeniable that Christianity would appear on the stage of history as a *negation* of Judaism in a much deeper sense than its pagan predecessors; that its theological polemics against Judaism were to be vital to its own identity far more than was the case for any other religion or culture. No other religion, indeed, makes the accusation that Christianity has made against the Jews, that they are literally the *murderers* of God. No other religion has so consistently attributed to them a universal, cosmic quality of evil, depicting them as children of the Devil, followers of Antichrist or as the "synagogue of Satan". The fantasies concerning Jews which were developed in medieval Christendom, about their plotting to destroy Christianity, poison wells, desecrate the host, massacre Christian children or establish their world dominion, represent a qualitative leap compared with anything put forward by their pagan precursors. Such charges, beginning with deicide, are peculiarly *Christian*, though in the twentieth century they have been taken up by Islam as well as by secular political religions such as Nazism or Bolshevism which have exploited the fiction of a Jewish world conspiracy.

Thus it is evident that Christian anti-Judaism and antisemitism did add a wholly new theological and *metaphysical* dimension to antisemitism which was absent in its pagan forerunners and quite distinct from the stigmatising or persecution of other minority groups. The pervasive influence of Christianity (from the fourth century A.D.), on government, culture and society led to the marginalisation of the Jews and their institutionalised oppression. The Christian theology which had usurped the Divine Promises to the Jews and proclaimed the Church as God's Chosen Elect, cast Israel in the role of God's forsaken, rejected and abandoned people – condemned to wandering and exile.

In the writings of the Church Fathers the negation of the Jews' religious and cultural values became a central motif. An overwhelmingly negative stereotype of the "deicide people" was transmitted through theological writings, the sermons of the clergy, the mystery and Passion plays, folklore, ballads and the plastic arts. This hostile collective stereotype of a Jewish people bearing the mark of Cain, a nation of Christ-killers and infidels in league with the Devil, became deeply embedded in the Western psyche following the massacres of Jews during the Crusades. During the next few centuries, new and even more irrational myths were added, that of the Jew as a ritual murderer, desecrator of the Host wafer, an agent of Antichrist, usurer, sorcerer and vampire. As Christianity spread among all the peoples of Europe, this devastating image crystallised until it was an integral part of European and Western culture, a fact which more than any other accounts for the pervasiveness of antisemitism to this day.

Jew-hatred no longer required any connection with real human relationships, indeed it no longer needed the presence of Jews at all. The stereotype had acquired a cultural dynamic of its own, as in medieval England after the expulsion of 1290, in Spain after the mass Jewish exodus of 1492, or in the "Judaising" persecutions of Muscovite Russia. Even today, in post-Holocaust societies like Poland, Austria or Rumania where there are very few Jews left, one finds a similar phenomenon of "antisemitism without Jews." Nothing could make clearer the fallacy that antisemitism can be simplistically viewed as a "natural" or even a "pathological" response to a *concrete* Jewish presence, to Jewish activities, behaviour or traditions.

The common denominator in all these societies is of course the impact of the Christian legacy and its

translation over centuries into legalised discrimination, Jewish servitude, ghettoisation and the narrow economic specialisation of Jewry. Even where Jews converted in large numbers, as in late medieval Spain, the descendants of the converts were regarded with hostility and suspicion, leading to the Inquisition and "purity of blood" statutes that pointed the way to modern racial antisemitism. Not even the rise of humanism during the Renaissance and Reformation could successfully throw off the impact of the medieval image of the Jew. A reformer like Erasmus never dreamed of applying his humanist teachings on toleration to the Jews, who simply remained beyond the pale as far as he was concerned. Martin Luther, for his part, reiterated all the medieval myths about Jews, reinforcing rather than undermining them with an apocalyptic fury and vehemence all his own. Thus Luther's assault on the Papacy and the whole fabric of the Catholic Church, instead of liberating the Jews made his Protestant followers more suspicious of them. Had they not refused to convert even after the great German Reformer had revealed to them the pure, unadulterated word of God? Were they not secretly encouraging the "Judaising" Christian sects in Central Europe? Were not the stubborn Jews in league with the Muslim Turks and perhaps even with Rome in seeking to destroy the new Church from within?

If the Reformation failed to bring any diminution of antisemitism, the eighteenth-century Enlightenment offered, at least on the face of things, a more promising prospect. There were Enlightenment writers who condemned the persecution of Jews as a way of attacking Christian intolerance. Their anticlericalism and concern for universal principles of human rights led them to a new conception of the status of the Jews, which found expression in the French Revolution of 1789. The Jews were not to be emancipated as a community but as *individual* human beings, the assumption being that, once oppression was removed, their distinctive group identity would disappear. There was no sympathy among the French revolutionaries for Judaism as such, which was generally viewed in Voltairean terms as a barbarous superstition.

The Enlightenment and the French Revolution

demonstrated that anti-Judaism and antisemitism did not require a specifically Christian source of inspiration and could even be animated by anti-Christian sentiments. Enlightened Europeans and their radical successors in the nineteenth century, on the Left as well as the Right, were nevertheless still influenced by Christian stereotypes when they attacked Judaism or denounced the "Jewish" origins of Christianity. Even wholly secularised antisemites like Voltaire, Bruno Bauer, Richard Wagner and Eugen Dühring always assumed that Christianity was a superior religion to Judaism and did not hesitate to draw on Christian teachings to reinforce their own cultural or racist perspectives. They inherited the pervasiveness of the Christian antagonism to Jewry while no longer believing in its scheme of salvation, which had still retained an overriding commitment to the conversion of the Jews. This development opened up a dangerous situation whose demonic possibilities only became fully apparent with the rise of Nazism. For although Christianity had provided the seedbed on which Nazi racialist doctrines concerning the Jews could flourish, the Church still provided the Jews with an exit. If a Jew converted he was saved. There was no need for the extermination of the Jews because they had their place, even if it was a subordinate and degraded one, in the Christian world-order.

The Nazis took over all the negative anti-Jewish stereotypes in Christianity but they removed the escape clause. There was no longer any way in which even fully assimilated or baptised Jews could flee from the sentence of death which had been passed by the inexorable laws of race. In that sense, the "Final Solution," the purification of a world that was deemed corrupt and evil because of the very existence of the Jews, went beyond even the most radical Christian solution to the "Jewish Question." Hitler and Nazism grew out of a Christian European culture, but that does not mean that Auschwitz was pre-programmed in the logic of Christianity. Indeed, one could argue that the decline of religious belief by removing all moral restraints actually intensified the antisemitism which had been incubated for centuries under its protective shield. If anything, this released an even more virulent Germanic strain of the same virus which ultimately turned on Christianity itself as one of the prime symptoms of the so-called 'Judaisation' of Western civilisation. . . .

ANTISEMITISM IN CENTRAL EUROPE

THE ROLE WHICH JEWS PLAYED in the German-speaking culture of Central Europe from the middle of the nineteenth century until the rise of Hitler was unprecedented in its scale and quality. Indeed it is difficult to imagine the culture of modernity without the contributions of Marx, Freud, Einstein, Kafka, Mahler, Schoenberg, Wittgenstein and many others whose parents or grandparents had only recently been emancipated from life in the ghettos of Central Europe. Without the German-Jewish "symbiosis" there would have been no great cultural peaks like fin-de-siècle Vienna or Berlin during the Weimar Republic. Paradoxically, the Jews became victims of their very success in penetrating and remoulding the agenda and the cultural axes of modernity in Central Europe. Identified by conservative and radical reactionary forces with the credo of liberalism or Marxism – with being standard-bearers of Western ideals of freedom, equality and social democracy – they were fated to be the first victims of the great counter-revolutionary backlash which culminated in National Socialism.

So deeply were Jews implicated in reshaping the culture, economy and politics of societies like Germany and Austria whose democratic traditions were weak and whose own national identity was insecure, that the antisemitism which developed in Central Europe assumed a uniquely racial and extremist quality. Racial antisemitism, grafted on to an older and still powerful Christian legacy of hate, served here to uproot at its very core the modern dream of assimilation, replacing it first with segregation, then expulsion and finally mass extermination of the Jews.

Already in 1819, post-Napoleonic Germany, shaken by economic crisis and political upheaval, had experienced the anti-Jewish outbreaks known as the "Hep! Hep!" riots (a derogatory rallying cry against Jews). The goal of the agitation was to return the Jews to their previous ghetto status, following their entry into certain occupations – such as the civil service and the legal profession – which had been made possible by the Napoleonic conquest of Germany. Not only the mob but also the "educated" burgher classes, university professors like Friedrich Rühs and Jakob Fries, and student leaders, railed against acceptance of Jewish civic equality within a Christian state. A new kind of "Teutomania" came into being, rejecting the ideals of the French Revolution as "alien" to Germany, adopting a mystical cult of the German nation as an *Urvolk* "natural folk," deploring the commercialisation of urban life and attacking the Jews as despoilers of the German people (*Volksausplünderer*).[1] Throughout the nineteenth century German antisemitism would feed on this explosive ideological mix of romanticism, anti-capitalism, *völkisch* nationalism and hatred of Western liberal democracy.

Even radical intellectuals in Germany during the first half of the nineteenth century – like the Young Hegelians, Arnold Ruge, Bruno Bauer and Karl Marx – made, as we have seen, their own distinctive contribution to the subsequent emergence of a secular, anti-Christian antisemitism. They condemned the "fossilised," antihistorical character of Judaism, its religious separatism and its "exploitative" character, which, according to the radical Hegelians, had permeated bourgeois Christian society with a Judaic ethos. This depiction of Judaism as something alien and inferior which has nevertheless succeeded in "Judaising" European society and culture finds its apogee in Richard Wagner's antisemitic tract, "*Das Judentum in der Musik*" (1850). Drawing on both the radical Hegelian and romantic nationalist traditions, Wagner identifies the "spirit of Judaism" with that of modernity – understood not as progress but as an expression of decadence and artistic decline.[2] As it was for the young Marx in the economic arena, so for Wagner, "liberation from Jewry" becomes the goal of redemption in the creative sphere.

But the great composer, one of the most influential antisemites of the modern age, goes much further than his contemporaries in his backlash against Jewry and the "abstract rationalism" which underpins their emancipation. For Jewry's entry into modern society is perceived by Wagner as the infiltration of a wholly alien and antagonistic group whose success symbolises the spiritual and creative crisis of German and European culture. The Jews represent the "evil con-

science of our modern civilisation" or, to quote another phrase much repeated by the Nazis, "the plastic demon of the decline of mankind." They embodied the corrupt, money-making principle of the new bourgeois world which Wagner held responsible for its artistic decay.[3] The modern, educated, assimilated Jew is depicted by Wagner, already in 1850, as "the most heartless of all human beings," alien and apathetic in the midst of a society he does not understand, whose history and evolution are indifferent to him. The Jew, wholly divorced from the *Volksgeist* ("spirit of the race"), has no passion, no soul, no "inner capacity for life," no true music or poetry. He is a cold, loveless, purely cerebral being. Contemporary German-Jewish artists like the composers Felix Mendelssohn and Meyerbeer, the poet Heinrich Heine or the radical writer Ludwig Boerne, are dismissed as arid, sarcastic and self-negating in their life and work.[4] The only redemption from this sterility lies in the "going under" of Jewry, its complete dissolution and disappearance.

Wagner's essentially racist vision of Jewry would have a profound influence on German and Austrian antisemites, including the English-born Houston S. Chamberlain, Lanz von Liebenfels and above all on Adolf Hitler himself. Richard Wagner gave to German antisemitism a metaphysical pseudo-profundity, an aesthetic rationale rooted in the pagan world of classical Greece and a mythical quality which also finds expression in some of his operatic works as well as in his writings. The later Wagner, influenced by the racist philosophy of the French diplomat and historian Comte de Gobineau, is already a theorist of blood purity and the need to cleanse European civilisation from the spiritual and physical pollution of the Jews. In 1881 he writes to Ludwig II of Bavaria: "I hold the Jewish race to be the born enemy of pure humanity and everything noble in it. It is certain that it is running us Germans to the ground, and I am perhaps the last German who knows how to hold himself upright in the face of Judaism, which already rules everything."[5]

It was in the late 1870s, in the decade immediately following formal Jewish emancipation in both Germany and Austria, that such ideas became commonplace and served as the basis for organised political antisemitism in Germany. It was the stock market collapse of 1873 in Vienna and then Berlin which provided the trigger by provoking an economic crisis which adversely affected the lower middle classes. It was against this background that radical German journalists like Otto Glagau and Wilhelm Marr wrote popular antisemitic tracts, and Prussian conservative publicists lashed out against the rule of the National Liberals ("Manchesterism" as it was often called), of Jewish financiers and of the German Jewish-liberal press.[6] Both Glagau and Marr suggested that "the social question is nothing but the Jewish question" and the latter sought in 1879 to create an Antisemitic League – the first of its kind in Europe. His highly pessimistic book *The Victory of Judaism over Germanism* (1879), which put forward the thesis that "Germanism" was lost, since the Jews were already constructing their Jerusalem on the ruins of the new Germany, went through several editions and aroused extensive press comment.[7]

Far more effective than Marr, however, was the Lutheran court-preacher Adolf Stoecker, who in 1879 organised Berlin's first genuine antisemitic movement. Stoecker's bitter critique of Judaism and of modern German Jewry's "domination" of the press and the stock exchange combined traditional Lutheran theology with an anticapitalist appeal designed to win over the working-class to Throne and Altar. Although Stoecker's Christian-Social Party failed in this objective, he remained one of the main propagators of a modern political antisemitism founded on Christian ideology in the Second German Reich.[8] His Catholic counterpart in Vienna, Karl von Vogelsang (an ex-Protestant German expatriate) who founded the conservative newspaper *Das Vaterland* in the 1870s, played a similar role in laying the ideological-political foundations of Austrian antisemitism. Here, too, the assault on the Jews derived from a sharp critique of the Liberal hegemony and capitalistic exploitation of labour, combined with fear of secularising trends in modern society and the resulting decline of Christian belief.

Racial antisemites like Eugen Dühring (a Berlin philosopher and economist), Theodor Fritsch and the Hessian peasant leader Otto Boeckel took an even more intransigent, uncompromising view of the

threat posed by emancipated Jewry to German society.[9] Moreover, they regarded Christianity as itself part of the problem since it was a "Semitic" religion which had imposed the "alien yoke" of the Old and New Testaments on the Germanic race, thereby inhibiting and distorting its natural instincts, its strength, virility and heroic virtues. This racist trend of antisemitism had considerable appeal to university students in Germany and Austria, who in the early 1880s already began to exclude Jews from membership in their fraternities (*Burschenschaften*). In an age of formal equality when Jews had emerged as dangerous competitors in the liberal professions, especially journalism, medicine and law, racism had obvious attractions. It provided a way of reconstructing the social boundaries that had fallen with the ghetto walls – replacing them with new biological criteria based on blood and descent. In a secular, scientific and positivist age, "race" distinctions still had a certain objective, neutral quality to them and seemed more persuasive to many pseudo-intellectuals than outdated Christian theological concepts in which they no longer believed. Above all, the notion of race had a certain finality to it, suggesting that negative Jewish qualities were fixed and unchanging – hence not amenable to assimilation, conversion or any other attempts at social integration.

Anti-Jewish stereotypes had, of course, preceded racial thinking by centuries and existed quite independently of the emergence of this new ideology in the late nineteenth century. One could, like Paul de Lagarde, one of Germany's most prominent Orientalists and Bible scholars, radically negate Jewish existence without espousing racism.[10] De Lagarde, in calling for a Germanic Christianity which would completely eradicate its "Jewish" components, was one of the few nineteenth-century intellectuals to openly favour expulsion or imply approval for the physical destruction of German Jewry.

More influential at the time was the conservative nationalist historian, Heinrich von Treitschke, who had welcomed the Berlin antisemitic movement in 1879 with the famous slogan "The Jews are our misfortune" "(*Die Juden sind unser Unglück*).[11] Von Treitschke gave academic legitimacy and respectability to what had hitherto seemed to be a rather disreputable, vulgar street movement. His demand for the total, unconditional surrender by German Jews of any distinctive Jewish identity did not openly employ racial arguments, but he did suggest that they remained an "alien" element in the German population who were largely to blame for the antisemitic response which their emancipation had aroused. Von Treitschke, like other Prussian conservatives, especially detested the "progressive" role which German Jews had played in promoting liberal ideas, radicalism and Social Democracy. Already in the Second Reich it had become fashionable to blame Jews for the policies of National Liberalism (Lasker, Bamberger), for stock-exchange capitalism (Rothschild, Bleichröder) and for revolutionary Marxism (Marx, Lassalle, Rosa Luxemburg). But what concerned the mandarin class in particular was their sense of Jews intruding into, subverting and ultimately controlling German intellectual and cultural life. This fear was rationalised as a desire to defend the semi-feudal, organic and "idealist" values of Germandom against the vulgar "materialism" with which Jews were supposedly corrupting the new capitalistic Germany. One finds such anxieties echoed across the political spectrum from radical economists like Werner Sombart to conservative monarchists like Houston S. Chamberlain.[12]

It was rare to find a German intellectual like Friedrich Nietzsche, who not only admired the Jews for their spiritual mastery and grandeur, while detesting "the stupidity, crudity and pettiness of German nationalism," but vehemently dissociated himself from the "damnable German antisemitism, this poisonous boil of *névrose nationalé.*"[13] The German philosopher who took an axe to the Christian religion (he was also highly critical of the Jewish "slave rebellion in morals") deplored "these latest speculators in idealism, the anti-Semites, who today roll their eyes in a Christian-Aryan bourgeois manner and exhaust one's patience by trying to rouse up all the horned-beast elements in the people."[14] The problem was essentially a digestive one, for the German type, so Nietzsche believed, was "still weak and indefinite, so it could easily be blurred or extinguished by the stronger race." He had no doubt that the Jews were indeed "the strongest, toughest, and purest race now living in Europe," who could gain mastery over it if

they so wished.[15] Yet, as Nietzsche stressed, they desired nothing but accommodation and absorption, to put an end to their centuries of wandering – to which purpose the German philosopher suggested that "it might be useful and fair to expel the antisemitic screamers from the country."[16]

The German antisemites in Nietzsche's day never constituted a major threat to the established social and political order. Their organisations were too divided among themselves, too limited in their electoral appeal and lacking in charismatic political leaders to obtain more than an ephemeral success at the polls. At the peak of their appeal during the Second Reich there were sixteen antisemitic deputies sitting in the Imperial Parliament – half of them from Hesse.[17] On the eve of the First World War party political antisemitism was clearly declining, but it would be very misleading to measure the impact of anti-Jewish feelings by such a narrow criterion. The influential Conservative Party adopted an openly anti-Jewish paragraph in its Tivoli Programme of 1892 and the ideologically affiliated Agrarian League (Bund der Landwirte) was a powerful ultraconservative and antisemitic pressure group.[18]

If purely antisemitic rabble-rousers like Otto Boeckel, Hermann Ahlwardt and Liebermann von Sonnenberg were ultimately unsuccessful, this was not so true of right-wing, imperialist lobbies like the Pan-Germanic League (Alldeutscher Verband), the Deutschnationaler Handlungs gehilfenverband (a white-collar trade union), the Akademischer Turnerbund (a gymnastics club) or the Verein Deutscher Studenten – an antisemitic students' movement. The impact of such lobbies and interest-groups, imbued with an antiliberal, *völkisch*-national and antisemitic outlook, was considerably greater than that of ephemeral anti-Jewish political parties which rose and fell in accordance with the vagaries of the economy and the political system as a whole.[19] Moreover, as we have seen, organised antisemitism, which had first emerged in Germany after 1873, had a strong underpinning in cultural and religious stereotypes that remained entrenched in almost all sectors of the population. Once this potential was activated by the effects of defeat in the First World War, by inflation, massive economic depression, chronic political instability and the rise of a powerful mass movement of the Right, German antisemitism was rapidly transformed into a formidable political force.

Before 1914 it was, however, in German Austria and above all in Vienna that antisemitism first displayed its vote-catching efficacy. The Jews of Vienna, who formed about 8 per cent of the population, were heavily over-represented in the liberal professions, especially journalism, law and medicine – half of the students in the medical faculty in 1910 were Jewish. The Jews dominated the liberal educated class in fin-de-siècle Vienna and, even more than in Germany at that time, they seemed to be the creators, the critics, the impresarios and managers of German high culture. For Stefan Zweig they contributed nine-tenths of everything important in Viennese culture – an exaggeration, no doubt, but one containing enough truth to arouse the rage of the Austrian antisemites from Lueger to Hitler who denounced the "Judaisation" of the press, art, literature and the theatre. The challenging innovations of Viennese Jews in psychoanalysis (Freud, Adler, Reich), in music (Mahler, Schoenberg), in literature, criticism and philosophy (Schnitzler, Salten, Beer-Hoffmann, Kraus) simply intensified the resentment of many Catholic Austrians.[20] Anti-Jewish theologians like August Rohling, author of the notorious *Der Talmudjude,* and Joseph Deckert railed against a "Semitic" conspiracy of powerful Jews who aimed at the subversion of the Catholic faith and even practised, so they alleged, ritual murder as part of their hatred of Gentiles and insatiable drive for domination in Austria.[21] Antisemitic politicians like Schneider, Gregorig, Pattai, Lueger and Schoenerer disseminated these and other baseless slanders to a mass audience.

To some extent this fin-de-siècle Austrian antisemitism was a displaced reaction against the liberal capitalism which threatened those declining social strata – especially the Viennese artisans – with economic decline into the proletariat. Jewish industrialists and bankers as well as migrant pedlars from Galicia were seen as two sides of the same threat posed by capitalist modernisation to the traditional way of life of the lower middle classes. While the multi-national Habsburg state valued the contribution made by Jewish enterprise to building up the

railroads, financing the coalmines, pioneering sugar-refining, establishing the beer industry, developing the iron and steel industry, the banking system and the metropolitan press, ordinary Austrians resented the dizzying ascent of the Jews in wealth and social status within one generation. It was all too easy and convenient to ascribe this success story to money-grabbing "materialism," dishonesty in business dealings or to a malevolent conspiracy to subjugate and oppress the Catholic majority.

The immensely popular resonance of anticapitalist antisemitism among the Viennese found its best expression in the spectacular career of Karl Lueger, the first democratic politician to triumph anywhere in Europe on an explicitly anti-Jewish platform.[22] Elected Mayor of Vienna in 1897, at the head of the Christian-Social Party, he retained power until his death in 1910 and was the first political role-model for the young Adolf Hitler, who admired him as "the greatest German *Bürgermeister* of all times." Lueger's attack on the Jews was a central part of his general assault on Liberal political hegemony in city politics and later of his defence of bourgeois class interests against the rising Social Democrats – most of whose intellectual leadership was Jewish, beginning with its founder Victor Adler. Lueger denounced Jewish influence in Hungary (coining the abusive term "Judeo-Magyars"), in Austrian banking, industry and commerce, in the Viennese Press, in medicine and the liberal professions. His Christian-Social party called openly for segregation in the school system (though this was never implemented), for banning the immigration of foreign Jews and for the restriction of Jewish influence in public life. Although officially Catholic in its discourse, the party had prominent agitators in its ranks, including Schneider, Gregorig and priests like Father Deckert and Joseph Scheicher, whose populist antisemitism was as incendiary as that of any beer-swilling Pan-German racists. After his election to office in 1897 Lueger himself was more covert in his anti-Jewish rhetoric, limited as he was by Franz Joseph's imperial authority, which upheld the equality of all religious faiths and of all Austrian citizens before the law. Nevertheless, Lueger did not disown the more extremist Jew-baiters in his movement and did on occasion resort to racist remarks as well as carrying on surreptitious discrimination against Jewish employees of the municipality.[23]

Although himself the holder of an academic degree, Dr Lueger did not hesitate to indulge in the crass anti-intellectualism so often directed by the more plebeian members of his party against Jews, free thinkers or socialists. Thus he frequently denigrated the universities and medical schools for being "Jew-infested" strongholds of atheism, free thinking, revolutionary subversion and the undermining of Christian morality. At the time of the 1905 Russian revolution, he threatened the Jewish community that if they supported the Social Democrats a pogrom could result. "I warn the Jews most expressly; for the same thing could perhaps happen as in Russia. We in Vienna are not anti-Semites [sic!], we are certainly not inclined to murder and violence. But if the Jews should threaten our fatherland, then we will show no mercy."[24]

The Christian-Social Party, he declared on another occasion, was determined that the "Christian *Volk*" and not the alien Jews should be masters in their own house. His movement advocated "Christian solidarity" accompanied by an economic boycott of Jewish businesses to achieve this end, though such calls were rarely observed. It constantly campaigned against the *Verjudung* ("Judaisation") of Austrian culture, though here too it met with little practical success. But it was more effective in implanting antisemitism in the hearts and minds of the younger generation, in making its discourse respectable and normal in public life, in linking it with a traditional, sentimental, religiously oriented Austrian Catholic patriotism.[25]

Lueger's conservative antisemitism was not incompatible with the toleration of baptised Jews or collaboration with wealthy, powerful Jewish capitalists whom the municipality needed to help fund its more ambitious projects for modernising Vienna. This pragmatic, opportunist approach had always been typical of Lueger's politics and it did not change after he had embraced antisemitism as an integral part of his platform and ideology. He understood the value of antisemitism as a tactical weapon for attaining power but also recognised, unlike many of his rivals and his more extreme supporters, its limits once in office. His "war against the Jews" was carried out

within the framework of a conciliatory, supranational Habsburg dynasty which deplored antisemitism as the politics of the street; mass violence within this *Rechisstaat* (a state based on law) was rare, except in moments of crisis in Hungary, Galicia or Bohemia. There were no major economic crises such as characterised the post-1918 era in Austria. Nor were there any pogroms in Habsburg Vienna despite the hysterical diatribes of the more rabid Austrian antisemites. Viennese Jews were not stripped of their civil rights; there was no expropriation of Jewish wealth and, for all the anxiety and insecurity which antisemitism aroused, Jews continued to make a brilliant contribution to German-Austrian culture.

Nevertheless, Austrian antisemitism – that of Lueger and of his great rival, the Pan-German Georg von Schoenerer – provided the first model for Adolf Hitler's own war against the Jews, demonstrating to him its possibilities as a method of mobilising the masses against a single, highly visible and vulnerable enemy. It was in pre-war Vienna that the young Hitler would discover the "Jewish Question" and begin to link it inexorably with capitalism, Marxism and the struggle for existence of the German nation. From Austrian Pan-Germanism Hitler took the biological, racist foundation of his world-view, and from Lueger he would learn how to use antisemitism as a political tool.[26]

Notes

1. Eleanore Sterling, *Judenhass: Die Anfänge der politischen Antisemitismus in Deutschland (1815–1850),* (Frankfurt a.M, 1969).
2. O. D. Kulka, "Richard Wagner und die Anfänge des modernen Antisemitismus," *Bulletin des Leo Baeck Instituts,* 4, (1961), 281–300 on the connection between Wagner's political radicalism and racial antisemitism. See also Hartmut Zelinski, *Richard Wagner – ein deutsches Thema. Eine Dokumentation zur Wirkungsgeschichte Richard Wagners, 1876–1976* (Vienna/Berlin, 1983).
3. R. Wagner, *Das Judenthum in der Musik* (Leipzig, 1869), 10–12.
4. *Ibid.,* 31–32.
5. Letter to Ludwig II, 22.XI.1881. Quoted in J. Katz, *The Darker Side of Genius: Richard Wagner's Antisemitism* (London, 1986), 115. Katz's book is useful but unfortunately fails to grasp the passion and depth of Wagner's hostility to Jews. On this point, see Margaret Brearley, "Hitler and Wagner: the Leader, the Master and the Jews," *Patterns of Prejudice,* Vol. 22, No. 2 (1988), 3–21.

6. Paul W. Massing, *Rehearsal for Destruction: A Study of Political Antisemitism in Imperial Germany* (New York, 1949); P. G. J. Pulzer, *The Rise of Political Antisemitism in Germany and Austria* (London, 1988, revised ed.).

7. See the informative but otherwise disappointing biography by Moshe Zimmermann, *Wilhelm Marr: The Patriarch of Antisemitism* (New York, 1986).

8. Adolf Stoecker, *Christlich-Sozial: Reden und Aufsätze* (Berlin, 1890, 2nd ed.); Hans Engelmann, *Kirche am Abgrund: Adolf Stoecker und seine antijüdische Bewegung* (Berlin, 1984), 120–72.

9. U. Tal. *Christians and Jews in Germany: Religion, Politics and Ideology in the Second Reich, 1870–1914* (Ithaca/London 1975); Birgitta Magge, *Rhetorik des Hasses: Eugen Dühring und die Genese seines antisemitischen Wortschatzes* (Neuss, 1977).

10. Fritz Stern deals with de Lagarde in *The Politics of Cultural Despair: A Study of the Rise of German Ideology* (Berkeley, 1961).

11. For Treitschke's articles and the response which they drew, see W. Boehlich (ed.), *Der Berliner Antisemitismusstreit* (Frankfurt a.M, 1965).

12. Werner Sombart, *Die Zukunft der Juden* (Leipzig, 1912), 52; Paul Mendes-Flohr; "Werner Sombart's 'The Jews and Modern Capitalism': An Analysis of Its Ideological Premises." *LBIYB*, XXI (1976), 87–107. Also Geoffrey C. Field, *Evangelist of Race: The Germanic Vision of Houston S. Chamberlain* (New York, 1981).

13. *Basic Writings of Nietzsche*. Translated and edited with commentaries by Walter Kaufmann (1968), appendix, 798.

14. *Ibid.*, 594.

15. *Ibid.*, 377.

16. *Ibid.* Nietzsche does, of course, also criticise the Jews, whose historic legacy he denounced as being responsible for "the slave-revolt in morals." This aspect of Nietzsche's approach to Judaism was as distorted as later efforts to turn him into a spiritual godfather of German Nazism.

17. Robert S. Wistrich, *Socialism and the Jews: The Dilemmas of Assimilation in Germany and Austria-Hungary* (London/Toronto, 1982).

18. Hans Jürgen Pühle, *Agrarische Interessenpolitik und preussischer Konservatismus im wilhelminischen Reich* (Hanover, 1966).

19. Werner Jochmann, "Struktur und Funktion des deutschen Anti-semitismus," in W. E. Mosse and A. Paucker (eds.) *Juden im Wilhelminischen Deutschland 1890–1914* (Tübingen, 1976), 389–477.

20. Robert S. Wistrich, *The Jews of Vienna in the Age of Franz Joseph* (London, 1989).

21. On the Rohling affair, I. A. Hellwing, *Der konfessionelle Anti-semitismus im 19. Jahrhundert in Österreich* (Vienna, 1972).

22. Robert S. Wistrich, "Karl Lueger and the Ambiguities of Viennese Antisemitism," *Jewish Social Studies* (1983), 45, 251–62.

23. Richard S. Geehr, *Karl Lueger: Mayor of Fin de Siècle Vienna* (Detroit, 1990), 293.

24. *Ibid.*, 200.

25. Wistrich, *op. cit.*, 258–61.

26. Robert S. Wistrich, "Georg von Schoenerer and the Genesis of Modern Austrian Antisemitism," *The Wiener Library Bulletin* (1976), Vol. XXIX. New Series, Nos. 39/40, 21–29.

Richard Wagner **Judaism in Music**

THE JEW SPEAKS THE LANGUAGE OF THE COUNTRY IN whose midst he dwells from generation to generation, but he speaks it always as an alien . . . The general circumstance that the Jew speaks modern European languages merely as learnt, and not as mother tongues, must necessarily debar him from all capability of therein expressing himself idiomatically, independently, and conformably with his nature. A language, with its expression and its evolution, is not the work of scattered units, but of an historical community: only he who has unconsciously grown up within the bond of this community, takes also any share in its creations. But the Jew has stood outside the pale of any such community, stood solitary with his Jehovah in a splintered, soilless stock, to which all self-sprung evolution must stay denied, just as even the peculiar (Hebrew) language of that stock has been preserved for him merely as a thing, defunct. Now, to make poetry in a foreign tongue has hitherto been impossible, even to geniuses of highest rank. Our whole European art and civilisation, however, has remained to the Jew a foreign tongue; for, just as he has taken no part in the evolution of the one, so he has taken none in that of the other; but at most the homeless wight has been a cold, nay more, a hostile looker-on. In this Speech, this Art, the Jew can only after-speak and after-patch – not truly make a poem of his words, an artwork of things. In particular does the purely physical aspect of the Jewish mode of speech repel us. Throughout an intercourse of two millennia with European nations, Culture has not succeeded in breaking the remarkable stubbornness of the Jewish *naturel* as regards the peculiarities of Semitic pronunciation. The first thing that strikes our ear as quite outlandish and unpleasant, in the Jew's production of the voice-sounds, is a creaking, squeaking, buzzing snuffle: add thereto an employment of words in a sense quite foreign to our nation's tongue, and an arbitrary twisting of the structure of our phrases – and this mode of speaking acquires at once the character of an intolerably jumbled blabber; so that when we hear this Jewish talk, our attention dwells involuntarily on its repulsive *how*, rather than on any meaning of its intrinsic *what*. How exceptionally weighty is this circumstance, particularly for explaining the impression made on us by the music-works of modern Jews, must be recognized and borne in mind before all else. If we hear a Jew speak, we are unconsciously offended by the entire want of purely-human expression in his discourse: the cold indifference of its particular "blubber" never by any chance rises to the ardour of a higher, heartfelt passion. If, on the other hand, we find *ourselves* driven to this more heated expression, in converse with a Jew, he will always shuffle off, since he is incapable of replying in kind. Never does the Jew excite himself in mutual interchange of feelings with us, but – so far as we are concerned – only in the altogether special egoistic interest of his vanity or profit.

Richard Wagner, "Judaism in Music" **Prose Works**, Translated by William Ashton Ellis, 8 vols. London: Kegan Paul, Trench, Trübner and Co., 1894. vol. 3, 82ff.

RICHARD WAGNER **What Is German?**

IN THIS SINGULAR PHENOMENON, this invasion of the German nature by an utterly alien element, there is more than meets the eye. Here, however, we will only notice that other nature in so far as its conjunction with us obliges us to become quite clear as to what we have to understand by the "German" nature which it exploits.—It everywhere appears to be the duty of the Jew, to show the nations of modern Europe where haply there may be a profit they have overlooked, or not made use of. . . . Adorable and beautiful is that foible of the German's which forbade his coining into personal profit the inwardness and purity of his feelings and beholdings, particularly in his public and political life: that a profit here, as well, was left unused, could be recognisable to none but a mind which misunderstood the very essence of the German nature. . . . The Jew set right this bungling of the German's, by taking German intellectual labour into his own hands; and thus we see an odious travesty of the German spirit upheld today before the German Folk, as its imputed likeness. It is to be feared, ere long the nation may really take this simulacrum for its mirrored image: then one of the finest natural dispositions in all the human race were done to death, perchance forever.

We have to inquire how to save it from such a shameful doom, and therefore first of all will try to signalize the characteristics of genuine "German" nature.—

Once more let us briefly, but plainly recite the outer, historical documents of German nature. "Deutsche" is the title given to those Germanic races which, upon their natal soil, retained their speech and customs. . . . In rugged woods, throughout the lengthy winter, by the warm hearth-fire of his turret-chamber soaring high into the clouds, for generations he keeps green the deeds of his forefathers; the myths of native gods he weaves into an endless web of sagas. He wards not off the influences incoming from abroad; he loves to journey and to look; but, full of the strange impressions, he longs to reproduce them; he therefore turns his steps toward home, for he knows that here alone will he be understood: here, by his homely hearth, he tells what he has seen and gone through outside. Romanic, Gaelic, French books and legends he transposes for himself. . . . But his is no more idle gaping at the Foreign, as such, as purely foreign; he wills to understand it "Germanly." He renders the foreign poem into German, to gain an inner knowledge of its content. Herewith he strips the Foreign of its accidentals, its externals, of all that to him is unintelligible, and makes good the loss by adding just so much of his own externals and accidentals as it needs to set the foreign object plain and undefaced before him. In these his natural endeavours he makes the foreign exploit yield to him a picture of its purely-human motives. . . .

Who would seize the wondrous individuality, the strength and meaning of the German spirit in one incomparably speaking image, let him cast a searching glance upon the else so puzzling, well-nigh unaccountable figure of Music's wonder-man *Sebastian Bach*. He is the history of the German spirit's inmost life throughout the gruesome century of the German Folk's complete extinction. See there that head, insanely muffled in the French full-bottomed wig; behold that master, a wretched organist and cantor, slinking from one Thuringian parish to another, puny places scarcely known to us by name; see him so unheeded, that it required a whole century to drag his works from oblivion; finding even Music pinioned in an art-form the very effigy of his age, dry, stiff, pedantic, like wig and pigtail set to notes: then see what a world the unfathomably great Sebastian built out from these elements! I merely point out that Creation; for it is impossible to denote its wealth, its sublimity, its all-embracing import, through any manner of comparison. If, however, we wish to account for

RICHARD WAGNER, "WHAT IS GERMAN?" **PROSE WORKS**, TRANSLATED BY WILLIAM ASHTON ELLIS, 8 VOLS. LONDON: KEGAN PAUL, TRENCH, TRÜBNER AND CO., 1894. VOL. 4, 158FF.

the amazing rebirth of the German spirit on the field of poetic and philosophic Literature too, we can do so only by learning from Bach what the German spirit is in truth, where it dwelt, and how it restless shaped itself anew, when it seemed to have altogether vanished from the world. . . .

Yet Bach's spirit, the German spirit, stepped forth from the sanctuary of divinest Music, the place of its new-birth. When Goethe's *Götz* appeared, its joyous cry went up: "That's German!" And beholding his likeness, the German also knew to shew himself, to shew the world, what Shakespeare is, whom his own people did not understand. These deeds the German spirit brought forth of itself, from its inmost longing to grow conscious of itself. And this consciousness told it – what it was the first to publish to the world – *that the Beautiful and Noble came not into the world for sake of profit, nay, not for the sake of even fame and recognition.* And everything done in the sense of this teaching is "*deutsch*"; and *therefore* is the German great; and *only what is done in that sense, can lead Germany to greatness.*

MARION PRITCHARD

THE NETHERLANDS... 1942 – Marion Pritchard was studying to become a social worker when Germany invaded the Netherlands. When it gradually became clear that the Jews were going to be persecuted, she began to think about how to help.

In 1942 she was asked by a friend, "Miek," who was also a member of the organized resistance, to find a hiding place for a Jewish friend and his three small children. When Marion could not find a place, Miek persuaded his mother-in-law to let Marion, Fred Pollak, and his children Lex, Tom, and Erica move into the servants' quarters of her house in the country. They stayed there until the end of the war.

They had many scary episodes. The most traumatic event occurred when a local Dutch Nazi policeman led three German Nazis to the house. They did not find the hiding place, but had learned that sometimes if they came back an hour later the Jews would come out of their hiding place and could easily be found. The baby started to cry so Marion let the children out of hiding. The Dutch Nazi returned and Marion felt she had no choice except to kill him.

After the war, Marion joined the United Nations Relief and Rehabilitation Administration and worked in a Jewish Displaced Persons camp in Bavaria.

Photo of Marion Pritchard with Erica Pollak.
(JFR Photo Archives)

CHAPTER 2 **World War I and the Interwar Period**

Adolf Hitler at a Nazi party rally, Nuremberg, Germany. Circa 1928. (Heinrich Hoffman Collection, courtesy of National Archives)

Debórah Dwork **Introduction**

"**I HAVE NOT BEEN IN A BATTLE;** nor near one, nor heard one from afar, nor seen the aftermath. I have questioned people who have been in battle – my father and father-in-law among them; have walked over battlefields, here in England, in Belgium, in France, and in America; have often turned up relics of the fighting . . . I have read about battles, of course, have talked about battles, have been lectured about battles and, in the last four or five years, have watched battles in progress, on the television screen. I have seen a good deal of other, earlier battles of this century on newsreel, some of them convincingly authentic, as well as much dramatized feature film and countless static images of battle: photographs and paintings and sculpture of varying degrees of realism. But I have never seen a battle. And I grow increasingly convinced that I have very little idea about what a battle can be like."[1] With this passage, the military historian John Keegan began his book, *The Face of Battle.* Keegan went on to analyze three military encounters, including the bloody and infamous Battle of the Somme during World War I, during which the British lost some 60,000 men, 21,000 of whom were killed in the first few minutes.

World War I wreaked havoc and destruction throughout the length and breadth of Europe. Nearly every European country was economically impoverished, politically unstable, and socially in turmoil by the end of the war, and the situation did not improve thereafter. France, Britain, and Germany were bled white from the loss of men of military age, and neither the victors nor the vanquished were satisfied with the postwar peace. At the time, it was called the "war to end all wars." We now know that 1914 marked the beginning of what a number of historians think of as a thirty-one-year war that ended in 1945. Yet, as John Keegan has rightly observed, we cannot imagine even a single battle.

The aim of this chapter is to illustrate the importance of World War I for contemporary Europeans – politicians and public alike – and to delineate just a few of its bitter consequences. The postwar period was a time of tremendous political, social, and economic turmoil. Many of the structures that had governed Europe were overthrown, and a great number of people looked either to the extreme right or the far left of the political spectrum for stability and inspiration. Within fifteen years after the First World War, the Russian Revolution was fought, the fascist leader Benito Mussolini came to power in Italy, and Hitler's National Socialist (Nazi) party came to power in Germany. World War I and the interwar period were the seedbed of Nazism. Why did Germans turn to this form of government; why were they attracted to and persuaded by Nazi ideas and plans? Why, in short, were they so frustrated by life under a democratic

Many of the structures that had governed Europe were overthrown after World War I and a great number of people looked either to the extreme right or the far left of the political spectrum for stability and inspiration.

government that they turned to Hitler? And why did their European neighbors do so little to stop their aggression and militarism?

France, Germany's traditional enemy, was exhausted by World War I. In an excerpt from Eugen Weber's social history of France during the 1930s, *The Hollow Years*, Weber has described the French post-war reaction to the great loss of young lives in uniform: the war-weariness, and the resolve not to put their men in uniform again. As Weber has made poignantly clear, what the French wanted most was to avoid another conflict with Germany.

If the French, who had won the war, were far from jubilant, the vanquished Germans were overburdened and angry. When Germany lost the war, it also lost whatever stability it had enjoyed for half a century. Disillusioned by military defeat and desperate for an armistice, German politicians forced their emperor to abdicate. Before a constitution could be written or the details worked out, one of these politicians proclaimed the birth of a republic: the Weimar Republic. Masses of Germans, however, felt humiliated by the terms of the Treaty of Versailles, which the allies imposed on them at the conclusion of World War I. The politicians, they believed, had stabbed the soldiers in the back by coming to terms with France, Britain, and the United States; they had sold out. As Debórah Dwork and Robert Jan van Pelt show in an excerpt from their book *Auschwitz*, the Nazis added an extra element to this theme: it was sabotage by the Jews.

The fifteen-year history of the Weimar Republic was marked by poverty and despair. In *Germany and the Germans*, published in 1931 and written a few years earlier, Eugen Diesel captured his countrymen's experience of the disastrous war and the demoralization that followed. For Germans, the postwar period was bleak, and the future held little promise. They felt, as Klaus Fischer put it in his book, *Nazi Germany*, "the trauma of military defeat and economic ruin."

Germans fought over solutions to such practical problems as unemployment, and to what they felt to be an international assault on their identity and integrity as Germans. One of these solutions, the Artaman "back to the land" movement (discussed in the excerpt from *Auschwitz*) need not have been sinister. Fed up with the complexities of city life and seeking a simple, unsophisticated existence, many young people sought refuge in the countryside. But their utopian vision harbored the shadow of disaster, although they themselves did not yet realize how vicious their ideology was. The land for which they yearned was in the east. Germany had fought a war on two fronts, one in the west and a second in the east. And while the German army surely had been defeated on the western front, the Artamans and millions of their countrymen felt their army had won on the eastern front. As a result of the Treaty of Versailles, however, that territory now belonged to Poland. And who, according to the Artaman Society and many other Germans, was entitled to this land? Certainly not the Poles; rather, only those who were

> Masses of Germans, however, felt humiliated by the terms of the Treaty of Versailles, which the allies imposed on them at the conclusion of World War I.

physically perfect and genetically Germanic. *Lebensraum* (living space) for the *Volk* (the German people) was their slogan.

Polish citizens of the newly re-created Poland were as nationalistic as their German neighbors. What they wanted was a Poland for the Poles: a nation-state of one people with a shared language, culture, and history, not a multicultural society. But when the borders of their new country finally were set, Ukrainians, Byelorussians, Jews, and Germans accounted for one-third of the population. These minority groups demanded minority rights – autonomy, if not independence. Ezra Mendelsohn has analyzed the Poles' dilemma in a chapter of his book, *The Jews of East Central Europe Between the Wars.* The Polish Socialists counseled tolerance. The right-wing Endek movement became ever more strident in their pro-nationalist and anti-minority, especially antisemitic, policies. In 1935, Poland veered sharply to the right. In that same chapter of his book, Mendelsohn has also described the attempt by Poland's multifaceted Jewish community to shape its identity in the ever more threatening political and economic climate of the inter-war years. And in the book's Introduction, he offers a glimpse of the Jewish experience during that period in some of the other countries of Eastern Europe.

Italy had embraced ultra-right-wing politics over a decade earlier. Like France, Germany, and Poland, Italy too faced poverty, unemployment, and political instability after World War I, and Benito Mussolini and his National Fascist Party (PNF) seemed to offer the country progress, development, and action. Mussolini would return Rome to its ancient glory; Italy would lead the world in science, industry, and technology, and Fascists would drain the marshes and grow wheat for bread – indeed, under Mussolini even the trains would run on time. The Fascist,

Benito Mussolini reviewing his troops on the seventh anniversary of the *fascisti* march on Rome. Mussolini, who sought to revitalize Italy after World War I, came to power in 1922. His fascist program influenced Adolf Hitler's politics of absolute power. Italy and Germany fought as allies in World War II. November 6, 1929. (AP/Wide World Photos)

Benito Mussolini, and the Nazi, Adolf Hitler, both used a nostalgic view of a glorious past to whet the popular appetite for their political parties' programs. And they agreed on many issues: high birth rates (for Italians and Germans, respectively), more land, the value and virtue of militarism. Most of all, they both demanded absolute power. Adults were won, wooed, or intimidated. Children were socialized, politically socialized, and indoctrinated. The state school system and the mandatory

Social and political turbulence were the hallmarks of interwar Europe. It was in the context of these conditions that Germany invaded Poland on September 1, 1939, and World War II began.

state-run youth groups offered young people precisely what their impoverished parents could not give them: food, clothing, school supplies, summer camp, and vocational and professional training. In an excerpt from her book, *Believe, Obey, Fight*, Tracy Koon shows how Italian children were socialized into becoming fascists, taught to think, act, write, even dress in accordance with fascist ideas, through the public education system and the youth-group arm of the Fascist party.

Taken together, these readings indicate the many reverberations of the First World War within postwar European society, and they underscore that most of Europe was in turmoil. The readings in this chapter focus on Germany, France, Poland, and Italy, but social and political turbulence were the hallmarks of interwar Europe. Indeed, large chunks of the continent were politically reshaped and reconfigured: the establishment of the Soviet Union in the wake of the Russian Revolution; the dissolution of Serbia, Montenegro, and the Austro-Hungarian Empire; and the creation of the sovereign states of Hungary, Czechoslovakia, Yugoslavia, Lithuania, Latvia, Estonia, and Poland.

It was in the context of these conditions that Germany invaded Poland on September 1, 1939, and World War II began.

Note

1. John Keegan, *The Face of Battle* (London and New York: Penguin, 1988), 13.

Eugen Weber A Wilderness Called Peace

Solitudinem faciunt, pacem appellant
They make a wilderness, and call it peace
—Tacitus

THE 1930s begin in August 1914. For fifty-one months thereafter, 1,000 Frenchmen were killed day after day, nearly 1 of every 5 men mobilized, 10.5 percent of the country's active male population. That was more than any other Western belligerent would suffer: The British counted half as many dead and missing, Germans and Austro-Hungarians, who had incurred heavy losses, never got as far as 10 percent. About 1,400,000 French lost their lives; well over 1,000,000 had been gassed, disfigured, mangled, amputated, left permanent invalids. Wheelchairs, crutches, empty sleeves dangling loosely or tucked into pockets became common sights. More than that had suffered some sort of wound: Half of the 6,500,000 who survived the war had sustained injuries. Most visible, 1,100,000, were those who had been evidently diminished and were described as *mutilés*, a term the dictionary translates as "maimed" or "mangled," and English usage prefers to clothe in a euphemism: "disabled."

Precise figures are unavailable, and anyway, on that sort of scale, they mean either too little or too much. Statistics, above all, offer general impressions that do not take stock of particular cases, like that of Eugène Haensler, a priest, gassed in the war, who died only in 1930 of tuberculosis contracted as a result of his poisoning. Or the amnesiac veteran whom the press discovered in 1936 living in Rodez and featured as "The Living Unknown Soldier." Or the Provençal infantryman Jean Giono, one of eleven members of his company to survive Verdun. Or Jean Giraudoux, wounded several times but wounded more severely still by clumsy surgeons, living for years with enteritis, diarrhea, nervous nightmares, to note: "fatigue, fatigue. . . ." Heroic endurance left behind postheroic letdown and depression.[1]

There was Eugène Dabit, who volunteered for the artillery in 1916, when he was eighteen. Appalled by the physical and moral horrors of the war, he tried to get out of it by simulating madness, then almost threw himself under a train (but didn't), finally came through with only a superficial wound. Returned to civilian life, he remained, as he said, "*malade de la guerre*" – sick with the war, for the rest of his life. "Almost every night since my demobilization, images of the front came back to haunt me, and – a still worse nightmare – I dreamed that hostilities were starting again."[2] Dabit wrote several novels, one of which, *Hôtel du Nord* (1929), brought him real success even before Marcel Carné turned it into a film. But through the thirties his private journals reflect a constant dread: War is coming. Can he escape? In August 1936, thirty-eight years old, Dabit made his escape: to death.

For the unafraid, another kind of deterioration lay in wait. In 1934 Roger Vercel, a frontline officer for four years, won the Prix Goncourt for *Le Capitaine Conan,* the story of a true fighter hero who ends up gross and full of bile, drinking himself to death in a provincial dump. It was people like him who won the war, Conan tells the narrator. "If you should run across them, look closely: they'll be like me." Not all of them were. Far from it. But in the *Gazette des tribunaux,* France's *Police Gazette,* case after case of officers, once decorated for their bravery, now dragged into court for fraud or other crimes, bears out Conan's bitterness.[3] . . .

As one might expect, few veterans cherished warm feelings for the kind of conflict they had by luck escaped or for the military institutions they had enjoyed but little. They had gone off to a fresh and joyous war. They were to be maimed or killed in ignoble butcheries like that which, between July and November 1916, killed 1,200,000 Germans, French, and British soldiers in the cold, rain, and mud of the Somme: more than at Verdun. Most of them, like the future *inspecteur des finances* Jean Appert, who served in the infantry, remembered their service as a massacre and their superiors as stupid. When they marched past, lapels clinking with decorations, they refused to march in step, the better to assert that they were no longer soldiers. Patriotic still, they were not militaristic. They were against military authority, against regular officers, against the murderous nonsense of war. In 1930 a member of the prime minister's cabinet reported to André Tardieu that they were "as intoxicated with pacifism as the [political] parties."[4] As a privileged young woman, the daughter of a conservative senator, noted on the eve of the following conflict, "Father served in the other war. His memory of it is so awful that he speaks of it only reluctantly, that is never. Mother, who was left alone with four children, has kept a sort of grudge ever since. They don't really believe in another war. It seems much too crazy."[5]

The land around them bore witness to the madness. In 1935, when Jean de Lattre, the future general, drove to Metz with his wife, Simone, to take over the 151st Regiment of Infantry, they passed through the Verdun area, where in 1916 a thousand soldiers died per square meter and where de Lattre himself had fought. Nineteen years after the carnage, vast areas, Simone noted, lacked all vegetation; the landscape looked chaotic, nightmarish, marked by a few blackened tree trunks and great lunar craters full of stagnant water. By then the Douaumont ossuary, built with privately raised funds and with American aid, offered a cold reminder of four hundred thousand dead. But for many years after the Armistice the great swath, four hundred miles long, ten or twenty miles wide, where the front had been lay desert, desolate. The ruins ran from the North Sea to Champagne and beyond. A decade barely sufficed for the rebuilding, and some sites that once were villages remained no more than place-names on a post. In the 1930s, when the war zone had been largely rebuilt, 10 percent of the dwellings and 10 percent of the factories in it had not been raised back. In 1933 a businessman from Toledo, Ohio, visiting the north of France was struck by the "devastation." In the Ardennes in 1938 one man had only just finished restoring his war damage. And cases of housing damage suffered over twenty years before were still before the courts in 1939.[6] The First World War was very

contemporary history even as the Second loomed ahead.

By the time reconstruction had been officially completed, in 1931, every village and every town in France had raised its monument to the fallen on which interminable lists of names, sometimes two or three per family, marched in dour columns. There are plenty of villages today where the number of World War dead is greater than that of the men remaining there.[7] . . .

Between 1914 and 1918 over thirty-five thousand teachers had been mobilized, more than a quarter of the teaching force. Of these, nearly one in four had died. Léon Emery, a militant pacifist, remembered that of his normal school class of thirty in pre-1914 Lyons, ten had been killed and several more severely injured. No other professional group seems to have known such losses. Be it the butchery, be it an older antimilitarist tradition or equally well-entrenched hostility to the bourgeois state, most French schoolteachers between the wars were pacifist. Before 1914 they had taught love of the fatherland, which could well mean laying down one's life for it. Now they revised their creed, and their schoolbooks, too. Schoolbooks had to be expurgated, and editors had to join in the task, else teachers – free to select their texts – would refuse to use books written on the wrong lines.[8]

Most teachers' unions were dedicated to weaning children from chauvinism and any glorification of war by teaching a new kind of history and civics that would inculcate respect for humankind and love of peace. The first step in this had to be a revision of the old, dark vision of the German neighbors traditionally presented as malevolent and aggressive. This theme had been discredited by the exaggerations of wartime propaganda. What we call brainwashing the French describe as headstuffing – *bourrage de crâne*. The trouble with this sort of thing, whatever you call it, is that excess breeds counterexcess. Intellectuals had learned that descriptions of enemy evil were not to be trusted. They were going to treat news from Nazi Germany with the same skepticism. Minds that were truly enlightened rejected the image of an evil Germany, assimilated criticism of Germans to warmongering, and suspected those who blamed Germans for evils perpetrated in the present as much as those who blamed them for evils past.[9]

Tales of villainy had been trumped up or exaggerated; now their kind was condemned as calumny. Talk of heroism had been overdone; now it was dismissed as a big lie. Calls for patriotism had led to chauvinism and then to butcheries; now they were denounced as dupery. It was time for history to be brought up-to-date, rewritten in a more equitable vein and one more conducive to international understanding. In the mid-1920s a fair-minded historian, Jules Isaac, revised Albert Malet's widely used history texts for secondary schools. The patriotic *revanchard* Malet had been killed in Artois in 1915. Son and grandson of army officers, Isaac, who had been wounded and decorated at Verdun, rewrote the texts of his predecessor to present both France and its enemies in a more balanced light: Napoleon's wars had been aggressions, too; German responsibilities for the Great War were less exclusive than the Treaty of Versailles would have them. In 1933 his equally influential *Le Problème des origines de la guerre* explicitly dotted the *i*'s and crossed the *t*'s of his argument, suggesting – as American revisionists were also doing – that the French too bore some responsibility for the outbreak of war in 1914. More important still, Isaac told his readers, enmity between nations was not historically or geographically determined, conflict was not inevitable, mutual understanding and international cooperation could surmount circumstantial hostility.

Imbibed by generations of teenagers, this revisionist history made unconditional patriotism ("my country right or wrong") less acceptable, certainly no excuse for war. At the same time, children who once were stuffed with ideas of martial glory were now being taken, class by class, to see antiwar films and then invited to put down their impressions. In July 1937 an educational publication surveyed schoolchildren's views. "War is a scourge," answered an eleven-year-old boy; "War is a horror," answered a nine-year-old girl.[10] That they were right is irrelevant. That there's no evidence of a "but" that might be used to qualify their convictions, of a sense that in some circumstances even calamities have to be faced, is significant.

Children brought up in such a moral atmosphere, like Christian de Lavarenne, born in 1911, looked upon war as ultimate evil, upon its harbingers with horror. Son of an officer killed in the war, member of a family whose menfolk became officers from father to son, Lavarenne believed an understanding with Germany essential and watched the rise of Nazism "with terror." Not a recipe for firmness or, really, for straight thinking. His point of view reminds us that pacifism, or something akin to it, was not limited to the Left. Though those who stood in the center or to the right of the political spectrum had been more given to bellicose talk through the 1920s, most of their troops continued pacific. By the 1930s the leaders had learned to follow their followers. In 1933 we find the marquis Régis de Vibraye, great landowner and generous supporter of the royalist Action Française, telling the management of a peace association that a Germany ruled by Nazis did not preclude understanding between the two countries.[11] Vibraye represented a new current of "integral pacifism," more suspicious of German refugees than of Germany's rulers, more opposed to parliamentary institutions than to Nazism.

Between pacifists from the Left, determined to dismiss whatever did not fit their beliefs in international understanding, and pacifists of the Right, who feared the nefarious manipulations of anti-Nazis eager to use the French as cat's-paws, there was ground for accommodation. Both looked askance at the republic and its institutions, the ones because they were not democratic enough, the others because they were too democratic. Both denounced ruling cliques as irresponsible and corrupt. Both hated war and, after war, the carnage of alcoholism and syphilis, the vectors of decadence: *bistrots*, brothels, homosexuals, drugs, degenerate art. Both suspected capitalism and its mealy-mouthed lackeys of every ilk: moderates, Masons, and Jews.[12] Both felt it a moral duty to face the state with sterile hostility, and both carried out this duty with stubborn fervor. As Raymond Aron (a "passionate pacifist" in his youth) found occasion to comment later, "resisting power when power is moderate: an excellent method to accelerate its ruin."[13] Moderate power makes revolt easy; moderate power encouraged immoderate opposition. In a France that was immoderate only in its moderation, opponents on all sides found many maledictions they could pronounce in common.

Notes

1. Alphonse Haensler, *Curé de campagne* (Paris, 1980), 160 (hereafter, when not indicated, the place of publication is Paris); *Paris-Soir-Dimanche,* Jan. 19, 1936; Jean Giono, "Refus d'obéissance," in *Récits et essais* (1989); Claudine Chouez, *Giono par lui-même* (1956), 23; Jacques Body, *Giraudoux et l'Allemagne* (1975), 181–84.

2. Pierre-Edmond Robert, *D'un Hôtel du Nord l'autre* (1986), 29, 31, and Eugène Dabit, *Journal intime (1928–1936)* (1939), 22, 88, 141, 173, 220, 256, 273–74, 286, 300–01, 349–50.

3. Roger Vercel, *Capitaine Conan* (1934), 254; *Gazette des Tribunaux,* Jan. 7, 8, 1937.

4. Jean Appert, interview, Archives Orales du Comité pour l'histoire Economique et Financière (hereafter AO), I, I; Prost, *Archives,* 86; Michel Missoffe, *André Tardieu* (1957), 36. Janine Bourdin, *La France et les Français,* 102, quotes the *Journal des mutilés et combattants* (Oct. 9, 1938), admitting that veterans had "doubtlessly emphasized too much their horror of war. . . ."

5. Edmée Renaudin, *Sans fleur au fusil* (1979), 15. Eric Mension-Rigau, *L'Enfance au château* (1990), 39, remarks how the bloodletting of the war unhinged and unsettled the upper classes. One man born in 1915 lost two of three uncles on one side of the family, three out of four on the other side, the fourth being a *grand mutilé.*

6. Simone de Lattre, *Jean de Lattre, mon mari* (1971), 75; NA, 851 1442–2, 1933; Renaudin, *Sans fleur.* 29; *Gazette des Tribunaux.* March 24, 1939. In November 1991 the mass grave in which Lieutenant Henri Alban Fournier – better known as the writer Alain-Fournier – and twenty of his comrades of the 288th Infantry Regiment lay buried was identified and dug up at Saint-Rémy-la-Calonne, in the Meuse forest where they had fallen seventy-seven years before, on September 22, 1914.

7. Pierre Laborie, *Résistants, Vichyssois et autres* (1980), 47.

8. Jean Vial, *L'Instituteur* (1980), 215; Léon Emery, *Correspondances.* (Carpentras, 1982), I, 89; Judith Wishnia, *The Proletarianizing of the Fonctionnaires* (Baton Rouge, 1990), 288; André Delmas in Bourdin and Rémond, *La France,* 214.

9. Simon, *Grande Crise,* 28–30; Jean-François Sirinelli, *Intellectuels et passions françaises* (1990), 77; Janet Teissier du Cros, *Divided Loyalties* (London, 1962), 77. On the other hand, some pacifists changed their minds in extremis. Pierre Brossolette and Jean Prévost, militantly antimilitarist at the Ecole Normale, died in the Resistance. Raymond Aron, who had been "passionately pacifist," ended up in London with General de Gaulle. Others, like Félicien Challaye, Georges Demartial, René Gerin, continued to blame France for the sins of the Germans even under the German Occupation.

10. *Marie-Claire,* Supplement *Nos Enfants* (July 1937).

11. AO, Christian de Lavarenne, I, I; Vibraye in Norman Ingram, *The Politics of Dissent. Pacifism in France 1919–1939* (Oxford, 1991), 95–96.

12. Ingram, 98, 181, 185, quotes a number of pacifist militants denouncing the Jewish press, "the bluff of anti-Semitism," the "occult links between Blum, the Socialists, Jewish finance and arms manufacturers." There are many ways to skin a cat.

13. Raymond Aron, quoted in Sirinelli, *Intellectuels.* 484, 486; see also *Le Spectateur engagé* (1981), 26.

DEBÓRAH DWORK AND ROBERT JAN VAN PELT Germany's Turn to the East

THE GERMANS WERE FORCED to seek an armistice in November 1918. "And so it had all been in vain," Adolf Hitler wrote in *Mein Kampf.* "In vain all the sacrifices and privations; in vain the hunger and thirst of months which were often endless; in vain the hours in which, with mortal fear clutching at our hearts, we nevertheless did our duty; and in vain the death of two millions who died." He called on their graves to open "and send the silent mud- and blood-covered heroes back as spirits of vengeance to the homeland which had cheated them with such mockery."[1]

The German generals articulated the same sentiment in another register. Unwilling to admit military failure, they repeatedly proclaimed that revolution on the home front and not defeat on the battlefield had caused the collapse. Germany would have remained unvanquished, Field Marshal von Hindenburg testified in a Reichstag inquiry, had it not been "for a secret intentional mutilation of the fleet and the army." Quoting the English general Sir John Frederick Maurice, Hindenburg declared, "The German army was stabbed in the back."[2]

The Weimar Republic was not "Germany." The government that had signed the Versailles treaty was not "Germany." The millions of civilians who wanted if not to forget the war then at least go on with their peacetime lives were not "Germany." The "true" Germany was to be found not on a map or in civil society but within the soul of each German soldier, the veterans, conservatives, and nascent National Socialists blazed. This "Deeper Germany," or "Inner Reich," was unconquerable, even if the German Reich had been defeated and her soldiers had died. To the contrary: her size and actual existence were measured by the number of soldiers who had fallen on her behalf. In the trenches the soldiers had formed the real Germany; in their graves they embodied the eternal Germany.[3]

This heroic interpretation of Germany was coined during the war and it originally applied to all soldiers, but between 1918 and 1933 extremist groups antagonistic to the Weimar Republic successfully monopolized the idea and refashioned it: the true Germany resided in those who opposed the state that, by signing the Versailles treaty, had betrayed the sacrifice of two million soldiers. . . .

The true Germany was to be found in the soldiers who had refused to surrender, and her greatest enemies were those who were believed to have actively sabotaged that resistance to the treaty. Millions of Germans called on their government to refuse to sign. "All over Germany, in every region and every social circle, a storm of anger suddenly ignited over the enormous arrogance of the peace terms," a National Socialist study of the history of the German Jews reported. "Everyone was caught in this mood. But in that hour of destiny it was primarily the Jews who were already prepared to sabotage the will to resist, and who thus broke the united front. In that hour they attacked the German nation in the back."[4]

Once conservatives in general and National Socialists in particular had determined the line of a Jewish stab in the back, they found evidence for the deed everywhere they looked. From the Reichstag to the Prussian diet to the daily papers, it was the Jews who spoke in favor of the treaty and who urged the government to sign. And sign they did; they had no muscle to support defiant rhetoric. Nevertheless, according to right-wing Germans, the Jews had weakened the national resolve. "We may, without any reservation, come to the historical judgment that without these Jewish writers and politicians the Reichstag would have decided differently, that is, against signing and in favor of rejection, and that no German government would have been willing to sign it."[5]

Claiming to speak for the two million dead soldiers of the Great War, absorbing the legacy of the

Baltic campaign, the anger about the Versailles Treaty, and exploiting the death of sixteen men in the failed putsch of 9 November 1923, Adolf Hitler – one of the millions who had suffered in the trenches – successfully arrogated to himself and his movement the status of the True Germany. He and his followers, the incarnation of the nation, had remained loyal and true to Germany while their fellow countrymen, preferring to forget the four years of war, had given up and given in.[6]

Hitler, the man who had been most loyal to the country, stood at the center of the True Germany. Those who were most loyal to him formed the innermost circle around the core. Heinrich Himmler, known in party circles as *der treue Heinrich,* the loyal Heinrich, perceived this before anyone else, and used it almost flawlessly to bring a marginal party organization, the SS, and himself to prominence. Established in 1925, the original role of the SS, *Schutzstaffeln,* or Protection Squads, was to provide security for party meetings. At the 1926 party rally in Weimar, Hitler entrusted the 200-strong SS with the Blood Flag, the standard stained with the blood of men shot in the melee of the putsch. The Blood Flag was the movement's holy relic, a symbol not of political miscalculation but of those who had fallen "with loyal faith in the resurrection of their people," as Hitler wrote in the dedication of his *Mein Kampf.*[7]

When the SS became the guardian of the Blood Flag it also became the steward of loyalty. Himmler, appointed by Hitler to lead the SS, appreciated the symbolism of the flag and understood the enormous potential of being identified with the virtue of loyalty.[8] He immediately orchestrated the presentation of the SS man as elect precisely because of his loyalty, limiting admission to the "best physically, the most dependable, and the most loyal men in the movement."[9] The SS were indoctrinated to owe unconditional loyalty to the person of Adolf Hitler, and their oath of allegiance proved it: "We swear to you, Adolf Hitler, as Führer and chancellor of the German Reich, our loyalty and bravery. We swear to you, and our superiors appointed by you, obedience to death. So help us God!"[10] Their motto was *"Meine Ehre heisst Treue,"* or My honor is loyalty. Loyalty was the center of their universe.

For Himmler loyalty transcended total obedience to commands given; it signified his duty to anticipate orders. Hitler was his liege, and loyalty to his liege meant total identification of his own aims with those of Hitler. The latter, his rock and his redeemer, did not need either to command or to review the loyal retainer's deeds. Himmler responded "with alacrity to every hint and signal from Hitler," the prominent Holocaust historian Christopher Browning has observed. "Himmler's stock rose precisely because he, more than any of his rivals, had the capacity to interpret Hitler's signals and ideological exhortations and to cast them into concrete programs."[11]

One such program was Himmler's racially perfect SS community. "It remains one of the greatest and most decisive achievements of the Reichsführer-SS," the official SS historian Gunther d'Alquen noted, "that he integrated and clearly applied, with both courage and logical consistency, the theoretical insights of the National Socialist ideology in this field to that which he had been entrusted to organize."[12] The SS were selected according to racial criteria and they were obliged to contribute to the future of the race by producing many racially pure children. In his Marriage Order of 31 December 1931, Himmler required potential brides of SS men to be screened carefully; SS men needed his permission to marry. The SS took great pride in the Marriage Order, as it affirmed the loyalty of the individual to his leader. "This drastic order" proved "the self-confidence of this voluntary community," d'Alquen explained, as it meant the complete and to others "incomprehensible intrusion in the so-called personal freedom of the individual."[13]

Himmler's SS selection procedures and Marriage Order translated Hitler's theories into practice. It was but one instance of his interpretation of the musings of Hitler the prophet and, after the latter's election, his anticipation of the wishes of Hitler the ruler. It was not a hardship; to a large degree, his agenda and Hitler's coincided. In the 1920s and 1930s, in no other domain was this so clear as in their shared belief in the regeneration of Germany in the East.

Faced with geographical, political, and economic collapse in the wake of defeat, many Germans believed that only the comprehensive reorganization of society would lead to recovery. They blamed the revolution of 1918, the political unrest of the years that followed, and the inflation of 1923 on the modernization of German society and the concomitant disintegration of traditional patterns of authority and loyalty. By the mid-1920s ordinary Germans in the urban areas had faced years of food scarcity, and sometimes even hunger. The metropolis, where the revolutionaries had clustered and the food lines had formed, became the symbol of all that was wrong with the country. The flight from the countryside swelling the city population was the cause of their problems, and it was a move from the rural East to the urban West. Anti-metropolitan sentiment began to merge with theories about the need to settle and strengthen the German East, and the Artaman Society unified these two ideas.

The society was founded in 1923 by Dr. Willibald Hentschell, whose ambition was to renew the German race by resettling urban young people in the countryside.[14] He urged German youngsters to become men, *Manen* in Old Middle German, of the fields, *Art*, or *Artamanen*. The young Heinrich Himmler joined the Artamans and quickly became the Artaman gauleiter, provincial leader, of Bavaria. In 1931 he was the official liaison between the Artamans and the National Socialists, who eventually absorbed the society in the Hitler Youth Land Service. Artaman ideals were to have a profound influence on Himmler's policies in Poland after 1939. And, as it was in the Artaman Society that he met the former Baltic volunteer Rudolf Höss, whom he later appointed commandant of Auschwitz, the theories of that organization provide an important context for the history of the concentration camp. Höss recalled the Artaman Society fondly as "a community of young patriotic people." United in their ambition to escape urban tensions, they sought "the natural way of life" in the country. "They hoped to return to the soil from which their ancestors had come forth, to the fountain of life of the German people, to the healthy farming community. This was also my way, my long-sought goal."[15]

The Artamans presented the East as the permanent solution to all that ailed Germany. "Germany's future, Germany's young power is in the East. Our destiny is not determined at the Rhine and the Ruhr, but at the Vistula and the Memel," they proclaimed.[16] As both the Vistula and the Memel flowed largely in the foreign territories of Poland and Lithuania, the Artaman ideology had an irredentist, if not belligerent, character. Nevertheless, that is precisely where long-range Artaman planning envisioned settlement. As the Artaman leader Wilhelm Kotzde put it, "Either we will go to the East, as our ancestors did once before in the twelfth century, or we will be erased as a people from world history."[17]

Walther Darré brought many Artaman ideas into theoretical focus and introduced them into mainline National Socialist thinking. A graduate of the German Colonial School at Witzenhausen, Darré had come to the conclusion by 1926 that the attempt to establish a colonial empire overseas had been a disastrous mistake.[18] Like many of his generation, Darré felt that Germany's failure before 1918 to reverse the Polonification of its eastern border region through policies of "inner colonization" had led to the loss of these lands to the new Polish republic. But his perspective was not limited to the pragmatics of power politics. He also trusted that such "inner colonization" would help to reverse the alienation of the German from his land. Darré believed that the Nordic race, which included the German people, was a peasant stock and that it was only as peasants that Germans would live in harmony with nature. In 1929 he published an impassioned plea for a return to the land.[19] Determined to live his doctrine, Darré joined an organization that appeared to provide the most promising means to achieve his own dream of a Nordic peasant state on German soil: Hitler's National Socialist movement.

From the moment that he became a member of the movement, Darré wielded great influence on the formation of National Socialist agricultural policy, and in June 1930 he was appointed head of the party's Agricultural Organization. One of his allies was that other agriculturalist – the thirty-year-old Reichsführer-SS Heinrich Himmler. Darré's vision of a Nordic peasant state paralleled Himmler's, and he joined the SS to become Himmler's closest adviser on the rooting of a people, or *Volk*, in the earth; as they called it, blood and soil.

According to the National Socialists and their many fellow travelers, Germany did not have enough land to bring the population into harmony with the soil. The space the country needed was in the East. "The fate of Germany is rooted in the East. . . . National Socialism has once more turned the face of the whole people clearly and with conviction to the East, leaving behind us the pernicious influence of the dissolving and decomposing mental sphere of the West," Darré bubbled.[20] The East, however, was a land in trouble. "We look on with dumb resignation while formerly purely German cities – Reval, Riga, Warsaw, and so forth—are lost to our folk." Predicting that even Breslau, Berlin, Stettin, or Dresden could be lost to the Slavs, Darré foresaw great conflict. "Our people must prepare for the struggle and also for this, that in that battle there can be only one outcome for us: absolute victory! The idea of blood and soil gives us the moral right to take back as much eastern land *as is necessary to achieve harmony between the body of our people and geopolitical space.*"[21]

The Artaman perspective of the German East as paradise lost was supported by the scientific theory of geopolitics, according to which the East was the horizon of Germany's future. What the National Socialists admired and called geopolitics was based on the work of the brilliant German geographer Friedrich Ratzel, who in the late nineteenth century had explored the relationship between the political history of states and the geographical conditions of the ground they occupied. Ratzel was interested in the conditions that allow states to thrive. *Raum* (space) or, as he interpreted it, *Lebensraum* (living space) was essential. Ratzel's space was not so much a physical, geographical concept as a vision, a task, and a vocation. The prominent German cartographer Arthur Hillen-Ziegfeld expressed this idea succinctly in 1934. "German living space is a challenge to our people. It is not an unchanging fact, but an eternal task."[22] Geopolitics was therefore a science that concerned itself with spatial conditions and spatial requirements. With the questions "Are the space needs of a state met? If not, how can they be brought into accord with geographical conditions?"[23] the German geopolitical scholar Otto Maull summarized the imperial scope of his discipline.

By the end of the 1930s living space had become, in the words of the German émigré Hans Weigert, "the national obsession of the German people, strong enough to upset, in our day, the balance of the world."[24] The popularity of the doctrine was undoubtedly the result of Hitler's enthusiasm for the geographer and retired major general Karl Haushofer, who had constructed a massive edifice of speculation on the foundations laid by Ratzel.[25] Hitler had come in contact with Haushofer through Rudolf Hess, who was an aide of the former and a student of the latter. Under the influence of Haushofer, Hitler devoted significant parts of *Mein Kampf* to geopolitical speculation. He proposed, for example, that "for Germany . . . the only possibility for carrying out a healthy territorial policy lay in the acquisition of new land in Europe itself. . . . If land was desired in Europe, it could be obtained by and large only at the expense of Russia, and this meant that the new Reich must again set itself on the march along the road of the Teutonic Knights of old, to obtain by the German sword sod for the German plow and daily bread for the nation. . . . We take up where we broke off six hundred years ago . . . and turn our gaze toward the land in the east." This policy, he promised, would open "a great and mighty future."[26]

With such an endorsement, it is understandable that the medieval settlement of the East became a pivotal point in German historiography after 1933. "The German settlement of the East proved to be the central pillar in the total makeup of the German nation," the authors of a classic description of this Push to the East declared in 1937. "Its history mirrors, with penetrating clarity, German history in general. One must know it to understand the history of the German land and the German people and, consequently, for a correct and deep appreciation of the German character."[27] The central word was "settlement." According to the geopolitical doctrine of *Lebensraum*, the sole purpose of conquest was settlement. The powerful arrows on the geopolitical maps may suggest marching armies rather than plowing peasants, but to a German in the 1930s the identification of the German East with settlement was clear, and its historic place as the greatest feat in the nation's history was accepted without question.[28] . . .

Notes

1. Adolf Hitler, *Mein Kampf,* trans. Ralph Manheim (Boston: Houghton Mifflin, 1943), 204f.
2. Paul von Hindenburg, "The Stab in the Back," in Anton Kaes, Martin Jay, and Edward Dimendberg, eds., *The Weimar Republic Sourcebook* (Berkeley, Los Angeles, and New York: University of California Press, 1994), 15f.
3. N. Ernst Jünger, "Die totale Mobilmachung," in Ernst Jünger, ed., *Krieg und Krieger* (Berlin: Junker and Dünnhaupt, 1930), 28.
4. Institut zum Studium der Judenfrage, ed., *Die Juden in Deutschland* (Munich: Franz Eher, 1939), 111.
5. Ibid., 112.
6. Carl Lange, "Ehre der Nation, deutsches Volkstums und Würde des Menschentums," in Carl Lange and Ernst Adolf Dreyer, eds., *Deutscher Geist 1935* (Leipzig: R. Voigtländer, 1934), 273.
7. Hitler, *Mein Kampf,* 687.
8. In the official SS historiography, Himmler's appointment marks the true beginning of the SS; see Gunther d'Alquen, "Die SS: Geschichte, Aufgabe und Organisation der Schutzstaffeln der NSDAP," in Paul Meier-Benneckenstein, ed., *Wehrhaftes Volk: Der organisatorische Aufbau Teil II, vol. 2 of Das Dritte Reich im Aufbau* (Berlin: Junker und Dünnhapt, 1939), 204.
9. As quoted in Herbert F. Ziegler, *Nazi Germany's New Aristocracy: The SS leadership, 1925–1939* (Princeton: Princeton University Press, 1989), 38.
10. As quoted in Bernd Wegner, *The Waffen-SS: Organization, Ideology and Function,* trans. Ronald Webster (Oxford: Basil Blackwell, 1990), 16.
11. Christopher Browning, "Beyond 'Intentionalism' and 'Functionalism': A Reassessment of Nazi Jewish Policy from 1939 to 1941," in Thomas Childers and Jane Caplan, eds., *Reevaluating the Third Reich* (New York: Holmes & Meier, 1993), 216.
12. D'Alquen, "Die SS," 205.
13. Ibid., 206.
14. A good introduction to the Artaman Society and its ideology can be found in Klaus Bergmann, *Agrarromantik und Grossstadtfeindschaft,* vol. 20 of the *Marburger Abhandlungen zur politischen Wissenschaft* (Meisenheim am Glan: Anton Hain, 1970), 24/ff.; also Michael H. Kater, "Die Artamanen – Völkische Jugend in der Weimarer Republik," *Historische Zeitschrift* 213 (1971): 577ff.
15. Rudolf Höss, *Death Dealer: The Memoirs of the SS Kommandant at Auschwitz,* ed. Steven Paskuly, trans. Andrew Pollinger (Buffalo: Prometheus Books, 1992), 79.
16. As quoted in Ulrich Linse, ed., *Zurück, o Mensch, zur Mutter Erde: Landkommunen in Deutschland, 1890–1933* (Munich: Deutscher Taschenbuch Verlag, 1983), 331.
17. Wilhelm Kotzde, (report on the beginning of practical Artaman work) in *Der Falke* 5 (1924): 107.
18. See Anne Bramwell, *Blood and Soil: Walther Darré and Hitler's "Green Party"* (Bourne End, Bucks.: Kensal Press, 1985).
19. Walther R. Darré, "The Peasantry as the Key to Understanding the Nordic Race," in Barbara Miller Lane and Leila J. Rupp, eds., *Nazi Ideology before 1933: A Documentation* (Manchester: Manchester University Press, 1978), 105.
20. Walther R. Darré, preface in Heinrich Bauer, *Geburt des Ostens: Drei Kämpfer um eine Idee* (Berlin: Frundsberg, 1933), 5.
21. Walther R. Darré, "The Farmers and the State," in Miller Lane and Rupp, eds., *Nazi Ideology before 1933,* 133.
22. A. Hillen-Ziegfeld, "Deutscher Lebensraum," in Lange and Dreyer, eds., *Deutscher Geist 1935,* 71f.
23. Otto Maull, *Das Wesen der Geopolitik* (Leipzig and Berlin: Teubner, 1936), 31.
24. Hans Weigert, *Generals and Geographers: The Twilight of Geopolitics* (New York: Oxford University Press, 1942), 95.
25. The standard biography on Haushofer is Hans-Adolf Jacobsen, *Karl Haushofer: Leben und Werk,* 2 vols., Schriften des Bundesarchivs 24/I and 24/II (Boppard am Rhein: Harald Boldt, 1979).
26. Hitler, *Mein Kampf,* 139f., 654.
27. Rudolf Kötzschke and Wolfgang Ebert, *Geschichte der ostdeutschen Kolonisation* (Leipzig: Bibliographisches Institut, 1937), 19.
28. Ibid., 10.

Eugen Diesel **The Old Order**

The Disaster.

The army that was hurled against the enemy was a thing of incomparable splendour, with its model equipment, its cavalry and its aeroplanes, and the romance of heroism that surrounded it. It performed brilliant feats, and won here and there no inconsiderable victories. In the first months the traditional atmosphere of war – bivouacs and trumpets and decampments, etc. – engrossed the attention. One marked the places taken with little flags on the map, and the names of our generals were on everyone's lips. . . .

Millions met their death under a never-ceasing hail of shells, amid the careful calculation of rations and equipment, in thousands of kilometres of stinking trenches. Four times winter covered the scene of war with its mantle of white, and hunger yawned greyly over the German land.

By the time the machines had come to a standstill and the masses returned home, the nation had given the utmost proof of its strength, its power of resistance, its self-sacrifice and its endurance. But it had also shown in the moment of collapse that Germany, considered as a nation, as a people, as a community, was without any real political foundation, that it had been held together during the war by no ideal deeper than that of victory or at least of holding its own in the face of the enemy. The Revolution could not at one stroke fashion the new German type, for the fanfares of the collapse had proclaimed in strident tones the advent of the machine age. The old standards could not be maintained any longer, but to build up the new would require decades, and perhaps centuries.

The months between the Armistice and the signing of the Peace Treaty were like a sort of magic farewell to the past. To be out of the trenches was itself ground enough for happiness, and people's incomes were still untouched, and their homes still intact. The officers lived in the proud consciousness of a well-fought fight, and the nation at large built its hopes on the idealism of the American President. The presence of the troops imparted a feeling of security, and over and again the fires of revolution were speedily quelled. One found oneself once more among the circle of one's old acquaintances, and refreshed the memory amid the shootings and alarums with the music and drama and poetry of the age that was past. It was all there, before one's eyes and ears, even if at times it seemed a little strange and out of place.

But a second deluge was already on its way. The account was not yet settled. The stupendous burden of debt must be cleared off, voluntarily or involuntarily, sooner or later. While the terms of the Peace Treaty slunk ever nearer, the figures mounted up and up, and went on mounting up long after the treaty had been signed. The landslide began; panic-stricken crowds were sucked into the vortex of speculation; paper values and artificial prices swelled only to explode. The higher money rose in the economic scales, the lower sank tangible property; machines and railways, iron and coal, whirled about in a sort of modern industrial *danse macabre,* presided over by the spirit of Economics as though by some heathen god. In the panic everyone tried to exchange money for goods; and while money plunged into the yawning gulf, the whole of Germany seemed to hang by a thread over the abyss.

Germany after the Collapse.

And then one morning Germany woke up to find that the mark had been stabilized, and that the deluge of paper billions had come to an end at last, with only the ledgers and ruined nervous systems to tell the tale of what had been. At length the fever of speculation was stayed, hedged round by a legion of rapidly designed paragraphs and regulations, as if by a circle of

Eugen Diesel, **Germany and the Germans**, 233, 234–38, 255–58. Translated by W.D. Robson-Scott. Copyright © 1931 by The Macmillan Company.

bayonets. Uncanny, unaccountable, the new Germany, a Germany still in scaffolding, arises from the blood-spattered ruins of war, a piece of solid rock out of the morass of the inflation.

Grey and uncertain it lies before us, that land over which the purple once so proudly waved. But there is comfort for our soul's distress; still the cities stand intact about us, still the trees are green, the fields rich with grass and corn. Still the chimes ring out over the cathedrals and the railway cuts its way across the plain. Is not Munich still redolent of malt, as the forest is redolent of wood and snow, and the warm stable of living cattle? Are not the things that remain eternally the same carried over into the world of tomorrow?

No. For the land has been robbed of the windows through which it looked out upon the European scene, robbed of the doors through which its people were free to wander into every quarter of the globe. On its battlements the soldiers of the alien, white and black, keep watch with bayonets drawn. Now they advance ever further into German territory, interfere in the working of the infinitely complex organism of German industry. They shoot on those who overstep the new and unfamiliar frontiers and restrictions of this narrow and congested corner of Europe. Harmless citizens find themselves prisoners in their own land.

The lost territories, once sources of strength to Germany, are now pregnant with peril for the future. Out of their borders stream millions of Germans into what is left of Germany, a trunk shorn of its limbs. Life is difficult in their new homes; strangers crowded into an already congested and poverty-stricken population, their lot is indeed a hard one. Poorly fed and poorly clad, they swarm into the houses and factories and railways of this teeming land.

For Germany suddenly finds itself most seriously restricted for space with its sixty million inhabitants. In this distracted land it is difficult to know whether it is worth while to keep the factories going, whether one can do so without losing the remainder of the fortune that one has somehow managed to scrape together. For every penny that is not needed for one's absolutely immediate wants must be delivered over to the tax-collector. The fiscal authorities are indeed like a huge band of mowers who search even the rubble screes, lest they find perchance a single blade or two among the stones. All around the land is littered with the products of the fever of inflation, débris of the dreams of inflation visionaries, whom the people looked upon as geniuses for the space of three long years: engines and motor-cars of inferior metal, artificial leather, leaking motor-boats, clothes made half of paper, semi-poisonous food substitutes. In the midst of their hunger and distress the masses stream into the universities and technical schools in the pathetic hope that the lecture room will enable them both to master the chaos that surrounds them and to earn money for themselves. Once again the shop windows are bright with light and the opera plays to crowded audiences. But on all sides people are sinking into the mire of poverty. Respectable ladies, accustomed to comfort and culture and travel, find themselves forced, in order to avoid literal starvation, to rise betimes in the mornings to search for work at the factories, exposing themselves to the scorn of the regular workers, or else to tout round wares from door to door in the more unsavoury quarters of the town on behalf of some firm or other.

That newspaper headline, which read like a triumph and a victory, had sealed the fate of millions, had destroyed the mainstay of Germany, her middle class. Fear and anxiety brood over the land. Never before had the world witnessed such a scene of legally enforced distress.

All the feelers with which Germany had formerly sought out its sustenance over the face of the planet were now cut off: all its cables, steamship lines, consulates, harbours and business connections. Vast quantities of its pasture land, cattle, corn and mineral wealth had been taken from it. Thousands of ships and railway carriages fell into alien hands. And as for what was left still – the fields and factories and mines – it was difficult in the extreme to know what to do with them, how to get them into working order again. And to make matters worse, the millions to whom this vast industrial organization should give work and sustenance were ready at any moment to turn against it, crying out, as they did, not only for bread, but also for the millennium of power and splendour, the Marxian dream to which they had clung for seventy-five long years, and which in the midst of all this distress must be realized now or never.

But in spite of all these difficulties life still went on. One went back to one's work bench because there was nothing else to turn to; the tramways transported their passengers to and fro; the goods truck rattled across the land. Things settled down into the new ways, hesitatingly, but surely. But before those new ways can be understood, it must be borne in mind that since the war the full force of the age of technical science had broken over mankind. . . .

GERMANY'S TRIBULATION.

IT IS HARD TO REALIZE that some eighty-five per cent of the population have to live on an income of eighteen hundred marks per annum, and that only five or six per cent earn from three thousand six hundred to five thousand marks. One million seven hundred thousand families are without homes of their own, and a fifth of the whole population live in conditions which are very hotbeds of consumption, incest and every kind of vice. In Berlin only sixty-six per cent of severe tubercular cases have beds of their own to sleep in; the rest have to share their beds with healthy children and adults, who do not remain healthy for long in consequence. And only one consumptive in a hundred has a bedroom to himself! Every fifth child of the German cities is without a bed of its own; it has to live amid poverty and sickness, immorality, dirt and coarseness. Thus millions of people exist in conditions of utter horror, in half-lit dungeons, where six or eight or even fourteen or more human beings are crowded together amid rats and filth. In many parts of the big towns children who do not suffer from venereal disease are actually the exception. It sometimes happens that children are born in unheated attics only to die of cold there, and in many slum dwellings the walls drip with damp, and everything gets covered with mould and rot. In thousands of cases one small room has to serve as workshop, kitchen, living-room and bedroom for the whole family. Taking it all round, America has quite four times as much housing room for its population as Germany.

Thus the apparent gaiety of German life is played out against a background of the darkest hue. The whole nation is enveloped in distress; official interference is of no avail; the people live in a veritable hell of meanness, oppression and disease. The whole land is buried, as it were, under a monstrous rubbish-heap of crushed hopes, vain labour, and misdirected schemes. But nothing is more worthy of admiration than the patience and industry of this unfortunate people. What might it not achieve if only it were free, if only it got the proper return for its labour, if the demon of mechanization were less a curse than a blessing, and if the nation ceased expending its brains and energy in the creation of ever more official departments!

There is certainly no lack of assiduous zeal; every second Prussian subject is engaged on some professional activity. But there are millions of unemployed, far more than the official statistics show, for they leave out of account all the small peasants and business men, all the doctors and other professions which only earn one-third of what they did before the war and now have to live in the utmost want, to starve or else run into debt. There are working women in Berlin who earn only forty-eight marks a month; in the Erzgebirge there are mothers of families who toil till late in the night in order to increase their monthly earnings by seven marks. True, the eight-hour day is on the statute book, but it obtains only in those places where rigid supervision is possible.

In between the proletariat and the industrialist, the middle classes with their fixed salaries and the millions with their fixed scale of wages, a class of unsavoury opportunists and speculators has grown up. This class penetrates into every nook and cranny of the land in its search for something to exploit, and its money-grabbing manners have affected ordinary business dealings no less than the relations between landlady and lodger, more especially, perhaps, in Berlin. These are the people who deal in second-hand goods of all kinds, who hawk round patent medicines of doubtful character, who borrow money of their acquaintances for some hare-brained scheme or other. But it is characteristic of the age that even those in high places, the general managers and heads of departments, spend a vast amount of their time in completely profitless labour. There are a hundred failures to every venture that really comes off. Hundreds of thousands of people, doctors, authors, manual labourers, shop-keepers, are always hovering on the brink of disaster; and to keep check of these disasters or hairbreadth escapes, as the case may be, ever more officials and authorities are needed. And the never-failing vampires and vultures of the law are always standing by in readiness to make a living from settling up the bankrupt estates and liquidated companies.

In a country in which it is a great achievement to be able to live like respectable people and educate one's children, most of the children realize full well that they have little to expect from their homes. And so the revolt against the older generation is particularly marked in Germany. The children are quick to learn self-reliance, quick to follow the ideals of the new age. What does it matter that they become waiters, dancers, film actors, typists, mannequins or adventurers? By so doing they escape from the older generation, which is still brooding over the money it has lost, still gloating over the fact that most other people are in no better case.

Men and women searching for coal as unemployment and inflation soared in post-World War I Germany. The war and the harsh provisions of the Versailles Treaty wreaked havoc on the German economy. 1922. (ullstein bild)

A breadline in Warsaw as World War I came to an end. The war weakened the national economies of many European countries, thus creating high rates of unemployment and poverty throughout Europe. 1917. (Courtesy of American Jewish Joint Distribution Committee)

With the collapse of the German economy in 1923, the Weimar government resorted to printing more and more paper money. The resulting runaway inflation made this one-billion mark note nearly worthless. In 1923 an egg in Germany cost 80 million marks while a pound of butter cost six billion marks. November 1923. (ullstein bild-Riehn)

With the unchecked inflation of the 1920s, many Germans sold their coins as junk metal. Here a man is exchanging aluminum coins for many times their face value. September 11, 1923. (AP/Wide World Photos)

Run at Berlin's banks. An immense crowd of frightened depositors in front of one of Berlin's banks early in the morning of July 16, 1931. (AP/Wide World Photos)

Women in Berlin wait in line to barter potato peels in exchange for wood chips to use for heating fuel. January 9, 1929. (ullstein bild, courtesy of USHMM Photo Archives)

Unemployed Germans and their families wait to receive a hot meal at a soup kitchen in Berlin. 1931. (ullstein bild, courtesy of USHMM Photo Archives)

KLAUS P. FISCHER — The Trauma of Military Defeat and Economic Ruin, 1919–23

THE END OF THE SECOND REICH

THE GERMAN PEOPLE were ecstatic when war was declared in August 1914, and many soldiers shared Adolf Hitler's euphoria about the impending thrill of combat. The parties of the left joined with their political antagonists by pledging themselves to suspend civil dissent until victory was achieved. The emperor proudly proclaimed a *Burgfrieden* (cessation of party strife) and said: "I no longer recognize parties; I recognize only Germans."[1] Intoxicated by this mood of nationalistic fervor, most Germans looked upon the war as a pleasant diversion from the boredom of civilian life and expected it to be all over by Christmas.

However, the war was not won by Christmas of 1914; it had turned, instead, into a seesaw battle of attrition with such staggering losses in men and materiel that even cold-hearted militarists gasped when they saw the casualty lists. The home front increasingly began to show cracks. The parties on the left, having voted for war credits, expected significant social and political concessions from the ruling elite; but when these were not forthcoming, political dissension reopened with a vengeance. It is still remarkable, however, that support for the war continued as long as it did, a fact that could only be attributed to an excessive delight in war, official insensitivity to suffering, and a misguided belief on the part of the German people that their leadership would richly reward them with the fruits of military victory.

The stark geopolitical and military reality pointed inevitably toward ignominious defeat. This should have been apparent to the German high command from the beginning. Germany was fighting on two major fronts against an enemy of decided numerical and productive superiority – an enemy, moreover, who possessed the geopolitical means of strangling Germany's tenuous lifeline by imposing a crippling economic blockade. Such a deadly threat required careful coordination of overall strategic policy, especially with Germany's partners in the alliance, and

close cooperation between civilian and military authorities. Neither of these essential factors for success existed.[2] Not only did the German high command lack a strategic plan for coordinating the war, but it increasingly began to subvert the power of the civilian government. This became especially serious when Paul von Hindenburg and Erich Ludendorff assumed supreme command of the German war effort in August 1916. Having crippled the Russians at Tannenberg and the Masurian Lakes, Hindenburg and Ludendorff became superhuman heroes in the eyes of the German public, and their reputations so dwarfed that of the emperor or any civilian that few dared to question the wisdom of their policies. Neither the emperor nor the chancellor, Bethmann Hollweg, was able to control Germany's military autocrats – first Field Marshal von Moltke, then General Falkenhayn, and finally the team of Hindenburg and Ludendorff. As early as the winter of 1914, the emperor had already complained that "the General Staff tells me nothing and never asks me advice. If people in Germany think that I am the Supreme Commander, they are gravely mistaken. I drink tea, saw wood, and go for walks, which pleases the gentlemen."[3]

The generals not only reduced the emperor to a position of political impotence but also rode roughshod over the chancellor, the cabinet, the Reichstag, industrialists, and trade unionists. All this proved highly popular with most Germans, provided, of course, that the military could hoodwink them into believing that victory was just around the corner.

The truth was that these military geniuses bungled from one disaster into another. In 1914 their much-vaunted Schlieffen Plan had failed to deliver the knockout blow in the west; in 1915 and 1916 they sacrificed a million men in futile battles on the western front; in 1916 their effort to challenge Britain's fleet failed off Jutland; in 1917 they committed three blunders that almost certainly guaranteed defeat: they threw away whatever chances they had to conclude a moderate peace with the Western powers, authorized unlimited submarine warfare and thus made inevitable the entrance of the United States into the war, and foolishly shipped Lenin from Switzerland into Russia to engineer the Russian Revolution. Finally, in 1918 they committed Germany's last reserves in a series of futile battles, and, facing certain defeat, they appointed civilians to arrange for a ceasefire and later blamed civilians for having "stabbed" the German army in the back.[4]

The defeat of a proud and arrogant nation, which up to the very last months of the war believed that final victory was within its grasp, is bound to cause a collective trauma with far-ranging consequences. Having been conditioned by four years of wartime propaganda to believe that victory was inevitable, most Germans refused to accept the reality of defeat. The generals subsequently blamed their failures on defeatism and sabotage at home, while others with political ambitions preferred to blame the defeat on conspirational forces – Communists, pacifists, Jews. Adolf Hitler later referred to these amorphous forces as the "November Criminals"; they were supposed to have stabbed the German army in the back and thus produced all subsequent calamities.

In the fall of 1918, however, most Germans were too numbed by four years of bloody war to think about who was responsible for it all. The war had devoured almost two million young lives and permanently crippled as many more. A generation of young people had bled to death on the battlefields of western and eastern Europe; and those who survived were permanently scarred by their wartime experiences, lacking the psychological resources needed to build a stable and peaceful society. Four ancient empires had collapsed: the German, Austro-Hungarian, Russian, and Ottoman. With the collapse of these ancient monarchies disappeared old symbols of authority that were not so easily replaced. The trauma of defeat and the collapse of ancient authorities opened the floodgates to years of violence, revolution, and extremism. It is against this postwar chaos, which extended into the 1920s and was later rekindled by the Great Depression, that the growth of political pathology must be seen. In Germany, as elsewhere in Europe, a generation of political extremists roamed the political landscape in search of a messianic leader who could redeem them from meaningless sacrifices on the battlefield and restore a collective sense of purpose that had disappeared with the old authorities.

When Germany faced inevitable defeat, those who had been most responsible for the disaster – the leaders of the military establishment – deftly stepped aside and let the new democratic leaders take the blame. As early as September 29, 1918, the day the Hindenburg line cracked, the German high command finally awoke to the reality of defeat. The Second Reich was drawing to a close. The emperor was by now a virtual nonentity, as he had been during most of the war; and when the military high command asked Chancellor Hertling to open negotiations for an armistice, it became painfully obvious even to die-hard supporters of the monarchy that President Woodrow Wilson and the Western allies did not want to negotiate with the kaiser and his military autocrats. The old order had become a diplomatic liability because Woodrow Wilson, enamored by lofty democratic sentiments, insisted that he would not bargain with the emperor or the military but only with the true representatives of the German people. This amounted in some way to an incitement to revolt or, at the very least, to a strong expectation, backed up by menacing threats, that the German people replace the monarchy with a more acceptable democratic government.[5]

The Allied powers, of course, were not the only catalysts of sweeping changes in Germany. By the middle of 1918, the Allied blockade was exacting a grim toll in the form of widespread starvation, food riots, political strikes, and plain lawlessness, made all the more serious by a worldwide influenza epidemic that killed twenty million people. In Munich, a young scholar named Oswald Spengler summed up much of this apocalyptic mood by finishing the last chapter of his *Decline of the West* by candlelight, often sitting atop a chair he had put on his desk because it was warmer near the ceiling. In Berlin, banks were failing, food rations were reduced even further, people died of the influenza virus, and the kaiser's credibility had reached rock bottom. Although the emperor dismissed Chancellor Hertling, who was widely regarded as a stooge of the military, the appointment of Max von Baden, his liberal cousin, did not improve his popularity.

Meanwhile, the generals left military headquarters at Spa for Berlin, where the major decisions were being made. Before they departed Spa, they issued a strident proclamation calling for the end of negotiations because President Wilson's terms, they felt, were unacceptable. A turbulent conference between the government and the military followed. This time the military lost. Ludendorff tendered his resignation and was replaced by General Groener, Max von Baden now sent his final note to Wilson, informing him that the German military was now fully subject to civilian control. The American president replied on November 5, stating that peace could be made in accordance with his Fourteen Points although he made one important reservation: Germany, he insisted, would be held liable for all damage done to Allied property. This was an ominous indication of what was in store for Germany: the imposition of "war guilt," reparations payments, and territorial losses.

On November 8, 1918, the German armistice commission, led by Matthias Erzberger, a leading Catholic Center politician and a catalyst of the peace resolutions in the Reichstag, arrived in the French village of Rethondes in the forest of Compiègne to parley with Marshal Ferdinand Foch, the supreme generalissimo of the Allied armies on the western front. Negotiating in a railroad car, later used by Hitler to dictate peace to the French in 1940, Foch presented several tough conditions to the German side before fighting would cease. The Germans were given two days, November 9 and 10, to respond to the Allied proposals. This presented a real problem to the German delegation because during the course of these two days the German emperor resigned, a republic was proclaimed, and Max von Baden handed over all of his authority to an interim president, Friedrich Ebert. In view of these events, the French wondered whether they were really dealing with the legal representatives of Germany. However, on November 10, Ebert sent a message agreeing to the armistice terms. The next day, November 11, the armistice was signed.

The terms of the armistice were anything but le-nient. Germany was given two weeks to withdraw from Alsace-Lorraine and from all other invaded territory. All German territory west of the Rhine was to be occupied by Allied troops. The Germans were to evacuate East Africa. Germany also forfeited an enormous amount of cannons, machine guns, planes, and trucks. All submarines were to be surrendered, and the whole German fleet was to be put into Allied hands. The treaties of Brest Litovsk and Bucharest made with Russia and Romania respectively, were declared null and void. Finally, Germany was to free Allied prisoners even though the Allies were not required to free German prisoners. The armistice was clearly designed to convince the Germans that they had lost the war. All was now quiet on the western front.

Inside Germany, however, all was not quiet on any front. While the German delegation agonized over the terms of the armistice in their railroad car in the forest of Compiègne, total confusion broke out in Germany. On November 9, Kaiser William abdicated his throne and a republic was proclaimed by the Social Democrat Phillip Scheidemann. The kaiser's hasty departure for exile in Holland left a political vacuum that several factions, including the Communists, attempted to fill. The Russian defeat in war had brought the Bolsheviks to power, and there were good reasons to suspect that similar developments might occur in Germany. This is certainly how Lenin perceived the situation from his vantage point in Moscow in November 1918. The Bolshevik autocrat spoke of Russia and Germany as twins and looked to the more industrialized Germany as his advanced outpost in the coming struggle with capitalism. Directly and indirectly, the Russian Communists gave enthusiastic support to their German comrades in hopes that a communized Germany would be the catalyst for a communized Europe.

Lenin's euphoria seemed confirmed by the events taking place in Germany in the fall of 1918. Even before the kaiser's government collapsed on November 9, 1918, councils of workers and soldiers had sprouted all over Germany. On October 28, 1918, mutinous sailors in Kiel refused to obey an order to steam out into the North Sea for another encounter with the British navy. Instead of launching their ships, the sailors turned their hoses on the fires in the boiler rooms, sang revolutionary songs, hoisted red flags over their ships, and then proceeded to take over the city of Kiel. The sailors' mutiny, in turn, inspired a rash of revolts throughout Germany that the government, paralyzed by defeat and general demobilization of troops, was unable to control. Besides Kiel, other north German ports soon fell into the hands of left-wing radicals who were not so much interested in revolution as they were in ending the war and improving working conditions within the navy.

The mutiny of the German sailors was the beginning of the end for the old imperial order. On November 8, the Independent Socialist Kurt Eisner, supported by councils of workers, soldiers, and peasants, overthrew the royal government in Bavaria and proclaimed a Socialist republic. Two days later, all eyes turned to the German capital, where a six-man council of people's commissars proclaimed itself the executive branch of the new German government.

Thus, in the first two weeks of November 1918 a reenactment of the Russian Revolution seemed to be taking place in Germany. This is certainly how a temporarily blinded young corporal by the name of Adolf Hitler, who was recovering from a poison gas attack at Pasewalk in Pomerania, perceived the political situation. In reality, the fear of a Communist revolution was much exaggerated because the German situation did not resemble the Russian. In Russia, the urban working class was proportionally much smaller than the German working force; it was also less disciplined along formal union lines and lacked the tradition of skilled craftsmanship that predisposed the German worker toward a more conservative political outlook. Both the Russian peasants and workers hated the tsarist regime and longed for its violent overthrow. Under the impact of a disastrous war, an elite cadre of revolutionaries skillfully mobilized these seething resentments and, taking advantage of the blunders of the first or moderate revolution of March 1917, staged a second revolution that put an end to the traditional order in Russia. The Bolsheviks imposed a one-party dictatorship on Russia and gradually assembled the instruments of mass control that such a rule inevitably necessitates: a revolutionary army (the Red Army), a secret police (Cheka), forced labor

camps for political opponents, and a pliant cadre of government officials executing the will of the reigning autocracy.

By contrast, in Germany there was only one revolution, and that one left the traditional social structure essentially undisturbed.[6] The decisive political shift of power in Germany had taken place during the last month of the war when the ruling elites, composed of the aristocracy, the upper middle class, and the High Command of the Armed Forces, were politically displaced for the moment by the forces of social democracy, especially by the parties in the Reichstag that commanded the loyalties of the workers and portions of the middle classes.

The largest of these left-wing parties was the Social Democratic Party. Founded in 1875, the party had gone through a hectic period of external persecution and internal dissension. In 1914 the party had reluctantly voted to support the war effort; but in doing so, it had spread further dissent into the rank and file, precipitating a walkout by the dissidents who formed a new party in 1917 called the Independent Socialist Party. The aim of this new radical party was to establish genuine socialism in Germany and bring an immediate halt to the despised war. The Independent Socialists were supported by the more radical Communists who had been organized into the Spartacist League by two remarkable revolutionaries – Rosa Luxemburg and Karl Liebknecht. Supported by many disenchanted workers, particularly the shop stewards, these Spartacists, named after the ill-fated Roman slave leader Spartacus, called for a Communist regime modeled on Bolshevik rule in Russia; they favored immediate revolution, expropriation of industry and landed estates, and the establishment of "soviets" or workers' councils. Their leader, Karl Liebknecht, was the son of Wilhelm Liebknecht, friend of Karl Marx and one of the founding fathers of the Social Democratic Party. Karl Liebknecht broke with the party in 1914 because he could not go along with its support of the war. Liebknecht was a short, slender man who wore a pince-nez, sported a military moustache, and gave the overall impression of a minor clerk in the civil service rather than a dangerous subversive. Yet Liebknecht was a man of unshakable determination and revolutionary zeal; his hatred of the Prussian military caste had earned him a jail sentence before the war for maligning the military establishment. After he voted against further war credits, his own party disavowed him and ultimately expelled him from its ranks. The military also retaliated against him by drafting him into a punishment battalion; but since he was a member of the Reichstag, he enjoyed certain immunities that allowed him to spread propaganda against the war.

In the Reichstag, Liebknecht was one of the few courageous deputies who frequently attacked Germany's military autocrats for their conduct of the war. He also published a radical newsletter called *Spartacus* and recruited disenchanted workers for his Spartacist League. On May 1, 1916, he organized a demonstration against the war at the Potzdammer Platz in Berlin, denouncing the war-mongers in the government and calling for a violent overthrow of the government. This seditious activity promptly earned him a four-year jail sentence. In October 1918, however, Liebknecht was released from prison as a result of a general amnesty and quickly returned to Berlin to resume his revolutionary activities. When he arrived in Berlin, he was welcomed by huge crowds and celebrated like a conquering hero. One government minister, startled by this remarkable change in public opinion, observed: "Liebknecht has been carried shoulder-high by soldiers who have been decorated with the Iron Cross. Who could have dreamt of such a thing happening three weeks ago?"[7]

With a sizeable part of the German left rallying around Liebknecht and his second-in-command, the gifted ideologue Rosa Luxemburg – a stout, crippled, but combative agitator in her middle forties – the Majority Socialists (Social Democrats) struggled to maintain their control over the German workers. Ostensibly Marxist in their orientation, the Majority Socialists showed little interest in ideology and even less in subverting the social order for Communism. In their lifestyles, the Majority Socialists were *petit bourgeois;* they wanted to raise the general standard of living for the working people in the context of a modern democratic society. Their leader, Friedrich Ebert, typified these relatively moderate expectations. Born in 1871, the son of a humble Catholic tailor, Ebert was apprenticed as a journeyman saddlemaker and, by dint of hard work, gradually rose to the chairmanship of the saddlers' union in Bremen. His good sense, jovial character, and pragmatic outlook made him popular among the rank and file and led to his election to the Bremen city council before he was thirty. In 1904 he became cochairman of his party's convention; and a year later, he was appointed secretary to the central committee of the party in Berlin. In 1912 Ebert became a deputy of his party to the Reichstag; in 1913 he succeeded August Bebel as head of the German Social Democratic Party (SPD).

The Majority Socialists admired Ebert's tact and diplomatic aplomb; they liked his flexibility on ideological issues. In fact, Ebert was not doctrinaire on ideological questions; he was, by conviction and temperament, a revisionary Socialist who strongly believed in parliamentary democracy, preferably in republican but under certain conditions also in monarchical form. His bête noire was lack of organization and lack of good order. He believed that everything should be done according to some acceptable protocol and that decisions should never be forced on constituted authorities by the irrational actions of crowds and rabble-rousers.[8] This is why Ebert threw his authority behind the government of Prince Max von Baden in October 1918, because he genuinely feared a social revolution that would lead, as in Russia, to a Bolshevik coup. The prospect of a Bolshevik revolution filled Ebert and his colleagues, including his right-hand man, Philipp Scheidemann (1863–1939), with horror.

The center of political gravity was thus shifting in the fall of 1918 from the imperial elites to the Majority Socialists. The crucial day was November 9, 1918. In order to prevent the Independent Socialists and the radical Spartacists from gaining control over the working population of Berlin, the Majority Socialists demanded the abdication of Kaiser William, who had moved to army headquarters at Spa for his own protection.

Berliners were in a state of nervous tension on November 9, 1918, sensing that something historic was about to happen. The streets were filled on this day because the Independent Socialists, backed by the Spartacists, had called a general strike. Although crowds milled about in expectation of some major event, relatively little violence occurred. There were some ugly scenes, however, of enlisted soldiers attacking their officers and tearing off their insignia of rank. What most Berliners expected on that day was the abdication of the emperor. Although this was a foregone conclusion, it seemed to drag on interminably. When the Majority Socialists, after repeated inquiries to the chancellery, did not receive definitive news of the emperor's abdication – for William was still toying with the idea of reasserting his control – they made good on their earlier threat of withdrawing their representatives from Max's cabinet. The man who now forced everybody's hands and decided the fate of postwar German politics was Max von Baden. On his own authority, he announced the kaiser's abdication and called for elections to a constituent assembly and the establishment of a regency. Max von Baden then resigned in favor of Friedrich Ebert. The emperor, who was still at Spa with his high-ranking military leaders, referred to this decision by his cousin as "bare-faced, outrageous treason," but his support among the German people had eroded to such an extent that even Groener had to remind him that, with no army behind him, the oath his soldiers had sworn to him was now meaningless. After a final but fruitless argument with his generals, William boarded a special train that carried him into exile in Holland. He never saw Germany again.

GERMANY IN REVOLUTIONARY TURMOIL

AT NOON ON NOVEMBER 9, 1919* while Philipp Scheidemann was eating a bowl of potato soup in the Reichstag dining hall, a crowd of soldiers rushed into the hall and accosted him with the ominous news that Liebknecht was already speaking from the balcony of the imperial palace and was ready to proclaim the Soviet Republic of Germany. Recalling his horrified reaction, Scheidemann later wrote:

> Now I clearly saw what was afoot. I knew his [Liebknecht's] slogan – supreme authority for the workers' councils. Germany to be therefore a Russian province, a branch of the Soviet. No, no, a thousand times no![9]

*sic, 1918, Ed.

Scheidemann then rushed to one of the large windows of the Reichstag and addressed a throng of cheering Berliners with the startling news that "the accursed war is at an end. . . . The emperor has abdicated. . . . Long live the new! Long live the German Republic!"[10]

When Scheidemann made this startling announcement, the news of the emperor's abdication had not been released, and even Liebknecht had not fully marshaled his forces. Thus, when Friedrich Ebert heard that his second-in-command had proclaimed a republic, "His face turned livid with wrath," as Scheidemann later recalled. Ebert banged his fist on a table and yelled at the embarrassed culprit: "You have no right to proclaim a Republic!"[11] Germany had received a republic by accident; and the fact that it was proclaimed by a Socialist would stigmatize it from the moment of its birth.

Later that day, Liebknecht's troops managed to occupy the deserted imperial palace, and it was from there that Liebknecht proclaimed a free Socialist republic, promising "to build a new order of the proletariat." By nightfall no one knew who was really in power in Berlin because two republics had been proclaimed successively. The issue, however, was actually decided on that very evening. As Friedrich Ebert tried to work out the implications of the day's events in his mind in the chancellor's private office, one of the office phones, which turned out to be a secret line to military headquarters at Spa, began to ring. Unaware of this secret line, Ebert was startled to hear General Groener, Ludendorff's successor, on the other end of the line. The general briefly recapitulated the day's events at Spa: he informed Ebert that the emperor had abdicated and was on his way to Holland and that an orderly withdrawal of Germany's front-line armies would commence immediately. In response to Ebert's question as to where the army stood in the present crisis, the general replied that the army would support Ebert's government if, in turn, the new government would support the officers' corps, maintain strict discipline in the army, and oppose Communism. Much reassured, Ebert agreed to these friendly overtures; by doing so, he concluded that much criticized marriage of convenience between the fledgling democratic republic and the traditional military-industrial complex. Although this pact saved both parties from the extreme elements of the revolution, it also, as John Wheeler-Bennett has pointed out, doomed the Weimar Republic from the start.[12] By agreeing not to tamper with the traditional structure of the German army, Ebert and his Majority Socialists unwittingly helped to perpetuate a military establishment that despised the democratic process. Throughout the Weimar Republic the military became a frequent rallying point for right-wing extremists who wanted to destroy the democratic republic.

Yet without the support of the army Ebert's government would probably not have survived the attacks launched against it by the extreme revolutionary left. By Christmas of 1918, Ebert was skating on very thin ice indeed; his cooperation with the military had exposed him to charges of counterrevolutionary activities. Playing for time, he invited three Independent Socialists to join his newly formed cabinet and temporarily endorsed the radicals' claim that all sovereignty resided in the council of soldiers and workers. Privately, he made it clear that he abhorred government by councils of workers and soldiers. The present situation, as he saw it, called for a sound constitutional method by which power would be transferred to a publicly elected constituent assembly that would then proceed to frame a constitution acceptable to the nation.

Ebert's hopes of a peaceful and orderly transition to parliamentary government required the restoration of law and order, and the most effective means of bringing this about still resided in Germany's armed forces. Unfortunately, many army units were melting away quickly in the wake of the general withdrawal from enemy territories and the impending plans to demobilize most of the units. Even in defeat, however, the army managed to preserve its dignity. General Groener succeeded so brilliantly in marching almost two million troops home to Germany that it created the illusion, especially in Berlin, that the German army had not really been defeated at all. On November 11, the day the armistice was signed in France, the vanguard of eleven army divisions staged a spectacular parade by marching up Unter den Linden to the sounds of cheers and hurrahs, with the band striking up "Deutschland, Deutschland, über Alles." Ebert himself reviewed the troops from a specially erected platform, declaring, "I salute you who return unvanquished from the field of battle."[13] The aura of militarism was still so powerful that not even a Socialist could admit publicly that the German army had been defeated.

In the general confusion following the tenuous transfer of power from the old ruling elites to the make-shift cabinet assembled by Friedrich Ebert, the ingrained German sense of order had prevented not only a complete political breakdown but a possible Communist seizure of power as well. Moreover, in order to avoid the collapse of German industry, representatives of employers sat down with trade unionist leaders and worked out mutually beneficial agreements that recognized the existence of independent trade unions and their right to collective bargaining. Finally, to safeguard the integrity of the civil service system, Ebert called upon all state officials to remain at their posts, a measure for which he was much criticized because the managerial elite of the old civil service was bound to be hostile to democracy. Yet only a small minority of Socialists, consisting largely of radicalized shop stewards and Spartacists, resisted these stabilizing policies set forth by Ebert and his Majority Socialists. Even within the councils of workers and soldiers there was determined opposition to following the Russian example of violent or "root-and-branch" revolution. . . .

WEIMAR AND VERSAILLES

BETWEEN 1919 AND 1933, Germany was subject to two major documents: the Treaty of Versailles, which determined how Germans responded to foreign powers, and the Weimar Constitution, which regulated the political life of Germans until Adolf Hitler decided to tear up both documents. Although the Weimar Constitution was one of the most democratic constitutions in the world in 1919, Richard Watt's clever judgment that the constitution began and ended as a document in search of a people remains a sad and tragic fact.[14] By the same token, one could argue that the Treaty of Versailles was also a document that began and ended in search of a single people willing to accept all of its provisions. Neither of these documents proved to be acceptable to the German people, and the fourteen-year history of the Weimar Republic (1919–33) witnessed persistent attempts, especially by the parties of the extreme ends of the political spectrum, to repudiate both. . . .

The provisions of the Versailles Treaty can be seen as treating three basic themes: territorial losses, reparations, and punitive actions aimed at reducing Germany to the level of a minor power. Concerning outright territorial losses, Alsace-Lorraine, as expected, reverted to France, and all German overseas possessions were parceled out among the victors. Acrimonious discussions occurred over the fate of the Rhineland, with the French demanding that the left bank of the Rhine be detached from the rest of Germany and set up as an independent state. Although this extreme proposal was rejected, the peacemakers did agree to detach the left bank of the Rhine along with fifty kilometers of territory on the right bank of the river. Such territory was designated a neutral zone; within that zone Germany was prohibited from establishing any military presence. Moreover, this "demilitarized zone" was to be occupied by Allied troops for a period of fifteen years. The Saar Valley, with its rich coal deposits, was to be placed in French hands for the same period of time; its citizens would then be given a choice whether they wanted to join Germany or France.

To the east, the Allied powers wanted to set up strong buffer states against Bolshevism. As a result, those parts of the former German Empire that had been populated by Poles were assigned to the new state of Poland, and those parts that had been populated by Czechs or Slovaks were given to the new state of Czechoslovakia. Unfortunately, large numbers of Germans would now find themselves living in Poland and Czechoslovakia. In the case of Poland, the peacemakers decided to give the new state access to the Baltic Sea, but by cutting a "corridor" to that sea, they cut off East Prussia from the rest of Germany. The city of Danzig, located at the end of the corridor, became a "free city," politically independent but economically available to Poland. The problem of Danzig and the corridor, involving disputed territory and ethnic conflicts, would poison the relationship

between Germany and Poland in the inter-war period, ultimately providing Hitler with a pretext for triggering World War II.

The fate of other territories, east or west, was to be decided by democratic plebiscites. Upper Silesia, a rich mining area, was annexed by Poland after a disputed plebiscite, while the rest of Silesia went to Germany. Although plebiscites were regarded by the Allies as an expression of national self-determination, they were not always honored when the decision was likely to run counter to the expected outcome of the victors. Thus, when the Austrians wanted to join Germany, the peacemakers set aside self-determination in favor of national self-interest, prohibiting the *Anschluss* on the grounds that this would add too much territory and too many people to Germany. The same argument was made in respect to the Sudetenland and the Tyrol. Over three million Germans lived in the mountainous provinces of Bohemia and Moravia – two regions that the peacemakers had given to the new state of Czechoslovakia, ostensibly to provide the Czechs with more defensible frontiers. The Germans who lived in these regions were called Sudeten Germans after the mountain belt separating Bohemia and Silesia. Strictly speaking, these Germans had formerly belonged to the Habsburg Empire, but now found themselves as a minority within the new Czechoslovakian state. The same was true of those Germans living in the South Tyrol, for when the Brenner Pass was given to the Italians for strategic military reasons, the Germans in the South Tyrol now suddenly found themselves living in Italy.

The clauses of the Versailles Treaty dealing with reparations were the most punitive because they were based on the self-serving belief that Germany was solely responsible for having caused the war. The peacemakers' claim that Germany was responsible for the war was summed up in Article 231 of the treaty, subsequently referred to by the Germans as the "war guilt" clause:

> The Allied and Associated Governments affirm and Germany accepts the responsibility of Germany and her allies for causing all the loss and damage to which the Allied and Associated Governments and their nationals have been subjected

as a consequence of the war imposed upon them by the aggression of Germany and her Allies.[15]

In practice, this statement declaring Germany guilty of having caused all the damage and suffering of World War I was intended to be a moral justification for reparations. The peacemakers were determined to hold Germany liable for all the material damage caused by four years of devastating warfare; but since they could not translate this claim into a measurable or sensible amount of money, the treaty remained silent on the full amount of payments the Germans were expected to dole out to the victors. In the meantime, the treaty forced Germany to pay five billion dollars in gold before May 1, 1921, and to relinquish extensive deliveries of coal, chemicals, river barges, and most of the German merchant marine fleet. The German delegation at Versailles was further informed that a special Inter-Allied Reparations Commission would be convened to settle Germany's final obligations. The German counterargument that this amounted to a blank check, obligating Germany in advance to pay any amount the victors wanted to impose, was categorically rejected by the Allies without explanation.

No other provisions of the Versailles Treaty poisoned the postwar period as much as the articles of the treaty that concerned reparations; and when the Inter-Allied Reparations Committee finally announced the total bill in 1921, a staggering sum of thirty-five billion dollars in gold, even Allied statesmen doubted that Germany could afford such exorbitant obligations. No Hitlerian demagogue was required to point out that such vindictive measures would cripple Germany's economy. Similar arguments were already being made on the Allied side, notably by John Maynard Keynes, then a young Cambridge economist and a member of the British delegation to the Paris Peace Conference. In a dispassionate work of analytical reasoning entitled *The Economic Consequences of the War* (1921), Keynes persuasively argued that reparations really aimed at the destruction of economic life in Germany and that by doing so, they would ironically also threaten the health and prosperity of the Allies themselves.[16] He argued that already before the war, German trade had

shown a large deficit because imports far exceeded exports, but he added that Germany had balanced its international trade account by "invisible exports" such as selling rights to the use of German shipping, selling interest in German investments abroad, selling insurance premiums, and so on. The treaty, however, impaired payments to Germany from abroad, thus in turn making it impossible for the Germans to pay off the vast reparations demanded of them. This was made all the more difficult now by

the almost total loss of her colonies, her overseas connections, her mercantile marine; and her foreign properties; by the cession of ten percent of her territory and population, of one third of her coal and of three-quarters of her iron ore; by two million casualties among men in the prime of life; by the starvation of her people for four years; by the burden of a vast war debt; by the depreciation of her currency to less than one-seventh its former value; by the disruption of her allies and their territories; by revolution at home and Bolshevism on her borders; and by all the unmeasured ruin in strength and hope of four years of all-swallowing war and final defeat.[17]

Keynes denounced the peacemakers as hypocrites and political opportunists whose pious promises of a just and lasting peace had led only to "the weaving of that web of sophistries and Jesuitical exegesis that was finally to clothe with insincerity the language and substance of the whole treaty."[18] He recommended the reconstruction of the German economy as a precondition to a general European recovery. Helping the Germans back on their feet, however, would require a scaling down of reparations, cancellation of war debts, reduction of inflation, and massive reinvigoration of German industry through international loans. Keynes even proposed an extensive free common market under the aegis of the League of Nations. His immensely stimulating and controversial ideas were roundly condemned by the defenders of the Versailles Treaty because they amounted, in essence, to a repudiation of the treaty at the moment of its birth.

Equally as shattering as the economic provisions

of the Versailles Treaty were the terms relating to the future of the German military. The German army was to be reduced in size to a volunteer force of one hundred thousand men. Of these one hundred thousand, no more than four thousand could be officers, and their term of service was limited to twenty-five years, while that of the enlisted personnel was limited to twelve years. The strength of this small volunteer force was to be further impaired by depriving it of tanks, aircraft, and other "offensive" weapons. Similarly, the German navy was to be dismantled except for a token surface-vessel force not exceeding ten thousand tons. The German battle fleet was to be delivered into Allied hands, but when the German officers who had taken the fleet to the naval harbor of Scapa Flow in the Orkney Islands learned of the fate that was in store for their ships, they cheated the Allies of their prize by scuttling fifty of the sixty-eight ships.[19]

Finally, with an eye toward the heart of the German military establishment, the treaty called for the abolition of the general staff, the war college, and all cadet schools. Adding insult to injury, the peacemakers also demanded that Germany hand over the kaiser and other war leaders for trial on charges of violating the laws of war.

POLITICAL CHAOS, PUTSCHES, AND THE END OF MONEY

THE IMMEDIATE IMPACT of the Versailles Treaty on Germany was twofold: it led to the first cabinet crisis within the new democratic government, and it inspired a soldiers' revolt against the republic. The first of these events occurred when the Scheidemann cabinet received the terms of the treaty, found the provisions unacceptable, and resigned on June 20, 1919. More serious was the military's reaction to the treaty. As previously noted, the provisions dealing with the future of the German military were devastating, especially on the German officers' corps. When the implications of the treaty had been fully recognized, several leaders of the German military, notably General Walter Reinhardt, commander of the provisional Reichswehr, began to think seriously about armed

resistance. These still inchoate plans, however, did not immediately come to fruition because even the most die-hard generals realized that opposition to the Allies was hopeless. Some military leaders now shifted their rage to the hapless republican government, blaming it for being pliantly submissive to the will of the Allied powers.

The republican government, in the meantime, was under intense pressure from the Allied powers to reduce the German army to a peacetime force of one hundred thousand men and to disband all paramilitary (Free Corps) forces that were still roaming the country. This only served to fuel the military's resentments, resulting in a series of mutinous acts aimed at overthrowing the government. The most serious of these acts came in March 1920 when several army officers conspired to overthrow the Weimar Republic. . . .

Germany's economic position was deteriorating daily as a result of runaway inflation. These inflationary difficulties stemmed primarily from a series of imprudent government fiscal policies that originated in World War I.[20] The German government did not try to finance the war by taxation but rather by floating internal bonds. In addition, the government also removed restrictions on the circulation of notes not covered by gold reserves; it further authorized the establishment of Loan Banks with the right to extend credit on collateral that had not previously been approved for Reichsbank loans under existing regulations. These Loan Banks extended liberal credits to a variety of borrowers – the federal states, municipalities, and newly founded war corporations. Funds were simply provided by printing paper money.

As war costs increased, the government resorted more and more to the printing presses, driving up the amount of currency in circulation and devaluating the mark. By 1918 the mark stood at half the gold parity of 1914. The war hid the problem of inflation, but the pressures of defeat, coupled with the economic burdens imposed on Germany by the Versailles Treaty, brought the problem to the surface in dramatic terms. The whole German economy was now cracking under the impact of years of deficit spending and burdensome obligations imposed by the Allies.

The immediate cause of the collapse of the German economy was the invasion of the Ruhr by the French on January 11, 1923. The French prime minister, Raymond Poincaré, was a Germanophobe who strongly believed that the Germans were willfully deceiving the Allies that they could not faithfully meet their financial obligations. The French had already spent billions of francs in restoring their wartorn areas, expecting the Germans to pay for every penny of it. Poincaré adamantly rejected Cuno's request for a moratorium on reparations payments and then tried to galvanize other Allied powers into supporting military intervention. Neither the British nor the Americans, however, believed that an Allied invasion of the Ruhr was justified. Poincaré pressed on regardless, merely waiting for a legal pretext. This came when the Reparations Commission declared Germany in default on the delivery of 140,000 telegraph poles.

On January 11, 1923, a French-Belgian force invaded the Ruhr, seized its industries and mines, and stirred up separatist feelings aimed at further weakening the unity of the Reich.[21] French occupying troops acted harshly and brutally. Bloody clashes were the order of the day. The German government responded to the French invasion with a policy of "passive resistance," which meant that all economic activity came to a standstill in the Ruhr. The German economy now became unglued because the government, in an effort to subsidize the Ruhr workers who had gone on strike, resorted to printing more and more paper money. Inflation reached fantastic heights; unemployment soared. Even with the best intentions, the German government simply could not meet all of its social obligations; it was already chafing under the weight of its obligations to the Allies, to its war veterans, to the unemployed, to the aged.

Germans were caught in a vortex from which there seemed no escape. The world was upside-down: a simple penny postage stamp cost 5 million marks, an egg 80 million, a pound of meat 3.2 billion, a pound of butter 6 billion, a pound of potatoes 50 million, a glass of beer 150 million. Prices changed from day to day, prompting people to rush to the stores armed with satchels of worthless money to buy simple necessities.

To many Germans this period seemed like an economic apocalypse. Konrad Heiden has referred to it as the "end of money,"[22] the end of roseate visions of material affluence, and the end of all secular faiths in progress. We might add that it also seemed like the end of faith in government, its good word, and its assurance that the savings of ordinary citizens would be protected. For nine years, Germans had sacrificed their lives and their savings to the government. In return, the government had squandered a third of the national wealth in a futile war as a result of which war loans, savings, and investments were now worthless. The savings of thrifty middle-class Germans were wiped out. It was not uncommon for German savers to receive polite letters from bank managers informing them that "the bank deeply regrets that it can no longer administer your deposit of sixty-eight thousand marks, since the costs are all out of proportion to the capital. We are therefore taking the liberty of returning your capital. Since we have no bank-notes of small enough denominations at our disposal, we have rounded out the sum to one million marks. Enclosure: one 1,000,000 mark bill."[23] To add insult to injury, the envelope was adorned by a canceled five million mark postage stamp.

While the majority of middle-class Germans were ruined by the collapse of 1923, never fully regaining their trust in the government, a few clever financial manipulators grew fabulously wealthy by securing massive bank credits, promptly investing in "physical values" (real estate, businesses), and repaying the debts with devalued money. It was in this manner that Hugo Stinnes, already a wealthy man before 1923, bought up at random large numbers of businesses, including banks, hotels, newspapers, paper mills, and so on.

Stinnes affected the frugal mentality of the clerk and coal miner he had once been, but there were hundreds like him who spent garishly and contributed much to the growing atmosphere of moral decadence and cynicism, an atmosphere that has been so vividly captured in the music, art, and popular entertainment of the 1920s. While a few grew rich, the country as a whole steadily deteriorated. Unemployment increased, farmers hoarded their produce, manufacturing dropped, and millions of thrifty savers lost all of their savings.

Since Cuno did not offer a solution to the crisis, the Social Democrats withdrew their support and called for stronger leadership. On August 12, 1923, Ebert appointed Gustav Stresemann, leader of the German People's Party, as chancellor of the new government. The new chancellor, destined to become one of the most important statesmen of the Weimar Republic, faced staggering problems: the Ruhr was occupied by the French; Communist-Socialist regimes had taken power in Thuringia and Saxony; Communist insurrections plagued Hamburg; Bavaria had fallen into the hands of right-wing reactionaries who threatened to secede from the Reich; Germany's eastern borders were threatened by the Poles; and the mark stood at 4.6 million to the dollar. It was in this volatile atmosphere that an obscure corporal of World War I, leader of a growing right-wing party, determined to overthrow the Weimar Republic. His name was Adolf Hitler.

Notes

1. Quoted by Alan Palmer, *The Kaiser: Warlord of the Second Reich* (New York: Scribner's, 1978), 175.
2. Gordon Craig, *War, Politics, and Diplomacy* (New York: Praeger, 1966), 46–57.
3. Georg Alexander von Müller, *Regierte der Kaiser? Kriegstagebücher, Aufzeichnungen und Briefe des Chefs des Marine-Kabinetts Admiral Georg Alexander von Müller 1914–1918,* ed. Walter Görlitz (Göttingen: Musterschmidt, 1959), 68.
4. For the origins of the stab-in-the-back legend (*Dolchstosslegende*), see John W. Wheeler-Bennett, *Wooden Titan: Hindenburg* (New York: W. Morrow, 1938), 238.
5. Erich Eyck, *A History of the Weimar Republic,* trans. Harlan P. Hanson and Robert G. L. Waite, 2 vols. (Cambridge, Mass.: Harvard Univ. Press, 1962), 1:37–39.
6. A good summary of scholarly views on the German revolution of 1918–19 is contained in Reinhard Rürup, "Problems of the German Revolution of 1918–19," *Journal of Contemporary History* 3 (1968) 109–35. The most acute analysis of the survival of prewar institutions (armed forces, civil service, education) into the postwar period is Dietrich Bracher, *Die Auflösung der Weimarer Republik: Eine Studie zum Problem des Machtverfalls in der Demokratie* (Villingen, Schwarzwald: Ring-Verlag, 1960).
7. Scheidemann quoted by Karl W. Meyer, *Karl Liebknecht: Man without a Country* (Washington D.C.: Public Affairs Press, 1957), 127.
8. Golo Mann, *The History of Germany since 1789,* trans. Marian Jackson (New York: Praeger, 1968), 332.
9. Philipp Scheidemann, *The Making of New Germany: The Memoirs of Philipp Scheidemann,* trans. J. E. Mitchell (New York: Appleton, 1929), 2:262.
10. Ibid., 2:264.
11. Ibid.
12. Wheeler-Bennett, *Nemesis of Power,* 21.
13. Friedrich Ebert, *Schriften, Aufzeichnungen und Reden* (Dresden: C. Reissner, 1926), 2:127–30.
14. Richard M. Watt, *The Kings Depart: The Tragedy of Germany: Versailles and the German Revolution.* (New York: Simon & Schuster, 1968) 314.
15. U.S. Senate, *Treaty of Peace with Germany,* 66th Cong., 1st sess., 1919, Senate Doc. 49.
16. John Maynard Keynes, *The Economic Consequences of the War* (New York: Harcourt, Brace & Howe, 1920), 15–16.
17. Ibid., 187.
18. Ibid., 51.
19. For the fate of the German navy, see Langhorne Gibson and Paul Schubert, *Death of a Fleet* (New York: Coward-McCan, 1932).
20. On the complexities of the German economic collapse of 1923 there is an excellent summary of views in Fritz Ringer's documentary collection entitled *The German Inflation of 1923* (New York: Oxford Univ. Press, 1969).
21. On the Ruhr question, see Paul Wentzcke, *Ruhrkampf: Einbruch und Abwehr im Rheinisch-westfälischen Industriegebiet* (Berlin: R. Hobbing, 1930).
22. Konrad Heiden, *Der Fuehrer: Hitler's Rise to Power* (Boston: Houghton Mifflin, 1944), chap. 7.
23. Ibid., 127.

Ezra Mendelsohn **Poland**

The resurrection of Poland as a free, sovereign state in 1918 was postwar Eastern Europe's most popular and dramatic example of the triumph of the national principle. Unlike the Czechs, Slovaks, Romanians, Lithuanians, and Latvians, the Poles had enjoyed a long and unbroken history of political independence, which came to an end only in the second half of the eighteenth century. The collapse of statehood, however, by no means signaled the collapse of Polish nationalism. In contrast with the situation among most of the peoples of Eastern Europe, the Polish ruling class (*szlachta*) remained intact and succeeded in maintaining the continuity of Polish culture even when the Polish state was no longer in existence. Poland, therefore, was never a peasant nation, although peasants constituted the bulk of the population. During the nineteenth century, moreover, in the wake of industrialization in the Polish lands, a small but significant Polish bourgeoisie and proletariat emerged. Polish national institutions – universities, the Polish Catholic church, even parliaments – also flourished, though certainly not everywhere in the Polish lands and sometimes only for short intervals. The anomaly of a vibrant, powerful people without a state of its own was obvious throughout the nineteenth century, and the Polish cause was enthusiastically adopted by many people and organizations which were far less interested in, or enthusiastic about, the national struggle of the Ukrainians or of the Romanians. Indeed, the "Polish question" became one of the most important and explosive issues in European politics, and its apparent resolution in 1918 was greeted with joy by Poland's many friends and with relief by those who saw in Poland's partition a source of political instability in Europe. If many greeted the creation of Czechoslovakia, Yugoslavia, and the independent Baltic States with skepticism, it was clear to most observers that the creation of an independent Polish state had righted an old and shameful wrong. By the same token, Poland's prospects, thanks to its strong national tradition and cultural and institutional continuity, seemed much brighter than those of the other new East European states. It was therefore hoped that a strong, stable Poland would act as the cornerstone of a stable East Central Europe.

During the nineteenth century the lands which had once constituted the Polish state belonged to the Prussian (later German), Russian, and Austro-Hungarian states. . . .

The sudden and unexpected collapse of the three partitioning powers in 1917–1918 made the rebirth of a Polish state inevitable. The borders of the new state, however, were the subject of lengthy diplomatic and military maneuvers, and were not permanently settled until 1923. The new borders did not satisfy those Polish maximalists who hoped for a return to the vast territories of the prepartition Polish state, but they were large enough to satisfy most nationalists. In the east the Poles made good their claims to Vilna (Wilno), and while they failed to annex Kiev, once a Polish city, they did annex the province of Volynia, previously part of the Russian Ukraine. These and other eastern areas were generally known during the interwar period as the "kresy" (borderlands). All of formerly Habsburg Galicia, including its heavily Ukrainian eastern half (whose capital was Lwów), was incorporated into the new state, as was nearly all of Congress Poland. In the west, Poland obtained part of Upper Silesia (after a plebicite in 1921), part of Austrian Silesia (shared with the new state of Czechoslovakia), Poznań, and part of Pomorze. (Danzig, also claimed by Poland, was made a free city.) The national appetite for borders which contained such Polish ethnic islands in non-Polish seas as Vilna and Lwów, as well as extensive territories in mixed Polish-German regions, rendered the new Poland not a nation-state but, rather, a state of nationalities. . . .

Ezra Mendelsohn, **The Jews of East Central Europe Between the World Wars**, 11–12, 13–14, 36–37, 82–83, 259, 261. Copyright © 1983 by Ezra Mendelsohn. Reprinted by permission of Indiana University Press.

According to the census of 1921, the population of Poland was 27,176,717; approximately one-third of this number were non-Poles. The largest non-Polish nationality was the Ukrainian group, followed by Jews, Belorussians, and Germans.[1] The Slavic minorities – Ukrainians and Belorussians – possessed a territorial base in the kresy and in eastern Galicia as well as aspirations for political independence. Indeed, the Galician Ukrainians, whose national consciousness was particularly strong, had proclaimed the independent West Ukrainian Republic in 1918, and, although this state was crushed by Polish arms, the hope of establishing a great Ukrainian state lived on. Ukrainian and Belorussian nationalism was particularly dangerous for the Poles, since both these nationalities might well be tempted to look eastward, to the Ukrainian and Belorussian Soviet republics, for inspiration and assistance. Thus the problem of the Slavic national minorities was inextricably connected with the threat of Soviet irredentism and the spread of Communism within Poland. By the same token, the German population of the western regions was naturally suspected of hoping and working for the return of German rule. It was less logical to accuse the Jews of plotting either to establish their own state within Polish borders or to destroy the Polish state through the intervention of its allies abroad, but such accusations were the stock in trade of numerous Polish anti-Semites. In short, for many Poles the national-minorities problem constituted a serious challenge to the integrity of the state, and the question of how to deal with it became a major issue in interwar Polish politics. . . .

The basic issue which confronted Polish politicians was whether Poland was a multinational state by definition or a Polish nation-state despite the undeniable existence of numerous non-Poles. Adoption of the first position implied granting extensive national rights to the "territorial minorities" in the east, the Ukrainians and the Belorussians, as well as giving special status to the German minority in the west. It also implied a greater willingness, at least, to consider the Jews' demands for national autonomy. If, on the other hand, Poland was to be regarded as a nation-state, the implications were quite different. In this case the nationalities would not receive special rights,

efforts would be made to polonize the country, and the interests of the Polish element within the population would be promoted at the expense of the non-Poles. It was this latter position which was adopted by the great majority of Polish political parties and was, in fact, implemented. The Ukrainians and the Belorussians were often regarded as an "ethnic mass" which, with the right treatment, eventually could be merged with the Polish nation. Ukrainian demands for autonomy in eastern Galicia were turned down, as were their requests to establish a Ukrainian university in Lwów. Ukrainian- and Belorussian-language elementary schools were permitted to exist but were under strong pressure to polonize; their numbers declined over the years. Members of these Slavic nationalities did not have an easy time in pursuing careers in the Polish civil service, and they encountered discrimination in all walks of life. The Germans, too, faced similar discrimination and received little satisfaction so far as their nationalist demands were concerned. True, negotiations were occasionally held between the Poles and the various nationalities (including the Jews), but the "agreements," if reached, failed to endure. The fact is that most Polish leaders adhered to the slogan "Poland for the Poles." The non-Poles would have to conform, suffer in silence, and in the end either emigrate or undergo polonization.[2] The Polish nation, it was felt, had not shed its blood and sacrificed its sons in order to establish a state in which vast territories and important financial resources would be controlled by non-Poles. . . .

In this new state, beset with seemingly intractable internal and external problems, only nationalism and the Catholic church served as unifying factors. Both Polish nationalism and Polish Catholicism were by their very nature exclusive, anti-pluralistic, and anti-Semitic. And, since there was little in the way of a tolerant, pluralistic, liberal political tradition in modern, as opposed perhaps to medieval, Poland, nothing stood in the way of the triumph of extreme national-religious intolerance from which all the minorities in the state suffered and which, because of the special nature of the anti-Jewish tradition and the economic vulnerability of the Jews, was particularly threatening to the Jewish minority.

It is true that the Polish state, unlike Hungary

and Romania, refrained from enacting anti-Jewish legislation in the late 1930s. It is also true that in Poland, unlike in most other East European countries, there was considerable opposition to the extreme anti-Semitism of the late 1930s. But, in the development of Jewish-gentile relations, there was little essential difference between Poland and the other major states of the region, with the important exception of Czechoslovakia. The combination of traditional hatred of Jews, the triumph of nationalism, internal weakness, and the role of the Jewish question in the struggle for power between the moderate right and the extreme right typified the situation not only in Poland, but in other East European states as well. In this respect, as with regard to internal Jewish developments – acculturation, economic decline, political divisiveness, the failure of national autonomy and Zionism to solve the Jewish question – Poland may serve as a paradigm of the Jewish experience in interwar East Central Europe. It remains only to add that,

when Hitler's soldiers, aided by Soviet troops, stamped out Polish independence in 1939, Nazi anti-Semitism, though far more extreme and thorough than the Polish variety, struck a highly responsive chord among large sections of the Polish population. In this respect, too, Poland was typical of East Central Europe.

Notes

1. For data and a discussion of the difficulties of ethnic statistics, see Rothschild, *East Central Europe,* 34–36.
2. See the following Polish studies: Andrzej Chojnowski, *Koncepcje polityki narodowościowej rządów polskich w latach 1921–1939* (Wrocław, etc., 1979); Jerzy Tomaszewski, "Konsekwencja wielonarodowościowej struktury ludności Polski 1918–1939 dla procesów integracyjnych społeczeństwa," in *Drogi integracji społeczeństwa w Polsce XIX–XX w.,* ed. Henryk Zielinski (Wrocław, etc., 1976), 109–38. See also Alexander Groth, "Dmowski, Piłsudski, and Ethnic Conflict in Pre-1939 Poland," *Canadian Slavic Studies* 3 (1969):69–91; Joel Cang, "The Opposition Parties in Poland and Their Attitude towards the Jews and the Jewish Question." *Jewish Social Studies* 1, no. 2 (1939):241–56.

Campaign poster for the *German-Soziale Partei* warning Germans against Communist rule. The illustration shows a multi-headed beast with large claws. One of the heads has the face of Lenin. The text reads:

The International under Marxism
brings only crisis, hunger, misery, [and] decay.
Away with this insanity!
Away with the Jews – and the dominance by foreigners!
Away with class struggle and party quarrels!
Unite yourselves, Germans! Vote for the Jew-free
German-Social party.

1924. (Deutsches Historisches Museum, courtesy of USHMM Photo Archives)

Henry Ford giving an address in support of Herbert Hoover during the 1932 presidential campaign. Ford, one of America's leading industrialists in the early twentieth century, used his newspaper, *The Dearborn Independent*, to publish the nineteenth century antisemitic forgery, *The Protocols of the Elders of Zion*. Hitler was so impressed by Ford that he awarded him the medal of the Grand Cross of the German Eagle. Ford publicly repudiated his antisemitism only when challenged by a libel suit brought against *The Dearborn Independent* in 1927. October 19, 1932. (From the collections of Henry Ford Museum and Greenfield Village)

An early photograph of members of the Nazi Party. Julius Streicher, seated front center, later became publisher of *Der Stürmer*, an antisemitic newspaper. 1922. (Joanne Schartow, courtesy of USHMM Photo Archives)

Ezra Mendelsohn **Jewish Life Between the Wars**

INTRODUCTION

THE INTERWAR YEARS in East Central Europe, a short but well-defined period no longer than a single generation, witnessed the dramatic and unexpected triumph of the national principle and the formation of such new states as Poland, Czechoslovakia, Latvia, and Lithuania. During these years previously subjugated nationalities struggled to overcome staggering difficulties and to establish viable states that, so it was hoped, would never again be brought under foreign domination. That their efforts, made possible by the collapse of German, Russian, and Austro-Hungarian power, were doomed by the rise of Nazism and of the Soviet Union should not obscure the considerable achievements of the 1920s and 1930s as the largely peasant peoples of East Central Europe firmly established their national identities and made strong claims for equal acceptance in the family of European nations. Indeed, despite the general failure to cope with seemingly intractable economic, social, and political problems, and despite the rise of local fascist movements in the 1930s, in some ways this period constitutes a golden age wedged between pre–World War I oppression and post–World War II Communist domination.

For the student of modern Jewish history, East Central Europe during the interwar years is of particularly dramatic interest. For one thing, these years may be justly regarded as a period of grim rehearsal for the tragedy of East European Jewry during World War II. In most of the new states, relations between Jews and gentiles were bad from the very beginning (Czechoslovakia and the Baltic States are notable exceptions), and in all of them these relations deteriorated sharply during the 1930s. In Hungary Jewish emancipation was actually revoked, while in Poland and Romania the emancipation won in 1918–1919 proved to be no guarantee of equality. Almost everywhere the "Jewish question" became a matter of paramount concern, and anti-Semitism a major political force. . . .

A second major consideration is internal developments within the Jewish communities. During the 1920s and 1930s modern Jewish political movements, largely the creation of tsarist Russia, flourished in Eastern Europe as they never had before and as they never would again. In some countries, most notably Poland, secular Jewish nationalism and Jewish socialism were transformed almost overnight into mass movements that were able to wrest control of the Jewish community from its more traditional leaders. The Jewries of Poland, Galicia, Lithuania, Bessarabia, and Bukovina underwent what might be termed a process of politicization and nationalization not unlike that which was affecting their gentile neighbors. Even the Orthodox population, traditionally strong in Eastern Europe, organized itself into modern political parties that adopted many of their secular adversaries' characteristics. Along with the striking politicization of East European Jewry went efforts to implement the tenets of the now triumphant ideologies. In fact, East Central Europe between the wars was the major testing ground for modern Jewish politics: thus the remarkable, though ultimately unsuccessful, efforts to establish extraterritorial national autonomy for the Jews, one of the chief aims of most Jewish nationalist parties; thus Zionist efforts to promote mass emigration (*aliyah* in Hebrew) to Palestine, which for the first time became a practical option for large numbers of Jews fleeing Eastern Europe. And then there was the attempt made by the Jewish left both to promote a proletarian Jewish culture and to forge alliances with the non-Jewish left in order to topple the "bourgeois" states of the region and to replace them with socialist or Communist regimes. Finally, the antinationalist Orthodox Jewish parties sought to perpetuate the old Jewish way of life by establishing new institutions and by instituting working relationships with the various regimes. . . .

EZRA MENDELSOHN, THE JEWS OF EAST CENTRAL EUROPE BETWEEN THE WORLD WARS, 1–8, 23–25, 27, 28–30, 32–36, 43, 47–49, 63–74, 76, 259–265. COPYRIGHT © 1983 BY EZRA MENDELSOHN. REPRINTED BY PERMISSION OF INDIANA UNIVERSITY PRESS.

The demographic . . . decline of East European Jewry [and] . . . the more important process of economic decline . . . resulted by the 1930s in the impoverishment of hundreds of thousands of Jews in Poland, Romania, and the Baltic States. An additional theme . . . has to do with the different though related processes of acculturation (by which is meant the Jews' adoption of the external characteristics of the majority culture, above all its language) and assimilation (by which is meant the Jews' efforts to adopt the national identity of the majority, to become Poles, Hungarians, Romanians "of the Mosaic faith," or even to abandon their Jewish identity altogether). Were the Jews in these lands growing closer to their neighbors, or further apart? And did the Jews' willingness or lack of willingness to acculturate and assimilate have any impact on attitudes toward them? These are among the most vital questions the historian of postemancipation Jewry can ask, along with the no less important question as to the efficacy of the various Jewish political proposals for solving the Jewish question.

East Central Europe is a notoriously difficult region to define, and it has been defined differently by different scholars.[1] . . . [In] Poland, Hungary, Czechoslovakia, Romania, Lithuania, Latvia, and Estonia . . . resided the major Ashkenazi (i.e., of German origin) Jewries, almost all of which, except for pre–World War I Romanian Jewry, had previously resided either in tsarist Russia or in Habsburg Austria-Hungary. The relatively small Jewish communities of Bulgaria and Yugoslavia. . . contained a strong Sephardic (i.e., Spanish) component.[2] Even within this rather limited area there was enormous diversity, both in general and among the various Jewish communities. Considering first the general context, we are confronted with a complex picture of different religious, cultural, and political traditions along with different social patterns and widely varying degrees of economic development. The predominant religion was Roman Catholic (in Poland, Czechoslavakia, Hungary, and Lithuania), but Romania was largely Greek Orthodox. The Uniate church was important in certain regions in Czechoslovakia, Poland, and Romania, while there were significant Protestant enclaves as well, represented by some German

minorities (as in the Baltic States) or by non-German remnants of the once powerful Reformation in Eastern Europe, as in Hungary and Czechoslovakia. Religious loyalties, in this part of the world, sometimes implied other loyalties as well – to Rome and the West, as in the case of the Catholic Poles, to Moscow and the East, as in the case of some Ukrainians in Subcarpathian Rus and Bessarabia, and of some Belorussians in Poland. The existence of strong Catholic, Uniate, Orthodox, and Protestant churches lent to the area the character of religious pluralism, which did not, however, as the Jewish experience demonstrates, necessarily result in an atmosphere of religious tolerance. The same may be said of the ethnic diversity of the regions; the mix of Slavs, Magyars, Romanians, Balts, and Germans by no means encouraged national tolerance, as we shall have occasion to observe during the course of this study.

Religious and ethnic diversity was paralleled by economic and social diversity. The western regions of Czechoslovakia, namely Bohemia and Moravia, were among the most advanced in Europe, and such cities as Budapest and Riga were hardly less modern than was Prague. On the other hand, East Central Europe contained some of the most primitive economies in Europe, in such areas as Subcarpathian Rus, eastern Galicia, and Bessarabia. The gentry-peasant societies of the more backward lands of the region stood in sharp contrast to the bourgeois character of the Czech lands. Political divisions were no less apparent, the most striking being between former Russian and former Habsburg territories. The Baltic States, central and eastern Poland, and Bessarabia had all been part of the tsarist empire and were strongly influenced by its autocratic political traditions. The Czech lands, Slovakia, Galicia, Subcarpathian Rus, Transylvania, Bukovina, and, of course, Hungary had all been part of the Habsburg empire. Here a further division is necessary, namely, between those territories that had been a part of the Hungarian half of the Habsburg empire (Transylvania, Subcarpathian Rus, and Slovakia) and those that had not been. These divisions had important cultural as well as political implications, since they determined in which regions Russian, German, or Hungarian culture was widespread.

Despite this evident diversity, certain shared

characteristics imparted to East Central Europe a large measure of unity. Most obvious was the fact that, with the already noted exception of the Czech lands, this was an economically and socially backward region that did not make great economic progress during the interwar years. The majority of the inhabitants were peasants, the percentage of city dwellers was low, and cities were often regarded as foreign enclaves by a hostile peasantry and by the gentry-derived intelligentsia. There was little industrialization, and the commercial class was often "nonnative." The old elites – landowners, the clergy – retained considerable power, although they had to share it with the emerging intelligentsia and bourgeoisie, and sometimes even with the rapidly organizing peasantry. To the problems of how to overcome backwardness and poverty was added another shared by most East Central European lands – political inexperience.

The new states faced the extraordinarily difficult task of nation-building after centuries of dependence, a task made all the more difficult by the degree of external hostility to their still fragile independence. The Baltic States had virtually no memories of independence; there had never been a Czechoslovakia, and Poland had been wiped off the map of Europe in the late eighteenth century. Romania had existed as an independent entity before World War I, but after its great postwar territorial acquisitions it was a virtually new state. Hungary had been an equal partner in the prewar Habsburg empire; now, greatly reduced in size, it too was something of a new state. Similar problems, together with similar economic and social structures, helped to produce a fairly homogeneous political situation in the region. All these states were anti-Communist and antirevolutionary, and most perceived the Soviet Union as their most dangerous antagonist. Most began their lives as democracies, at least on paper, and all, with the familiar Czechoslovak exception, moved to the right during the interwar years. This was only to be expected, given their anti-Soviet orientation, the control exerted by the traditional elites, and the weak if not nonexistent traditions of democracy and liberalism. In most of these lands the principal political struggle was not between left and right (the left tended to be quite weak), but rather between right and extreme right. The principal internal threat to the stability of such countries as Poland, Hungary, and Romania in the 1930s emanated from the so-called native fascist movements, such as the Iron Guard in Romania and the Arrow Cross in Hungary. This struggle, in which the Jewish question played a great role, had fateful consequences for the local Jewish communities.

Another major problem that plagued all the lands of East Central Europe was that of the minority nationalities. Despite the triumph of the national principle after World War I, the political boundaries in East Central Europe were not, and indeed could not, be drawn according to strictly ethnic criteria. Most of the countries discussed here regarded themselves as nation-states, but in fact they were not. One-third of the population of Poland, for example, was non-Polish. The minorities were often regarded as threats to the status quo and as disloyal elements interested in redrawing the frontiers in order to accommodate their own national interests. There was something to these accusations. The German minority in Czechoslovakia was transformed into a pro-Nazi force during the 1930s, and the Hungarian minority in Romanian Transylvania wished to live under Hungarian sovereignty. Many Ukrainians of Galicia and other regions in Eastern Europe wanted a state of their own, and some were sympathetic to the Soviet Ukrainian republic. The determined efforts of such countries as Poland and Romania to establish centralized states and to promote the interests of the dominant nationality inevitably clashed with the grievances, real or imagined, of the national minorities. This led to the flourishing of extreme nationalism, which may be regarded as the ruling ideology of East Central Europe between the wars. In this region nation was exalted over class, and unbridled nationalism was rarely tempered by social idealism. Moreover, the existence of the national-minorities problem constituted a standing invitation to intervention on the part of foreign powers interested in upsetting the Versailles settlement. Germany, Italy, and Soviet Russia all promoted various irredentist movements in Eastern Europe, thus greatly contributing to the region's instability.

From the Jewish perspective, the East Central European environment as it has been described here offered little grounds for optimism. Generally Jews have flourished in lands of cultural and religious tolerance, political liberalism, stability, and economic growth. In interwar East Central Europe they were confronted, rather, with chauvinism and intolerance, instability, economic stagnation, and extreme right-wing politics. Moreover, the traditional safety valve of emigration had been blocked by the new restrictions inaugurated by the United States and other Western nations. Many observers were quick to point out, even at the beginning of this period, that the old multinational Habsburg empire was a much more favorable environment from the Jewish point of view than were the successor states, and some went so far as to insist that even the tsarist empire was preferable. It can be argued, too, that the neighboring Soviet Union was a much more friendly place for the Jews than were most of the new East European states. In the Soviet Union the dominant ideology was based on class rather than nation, the old conservative (and anti-Semitic) elites had been destroyed, and economic dynamism was beginning to transform a typically backward East European state into a modern, industrialized colossus. In comparing the fate of the Jews in the Soviet Union with that in East Central Europe during the interwar period, one might conclude that in the latter the environment was bad for the Jews while not necessarily being bad for Judaism – that is, collective Jewish religious, cultural, and even political expression – whereas in the former Jews as individuals were able to prosper while Judaism as a religion, and indeed all forms of specifically Jewish creativity, withered away. We shall see that in certain countries of East Central Europe, most notably Poland, the hostile environment was no impediment to the flourishing of Jewish culture of either the secular or the religious variety.

If East Central Europe was far from being a unified region, despite certain characteristics common to most of its countries, the same was true of the Jewries of East Central Europe. Not only was there no such thing as "East Central European Jewry," but also it made little sense to speak of "Czechoslovak Jewry," "Romanian Jewry," or even "Polish Jewry." There was a world of difference between the basically middle-class, acculturated Jewish communities of Bohemia

and Moravia in western Czechoslovakia and the poverty-stricken, Yiddish-speaking, Orthodox Jewry of Subcarpathian Rus in eastern Czechoslovakia. And there was little to unite the Jewish community of Wallachia, in old, pre–World War I Romania, with the Jewish community of Bessarabia, annexed to Romania after the war. The same can be said of the Jews of central (or Congress) Poland and of Polish Galicia, or of the Jews in northern and southern Latvia. In fact, only in Lithuania, Hungary, and Estonia were there fairly homogeneous Jewries. Viewed broadly, two basic "types" of Jewish communities in East Central Europe emerge – a "West European type" and an "East European type." The East European type was characterized by the relative weakness of acculturation and assimilation, the preservation of Yiddish speech and religious Orthodoxy (sometimes of the extremely conservative Hasidic variety), and a lower-middle-class and proletarian socioeconomic structure. A typical East European Jewish community had a high birth rate and a low rate of intermarriage, and, while it was largely urban in nature, many of its members still lived in the old-style *shtetl* (small Jewish town). In such a community a certain degree of acculturation and secularization had occurred, but such acculturation and secularization, which took place gradually in the context of socioeconomic backwardness and general anti-Jewish hostility, most typically led not to assimilation, but to modern Jewish nationalism of one form or another. There existed in this type of community two legitimate forms of Jewish identity – religious (meaning almost always Orthodox, since Reform Judaism was virtually unknown) and national (usually secular national). Finally, East European Jewish communities usually constituted a rather large percentage within the general population, especially within the urban sector, and played a highly conspicuous role in local economic life, particularly in commerce. In lieu of a "native" middle class, these communities were often correctly identified as the local equivalent of a bourgeois class.

The West European type was characterized by a high degree of acculturation, aspirations toward assimilation, and a general tendency to abandon both Yiddish and Orthodoxy, accompanied by a readiness to embrace some form of Reform, or liberal, Judaism.

From a socioeconomic point of view, such Jewish communities tended to be middle class; from a demographic point of view, they were highly urbanized, though they rarely constituted a remarkably high percentage within the general urban population. The typical West European Jewry possessed a low birth rate and often a high rate of intermarriage; its sense of Jewish identification was usually religious, not national secular.

The West European type of Jewish community obviously closely corresponds to the Jewries of such Central and West European countries as Germany, France, and England. In East Central Europe it was found in Bohemia and Moravia (the so-called Czech lands), in Hungary, in certain parts of Latvia, and in Romanian Wallachia. The East European type was found in Galicia, central (Congress) Poland, Polish Lithuania, independent Lithuania, Subcarpathian Rus, Bukovina, Bessarabia, and southern Latvia. Other regions, notably Slovakia and Moldavia, possessed Jewish communities of a mixed type, somewhere between the Eastern and Western varieties. There is an obvious correlation between the degree of economic development and the type of Jewry. Usually, though not invariably, the more developed the region, the more Western the type of Jewry; the less developed, the more Eastern. But if all the Jewries in Central and Western Europe were of the Western type, in East Central Europe, geography notwithstanding, there were besides the predominant East European type some Jewish communities quite similar in most respects to those of Germany and France.

The implications of this typology for the internal development of the various Jewish communities of East Central Europe were very important. In the East European communities, autonomous Jewish culture flourished during the interwar years, as did the new Jewish politics. In these communities Zionism, Jewish socialism, and modern Hebrew and Yiddish schools and literature thrived, along with a new Jewish leadership based on mass support from within the community. Here, too, were voiced demands for Jewish national autonomy. In the West European–type communities, on the other hand, autonomous Jewish politics and culture were much less in evidence. Jews participated much more in the cultural life of the majority nationality and were much less attracted to the various forms of modern Jewish nationalism. Their leaders were quite different, as were the policies they followed. It is extremely doubtful, however, if the type of community had much to do with Jewish-gentile relations.

In modern Jewish history in the Western world, the classical pattern has been progression from nonacculturation and nonassimilation to acculturation and efforts to assimilate, from the physical and spiritual ghetto to integration, of one sort or another, into the broader society. In interwar East Europe this pattern is not in evidence. The East European–type communities, despite a certain, and sometimes even an impressive, degree of acculturation during the 1920s and 1930s, remained basically Yiddish speaking, lower middle class and proletarian, and strongly influenced both by religious Orthodoxy and by modern separatist Jewish nationalism. Once again we may contrast this situation with that of Soviet Jewry, a typical East European community at the outset of the interwar period, but well on its way to becoming a West European–type community by the end of the 1930s. This dramatic change was a function of the ruling ideology and of the economic dynamism of the Soviet state. In East Central Europe the combination of intolerant, anti-Semitic nationalism, right-wing politics, and economic stagnation made such a change impossible. . . .

The Jews of Poland: Demography, Economic Structure, National Identity

During the interwar period the Polish state conducted two censuses, the first in 1921 and the second ten years later. According to the first census there were 2,855,318 Jews (by religion) in Poland, or 10.5 percent of the population. By 1931 the number had grown to 3,113,933, but the percentage had dropped to 9.8. This was by far the largest Jewish community in non-Communist Europe, and also the community that made up the highest percentage within the general population. . . . Even more impressive was the extremely high percentage of Jews in Polish cities. . . . In 1921 the Jews constituted nearly one-third of the entire urban population of the country, and in the eastern provinces of Volynia and Polesie over one-half. Such numbers were interpreted by Polish anti-Semites as proof that Polish cities were dominated by "foreigners," against whom a holy war must be waged by the native middle class. . . .

Despite their strong urban bias, the result of rapid urbanization during the nineteenth century, many Polish Jews remained in the countryside. In 1931, 23.6 percent of all Jews resided in villages. . . .

No dramatic changes occurred in the Jewish demographic structure during the interwar period. . . .

The economic structure of the Jewish population naturally reflected the urban character of the community. If most Poles were employed in agriculture, the overwhelming majority of Jews were employed in commerce, industry, and the professions. Moreover, if most Poles in the nonagrarian sector tended to be engaged in industry, most Jews, at least in 1921, were employed in commerce. This meant that Jews were relatively more dominant in the latter category than in the former. . . .

In general, the Jewish population in interwar Poland may be termed lower middle class and proletarian, with a numerically small but important intelligentsia and wealthy bourgeoisie. . . . The Jewish proletariat, as we have already seen, was not a proletariat of the great factories and mines; it was, rather, a proletariat consisting almost entirely of craftsmen employed in light industry. The typical Jewish worker was a shoemaker, baker, or tailor who worked in a small shop, possibly with a few other journeymen, but often alone. . . .

It was often asserted, with some degree of accuracy, that Jews preferred to be self-employed and resisted being absorbed into the factory proletariat. More important was the fact that Jews were rarely employed in non-Jewish firms, and relatively few Jews owned large factories. The problem of Saturday work was also of importance in this regard, since Jews usually refused to work on the Sabbath, and any factory that employed both Jews and non-Jews would therefore have to close down two days a week. Finally, that non-Jewish workers often regarded factory jobs as their monopoly and resisted Jewish incursions was a natural phenomenon in light of the existence of chronic unemployment.[3] In the 1930s there were

some signs in Poland that the situation was changing, as more and more Jews, driven by economic necessity, sought work in factories. But until the very end the Jewish working class, though large and politically as well as socially important, remained a most un-Marxian unit, in the sense that it was far from being a working class of the great industrial establishments.

If the typical Jewish worker was a tailor, the typical Jewish "merchant" was a small shopkeeper, or owner of a stall in the local market, working alone or with the help of his family. Of all Jews active in commerce in 1931, 78.6 percent were self-employed and did not employ workers (among non-Jews the percentage was significantly lower, 42.5).[4] There were, of course, wealthy Jewish merchants, just as there were wealthy Jewish industrialists, and in general the Jewish bourgeoisie played an important role in the Polish urban economy.[5] But great Jewish industrialists, merchants, and bankers were much more prominent in the economic life of nineteenth-century Russian Poland than they were in the interwar period, when the state came to play a dominant role in economic life and did its best to exclude Jews from positions of influence. . . .

The Jewish economic condition in Poland at the outset of the interwar period, as in other economically backward regions of Eastern Europe, was undeniably gloomy. On the one hand, it could be asserted, and often was, that Jews "dominated" the economy; on the other, the community itself was poor, existing to a dangerous extent on foreign relief funds and cursed with an unhealthy economic structure. One of the great questions that faced the Jewries of independent Poland was whether the economic performance of the new state, and its economic and social policy, would permit the kind of economic breakthrough into the ranks of the middle class that had been experienced by the Jews of Central and Western Europe and that would be experienced by the Jewish communities of North America and the Soviet Union during the interwar period. The future of Polish Jewry depended to a great extent on the answer to this fateful question. . . .

The data from the 1931 census on language affiliation reveal that . . . 79.9 percent of Polish Jewry declared Yiddish to be its mother tongue, and 7.8

percent obeyed the command of the Zionist movement and declared (falsely) its mother tongue to be Hebrew. Those who described themselves as Polish speaking from childhood obviously belonged to the acculturated segment of the Polish Jewish community. . . .

The data presented portray a Jewish community that despite its evident heterogeneity was basically lower middle class and proletarian, and both unassimilated and unacculturated—although, as we shall see, by the 1930s acculturation was making rapid strides forward. It was not only largely Jewish in speech and in national feeling, but also, of course, deeply rooted in traditional religious Judaism, whether of the Hasidic or anti-Hasidic (misnagdic) variety. . . .

The Jewish Question in the New Poland: Jewish Demands, Polish Responses

. . . The Jewish effort to win recognition as a national minority was above all a struggle to win such recognition in the new Polish state, which both was the largest of the successor states of Eastern Europe and contained by far the largest Jewish population. It was apparent to all that Poland was a test case for this rather new concept, upon which so many Jewish leaders pinned such extravagant hopes.

One of the hallmarks of the new Jewish politics in Eastern Europe . . . was the principle that the Jews were a nation like all other nations. The fact that they had no territory of their own was not regarded as an indication that they were no less a legitimate national entity than the Ukrainians or the Poles. Whether or not the Jews ought to aspire to a territory and state of their own was a bone of contention among the competing Jewish political parties, but most Jewish nationalists, whether Zionist or anti-Zionist, believed that so long as Jews lived in the East European diaspora they should enjoy both civil and national rights. . . .

Jewish national autonomy meant different things to different people. Its most fundamental meaning was that the Jews, like other minority nationalities, whether territorial or extraterritorial, should be granted the right to develop their national life with the help of public funds. In practical terms this meant above all the right to establish state-supported Jewish schools conducted in Jewish languages (either Yiddish or Hebrew). More far-reaching plans called for state support for a wide range of Jewish cultural, social, and economic institutions and, on the political level, for a state-recognized official Jewish democratic body whose elected leaders would represent the Jews in parliament and in the government. Some Jewish nationalists even demanded that the Jewish national representation in parliament be guaranteed in accordance with the Jewish proportion of the general population. . . .

It is important to emphasize that not all East European Jews were interested in the various schemes for Jewish national autonomy. This was obviously true of the assimilationist sector, and it was true of many acculturating Jews as well. It was also true of most Orthodox Jews. The last were naturally hostile to all secular ideologies, and the fact is that almost all the adherents to Jewish national autonomy had in mind secular national autonomy—secular Jewish national schools, for example. . . . That the religious leadership of the Polish Jewish communities could no more support the secular ideology of national autonomy than they could support the Marxist ideology of the Jewish socialist Bund was a fact known, and exploited, by the Polish government.

Jewish demands for national autonomy in Poland were set forth by Jewish leaders at the Paris peace conference of 1919, at which time these leaders attempted to persuade both the great powers and the Polish politicians that the granting of such demands would serve both the Jewish and the Polish interests. . . .

In the end, Poland signed (in June 1919) a Minorities' Treaty with the victorious powers, of which two articles specifically mentioned the Jews. The first called upon the Polish government to allow for the existence of Jewish schools, controlled by Jewish authorities and funded by the state. The second forbade the government to compel the Jews to violate their Sabbath. . . .

The Poles bitterly resented having been coerced into signing the Minorities' Treaty. They regarded it as an intolerable act of interference on the part of the great powers and blamed the Jews for having engineered its acceptance. . . . The secular national Jewish leadership, on the other hand, regarded its passage as a great victory. It was, so thought the optimistic Zionists, a "magna carta" in that it specifically referred to the Jews as a minority with national, not only religious, rights. It signified, so they thought, the beginning of a new era in Polish-Jewish relations and a foundation upon which the glorious edifice of Jewish national autonomy in Poland would be erected.[6] From our vantage point, however, such optimism is difficult to understand. . . . Polish nationalism was so strong, and the Polish cause so universally supported, that Jewish help was seen as superfluous. Moreover, for most Polish leaders it was also undesirable. . . . Far from being regarded as potential allies, as they were in Lithuania and in Bohemia, the Jews were generally regarded as enemies of the Polish cause. Their effort to force Jewish national autonomy down the Poles' throats with the aid of foreign powers was seen as yet another example of their basically hostile attitude toward the Polish state. . . .

The Jewish Response: Jewish Politics in Poland in the 1920s

. . . When viewed as a whole, Jewish politics in Poland possessed certain special characteristics. For one thing, the degree of divisiveness and factionalism was surprisingly great, all the more so in view of the relatively homogeneous nature of the Jewish social structure. The Jews, unlike the other national groups of the region, possessed neither a peasantry nor a landed aristocracy and thus were spared political parties based on these two groups. Nonetheless, the number of Jewish political organizations in independent Poland was remarkable. To be sure, political divisiveness in Eastern Europe was not a Jewish monopoly, but there were certain specific reasons for its prevalence among the Jews. The question of where the Jewish problem was to be solved, "here" or "there," did not confront any other national group in the region, and neither, except in a few marginal cases, did the question of linguistic orientations. Moreover, the question of which identity to assume, secular national or religious, was more acute among the Jews than among the other nationalities. Finally,

since the Jews enjoyed no political power, there was little incentive to prevent political factionalism. The absence of real rewards for sticking together meant that ideological differences led almost inevitably to organizational splits. On the other hand, traditional notions of Jewish unity and the fact that the anti-Semites often made no distinctions among Jews usually failed to lead to Jewish political unity.

Along with divisiveness went a remarkably high degree of political mobilization within the Jewish community. Not all Jewish parties were mass organizations; some, in fact, were the creations of one man and a typewriter. But on the whole the historian of interwar Polish Jewry cannot fail to be struck by the fact that Polish Jewry, especially Polish Jewish youth, was highly politicized. An important collection of hundreds of autobiographies of Jewish teenagers, available in the archives of the Jewish Scientific Institute (Yivo) in New York, demonstrates that for young Polish Jews, particularly in the 1930s, joining a political youth movement or party was the norm, the expected thing to do. Why was this the case? One obvious reason was the very acuteness of the Jewish question itself, which obliged many Jews, young people particularly, to seek solutions in the political arena. If political activism is a function of extreme situations, we should not be surprised that so many Jews turned to politics. The Jewish dilemma in Poland, in both its economic and its political aspects, also had the effect of lessening the traditional authority of the parents and of religion in the Jewish household. Economic collapse and violent anti-Semitism, along with the secular, democratic, and modernizing character of the new Polish state, meant that Jewish children were less likely to look to their parents or to their rabbis for guidance and more likely to place their hopes in one or another of the new political organizations, both Jewish and non-Jewish. They were, in other words, more likely to "run away" to the Pioneer, to the Bund, or to the Polish Communist Party. Parental opposition, once formidable, weakened during this period and was usually not strong enough to dissuade them. The generational war between parents and children often took the form of a war over the political orientation of the youth, whose rejection of parental attitudes and whose growing indifference to religious authority resulted in the swelling of the ranks of the Jewish parties.

Another characteristic of Jewish politics in Eastern Europe was that the party or the youth movement . . . served as a kind of substitute both for the family and for the secular state, which notably failed to treat its Jewish citizens equally and was not interested in granting them the kind of services they needed. To be a Bundist or a member of Poale Zion was to belong to a separate world with its own cultural, social, and economic institutions. The parties, therefore, were important in aiding Polish Jews in compensating for their alienation from the anti-Semitic, Catholic, Polish nationalist state.

All the major Jewish parties in Poland, with the important exception of Agudes yisroel, were committed to what they termed the "new Jewish politics." This signified that they had broken once and for all with the old Jewish political traditions of seeking a modus vivendi, at all costs, with the authorities. They denounced such traditional behavior as demeaning. . . . The "new Jew," they reasoned, possessed national pride and would proudly demand his rights as a Jew and as a free man. Adherents to the new Jewish politics would therefore not be afraid to anger the gentiles. It was this point of view that lay behind Jewish political activity at the Paris peace conference, where Jewish national rights were demanded even though such demands obviously angered the Poles. And the fact that Agudes yisroel rejected this stance in favor of time-honored Jewish political practices made this religious party the object of disgust and scorn in Zionist, Folkist, and Bundist circles. The new Jewish politics flourished in interwar Poland as nowhere else in the diaspora. . . .

Aspects of Jewish Cultural Life

Just as interwar Poland became the center of autonomous Jewish politics in the Jewish diaspora, so it also became the center of autonomous Jewish culture, whether secular or religious, whether in Hebrew or in Yiddish. The yeshivas for which Poland had been so famous in the Jewish world continued to flourish, and new institutions of traditional Jewish learning were founded by the two new religious parties,

Agudes yisroel and the Mizrachi.[7] Along with the preservation of traditional Jewish culture went the remarkable experiment to create in Poland a secular Jewish national culture based on Yiddish which was designed to serve as one of the cornerstones of Jewish national autonomy. Never before in modern Jewish history, and for that matter never again, would this version of autonomous Jewish culture make such deep inroads into Jewish life. If in the Soviet Union the regime clamped down on Yiddish culture in the 1930s, and if in America acculturation and assimilation sentenced Yiddish to a gradual but inevitable decline, Poland remained the ideal setting in which the "folk language" and the "folk culture," in its new, modern form, could thrive. . . .

One dramatic example of the success of Yiddish culture in Poland was the Yiddish press, with its two mass-circulation dailies in Warsaw (*Haynt* and *Moment*) and hundreds of other daily and weekly newspapers in the provinces. Jewish newspapers also appeared in Hebrew and in Polish, but neither of these languages, especially not the former, could compete with Yiddish.[8] Another example was the flourishing of the Yiddish theater.[9] Interwar Poland also became a great center of Yiddish literature. . . . producing such talented authors as Y. Y. Trunk (1887–1961), Oizer Varshavsky (1898–1944), and I. J. Singer (1893–1944). It was also the milieu in which the most famous of modern Yiddish writers, Isaac Bashevis Singer (b. 1904, known simply as Bashevis in Yiddish), made his literary debut.[10] Along with literature went the development of Yiddish literary criticism and new efforts to promote an understanding of Jewish history and culture. In 1925 the Jewish Scientific Institute (Yivo) was founded in Vilna, mostly by secular Yiddishist intellectuals sympathetic to the Folkists or to Jewish socialism. The Yivo quickly became the main scholarly institution of the secular Yiddish cultural movement, and its various publications helped lay the foundation for modern academic work on Yiddish language and literature. It also encouraged work on East European Jewish history. . . .

For those Jewish intellectuals committed to the cause of secular Yiddish culture, education was surely the single most important issue, and it is not surprising that tremendous efforts were made to educate the young generation in this spirit. In 1921 a conference in Warsaw created the Central Jewish School Organization (known as Tsisho after its Yiddish initials), which aimed at establishing elementary and high schools that would use Yiddish as the language of instruction and promote a national, diaspora-centered, secular Jewish culture. From the very beginning the Tsisho school system was highly politicized, and it was riddled by political conflicts among Bundists, Zionist socialists, Folkists, and even Communists. Its leaders endlessly debated such questions as whether or not its goal was to produce "class-conscious socialists" and whether or not to allow the teaching of Hebrew. Its greatest dilemma, however, was the nature of the new secular Yiddish culture it sought to promote in the classroom, for such a concept was obliged to reject not only the Jewish religion, but Hebrew culture as well, and to replace it with the still very young Yiddish secular culture of Eastern Europe. There were no models in the Jewish historical experience for the kind of schools that Tsisho wanted to establish, and its revolutionary character – revolutionary both in the sense of its socialist ideology and in the sense of its radical departure from traditional Jewish education – doubtless alienated many parents. The success of Tsisho was also hampered by other problems that it shared with most other Jewish school systems – government harrassment and the state's refusal to share the financial burden. . . .

By 1934–1935 the grand total of pupils attending Tsisho institutions was 15,486.[11] This was, of course, a very small minority of all Jewish pupils in Poland and a far cry from the hopes of the ideologues of the new Yiddish secular culture. The extremely high pedagogical level of the Tsisho school system, which was generally acknowledged, could not conceal its failure to attract the young generation. . . .

Granted the existence in interwar Poland of a Yiddish literary "renaissance," how deep were its roots?[12] It would appear that, despite the unparalleled flourishing of the Yiddish press, theater, and literature, the secular Yiddish movement encountered grave difficulties both because of its militant secularism and because, in the final analysis, many Jews must have asked themselves just what their children would gain by acquiring a Yiddish education. It was all very well to study the works of Sholem Aleichem and [Y. L.] Perets, and to learn how to write a proper Yiddish sentence, but what good would this be to someone growing up in Poland? . . .

If modern Yiddish culture in the interwar period found a center in Poland, modern Hebrew culture fared less well. The Hebrew press, supported by the Zionist movement, was not nearly so successful as its Yiddish rival, and the new Hebrew theater and literature were now concentrated in Tel Aviv and Jerusalem rather than in Warsaw and Vilna. Hebrew, of course, was not a spoken language of Polish Jewry, and in an age of mass-circulation newspapers and novels, the small, cultural elite which had traditionally supported Hebrew culture could not compete with popular tastes and habits. Nonetheless, the idea of promoting a modern Hebrew culture in Poland did lead to the establishment of the remarkable Tarbut school system. The Tarbut (the word means culture in Hebrew) school system, which was backed by the General Zionist and other, moderate left-wing Zionist parties, took upon itself the awesome task of making Hebrew a living language for Jewish elementary and high school pupils. In the Tarbut schools the language of instruction for all subjects save Polish language and history was Hebrew; with the establishment of Tarbut kindergartens and high schools it became possible for Polish Jews to spend their entire educational career in a Hebrew-speaking environment. . . .

From a linguistic point of view, the Tarbut schools were more alien to Polish Jewry than were the Tsisho institutions, but the Zionist schools were less radical politically and more closely related to traditional Jewish education. This, along with their Palestinian orientation, made them rather more popular among the Jews. . . . By 1934–1935 the number of pupils had risen to 37,000. Like Tsisho, Tarbut was mainly a phenomenon of the kresy [borderlands], and in the various towns of the eastern borderlands the Tarbut school system became a focal point of local Zionist activity, especially for the various youth movements. It was much less successful in Congress Poland and in Galicia, where the more acculturated and the more Hasidic elements within the Jewish population were both unfriendly to its brand of Jewish education. . . .

A glance at the statistics of Jewish schools and the division of Jewish youngsters among the various systems reveals two important facts. First, the most attractive Jewish school system in interwar Poland was that of Agudes yisroel (the Khoyrev schools for boys, and the Beys yankev schools for girls), despite the great popularity of the new Jewish politics and the undoubted process of secularization within the Jewish community. According to one set of statistics, the number of students in the Khoyrev and Beys yankev schools reached nearly 110,000 in 1934–1935, as compared with slightly over 50,000 pupils in the Tsisho and Tarbut networks. . . . In their choice of a Jewish school, therefore, Polish Jewish parents revealed a markedly conservative character, preferring the traditional religious schools to the Bundist or Zionist alternatives. Second, the majority of all Jews of school age attended Polish state schools rather than Jewish private ones. According to [Chaim] Kazdan, about 60 percent of all Jewish pupils studied in state schools, although it should be emphasized that this figure includes Jewish pupils in those state schools that catered exclusively to Jews (the so-called Szabasówki, which exempted Jews from writing on Saturday) and that many Jewish pupils studied both in Jewish and in state schools.[13] On the high school level the majority of Jewish pupils attended Jewish schools, since Polish high schools, unlike Polish elementary schools, discriminated against Jews.

The reasons for the preference of state over Jewish education among Polish Jews are obvious. Polish state schools, after all, were free. And even if they were sometimes anti-Semitic, they dispensed a Polish education. . . . The new Jewish generation was at least to some extent becoming culturally polonized, whatever the findings of the 1931 census, and in this sense the old Polish Jewish assimilationist dream of a Polish-speaking Jewry was realized during the interwar period. . . .

The ever-growing encroachment of Polish on Jewish life did not mean that the Jews were assimilating into Polish society. It did, however, indicate the severe obstacles confronted by the adherents to Jewish national cultural autonomy everywhere in Poland, with the exception of the still not polonized kresy.

Moreover, the continued cultural conservatism of the Jewish population, demonstrated by the strength of the Orthodox school networks, showed that the efforts of Tsisho and Tarbut activists to formulate a new, secular Jewish culture based either on Yiddish or on Hebrew were also unsuccessful. . . . It is legitimate to wonder whether, in the long run, the very concept of secular national Jewish culture was viable in the Jewish diaspora. It is safe to assume that, had independent Poland survived for another twenty years, modern Yiddish and Hebrew culture and schools would have inevitably declined, to be replaced by Jewish cultural creativity in the Polish language.

Before the war some Jews had played a major role in Polish cultural life, and this trend continued into the interwar period. Indeed, only in Hungary, and of course in interwar Soviet Russia, did Jews penetrate so deeply into the cultural life of the majority nationality in Eastern Europe. . . . The presence of a small but important Polish Jewish cultural elite demonstrates the heterogeneous character of Polish Jewry. . . .

The 1930s: The Reemergence of Violent Anti-Semitism and the Jewish Reaction

During the 1930s, and particularly in the last four years of Poland's existence as an independent state, violent anti-Semitism made a dramatic reappearance. It was accompanied by redoubled efforts to strike at the Jews' economic interests and to remove the Jews, as many as possible, from Polish economic and intellectual life. A complex combination of factors, having to do with the transition from democracy to right-wing authoritarianism, economic depression, and events outside Poland's borders, was responsible for these ominous developments. In Poland, as in most other states of East Central Europe, the last decade of the interwar period witnessed a struggle for power between moderate and extreme right-wing nationalists in the context of an economic crisis and the rising influence of Nazi Germany. The Jewish question, in Poland as elsewhere, proved to be an integral part of a political struggle the outcome of which was to determine who would rule the country.

The first great blow to Poland's democratic form of government was Piłsudski's coup d'etat of 1926. . . . [During] Piłsudski's ten years in office as the supreme arbiter of Poland's fate, he was successful in holding the extreme anti-Semites in check and welcomed the participation of Jews in his government lists during elections to the Sejm. . . .

However, Piłsudski and his camp, popularly known as the Sanacja (cleansing), took no steps to alter the state's basic attitude toward the Jews, just as they did little to win the affection of the Ukrainians and Belorussians.[14] The Jews continued to receive virtually no state funds for their cultural institutions, and they remained the victims of wide-ranging economic discrimination. The Great Depression, which struck Poland with a vengeance in 1929, rendered the impact of this economic anti-Semitism all the greater. In short, despite Piłsudski's refusal to embrace anti-Semitic slogans, the Jewish crisis intensified. If the Jews sincerely mourned Piłsudski after his death in May 1935, they mourned him as the lesser evil, as a man much to be preferred to his National Democratic and fascist-leaning opponents. . . .

The roots of the unprecedented wave of anti-Semitism that characterized the post-Piłsudski period are certainly to be found in pre–1935 Poland. One is the economic crisis, which heightened social tensions and inevitably worsened Polish-Jewish relations. Another important factor was the rise of Nazism in Germany. Polish nationalists had much to fear from a resurgent Germany, but they were greatly impressed by Hitler and by the prominent role of anti-Semitism in the Nazi ideology. Of particular significance was the influence of Nazism on the younger National Democrats. In 1934 some right-wing radical youths split off from [Roman] Dmowski's party* and formed the National Radical Camp (ONR), clearly based on the Nazi model; its members were described by Moshe Kleinbaum (Sneh), a leading Zionist, as "Polish Hitlerites."[15] And the National Democratic movement itself, called since 1928 the National Party, veered ever more sharply to the right, its anti-Semitism "greatly encouraged by the impunity with which Hitler was able to deprive of political rights the wealthiest and most powerful Jewish community in

Europe."[16] As was the case elsewhere in East Central Europe, particularly in Romania, the universities became centers of anti-Jewish agitation and riots, much of it in emulation of the Nazis. . . .

While the right-wing opposition took comfort from Hitler's triumph, the Polish government took steps to come to terms with the new regime on its western border. In 1934 Poland and Germany signed a nonaggression pact, thus signaling the Polish government's apparent belief that it had nothing to fear from Hitler. This in turn naturally increased Nazi influence within Poland. In July of the same year, Goebbels visited Poland and lectured at the University of Warsaw. Many Polish dignitaries, including the prime minister, attended his lecture, which dealt, among other things, with the National Socialist attitude toward the Jewish question.[17] . . .

After the death of Piłsudski, Poland was ruled by a small circle of Piłsudski loyalists who lacked their revered leader's charisma and who enjoyed little popular support. . . .

The most serious threat to the rule of the "colonels," as Piłsudski's followers were called, came from the right—from the National Party and its fascist offshoot, the ONR. In the struggle, which took place in the context of growing social unrest and an increasingly dangerous international situation, the Jewish question became a major issue, as each side, seeking popular support among the impoverished Polish masses, attempted to outdo the other in its devotion to the anti-Jewish campaign.[18]

During the post-Piłsudski years the government's attitude toward the Jewish question was fairly clear. In the short run, the Jews' role in the Polish economy and in all other walks of life was to be drastically reduced. In the long run, emigration was the only solution. In a declaration of 1937 the government, which refused to allow Jews to join the ruling party, defined its Jewish policy as follows:

> We have too high an idea of our civilization and we respect too strongly the order and peace which every state needs to approve brutal anti-Semitic acts which harm the dignity and prestige of a great country. At the same time, it is understandable that the country should possess the in-

---

*The right-wing Polish National Democratic Party or "Endek" party, *Ed.*

stinct compelling it to defend its culture, and it is natural that Polish society should seek economic self-sufficiency.[19]

This last reference to "self-sufficiency" meant that the government lent its official sanction to unbridled economic anti-Semitism. This policy was given its most famous formulation by Prime Minister Slawoj-Składkowski, who said in 1936, "Economic struggle [against the Jews] by all means [*owszem*]—but without force."[20] But the main thrust of official policy toward the Jews was to promote the cause of Jewish emigration. The problem was, of course, that it was not clear where the Jews could go. The Polish government did its best to soften British opposition to emigration to Palestine, and, if Zionism meant Jewish emigration to that country, no one was more Zionist than Poland's leaders in the late 1930s. . . .

Both economic anti-Semitism and "pro-Zionist" leanings were very much present in pre-1935 Poland, and neither can be regarded as a new departure. What was new was the government's open and vocal espousal of these principles, the immediate causes of which were its weakness, its fear of the extreme right, and its antidemocratic tendencies. In its Jewish policy it received the full support of the Polish Catholic church, long a bastion of anti-Semitism and, of course, an institution of great influence and authority. The church was a veteran supporter of the National Democrats, and some priests were among the most active propagators of anti-Semitism in the country. In 1936 Cardinal August Hlond, head of the Polish hierarchy, published a special pastoral letter on the Jewish question in which he opposed Nazi racist doctrines but condemned the Jews as atheists and revolutionaries. He also lent the authority of the church to economic anti-Semitism.[21]

The main difference between the attitude of the extreme right-wing opposition and that of the government and the church to the Jewish question had to do with means, not ends. While the political and religious establishments deplored violence, the right embraced it. And if the church, at least, resisted Nazi racism, thereby seeking to protect Jewish converts to Catholicism, the right had no such scruples. Both establishment and opposition, the Endeks and the

Sanacja, agreed that "Jewish influence" in Poland must be done away with. What this meant was clear, although how it was to be achieved was not. The centrist Peasant Party, an amalgam of the various peasant factions of the 1920s, also lent its voice to the anti-Jewish chorus. . . .

This left the Polish Socialist Party [PPS] as the only important political organization clearly opposed to anti-Semitism, and even within its ranks there was no unanimity on the Jewish question. . . . Nonetheless, in Poland, as was not the case in Hungary, a political organization of considerable and even growing strength set its face clearly against the government-inspired anti-Semitic campaign. Gentile opposition to anti-Semitism, therefore, was not restricted, as it was in other countries, to a courageous but lonely and isolated group of intellectuals and priests who viewed with alarm the emergence of virulent racism on the Nazi model. . . . But it is also true that the PPS was too weak to blunt the anti-Semitic campaign. Its stand, therefore, was of greater moral than practical significance.

The war against the Jews during 1935–1939 took many forms, ranging from legislative efforts to brutal attacks. In 1936, for example, legislative action was initiated in the Sejm to outlaw *shkhite* (ritual slaughter). This attack on one of the most fundamental aspects of Jewish religious practice caused a tremendous storm in the Jewish world, where it was interpreted as a first step toward revoking Jewish emancipation. A law forbidding *shkhite*, closely modeled on Nazi German legal precedents, was actually passed by the Sejm in 1936, but was eventually amended by the government to allow a certain amount of ritually slaughtered meat for Jews in areas where they made up more than 3 percent of the population.[22]

Another dominant theme in the anti-Semitic movement was the effort to establish "ghetto benches" in Polish universities. In some of these institutions the Jewish students, whose number was rapidly dwindling, were required to attend lectures in segregated areas of the classroom; this system was inaugurated at the Lwów Polytechnicum in 1935, and later at the University of Vilna. From 1937 on, physical attacks against Jewish students became ever more common, and several Jewish students were actually murdered. The ghettoizing of Jewish students was the first skirmish in the campaign to segregate (and eventually oust altogether) Jews in the white-collar professions. In 1937 various associations of doctors and journalists adopted the "Aryan paragraph," thereby making Jewish membership impossible.[23]

Most serious, however, was the economic boycott of Jewish businesses, an age-old tactic that now resurfaced with explicit government support. Bands of anti-Semitic enthusiasts invaded the marketplaces of Polish towns and villages and warned Christian Poles not to do business with Jewish merchants. Behind them stood a well-organized movement, spearheaded by National Democrats but supported by the various Polish economic organizations of merchants and artisans. Christian businessmen were supplied with special signs attesting to their "Aryan" nature, which were displayed for all to see. Pressure (not all of it gentle) was brought to bear on Christian Poles not to do business with Jewish firms, not to deal with Jewish agents, and not to rent apartments to Jews. The right-wing press often published the names of Christians who failed to obey the boycott. Thus in 1937 the *Warszawski Dziennik Narodowy* informed its readers that a certain Von Richwald had purchased a radio from a Jewish store in Poznań Province and that a civil servant from Radom had taken a ride in a Jewish cab.[24]

The enforcers of the boycott had frequent recourse to violence. Jewish stalls in marketplaces and at fairs were destroyed; Jewish storekeepers and artisans in little towns were terrorized and forced to abandon their shops. In such an atmosphere it did not require much for attacks on Jewish shopkeepers to degenerate into pogroms directed against the entire local Jewish population. From 1936 on, such pogroms were a common occurrence, once again reviving a phenomenon familiar in Poland during the prewar period. . . . According to a list prepared by Yankev Leshchinski, during 1935–1936 1,289 Jews were wounded in anti-Semitic attacks in over 150 towns and villages in Poland, a number based on reports in the Polish press and probably much too low. "Hundreds of Jews were killed."[25]

The impact of all this on the Jewish population,

both from the economic and psychological point of view, was enormous. During the 1930s, the period of the Great Depression when the entire population of Poland underwent a process of pauperization, it began to appear as though not only the Polish Jewish youth had "no future" in the country, but that the entire Jewish community was in dire peril. The most telling aspect of the economic crisis was the decline in the number of Jewish-owned stores. During the years 1932–1937 the Jewish economist Menakhem Linder carried out a study of the Jewish-owned shops in eleven towns in the Białystok region. . . . In 1932 there were 663 Jewish-owned shops in these towns, which constituted 92.0 percent of the total number of shops; by 1937 there were 563 Jewish-owned shops, which constituted 64.5 percent of the total number. The figures show that the crucial year in this decline was 1936–1937, the reason being the renewed boycott. The decline was nationwide, although it was particularly evident in the eastern borderlands, where Jewish domination of commerce was so pronounced. By 1938, according to one authority, the share of Jewish-owned enterprises in Polish commerce had sunk below 50 percent, and no end to the precipitous decline was in sight. . . . [26]

The Great Depression, the anti-Semitic campaign, and the competition of a "native" bourgeoisie and of peasant cooperatives combined to push more and more Jews below the poverty line. As early as 1934 the percentage of Jews who appealed for some form of relief during the Passover holiday was alarmingly high—in Galicia nearly one-third of the Jewish population, in fifty-eight selected urban localities needed such aid.[27] And the worst was yet to come. The vigorous, even heroic efforts of foreign Jewish relief organizations to halt the economic decline saved many Jews from starvation, but were unable to reverse the trend.[28] By the eve of World War II, Polish Jewry was an impoverished community with no hope of reversing its rapid economic decline. There was, of course, no lack of poverty among the Christian population, but in the Jewish case the "artificial" causes of the crisis, when added to the repercussions of the general economic crisis, made the situation particularly intolerable.

The psychological impact of the crisis of the 1930s is more difficult to measure, but it was obviously great, perhaps greater, because of the anti-Semitic component, than it was among non-Jews. One indication of its scope was the rise in the number of suicides among Polish Jews.[29] Another was signs of apathy and despair that the celebrated Jewish scholar Maks Vaynraykh found in his study of autobiographies of Jewish Polish youth. For many members of the new Jewish generation, on the whole better educated and more ambitious than the prewar generation, the situation in the 1930s was one of absolute gloom. One youth wrote, "If one were to ask me to give a single definition of the period in which I live, I would answer: a hopeless generation."[30]

Notes

1. The best survey of this region is Joseph Rothschild, *East Central Europe between the Two World Wars* (Seattle and London, 1974), which includes Poland, Romania, Czechoslovakia, Hungary, Bulgaria, Yugoslavia, Albania, and the Baltic States. Antony Polonsky, *The Little Dictators: The History of Eastern Europe since 1918* (London and Boston, 1975) includes Austria but omits the Baltic States and Albania. Alan Palmer, *The Lands Between: A History of East-Central Europe since the Congress of Vienna* (London, 1970), includes Greece, omits Austria, and has little material on the Baltic States. Alan Palmer and C. A. Macartney, *Independent Eastern Europe* (London and New York, 1962), has the broadest conception of all, going so far as to include Turkey and Finland. On the other hand, the old classic, Hugh Seton-Watson, *Eastern Europe between the Wars, 1918–1941,* 1st ed. (Cambridge, 1945), emphasizes only Poland, Czechoslovakia, Hungary, Romania, Yugoslavia, and Bulgaria.

2. A strong case could be made for including Austria, which was also, of course, a successor state of the Habsburg empire. But I would argue that the cultural, economic, and social characteristics of the Austrian Jewish community, so similar to those of German Jewry, make it much more a Central than an East Central European Jewry.

3. For a discussion of this question, see Ezra Mendelsohn, *Class Struggle in the Pale* (Cambridge, Eng., 1970), 19–23.

4. Refael Mahler, *Yehude polin ben shte milhamot w Polsce w okresie miedzywojennym* (Warsaw, 1963); 133.

5. Janusz Zarnowski, *Spoleczenstwo drugiej rzeczypospolitej* (Warsaw, 1973) 391.

6. For the quotation see Ezra Mendelsohn, *Zionism in Poland: The Formative Years, 1915–1926* (New Haven and London, 1981) 107. See also Schlomo Netser, *Maavak yehude polin al zekhuiyotehem ha-ezrahiyot ve-ha leumiyot (1918–1922)* (Tel Aviv, 1980), 162.

7. Sh. Z. Kahana, "Ha-moreshet ha-masoratit shel yehude polin," *Sefer ha-shana/yorbukh* 2 (1967): 34–70; Yitshak Levin, "Yeshivat hokhme lublin," ibid., 381–88; Shmuel Mirski, ed., *Mosdot tora be-iropa be-vinyanam u-ve-horbanam* (New York, 1956), 1–413, 561–603.

8. For bibliographies of the Yiddish press, see Yisroel Shayn, *Bibliografie fun oysgabes aroysgegebn durkh di arbeter parteyen in poyln in di yorn 1918–1939* (Warsaw, 1963); idem, "Bibliografie fun yidishe periodike in poyln," in *Studies on Polish Jewry,* ed. Joshua Fishman, (New York, 1974), 422–83. For studies of the Jewish press, see *Fun noentn over,* vol. 2 (New York, 1956), which deals with the Jewish press in Warsaw; Khaim Finkelshtein, *Haynt, a tsaytung bay yidn, 1908–1939* (Tel Aviv, 1978). See also David Flinker et al., ed., *Itonut yehudit she-hayta* (Tel Aviv, 1973), and Marian Fuks, *Prasa żydowska w Warszawie 1823–1939* (Warsaw, 1979).

9. See Mikhol Vaykhert, *Zikhroynes, Varshe,* vol. 2 (Tel Aviv, 1961), for a memoir on the Yiddish theater in Poland. See also Yitskhok Turkov-Grudberg, "Dos yidishe teater in poyln tsvishn beyde velt-milkhomes," *Sefer ha-shana/yorbukh* 2 (1967):325–58.

10. Dov Sadan, *Sifrut yidish be-folin ben shte milhamot ha-olam* (Jerusalem, 1964); Y. Y. Trunk, *Di yidishe proze in poyln in der tkufe tsvishn beyde velt-milkhomes* (Buenos Aires, 1949); Nakhmen Mayzel, *Gevn amol a lebn* (Buenos Aires, 1953).

11. Mendelsohn, *Zionism in Poland,* 205; Khaim Shloyme Kazdan, *Di geshikhte fun yidishn shulvezn in umophengikn poylna* (Mexico City, 1947), 549. For somewhat lower figures, see Stanisław Mauersberg, *Szkolnictwo powszechne dla mniejszości narodowych w Polsce w latach 1918–1939* (Wrocław, etc., 1968), 167.

12. The word "renaissance" is used by Trunk, *Di yidishe proze,* 17.

13. Kazdan, *Di geshikhte fun yidishn shulvezn,* 550–51.

14. Chojnowski, *Koncepcje polityki narodowosciowej rządów polskich w latach 1921–1939* (Wrocław, etc., 1979) 69–83.

15. Emanuel Meltser, *Yahadut polin ba-maavak ha-medini al kivma be-shnot 1935–1939* (Ph.D. diss., Tel Aviv University, 1975) 13. See also Roman Wapiński, *Narodowa Demokracja 1893–1939* (Wrocław, etc., 1980), 299–329.

16. Antony Polonsky, *Politics in Independent Poland* (London, 1972) 370.

17. Yosef Teeni, *Aliyat Hitler la-shilton ve-hashpaata shel ha-antishemiyut al matsavam shel yehude polin ba-shanim 1933–1939* (Ph.D. diss., Hebrew University, 1980), 61. See also Meltser, "Yahse polin-germaniya ba-shanim 1935–1938 ve-hashpaatam al baayat ha-yehudim be-folin," *Yad va-shem, kovets mehkarim* 12 (1977):145–70.

18. For a good analysis of the situation, see Edward Wynot, " 'A Necessary Cruelty': The Emergence of Official Anti-Semitism in Poland," *American Historical Review* 76, no. 4 (October 1971):1035–58. See also Korzec, *Juifs en Pologne,* 239–74.

19. As quoted in Polonsky, *Politics,* 424.

20. As quoted in Trunk, "Der ekonomisher antisemitizm in poyln tsuishn di tsvey velt-milkhomes," in *Studies,* ed. Friedman, 65. See also Meltser, *Yahadut polin,* 45–46.

21. Teeni, *Aliyat Hitler,* 11–12.

22. Meltser, *Yahadut polin,* 12.

23. Ibid., 99–105; Korzec, "Antisemitism in Poland as an Intellectual, Social, and Political Movement," in *Studies on Polish Jewry [shtudies vegn yidn in polyn]* 1919–1939, ed. Joshua Fishman (New York, 1974), 94–98.

24. Trunk, "Der ekonomisher antisemitizm," 52. On the boy-

cott, see ibid., 48–60; Meltser, *Yahadut polin*, 42–50, 190–205.

25. Trunk, "Der ekonomisher antisemitizm," 54; Yankev Leshchinski, "Ha-praot be-folin," *Dapim le-heker ha-shoa ve-ha-mered* 2 (February 1952):37–92; Leshchinski, *Erev khurbm* (Buenos Aires, 1951).

26. Meltser, *Yahadut polin*, 204.

27. Sh. Berkovich, "Ankete vegn der peysekh untershtitsungsaktsie in yor 1934," *Dos virtshaftlekhe lebn* 4–5 (1934):6. See also Leshchinski, "Di poyperizirung fun di yidishe masn in poyln," *Yivo bleter* 6, no. 2 (March–April 1934):201–28.

28. On the work of the Joint Distribution Committee in Poland in the 1930s, see Yehuda Bauer, *My Brother's Keeper: A History of the American Jewish Joint Distribution Committee 1929–1939* (Philadelphia, 1974), 190–209.

29. Leshchinski, *Erev khurbm*, 142–49.

30. Quoted in Maks Vaynraykh, *Der veg tsu unzer yugnt* (Vilna, 1935), 210.

Tracy H. Koon **Believe, Obey, Fight**

INTRODUCTION

TOTALITARIAN OR ONE-PARTY SYSTEMS adopt a whole array of primary and secondary agents in the socialization process. Foremost among the primary agents is the family and, as an extension of early familial relationships, the encouragement of imitation among the young of adult leader roles. As the child's ideas become more abstract and take on cognitive substance, the secondary agents of socialization become more influential. First among those secondary agents is the school system, a crucially important tool in the political education of children. The formal instruction imparted in totalitarian states is characterized by a great degree of "manifest political socialization," the inclusion of an explicitly political content in the school curricula. There is a greater degree of uniformity and coercion in such systems than is present in pluralist societies.

The expressly political content of the formal school curricula is supplemented by the tenets of state-run youth groups and by a wide array of state-sponsored propaganda aimed at the young. The groups attempt to reinforce a sense of belonging with badges of social acceptance: slogans, rituals, and uniforms are the external signs of community. The goal is a collective identity, total immersion in a new group that is bolstered by continual condemnation of the enemy, the unholy "them" as opposed to the "us." Refusal to belong produces crisis, the necessity of asserting diversity and separateness when all the pressures on the child are pushing in the direction of sameness and togetherness.

For the Italian Fascist regime, youth was a central and essential concern. Fascism was portrayed as a movement of the young, the daring, the audacious. Italy under fascism would fulfill its glorious destiny as a youthful and virile nation struggling against the decadent and fossilized remnants of the old Europe for its rightful heritage. The word "youth" occurs ad nauseam in Fascist propaganda; the choice of

"Giovinezza" as the Fascist anthem points up the fact that the mystique of youth was one of the key myths of the movement.

The young were courted more assiduously than any other social group in Fascist Italy. They were the regime's best hope for the future; they had to be molded for their roles as future defenders of the faith and high priests of the new political cult. The political socialization of youth was, therefore, a fundamental prerequisite for the continuation of the regime: Fascist leaders hoped that the indoctrination of youth would create a new political culture and produce stability and continuity. . . .

Fascism proclaimed itself a revolution: it would produce both a new Italy and a new Italian, a political and economic revolution that would sweep away injustice and class struggle and effect a spiritual and moral revolution in the character of the Italians. It was portrayed not as a reaction against Marxism but as a revolutionary alternative to Marxism that would achieve social harmony and productivity in the context of national self-assertion. Fascism was the third way, a rejection of the materialism and egoism of socialism and liberalism that would through the corporate state recognize the needs of the individual but harmonize them with the needs of the community. Fascism would be a true Socialist regime serving national purposes, designed not to destroy the capitalist system but to make it work for the good of all under the overarching control of the state, a syndicalism inspired not by pacifism and internationalism but by love of country and national solidarity. In this way fascism could reject socialism but promise social justice and reform – social change within the law instead of the anarchy and chaos of the leftists. In posters and propaganda tracts the regime played on this as the fundamental distinction between the Socialist revolution and the Fascist revolution. Leftist revolution would produce destruction, chaos, desolation, strikes, and poverty. The Fascist images were quite different: flowering and fertile fields, happy and productive workers, stabilization of the *lira*, order, and trains running on time.[1]

In all of these revolutionary endeavors youth was to play a key role. If the regime's militaristic rhetoric appealed to the youthful thirst for glory and adventure, the myth of the Fascist revolution, the "new order" that fascism would bring to Italy and to Europe, appealed to the idealism and the social conscience of the young.

Mussolini seemed to have little faith in the older generations, but in his autobiography he exclaimed: "I have trust in young people. Their spiritual and material life is led by quick attentive minds and by ardent hearts."[2] The March on Rome was presented as a revolutionary seizure of power that had begun the process of renewal in Italian society, a renewal in which the youth had a special role to play. The rhetoric of the regime seemed to promise construction, building, and a zest for the future – all of this tied to the dynamic image of the leader who offered to the young a way to channel their spirit of rebellion into politically productive outlets. The countless images of Mussolini in the fields and factories seemed to give credence to his promise that in ten years Italy would be unrecognizable.

Under fascism Italy was to be viewed no longer as a land of spaghetti-eating and mandolin-strumming romantics but as a land of sobriety, hard work, and seriousness of purpose. The party and the Duce had revolutionized Italy, and all was working according to his will. To maintain this image, the press office forbade the mention of any internal conflicts. Newspapers could not carry stories of crimes of passion, suicides, or obituaries, which were not in the Fascist style. Nor did Italians read stories of epidemics, natural calamities, or even bad weather. The new Italian would be physically and mentally hard and fit, lean and sinewy and ready for combat. "I have no pity for the fat," Mussolini was quoted as saying. "If you eat too much you steal from the Fatherland," read another propaganda poster.[3] . . .

Fascism promised to rally the people in a great national revival. In fact the regime was predicted on depoliticization of the masses, whose participation in

the political process was reduced to ritual cries of support for policies decided on high, to orchestrated demonstrations of faith in the Duce. The dynamism of the early movement was reduced to a few formulas, repeated incessantly. The ideals of creativity and activism were transformed into the dead weight of dogma. Slogans about renewal and construction were reduced to the immobility of the catechism. The tone became ever more exalted as the years passed, the ideas ever more barren. The great revolution was in the end reduced to the cult of one man, the study of Fascist "mysticism:" "The font, the only font of our mysticism . . . is Mussolini, exclusively Mussolini. This is our fixed point . . . fascism for us mystics is Mussolini, only and exclusively Mussolini."[4]

For the youth this contrast between revolutionary rhetoric and reality had especially important consequences. Giuseppe Bottai insisted that to avoid paralysis and decay, the PNF [Partito Nazionale Fascista] had to allow the young to assume real power in the Fascist party. They should be free, he warned, to rethink fascism and to make their own contributions to keep the regime in tune with the needs of a changing world. In 1929 he asked: "Is the Revolution therefore completed? Is nothing left but to accept the closed cycle of its history as it exists in the institutions, laws, the concretized regime?"[5] Bottai refused to believe that the revolution did not have a future, and many young people, too, clung tenaciously to the belief that, appearances to the contrary, the real battle for a new society was still ahead.

Fascism promised that it would build upon the spirit of rebellion and the youthful activism that had brought it to power, that it would provide real outlets for their spirit of criticism, their desire to create, to reform. In a special edition of *Popolo d'Italia* in 1932, Arturo Marpicati, then vice-secretary of the PNF, claimed that the "Fascist state considers . . . the educational mission as fundamental among its functions, and it has assumed this mission with ardor. To the youth it entrusts the duty of perpetuating the faith and continuing the work of fascism."[6] The regime promised to fulfill its motto of *largo al glovani* – "make way for the young" – but proceeded to erect an educational system and youth organizations that aimed at suppressing all evidence of intellectual independence and courage and at producing blind believers armed with a catechism of Fascist responses. In this sense the Fascist revolution for the young was best summarized with the motto "Believe, Obey, Fight" or, perhaps more to the point, "Mussolini is always right." . . .

THE REGIME AND THE TEACHERS

ONE OF THE MAIN LINES OF ATTACK in the government's campaign to fascistize the school was the drive to control and organize the teachers. Despite (or perhaps because of) his own experience in the schools, Mussolini was suspicious of teachers who could easily "awaken doubts and play politics" by the timely use of an allusion or an opinion from the lectern. The teacher, he said, "has a political office and must be a Fascist."[7] Teachers in the Fascist state were, in the words of another commentator, to be "apostles and priests."[8] Agnosticism had no place in the realm of the intellectuals any more than it did in the political sphere; culture under fascism had to be Fascist culture – meaning culture serving the needs of the regime.[9] . . .

One of the most effective means of shaping a loyal teaching cadre was simply to eliminate all those teachers who did not conform. The December 1925 law on public employees allowed the regime to carry out a purge of the teaching corps that was apparently accomplished on quite a large scale.[10] After February 1929 elementary and secondary school teachers were required to take an oath of loyalty to the regime – one way of offsetting the apparent gains made by the church that same month in education.[11] Political merits were considered routinely in salary and promotion decisions, and as Mussolini's demographic campaign gained momentum, teachers were often given bonuses for marrying or producing offspring. In 1933 membership in the PNF became a prerequisite for employment in the state administration, including the schools.[12] This law did provide that those who were already employed were not bound to request membership, but the regulation was applied so rigidly that by the mid-thirties the civil servants who "did not have a party card could be counted on one's fingers."[13]

The regime also exerted pressure on teachers, especially primary school teachers, to participate as group leaders and officers in the PNF's youth organizations. By the late 1920s teachers who expected to be promoted had to devote considerable time and energy to these activities. The aim was identification of the school and regime: fascistization of the academic institutions by blurring the lines between the school and the party. In rural areas, where the schools were run directly by the ONB*, it became increasingly rare to find elementary school teachers who did not also serve as officers of the youth groups. This was less true in urban areas, but even there the party made an all-out effort to see that as many teachers as possible became identified with the regime's youth program.

As party members, teachers were obliged to attend the meetings of the local *fascio*, march in parades wearing the black shirt, and come to class wearing the PNF insignia. By 1926 the Roman salute was imposed on all state employees. After 1934 every elementary school teacher was also required to wear the uniform of the PNF or the Fascist militia during school hours to impress upon the student that he or she was no longer a teacher but an "officer, educator, commandant of his students . . . who prepares them in and out of school for service to the Fascist Fatherland."[14] Failure to discharge any of these obligations with the proper dedication and enthusiasm meant withdrawal of the party card and unemployment. . . .

In August 1931 all university professors were required to sign the following oath: "I swear to be loyal to the King, to his royal successors, to the Fascist Regime, to observe loyally the Constitution and the other laws of the State, to exercise the profession of teacher and to carry out all academic duties with the aim of training upright and hardworking citizens who are devoted to the fatherland and to the Fascist Regime. I swear that I neither belong to nor shall belong to associations or parties whose activities do not harmonize with the duties of my profession."[15] Recalcitrant professors were subject to unsubtle pressure from university rectors for several months, and in December Pope Pius XI threw the weight of the church into the balance by approving the oath for Catholics provided they make a mental reservation that it

Opera Nazionale Balilla – an early youth organization in fascist Italy, *Ed.*

would not conflict with their duties to God or the church.[16]

On 20 December 1931 the names of those men refusing to take the oath were published: only 11 or 12 out of some 1,250 refused to bow, though two others did retire from their positions rather than swear the oath and one apparently continued to teach without signing. Those who would not capitulate were dismissed from their positions.[17] Clearly many of those who did sign were motivated more by practical considerations than by faith. Many saw refusal to sign as a futile gesture and, following the counsel of Croce, accepted the oath in order to avoid abandoning the universities and the students to the servile Fascists. There were probably few committed Fascists among the university professors, but there were also few instances of open political resistance, especially as the regime tightened its control during the 1930s. . . .

Introduction of the *LIBRO UNICO*

IN 1929 THE REGIME introduced state textbooks in all public and private elementary schools. This state text, or *libro unico*, was a trump card in the regime's program to fascistize the schools and socialize the young – a truly mass medium that reached virtually all children educated in Italy between 1930 and 1943. . . .

The law requiring the adoption of the state texts passed under Minister Giuseppe Belluzzo in January 1929.[18] One scholar of the period has referred to the adoption of the *libro unico* as "the most drastic step in the field of education taken by Fascism after the foundation of the ONB."[19] The move did speed up the tempo of fascistization in the schools and silence once and for all [Giovanni] Gentile's* call for freedom of teaching.

The regime established a ministerial commission to direct and coordinate the compilation of the necessary texts. This commission chose authors in all fields, though it was the duty of the minister to see that all books approved were "pedagogically sound and imbued with the true Fascist spirit." Mussolini was extremely interested in the publication of these texts and became personally involved in the choice of authors. The first texts were presented to him by Minis-

ter Balbino Giuliano on 21 April 1930, 2,684 years to the day after the founding of Rome.[20]

Publication of the texts was an enormous undertaking. In the first year they were used in the school (1930–31), the state arranged for the printing of 5,445,000 books. Primers and religion texts were provided for the first two grades and combined texts on history, geography, arithmetic, and science for the last three grades. The church was actively involved in the selection of the religion texts, because all such material had to be approved by an ecclesiastical committee. . . .

A SAMPLE OF STATE TEXTBOOKS FOR THE ELEMENTARY SCHOOLS

AN EXAMINATION of some of the state textbooks sheds considerable light on the fascistization program in the elementary schools. The textbooks examined here were used in grades one through five in all Italian schools from 1938 to 1944 (these last edited by the Allied Commission). Studies of such school texts for earlier periods indicate that the tone and content of the volumes were substantially the same as in the later years. The law on the *libro unico* had stipulated that the books should be revised every three years, but the first real revisions came after 1935 to keep the books in tune with the regime's imperial and racial policies. As Fascist policy evolved, pages were added to the texts, most frequently in the readers and in history and geography sections. The material chosen here is representative of the reading matter presented to schoolchildren in classrooms all over Italy in these years, and should serve to highlight the main propaganda interests of the regime and the view of politics and society inculcated in Italian youngsters from their earliest days in school.[21]

In general, the books were of good quality technically, profusely illustrated and enlivened with an eye-catching use of color. The distinctly Fascist content of the books increased after the first-year primer, which concentrated on phonics. In the higher grades the nationalistic and militaristic tenor of the stories and lessons was striking. In addition to the compulsory Fascist themes, most of the books also stressed

*Mussolini's first minister of public instruction, *Ed.*

the simple virtues; elementary notions of hygiene and nature were included in all the books, though emphasized especially in the texts destined for the rural schools, which had separate books after 1938. Even in the sections not dealing directly with religion, there was a considerable amount of Catholic influence: stories about religious holidays, lives of the saints, and simple stories and prayers about Jesus and the Virgin Mary.

The children reading these state textbooks were to be left with one overriding impression: the world revolves around Italy, and Italy, in turn, revolves around Benito Mussolini and the Fascist party. Flags and symbols of the fatherland abounded. Cheek by jowl with these national or royal symbols were those of the PNF. In these texts there was no distinction made between patriotism and fascism; service to fascism was portrayed as a patriotic duty. The presence of both king and Duce in these textbooks served also to stress the unity and community that fascism had supposedly realized in Italy.

The genius and goodness of Mussolini were praised in a litany that became a grotesque exaltation of the Duce as a wise father come up from poverty and misery to guide the fortunes of all Italians. Veneration of this benevolent leader was religious in tone: he was portrayed as omnipotent and omniscient (knowing, for example, what a small boy wanted for his birthday and sending it to him personally). Stories compared him to the saints and told tales of children who became better for having visited his sacred birthplace or for having glimpsed him as he spoke from the balcony in Piazza Venezia. Another recurrent theme was that of the Duce as indomitable war hero; the Great War, it would seem, was fought at his bidding and under his direction. In the pages of these schoolbooks, the Duce was brave and felt no pain; around him flocked the most shining flowers of Italian youth, the heroes of the Fascist revolution whose often gory tales were also told and retold.

Later on the children began to read about the glories of his (or rather His) regime. They saw color pictures of rosy-cheeked men, women, and children all dressed in their PNF uniforms; they learned about the orderly and clean new cities that the genius of the Duce had created where once there had been only

swamps. Fascism, the texts reiterated in simple terms, had produced social justice for all, and the old distinctions of rich and poor had disappeared. Mussolini became something of a magician who, having proclaimed the policy of autarky, then produced wool (or *lanital*, as it was called) out of ordinary milk, and waving fields of grain from the poor earth of Italy.

The regime's demographic campaign appeared in countless subtle and not so subtle ways in the pages of these texts: in most of the families in the readers there were many children, little girls were given dolls to prepare them for their job as (very young and very frequent) mothers, and stories ended with traditional formulas such as "God bless you and give you male children." The result of this boom in procreation was, naturally, overpopulation, which just as naturally was to be solved by expansion and colonization in the underpopulated and undercivilized areas of the world.

Another key theme was that of Fascist militarism and the new power of Italy. In these books all the young children ardently desired one thing above all: to put on their uniforms and march around with play rifles in preparation for the day when they could become real soldiers in the army of the Duce. They were fascinated by the strength and power of the young black shirts and mesmerized by tales of the heroism and derring-do of the Fascist legions in Ethiopia, Spain, and Albania. They learned to repeat the war cries of their big brothers and marched around town shouting, *Bombe a mano, carezze di pugnal!* ("Grenades and caresses from the dagger!"). Nationalism became chauvinism in these texts, especially in the frequent discussions of the African war. The Abyssinians were presented as bloodthirsty barbarians; their emperor was portrayed as a corrupt and ferocious slave-trader. The highlight of such stories was the bravery of the Italians, who responded to the perfidious British and French by rallying around their Duce in iron-willed opposition to sanctions. All of this is easy enough to ridicule, but it was the standard – in many cases the only – intellectual fare for millions of Italian children.

Religion lessons for the first and second grades were included in the readers; in the upper three grades there was a separate section on religion in the combined texts. In the later grades the material devoted to religion usually constituted about 20 percent of the textbook. Often the religious pictures and lessons seem out of place, juxtaposed as they are with stories and songs aimed at filling the child's mind with militarism and violence. "In the minds of the children," wrote Herman Finer, "Christ and Mussolini are brothers who speak the same language and hold positions of equal importance in the scheme of the universe, perhaps with Mussolini a little in the lead, since he is, after all, a living being and Christ is somewhere behind the clouds."[22] . . .

On the cover of the 1942 second-grade text for the urban schools there was the ever-present *figlio della lupa* writing "WIN" on the walls. The text, not surprisingly, given the date of publication, was decidedly militaristic and racist in tone. One especially distasteful story was "The White Soul of Black John," about a missionary who came home from Africa with a native boy who, the priest explained, "is black outside but white inside . . . he loves Italy which has taught him to know the Lord. When he came to the missions he was little more than a beast: he went about nude and ate raw meat. Now he reads, writes, and wants to become a missionary like me to help his black brothers to find their white souls." The children were not convinced, and one asked if the little African boy should be put in the laundry to make him clean again. This story was not removed from the 1944 version of the textbook.[23]

In the 1942 rural text, second-graders read the approved version of the Fascist revolution. Years ago, ran the story, Italy was a "beautiful and flowering garden," but in the garden there were a lot of wolves who wanted to destroy everything, "evil men who wanted to ruin the Fatherland." But then "to save everything one Man rose up and put himself at the head of an army of courageous men," who undertook a "glorious march during which the evildoers hid trembling with fear." Benito Mussolini, "the man who had defended the Fatherland so nobly, became Head of Government and DUCE OF ITALY."[24] . . .

Voltaire once said that history is a series of accumulated imaginative inventions, and this definition certainly applies to the content of the state textbooks during the Fascist period. As taught in these school books, history was totally Italocentric, viewed in rela-

tion to the arrival of the man of providence and reduced to incomprehensibility because it ignored the role of other nations. History thus became a series of convenient myths directed toward a practical aim: producing consensus and enthusiasm for the regime among Italian schoolchildren. Separate sections on history in the mass-produced textbooks began with the third grade. The entire year's study was little more than an ode to the regime and a repetition of all the most commonly used Fascist myths. Mussolini was always portrayed as Italy's savior: "The deserters, traitors and cowards . . . sought to render vain the sacrifices of our 600,000 dead. . . . Our beautiful tricolor was reduced to a rag by sacrilegious hands . . . while another flag, a red one symbolizing destruction, was waved and carried in triumph. . . . Then Benito Mussolini – the Man sent by God – determined to save the Fatherland from the Communist danger."[25]

The perfidy of the British and French, which had been a favorite propaganda myth of fascism since the Ethiopian war, was also blamed for the outbreak of the Second World War. After twenty years of trying to stifle the aspirations of the Italians, so the stories went, these ex-allies also tried to strangle the Germans, who, under the admirable leadership of Adolf Hitler, had set themselves to the task of reconstruction. But the selfish states, "who for some time had been used to bossing the whole world around," could not permit Germany to realize its rightful place in the world. After nine months of nonbelligerence the Italians joined in the conflict and, faithful to the orders of the Duce, "won everywhere: on land, on the sea, in the air." The conclusion of the chapter on World War II left the youngsters with food for thought: "The most luminous and complete victory will smile upon the forces of the Axis because their cause is just and holy." These words must have rung hollow by 1943 when Italian schoolchildren saw a much different reality all about them.[26]

Notes

1. Vittori, *C'era una volta il duce*, figs. 32–34.
2. B. Mussolini, *Autobiography*, 280–81.
3. *Il Resto del Carlino*, 29 April 1924; Vittori, *C'era una volta il duce*, back cover.
4. Nicolò Giani, "Civiltà fascista, civiltà dello spirito," quoted in Guido Quazza et al., *Fascismo e società italiana* (Turin:

Einaudi, 1973), 235–36. On the School of Fascist Mysticism see also Marchesini, *Scuola dei gerarchi*, and "Episodio della politica culturale," 90–122.

5. Bottai editorial in *Critica fascista*, 1 January 1929, quoted in Ledeen, *Universal Fascism*, 67. On Bottai and the youth see Guerri, *Giuseppe Bottai*, especially 133–46.

6. Marpicati, "Azione educativa."

7. Quoted in Cantarella, "Situation of the Learned Class," 48.

8. Marciano, *Concetto fascista*, 39.

9. On the intellectuals under fascism see Mangoni, *Interventismo della cultura*; A. Hamilton, *Appeal of Fascism*; Garin, *Intellectual italiani*; Carpanetto Firpo, "Intellettuali e mass-media," 356–76; Vita-Finzi, "Italian Fascism and the Intellectuals," 226–44; Tannenbaum, *Fascist Experience*, 279–302; Manacorda, *Letteratura e cultura*; and Bordoni, *Cultura e propaganda*.

10. Lyttelton, *Seizure of Power*, 408; ACS, PCM, Gabinetto, Atti (1931–33), fasc. 5/5-6829.

11. Natale, Colucci, and Natoli, *Scuola in Italia*, 138.

12. Royal Decree of I June 1933 (no. 641).

13. Salvatorelli and Mira, *Storia d'Italia*, 2:745.

14. MEN, *Bollettino dell'Opera Nazionale Balilla*, 15 November 1934.

15. The text is reprinted in Delzell, *Mediterranean Fascism*, 147, and Marraro, *New Education in Italy*, 72. The oath was article 18 of the Law of 28 August 1931 (no. 1227).

16. The pope's defense of the oath appeared in the *Osservatore romano* on 4 December 1931. See Binchy, *Church and State*, 464–65; and Borghi, *Educazione e autorità*, 247–49.

17. All sources agree that these university professors refused to swear the oath and were removed: at the University of Milan, Giuseppe Antonio Borgese (professor of aesthetics) and Piero Martinetti (philosophy); in Turin, Mario Carrara (criminal anthropology), Senator Francesco Ruffini (church law), Lionello Venturi (history of art); in Rome, Ernesto Buonaiuti (history of Christianity), Gaetano De Sanctis (ancient history), Giorgio Levi della Vida (Semitic languages); in Pavia, Giorgio Errera (chemistry); in Bologna, Bortolo Negrisoli (surgery); and in Perugia, Edoardo Ruffini-Avondo (history of law). Some sources also add Michele Giua, professor of chemistry at the University of Turin. In addition, two professors asked for retirement: Vittorio Emanuele Orlando, professor of constitutional law in Rome, and Antonio De Viti De Marco, professor of financial science in Rome. Guido De Ruggiero refused to sign the oath but apparently kept his position. See Zangrandi, *Lungo viaggio*, 356; De Felice, *Mussolini il duce*, 1:109; Borghi, *Educazione e autorità*, 295; Friends of Italian Freedom, "Oath of the University Professors," and "Controversy Concerning the Oath"; and Salvemini, "Teachers' Oath," 523–37.

18. Law of 7 January 1929 (no. 5). For a draft of the law see Senato del Regno, Camera del Deputati, *Bollettino Parlamentare*, 3 vols. (1929), 2:295.

19. Minio-Paluello, *Education in Fascist Italy*, 171.

20. ACS, PCM, Gabinetto, Atti (1931–33), busta 678, fasc. 3–5/4023.

21. For other studies of the state textbooks bearing on this discussion see Schneider and Clough, *Making Fascists*, 94–100; and Finer, *Mussolini's Italy*, 475–78. Texts used in the midthirties are discussed in Minio-Paluello, *Education in Fascist Italy*, 171–75; C. Hamilton, *Modern Italy*, 2–25; Leeds, *Italy under Mussolini*, 57–59; and Ricuperati, *Scuola italiana*, 47–102. Two valuable articles on the same topic are Garofalo, "Veleno sui banchi," 1430–38; and Abad, "Fascist Education," 433–38. An indictment of the content and approach of these state texts can be found in Flora, *Appello al Re*, 48–53.

22. Finer, *Mussolini's Italy*, 183–84.

23. Ballario and Angoletta, *Quartiere Corridoni*, 160.

24. Belloni and Bernardini, *Libro per la seconda classe*, 22.

25. *Libro della terza classe*, 69, 116, 118–21.

26. Ibid., 188–93.

FRIEDA ADAM

BERLIN, GERMANY... SEPTEMBER 1942 – In 1938, Erna Puterman was working as a seamstress in Berlin where she met Frieda Adam, a co-worker. The two teenage girls became friends. Even when Erna was forced to change jobs, Frieda continued her friendship with Erna – Frieda refused to be intimidated by the anti-Jewish laws and climate.

Life became increasingly difficult and harsh for the Jews of Germany. In September 1942, Erna's mother was arrested and later sent on one of the early transports to Auschwitz. Erna was left to care for her brother who was deaf. Not knowing what to do, Erna went to Frieda for help and advice.

Frieda's response to Erna was immediate, "As long as there is food for us, there will be food for you, too." Thus in September 1942, Erna and her brother went into hiding for more than two years. Frieda had three small children ages 6, 4, and 2 and a husband in the German Army. Frieda said of her husband, "He was an evil man. Everyone was evil back then." When Frieda's husband discovered that she was hiding two Jews, he began to blackmail her. Late in 1944, Frieda was forced to find Erna and her brother another place to hide. They all survived the war.

Photo of Frieda Adam (left) *with Erna Puterman* (right), *Berlin, 1939. (JFR Photo Archives)*

CHAPTER 3 **The National Socialist Regime**

Newly-appointed Chancellor Adolf Hitler greets German President Paul von Hindenburg as Hermann Göring (at left in helmet) and other high-ranking Nazi officials look on. Circa January 30, 1933. (Imperial War Museum [NYP22518] courtesy of USHMM Photo Archives)

DEBÓRAH DWORK **Introduction**

FIELD MARSHAL PAUL VON HINDENBURG, Germany's revered military hero of the First World War, was persuaded to come out of retirement in 1925 to run for the presidency of the Weimar Republic. His first years in office were a relatively stable time in the history of the republic, but by 1930 Germany was in turmoil as great as the country had experienced in the immediate postwar era. The Social Democratic government of chancellor Hermann Müller fell in the spring of 1930, and his successor, the centrist politician Heinrich Brüning, lasted but two turbulent years. In the election that followed in July 1932, the ultraconservative, rabidly nationalistic, and intensely antisemitic National Socialists (Nazis) won 230 of the 608 seats in the Reichstag (the German Parliament) and became the largest party in Germany's governing body.

It was Hindenburg's job as president to appoint a chancellor, and it was customary for the leader of the party with the greatest number of seats in the Reichstag to be asked to hold this office. Hindenburg, however, overlooked Adolf Hitler, the head of the Nazi party. Hitler was too crude a politician for Hindenburg's taste: too divisive and too vitriolic. The president recognized Hitler's popularity and power, but he did not believe that Hitler's agenda would serve the nation well. Deeply conservative, Hindenburg distrusted the naked violence of the Nazi ideology. He therefore appointed the charming, intellectual nonentity Franz von Papen, but the heavily Nazi new Reichstag did not confirm his choice. Hindenburg then dissolved the government and set new elections for November. Once again the Nazis did well, winning 196 of the 584 seats, and once again Hindenburg ignored the Nazi leader and appointed the crafty General Kurt von Schleicher as chancellor.

Von Schleicher was determined to stop Hitler, and he failed utterly. Once again the government fell, and this time the by-then eighty-five-year-old Hindenburg, who had slipped into senility just when Germany needed him most, asked Adolf Hitler on January 30, 1933 to form a coalition government in which Hitler would be chancellor and von Papen vice-chancellor. Von Papen was confident he could control Hitler, but the Nazis had no compunctions about using both propaganda and terror to attain power. They needed a two-thirds majority in the Reichstag to change the constitution legally, and they began a campaign to ensure that they would win the requisite seats by the time of the new elections on March 5. Using whatever means were necessary, the Nazis meant to convince the majority of upright German citizens that a fully National Socialist government was the only way to prevent Germany's descent into Communist chaos.

The National Socialists' trump card was the Reichstag fire of February 27, 1933. This deliberate arson against the German parliament

> The Nazis used both propaganda and terror to attain power.

building was quickly and conveniently blamed on the Communists, and it created the atmosphere of apprehension that encouraged Hindenburg to sign an emergency decree "as a protection against Communist acts of violence endangering the state." In the week between the fire and the election, many of the Nazis' political opponents were arrested, taken into so-called protective custody, and detained in hastily erected protective custody camps or, as they were also called, *Konzentrationslager*, concentration camps. Remarkably, the Nazis did not win a majority in the March elections. But with eighty-one Communist deputies under arrest or in flight, and with the support of Reichstag deputies from the Nationalist and Catholic parties, Hitler attained an effective majority to suspend the constitution. It was the end of the Weimar Republic.

The purpose of this chapter is to explore the development of the tentacles of the Nazi state that led to the Holocaust: the growth of the police apparatus and the establishment of concentration camps; the policy and practice of antisemitism; and the institutionalization of state-run, state-mandated murder. National Socialist rhetoric and propaganda espoused the centrality of Hitler's visionary leadership, but the actual structure and operation of the regime was hardly based on unity of purpose. On the contrary: the Nazi power structure did not develop as a result of a unified leadership with clear concepts and consistent policies but emerged from the confused interaction of many separate, mostly inconsistent, and often opposing aims.

In the institutional jungle that evolved, only rivalry and conflict could be taken for granted. According to the late historian Martin Broszat, most of the top leaders appreciated the endemic struggle for power within the Nazi hierarchy. They thought it increased efficiency, kept their underlings in check, and produced compromises and mutual arrangements that seemed to stabilize the regime. For Hitler it was ideal. So long as the ministerial bureaucrats and the generals argued among one another, he remained the ultimate arbiter of power.

The growth of the concentration camp system was shaped by this endemic struggle. The legal basis for the camp system – as Wolfgang Sofsky has explained in a chapter from his book, *The Order of Terror* – was President Hindenburg's emergency decree mentioned above, "For the Protection of People and State." As we have seen, the decree was intended as a "defense against Communist acts of violence," but it was used to defend mass arrests of opponents of National Socialism and the creation of "protective custody camps." Initially, these

Hitler youth salute at a May Day rally in Berlin. May 1, 1933. (Courtesy of USHMM Photo Archives)

concentration camps were meant for political enemies, but as the National Socialists became more firmly entrenched and the boundaries between state, society, and party dissolved, the focus shifted. With a vanishingly slim legal cover, the Nazi party police, the *Schutzstaffel,* or SS, began to incarcerate people whose very existence was supposed to damage the national community: vagabonds, drug addicts, and beggars. For Heinrich Himmler, the chief of the SS, the camps became a tool to clean up the cities. They also became a tool for Himmler to fill SS coffers. Himmler had joined the Nazi party in 1923, and the SS was established two years later in 1925. Originally an unimportant organization to provide security for party meetings, the SS was quickly developed into an elite police force by the utterly loyal, devoted, and fanatic Himmler. Within a decade, his SS had become a virtual state within the state, and Himmler needed money for his black-shirted empire.

By 1937 Himmler was in a position to exploit the economic potential of camp inmates. By that time the concentration camps had become largely superfluous as an instrument of terror against actual or potential political opponents. They were ready to be filled with the so-called "asocials" (vagrants, tramps, drug addicts, beggars) caught by any one of the many branches of Himmler's now extensive police apparatus in their raids to cleanse the German streets. These asocials formed a stable labor pool for an SS-owned building material industry. Unlike the original political prisoners who were supposed to be "reeducated" in the "protective custody" camps, these inmates were slaves.

The definition of "asocials" to be caught and incarcerated in the camps was expanded and altered from time to time. Himmler's circular of January 26, 1938 ordered the internment of "work-shy elements," which were defined as "men who are old enough to work and who have been certified as fit by an official doctor or who will be certified fit and who can be proved to have rejected offers of work on two occasions without just cause or have accepted work only to abandon it again shortly afterwards without adequate reason." On June 1 of that year, a new edict from Himmler ordered a comprehensive swoop of asocials. Now included were "Vagabonds at present moving from place to place without work; Beggars, even if they have a permanent domicile; Gypsies and persons traveling in Gypsy fashion who have shown no desire for regular work or have violated the law; Pimps who have been involved in criminal proceedings – even if they were acquitted – and who still move in pimp and prostitute circles, or persons strongly suspected of being pimps; Persons with several convictions for creating disorders, doing bodily harm, causing brawls, breaking the peace, etc., who have thus demonstrated that they are not prepared to fit into the national community." It also included another group of people to be arrested: all male Jews with previous criminal records.[1] This was the first significant role of the camps in the National Socialist assault on the Jews.

Between 1933 and 1939 the National Socialist regime had marginalized German Jews with extraordinary rapidity through a policy that began with a definition of who was a Jew and continued with the

Between 1933 and 1939 the National Socialist regime marginalized German Jews with extraordinary rapidity through a policy that began with a definition of who was a Jew.

progressive financial expropriation through dismissals from work and forcing Jews to sell their businesses for a pittance to so-called "aryans" (people the Nazis considered members of the "Nordic race," which in practice translated into "racially pure" Germans and other Northern European peoples). Jews were also burdened with special taxes, and their bank accounts were blocked. At the same time as Jews were driven into economic despair, they were faced with increased social isolation through various decrees ranging from a quota for Jewish students at German universities (1933), to the prohibition of German-Jewish marriages and German-Jewish extramarital relations (1935), to the expulsion of all Jewish children from German schools (1938). (See William Carr's essay *"Nazi Policy Against the Jews."*) This legal assault on the rights and privileges of Jewish Germans, and their loss of place, position, and role in society, was accompanied by a pervasive antisemitic rhetoric in political posters, newspaper articles, editorials, cartoons, radio broadcasts, and written tracts of all sorts. Jews were portrayed as conspirators who sought to undermine German unity through communist agitation and capitalist manipulation, and who attempted to destroy not only the German spirit through "gutter journalism" but also the German body through carnal behavior.

Until 1938, to be a Jew was not reason enough to be committed to a concentration camp. The camps were meant for communists, socialists, asocials, and others who, according to the Nazis, did not fit into the national community. There were, of course, many Jews among them, and when their political affiliation or social behavior landed them in a camp, they usually were treated considerably more harshly than the other inmates. Often separated from the main body of prisoners, they had less chance of being released. Nevertheless, they were not there because they were Jews.

This changed abruptly on November 9, 1938, with the November Pogrom or so-called *Kristallnacht*, the Night of Broken Glass. (See the chapter from Marion Kaplan's book on Jewish life in Nazi Germany, *Between Dignity and Despair.*) That night National Socialists orchestrated a violent rampage throughout Germany against Jewish-owned property – synagogues, businesses, and homes – and Jewish people, "in response" to the assassination in Paris of Ernst vom Rath, a German embassy official, by a young Jew named Herschel Grynszpan. In the early hours of November 10, some 26,000 Jewish men were swept out of their homes and in transport after transport dispatched to concentration camps. The purpose of the destruction and the dragnet was to terrorize the Jewish community: most of the Jewish internees eventually

Germans pass by the broken window of a Jewish-owned business smashed during the November Pogrom. November 10, 1938. (National Archives, courtesy of USHMM Photo Archives)

were released after they had promised to leave the country. Shortly thereafter, the Nazis opened a Central Office for Jewish Emigration to streamline the departure procedures for, and to maximize the financial depredation of, their unwanted neighbors. (But where were the Jews to emigrate? See Chapter 4.) They had been let go this time, but the message was clear: To be a Jew was sufficient cause for incarceration.

Incarceration, but not yet annihilation. The November Pogrom marked the end of the beginning, but it was not yet the beginning of the end. The German government had sponsored a ferocious pogrom. And German people had participated in the brutality both by taking part and by doing nothing either at the time or afterwards, when the government insisted that the Jews pay for the damage the authorities themselves had organized. But in the 1930s the Nazi regime was not yet genocidal.

As Debórah Dwork and Robert Jan van Pelt explain, however, in an excerpt from their book *Auschwitz*, developments in science and medicine moved the regime along that path. In the nineteenth century, Germans like Ernst Haeckel had

Newly arrived prisoners, with shaven heads, stand at attention in their civilian clothes during a roll call in the Buchenwald concentration camp. Some still have their suitcases and other bags with them. These prisoners were among the more than 10,000 German Jews arrested during the November Pogrom and sent to Buchenwald. Another 20,000 German Jews arrested at the same time were imprisoned in two other concentration camps, Dachau and Sachsenhausen. Circa November 10, 1938. (American Jewish Joint Distribution Committee, courtesy of USHMM Photo Archives)

adopted the English biologist Charles Darwin's theory of natural selection and survival of the fittest to create a new philosophy of social planning. If natural selection determined the life of species in the plant and animal world, Haeckel argued, then it also affected human beings. And if natural selection wasn't having the desired effect on the nation's populace, it was legitimate to aid the process through artificial selection. In other words, if natural selection did not kill degenerate people, the state should step in and complete the purpose of nature.

Haeckel's recommendations found little acceptance at first. But in the early years of the twentieth century, criticism of the explosive growth of medical expenditure and fear that the working class would continue to grow and that socialism would ensue encouraged middle-class acceptance of Haeckel's peculiar interpretation of Darwin's ideas. Combined with the racist views of Richard Wagner and Houston Stewart Chamberlain (see Chapter 1), the policy of "Racial Hygiene" explicitly called for the killing of the "unfit."

Hitler certainly thought it was a wonderful idea. In *Mein Kampf*, the book that became a kind of Nazi bible because it was written by Hitler himself during his brief imprisonment in 1924 for attempting to overthrow the Weimar Republic by force, he demanded that the state adopt ruthless policies with regard to the "imperfect." Within months of taking power he decreed the sterilization of all those who were mentally handicapped, schizophrenic, manic-depressive, hereditary epileptics, blind, deaf, or alcoholic, and the castration of serious moral offenders. In 1935 Hitler went further and prohibited people who had been diagnosed with a serious contagious disease (like tuberculosis), a mental disorder, or various hereditary diseases from marrying. Finally, in 1938, Hitler turned his attention to euthanasia. He had begun to receive an increasing number of letters from family members of mentally handicapped people requesting the "mercy death" of loved ones. Hitler was intrigued by the entreaty of a certain Mr. Kauer from Leipzig. Kauer's child had been born blind, appeared idiotic, and was missing a leg and part of an arm. Hitler instructed his personal physician, Dr. Karl Brandt, to examine the child and, if the father's description was correct, to kill the youngster. Brandt obeyed. Hitler was pleased, and authorized other cases to be treated in the same way. In the summer of 1939, men on Hitler's personal staff established a new organization to kill infants and children up to age three who suffered from a range of physical and mental disabilities.

> In the summer of 1939, men on Hitler's personal staff established a new organization to kill infants and children up to age three who suffered from a range of physical and mental disabilities.

In all, some 5,000 children were killed and, having crossed that moral line, Hitler ordered preparations to kill adults "unfit for life." In mid-October 1939 he issued an informal authorization written on his personal notepaper. It was backdated to September 1 – the day the war had begun. This operation, code-named T-4 after its headquarters at Tiergartenstrasse 4, began at the end of 1939. For the National Socialists it was an unqualified success. In 1939 between 65,000 and 75,000 candidates had been identified. When Hitler stopped the program on August 24, 1941, the organizers congratulated themselves that "70,273 persons have been disinfected." And while the 70,273 victims amounted to one in five of all institutionalized patients, it included all Jewish patients.

Despite Hitler's order, the murder of mental patients continued on a decentralized basis and primarily – but not exclusively – through starvation. This left the T-4 corps with little to do. They were not unemployed long. Within three months of the official end of the program, their expertise and at least a quarter of the personnel had been relocated to the east of Europe where they put their experience to use murdering Jews.

Note

1. Himmler edict of June 1, 1938, quoted in Martin Broszat, "The Concentration Camps, 1933-1945," in Helmut Krausnick et al., *Anatomy of the S.S. State,* trans. Richard Barry, Marian Jackson, and Dorothy Long (New York: Walker, 1968), 455.

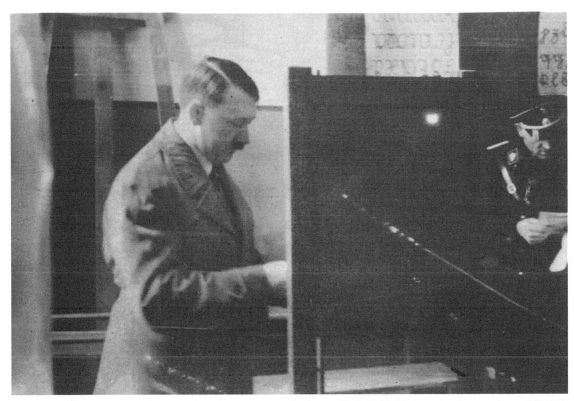

Adolf Hitler casts his vote at a Berlin polling station set up in a schoolroom. March 1933. (National Archives, courtesy of USHMM Photo Archives)

Massive rally of Hitler Youth honoring unknown soldier. August 23, 1933. (AP/Wide World Photos)

Wolfgang Sofsky # On the History of the Concentration Camps

THE ORGANIZATIONAL HISTORY of the German concentration camps began in an atmosphere marked by improvisation, rivalry, arbitrary decisions, and revenge.[1] On the night of February 27, 1933, the Reichstag was set ablaze; the following day, the Emergency Decree for the Protection of the Nation and State abrogated the rights to freedom enshrined in the Weimar constitution. This created the legal basis for putting political opponents behind bars for longer periods. The secret police and their auxiliaries in the SA (*Sturmabteilung*, the elite paramilitary "storm trooper" units of the Nazi Party) and SS were empowered to order *Schutzhaft* (protective custody) without a court decision. Even before the burning of the Reichstag, the police in Prussia had taken an oath to uphold National Socialist principles of struggle, and the paramilitary Nazi units had been granted police authority. During initial raids on the night of the conflagration, numerous communist functionaries and parliamentary representatives were arrested. On March 23, the so-called Enabling Act (*Ermächtigungsgesetz*) made the civil state of emergency a permanent fixture; two days later, the police and the SA occupied forty-six trade union office buildings; on April 1, the first nationwide boycott was instituted against Jews. On April 7, the regime removed undesirable officials from the civil service by passing the Civil Service Law (*Berufsbeamtengesetz*); two weeks later, "non-Aryan" doctors were denied permission to practice in hospitals. On May 2, the unions were dissolved. On May 10, books were set afire on pyres in university towns. On June 22, the SPD (Social Democratic Party) was banned; other political parties were disbanded under coercion at the end of the month. After members of the left opposition were hauled in, the wave of arrests now extended to members of the bourgeois center: clerical workers, civil servants, and journalists. In May, the number of those arrested dropped, only to crest again during the summer. On July 31, at least 26,789 persons were in protective custody in the Reich; of these, 14,906 were in Prussia, 4,152 in Bavaria, and 4,500 in Saxony.

In the wake of the political consolidation of the regime, arrests declined once again in the following months. In November 1933, some 11,000 were incarcerated in Prussian concentration camps. In the spring of 1934, after a large-scale Christmas amnesty, there were just under 5,000 in the camps; by the beginning of August, their numbers had dropped to 1,243. There was a similar development in Bavaria. In December 1933, there were 3,855 prisoners registered in protective custody; ten months later, that figure had declined by more than half, to some 1,700. Between February 1933 and August 1934, some 50,000 individuals were remanded to protective custody in the two states for varying periods of time; some 3,000 were not released again.

The establishment of the first concentration camp was not centrally guided by the new government in Berlin; it came about on the initiative of subordinate offices and local party groups. Most camps were under the authority of state agencies, the political police, the state ministries of the interior, or the administrative heads of various government districts (*Regierungspräsidenten*). Prison facilities had been set up by local party leaders; these remained totally shielded from any state supervision. Many prisoners were not even brought to the overcrowded jails of the justice system by units of the SA and the SS; they were initially confined in the jail facilities, meeting halls, basements, or indoor riding rings of those groups. Later, the prisoners were transferred to newly comandeered quarters. Improvised terror in these provisional jails, although it was generally only of short duration, anticipated later developments. These were sites for beating and torture pure and simple, settings for vengeance against actual or presumed opponents of the regime. The party groups also enjoyed appreciable influence in the camps under the supervision of the civil administration or the regular police. The groups were often in close cooperation with government offices, which increasingly were staffed by party members. Where, due to administrative rivalries, that did not immediately come to pass, the SA and the SS largely retained the local right of disposal over the prisoners. As the official auxiliary police, they provided the supervisory and guard personnel in most of the state concentration camps.

In Bavaria, there was no competition between provisional SA camps and the offices of the interior and justice ministries.[2] From its inception, the camp at Dachau (twelve miles northwest of Munich) was under state supervision. On March 9, Reichsführer-SS, Heinrich Himmler had advanced to the post of police commissioner of Munich. On April 1, he was appointed commander of the Bavarian political police, which was separated from the police bureaucracy as a special ministerial agency. This provided the basic outlines of the model for the later fusion of the secret police and the SS. Himmler was in charge of both the police admissions office and the guard units in Dachau, the first camp under exclusive SS supervision. Equipped with this control, Himmler could parry attempts by the Bavarian justice authorities to intrude, and could also block efforts by the Reich governor in Bavaria further to limit the numbers of detainees in protective custody. Between June 1933 and November 1934, the number of Dachau inmates fluctuated between twenty-seven hundred and seventeen hundred. Despite the lack of a proper infrastructure, the camp had been designated as a central facility to house all detainees in protective custody in Bavaria.

A similar move toward centralization in Prussia proved abortive, initially because of the rivalry between administrative offices. The state interior ministry took over camp administration, and in mid-March made plans for a central camp complex to house ten thousand prisoners in the Emsland, the rather remote area west of Bremen between the Ems River and the Dutch border. Inmates were to be deployed as laborers to drain the nearby moors.[3] In order to curb the local power of the SA and the SS, the Prussian interior minister, on October 14, granted

formal recognition as state facilities for protective custody to the Papenburg, Sonnenburg, Lichtenburg, and Brandenburg camps and also to the political departments in the Brauweiler Institute near Cologne and the Provincial Workhouse at Moringen (north of Göttingen), which were linked to the Gestapo (*Geheime Staatspolizei*, the secret state police). However, the power to decide on the admission of detainees lay not with the interior ministry, but with the Gestapo. It had been separated from the general administration as an independent prosecuting agency and placed under the personal supervision of Hermann Göring, the Prussian chief minister. Attempts by the interior ministry to set up an administrative structure headed by a director foundered because of opposition by SS guard units. Thus, rivalry between competing agencies prevented the uniform planning of the camp system. The SA camps were gradually disbanded; at the same time, however, protective custody was removed from ministerial supervision and made the exclusive domain of the Gestapo and the local SS units. On April 20, 1934, Himmler assumed control of the political police in Prussia. The SA no longer had any camps of its own; its guard personnel were under the control of the justice administration. Now the SS could set about revamping the system of concentration camps.

Although the number of prisoners was steadily declining and they still could have been transferred to the regular justice system, Himmler (whose plans were always approved by the Führer) ordered the Dachau commandant Theodor Eicke in May 1934 to begin reorganizing and expanding the camp system. This foreshadowed a fundamental functional change in the concentration camps. Instead of a temporary instrument of repression necessary for the consolidation of the new regime, these camps were now to be permanent facilities for the preventive detention of anyone whom those in power might define as opponents. Eicke replaced commandants, and he withdrew the guard units from the general SS, combining them into barracked guard formations. At the same time, he dissolved the remaining prison facilities and concentrated the prisoners in a small number of camps. In the early summer of 1935, the inspector of concentration camps and commander of SS guard units (*Inspekteur der Konzentrationslager und Führer der SS-Wachverbände*) was in charge of six camps with approximately thirty-five hundred prisoners: along with Dachau, the Esterwegen, Lichtenburg, Sachsenburg, and Moringen camps, as well as the Columbia House in Berlin-Tempelhof. Beginning in 1935, the new supervisory agency, the *KZ-Inspektion* (concentration camp directorate), was initially located in the Gestapo offices in Berlin. In August 1938, Eicke's staff was relocated to Oranienburg, not far from Sachsenhausen, a camp set up in 1936. The *Inspektion* remained there until 1945.

This office was relatively small.[4] In 1935, its staff numbered eight SS members and five police officers. One year later, some thirty positions were approved for the leadership staff of the Death's Head units. Nonetheless, the *KZ-Inspektion* enjoyed a basically free hand in its decisions. The organizational principle of dual and personal subordination, typical of the SS bureaucracy, favored protected privilege and promoted independent concentrations of power; those in the *KZ-Inspektion* were able to act with a high degree of independent initiative and make decisions not bound by rules. As camp inspector, Eicke belonged to Heydrich's secret state police; as head of the Death's Head units, he was responsible solely to the central office of the SS. State and party functions were united in one man. As soon as one supervisory authority attempted to control affairs, Eicke was able to fall back on the other side of his dual competency. In cases of conflict, he brought all his bundled authority to bear, or circumvented the offices above him, turning directly to Himmler. Despite this, his position was controversial. The concentration camps remained an object of debate and contention in the organizational field.[5] Now it was no longer the justice authorities or the SA who disputed the right of the camp SS to exercise full control. The SS administrative office headed by Oswald Pohl, as well as the later SS personnel office and the surgeon-general SS, all had the opportunity to influence the activities of Eicke's inspection agency. Moreover, relations between the *Inspektion* and Heydrich's Gestapo were apparently also tense. The Gestapo decided on the admission and release of prisoners, and maintained a Political Department in each and every camp as a Gestapo base.

Many members of the camp SS viewed that department with nothing but mistrust. Externally, vis-à-vis the authorities, they closed ranks and demonstrated unity as soon as the interests of the SS were involved. Internally, however, there was a welter of personal rivalries, not only between Heydrich and Eicke, but also between the camp commandants and local officers of the Gestapo or the criminal police.

Along with the establishment of a central bureaucracy, the reorganization of the SS camps was one of Eicke's principal tasks. The consolidation during the years 1934 through 1936 led to the formalization of the camp administration and to a certain standardization in the detention system. A pattern of distribution of tasks and competencies had already crystallized. That pattern was to remain in place until the end of the war. The sentry and escort service was separated from the administration, and the bureaucracy was structured according to a uniform scheme.[6] This formal structure stabilized the framework of positions. The organization of the concentration camp was rendered independent of any changes in personnel and their initiatives. Consolidation thus meant not only the concentration of prisoners under a unified leadership, but also the institutionalization of the camp as a social system.

In keeping with this was the internal standardization of camp operations according to the "Dachau model."[7] Dachau at this time was not merely an important practical training center for the camp SS, where the careers of many SS leaders began, men who would carry the *habitus* of the "Eicke school" to other camps. Dachau was more: it served as the paragon for the reorganization of the entire system of concentration camps. The model encompassed four components: classification of the prisoners; labor as an instrument of terroristic detention; a graduated system of penalties that could be imposed officially as well as informally; and military law for grave offenses such as mutiny or attempted escape (although it also served as a cover for spontaneous and concealed killings). Eicke introduced the 1933 regulations governing guard service in other camps as well; these regulations essentially remained in force until the end of the war. The disciplinary and penal codes for the prisoner camps were altered in order to curtail the arbitrary decisions of the commandants, yet no limits were set on mistreatment and cruel harassment. The rules established terror as a principle, at the same time opening the door to arbitrary caprice. They indicated to the guard personnel the scope and latitude of what was permissible. The Dachau model was more than a catalog of codified, standard rules and regulations; it was a paradigm for the everyday practice of terror, which the camp personnel was able to carry out according to its own experience, habits, and whim.

Until 1936, preventive detention was primarily a way to abet the internal consolidation of the regime. The Gestapo engaged in a policy of arrest aimed at frightening and intimidating the population – a strategy of deterrence. In every locality, a few individuals suddenly disappeared; most returned after a certain period of time, depressed and frightened. This gave rise to a climate of paralyzing fear. What snippets of information people heard about the camps sufficed to suppress opposition. Often, legends of horror circulated that surpassed even the stark reality of the camps. The concentration camps, far from being a well-kept state secret, were publicly known institutions. The release of a relatively high number of persons from custody was a shrewd way to consolidate further the grip of the regime.

All this changed fundamentally in 1936. The SS began with the planning and construction of new concentration camps. Year by year, sites of absolute power were established that would continue in operation until the war's end: Sachsenhausen (in the town of Oranienburg, north of Berlin) in 1936, Buchenwald (outside Weimar) in 1937, Flossenbürg (between Weiden and the Czech border in northeastern Bavaria) in 1938. Immediately after the invasion and *Anschluß* (annexation) of Austria in 1938, the Mauthausen camp was set up near Linz; in 1939, the women's camp of Ravensbrück was established (fifty miles north of Berlin). The only camp from the first phase that still existed was Dachau; all the others had been disbanded. Prisoners from Esterwegen (in Emsland) and the Columbia House were transferred to Sachsenhausen, Sachsenburg prisoners were sent to Buchenwald, and the women from Lichtenburg were relocated to Ravensbrück. After consolidation and contraction, the system was readied for the next phase

of expansion. The new barracks camps were to be made available for the heightened security measures anticipated in the event of war; they were to have an expandable absorption capacity, and contribute to the four-year plan by deploying inmates as laborers in SS enterprises. Now, the location of the camps was not determined by the availability of prisons, workhouses, fortified palaces, or castellated monasteries; rather, the decisive factors were production facilities for building materials, granite quaries, and tile and brick factories.

Although the political opposition had long since been eliminated, a development arose with the establishment of the new camps that gradually extended terror to encompass more groups. A new category was added to that of the political adversary: the *Volksschädling* (pest harmful to the people). The camps changed from a locus of political repression into an instrument for racial-ethnic (*völkisch*) social policy, a dumping ground to which the SS dragged all those it considered noxious or superfluous.[8] Preventive detention was redefined as an unlimited "substitute penalty" that could be imposed on anyone the police labeled a social outsider. Already in 1934, there were some 350 "work-shy" prisoners in Dachau; in 1935, Lichtenburg had 325 "homosexuals" in detention, while 476 "professional criminals" were confined in the Esterwegen camp. These categories of prisoners were to gain even more importance in the subsequent period. On June 17, 1936, Himmler took over the criminal police. One year later, with the setting up of the central Reich Office of the Criminal Police, the organizational basis had been created for new waves of persecution. In March 1937, some two thousand "professional and habitual criminals" and "dangerous sexual offenders" were taken into preventive custody; these persons were already listed in specially prepared files. At year's end, the circle of individuals targeted for detention was expanded to include social outsiders. Local labor offices and Gestapo head offices were ordered to take the initiative in recording the particulars of "work-shy" and "asocial" persons (*Asoziale*) and recommending them for detention. This collective category included beggars, "vagrants," "ruffians," those suffering from venereal disease, prostitutes, homosexuals, alcoholics, "psychopaths," "traffic offenders," "fault-finders," and Gypsies – in short, anyone and everyone who had fallen out of favor with some authority or with an informer in the neighborhood. The first "Operation against Asocial Elements" (*Asozialen-Aktion*) in April 1938 led to the arrest of some fifteen hundred persons. In June, Heydrich ordered every district office of the criminal police to send at least two hundred able-bodied men as well as all Jews with previous convictions to the Buchenwald camp. Camps were no longer being set up because prisoners could not be accommodated elsewhere. On the contrary: persons were taken into custody in order to fill the waiting camps and secure laborers for the SS factories. At the beginning of 1937, the total population of the camps was seventy-five hundred prisoners; by October 1938, it had more than tripled, to twenty-four thousand. The forced recruitment of workers was cited as a reason for the mounting search, along with the need to create social order in the folk community (*Volksgemeinschaft*). However, the makeup of the prisoner population in the camps shifted. Political prisoners were now in the minority. Until the middle of the war, some two-thirds of all non-Jewish German prisoners were in the catchall category *Asoziale*.

Several thousand more political prisoners were incarcerated in the wake of the occupation of Austria and the Sudetenland. After the Crystal Night (*Reichskristallnacht*) pogrom of November 9–10, 1938, the SS rounded up some thirty-six hundred Jews and sent them to the camps, which were totally unprepared for such large numbers of detainees.[9] The Jews were plundered there, jammed together in special sections, and left without medical care, adequate clothing, or food. Although most were released after a short time, this mass arrest can arguably be classified as the first annihilation operation. The number of deaths in the severely overcrowded emergency quarters reached several hundred over a period of two months; this was a scale previously unknown among camp detainees. Many were murdered; others succumbed to the constant torment, agony, and strain. Yet that contradicted the official aim of the operation. These arrests had been conceived as a means of exortion. Those Jews who pledged to emigrate and signed an agreement regarding the "Aryanization" of their assets were generally released after several weeks. In the spring

and summer of 1939, the number of prisoners declined once again. In the wake of the pogrom, there had temporarily been as many as 60,000 inmates in the camps; at the end of August 1939, the camp population had declined to approximately 21,400.

The outbreak of the war led to a radical caesura. It did not change the principles of organization, but it altered the functions of the camps and the structure of prisoner society. Detention was intensified, food rations were reduced, everyday routine was rendered more strict, time for roll call was extended at the expense of free time. In the first winter of the war, death rates soared, reaching previously unknown levels, and the camps filled with foreign prisoners from the occupied countries. The further the German troops advanced, the smaller the percentage of German prisoners in the camps. During the war, they constituted only 5 to 10 percent of the total prisoner population. Most of the foreign prisoners were from Poland and the Soviet Union, where they were seized and taken to the camps directly after occupation. The waves of arrests in northern and western Europe were initially limited to isolated reprisal operations against "saboteurs" and resistance fighters. These also included prisoners taken in so-called *Nacht-und-Nebel* ("night and fog") operations.[10] In September 1941, Hitler ordered the seizure of any persons considered "suspicious"; they were to be brought across the border into the Reich and then made to vanish into the "night and fog" without a trace. Most were interned in the camps at Natzweiler (in Alsace) and Groß-Rosen (in Silesia). Despite the indiscriminate raids and searches in western Europe, summary arrest was initially restricted to the occupied territories with Slavic populations. Here, the more important factor was the racist population policy, which outweighed that of suppression of the opposition.

The internationalization of prisoner society increased internal social differentiation, leading to profound contrasts between the various national groups. German prisoners rose in the social pecking order, and accounted for the majority of functionaries in prisoner self-administration. At the bottom of the heap were the "non-Aryan" categories: along with the Jews, principally Poles and Russians. The number of prisoners surged, quickly reaching the level of the winter of 1938, and stabilized at some 60,000; by August 1942, the figures had risen again, nearly doubling, to approximately 115,000.[11] Overcrowding became a permanent feature. The concentration camp changed into a mass society; annihilatory pressures mounted rapidly, though the tempo and scope differed in the individual camps. This is reflected in figures for new admissions and deaths in several main camps (see table 1).[12]

The batching of new prisoners varied from camp to camp. At the end of June 1939, Buchenwald had 5,523 prisoners; by the end of the year, that figure had more than doubled with the admission of 2,500 Jews from Austria, the transfer of 2,200 prisoners from Dachau, and the admission of 2,098 Poles. However, the new admissions were largely offset by the numerous deaths and transfers, so the camp population leveled out at the end of 1942 at below 10,000. In Sachsenhausen, some 6,500 were confined at the outbreak of the war. Shortly thereafter, in September 1939, 900 Polish and stateless Jews from the Berlin area were taken to the camp; at the beginning of November, 500 Poles were interned. At the end of that month, 1,200 Czech students were added, and approximately 17,000 persons, mainly Polish nationals, were admitted as inmates in the period from March to September 1940. Despite the high number of new inmates, the camp population here too stabilized at the level of roughly 10,000 prisoners. That was because of the high mortality rate as well as the transfer of large numbers of Poles to Flossenbürg, Dachau, Neuengamme (in the Bergedorf section of southeastern Hamburg), and Groß-Rosen.

Mauthausen began to expand a year later, but at a faster pace. The camp population did not rise significantly until March 1940, with the transfer of the first Polish prisoners from Buchenwald. About eight thousand Poles were incarcerated in Mauthausen that year, augmented from 1940 to 1942 by some seventy-eight hundred Republican Spanish prisoners. Although the mortality figures the first year resembled those in Sachsenhausen, the annihilatory pressure in subsequent years at Mauthausen far exceeded that in any other main camp. Along with Auschwitz and Majdanek, Mauthausen and the neighboring camp, Gusen, were the centers for mass annihilation within the concentration camp system. Dachau went through a special trajectory of development. From September 1939 to March 1940, the camp was closed, and most inmates were transferred to Buchenwald, Mauthausen, and Flossenbürg. After return transfers, the camp population at the end of March was less than three thousand; it rose rapidly once more to some ten thousand by the end of that year, thus again rivaling the size of Sachsenhausen.

The soaring numbers of prisoners led to overcrowding in the old camps, which originally had been planned to house only five thousand inmates each. Therefore, the SS set up additional camps in 1940 to absorb the influx of prisoners from the occupied countries. In June 1940, the first Polish prisoners were admitted to the old military barracks at Auschwitz. Initially, Auschwitz had only been planned as a quarantine and transit camp to handle some ten thousand inmates. By mid-1941, however, more than seventeen thousand had been registered. In March of that year, work commenced on the construction of the largest camp complex at Birkenau,

TABLE 1

NEW ADMISSIONS AND DEATHS IN FOUR CAMPS, 1937–1945

	BUCHENWALD		SACHSENHAUSEN		MAUTHAUSEN		DACHAU	
	ADM.	DEATHS	ADM.	DEATHS	ADM.	DEATHS	ADM.	DEATHS
1937	2,912	48	750	38	–	–	2,015	69
1938	20,122	771	8,300	229	1,080*	36	18,681	370
1939	9,553	1,235	9,144	819	2,800*	445	3,932	300
1940	2,525	1,772	18,925	3,892	11,000*	3,846	22,675	1,515
1941	5,890	1,522	8,662	1,816	20,000*	8,114	6,153	2,576
1942	14,111	2,898	16,590	4,968	20,387*	14,293	12,572	2,470
1943	42,177	3,516	20,031	3,807	21,028	8,481	19,358	1,100
1944	97,866	8,644	50,560	2,347	65,645	14,766	78,635	4,794
1945	43,823	13,056	54,794	15,000*	24,793	52,814*	30,958	15,384

*Estimated figures

three kilometers from Auschwitz; it eventually had 250 barracks, and temporarily housed more than a hundred thousand inmates. The SS had the death factories built close by; these were put into operation in the first half of 1943.

In addition, Neuengamme, which had been functioning as a satellite of Sachsenhausen since 1938, was upgraded in 1940 to a separate concentration camp. The plan was to concentrate prisoners from northern and western Europe there. Two months later, in August 1940, the Groß-Rosen camp was set up in Lower Silesia; initially it was also a satellite of Sachsenhausen, but it became a separate, full-fledged camp on May 1, 1941. That was also the date of the establishment of Natzweiler in Alsace, where many of those seized in *Nacht-und-Nebel* operations were interned. In January 1942, Stutthof (near Danzig) was added to the list of concentration camps; it had been in operation since 1939 as a camp for civilian prisoners. One year later, the SS established Herzogenbusch in the Netherlands;[13] its inmates included people in preventive detention, prisoners of the German police in custody awaiting trial, and Dutch Jews. After a short stay, most were deported via Westerbork to Sobibór and Auschwitz.

Until 1939, the concentration camp system served primarily to eliminate political opponents, isolate social outsiders, and terrorize the population. Labor deployment was of secondary importance; it tended to be used more as a means than as an end of imprisonment. In the subsequent period, little changed in this regard at the local level. However, economic considerations became ever more important in the thinking in the top echelon of the SS leadership. The decisive factor in selecting the location for the camps at Natzweiler and Groß-Rosen, as earlier in the case of Mauthausen and Flossenbürg, was the proximity of a granite stone quarry. In the spring of 1941, I. G. Farben began with the construction of a Buna plant in Auschwitz. Initially, the main camp, seven kilometers away, furnished a pool of laborers, until the Monowitz camp was opened in 1942 directly at the construction site in order to shorten the route to work. The SS tried to gain complete control over the entire production cycle for goods vital to the war effort, though that policy met opposition from

private industry and [Albert] Speer's Armaments Ministry.[14] After several rounds of negotiations, an agreement was reached in the summer of 1942 not to transfer skilled workers from industrial firms to the camps, but rather to hire out prisoners to private firms and set up external camps near the armaments plants. The model for this mode of cooperation was the Buna camp at Monowitz. This local differentiation in the concentration camp system did not take hold on a larger scale until 1943.

During the early phase of the war, a second functional shift spread more rapidly: the transition from terroristic arrest and confinement to execution and mass annihilation. The concentration camp was transformed into a place of execution, first for individual "war saboteurs" and criminal prisoners the police wished to dispose of without trial, and then for registered prisoners as well. Finally, in the fall of 1941, that came to include thousands of Soviet prisoners of war who, after the invasion of the Soviet Union, had been captured and incarcerated in segregated sections of the camps.[15] The mass killing of POWs marked a new stage of power in the history of the camps. Not only were the prisoners systematically starved; new procedures for killing were also devised. In Buchenwald, some eighty-five hundred POWs were killed serially by a single shot to the nape of the neck (*Genickschuß*) in a facility specially constructed for the purpose. In Sachsenhausen, some thirteen thousand were killed in a similar fashion. In Auschwitz, the first experiments were conducted in September 1941 on a group of six hundred POWs using the poison gas Zyklon B. A bit later, execution orders were eased once again in order to pursue another tack: working the prisoners to death in the stone quarries. Not until the end of 1942 did the top echelon shift completely to deploying prisoners as forced laborers, dissolving the segregated camp sections and integrating the few survivors into the normal routines of camp life (and death).

The numbers of the dead surged, not only as a result of the executions, but particularly due to the cycle of "indirect" mass annihilation. Food rations for the prisoners deteriorated rapidly. The chronic hunger in the camps led to physical exhaustion, aggravating susceptibility to infections. This reduced performance and led to ever more brutal mistreatment; that in turn acted further to diminish an individual's labor power and chances for survival. The willful infliction of misery and violence were intermeshed. The SS murdered in order to come to grips with overcrowding in the camps and create room for new able-bodied prisoners, yet the latter were soon caught up in the same lethal cycle of emaciation, disease, exhausting labor, and violence.

From 1942 on, the second half of the war was marked by several parallel developments: the mass annihilation of European Jewry, labor deployment in the arms industry and in the construction projects of the special staffs for rocket and aircraft production, the establishment of hundreds of *Außenlager* (external subcamps), and the rapid rise in the number of prisoners. At the start of the war, the total inmate population was still some 24,000.[16] In 1941, that had surged to approximately 60,000; in August 1942, the figure reached 115,000, climbing to more than 200,000 in May 1943. In August 1944, the number of prisoners reached 524,268;[17] by January 1945, it had swelled once again, to 714,211, including 202,764 women.[18] In order to fill the camps with fit laborers, the SS initially fell back on prisoners in the clutches of the justice system. In mid-September 1942, Himmler and Thierack, the Reich minister of justice, reached an agreement that all imprisoned "security detainees," Jews, Gypsies, Russians, Ukrainians, Poles with sentences of more than three years, and Czechs and Germans serving sentences of more than eight years should be interned in the camps – for the expressly stated purpose of "extermination by work" (*Vernichtung durch Arbeit*).[19] Of the 12,658 prisoners from the justice system transferred during the winter of 1942–43 to the camps, primarily to Gusen, 5,953 (more than 47 percent) had perished by the following April.[20] However, in the eyes of the SS, by far the largest reservoir was the millions of foreign civilian workers in the Reich, especially Poles and Russians.[21] Any of these "foreign workers" (*Fremdarbeiter*) who caught the attention of the authorities was no longer handed over to the justice system, but was sent by the Gestapo to a labor-education camp or transported directly to a concentration camp. In this way, tens of thousands of Polish and Russian con-

scripted foreign laborers were sent every month to the camps. They were no longer registered in separate files; their numbers were only reported to the admissions office (the RSHA – *Reichssicherheitshauptamt*, the Reich Security Main Office) as a global figure. Once this reservoir was exhausted, Hitler gave permission in April 1944 for an exception to the program of genocide, allowing some 100,000 Jews to be brought into the Reich from the East to work in armaments production and bunker construction.[22] Thus, for example, some 108,000 were selected from the 458,000 Hungarian Jews in Auschwitz, and then transported in contingents of 500 persons each to work as laborers in the Reich.[23] Under pressure of a labor shortage, the regime deviated for a short time from the policy of mass annihilation.

The measures of annihilation directed against the Jews had already reached their most radical stage in the winter of 1941–42. In occupied Poland, the Jews were initially herded into forced ghettos, where intentional selections were subsequently carried out.[24] Those fit to work were systematically destroyed by means of labor, terror, and enforced misery in the newly established "forced-labor camps" (*Zwangsarbeitslager*); the others were deported immediately to the death camps. In December 1941, mobile extermination vans, using engine exhaust gases, began functioning in Chelmno (the first extermination camp, between Lodz and Posen in the so-called Warthegau); in the spring and summer of 1942, construction was begun on the death factories of Operation Reinhard: Belzec, Sobibór, and Treblinka. These killing facilities were not under the direction of the *Inspektion*, but were controlled by the local SS leadership of Lublin District in the *Generalgouvernement*, the largest administrative unit of occupied Poland. By contrast, the Baltic camp complexes in Riga-Kaiserswald, Vaivara, and Kaunas were under the administration of the *Inspektion*; they were set up in the summer and fall of 1943 for the internment of able-bodied Jews who had not been exterminated in the ghetto liquidation operations in Riga, Daugavpils, Vilna, and Kaunas.[25] Only the camp at Riga housed non-Jewish prisoners as well: some four hundred "Aryan" inmates with German citizenship, along with a small number of Poles. Moreover, seven hundred political prisoners from Estonia were interned in the facility at Klooga, a subcamp of Vaivara, along with eight hundred Soviet POWs. All other prisoners were Jewish; they either perished because of harsh labor and poor conditions or were shot after being selected. Only some twenty-five hundred inmates out of the total inmate population of fifty thousand in these camps survived to the end of the war. Auschwitz and Majdanek were also under the supervision of the Oranienburg *Inspektion*. Here, the policy of genocide intersected with the program of labor deployment. That policy's historic focus was the notorious "ramp" at Birkenau, where most incoming transports were subjected to the filter of selection, and the SS sorted Jewish workers according to the camps' momentary needs and absorption capacity. Prisoners selected were admitted to the camp; they were then worked to death. Despite the labor shortages, genocide clearly had priority, although this meant the loss of millions of Jewish workers.

The conversion of the concentration camp system to meet the needs of labor deployment was carried out primarily by a new agency of the SS, set up in 1942. On February 1, 1942, all SS matters pertaining to administration, economy, and construction were gathered together in a new office, the WVHA – the *Wirtschafts- und Verwaltungshauptamt* (Economic and Administrative Main Office), run by the previous head of SS administration, Oswald Pohl.[26] With a bureaucracy of fifteen hundred to seventeen hundred persons, the WVHA formed the counterweight within the SS to the RSHA, the central prosecuting authority of the criminal police and the Gestapo. Along with responsibility for troop administration and supplies for the units of the Waffen-SS, this office for SS industrial and commercial interests encompassed three branches (*Amtsgruppen*): "Construction" (C), "Economic Enterprises" (W), and, from March 5, 1942 on, *Amtsgruppe* D, the *KZ-Inspektion* located in Oranienburg. Pohl was thus entrusted with the central leadership of the camps and the task of removing the system from the grasp of the Armaments Ministry and Fritz Sauckel, the GBA – *Generalbevollmächtigter für den Arbeitseinsatz* (plenipotentiary for labor deployment). Using the most brutal methods, Sauckel had been recruiting civilian *Ostarbeiter* (Eastern workers) in the Soviet Union. The aim of in-

tegrating the camps into the economic central office for SS enterprises was not only to economize; it also had a strategic intention: to make sure the camps stayed within the sphere of power of the SS. Despite formal subordination to the WVHA, the *Inspektion der Konzentrationslager*, under Richard Glücks, Eicke's successor, continued to be a relatively independent agency.

The internal organizational structure of Branch D was largely in keeping with the tried and tested division of labor in the camps. The Central Office DI dealt with basic questions pertaining to the treatment of prisoners, in conjunction with the admissions agency, the RSHA. Office DII handled labor deployment: DIII supervised medical services. DIV was in charge of material equipment for the camps; de facto, however, it had only coordinating functions, because Branch C was responsible for all construction operations within the WVHA, while Office BII oversaw the provision of uniforms for the guard personnel and prisoners. Each office head had immediate authority to issue orders in his specific area of competence. Thus, the organizational principle of dual subordination was also operative in the case of the camp administrations. The labor-deployment leaders, camp doctors, and administrative heads received their orders both from the local SS command post and from the relevant central office. The local headquarters had no monopoly on command authority; orders from above could be sent directly from the special offices in the WVHA to the camps, bypassing the local SS headquarters.[27] The more important labor deployment became, the greater was the influence that accrued to Office DII. This office handled negotiations with the firms and the Armaments Ministry, deciding on the selection of workers and the establishment of new camps. In this way, Maurer, for many years a close associate of Pohl and the head of Office DII, was able to become the actual inspector of concentration camps – in contrast with Richard Glücks, who was nominally in charge of *Inspektion*.[28]

The policy of labor deployment opened up the camp system to external beneficiaries, interministerial special staffs, and a host of private munitions firms.[29] Yet it should be borne in mind that the concentration camps were not integrated into the total war economy until rather late, and then only with various misgivings. Although the top leadership echelon had touted the utility of labor deployment as early as the end of 1941, it was not until 1943 and 1944 that hundreds of satellite camps were set up: the drastically deteriorating military situation left no other option. The turbulence and exigencies of the final phase of the war were what sparked the dramatic expansion of the system – not the policies of the *Inspektion*. In December 1942, there were only 82 external work Kommandos (*Außenkommandos*); 29 of these were in Dachau alone. A year later, the total had climbed to 196. Most of the satellite camps were not set up until 1944; in June of that year, there were 341, and by January 1945, there were 13 main camps with a total of 662 *Außenkommandos*.[30] This local differentiation undermined the principle of the closed, single, self-contained camp. The concentration camp was transmuted into an enterprise for hiring out laborers. The main camps now formed the center of an organizational unit with numerous branches and external satellites. However, labor deployment in this framework brought no lessening of the threat of annihilation for the prisoners. Their work was not slave labor, but terror labor (*Terrorarbeit*),[31] performed under the most miserable and harrowing conditions. Even if labor had not been planned and engineered everywhere as a means of annihilation, it nonetheless became a major cause of death.

The final period coincided with the advance of the Allied armies and the dissolution of the concentration camp system. In July 1944, Majdanek was the first large camp to be vacated. In the preceding months, transports with thousands of prisoners had left Majdanek for Groß-Rosen, Ravensbrück, Bergen-Belsen, and Auschwitz. The final contingent of 1,000 prisoners set off on foot to Auschwitz; six days later, only 698 arrived at their destination.[32] From August 1944 to January 1945, Auschwitz also was dissolved in stages. Some 65,000 prisoners were freighted off in transports to the Reich; during the week of January 17–23, 1945, the remaining 60,000 were herded onto the roads leading west. Thousands perished during these forced marches. Many were shot dead; others, too feeble, collapsed and froze to death in the snow. Of the 800 prisoners who set out from the sub-

camp Janinagrube, 600 died on the eighteen-day trek to Groß-Rosen. On January 18, a column of 3,000 prisoners set out from Birkenau; at the end of March, 280 of them arrived at their destination, Geppersdorf near Görlitz. Some 29,000 Jews were evacuated by ship and train from Danzig and Stutthof, but only 3,000 survived to reach Ravensbrück and Sachsenhausen.[33]

The deeper the Allies penetrated, the more rapidly the network of the camps crumbled. In this process of dissolution, prisoners were caught up in a maelstrom, driven ever more quickly from camp to camp. The intention was that no prisoner should fall into the hands of the liberators. Down to very last minute, prisoners were deployed on construction projects "vital to the war effort": building railroad embankments, repairing bridges, digging bunkers, or erecting tank barriers. The harried columns were marched back and forth from camp to camp. A few examples: in Neuselz on the Oder, a contingent of 1,000 Jewish women set off on foot on January 26; after forty-two days on the road, 200 of them reached Flossenbürg in eastern Bavaria. Eight days later, the survivors were herded onto a train to Bergen-Belsen. On April 15, a last prisoner train was sent from Neuengamme via Nuremberg to Ebensee on Lake Traun in the Austrian Salzkammergut. That same day, 17,000 women from Ravensbrück and 40,000 men from Sachsenhausen were herded off on a march heading west. In Brandenburg, thousands died of exhaustion or were massacred by their guards. On April 15, British troops liberated Bergen-Belsen, where they found 10,000 unburied corpses rotting in the spring air. On May 5, a United States armored unit reached Mauthausen; the following day, Ebensee was the last camp to be liberated.[34]

It is impossible to determine precisely how many died in the camps and on the death marches. Camp records, insofar as they exist, were not kept according to uniform rules, and they exhibit numerous gaps.[35] SS figures on monthly mortality served as an official indicator of living conditions in a camp. However, they must be evaluated as "political statistics," manipulated totals with which local SS headquarters wished to present themselves in as favorable a light as possible to the central authority.[36] If there was an order to reduce mortality rates, the camp command posts tried to pass on sick and exhausted prisoners from one camp to another by transport. In this way, figures for the dead could be reduced at the point of dispatch; the transports were often not even registered at their destination. Prisoners died en route or were killed immediately after arrival, and thus disappeared, unrecorded. The central administration operated in a similar manner. If it appeared to be convenient to present a low number of dead to a superior office, only the cases of "natural death" were counted. If, on the other hand, there was an order instructing the camps to maintain labor power, all deaths were tallied, so as to document and underscore the catastrophic living conditions responsible for their difficulty in maintaining the desired level of labor. Within the concentration camp system, the accountancy of death was an instrument for death's manipulation; in the hierarchy of bureaucratic offices and channels, such bookkeeping served as a tactical means of proof.

Table 2 can nonetheless provide a picture of the annihilatory pressure in the various camps. It includes only those camp complexes for which there are relatively reliable figures, or at least plausible estimates

TABLE 2
ADMISSIONS AND DEATHS IN SELECTED CAMPS, 1933–1945

		ADMISSIONS	DEATHS
CAMP			
DACHAU	(1933–45)	206,206	31,591
BUCHENWALD	(1937–45)	238,979	56,545
MAUTHAUSEN	(1938–45)	197,464	102,795
NEUENGAMME	(1938–45)	106,000	55,000
FLOSSENBÜRG	(1938–45)	96,217	28,374
GROß-ROSEN	(1940–45)	120,000	40,000
AUSCHWITZ	(1940–45)	400,000	261,000
MAJDANEK	(1941–45)	250,000	200,000
DORA-MITTELBAU	(1943–45)	60,000	20,000
BERGEN-BELSEN	(1943–45)	125,000	50,000
CONCENTRATION CAMP SYSTEM	(1933–45)	(1,650,000)	(1,100,000)
EXTERMINATION CAMP			
CHELMNO	(1941–43)		225,000
BELZEC	(1942–43)		600,000
SOBIBÓR	(1942–43)		250,000
TREBLINKA	(1942–43)		974,000
AUSCHWITZ	(1941–44)		1,100,000

based on the present state of research.[37] Even if one assumes a large margin of error, proceeding on the basis of a highly restrictive assessment of these statistics, it is evident that approximately two-thirds of the pris-

oners in the concentration camps did not survive. If the more than three million Jewish victims in the death factories of Operation Reinhard, Chelmno, and Auschwitz-Birkenau, who were liquidated immediately after arrival, are added to these figures, the total rises to far more than four million persons who perished in the concentration and extermination camps.

Notes

1. See Broszat, 13–37; Pingel, 23–35; Worsmer-Migot, 63–138; Tuchel, 35–158.
2. Before the establishment of Dachau, the camp known as Heuberg in Swabia was set up as a central camp for the state of Württemberg (see Schätzle, 15ff.; Lechner, 61–62). In Saxony, sections of the prisons in Dresden and Zwickau, the workhouse at Coldlitz, and the camps known as Hohenstein and Sachsenburg were run as state concentration camps. On the Hamburg detention facilities Fuhlsbüttel and Wittmoor, see Timpke; Klawe. On additional early concentration camps, see Stokes; Wollenberg; Finckh; Lechner; Haardt; Vogt. Schwarz (139ff.) mentions a total of fifty-nine concentration camps in the early phase.
3. Regarding the early history of the Emsland camps, see Kosthorst and Walter, 29ff.; Suhr, 27ff.
4. For more detail, see Tuchel, 205–96.
5. See Broszat, 64–65; Aronson, 111–12; Höhne, 188ff. On the basis of documentation, Tuchel (212ff.) has raised fundamental doubts about the thesis, frequently encountered in the secondary literature, regarding the rivalry between the Gestapo and the *KZ-Inspektion*. However, one cannot conclude from their evident external cooperation that there was completely harmonious internal cooperation. In the sociology of organizations, it is well known that struggles over secret plots and intrigues rarely become a matter of formal record. Moreover, Tuchel does not give adequate attention to the local tensions in the camp administrations or the lines of conflict that later emerged between the RSHA and the central *Inspektion*, incorporated in 1942 into the WVHA.
6. For more detail, see chap. 9.
7. See Broszat, 46–55; Pingel, 35–42; Richardi, 119–54.
8. On the following, see Broszat, 66ff., 76ff.; Pingel, 70ff.; Schwarz, 26ff.; Tuchel, 312ff.
9. However, these were not the first Jewish prisoners. As early as 1933, the SS had placed all Jews in Dachau, who made up roughly 10 percent of the camp population, in a separate *Strafkompanie*. Although initially taken into custody and interned primarily because they were active on the political left – not because they were Jews – these individuals were a preferred target for harassment and mistreatment from the beginning. It was only after the November 1938 pogrom that Jews were also confined as prisoners in other camps. Right from the start, they were at the bottom of the heap, the lowest in the prisoner pecking order.
10. See Wormser-Migot, 203ff. *Nacht-und-Nebel* operations occurred "under cover of the night."
11. See Billig, 72; Pohl to Himmler, September 30, 1943, Nbg. Dok. PS-1469.

12. See Kogon, 173; Carlebach et al., 1984, 172ff.; Komitee der antifaschistischen Widerstandskämpfer der DDR, 143ff.; Hrdlicka, 46; Pingel, 81, 181ff., 259, 301; Marsalek 1980, 119ff., 131ff., 155ff.; Kimmel, 385; KZ-Museum Dachau, 204; Billig, 75. As a rule, these figures represent the deaths officially registered in the camps. They do not contain the Soviet POWs who were executed, or the victims who died on the death transports or death marches in the war's final phase. On the numbers of dead more generally, see n. 37 below.

13. See Stuldreher, 152ff.

14. Pingel, 125–26.

15. Ibid., 199ff.; Streit, 44ff., 83ff.

16. Pohl to Himmler, April 30, 1942, Nbg. Dok. R-129.

17. Report on Strength, Burger (Head, Office DIV) to Loerner (Head, Office B), August 15, 1944, Nbg. Dok. NO-1990.

18. "Aufstellung über die Zahl der Wachmannschaften und Häftlinge in den Konzentrationslagern, Januar 1945" (List of the Number of Guards and Prisoners in the Concentration Camps, January 1945), BA Koblenz NS 3/439.

19. Memo from Thierack on discussion with Himmler, September 18, 1942, Nbg. Dok. PS-654; Herbert 1985, 244ff.

20. See Broszat, 126; Marsalek 1980, 124.

21. See Pingel, 129; Herbert 1987, 226ff.; Herbert 1985, 154ff.; Herbert 1990, 143ff.; Kaienburg, 302ff.

22. Hilberg 1982, 631.

23. Herbert 1987, 231–32; Herbert 1990, 172ff.

24. Schwarz 1990, 103ff.; Hilberg 1982, 156ff.

25. See Streim; Schwarz, 169–70, 186ff., 196ff.; on the forced ghettos in the Soviet Union, see also Hilberg 1982, 243ff.

26. See Georg, 25ff., 38ff.

27. For more detail, see chap. 9.

28. See Höß, 136.

29. See chap. 15.

30. These figures are based on calculations using the most complete list of camps compiled to date; see Schwarz.

31. See chaps. 14 and 16.

32. See Marszalek, 243–44.

33. Gilbert, 214ff.

34. See Marsalek 1980, 329ff.

35. Anyone trying to calculate the number of admissions must grapple with the problem of discontinuous accounting: in various camps, registration numbering for dead, released, and transferred prisoners was not continuous, but was repeatedly begun anew. On this, see Billig, 81; Marsalek 1980, 140.

36. On the statistical manipulation of figures for the dead by the SS offices, see Kárný 1987, 140ff. On methodological problems in connection with the statistical recording of deaths, see Pingel, 16; Billig, 68ff.; Kogon, 175ff.

37. On Dachau, see KZ-Museum Dachau, 204–5; the figures here are the number of admissions and deaths ascertained and documented by the Red Cross. They do not contain persons admitted to camps during the war for the purpose of execution, the 800 Soviet POWs executed in Dachau on the basis of the Commissar Order (*Kommissarbefehl*) (Kimmel, 405), or the victims who perished on the death marches in the late winter and early spring of 1945. Billig (82, 98–99) arrives at a figure of 78,000. This estimate is more than double that of the Red Cross, and is probably too high, even if one takes the high rate of mortality in the camp complex known as Kaufering into consideration. On Buchenwald, see Internationales Buchenwald-Komitee, 83–84. The figure here includes the 8,500 Soviet POWs executed there. Kogon (173) arrives at a total of 33,462 deaths on the basis of the records of the prisoner hospital, but that number does not include those who died on the death marches or death transports. He puts the total number of dead for Buchenwald at some 55,000. On Mauthausen, see Marsalek 1980, 141, 155–58. On Neuengamme, see Bauche et al., 162. On Flossenbürg, see Siegert, 490–91. This figure also includes the approximately 800 Soviet POWs executed there as well as the approximately 6,900 who died on the evacuation marches; it does not contain the roughly 2,000 persons admitted in 1944–45 to be executed who were never registered. On Groß-Rosen, see Konieczny, 20, 24. On Auschwitz, see Piper, 94ff. These figures refer only to those persons who were registered in the camp, and do not include the victims from ramp selection or those who perished during evacuation transports. On Majdanek, see Marszalek, 77, 133; Scheffler, 148. On Dora-Mittelbau, see Bornemann and Broszat, 197–98; Pachaly and Pelny, 105ff. This figure contains the 12,813 deaths listed in the card file of the hospital section, as well as the victims who perished on the death marches and those dead who were not even recorded in the admission report lists. On Bergen-Belsen, see Fassina, 38; Kolb 1985, 40. On the concentration camp system, see Billig, 96ff. In Billig's estimate, the dead in the concentration camps (not including the extermination camps) for the period from 1933 to the end of 1944 amounted to some 800,000. During the first several months of 1945, the period of the death marches, some 300,000 more perished. Kogon (177) places total admissions at 1,540,350, and the number of victims at 1,180,650. To date, the Red Cross has been able to document the names of some 450,000 dead. On the extermination camps, see Benz 1991 (17) and Golczewski (464ff., 495). Piper estimates the total number of victims in the entire Auschwitz camp complex to have been at least 1,100,000, including some one million Jews. This total figure comprises both those victims who were murdered in the gas chambers directly after arrival at the ramp and thus not registered (about 900,000) and the victims from the concentration camp already referred to above. It is important to bear in mind that the figures for victims in the concentration and extermination camps should not be confused with the total number of victims who perished in the Nazi genocide of the Jews. Jews were not only murdered inside the camp system; they were also killed by the mobile death squads of the SS *Einsatzgruppen* and in the forced ghettos, which were not part of the concentration camp complex.

Reichminister Joseph Goebbels delivers a speech to a crowd in Berlin urging Germans to boycott Jewish-owned businesses. He defends the boycott as a legitimate response to the anti-German "atrocity propaganda" spread abroad by "international Jewry." April 1, 1933. (National Archives, courtesy of USHMM Photo Archives)

Four Nazi troops sing in front of the Berlin branch of the Woolworth Co. store to support the boycott of Jewish businesses in Germany. The Nazis mistakenly believed the founder of the Woolworth Co. was Jewish. March 1933. (AP/Wide World Photos)

Three Jewish businessmen are paraded down Brühlstrasse in central Leipzig, Germany, carrying signs that read: "Don't buy from Jews; shop at German stores!" 1935. (William Blye, courtesy of USHMM Photo Archives)

German Jewish prisoners hauling supplies in Dachau, one of 50 concentration camps opened by the Nazis in 1933 to which political opponents were sent. May 24, 1933. (Bildarchiv Preussischer Kulturbesitz, Berlin, courtesy of USHMM Photo Archives)

Public burning of "un-German" books by the SA (Storm Troopers) and German students in Berlin. May 10, 1933. (Bundesarchiv Bild 102/14 597)

WILLIAM CARR **Nazi Policy Against the Jews**

FOR NEARLY TWENTY YEARS after the collapse of Hitler's Reich first revealed the full horrors of the Holocaust it was widely supposed that genocide on this enormous scale must have been the last stage of a deliberate Nazi policy, a long-matured master plan which aimed all along at the physical annihilation of European Jewry. In the monolithic Nazi State where all power was allegedly concentrated in the Führer's hands, his vitriolic hatred of all things Jewish would have been sufficient on its own to explain the murder of six-and-a-half million Jews.

Not until the 1960s did historians generally accept that the Nazi State was no monolith but a mosaic of conflicting authorities bearing more resemblance to a feudal State, where great vassals were engaged in a ruthless power struggle to capture the person of the king who in his turn maintained his authority by playing one great lord off against another. The clear implication was that Nazi anti-Semitism must also have reflected the twists and turns of the power game and that Hitler's paranoid hatred of Jewry could only have been one – albeit most important – factor in a complex historical equation. Some historians now suggest that the Holocaust itself was not the final phase of a long-cherished plan but a piece of improvisation in an unexpected situation.

On one point all are agreed; Hitler and his followers were paranoid in their determination to turn Germany's half a million Jews into pariahs. Forming less than 1 per cent of the total population – and declining numerically – the Jews had resided in Germany for generations and had been for the most part assimilated into the life of the community. Only 20 per cent were the so-called "Eastern Jews" who emigrated to Germany from the disturbed areas of Eastern Europe after the First World War, still retained their distinctive Jewish garb and tended to live together in certain quarters of the great cities. Certainly Jews were prominent in the cultural and economic life of Berlin. And in certain professions there was a higher proportion of Jews than Aryans. For example, 17 per cent of all bankers were Jews – a much lower percentage than in the closing years of the nineteenth century; 16 per cent of all lawyers – but rarely was a judge Jewish; and 10 per cent of all doctors and dentists – but few held university or hospital posts. In the clothing and retail trades Jewish influence was pronounced. But in no way could it be argued that the Jews "dominated" the cultural or economic life of Germany as the Nazis claimed. Nor were the Jews particularly wealthy; many of them were as poor as their Aryan neighbours, despite a well-earned reputation for hard work.

Nevertheless for rank-and-file Nazis the Jew had become a grotesque nightmare figure far removed from the reality of everyday life. In the viciously anti-Semitic literature pouring out from Nazi presses the Jew was denounced as the root cause of all Germany's ills and depicted as a sub-human figure burrowing away at the moral and economic foundations of the State and dedicated to the destruction of the whole world. In the cosmic confrontation between "Good" and "Evil" the Aryan race led by the German people was destined to save mankind from the horrors of the "Jewish-Bolshevik" yoke, as exemplified by Russian Communism. No doubt anti-Semitism was a useful ploy to deflect the party's attention away from the Nazi leadership's partnership with the detested old order. But basically the crude and vicious anti-Semitism of [Julius] Streicher's *Der Stürmer* was a psychological necessity for many party members, especially those in the Brownshirts and in Himmler's SS, who desperately needed "outgroups" – including gypsies and Jehovah's Witnesses – on whom they could vent their personal frustrations.

However much Hitler sympathised with this crude and visceral anti-Semitism, once he was in office he was obliged to try and contain rank-and-file outbursts in the interests of political stability, public order and economic recovery. Thus, when the Brownshirts went on the rampage after the Nazi electoral victory in March 1933 assaulting Jews and ransacking shops, he sought to canalise their energies through a centrally coordinated boycott of Jewish shops. Under pressure from President [Paul von] Hindenburg and Foreign Minister [Konstantin von] Neurath this boycott was limited to one day and never extended because of public apathy, foreign reactions and the danger of damaging a fragile economy. The reduction of unemployment had so high a priority that in July the Cabinet agreed to continue offering public contracts to Jewish firms. Similarly, when legislation was enacted in April to dismiss Jewish civil servants, Hitler had reluctantly to yield to Hindenburg's demand that all Jews appointed before 1914, all those who had fought in the First World War or whose fathers or sons had died in the war be exempt, a concession which partially emasculated the measure.

For the next two years the Jews enjoyed a period of relative freedom from persecution. This changed in the course of 1935. Certainly Hitler was in a much stronger position to give vent to his rabid anti-Semitism. Since Hindenburg's death he had been head of State and in 1934 had brought the Brownshirts sharply to heel. But it seems likely that a significant recrudescence of anti-Semitic agitation amongst rank-and-file Nazis forced him to give the Jews another turn of the screw.

Rank-and-file demands for a "Jew-free economy" he had to resist as long as the contribution of Jewish firms to economic recovery was important. Where he did give way was in an area which, as the pornography of Streicher's *Der Stürmer* amply demonstrated, fascinated many anti-Semites: sexual relations between Jews and Gentiles. In the Law for the Protection of German Blood announced at the Party Rally in Nürnberg in September, marriage between them and sexual relations outside marriage were forbidden. Under the so-called Nürnberg Laws Jews were also to be denied German citizenship and were forbidden to fly the German flag. It is significant that Hitler encountered no resistance from his civil servants. Indeed they positively welcomed legislation which by placing anti-Semitism on a sound legal foundation would prevent – they hoped – further disorderly street scenes so disturbing to tidy-minded bureaucrats.

Up to the end of 1937 Jews had managed to keep control of their businesses and could still use most of the amenities open to other Germans. Signs of a more radical anti-Semitic policy multiplied in the winter of 1937/8. At the Party Rally in September Hitler made an outspoken attack on Jews for the first time in two years. As the German economy moved into top gear, the big industrial concerns, eager to take over their Jewish competitors at knock-down prices, pressed the government to proceed to the "Aryanisation" of the economy. To induce Jewish firms to sell out, Goering, plenipotentiary for the Four-Year Plan and the friend of big business, reduced their raw materials allocation and after the spring of 1938 they received no further public contracts. Following the *Anschluss* with Austria, Goering issued a decree ordering Jews to register all property above 5000 Marks in value and forbidding them to sell it without permission. In the summer of 1938 Jewish doctors, dentists and lawyers were forbidden to offer their services to Aryans. Even the names to be given Jewish children were specified in a new directive. Jews with other names had to add Israel or Sarah to them. Jews were now obliged to carry identity cards and from October all Jewish passports were stamped with the letter J.

After *Reichskristallnacht* (Night of broken glass) on November 9th–10th, 1938, the position of German Jewry deteriorated more rapidly still. On that night ninety-one Jews were murdered, 20,000 thrown into concentration camps, synagogues were burnt down all over Germany and thousands of Jewish shops vandalised (the broken glass littering the pavements gave its name to the incident) in an unprecedented outburst of savagery carried out by party activists and carefully orchestrated from Josef Goebbels's Propaganda Ministry. World opinion was profoundly shocked by the spectacle of a pogrom in a hitherto civilised country; the trade boycott on German goods intensified; and Franklin Roosevelt withdrew Ambassador [William] Dodds from Berlin.

World opinion, alas, could do little to alleviate the plight of the Jews. A spate of discriminatory decrees were issued aimed at creating a "Jew-free" economy. Jews were now forbidden to practice trades or to own shops or market stalls or manage businesses. Jewish shops, firms and real estate holdings were "Aryanised" – that is compulsorily sold to Aryan competitors. In later decrees Jews were totally excluded from schools and universities, cinemas, theatres and sports facilities. In many cities, where of course the bulk of the Jewish population was resident, Jews were forbidden to enter designated "Aryan" areas. This legislation was enforced zealously by local fanatics so that by the outbreak of war the Jew was well on the way to becoming the pariah in German society towards which the Nazi party had been working for so long.

The radicalisation of the regime's anti-Semitic policy on the eve of war cannot, however, be attributed simply and solely to Hitler's vindictive attitude but has to be seen against the political background. In the winter of 1937/8 as the pace of German foreign policy began to accelerate, the balance of power inside Germany shifted generally towards the more radical elements in the Nazi party. In November 1937 with the dismissal of Economics Minister [Hjalmar] Schacht the last obstacle to Goering's ascendancy in the economic field was removed. Whereas Schacht had been acutely conscious of the unfavourable international repercussions "Aryanisation" was bound to have, Goering, a close friend of Hitler, was contemptuous of foreign opinion and determined to create a "Jew-free" economy as quickly as possible. In the spring of 1938 Generals [Werner von] Blomberg and [Werner von] Fritsch, opponents of Hitler's forward foreign policy, were removed and Hitler assumed command of the Wehrmacht. The foreign office, too, came under Nazi control when Foreign Minister Neurath was replaced by the ardent Nazi and admirer of Hitler, Joachim von Ribbentrop.

Intensification of the persecution of German Jewry served another function as well: it helped unify a leadership divided by *Reichskristallnacht*. It was not Goering but Goebbels who triggered off the pogrom. In an intrigue typical of life at the top in Nazi Germany he sought to ingratiate himself with Hitler, who was annoyed by the Propaganda Minister's amorous liaisons. When an embassy official in Paris was murdered by a Jewish boy Goebbels played up the anti-Semitic theme in the press and, dashing to Munich

where Hitler was taking part in the annual celebration of the 1923 Putsch, secured his consent for "spontaneous action" on the streets.

"The SA should have a last fling," he is supposed to have exclaimed. But Goering, Himmler and [Reinhard] Heydrich, the enemies of Goebbels, were deliberately kept in the dark. Goering at once protested vehemently to Hitler at the wanton damage done by the activists while Himmler and Heydrich deplored the deleterious effect the pogrom was likely to have on their low-key emigration policy. Though Hitler's sympathies lay with the radically-minded Goebbels, he soon fell in with Goering's suggestion that the time had come for a properly co-ordinated and centrally controlled onslaught on Jewish property. In the end the Nazi leaders forgot their differences and co-operated amicably in the intensified persecution of the common enemy. But Goering, not Goebbels, was put in overall charge of the operation which ensured that his industrial friends were the main beneficiaries of Aryanisation and not the small businessmen whom the Nazis were supposed to favour.

As the war clouds gathered ominously in Europe in 1939, Hitler gave vent to his paranoid hatred of Jewry. In January he told an enthusiastic Reichstag that if

> International Jewish finance inside and outside of Europe succeeds in involving the nations in another war, the result will not be the bolshevization of the earth and the victory of Judaism but the annihilation of the Jewish race in Europe.

The same month he informed the Czech foreign minister that "we are going to destroy the Jews. They are not going to get away with what they did on November 9th, 1918" (i.e. when they allegedly "betrayed" Germany by masterminding the German Revolution). These and other comments in the spring of 1939 are interpreted by "intentionalist" historians as proof that the physical destruction of Jewry was still Hitler's aim in 1939, as it had been from his first entry into politics in 1919. But it is questionable whether one can assume that because the Holocaust happened every utterance of Hitler's – a man notoriously given to wild talk – must have been leading up to a grand climax in the gas chambers of Auschwitz.

It would seem, on the contrary, as if the Nazis had no very clear idea where they were going in their anti-Semitism, and that Hitler's tendency to side with the big battalions – when they identified themselves – applied in this as in many other areas of State activity. Hence his willingness to support the emigration policy favoured, oddly enough in view of what followed, by the dreaded SS.

As early as 1934 a sub-section of the SS – the SD or Security Department – whilst anxious to reduce Jewish influence in German life, realised the sporadic Brownshirt outbursts against Jews did harm to the German image. Instead they proposed to solve the "Jewish question" by pursuing an orderly and systematic policy of mass emigration. Since Himmler's star was in the ascendancy in 1936 he sought to extend his empire by acquiring the exclusive right to handle Jewish affairs.

Emigration was not particularly successful. Only 120,000 of Germany's 503,000 Jews had left the country by the end of 1937. Many even returned deluded by the regime's cautious tactics into believing the worst was over. In March 1938 the SS had their big chance when the annexation of Austria added 190,000 Jews to the existing total. This increase appalled anti-Semites anxious to be rid of Jews, not to take in more. Operating from a central office in Vienna Adolf Eichmann of the SD succeeded in forcing 45,000 Jews out of Austria within six months, using confiscated Jewish property to finance their emigration. Goering, who still had overall responsibility for anti-Semitic measures, was greatly impressed by Eichmann's ruthless efficiency. In January 1939 he gave the policy his approval and delegated its execution in Germany to Reinhard Heydrich, chief of the Reich Security Main Office.

In the course of 1939, 78,000 Jews were forced out of Germany and 30,000 out of Bohemia and Moravia. As it was increasingly difficult to find countries willing to receive Jewish refugees, the SD even worked with Zionist organisations to ship as many Jews as possible illegally to Palestine where the British authorities, anxious not to offend Arab susceptibilities, sought to prevent them landing. As emigration to Palestine obviously helped to create the nucleus of a future Jewish State, SS policy was opposed both by the foreign office and by the *Auslandsorganisation*, a Nazi agency led by Gauleiter Bohle, both of which favoured dispersal of Jews throughout the world. Hitler, who invariably watched power struggles from the sidelines intervening only rarely and reluctantly did, in fact, support the SS against their rivals.

The outbreak of the war opened up a new and more terrible chapter in the history of the persecution of the Jews. That Hitler was capable of the most cold-blooded crimes was amply demonstrated in September 1939, when he ordered five *Einsatzgruppen*, or action squads, into Poland in the wake of the German armies with instructions to murder tens of thousands of officials, priests and intellectuals in an attempt to deprive the Poles of their ruling class.

While the battles were still raging in Poland the outlines of a new "solution" of the "Jewish question" were taking shape. Hitler informed close associates of plans to remould Eastern Europe on racial lines, turning their peoples into slaves serving a master race of German settlers. As a first step, the three million Polish Jews must be put in ghettos in specified towns in Eastern Poland and finally resettled in a huge reserve south of Lublin. Early in October Himmler was given special powers as Reich commissioner for the strengthening of Germanism in the East, a crucial appointment which placed the Jews completely at the mercy of the SS. Between December 1939 and February 1940, 600,000 Jews from Danzig – West Prussia and the *Wartheland* (the territories annexed to the Reich) were brutally uprooted, forced into cattle trucks and dumped in the *Generalgouvernement* (the remainder of German-occupied Poland governed by Hans Frank). As he already had 1,400,000 Jews under his jurisdiction, he protested to Goering at the strain placed on limited food supplies. The latter, with Hitler's approval, agreed that further transports must have Frank's approval. As this was not forthcoming, Nazi plans came to an abrupt halt. Meanwhile, as it took time to enclose the Jews in ghettos, interim measures forbade them to change residence, subjected them to a curfew, obliged them to wear a yellow star on their clothing and compelled them to perform forced labour for the German conquerors.

Quite why the Lublin resettlement plan was

abandoned is unclear. Perhaps the preparations for the Scandinavian and then the Western campaign absorbed Hitler's attention, for it seems unlikely that Frank's intervention was decisive. What is interesting, in view of the belief of "intentionalist" historians that the Nazis never wavered in their determination to annihilate the Jewish race physically, is the so-called Madagascar Plan. In the summer of 1940, during the closing stages of the French campaign, Nazi leaders seem to have given serious consideration to transporting the four million Jews of Western Europe to this French island, whilst leaving the Eastern Jews in Poland as a deterrent to American intervention in the war.

The Madagascar Plan had been a favourite with anti-Semites in the 1920s. Himmler was immediately enthusiastic. Eichmann, now in the notorious section IV at the Reich Security Main Office, spent many hours in the Tropical Institute in Hamburg studying climatic conditions in Madagascar. With Hitler's approval a plan of action was drafted. During the summer Hitler mentioned Madagascar to several influential figures including Mussolini and [Constanzo] Ciano. The plan was killed stone dead by Britain's refusal to capitulate as so confidently expected by the Nazis. As long as Britain controlled the seas, the transportation of Jews to Madagascar was simply impracticable.

There is no doubt that Hitler's decision to attack Russia, finalised in December 1940, had the most profound implications for the future of European Jewry. For Hitler warned his staff that the impending campaign must be fought on racial lines. "We must depart from the attitude of soldierly comradeship," he told his commanding generals ". . . we are talking about a war of annihilation . . . commissars and members of the GPU (secret police) are criminals and must be dealt with as such . . ." Just before the attack in June 1941 he signed the Commissar Order requiring his generals to have captured commissars shot forthwith. To carry out these instructions four new action squads, composed of SS, criminal police and security police, operated behind the German lines. Although Heydrich's instructions to the higher SS and Police Officers in charge of captured Russian territory only specified "Jews in the service of party and

State," it seems very likely that the action squads were encouraged to execute all the Jews they could lay their hands on – which is exactly what happened. By the winter of 1941/2, 500,000 Jews had already been shot in this first mass extermination of the war. This episode more than anything else probably sealed the fate of European Jewry.

At this point historians differ in their interpretations. Several, including Christopher Browning, Gerald Fleming, Eberhard Jäckel and Andreas Hillgruber, argue that Hitler decided on the Final Solution sometime in the summer of 1941 whilst others, principally Uwe Dietrich Adam, Martin Broszat and Hans Mommsen, maintain that the decision was arrived at only in the late autumn. Behind what may seem a disagreement about a relatively minor matter of timing, lie fundamental differences about Hitler's role in the Third Reich and, specifically, about his role in the genesis of the Holocaust.

The Mommsen-Broszat school occupy a "structuralist" position, i.e. whilst not disputing that Hitler exerted considerable influence on the course of events, they do not believe he was always the prime mover. The Holocaust, in their view, was not planned by Hitler from the very beginning but developed out of a deteriorating situation not anticipated by the Nazis though probably rendered inevitable by the spiralling radicalism of their visceral anti-Semitism.

On rather thin evidence they argue that the Final Solution was preceded by yet another solution: the resettlement of European Jewry east of the Urals after Russia's defeat, which was confidently expected to be a matter of weeks only. Stiffening Russian resistance wrecked that plan. Yet in October 1941, precisely when it was becoming apparent that the Blitzkrieg had failed, Hitler ordered the transportation of Jews to the eastern territories to begin again. As there was no way out over the Urals and as more and more Jews were forced into the ghettos of Eastern Poland, resources were strained to breaking point and epidemics started to break out. The response of local SS leaders was to begin, on their own initiative, to murder Jews either by shooting or by using mobile gas vans. Sometime in October or November Himmler informed Hitler of this evolving situation and the latter approved the extension of these practices to encompass the whole of European Jewry. It is even conceivable that the initiative was taken not by Hitler but by Himmler.

The explanation offered by Fleming, Jäckel, Hillgruber and others is an "intentionalist" one, i.e. that Hitler made his decision in the summer of 1941 under no structural pressure but because he believed a Russian collapse imminent and felt that the moment had come to realise a life-long ambition. Whether he gave a specific order to this effect – no written order has ever been found – or more likely supplied "a prompting initiative" is an open question. At all events, on July 31st Goering ordered Heydrich to complete the task he had given him in January 1939 by "bringing about a complete solution of the Jewish question within the German sphere of influence in Europe," and requested him to draft a plan to this effect. Significantly enough at the Wannsee Conference, where the details of the Holocaust were worked out, Heydrich referred specifically to this directive as the justification for the meeting.

The evidence, including that of SS men such as Eichmann and [Rudolf] Höss, commandant of Auschwitz, suggests that throughout the summer and autumn of 1941 the SS were working feverishly on the new project. Restrictions already placed on Polish Jews were now extended to German Jews. On September 1st all Jews were ordered to wear a yellow star and forbidden to leave their area of residence without permission. In October Himmler completely banned further Jewish emigration. So when Hitler spoke to Himmler in October/November, he merely approved an existing extermination plan. The undeniable chaos in Eastern Poland in the autumn and the localised shootings and gassings came about not because a "resettlement plan" had been wrecked – the intentionalists deny the existence of such a plan, believing that Hitler kept Goebbels and [Alfred] Rosenberg in the dark and spoke to them of "resettlement" when he had "extermination" in mind – but because an impatient Führer ordered deportations from Germany to begin before the extermination installations had been completed.

What is not in doubt is that in January top SS officials met in the Berlin suburb of Wannsee under Heydrich's direction to work out the final details of the Holocaust. Though the participants, characteristically, preferred to avoid the term "extermination" the intention was clear enough: the Jews were to be worked to death or gassed. Following the conference, work was accelerated on the building of gas chambers and crematoria at several sites in Eastern Poland: Belzec, Sobibor, Treblinka, Majdanek and Auschwitz-Birkenau. For two years the transports continued to roll eastwards from all corners of Europe and the murder squads continued their grisly task until the advancing Russian armies drove the Germans out of Poland. In all, between five and six-and-a-half million Jews perished in one of the most frightful episodes in history.

Finally, we come to the all-important question: How could members of a highly civilised nation like the Germans have committed such horrible crimes? There is no adequate answer. All one can do is point to certain factors in the historical equation. Naturally the Nazis tried to shroud the operation in secrecy by carrying it out in a remote part of Poland. All the same, rumours did circulate about dreadful deeds in the East. No doubt many Germans were pretty indifferent to the fate of the Jews even if they did not believe what they heard. Because of the Nazis' much-publicised resettlement plans, tens of thousands of people were being moved around Europe like pieces on a chessboard, so that some Germans – including those who rounded the Jews up and transported them eastwards – may have suppressed their doubts and tried to believe that the deportations had no sinister implications.

Above all, one must not forget that a dictatorship gradually corrupts the moral fibre of its citizens: to ask too many questions, let alone protest, was to risk arrest and possibly death. But in the twilight atmosphere in the corridors of power where ambitious men were struggling to build up personal empires there were always plenty of willing hands to do the Führer's bidding. In the SS Hitler had a perfect instrument for mass murder.

To what extent the members of the murder squads were sadists, pathological cases, promotion-seekers or automatons with a grossly distorted sense of duty is a complex matter. What is certain is that without these hardened and experienced killers the

Holocaust could not have taken place. Finally, Hitler's constant encouragement ensured that the grisly work continued at a time when Germany's military position was deteriorating and it was plainly an act of madness to divert precious resources to mass murder. That the Holocaust did continue is the ultimate proof of the irrationality at the heart of National Socialism.

Judges and clerks of the Berlin courts swear allegiance to Hitler and their loyalty to Nazi principles. As a symbol of their subservience, the eagle and swastika were worn on the breast of the traditional judge's robe. October 1936. (ullstein bild-Bunk, courtesy of USHMM Photo Archives)

A Jewish man and a Christian woman in Hamburg accused of intimate relations. The woman's sign: "I am the biggest pig around here because I make it only with Jews." The man's sign: "I am a Jewboy who always takes German girls to my room." 1935. (Courtesy of Yad Vashem Photo Archives)

Nazi mass rally in Berlin at which the party promised a Germany "cleansed of Jews." One slogan reads: "The Jews are our misfortune" and the other reads: "Women and girls! The Jews are your seducers!" August 15, 1935. (Nederlands Instituut voor Oorlogsdocumentatie, courtesy of USHMM Photo Archives)

1936 Berlin Olympics. View of the opening ceremony as the American Olympic team enters the stadium. Despite calls to boycott the Berlin games because of Germany's increasing antisemitic policies, the American Olympic Committee decided to send the U.S. team. After Jesse Owens, an African-American runner, won four gold medals, Hitler refused to shake his hand. Two Jewish-American runners, Marty Glickman and Sam Stoller, were thrown off the U.S. 400-meter relay team by the American track coaches moments before the race. August 1, 1936. (AP/Wide World Photos)

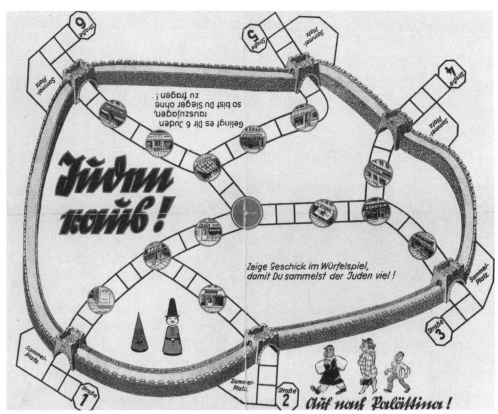

Children's board game *Juden Raus!* (Jews Out!) 1938. (Courtesy of the Leo Baeck Institute, New York)

Adolf Hitler, sitting in an open car, in conversation with a member of the Hitler Youth. Albert Speer, Hitler's favorite architect and later Minister of Armaments, watches from the back seat. 1935. (Bildarchiv Preussischer Kulturbesitz, Berlin, courtesy of USHMM Photo Archives)

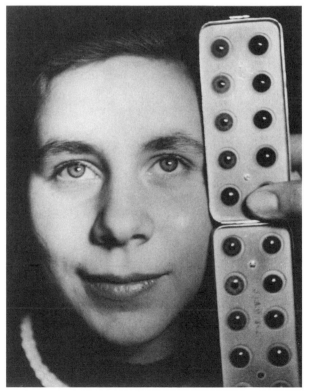

A racial hygienist determines the color of a woman's eyes using a special eye color measuring tool. 1937. (Bildarchiv Preussischer Kulturbesitz, Berlin, courtesy of USHMM Photo Archives)

The November Pogrom and Its Aftermath

MARION A. KAPLAN

The store was boarded up . . . Our home no longer offered us . . . security.
Our family was now scattered in three different locations.

— Shlomo Wahrman

THE NOVEMBER POGROM struck like lightning, suddenly shattering everything it touched, shocking those who suffered it. Although it represented the intensification of the political disenfranchisement, economic strangulation, and social segregation that had begun in 1933, no one expected the widespread violence – a pogrom of the sort connected only with czarist Russia. The public manifestations of Jewish life in Germany stood covered with broken glass. Businesses and synagogues were ransacked, Jewish livelihoods destroyed. The Nazis also destroyed private, interior spaces. Homes, which had previously felt safe, were transformed into nightmares of smashed furniture and torn feather beds. Jewish men, often humiliated and beaten, were now forced into concentration camps. Jewish women remained behind, trying frantically to free their men, repair their homes, and help their families flee for their lives.

THE BACKGROUND TO NOVEMBER 1938

THE NAZIS STEPPED UP THEIR PERSECUTION of Jews in 1938. In March the German annexation of Austria sparked the public abuse of Jews and the looting and pillaging of their shops and homes in Austria. In annexing Austria, the Reich had added 200,000 Austrian Jews, canceling out the reduction of German Jews by recent emigration. In Germany that same month, the Nazis enacted the "Law Regarding the Legal Status of Jewish Communities," the first major piece of anti-Jewish legislation since the Nuremberg Law. This law deprived Jewish congregations of legal protection and subjected them to the administrative control of the regime. In addition, they could no longer tax members, a restriction intended to reduce them to penury. The law proclaimed a renewed attack upon Jews.

The noose tightened in the spring, when Jews and "Aryan" spouses of Jews had to assess and report the value of their domestic and foreign property worth over 5,000 marks: "From here it was only a short step to the outright seizure of Jewish property." Jews would have to inform the government of whatever they planned to take abroad and were forbidden from taking valuables out of the country. As if preparing its inventory of sites to be ransacked, the government required the registration and identification of all Jewish commercial establishments in June. A Jewish teenager recalled his fury upon first noticing a sign labeling a "Jewish" store. He tried to erase it. The Jewish owner chased him away, since he had to identify himself as specified by the new regulation.[1] By June, fresh boycotts intensified.

Most ominously, the government rounded up Jewish men and sent them to concentration camps. First it singled out "foreign" Jews. As a result of Germany's intentionally difficult and exclusionary naturalization laws, many of these so-called foreign Jews had actually resided in Germany for generations; about 40 percent were born there[2] but had not achieved citizenship. In February the government ordered the expulsion of "Soviet Jews" – often people whose grandparents had come to Germany at the beginning of the century. Those who had not emigrated by May were sent to concentration camps, from which they would be released only when they had emigration papers in hand.

In its "June Action" the Gestapo arrested about 1,500 so-called antisocial Jewish men, sending them to concentration camps. Most of these men had previously been convicted of minor legal infractions – some 500, for example, of traffic violations. The pettiness of these "crimes" notwithstanding, 146 died at Buchenwald alone while wives, families, and friends exerted major efforts to have the others freed. They, too, would be set free only when they could prove readiness to emigrate. That same summer, the Nazis destroyed three synagogues – in Munich, Nuremberg, and Dortmund. In addition, all Jews were required to have the letter *J* stamped on their passports as of the fall. In January 1939 they would receive a new identity card, also stamped with a *J*. The *J* marked them as easy prey and made looking for housing or jobs impossible, since no one would rent to or hire a Jew.[3]

It was the deportation of Polish Jews – many of them also resident in Germany for generations – that sparked the incident that led to the November Pogrom. Germany expelled 17,000 Polish Jews on October 27 and 28, 1938, sending them to the Polish border. Poland denied them entry. They languished in a no-man's-land between two borders, in the cold and without food or shelter, while their families and communities became more and more desperate. The deportation of the Polish Jews, usually mentioned only as a prelude to and then overshadowed by the November Pogrom, sent shock waves through the entire Jewish community in Germany.

The manner in which the Polish Jews were deported foreshadowed the brutality to come: officials picked them up without warning, gave them a few moments to pack necessities, allowed them to take only ten marks, and then herded them away. For the first time, the Nazis swept up Jews without regard for age or sex. Various states and cities such as Hamburg, Frankfurt, and Munich rounded up whole families. In Württemberg and Saxony, women and children made up the majority of deportees. One deportee wrote:

> Everyone . . . was loaded onto the wagons. . . . Crying women and children, heartrending scenes. . . . [A]rriving at the border at 5 P.M., we were shoved across it. . . . For three days we were on the platform and in the train station, 8,000 people. Women and children fainting, unconscious, incidents of death, faces yellow as wax. . . . Women and children half-dead. On the fourth day help finally came . . . from the Warsaw Jewish Committee.[4]

Whatever food, clothing, or succor the deportees received came from other Jews. Jewish communities in Germany, too, helped the Polish Jews. In Munich,

a leader of the League of Jewish Women quickly organized members to race to the homes of the deportees in order to pack some clothing and food for them. One volunteer discovered five terrified children whose parents had hidden them from the roundup. The oldest was ten. The volunteer slipped them out of the apartment and brought them to an orphanage, preventing their immediate deportation. Those involved in relief activities all felt the imminent threat to themselves. In Hamburg, the women who brought food to the trainloads of Polish deportees returned saying, "And who will bring *us* bread and butter at the train?"[5]

THE POGROM

AS THE PITIABLE DEPORTEES languished in the cold, wet, no-man's-land between Poland and Germany, young Herschel Grynszpan, whose parents and sister were among them, was driven to despair. He shot Ernst vom Rath, a diplomat at the German embassy in Paris. The Nazis used the death of vom Rath as a convenient excuse to launch their largest pogrom to date. Organized by the government and Nazi organizations and supported by mobs, the attacks began around 3 A.M. on November 9/10.[6]

Destruction and Persecution

Assailants wielding hatchets and axes ravaged Jewish homes and businesses, while others used incendiary bombs and dynamite to demolish synagogues. Mobs destroyed holy items and books and plundered Jewish homes while forcing Jews to watch. Rowdies rounded up Jews – women and men – half dressed or in their pajamas and herded them into the marketplace or main squares to taunt them. Firemen and police looked on or prevented aid as synagogues and other Jewish property burned, attempting only to save neighboring "Aryan" buildings from destruction.

In the frenzy of this "public degradation ritual," the Nazis went beyond plundering and terrorizing Jewish women and men. They also invaded Jewish hospitals, old-age homes, and orphanages. In Königsberg, a band forced the children of the Jewish orphanage out onto the street in their nightclothes. The freezing children huddled close to the burning synagogue to warm themselves. When Nazis stormed an orphanage in Dinslaken, in the Rhineland, the director ordered the children, aged six to sixteen, outside, assuming that the troopers would not dare harm the children out in the open. Despite the cold, the children scrambled into the street, without coats, running after the director to the town hall to obtain police protection. They encountered about ten police and a crowd of eager onlookers. "We do not give protection to Jews," the police chief announced, "Get out with those children or I'll shoot."[7]

The next morning the SS forced Jews to sweep up the broken furniture, destroyed household items, feathers, and glass that littered the streets. The SS stood around, laughing and taunting. Moreover, the job was left to a community deprived of most of its able-bodied men. The Nazis had systematically rounded up Jewish men and imprisoned them in concentration camps: 11,000 to Dachau; 9,845 to Buchenwald; 9,000 to Sachsenhausen. There, brutality and humiliation reigned. Guards prevented Jewish men from washing and drinking water while subjecting them to long days of torturous exercise, standing at attention, or sitting in the sun without permission to move. The Jewish men suffered sickness, madness, and death. The lucky ones were released if they could prove they were about to emigrate and agreed to sell their businesses for minute sums. The first group left after six days; others stayed for months. The men who were lucky enough to return from internment, with shaved heads and frozen limbs, were often physically and psychologically ravaged. Gerdy Stoppleman's husband left Sachsenhausen in March 1939: "More than his body, my husband's mind was deeply affected. Almost every night he experienced Sachsenhausen concentration camp anew in nightmares so alarming that I feared for his sanity." Still, others faced even worse: "On a daily basis one heard that the ashes of a dead person had been delivered to this or that family. These urns were sent cash on delivery (for which the post office took the sum of 3.75 marks)."[8]

Threatened with worse punishment if they told anyone of their suffering in the camps, many Jewish men were too terrified to tell their families. Others wanted to repress their experiences. Ingeborg Hecht's father, however, described his ordeal in Sachsenhausen: "In a low voice, punctuated by the hollow cough that lingered with him for a long time to come, he recounted his terrible experiences. If he hadn't been our own father, a qualified lawyer, and in his right mind, we would never have believed him."[9]

The November Pogrom claimed the lives of at least one hundred Jews, not counting the camp deaths or suicides occurring shortly thereafter. The pogrom also destroyed hundreds of synagogues and countless homes and shops. Damage was estimated at several hundred million marks: the broken glass alone was valued at 24 million marks. Jews were made to pay a fine of 1 billion marks as punishment for the vom Rath assassination. The government, not the Jews, would collect on insurance payments for damages incurred. The Nazis used the pogrom not only as the occasion to accelerate their plunder of the Jewish community but also to dismantle the Central Organization of Jews in Germany. In 1939, the government forced the Central Association of Jews in Germany (*Reichsvereinigung der Juden in Deutschland*) upon the Jewish community. It would oversee emigration, education, and social welfare programs and would represent all individual Jews in Germany. The Gestapo, not the Jewish community, would appoint its leadership.

German Reactions

The November Pogrom provides examples of the contradictory behavior of Germans toward Jews – a mixture of rampant viciousness, studied ignorance, and occasional kindness. Many Germans joined mobs to attack and burn Jewish homes, businesses, and synagogues. Others chose to take advantage of their Jewish neighbors. In Bavaria, for example, an "Aryan" neighbor offered a Jewish woman and her mother a "deal" after the arrests of their husbands. The Jewish woman should sign over the deed of her house to him and leave Germany. Should they decide to return, he would give it back to them! She declined. Ingeborg Hecht's neighbor chose to make excuses: she gave Ingeborg a big bag of groceries for her father upon his return from Sachsenhausen, assuring her that "the Führer knows nothing of this."[10]

One Jewish woman recalled the events as a mixture of mobs and helpers:

> While I was sweeping up some of the debris, I noticed another mob of hoodlums, among them women. They were armed with axes as they approached [and] proceeded to ransack the entire house. . . . I thought of Anna K., the former parlor maid. . . . Soon we were on our way in hope that there would be some straw bed in her barn. . . . She had two such beds, but we would have to leave early the next day . . . because her brother had become a member of the SA.

Mally Dienemann of Offenbach am Main was deeply touched when her non-Jewish landlady helped clean up her apartment: "Her devotion and guilt . . . knew no bounds. These simple people . . . brought me flowers when I was alone . . . and other Jews must have also known such people in one form or another. For officially we were all supposed to starve during these November days."[11]

What were the reactions of Germans not immediately involved either in the destruction or in helping Jews? While most approved of, or went along with, "moderate" antisemitism, many disapproved of the open barbarism of the November Pogrom: "Shame at the act, shock at its extent, and regret for the property destroyed converged to create a negative reaction." Even if Nazi Party members approved, the large majority of the population condemned the violence — even those who had previously endorsed "moderate" antisemitic measures. Still, there are almost no cases of public opposition to it. In the wake of Hitler's triumphs (incorporating Austria and dismembering Czechoslovakia) and in the shadow of an increasingly terrorist state (in which there were also no protests against the arrest or murder of political opponents), the pogrom was met with silence. In addition, when Germans watched what was happening to Jews they became still more mute, fearing for their *own* lives and property. Some thought the pogrom would only start with Jews and soon spread to other opponents of the system. When neighbors in the small town of "Sonderburg" saw the furniture and possessions of a Jewish family being tossed from a second-floor window – watching in horror as the feathers from the down quilts floated in the air – they tightened their shutters, secured their doors, drew their curtains, and trembled for themselves.[12]

As it was happening, the Nazis referred to the pogrom as the "Jew Action," a typically bureaucratic euphemism. Afterward it became known as "Crystal Night" (*Kristallnacht* or *Reichskristallnacht*) – a term commonly used through the late 1980s. Although the origin of the term is unclear, many Germans used this euphemism to describe the tons of shattered glass spread over public areas, streets, and squares, from the ruined homes and shops of Jews.[13]

A powerful image, mentioned often in Jewish women's memoirs, is that of flying feathers – feathers covering the internal space of the home, hallway, and front yard or courtyard. As in Russian pogroms at the turn of the century, the mobs tore up feather blankets and pillows, shaking them into the rooms, out the windows, and down the stairways. Jews were deprived of their bedding and the physical and psychological sense of well-being it represented.[14] Broken glass in public and strewn feathers in private spelled the end of Jewish security in Germany.

WOMEN'S ROLES AND REACTIONS DURING THE POGROM

THE IMAGE OF FEATHERS FLYING is one of a domestic scene gravely disturbed. This was women's primary experience of the November Pogrom. The marauders beat and arrested men. Although some women were publicly humiliated, bloodied, beaten, and murdered,[15] most were forced to stand by and watch their homes torn apart and their men abused. Later, women anguished as their men disappeared into concentration camps and many strove, heroically, to free them.

Personal testimonies show the massive terror. In the small town of "Sonderburg," for example, with 4,000 inhabitants and only 150 Jews, one Jewish woman recalled:

> It was around 6 o'clock in the morning when five young fellows came in . . . one from Sonderburg

who had worked with me at . . . the department store for at least ten years. He didn't do anything, he only sent the others in and they destroyed everything. . . . They . . . told me to go to the window, then they came with an axe but instead of hitting me, they hit the windows. A couple of hours later . . . children came by and threw stones in. . . . The man who worked with me said nothing: I looked at him . . . but he lowered his face. Among the four was the veterinarian and he came to my father's bedroom and said, "Mein Herr, following orders, we must destroy your house. You and your wife, go out."

The veterinarian had known her father from community sports events. Another woman recalled her experiences as an eleven-year-old in "Sonderburg": "Men . . . ran around axing all our furniture and throwing things out the window. They smashed the closet door and broke all my toys. Afterward, we hid in a closet in a neighbor's apartment." In Berlin, where the pogrom spread unevenly at first, Toni Lessler described the children arriving at her school from various neighborhoods exclaiming that the synagogues were burning. Fearing that they might be attacked at school, she sent them home with their teachers. Many arrived home to find only their distraught mothers: ninety-two of their fathers had been sent to concentration camps. After the pogrom, Jewish schools limped on, taught and directed, for the most part, by women and a few elderly male teachers.[16]

Although the ravage was thorough, in large cities a few escaped the worst because of oversights by the Nazis, because some buildings were protected by "Aryan" owners, because the vandals did not have enough time to get to them, or because, having been forewarned, some families split up and hid. In Leipzig, for example, as arrests of men continued after the pogrom, the Wahrman family split three ways: the father stayed with friends; the mother, aunt, and daughter went to (non-Jewish) neighbors; and the two young sons hid with other neighbors. Eleven years old at the time, one son later recalled: "How sad it was. . . . The store was boarded up. . . . Our home no longer offered us safety and security. Our family was now scattered."[17]

Those fortunate few who managed to escape still experienced days of terror, often trying to distract themselves or calm their families with the kind of avoidance behavior they had used in previous situations. One woman wrote: "We were at the piano and played a Mozart concerto. Often our eyes went to the window, but we did not stop. . . . We did not want to admit disturbing reality. We wanted to spare our nerves."[18]

Immediately after the cataclysm, with men imprisoned, many women continued to hide from further persecution; others had no way of remaining in their ransacked homes. Deprived of their men, women gathered together for consolation, encouragement, and advice. One young woman joined her fiancée's mother in Mannheim, "who had found refuge with about twenty other women and girls in one relative's apartment. All the men were already in Dachau." In another small town, where all the Jews had been herded together and then separated by sex, an observer noted: "We met nothing but young wives and mourning mothers" lingering in the area where the men had been imprisoned. Visiting a local hospital, she saw many women lying in the reception area, "all of them had escaped from small towns [where they would have been recognized] just in time, but did not know any longer where to go."[19] Eventually, most women returned home to clean up the wreckage and salvage a few objects or pieces of clothing. Since most of the dishes, pottery, or porcelain had been smashed, clothing slashed, and furniture axed, cleanup involved throwing away most items or saving shards of family treasures.

The most crucial task confronting Jewish women was to have their men freed. Since 1933, women had frequently represented their husbands to the authorities; now they would have to rescue them. Wives of prisoners were told that their husbands would be freed only if they could present emigration papers. Although no statistics are available to indicate their success, these women displayed extraordinary nerve and tenacity in saving a large number of men and in facilitating a mass exodus of married couples in 1939. Many women summoned the courage to overcome gender stereotypes of passivity in order to find any means to have husbands and fathers released from camps. Charlotte Stein-Pick wrote of the November Pogrom: "I tried . . . day in and day out, to find a connection that could lead to my husband's release. I ran to Christian acquaintances, friends, or colleagues, but . . . people shrugged their shoulders, shook their heads and said 'no.' And everyone was glad when I left. I was treated like a leper, even by people who were well-disposed toward us." Undaunted, Stein-Pick entered Nazi headquarters in Munich, the notorious Brown House, to request her husband's freedom based on his status as a war veteran. There she was shown her husband, twenty pounds thinner, and begged repeatedly for his release. The Nazis demanded that she explain the finances of her husband's student fraternity, of which he was still treasurer. She did. Upon his release, she had to return to the Brown House monthly to do the fraternity's bookkeeping until she emigrated.[20]

Ruth Abraham impressed not only her family but also the SS with her determination and bravery. During the November Pogrom, she pulled her fiancé out of hiding and led him through the teeming crowds: "His store was in ruins and I found him hiding behind a pillar." She then traveled to Dachau to ask for the release of her future father-in-law. She arrived at the concentration camp in a bus filled with SS men. She assumed that because of her "Aryan" looks she was taken for a member of the League of German Girls. She requested an interview with the commandant and begged for the elderly man's freedom. After three days and the intercession of a Nazi Party member, she succeeded. Again she attributed her success to her looks, since the men she met refused to believe that she was a "full Jew" and seemed to take pity on her. Abraham's unconventional behavior found a conventional reward: the couple married immediately. The rabbi who performed the ceremony had bandaged hands, an indication of the treatment he had received in a concentration camp.[21]

Some women saw not only to their husband's release and the necessary papers but also to the sale of their joint property. Accompanying her husband home after his imprisonment, one wife explained that she had just sold their house and bought tickets to Shanghai for the family. Her husband recalled that anything was fine with him, as long as they could es-

cape from a place in which everyone had declared "open season" on them.[22] Expressions of thankfulness tinged, perhaps, with a bit of surprise at women's heroism can be found in many men's memoirs. They were indebted to women even after their ordeal, when many men were too beaten in body and spirit to be of much use in the scramble to emigrate.

The testimonies of both men and women emphasize women's calm, dry-eyed, self-control in the midst of turmoil. For example, a Jewish community leader wrote: "The highest praise . . . goes to our wives who, without shedding one tear, inspired the hordes, some of whom had beaten their men bloody, to respect them. Unbroken, these women . . . did everything to have their men freed." Charlotte Stein-Pick recalled her husband's counsel on the day of the pogrom: " 'Just no tears and no scene.' . . . But even without this warning I would have controlled myself." Hanna Bernheim, remembering the pain of giving up prized family heirlooms to the Nazis some months after the pogrom, reflected on the dignity and self-control of Jews around her and on her own form of defiance: "I was glad that the Jews I saw behaved well, they didn't show any excitement noticeable to strangers. And I told an acquaintance I met loud enough for the employees to understand it, that I had never cared for these things." When the Nazis confiscated all her valuable ritual objects and jewelry, a Hamburg woman wrote in a poem that expressed her grief and her quiet defiance, "I will separate myself without tears."[23] This stoic calm in the face of danger was not merely a proclamation of female stalwartness to counter the stereotype of female "frailty." German-Jewish bourgeois upbringing had always valued decorum, and so women maintained their dignity as part of their Jewishness in the face of general dishonor. Jewish women's heroism reproached "Aryan" savagery and suggested a new task for women. Traditionally men had publicly guarded the safety and honor of the family and community; suddenly women found that they stood as the defenders of Jewish honor and pride – and of Jewish life itself.

On their own, many women faced the dizzying procedure of obtaining proof of immediate plans to emigrate in order to free a relative from a concentration camp. They had to decide whether to send children abroad while they organized their papers, settled on a destination (if they had not already discussed this previously), sold property, and arranged the departure. In spite of their apparent calm, the inner stress for women was massive.

EMIGRATION

THE NOVEMBER POGROM decisively tipped the balance toward emigration. For those in camps, the only way out was proof of readiness to emigrate, and for those not in camps, the violence influenced their decisions. Psychologists who studied refugee memoirs determined that almost 40 percent of memoir writers did not give up psychologically until 1938 or 1939. It was only after the pogrom that Jews were finally convinced that they faced physical danger. After November 1938, "essentially everyone tried to find a possibility of emigrating."[24]

Obstacles to Emigration

In the period following the pogrom, emigration became the highest priority within the Jewish community. Still, immigration restrictions in foreign countries and Nazi bureaucratic and financial roadblocks stymied Jews. Countries of potential refuge thwarted Jewish entry. Elisabeth Freund described her and her husband's many attempts to leave Germany:

> It is really enough to drive one to despair. . . . We have filed applications for entry permits to Switzerland, Denmark, and Sweden . . . in vain, though in all these countries we had good connections. In the spring of 1939 . . . we obtained an entry permit for Mexico for 3,000 marks. But we never received the visa, because the Mexican consulate asked us to present passports that would entitle us to return to Germany, and the German authorities did not issue such passports to Jews. Then, in August 1939 we did actually get the permit for England. But it came . . . only ten days before the outbreak of war, and in this short time we were not able to take care of all the formalities. . . . In the spring of 1940 we received

> the entry permit for Portugal. We immediately got everything ready and applied for our passports. Then came the invasion of Holland, Belgium and France. . . . A stream of refugees poured into Portugal, and the Portuguese government recalled . . . all of the issued permits. . . . It was also good that in December 1940 we had not . . . paid for our Panamaian visas, for we noticed that the visas offered us did not . . . entitle us to land in Panama.

Freund was frustrated with friends who urged them to leave Germany: "As if that were not our most fervent wish." She agonized: "There are no more visas for the U.S.A. My husband has made one last attempt and asked our relatives in America by wire for the entry visas for Cuba. . . . No other country gives an entry permit to German Jews any longer, or is still reachable in any way."[25]

Once they received permission to *enter* a foreign country, Jews still had to acquire the papers to *exit* Germany. "Getting out . . . is at least as difficult as getting into another country and you have absolutely no notion of the desperation here," wrote sixty-six-year-old Gertrud Grossmann to her uncomprehending son abroad. Getting the required papers took months of running a bureaucratic gauntlet, which many women faced alone, meeting officials who could arbitrarily add to the red tape at whim: "There was no rule and every official felt like a god."[26]

Bella Fromm summarized the plight of all German Jews: "So far I have gathered a collection of twenty-three of the necessary documents. I have made a thorough study of the employees and furniture in fifteen official bureaus . . . during the hours I have waited." Bewildered, she reported that she did not yet have all the papers she needed – and this was a few months before the November Pogrom. Afterward, Mally Dienemann, whose sixty-three-year-old husband languished in Buchenwald, raced to the Gestapo to prove they were ready to emigrate. Next she rushed to the passport office to retrieve their passports.

> After I had been sent from one office to another . . . I had to go to . . . the Emigration Office in

Frankfurt, the Gestapo, the police, the Finance Office, [send] a petition to Buchenwald, a petition to the Gestapo in Darmstadt, and still it took until Tuesday of the third week, before my husband returned. . . . Next came running around for the many papers that one needed for emigration. And while the Gestapo was in a rush, the Finance Office had so much time and so many requests, and without certification from the Finance and Tax offices . . . one did not get a passport, and without a passport a tariff official could not inspect the baggage.[27]

Finally arriving in Palestine in March 1939, Rabbi Dienemann died from his ordeal.

By 1939, new arbitrary laws slowed emigration even more. Even with a U.S. affidavit in hand, Else Gerstel could not simply leave "immediately," as her brother abroad urged. "It was impossible even to buy the ship tickets before we had the official permits. And that meant to pay taxes which were much higher than everything we owned. There were several months of red tape, desperate struggle." The elderly were physically ill equipped to endure the strains of this paper chase. Gertrud Grossmann confided by letter: "I dread going to the consulate and possibly standing around there for hours, which is physically impossible for me." The situation deteriorated so much that by 1940 she wrote her son: "Your emigration [in 1938] was child's play compared to today's practically insurmountable difficulties."[28]

As the government harassed the desperate Jews, individual Germans sought to enrich themselves at Jewish expense and Jews, often women, since the men were in camps, regularly encountered corruption. Charlotte Stein-Pick, anxious to get her husband out of a camp and expecting to receive visas from the American consulate imminently, was shocked to learn that there were Germans at the embassy who expected bribes in order to forward her papers. She went to a lawyer, who informed her that it would take 3,000 marks to pay off the swindlers: "I ran around bewildered. . . . In spite of everything, we German Jews still continued to resist believing the terrible corruption which National Socialism brought with it." In a respectable shipping company's elegant office on

Berlin's exclusive boulevard, Unter den Linden, another desperate woman had to hand over a 100-mark payoff for a place on a ship's waiting list. Moreover, she had to participate in the expensive farce of paying for round-trip tickets because, even though the Germans would have blocked their reentry, her family's visas to Cuba had to be tourist visas. Since this family had hidden money before the government blocked it, she was able to pay for the trip.[29] A situation like this was frustrating and nerve-racking before the war; it could cost Jewish lives thereafter.

Even before the pogrom, the government had no intention of letting Jews escape with their money or property. Afterward it blocked bank accounts more stringently and robbed potential emigrants more thoroughly. In Berlin, the Gestapo set up a special "one-stop" emigration bureau where: "the emigrating Jew was fleeced, totally and completely, in the manner of an assembly line." When they entered they were "still . . . the owner[s] of an apartment, perhaps a business, a bank account and some savings." As they were pushed from section to section "one possession after the next was taken." By the time they left, they had been "reduced to . . . stateless beggar[s]," grasping one precious possession, an exit visa.[30]

Nazi avarice is illustrated by the experience of the Bernheim family. They left in July 1939, falling prey to the Nazi decree of February 1939 that expropriated all valuable stones and metals from Jews. Thus, before emigrating, Hanna Bernheim packed a suitcase and headed for a Nazi "purchasing post" to give up her valuables:

> There were many people who had three, five suitcases, full of marvelous things: old [bridal] jewelry, Sabbath candles and goblets . . . beautiful old and modern plates. . . . The young officials were in high spirits. . . . These treasures, often collected by generations, were thrown together. . . . They were small-minded enough to take jewelry not at all precious as to the . . . value, but precious to us as souvenirs of beloved persons.

Shortly thereafter, at the airport, agents examined Bernheim's hat box and confiscated a brass clock, toiletries, and underwear. The guard even insisted on a body search. She recalled: "The propellers started . . . and I could only beg the woman to do the examination immediately. She was nice and correct, helped me with dressing, and the French pilot waited. And so I flew out of . . . hell."[31] Nazi insatiability was so great that a dentist warned one woman to see him before departing "and have him cover a gold crown and filling I had with a white coating. A patient of his had missed her ship while the gold in her mouth was removed by a Nazi dentist."[32]

Despite chaos and barriers, the largest number of Jews to leave in one year emigrated directly after the November Pogrom, reaching 78,000 in 1939. The United States, Palestine, and Great Britain took the most German Jews, but Jews left no escape route untried, as the 8,000 who fled to Japanese-occupied Shanghai show. By September 1939, about 185,000 (racially defined) Jews still remained in Germany; their numbers sank to 164,000 by October 1941, when Jewish emigration was banned. Another 8,500 managed to escape between 1942 and 1945. Exact figures of those who left Germany as a result of racial persecution cannot be established, but a good estimate is between 270,000 and 300,000 Jews. That is, close to three-fifths of German Jews managed to flee Germany. Yet approximately 30,000 of those who got out were later caught by the Nazis in other European countries. Ultimately, about half of those Jews who had lived in Germany in 1933 could save themselves through emigration to safe countries. Their friends and relatives who remained behind were murdered.[33]

Packing for Good

When Jews finally reached the stage of packing, they believed their departure would be permanent. Women took charge. As Berta Kamm put it: "Only a woman knows how much there is to deliberate and resolve in such a rushed departure." Packing was so clearly considered "women's work" that some women stayed behind to do it, sending men and children ahead. Packing quickly became an art as Nazi rulings and red tape skyrocketed. To emigrate with one's belongings, one had to receive a permit from the Finance Department. This permit was obtainable only after preparing lists of all the items one wished to take. Lisa Brauer spent an entire week writing "endless lists, in five copies each . . . every item entered, every list neatly typed, and in the end I could only speak and breathe and think in shoes, towels, scissors, soap and scarves." Another woman recalled how "a science of emigration advisement came into being [and these advisers] prepared the lists. For example, one was not allowed to say 'one bag of sewing supplies,' but had to detail every thimble, every skein of wool, every snap." Also one could not take just anything: "Only those things were allowed which had been purchased before 1933." Other items could be taken only in limited amounts and only "if the complete purchase price was paid to the Gold-Discount-Bank once again."[34]

After completing the lists, and often with ship or plane tickets in hand, Jews had to await the authorization of the Finance Department. Despite official policy encouraging emigration, the Nazi bureaucracy dawdled and delayed Jewish emigration. Again, connections and bribes seemed to speed up the process and, again, women had to master the world of officialdom and the art of bribery. To obtain the necessary papers before her boat departed, Lisa Brauer begged for assistance from a former student who she knew was married to someone in the Finance Department. She arrived at the student's door early one morning, when it was still dark, "to avoid being seen and recognized by curious neighbors." Shortly thereafter, a clerk from the Finance Department appeared at her home. Brauer offered him any books in her library. "Three days later I got my appointment at the Finance Department."[35]

With the arduous packing accomplished and papers in hand, some families sent the freight containers, known as "lifts," to interim stations, frequently ports in Holland. They remained there until the family knew its final destination. Some families lost their possessions when access to their containers was cut off by the German invasion of Holland. But others could not even consider packing most of their possessions, since the giant containers and the surcharge demanded by the Nazis for every item cost too much. One man recalled "that these giant containers . . . stood in front of many houses in my neighborhood, with the designation . . . New York or Buenos Aires or

Haifa. However, most emigrants could not afford such costly things and traveled to foreign lands with only a few suitcases."

Many emigrants, mourning their loss, sold their homes and furnishings for a pittance. Lisa Brauer, trying to create what she viewed as a dignified moment amid her misfortune, set the table with coffee and cake and invited neighbors to purchase items: "Only a few . . . took advantage and tried to grab as much as they could carry." Dismantling her home after the November Pogrom, Alice Baerwald wrote: "It was so terribly difficult to destroy . . . what one had created with so much love." She had cultivated every plant around the house: "Flowers, nothing but flowers, that was my joy. . . . My children had played and laughed here and romped in the grass with the dogs. And now suddenly to sell to total strangers." The city of Danzig decided the price of her house and chose the buyer. She then sold the contents of her home to "Aryan" purchasers, many of whom complained of *their* plight. Since Nazi ideology asserted that Germans suffered because of Jews, many Germans could simultaneously ignore Jewish suffering, exploit Jews, and lament their own lot. A pastor's wife proclaimed, "We're suffering just as much as you," but Baerwald retorted, "only with the difference that you're buying and I'm selling."[36]

It was clear to the emigrants that their German neighbors were benefiting greatly from their misery and doubtlessly clear to these Germans as well. Placing an ad in the paper, Lotte Popper tried to sell her "bedroom, living room, kitchen furniture." The ad was simply one among many other ads by Jews. She commented: "Yes, the Aryans had it good. They could now beautify their homes cheaply with the well-cared-for furniture of emigrating Jews." Only "the stupid among the populace were persuaded not to buy anything which had been used by Jews. The others, however, crowded the auction rooms, for the belongings [of Jews] were to be had for a song."[37]

Packing gave some women the chance to smuggle valuables out of the country. What their ingenuity managed to salvage was paltry compared with what the Nazis stole from them. Still, it helped some families subsist for a short time when they arrived penniless at their destination and saved precious mementos. While most women packed feverishly under the scrutiny of one or two officials,[38] some women managed to bribe these officials. One woman, who smuggled gold, silver, and jewelry into her bags, commented on the officials who demanded huge payoffs to make this possible: "This corruption of the Germans, which grew into the monstrous, rescued the lives and a modest existence for many people, particularly Jews." A few women bribed officials without consulting their husbands. They knew full well that their plans would have been vetoed, but they hoped to save some valuables for their immediate needs abroad. Else Gerstel, the wife of a judge, hid silverware with "Aryan" friends until the night before she packed. She then paid off packers to hide the silver while "seven Gestapo men were watching." She also smuggled other valuables in a secret compartment of her desk, built especially for this purpose: "I had risked of course the concentration camp and my life, probably all our lives. Alfred had no idea of what I had done. The night before we arrived in Cuba I whispered the whole story in his ear."[39]

Other women smuggled jewelry or money abroad for their relatives. Visiting her grandchild in Switzerland, one grandmother smuggled jewelry on each trip. Alice Baerwald, a resident of Danzig, agreed to smuggle her sister-in-law's jewelry from Berlin to Danzig in order to mail it to her when she emigrated. It was not yet forbidden to send one's own jewelry from Danzig, a "free city" according to the Treaty of Versailles, and she could claim it belonged to her. Then other elderly family members begged her to take their jewelry to Danzig too. None of them wanted to become dependent upon their adult children once they arrived abroad. Even more fearfully, she agreed, noting that "if someone caught me, I'd be finished." A few years later, she reflected: "One lived . . . in such danger that one . . . forgot completely that there could still be a normal life elsewhere. . . . Naturally one did many forbidden things, but because, in fact, everything was forbidden to us Jews, one had absolutely no choice."[40]

Women committed "illegal" acts not only to support their families but also to help the community at large. Beate Berger, for example, smuggled money from Berlin to Palestine in order to buy land for a children's home. Faithful friends, too, helped Jews take valuables abroad. The patient of one Jewish doctor, who was driven to commit suicide because of Nazi persecution, helped the doctor's widow smuggle jewelry and fur coats to Switzerland. She even accompanied the family to the border to assure their safety.[41]

While for many, "packing reduced a lifetime of possessions into three suitcases," for others, the clothing, shoes, and linens they packed had been donated by the Jewish Winter Relief Agency. Having sold the little they had to pay for their voyage, they had nothing left to take with them. The Jewish organization proclaimed: "They should not be uprooted and arrive in a foreign country with the mark of poverty stamped upon them."[42]

Final Farewells

In fear for their lives, some people fled immediately after the pogrom. Alice Oppenheimer, with exit papers in hand and a husband in Buchenwald, packed bags for her five children and looked up the next train to Switzerland. It would leave on a Saturday. Because she was religiously observant, she phoned a rabbi for his advice regarding travel on the Sabbath. He told her to disregard the prohibition against travel since her life was in danger. She left with only some jewelry to sell in Italy in order to tide the family over until its departure for Palestine: "I could sell only a few articles, and those I practically gave away. I had to have some money in hand. How else could I proceed with five children? [In Italy] I bought a loaf of bread for them and said: 'I cannot give you any more to eat, or I won't have enough money.' " Several days later they embarked for Palestine, where they met up with the sixth child. Her husband also joined them, freed after sixteen days in a concentration camp because of his Palestine certificate. Oppenheimer remarked that the camp had "transformed a still youthful man into an old man whom I failed to recognize when he finally landed by boat at Tel Aviv."[43]

For those lucky enough to leave Germany, most faced painful farewells with friends and relatives. "More and more, one learned to say farewell," wrote

one woman, as she listed friends who had scattered over the entire world. Moreover, all worried that those left behind would face increasing torment, and neither side knew whether they would ever see each other again. Fleeing shortly after the pogrom, Toni Lessler said her farewells in the only public place left for Jews, the railroad station café. There, no one noticed a few Jewish people visiting with each other. Referring to the Zoo station in Berlin, Lessler wrote:

> As we looked around . . . we saw similar groups to ours . . . friends and relatives who were taking leave from one another, none of whom could find any other meeting place than this dismal train station . . . in the midst of renovation and which offered the most inhospitable sojourn imaginable. I am unable to say how many tears were shed that evening.

When Elisabeth Freund finally escaped, shortly after Germany invaded the Soviet Union, her good-byes were excruciating. In the midst of real terror, having experienced bombings, forced labor, and the removal of Jews to tighter quarters, she tried not to break down: "Just no tears. One must not start that, otherwise one cannot stop. Who knows what will become of these people. In a situation like this, one can no longer say farewell in a conventional way."[44]

Individuals took leave in their own personal ways of what had been the *Heimat* – an almost untranslatable, nostalgic word for a romanticized homeland. In 1962, Ann Lewis and her parents described their feelings as they embarked for England. Ann, ten years old at the time, recalled the farewell at the train station:

> Relatives and friends – perhaps twelve or fifteen people – had gathered to see us off. . . . Everyone had brought presents . . . flowers, chocolate, sweets, magazines, books. . . . I have never forgotten this picture of the little knot of our friends and relations, standing close together as if to give each other mutual comfort, waving to us as the train carried us away. Sometimes I am surprised how often it comes into my thoughts. Although this leave-taking occurred when I was still so

young, it marked the most important turning-point of my life . . . the fundamental break with my roots.

Her mother wrote:

We are waiting at Bahnhof Zoo. . . . Many relatives and friends are there with flowers and presents. The train comes into the station, we get in, the children are excited and are looking forward to opening their presents – the train begins to move, we wave. Everything vanishes, we sit down – try not to think – dull apathy – mind a complete blank, vacant, oppressed, not a single tear. Courage – we *must* win through.

Her father wrote:

It is comfortable in the compartment . . . the luggage-racks are crammed with suitcases. . . . The four . . . are silent . . . the two adults, their faces looking serious and tired, are gazing with unseeing eyes through the windows, deep in thought. . . . Barely a quarter of an hour from now . . . Germany will lie behind them – Germany, the country which had been their home, where they had experienced happiness and suffering, the land whose language they had spoken – Germany, the country whose landscape was so dear to them . . . the Germany of poets, of thinkers and of the great composers.[45]

Strikingly, even as both parents experienced relief, their farewell thoughts echoed the general orientation of women and men when contemplating emigration: most women covered their pain and maintained a courageous front, while many men looked back, mourning for the country and culture they had once loved and had now lost. Adding to these differences . . . were more immediate concerns: women looked forward to a safer environment for their families, while men agonized about how to support them.

It was terribly distressing for Jews to leave their homeland, family, and friends, especially when they saw the present suffering and feared for the future of those left behind. They also worried about how they would fare abroad. Their anguish notwithstanding, these émigrés were the lucky ones, and not only in hindsight. When Toni Lessler confided to a friend that "emigrating is terribly hard," he responded tearfully, "Remaining here is much harder!"[46]

Who Stayed Behind?

A gender analysis of the desire to emigrate highlights women's and men's unique expectations, priorities, and perceptions. Women wanted to leave well before their men. Paradoxically, it does not follow that more women than men *actually* left. To the contrary, fewer women than men left Germany. Why?

Although life was becoming increasingly difficult in the 1930s, there were still compelling reasons to stay. First, women could still find employment in Jewish businesses and homes. They could also work as teachers in Jewish schools, as social workers, nurses, and administrators in Jewish social service institutions, and as clerical workers for the Jewish community. And older, educated women found jobs in cultural and social service fields within the Jewish community. Hedwig Burgheim, for example, found challenging and important work. In 1933, she was forced to resign as director of a teacher training institute in Giessen. Thereafter she directed the Leipzig Jewish Community's School for Kindergarten Teachers and Domestic Services, which trained young people for vocations useful in lands of emigration. After the November Pogrom, her own attempts at emigration having failed, she taught at the Jewish school and, by 1942, headed the old-age home in Leipzig. Along with its residents, she was deported in early 1943 and died in Auschwitz. Martha Wertheimer, a journalist before 1933, also found her skills in demand thereafter. She plunged into Jewish welfare work, while also writing books and plays, contributing to the Jewish press, and tutoring English to earn extra money. She escorted many children's transports to England; worked twelve-hour days without pausing for meals in order to advise Jews on emigration and welfare procedures; took great joy in leading High Holiday services at the League of Jewish Women's Home for Wayward Girls; and organized education courses for Jewish youth who had been drafted into forced labor. Ultimately, she wrote a friend in New York that, despite efforts to emigrate, she was no longer waiting to escape: "A great dark calm has entered me, as the saying of our fathers goes *'Gam zu le'tovah'* ('this, too, is for the best')." She continued: "It is also worthwhile to be an officer on the sinking ship of Jewish life in Germany, to hold out courageously and to fill the life boats, to the extent that we have some."[47]

While the employment situation of Jewish women helped keep them in Germany, that of men helped get them out. Some men had business connections abroad, facilitating their immediate flight, and others emigrated alone in order to establish themselves before sending for their families. Among Eastern European Jews who returned east between 1934 and 1937, for example, the majority were male, even though almost half of them were married. A handful of men, some with wives, received visas to leave Europe from groups hoping to save eminent intellectuals and artists. Women's organizations agreed that, if there was no choice, wives should not "hinder" husbands from emigrating alone, but they argued that it was often no cheaper for men to emigrate without their wives.[48]

Before the war, moreover, men faced immediate physical danger. Men who had been detained by the Nazis and then freed, as well as boys who had been beaten up by neighborhood ruffians, fled Germany early. After the November Pogrom, in a strange twist of fortune, the men interred in concentration camps were released only upon showing proof of their ability to leave Germany immediately. Families – mostly wives and mothers – strained every resource to provide the documentation to free these men and send them on their way while some of the women remained behind. Alice Nauen recalled how difficult these emigration decisions were for Jewish leaders:

> Should we send the men out first? This had been the dilemma all along. . . . If you have two tickets, do you take one man out of the concentration camp and his wife who is at this moment safe? Or do you take your two men out of the concentration camp? They took two men out . . . because they said we cannot play God, but these are in immediate danger.

Even as women feared for their men, they believed that they themselves would be spared serious harm by the Nazis. In retrospect, Ruth Klüger reflected on this kind of thinking and the resulting preponderance of women caught in the trap: "One seemed to ignore what was most obvious, namely how imperiled precisely the weaker and the socially disadvantaged are. That the Nazis should stop at women contradicted their racist ideology. Had we, as the result of an absurd, patriarchal short circuit, perhaps counted on their chivalry?"[49]

Despite trepidations, parents sent sons into the unknown more readily than daughters. Bourgeois parents worried about a daughter traveling alone, believing boys would be safer. Families also assumed that sons needed to establish economic futures for themselves, whereas daughters would marry. In 1935, one family sent its son to Palestine because "it was proper for a young man to try to leave and find a job elsewhere." His parents were reluctant to send their daughter abroad. Like other young women, socialized to accept their parents' judgment, she consented to remain behind and even made it "possible for him to go abroad by supporting him financially." As more and more sons left, daughters remained as the sole caretakers of elderly parents. One female commentator noted the presence of many women "who can't think of emigration because they don't know who might care for their elderly mothers . . . before they could start sending them money. In the same families, the sons went their way." Leaving one's aging parent – as statistics indicate, usually the mother – was the most painful act imaginable. Ruth Glaser described her own mother's agony at leaving her mother to join her husband, who had been forbidden reentry into Germany: she "could not sleep at night thinking of leaving her [mother] behind." Men, too, felt such grief, but more left nonetheless. Charlotte Stein-Pick wrote of her husband's anguish: "This abandonment of his old parents depressed him deeply. . . . He never got over this farewell. . . . To be sure, he saw that we could never have helped them, only shared their fate. I almost believe he would have preferred it."[50]

As early as 1936, the League of Jewish Women noted that far fewer women than men were leaving and feared that Jewish men of marriageable age would intermarry abroad, leaving Jewish women behind in Germany with no chance of marrying. Still, the League was not enthusiastic about emigration to certain areas because of anxiety about the possibility of forced prostitution. The League of Jewish Women also turned toward parents, reminding them of their "responsibility to free their daughters" even though daughters felt "stronger psychological ties to their families than sons do, [which] probably lies in the female psyche." As late as January 1938, one of the main emigration organizations, the Aid Society, announced that "up to now, Jewish emigration . . . indicates a severe surplus of men." It blamed this on the "nature" of women to feel closer to family and home and on that of men toward greater adventurousness. It also suggested that couples marry before emigrating, encouraged women to prepare themselves as household helpers, and promised that women's emigration would become a priority. Yet only two months later the Society announced it would expedite the emigration of only those young women who could prove their household skills and were willing to work as domestics abroad.[51] Jewish organizations also provided less support to emigrating women than to men.[52]

That some women and men took the advice to marry before going abroad, or came upon the idea on their own, can be seen from marriage ads in Jewish newspapers. These ads frequently included the requirement that the future spouse be amenable to emigration. For example, in 1936, one woman sought a "marriage partner . . . with the possibility of emigration," while another woman gave the value of her dowry in Swiss francs. A businessman offered a "pretty, healthy, and young woman" the opportunity of emigrating to Palestine together. By 1938, almost every ad announced the desire or ability to emigrate, occasionally boasting "affidavit in hand." Some may have entered into phony marriages before emigrating to Palestine. Since a couple, that is, two people, could enter on one certificate, a quick marriage of convenience, to be continued or broken upon arrival, saved an extra life.[53]

Families were often reluctant to consider Palestine, and the kibbutz, as an alternative for daughters. One survey of graduating classes from several Jewish schools in late 1935 showed that 47 percent of the boys but only 30 percent of the girls aimed for Palestine. Statistics for the first half of 1937 indicate that of those taking advantage of Zionist retraining programs, only 32 percent were female. Overall, fewer single females than males emigrated to Palestine: between 1933 and 1942, 8,209 "bachelors," compared with 5,080 "single" females, entered from German-speaking lands.[54]

Those young women who actually wound up in Palestine preferred the cities. The majority of German-Jewish girls and young women did not take available positions on kibbutzim or in agricultural training centers but rather took jobs as cooks or milliners. Better jobs, such as social workers, kindergarten teachers, and nurses, were much harder to find. While emigration consultants encouraged young women to take up the adventures of kibbutz life, articles appearing on Palestine, often written by committed Zionists, must have given pause. In one such article, the male author described a situation in which eight young women cared for fifty-five young men. They cooked, washed "mountains" of laundry, darned hundreds of socks, and sewed ripped clothing, working long days and into the night. But even more was expected of them. They were to do the emotional housework as well:

> A friendly word at the right time will bring a young man to his senses who once had a dozen shirts . . . and now noticed that his last carefully maintained shirt was taken by another. . . . Whether the kibbutz thrives is up to the girls! They have to mother one, be a comrade to the other . . . and have the endlessly difficult task of always remaining in a good mood [and] smiling.

Such reports, plus the numerous news items regarding Arab-Jewish discord, left most young women looking elsewhere for refuge.[55]

The growing disproportion of Jewish women in the German-Jewish population also came about because, to begin with, there were more Jewish women than men in Germany. In 1933, 52.3 percent of Jews were women, owing to male casualties during World War I, greater marrying out and conversion among

Jewish men, and greater longevity among women. In order to stay even, a greater absolute number of women would have had to emigrate. The slower rate of female than male emigration, however, meant that the female proportion of the Jewish population rose from 52.3 percent in 1933 to 57.5 percent by 1939. After the war, one woman wrote:

> Mostly we were women who had been left to ourselves. In part, our husbands had died from shock, partly they had been processed from life to death in a concentration camp and partly some wives who, aware of the greater danger to their husbands, had prevailed upon them to leave at once and alone. They were ready to take care of everything and to follow their husbands later on, but because of the war it became impossible for many to realize this intention and quite a few of my friends and acquaintances thus became martyrs of Hitler.[56]

A large proportion of these remaining women were elderly. Age, even more than being female, worked against timely flight; together they were lethal. Between June 1933 and September 1939, the number of young Jews in Germany under age thirty-nine decreased by about 80 percent. In contrast, the number of Jews over sixty decreased by only 27 percent. As early as 1936, a Jewish woman released from prison for her work in the communist resistance recuperated in a sanatorium. She remarked upon its "dismal milieu": "The guests [were] nearly all old people who had remained behind by themselves. Their children were either in prison camps or in Palestine, the U.S.A., and still farther away. . . . [They] longed for death." By 1939, the proportion of people over sixty had increased to 32 percent of the Jewish population; by 1941, two-thirds of the Jewish population was past middle age. In Berlin alone, the number of old-age homes grew from three in 1933 to thirteen in 1939 and to twenty-one in 1942. Already in 1933, the elderly had consisted of a large number of widows, the ratio being 140 Jewish women over the age of sixty-five to 100 men. By 1937–38, 59 percent of the recipients of Jewish Winter Relief aged forty-five and over were female. In 1939, 6,674 widowed men and

28,347 widowed women remained in the expanded Reich.[57]

In short, in slightly less than eight years and drastically increasing after the November Pogrom, two-thirds of German Jews emigrated (many to European countries where they were later caught up in the Nazi net), leaving a disproportionate number of old people and women. Jewish newspapers featured articles about old women whose children had emigrated, whose living quarters were small, whose help had disappeared, whose finances were meager. Thrown together, sometimes in old-age homes, sometimes as paying guests in the homes of other Jews, these women passed their days reliving memories of better times. Financial worries plagued them, but they were even more tormented by not knowing their children's exact whereabouts or circumstances. They constituted a "community of old people, who supported . . . and consoled each other." When Elisabeth Freund, one of the last Jews to leave Germany legally in October 1941, went to the Gestapo for her final papers, she observed: "All old people, old women" waiting in line.[58]

Notes

Epigraph: Wahrman, *Forget*, 116–18.
1. Property decree of April 26, 1938. "Seizure" in Schleunes, *Twisted Road*, 221; teenager in Lange, *Davidstern*, 23.
2. Maurer, "Abschiebung," 62.
3. Buchenwald and synagogues in Thalmann, *Crystal*, 16–20; wives in Behnsch-Brower, LBI, 4–5.
4. Letter of Nov. 19, 1938, from Otto Buchholz, quoted by Maurer, "Abschiebung," 52–53. See also: Sybil Milton, "The Expulsion of Polish Jews from Germany, October 1938 to July 1939," LBIYB, 1984; Yfaat Weiss, " 'Ostjuden' in Deutschland als Freiwild. Die nationalsozialistische Aussenpolitik zwischen Ideologie und Wirklichkeit," *Tel Aviver Jahrbuch für deutsche Geschichte* 25, (1994), 215–33.
5. Munich in Stein-Pick, LBI, 34; Hamburg in Meyer-Gerstein, LBI, I, 41. See also: Wahrman, *Forget*, 90; Maurer, "Abschiebung," 62–63.
6. Anti-Jewish actions began around November 8, escalating dramatically during the actual pogrom and continuing through November 11. Lauber, *Judenpogrom*.
7. Peter Loewenberg, "The Kristallnacht as a Public Degradation Ritual," LBIYB, 1987; Königsberg in *Sopade*, 1939, 219–20; Dinslaken in Thalmann, *Crystal*, 84–85. On another Jewish orphanage, see: Benz, "Rückfall," 34.
8. Jewish women organized emergency aid near the concentration camps as men were released. See *Sopade*, 1939, 924. "Sanity" in Stoppleman, LBI, 5; urns in Littauer, Harvard, 33.

9. Hecht, *Walls*, 59.
10. Neighbor in Stein-Pick, LBI, 40; Hecht, *Walls*, 59.
11. "Sweeping" in *LBI News*, no. 56 (1988), 4–5; Dienemann, Harvard, 34.
12. "Shame" and "moderate" in Bankier, *Germans*, 85, 87; "Sonderburg" in Henry, *Victims*, 116–18.
13. Pehle, "Preface," *November*, vii–viii.
14. Albersheim, Harvard, 28; Axelrath, Harvard, 43; Baerwald, Harvard, 72.
15. Women were not "exempt" from violence. See: Albersheim, Harvard, 63; Baerwald, Harvard, 58; Anonymous, LBI, 5; Henry, *Victims*, 116–17; Baumann, "Land," 38; Günther Haselier, *Geschichte der Stadt Breisach am Rhein* (Breisach, 1985), 450; Moritz, *Verbrechen*, 94–97, 232–33; *Sopade*, 1939, 920; Sauer, *Dokumente*, II, 25–28; Lauber, *Judenpogrom*, 110–14, 221–33; Thalmann, *Crystal*, 70, 81. Also, women were taken hostage for husbands: Lixl-Purcell, *Women*, 71; *Sopade*, 1939, 922. Finally, the aged, female and male, were not spared physical brutality either; *Sopade*, 1938, 1340. Four Nazis who had assaulted Jewish women were, interestingly, expelled from the Party, whereas twenty-six men who had killed Jewish men received no punishment. Hilberg, *Destruction*, I, 46.
16. "Sonderburg" in Henry, *Victims*, 117–18; Lessler, LBI, 32; Epstein, LBI, 8 (describing the Philanthropin in Frankfurt am Main).
17. Wahrman, *Forget*, 116–18.
18. Allport, "Personality," 6.
19. Mannheim in Abraham, LBI, 3; small town Anonymous, LBI, 4–5.
20. Stein-Pick, LBI, 41–45.
21. Abraham, LBI, 3–5.
22. "Open season" in Limberg, *Durften*, 325.
23. "Praise" in Gompertz, LBI, 10; Stein-Pick, LBI, 39; Bernheim, Harvard, 56, 63; Hamburg (Paula Kleve) in Gillis-Carlebach, *Kind*, 238. See also: Albersheim, Harvard, 33.
24. Psychologists in Allport, "Personality," 4; "everyone" in Lange, *Davidstern*, 27.
25. Freund in Richarz, *Life*, 413–15.
26. Letter from Gertrud Grossmann, Jan. 17, 1939; "god" in Bernheim, Harvard, 51.
27. Fromm, *Blood*, 238 (July 20, 1938); Dienemann, Harvard, 35.
28. Post-1939 laws in Bernheim, Harvard, 63–64; Gerstel, LBI, 76. See also: Nathorff, LBI, 127–33; letters from Gertrud Grossmann, Jan. 3, 1939; Feb. 22, 1940. The government continued to add new impediments to emigration. In 1941, it forbade the emigration of combat-fit Jewish men between the ages of eighteen and forty-five. It also forbade the emigration of women between those same ages. Freund, LBI, 166.
29. Stein-Pick, LBI, 37; also bribes to have husbands released from camps in Moses, Harvard, 44; payoff in Brauer, LBI, 51.
30. Alexander Szanto in Barkai, *Boycott*, 152.
31. Bernheim, Harvard, 55–56, 66; see also Lessler, LBI, 33.
32. Gerstel, LBI, 76, 80, 86.
33. Strauss, "Emigration," I, 317–18, 326–27.
34. Kamm, Harvard, 27, 31; "women's work" in Freyhan, LBI, 7; Brauer, LBI, 56; "before 1933" in Freund, LBI, 144–45.

See also: Bab, LBI, 198; Limberg, *Durften*, 203.
35. Brauer, LBI, 57.
36. Containers in Lange, *Davidstern*, 30; Brauer, LBI, 55; Baerwald, Harvard, 65–67.
37. Popper, Harvard, 75; "stupid" in Honnet-Sichel, Harvard, 80.
38. Brauer, LBI, 54, writes of a bailiff (*Gerichtsvollzieher*) and Freund, LBI, 178, of a custom's official (*Zollbeamter*) coming to the home. See also: Glaser, LBI, 71.
39. "Corruption" in Moses, Harvard, 44–45; Gerstel, LBI, 77–79.
40. Grandmother in Glaser, LBI, 38; Baerwald, Harvard, 73, 75. Blocked accounts and prohibitions re. money in Walk, *Sonderrecht* (April and Dec. 1936); Barkai, *Boycott*, 100, 138.
41. Berger in Scheer, *Ahawah*, 265; patient in Lixl-Purcell, *Women*, 53.
42. "Packing" in Vogel, *Forget!*, 202; "uprooted" in Schwarz, "Tschaikowsky," 119.
43. Lixl-Purcell, *Women*, 78.
44. "Farewell" in Bab, LBI, 193; Lessler, LBI, 34; Freund in Richarz, *Life*, 423.
45. Lewis, LBI, 275–77.
46. Lessler, LBI, 33.
47. *JWS*, 1937, 7–13; 27, 78–81; Barkai, "Existenzkampf," 163; Burgheim, archives, LBI; Hanno Loewy, ed., *In mich ist die grosse dunkle Ruhe gekommen, Martha Wertheimer Briefe an Siegfried Guggenheim* (1939–1941), Frankfurter Lern-und Dokumentationszentrum des Holocaust (Frankfurt am Main, 1993), 6, 9, 13, 15, 22, 37.
48. Returning east in Maurer, "Ausländische," 204; "hinder" in *BJFB*, December 1936, 5.
49. Men beaten in Eisner, *Allein*, 8; Nauen (whose father was secretary of the Hilfsverein in Hamburg Research Foundation, 15; Klüger, *leben*, 83.
50. "Proper" in Morris, "Lives," 43; "the sons" in *BJFB*, April 1937, 5; Glaser, LBI, 26, 71; Stein-Pick, LBI, 46. Another daughter who remained with her parents in Erika Guetermann, LBI.
51. *BJFB*, Dec. 1936, 1. Bundesarchiv, Coswig: 75C Jüd. Frauenbund, Verband Berlin, folder 37. Protokoll der Arbeitskreistagung vom 2 Nov. 1936; Aid Society (Hilfsverein) in *CV*, Jan. 20, 1938, 5; March 3, 1938, 6.
52. For example, in 1937, of the 7,313 émigrés supported by the emigration section of the Central Organization of Jews in Germany, there were approximately 4,161 men and 3,041 women. The Hilfsverein supported 3,250 men and 2,512 women. The Palestine Bureau supported 911 men and 529 women. *Informationsblätter*, Jan./Feb. 1938, 6–7. Overall immigration into the U.S. showed a higher proportion of men, evening out only in 1938–39. See: *AJYB 5699 (1938–39)* (1938), 552–554; *5701 (1940–41)* (1940), 608–9; *5702 (1941–42)* (1941), 674–75; Quack, "Gender," 391; Backhaus-Lautenschläger, *standen*, 30 (who claims more women than men entered between 1933 and 1941, although this encompasses Jews and non-Jews).
53. Businessman in *IF*, March 5, 1936; "affidavit" in *IF*, Oct. 13, 1938, 16; see also Klemperer, *Zeugnis*, I, 462 (Feb. 1939). Phony marriages in Wetzel, "Auswanderung," 453; Kliner-Fruck, "*Überleben*," 140; Backhaus-Lautenschläger, *standen*, 62.

54. Surveys in *JWS*, 1935, 188. The programs included: Hechaluz, Habonim, and Makkabi Hazair. *Informationsblät-ter*, Aug./Oct. 1937, 60. Palestine statistics in "Jewish Immigration from Germany during 1933–1942 (includes Austria . . . Czechoslovakia and Danzig . . .)," reprint from "The Jewish Immigration and Population" issued by the Dept. of Statistics of the Jewish Agency.

55. *JWS*, 1933–34; "friendly word" in *IF*, Jan. 16, 1936, 15; June 25, 1936, 9.

56. "Mostly" in Lixl-Purcell, *Women*, 92. Women were also a majority of the Jewish populations of German-dominated Europe: Hilberg, *Perpetrators*, 127; *IF*, Feb. 27, 1936; Blau, "Population," 165.

57. On age, see Strauss, "Emigration," I, 318–19, and Blau, "Population," 165; "dismal" in Rothschild, LBI, 125–26; old age homes in Gruner, "Reichshauptstadt," 242, 251; Winter Relief in Vollnhals, "Selbsthilfe," 405, and *BJFB*, Oct. 1938, 4.

58. Disproportionate number of elderly women in Richarz, *Leben*, 61; *JWS*, 1937, 96–97, 161–63, 200–01; Klemperer, *Zeugnis*, I, 475; *IF*, Jan. 16, 1936; Freund, LBI, 146.

German children pore over an antisemitic schoolbook, "The Poisonous Mushroom." Like a companion volume titled "Trust No Fox" (held by the girl at left), it sought to instill hatred of Jews in the very young. After January 1, 1938. (Stadtarchiv Nuernberg, courtesy of USHMM Photo Archives)

Jewish deportees line up for soup at a mobile cooking facility in the Zbaszyn refugee camp. On October 27, 1938 the Germans began to arrest and expel Jews of Polish nationality living in Germany. During the first two days of the expulsion, 6,100 Jews arrived in Zbaszyn, a small Polish town on the border with Germany. Sources estimate a total number of 10,000 Jews were expelled. November 1938. (Yad Vashem Photo Archives, courtesy of USHMM Photo Archives)

Hitler at a mass rally. 1934. (Courtesy of Yad Vashem Photo Archives)

162

The front page of the *Philadelphia Inquirer* reporting that Jews would have to pay a one-billion *Reichsmark* fine for the destruction caused during the November Pogrom. November 14, 1938. (Courtesy of USHMM Photo Archives)

Postcard of the synagogue in Landau in der Pfalz, Germany before its destruction on the night of the November Pogrom. Circa 1900. (Landau in der Pfalz, Archiv und Museum, courtesy of USHMM Photo Archives)

Fire consumes the synagogue in Landau in der Pfalz, Germany on the night of the November Pogrom, November 9, 1938. (Landau in der Pfalz, Archiv und Museum, courtesy of USHMM Photo Archives)

Debórah Dwork and Robert Jan van Pelt **The Third Reich**

In early-twentieth century Germany, the rhetoric of degeneration, criticism of the explosive growth of medical expenditure, and fear of the proletariat had converged into a call for "racial hygiene."[1] Its most important advocate, the physician Alfred Ploetz, argued that the primary and most important task of the physician was to prevent the wholesale degeneration of Germany into one large asylum. In this, the most crucial crisis that the German people had ever faced, the rights of the individual were of no consequence if they conflicted with the interests of the community.

Ploetz was supported by the respected and influential biologist Ernst Haeckel, who had been an early apostle of Darwinism among the Germans. Ignoring Darwin's injunction that civil society could not and should not be interpreted in terms of "selection" and "struggle for existence," Haeckel insisted that if selection determined the life of bacteria and bees, it also affected human beings: "artificial" selection should aid the process of natural selection. Indeed, Haeckel argued, if natural selection did not kill degenerates, human beings should step in. To illustrate what he had in mind, Haeckel adduced the example of Sparta. "A remarkable instance of artificial selection in man, on a great scale, is furnished by the ancient Spartans, among whom, in obedience to a special law, all newly-born children were subject to careful examination and selection. All those that were weak, sickly, or affected with any bodily infirmity, were killed. Only the perfectly healthy and strong children were allowed to live, and they alone afterwards propagated the race. By this means, the Spartan race was not only continually preserved in excellent strength and vigour, but the perfection of their bodies increased with every generation."[2] Haeckel lamented that any attempt to follow the Spartan example would be stopped by the same humanitarians who so easily accepted the destruction of thousands of young, vigorous men in war. In other words, if one accepted the

selection of the physically fit and the rejection of the unfit at the recruiting office, then one should accept it in absolute terms at the crib.[3]

Inspired by Haeckel, Ploetz recommended the Spartan practice; he suggested that a commission of racial hygienists examine every young person who wished to marry and have children and grant permission for marriage and procreation. The commission was then to examine newborn babies and kill those it found unfit. "The parents," Ploetz observed, "will not permit rebellious feelings to overcome them but, having renewed their qualification to procreate, fresh and merry will attempt to do so a second time."[4]

The judicial and medical establishment remained aloof from Haeckel and Ploetz until the carnage of the First World War, the subsequent revolution, and the economic difficulties of the postwar years led a few prominent lawyers and physicians to reconsider the merits of a radical shift in policy regarding the insane, the incurably sick, and the totally invalid. A catalyst in this change of opinion was the publication in 1920 of the very readable sixty-two-page *The Destruction of Life Unworthy of Life,* by Karl Binding, one of Germany's most eminent legal scholars, and the well-known neuropathologist Alfred Hoche. Reflecting on the war, which had wasted "the most valuable and self-sufficient lives full of energy and vigor," the authors compared it to the massive energy spent to sustain "worthless lives" in asylums. Now more than at any other time in Germany's history, the country needed every citizen to be 100 percent productive. "There is no place for those who can only manage 50 percent, 25 percent, or 12.5 percent of the normal contribution. The task which faces us as Germans will demand the highest mobilization of all possibilities for a long time to come."[5] It was time to bring an end to the practice of maintaining even the most socially worthless existence and to reconsider the merits of the "barbaric" practices of killing the unfit. And

Hoche confidently predicted that "a new period" would come when "on the basis of a higher morality" an "exaggerated concept of humanity and an exaggerated view of the value of human life" would no longer hold.[6]

Binding and Hoche's ideas were echoed a few years later by no one less than Adolf Hitler. Sentenced to five years imprisonment for his role in an attempted coup d'état in Bavaria, Hitler settled into prison life comfortably and sat down to write his vision for Germany. He had no doubt that the state should adopt ruthless policies with regard to the unfit. "It is a half-measure to let incurably sick people steadily contaminate the remaining healthy ones," Hitler wrote in *Mein Kampf*.[7] Strict application of the laws of racial hygiene had allowed 6,000 Spartans "of high racial value" to rule 350,000 Helots. "This was the result of a systematic race preservation; thus Sparta must be regarded as the first folkish state. The exposure of sick, weak, deformed children, in short their destruction, was more decent and in truth a thousand times more humane than the wretched insanity of our day which preserves the most pathological subject, and indeed at any price, and yet takes the life of a hundred thousand healthy children in consequence of birth control or through abortions, in order subsequently to breed a race of degenerates burdened with illnesses."[8]

Not long after these words were written, the Prussian aristocrat Reich President Paul von Hindenburg appointed their author Reich Chancellor, and the German nation confirmed his choice in a national election.

Hitler's first major social program was the Law for the Prevention of Hereditarily Ill Offspring. [Heinrich] Himmler understood it was the Führer's wish to establish a racially pure, physically perfect people. The policies Himmler had set for the SS were now adapted and adopted for the nation. Ordering the sterilization of the mentally handicapped, schizophrenics, manic-depressives, hereditary epileptics, and the blind, deaf, or alcoholic, this edict was followed by the Law against Dangerous Habitual Criminals, which provided for the castration of serious moral offenders. Initial estimates suggested that some

400,000 people would be sterilized or castrated, but these measures did not go far enough for Hitler. As Himmler had foreseen, marriage itself was to be regulated: the Law to Preserve the Hereditary Soundness of the German People forbidding the marriage of people who had, or had been diagnosed as having, a dangerous contagious disease, a mental disorder, or various hereditary diseases, was passed in 1935.

The new laws and policies were not kept secret from the general public. To the contrary; using the educational curriculum of National Socialist organizations like the Hitler Youth, schoolbooks, articles, and films, the government rallied the population behind its increasingly ferocious and far-reaching racial hygiene policies. A Hitler Youth instruction book, *About the German Nation and Its Living Space*, for example, warned that the increase of the "less worthy" was six times that of healthy people. "Most of these congenitally diseased and less worthy persons are completely unsuited for life. They cannot take care of themselves, and must be maintained and cared for in institutions." Claiming that 1.2 billion marks was "lost" annually in this way, the authors asked, "How many gymnasia, swimming pools, homesteads, and kindergartens could have been built with this money?"[9] New schoolbooks introduced the economics of racial hygiene in math problems: "The construction of an asylum costs 6 million marks. How many new houses at 15,000 marks apiece can be built for this sum?"[10]

Similar arguments were presented in films like *Victims of the Past* (1937). On Hitler's explicit instruction that everyone see this twenty-four-minute movie, it was shown as a trailer in all German cinemas during the Führer's birthday month of April.[11] "Hereditarily healthy people lived in narrow, dark alleys and half-collapsed tenements, while palaces for idiots and imbeciles were built," the narrator lamented, as scenes of squalid slums were followed by views of monumental asylums.[12] Sequence after sequence showing the life of inmates unable to communicate or feed themselves and requiring the constant attention of "racially valuable" nurses were accompanied by dire warnings. The future of the nation was at risk. In the previous seventy years the German population had increased by 50 percent while the number of people with hereditary illnesses had risen 450 percent. "If this development continues, fifty years from now one in five people will suffer from hereditary disease," the audience was told.[13] Reviewers praised the film for revealing the great threat the German people faced. . . .

In late 1938 an increasing number of letters arrived at the National Socialist Party office that handled Hitler's private business, including personal appeals to him by family members of mentally handicapped people requesting the "mercy death" of their loved ones: Hitler was intrigued by the entreaty of a certain Mr. Kauer from Leipzig. Kauer's child had been born blind, appeared idiotic, and did not have a leg and part of an arm. Hitler instructed his personal physician, Dr. Karl Brandt, to examine the child and, if the father's description was correct, to kill the youngster. Brandt obeyed. Hitler was pleased, and authorized Brandt and Philipp Bouhler, the head of the department receiving the letters, to treat similar cases in the same way. They were happy to oblige and in August established the Reich Committee for the Scientific Registration of Serious Hereditarily and Congenitally Based Illnesses. That same month the Reich Ministry of the Interior decreed that midwives and physicians had to report infants born with various conditions to the Reich committee. Investigators on the committee examined the information submitted, and authorized the murder of "positive" cases in special pediatric departments established in thirty asylums.

The facility in the asylum at Egelfing-Haar, near Munich, was among the first to open. Its director, Dr. Hermann Pfannmüller, hosted a large site visit of officials of the National Socialist Party, the army, and the SS on 16 February 1940. "Dr. Pfannmüller approached one of the fifteen cots which flanked the central passage to the right and left," a member of the delegation remembered after the war.

> We have here children aged from one to five," he pontificated. "All these creatures represent for me as a National Socialist "living burdens" . . . a burden for our nation. . . . In this sense, the Führer's action to free the national community from this overburdening is quite simply a national deed, whose greatness non-medical men will only be able to assess after a period of years if not decades. We do not carry out the action with poison, injections or other measures which can be recognised . . . for then the foreign press and certain circles in Paris or London would only have new opportunities for propaganda against us. . . . No, our method is much simpler."
>
> With these words he pulled a child out of its cot. While this fat, gross man displayed the whimpering skeletal little person like a hare which he had just caught, he coolly remarked: "Naturally, we don't stop their food straight away. That would cause too much fuss. We gradually reduce their portions. Nature then takes care of the rest. . . . This one won't last more than two or three more days.[14]

Five thousand children were killed in this way.

Satisfied with the pediatric program, Hitler instructed Bouhler's department to organize the murder of adults unfit for life.[15] After consultation with Albert Widmann, the chief of the Chemical Department of the Criminal Technical Institute, Bouhler's deputy, Viktor Brack, recommended the use of bottled carbon monoxide produced by BASF. At a meeting attended by, among others, Professor Werner Heyde, a well-known psychiatrist, a friend of Himmler's, and the leader of the operation; Professor Hermann Paul Nitsche, also a psychiatrist and the director of the Sonnenstein asylum near Dresden; a police officer, Paul Werner; and chaired by Brack, the decision was taken to kill between 65,000 and 75,000 asylum inmates by carbon monoxide poisoning.[16]

The first experimental gassing was conducted by Widmann in an unused prison in the town of Brandenburg eight weeks later. Christian Wirth, a police officer from Stuttgart, had built the gas chamber, installed the gas cylinders, and designed the fake showers. One of Widmann's collaborators recalled after the war that the gas chamber was "similar to a shower room which was approximately 3 metres by 5 metres and 3 metres high and tiled. There were benches round the room and a water pipe about 1″ in diameter ran along the wall about 10 cm off the floor.

There were small holes in this pipe from which the carbon monoxide gas poured out. The gas cylinders stood outside this room."[17] Between eighteen and twenty patients were brought to an anteroom, undressed, and led into the gas chamber. The door was locked, Widmann turned the valve, and the patients died within minutes. Their bodies were cremated in two mobile incinerators brought in for the occasion.

The operation, code-named T4 for the operation's headquarters at Tiergarten 4, began a few weeks later with the gassing of a first transport of inmates to the Grafeneck asylum (west of Ulm). Brandenburg came into operation in February, followed by Hartheim (near Linz), and Sonnenstein (near Dresden) in May, Bernburg (south of Magdeburg) in September, and Hadamar (north of Frankfurt) in January 1941.[18] The procedure was always the same. Institutions sent information on their patients to the Reich Committee. Three physicians assessed each file; the names of those judged "positive" were put on a list which was sent back to the asylum. The patients were transported to one of the six killing centers on buses with darkened windows. Stripped naked upon arrival, they were conducted to a room where a physician checked their files. "Someone then stamped them," a stoker in the crematorium at Hartheim recalled. "An orderly had to stamp them individually on the shoulder or the chest with a consecutive number. The number was approximately 3–4 cm in size. Those people who had gold teeth or a gold bridge were marked with a cross on their backs." They were then led into the gas chamber and killed. After an hour and a half, the fans were turned on, and the stokers went in to move the corpses to the mortuary which "was a difficult and nerve-racking task. It was not easy to disentangle the corpses, which were locked together, and drag them into the mortuary." When the incinerator was ready, the gold was removed from the corpses marked with a cross. Then the body was laid on a pan, "pushed in and left there just like with a baking oven."[19]

The victim's family received a letter a few weeks later informing them that their relative had been transferred to a new asylum and fallen ill and that "all attempts by the doctors to keep the patient alive were unfortunately unsuccessful." After the usual condolences, the letter explained that "in accordance with police instructions we were obliged to cremate the corpse immediately. This measure is designed to protect the country from the spread of infectious diseases which represent a serious threat in war time and we must strictly abide by it."[20]

Inmates from asylums in East and West Prussia and the Wartheland were not brought to a T4 death chamber. They were gassed in a special truck operated by a Sonderkommando, or Special Squad, headed by Herbert Lange. Stationed in Posen, Lange had the job of driving to an asylum, presenting a list of names to the staff, and loading the inmates into the airtight cargo area of a large Kaiser's Coffee truck. After they had left the grounds of the asylum, the driver opened the valves of the carbon monoxide cylinders stored in his cabin and connected to the cargo area, and killed his passengers.[21]

From the perspective of its management, operation T4 was an unqualified success. In 1939 Bracht and his colleagues estimated that 65,000 to 75,000 asylum inmates were candidates for death. When Hitler stopped the program on 24 August 1941, the T4 officials congratulated themselves that "70,273 persons have been disinfected."[22] They also took pride in the 885,439,800 marks they calculated they had saved the Reich.[23] Their report did not mention that, at the termination of the operation, its personnel had been offered jobs in the East. Nor did it mention that while the 70,273 victims amounted to one in five of all institutionalized patients, it included all Jewish inmates. Their papers had not been given even a cursory glance.

Notes

1. Max Nordau, *Degeneration* (Lincoln and London: University of Nebraska Press, 1993), 2, 537; Hans-Walter Schmuhl, *Rassenhygiene, Nationalsozialismus, Euthanasie: Von der Verhütung zur Vernichtung "lebensunwerten Lebens," 1890–1945* (Göttingen: Vandenhoeck & Ruprecht, 1987), 76f.
2. Ernst Haeckel, *The History of Creation: or, The Development of the Earth and Its Inhabitants by the Action of Natural Causes,* trans. E. Ray Lankester, 2 vols. (New York: D. Appleton, 1876), 1:170f.
3. Ibid., 173.
4. Alfred Ploetz, *Die Tüchtigkeit unserer Rasse und der Schutz der Schwachen* (Berlin: S. Fischer, 1895), 144f.
5. Alfred Hoche, "Ärztliche Bemerkungen," in Karl Binding and Alfred Hoche, *Die Freigabe der Vernichtung lebensun-*

werten Lebens: Ihr Mass und ihre Form (Leipzig: Felix Meiner, 1920), 55.

6. Ibid., 100f.

7. Adolf Hitler, *Mein Kampf,* trans. Ralph Manheim (Boston: Houghton Mifflin, 1943), 255.

8. Adolf Hitler, *Hitler's Secret Book,* introd. Telford Taylor, trans. Salvator Attanasio (New York: Grove Press, 1961), 18.

9. Harwood L. Childs, ed., *The Nazi Primer: Official Handbook for Schooling the Hitler Youth* (New York and London: Harper, 1938), 69f.

10. Hans-Walter Schmuhl, *Rassenhygiene, Nationalsozialismus, Euthanasie: Von der Verhütung zur Vernichtung "lebensunwerten Lebens," 1890–1945* (Göttingen: Vandenhoeck & Ruprecht, 1987), 175.

11. Karl Ludwig Rost, *Sterilisation und Euthanasie im Film des "Dritten Reiches"* (Husum: Matthiesen, 1987), 67ff.

12. Ibid., 234.

13. Ibid., 237.

14. As quoted in Noakes and Pridham, eds., *Nazism, 1919–1945,* 3:1008.

15. Christopher R. Browning, *Fateful Months: Essays on the Emergence of the Final Solution,* rev. ed. (New York and London: Holmes & Meier, 1991), 58ff.

16. As quoted in Noakes and Pridham, eds., *Nazism, 1919–1945,* 1010f.

17. As quoted ibid., 1019.

18. Klee, *"Euthanasie" im NS-Staat,* 207.

19. As quoted in Noakes and Pridham, eds., *Nazism, 1919–1945,* 3:1025f.

20. As quoted ibid., 1028.

21. Browning, *Fateful Months,* 59.

22. As quoted in Noakes and Pridham, eds., *Nazism, 1919–1945,* 3:1040.

23. As quoted ibid., 1042.

Viennese Jews forced to scrub the city pavements. March 1938. (Courtesy of Yad Vashem Photo Archives)

A woman, forced to wear a sign around her neck, is led through the streets of Vienna by Austrian Nazis. The sign reads: "I am a Christian swine and I buy from Jews." November 10, 1938. (Bildarchiv Preussischer Kulturbesitz, Berlin, courtesy of USHMM Photo Archives)

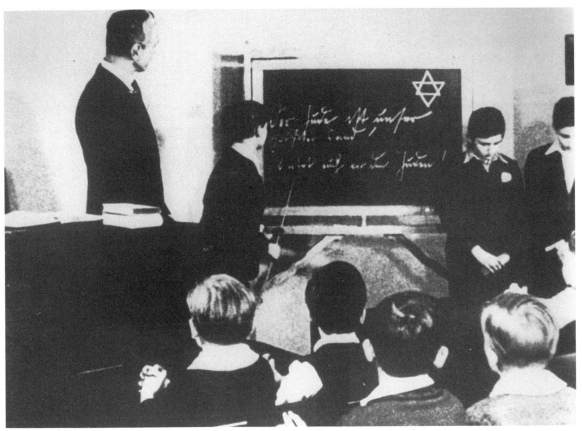

Jewish students are humiliated in front of their classmates. The boys are forced to stand next to a blackboard on which an antisemitic slogan has been written, while another student reads the words aloud, "The Jew is our greatest enemy!" Vienna, 1938. (Institute of Contemporary History and Wiener Library Limited, courtesy of USHMM Photo Archives)

A crowd of Viennese children looks on as a Jewish youth is forced by Austrian Nazis to paint the word *"Jude"* on his father's store. March 1938. (Österreichische Gesellschaft für Zeitgeschichte, courtesy of USHMM Photo Archives)

Huge pictures of Reichsführer Adolf Hitler and slogans reading "For Greater Germany and Hitler" on streetcars were used in Vienna to arouse greater interest in the April 10th plebiscite which officially annexed Austria to Germany. April 15, 1938. (AP/Wide World Photos)

Nazi troops form a human chain on the steps of the University of Vienna to prevent Jews from entering. The action by the Nazis led to a day of student antisemitic riots, which had to be suppressed by the police. Circa 1938. (National Archives, courtesy of USHMM Photo Archives)

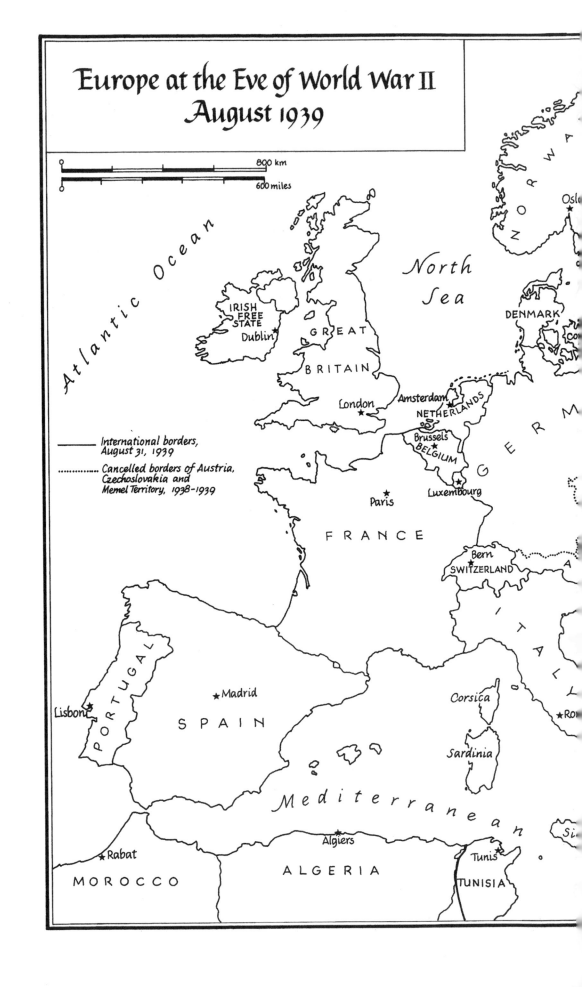

Europe at the Eve of World War II
August 1939

800 km

600 miles

Atlantic Ocean

North Sea

NORWAY

Oslo

DENMARK

IRISH FREE STATE

Dublin

GREAT BRITAIN

London

Amsterdam

NETHERLANDS

Brussels

BELGIUM

GERMANY

Luxembourg

Paris

Bern

SWITZERLAND

International borders, August 31, 1939

Cancelled borders of Austria, Czechoslovakia and Memel Territory, 1938-1939

FRANCE

PORTUGAL

Lisbon

Madrid

SPAIN

Corsica

ROME

Sardinia

ITALY

Mediterranean

Rabat

Algiers

Tunis

MOROCCO

ALGERIA

TUNISIA

ELIETTE CARAPEZZI ENARD

PAU BASSE PYRENEES, FRANCE... SEPTEMBER 1942 – "My family was on the St. Louis, that doomed ship which no country seemed to want. We made our way to southern France, like so many refugees from Germany. We were from Berlin.

"In May 1939, my mother and father rented a small apartment in the home of Eliette Enard. In September 1942, my parents and I were arrested and taken to the Gurs camp. The *Oeuvre de Secours aux Enfants* (OSE), the main Jewish organization working to safeguard children in France, was operating in Gurs. The OSE would take children out of the camp and place them in convents and homes throughout the region, passing them off as Christians.

"I was taken out of Gurs and placed with the Enards. I was so sick and malnourished. My French mother, Eliette, nursed my wounds and brought me back to health. I lived in a very loving atmosphere for four years as a member of their family. My parents died in Auschwitz in 1942.

"In 1946, Eliette took me to Paris where she gave me to the OSE, which arranged to send me to the United States to live with my aunt and uncle in New York City."

This was the testimony given by Judith Steel, the little girl saved by Eliette.

Photo of Eliette with Judith Steel. (JFR Photo Archives)

CHAPTER 4 **Refugee Policy**

St. Louis passengers, granted a temporary haven in Belgium, prepare to disembark at the port of Antwerp. From a page of an illustrated feature article on the St. Louis refugee ship published in the weekly newsmagazine, *Paris Match*. June 17, 1939. (Clark Blatteis, courtesy of USHMM Photo Archives)

On May 13, 1939, over 900 Jewish passengers sailed from Hamburg, Germany aboard the St. Louis in search of safe haven. Turned away by Cuba and the United States, the ship was forced to return to Europe. Four European countries (Great Britain, France, Belgium, and the Netherlands) accepted the passengers, but within a few months war broke out in Europe and the refugees in three of these countries found themselves once again under German rule. Many of them were killed during the Holocaust.

Debórah Dwork **Introduction**

JACQUES KUPFERMANN'S ARTISTIC ABILITIES SAVED HIS LIFE. I met him in England some twenty-five years ago, when he was forty-six years old. I admired his work, we had a vague family connection, and we became friends. He lived at that time in Maidenhead, a beautiful area on the Thames River. One autumnal Sunday I asked about his childhood, his parents, and his painting. He was born in Vienna in 1930, he said. His parents were from the eastern reaches of the Austro-Hungarian empire, which had become Poland, and it was with Polish passports that they had emigrated to the capital city of the former empire. From his early youth it was clear that Jacques had artistic talent and, at hardship to themselves, his parents arranged for him to have lessons to develop his abilities. His teacher, it turned out, was an Austrian Nazi.

As happens in close human relationships, Jacques's teacher's feelings were complicated. In Jacques's memory, she spoke quite frankly to the Kupfermann family as early as 1937. Austria would join Germany, she predicted, and the situation for the Jews would not be pleasant. She urged Mr. and Mrs. Kupfermann to obtain emigration papers and immigration visas for themselves and for their child. With their Polish passports, they came under the quota for Poland, which was small and had a long waiting list to be admitted to the United States. With his Austrian passport, Jacques came under the quota for Austria, which was proportionally more generous and had a shorter queue. By 1938, Jacques's parents' visas had not yet been issued. The situation had become desperate and tense. Jacques's teacher told his parents to wait no longer; the boy had talent, he should be spared. He was sent to relatives in the United States. His parents were caught in Europe. Time had run out, and their son never saw them again.

The goal of this chapter is to delineate how this tragedy happened.

Austrians wildly acclaim the conqueror Adolf Hitler, who annexed Austria to Germany in a bloodless coup. Here Viennese police are shown hard pressed to hold back the enthusiastic throng as Hitler approached on his triumphal ride through Vienna's streets. March 15, 1938. (AP/Wide World Photos)

Why weren't the parents admitted into the United States with their child? And if the entire family could not go to the United States, wasn't another country prepared to accept them? What options did the Kupfermann family – and millions of other Jews – have to leave Europe after Hitler came to power in 1933? Who formulated immigration policies, and who enforced them?

By the late 1930s, hundreds of thousands of Central Europeans sought to flee their homelands in search of safety. Communists, Social Democrats, and Jews in Germany and German-occupied Austria and Czechoslovakia stood on line at embassies, consulates, shipping companies, and government offices, desperate for papers: exit visas, entry visas, transit visas, receipts for tax payments, clearance forms, ship tickets, train tickets. Jews in right-wing, nationalistic Poland and Rumania joined them. After the death in 1935 of the slightly moderate dictator and much-loved former military hero, Jozef Pilsudski, an undeclared war against the Jews was waged in Poland, with organized pogroms, random acts of street violence, economic boycotts, and the institution of "bench ghettos," special seating areas for Jewish students at the universities. In Rumania, the extreme-right-wing government of Octavian Goga in 1937 endorsed radical political antisemitism, and some fifty-thousand Jews fled the country annually for the next few years.

Warsaw University student ID booklet issued for Cypa Gorodecka. The stamp above the photo-graph reads: "Sit in odd numbered benches only." Jewish students in Poland were required to sit separately from non-Jews. October 15, 1934. (Adam and Krystyna Drozdowicz, courtesy of USHMM Photo Archives)

The sheer number of people seeking asylum and the paucity of places willing to receive them created a refugee crisis of international proportions. At President Roosevelt's invitation, a multinational conference was convened at the French resort town of Evian-les-Bains in July 1938. We now know that the Evian conference was designed to protect America's image, not to help the Jewish and political refugees of Europe. (See Henry Feingold's chapter "Roosevelt's New Deal Humanitarianism," from his book, *Bearing Witness: How America and Its Jews Responded to the Holocaust*.) The unemployment rate in the United States had just reached an all-time high, and politicians and the public feared both immigrant competition for jobs and the financial burden of supporting them. The Great Depression had impoverished millions of families and had robbed the country of hope and security. Many Americans were isolationists; they wanted nothing to do with Europe and its problems. It was America's duty to take care of Americans, not to resolve European conflicts or to open its doors to foreigners. Politicians in Washington reflected the mood of their constituencies at home, and many advocated a policy of restrictionism to keep the number of immigrants as low as possible.

Nevertheless, America had the time-honored reputation as a refuge for the oppressed. The Evian Conference was meant to sustain this image, not to effect any change in practice or to liber-

A political cartoon published in the Sunday, July 3, 1938 edition of *The New York Times:* "Will the Evian Conference guide him [the Jewish refugee] to freedom?" (Courtesy of USHMM Photo Archives)

alize policy. President Roosevelt accordingly issued invitations to twenty-nine countries, despite the fact that the League of Nations (the predecessor to the United Nations) already had three agencies to deal with different aspects of the refugee problem, that Germany's neighbors already carried a heavy refugee load and were hardly ecstatic about an initiative by a non-European country that had not taken refugees, and that Britain was already under conflicting Arab and Jewish pressures because of her policy delimiting the immigration of Jews into Palestine. To allay fears that the United States would demand great concessions, the invited nations were told that "no country would be expected to receive a greater number of emigrants than is permitted by its existing legislation." All new programs were to be financed by private agencies, not public monies. And finally, the stated purpose of the meeting was to facilitate the emigration of "political refugees" (not Jews) from Germany and Austria.

The conference was a dismal failure and a grave disappointment to Jews desperate to leave Europe. But neither they nor anyone else realized at the time how tragic its results would be. No one was ready to take responsibility for finding safe havens for the refugees and, as everyone refused to act, each country was given tacit international permission to keep its doors closed. The historian David Wyman has called this policy "the abandonment of the Jews" and his book by that name examines America's failure to help. One of the two chapters from that book excerpted here explains how the "paper walls" erected by the State Department – the required paperwork – became a serious impediment to immigration, devised by bureaucrats who certainly intended them to be a means of keeping out refugees. The visa application to be completed by American sponsors of Europeans hoping to be allowed entry into the United States was a two-sided document over four feet long, and six copies had to be submitted. No reasons were given to explain a rejection and, if unsuccessful, the sponsor could not reapply for another six months. American programs to save endangered Jews were, as David Wyman has shown, nothing more than "paper plans," and in a second chapter from his book *The Abandonment of the Jews*, Wyman has focused on the moral issue of responsibility.

Bernard Wasserstein has been equally critical of the British, who had been given a mandate by the League of Nations after the First World War to administer Palestine and other areas conquered by the Allies that had been under Turkish control. As the mandatory authority in Palestine, the British controlled immigration to the land where many Jews sought to create a National Home and many more sought safety. The Jews had good reason to do so. Toward the end of World War I the British government had issued the Balfour Declaration (November 1917) that recognized, in principle, the eventual establishment of a Jewish National Home in Palestine. A month later, the British general Edmund Allenby entered Jerusalem and his troops soon occupied the entire country. Palestine thus passed from Turkish to British rule. When the League of Nations confirmed British authority in 1922 with a Mandate for Palestine, the League Council included the text of the Balfour Declaration. In the years immediately after World War I, it seemed as if Palestine would become a Jewish homeland and to the persecuted Jews of interwar Europe, Palestine thus appeared to be a place of refuge. And it was: between 1922 and 1929, some 70,000 and, from 1932 through 1935, another 143,500 Central and East European Jews emigrated to Palestine.

Palestinian Arabs fiercely opposed a Jewish National Home in Palestine, however. Faced with violent riots in the streets of Jerusalem that escalated in April 1936 into a full-scale Arab rebellion, and with the threat of war in Europe looming on the horizon, the British decided to pacify the local Arab population by reducing Jewish immigration dramatically. Negotiations about the possible partition of Palestine into two states, one for Arabs and one for Jews, as well as about the number of immigrants to be admitted prior to the establishment of such states, continued until May 1939, when the British issued a White Paper laying out their policy. Under this policy, for each of the next five years, ten-thousand Jews would be allowed into Palestine annually. Furthermore, given the grave dangers many Jews in Europe faced, an additional twenty-five-thousand Jews would be admitted immediately. That was all. In an excerpt from *Britain and the Jews of Europe*, Bernard Wasserstein has argued that during the first two years of the war the primary obstacle to Jewish emigration from Nazi-controlled areas of Europe was not the German government, but the British and the Americans. It was they who "sealed the escape routes."

If the participants at the Evian Conference could rightly say that in 1938 they did not know the fate to which their failure to act would consign the Jews of Europe a few years later, the delegates to the

---

If the participants at the Evian Conference could rightly say that in 1938 they did not know the fate to which their failure to act would consign the Jews of Europe a few years later, the delegates to the Bermuda Conference in April 1943 were called to meet precisely because they knew about the mass murders. And still they accomplished little.

Bermuda Conference in April 1943 were called to meet precisely because they knew about the mass murders. And still, as the excerpt from Michael Marrus's book, *The Unwanted,* makes clear, they accomplished little. "Caution quickly triumphed over imagination." Refugee policy, both national and international, was a disaster for the Jews. Help did not come from the politicians.

Refugee policy was a disaster for the Jews.

Henry L. Feingold # Roosevelt's New Deal Humanitarianism

THE STORY IS TOLD of two concentration-camp inmates who by some miracle succeed in escaping, only to be recaptured. They are placed against a wall for summary execution, but before dispatching them, the officer in charge, as is the custom, asks if they have any last requests. In his last agony, one of the men requests a blindfold, whereupon the other nervously whispers to him "Don't make trouble!"

Much of the early discussion of the Holocaust centered on the reaction of the victims: Why did they not resist? Why did they not "make trouble"? We tended to forget that, whether they fought heroically in the Warsaw ghetto or went passively to their fate at Babi Yar, they remained victims. It was almost as if we were seeking a kernel of courage that would prove to us that death could not be produced in factories. European Jewry would be the Luddites of the twentieth century. Meanwhile, this preoccupation with the role of the victims had the unfortunate effect of momentarily obscuring the posture of the third parties – the Vatican, the neutrals, the Roosevelt administration, the International Red Cross, the rescue agencies. Victims remain victims whether they ask for blindfolds or not, but the role of witnesses is not preordained; their ambit of action is far greater because they were not locked into the Final Solution. What did they do? What follows is a brief description of one of the third parties – the Roosevelt administration – in relation to the Holocaust and some attempt to make sense of it.

THE HISTORIOGRAPHICAL CONTEXT

HOLOCAUST OBSERVERS SUCH AS [Gerald] Reitlinger, Hilberg, and, more recently, Gideon Hausner have made short shrift of the rescue story, dismissing it as at best nonexistent and at worst as tending to play an adjunct role to the operations of the Final Solution. The rescue story is, indeed, a tragic one, replete with incredible ineptness and indifference. But to observe that not enough was done is simply to recite a self-evident truth. Enough can never be done where such catastrophes are concerned. Moreover, such recitations, tinged as they are with righteousness, are not concerned with the reason for the failure or even the context in which it occurred. Yet, such failures often have more to tell us than the successes we experience. After one concludes that not enough was done – and such a conclusion is inescapable – the rescue story can serve for more than simply another sermon about man's inhumanity to man.

In addition to offering an opportunity to examine the authenticity of New Deal humanitarianism, there is in the rescue issue a model of special-interest pleading by a hyphenate group that seemed well equipped to exert pressure. Why did the Jews fail while the Irish "twisted the lion's tail" successfully during the last decades of the nineteenth century? Moreover, the rescue issue offers some fascinating insights into Roosevelt's administrative style. It is replete with overlapping agencies in perpetual conflict and with violent personal antagonisms, which can be traced to the president's uncertain mandate. To trace Roosevelt's devious path between those who insisted that refugees presented a threat to American security and those who insisted that the humanitarian roots of the New Deal had to be watered with something more than mere rhetoric presents us with a superb picture of Roosevelt the fox rather than the lion. And for American Jews, what Roosevelt did and did not do during the Holocaust has a special interest. What they really want to know is whether Roosevelt loved them as much as they loved him. One almost hesitates to burst the bubble.

FROM HENRY L. FEINGOLD, **BEARING WITNESS: HOW AMERICA AND ITS JEWS RESPONDED TO THE HOLOCAUST**, 73–93, 282. (SYRACUSE: SYRACUSE UNIVERSITY PRESS, 1995). BY PERMISSION OF THE PUBLISHER.

PHASE ONE: THE EVIAN INITIATIVE AND BEYOND

ROOSEVELT'S INTEREST IN RESCUE began in earnest with the astonishing and unexplained invitation to thirty-two nations to meet at Evian, France, to bring order into the chaotic refugee situation brought on by Berlin's extrusion policy. The invitation, extended during March 1938, was astonishing because Roosevelt chose to intrude into a situation in which he was virtually powerless to act, bound as he was by a highly restrictive immigration law. The invitation to Evian was in fact so carefully circumscribed that the conference was actually preordained to failure. No nation, cautioned the invitation, would be required to change its immigration regulations. Certainly, the United States would not. Roosevelt had no intention of directly confronting the restrictionist elements in Congress. And so the American delegation went to Evian with no bargaining power at all, and no amount of verbal maneuvering by Myron Taylor, the former head of United States Steel whom Roosevelt selected to lead the delegation, could conceal the impression that the administration would ultimately embarrass itself by sponsoring an exercise in futility.

Long-winded Latin-style oratory was a prominent feature of the deliberations. Virgilio Molina, the Dominican delegate, trusted "that our conference will be like a peaceful, limpid lake, whose health-giving waters assuage the thirst and add to the fertility of the lands that border it."[1] Ironically, the Trujillo regime was the only one to make a substantial resettlement offer, which became the refugee colony in Sosua. But even here, the offer was based more on a peculiar racist breed of thinking rather than a concern with the plight of the hapless Jewish refugees. Little was done to hide the Roosevelt administration's disappointment at the results of the conference. The hope was that Latin America would offer the havens that the United States could not. Had not the great Argentinian educator and statesman Domingo Sarmiento urged his countrymen to emulate the generous immigration policy of the United States? But by 1938, the policy of the United States had changed, and it was this change that the Latin American republics preferred to emulate. The failure to find suitable mass-resettlement havens became the rock on which the first phase of the rescue effort foundered.

Despite the failure at Evian, the administration chose to sustain its initiative. The decision was all the more remarkable because it was apparent that France and England, already burdened with growing numbers of refugees, were in no mood to open further the Pandora's box of resettlement and, for that reason, strongly supported the relatively innocuous League of Nations Refugee Commission, which was distinguished by its inability, as a League agency, even to deal with Berlin on refugee matters. In 1935, American High Commissioner James G. McDonald, later to be appointed by Roosevelt to head the President's Advisory Commission on Political Refugees (PACPR), had dramatically resigned from the League Commission because of its impotence.

The Intergovernmental Committee on Political Refugees (IGC), which grew out of the Evian conference, was, therefore, a peculiarly American contribution to the solution of the refugee crisis and was pushed with some vigor by the Roosevelt administration. Its primary goal was to come to some agreement with Berlin, so that order might be imposed on the chaotic refugee situation. In 1938, it was believed in Washington, no less than in London, that the men in Berlin were after all, reasonable and could be talked to. The dream of an equitable solution to the refugee problem via negotiations was an integral part of that species of reasoning that led in September to Munich.

Eventually, Berlin did in fact agree to negotiate. From January to March 1939, George Rublee, an old Groton crony of the president's, assisted by the State Department's Robert Pell, partook in long and difficult negotiations first with the Nazi financial wizard Hjalmar Schacht and then with Helmut Wohlthat, an official in the Economic Affairs Ministry. To the dismay of some and the astonishment of others, Rublee actually succeeded in wresting a Statement of Agreement from Berlin. The agreement, an informal arrangement, was far from a humane solution to the German refugee problem and was soon dubbed a "ransom offer" by Dorothy Parker. That label gave to Holocaust history a ghoulish symmetry. It began with an offer to ransom German Jewry and ended with an offer to ransom the Jews of Hungary.

In fact, the Statement of Agreement was more than a simple ransom deal. It bore a startling resemblance to the *Ha'avara* agreement that the Jewish Agency had with Berlin. It required the forced sale of capital goods, the establishment of a trust fund from confiscated German Jewish capital, and an outside agency representing "international Jewry" that would purchase capital goods from the Reich that could then be used for resettlement purposes by the receiving nation. In turn, for such a forced sale of German goods, which incidentally would go far to shore up the Reich's precarious exchange balance, Berlin would permit an orderly, phased emigration of the Jewish community, protection for the aged and infirm who would be allowed to remain in Germany, and even some guarantees that overt persecution would be eliminated. Success in carrying out the agreement would depend on three factors: continued stability in Germany, the willingness of outside Jews to cooperate, and the availability of resettlement havens. None of these requirements could be fulfilled. Hitler's abrupt dismissal of Schacht in the midst of the negotiations indicated that events in the Reich were already out of control. Nor would the organization of an international Jewish corporation and the location of resettlement havens prove more successful.

We have a fairly good description of the agonizing decision that had to be made by the American, British, and French Jewish communities in Lewis Strauss's *Men and Decisions*. Involved was the question of whether these Jewish communities, not called upon to participate in the negotiations, should now make themselves over to fit the anti-Semitic image of "International Jewry" that Berlin fantasized. An international corporation to act as financial agent would first have to be created, and millions of dollars would have to be raised. Most galling was the suspicion that Washington and London, half sharing the notion that there was such a thing as international Jewish finance, were urging Jewish leaders to cooperate in subsidizing a government that had vowed to destroy Jews. Jewish leaders were wary of establishing a precedent of aiding Berlin to eliminate a particularly splendid community. The problem of the Jews' cooperation in their own destruction came to the fore three years before the decision to liquidate them and was actively

abetted by Washington and London. Jews were shocked by the malevolence of the proposal, and they were also aware that in the wings waited Poland and Romania, anxious to "sell" their Jews. Would it not be better to follow the League precedent of protecting unpopular minorities where they lived rather than starting the sticky business of mass resettlement, especially when there was no place to move to? By the time even a nominal compliance with the agreement had been hammered out, the war was upon them. German Jewry was resettled – eastward.

THE SECURITY PSYCHOSIS AND THE VISA DEBACLE

YET, THOUSANDS HAD BEEN ABLE to leave the Reich and Austria and would continue to be able to do so for some time. It was this stream of refugees that became a primary concern for the administration. Ultimately, the preoccupation with those who in effect were already rescued would become a gambit in foiling the rescue effort. Washington, as late as June 1943, insisted on focusing on these political refugees exclusively as it closed its eyes to the genocide operation. Not until January 1944 did rescue advocates finally succeed in broadening the administration's focus to include those who faced certain death in the camps.

By 1938, some pressure had developed to liberalize the rigid administrative procedures first initiated by Herbert Hoover at the outset of the depression. From time to time, pronunciamentos emanated from the White House declaring a liberalization of the visa procedure. But it soon became apparent that a gulf existed between the aspirations of the White House and what was happening on the operational level. By a fluke in the immigration law, the consuls had the final say on who could get the visas. With the middle-echelon officialdom of the State Department, they shared opposition to a new influx of immigrants and, in some cases, a barely concealed distaste for Jewish refugees. Thus between 1938 and 1941, when the need for visas was crucial and despite professions to the contrary, visas were consistently underissued.

Nevertheless, the private rescue agencies did succeed in communicating to the administration the urgent need to salvage the cultural and scientific elite of Europe. Accordingly, Roosevelt ordered a special visa procedure whereby the various sponsoring groups within the country compiled lists of rescue clients whose names would then be given to the President's Advisory Commission on Political Refugees, which acted as a conduit to the State Department. In theory, such people would then be given priority in visa consideration. In practice, the State Department had begun by 1940 to wage a relentless campaign to restrict such lists. Only now are researchers finally beginning to compile data that will allow some estimate of the extent to which the American cultural and scientific boom of the fifties and sixties was based on the imported refugee intellectual capital of the war years.

Certainly, the persons in the State Department who administered the visa regulations were barely cognizant of such a potential national asset. They were more inclined to view the refugee as an economic burden or a security risk and, therefore, spared no effort to close the doors. The high point of the resistance is well illustrated by the case of the *SS Quanza*, which arrived in Norfolk in September 1940 with a cargo of refugees who had been refused entrance to Mexico. The Mexican authorities had issued new visas to some passengers that would allow them to enter any haven but Mexico. When the *Quanza* docked, ostensibly to refuel, a direct confrontation occurred between those who favored leniency for the admission or at least landing, of these refugees and those around Breckinridge Long, a newly appointed assistant secretary and head of the newly created Special Problems Division of the State Department, who were determined to halt the flow of refugees at any cost. It was one thing to urge Havana to accept the refugees of another steamer, the *St. Louis*, and quite another to bring them here. The violent temper tantrum thrown by Long after he learned that, after screening, most refugees had, after all, been found qualified for visas, went far in helping to identify him as the source of much of the resistance to a more humanitarian refugee policy. The *Quanza* victory was a temporary one. By mid-1941, Long was able to write gleefully in his diary that he had been almost completely successful in halting the flow of all refugees.

The instrument employed to bring the flow of refugees to a halt may be labeled the security gambit. It involved a playing on the fear that Berlin had infiltrated the refugee stream with agents. Even Roosevelt contributed to the security panic by referring in a speech to the Trojan horse tactic by which the Nazis had ostensibly gained the upper hand in France. If Berlin had attempted to shore up its exchange balance by attempting to blackmail Jews, could one reasonably expect that they would forego the opportunity that the refugee stream offered to penetrate the security of the United States? A spate of Hollywood spy thrillers generously abetted that kind of thinking in the mind of the American public. As patently ludicrous as such fears were, it was difficult for rescue advocates to counteract them without placing in jeopardy their own credentials as loyal citizens. The Zionist thrust had generated apprehension about dual loyalties in the Jewish community, so that rescue advocates were perhaps too finely attuned to the loyalty question. In any case, the rescue agencies were completely overwhelmed by the security gambit. Even Stephen Wise assented to stricter visa controls in 1941. Men like Breckinridge Long took considerable pride when they looked back at their work. The rescue effort that began with such loud trumpeting seemed to have fizzled by mid-1941.

THE RESETTLEMENT DILEMMA

THE ABSORPTION OF MORE REFUGEES into the United States became an academic question once it became apparent that Hitler's scheme would ultimately involve all of European Jewry. The nub of the problem was from the beginning concerned with the possibility of finding and developing a suitable resettlement area. Few expected that over 10,000,000 Jews could be infiltrated into existing states. But the Evian conference had already demonstrated that a parallel reluctance existed for offering mass resettlement havens. The administration pressed for such schemes at the Washington conference of the officers of the IGC in October 1939. Roosevelt, playing his favorite role as statesman and amateur geographer, proposed to Paul Van Zeeland, the new head of the Coordinating Foundation, a grandiose plan for resettling millions. This – even as the French and the British were showing distressing signs that they would not be able to withstand the Nazi juggernaut and might soon themselves become candidates for refuge.

Perhaps the most interesting scheme generated by Roosevelt's enthusiasm was the Baruch-Hoover idea of establishing a United States of Africa, where all refugees would be accepted. Undaunted by the warnings of America's leading geographer, Isaiah Bowman, that mass resettlement of a highly urbanized group was chimerical, and forsaking the warnings of Myron Taylor that Jews did not welcome pioneering resettlement schemes, the administration pressed ahead with a plan to make Angola or perhaps Rhodesia into a refugee republic. America's own experience as a successful resettlement operation was too strong to overcome. While Roosevelt was focusing on Africa as the most likely place where new "huddled masses" could be settled, Whitehall was showing increasing interest in British Guiana in the American sphere. Neither side seemed particularly enthusiastic about committing its own sphere to resettlement. Roosevelt's enthusiasm showed a suspicious increase the further such resettlement schemes were away from home. When Harold Ickes pushed for resettlement in Alaska or the Virgin Islands, the idea was rejected by the administration.

The question of whether resettlement of European Jewry would work, an idea that Berlin, had also toyed with between 1939 and 1941, was never put to the test. The Wannsee conference held in the suburbs of Berlin in January 1942, came after Hitler had abandoned the idea that a solution by resettlement was possible. The "Statement of Agreement" came to naught, and the question of whether Berlin might have opted in favor of resettlement had such havens been made available remains to plague us today. Nazi preoccupation with a resettlement solution is hinted at by the camouflage terminology under which the Final Solution was carried out. How many Jews entered the cattle cars under the impression that they would be resettled somewhere in the East? Paradoxically, Berlin's decision for mass murder solved not only its Jewish problem but also the Allies' refugee problem. Each cattle car that rolled eastward meant that many fewer refugee clients.

*Secretary of the Treasury, *Ed.*

THE DEPARTMENT OF STATE AND AMERICAN JEWRY

THE CHIEF ARCHITECT of the State Department's rescue policy was Breckinridge Long. Little need be said about him except that his diary, housed in the Manuscript Division of the Library of Congress, can be read with great profit by a psychoanalyst. He viewed his fight against the refugees as primarily a battle against Jewish Communist agitators who were trying to ruin his political career. It was Long who directed the antialien battle in Congress through his friends Senators Richard Russell and Robert Reynolds and Congressman Martin Dies. One of Long's favorite tactics was simply to deny that there was a problem which concerned Jews specifically. As late as April 1943 the State Department used the term "political refugee," despite ample evidence that the Nazis talked of nothing but Jews. While Berlin was "converting" all its enemies, including Roosevelt, to the Jewish faith, the State Department was reconverting Jews to a bland category labeled "political refugees." To avoid having to submit to a more active rescue policy, all one had to do was to deny that the Final Solution existed. Like Berlin, the Roosevelt Administration early discovered the effectiveness of a camouflage terminology to disguise its real purpose or lack of it. The now well-known attempt by the State Department to suppress news of the Final Solution that emanated from Gerhart Riegner, agent of the World Jewish Congress in Bern, fits into the same category.

Of course, it was naïve to imagine that news of such a massive operation could be hidden indefinitely and ultimately, the attempt to do so boomeranged on the department. It was [Henry] Morgenthau's* file detailing the State Department's deliberate sabotage that went far in convincing Roosevelt to create a special board in 1944. By the final months of 1942, the lid was off, and news that a mass-murder operation was in progress shocked the Jewish community. The result was a protracted period of agitation by American Jewry, which was designed primarily to redirect the rescue effort into more active channels.

As in the first phase, American Jewry dissipated much of its formidable organizational resources in internal bickering, until it seemed that it was more anxious to tear itself apart than to rescue its coreligionists. This internal organizational deadlock in the American Jewish community had a negative effect on its ability to focus pressure on the administration. One might almost say that the paralytic reaction pattern noted by Hilberg for European Jewry had its American counterpart. Reading the various organizational positions today can be a frightening experience. That a community that desperately needed unity to operate nevertheless remained divided and thus was never able to speak to Roosevelt with one voice is no small tragedy. The issues that divided Jewry seem amazingly irrelevant today. They are too complex to go into here, but one can nevertheless wonder whether the organizations allowed themselves the luxury of fiddling while Jews burned.

Little attempt seemed to have been made to activate the numerous Jews who had won high places in the Roosevelt administration. The silence of the *shtadlanim* is one of the most puzzling aspects of the rescue story. It was not until Henry Morgenthau Jr., secretary of the treasury and Roosevelt's good friend, was drawn into the rescue effort that rescue advocates succeeded in removing it from the State Department, where sabotage and sheer bureaucratic viscosity had brought the effort to a virtual standstill. Sam Rosenman opposed certain resettlement schemes in 1941 because they smacked too much of a re-ghettoization of the Jews. There is almost no information in the archives on the activities of such men as Felix Frankfurter, David Lilienthal, Isador Lubin, Sidney Hillman, Herbert Lehman, and David Niles. Yet, they represented one of the keys to a more successful effort.

THE BERMUDA CONFERENCE

IN THE EARLY MONTHS OF 1943, public pressure to rescue Jews reached a crescendo. In New York's Madison Square Garden, a rally was held on March 1 under the motto "Stop Hitler Now." In London, the agitation was, if anything, even stronger because of the role of Whitehall's Palestine policy. It was this pressure that brought Anthony Eden to suggest, while visiting in Washington in March, that a new refugee

conference would go far in alleviating London's painful embarrassment. At first, the State Department was reluctant, but as the agitation increased, it saw the wisdom of the Eden gambit. Diplomatic preparations for a new refugee conference to be held in inaccessible Bermuda were begun.

There can be little doubt today that the primary objective of the Bermuda conference, which was held in April, was to deflect the growing agitation over rescue policy. The agenda, carefully prepared by Long, dealt exclusively with the problem of "political refugees." In 1943, that meant rescue of those who were already fortunate enough to be in the refugee stream and had perhaps found a precarious safety in Spain or North Africa. Those in the death camps were simply to be written off. Long, although he denied this at the November congressional hearings, specifically ruled out any attempt to negotiate with Berlin or the satellites through neutral intermediaries. Mostly, Long wanted to refurbish the IGC, an agency that had never really functioned after the outbreak of the war in 1939. Solomon Bloom, the Jewish chairman of the House Foreign Affairs Committee, was shrewdly selected to still the cry of rescue advocates. Later, he was tagged as the administration's *shabbes goy* (a non-Jew retained to perform tasks on the Sabbath forbidden to observant Jews) for allowing himself to be used in a conference that was generally acknowledged to be a callous mockery of the victims rather than an attempt to rescue them. The sheer malevolence in using such a tactic while a mass-murder operation was in progress served to intensify rather than to still the agitation among rescue advocates.

In the Jewish community, a new organization led by Peter Bergson and called the Emergency Committee to Save the Jewish People of Europe began to gain influence on the periphery of Jewish organizational life. It displayed a special flair for publicity and politics that made it the bane of the mainline organizations. Although it contributed to intensifying the organizational strife within American Jewry, it also succeeded in having introduced into Congress two rescue resolutions that sought to remove the rescue operation from the State Department and to create a new agency for that purpose. Hearings on the rescue resolutions were held in November. Breckinridge Long requested to be allowed to testify in executive session. It is difficult to account for the fiasco that followed. Long suffered severely from ulcers and hypertension, and the now-constant pressure on him emanating from "the radical boys" may have caused him to lose his usual aplomb. He presented the committee with a vastly exaggerated figure of the number of refugees admitted and insisted, despite his own well-known strictures, that the IGC had plenary power to negotiate with the enemy through an intermediary. When the testimony became known, rescue advocates became aware that Long himself had given them all the evidence necessary to prove that deliberate procrastination on rescue had been the policy of the State Department. With the help of Congressman Emmanuel Cellar and others, Long's role was publicly exposed. It became the lever by which he was finally pried from continuing in his key rescue post.

CHANGING THE RESCUE GROUND RULES

IT WAS MORGENTHAU who delivered the *coup de grâce*. He carried a carefully collected file of evidence on the State Department's sabotage, giving special prominence to the deliberate attempt to squelch news of the Final Solution, to Roosevelt. In January 1944, the president startled rescue advocates by announcing the establishment of the War Refugee Board. Headed by John Pehle, an assistant secretary and director of the Foreign Funds Control Division of the Treasury, the new agency was in fact, if not in theory, almost exclusively a Treasury Department operation; and its charter, which gave it special powers, followed generally along the lines recommended by the private rescue agencies.

An energetic rescue operation was initiated employing not only the fragile underground apparatus in occupied Europe but also developing new techniques in psychological warfare that would prove particularly successful in the satellites. The establishment of the WRB was followed in June by a second breakthrough on the heretofore frozen immigration front. The administration adopted a scheme of temporary havens for refugees. The momentum for the idea,

which was as old as the rescue effort itself, was furnished by Samuel Grafton, the syndicated columnist for the *New York Post*, who dubbed the idea "free ports." Using the clever analogy of comparing such interned refugees as having the same status as goods awaiting transshipment, the refugees accepted would simply not be registered as immigrants because they would be interned here temporarily until they could be sent back to their country of origin. Paradoxically, the legal precedent was furnished by an action of Breckinridge Long, who in the throes of the security psychosis, had accepted for internment thousands of unfriendly aliens from Latin America outside the quota system. The adoption of free ports, while it circumvented the immigration law only symbolically, marks the high-water mark of the American rescue effort.

When the victory did come, it had rather an empty taste. More than 4,000,000 Jews were already in ashes, and until an effective instrument could be fashioned to save Hungarian Jewry, over 1,000,000 additional Jews would lose their lives. The four years that it had taken to remove the operation from the State Department were crucial. The time lost could not be regained, nor could the dead be brought back to life.

ANALYSIS: NEGATIVE

FURNISHED WITH A BRIEF DESCRIPTION of what transpired within the Roosevelt administration during the Holocaust years, we are now prepared to make some general observations and draw some conclusions, not about victims but about third parties.

We begin by observing that after the failure of the first phase of the rescue effort, which, as we have seen, contributed to Berlin's decision to liquidate European Jewry, the possibility of large-scale rescue became more remote. In a sense, the battle was lost in the first round. After January 1942, it would have taken an inordinate passion to save lives, a huge reservoir of good-will to achieve mass rescue. Such good-will was not forthcoming. There was no crisis of will; there was simply an absence of it. The energy and organization that went into the administration's rescue effort, even after the establishment of the WRB, never remotely approached the expenditure Berlin was willing to make to see the Final Solution through to the bitter end. Even after Miklós Horthy's amazing offer to halt the deportation of Hungarian Jewry in July 1944 and Heinrich Himmler's remarkable change of mind, there was an Adolf Eichmann to make certain that the ovens of Auschwitz were well stocked. The operation of the Final Solution had achieved a momentum of its own in 1944 that not even Berlin could stop.

Once it is understood that rescue required a commitment and a price that Roosevelt was unwilling or unable to make, the puzzling activities of the administration become comprehensible. Roosevelt and many in the administration wanted to rescue Jews – if only the price were not so high and the possibility so remote. In the absence of active measures, humanitarian rhetoric was substituted for action. Virtually every action taken before the establishment of the WRB – the Evian and Bermuda conferences, the search for resettlement areas, the liberalization of the visa procedures, and even the establishment of a temporary refugee haven in Oswego, New York, in August 1944 – should be viewed as humanitarian gestures without serious intention of carrying them through. There is a double irony here; for although London and Berlin soon learned to dismiss the American initiative as a political gesture made for domestic consumption, American Jewry rarely directly questioned the sincerity of Roosevelt. They preferred to attack the State Department, which was being used by Roosevelt as a foil. It was one of the few instances in which Roosevelt found some use for the department. Roosevelt, in fact, had been fully briefed on the rescue issue and knew precisely what was happening. Like all love, the Jewish "love affair" with the New Deal showed a distressing tendency to be blind.

Then, there is the question of Breckinridge Long. I have never heard historians attribute anything to simple *finster mazel* (black luck), but here is certainly a case that deserves examination. Long, an early admirer of Hitler and Mussolini, a charter member of the American version of the Cliveden set, came to head the special Problems Division of the State Department almost by accident. He actually was consid-

ered as a possible replacement for Joseph Kennedy in London or for Hugh Wilson in Berlin. It was the caprice of this single individual that could make the difference between life and death. He was utterly devoted to foiling the rescue effort and was everywhere successful until Morgenthau was activated as a countervailing force within the administration. During the seventy-sixth, seventy-seventh, and seventy-eighth Congresses, dozens of antialien bills were introduced, which had the effect of reinforcing Roosevelt's sensitivity to the restrictionist element in Congress. Roosevelt thought his hands were tied by the continued strength of the restrictionists; and in case he forgot, Long was always there to remind him because Long himself was on very friendly terms with this group and able to suggest to them the legislation he considered necessary to plug the loopholes in the immigration law. Much of the initiative for the alien registration and other security laws emanated from Long.

Roosevelt, of course, had other problems besides the real or imagined strength of the restrictionists. He was a superb politician and prided himself on his fine political touch. His political antennae were astute, and when the label "Jew Deal" began to be heard across the land, he may have overreacted. Roosevelt was reputed to have appointed more Jews to high places than any previous president. He had stuck his political neck out for the appointment of Felix Frankfurter to the Supreme Court. But the "Jew Deal" label nettled and had its effect on the rescue initiative. The rescue of a foreign minority, whose coreligionists in the United States were not overly popular, represented a distinct political risk. The "political refugee" label, which gave Berlin considerable help in disguising the nature of the Final Solution, may have been maintained to avoid an overclose association with a Jewish problem and, therefore, not prove counterproductive for rescue purposes. In 1938, there was in fact a sizable minority of non-Jews in the refugee stream, so that this policy had some justification. But Roosevelt continued to insist on the interdenominational image even when it was clearly no longer feasible. Thus, when Rublee returned to the White House with the Statement of Agreement, Roosevelt expressed regret at the specific mention of the unmentionable – Jews. Before he made public his intention to establish a temporary haven in Oswego, Robert Murphy, his agent in North Africa, was given specific instructions to select a "good ethnic mix." One may read the memoranda in the State Department archives on the Holocaust and never know that the whole tragic business had something to do with Jews.

Less explicable is the administration's reluctance to use psychological warfare techniques, such as threats of retribution. A statement by Washington that the massive raid on Hamburg in July 1943 was in retribution for Treblinka or Auschwitz would have contributed substantially to opening a dialogue on the Final Solution. As it was, the cattle cars rolled to Auschwitz amidst an eerie silence. Crimes against Jews were consistently omitted from war-crime statements. Not until March 1944 could Roosevelt be prevailed upon to make some correction in the Moscow statement on war crimes, which promised dire vengeance for crimes against Cretan peasants but not specifically against Jews. Ostensibly, the silence was maintained for fear that such threats would actually lead to a Nazi escalation of terror. Berlin, it was believed, was fully capable of exacting retribution on the people of occupied Europe for what was being done to her from the air. It was a game in which Berlin held all the cards. But for European Jewry, at least, one is hard pressed to imagine what greater terror than Auschwitz might have been conceived. And the consequences of the policy of silence were tragic. Men like Joseph Goebbels fully believed that the Allies approved or were at least indifferent to the fate of the Jews. When one reads Anthony Eden's reference to "surplus people" in the State Department archives or Lord Moyne's infamous reply to Joel Brand when informed about the possibility of rescuing the Jews of Hungary ("Save a million Jews? What shall we do with them? Where shall we put them?"), Goebbels was after all not so far off the mark. At one point, for example, Breckinridge Long argued vehemently against relief shipments to the camps because that would relieve Berlin of this responsibility and thus help their war effort.

Bombing the crematoria and the rail networks leading to the camps would have gone even further in making clear Allied opposition to genocide. More im-

portant, it could have disrupted the actual killing process, which was everywhere dependent on a fragile coordination between available transportation and the capacity of the crematoria. But here, too, there was a strange reluctance to proceed. John J. McCloy, then assistant secretary of war, dismissed a joint request by the World Jewish Congress and the WRB to bomb the crematoria on the grounds that he could not divert needed air power on projects of such "doubtful efficacy." Moreover, it might "provoke even more vindictive action by the Germans." The refusal to consider such bombings marks a separate calamity within the larger tragedy of the Holocaust. The Hungarian rescue case establishes beyond doubt that the mere threat of bombing that emanated from within Hungarian underground sources was sufficient to frighten Budapest half to death and was instrumental in leading to the halting of the deportations. The satellites were sensitive barometers to how the winds of victory were blowing. After Stalingrad (February 1943), the need to dissociate themselves from the Final Solution must have been fairly apparent.

A word should be added concerning the role of American Jewry. When the catastrophe descended, the deep fissures between its "uptown" and "downtown" elements had barely been bridged. Jews, anxious above all to move into the mainstream of American life, did not accept the mantle of leadership, ensconced for centuries in Europe, with alacrity. American Jewry was divided and hesitant about exerting pressure through its *shtadlanim*. One has only to read Long's description of the numerous Jewish delegations, each representing another set of clients, to realize how tragic its posture was. It is, of course, easy to talk from hindsight. The role that fell to American Jewry was a difficult, perhaps an impossible, one to fulfill. They had the unenviable task of trying to change the administration's rescue ground rules, which were frozen solid by an immigration law thought immutable, and which, incidentally, a majority of American Jews had supported in 1938. They had to counteract a hysterical fear of the prowess of German espionage. No hyphenate group had ever been faced with the prospect of total annihilation of its European brethren, and although there was great urgency to use its influence, the instruments for doing so had to be developed from scratch. Moreover, the delivery of a voting bloc, the most potent weapon in any political arsenal, was practically denied to the Jewish leadership. The Jewish "love affair" with Roosevelt had, in contrast to other ethnic groups, become more ardent after the election of 1936. Jewish leadership could not gain leverage by threatening the withdrawal of votes and, therefore, was forced to depend on the less-certain rewards for political loyalty. As in the international arena, American Jewry lacked political organization and power. Jews loved the New Deal because of its humanitarianism, and ironically, it would be Jews who would require most evidence of its authenticity. For the most part, this evidence was denied to them. The most interesting facet of Arthur Morse's *While Six Million Died* is that he still reads the New Deal as did the Jews of the thirties. Most of American Jewry still does. The assumption is that the New Deal, *especially* the New Deal, ought to have been able to make a more humane response to the Holocaust. It is forgotten that there was the internment of the Japanese, an action that bears some parallels to Berlin's treatment of the Jews.

Something needs to be said also about the posture of American Zionism. Its startling growth as the catastrophe reached its apogee led its leaders to believe that the Jewish community should be unified under its auspices. But other organizations stubbornly refused to follow the Zionist lead and protected their organizational integrity against a real or imagined assault. For the Zionists, the rescue issue posed a special dilemma. The emergency had given the old territorialists a renewed lease on life. Roosevelt, we have seen, was specially taken with visionary resettlement schemes. For Zionists, a national homeland in Palestine was so clearly the answer to the refugee-rescue problem that to consider resettlement elsewhere was viewed as criminal heresy. The merest suggestion by the Bergson group that the rescue goal and the national commonwealth goal were working at cross purposes to the detriment of both, brought storms of invective from the Zionist leadership. Yet, a decision to divert some support to resettlement schemes outside of Palestine might have made a difference. The Zionist movement had, after all, fashioned the only major successful mass resettlement experiment in the

twentieth century. It possessed the zeal and the pioneering skill that would have helped overcome the serious demographic difficulties that interfered with resettlement elsewhere. Many more might have been rescued had there been more Sosuas, and more Sosuas might have been developed in Latin America had there existed an ability to pioneer. For the Zionists, the decision was an agonizing one. Resettlement outside Palestine was even under the most favorable circumstances only remotely possible, while, in contrast, the *Yishuv** was firmly established. Palestine was the logical area for resettlement, they reasoned, and to divert funds and energy from it would have been a liability to the pioneering operation. An agonizing choice had to be made. There were not enough resources and energy to do both; and yet, for mass rescue to become a reality, not only would both have had to take place but, in addition, a massive campaign to encourage infiltration to established states would also have been necessary. The Zionist movement made the only choice it could make and in doing so left itself open to the charge of complicity.

Unfortunately, the strife between Zionist and other groups did not remain merely academic. The makeshift, largely Zionist-organized rescue operation that had been established on the periphery of Nazi Europe was often plagued by bickering between the different agents. Almost always the issue was who should get the credit for rescuing the handful that were brought out. The bitter recriminations that could be heard in Lisbon, Ankara, Stockholm, and even Bern possess an irony all their own; for although Berlin endlessly projected a picture of a well-coordinated international Jewish conspiracy, the rescuers were plagued by questions of which Jews should be saved and who should get the credit.

MITIGATING CONSIDERATIONS

OUR PICTURE WOULD BE INCOMPLETE if the mitigating circumstances that contributed to the failure of the Roosevelt administration to become a more energetic rescue agent were not given mention. Some of the realities of the American political scene during the war have already been described, and the crucial impor-

*Hebrew word for the Jewish community in Palestine, *Ed.*

tance of the rescue failure between 1938 and 1942 has been highlighted. Between 1942 and 1944, the possibility of mass rescue was severely circumscribed by Berlin, so that one can give no assurance, even had Washington acted, that the Final Solution could have been entirely prevented. Two variables were never under Allied control: Nazi determination to liquidate European Jewry and physical control of the scene of the depredations. The potential for rescue varied from country to country and was dependent on the degree of Nazi control. Jews directly under the Nazi heel, like those in the *général-gouvernement*, had far less opportunity for rescue than those living in the co-belligerent states like Italy and Hungary or favorite satellites like Denmark. One is hard pressed, for example, to discover a way in which the Jewish community of Poland might have been rescued even under the most fortuitous circumstances.

Admittedly, one feels wary about quibbling over legal technicalities when an operation of mass murder is in question, but there can be little doubt that legal questions played a crucial role in the posture of the third parties. Arthur Morse assumed that the Roosevelt administration was not true to its humanitarian precepts when it undertook only a listless rescue effort. Even if this assumption about the New Deal were fully acceptable, it would have only a peripheral significance as far as mass rescue of European Jewry is concerned. Few nation-states are able to muster concern about the fate of a foreign minority. They have enough trouble making human responses to their own minority problems. On the foreign scene, nation-states, if they do have souls at all, are probably more demonic than saintly. We tend to forget that even the American government under Roosevelt was a human-made institution, not human itself. It had no natural soul and little concern about morality. But things were entirely different when there was a clear legal responsibility to do something. Hungary did protect Hungarian Jews living in France from deportation and even protested their having to wear the telltale yellow star. Turkey and Spain gave similar protection to their Jews. The American government went to considerable lengths to protect the property of American Jews in Germany. When the nation-state had a clear legal responsibility, it could act. Some-

times, the knowledge of this possibility could be used for rescue. Often, Latin American legal papers made the difference between life and death, for, paradoxically, even the Nazis in the midst of their bloody operations retained certain legal niceties.

Perhaps, if a broader segment of the American people had joined in the agitation, the Roosevelt administration might have responded sooner. But here, too, rescue advocates were persistently stymied by a failure to gain credibility. The idea that a mass-murder operation, using modern production techniques, was in progress simply beggared the imagination. It played havoc not only with the victims, who could not bring themselves to believe the unbelievable, but with the rescue agents as well. How does one react to such a datum except by asking over and over again whether it is true? A Roper poll taken in December 1944 showed that the great majority of Americans, although willing to believe that Hitler had killed some Jews, could not accept the idea that a mass-murder operation in which millions had died, had occurred. Apparently, there is such a thing as a saturation point as far as atrocity stories are concerned. In the American mind, the Final Solution took its place beside the Bataan death march and the Malmédy massacre, in which seventy US prisoners of war were killed by Germans. It was just another atrocity in a particularly cruel war. It was a supremely difficult task to break through the curtain of disbelief, and the role of the State Department in suppressing the details of the story did not make the task easier.

Then, too, the Roosevelt administration was but one of many components that had to be activated for a successful mass-rescue operation. There were also the Vatican, the Committee of the International Red Cross (CIRC), the neutrals, the other Allied governments, the governments-in-exile, and the people in the occupied areas. A more energetic leadership from Washington would have invigorated the flagging rescue effort, but no one can be certain to what extent. All maintained their own measure of commitment and did not necessarily follow Washington's lead, that was especially true in the case of resettlement in the Latin American republics, the unsuccessful Taylor mission to the Vatican, and the failure to activate fully the International Red Cross until mid-1944. In the case of the Vatican and the CIRC, even after Washington stopped saying "do as I say, not as I do," the two rescue components remained reluctant to participate fully. The existence of so many independent components made for problems of coordination and unity. The IGC, which was established after the Evian conference, was supposed to furnish such coordination, but, as we have seen, it became instead the first casualty of the general lack of will and ultimately was used by the State Department and Whitehall as a foil for rescue. The early rescue effort was literally strangled in a sea of red tape, which itself was a reflection of the lack of will. The classic example of this is the diplomatic game played between Britain and the United States over the resettlement question. They played a game that might be called "who has the moral onus now?" The need to have a collective effort meant in practice that no one really felt the responsibility to do anything. Collective failure, like collective guilt, has an allure all its own. It is far easier to bear.

Finally, even if all the problems that beset the rescue effort had been magically solved – if Breckinridge Long had been converted to the cause of rescue, if London had abandoned its inhumanely political attitude toward Palestine, if the divisions within American Jewry had been healed, if the pope had spoken out, if the CIRC had had been more courageous in interpreting its role – we still have no guarantee that mass rescue could have been realized. Certainly, more might have been saved, especially in the satellites. Something like such a miracle took place in Hungary in 1944: virtually all the components of a complete rescue effort were fully activated. Yet, within full view of the world and when Berlin knew that the war was lost, the cattle cars rolled to Auschwitz as if they had a momentum all their own. Over half of Hungary's Jewish community went up in smoke.

Apparently, even the passionate will to save lives was not enough. Something else was also required, something to soften the hearts of those in Berlin who were in physical control of the slaughter. The production of such a miracle was never in the hands of the Washington policymakers. Perhaps it was in the realm of a higher kingdom. Its strange indifference has become the overriding preoccupation of the theologians.

Note

1. *Proceedings of the Intergovernmental Committee,* Evian, July 6–15, 1938.

Renee Haase, a displaced child in Shanghai. Circa 1947. (Lutz Haase, courtesy of USHMM Photo Archives)

Lutz Haase was born in Wrzesnia, Germany in February 1914. After World War I, Wrzesnia became part of Poland. Lutz's parents chose to remain German citizens and they moved with their son first to Nuremberg and later to Berlin. Lutz was arrested during the November Pogrom, November 10, 1938, and sent to Oranienburg concentration camp, where he was assigned to a labor group. After two years of hard labor, too weak to continue working, he was condemned to an underground bunker where few survived for more than a day. Just before the execution of this death sentence, he was approached by SS Obergruppenstürmführer Heinz Schultz, a former art school classmate, who remembered that Haase had given him advice on stamp collecting. Schultz enabled Haase to leave both the camp and the country.

On October 22, 1940, the day Berlin was bombed for the first time, Haase traveled by train from Berlin to Moscow; there he took the Transiberian train to Manchuria. He settled in Shanghai, where he worked with the Allied underground and served as a member of the civil guard protecting Shanghai residents. He also ran a bookbinding business and print shop and he got married. He and his wife Margot had a daughter, Renee, in Shanghai in 1945. The family left Shanghai for Canada in 1949.

Helga Kreiner, a little girl who was a member of the first *Kindertransport* from Germany, clutches her doll while waiting in a lounge after her arrival in Harwich, England. Between December 1938 and September 1939, close to ten thousand unaccompanied refugee children from central Europe were permitted entry into Great Britain. They arrived in a series of transports that came to be known as the *Kindertransports*. Seventy percent of these children were Jewish and were chosen by the central Jewish organizations in Germany, Austria, and Czechoslovakia. December 2, 1938. (Bibliotheque Historique de la Ville de Paris, courtesy of USHMM Photo Archives)

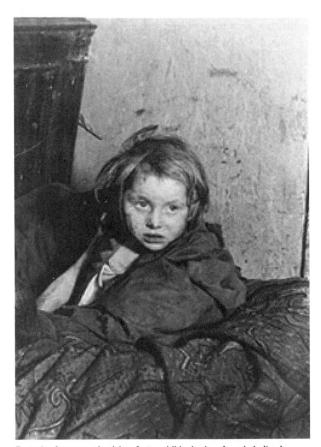

Portrait of a young Jewish refugee child who has found shelter in Mukachevo (former Soviet Union). (Roman Vishniac *Mukachevo*, 1938 (detail) Gelatin silver print Collection of the International Center of Photography © Mara Vishniac Kohn, courtesy the International Center of Photography)

DAVID S. WYMAN **The Abandonment of the Jews**

PAPER WALLS AND PAPER PLANS

STATE DEPARTMENT POLICYMAKERS planned the Bermuda Conference in part to help check pressures for increased immigration to the United States. They also intended it to inject enough life into the Intergovernmental Committee to make it appear capable of taking over responsibility for the refugee problem. What were the State Department's immigration policies? What roles did the Intergovernmental Committee assume? Both questions are important to understanding America's response to the Holocaust.

Paper Walls: American Visa Policies

In 1938, increased German persecution of the Jews led President Roosevelt to ease the extremely restrictive immigration policy of the Great Depression and open the European quotas for full use. This step did not, however, set off mass migration to the United States, for the combined quotas of the affected countries amounted to under 40,000 per year. Furthermore, in mid-1940 the policy was reversed. Claiming the Nazis were infiltrating secret agents into the refugee stream and forcing some authentic refugees to spy for Germany, Breckinridge Long, with the cooperation of the Visa Division, suddenly tightened the requirements for entry. This step slashed admissions by half.[1]

In July 1941, refugee immigration was cut again, to about 25 percent of the relevant quotas. Behind this decline was the "relatives rule," a State Department regulation stipulating that any applicant with a parent, child, spouse, or sibling remaining in German, Italian, or Russian territory had to pass an extremely strict security test to obtain a visa. The State Department explained that cases had come to light of Nazi and Soviet agents pressuring refugees to engage in espionage under threat of retaliation against their relatives.[2]

Another innovation in July 1941 required a systematic security review of *all* immigration applications by special interdepartmental committees. (Each committee included representatives of the Visa Division, the Immigration and Naturalization Service, the FBI, Army Intelligence, and Naval Intelligence.) Applications that received unfavorable recommendations from the special committees were rejected. For favorably recommended cases, the State Department sent "advisory approvals" to its visa-issuing consuls abroad. Normally, the consuls then granted the visas. But they were not required to do so; legally, the final decision was theirs.[3]

The President's Advisory Committee on Political Refugees met with Roosevelt to protest the sweeping new policies. It requested substantial modification of the "relatives rule" and the establishment of a review board to reevaluate cases rejected by the interdepartmental committees. No meaningful change was made in the "relatives rule," but a complex appeal process was instituted in December 1941.[4]

Under the new system, cases turned down by the interdepartmental committees were considered by Review Committees consisting of higher officials from the same five agencies represented on the original committees. The applicants' American sponsors were permitted to testify in person before the Review Committees. Cases rejected by the Review Committees went to the Board of Appeals, which consisted of two private citizens appointed by the President. If a Review Committee or the Board of Appeals ruled favorably, the State Department dispatched advisory approval to the consul nearest the applicant.[5]

After Pearl Harbor, visa procedures were even more stringently tightened for a large category of refugees, those who had been born in enemy countries or had been longtime residents there. Visa applications for these "enemy aliens" had to pass through all three security-screening levels. In addition, no enemy alien could receive a visa without proof that his admission would bring "positive benefit" to the United States.*[6]

Strict enforcement of these regulations led to severe difficulties for many refugees. A mother and her twelve-year-old daughter were stranded in Vichy, France. The father, an Austrian, was in Cairo with the Allied military forces. The mother was an American citizen and wanted to take the daughter to safety in the United States. But the girl could not obtain a visa because her Austrian birth made her an enemy alien.[8]

Another incident involved a German refugee in France, who was sent to Auschwitz in the great deportations of 1942. Her visa had been approved in Washington in November 1941. But before she received it, the United States entered the war, and as an enemy alien she had to begin the procedure all over again. In October 1942, a Unitarian Service Committee report noted, "In spite of what seemed to be a favorable reception of her case when it was presented by her niece in Washington, the visa was refused and this meant her case could not be reopened for six months. There was nothing we could do. A few days ago came word of her deportation."[9]

By early 1942, private refugee-aid organizations had recognized that State Department stringency regarding visa issuance far surpassed legitimate concern for protecting the nation from subversion. Their observations were summarized by George Warren of the President's Advisory Committee, who described the immigration process as "one of incredible obstruction to any possible securing of a visa." He had earlier disclosed the source of arbitrary exclusion of refugees as "a group in the State Department . . . which of itself sets up new tests for immigration visas."†[10]

During 1943, it became clear to the private agencies, through their day-to-day contacts with the Visa Division concerning refugee cases, that the State Department had gone beyond the law in blocking immigration. The agencies did not publicize the point, for that would have ended their effectiveness in dealing with the State Department. They did press quietly, but unsuccessfully, for modification. And they recorded the situation in numerous documents still in their archives. In January, Warren pointed to a persistent effort to shut the doors, which he attributed to anti-alien attitudes in the State Department. He noted that "conditions are becoming tougher all the time" for obtaining American visas, especially for refugees in Spain. (At that time, German occupation of Spain looked quite possible.) Four months later, Warren confirmed that State Department opposition to refugee entry remained strong. By December 1943, he saw nearly no hope for much further immigration. He described it as "almost a frozen situation." A representative of the American Friends Service Committee reported a discussion he had with top officials of the Visa Division: "Everybody was very polite, but the resistance to be overcome is evidently enormous." The records of the National Refugee Service, a leading Jewish aid agency, reveal continual anxiety about "the anti-immigration attitude of the State Department."[11]

Alongside official regulations such as the "relatives rule" and the special requirements for enemy aliens, the State Department raised additional obstacles. One was the unnecessarily long time, usually around nine months, required to move applications through the screening machinery. For those in the enemy-alien category, the wait was longer and approval unlikely. Furthermore, even when an applicant faced immediate danger, the State Department would not expedite the case.[12]

Another bureaucratic wall was the visa application form put into effect in July 1943. More than *four feet* long, it had to be filled out on both sides by one of the refugee's sponsors (or a refugee-aid agency), sworn under penalty of perjury, and submitted in six copies. It required detailed information not only about the refugee but also about the two American sponsors who were needed to testify that he would present no danger to the United States. Each sponsor had to list his own residences and employers for the preceding ten years and submit character references from two reputable American citizens whose own past activities could be readily checked.[13]

Two entirely arbitrary barriers were added in the fall of 1943. The presumption that a refugee was "not in acute danger" began to enter into visa refusals. Persons who had reached Spain, Portugal, and North

---

*At about the same time, the State Department persuaded Latin American governments to halt nearly all immigration from Europe. The reason given was the need to safeguard hemispheric security. Yet the department's information sources had no reports of Nazi agents or subversive activities among refugees in Latin America.[7]

†Warren, who worked closely with several of the private organizations, also held a post in the State Department. He was a person of measured opinions who normally gave the State Department the benefit of the doubt.

Africa were considered to be in that category. This arrangement permitted the State Department to close the doors at will. Where Jews *were* in acute danger, in Axis-held territory, there were no American consuls to issue visas. But those who escaped to countries where consuls continued to operate were "not in acute danger" and for that reason could be kept out of the United States.[14]

After agreement was reached to establish a refugee camp in North Africa (but many months before it opened), the State Department attached a new restriction to some advisory approvals sent to consuls in Spain. It stipulated that a visa would be granted, but only if the refugee could not be included with those going to the camp. A Quaker representative in Lisbon reported that this step "practically suspended the granting of visas" to refugees in Spain.[15]

The State Department also plugged any holes the refugee-aid organizations might find in the barricades. In 1943, Quaker and HIAS* personnel in Casablanca attempted to open a refugee outlet through that port. Despite the State Department's unremitting insistence that American ships were totally occupied in the war effort and could not possibly assist in moving refugees, the relief workers discovered that the military authorities in Casablanca thought otherwise. They were willing to take refugees on ships returning empty to the United States, provided they had visas and quota numbers. The American consulate in Casablanca agreed to cooperate. Fourteen refugees reached New York via military transport. Then the State Department's Visa Division halted this apparent breakthrough by refusing to dispatch quota numbers for people in North Africa until after they had assurance of transportation. The military in North Africa would not assure transportation until the refugees had their quota numbers. "So there we are," concluded a frustrated relief worker in Casablanca.[16]

Another tactic was used to hamper the prospects of reactivated visa cases. Unsuccessful visa applications were eligible for reconsideration six months after rejection. But the State Department would never give reasons for the original refusals. Sponsors and refugee-aid agencies were thus left to guess at how to revise the applications. Should one or both of the sponsors be changed? Were the financial guarantees insufficient? Or was the difficulty something unalterable, such as the applicant's birth in Germany? The private agencies expended considerable effort – with little success – trying to fathom State Department reasoning and to adapt reapplications to it.[17]

A constant obstacle to refugee admission was prejudice on the part of many members of the security-screening committees. The Review Committees openly displayed biased attitudes in the hearings they were required to grant to applicants' sponsors. An official of the National Refugee Service described these interviews as "a pretty bad experience, as some are very strictly prejudiced about letting anyone in." The Friends Committee learned that, frequently,

> time is consumed heckling and questioning the affiant [sponsor] on his own personal affairs, his habits, the books he reads, his activities and friends, while the Board fails to learn the important facts regarding the prospective immigrant.

The Review Committees also concentrated excessively on possible Communist or other leftist connections of the sponsors.[18]

Reliable people who testified before Review Committees as sponsors of refugees reported being asked:

> Are you Jewish by race and faith?
> Do you belong to any political group or organization in this country?
> Have you read Tolstoy?
> Did the Social Democratic Party want to change the government?
> Would you call yourself a socialist?
> What are your political convictions now?

Some questions astonished the sponsors, as in this incident reported by Dorothy Detzer, executive secretary of the Women's International League for Peace and Freedom:

> There was a Czech soldier who was at Dunkirk. His wife was in Southern France. When the British evacuated, he went with them and is now

---

*Hebrew Sheltering and Immigrant Aid Society, a foremost Jewish migrant-assistance agency.

in England. His mother-in-law is in the United States and is trying to get a visa for her daughter who is still in France, and the military man on the committee asked: "Well, when your son-in-law left Dunkirk with the English, why didn't he get his wife to come up from Southern France to go with him?"[19]

The private agencies concluded that several members of the screening committees were "making absurd interpretations of facts in individual cases." The President's Advisory Committee checked and found that representatives of the FBI and Army and Navy intelligence were especially difficult, seemingly following a "policy of excluding all the aliens that they can." But repeated efforts both to rectify this bias and to improve the conduct of the hearings achieved nothing.[20]

One moderating influence in the visa-screening system was the Board of Appeals. Its original members were Dr. Frederick P. Keppel, formerly president of the Carnegie Corporation, and Robert J. Bulkley, previously a senator from Ohio. Keppel, especially, worked hard to move the visa system away from excessive suspiciousness and toward the tradition of America as a haven for the oppressed. But the possibilities were limited, as Keppel noted in a memorandum regarding such talented refugees as scientists, writers, artists, scholars, and dramatists:

> Case after case comes to our Board, with the unanimous recommendation of the Interdepartmental Review Committee, to exclude an applicant of the type I have in mind on the basis of vague and unsubstantiated charges of communistic, or less often, Nazi sympathies on the part of the applicant or his sponsors. We can and do reverse some of these recommendations, . . . but we are naturally reluctant to run our percentage of reversals too high.

The Board of Appeals overruled about one-quarter of the negative recommendations made by the Review Committees.[21]

Case notes left by the Board of Appeals reveal some of the reasoning behind Review Committee de-

cisions. One person was disapproved because he was born in Germany, although he had not been there for thirty years. A Socialist was rejected because a Review Committee saw an important similarity between Socialists and Communists. Another applicant was turned down because of a negative security report on a sponsor; but the sponsor was working for the Office of Strategic Services.[22]

The Board of Appeals managed to remove one obstacle from the path of visa applicants. Regulations stated that no enemy alien could be admitted without proof that his presence would be of "positive benefit" to the United States. Keppel and Bulkley opened the way for virtually any upright refugee to pass this test. They ruled that "the Board found benefit in maintaining the traditional American policy of providing a haven of refuge for decent people who are in distress and peril." Until his death, in September 1943, Keppel persisted in efforts to offset the anti-immigration bias that prevailed in the visa decision machinery.[23]

In mid-1944, visa procedures were simplified a little. In May, the State Department set up a new committee to screen the cases of applicants who were not enemy aliens. If a file contained "no derogatory information" and the new committee made a favorable recommendation, an advisory approval went directly to the consul, bypassing all three regular review committees. In July, a briefer application form was instituted. These changes expedited visa decisions. But refugee immigration did not increase. The modifications, though they made the procedure less onerous, were superficial.[24]

In justifying its stringent restrictions, the State Department stressed the necessity of keeping subversive elements out of the United States. The nation's security was, of course, essential. But the problem as it related to refugees was greatly exaggerated.

Nazi agents infiltrated among the refugees would have been found out and exposed by the many anti-Nazis who accompanied them. This did not have to be left to chance either. It was suggested at the time that applicants could be screened by committees of refugees, either overseas or in American detention centers. Questionable cases would go through more complete investigation. The Unitarian Service Committee, in fact, did this on its own in Lisbon.

Refugees who came to the Unitarians for help in reaching the United States were screened by two Germans who, as former prisoners of the Nazis, were familiar with Gestapo methods.[25]

The other danger cited by the State Department was that the Nazis would force genuine refugees to spy for Germany under threat of harm to close relatives still in Axis territory. Keppel, Bulkley, and their legal adviser, Dean F. D. G. Ribble of the University of Virginia Law School, exposed the fallacy of that argument:

It does not seem likely that hostage pressure can be used as an effective means of compelling anti-Nazis in the United States actively to serve the Nazi cause. The reason lies in the simple fact that such service ordinarily would necessitate collaboration on the part of Nazi agents. That collaboration, even though it might not completely reveal the identity of a Nazi agent, would necessarily give a clue to his identity. The anti-Nazi subjected to pressure and necessarily filled with hate of the Nazi power might readily turn his knowledge over to the proper American authorities. In other words, the chance that Nazi agents will disclose themselves by their use of hostage pressure to make persons in the United States cooperate in Nazi plans seems so great that a realistic appraisal indicates such methods would scarcely be used.[26]

It is not possible to analyze the information that government agencies collected about refugees suspected of subversive intentions. Intelligence records concerning private individuals are not available for research. But the examples that appear in State Department and other sources are exceedingly few and not convincing.[27]

In one celebrated case, a Jewish refugee arrested in Cuba possessed plans of a U.S. air base near Havana. The Cuban court, however, declared the plans valueless and found no connection with German operatives. Occasionally, American military intelligence abroad sent back reports of Axis agents disguised as refugees. But in the instances found in the records, all impostors were detected and dealt with overseas.[28]

Two German brothers, refugees who reached North Africa, applied for American visas. Despite the endorsement of American officials in the area, the support of the Quakers and the Joint Distribution Committee*, and a clean report from American military intelligence in North Africa, the applications were turned down in Washington. The difficulty was a statement by the French administration in North Africa that the two might possibly be spies. This suspicion had arisen because a person with a grudge against one of the brothers had denounced them to French authorities. On such evidence, people were judged dangerous and kept out of the United States.[29]

A report by the U.S. Office of Censorship regarding three highly reputable Jewish refugee-aid organizations – the Joint Distribution Committee, HIAS, and HICEM (the European affiliate of HIAS) – reveals some of the ignorance and dubious logic that fed State Department suspicions. The Censorship Office disclosed that "it is reliably reported" that HICEM "is extensively used by the Germans as a medium through which agents can be placed in any part of the world." This unsubstantiated assertion was contravened in the same report by a statement that British intelligence in Bermuda, which closely monitored HICEM-HIAS messages, was not suspicious. Yet the writer concluded that, because the Joint Distribution Committee and HIAS had close ties with HICEM, "it necessarily follows" that they "have been used in the same manner" and should be viewed "with no less suspicion."[30]

The chance that a refugee, or a Nazi agent disguised as a refugee, could have successfully carried out subversive activities once in the United States was extremely small. The American government was highly effective in controlling Nazi espionage and sabotage during World War II. In the famous case of the eight saboteurs landed by U-boats on Long Island and the Florida coast in June 1942, detection and capture came shortly after their arrival. The Nazis had no more success with the spy Herbert Bahr, an American citizen whom they sent to the United States on the exchange ship *Drottningholm*. Planted among other Americans being repatriated from Germany, Bahr was arrested before he left the ship. Throughout the war, reports by the attorney general and the FBI empha-

*Also known as the American Jewish Joint Distribution Committee (JDC), *Ed.*

sized that no instance of foreign-directed sabotage had occurred in the United States and that enemy espionage was effectively throttled.[31]

The conclusion is that a legitimate need, guarding the nation against subversion, was used as a device for keeping refugee entry to a minimum. Many thousands were turned away who could have come in without risk to the war effort. When Treasury Department lawyers covertly looked into State Department immigration procedures during 1943, they were led to make the following conclusions:[32]

> Under the pretext of security reasons so many difficulties have been placed in the way of refugees obtaining visas that it is no wonder that the admission of refugees to this country does not come anywhere near the quota. . . .
>
> If anyone were to attempt to work out a set of restrictions specifically designed to prevent Jewish refugees from entering this country it is difficult to conceive of how more effective restrictions could have been imposed than have already been imposed on grounds of "security." . . .
>
> These restrictions are not essential for security reasons. Thus refugees upon arriving in this country could be placed in interment camps similar to those used for the Japanese on the West Coast and released only after a satisfactory investigation. Furthermore, even if we took these refugees and treated them as prisoners of war it would be better than letting them die.[32]

One positive note in the State Department's response to the Holocaust was its permission in September 1942 for 5,000 Jewish children trapped in France to enter the United States. This offer, made at the time of mass deportations from France, was obtained through pressure by Eleanor Roosevelt, the President's Advisory Committee, and the refugee-aid agencies. The project failed because of stalling by the Vichy government.[33]

Among the Jews who evaded deportation by fleeing across the Pyrenees were perhaps 200 children. Most were in Spain; some were in Portugal. American refugee-aid organizations feared German occupation of the two countries and a repetition of the events in France. They were also disturbed because Spain's policy of interning these illegal refugees in prisons applied to children as well as adults. The private agencies and the President's Advisory Committee therefore appealed to the State Department to assign 200 of the 5,000 visas to these children and to expedite their evacuation by instructing American consuls to waive the red tape usually involved in visa issuance.[34]

Sumner Welles agreed in December 1942 to do so. He also offered to include the children's mothers. But this generous impulse was undermined before any visas were granted. The State Department ruled that the mothers would have to go through the regular visa-approval process. That meant they had very little chance of reaching the United States, for even though the quotas were already far undersubscribed, 1943 saw further severe tightening of immigration restrictions. And so it happened, to cite but one example, that fourteen-month-old Max reached America in the care of his sisters, nine and twelve years old. His mother, who had somehow smuggled her baby boy and her daughters over the Pyrenees after her husband was deported, remained in Spain.[35]

Even the agreement to bring the children out ran into trouble. The Visa Division tried to restrict the program to children whose parents had both been deported, but backed down following protests from the private agencies. Then it stalled on dispatching the necessary instructions to the American consulates; and when it did send them, they were confusing and vague. Almost immediately after clarified directions finally arrived at the Lisbon consulate, thirty-one children sailed to a new life in the United States. A second group of twenty-one followed a few weeks later, completing the Portuguese side of the project.[36]

The American consulates in Spain took no such expeditious action. After receiving workable instructions, the Barcelona consulate delayed for two months by insisting on technicalities supposedly waived for the children. For instance, some were required to produce unavailable French passports. Then, in the midst of the processing, the consul sought to postpone the project again because other demands on his time had arisen.[37]

When the first group of thirty-five children from

Spain finally sailed, it included twenty-one with visas issued in Barcelona. But an equal number had been turned down there. A frustrated JDC representative wrote to New York that the consulate in Barcelona "instead of facilitating the project apparently is doing everything possible to limit its scope."[38]

The President's Advisory Committee and the private agencies urged the Visa Division to remedy the situation in Spain, but nothing changed. In May, Eleanor Roosevelt pressed Sumner Welles about the children. His reply was entirely noncommittal. A month later, the Quakers reported a continued "lack of action on the part of Barcelona." In September, Madrid was a center of difficulty. The consulate there, by raising technical barriers, had stopped the visas of three of the thirteen children who had been readied for departure. Two of them, a brother and sister whose father was dead and whose mother's whereabouts were unknown, got out two months later. Apparently the other, an orphaned boy of fourteen, did not.[39]

In all, about 125 children left Spain and Portugal for the United States during 1943 under the special program. Another dozen followed before the war ended in Europe. At no time was shipping a problem. Portuguese passenger vessels were sailing regularly to the United States only partially booked.[40]

In Lisbon, the American consulate's cooperative approach toward the children's project also characterized its dealings with adult refugees. Quaker relief workers described the American vice-consul in Lisbon as "splendid and cooperative" and the rest of the consultate – and the legation, too – as very helpful.[41]

No such sensitivity was found in Madrid or Barcelona. Consuls there not only resisted the children's project, but did what they could to stifle adult immigration to the United States. Their interference was crucial; after November 1942, Spain and Portugal were the only countries in continental Europe where American consuls still issued visas. Jewish refugees had encountered obstructionism at Barcelona since the fall of 1941. But in 1943 the difficulties reached extremes, as consuls held back the visas of a substantial number of refugees who had been cleared by the screening process in Washington.[42]

In June 1943, Howard K. Travers, chief of the Visa Division, admitted to a Friends representative that the Madrid and Barcelona consulates were withholding visas from refugees who had advisory approvals. The Quaker pointed out that Spanish officials were disturbed that refugees were not moving on; Travers agreed to press the consulates for an explanation. Six weeks later, Travers said he had received no response but would try again. Two more weeks passed without any word. At that point, in August, the available record runs out. Some of the visas in question had been approved in Washington as far back as February; yet none had been granted, and no explanation could be obtained. It is difficult to believe that in eight weeks the State Department could not get an answer from subordinate personnel overseas. One has to suspect that the Visa Division was a party to this subversion of the visa process.[43]

Two documents will suffice to illustrate attitudes current among American diplomats in Spain. The first, a June 1943 report by Robert Brandin, a middle-level official at the embassy in Madrid, sharply criticized the Joint Distribution Committee for its efforts to help Jewish refugees immigrate to the United States. Furthermore, from Brandin's standpoint, a refugee who obtained advisory approval from Washington had won "only half the fight since the individual consul still has the final say." Proof appeared in Brandin's report: only 64 percent of the advisory approvals sent to Madrid that year had resulted in the issuance of visas.*[44]

The second document is a record of a conversation in April 1944 between a Quaker representative and Mary Evelyn Hayes, the wife of Carlton J. H. Hayes, the American ambassador to Spain. Mrs. Hayes mentioned that the ambassador was antagonistic toward the Joint Distribution Committee. She also said the consuls in Madrid were very annoyed that "the Jews always seem to know more than anyone else." The consuls' complaint actually grew out of the JDC's use of cablegrams to inform refugees of their visa status, while the State Department relayed the same data to the consulate by much slower airgrams. The animosity was also unquestionably fueled by the JDC's occasional success in persuading the Visa Division to put pressure on the consuls to issue visas.[46]

---

*Statistics in Brandin's report sharply contradicted the State Department's continual insistence that the refugee problem was not essentially a Jewish one. Of 117 advisory approvals, noted Brandin, 114 were for Jews. In Washington, the visa Board of Appeals, drawing on other evidence, made the same point in a report to the President.[45]

Only the close of the war in Europe brought an end to Washington's complex security-screening machinery. On July 1, 1945, the visa system reverted to pre-war procedures.[47]

What were the quantitative results of America's wartime immigration policy? Between Pearl Harbor and the end of the war in Europe, approximately 21,000 refugees, most of them Jewish, entered the United States.* That number constituted 10 percent of the quota places legally available to people from Axis-controlled European countries in those years. Thus 90 percent of those quotas – nearly 190,000 openings – went unused while the mass murder of European Jewry ran its course.[†48]

The quota limits were mandated by law. But the severe restraints that the State Department clamped on immigration were not. They took the form of administrative regulations and, at times, purely arbitrary State Department innovations. President Roosevelt had the legal power at any time to modify the restrictions and open the quotas to full use. He did not do so, possibly out of concern that restrictionists in Congress might lash back and enact the restrictions into law. More likely, he was just not interested and found it convenient to leave immigration policy to Breckinridge Long and his associates.[50]

Late in 1945, a *New York Times* writer summarized the effect of America's wartime immigration policies: "The United States, once the haven of refuge for the oppressed peoples of Europe, has been almost as inaccessible as Tibet." He was, of course, exaggerating – but not by much.[51] . . .

RESPONSIBILITY

AMERICA'S RESPONSE TO THE HOLOCAUST was the result of action and inaction on the part of many people. In the forefront was Franklin D. Roosevelt, whose steps to aid Europe's Jews were very limited. If he had wanted to, he could have aroused substantial public backing for a vital rescue effort by speaking out on the issue. If nothing else, a few forceful statements by the President would have brought the extermination news out of obscurity and into the headlines. But he had little to say about the problem and gave no priority at all to rescue.[51a]

In December 1942, the President reluctantly agreed to talk with Jewish leaders about the recently confirmed news of extermination. Thereafter, he refused Jewish requests to discuss the problem; he even left the White House to avoid the Orthodox rabbis' pilgrimage of October 1943. He took almost no interest in the Bermuda Conference. He dragged his feet on opening refugee camps in North Africa. He declined to question the State Department's arbitrary shutdown of refugee immigration to the United States, even when pressed by the seven Jews in Congress.[52]

In November 1943, on the eve of Roosevelt's departure for Cairo and Tehran, stirrings in Congress briefly drew his attention to the rescue question. When he returned six weeks later, he faced the prospect of an explosive debate in Congress on administration rescue policies and the probable passage of legislation calling on him to form a rescue agency. Not long afterward, he established the War Refugee Board [WRB]. His hand had been forced by the pressure on Capitol Hill and by the danger that a major scandal would break over the State Department's persistent obstruction of rescue.

After creating the board, the President took little interest in it. He never acted to strengthen it or provide it with adequate funding. He impeded its initial momentum by delaying the selection of a director and hindered its long-term effectiveness by ruining the plan to appoint a prominent public figure to the post. When the board needed help with the recalcitrant American ambassador to Spain, Roosevelt kept hands off. At the urging of the WRB, the President did issue a strong war-crimes warning in March 1944. But he first diluted its emphasis on Jews. His

---

*A sizable proportion of them were people who had already reached safety in the Western Hemisphere and had waited there for over a year for an opportunity to move on to the United States. Exact statistics are not available, but in late 1942 and in 1943 about 40 percent of the refugees admitted to the United States were in that category.[49]

†The year-by-year numbers follow, based on fiscal years that ended on June 30. The figures for fiscal 1941 are presented for purposes of comparison; that year closed just as the stringent immigration restrictions of July 1941 were imposed. The first five months of fiscal 1942 preceded America's entry into the war, so immigration in those months is not included in the overall wartime total of 21,000.

FISCAL YEAR	1941	1942	1943	1944	1945
REFUGEE IMMIGRATION	28,927	11,702	5,944	5,606	4,793
PERCENTAGE OF QUOTAS USED	47.5	19.2	9.8	9.2	7.9

(refers to quotas assigned to countries of Axis-dominated Europe)

subsequent handling of the UN War Crimes Commission and his treatment of Herbert Pell were hardly to his credit.

Even when interested in rescue action, Roosevelt was unwilling to run a political risk for it, as his response to the free-ports plan showed. The WRB's original rescue strategy depended on America's setting an example to other nations by offering to open several temporary havens. The President, by agreeing to only one American camp, signaled that little was expected of any country. A more extensive free-ports program would probably have strained relations with Congress. It might also have cost votes, and 1944 was an election year.

It appears that Roosevelt's overall response to the Holocaust was deeply affected by political expediency. Most Jews supported him unwaveringly, so an active rescue policy offered little political advantage. A pro-Jewish stance, however, could lose votes. American Jewry's great loyalty to the President thus weakened the leverage it might have exerted on him to save European Jews.[53]

The main justification for Roosevelt's conduct in the face of the Holocaust is that he was absorbed in waging a global war. He lived in a maelstrom of overpowering events that gripped his attention, to the exclusion of most other matters. Decades later, Dean Alfange doubted that he actually realized what the abandonment of the European Jews meant: "He may not have weighed the implications of it to human values, to history, to a moral climate without which a democracy can't really thrive."[54]

Roosevelt's personal feelings about the Holocaust cannot be determined. He seldom committed his inner thoughts to paper. And he did not confide in anyone concerning the plight of Europe's Jews except, infrequently, Henry Morgenthau. There are indications that he was concerned about Jewish problems. But he gave little attention to them, did not keep informed about them, and instructed his staff to divert Jewish questions to the State Department.* Years

later, Emanuel Celler charged that Roosevelt, instead of providing even "some spark of courageous leadership," had been "silent, indifferent, and insensitive to the plight of the Jews." In the end, the era's most prominent symbol of humanitarianism turned away from one of history's most compelling moral challenges.[55]

The situation was much the same throughout the executive branch. Only the Treasury reacted effectively. Oscar Cox and a few others in the Foreign Economic Administration did what they could. But their impact was minor. Secretary Ickes and a small group in the Interior Department were greatly concerned; however, they were not in a position to do much. The War Shipping Administration assisted the WRB with a few transportation problems. The record of the rest of the Roosevelt administration was barren.[57]

Callousness prevailed in the State Department. Its officers, mostly old-stock Protestants, tended strongly toward nativism. Little sympathy was wasted on East Europeans, especially Jews.[58]

Secretary Hull did issue public statements decrying Nazi persecution of Jews. Otherwise he showed minimal interest in the European Jewish tragedy and assigned no priority to it. Ignorant of his department's activities in that area, and even unacquainted with most of the policy-makers, he abandoned refugee and rescue matters to his friend Breckinridge Long. Long and his co-workers specialized in obstruction.[59]

Even after Sumner Welles confirmed the accounts of genocide, State Department officials insisted the data had not been authenticated. They sought to silence Stephen Wise and other Jewish leaders. They tried to weaken the United Nations declaration of December 1942. In early 1943, in order to stifle pressures for action, they cut off the flow of information from Jewish sources in Switzerland.

These people brushed aside the Rumanian offer to free 70,000 Jews. With the British, they arranged

---

*Roosevelt's grasp of Jewish issues tended to be superficial. To note but one example, during the Casablanca Conference he spoke for keeping the number of Jewish professionals in North Africa proportional to the Jewish population there. This, he stated, would avoid the "understandable complaints which the Germans bore towards the Jews in Germany, namely, that while they represented a small part of the population, over fifty percent of the lawyers, doctors, school teachers, college professors, etc., in Germany were Jews." (Quotation from the clerk's summary of the discussion.)

In reality, Jews had composed 1 to 2 percent of Germany's population. They had occupied 2.3 percent of professional positions. In the extreme cases, lawyers and medical doctors, Jews made up 16.3 and 10.9 percent respectively. They held 2.6 percent of the professorships and 0.5 percent of the schoolteacher positions.[56]

the Bermuda fiasco, another move to dampen pressures for action. Rescue plans submitted to the State Department were strangled by intentional delays. Or they were sidetracked to the moribund Intergovernmental Committee on Refugees.

The State Department closed the United States as an asylum by tightening immigration procedures, and it influenced Latin American governments to do the same. When calls for a special rescue agency arose in Congress, Long countered them with deceptive secret testimony before a House committee. After the WRB was formed, the State Department cooperated to a degree, but the obstructive pattern recurred frequently. It is clear that the State Department was not interested in rescuing Jews.

The War Department did next to nothing for rescue. Secretary Stimson's personal opposition to immigration was no help. Far more important, however, was the War Department's secret decision that the military was to take no part in rescue – a policy that knowingly contradicted the executive order establishing the WRB.

On the basis of available evidence, the Office of Strategic Services [OSS] took minimal interest in the extermination of the Jews. Its information about the Holocaust was frequently out-of-date and did not lead to countermeasures. In April 1944, the OSS obtained the first detailed account to reach the West of the mass murder of Jews at Auschwitz. Prepared eight months earlier by Polish underground sources, the document in many ways foreshadowed the Vrba-Wetzler report. The OSS did nothing with it.[60]

When the Vrba-Wetzler account first arrived in Switzerland, in June 1944, part of it was delivered to Allen W. Dulles of the OSS with a plea that he immediately urge Washington to take action. Dulles instead passed the material to the WRB in Bern, noting that it "seems more in your line." Nearly a year later, the OSS received a copy of the Vrba-Wetzler report that had reached Italy. By then, the document had been widely publicized in the West for many months. Yet the OSS treated it as new information![61]

In general, the OSS was unwilling to cooperate with the WRB. At first, at OSS initiative, there was some collaboration overseas between the two agencies. Before long, however, top OSS officials issued

orders against further assistance to the board, apparently following intervention by the State Department. Once more, the executive order that set up the WRB was contravened.[62]

The Office of War Information [OWI], for the most part, also turned away from the Holocaust. It evidently considered Jewish problems too controversial to include in its informational campaigns aimed at the American public. Its director, Elmer Davis, stopped at least two plans for the OWI to circulate the extermination news to the American people. During the last year of the war, the OWI did disseminate war-crimes warnings in Europe for the WRB. But Davis was cool even toward that. And in late 1944, when the board released the Vrba-Wetzler report to the press without prior approval by his agency, Davis protested angrily.[63]

The President's Advisory Committee on Political Refugees (PAC) was a quasi-governmental group of eleven prominent Americans appointed by Roosevelt in 1938 to assist in developing refugee policies. Reflecting the inclinations of James G. McDonald, its chairman, and George L. Warren, its executive secretary, the PAC worked cautiously behind the scenes. Almost without access to Roosevelt, it dealt mainly with the State Department, to which its leadership usually deferred.[64]

The PAC was instrumental in persuading the Roosevelt administration to make visas available for 5,000 Jewish children in France whose parents had been sent to Poland in the mass deportations of 1942. The Nazis never permitted them to leave, however. After that, the committee was virtually inoperative, although it did apply tempered pressure for modification of the stringent visa policies and it endorsed the free-ports plan.[65]

One reason for the PAC's weakness was its uncertain financing. It was a presidential committee, yet it received no government funds. The American Jewish Joint Distribution Committee furnished most of its tiny budget of about $15,000 per year. For a time, Zionist organizations paid half the costs, but they stopped contributing in 1941. The American Catholic and Protestant refugee-aid committees each provided a total of $500 during the PAC's seven years.[66]

Important individuals who had access to the President and might have pressed the rescue issue with him did little in that direction. Vice President Wallace kept aloof from the problem. His closest encounter took place on the Capitol steps in October 1943 when he delivered a brief, noncommittal speech to the pilgrimage of Orthodox rabbis.

Eleanor Roosevelt cared deeply about the tragedy of Europe's Jews and took some limited steps to help. But she never urged vigorous government action. She saw almost no prospects for rescue and believed that winning the war as quickly as possible was the only answer.[67]

Except for Morgenthau, Jews who were close to the President did very little to encourage rescue action. David Niles, a presidential assistant, briefly intervened in support of free ports. The others attempted less. Bernard Baruch – influential with Roosevelt, Congress, the wartime bureaucracy, and the public – stayed away from the rescue issue. So did Herbert Lehman, director of UNRRA [United Nations Relief and Rehabilitation Administration]. Supreme Court Justice Felix Frankfurter had regular access to Roosevelt during the war, and he exercised a quiet but powerful influence in many sectors of the administration. Although he used his contacts to press numerous policies and plans, rescue was not among them.[68]

As special counsel to the President, Samuel Rosenman had frequent contact with Roosevelt, who relied heavily on him for advice on Jewish matters. But Rosenman considered the rescue issue politically sensitive, so he consistently tried to insulate Roosevelt from it. For instance, when Morgenthau was getting ready to urge the President to form a rescue agency, Rosenman objected. He did not want FDR involved in refugee matters, although he admitted that no one else could deal effectively with the problem. Rosenman also argued that government aid to European Jews might increase anti-Semitism in the United States.[69]

The President, his administration, and his advisers were not the only ones responsible for America's reaction to the Holocaust. Few in Congress, whether liberals or conservatives, showed much interest in saving European Jews. Beyond that, restrictionism, especially opposition to the entry of Jews, was strong on Capitol Hill.[70]

Congressional attitudes influenced the administration's policies on rescue. One reason the State Department kept the quotas 90 percent unfilled was fear of antagonizing Congress. It was well known to private refugee-aid agencies that some congressional circles were sharply critical of the administration's supposed "generosity" in issuing visas. The State Department was sufficiently worried about this that, when it agreed to the entry of 5,000 Jewish children from France, it forbade all publicity about the plan. As a leader of one private agency pointed out, "Officials are extremely anxious to avoid producing a debate in Congress on the wisdom of bringing large groups of children to the United States." Yet the immigration quotas to which the 5,000 visas would have been charged were undersubscribed by 55,000 that year.[71]

Except for a weak and insignificant resolution condemning Nazi mass murder, Congress took no official action concerning the Holocaust. The only congressional debate to touch at all on the question was little more than an outburst by Senator Scott Lucas against the Committee for a Jewish Army for its public denunciation of the Bermuda Conference.

Late in 1943, the Bergsonite Emergency Committee persuaded a dozen influential members of Congress to endorse a resolution calling for a government rescue agency. The connections and prestige of these legislators attracted substantial additional backing. Public interest in the issue was also rising. The resulting pressure figured crucially in Roosevelt's decision to establish the War Refugee Board. But even then, the newly formed board, assessing the climate on Capitol Hill, concluded that congressional indifference toward the European Jews ruled out the possibility of appropriations for rescue programs. The WRB turned instead to private sources for funding.

Of the seven Jews in Congress, only Emanuel Celler persistently urged government rescue action. Samuel Dickstein joined the struggle from time to time. Four others seldom raised the issue. Sol Bloom sided with the State Department throughout.

One reason for the government's limited action was the indifference of much of the non-Jewish public. It must be recognized, though, that many Christian Americans were deeply concerned about the murder of European Jewry and realized that it was a momentous tragedy for Christians as well as for Jews. In the words of an official of the Federal Council of Churches, "This is not a Jewish affair. It is a colossal, universal degradation in which all humanity shares." The message appeared in secular circles as well. Hearst, for instance, stressed more than once in his newspapers, "This is not a Christian or a Jewish question. It is a human question and concerns men and women of all creeds."[72]

Support for rescue arose in several non-Jewish quarters. And it came from leading public figures such as Wendell Willkie, Alfred E. Smith, Herbert Hoover, Fiorello La Guardia, Harold Ickes, Dean Alfange, and many more. But most non-Jewish Americans were either unaware of the European Jewish catastrophe or did not consider it important.

America's Christian churches were almost inert in the face of the Holocaust and nearly silent too. No major denomination spoke out on the issue. Few of the many Christian publications cried out for aid to the Jews. Few even reported the news of extermination, except infrequently and incidentally.

On the Protestant side, Quakers and Unitarians responded to the moral challenge through their service committees. But both denominations were tiny. An even smaller organization, the Church Peace Union, persistently but vainly pressed the churches to take a stand and urged the government to act. Mercedes Randall of the Women's International League for Peace and Freedom published *The Voice of Thy Brother's Blood*, a booklet calling for action on "one of the most urgent matters of our time." The only comprehensive discussion of the European Jewish disaster issued by an American Christian source during the Holocaust, Randall's essay closed with a clear warning:

> If we fail to feel, to speak, to act, it bespeaks a tragedy more fateful than the tragedy of the Jews. . . . We have passed by on the other side. . . . Shall we have to live out our lives with that terrible cry upon our lips, "Am I my brother's keeper?"

(The Women's International League had to turn to Jewish sources for financial help to print 50,000 copies and distribute them to newspaper editors, radio commentators, and other opinion leaders.)[73]

The Federal Council of Churches compiled a mediocre record, yet it stood in the forefront of the Protestant effort to help. Besides several public calls for rescue, it sponsored the only nationwide attempt at Christian action, the Day of Compassion of May 1943. But even that event, which most local churches ignored, took place only because Jews urged it on the council and Jewish organizations did much of the necessary work.[74]

The *Christian Century*, a highly influential Protestant weekly, reacted to the first news of extermination by charging that Stephen Wise's statistics were exaggerated. (His estimates were actually far too low.) Thereafter, it reported on the Jewish catastrophe only occasionally, and only rarely did it speak out for rescue action. Such social-action-oriented periodicals as the *Churchman* and Reinhold Niebuhr's *Christianity and Crisis* published even less on the Jewish tragedy. Yet these three journals carried more news on the issue than most Christian periodicals. The bulk of the Protestant press was silent, or nearly so. And few cries for action arose from the pages of any part of Protestantism's print media.[75]

Indicative of the feeble Christian response to the Holocaust was the plight of two American committees established to assist Christian refugees, most of whom were of Jewish descent. Neither organization could rely on its vast parent church to fund its tiny program. The Protestant agency, the American Committee for Christian Refugees (ACCR), leaned heavily on the Jewish Joint Distribution Committee for financial support from 1934 through 1940. When those funds dried up, the ACCR survived by severely reducing its already limited services. It regained a semblance of effectiveness only in mid-1943 with an infusion of money from the National War Fund.*[76]

The Catholic Committee for Refugees (CCR) was organized in 1937 by the American Catholic bishops. But the church did not adequately support this very modest operation, either with funds or by lending its prestige to the committee. In its first years, the CCR needed financial help from the Joint Distri-

---

*The National War Fund, formed under government supervision in 1943, established a united nationwide campaign for private fund appeals related to the war effort. Among the groups it benefited were government-approved private war-relief agencies. This large-scale, broad-based fund-raising system proved a bonanza to small, foundering agencies.[77]

bution Committee. Even so, it was all but ineffective until mid-1943, when the National War Fund assumed virtually all of its expenses.[78]

Two important Catholic periodicals, *America* and *Commonweal*, did speak out from time to time on the extermination of the Jews and called for action to help them. But the rest of the Catholic press was almost silent on the issue, as was the American church itself. No Catholic pressures developed for a government rescue effort. The National Catholic Welfare Conference (NCWC), which acted for the American bishops in social and civic matters, was America's leading organization for Catholic social welfare. It might have led a Catholic drive for rescue action. But it made no move in that direction. Instead, as can be seen in the records of its Bureau of Immigration and in the reactions of its general secretary, Msgr. Michael J. Ready, the NCWC was consistently negative toward immigration of Jewish refugees.[79]

The Bureau of Immigration was responsible for helping Catholic refugees come to the United States. The correspondence of its personnel shows little sympathy for European Jews. It also reveals a distrust of Jews generally and a particular suspicion of American Jewish organizations. They were viewed as too aggressive in assisting Jewish refugees and too little concerned about persecuted Catholics. The Bureau of Immigration was the only refugee-aid organization that encountered no problems with the State Department concerning visa issuance and visa policies.[80]

Until the end of 1943, Catholic refugees passing through Spain and Portugal, or stranded there, turned to American non-Catholic organizations for aid. Jewish, Unitarian, and Quaker agencies provided support funds and ship passage to needy Catholics, whether of Jewish descent or not. After two years of requests that they share the burden, American Catholic leaders investigated the situation in late 1943. By then the American bishops, in order to channel National War Fund money into Catholic relief projects, had established a new branch of the National Catholic Welfare Conference, the War Relief Services. When those funds became available, the War Relief Services – NCWC started to send money to Portugal. Soon afterward, it opened its own office in Lisbon to assist Catholic refugees. The NCWC

also began to contribute to the Representation in Spain of American Relief Organizations, a Jewish-Protestant venture that for over a year had been caring for Catholics along with other refugees.[81]

At the heart of Christianity is the commitment to help the helpless. Yet, for the most part, America's Christian churches looked away while the European Jews perished. So did another part of the public that might have been expected to cry out for action, American liberals. The *Nation* and the *New Republic* did speak, throughout the war, warning of what was happening and pressing for rescue. From time to time, some prominent individual liberals also urged action. But rescue never became an important objective for New Dealers or other American liberals. Even as thoroughly liberal an institution as the New York newspaper *PM*, though it did call for rescue, did not make it a major issue.[82]

The AFL and the CIO frequently endorsed Jewish organizations' appeals for rescue. In a notable change in labor's traditional restrictionism, both unions began in 1943 to urge at least temporary suspension of immigration laws to open the doors for Jewish refugees. But there was no movement to arouse the rank and file, to build active support for rescue on that broad base.[83]

Most American intellectuals were indifferent to the struggle for rescue. Dorothy Thompson and Reinhold Niebuhr were exceptions, as were those who helped the Bergsonite Emergency Committee. Overall, Jewish intellectuals remained as uninvolved as non-Jews. To note one example among many, Walter Lippmann, a highly influential news columnist who dealt with practically every major topic of the day, wrote nothing about the Holocaust.[84]

American Communists contributed virtually nothing to the rescue cause. In the wake of the Bermuda Conference, they publicly agreed with the diplomats: "It would be foolhardy to negotiate with Axis satellites for the release of Hitler's captives." They insisted throughout the war that the only answer for European Jewry was the swiftest possible Allied victory. Nor would they tolerate criticism of the President for his limited rescue steps. "Roosevelt," they argued, "represents the forces most determined on victory"; those concerned about the Jews should "speak helpfully" about him or keep silent. This, of course, coincided with the Communists' view of what was best for Soviet Russia.[85]

An organization formed in early 1944 by the American Jewish Conference seemed to open the way for effective action by prominent non-Jews. The National Committee Against Nazi Persecution and Extermination of the Jews, with Supreme Court Justice Frank Murphy as chairman, included such distinguished Americans as Wendell Willkie and Henry Wallace and other political, religious, and business leaders. But this all-Christian committee failed to attract adequate funding and amounted to little more than a paper organization. Moreover, it did almost nothing to advance its main objective, "to rally the full force of the public conscience in America" against the extermination of the Jews and for vigorous rescue action. Instead, the Murphy committee channeled its meager resources into what it announced as its second priority, combating anti-Semitism in the United States. Murphy and others contributed, in speeches and in print, to the battle against American anti-Semitism. But the rescue issue fell by the wayside.[86]

One reason ordinary Americans were not more responsive to the plight of the European Jews was that very many (probably a majority) were unaware of Hitler's extermination program until well into 1944 or later. The information was not readily available to the public, because the mass media treated the systematic murder of millions of Jews as though it were minor news.

Most newspapers printed very little about the Holocaust, even though extensive information on it reached their desks from the news services (AP, UP, and others) and from their own correspondents. In New York, the Jewish-owned *Post* reported extermination news and rescue matters fairly adequately. *PM's* coverage was also more complete than that of most American papers. The *Times*, Jewish-owned but anxious not to be seen as Jewish-oriented, was the premier American newspaper of the era. It printed a substantial amount of information on Holocaust-related events but almost always buried it on inner

pages.* The *Herald Tribune* published a moderate amount of news concerning the Holocaust but seldom placed it where it would attract attention. Coverage in other New York City newspapers ranged from poor to almost nonexistent.[87]

The Jewish-owned *Washington Post* printed a few editorials advocating rescue, but only infrequently carried news reports on the European Jewish situation. Yet, in October 1944, it gave front-page space for four days to a series attacking the Bergson group. (Inaccuracies soon forced a retraction.) Nothing else connected with the Holocaust even approached comparable prominence in the *Post*. The other Washington newspapers provided similarly limited information on the mass murder of European Jewry.[88]

Outside New York and Washington, press coverage was even thinner. All major newspapers carried some Holocaust-related news, but it appeared infrequently and almost always in small items located on inside pages.[89]

American mass-circulation magazines all but ignored the Holocaust. Aside from a few paragraphs touching on the subject, silence prevailed in the major news magazines, *Time*, *Newsweek*, and *Life*. The *Reader's Digest*, *American Mercury*, and *Collier's* released a small flurry of information in February 1943, not long after the extermination news was first revealed. From then until late in the war, little more appeared. Finally, in fall 1944, *Collier's* and *American Mercury* published vivid accounts of the ordeal of Polish Jewry written by Jan Karski, a courier sent to Britain and America by the Polish resistance. Karski described what he himself saw in late 1942 at the Belzec killing center and in the Warsaw ghetto.† Except for these and a few other articles, the major American magazines permitted one of the most momentous events of the modern era to pass without comment.[90]

Radio coverage of Holocaust news was sparse. Those who wrote the newscasts and commentary programs seem hardly to have noticed the slaughter of the Jews. Proponents of rescue managed to put a little information on the air, mainly in Washington

---

*To note one typical example, the *Times* on July 2, 1944, published "authoritative information" that 400,000 Hungarian Jews had been deported to their deaths so far and 350,000 more were to be killed in the next three weeks. This news (which was basically accurate) received four column-inches on page 12. The *Times* found room on the front page that day to analyze the problem of New York holiday crowds on the move.

†In July 1943, Karski saw Roosevelt, told him what he had witnessed at Belzec, and informed him that the Germans unquestionably intended to exterminate all the Jews in Europe and were well on the way to doing so.[91]

and New York. Access to a nationwide audience was very infrequent. The WRB even had difficulty persuading stations to broadcast programs it produced.[92]

American filmmakers avoided the subject of the Jewish catastrophe. During the war, Hollywood released numerous feature films on refugees and on Nazi atrocities. None dealt with the Holocaust. Despite extensive Jewish influence in the movie industry, the American Jewish Congress was unable to persuade anyone to produce even a short film on the mass killing of the Jews. The very popular *March of Time* news series did not touch the extermination issue, nor did the official U.S. war films in the *Why We Fight* series.[93]

There is no clear explanation for the mass media's failure to publicize the Holocaust. Conflicting details and inconsistent numbers in the different reports from Europe may have made editors cautious. But no one could have expected full accuracy in data compiled under the difficulties encountered in underground work.

Another problem was the fabricated atrocity stories of World War I. This time, editors were very skeptical. Yet, well before word of the "final solution" filtered out, numerous confirmed reports of Nazi crimes against civilian populations had broken down much of that barrier to belief.[94]

The way war news flooded and dominated the mass media may have been a factor. Holocaust events merged into and became lost in the big events of the world conflict. For example, information on the destruction of the Hungarian Jews was overwhelmed by news about preparations for the cross-channel invasion, the invasion itself, and the dramatic reconquest of France that summer.

It is possible that editors took a cue from the *New York Times*. Other newspapers recognized the *Times*'s superior reporting resources abroad and looked to it for guidance in foreign news policy. A perception that the Jewish-owned *Times* did not think the massive killing of Jews was worth emphasizing could have influenced other newspapers. Again, Roosevelt's failure until March 1944 to mention the extermination of the Jews in his press conferences may have led editors to conclude that the issue was not a major one.[95]

The mass media's response to the Holocaust undoubtedly was also affected by the complicated problem of credibility. Publishers and broadcasters feared accusations of sensationalism and exaggeration. They may also have had difficulty themselves in believing the reports. Annihilation of an entire people was a concept that went well beyond previous experience. Moreover, extermination of the Jews made no sense, because it served no practical purpose. The German explanation that Jews were being deported to labor centers seemed more plausible.*[96]

The problem of disbelief may be illustrated by a conversation in December 1944 between A. Leon Kubowitzki of the World Jewish Congress and Assistant Secretary of War John McCloy. Kubowitzki recorded the episode:

> "We are alone," he [McCloy] said to me. "Tell me the truth. Do you really believe that all those horrible things happened?"
>
> His sources of information, needless to say, were better than mine. But he could not grasp the terrible destruction.[98]

On a broader level, the enigma was reflected in the way that military leaders, government officials, newsmen, and members of Congress reacted to what was found when American and British forces liberated German concentration camps in spring 1945. They were stunned. Yet most had been exposed for a long time to information about the camps and the extermination of the Jews – information augmented by two striking disclosures released as recently as August and November 1944.

In August, a month after the Red Army captured the Majdanek killing center, near Lublin, Soviet authorities permitted American reporters to inspect the still-intact murder camp – gas chambers, crematoria, mounds of ashes, and the rest. One American voiced the reaction of all who viewed Majdanek: "I am now

---

*On the other hand, many observers had no real difficulty believing the extermination information. To name only a few of them: the Jewish leadership, editors of the Catholic periodicals *Commonweal* and *America*, the foremost British church leaders, Treasury Department officials, and even State Department policymakers.[97]

prepared to believe any story of German atrocities, no matter how savage, cruel and depraved."[99]

The newsmen sent back detailed accounts, which were widely published in American newspapers and magazines, in many cases on the front pages. A few reports pointed out that Jews were the main victims, but most mentioned them only as part of a list of the different peoples murdered there. And none of the correspondents or their editors connected Majdanek with the extensive information available by then about the systematic extermination of European Jewry. Author Arthur Koestler had tried to explain the phenomenon earlier that year. People, he wrote, can be convinced for a while of the reality of such a crime, but then "their mental self-defense begins to work." In a week, "incredulity has returned like a reflex temporarily weakened by a shock."[100]

The second disclosure, released to the press by the War Refugee Board in November, was the Vrba-Wetzler report of mass murder at Auschwitz. It had reached [Roswell] McClelland* in Switzerland in June. He soon telegraphed a condensation to the WRB in Washington, but was unable to forward the complete text until mid-October.†[101]

The full Auschwitz report – officially issued by a government agency – received prominent notice throughout the country, including Sunday front-page coverage in many newspapers. News accounts were long and graphic; many newspapers followed up with editorials. Radio also spread the information.‡[103]

Despite the reports on Majdanek and Auschwitz (and numerous other accounts of extermination), many well-informed Americans failed to comprehend what was happening. This explains, in part, the wave of amazement that resulted when German concentration camps were opened in April 1945. Military men were appalled and astonished at what they saw. Hardened war correspondents found the horror "too great

for the human mind to believe." General Eisenhower called the "barbarous treatment" inflicted on inmates "almost unbelievable."[105]

To dispel any doubts about the accuracy of reporters' accounts, Eisenhower requested that a dozen congressmen and a delegation of American editors fly to Germany to look at the camps. The legislators emerged from Buchenwald "shocked almost beyond belief." Editors, expecting to find that correspondents had overstated the situation, came away convinced that "exaggeration, in fact, would be difficult."[106]

Failure to grasp the earlier information about Nazi camps was the key cause for this astonishment. Another reason was that camp conditions, ordinarily deplorable, sank to appalling depths during the last part of the war. As the Third Reich crumbled, administration systems broke down. Transportation of food and supplies failed. And as they retreated, the Germans shifted thousands of inmates from outlying camps to the already overloaded ones in the interior of Germany. Conditions were abysmal: massive starvation, unchecked disease, terrible crowding, thousands of unburied corpses."[107]

Ironically, these camps (Buchenwald, Belsen, Dachau, and so on) were not among the most destructive. They were not extermination camps. The horrors that took place within their confines were on a different plane from the millions of murders committed at Auschwitz, Majdanek, and the four other killing centers, all situated in Poland.

The American press, which for so long had barely whispered of mass murder and extermination, exploded with news of the German camps. For over a month, stories ran in all the newspapers and news magazines, frequently on the front pages, accompanied by shocking photographs. And newsreels, made by Hollywood studios from Army Signal Corps footage, confronted millions of American

---

*Director of the American Friends Service Committee's refugee-relief program, *Ed.*

†The delay apparently resulted from the low priority the American legation in Bern gave to WRB matters. The long wait may have been costly. The full report hit with much more force than the telegraphed summary had. It convinced Pehle for the first time that he should put strong pressure on the War Department to bomb the Auschwitz gas chambers. If it had arrived earlier, it might have heightened the urgency of rescue efforts.[102]

‡Shortly before the document was available to the press, the editors of the Army magazine *Yank* asked the WRB for material for an article on atrocities. The board supplied a copy of the Auschwitz report. *Yank*'s editors decided not to use it. It was "too Semitic." They wanted "a less Jewish story," one that would not stir up the "latent anti-Semitism in the Army."[104]

moviegoers with stark scenes of the carnage.[108]

During spring 1945, American newspaper editors blamed the false atrocity stories of World War I for their earlier skepticism about Nazi war crimes. One of the congressmen who saw the camps explained that "it was always a question whether the reports were propaganda and now they can be confirmed." In fact, after the Nazis obliterated the Czech village of Lidice, in mid-1942, the press had not hesitated to publicize German atrocities against occupied populations. But it had consistently pushed information about Europe's Jews into the inner pages, or omitted it entirely. This minimized a substantial body of evidence that pointed to a hard-to-believe fact — the systematic extermination of a whole people.*[109]

In the last analysis, it is impossible to know how many Americans were aware of the Holocaust during the war years. Starting in late 1942, enough information appeared that careful followers of the daily news, as well as people especially alert to humanitarian issues or to Jewish problems, understood the situation. Probably millions more had at least a vague idea that terrible things were happening to the European Jews. Most likely, though, they were a minority of the American public. Only three opinion polls (all by Gallup) asked Americans whether they believed the reports about German atrocities, and only one of them dealt directly with Jews. The first survey, in January 1943, specifically referred to news reports of the killing of two million Jews. Forty-seven percent thought the reports were true. (Twenty-nine percent did not, and 24 percent gave no opinion.)[111]

Late in the war, in mid-November 1944 and again in May 1945, the pollsters asked whether reports that the Germans had murdered "many people in concentration camps" were true. The November poll indicated that 76 percent believed the information was accurate. By early May, following three weeks of steady news about the liberated concentra-

tion camps in Germany, the figure had risen to 84 percent. On the face of it, public knowledge of Nazi atrocities had reached a high level by November 1944. But the last two polls furnish no real evidence about awareness of the extermination of the Jews, because Jews were not mentioned in either of them.[112]

Throughout the war, most of the mass media, whether from disbelief or fear of accusations of sensationalism or for some other reason, played down the information about the Jewish tragedy. As a result, a large part of the American public remained unaware of the plight of European Jewry. Hesitation about giving full credence to reports of the systematic extermination of an entire people may be understandable. But those who edited the news surely realized, at the very least, that European Jews were being murdered in vast numbers. That was important news. But it was not brought clearly into public view.

Popular concern for Europe's Jews could not develop without widespread knowledge of what was happening to them. But the information gap, though extremely important, was not the only limiting factor. Strong currents of anti-Semitism and nativism in American society also diminished the possibilities for a sympathetic response. A quieter, more prevalent prejudice, a "passive anti-Semitism," was another major barrier to the growth of concern. It was reflected in opinion surveys taken by the Office of War Information. They showed that the impact of atrocity information on the average American was seven times stronger when it involved atrocities in general than when it referred specifically to atrocities against Jews. A Christian clergyman with extensive connections in Protestant circles reached a similar conclusion: "Not only were Christians insensitive and callous [about rescue]; . . . there was an anti-Semitism there, just beneath the surface."†[113]

The American government did not respond decisively to the extermination of Europe's Jews. Much of

---

*To some extent, the pattern continued during spring 1945. News reports about the liberated camps mentioned Jews among the various types of victims, but the fact that they were the main victim did not come across clearly.

The crowning irony occurred in May, when the Soviets released an official report on their investigations at Auschwitz. The long summaries sent from Moscow by American reporters did not mention Jews, although most of those killed at Auschwitz were Jews. One reason was probably Soviet unwillingness to distinguish Jews from other citizens. Also, apparently, the American correspondents were unaware of or disbelieved earlier reports on Auschwitz, including the much publicized one released by the WRB the preceding November.[110]

†Another obstacle to American concern for the European Jews was the preoccupation of most people with the war and with their personal affairs. Public opinion research disclosed that typical Americans, still acutely aware of the Great Depression, were mainly concerned about their jobs and their job chances after the war. They also worried about their boys and men away from home. And they gave a lot of attention to such questions as how to spend and save and when they could drive their cars for fun again. These personal matters crowded out even headline issues, except for the progress of the war.[114]

the general public was indifferent or uninformed. What about American Jews – how did they meet the challenge?*

American Jewish leaders recognized that the best hope for rescue lay in a strong effort to induce the U.S. government to act. The obvious approaches were two: appeals to high government officials and a national campaign to publicize the mass killings with a view to directing public pressure on the Roosevelt administration and Congress. Jewish leaders made progress in both directions, but their effectiveness was severely limited by their failure to create a united Jewish movement and by their lack of sustained action.[116]

A unified effort by the main Jewish organizations did take place for two weeks in late 1942, coordinated by the "Temporary Committee." For ten additional weeks, from early March to mid-May 1943, cooperative action resumed under the Joint Emergency Committee on European Jewish Affairs. During those twelve weeks, some advances were won, but that amount of time was too brief to budge the Roosevelt administration. Besides, none of the cooperating organizations gave top priority to the rescue problem. And they refused the Bergsonites' requests to be included in the effort.[117]

The basis for united action existed throughout the war. All Jewish organizations agreed on the need for rescue and the need to abolish the White Paper and open Palestine to European Jews. But the split over the issue of Zionism proved unbridgeable. It was the chief obstacle to formation of a united drive for rescue.[118]

The outcome was that non-Zionist organizations (American Jewish Committee, Jewish Labor Committee, B'nai B'rith, and the ultra-Orthodox groups) went their separate ways and accomplished little in building pressure for rescue. The Zionists, who were the best organized of the Jewish groups, were more effective in pushing for rescue action. But the major part of their resources went into the effort for a postwar state in Palestine.[119]

The Bergsonite Emergency Committee tried to fill the gap in the rescue campaign. Its work was vital in finally bringing the War Refugee Board into existence. But the Bergsonites were too weak to generate enough pressure after the formation of the board to force the Roosevelt administration to give it the support that it should have had. The situation was not helped when they divided their limited energies by launching their own statehood movement through the Hebrew Committee for National Liberation and its partner, the American League for a Free Palestine.[120]

The fact that the tiny Bergsonite faction accomplished what it did toward the establishment of the WRB is compelling evidence that a major, sustained, and united Jewish effort could have obtained the rescue board earlier and insisted on its receiving greater support than it did. Such an effort could have drawn on substantial strengths. The Zionist groups had mass followings, organizational skills, some financial capability, a few prestigious leaders, and valuable contacts high in government. The American Jewish Committee combined wealth and important influence in high places. The Jewish Labor Committee was backed by a sizable constituency and could count on help from the American Federation of Labor. B'nai B'rith held the allegiance of a broad cross section of American Jews. Agudath Israel represented a very active element of Orthodoxy. And the Bergson group offered energy, publicity skills, fund-raising proficiency, and the capacity to win friends in Congress and elsewhere in Washington.

Along with the lack of unity, American Jewry's efforts for rescue were handicapped by a crisis in leadership. The dominant figure, Stephen Wise, was aging, increasingly beset by medical problems, and burdened with far too many responsibilities. Abba Hillel Silver's rise to the top was slowed by his rivalry with Wise and by his own tendency to create enemies. He was, nonetheless, a forceful leader; but his single-minded commitment to postwar Jewish statehood meant that he did not participate in the campaign for government rescue action. No other leaders approached the stature of these two.[121]

The scarcity of fresh, innovative leadership aroused concern at the time. In 1944, the editor of the Brooklyn *Jewish Examiner* asserted that "not a new personality with the possible exception of Henry Monsky has come to the fore in the past decade." As evidence he listed the leading Jewish spokesmen of

---

*Most American Jews who maintained connections with Jewish life probably knew about the ongoing extermination. The Yiddish daily press, which reached 30 percent of American Jewish families, reported on it frequently. Many of the periodicals sponsored by the numerous Jewish organizations emphasized the terrible news. Anglo-Jewish weekly newspapers, published in most sizable cities and in all regions of the United States, provided substantial coverage (drawn mainly from Jewish press services). And information must have spread by word of mouth at synagogues and other centers of Jewish activity. Wide Jewish knowledge of the extermination is evidenced by the fact that hundreds of thousands of American Jews attended rallies and mass meetings for rescue held throughout the United States.[115]

1933 and pointed out that, except for two who had died, "the names today are the same; there are no new ones." A tendency among second- and third-generation American Jews to minimize their Jewishness may have hindered the emergence of strong new leadership during the 1930s and 1940s.[122]

An additional problem was the inability of American Jewish leaders to break out of a business-as-usual pattern. Too few schedules were rearranged. Vacations were seldom sacrificed. Too few projects of lesser significance were put aside. An important American Zionist remarked years later that the terrible crisis failed to arouse the "unquenchable sense of urgency" that was needed. Even from afar, this inability to adapt was painfully clear. In late 1942, Jewish leaders in Warsaw entrusted a message to Jan Karski, the Polish underground agent who was about to leave for Britain and the United States. It called on Jews in the free nations to turn to unprecedented measures to persuade their governments to act. But the Polish Jews had no illusions. Before Karski departed, one of them warned him:

> Jewish leaders abroad won't be interested. At 11 in the morning you will begin telling them about the anguish of the Jews in Poland, but at 1 o'clock they will ask you to halt the narrative so they can have lunch. That is a difference which cannot be bridged. They will go on lunching at the regular hour at their favorite restaurant. So they cannot understand what is happening in Poland.*[123]

Despite the obstacles and failures, American Jews were responsible for some important achievements. Finding the mass media largely indifferent, they devised ways to spread the extermination news and create limited but crucial support among non-Jews. This, combined with pressures from the American Jewish community, helped bring the War Refugee Board into existence.

American Jewish organizations also carried out valuable rescue and relief work overseas. During World War II, the American Jewish Joint Distribution Committee provided more aid to European Jews than all the world's governments combined. In doing

so, it paid for nearly 85 percent of the work of the War Refugee Board. The Hebrew Sheltering and Immigrant Aid Society dealt effectively with migration and ocean transportation problems. The World Jewish Congress, though chronically short of funds, undertook important rescue projects in collaboration with overseas Zionist organizations and anti-Nazi underground movements. Vaad Hahatzala, grounded in the requirements of Jewish law for the preservation of human life, turned to all available rescue tactics, however unconventional. Other American Jewish organizations contributed, though on a smaller scale.[124]

In the end, American Jewish groups and their overseas affiliates were central to most of the WRB's direct-action projects. This fact, while reflecting great credit on American Jewry, must cast a shadow over the rest of the nation. Voluntary contributions from American Jews – in the millions of dollars – funded these organizations and thus most of the limited help that America extended to Europe's Jews.

Notes

1. Wyman, 43, 49, 168–82, 194.
2. Ibid., 193–4, 199, 200, 204; "Quota Immigrants Admitted" (nd), NRS, 506.
3. Wyman, 193–96, 202.
4. Ibid., 200–1.
5. Ibid., 201–2.
6. Ibid., 203; Mayerson to Sapper, 12/24/41, NRS 991; Welles to McDonald, 2/17/42, JM, P50.
7. Bernstein & Dijour to Taylor, 4/24/42, JM, P55; McDonald & Warren to Welles (draft), 3/11/43, JM, P67; NYT, 5/14/42, 6; FR 1942, v 1, 450–7; BC Mins, 4/25, AM; Office of Censorship, Daily Rpt #7000 [9/42], SD, R/3489.
8. Cohu's ltr of 6/3/42 from Marseille, AF, RS 1. Several other examples in McClelland to Rogers, 3/14/42, AF, RS 1.
9. Niles, Case Com Rpt, 10/13/42, USC, Case Com.
10. The obstruction is clearly seen in the archives of AFSC, JDC, and NRS. Warren's remarks: CEP Jour, 5/5/42; JPC 3050.
11. JPC 3274, 3379, 3436–37; Kaplan, MASC Mtg, 1/12/43, NRS 326; [1st] Draft Mins Mign & Alien Status Sub-Com, 2/17/43, NRS 325; Schauffler, Re Visa Policy, 12/21/43, AF, GF 4; Vail, Trip to Wn, 3/12/43, AF, FS 3.
12. JPC 3340; Mins of MASC, 5/11/43, Kaplan draft, NRS 326; IR, 10/28/43, 327; Rogers to Hiatt, 10/2/42, AF, RS 3; JPC 3282.
13. IR, 10/28/43, 309–55.
14. CR, v 90, 666.
15. Excerpts & Summary of Rpt on Spain from Conard, 11/20/43, AF, RS 6.

*To some extent, the anti-Semitism of the time was another factor limiting American Jewish action for rescue. It undoubtedly put Jews on the defensive and kept some from speaking out. It should not be overemphasized, however. Many thousands of Jews were publicly vocal on a variety of controversial issues.

16. Schauffler to Heath, 1/5/43, 2/12/43, Heath to Vail, 1/19/43, AF, RS 2; Heath to Wriggins, 1/18/43, AF, RS, Ctry FNA, Fr Morocco, Casa; Schauffler to Hartley, 6/18/43, AF, RS 7; Mins of Mtg on 12/30/43 with Katzki, JDC, G/E, Germany–NRS; Schauffler to Pickett, Vail, et al, 4/13/43, AF, FS, C/O, HIAS; Translation-Excerpts, 8/9/43. u/c Dijour to Schauffler, 10/7/43, AF, RS, Ctry FNA, Genl.

17. Mayerson to Abrahamson, Monthly Rpt, 10/7/42, NRS 459; numerous individual cases in NRS 575; Schauffler to Judkyn, 11/9/43, AF, RS 3.

18. Pickett to Warren, 5/27/42, AF, GF 1; 54th Mtg of PAC, 6/18/42, JM, P66; [1st] Draft Mins Mign and Alien Status Sub-Com, 2/17/43, NRS 325; Mins of MASC, 5/11/43, Kaplan draft, NRS 326; Rogers, Rpt, Ref Div, For Serv Section, Jan–May 1942, AF, RS, Rpts & Discussions.

19. Rogers to Vail, 5/20/42, with enclosure, Rogers to Warren, 6/4/42, AF, GF 1; Detzer to Baer, 6/16/42, WIL, Ref Com, 1938–43, Cases, Schottlaender.

20. JPC 3379; Chamberlain to Schauffler, 3/12/42, AF, GF, For Serv, Switz; Warren to PAC, with enclosures, 5/8/42, Warren to PAC, 5/11/42, 54th Mtg of PAC, 6/18/42, JM, P66.

21. DSB, 9/10/44, 277–78; JPC 3379; "Keppel Study," 8/23/43, NRS 570; anon memo (probably Keppel to Berle), 8/3/42, Travers to Long, 8/4/42, BLP, B 211, Visa Bd of Appeals; JPC 3340–4.

22. Visa Bd of Appeals, Rpt, 11/9/42, BLP, B 211, Visa Bd of Appeals.

23. BKR Rpt, 13; Summary of Proceedings – Special Mtg NRS, 1/23/43, AF, RS, C/O, NRS (Mins); Schauffler/Rogers to Conard, 3/27/42, AF, RS, Ctry Port, Ltrs to; NYT, 9/9/43, 25.

24. DSB, 9/10/44, 274; SIB, 6/16/44, NRS 1391; *Rescue*, 6/44, 3; IR, 7/18/44, 228–29; Petluck to Mign Staff, 8/2/44, NRS 587.

25. Maurice Davie, *Refugees in America* (1947), 194; Loewenstein, Suggestions for a Better Verification, 9/14/42, SD, R/3179; Elisabeth A. Dexter, "Last Port of Freedom," draft MS (1942), ch I, 9; Chr R, 9/42, 331.

26. BKR Rpt, 14.

27. MD 694/191; Warren-Jarvik interview, 1/22/79.

28. NYT, 10/15/42, 9; Teleg No. 78 from Tangier to MILID, Wn, 2/23/43, BLP, B 195, Foreign Territories; ltr from War Dept, 5/1/43, SD, R/3805.

29. Schmidt file in AF, OF, N Afr; memo by Heath, 9/22/43, AF, RS 2; Heath to Kimberland, 5/9/44, AF, RS, Ctry FNA, Algeria, Ltrs to; Schauffler, memor re Schmidt, 11/16/43, AF, FS 3.

30. Office of Censorship, Daily Rpt #7000 [9/42], SD, R/3489. The actual facts concerning HICEM are found in Warren, memo on HIAS-ICA, u/c McDonald to Hull, 3/13/42, JM, P50. SD views concerning subversives among refugees are seen in FR 1942, v 1, 450–56.

31. Standish to Lesser, 3/27/44, W 10, Imgn Memos; NYT, 6/28/42, 1, 7/30/42, 1, 34, 7/1/42, 1, 7/10/42, 1, 12/6/42, 59, 7/26/43, 32, 7/16/44, 7, 12/31/44, 16, 3/19/45, 19, 12/8/45, 3; Louis de Jong, *The German Fifth Column in the Second World War* (1956), 215–21.

32. Greenstein, Summary of Invitation Cf, 10/18/41, AF, GF, C/O, NRS; MD 693/217–18.

33. Ch 2. Baerwald to Beckelman, 9/8/42, JDC, Refs, Children;

Notes, Mtg of US Com, 9/21/42, Hyman to Levy, 10/22/42, JDC, France, Children. Even here, though, the Visa Division raised several technical difficulties (Stmt by Warren, 9/14/42, AF, GF, US Govt, PAC).

34. Schwartz to Leavitt, 12/21/42, 1/13/43, Leavitt to Hayes, 1/29/43, McDonald & Warren to Welles, 12/1/42, JDC, Refs, Children; Conard to Pickett, 11/21/42, AF, OF, Port, 1000 Group.

35. Frawley to Pickett & Vail, 12/8/42, AF, GF 3; Mtg of MASC, 12/9/42, NRS 452; JPC 3223, 3283; USCOM, Rpt of Exec Dir to Bd of Dirs, 5/12/43, AF, RS, C/O, USC-CEC, Rpts; Radio Script, 5/7/43, JDC, Refs, Children.

36. Mtg of MASC, 12/9/42, NRS 452; BC Mins, 4/25, AM; Frawley to Pickett, Vail, et al, 12/24/42, AF, GF 5; SS to Lisbon, 12/26/42, W 44, Evacn of Children from France; Frawley to Pickett, Vail, et al, 1/6/43, AF, RS 10; Schwartz to Leavitt, 1/4/43, 1/18/43, JDC, Refs, Children; Frawley to Leavitt, 1/13/43, JDC, France, Children; Ben Schauffler to Lang, 1/6/43, AF, OF, Port, USC CEC; Rpt by Escort of 21 on Serpa Pinto, 3/20/43, AF, RS 8; JDC, Loose-Leaf Memo #32, 3/22/43, NRS 1302.

37. Katzki to Leavitt, 2/27/43, Wriggins to AF, 4/2/43, 4/6/43, JDC, Refs, Children.

38. JDC, Loose-Leaf Memo #34, 5/21/43, NRS 1302; Katzki, Lisbon, to JDC, 4/28/43, AF, RS 10.

39. Memo of telephone message from Warren, 4/12/43, HW to MF, 6/10/43, Olsen to Frawley, 9/30/43, Conard to Lang [12/43], AF, RS 8; Conard to Pickett, 9/24/43, AF, RS, Children, US Com, Case Lists; Thompson to Welles, 5/20/43, ER 894/70; Welles to Thompson, 5/28/43, ER 1703/100; Katzki to Leavitt, 9/24/43, JDC, Refs, Children.

40. Olsen to JDC (Leavitt), 6/14/45, JDC, Refs, Children; Conard, Rpt to AF for Dec 1943 to Aug 1944, 8/15/44, AF, RS 4; Gallagher to Olsen, 4/25/45, AF, FS, DP Servs, Children, USCCEC; BC Mins, 4/25, AM.

41. Conard & Wriggins, AF Lisbon Office Mid-Aug Rpt, 8/13/42, along with several letters also in this file, AF, RS 4 (1942); Conard to Vail, 6/10/43, Conard to Schauffler, 8/25/43, Wriggins to Schauffler, 8/10/43, AF, RS 4 (1943).

42. Rpt of the Secy to Exec Com Mtg of JDC, 10/22/41, JDC, Rpts; Katzki to Leavitt, 2/26/43, 2/27/43, 4/14/43, JDC, Refs, Children; Schauffler to Conard, 6/22/43, AF, RS 6.

43. Schauffler to Pickett, Vail, et al. 6/11/43, AF, GF 4; Schauffler to Conard, 6/22/43, Schauffler to Rogers, 7/26/43, Rogers to Travers, 8/10/43, Excerpts & Summary of Rpt on Spain from Conard, 11/20/43, AF, RS 6.

44. Brandin, memo on JDC, 6/28/43, CH, B 6, Ref Orgzns.

45. Ibid.; BKR Rpt, 23.

46. Notes on Lois Jessup's talk with Mrs. Carlton J. H. Hayes, 4/28/44, AF, FS, AF, Wn Trips.

47. IR, 6/14/45, 154–56.

48. Based on 26 nations with annual quotas totaling 60,888 (Status of Quotas as of 10/31/45, NRS 502). Statistics from *Annual Report of the Immigration and Naturalization Service* (1946), 72. An estimated 5,000 entered during the portion of fiscal 1942 that followed American entry into the war (Kovarsky to Levy, 7/13/42, NRS 505; IR, 2/27/42, 83). The total eligible from Pearl Harbor to V–E Day was 208,000.

49. MR, 4/44, 13, 6/45, 158, 8/45, 189.

50. BLD, 399.

51. NYT, 12/30/45, IV, 10.

51a. Parts of this chapter are supported by data presented in the foregoing chapters. For the most part, only new sources of information will be cited in the notes for this chapter. Wise to FDR, 3/4/45, FDR, PPF 3292, Wise.

52. MD 701/250. In July 1943, FDR did speak briefly about the Riegner plan with Stephen Wise. But this was subsidiary to their main discussion. The President also saw the seven Jewish congressmen in April 1943. See ch 4, source note 42.

53. Led by Stephen Wise, millions of American Jews venerated FDR (eg, Wise, ch 13; Celler to FDR, 12/15/44, PSC 3/63; Neumann, *Arena*, 184, 200, 206–7; JO, 1/42, 2; NYT, 6/29/43, 13). To note but one typical example, Louis Levinthal, president of ZOA, drew consolation in the wake of the Bermuda fiasco from his belief that "we do have genuine, loyal friends, in government and outside of government circles, and none more genuine, more loyal than our beloved President, Franklin Delano Roosevelt" (NP, 5/7/43, 15). Helen Fein provides insight into the Jewish relationship with FDR in *Patterns of Prejudice*, 9/73, 22–28. Also relevant is Fuchs, *Political Behavior*, 71–75, 99–107.

54. Burns, 397; Alfange-Wyman interview, 3/22/79.

55. MD 106/275–6, 147/375, 151/32, 155/41–42, 692/288–90, 694/191; MPD, v 5, 1200–1, 1338–41; Hull, *Memoirs*, 1530–31; Convsn ER with Rosenheim et al, 10/14/44, JM, 324 ER; NG, Interview with Rosenman, 10/6/43, AHS, Ma I–93, Rosenman; Celler speech, 10/23/75, at J Hist Soc of NY.

56. FR, *The Conferences at Washington, 1941–1942, & Casablanca, 1943* (1968), 608, 611; Wyman, 27, 232; Davie, *Refugees in America*, 6.

57. OC, B 101, Refugee file; HID, 9789, 10187, 10190; Kingdon to Ickes, 2/1/45, Ickes to Rogers, 12/9/43, HI, Associations; CW, 1/18/43, 2; Lubin to Hassett, 3/8/45, 3/12/45, FDR, OF 700.

58. Eg, Flournoy to Travers & Holmes, 3/30/45, SD 150.01 Bills/3-3045; Martin Weil, *A Pretty Good Club* (1978), esp ch 2.

59. NYT, 10/31/42, 5, 9/11/43, 8, 6/27/44, 6, 7/15/44, 3; MD 692/291, 695/31, 696/87.

60. Description of Conc Camp at Oswiecim, 8/43, u/c Belin to Langer, 4/10/44, RG 226, R & A 66059.

61. Dulles to McC, 6/15/44, with enclosures, W 61, Extmn Camps; OSS R & A Field Memo 257, 5/10/45, OSS Records 1944, Hoover Institution; CJR, 10/44, 524. Visser't Hooft (*Memoirs*, 168) gives further evidence of Dulles's indifference. Werner Rings's account of events in Switzerland connected with the Vrba-Wetzler report, including Dulles's reaction to it, is heavily flawed (*Advokaten des Feindes* [1966], 144–46).

62. Lesser to Pehle, 4/18/44, JBF, Memo beginning, "1. The WRB established by," 4/20/44, W 50, OSS.

63. Margoshes in *Day*, 3/19/43, 1; Allan Winkler, *Politics of Propaganda* (1978), index; Allan Winkler to Eliyho Matzozky, 12/28/78 (copy in Wyman files); Mannon, Memo for Files, 11/22/44, Davis to Pehle, 11/23/44, W 6, Ger Extmn Camps; Mtg of PC, 12/17/42, WJC, U185/3; WJC, *Unity in Dispersion*, 163.

64. Wyman, 48; MD 696/204, 206, 219, 697/17; Ltrs to Shad Polier, 1/39, in Memo to File re Ref Children, 5/13/75, private files of Justine Wise Polier; McDonald to Welles, 8/8/41, JM, P50; McDonald to Grew, 5/21/45, JM, P3; McDonald to Rosenheim, 2/25/43, JM, P49; McDonald to Taylor, 6/3/43, JM, P55; 57th Mtg of PAC, 3/9/43, JM, P67; Schauffler to Branson et al, 11/6/44, AF, RS 11; Schauffler, Re Visa Policy in SD, with enclosure, 12/21/43, AF, GF 4.

65. 55th Mtg of PAC, 9/9/42, Warren to PAC, 10/16/42, 56th Mtg of PAC, 12/1/42, Warren to McDonald, 2/2/42, 54th Mtg of PAC, 6/18/42, JM, P66; JPC 655–66; Warren to McDonald, 5/9/44, McDonald to FDR, 5/12/44, JM, P68. The last recorded meeting of the PAC took place in Dec 1943. It met only 10 times between Pearl Harbor and V-E Day.

66. Warren to McDonald, Wise, & Baerwald, 1/18/41, Warren to McDonald & Baerwald, 5/3/41, JM, P65; Lourie to Warren, 11/10/41, JM, P66; JDC file G/E, Austria, Intergovernmental Advisory Com 1938–43, esp Baerwald to Warren, 12/24/41, McDonald to Leavitt, 1/14/43, Buchman to Rosner, 1/19/43, Baerwald to Bressler & Hyman, 5/20/38, Morrissey to Speers, 3/19/41.

67. Convsn ER with Rosenheim et al, 10/14/44, JM, 324 ER; McDonald to ER, 9/5/41, JM, P43; ER to Welles, 3/9/42, Boettiger to Thompson, 8/31/42, ER 853/70; FDR to Undersecy of State, 12/10/42, with note ER to FDR, FDR, OF 76C; MD 692/288, 694/86; printed EC brochure, cover missing, 12, PSC 9/69.

68. Niles: MD 726/146–47. Baruch: Jordan Schwarz, *The Speculator: Bernard M. Baruch in Washington* (1981), 306–8, 417–26, 437, 446–47, 457–59, 467–74, 559–66. Lehman: nothing on rescue appears in the relevant archives or in Nevins, *Lehman & His Era*. Frankfurter: MD 696/122–3; Frankfurter Papers genly; Bruce Murphy, *The Brandeis/Frankfurter Connection* (1982), chs 6–8 genly & esp 243–45, 252–57, 273–74, 287–96, 308–10. Laqueur's statement (*Terrible Secret*, 94) that Frankfurter raised the extermination issue with FDR in 1942 is wrong; it is apparently based on the same error by Feingold (*Politics of Rescue*, 170, 333). Cf Voss, 248–51.

69. MD 693/205–6, 209–10, 694/190, 707/243; Stettinius to Early, 3/8/44, FDR, PSF, Refs; SIR to Watson, 3/17/44, FDR to Wise, 7/30/44, with attached note, FDR, PPF 5029; NG, Interview with Rosenman, 10/6/43, AHS, Ma I-93, Rosenman. Also see Samuel Hand, *Counsel & Advise: A Political Biography of Samuel I. Rosenman* (1979), 139–40, 233.

70. Berlin, Confidential Memo, 2/24/43, AHS, Ma I-62; BC Mins, 4/25, AM; RR, 63–64; Travers to Foster, 4/6/45, SD 150.01 Bills/3-3045; Joy to Burton, 5/4/44, Burton to Joy, 5/7/44, USC, Sen Burton; Biddle to FDR, 12/29/44, FDR, OF 3186; Schauffler, Re Visa Policy in SD, 12/21/43, AF, GF 4; JPC 3246, 3379–80; Kaplan, MASC Mtg, 1/12/43, NRS 326; NYT, 9/22/42, 16; CR, v 89, 8594–5; Com Mtg with Shaughnessy, 11/20/44, Legis 16453; BMM, Memo for Record, 10/20/43, Mohler to Ready, 10/20/43, BI 83, Refs – Restrictions on Admission as Visitors, R-4.

71. [1st] Draft Mins Mign & Alien Status Sub-Com, 2/17/43, NRS 325; Kaplan, MASC Mtg, 1/12/43, NRS 326; Dubin, Rpt on discussion with Travers, 12/5/45, NRS 558; JPC 3246, 3274; Frawley to Vail et al, 10/8/42, Frawley to Pickett & Vail, 12/8/42, AF, GF 3.

72. CW, 1/8/43, 13; *NY Daily Mirror*, 12/10/43, 25; NYJA, 9/4/43, 4.

73. Randall to Dear Friend, 7/43, Randall & Black to Swing, 5/26/44, WIL, Ref Com, 1938–43, Releases; Randall, *The Voice of Thy Brother's Blood* (1944) (quote from p 30); Randall to ER, 6/28/44, ER 2946/190 Misc; CM, Admin Com, 5/25/44; Digest of Mins of Int Com, 3/21/44, AJHS, I-67, B 6.

74. NYT, 12/21/42, 17, 3/17/43, 8, 4/26/43, 17; Voss-Wyman interview, 2/11/78.

75. CC, 12/9/42, 1518–9; Hilberg, 337; *Shoah*, spr 1981, 20. The general statement on the near silence of the Protestant press is based on my analysis of ten periodicals: *Christendom, Christian Century, Christian Register, Christianity and Crisis, Christianity and Society, Churchman, Federal Council Bulletin, Lutheran, Religion in Life, Religious Digest.* (The last, while not strictly a Protestant magazine, was heavily Protestant in emphasis.)

   Robert Ross, in *So It Was True: The American Protestant Press and the Nazi Persecution of the Jews* (1980), asserted that "the whole story" of the Nazi extermination of the Jews was published "extensively, continuously, and often comprehensively in the American Protestant press" (258). A close reading of his book, however, shows that what Ross actually demonstrated regarding the extermination period (mid-1941 to spring 1945) is the following: (1) two tiny-circulation publications issued by organizations dedicated to converting Jews to Christianity provided fairly thorough (but far from extensive) coverage; (2) the *Christian Century* and a very few other mainline Protestant periodicals published occasional (and often inconspicuous) reports; and (3) some 25 other Protestant journals said even less, or nothing at all.

   The major problem with Ross's assessment of the data is that he added up *all* the references to Nazi actions against Jews that appeared in some 30 periodicals, and considered that to be such extensive reporting that American Protestants in general were exposed to the whole story. For instance, he found that in 1943 over 100 references appeared in the 31 periodicals he studied. But he did not take cognizance of the fact that few Protestants were reading more than one or two of the magazines. Seen another way, his findings show that, on the average, each periodical carried only a little over three references to the Jewish catastrophe during the entire critical year of 1943 and that no publication had more than nine. Furthermore, as Ross himself noted, many of the reports were only brief items. This is hardly extensive press exposure. Moreover, as he also showed, these Protestant periodicals printed many more references in 1943 than in any of the other extermination years. (*So It Was True*, 152–284, esp 164, 169–70, 183, 188–92, 197–202, 217, 220–25, 254–59, 264, 276, 280, 284; also the source notes for these pages.)

76. Mins of Mtg with Pehle, 2/10/44, JDC, WRB; Staff planning cfs, 6/14/44, 7/13/44, AF, FS, Planning Com (Policy); W S Bennet to A W Bennet, 5/10/46, A. W. Bennet Papers, B 25, F 1, J Affairs; *Newscast* (ACCR), 2/41, 5, 3/41, 5, 4/41, 2, 9–10/44, 2, 1–2/45, 2; Mohler to Mulholland, 8/5/40, BI 87, R-8; Leiper to Pickett, 4/3/40, ACCR, Rpt of Com on Orgzn, 11/26/40, AF, GF, C/O, ACCR; AJHQ, 12/71, 125–27; Cavert to Dexter, 9/15/43, FCC, B 9, Genl

77. NCWC, *Progress Rpt 1943: WRS – NCWC* (1943), 1; Chr R, 5/43, 179.

78. J. F. Rummel, *Tenth Annual Rpt of the Catholic Com for Refs* [1946], 27; Staff planning cfs, 6/14/44, 7/13/44, AF, FS, Planning Com (Policy); Mulholland to Mohler, 1/22/37, Mohler to Mulholland, 2/13/37, 11/9/37, BI 80, Refs-CCR 1937, R-1; Mohler to Mulholland, 8/5/40, BI 87, R-8; AJHQ, 12/71, 127; SW to Mohler, 6/5/41, Mankiewicz to Dear Sir, 6/11/41, Burger to Mohler, 8/22/41, BMM, Memo for Record, 9/10/41, BI 80, Refs-CCR 1941, R-1; J. F. Rummel, *Seventh Annual Rpt of the Catholic Com for Refs* [1943], 13, 24. In 1944, the Natl War Fund supplied 90% of CCR's expenses and 77% of ACCR's (J. F. Rummel, *Eighth Annual Rpt of the Catholic Com for Refs* [1944], 25; J. F. Rummel, *Ninth Annual Rpt of the Catholic Com for Refs* [1945], 26; *Newscast*, 1–2/45, 2).

79. *America*: eg, 9/19/42, 654–55, 658, 3/13/43, 630, 6/12/43, 266, 9/9/44, 550, 10/7/44, 10–1, 5/26/45, 145; *Commonweal*: eg, 12/11/42, 204–5, 12/18/42, 220, 2/19/43, 435, 6/4/43, 181–88, 5/12/44, 76–77, 6/9/44, 172, 3/23/45, 558. Other Catholic publications analyzed were *Catholic Action, Catholic Digest, Catholic Mind, Catholic Worker, Catholic World, & Review of Politics.* The *Catholic Mind* printed 2 or 3 inconspicuous references to the mass murder of European Jews (2/44, 120, 8/44, 450, 11/44, 664). The *Catholic Worker* published 2 articles calling for rescue (5/43, 1, 6/43, 1, 9). Regarding the National Catholic Welfare Conference and its Bureau of Immigration: BMM, "Summarization of correspondence . . . to Archbishop Rummel," 2/25/41, BI 82, Ref Problems, R-3; Mohler to Ready, 9/8/44, BMM, Memo for Record, 9/6/44, BI 98, WRB, W-1; Mulholland to Mohler, 9/7/34, BI 40, Jews-Jewish, J – 1; Mulholland to Mohler, 3/26/38, BI 80, Refs-CCR 1938, R-1; Mohler to Mulholland, 5/3/38, BI 82, Refs, German-Austrian 1938, R-3; Mohler to Ready, 10/20/43, BI 83, Refs, Restrictions on Admsn, R-4; Mohler to Mulholland, 11/29/44, BI 81, Refs, Child, USCCEC, R-2; Carroll to Pehle, 3/22/44, W 17, NCWC; Haim Genizi, "The Attitude of American Catholics toward Catholic Refugees from Nazism: 1933–1935," in *Proceedings of the Seventh World Congress of Jewish Studies Holocaust Research* (1980), 27–29, 37–38.

80. Mulholland to Mohler, 8/31/44, 3/13/45, Mohler to Mulholland, 9/6/44, 12/7/44, 4/28/45, 6/11/45, BI 98, WRB, W-1; Mulholland to Mohler, 7/25/39, BI 79, Quotas, Q-1; Mohler to Mulholland, 5/25/34, Mulholland to Mohler, 4/6/37, 3/16/39, Mohler to Mulholland & Calleros, 4/12/38, BI 82, Refs, German, R-3; Buckley to Mohler, 8/4/41, BI 6, Religious; Mohler to Mulholland, 6/7/43, BI 84, R-5; Mohler to Ready, 9/22/41, BI 83, Refs, Eur, PAC, R-4; Mohler to O'Boyle, 3/7/45, BI 35, IMS, I-5.

81. Richie to Rogers, 5/28/42, Wriggins to Schauffler, 7/17/42, Wriggins to Rogers, 4/9/43, 6/3/43, Conard, Rpt to AF, 8/15/44, AF, RS 4; Jessup, Cf with Swanstrom, O'Conner, & Amiel, 2/9/44, A Short Sum of Program of Office of RSARO, 7/18/44, Conard, Rpt on Visit to Spain, 10/16/44, AF, RS 5; USC, Catholic Orgzns folder; Brandt, Convsn with Swanstrom, 10/7/43, BLP, B 202, Refs; Mohler to O'Boyle, 12/22/43, CH, B 6, Ref Orgzns; Egan & Amiel to

O'Boyle, 3/28/44, Amiel to O'Boyle, 5/23/44, W 17, NCWC; Catholic Refs in Lisbon (nd), BI 84, R-5; NCWC, *Progress Rpt 1943: WRS – NCWC* (1943), 1, 3, 6, 8–9; NCWC, *Rpt to Board of Trustees WRS – NCWC: Aug 1943–Sept 1944* (1944), 13–4, 26.

82. *PM*'s news coverage of Holocaust-related developments was relatively thorough from November 1942 through the Bermuda Conference. After that it was sporadic. For instance, it had almost nothing on the Oct 1943 Washington pilgrimage of 400 rabbis, on the Rescue Resolution hearings, or on the emergence of the WRB.

83. Eg, Schoenberg & Gallo to Bloom, 11/19/43, Legis 16432; Robertson to FDR, 5/26/43, FDR, OF 76C; JTA, 12/16/43, 4; JF, 4/43, 3, 11/43, 10–12; Held et al to FDR, 5/4/44, Green to FDR, 5/8/44, FDR, OF 3186; N. A., Notes on Informal Cf, 6/24/43, JDC, Refs, Gen.

84. Ans, 8/43, 6, 12, 15, 11/44, 18; *The Work Is Still Ahead* [12/44], 6–7, PSC 6/27; CW, 2/5/43, 5; Ronald Steel, *Walter Lippmann & the American Century* (1980), 330–33, 373; Roger Manvell, *Films & the Second World War* (1974), 196–99; CC, 12/29/43, 1545; *Commonweal*, 9/24/43, 563.

85. *Daily Worker*, 7/12/43, *Morning Freiheit*, 7/12/43, PSC, S 16; *New Masses*, 5/11/43, 3–4, 11/30/43, 4, 8/15/44, 18–19.

86. Mins of Exec Com, 11/6/43, Digest of Mins of Int Com, 11/23/43, 3/21/44, AJHS, I-67, B 6; CfR 7; NYT, 1/31/44, 5, 8/13/44, 19; LAT, 5/31/44, II, 3; SFE, 8/18/44, 7, 8/30/44, 3; Peterson to Proskauer, 5/24/44, AJC, PEC; MD 707/220; CW, 1/21/44, 20, 1/28/44, 16; J. Woodford Howard, Jr., *Mr. Justice Murphy: A Political Biography* (1968), 353; Scott to Smith, 5/22/44, TH 2; NJM, 6/44, 321; CJR, 12/44, 630; *Liberty*, 1/6/45, 15ff; Chr R, 8/44, 281–83.

87. Based on extensive sampling of the NYC daily press.

88. Based on a thorough analysis of WP & a sampling of other Washington newspapers. Specific references: WP, Oct 3–6 & 8, 1944, & 10/13/44, 16.

89. Based on a thorough survey of BG, CT, DN, DP, KCS, LAT, SFE, and ST; and a sampling of many other newspapers.

90. *Life* had almost nothing; *Time* and *Newsweek* had only a few, mostly minor, items (eg, *Life*, 10/11/43, 93, 8/28/44, 34, 9/18/44, 17–18; *Time*, 12/28/42, 24, 3/1/43, 30, 3/8/43, 29–30, 5/31/43, 24, 9/6/43, 26, 1/10/44, 78, 9/11/44, 36; *Newsweek*, 12/14/42, 104, 12/28/42, 46, 3/8/43, 48, 3/15/43, 36, 5/24/43, 54, 9/13/43, 40, 12/6/43, 22, 9/11/44, 64, 67, 12/4/44, 59). RD, 2/43, 107–10; *Am Mercury*, 2/43, 194–203, 11/44, 567–75; *Collier's*, 2/20/43, 17ff, 2/27/43, 29ff, 8/28/43, 62, 4/22/44, 30, 10/14/44, 18ff; *Saturday Evening Post*, 6/12/43, 16ff, 10/28/44, 18ff; NP, 3/19/43, 21, 7/16/43, 15. Karski's articles were adapted from *Story of a Secret State*, his book on the Polish underground, published in fall 1944 for the Book-of-the-Month Club (Scherman to Pehle, 12/13/44, W 6, Ger Extmn Camps).

91. Ciechanowski, *Defeat in Victory*, 180, 182.

92. Eg, 1943 Radio Scripts, JM, Manuscripts & Speeches file; PC Mtg Mins, 12/29/42, WJC, U185/2; Murphy to Weinstein, 4/4/44, W 22, Radio/Misc; Pehle to Green, 4/7/44, W 22, Radio/A. Green.

93. Manvell, *Films & the Second World War*, 167–83; CC, 5/19/43, 622, 10/6/43, 1150, 1/5/44, 31, 3/8/44, 319, 5/31/44, 679; Shultz to J W Wise, 1/6/43, WJC, 268/V;

Activities of AJCg & WJC with Respect to Hitler Program [1/43]. WJC, U185/2; Suid-Wyman interview, 11/15/78; CW, 11/20/42, 5; Raymond Fielding, *The March of Time, 1933–1951* (1978), index; David Culbert to David Wyman, 10/31/78. Feature films dealing with refugees and/or Nazi atrocities included *Watch on the Rhine, Hangmen Also Die, North Star, The Last Chance, None Shall Escape, The Seventh Cross, Diary of a Nazi, Edge of Darkness, The Hitler Gang*. In the last, the narrator did speak, near the end, of the extermination of whole peoples: the Jews, the Poles.

94. Ch 2 above.

95. This is discussed by Robert Weintraub in *J Week*, 10/26/80, 32. Several newspapers used NYT copyrighted articles on events overseas.

96. Arthur Koestler published a penetrating essay on this problem in NYT, 1/9/44, VI, 5. Other useful discussions include those in YVS, v 7, 53–5 (by Louis de Jong), & in Walter Laqueur's *The Terrible Secret*, esp 2–3, 199–206.

97. *Commonweal*, 10/16/42, 604, 12/11/42, 204–5, 12/18/42, 220, 2/19/43, 435, 3/26/43, 566, 6/4/43, 181–88, 11/12/43, 93; *America*, 9/19/42, 654–55, 658, 3/13/43, 630, 6/12/43, 266, 5/26/45, 145; chs 2, 3, 6, 10 above; Berle, Memo of Convsn with Vahervuori, 12/8/42, SD, R/3495½; BG, 5/3/43, 1, 11; Reams to Stettinius, 10/8/43, BLP, B 202, Refs.

98. *YV Bulletin*, #6/7, 1960, 25–26.

99. NYT, 8/30/44, 9.

100. Eg (all on 8/30/44): NYT, 1, 9; WP, 2; SFE, 1, 6; DN, 1; LAT, 4; CT, 6. Also, *Time*, 8/21/44, 36, 38, 9/11/44, 36; *Newsweek*, 9/11/44, 64, 67; *Life*, 8/28/44, 34, 9/18/44, 17–18; *Sat Eve Post*, 10/28/44, 18ff. *Newsweek*'s report did state that about half of the 1,500,000 killed at Majdanek were Jews. And *Life* reported that most of the victims were Jews. In his book *Six Presidents, Too Many Wars* (1972), Bill Lawrence mentioned that his report (to the NYT) had specified that most of the Majdanek victims were Jews, but the Russian censors had cut that part out (100). Unlike the press, State Department officials recognized the connection of Majdanek with the Holocaust (NYT, 9/11/44, 10). Koestler: NYT, 1/9/44, VI, 5.

101. GEC; McC to Pehle, 10/12/44, W 61, Extmn Camps; MD 750/354–60, 751/239. The version released by the WRB also included the report of a Polish military officer who had escaped from Auschwitz. A summary of the data appeared in some US newspapers in July 1944, but it attracted little notice. (NYT, 7/3/44, 3, 7/6/44, 6; *Wn Star*, 7/3/44, 2; ST, 7/3/44, 2; KCS, 7/3/44, 12.).

102. Roswell McClelland to David Wyman, 9/18/80; Pehle to McCloy, 11/8/44, W 6, Ger Extmn Camps; MD 790/135–6.

103. MD 799/231–36, 802/254; W 5, Ger Extmn Camps, Newspaper Clippings folders. Eg, NYT, 11/26/44, 1, 24; WP, 11/26/44, 1, 11; *Collier's*, 1/6/45, 62.

104. Mannon to Pehle, 11/16/44, W 6, Ger Extmn Camps.

105. All in 1945: SFE, 5/2, 8; LAT, 4/21, 1; KCS, 4/23, 6; ST, 4/25, 1; DP, 4/25, 24; NYT, 4/22, 13, 4/27, 3.

106. All in 1945: NYT, 4/21, 5, 4/23, 5; DP, 4/23, 22, 5/15, 1; LAT, 4/22, 1, 2, 4/27, 7, 4/28, 1, 5/15, II, 1, 5/16, II, 4, 5/18, II, 1; KCS, 5/13, 1; CT, 4/23, 4, 4/29, 20; SFE, 4/29, 1, 5/16, 7; DN, 5/10, 2, 5/16, 1.

107. Hilberg, 632–33.

108. Eg, NYT, 4/25/45, 3; CT, 4/26/45, 3; DN, 4/26/45, II, 10, 5/2/45, 11.

109. Based on analysis of the 10 newspapers listed in ch 2, source note 12. Quotation is from SFE, 4/22/45, 4.

110. *1st para*: eg, NYT, 4/18, 8, 4/23, 5, 4/28, 6; WP, 4/10, 1–3, 4/16, 1, 4, 4/18, 1, 2, 4/21, 1, 3, 4/24, 1, 7, 4/28, 1; *Collier's*, 6/16, 14, 28, 6/23, 16ff (all in 1945). *2nd para*: NYT, 5/8/45, 12; LAT, 5/8/45, 4; WP, 5/8/45, 3; NYT, 8/4/79, 2; *J Advocate* (Boston), 9/28/78, II, 23.

111. Cantril, 383.

112. Cantril, 1070–1; WP, 12/3/44, 1. In the November poll, 12% thought the information was not true, and 12% had no opinion. In May, 9% thought the reports partly true but exaggerated, 3% considered them untrue, and 3% did not answer. Those who said they believed the reports were asked for their "best guess" as to how many had been murdered. In November, the most typical answer was 100,000. In May, it was 1,000,000.

113. Ch 1 above; ch 14 above, section on Ft Ontario; Mtg of PC, 12/17/42, WJC, U185/3; Voss-Wyman interview, 2/11/78.

114. NYT, 5/14/44, VI, 9.

115. See pages 62–3; IR, 10/13/43, 291, 297; *N. W. Ayre &*

Son's Directory of Newspapers & Periodicals (1943); Matzozky, "Am J Press Reaction"; RYP genly; AJYB, v 46, 473–81. Mass meetings were covered in chs 2 and 5 and elsewhere above. Also, many thousands of Jews sent letters and telegrams to Washington concerning rescue. (Seen in FDR Papers, WRB Papers, and elsewhere. Also, MPD, v 5, 1340.)

116. Ch 4 above.

117. Chs 4–6 above.

118. Ch 9 above; Adler, "American Jewry & That Explosive Statehood Question," 12, 16–17; AJYB, v 44, 476–77.

119. Ch 9 above; Adler, "American Jewry," 7.

120. Chs 8 & 11 above.

121. Ch 9 above; Voss-Wyman interview, 2/11/78; AJH, 3/81, 310–30.

122. Mds, 3/64, 9; *Reconstructionist*, 1/21/44, 3–4; *J Examiner*, 1/14/44, 4.

123. Mds, 3/64, 9; Neumann, *Arena*, 189; GCM, 11/12/42, 12/3/42; Meltzer, Convsn with Goldmann, 7/14/43, SD, R/4063; Lesser, Memo for Files, 7/21/44, W 70, J. Brandt; *In the Dispersion*, winter 1963–64, 6–7; *Reconstructionist*, summer 1983, 4; *Martyrdom & Resistance*, 11/83, 11; *YV Bulletin*, 4/57, 4; *PM*, 5/18/43, 9; JF, 6/43, 3.

124. JDC's share of funding is based on data on pages 213–14.

Jewish refugees (mostly children) arriving in France from Germany. Many of those Jews who managed to escape Germany in the 1930s were caught in the net of German occupation as it engulfed Europe. 1933–1936. (YIVO Institute for Jewish Research, courtesy of USHMM Photo Archives)

Jewish refugees from Italy, who fled over the border into France following the adoption of antisemitic legislation by the Italian fascist government, eat a meal at a shelter in Nice. March 16, 1939. (Bibliotheque Historique de la Ville de Paris, courtesy of USHMM Photo Archives)

Jewish emigrants sit on bunks in cramped sleeping quarters aboard a ship bound for South America. Circa 1933–1940.
(Deutsches Historisches Museum)

Departure of Sol and Henrietta Meyer and their son Harvey from a train station in Germany en route to the United States. 1939.
(Jill Berg Pauly, courtesy of USHMM Photo Archives)

Bernard Wasserstein **Sealing the Escape Routes**

During the first two years of the war the German Government was not the primary obstacle to Jewish emigration from Nazi-controlled areas of Europe. Not all Jews, of course, were permitted or able to emigrate. Those incarcerated in concentration camps, prisons, or ghettos had little opportunity of escape. Much often depended on the whim of a bureaucrat and the venality or soft-heartedness of a police or customs official. Jews who left Germany were forced to surrender their property and were often subjected to brutal treatment before departure. Some tens of thousands of Jews managed to escape: in 1940 36,945 Jews entered the USA, and 8,398 were admitted to Palestine; a few thousand more reached Argentina, Canada, and other countries.[1] But these numbers constituted only a small fraction of the vast multitudes desperately seeking an escape route from Nazi-dominated Europe. That the great majority of Jews failed to emigrate was primarily due to the extreme reluctance of all countries to admit them. The only two countries, indeed, to which any significant numbers of Jews could still emigrate after the outbreak of the war were the USA and Palestine. But even in these cases the door was now almost closed. Fifty-two percent of all immigrants to the USA in 1939 and 1940 were Jewish; the Jewish proportion of the total was the highest in American history; but in absolute terms the numbers admitted (43,450 in 1939 and 36,945 in 1940) fell far short of the peak years of Jewish immigration between 1899 and 1914 when about 1,300,000 Jews had arrived (out of a total immigration to the USA in those years of 13,700,000). The main obstacle to larger Jewish immigration was the quota system imposed under American law, which laid down the numbers of immigrants of each national origin to be admitted in any year. The law prevented many applicants from qualifying for admission, and long queues developed for visas several years in advance. In spite of the intense pressure for visas, there was formidable public and congressional opposition to any change in the immigration laws. The interpretation of the law by the State Department was, in general, stringent and restrictive, particularly toward refugees "likely to become a public charge." After July 1940 hardly any visas were issued to applicants from Germany.[2]

Throughout the war the British and United States Governments continued the futile search among the waste places of the earth for suitable havens for Jewish refugees. In the course of 1940 there was extensive discussion in the Foreign Office about the possibility of reviving the scheme for a "second Jewish National Home" in the interior of British Guiana; the provision of such a refuge was seen, as one Foreign Office official put it, as "desirable . . . to salve the conscience of H.M.G. [His Majesty's Government] in relation to European Jewry."[3] But the Colonial Office insisted that Britain was "under no *special* obligation to assist the settlement of Jewish refugees within the United Kingdom or the Colonial Empire." It was pointed out that the scheme "would be open to objection on the ground that the British subjects in the West Indian area were in greater need of and had a far stronger claim to such assistance." And the fear was expressed that "any reference to the establishment of a Jewish National Home, however vague, would give rise to strong opposition in British Guiana . . . [and] to difficulties comparable with those experienced in Palestine."[4] The project was abandoned. Exotic proposals for Jewish refugee settlement in a number of improbable places, among them North-West Australia, Eritrea, Ethiopia, and the Mindanao area of the southern Philippines, flourished briefly in the official files, and were speedily consigned to the oblivion of the archives. The United States Government was particularly attracted to the notion of large-scale Jewish settlement in Angola; the Government of Portugal (which ruled Angola) betrayed no interest in the idea. A suggestion that Jews might settle in Alaska was similarly discarded. For a time much faith was placed in the prospects for Jewish refugee settlement in the Dominican Republic, whose government manifested considerable enthusiasm for Jewish immigration. With the active support of the Inter-Governmental Committee and of the U.S. State Department, an agreement was signed in January 1940 between the Dominican Government and the Dominican Republic Settlement Association [DORSA], an American-financed company: the agreement provided for the immigration of up to 100,000 refugees who were to be settled under the auspices of DORSA. By June 1942 a total of 472 settlers had been established (at a cost of $3,000 a head). Plans for expansion of the settlement were abandoned after the disappointing beginning.[5] Repeated efforts by the British Government to induce Dominions and colonial governments to accept some Jewish refugees met with frustratingly negative replies. In a typical comment, in January 1941, on a Foreign Office query about the possibility of Jewish emigration to the colonies, a Colonial Office official wrote:

> Apart from the obvious difficulties in the way of their getting to any Colony, the hard fact remains that they are not wanted by any Colonial Government for a number of very good reasons, the most important of which perhaps are that they are certain sooner or later to become a charge on public funds . . . The introduction of a body of people, however small, which is entirely alien in every sense of the word, would be greatly resented by the working classes in the Colony and might well lead to serious trouble . . . I am thinking particularly of the West Indies.[6]

Such replies evoked a feeling akin to despair in the Foreign Office, where one official minuted: 'This was to be expected. I don't know what is wrong with the colonial Empire, but its absorptive capacity seems to be nil.'[7]

As the door of the USA closed, as the British Empire was discovered to be filled to capacity, as the far-fetched settlement programmes for obscure regions collapsed, as all sovereign states closed their borders to

all but a trickle of refugees, and as the vise tightened round European Jewry, thousands of Jewish refugees, fearing for their lives, struggled to reach any safe destination. In the course of 1940 and early 1941 over two thousand Jews travelled over the Trans-Siberian railway to Kobe in Japan, whence they made their way to Shanghai, swelling further the Jewish refugee population there. The *Yeshiva* of Mir arrived in Shanghai *en bloc*, having been issued with visas to Curaçao in the Dutch West Indies, by a sympathetic Dutch Consul in Kaunas, Lithuania; they were able to make the journey after receiving Japanese transit visas from the Japanese consul. But immigration restrictions to Shanghai, first imposed by the Japanese occupiers in August 1939, were after 1941 stringently enforced.[8] Except for Jews in Lithuania, able somehow to obtain Soviet transit visas, Shanghai was, after the outbreak of the war, no longer a practicable destination. There appeared to be only one alternative: Palestine. During the autumn and winter of 1939–40 boats heavily laden with Jewish refugees continued to set out for Palestine from ports on the Black Sea and the Aegean. The Jewish Agency's Immigration Department, with its network of Palestine Offices (which, in some cases, were permitted to operate in Nazi Europe), was officially charged with the administration of legal immigration to Palestine in cooperation with the Government of Palestine; but its officials simultaneously organized part of the illegal (or as the Agency preferred to term it, "uncertificated") influx. Larger numbers of illegal immigrants were organized by the Revisionist Zionists and by shady figures from the Roumanian and Greek underworld who perceived an opportunity to combine humanitarianism with an easy penny.

The reaction of the British Government was to implement the immigration provisions of the White Paper policy. . . . The White Paper had laid down that a total of 75,000 Jewish immigrants were to be admitted in the course of five years: the policy was applied with retroactive effect from April 1939. However, so strict was the application of the policy that, in spite of the great outward pressure from Europe in 1939 and 1940, the numbers admitted fell far short even of the figure set by the White Paper. In July 1939 the Government had announced that because of the large number of illegal immigrants who were arriving in Palestine no quota at all would be issued for legal immigration in the six months October 1939 to March 1940. Upon the outbreak of the war the principle was enunciated that no refugees from Germany or from German-occupied territory were henceforth to be admitted to Palestine. "So far as we and France are concerned," minuted a Foreign Office official, "the position of the Jews in Germany is now of no practical importance."[9] As a result of insistent Zionist pressure, the Colonial Office conceded that persons in enemy territory who already held Palestine immigration certificates would be allowed to proceed.[10] With the cooperation of the neutral Italian Government, and the full acquiescence of the Germans, 2,900 certificate-holders (including 1,019 from Prague, 717 from Berlin, and 448 from Vienna) were transported to Palestine via Trieste by an Italian shipping line.[11] But this was the only significant exception to the rule. For the six months April to September 1940, a quota of 9,060 certificates was authorized; but under half that number were actually admitted to Palestine. From October 1940 until June 1941 legal immigration was again suspended. In fifteen of the first thirty-nine months of the war no legal immigration schedules were issued. The result of these measures was that by the end of 1942 (when three-quarters of the five-year period laid down by the White Paper had already passed) barely half of the 75,000 immigrants theoretically permitted under the White Paper had been admitted to Palestine: since April 1939 a total of 38,930 had arrived; of these a majority, 19,925, were illegal immigrants.[12]

In order to counter the "invasion," as it was termed, of illegal immigrants, the Government considered every possible diplomatic, legal, and military means at its disposal. In an effort to block the escape routes from central Europe which were used by illegal immigrants, energetic diplomatic action was undertaken by the Foreign Office to try to persuade the governments of south-east European states to cooperate. The Bulgarian Government was warned in December 1939 that "in the event of any further instances of Bulgarian ships being involved in the illegal immigration traffic with Palestine, His Majesty's Government will expect [the] Bulgarian Government to

take [the] immigrants back."[13] Under pressure from the British Embassy in Bucharest, the Roumanian Government promised that Roumanian vessels would be prevented from carrying Jewish refugees down the Danube.[14] In February 1940 the Yugoslav Government, as a result of similar representations by the British Government, promised "to exercise a strict control over the passports of all Jews who are embarking on vessels under the Yugoslav flag . . . taking a particular care that the passports are labelled with the necessary letter "J" and that in every respect they are provided with all the necessary visas and other formalities allowing the bearer to proceed to and disembark in Palestine." The Yugoslav Foreign Ministry added that the measures were being taken "with the sole object of responding to the urgent requests made by the British Government . . . although such a measure will inevitably deprive our shipping companies of a very substantial sale of transport tickets." The Foreign Office instructed the British Ambassador in Belgrade to convey "an expression of the appreciation of H.M. Government" to the Yugoslavs.[15] The Panamanian Government was induced to take preliminary steps toward the cancellation of the Panamanian registration held by many of the ships engaged in the illegal traffic.[16] The Liberian Government was asked to prevent the circulation of bogus Liberian entry visas.[17] Summarizing the diplomatic action taken, a Foreign Office memorandum stated:

The Foreign Office has asked countries of transit to refuse transit visas; . . . it has asked the nations where the owners of such [illegal immigrant] ships reside to take action against them; it has asked the nations whose ports are used by such ships to put administrative difficulties in the way of their sailing; and it has explored the possibilities of evading the legal provisions concerning freedom of transit on the Danube and through the Straits in order to enable the riparian governments at our request to hinder the traffic. Representations have been made to twelve European and Mediterranean governments and to several American governments. In Roumania, Turkey, Greece, Bulgaria and Yugoslavia these representations have been carried to a point which has made the question of illegal immigration a factor constantly present in our relations with those countries.[18]

Yet this far-reaching British diplomatic effort to stanch the flow of refugees out of Europe had only a limited effect: it raised the prices paid for tickets to shipping agents and in bribes to officials of Balkan and other states, but it did not stop the illegal movement.

Notes

1. Gurevich, *Statistical Handbook*, 116.
2. Wyman, *Paper Walls, passim.*
3. Minute by R. T. E. Latham, 26 Dec. 1940, PRO FO 371/24568/47 (E 1063/1063/31).
4. Colonial Office memorandum, June 1940, PRO FO 371/24568/160 ff. (W 1063/1063/31).
5. Dana G. Munro *et al., Refugee Settlement in the Dominican Republic*, Washington 1942.
6. K. E. Robinson to P. J. Dixon (Foreign Office), 13 Jan. 1941, PRO FO 371/30000 (R 425/122/37).
7. Minute by E. M. Rose [?], 20 Jan. 1941, ibid.
8. David Kranzler, 'The Jewish Refugee Community of Shanghai, 1938–1945', *The Wiener Library Bulletin*, 1972/3, vol. XXVI, nos. 3/4, new series nos. 28/9, 28–37; Yehuda Bauer, 'Rescue Operations Through Vilna', *Yad Vashem Studies*, vol. IX, Jerusalem 1973, 215–23.
9. A. W. G. Randall minute, 5 Sept. 1939, PRO FO 371/24078 (W 13132/45/48).
10. M. MacDonald to G. Weizmann, 3 Oct. 1939, PRO FO 371/24095/54 (W 14438/1369/48).
11. H. Barlas, *Hatzalah Bimei Shoah*, Tel Aviv 1975, 20–3.
12. Hurewitz, *Struggle for Palestine*, 109, 138–9.
13. Foreign Office to Rendel (Sofia), 6 Dec. 1939, PRO FO 371/24096/347 (W 17689/1369/48).
14. Sir R. Hoare (Bucharest) to Sir R. Campbell (Belgrade), 30 Jan. 1940, PRO FO 371/25238/405 (W 1384/38148).
15. Translation of Note Verbale from the Yugoslav Ministry of Foreign Affairs', 19 Feb. 1940, PRO FO 371/25240/86 (W 3207/38/48); Foreign Office to Belgrade (draft), 29 Feb. 1940, PRO FO 371/25240/87 (W 3207/38/48).
16. Panamanian Ministry of External Affairs to British Envoy Extraordinary, 13 Dec. 1939, PRO FO 371/25238/215 (W 318/38/48).
17. Foreign Office to Monrovia, 11 Apr. 1940, PRO FO 371/25241/143 (W 5819/38/48).
18. Memorandum by J. E. M. Carvell, Feb. 1940, PRO FO 371/25239/150 (W 2500/38/48).

Two women sit in despair in their cabin on the SS Flandres after hearing the news that they and their fellow Jewish refugees will not be allowed entry into Cuba. On May 16, 1939, ninety-seven German and Czech Jewish refugees sailed aboard the French liner, Flandres, for Havana. When the ship arrived, however, Cuban authorities ruled that only six of the passengers had proper visas and would be allowed to remain in the country. When Mexico also denied entry to the remaining refugees, the ship was forced to recross the Atlantic. The passengers disembarked in St. Nazaire, and were given temporary sanctuary in the west of France. June 8, 1939. (Bibliotheque Historique de la Ville de Paris, courtesy of USHMM Photo Archives)

Members of the *Yishuv* (the Jewish community in Palestine) take to the streets in protest against the British White Paper restricting Jewish immigration to Palestine. May 18, 1939. (The Photo Archives of Keren Kayemet, LeIsrael Jewish National Fund, courtesy of USHMM Photo Archives)

Michael R. Marrus **Rescue Efforts**

During the last days of 1942, the Allied governments finally issued an official condemnation of Nazi genocide against the Jews. Since the preceding summer, incontrovertible evidence of mass murder inundated British and American officials; from various quarters at once pressure mounted for a public pronouncement on the matter. On 17 December such a statement was formally released, made on behalf of Britain, the United States, the Soviet Union, the French National Committee, and the governments in exile of Belgium, Holland, Luxembourg, Norway, Czechoslovakia, Greece, Yugoslavia, and Poland. Immediately, the declaration was released to Nazi-occupied Europe in twenty-three languages. Numerous reports indicated, the statement began, that the Nazis "are now carrying into effect Hitler's oft-repeated intention to exterminate the Jewish people in Europe." After a graphic description of the slaughter and an estimate that the victims numbered "many hundreds of thousands of entirely innocent men, women and children," the declaration solemnly called for the punishment of the perpetrators of these crimes. Along with retribution, however, many who were moved by these words demanded some sort of rescue. Something, they urged, had to be done for the Jews who still survived. In practical terms, this sentiment focused on the possibility of evacuating endangered Jews to some place of refuge, perhaps to a neutral country like Sweden.[1]

Appeals for some sort of rescue reached Allied capitals at the very moment when the Nazis were beginning to lose the military initiative in the field. If there was a turning point in the European conflict, this was undoubtedly it: in October 1942 the battle of El Alamein in the Egyptian desert sent a great shock through the Wehrmacht; the tremendous battle of Stalingrad, which ended on 2 February 1943, shattered the entire German Sixth Army of a half million men and kept the oil-rich Caucasus out of Nazi hands. The following summer the British and Americans landed on the coast of Sicily, soon to begin the fight up the Italian boot. Meanwhile, the Soviets sent thousands of tanks against the Germans at Kursk-Orel, beginning a westward drive that never stopped. By the end of the year the Russians reached the old frontiers of Poland. These military moves provided the backdrop before which rescue advocates issued their call for action. Allied victories not only cleared territory, occasionally liberating civilian refugees, but they also prompted neutrals and even some cobelligerents with the Reich to cooperate with evacuation schemes.

Despite the new opportunities, however, the results were meager. The Bermuda Conference on the refugee problem held in April 1943 in effect postponed serious efforts; the spectacular Danish rescue of several thousand Jews in October was an exceptional instance of rescue, made possible by unique circumstances of time and place. Only toward the end of the war did the Allies shift their priorities from the fighting itself, and only in early 1944 did serious refugee assistance begin, with the establishment of the American War Refugee Board.

New Prospects in 1943

In the months following the Allied declaration of December 1942, the plight of European Jews and the possibilities of rescue tugged at British and American opinion. Major Jewish organizations in the United States formed a Joint Emergency Committee on European Jewish Affairs to press for action. Nipping at the heels of this body and drawing on many unaffiliated Jews was a much more radical group, eventually known as the Emergency Committee to Save the Jewish People of Europe. Led by Peter Bergson, then a Zionist Revisionist activist and organizer of its underground army, the Irgun, the Emergency Committee helped keep the pot boiling with provocative demonstrations, full-page newspaper advertisements, and intensive congressional lobbying. On 1 March 1943 a huge rally in Madison Square Garden in New York announced a twelve-point program for rescue, calling for negotiations with Germany and her satellites for this purpose and resettlement of the refugees. From Geneva, the World Jewish Congress and the World Council of Churches issued a similar appeal, asking that neutral states grant temporary asylum to Jewish refugees and that Britain and the United States guarantee their reemigration after the war. In Britain, meanwhile, public opinion may have been even more aroused by news of the Holocaust than in the United States. In striking contrast to the phlegmatic commentary in the Foreign Office, angry calls for action sounded in Parliament, the newspapers, and church pulpits. Sir Neill Malcolm, former League of Nations high commissioner for refugees, added his voice to the chorus demanding the admission of more refugees to Britain and the colonies; Eleanor Rathbone, an Independent M.P., bombarded Whitehall with a twelve-point program of her own, including a wide variety of concrete measures to facilitate the arrival of Jewish refugees.[2]

But caution quickly triumphed over imagination. In diplomatic correspondence with Washington in early 1943, the British responded to the mounting pressure at home by suggesting a private Allied meeting on the refugee question. London explained how complicated it felt the problem of refugees to be. There was a danger of "raising false hopes." Notably, the British worried that the Nazis or their satellites "may change over from the policy of extermination to one of extrusion, and aim as they did before the war at embarrasssing other countries by flooding them with alien immigrants." Something, nevertheless, had to be done to assuage the aroused public feelings and to secure additional havens for refugees. Officials in Washington agreed with the British that it would be impolitic to put too much emphasis on Jews: "The refugee problem," they said, "should not be considered as being confined to persons of any particular race or faith. Nazi measures against minorities have caused the flight of persons of various races and

faiths, as well as other persons because of their political beliefs." They concurred that a meeting would be useful. But on the concrete proposal they delayed.

When the British finally threatened to move on their own, the State Department launched what eventually became the Bermuda Conference of April 1943. The Americans first proposed Ottawa as a site for the meeting; but the Canadians, fearful that their own extremely restrictive refugee policy would become the object of critical examination, refused to go along.[3] Concerned in his own right that such a meeting might become a sounding board for appeals to open American gates, a State Department official, Breckinridge Long, a staunch opponent of accepting Jewish refugees, told Whitehall that the meeting was not to propose drastic solutions; the principal goal, it became plain, was to relieve the pressure of prorescue opinion. The Americans knew London to be extremely sensitive to the public relations issue and eager to appear as a champion of the Jews in Europe. In reality, the British were extremely sensitive to their declining influence on Washington and their increasing dependence on the United States. They feared being drawn in the wake of the Americans and exuded caution over the prospects of the conference. Foreign Secretary Anthony Eden was extremely nervous about having too many Jews thrust on the Allies, was defensive about Jewish emigration to Palestine, and concerned about the availability of shipping space. Meeting with Roosevelt, Secretary of State Cordell Hull, and Under Secretary Sumner Welles at the end of March, Eden helped set the tone of the conference. In particular, he poured cold water on the suggestion that the Allies pursue the possibility of evacuating threatened Jewish refugees from southeastern Europe. Although London and Washington agreed to go forward with the Bermuda meeting, therefore, all parties approached it with their guard up, eager to see the gathering transpire without surprises and without any alteration of existing policy.

The Bermuda Conference largely achieved this aim. The Americans put no pressure on Britain over the White Paper quotas for Palestine; the British did not ask the United States to raise its own immigration ceilings. Jewish representatives and inquisitive reporters were kept at bay, and discussions were held in private. No report of the proceedings was ever published. The conference rejected suggestions for negotiations with the Germans or the dispatch of food and assistance to the Jews of Europe. The delegates determined flatly that "no shipping from the United Nations sources could be made available for the transport of refugees from Europe." Although fulsome in praise of what the British and Americans had already done for refugees, the conference report indicated no new prospects for resettlement. The conference did recommend the revival of the dormant Inter-Governmental Committee on Refugees (IGCR) with urgent new tasks. The IGCR ("this decorous and entirely ineffectual instrument" as Ira Hirschmann called it) was to try to obtain neutral ships to move refugees and to secure new places of refuge. The British and Americans were to negotiate the release of refugees held in Spain and consider their removal to North Africa. In an important declaration intended to encourage governments of neutral countries to accept more refugees, the participants announced that they would receive all their nationals at the end of the war and create conditions "as will enable all [refugees], of whatever nationality, to return to their homes."[4]

On both sides of the Atlantic, refugee advocates realized how meager were these results. Congressman Emmanuel Celler of New York denounced the meeting as "a diplomatic mockery of compassionate sentiments and a betrayal of human interests and ideals"; Rabbi Stephen Wise, head of the American Jewish Congress, pressed for a meeting with Roosevelt about the "inexplicable absence of active measures to save those who can still be saved." In London, overwhelmed by the news of the Warsaw Ghetto uprising and the failure of the conference, the Bundist representative on the Polish National Council, Shmuel Zygielboim, committed suicide, protesting the failure of the Allies to act. Eleanor Rathbone, leader of the National Committee for Rescue from Nazi Terror, told the House that the results were "pitiably little."[5]

The conference failed to accomplish much even in areas where there appeared to be constructive agreement. On the matter of encouraging neutrals' acceptance of refugees, for example, London and Washington each wanted an exception made. At the suggestion of the American ambassador in Madrid,

Carlton Hayes, the State Department argued that pressure on Spain would be counterproductive; similarly, the British urged their own exception, Turkey, fearing that Jews arriving there would head for Palestine. Trouble also arose over the establishment of a temporary refuge in North Africa. On this issue, American fears of adverse reactions in the Moslem world to the concentration of Jewish refugees seem to have been decisive. Thus, American military authorities objected to the establishment of even a small camp in North Africa to drain off the accumulation of refugees in Spain. Churchill forced the issue later that summer, and Roosevelt did promise a camp for a few thousand refugees from Spain. More delay followed, however, because of French objections. The results, in the end, were derisory – a few hundred refugees reached North Africa by the end of June 1944, at which point the liberation of France was well under way.[6] Finally, the Inter-Governmental Committee stirred into life in the summer of 1943 with Sir Herbert Emerson as director. Its staff and budget were enlarged, and its membership broadened to include even the Soviet Union. But the IGCR was essentially a political organization without a political mandate; it had no relief machinery of its own and no real power to negotiate with neutral or enemy states. The committee channeled most of its relief funds through the Joint Distribution Committee and provided a secret conduit for sending relief assistance into Rumania. In every important respect, the Allies kept the IGCR on a tight leash. As historian Bernard Wasserstein notes, "the Committee failed to acquire sufficient independent authority to play any significant role in the succor of refugees from Nazi Europe; it remained a bureaucratic monument to the spirit of futility at Evian, where it had been born."[7]

For Peter Bergson and the Emergency Committee in the United States the dramatic evacuation of almost 7,500 Jewish refugees from Denmark in October 1943 pointed to other possible rescue activities. The committee published a full-page advertisement in *The New York Times* with this message, headlined "It Can Be Done."[8] In reality, however, the Danish rescue was an extraordinary achievement, conceivable only in the particular circumstances of Danish geography and conditions of occupation.

Unlike the other defeated states of Western and Eastern Europe, the Danes were largely left alone by Hitler after their prompt surrender in the spring of 1940. In exchange for economic cooperation with the Reich, Denmark kept her king, her government, and even an army, maintaining a nominal degree of independence in internal affairs. For three and a half years, eight thousand or so local Jews lived in relative tranquillity. The Nazis remained unhappy about this, but feared provoking the democratically minded Danes over the issue. Stretched thinly across Europe and disinclined to launch an expensive policy of repression, the Germans kept their hands off Danish affairs. All this changed in the late summer of 1943, when the Nazis, under heavy air bombardment and suffering grave reverses in Russia, increased their economic exactions. Following strikes, riots, and some sabotage, the Germans proclaimed a state of emergency, sweeping aside the Danish government and proclaiming martial law. Nazi persecution of Jews and political dissidents came together with a sudden clamping down on Danish society. The Danes, who had formerly constituted the Germans' "model protectorate," now fought them on every front – including a proposed deportation of the country's Jews for the Final Solution.

In the famous rescue of Danish Jews, geography was paramount: the evacuees were overwhelmingly concentrated in Copenhagen, directly across a narrow stretch of water from the Swedish sanctuary. Timing was also critical. In the second half of 1943, persecutions of Jews were linked to the crushing of Danish independence because the two emerged at precisely the same moment. The autumn of 1943, moreover, was an obvious time for action. Danish resistance, like resistance everywhere in Europe, drew strength from the news of spectacular German misfortunes of the previous summer – the massive Allied bombing over the heartland of the Reich, the invasion of Sicily and the collapse of Mussolini, and the great tank battles in Russia.

Even with these circumstances, large-scale rescue was only possible because of the proximity of Sweden and the Swedish willingness to receive refugees. On more than one occasion Stockholm had used its neutrality on behalf of victims of Nazi terror. Represent-

ing Dutch diplomatic interests in Berlin, the Swedish ambassador to Germany repeatedly inquired about the fate of Jews deported from the Netherlands. Swedish diplomats had intervened on behalf of Norwegian Jews in December 1942, declaring to the Germans their willingness to receive those about to be deported. Although the Nazis refused, the Swedes persisted. In addition, the Swedes knew that they did not act alone. As soon as he heard of the impending deportations, the Danish ambassador to Washington, Henrik Kauffmann, wrote to Secretary of State Cordell Hull, requesting help for Danish Jews and others persecuted by the Nazis; he also immediately cabled Stockholm, notifying the Swedes that Denmark would reimburse Sweden for all rescue costs. The State Department similarly encouraged Stockholm to receive the refugees. The Swedish government, therefore, did not hesitate in October 1943. As soon as the Swedes learned of the impending deportation, their representative in Berlin offered to accept into Sweden all the Jews in Denmark. When the Germans failed to reply, the government released its offer to the press. According to one historian, the Swedish ambassador warned the Nazi Foreign Office "of the indignation and the serious anti-German repercussions which a persecution of Jews in Denmark would provoke in Sweden."[9] Swedish officials encouraged the Danes involved in the rescue and cooperated in the logistical effort that brought the evacuees to Malmö. In Sweden, the Danes were permitted to organize relief committees up and down the coast. At the end of 1943, British representatives in Stockholm reported 11,600 Jewish refugees in Sweden, among them practically the entire Danish Jewish community.[10]

The months following the Bermuda Conference saw a clear shift away from the exclusionist forces of the State Department, led by Assistant Secretary Breckinridge Long, in favor of the advocates of rescue and assistance for refugees. Agitation on behalf of rescue, particularly with a focus on Palestine, increased within American Jewry. "You can't imagine the flood of correspondence that has poured in from all over the country," Long complained to Carlton Hayes in May 1943.[11] Protest mounted with the news of German reverses; and refugee advocates in the United States, notably the Bergson group, became more bold. At the same time, the various governments in exile, sensing now that the day of retribution was drawing near, pressed for declarations on war crimes and warnings about harm done to civilians. Among those moved by the accumulating evidence of the Final Solution was Treasury Secretary Henry Morgenthau, Jr., an assimilated Jew, whose father had called attention to the slaughter of Armenians in 1915, when he was American ambassador to Turkey. At the end of 1943, Morgenthau prepared a confidential report to Roosevelt, calling for rescue of Jews threatened by mass murder. Originally entitled "Report to the Secretary on the Acquiescence of this Government in the Murder of the Jews," the document contained a bitter attack on the dilatory State Department refugee policy. Aware of the depth of such feeling, which now extended significantly beyond the Jewish community, Roosevelt was ready to do something concrete. Following their meeting in mid-January 1944, the president authorized the Secretary of the Treasury to create the War Refugee Board (WRB) to pursue evacuation possibilities and provide relief and assistance. Operating unofficially under Morgenthau's department, conveniently outside the State Department, the WRB was given broad authority to plan rescue operations, evacuate and care for refugees, and negotiate with foreign governments. Roosevelt put John Pehle, thirty-four years old and an energetic Treasury Department official, in charge of the board. Ira Hirschmann, its first full representative, fresh from an important post at Bloomingdale's in New York, immediately sensed that this was an instrument with authority: "Here at last was not a gesture, but a powerful weapon forged by the people of the United States." Underlining the new priority, the director of the WRB was to report to the president "at frequent intervals concerning the steps taken for the rescue and relief of war refugees." Financed mainly through private agencies, the WRB, nevertheless, received a million dollars immediately from Roosevelt's emergency fund and considerably more within a few months.[12]

Notes

1. See Walter Laqueur, *The Terrible Secret: An Investigation into the Suppression of Information About Hitler's 'Final Solution'* (London, 1980), 224–28; Wasserstein, *Britain and the Jews of Europe*, 173–74; Gilbert, *Auschwitz and the Allies*, 101–04.
2. Feingold, *Politics of Rescue*, 174–78; Wasserstein, *Britain and the Jews of Europe*, 177–88; Eleanor F. Rathbone, *Rescue the Perishing: An Appeal, A Programme and a Challenge* (London, 1943); Dina Porat, "Al-domi: Palestinian Intellectuals and the Holocaust," *Studies in Zionism*, 5 (1984), 97–124.
3. Irving Abella and Harold Troper, *None Is Too Many: Canada and the Jews of Europe, 1933–1948* (Toronto, 1982), 130–31.
4. War Cabinet document on the Bermuda Conference, 4 May 1943, Annex No. 5, PRO: FO371/5770/WR67; Monty N. Penkower, "The Bermuda Conference and Its Aftermath: An Allied Quest for 'Refuge' During the Holocaust," *Prologue* (Fall 1982), 145–73; Hirschmann, *Life Line*, 16.
5. Feingold, *Politics of Rescue*, 208; Gilbert, *Auschwitz and the Allies*, 267.
6. Avni, *Spain, the Jews, and Franco*, 117 ff.
7. Wasserstein, *Britain and the Jews of Europe*, 218.
8. Feingold, *Politics of Rescue*, 208; Monty N. Pentkower, "In Dramatic Dissent: The Bergson Boys," *American Jewish History*, 70 (1980–81), 281–309.
9. W. M. Carlgren, *Swedish Foreign Policy During the Second World War*, trans. Arthur Spencer (London, 1977), 158; Valentin, "Rescue and Relief Activities," 235–38.
10. Harold Flender, *Rescue in Denmark* (New York, 1963), 237–38; Wasserstein, *Britain and the Jews of Europe*, 216.
11. Feingold, *Politics of Rescue*, 208.
12. Ibid., 246; Monty N. Pentkower, "Jewish Organizations and the Creation of the U.S. War Refugee Board," *Annals, American Academy of Political and Social Science*, 450 (1980), 122–39. Hirschmann, *Life Line*, 19; Bauer, *American Jewry*, chap. 17; *Final Summary Report of the Executive Director, War Refugee Board* (Washington, D.C., 1945).

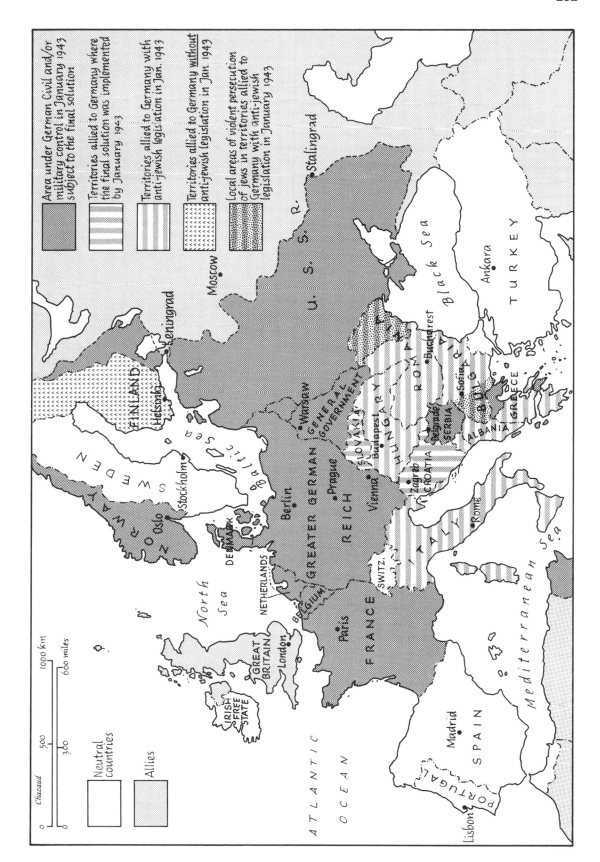

EUROPE, JANUARY 1, 1943

Chazaud

| Area under German Civil and/or military control in January 1943 subject to the final solution |
| Territories allied to Germany where the final solution was implemented by January 1943 |
| Territories allied to Germany with anti-jewish legislation in Jan. 1943 |
| Territories allied to Germany without anti-jewish legislation in Jan 1943 |
| Local areas of violent persecution of jews in territories allied to Germany with anti-jewish legislation in January 1943 |

Neutral countries

Allies

0   500   1000 km
0   300   600 miles

PREBEN MUNCH NIELSEN

COPENHAGEN, DENMARK... OCTOBER 1943 – After the Germans occupied Denmark in 1940, Preben joined the resistance as a courier. In October 1943, when the Gestapo began the roundup of Danish Jews, Preben and his group in the resistance began to help the Jews by hiding them in houses near the shore and bringing them to waiting boats. Under cover of darkness, Preben and his friends took up to 12 Jews at a time across the straits to Sweden. In a three-week period, Preben and his group helped to transport 1,400 Jews to Sweden. He fled to Sweden in November 1943, returning home in May 1945.

As Preben said, "It was a matter of decency, we had no choice."

The Danish rescue boat on display at the U.S. Holocaust Memorial Museum is one of the boats used by Preben's resistance group.

(JFR Photo Archives)

CHAPTER 5 **Gentile Life under German Occupation**

Adolf Hitler and his entourage in front of the Eiffel Tower shortly after the fall of France. With Hitler are Albert Speer, Wilhelm Keitel, Martin Bormann and other Nazi officials. June 28, 1940. (Bildarchiv Preussischer Kulturbesitz, Berlin, courtesy of USHMM Photo Archives)

DEBÓRAH DWORK **Introduction**

EARLY IN THE MORNING OF SEPTEMBER 1, 1939, German troops attacked Poland without warning. With their much larger army and more sophisticated weaponry, the Germans defeated the Poles in less than three weeks, despite the latters' heroic attempt to defend their homeland. It was the brutal beginning of a vicious five-year occupation, during which gentile Poles suffered horribly and Polish Jewry was annihilated.

As the war stretched across the continent, occupation regimes of varying degrees of severity were instituted in the countries Germany conquered: Poland in 1939, followed in 1940 by (chronologically) Denmark, Norway, the Netherlands, Luxembourg, Belgium, and France. France was divided into two zones: the "Occupied Zone" to the north was under direct German administration, while the so-called "Free Zone" in the south was still under French governance. The headquarters of the "Free Zone" was in the resort town of Vichy, from which the newly constituted state derived its name: Vichy France. Vichy France was occupied by Germany two years later (1942), after the German armies had conquered both Yugoslavia and Greece in 1941, and had invaded and occupied vast stretches of the Soviet Union that same year. Germany's allies, Italy and Hungary, were occupied by Germany when their governments sought to make a separate peace with the Allies in 1943 and 1944, respectively. In each and every case, no matter how harsh or lenient the occupation regime was for the gentiles, Jews ultimately were marked for death.

The life of the Jewish population under German rule is the subject of chapter 6; our concern in this chapter is the conditions under which the gentiles lived during the war years. What was life like for them? How were they treated by the Germans? Were they governed by their own countrymen, albeit under German military occupation, or were they subject to direct rule by the German invaders? And what about their daily concerns? Could they go about their business as they normally did? Did children attend school as usual? Did people socialize, shop, work, and go to the movies as they had done before?

The Poles learned immediately that life most certainly would not go on as before. According to Nazi racial ideology, all Slavic peoples, including the Poles, were an inferior breed, although not in the vermin class of the Jews. The Poles were fit for little, the Germans maintained. They would be the serfs, the brute labor force, in the New Europe that Nazi ideology envisioned. During the war, some two million Poles were sent to work as slave laborers into what the Germans now called "Greater Germany;" i.e., Germany itself and the lands the Germans had chosen to include within their newly enlarged borders. Polish

Early in the morning of September 1, 1939, German troops attacked Poland without warning. It was the brutal beginning of a vicious five-year occupation, during which gentile Poles suffered horribly and Polish Jewry was annihilated.

intellectuals were not to be tolerated at all; during the five years of German rule, nearly 10 percent of the Polish gentile population was killed or died of hunger or disease, and the intelligentsia suffered disproportionately.

Poland itself was divided twice. First, in accordance with a secret German-Soviet agreement, the Soviets invaded from the east seventeen days after the Germans had attacked from the west. The country was split between them with the new border along the Bug River. The Germans then annexed the western part of German-occupied Poland to Greater Germany, deporting hundreds of thousands of Poles and Jews from that area and dumping them into the newly created "Government General," as the remaining German-occupied Polish territory was called. A description of one such deportation has been included here. Written at the time the events took place in 1940, this report was part of a compendium of documents and photographs published in London in 1942 to present "the black record of German barbarism" to the English-speaking world. Appropriately named

Poles forced from their homes by German police carry their belongings to a train station during a resettlement action. 1940–1941. (Glowna Komisja Badania Zbrodni Przeciwko Narodowi Polskiemu, courtesy of USHMM Photo Archives)

The Black Book of Poland, this compilation delineates, in the words of the editors, "the terrifying picture of oppression to which Poles are subjected."

The editors did not exaggerate. The German occupation of Poland was a reign of terror that left little of prewar Poland intact. The Polish government, refusing to hand over power to the Germans, fled to England. Unlike the French, the Danes, or the king of the Belgians, who cooperated with the Germans to varying degrees when France, Denmark, and Belgium were invaded, the Polish government refused to collaborate. By the end of the war, there were several governments-in-exile in London, and they became a powerful focus for patriotism and resistance. The Poles and, later, the Norwegians, Dutch, Luxembourgers, Yugoslavs, and Greeks knew that their statesmen and their sovereigns were alive and well, waiting and working to return.

But Poland was the first country to be invaded by the Germans in World War II, and therefore the Poles were the first to face the violent dissolution of the world they had known. Their country was carved up among the Soviet Union, Greater Germany, and the newly constituted Government General which covered what remained of Poland; their government was in exile in London; the Polish armed forces were also in exile; and the leaders of their communities and society (the prominent businessmen, politicians, professors, etc.) were targeted for "liquidation" – a euphemism for murder.

In the annexed territories, urban Poles were subjected to a reign of terror from the beginning; rural Poles felt the Germans' brutality shortly thereafter. As the occupation continued, Poles in the Government General were subjugated as viciously as their countrymen to the west. As *The Black Book of Poland* excerpts illustrate vividly, every aspect of life was affected: the deportations of hundreds of thousands of people, the institution of forced labor, the intentional destruction of Polish culture, including a prohibition on teaching Polish children the Polish language, and the constant terror of random violence and mass murders. Daily life – going to work, attending school, even purchasing food – was an ordeal. Food, for example, was severely rationed, and the Poles were legally entitled to little. The fruit, vegetables, grain, and livestock of Poland were shipped home to Germany to enrich the Germans' meals. With ration coupons that barely supported a substandard diet, the Poles were left to starve to death slowly. The only way to obtain enough food to survive – let alone to ensure the growth of one's children – was to break the Germans' laws by buying food illegally, without ration coupons and at high prices on the "black market." It was economically advantageous for farmers to sell their products surreptitiously, and the rest of the population needed the foodstuffs they sold. But the risk for both buyer and seller could not have been greater. There was only one penalty for failure to comply with the Occupation regime: death by immediate execution.

France, like Poland, also was divided after the German invasion in May 1940. As noted above, the northern part of the country was occupied by the German army, while the southern part, the "Free Zone," was defeated but not occupied. Unlike in Poland, however, the full weight of the German presence was not felt for some time. On the contrary: on June 17, 1940, the eighty-four-year-old hero of the First World War, Field Marshal Philippe Pétain, announced to the nation that he would seek an armistice with the Germans. He had agreed to head a new government, he explained, and the French should lay down their arms. The armistice was signed five days later and when the French government, the senators, and deputies, met in the spa town of Vichy on July 10, they voted overwhelmingly to give full powers to Pétain.

In theory, Pétain's power extended into the northern zone, but in practice it was only in the south that he suffered little German interference. Nevertheless, the extent of the German occupying presence was significantly different in France, both north and south, than in Poland. And to most French people it initially appeared that "occupation" was a delimited military phenomenon, not a social, political, and economic stranglehold. The French had a legitimate national government on French soil, duly authorized by elected representatives. Their army was reduced to one hundred thousand men – but they had an army, and no claim was made on the navy. The Mediterranean coast was left under Vichy control, which permitted the French access to their North African territories. Marshal Pétain's government in Vichy

> Every aspect of daily life was affected: the deportations of hundreds of thousands of people, the institution of forced labor, the intentional destruction of Polish culture, including a prohibition on teaching Polish children the Polish language, and the constant terror of random violence and mass murders.

had its own deeply conservative national agenda, the "National Revolution," which it pursued largely unimpeded for several years. Vichy's policy with regard to Germany, as Pétain unabashedly announced, was "collaboration."

By the second year of German rule, however, many French people had come to realize that they were, in fact, both defeated and occupied, and that the occupation did not have delimited, specific goals but was a ubiquitous, seemingly omnipotent authority. As a young Parisian named Paul Simon wrote in early 1942, "In 1871 [after the Franco-Prussian War] the Germans occupied only; this time they are interfering in everything. They have installed themselves in the railways, public administration, police forces, banks, insurance companies, press, wireless, films, law and education. They are everywhere, even in the so-called unoccupied zone, and in the colonies. . . . They are . . . suppressing all liberty, even of thought. . . . A regime of tyranny has been set up . . . and every day fresh executions take place."[1]

Both men and women were affected, but not necessarily in identical ways. One and a half million Frenchmen were prisoners of war, and the women left at home had the double burden of working and taking care of their families. Finding food for meals and the fuel with which to cook it were burdensome challenges, as were the vain attempts to keep family, clothes, and home clean without soap. An excerpted chapter from Margaret Collins Weitz's book, *Sisters in the Resistance*, explores the special difficulties French women faced within the context of the Occupation and the Vichy regime.

Hitler had appeared to offer France a partnership, a "collaboration," in his New Order; in fact he was interested only in exploitation. But if the Poles were of no consequence and the French of little consequence, the Danes, by contrast, were of significant consequence. It was to Denmark that the offer of partnership and collaboration was sincerely extended. The Danes, after all, were "Aryans." They were also cooperative.

Denmark was invaded in April 1940 and quickly surrendered. As an excerpt from Leni Yahil's book, *The Rescue of Danish Jewry*, explains, the Danish king remained on the throne and many aspects of prewar civilian life remained intact and undisturbed for three and a half years. It was the most lenient form of occupation; a "model protectorate" according to Hitler. Unlike in Poland where the prewar political elites, administration, and structures were shattered immediately, or in France where the death of the prewar republic became clear with time, in Denmark the prewar democratic internal institutions remained intact. For gentile Poles, daily life during the war was catastrophically different from what it had been

King Christian X of Denmark rides down a Copenhagen street shortly after the German occupation. April 11, 1940. (AP/Wide World Photos)

before. For most gentile French men and women, the depth of the schism between pre-Occupation and Occupation life soon emerged despite the Vichy regime. But in Denmark, daily life in wartime remained remarkably the same as it had been before the Occupation. This served the Danes well when their Jewish countrymen were threatened in October 1943.

Note

1. Quoted in H. R. Kedward, *Occupied France: Collaboration and Resistance, 1940–1944* (Oxford and New York: Basil Blackwell, 1985), 10.

Daily life in wartime Denmark remained remarkably the same as it had been. This served the Danes well when their Jewish countrymen were threatened in 1943.

THE GERMAN-SOVIET PARTITION OF POLAND, 1939–1941

Poland, September 1939

Polish territories annexed by the German Reich, 1939

General Government 1939–1941

Vilna land, annexed by Lithuania, 1939–1941

Eastern Poland, annexed by the Soviet Union, 1939–1941

Chazaud

THE POLISH MINISTRY OF INFORMATION **The Black Book of Poland**

MASS SLAUGHTERS AND EXECUTIONS UNDER THE OCCUPATION

In the "Incorporated" Territories

Immediately after their entry into Poland, the Germans set to work to exterminate the Polish intellectual classes. They at once murdered large numbers of Polish priests, landowners, officials, lawyers, professors, teachers, and doctors. Then came mass executions, which reached their greatest intensity in the period following October 15, 1939. **It appeared that the Germans had determined to exterminate entirely the leading elements in the western provinces of Poland.** In addition to the categories already mentioned, these murders also included merchants, artisans, labor leaders, Trades Union leaders, leaders of peasants' agricultural organizations, etc.

Especially during the first period, these murders were committed without even a parody of court procedure, without even the formulation of a charge. A Pole had only to be indicated as "inimically disposed toward the Germans" *(deutschfeindlich gesinnt)*. Poles were executed either publicly, usually in the marketplaces, or the Gestapo disposed of them secretly, often at night; very many were murdered in the prisons. Hundreds of hostages also were murdered. The most glaring cases in each of the Western provinces of Poland are given below.

Pomerania

At **Gdynia**, 350 of the leading men were arrested as hostages. First they were taken to Danzig, where they were made to do hard labor, then to Wejherowo. Many of these hostages were shot in the local prison, on the Polish Independence Day, November 11, 1939. Before the execution took place, these men dug their own graves. The shooting was carried out in relays, each group being obliged to witness the deaths of those who preceded them. The Gestapo agents killed their victims by a revolver shot in the head.

The attitude of these unfortunate men was heroic. They died crying: "Long live Poland!" There was not a suggestion of court procedure. No statement was made as to why these massacres took place.

Here are the names of some of the leading men, whose fate, after nearly two years, is unknown:

Messrs. Łęgowski, director of the port of Gdynia; W. Szaniawski, Governmental Vice-Commissioner for Gdynia, President of the Franco-Polish Association, former French officer, decorated with the Legion of Honor; Jagodziński, Counsellor of the Gdynia Governmental Commissioner's Office; Czarliński, President of the District Court; Kryczyński, Vice-President of the District Court; Schwarz, Konwiński, Kiedrowski, Judges; Kozłowski, Prosecuting Attorney; Linke, director of the Communal Savings Bank; Borysławski, director of the local branch of the Agricultural Bank; Józewicz, lawyer; Stanisław Borkowski, director of the Naval Department; Prelate Turzyński and his brother; Pinecki, a Danzig professor. . . .

THE TRAGEDY OF THE PEASANTS IN THE ŻYWIEC COUNTY (REPORT DATED THE END OF DECEMBER, 1940)

"IN THE AUTUMN OF 1940 the German authorities began the brutal deportation of the Polish peasant population from the County of Żywiec, in former Western Galicia, a district purely Polish from the ethnic point of view, and never inhabited by any considerable number of Germans.

"As they were threatened with transportation, the peasants refrained from planting potatoes, sowing winter rye and other autumn operations. Then the *Landrat* of Żywiec proclaimed that the deportations would not take place, and that everyone must carry out his agricultural work under pain of punishment

THE POLISH MINISTRY OF INFORMATION, **THE BLACK BOOK OF POLAND**, 28–30, 199–201, 417–18, 425–27, 443–46, 486–88, 490–92. COPYRIGHT © 1942 BY THE POLISH MINISTRY OF INFORMATION. G. P. PUTNAM'S SONS, NEW YORK, NY.

for deliberate sabotage. Despite this proclamation deportations began at the end of September 1940, being carried out in the following manner. Early in the morning a number of lorries, filled with armed S.S. men, would drive into a village. All the roads, bridges and even field paths were occupied by the S.S., who were armed with machine-guns which they trained on the village. Smaller detachments paid particular attention to the peasant farms, driving the inhabitants on to the road, and making them stand with their hands up, with machine-guns trained on them. Then they proceeded to search each individual and to go through the farm buildings. During this search small objects like watches, money and even wedding rings found their way into the pockets of the members of the S.S.

"The deportees were allowed to take with them only one suit of clothes and a little food. As they were driven out of their houses they were kicked and beaten with the butts of guns, neither old folk, women nor children being spared. In consequence several were wounded, and even killed, for example at Sól and Jeleśnia. Several women as they were trying to escape were shot among the farm buildings. One woman had her infant shot in her arms. Then they were kicked and knocked about, packed into lorries, and transported to concentration camps at Rajcza and Żywiec. There deportees from several villages were assembled and kept two or three days in the open fields in rain and frost, not being allowed any warm food or covering. There were terrible scenes of suicide and child births. Only after two or three thousand deportees had been collected were they packed into trains, with twenty złotys each in their pockets, and transported to the neighbourhood of Lublin, Warsaw, or Kielce in the 'Government General.'

"It should be mentioned that the journey in unheated trucks frequently lasted three days. On arrival at their destination they were divided into groups of ten or so, who were assigned to one farmer, this being equivalent to being condemned to a life of beggary. A few of the younger men and the stronger women were transported to Germany in special trains to do compulsory labour there.

"It should be said that in spite of the desperate position in which they found themselves, the population behaved heroically. When the lorries full of deportees drove through some place which had not yet been evacuated they sang the Polish National Anthem.

"When it transpired that the assurance that there would be no transportations was false, the people began to destroy their farm buildings and stock, so as to leave as little as possible for the Germans. They cut the throats of their fowls, sheep and goats and cattle. They scattered their feather quilts and pillows, throwing the feathers down the wells, they broke the windows, destroyed the tiled stoves, and chopped up the floorboards and doors. Every night chickens and geese were hung on the door of the police station, with the inscription underneath: 'They would rather be hanged than be eaten by the Germans.'

"The entire population of any particular village was not deported at once, for some inhabitants were left in peace. It appeared that this was done because the agricultural labourers left behind were wanted to dig potatoes and finish agricultural operations for the incoming Germans. But they were used principally to destroy the mountaineers' cottages. For in place of ten or twelve deported families the authorities established a single family of Germans from Volhynia, who spoke Polish or Ruthenian, and knew only a few words of German; they were given the fields and the livestock, etc., which had belonged to the deported Poles. In this way the authorities created farms of twenty to thirty Little-Polish *mórg* (one *mórg* is about half a hectare, or 1.3 acres). The German family was established in the best house, and all the other houses were destroyed and used for firewood. Those of the inhabitants who were not deported at first had their turn later, only a few families being left in each village. They were quartered in remote cottages, which lay high in the mountains. Two or three families were crowded into each cottage, for which they were compelled to pay a rent of seven to twenty marks. They were also deprived of the fields they had formerly possessed, and were allotted small holdings of one-half or three-quarters of a *mórg* of the worst soil high in the mountains. They were informed that even this land was only rented to them and not given outright.

"The villages in the County of Żywiec had a 98.5 percent Polish population at the last census. Today the district is completely changed in appearance. On the lonely roads one hears Ukrainian, and the densely built settlements are vanishing, only heaps of rubbish being left in their place. The transportations are continuing, and it has further to be added that even before they began some 20,000 people, mainly men, were in German or Russian captivity, or had been transported in masses to Germany for forced labour during the Spring of 1940." . . .

THE RESTORATION OF SLAVERY

THE GERMANS WERE NOT SATISFIED with invading Poland, murdering tens of thousands of the civil population by bombardment from the air, and introducing into the occupied territory a system of murder, persecution and robbery, which surpasses everything of this kind hitherto known in the history of mankind. Their rule in Poland is characterized by the constant aim of humiliating and degrading the Polish population, while at the same time the leaders of the Third Reich, the Press, and the German wireless deliberately and systematically attempt with cynical falsehood to blacken the Poles in the eyes both of the German community and of the whole world. The Poles in their own country are treated as people of lower class, as servants, and even as slaves. The doctrine that the Germans are a *Herrenvolk*, preached by so many German philosophers and historians ever since the beginning of the nineteenth century, has been applied to the full by the National Socialist regime in the occupied territories of Poland.

After almost 2,000 years of Christian civilization, slavery has been reintroduced in large areas of Central and Eastern Europe.

In the system of the German occupation in Poland we find all its characteristic features: the deportation of the population of whole provinces from their ancient homes, united with the robbery of all their property, movable and immovable, the deportation of hundreds of thousands of people, men and women, for forced labor in places from which they may not shift, the seizure of young girls and their deportation to brothels, mass executions, carried on, without any trial, under the auspices of the authorities, complete impunity for every functionary who may murder or torture Poles, the intentional deprivation of the Polish population of all means of access to the higher spheres of education and culture, the prohibition on teaching Polish children their native tongue, and the merciless extermination of the leading class of the nation.

Indeed, the representatives of the German authorities in Poland themselves assert that it is the destiny of the Polish people to serve the German *Herrenvolk*.

The chief German administrator at Łódź, Herr Übelhor, former mayor of the city of Mannheim in Southern Germany, made a speech typical of this attitude on November 11, 1939, that is to say, on the day which the Poles celebrate as the anniversary of the recovery of independence. He said inter alia:

> We are masters, as masters we must behave. The Pole is a servant *(Knecht)* and must only serve . . . we must inject a dose of iron into our spinal columns and never admit the idea that Poland may ever rise again. . . . Be hard.

Further on in his speech, which was published in the local official German *Lodzer Zeitung* (now called the *Litzmannstädter Zeitung*), Herr Übelhor announced that the Kościuszko monument at Łódź had been destroyed as a sign that:

"Poland will never return here."

The same Herr Übelhor, in a broadcast speech of December 2, 1939, repeated:

> Every Pole is a servant *(Knecht)* and every Pole must blindly and unhesitatingly carry out any order given to him by a German.

After more than a year's occupation, the speeches of the administrator of Łódź, the largest Polish city after Warsaw, had undergone no change. We quote words spoken by him and printed in the *Litzmannstädter Zeitung* of October 28, 1940:

> District President Übelhor declared that the Pole never changes: we shall never forget what he has done to us, and we must make him feel that

we are masters, and he must work for us. If he meets a German on the pavement, the Pole must step aside. As for the Jew, he must work with ever-increasing intensity, must toil and sweat to keep himself alive.

Mr. Übelhor's declarations are not at all exceptional. . . .

"A Lower Race Needs Less Food"

The Poles are systematically **hindered from obtaining sufficient food.** As we describe in more detail elsewhere, they get a food ration 50, 66, or often 75 percent less than the German population, who receive different ration cards. The Poles get no ration whatever of some foodstuffs which are indispensable. Milk, for example, in many places is reserved for German children. It is forbidden to sell chocolate to Poles in the "Government General": the well-known Polish chocolate factories of Wedel, Fuchs and others are compelled to produce exclusively for the Germans.

On January 31, 1940, Dr. Ley, the head of the German Labour Front *(Deutsche Arbeitsfront)*, made a speech in which he stated that a nation of "superior culture," as he considers the Germans to be, needs more space and a higher standard of life than races with a "lower culture," such as the Poles.

"A lower race," he said, "needs less food."

A regulation issued by the *Oberbürgermeister* (Mayor) of the city of Poznań, Dr. Scheffler, dated November 8, 1940, allows the **sale of fruit and milk only to German children and youth.**

Nor is that all. Food may be sold to Poles in the shops only after the Germans have been served, in special hours, often only in the afternoon, after the Germans have been served in the morning. The result is that very often, after waiting in front of the shops in long queues, Poles do not get anything, since the Germans have bought up everything.

Here is a notice of this kind printed in the *Litzmannstädter Zeitung* of November 22, 1940:

> At Łódź from 9 a.m. onwards Poles are to be served with milk only after Germans. Further, a police order reserves 30 eating houses for the ex-

clusive use of Germans, so that these German eating houses may receive goods which come in small quantities and therefore cannot be distributed among general customers.

In the same number of the *Litzmannstädter Zeitung* we find the following notice:

> The Poles are not allowed to enter shops between 8 and 10:30 A.M., or 3 and 4 P.M.

Special regulations direct that even at fairs and markets Poles are only to be served after Germans. The same is the case in all Government and municipal offices. Throughout the German-occupied area the order in which people are served is as follows: First *Reichsdeutsche*, after them *Volksdeutsche*, who are not citizens of the Reich, next Ukrainians, after them Poles, and last of all Jews.

Prohibitions

In the "incorporated" areas the **Poles are forbidden to go into public gardens, swimming baths and bathing beaches. They are restricted in their use of the railways, the long-distance buses, and the trams,** and even taxis, bicycles, horse cabs and light carriages. If they disobey they are **beaten and violently maltreated.** As a rule there is no defense; the German aggressor is always right.

On the most important tram routes in Poznań the leading **tramcars are reserved exclusively for German** use, and the Poles are allowed to use only the trailer cars. A regulation dated December 2, 1940, completely prohibits the use of trams by Poles between 7:15 and 8:15 A.M.

The situation is not much better in the "Government General."

The rear compartments of trams in Warsaw and other towns are reserved for Germans. The Poles are allowed to get on only in front, which causes crowding and numerous accidents, especially as the trams are almost the only means of travel in the towns, as motor buses and cars have been withdrawn from use. Poles are not allowed to travel by express trains; and in ordinary trains they may only go third class. The occupation authorities have forbidden Jews to travel by train at all. . . .

THE REAL AIM OF THE GERMAN AUTHORITIES

NOWHERE IS THE REAL AIM of the German authorities in Poland shown so clearly as in the field of culture. If we consider a nation to be a community bound together not only by a common language but also by common traditions and a common intellectual and artistic heritage, and possessing in addition a whole class of people who are occupied with questions of enlightenment, science and art, then we see clearly from the German proceedings in the occupied areas of Poland that they are systematically and with premeditation aiming at the complete annihilation of the Polish nation.

There are certain differences between the policy followed in the "incorporated" areas and in the "Government General," resulting from the fact that the "incorporated" territories are intended by Berlin for complete Germanization, whereas the "Government General" is to form a kind of Polish "reserve." But the fundamental aims of German policy are the same in both.

The following, in a few words, are these aims in the field of culture:

The destruction of the Polish intellectual classes: i.e., Polish scholars, professors, teachers, writers, artists, lawyers, engineers and doctors, by their murder or by torturing the great majority of them to death in concentration camps and by depriving the remainder of their livelihood;

The destruction or pillage of the monuments of Polish history and culture, and of everything which bears witness to the great past of the Polish nation;

The transportation out of the country of all valuable collections and objects connected with science or art;

The prevention of the Polish community from obtaining knowledge, by the closing of universities and secondary schools, organizations for popular education and libraries, and, in the "incorporated" territories, even of Polish elementary schools;

The paralyzing of all scientific, artistic and literary work, the closing of all cultural institutions, the prohibition of the publication of all kinds of Polish periodicals and books, and the destruction of Polish drama, cinema, music, and plastic arts*;

The abolition of the use of the Polish language in public and even in private life;

And finally the systematic lowering of the intellectual and moral level of the Polish community.

The aim which the German authorities keep in view is the **transformation of the Polish nation into a community composed only of manual workers, who are to be slaves, deprived of their own culture and national tradition, and forming a reservoir of labor** for the benefit of the German Reich. This aim, indeed, is not in the least concealed. Governor General Frank has repeatedly proclaimed the destruction of the Polish intellectual classes and expressed the conviction that every manifestation of Polish culture ought to be crushed.

"The Poles" – he says – "do not need universities or secondary schools; the Polish lands are to be changed into an intellectual desert" (*eine intellektuelle Wüste*). . . .

THE DESTRUCTION OF THE POLISH INTELLECTUAL CLASSES

THE INTELLECTUAL CLASS is undoubtedly the social class which, with the clergy, is most savagely attacked by the German occupiers of Poland.

In the **"incorporated" areas** it has been completely annihilated. Some of its representatives have been murdered, others were flung into prisons and concentration camps, and the remainder, robbed of everything they possessed, have been deported in cattle trucks to the "Government General." An area with almost eleven millions of inhabitants, of whom more than nine and a half millions are Poles, has been completely deprived of Polish professors, scholars, schoolteachers, judges, lawyers, doctors and engineers. These unhappy people were robbed of everything: their scientific laboratories, private libraries and art collections, their lawyers' offices, medical and dental surgeries, laboratories and clinics. No revolution or

---

*sic, fine arts, *Ed.*

war hitherto has led to such monstrous and un-examined robbery and to such mass deportation of a whole social class. The victims, deported without any means of livelihood, have been scattered mainly among the small towns and villages of the "Government General," where they live with their families in abject poverty. There is not the least hope for the great majority of them of getting any kind of employment.

The situation of the Polish intellectual class in the **"Government General"** itself is not much better. Many of its eminent representatives, as we have already stated in another place, have been murdered by the Germans; thousands are tormented and tortured in prisons and concentration camps, especially at Oświęcim, Sachsenhausen-Oranienburg near Berlin, Dachau in Bavaria and Mauthausen in Austria. Their families live in continuous uncertainty as regards the morrow. The manhunts and arrests carried out by the Gestapo are directed principally against the educated classes: thus, for example, in the course of a single night in July 1940, more than 100 Polish lawyers were arrested in Warsaw.

Eighty percent of the Polish intellectual classes have lost their sources of income and are sunk into poverty. Literary men and journalists are completely deprived of their means of existence by the closing of the whole Polish press, the prohibition of the publication of new books and the confiscation from book shops of many works already published. Plastic artists (painters and sculptors) can work only if they obtain a special license from the German authorities; and of course no one applies for such a license. Actors likewise have been unemployed since the closing of all the theaters. Some of them have become waiters in Warsaw coffee houses. Wide circles of former officials, school-teachers, engineers, etc., are doing manual work insofar as they can find any: some of them are breaking stones on the road, others are clearing away the debris of houses destroyed in Warsaw, and some are employed in small factories and workshops. These, however, form a comparatively small proportion; the remainder, deprived of the possibility of finding any employment, are selling the rest of what they possess and dying of hunger.

The most tragic fate, however, is that of the Pol-ish university professors. In their treatment German barbarism has reached its climax.

Professors of Polish Universities in Concentration Camps

The fury of the occupying authorities was directed particularly against the **University of Cracow,** one of the oldest in Europe, founded in 1364 by King Casimir the Great. For nearly six centuries this university has been the main center of Polish intellectual and cultural life and has produced a number of scholars of world fame. In modern times many of them have worked in the second great scientific institution at Cracow: The Polish Academy of Science and Letters.

Two months after the entry of the German armies, at the beginning of November 1939, all the professors of the University of Cracow and of the Mining Academy were invited by the German authorities to a meeting, which was to take place on November 6th in the University Aula. At this meeting – the invitation stated – a lecture was to be delivered by a German on the subject of "The attitude of the German Authorities to Science and Teaching." When the professors, invited in this treacherous manner, gathered in the Aula, Dr. Meyer, the chief of the Gestapo in Cracow, addressed them with the following declaration:

"In view of the facts that (1) the professors of the University were intending to begin lectures; (2) they had not interrupted their work in the scientific institutes and seminaria; and (3) the University of Cracow had been a bastion of Polonism for more than five hundred years, **all the professors in the Aula are arrested."**

Thereupon the agents of the Gestapo **attacked the amazed professors** and put them in police cars, pushing and kicking them brutally in the process. **Some were severely beaten.**

Of a total of one hundred and seventy-four professors and assistants arrested, only seven, very old or seriously ill, were set free.

The remainder, **one hundred and sixty-seven** in

number, were at first kept for a few days in prison at Cracow, and then **were deported** to Breslau, without being allowed even to take leave of their families. With them were deported also five students who happened to be in the Aula. Thus one hundred and seventy-two altogether were deported.

DESTRUCTION OF UNIVERSITIES, SCHOOLS, CULTURAL INSTITUTIONS, THE PRESS, AND OF THE INTELLECTUAL AND ARTISTIC LIFE

Universities and Schools

Polish universities and schools have met with a fate they had not known even in the worst times of former captivity.

All the universities and schools of the academic type in both portions of German-occupied territory have been closed and liquidated; and the German authorities have proceeded to deal in the same way with the higher schools.

In the "incorporated" territories all the elementary schools which use Polish as the language of instruction have also been liquidated. It is only in the "Government General" that a certain number of these schools have been left.

When the Poles in the "Government General" made efforts to open secondary schools, one of the highest officials of the Governor General's administration, a certain Wartheim, declared to the delegates that he did not propose to open secondary schools and still less universities, since in the territory of the "Government General" a Polish educated class was not needed. Governor General Frank declared that the Polish tribe, being a *Knechtenvolk*, did not require higher education. The elementary school was more than sufficient. Henceforth there are to be no higher schools in Poland.

Fate of the Polish Universities

In the area subsequently occupied by the Germans there were before the war four Polish universities: at Warsaw, Cracow, Poznań and Lublin, together with twelve well-organized schools of university type, eight of which were in Warsaw, namely: the Free Warsaw University, the Warsaw School of Engineering, the Principal School of Rural Economy, the Commercial Academy, the State Institute of Stomatology, the School of Political Science, the Higher School of Journalism, and the School of the Eastern Institute; three were at Cracow: the Mining Academy, the Academy of Fine Arts, and the Commercial Academy. In Poznań there was the Commercial Academy. (In the Soviet-occupied area there were two universities, in Lwów and in Wilno, besides The Lwów Engineering School, School of Veterinary Medicine and Academy of Foreign Commerce, and the School of Political Science in Wilno.) All these schools in the academic year 1938–39 had more than 45,000 students, male and female.

Today, as the result of the express prohibition of the German authorities, not one of these is active; indeed their formal liquidation has been announced. The official *Verordnungsblatt* of the "Government General" of November 2, 1940, announced the nomination by the German authorities of a special curator of universities and schools of university standing, whose task is to be the liquidation of all universities in the territory of the "Government General." The procedure in the "incorporated" territories is similar.

In actual fact the German authorities destroyed the universities and academies in Poland even before these proclamations were issued, in the very first months of the occupation. They forbade the universities to open at the beginning of the academic year, the buildings of the universities and academies were occupied by the military and civil authorities, the laboratories and libraries were pillaged and a large number of professors were imprisoned or placed in concentration camps. . . .

Secondary Schools

In the German-occupied territory there were about 550 secondary schools. All these were closed by the occupying authorities, a considerable proportion of their buildings being occupied by the army or the Gestapo and a large number of their teachers being imprisoned.

In the **"incorporated" area** the buildings of all the Polish secondary schools, state and private, together with all their equipment, were confiscated and the Polish libraries were destroyed. The Polish teachers were deported to the "Government General," or imprisoned and sent to concentration camps. Many of them were shot. The young people of school age were scattered; many secondary schoolboys were actually shot (there were dreadful massacres at Bydgoszcz and at Obłuże near Gdynia). Large numbers of young people of secondary school age, boys and girls, were deported for forced labor in the heart of Germany.

Besides the already existing German secondary schools in the "incorporated" areas, new ones were founded and housed in the confiscated buildings of Polish schools.

In the territory of the **"Government General"** the secondary schools began work in October, 1939, but in Warsaw on November 15 of the same year the Germans ordered teaching to stop; similar instructions were issued a little later in the provinces.

While military operations were still in progress the schools suffered grave losses in equipment and teachers, varying between 30 and 60 percent. The scientific collections and libraries of the schools were pillaged or laid waste by the Germans. Thus, for example, at Warsaw the scientific collections of the state secondary schools were thrown in disorder into the school museum in Hoża Street and afterwards were partially seized and carried off by the Germans. The school libraries were completely destroyed. The best school buildings (e.g. the building of the Batory Gymnasium and Lyceum at Warsaw) were given to newly created German schools.

The German authorities permitted the opening in the territory of the "Government General" only of trade schools, principally of handicrafts. This is in accordance with the policy of trying to change the Polish community into a reservoir of laborers and craftsmen to serve the needs of the German Reich.

Elementary Schools

In the **"incorporated" area,** as we have already stated, there are no elementary schools at all – in fact no schools where Polish is the language of instruction; the former Polish schools were treated in the same way as the secondary schools; their buildings and equipment confiscated, their Polish books burned, and their teachers shot, imprisoned, or sent to the "Government General."

Because the Polish children and young people are full of patriotism and national consciousness, the Germans endeavor to destroy them by every means in their power; by the organization of forced labor, by transportation into the center of Germany, and by deportation to the "Government General." The majority of Polish children are receiving no education. On the other hand, new German schools are open to which the children are compelled to go, to be Germanized there. These are not the German schools which existed for the German minority under the Polish government; they are special schools for Polish children, the purpose of which is the denationalization of these children.

The system of the teaching is, of course, National Socialist. The cult of Adolf Hitler and the falsification of history is the basis of the teaching, which recalls very much the communist schools, where religious teaching is replaced by the cult of Stalin.

Corporal punishment has been introduced into these schools, though it was unknown to Polish children before, and also the so-called *Militärhaltung*, whereby the children are compelled to stand at attention before the commissary who plays the part of inspector, and follow his every movement with their eyes. They are punished if they turn their eyes in another direction.

The teachers brought from Germany are unable to deal with the Polish children because they cannot understand their language. Consequently the German authorities have ordered Polish teachers who speak German to help in the teaching. The majority of them have refused their cooperation, and consequently have been sent to concentration camps. Those who yielded to threats and agreed are treated as assistants of an inferior class.

In the **"Government General"** in October 1939, permission was given for the opening of elementary schools, but a certain number were soon closed again; in Warsaw alone, for example, thirty elementary schools were closed in January 1940. In March of the same year permission was given for the reopening of these schools.

From that time onward the number of elementary schools has varied considerably, depending on the decisions of the central or local German authorities, whose motives are completely unknown. In consequence the number of children attending elementary schools is not much more than a half of what it was before the war; for example, in Warsaw in 1938 there were 380 elementary schools with 141,000 pupils, while at the beginning of 1941 there were only 175 schools with about 82,000 pupils. In these schools all textbooks of Polish as well as of History, Geography and Religion have been confiscated.

The teaching of History and Geography has been stopped altogether. It is forbidden to publish new textbooks and so there is a shortage of books even for the subjects which are permitted; and in consequence of the confiscation of the old books for teaching Polish the children in the villages frequently learn reading from their prayerbooks. All periodicals for children and young people have been prohibited (like all Polish periodicals in general).

The work at school is in general carried on under the worst possible conditions; a portion of the buildings have been destroyed by bombardment, and a further portion is occupied by German soldiers and officials. Because of the lack of fuel the temperature in the schoolrooms in winter is hard to endure. . . .

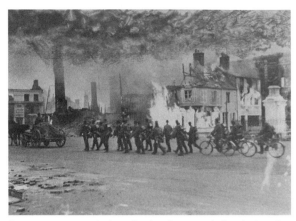

German troops march through a burning town during the invasion of Poland. September 1939. (Jerzy Tomaszewski, courtesy of USHMM Photo Archives)

Four days before the fall of Warsaw to the Germans, a German anti-tank gun is brought in position on main road immediately outside of Warsaw. September 23, 1939. (AP/Wide World Photos)

German troops tear down the border crossing at Sopot, near Danzig, as they invade Poland. September 1, 1939. (Archiwum Dokumentacji Mechanicznej, courtesy of USHMM Photo Archives)

The execution of Piotr Sosnowski, a priest from Byslaw, Poland, by the SS and *Selbstschutz* (the ethnic German self-defense militia in Poland) in a forest near Tuchola. October 27, 1939. (Glowna Komisja Badania Zbrodni Przeciwko Narodowi Polskiemu, courtesy of USHMM Photo Archives)

A group of Polish prisoners was taken to the Tuchola forest, ordered to empty their pockets and forced to dig a large grave. Father Sosnowski from the nearby village of Byslaw was allowed to give the men absolution. SS-Colonel Wilhelm Theodor Richardt then informed the prisoners that they were to be shot in reprisal for burning two barns owned by ethnic Germans. Six at a time were shot at the edge of the grave by a *Selbstschutz* firing squad. Ten Poles were left alive to fill in the grave. Altogether forty-five men, including Father Sosnowski, were killed in the *aktion*.

SS personnel lead a group of blindfolded Polish prisoners to an execution site in the Palmiry forest near Warsaw. October 1939 – December 1939. (Glowna Komisja Badania Zbrodni Przeciwko Narodowi Polskiemu, courtesy of USHMM Photo Archives)

Statues of Polish cultural figures removed by German authorities and hidden by Franciszek Luczyno in his masonry shop. 1939–1940. (Glowna Komisja Badania Zbrodni Przeciwko Narodowi Polskiemu, courtesy of USHMM Photo Archives)

A German soldier guarding church bells in Poland confiscated by the Germans. (Courtesy of Photo Archives, The Ghetto Fighters' House Museum, Israel)

Spectators watch as a Polish woman is led through the town square by two Jews wearing armbands. The sign around her neck states: "For selling merchandise to Jews." In Poland, the consequence for a non-Jew helping a Jew was death. [This woman is apparently being taken to an execution site.] After 1940. (Zydowski Instytut Historyczny Instytut Naukowo-Badawczy, courtesy of USHMM Photo Archives)

Polish civilians handing in radio receivers as ordered by the Germans. (Imperial War Museum, courtesy of Photo Archives, The Ghetto Fighters' House Museum, Israel)

Margaret Collins Weitz **France Under German Occupation**

Toward the end of the 1930s, when Hitler's deeds began to match his designs to institute the principles of Nazism set forth in his *Mein Kampf* (*My Battle*, 1925–1926), most French people continued to believe that France was not in serious danger. This indifferent reaction may be attributed partially to the internal crises the country had weathered after World War I, the war "to end all wars." The interwar years in France were characterized by tensions and social unrest. France suffered severe economic depression in the 1930s, and the country was still trying to regain a firm financial footing.

Following an attempted rightist coup in 1934, the Popular Front, a left-leaning government, was installed in 1936–1937. When the Popular Front broke up in 1937, its members followed their separate ideological bents. Many of the Socialists were pacifists, but the Communists were not; condemning imperialist nations, they focused on the class struggle of the workers against the ruling class as that struggle was defined and redefined for them by the Comintern from Moscow. The outbreak of civil war in neighboring Spain furthered dissension among the French. French efforts to confront the growing German aggression were met by British pressures for appeasement, the 1938 Munich accord being the most noted among these ultimately futile efforts to keep the peace. These factors all contributed to internal discord. Although, paradoxically, three women served as undersecretaries for the first time during the Popular Front government, French women did not gain the right to vote until the end of World War II, hence they did not yet have a voice in the political process.

In 1938, Édouard Daladier of the Radical Party put together a government that attempted to deal with the steadily deteriorating situation. Decree-laws were passed to circumvent the legislature, the elected delegates of the people. The Daladier government was convinced that Hitler could be appeased; France's ally Great Britain shared that belief even after the Germans invaded Czechoslovakia. When German troops marched into Poland on September 1, 1939, however, France and Great Britain honored their alliance and declared war on Nazi Germany two days later.

A long period of inactivity following Hitler's victories in Eastern Europe in the fall of 1939 lulled France into complacency. Rationing was not implemented and military preparations lagged. In the ensuing months, little happened except for brief French military incursions into the German Saarland and an unsuccessful Anglo-French expedition to defeat the Germans in Norway in late April 1940. This débâcle ended what the French termed the *drôle de guerre*, the phony war.

During the interwar period, the French High Command had not sufficiently studied or kept up with advances in military theory and technology. By the late 1930s, the French military was spending four times as much on fodder for horse-drawn artillery as it was on fuel for military vehicles![1] Excessive resources – and confidence – had been invested in the Maginot Line, a series of fortifications along France's eastern border. Few seemed aware of just how vulnerable a fixed fortification was; flexibility and maneuverability were now key factors in waging war. One exception was a young army officer named Charles de Gaulle, who advocated extensive use of tank units. His suggestions had been largely ignored by his countrymen – but not by their enemy. Consequently, when the German blitzkrieg overran Holland and Belgium in May 1940, the French High Command was caught off guard. There was opposition from the Allied forces, which included British troops and the belatedly called-up French reservists. Only the massive evacuation from Dunkirk saved several hundred thousand British and some French soldiers trapped by the German pincer strategy. The rest of the French

Margaret Collins Weitz, *Sisters in the Resistance: How Women Fought to Free France, 1940–1945*, 21–43, 314–17. Copyright © 1995 by Margaret Collins Weitz. This material is used by permission of John Wiley & Sons, Inc.

army – then the world's largest – fought in retreat. The French nation was devastated, in shock. The national administration collapsed. There were no contingency plans for the possible occupation of Paris. As German troops advanced on the capital in the early days of June, perhaps close to 10 percent of the nation fled southward, along with refugees from neighboring nations. This mass exodus – consisting mainly of women, children, and the elderly – was comparable to what occurred during the barbarian invasions in the Middle Ages. Every means of transport imaginable was used – from cars to carriages and wheelbarrows, all piled high with possessions and people. German war maneuvers and strafing of refugee columns added chaos and disruption to the French military's problems and the general demoralization of the people.

When the Germans invaded France, a young woman whom we will call "Annette" (since she requested anonymity) and her widowed mother joined those making the traumatic trip southward during the exodus. Her account provides some details of that fearful flight. Along the way, mother and daughter were sheltered and fed by peasants. At times they slept on kitchen floors. Finally they arrived at "Annette's" grandmother's home, only to have trouble convincing the family maid to let them in. They were so dirty and disheveled she took them for beggars! When funds ran out, "Annette" and her mother had to return to their apartment in Paris.[2] In addition to personal reminiscences, this mass movement and its consequences are treated in novels such as Jean-Paul Sartre's *La Mort dans l'âme*.

Historian and sociologist Evelyne Sullerot also has vivid memories of the exodus:

My mother was not with us when the Germans suddenly invaded France. She had gone to see my twenty-year-old brother who had been mobilized. Do you have any idea of what that means? Only twenty years between the two wars and we had lost an entire generation [of young men]. My brother was born in 1919, one year after the war ended. He had the name of a dead uncle. And now he was being called to fight in another world war. We, the younger children, had been left with our grandmother, separated from our mother. We were waiting for her in southwest France when the Germans arrived.

They came at night. We heard strange noises and voices. It was the Germans installing guns in our garden. So it was that one night I heard that language which I came to hate to such an extent that it is impossible to express. My grandmother (who knew German) told us, 'Those are the Germans.' It was extraordinary. They entered our garden; just like that. They seemed to belong to another race. It was a Panzer division. The soldiers were very tall – almost six feet – and dressed entirely in black with skull-and-crossbones insignias. They were superb, like angels of death – completely different from our friends, our comrades, from all that we knew.

My mother managed to join us a few days later. This was in June 1940. As it turned out, she was so anxious to rejoin us in the southwest that she traveled from the port city of La Rochelle inside a hearse – under all the flowers. A Protestant pastor arranged it. She came the rest of the way on foot. I wonder if you have any idea of the unbelievable situation in France at that moment. Ninety-nine out of every hundred French citizens were relieved that an armistice had been sought. It was frightening. Everyone had taken to the roads. We saw thousands fleeing, unbelievable scenes. All the Belgians, all of northern France had come to the southwest because they never dreamed that the Germans would penetrate that far. They had all streamed down. Food was scarce. A tomato was worth a fortune. It is difficult to imagine. People slept outdoors, on the beach. The beach was covered with families all in black. The old women were dressed in black. The peasants came with some of their livestock, with their carts, their wheelbarrows. The country was thrown into total confusion, like an anthill that had been knocked over.[3]

Career military officer Henri Frenay (who took "armistice leave" to found Combat, one of the major French Resistance movements) was very disturbed by the general mood. He found the French people "settling into defeat."[4] And Resistance martyr and historian Marc Bloch, in his moving analysis of France's *Strange Defeat* (1946), stated that he belonged to "a generation with a bad conscience" – a generation preoccupied primarily with returning to individual concerns after World War I. In Bloch's view, the French High Command capitulated long before it should have because it was ready to accept an appalling consolation: A regime it abhorred would be crushed to death in the ruins of France. This was the punishment Destiny meted out to a "guilty" nation.[5] Defeatism followed discouragement and disarray.

Paris was declared an open city and surrendered without resistance on June 14, 1940. Four days earlier, the French government itself had joined the exodus to the south and west. After a brief stop at Tours, in the château region of the Loire Valley, it reassembled in the port city of Bordeaux. Changes in cabinet and government followed. Politician Pierre Laval and several colleagues maneuvered to name Marshal Philippe Pétain head of the new French government. Although Pétain was in his eighties and had just returned from serving as French ambassador to Spain, his name inspired hope. He was the World War I victor of the Battle of Verdun. On June 17, Pétain went on national radio to inform the French public that he was offering the "gift of his person" to the French nation and asking the Germans for an end to the hostilities – the only defeated country to seek an armistice.

The following day, de Gaulle (who had been promoted temporarily to brigadier general a few weeks earlier) spoke to the French people from London via the BBC, assuring them that "the flame of French resistance must not die, and will not die." Few heard the speech and even fewer responded. Like the majority of the French, Geneviève de Gaulle heard Pétain's speech, but not that of her uncle.

> We heard the speech of Marshal Pétain on June 17, 1940, at our summer home in Brittany. My reaction was one of shame and anger. Perhaps someone was imitating the marshal. After all, there had been rumors of fifth-column activities designed to deceive the public. My conception of the hero of World War I was so different. But then my father observed that it was indeed Pétain.

The next day, smartly uniformed 'young war gods' arrived by motorcycle in the town where we had spent the night, but they did not stop long enough to take prisoners. It was a sad day: Veterans from World War I wept. Then an excited curé came running up. He had just heard an unknown French general speaking on the BBC who urged resistance, a certain General de Gaulle. 'That's my son,' exclaimed my eighty-year-old grandmother. Already in poor health, she died a month later. The German censors forbade any mention of the name *de Gaulle*, so the obituary notice gave only her maiden name, Jeanne Maillot. Nevertheless, she was well known in the area. In spite of transportation difficulties, there was a large crowd for the funeral services – many carrying wreaths. The local gendarmes gave her military honors. Her burial became a spontaneous, collective act of Resistance.[6]

Charles de Gaulle was among a small group of French who fled to England or one of France's colonies in order to carry on the fight. Ten days later, Britain's Churchill government recognized him as head of the Free French Forces (FFL), the London-based French who vowed not to accept the armistice. De Gaulle was forced to devote considerable time trying to assert his authority, particularly vis-à-vis the United States. Throughout the war, he had to contend with power struggles among the French military who, while in agreement about continuing the fight against the Germans, were often in disagreement over the tactics to be used and the leaders to be chosen. There were tensions among de Gaulle's Free French as well as between de Gaulle and the different Resistance groups formed by those who had remained in France.

The Vichy government openly blamed the general for having, in its view, "abandoned" France. De Gaulle was, in fact, tried in absentia at a June 23 court-martial, convicted of desertion and treason, and sentenced to death. Having a French leader in exile recognized by Great Britain complicated the situation for the French remaining in metropolitan France. No other occupied country had set up a new government on home territory functioning with German approval. French citizens had been brought up to respect legal authority, and Pétain claimed to have been legally invested. This point is still debated in France today. Furthermore, the United States recognized Pétain's government by accrediting Admiral William Leahy as American ambassador to Vichy. To many French, America's recognition was further proof of the legitimacy of the Vichy regime.

Pétain and his entourage moved to the spa town of Vichy in midsummer 1940, a "temporary" situation that lasted until the liberation of France in 1944. There he presided over the demise of the Third Republic. Under Laval's leadership, the National Assembly voted itself out of existence – without debate – on July 10, 1940, and granted Pétain full powers. According to terms of the Franco-German armistice, which went into effect on June 25, France was obligated to pay exorbitant Occupation costs: the nearly two million French prisoners of war were not released.

With the armistice, France was divided into two major zones.* The occupied zone, encompassing the northern three-fifths of the country, had a larger population and greater resources than the so-called free zone in the south, which included Vichy. The fateful word *collaborate* appears in the text of the armistice agreement: French officials and public servants were to "conform to the decisions of the German authorities and collaborate faithfully with them."

The army had fought six weeks, with high losses. Almost 100,000 died and more than 200,000 were wounded. Consequently, the vast majority of the French population tended to view the defeat with relief. France would be spared the extensive death and destruction that characterized World War I. The French people looked forward to stability, to a return to normal life. Yet the situation in France at the outset of the Occupation was far from clear. The eighty-four-year-old hero of World War I headed a new government. Although most felt that Pétain would once again outfox the Germans, some refused to accept accommodation and surrender. *Résistante* Lucie Aubrac recounts the population's confusion.

In the beginning of the Occupation, there were few French willing to undertake risks and join the Resistance. France – unlike, say, Holland or Denmark – had a national government collaborating with the German occupiers. In France the situation was ambiguous. Moreover, it was compounded by French patriotism and nationalism. Marshal Pétain, the head of the government, was a man over eighty and a hero of the preceding war. The French respect age and authority, in addition to their fierce patriotism. It was not easy to join a Resistance group. It was voluntary – and not very glorious at that. There were no uniforms, no military preparation, and no idea of what you would be asked to do. And there was no tradition of women in the military.[7]

Like-minded individuals met to discuss the situation and determine how best to continue the struggle. The aim and nature of their efforts were in large measure determined by location. Those in the occupied zone, where collaborationists were in charge, had to deal with the German presence. There early Resistance was essentially urban, and directed against the Nazis. In the absence of uncensored information, those in the north attributed Vichy's increasingly disconcerting measures to German pressure. Even late in the war (and, for some of Pétain's supporters, to this day), the French in the northern zone accepted the myth of the grand old man playing a double game and doing his best to save France. A 1942 prefect's report from the department of Haute-Vienne claimed that Pétain's "game" was too subtle to be understood.[8] In reality, as historian Robert Paxton convincingly shows, Vichy "sought neutrality, an early peace, and a final settlement on gentle terms with Germany."[9] There was little truth to the postwar myth of Vichy's passivity. For scholar Tony Judt, Pétain embodied "the incompetence of the French High Command, the deep-rooted anti-Semitism of his class and caste, [and] the instinctive desire of many of the French to wait out the war."[10]

Pétain set about implementing what was termed

*The exceptions were the provinces of Alsace and Lorraine, which were annexed, forbidden zones in the northeast and along the coasts, and an area in the southeast that was under Italian control until 1943.

a *National Redressment* or *Revolution*. His regime blamed the Popular Front coalition for France's ignominious defeat. More generally, the hated Third Republic (1871–1940) was held responsible for France's decline and decadence, decried in the literature of the period. Under the guise of patriotism, men who had not been elected to office now set about imposing their vision of France – what France specialist Stanley Hoffmann terms the "revenge of the minorities." A Vichy regime composed of traditionalists, industrialists, financiers, lawyers, technocrats, much of the Catholic hierarchy, military figures seduced by Pétain's reputation, reactionaries, and opportunists sought revenge against those they charged with France's defeat: leftists, Communists, trade unionists, civil libertarians, Freemasons, and Jews. A 1942 prefect's report from Montpellier (AN F/1C III 1156) explicitly states that those in favor of Pétain's government feared a return of the prewar regime.

Without an assembly to hinder him, Pétain instituted a series of statutes and decrees aimed at strengthening the French state. An ever-expanding administration helped implement these so-called laws signed into existence by Pétain.* Pétain's government made overtures to the Third Reich, suggesting a policy of "faithful collaboration," although initially the Germans responded lukewarmly to the marshal's invitation to walk down "the path of collaboration" together. It was in Germany's interest for France to contribute to the Reich's extensive needs. Vichy replaced the republican motto of "Liberty, Equality, Fraternity," with "Work, Family, Country" and changed the name of the French Republic to that of *l'État Français*, the French state, making it more consistent with Germany and Italy's status and underscoring the break with the Third Republic and republican traditions. The nation was to be purified and its moral tone strengthened; harmful individualism would be suppressed. In a June 25, 1940, message, Pétain convoked the nation to an intellectual and moral healing. Such broad changes were made possible by the acquiescence of a demoralized country coming to terms with defeat.

Efforts to purify the French state focused on the Jews, traditional scapegoats. In their authoritative study, *Vichy France and the Jews*, Michael Marrus and Robert Paxton show that Vichy inaugurated its own anti-Semitic policies before any German text regarding the Jews in France had been published, and without having received direct orders from the Germans. And, Paxton points out, as long as Vichy could determine the treatment of French Jews, the regime followed a Catholic and national anti-Semitic tradition.[11] The Germans wanted Jews in the occupied zone sent to the unoccupied zone. Vichy did not want them and started a rival anti-Semitic program in the hope of asserting its authority and preempting German legislation. Jews residing in France – not just the large number who fled there from Eastern Europe during the 1920s and 1930s, but also those holding French citizenship – were subject to special anti-Semitic statutes. Scarcely had the Vichy regime been installed when it set up a commission to review each case of French citizenship granted since 1927. More than fifteen thousand people had their citizenship revoked, including more than six thousand Jews who now automatically became foreigners without protection, hence vulnerable to persecution. Indigenous Jews in Algeria, who had been granted citizenship by the 1870 Crémieux decree, lost it overnight under a law enacted on October 7, 1940.

While German legislation referred to Jews by their religion, the Vichy law of October 3, 1940, defined them by race and promulgated a more restrictive definition than did the Nazis. The following day, a decree was issued permitting prefects to intern foreign Jews or assign them to forced residence. Approximately 25,000 foreign Jews ultimately were rounded up and sent to special French camps where conditions were often harsh – in some instances, worse than the Nazi concentration camps of the time. Under the Third Republic, French detention centers had been opened for foreigners judged undesirable: refugees from the Spanish Civil War; political refugees from Germany; Jews and gypsies from other countries. The history of these camps is becoming better known, and it is not an edifying chapter in French history. Madeleine Barot of the Protestant relief agency

---

*The legal community accepted Vichy's "laws" virtually without protest.

CIMADE and Sabine Zlatin were among those who tried to help the unfortunate internees.

When the war broke out, those viewed as foreign enemies – a threat to France's security – were interned. To this group were added the increasing number of foreign refugees without legal status. Austro-Hungarian Jewish writer Arthur Koestler described their precarious situation as a "new, refined form of torture," when writing of his internment (1939–1940) in the French camp of Le Vernet near the Spanish border (*Scum of the Earth*, 1941). German philosopher Hannah Arendt was imprisoned with other women at Gurs, in southwestern France. Both eventually managed to leave the country. France soon had ninety camps that, while officially described as internment centers, already were being referred to as "concentration" camps by authorities. Jews of foreign citizenship were sent either to existing camps, such as Gurs, or to new centers such as Rivesaltes, in the Pyrénées region. According to Anne Grynberg (*Camps de la honte, Camps of Shame*, 1991), there were approximately forty thousand Jews in these southern-zone camps by 1941.

Additional anti-Jewish legislation followed. Vichy passed a law in December 1942 that required Jews to have their identity and food cards stamped with the designation *Jew*. This was yet another way of keeping them under control. According to Marrus and Paxton, Vichy's aim was to limit immigration, encourage Jews in the Southern zone to leave, and reduce the foreign – or what was viewed as the non-assimilable – element in French economic and cultural life. The profound indifference of Pétain and Laval to the plight of the Jews left the door open to anti-Semitic extremists. Additionally, the pursuit of Jews attracted those who sought employment and enrichment. Along with their jobs, Jews lost their property – art and jewelry, homes and businesses; ultimately, many also lost their lives.

A July 1940 decree forbade Jews – even native-born ones – from holding positions in the French national administration, in metropolitan France as well as overseas. The October 3, 1940, law virtually excluded Jews from the professions, as a 2 percent cap was placed on the number of Jews who could continue practicing medicine, law, and teaching. Those

pressuring the government to enforce this legislation included the national union of students and the orders of the professions.[12] Among those who found this legislation unacceptable was Violette Morin, a student at the University of Toulouse in southwest France:

> My family was Catholic and devoted to republican traditions and values. There were few foreigners in that area. I was somewhat insular and naive about the country's policies regarding strangers. Then I went to Paris for university studies. There I worked with the Vigilance Committee of Antifascist Intellectuals (CVIA). When hostilities broke out, I transferred to the University of Toulouse to continue my studies. Now aware of the so-called Jewish problem, I was outraged to learn that several of my favorite teachers had been relieved of their teaching responsibilities. Why? Because they were Jews. This I found unacceptable. An irrepressible feeling of revolt seized me. I looked for some way to combat those who imposed such decrees and joined a Resistance group.[13]

The list of exclusions was further extended by statute on June 2, 1941. The head of Vichy's Commission for Jewish Affairs would later boast that Jewish civil servants had been eliminated from state posts they had "invaded" "in the press, in the film industry, in all areas where their functions gave them power to control and manipulate minds."[14] This was in addition to their elimination from other areas, in particular those touching the national economy. All the legislation that so affected Jews was published in the *Journal Officiel*, along with mundane matters, such as the required dimensions for sports fields – yet another example of the "banality of evil."

Efforts were concentrated on counting and controlling the Jews, along with depriving them of their goods. With unusual efficiency and utilizing the latest technology, Vichy set up a coded card index of French Jews and their property in June 1941. An earlier German order (September 1940) charged the French with registering both French and foreign Jews in the occupied zone. For the first time in seventy years, information on ethnic background was required of French citizens. The extremely detailed information gathered in these surveys – and the assiduity and thoroughness with which the French undertook them – greatly facilitated the later Nazi decision to implement the Final Solution in France. Only 2,800 of the more than seventy-five thousand Jews deported from France returned.[15] But a quarter of a million survived, according to historian Susan Zuccotti, because of the silence or benign neglect of the majority of the French population.[16] As late as 1943, when compulsory labor laws (*Service du Travail Obligatoire*, STO) were passed, some in France resented the exemption of Jews. Previously viewed as victims, they were now seen as privileged. Postwar emphasis has focused on the large number (three-fourths) of war survivors among Jews – most native-born – residing in France when hostilities broke out. Yet one cannot overlook the Vichy state's early initiative in excluding those deemed "undesirable," passing restrictive anti-Jewish legislation, and acquiescing in German demands to hand over non-French Jews. The rationale behind these exclusionary policies was that they would protect France's own Jewish citizens, yet they betrayed France's historic commitment to the Enlightenment and the Rights of Man.

One result of these anti-Jewish decrees was the decision of some Jews to form their own Resistance group, the *Organisation Juive de Combat* (OJC). Others joined various movements and groups, both Communist and non-Communist. This was more consistent with the republican tradition of seeing themselves as French citizens first and foremost. As Stanley Hoffmann has noted, the traditional prewar view was that the French Republic does not recognize minorities. In whatever group, being Jews made them doubly vulnerable if captured. On the other hand, some believed they had more reason to resist and refused to accept their fate passively.

During the Nazi occupation, French police continued their work, at times in tandem with the much smaller German police contingents and the even smaller SS group stationed in France, few of whom knew French.[17] It was French police and their helpers who rounded up the primarily foreign Jews for internment or deportation (even children, whom the

Nazis had not requested) and helped pursue *résistants*. The biggest roundup of Jews took place on July 16, 1942. (July 16 was designated a national day of remembrance in France in 1993.) Close to thirteen thousand French and foreign Jews – including more than four thousand children – were rounded up in a carefully planned operation involving thousands of French police and auxiliaries, following minutely detailed instructions. For example, pets were to be left with concierges so *they* would not be "abandoned." Those without children were bused to the camp at Drancy, outside Paris, an antechamber to the German concentration and extermination camps. Children under sixteen and their parents were taken to the Vélodrome d'Hiver (or Vel' d'Hiv) in Parisian buses. In contrast to all the meticulous arrangements undertaken for the raid itself, little had been done to prepare for the more than eight thousand people crowded into the indoor racing rink in appalling conditions – oppressive heat, lack of food and water, and virtually no sanitary facilities. Teenager Annie Kriegel (shortly to join the Resistance) witnessed the roundup:

> We had been warned about it. And when I say "we," I mean most Jews. White Russians working at the Prefecture told their Jewish compatriots, who in turn alerted others. That day I was taking the oral examination for the *bac* at the Sorbonne. Mother appeared unexpectedly. She told me that rumors about a roundup, scheduled for that evening, were circulating in the neighborhood. She warned me not to return home. Instead, I was to try and find someone to take me in. Several people I approached could not take me in, for one reason or another. Someone suggested I go to a house that was said to be taking in Jews. So I went to an unpretentious house – at the corner of the rues Sévigné and Francs-Bourgeois in the Marais – where a woman answered the door and led me into a large room with perhaps fifty or more people. There was a heavy silence, like that in a dentist's office. I never learned who this woman was, what her affiliation was, or why she took in all those Jews. I found a spot in a corner and tried to sleep, although I was very frightened.

Young girls then were not as emancipated as they are today. I had seldom been anywhere without my mother or one of my brothers, so I was very frightened.

When I woke at dawn, I looked out the window. Things appeared calm, so I decided to return to our house. On the way there, I saw French policemen carrying suitcases from the dilapidated buildings on rue Duraigne. They were followed by entire families. A scene remains vivid: a typical French policeman, big, strong, rough-cut – crying. He was carrying suitcases and leading these families away, following orders. I kept on and then suddenly heard screams, screams like those one hears in hospital delivery rooms. It was all the human pain of both life and death. In a garage on rue de Bretagne, they were separating men and women before loading them into the buses. I sat down on a bench and thought about what I should do. There, on that bench, I left my childhood.[18]

The same might be said of the four thousand children taken to camps in Pithiviers and Beaune-la-Rolande (both near Orléans) where they and their mothers were transported after spending anywhere from three days to a week in deplorable conditions at the Vel' d'Hiv stadium. Since permission to deport the unrequested younger children had not yet arrived from Berlin, parents and children over fourteen were deported first, leaving the youngest children to fend for themselves. Annette Muller Bessmann describes her memories as a nine-year-old witness at Beaune:

> Everyone was assembled in the center of the camp. The children hung on to their mothers, pulling on their dresses. They had to separate us with rifle butts, with truncheons, with streams of icy water. It was a savage scramble, with cries, tears, howls of grief. The *gendarmes* [national police] tore the women's clothing, still looking for jewels or money. Then, suddenly, a great silence. On one side, hundreds of young children; on the other, the mothers and older children. In the middle, the *gendarmes* giving curt orders.[19]

That was the last Bessmann saw of her mother. Commenting on the testimony of Bessmann and others, historian Zuccotti terms the story of the bewildered, terrified, and abandoned children "the most horrifying, heartrending episode of the Holocaust in France, and the most shameful." Since that time, social worker Annette Monod has devoted her energies to raising the consciousness of the nation about the shocking events she witnessed that infamous day at the Vel' d'Hiv and what followed at Pithiviers. For her, bearing witness is a matter of Christian duty.

Not a single prefect and only a handful of French policemen resigned to protest anti-Jewish measures, although individual French policemen helped the Resistance in different ways. To this day, the role of the French police – which expanded considerably under Vichy – in implementing German and Vichy orders remains a delicate topic. French censors would not release *Nuit et Brouillard* (*Night and Fog*), a 1955 documentary on the Occupation, until a scene of a French policeman overseeing Jews at the Pithiviers camp was deleted from the film.[20] Between June 1940 and November 1942, French police operating in the so-called free zone hunted and pursued members of the Resistance. The police claimed they did so rightly, under orders from Pétain and Laval.[21] In January 1943, the Militia was formed. Those who joined swore to combat democracy, Jewish "leprosy," and Gaullist dissent – that is, the Resistance.

Catholics – more than 80 percent of the French population – did not have as long a tradition of resistance to persecution as did French Protestants. Catholic response to the defeat varied. In his study of the conduct of Catholics during the Occupation, Jacques Duquesne holds that for decades prior to the war, French Catholics behaved essentially as spectators of history.[22] Another observer notes that practically all of Catholic France was "anesthetized" when it came to the Jewish question. Philippe Burrin contrasts the steadfastness with which the church defended its interests and its laxity in responding to the persecution of the Jews. In 1988, Cardinal de Lubac condemned as a grave mistake the silence of Catholic authorities over the anti-Jewish legislation. Refusal to become concerned about worldly affairs was viewed as virtuous behavior by some. Catholic activists, however, did not accept the hierarchy's largely pro-Vichy position. Hearing of the projected armistice, Edmond Micheler, leader of a small group of liberal Catholics in the south, wrote what is presumed to be the first Resistance tract – reprinting texts by poet Charles Péguy – on June 17, 1940, one day before de Gaulle's call for resistance. One outcome of Catholics' participation in the Resistance was their contact with what Duquesne terms the "other": the Protestant, the Jew, the Communist, the atheist.

Education was a major component of Pétain's National Revolution. The marshal spoke to the French – as he did often – as a teacher insisting that schools must instill respect for moral and religious beliefs, particularly those beliefs that the French had held since the nation began – that is, Catholic beliefs. France's secular education system was blamed for the country's defeat. Conservatives and clerics alike saw an opportunity to change the system – one of the major achievements of the Third Republic – faulted for having instituted a clear separation between church and state. Public schools could now offer religious instruction during school hours. In early September 1940, Vichy struck down a 1901 law that required those belonging to religious orders to obtain government permission to teach. Municipalities were free to fund parochial schools. Vichy set the example by awarding Catholic schools a large grant in 1941, although stressing that it was "exceptional." After almost forty years of total prohibition, religious symbols (generally crucifixes) appeared in public schools in some regions, while busts of Pétain replaced those of Marianne – symbol of the French Republic – in public buildings. Following this and related moves, the Catholic newspaper *La Croix* urged Catholics "to express their *unreserved gratitude* to Pétain's government for revoking the iniquitous laws of the Third Republic."[23]

Vichy found that ideological commitment to the curriculum – such as adherence to the detailed instructions on the teaching of history – was more difficult to control. In practice, these directives often had the opposite result from that intended. Vichy's clericalism and demands for ideological conformity encouraged school inspectors and teachers alike to join the Resistance. With few exceptions, those in the public schools were against Pétain and his government's efforts to change their secular educational system. Early in the war, Danielle Mitterrand's father was fired for refusing to submit a list of "foreign" names to authorities. As it turned out, this freed him and his family to undertake Resistance work. Danielle Mitterrand explains:

> My parents were both teachers. They committed their lives to the republican ideals they believed in. They tried to extend the opportunities they received to others. My father [Antoine Gouze] held progressive ideas. He was freethinking, a Freemason, and nonreligious man with firmly held moral principles.
>
> I was enrolled in the Villefranche coed school, where my father was principal and teacher. France had surrendered and was divided into occupation zones. Then my father lost his job and, with it, our family home. [In France, the municipality was generally responsible for housing public-school teachers, whom the state provided and paid.] My father was fired because he would not give authorities the names of students who had foreign names, as required by a 1942 Vichy edict. Vichy wanted the names of Jews and other "foreigners," groups soon to be persecuted. As a dedicated teacher, my father believed his role was to educate the children in his classroom. Period. I left the school when he did. His colleagues gave me private lessons.[24]

Other teachers and inspectors refused to facilitate the forced-labor laws and would not submit the required lists of students eligible for mandatory work service on the coastal defenses the Germans built, or, more frequently, in German factories.

Linked to concerns with education was the cult of Pétain, the venerable father figure. The marshal spoke to the population "in the language of a father, a concerned father who at times needed to scold" his wayward children. Other variants were the adulation of Pétain in religious terms – like Christ expiating the sins of the nation – and Pétain the monarch, who would heal France.* The feast day of Saint Philippe became a national holiday. Double rations were issued and celebrations were held. A new act of faith was composed by the collaborationist newspaper *Le Franciste*: "Monsieur le Maréchal, I firmly believe in all the truths you teach, because you cannot err or deceive the people." An adaptation of the Lord's Prayer addressed to Pétain – "Our Father, Who is at our Head – was circulated widely. There was even a version of the Hail Mary substituting Pétain for the Virgin. The providential savior was described in 1941 as "officiating at a great Mass for the desperate."[25] Pastoral letters urged the faithful to submit and obey the new head of government. Resistance was a crime, preached a Jesuit in a Lenten sermon at Notre Dame Cathedral. Vichy's propaganda services diffused these texts. Thus, a climate was created in which it was held that "a Catholic who disapproves of any act of Marshal Pétain commits a sin." In October 1943, the assembly of cardinals and archbishops went so far as to condemn Catholic Resistance for its deplorable "policies of personal decisions and independence," recalling the exclusive authority of the hierarchy. A recent study on the Catholic Church's role during the Occupation holds that instead of limiting itself to the Pauline doctrine of obedience to the established government, the French Church used all its authority to urge Catholics to rally behind the "legitimate" head of state and to adhere to the program of the National Revolution.[26]

As with Hitler, the new messiah was greeted with religious fervor by large, enthusiastic crowds at his many public appearances. Schoolchildren saluted his picture and expressed their loyalty in song: "*Maréchal, nous voilà*" ("Marshal, here we are [to follow you]"). Prefaces to historical studies of Joan of Arc, Louis XIV, or Napoleon noted the similarities between these figures and Pétain. Clubs, organizations, and programs for young people were established, the best known being the *Chantiers de Jeunesse*. At these obligatory camps in the southern zone, young, non-Jewish French males attended lectures and worked on outdoor projects, the emphasis being on moral and physical development. The *Chantiers* were set up to occupy young men who normally would have been called up for military service, fol-

lowing Vichy's concern for the young – which it conveniently forgot in promoting the compulsory labor of the STO. The only female presence permitted was that of the nurse. Her role, as defined by General Paul La Porte du Theil, founder of the *Chantiers*, reveals the conservative view of French women then widespread:

> The nurses will remain in permanent contact with the young men, sharing their concerns, their difficulties, and guiding and counseling them – in a word, both sister and mother for them. [Nurses are needed in these camps] because a woman is much more kind and understanding than a man. A young man of twenty, when he feels ill, is but a child. He will be more appreciative of the maternal attentions that only a devoted nurse knows how to offer. [This implies that the nurse have] a correct attitude and appearance, and not permit any questionable conduct. [The young men must show her the respect for women] that has been lost and that we must restore in France. I well know that many women have lost [this respect] through their own fault, but it is not up to us to try them.[27]

The general's charitable stance in not throwing the first stone is undercut by his blame of women, a theme repeated in many Vichy directives: Through their vanity and selfishness (in not producing enough children), French women were responsible for the defeat. After the Liberation, women would again become public expiatory victims when women thought to have consorted with the enemy were punished.

Rural France played an important part in Vichy's ideology. Rural virtues were extolled: The land, France's sacred soil, "does not lie," proclaimed Pétain. Hitler, too, envisioned rural France playing a role by supplying Germany's ever-growing need for food and raw materials. Early in October 1940, Pétain sought to launch a family agricultural scheme destined to become the main social and economic base of France. As it turned out, the utopian peasant economy never materialized. France's pressing problems required more than "return to the soil."

---

*French kings had been credited with healing powers.

The Germans in the northern zone were on their best behavior during the early days of Occupation, and most of the French population, for their part, responded in kind. A proud Rennes prefect was able to report in late 1940 that the "Christian and patriotic population behave 'correctly' toward the occupier." Over and over in these official reports, prefects in charge of *départements* (administrative districts) warned that the economic situation was the major problem of occupied France – a problem that undercut German propaganda efforts. Because the Germans controlled the press and radio in the north and Vichy in the south, it was some time before the French realized that the ever-increasing shortages were the direct result of the enormous booty of clothing, food, and raw materials being sent to Germany. The Germans issued many requisitions and regulations, all demanding immediate attention.

Reactions to the German presence varied. Writing on the eve of D day, a prefect from Marseilles summarized the conduct of the populace at that time:

> Industrialists and prominent businessmen concentrate on protecting their goods and persons until the end of hostilities, which they assume will usher in a new era of prosperity. Small proprietors fear the Russians. Civil servants keep a low profile. Although they are concerned about their inadequate salaries, they hesitate to make their grievances known to the Vichy government. The clergy focuses increasingly on religious matters but is indignant over Allied bombings. Workers want the unions restored so they may enjoy a better life. Their salaries have not kept up with the cost of living.[28]

For most, food was *the* primary concern in France throughout the Occupation. One can appreciate the impact of major food shortages in a country where meals are the focus of daily life. Bread and meat were rationed by the end of September 1940; other commodities were added to the list of rationed products shortly thereafter. Allocations – determined by age and activity – diminished during the Occupation years.*

Simone de Beauvoir was among the many women for whom concerns about finding food became a major obsession during the war years: "I watched while the coupons were clipped from my rations books, and never parted with one too many. I wandered through the street rummaging . . . for unrationed food stuffs, a sort of treasure hunt, and I thoroughly enjoyed it."

The food shortage serves as a metaphor for de Beauvoir's only play, *Useless Mouths (Les Bouches inutiles)*, written during this period. De Beauvoir wanted to convey: ". . . the daily decisions and choices each French woman entrusted with the welfare of others had to make as she struggled to feed her family."[29]

Escalating prices reinforced the hardship of shortages. Intercepted telephone communications, such as this one between a grocery-store owner and his customer, reveal the impact of shortages and price increases on the population:

—Have you any coffee?

—None at all.

—Or some chicory?

—No.

—Macaroni?

—No pasta of any kind. No olive oil, either. You can't find coffee anywhere.

—This morning veal breasts went up a hundred francs. Ham, thirty francs more.

—Yes, everything is going up.

—It's difficult to know what's going on with the stores. Some sell wine for twenty-two sous, others for ten francs a liter.

The explanation behind these price variations is found in a conversation between a Paris wine merchant and his supplier in Burgundy:

*Rationing in France did not end until 1949 because the Germans had so pillaged and decimated French agriculture.

PARIS: Now can we change the date on the bottles if we don't have what was ordered?

BEAUNE: Yes, without hesitation. For ordinary Burgundy, you can price it as 7.25 francs.

PARIS: And the Burgundy *fleurie*?

BEAUNE: Sell it at 13 francs, instead of the former 9.60 price. If they are going to eliminate *vin ordinaire*, we'll sell it under a château label.

PARIS: And for the wine of . . . ?

BEAUNE: Oh that, we can't discuss it over the telephone. You never know [who might be listening]. By letter, it's safer. But even then. . . .[30]

Author Gertrude Stein's companion, Alice B. Toklas, devotes a chapter in her memoir-cookbook, *The Alice B. Toklas Cook Book* (1954), to food problems during the Occupation. An excellent cook, Toklas devised new recipes for what was available under rationing. Somehow, the two women managed to continue to entertain their friends. One was Hubert de R., who was in the Resistance. To satisfy his sweet tooth, Toklas concocted a raspberry dessert that "cried for cream" – as did they, she notes. Hubert de R. enjoyed the treat. As Toklas recounts, when sitting around the fire after dinner, he said:

"That dessert was made with gelatine, wasn't it? Where do you find gelatine these days? There is none in Savoie. My wife no longer has any." His knowing anything about gelatine surprised me. When as he was leaving I gave him twenty sheets to take to his wife, he was more grateful than the small gift justified. It was not until some time later [that] he told us for what he had wanted the gelatine. He had needed it desperately for making false papers.[31]

City dwellers "rediscovered" their country cousins. Reports from different regions reveal a growing contrast between rich and poor, between city dweller and peasant. Peasants were viewed as privileged, although this was hardly true for those with small holdings. City dwellers tended to believe the peasants received good prices for their crops and sold on the black market as well. While some did profit from the country's predicament, other peasants generously helped the Resistance with food and shelter. In his memoirs, Ephraïm Grenadou explains what he perceives as the dilemma of the French peasant. Parisians came to him and other farmers near Chartres, in the Beauce area, seeking food. The farmers preferred to sell to them – even though it was the black market – rather than have the Germans commandeer it.[32]

Simone Martin-Chauffier, a city dweller who sheltered Resistance members and Jews, had great difficulty feeding her family and her "guests." The inability to feed everyone was getting on her nerves. On one occasion, she even cooked a maggot-ridden ham friends were going to throw out; fire purifies all, she reasoned. Fortunately, she found Mme Martin, an obliging and well-provisioned peasant woman who lived near Mâcon. Unfortunately, the trip to her farm took the better part of a day, and the provisions were heavy:

Madame Martin asked us if we could plume and dress a duck. "You'll do well to learn because while I did it this time, I won't do it again" – which suggested other ducks. I tried vainly to thank her. Mme Martin continued: "I hope you will remember who supplied you [during the war] and who didn't. You don't need to shut the door twice in the face of us peasants." She had a way of saying "us peasants," which, under the appearance of modesty, reduced city folk to their deserved place as parasites. That said, Mme Martin conspicuously added some butter, white flour, several bottles of wine – "which I presume you appreciate more than milk" – and, surreptitiously, a cheese and small sausage. The price for all this was ridiculously low. [Mme Martin could have sold the food for much more to others not in the Resistance.]

As we got on the ferry, she asked us if we wanted to order a goose or a duck for Christmas! From that day on, Hélène [her teenaged daughter] and I returned each week. The Martins and their young son became our good friends. A visit once a week for two years creates ties. One day she told us she was certain that we would forget her once the war was over. I swore it wasn't true. Yet while I think of her often, I have only been to see her once in twenty years.[33]

Like other urban women, Martin-Chauffier came to appreciate the contribution of many peasant women. Largely apolitical, their reaction was one of patriotism, a love for *la douce France*.

Wherever they lived, the wealthy could supplement meager rations with black-market purchases. Most of the people, however, were obliged to spend a large portion of the family budget on food – when they could find it. Food prices tripled between 1939 and 1942; there was much privation. In 1938, posters had urged the population to consume more pastry because there was surplus flour; just a few years later, posters in Paris warned citizens about the health dangers of eating rats. Lucie Aubrac's hit squad killed and cooked crows. Desperate people ate cats and dogs – among other fare. At the heart of the matter was Germany's appropriation of a large part of France's extensive agricultural output.

Trials for infractions of rationing regulations increased dramatically. A woman identified only as Mme B. was sentenced to a month in prison for stealing ten potatoes and a bunch of parsley. Black marketeers, on the other hand, were generally treated with indulgence. An extensive black market developed for ration cards. This intensified the danger for the Resistance, which was forced to print false ration cards to supply its needs. Ultimately, perhaps, the food shortages and increased prices had their greatest impact on the nation's morals. Many French were forced to steal, further weakening Pétain's aim to strengthen the "true values." Occupation brought pillage, servitude, and famine.

French women stood in lengthy lines for commodities often unavailable, even with the required ration tickets. Some women hired themselves out to wait in queues. With newly acquired power and privilege, shopkeepers became feared figures. A housewife needed a large, roomy wallet for the many coupons and tickets needed for a wide range of articles: tickets for food; tickets for ersatz tobacco and wine; coupons for work clothes or even a bathing suit. In his multi-volume study of the Occupation years in France, Henri Amouroux observes that coupons were needed for shoes and detergents and soap products; for household articles made of iron; as well as for school supplies.

To add to the population's misery, the winters of the Occupation were among the coldest on record, and fuel was scarce. Because of the shortage of electricity, people often went without hot water; reading was difficult; elevators did not run. With clothing and fabrics rationed, women fashioned clothes from drapes and blankets, and everyone used newspapers to insulate garments. It was a matter of survival. As has been observed, for three years most of the French focused on surviving from day to day as best they could, obsessed with concerns about food and bombings, haunted by fears of the future, and convinced of France's impotence.

Notes

1. Tony Judt, *London Times Supplement*, Sept. 28–Oct. 4, 1990, 1020. The French High Command assumed that any German invasion would take the same route as the one used in World War I. Since France did not wish to antagonize its neighbors, the Maginot Line was not extended northward to the sea along the Franco-Belgian border. Instead, the Belgians were charged with defending that area. This need for maneuverability was ignored again when *maquis* units were installed in mountain hideouts in the last years of the Occupation – with tragic results.
2. Interview with "Annette," May 20, 1986.
3. Interviews and correspondence with Evelyne Sullerot, starting June 1983.
4. Henri Frenay, *La Nuit Finira* (Paris: Robert Laffont, 1973), 36. (*Night Will End*, New York: McGraw-Hill, 1975.)
5. Marc Bloch, *L'Étrange défaite: Témoignage écrit en 1940* (Paris: Editions Franc-Tireur, 1946), 215. (*Strange Defeat*, New York: W. W. Norton, 1968.)
6. Interview with Geneviève de Gaulle, May 24, 1983.
7. Interviews with Lucie Aubrac, previously cited, plus extended correspondence.
8. See Preface regarding the role of prefects.
9. Robert Paxton, *Vichy France: Old Guard and New Order 1940–44* (New York: Morningside ed. 1982), 46.
10. Judt, 1018.
11. Michael Marrus and Robert Paxton, *Vichy France and the Jews* (New York: Basic Books, 1981). References to the situation of the Jews are largely drawn from this authoritative work. The French edition, *Vichy et les Juifs*, contains the texts

of all the anti-Jewish legislation. Data from Paxton lecture, "Vichy and the Jews," at the Harvard University Center for European Studies, November 14, 1980. Pétain's private secretary, Henri du Moulin de Labarèthe, states in his memoirs that Vichy's anti-Jewish legislation was spontaneous, or "native": *Le Temps des illusions: Souvenirs juillet 1940–avril 1942* (Geneva: Éditions du Cheval Ailé, 1946), 280. For a more recent study of France's role in the persecution of Jews, which includes personal testimony, see Susan Zuccotti, *The Holocaust, the French, and the Jews* (New York: Basic Books, 1993).

12. The reviewer of a French book on the Jews' dismissal from French universities observed that the speed with which these regulations were implemented is still amazing – in contrast to the more customary plodding administrative pace.

13. Interview with Violette Morin, June 15, 1983.

14. Henri Amouroux, *La Grande Histoire des Français sous l'occupation*, I, 392. Commissioner Xavier Vallat deplored the "error" of the French Revolution in granting citizenship to Jews. In his view, this wandering race endeavors to take over wherever it travels with its dream of universal domination.

15. Marrus and Paxton, 343. Social worker Céline L'Hotte recounts how a nurse returning from Belgium was laughed at when she spoke of "extermination camps." Only in 1944 were the rumors given some credence and efforts made to do something. *Et pendant six ans . . .* (Paris: Bloud and Gay, 1947), 59.

16. Zuccotti, *The Holocaust*, 288.

17. There were three rival German police groups. Their aims were different, even conflicting at times. The average French person knew mainly the hated SS, the Gestapo. Those interviewed tended to refer to *all* German police as the Gestapo, whatever their affiliation. That designation has been kept in narratives, even in situations where it appears interviewees were dealing with other German authorities. French historian Jacques Delarue has written several books on the subject of the French police during the Occupation. According to German records, at the most there were five thousand SS men in France: *Die faschistische Okkupationspolitik in Frankreich (1940–1944)* (Berlin: Deutscher Verlag der Wissenschaften, 1990), 31–32, cited in Philippe Burrin, *La France à l'heure allemande 1940–1944* (Paris: Seuil, 1995), 97.

18. Interview with Annie Kriegel, June 21, 1983. See also her *Réflexions sur les questions juives* (Paris: Hachette, 1984). For a summary of the roundup of July 16, see Zuccotti, *The Holocaust*.

19. Annette Muller Bessmann, "Manuscrit-témoignage," 48 (*La Petite*, 101), quoted in Zuccotti, 112. For other testimony on the roundup, see Claude Lévy and Paul Tillard, *Betrayal at the Vel' d'Hiv* (New York: Hill and Wang, 1969).

20. Francine Duplessix Gray, "When Memory Goes," *Vanity Fair*, November 1983, 122. As indicated in chapter 1, the archives of the Paris Prefecture of Police remain closed.

21. In recent years, the two principal Vichy police chiefs, René Bousquet and Jean Leguay, were indicted – again. Bousquet was found guilty of collaboration in 1949, but after some years of "national indignity," he was given a suspended sentence. He went on to a very successful career in banking. Leguay, who was never tried, also had a very successful postwar career. The two were accused of rounding up and deporting more than forty thousand Jews. Leguay was indicted in 1979 and died a decade later without ever having his case tried. In the spring of 1993, while awaiting trial, Bousquet was killed by a man avid for celebrity. Not all accept this explanation, however, believing he was executed to protect others.

22. Jacques Duquesne, *Les Catholiques françaises sous l'occupation* (Paris: Grasset, 1986).

23. Duquesne, 43 (my emphasis).

24. Interview with Danielle Mitterrand, June 16, 1992.

25. Anatole de Monzie, *Ci-devant* (Paris: Flammarion, 1941), 253.

26. Burrin, 232; see also Duquesne, 56.

27. Cited by Pierre Giolitto, *Histoire de la jeunesse sous Vichy* (Paris: Perrin, 1991), 558–559.

28. An F/IC III, 1143, Bouches-du-Rhône, June 5, 1944.

29. Deirdre Bair, *Simone de Beauvoir* (New York: Summit, 1990), 263.

30. Jean-Louis Crémieux-Brilhac, *Les Français de l'an 40*, two volumes (Paris: Gallimard, 1990), I, 413–14, 430.

31. Alice B. Toklas, *The Alice B. Toklas Cook Book* (New York: Harper & Brothers, 1954), 206–7.

32. Ephraïm Grenadou, with Alain Prévost, *Grenadou, paysan français* (Paris: Seuil, 1966), 204. Grenadou describes the difficulties of a peasant trying to outsmart those who wanted to requisition his horses among other problems.

33. Simone Martin-Chauffier, *A bientôt quand même* (Paris: Calmann-Lévy, 1976), 210–11.

F RANCE, 1940–1944

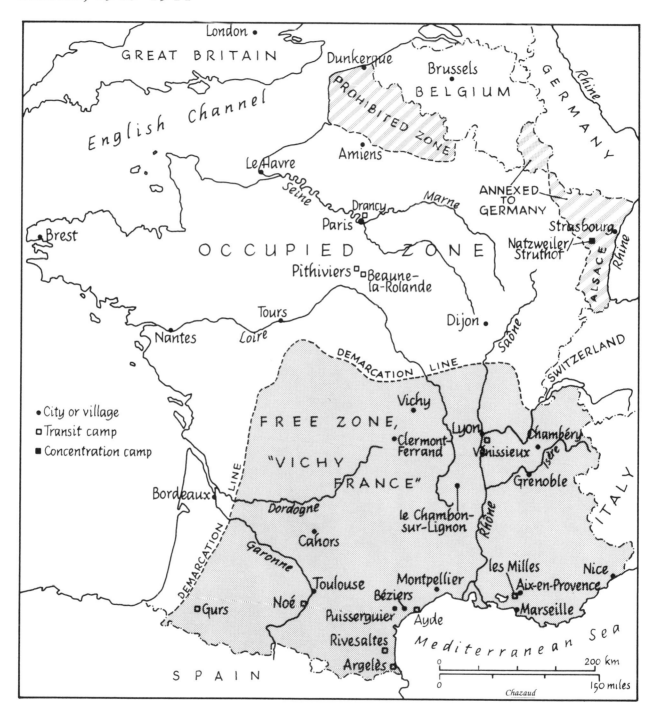

Leni Yahil **Under State Protection**

The Occupation and Its Characteristics

The German army invaded Denmark and Norway on April 9, 1940. The Danish people were taken completely by surprise; but the authorities too had largely ignored the many symptoms and warnings of the preceding period. The German attack rendered worthless the German-Danish nonaggression pact of May 30, 1939.[1] The Germans claimed that this step – a clear infringement of the pact – was necessary in view of the threat of an Allied invasion of Norway. The war situation on the northern front at the time was extremely complicated and could be interpreted in various ways, as indeed it was both during and after the war.[2] In any event, the Germans declared to the Danes that the country was threatened by an Anglo-French invasion and that it must therefore be Germany's duty to take the Nordic countries under its protection to prevent the war spreading to them.

The German minister, Cecil von Renthe-Fink, presented to the Danish foreign minister his government's official note, which demanded that the Danish government accept the German occupation with good grace. The note ended as follows: "In keeping with the good relations which have always existed between Germany and Denmark, the Government of the Reich assures the Royal Danish Government that Germany has no intention *now or in the future of encroaching upon the Kingdom of Denmark's territorial integrity or political independence*" (author's italics). The brief reply of the Danish government included its capitulation, and Foreign Minister P. Munch repeated the sentence of the German memorandum emphasized above, while protesting against the violation of Denmark's declared neutrality.[3] This quotation turned the passage from the German note, so to say, into the basis for the German-Danish agreement which regulated the cooperation between the occupier and the occupied. Thus the interpretation of this sentence, given in theory and practice by each of the two partners, served in the coming years as a yard-

stick for what the Danes called "the policy of negotiation."

During some three and a half years – until August 29, 1943 – Danish democratic government continued to function in accordance with the parliamentary system as laid down in the constitution – a government appointed by the king and responsible to the Rigsdag (Danish parliament). The Germans from time to time reaffirmed the special status of the Danish government,[4] but the Danes themselves examined the maintenance or breach of the agreement in the light of certain criteria. Those were the preservation of Danish independence, i.e., noninterference in the affairs of the army, navy, and police; full maintenance of the constitution and normal functioning of the parliamentary institutions and of the courts; freedom of the trade unions and political organizations; and freedom of political expression. The defenders of the policy of negotiation assert that – until the final crisis at any rate – they succeeded in preserving the country's territorial, national, and economic integrity, though they had to make concessions in all these spheres.[5] Their opponents point out, however, that the Germans undermined the democratic and independent Danish regime step by step, and that in fact none of the guarantees given by the Germans at the time of occupation were honored.[6] But there was, and is today, no divergence from the opinion that the main objective was not only to preserve the Danish people and its physical existence but also – and perhaps more important – to preserve its spirit and the basic values of its social and political life. At the time of the occupation it seemed to the nation's leaders that there was no other way of achieving this except by negotiation with the Germans. The majority of the population supported the government's policy, and only a tiny minority were then in favor of resistance. In the course of time, as concessions, infringements, and encroachments increased, internal debate became more critical and active opposition, particularly in 1943, gained in momentum.

Above all differences of opinion, however, the people and its leaders were conscious of a number of basic values, which were not merely subscribed to by everyone, but for which every Dane who associated himself with the essentials of the constitution was prepared to fight. These were the basic principles of freedom, equality, law, and justice. When in August 1943 the Germans demanded from the Danish government that it waive these principles and act against them, the government refused, and parliamentary rule was suspended.[7] Until then, the Danish authorities had conducted a policy of negotiations as the lesser evil and as camouflage for passive resistance. After the war, a pronouncement made at Christmas 1940 by the then prime minister, Thorvald Stauning (who died on May 3, 1942), was made public: "We will be forced to do many things," he said, "for which people will afterward spit at us, if we are to bring Denmark unscathed through this period."[8] It should nevertheless be understood that many Danes and some of the nation's leading figures at the time not only were convinced – as was Stauning himself – that Germany would win the war, but also regarded that country with sympathy. Support for this view may be found in the speeches both of Stauning and – more markedly – of Erik Scavenius, who was foreign minister from the summer of 1940 on.[9]

It was in fact one of the leaders of the Danish resistance movement, Professor Mogens Fog, who pointed out after the war that Denmark, unlike Norway, had no quisling government on one side with an underground movement on the other, and that it was the lawful authorities of the nation who proclaimed an agreement with the Germans and carried out a policy of collaboration.[10] The government could only follow this policy and guide the country through the devious ways of negotiation with the Germans as long as it knew that the majority of the people stood behind it. National unity and agreement were the government's bastion.[11] This striving for unity expressed itself in various arrangements and regulations. The need for internal solidarity was reflected in a sort of domestic armistice, which led in the summer of 1940 to the establishment of a broad coalition government of the five main parties under the Social Democrats, who had directed Danish policy during the ten preceding years. In addition, a new body – a sort of liaison office between the government and the Rigsdag – was set up. This was the Council of Unity (also called the Council of Cooperation and in the course of time referred to as the Council of Nine, after the number of its members). The council contained representatives of the five main parties (Social Democrats, Conservatives, *Venstre*, Radicals, and *Retsforbund*), and its task was to insure the unimpaired maintenance of parliamentary rule, whether the Rigsdag was in session or in recess. It seemed – and this was confirmed by experience – that in conditions of occupation this smaller body would be more apt to reach decisions on internal and external affairs than could the two houses of representatives through public debate. The statement establishing the council stated: "The parties represented in the Rigsdag, in their desire to preserve the existing constitution as the basis of political life, have decided to enact a measure of national Danish cooperation. The parties lay aside all disagreement and will unite to preserve the independence and integrity of our country, which are the principal wish of the people."[12] This body quickly became the central institution of political life. As stated, the council regarded as its primary duty the preservation of the country's national integrity and democratic independence.

This assignment was by no means simple. At the time of the occupation the Danish people were not cast in one mold. During the thirties the country had undergone economic difficulties and unemployment on a scale hitherto unknown.[13] Economic insecurity at home was complemented by the feeling of insecurity caused by the rise of the antidemocratic forces in Europe. The widespread use of force by the Fascists in Italy, in Spain, and of course in Denmark's mighty neighbor, Germany, as a solution for domestic and foreign problems; the failure of the League of Nations; the ineptitude of the democratic powers – all these factors aroused doubts and scepticism in the hearts of many, who wondered whether Denmark had chosen the right path by disarming at the beginning of the thirties and by continuing its traditional system of parliamentary rule and free debate on internal affairs. Nevertheless, Danish Social Democracy continued to gain in strength until, at the end of the decade, the party suggested a change in the constitution to unify the two houses of parliament. However, in the spring election of 1939 the party suffered a setback and the number of its seats in the Rigsdag was reduced. Then war broke out before the reform could be introduced.

Certain antiparliamentary, rather than antidemocratic, trends manifested themselves among the population. As in all periods of crisis, the deficiencies of the democratic system stood out: party differences, fruitless discussions, disunity at the critical moment, lack of decisiveness and action. This encouraged tendencies to seek less conventional methods. Nazism attracted very few even of the discontented, who abhorred systems of terror, but there were people who, while "not going so far as to abolish democratic rule, often enunciated vague concepts of other forms of government, which though designated as democratic were in reality more or less camouflaged imitations of Fascist regimes."[14] It is clear that a serious threat would arise were these tendencies to flourish when the country fell into Nazi hands – a situation which in itself not only seemed to prove the ineptitude of the Social Democratic parliamentary system but also opened up vistas for help and support from the occupying power, which, after all, wished to incorporate Denmark into its "New Order." It cannot be claimed that attempts in this direction were not made from both the Danish and the German side,[15] but they all failed in the end, and the legal and democratic institutions maintained their authority, with the support of the majority of the people.

Honor for this fact is due to the national spirit and love of freedom of the Danish people, without which the authorities could not have demanded the "preservation of law and order." This national discipline was achieved without any recourse to coercion. It is, however, doubtful whether the country's leaders, parties, and institutions could have united the people so completely had there not existed independent forces which made it their aim to emphasize and consolidate the "bases of Danish freedom."

These forces were to be found inside and outside the parties, among adults and youth, workers and stu-

dents, the organized and the unorganized. During 1940 and 1941 a large movement sprang up throughout the country, a movement of unity with the aim of preserving "the political, intellectual, and personal freedom of the people and the special cultural character of Denmark."[16] The movement spread from man to man, group to group, organization to organization, town to town, and party to party, and an umbrella organization – The Union of Danish Youth (*Dansk Ungdomssamvirke*) – was set up. It rose from the grass roots, from the young people themselves, assisted by the Council of Elders, a group of older people who helped both intellectually and materially. The movement generally assumed the form of cultural activity, for its own sake and without undertones, and aimed to strengthen the national consciousness by study of the country's nature, people, and history. In the course of time there was a natural transition to political topics, and the courses were also used as channels of communication for messages which the government was unable to bring to the notice of the people by newspaper or radio under the conditions of occupation. The state broadcasting system nevertheless cooperated with the movement by arranging suitable cultural programs, and one of its leading officials was a member of the Council of Elders.

The initiators and organizers of the Union of Danish Youth were true heirs of the celebrated Danish priest N. F. S. Grundtvig (1783–1872) and the Folk High School system which he bequeathed to the people. Even in his youth, and certainly by the 1840s, this unusual man had come to the conclusion that the classical system of education then practiced in Danish schools did not fulfill the needs of the people, and he organized new programs and even experimented with the establishment of a new type of school for adolescents from all sections of the population. During the grave crisis which swept over Denmark following its defeat in 1864, when the national consciousness was shaken to its very core, it was Grundtvig and his disciples who succeeded in giving the people a new cultural and national content. This inmost conclusion, drawn from disaster, and the inner mental and spiritual strength which these same schools gave to the people, without any motives of practical or material advancement, was what consolidated the Danish spirit of democracy and humanity. "Grundtvig had, after the misfortune of 1864, by his bluff Danish manner, strong biblical faith, and manly instinct for freedom, given Denmark a new aim in life, so vital that it influenced the whole of Nordic development. He has now [i.e., under the occupation] been, as it were, rediscovered." These words by the then aide-de-camp to the king[17] sum up a public phenomenon unparalleled as an example of the close connection between education and culture on the one hand and the national spirit of freedom and democracy on the other.

The movement enjoyed the active personal support of the coalition government's minister of education, Jørgen Jørgensen, who was also a member of the Council of Elders. In recognizing that the educational-cultural work in strengthening the "Danish mentality" had to be "a silent task, from man to man," he returned to the "popular-Christian sources which were the old foundation of the Folk High Schools."[18] In one of the early meetings of a small group to discuss these problems, he explained that the ideas of these schools were the basis which now had to be built upon. Similar thoughts were voiced at the time by various groups and sections. Besides the clergy, teachers were prominent among those who played an active role in this cultural-political activity. The movement would, however, possibly never have achieved its wide scope and made such deep inroads among the population had it not had as its leader a man who became within a very short time the symbol of the national conscience. This was the young theologian and professor of church history in the University of Copenhagen, Hal Koch.

Like many others who then took a leading part in the "cells of unity" everywhere, Hal Koch was previously unknown to the public at large and was not connected with any party or organization. He had, however, spent some of his student years in both Italy and Germany and had come to the conclusion that fascism and national socialism were not products of any national culture but were an international conspiracy against democracy. Recognizing that the main danger to the Danish people lurked within and that youth in that hour was in need of a guiding spirit, in the autumn of 1940 he held a series of lectures on

Grundtvig as a young man. In an interview published in *Berlingske Tidende* before the lectures started, he said:

> I have decided to give these lectures because I feel that we are at present in a state of terrible confusion – from all points of view: national, human, and Christian. . . . The task awaiting students on completion of their studies is not to get a job at a fairly good salary – but to live as Danes capable of building the life of the people. To this end they have to know the truth. Of course, the University should not be exploited for propaganda toward any particular form of life; but I think that it would be useful to present to the students the image of a man who more than others knew the meaning of living as a Dane.[19]

The lectures were open to students of all faculties. At the very first lecture the large auditorium was packed and long queues of students and visitors stood outside, so that the lecturer himself had the greatest difficulty in reaching the podium. In the course of time, Koch was obliged to hold each lecture twice. In his many talks and lectures, held all over the country in the years that followed, Hal Koch warned young Danes not to listen to big talk or imagine that the time had come for vigorous action. He urged self-criticism and self-recognition and tried to arouse the young to an interest in politics, but not to that form which divided into parties and groups, for he was after all the leader of a movement of unity. He wished to convert this same unity of youth into an instrument against Nazi and antidemocratic thought and attitudes. As he said:

> The task of the Union of Danish Youth is to politicize youth, that is, to arouse interest and spread knowledge regarding the country and public life until a feeling of responsibility has been created. . . . Politicization and responsibility of this sort are the only bases on which rule of the people can safely rest. . . . Until now there has been a tendency – in academic circles at least – to regard politics as an inferior occupation, and there has generally been little interest in public af-

fairs. If this trend continues, we are destined to have a regime of gangs, be they democratic or dictatorial. The aim is therefore – to arouse interest and responsibility as citizens among the best of our youth, those who will decide our future.[20]

In addition to planning lectures and organizing study groups and other forms of education and explanation, the Union of Danish Youth also issued a monthly *Newsletter to Youth Leaders (Lederbladet)*, a central organ where Koch summed up his opinions on general and topical questions. In 1942 he even published a booklet called *The Day and the Way* in which he expressed his opinions and observations and attempted to guide Danish youth through the political and moral labyrinth of the period. He stressed the general principles of humanity on which Danish society was based and which formed the foundation of politics. In practical terms, he concluded that the policy of negotiation should be supported, for in it he saw a guarantee of the democratic unity of the people. Although he considered it an error that the Germans had not been actively resisted at the time of the invasion, he opposed underground operations and acts of terror. Since national unity had not been forged in battle against the Germans, he considered it necessary to strengthen it by politico-educational means. He was not unaware of the doubtful, even dangerous, elements inherent in the policy of negotiation. Denmark, he pointed out in his book, though privileged in comparison with other conquered countries, had nevertheless paid a high price – the people no longer controlled their own home. "This has meant that we have said many a Yes and many a No which have not come from our own hearts, and that our talk has taken on a fateful hypocrisy."[21] Even in underground circles which rejected the policy of negotiation, Koch's book was recommended reading.

In every sphere – government, parliamentary life, among adults and youth – the striving for unity and for internal cohesion was paramount. There was an attempt to examine how best to survive the stern test of maintaining a democratic way of life, at a time when the country lay prostrate before the tradi-

tional enemy attempting to superimpose a totalitarian regime. Internal unity seemed the best, indeed the only, way of preserving national integrity against the dangers from without and within. . . .

The moderate attitude of the Germans toward the Danes is usually explained by the economic benefits that could be reaped from Denmark – and only from a tranquil Denmark whose internal affairs operated without disturbance.[22] The Danes were therefore allowed to continue their standard of living, and though they were obliged to introduce price controls and rationing, they were the only people among all the occupied areas whose standard of living was higher than that of the Germans themselves – even in the first years of the war.[23] The reason did not lie in German affection for the Danes but in their awareness that "surplus production in so decentralized a system as Danish agriculture, with its large number of independent farms, would evaporate completely"[24] if there did not exist what the Germans called *Lieferungsfreude* ("willingness to supply"). In May 1942 [De Gustav] Meissnei* also attributed the failure of the Danish National Socialists to the fact that the Germans were interested in working with the national government in order to insure economic cooperation.[25] S. Hartogsohn (one of the few Jews who remained openly in Denmark after October 1943 and continued, with German knowledge, to work as secretary of the National Bank[26]) stressed that the agricultural output the Danes were able to place at the disposal of the Germans far surpassed the calculations and assumptions of the Germans prior to the occupation. According to Danish calculations, 3.6 million Germans received their meat, pork, and butter rations from Denmark in 1942, 4.6 million in 1943, and 8.4 million in 1944.[27] At the height of the crisis in August–September 1943, the German Food Ministry explained to the Foreign Ministry that it was not interested in exploiting the situation to make greater demands; on the contrary, it would put up with the temporary upheavals in the hope that the plenipotentiary of the Reich would soon succeed in restoring the arrangements in Denmark to their former proportions.[28] The degree to which this policy

---

*Cultural and press attaché in the German legation, *Ed.*

bore fruit may be seen from the statistics given above, though account should also be taken of the fact that German rations were reduced.

Notes

1. The pact stated: "The Kingdom of Denmark and the German Reich will in no case resort to war or any other use of force against each other. In case any third power should take action of the nature described in the first paragraph against either contracting party, the other party will not in any way render support to such action" (cited in R. Lemkin, *Axis Rule in Occupied Europe*, 157, notes 1, 2). Cf. also the memorandum of the Danish government: IMT XXXVIII 901-RF, 61.
2. In the winter of 1939–40 both the Allies and the Germans planned an invasion of Norway. The Germans were first for two reasons: (1) Decision, planning, and implementation were more rapid than they were under the cumbersome procedure of the Allies, and (2) complete disdain for the declared neutral rights of the Scandinavian countries. See Royal Institute for International Affairs, *Hitler's Europe – The Scandinavian States and Finland*; Th. K. Derry, *The Campaign in Norway*; W. Hubatsch, *Die deutsche Besetzung von Dänemark und Norwegen 1940*; Winston Churchill, *The Second World War*, I, 999.
3. Memorandum of the German Reich to the government of Denmark, 4/9/40 – see *Beretning*, bilag IV, 14–18, 21; the German commander-in-chief's proclamation to the Danish army and people, *ibid.*, 13; and Lemkin, *op. cit.*, 377.
4. For example, on 12/20/40 the director of the German Foreign Ministry, Weizsäcker, explained to the head of the Reich Chancellery, Lammers, that in view of Denmark's special status, the plenipotentiary of the Reich only fulfilled the duties of a minister, as distinct from the tasks of the commissars in Norway and Holland: "He must carry out his duties through diplomatic methods." *Beretning*, bilag XIII, I, 25; also *Hitler's Europe*, II, 213–14.
5. Anders Vigen, *Erik Scavenius*, 23–24.
6. La Cour, *Danmark under Besættelsen*, I, 245.
7. For fuller details, see Chapter IV.
8. Evidence of Henning Dalsgaard, who was one of the "mediators" between the German authorities and the Danish government. He was accused of collaboration after the war but was acquitted. *Beretning*, bilag VIII, 147.
9. Stauning's speeches in *Frit Danmarks Hvidbog* (hereafter *Hvidbog*), I, 96, 105, 107, 108; Scavenius's speeches in *Besættelsestidens Fakta* (hereafter *Fakta*), I, 320, 654.
10. Introduction to *Hvidbog*, 10.
11. See S. H. Nissen and H. Poulsen, *Paa dansk Frihedsgrund*, 240.
12. Hartvig Frisch, *Danmark besat og befriet*, I, 361. It is natural that in the weighty Danish literature on the occupation period, varying conceptions and explanations are to be found, in accordance with the views and experiences of each author. It is not intended here to intervene in this internal Danish

discussion which is still in progress. Great effort is being made in Denmark to clarify the history of the occupation period with the help of the considerable documentary material in the Danish and German archives. See also the author's bibliography, *Denmark Under the Occupation*, WLB XVL, No. 4.
13. See W. Shirer, *The Challenge of Scandinavia, passim*; and Haim Yahil, *Scandinavian Socialism in Its Implementation* (Hebrew) Hakibbutz Hameuchad, Tel Aviv, 1966, *passim*.
14. Nissen and Poulsen, *op. cit.*, 35.
15. See below, Chapter III, note 35.
16. Nissen and Poulsen, *op. cit.*, 76.
17. Th. Thaulow, *Konge og Folk gennem Brændingen*, 187.
18. Nissen and Poulsen, *op. cit.*, 54–55.
19. *Ibid.*, 130.
20. *Ibid.*, 136–37.
21. Hal Koch, *Dagen og Vejen*, 7. On the problem of hypocrisy see the introduction to Chapter IV below.
22. The explanation of the French prosecutor at Nuremberg, Faure, that the behavior of the Germans in the first period was due to international considerations and to the hope of "Germanizing" Denmark from within through Nazi propaganda (IMT VI, 500) does not appear sufficiently plausible, though it was true that Ribbentrop was sensitive to international reaction to events in Denmark (see Chapter II, THE JEWISH QUESTION – A DANISH PROBLEM). Even less convincing is his view that the crisis of August 1943 was caused by "the disappointment of the Germans at the economic effort of the Danes" (*ibid.*, 506).
23. See RIIA, *Europe under Hitler*, 39.
24. Frisch, II, 24 (Jens Otto Krag, "Byerhvervene of krigsøkonomien").
25. Letter of Meissner to Luther, 5/12/42 (*Beretning*, bilag XIII, bind 2, 579): ". . . but it [i.e., Danish national socialism] lacks the great propelling impulse, which cannot be created as long as on the German side one is interested in insuring the economic cooperation between Denmark and Germany important for us through cooperation with the coalition government."
26. Evidence, summary of talk, Yad Vashem 027/13.
27. Krag, *op. cit.*, 46, note 18. According to Gudme, *Denmark*, 153, Danish agriculture was, under normal conditions, capable of supporting an additional twelve million persons. Leistikow (*op. cit.*, 349–50) emphasizes the damage caused to Danish agriculture by the loss of trade to England on the one hand and German exploitation on the other.
28. "Herr Backe [director of the Ministry of Food] has with this decision assumed that maintenance of Danish agriculture's production willingness and capacity is of such vital importance for Germany that everything in this sphere should be avoided which might cause lasting damage and make difficult the efforts of the Reich plenipotentiary to reestablish orderly conditions" – AA.ST.S. Akten betreffend Dänemark vom 24.3.43 bis 31.10; 43, Bd.4, JM/2470. The role of the director of the German Food Ministry at the height of the crisis will be referred to again in this work.

German planes bomb Athens, Greece. (Courtesy of Yad Vashem Photo Archives)

German troops invade Minsk, capital of Belorussia. June 1941. (AP/Wide World Photos)

Heinrich Himmler inspects a prisoner of war camp in the Soviet Union. Circa 1940-1941. (Heinrich Hoffman Collection, courtesy of National Archives)

People line up at a butcher shop in Brussels for their ration of one ounce of meat: beef, horse, dog, cat, or tripe. (UNIO, courtesy of Hoover Institution Archives: W.W. II Pictorial & Photo Willinger Collections)

TAMARA OSIPOVA

MINSK, BELARUS... AUGUST 1941 – After Minsk was occupied by the Germans in 1941, Tamara Osipova, a student, joined a partisan group made up of mostly students and teachers. From August 1941 to September 1942, these partisans fought against the Germans and worked to rescue Jews from the Minsk ghetto.

Tamara and her mother, Maria, went to the ghetto and smuggled out dozens of Jewish women and children. Putting their lives at risk, they often had to bribe local officials to save these Jews. Once out of the ghetto, they hid them first in their home. Maria was then responsible for obtaining forged identity papers while Tamara worked to get the children to the partisans in the woods.

Elena Krechetovich was one of the many women they smuggled out of the ghetto. After obtaining forged identity papers for Elena, Tamara and Maria were able to get her a job at the local hospital. Along with many others rescued by Tamara and Maria, Elena stayed in the Osipova's house and survived the war.

(JFR Photo Archives)

CHAPTER 6 **Jewish Life under German Occupation**

Portrait of Helen Verblunsky, a young girl in the Kovno ghetto (Lithuania) delivering milk to one of her mother's customers. Her mother Tova smuggled milk, which she obtained from Lithuanians in exchange for articles of clothing, into the ghetto. Helen looked after her younger brother Avramaleh while her parents worked on forced labor brigades. During the Children's *Aktion* on March 27, 1944, seven-year-old Avramaleh was forcibly taken from Helen. He never returned. Helen and her parents were deported to Stuthoff in July, 1944. Upon arrival, her father, along with all the other men, was shipped to Dachau. Helen and her mother never saw him again. Mother and daughter succeeded in staying together until liberation. 1941–1943. (George Kadish, courtesy of USHMM Photo Archives)

DEBÓRAH DWORK **Introduction**

FRIEDA MENCO-BROMMET was born in Amsterdam in 1925. Her mother
looked after their family of three (Frieda was the only child), and her
father was a window dresser and a teacher of window dressing. "We
had a family life," Frieda explained in an oral history recorded more
than forty years after the war. "I had four grandparents. Family. So, I
should say, kind of a middle class life . . . I knew I would study [at the
university when I got older]. Some day I would be able to study. That
was what we thought. And so my father had insurance for me and put
away money for me to study. So there were a lot of certainties. But the
certainties ended when I was fourteen years old. They never came
back again, of course."

During the late 1930s, as the European nations moved toward
increasingly belligerent positions, both gentiles and Jews were subjected
to the restrictions imposed by this preparatory state, and by the war and
occupation that ensued. Everyone was affected: the loss of adult male
family members to the armed services and female members to war-effort
work, ration coupons, bombardment, the actual presence of enemy
troops and the occupying forces, anxiety, evacuation, destruction,
death. Jews, like their gentile neighbors, suffered these disruptions and
terrors. But apart from that, and absolutely distinct from it, Jews began
to experience a nightmare all their own.

Chapter Five focused on the life of gentiles under German
occupation. The aim of this chapter is to look at the daily lives of Jews.
The focal word is *life*. When we think about the Holocaust, the
machinery of death and the actions of the perpetrators loom large.
They occupy the central stage, while the activities of the Jews day in
and day out – their occupations and preoccupations, hopes and fears,
plans and worries – are marginalized. "The Jews" all too often are seen
as a mass of living dead until they were in fact dead. The purpose of
this chapter is to present how life went on at home, in hiding, and in
ghettos until the moment of death or, far less frequently, liberation.

The destruction of the Jews began with a legal definition. Who,
after all, was a Jew? Was Judaism a religion, or did Jews constitute a
distinct race, with Judaism in their blood, so to speak? If "Jews" were
the people who practiced the Jewish religion, Jewish converts to
Christianity would no longer be Jews; they would be Christians. And
what of nonbelievers, born to practicing Jews? Were they Jews, too?
The Germans and their European allies, Italy and Hungary, were
adamant that Jews were a distinct race. Whether "Jews" practiced
their religion or not, whether they converted or were the children of
converts, was of no consequence: they were still Jews.

**The destruction of the Jews
began with a legal definition.**

283

According to National Socialist ideology, Judaism was inherited from parents and grandparents, and the fascist Italian government under Benito Mussolini and the ultra-conservative Hungarian government under Miklos Horthy concurred. The precise requirements for someone to be defined as a Jew differed slightly from country to country, but the principle of passage through the blood remained constant. In Germany itself, Jews were defined by the Reich Citizenship Law of November 14, 1935. The legislators began by establishing the Jewish identity of grandparents: "A grandparent is to be considered fully Jewish if he [or she] belonged to the Jewish religious community." It therefore followed that a "Jew" was a person "descended from at least three grandparents" who were "fully Jewish by race."[1] Children of such a person were also Jews (regardless of the religion of the other parent), as were the spouses (regardless of that spouse's own ancestry or religious beliefs). Italy, Germany's first ally, adopted similar legislation in its Provisions for the Defense of the Italian Race of November 17, 1938. The Italian regulations addressed the conversion issue explicitly in the first clause of the definition: "He is of the Jewish race who is born of two parents of the Jewish race, even if he belongs to a religion other than the Jewish faith."[2]

These legal definitions were ominous because they reflected a perception of Jews as the other, the stranger who, because of her or his birth, never could become part of the "Aryan" community, those whom the Nazis defined as physically perfect and genetically German. The definitions would have been meaningless, however, had they not been used in legislation to discriminate against the newly defined "Jews" and to privilege the "Aryans." Numerous laws and edicts were passed quickly to remove Jews from positions of "public influence" (as teaching and work in the press, radio, film, and the theater were called), to bar Jews from the civil and armed services, to appropriate their businesses, forbid them to work in a number of capacities in gentile enterprises, and to delimit their participation in the professions and in commerce.

Children studying in a clandestine school in the Kovno ghetto. These classes were held in a stable. The Germans outlawed education in the ghetto as of August 1942, but small numbers of children attended these clandestine schools. 1941–1942. (Eliezer Zilberis, courtesy of USHMM Photo Archives)

Jewish adults were faced with the daunting prospect of trying to continue to earn a living, to carry on within the regulations by radically restricting or restructuring their activities. Jewish physicians, for example, could no longer treat gentile patients, and Jewish patients could no longer be treated by gentile physicians: Jewish physicians therefore attempted to earn a living by treating Jewish patients. Similarly, when Jewish teachers could no longer work in, and Jewish children were thrown out of, the public schools, Jewish schools were established, staffed by Jewish teachers and attended by Jewish children. Some people who had owned businesses and shops tried to get by with Jewish clientele, while others defied the regulations and continued to trade – clandestinely and at great risk – with those gentile customers who were brave enough to deal with Jews.

Jewish children were not affected by the economic sanctions as their parents were. They may have felt or noticed the family's altered financial circumstances, but their daily lives for the most part remained unchanged. Their families were intact, they continued to eat and be dressed, and their own immediate activities and future plans were not threatened in any way they could feel. As an excerpt from *Children With A Star* explains, their insular world of childhood was shattered by the second wave of antisemitic legislation designed to segregate Jews from the rest of the population. Now they were no longer welcome in public places. They could not go to the movies or ice cream parlors; they could not play in the park or swim in the municipal pools. And they were thrown out of the public schools.

Rickshaw drivers travel with passengers through a busy intersection in the Warsaw ghetto. 1941. (Bundesarchiv Bild 101 I/134/778/12)

Expulsion from school, the sudden and shocking introduction of segregation in education, was the first of the legalized social abuses Jewish children suffered. It was neither the last nor the worst. On the contrary, it was but the beginning of a process of segregation and ostracism in which the external marking with the Star of David was another step.

Edicts and regulations harassed and mortified the Jewish population by regulating its movements in every facet of ordinary life. Little by little, their normal activities were curtailed and the parameters of their physical world were reduced. Jews could no longer participate in public institutions or go to public places. Transportation became increasingly problematic. Bicycles were appropriated, only the last car of the metro or trolley could be used, travel was allowed only at certain hours of the day, and then it was prohibited entirely. Their world continued to shrink. Curfews were introduced. Visits between Jews and gentiles were forbidden. Jewish friends were deported or disappeared. Jewish life became increasingly restricted to their own homes, gardens, courtyards.

Raul Hilberg, one of the first and, to this day, one of the greatest historians of the Holocaust, has distinguished four stages in the Germans' persecution of the Jews: identification, expropriation, isolation, annihilation. As we have seen, the first step was the establishment of a legal definition of who was a Jew. Once the Jews were identified, the second step was to expropriate their businesses, assets, and goods, to strip them of their savings and resources. Hard on the heels of the assault of financial expropriation came the assault of social segregation which stripped them of their contacts in and access to the gentile world. Nevertheless, for a time at the beginning of the occupation, Jews had their homes and their families, their loyal gentile friends and their Jewish friends. And then came the moment of departure: to go into hiding, to escape as a refugee, to go to the ghetto, to be deported. Now Jews were not only socially segregated from the world they had known, they were physically isolated from it. In a second excerpt from *Children With A Star* the daily lives of Jewish children in hiding and hidden (like Anne Frank) or in hiding and visible (passing as a gentile) are elucidated and analyzed.

An official visit of Luftwaffe officers with Adam Czerniakow, head of the Jewish Council *(Judenrat)* in the Warsaw ghetto, probably to demand a quota of Jews to work at the airfield facilities. Czerniakow committed suicide on July 23, 1942, after refusing to sign an order to deport children. Circa November 1940. (Hans-Joachim Gerke, courtesy of USHMM Photo Archives)

Relatively few Jews, however, went into hiding during the war. The great majority were forced into areas or specific streets the Germans designated as a ghetto. These ghetto communities were no longer under the local municipal authority. Physically cut off from the gentile population on the other side of the boundary, the Jews were now ruled by a "Jewish Council," a group of prominent Jewish men chosen by the Germans to carry out their orders and to deal with the myriad problems of what amounted to nothing less than a municipality with meager resources and grave problems. It was their job to establish an infrastructure for housing allocations, food distribution, hygiene services, medical care, and youth services, as well as to establish and maintain orphanages, hospitals, and apprenticeship schools (often the only education the Germans permitted for Jewish children). Established to "govern" the community, the German-imposed Jewish Councils (*Judenrat,* in German), as excerpts from Isaiah Trunk's book by that name explain, had multiple responsibilities but no power in relation to the German overlords. Extremely powerful within the ghetto, the Jewish Councils had neither authority nor leverage with the Nazis.

Daily life in the walled ghettos of Poland is described in excerpts from the diary of a middle-aged Jewish man, Chaim Kaplan, who did not survive the war and from a memoir by Janina Bauman, who integrated her own girlhood ghetto diary entries with her memories as an adult woman. Both Chaim Kaplan and Janina Bauman lived in Warsaw and were forcibly incarcerated in the ghetto in November 1940.

From the perspective of the Jews, to be forced into a ghetto was not without precedent. Historical examples were well known to them. It was only at the beginning of the nineteenth century (1824) that Jews won the right to reside outside the walled ghetto in Frankfurt (Germany), and the ghetto of Rome was not formally abolished until 1870. The inhabitants of the ghettos the Germans established in east European cities such as Warsaw, Vilna, or Lodz were familiar with the traditional Jewish quarters in which they now were compelled to live. The physical environment, the streets, synagogues, and markets had developed over the centuries to meet the Jewish community's needs; in the current situation it suggested that life was still possible. This was true even for the hundreds of thousands of refugee Jews evicted from their hometowns within a few months of the German invasion. Forced to flee to the larger cities, they arrived dazed and destitute, but they came to a place that was in one way or another familiar. The concept of a ghetto had a past in Jewish memory, and the ghettos themselves had a Jewish past.

As Kaplan's and Bauman's diaries reveal, at least initially there was hope for a Jewish future. Life went on. Chaim Kaplan tried to continue to earn a living through the illegal activity of teaching. Janina Bauman attempted to continue her education through the illegal activity of taking lessons. Both noted that despite the grinding misery of hunger, disease, random violence, and terrible uncertainty, the ghetto community carried on an extraordinary cultural and intellectual life. Jewish musicians, actors, poets, and writers continued to perform and to be creative. In this, the Warsaw ghetto was not unique; diaries from people in Vilna, Lodz, Kovno, and other ghettos, as well as oral histories from survivors, attest to extraordinary vitality in the face of unprecedented persecution. The atrocities Bauman and Kaplan witnessed and the insanity with which they lived were not unique to Warsaw either; they were common features of ghetto life under German occupation. Jews were shot at random as they went about their daily business, and people died of hunger and disease on the streets. Dragnet operations called *razzias* were staged without warning to round up workers for forced-labor details, to serve as hostages or, if the German authorities believed the ghetto population was too large, to be deported to killing centers and concentration camps.

In the end, existence in the long-term ghettos of eastern Europe led to death, not life. Jews died of infectious diseases, exposure to the elements, and starvation. If the number of people who died in each ghetto is considered in relation to that ghetto's average population, it is clear that all the inhabitants eventually would have suc-

In the end, existence in the long-term ghettos of eastern Europe led to death, not life.

cumbed to the lethal conditions of their daily lives. In Warsaw, 84,896 people, or 18 percent of the average population, died between September 1939 and August 1942; and in Lodz, 43,743 people, or 34.7 percent of the population, died between May 1940 and July 1944. The initially perceived stability of the physical environment of the Jewish quarter with its streets, synagogues, and markets had been a chimera.

In Warsaw, many young women and men began to realize that there was no way out; everyone was marked for murder. Massive German *Aktionen* (deportation dragnets) throughout the ghetto in September 1942 proved these forebodings to be true. All their struggles to survive day by day had come to naught: parents, wives, husbands, brothers, sisters, children, had been snatched up and deported. Those who remained in the ghetto were, for the most part, able-bodied, bereft, and desperate. They had no one and nothing left to lose. Armed resistance at least offered revenge, even if it did not promise survival. By the time the Germans mounted *Grossaktion* to clear Warsaw of Jews in April 1943, these young people were determined to act.

According to the historian Yisrael Gutman (an excerpt of whose book, *The Jews of Warsaw, 1939-1943*, has been included here), the number of actual fighters in the Warsaw ghetto uprising was not large. Some 500 combatants belonged to the Jewish Fighting Organization (ZOB), approximately 250 to the Jewish Fighting Union (ZZW), and an unspecified number to small, unaffiliated groups. They had few weapons and little ammunition. They were untrained in military matters and emaciated from years of starvation rations. Yet they defied a German contingent of 2,054 soldiers and 36 officers equipped with armored vehicles, tanks, cannons, flamethrowers, and machine guns. Holding out for at least a month, the Jewish resistance fighters had the satisfaction of inflicting significant losses and forcing the Germans to reckon with them as combatants prepared to kill.

The Warsaw Ghetto Uprising is one instance of one form of resistance by Jews. There were armed insurrections elsewhere, including revolts in the death camps of Birkenau, Sobibor, and Treblinka. And there were other kinds of resistance, such as the development of rescue operations, and cultural and spiritual initiatives to bind the community together, to hold fast to Jewish history, ethics, and customs. Notwithstanding this array of resistance activities,

Two destitute children in the Warsaw ghetto. June – August 1941. (Raphael Scharf, courtesy of USHMM Photo Archives)

however, the ghettos of eastern Europe were, from inception to liquidation, slow extermination centers.

But "slow" was not fast enough, and each ghetto was emptied in turn. The inhabitants who had survived the hunger, disease, forced labor, and loss of loved ones were congregated in a central square, marched to a train siding, and deported to a killing installation or concentration camp.

Notes

1. Ordinance reprinted in: Raul Hilberg, *Documents of Destruction: Germany and Jewry, 1933–1945* (Chicago: Quadrangle Books, 1971), 20–21.
2. Provisions reprinted in: Renzo de Felice, *Storia degli ebrei italiani sotto il fascismo* (Turin: Einaudi, 1972), 563.

Survivors of the ghetto ultimately were deported to a killing installation or concentration camp.

THE GERMAN OCCUPATION OF POLAND, 1941–1944

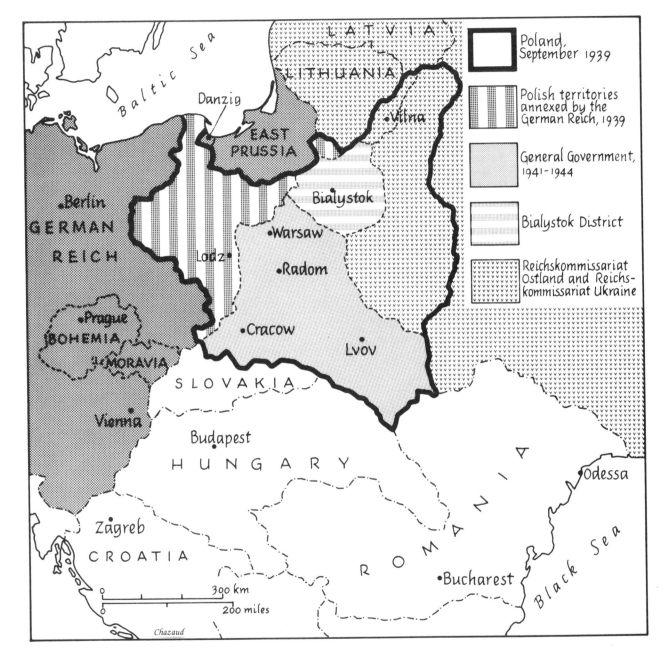

Poland, September 1939

Polish territories annexed by the German Reich, 1939

General Government, 1941–1944

Bialystok District

Reichskommissariat Ostland and Reichskommissariat Ukraine

Baltic Sea

LATVIA

LITHUANIA

Danzig

EAST PRUSSIA

•Vilna

Bialystok

•Berlin

GERMAN REICH

•Warsaw

Lodz•

•Radom

•Prague

BOHEMIA

MORAVIA

•Cracow

Lvov

Vienna•

SLOVAKIA

Budapest•

HUNGARY

Odessa•

Zagreb•

CROATIA

ROMANIA

•Bucharest

Black Sea

300 km

200 miles

Chazaud

DEBÓRAH DWORK **At Home and In Secret**

THE COMPLACENCY AND UNCONSCIOUSNESS of childhood was shattered by the restrictions on normal social life that came with the second wave of antisemitic legislation which was designed to ensure the social segregation of the Jewish population. The subculture of child life was deeply affected by these edicts and regulations; their reverberations resounded and ricocheted against the parameters of the children's daily activities. The first, and at least initially for many, most tremendous of these shocks was the expulsion of Jewish children from the state and state-supported schools. (Again, although the dates of institution differ, the basic pattern of antisemitic legislation was essentially the same throughout Nazi and Axis Europe.) Nearly all schools were included in this legislation as schools of religious denomination in Europe were supported by the state. In many ways, this was the equivalent within the realm of childhood to the economic and employment prohibitions which adults suffered: children go to school; adults go to work. To go to school was the absolute social norm of childhood, a fixed activity of their lives, of the world they inhabited. This is what they were told they would do when they came of age, this is what they saw older children doing, and this is what they themselves began to do.

This violent separation from the community they shared with their gentile friends raised two distinct but obviously related sets of issues, and engendered a two-part reaction. The immediate response was related to the trauma of ostracism and expulsion. Suddenly, from one week to the next, a basic structure of their experience collapsed – and collapsed for them alone. Their subsequent reaction centered on the question of Jewish identity. For the first time in many of these children's lives, they were forced to confront the concept of what being a Jew meant to them and to the society in which they lived. They had no choice but to understand that they were thrown out of

school solely because they were Jews. It was a legal and societally accepted sign that they were marked as different. No longer members of the community, they were strangers.

Given the implications and impact of this legislation, it is not surprising that its effects figure so prominently in the oral histories, memoirs, and diaries of Jewish children in Fascist and Nazi Europe. As Mariella Milano-Piperno, a well-to-do Jewish girl at the time, explained, her parents tried to "sweeten the pill" of Mussolini's Fascism for her, but after the passage in November 1938 of the racial laws which excluded her from school, she felt "marginalized." That was, she said, the heart of the matter for her. She was simply excluded and discarded. "The day that we could not return to school, I remember that I was ashamed before my companions, to tell them: I cannot come because I am a Jewish girl." And then the questions came. "Why? What did I do not to be allowed to go to school?"[1]

At that point her family (like other Italian Jewish families) had two choices for their older children: to send them to a Catholic or to a nondenominational private school. The former was problematic in that there the children had to follow the entire Catholic rite, and the latter was designed for students who had to repeat a year because they had failed in the public schools; i.e., for remedial education. In Rome, as in many other cities in Italy, a Jewish primary school (grades one through five for children aged six to ten) was already in existence, but there was little in the way of Jewish secondary education for girls and boys the age of Mariella Piperno. To meet that need, a number of Jewish communities established schools for their young people.[2] They were taught by the schoolteachers and university professors who had lost their jobs as a result of the same racial laws of November 1938. For the adults the problem was resolved: their children would receive a good education;

FROM CHILDREN WITH A STAR: JEWISH YOUTH IN NAZI EUROPE BY DEBÓRAH DWORK, 14–20, 68–77, 278–79, 288. YALE UNIVERSITY PRESS. COPYRIGHT © 1991 BY DEBÓRAH DWORK. USED BY PERMISSION OF THE AUTHOR.

they were in school. For the young people themselves the solution was not so simple or so easily accepted. Their perspective was entirely different; this issue was fundamental to their daily lives and raised questions of community and identity.

Mariella Piperno's family considered the matter carefully. They were anxious for their daughters to live as normal a life as possible and to continue to go to school with Catholic Italian children. Furthermore, her grandmother, who was rather elderly at the time, "remembered all that the Jews had suffered in the ghetto [of Rome] when it was closed [until 1870], and she remembered with terror that fact of being enclosed all together." She urged her granddaughters, " 'Now that we have obtained liberty, why don't you profit by it, revel in it! Why must you enclose yourselves once again?' "[3] For two months Piperno attended a nondenominational private school, but the education she received was too poor to be acceptable and she enrolled in the Jewish high school.

By all accounts La Scuola Ebraica di Roma, like its counterparts elsewhere, was an extraordinary institution. The school in Rome provided three separate courses: gymnasium/lyceum (or academic high school), a technical institute, and a teachers' training school. It functioned for five academic years, from 1938 through 1943, and according to Italian law it was accredited by the state. (The principal was a state employee and an "Aryan.") The broad range of education offered was only one aspect of this phenomenal high school. The reason it is remembered with such affection and esteem is because the teachers and professors provided a forum for, and encouraged participation in, discussion of the questions which were central to their being at that school at all. When we went to the Jewish School, Piperno explained, "we asked: 'Who are we? What does it mean to be Jews?' " They, who had been very assimilated before and lived among Catholics all their lives, faced these questions when they were together. And they learned that Judaism was not a religion alone. "This was the great discovery of the Jewish School: when we began to understand that to be Jewish was not only to be of the Jewish religion. A Jewish culture existed, a Jewish civilization existed, that, in other words, all that is meant by Judaism existed. And this was very important. In

my opinion, the Jewish School was like the opening of a book for us, and we began to read in this book which had been completely closed to us before." Furthermore, according to Piperno and her ex-schoolmates, their professors were quite simply excellent, and they received an incomparable education. This was true not only for the technical subjects like mathematics (which was taught by the well-known mathematician Emma Castelnuovo), but also for history and philosophy (taught by Monferrini) which, they said, they had to relearn completely as they previously had been taught according to Fascist ideology. The intellectual openness and the depth of inquiry fostered by the professors were appreciated by the students. The intense personal interaction among the young people, in that particular atmosphere and special situation, led to the development of close friendships which are still dear to them today.[4]

Many of the elements of the experience of the Roman Jewish children were similar to those of young Jews from Amsterdam in the Netherlands to Kolozsvár in Hungary. A school system was established everywhere that there was a sufficient hiatus between the introduction of antisemitic legislation affecting social life and the operation of the actual machinery of deportation. In the Netherlands, for example, the edict prohibiting Jewish children from attending schools was published in August 1941. As in Italy, the Jewish education apparatus was not extensive, and the Jewish Council (which had been appointed in February 1941, nine months after the invasion of the Netherlands) faced the problem of constructing an entire school system. Primary schools were established in several cities and towns, and high schools were set up by the Council in Amsterdam and The Hague. All Jewish children were compelled to attend these schools, and the onus of compliance was on the parent or guardian. (Many Catholic and Protestant schools would have been willing to continue to educate converted children, but it was the parents and not the school authorities who were threatened in consequence.)[5]

Like their Italian counterparts, Jewish children in the Netherlands were forced to confront their expulsion from school and, as a result, the issues of Judaism and Jewish identity. Again, the first reactions of shame and shock were followed by the sense of something new and interesting, and of being at ease. Salvador Bloemgarten, for instance, was sixteen when he began to attend the Jewish Lyceum (where Anne and Margot Frank also were students) in September 1941. He, like many other pupils, was there for only one academic year (although the Lyceum continued to function into 1943) because deportations from the Netherlands began in earnest in July 1942 and so children were picked up or went into hiding.[6] Indeed, those who began the second academic year in the Jewish schools remember it as a bizarre experience because each day new seats were empty; their companions had disappeared and the children who remained wondered when their inevitable turn would come.[7]

But that first year, from 1941 to 1942, was for many students, as Salvador Bloemgarten affirmed, "a wonderful year." The schools for Jewish students were set up like other educational institutions, with the usual classes, a headmaster, senior master, janitor, and so on. The education the Jewish pupils received was equal to that of gentile children; after the war the Dutch government recognized the graduation certificates the schools had issued. It is important to note, however, that while equal, the training was not precisely the same. First of all, the schools for Jewish students were closed on Saturdays and Jewish holidays, as well as Sundays. Then too, as the teachers recognized that their students would not either attend or finish school in the normal way, they deviated from the standard curriculum to offer programs they found interesting or enriching. Thus, at the Jewish Lyceum eight Friday afternoons in early 1943 were devoted to a series of lectures on the Romantic movement. Not only was this unorthodox; it also had its complications. At one session a group of musicians played a Schumann quintet for the students, but as the composer was a good "Aryan" the Jewish musicians were forbidden to play his work. They ignored the injunction.[8] On a more personal level, students who survived the war remember their school experiences with warmth, and with the sense that they felt comfortable in that environment. "It was a strange thing; all the assimilated Jews [now in a completely Jewish environment] felt very comfortable with each other, there was a good atmosphere, and we also had good teach-

ers [including] Dr Michman, who is now in Israel, and Presser as history teacher," Bloemgarten recalled.[9] Or as Mirjam Levi, who as a ten-year-old transferred to the newly created Jewish Montessori school in The Hague explained, "I remember a very amazing thing. . . . I remember when I was with these Jewish children in this Jewish school, very suddenly I felt very much at ease, and I felt that it was that we came from the same origin. I felt very good." She no longer had to be so careful about what she said and to whom. She felt that the children shared the same fate, had the same sort of family lives and, in that "intimate surrounding" she felt "free."[10]

The pattern for Jewish children in Kolozsvár was very much the same. Between the two world wars Kolozsvár, or Cluj as it was then (and is now) called, belonged to Rumania. Then, in 1940, the northern part of Transylvania (which included Cluj) was returned to Hungary, and its inhabitants became Hungarian. With the new citizenship came subjugation to the Hungarian racial laws, the Bill for the More Effective Protection of Social and Economic Life (May 1938) which defined who was a Jew and trammeled Jewish economic activity, and the Bill to Restrict Jewish Penetration in the Public Affairs and Economic Life of the Country (May 1939) which, among other measures, restored the Numerus Clausus Law of 1920 that had limited the admission of Jews to institutions of higher education to 6 percent.[11] This meant that a quota on Jewish students in the education system after the first four classes of elementary school was once again operant. As Sherry Weiss-Rosenfeld, who was eleven at the time, put it, "As soon as the Hungarians came, our life . . . changed. . . . We became, as children, totally segregated." She was supposed to start the first year of gymnasium and, like the great majority of Jewish children in Kolozsvár, she was denied admittance. "We didn't have any place to go. . . . We were left on the street with nothing to do." Jewish primary education already existed in the city, but a secondary school (which in Hungary began with the fifth grade at age ten) had to be organized immediately. As in the Netherlands and Italy, the students of this school remember their teachers, who had lost their state jobs through the same discriminatory legislation, as having been "excellent, excellent."[12] And again, these young people who had been legally separated from and rejected by the society in which they lived, were comfortable and at ease in the Jewish school. Gabor Czitrom was one of the few Jewish students to attend a non-Jewish school under the quota system the first year Kolozsvár became part of Hungary. It was a Calvinist institution, which he described as "a tolerant and excellent school. Nevertheless," he reflected, "we were two Jewish boys in a class of thirty. There we felt, and we were made to feel by a certain part of the class, that we were Jews – and stinky Jews too." This was his first encounter with this sort of abuse "as an institutional behavior." The following year Czitrom enrolled in the Jewish school: "I somehow went home. I was made to feel, quite distinctly, that I was out of place in this Calvinist school. . . . So going to the Jewish school, I definitely felt that I was going home. It was quite a natural move to go to a Jewish school with all the Jewish youth of my home town." At school, the students discussed politics and the war and, as in Rome, they were exposed to a dimension of Jewish culture other than religious observance. "What I found interesting," Czitrom observed, "was our religion teacher, a rabbi, who explained Biblical texts more on a literary and historical level than with its religious implication." That was something new; it was exciting and engaging at the time, and still worthy of note forty-five years later.[13] . . .

What was it like to be in hiding and hidden or in hiding and visible? What did these children do all day? With whom did they play? What were their hopes and fears, chores and tasks, occupations and preoccupations?

Each genre of experience, to have been in hiding (in hiding and hidden) and to have been "in hiding" (in hiding and visible) was problematic in its own way, but the former was more obviously, more bluntly and brutally so. To go into hiding meant that all, or nearly all, ties with society were severed. Whether in an attic in the city or a warren in the forest, the child literally was hidden from the mortal danger the rest of the world represented. Even the restricted sphere their lives had become was denied to them. They had been segregated from their former gentile playmates,

banished from the world they used to inhabit of school, cinema, and parks, and identified and isolated with the star of David as the "other," the "stranger." Finally forced to flee their very own homes, to separate from the few friends who remained to them and, very often, from their families too, these children began a new ever more estranged existence. Completely cut off from any community, without mobility or access to either goods or services (food, clothes, shoes, medicines, books, medical care, dentistry), their lives became straitened and circumscribed. "Now, at fifty-one years of age," Marco Anav, a Roman Jew, reflected about his period in hiding in 1944 with his family in a Catholic friend's apartment, "I can tell you that the most important thing about being in hiding was the lack of freedom; the fact of being confined; the fact of being enclosed in a room smaller than the one in which I am sitting now: the fact that when one knocked – you had to knock, one two three, because if you heard one, two, it was something else – Silence, children, be still!' " [14] Indeed, the most primitive of human needs, to wash and to go to the toilet, were practiced only with care and by plan. Moishe Kobylanski and his family hid in the countryside surrounding Gruszwica, their village in the Ukraine. From the end of 1942 until May or June 1943 they lived burrowed in a straw loft in a pigsty. "Bathroom facilities were excellent. You just went over there in the other end and you bundled everything up in straw. And when I went after food I took it with me and I went crazy to find a place to dump it." It was Kobylanski's job to forage for food and, at the same time, to remove the family's excrement. "The urine was easy. It was in a bottle and as soon as I walked out I dumped it. That was no problem. The faecal matter was a problem. I went where they had cattle manure, I found a place, and I tried to hide it there. But how does human excrement fit in with cattle manure? No good either. It was always a problem because I might leave evidence after myself."[15] In short, to be in hiding meant to be committed to an extraordinarily punitive prison cell, not because the child had committed a crime but because everyone else was acting criminally.

Each child's experience was unique, but certain aspects of life in hiding were almost universally shared. The first of these was a fundamental lack of comprehension of why events transpired as they did, and a concomitant, ever-present fear and tension. Their previous lives had not prepared them for this new existence. The children understood that the Germans and their allies were dangerous, but precisely what that danger signified was beyond their grasp. This was especially true for younger children who were more likely to perceive the peril as an inchoate insecurity rather than a specific and comprehensible calamity. "Why must I hide?" was the fundamental question. With no good answer (indeed, there was no rational, comprehensible answer), and only a dim (or clear) understanding that to do so meant to be safe, came great anxiety and trepidation. They did not understand why they were forced to leave their homes, their families, their friends, and they did not know what was safe and what dangerous. Precisely that which previously had represented security was now lost and abandoned. What was stable, where was shelter?

Judith Ehrmann-Denes was not yet four years old when her mother, eighteen-month-old brother, and she went into hiding in Budapest. One Sunday in the early spring of 1944 they went out, as was their custom, to visit relatives in the afternoon. When they returned they found their concierge, "who was a very, very nice lady," waiting for them in the courtyard. "She said, 'Don't come in, don't come in! The Nazis were here.' The *Hungarian* Nazis . . . the Arrow Cross. . . . They were there and they took all the Jews away [who were] living in the house. So we went that evening to my father's gentile friend. . . . We lived with them, and I couldn't understand why we were not going home. We were staying there. . . . I remember being there and not understanding. I remember anxiety all the time, which seeped over from my mother, who obviously had anxiety twenty-four hours a day. . . . That's all I remember is anxiety. And I thought life was like that. What does a three-year-old know? This is the way life is. You just have anxiety all the time, and fear."[16]

It was both physically and psychologically difficult to go into hiding. To be so completely removed from ordinary existence, to sever all normal activities, was a great shock which required radical adjustments.

As one man who was then a teenager explained, "It was all of a sudden a way of life without life [without living]."[17] Every act of daily life had to be considered consciously and adapted to fit the situation; the obstacles to surmount or circumvent were never-ending. To maximize her family's protection, Judith Ehrmann-Denes's mother obtained the original legal papers of a young gentile woman her own age who, like her, also had two children. Mrs Denes felt that this was insufficient, and she decided to transform her eighteen-month-old boy into a girl. "My brother was dressed as a little girl, because boys could be checked to see if they were circumcised or not." The Deneses hid with a number of Christian families in Budapest. They avoided contact with the outside world, but were not absolutely sequestered. "Nobody really knew us, and being that we were both 'girls' there was no way to check. People would just take the word. If somebody reported us and the Arrow Cross came by to check, there was not much they could do with two little girls. My brother had blond curly hair with a red bow so it just wouldn't even occur to them to think, 'That's a boy.' " The deception posed its own problems. "My brother, who by then had learned to stand up to pee, had to sit down again. And remember, there were no toilets. . . . So my brother had to learn to sit on the chamber pot again. Luckily he spoke real late, so he couldn't really talk. He put up a fuss about it, but nobody knew why, because my mother had to make sure that nobody knew it was a boy. And there were a lot of problems and anxieties that, God forbid, this kid should unzip or pull down his pants."[18]

While it was safer to be female than male because of the physical identification of Jewish identity by circumcision, older girls had their own biological difficulties. Herta Montrose-Heymans was fifteen when she went into hiding. Her family had moved from Germany to the Netherlands to escape persecution, but the Nazis caught up with them and in 1942 they were forced to go underground. In the winter of 1943 Heymans moved to an address where she spent the rest of the war years. She, her grandfather, and another elderly man lived with an older couple in a "tiny little working-class house" in Enschede, in the east of the Netherlands. "Menstruating was absolutely harrowing," Heymans recalled. "In those days, you had little pads that had to be washed. The land-lady couldn't hang them on the line, could she? The neighbors knew there was no young person living there."[19]

The essential problem was to leave no evidence or sign of one's presence, to live without trace or vestige of existence. This was accomplished through concealment and dissimulation. In Heymans's case, for example, not only was it impossible to dry her menstrual pads on the outside clothes line, it was also out of the question to hang out her grandfather's shirts. "Nobody was supposed to know that we were there," Heymans emphasized. "We couldn't hang two shirts out when there was only one man living there." They moved about the back rooms of the house quite freely, but "we whispered, we never spoke up really. It became second nature." What was not hidden was masked in one way or another. For instance, the host couple "had a harmonium which they played on Sundays especially. As I had started to learn to play the piano before I went to live underground, I learned to play the harmonium for them which gave them great pleasure." They of course pretended that one of them was playing. "There was a lot of pretense going on all the time."[20]

To obfuscate the actual situation became a way of life for both host and guest. Various stratagems were employed, ranging from obvious tactics to subtle maneuvers. As the guest children were not supposed to exist, they could not be seen. They were forbidden to go near the windows so as to prevent detection from the outside, and when visitors came they were restricted to a confined space and had to maintain complete silence. Often this meant that the children could not move. Hidden in a cupboard or behind a curtain, any change of position would have meant disclosure. Just as the children were not to be visible, they were not to be heard. Like Heymans, they learned to speak in whispers, or not at all. They could not laugh aloud or, forgetting themselves, cry out from a sudden pain. Nor could they do anything which by its noise would reveal their presence. Thus, if a child was alone she could not flush the toilet; if the host was in the front room, she could not wash up in the kitchen. Activities and sound had to be attributable to those who were known to be present in

the house (or barn, like Moishe Kobylanski or warehouse, like Anne Frank).

Obtaining goods and services for the children in hiding required thoughtful planning. If a child did not have ration coupons, food had to be purchased on the black market, which was very expensive. With ration cards (provided by the Resistance) the prices were controlled, but how could a housewife present coupons for three when her baker knew perfectly well that only two people had lived in her household for years? Women who had children hiding in their homes spent hours in queues in numerous shops in the effort to acquire the maximum their ration cards would allow without arousing suspicion. Bertje Bloch-van Rhijn and her family were hidden in the home of an elderly lady just outside Kampen in the east of the Netherlands. This woman "lived there alone, and it was very difficult to bring in food. Naturally, one could not come into the house with bags full of shopping. . . . The mistress of the house had a maid and a housekeeper, and the housekeeper was really too dumb to dance for the devil [as they say in Dutch]. The important point about Marietje [the housekeeper] is that she held her tongue in all the stores where she went to do the shopping. She always bought with a ration card and she had to go to many grocers to buy with the different ration cards she had got from the underground. She could not present more than one card in each shop since she had to maintain the pretense that she was shopping for [the mistress of the house]. So," van Rhijn concluded, "it's not nice of me to say that she was stupid."[21] Food was an essential and constant problem, but the contours of the dilemma and its solution remained constant for other goods as well. Books, for instance, were very important to many young people in hiding; reading was a way to pass the time and to escape the confines of their harshly delimited existence. Philip Maas and his parents were hidden by a working-class family who had used the public libraries long before their guests came to live with them. With the Maas family's arrival their needs increased. "They were members of two libraries and they very cleverly sometimes only took one or two books from one library while at the same time taking many books from the other."[22]

In short, both the children and those who hid

them strove to conduct themselves in such a way that the young people's presence would not be disclosed by their behavior either in the house or in dealings with the outside world. In these domains the children and their hosts had some measure of control. The operations of the Germans and their allies, however, could not be checked. A *razzia*, or search, had nothing to do with unwitting self-betrayal; it was an expected but unpredictable calamity. That it would occur was anticipated, but when was unknown. Very often, special hiding places were constructed to be used in such emergencies, and the children were drilled to ensure that they would disappear within seconds. Tiny hidden spaces within a wardrobe or closet, under the stairs or floor, in the attic or cellar were constructed with false walls and floors. The children remember rehearsing to get into them, as well as the terrifying times when they were necessary. When Herta Montrose-Heymans first went into hiding in 1942 she was with a cousin who was spastic. "How long we stayed in our first address I really can't remember. But as a child it was a terrific responsibility to look after this spastic child as well. As you must appreciate, we had regular exercises in hiding in certain hiding places which had to be done very, very quickly from the time the bell would go. You were given, say, a minute to hide either in the cupboard or. . . . In our first place, I remember we had to go under the floorboards which was all right for me because I was healthy, but my cousin couldn't walk very well. So it was all very harassing and complicated, and a terrific burden on a young girl of fifteen."[23] Like Heymans, Selma Goldstein was a German Jewish girl whose family fled to the Netherlands after *Kristallnacht*. She was ten years old when her family went into hiding in a small worker's house in Enschede.

> The room in which we stayed was not so small. It was a bedroom with two beds and a rather big wardrobe. In the wardrobe a second cupboard was made where we could hide. It was about 25 centimeters wide; a very tiny space. It was built into a little niche in the wall, but you could see it if you looked carefully because you could see that the space inside the wardrobe was not so large as that of the external wardrobe. Also, when you

knocked on it, you could hear that there was a space behind it. So it was not really a safe place to hide.

> Once it was used. Somebody was running away from the Germans and decided to come through our house. He jumped into the back garden and went through the back door, through the hall, through the front door, and left at the other street. The Germans were behind him, but the man with whom we were staying wanted to give this man a chance so he locked the front door so that in any case the Germans would have needed to open the front door and would waste time. But that did not happen. The Germans came into the house . . . and one of the girls of the family kept them busy talking while we got into our cupboard. We were in the cupboard and then the Germans thought that because the door was locked the man could not have left. They started to look very carefully to see if the man was there. I was so frightened I started to hyperventilate and my mother put a sock in my mouth.[24]

Despite the hosts' and the guests' precautions and care, situations constantly arose that made clear how compromised their lives were and how tenuous and fragile their arrangements. For example, the family with whom Philip Maas hid had two children, a girl of thirteen and a boy of eleven. The young boy had a friend who lived next door. "I slept in the little boy's room," Maas explained, "and the boy next door would knock on the wall to make contact with his friend and then also sometimes he would climb across the gutter from his room to mine. So then I had to close the window very quickly to prevent him from getting into my room – because I was sleeping there, and not his little friend as he thought. There were problems with that, because the neighbor boy did not know there was somebody hiding there – the little boy never told – and he expected to play as they normally did."[25] This predicament was comic, almost farcical, although of course it could have had literally fatal consequences. Other such unanticipated incidents were absolutely tragic. One year after Selma Goldstein and her parents went into hiding, her father died. "The problem was how to get him out of the house," Goldstein recalled. The people next door and the family across the road were Dutch Nazis. "So my father was sewn into a bed and the neighbors were told that the bed had to be cleaned. The bed was carried out of the house with my father in it. Then it was brought to a country estate out of town where a good policeman stood guard while my father was buried."[26] For Goldstein, the normal process of mourning the death of her father was replaced by the horrible dilemma of how to get rid of his body.

Given the practical problems of being in hiding and the physical constraints on their activities, what did the children do all day? Or, to put it more appropriately, how did they pass the time? "Our major activity was to think about food," Philip Maas reported. "From the moment we got to that hiding place food was a big problem and we talked about it all the time."[27] Several thousand kilometers away, in a pigsty in the Ukraine, Moishe Kobylanski and his family had the same concern.

We used to sit all day and debate where to go [to ask for food]. We sat there; we sat there every day and followed the ritual. First, there wasn't much to eat. . . . So we just sat, counted the hours and killed lice. Just sat around. Didn't do anything. What can you do? You were dreaming, talking about this and talking about that. Making plans [to forage for food], maybe tomorrow if it's quiet, if it's dark. My parents weren't peasants in the term of knowing the seasons, the moon schedule. . . . Is this the month there's going to be a full moon, or is it going to be a quarter-moon, half-moon? So you waited . . . I think this is going to be a quarter-moon so I'll be able to go because it doesn't shine so bright. The weather doesn't look too good; if it's a storm it's a good night to go hunting for food. That's how the day was taken up.[28]

In addition to dreaming and scheming about food, many children who were old enough took up hobbies. If they were able to obtain the materials, and were permitted to do so, children turned their energies to all genres of writing, art, and handicrafts.

Anne Frank, for instance, wrote short stories as well as her diary, which she rewrote in three versions. Philip Maas specialized in woodwork. Wood was brought to his hiding address and with it he constructed model windmills and fashioned pictures of marquetry. His pieces were very fine and intricate, and like Anne Frank's diary reworked several times. Sara Spier crocheted. "I made little things to put on the table and I gave them away. I made them from very thin thread because there was not much in the war. It was quite nice, like lace."[29] Frieda Menco-Brommet also crocheted. "I made curtains, and I made tablecloths too. And I never did those things again after the war."[30]

As might be expected, reading and studying were common activities for children of school age. With a paucity of alternatives and a plethora of time, intellectual pursuits were a natural choice. Furthermore, children expected to go to school. To continue with their education signified in a very basic and fundamental way that they meant to return to society, that they believed they would resume a normal life. "I took my schoolbooks with me, and my mathematics [exercises]," Spier remembered. "Every day I did again the last mathematics problems I had at school, just not to forget them, because I couldn't go on." She kept on studying, "but I missed my school very much because I loved to go to school. I was in a lyceum and you could choose at the end of the second year if you wanted to do *gymnasium* [university-track high school]. I had chosen classical languages which I always wanted to learn. And there was nobody to teach me. So I had my books and, well, I couldn't go on further because nobody could see what I did right or wrong. I just read, and read again what was written in the books."[31] Frieda Menco-Brommet was with her parents and so the educational process was more interactive. "During our two years in hiding my father and I spent our days together teaching each other. His English was much better than mine, so he taught me English. My French was better than his, I taught him French. We read the same books and we discussed them."[32]

One of the most important factors in determining what a child did all day was the culture of the host with whom she hid. Quite often, the people who took in children had their own ideas of what they considered appropriate activities. Thus, for example, Bertje Bloch-van Rhijn and her family were hidden with the mother of a university friend of Bertje's mother. The university friend had been well educated in her youth and her mother believed in the importance of schooling for young people. She had saved her children's books and toys, which proved a treasure for van Rhijn and her sister. "The lady of the house had a whole lot of books – she'd had three children – and she had schoolbooks, big history atlases, a complete set of Dickens, and lots of biographies." Indeed, the hostess's dedication to the van Rhijn girls' education led her to reveal the girls' existence to the directress of the local public library, fortunately without harmful consequences. "The lady of the house was a very well-read woman; she knew a great deal. She had a membership at the library, of course, and she went for us, naturally also for schoolbooks. She had to ask for them in one way or another and so the directress of the library knew.[33] Sara Spier's experience could not have differed more. While the van Rhijn girls were hidden at only a few addresses throughout the war, Spier was moved thirty-two times. And where the van Rhijn family was united in May 1943 and lived together until the end of the war, Spier was separated from her sister, brother, and parents, and the latter three were betrayed and deported. She mourned the loss of her family long before she knew of their death and, not knowing of their deportation, she missed their home life. She was hidden by people who had very different ideas about how to occupy oneself; they came from another culture and had their own mores.

The people who hid me were farm laborers, very simple, very nice, very sweet. But they didn't know anything about [high] culture or languages. Their life was very simple and they were Christian. So I came into a totally different milieu where there was no education and a different religion. I felt the difference very forcefully but of course I didn't say anything. I realized they were people who hid me and I couldn't say I didn't like their way of life. For example, they didn't read books. They were always knitting, or doing some embroidery, or busy in the kitchen, or busy in the garden, or doing something. But reading was something luxurious. They accepted that I had my schoolbooks, but when I would ask for some book to read, they said you can do something more useful.[34] . . .

Notes

1. Mariella Milano-Piperno, interview with author, Rome, Italy, 6 June 1985, transcript. 2.
2. According to De Felice, the establishment and maintenance of academic facilities was one of the two major activities of the Union of Jewish Communities, or l'Unione delle Communità, from 1940 on. See his discussion of this question, De Felice, *Storia degli ebrei*, 415–16.
3. Interview with Mariella Milano-Piperno, 3. In 1849 the ghetto rules had been reapplied, and all Jews who lived outside its former walls were forced to return to the confined area. The ghetto of Rome was without doors or gates, but nevertheless bounded by strict lines of demarcation. See: Sam Waagenaar, *The Pope's Jews* (London: Alcove Press, 1974), 270–74.
4. Interview with Mariella Milano-Piperno, transcript 3–5. The extent to which the people I interviewed throughout Europe agreed about the importance of the broad Jewish education they received as children, the excellence of their teachers, and the singularly deep and enduring friendships they formed at the Jewish School was astonishing. With regard to Italy, see also the published memoirs: Fabio Della Seta, *L'incendio del Tevere* (Trapani: Editore Celebes, 1969); Giorgio Piperno, "Fermenti di vita giovanile ebraica a Roma durante il periodo delle leggi razziali e dopo la liberazione della città," in Daniel Carpi, Attilio Milano, Umberto Nahon, eds., *Scritti in memoria di Enzo Sereni: Saggi sull'ebraismo romano* (Milan: Editrice Fondazione Sally Mayer, 1970), 293–313; and the report of the fiftieth anniversary of the founding of the Scuola Media Ebraica (Jewish middle school) in Trieste: Jane Boutwell, "Letter from Trieste," *The New Yorker* 26 December 1988, 76–80.
5. Jacob Presser, *Destruction of the Dutch Jews* (New York: Dutton, 1969), 76–80, [*Ondergang* (The Hague: Staatsuitgeverij 1965)].
6. Salvador Bloemgarten, interview with author, Amsterdam, The Netherlands, 18 June 1986, transcript 6. See also the description of the shadow of deportations which hovered over the Jewish Lyceum in: Presser, *Destruction of the Dutch Jews*, 142–43.
7. As Presser noted, the absentees "were not quite the ordinary absentees, as for the usual reasons some were never seen again. Thus, class 2B which, in the autumn of 1942, counted twenty-eight pupils was reduced to four in May 1943. The writer will never forget the look on his pupils' faces when names were called from the register and there was once again no voice to answer." Ibid., 258.
8. Ibid., 258–59.
9. Interview with Salvador Bloemgarten, 6–7. Jozeph Michman, to whom Bloemgarten referred, now lives in Israel and is an active scholar. Presser is the historian Jacob Presser, who devoted his professional life after the war to investigating and analyzing the tragedy of the Dutch Jews during the Second World War.

10. Interview with Mirjam Levi, 11–3.

11. Szaraz, "The Jewish Question," and Nathaniel Katzburg, "The Tradition of Anti-Semitism in Hungary," in Braham and Vago, eds., *The Holocaust in Hungary*, 21, 25.

12. Sherry Weiss-Rosenfeld, interview with author, Southfield, MI, 26 January 1987, transcript 2.

13. Gabor Czitrom, interview with author, Paris, France, 30 June and 1 July 1987, transcript 4, 5, 7.

14. Marco Anav, interview with author, 16 June 1985, Rome, Italy, transcript 9.

15. Martin Koby, interview with author, Ann Arbor, MI, 11 and 25 November 1987, transcript 49.

16. Judith Ehrmann-Denes, interview with author, Ann Arbor, MI, 28 January, 2 March, and 16 April 1987, transcript 3.

17. Salvador Bloemgarten, interview with author and Robert Jan van Pelt, Amsterdam, The Netherlands, 18 June 1986, transcript 11.

18. Interview with Judith Ehrmann-Denes, 2, 6.

19. Herta Montrose-Heymans, interview with author, Cardiff, Wales, 21 July 1985, transcript 11, 14.

20. Ibid., 11, 14, 12.

21. Bertje Bloch-van Rhijn, interview with author and Robert Jan van Pelt, Doetinchem, The Netherlands, 21 June, 1984, transcript 18, 21–22.

22. Philip Maas, interview with author and Robert Jan van Pelt, Hilversum, The Netherlands, 23 June 1986, transcript 12.

23. Interview with Herta Montrose-Heymans, transcript 7–8.

24. Selma Goldstein, interview with author and Robert Jan van Pelt, Doetinchem, The Netherlands, 22 June 1984, transcript 9–10.

25. Interview with Philip Maas, transcript 10, 16.

26. Interview with Selma Goldstein, transcript 5–6.

27. Interview with Philip Maas, transcript 12.

28. Interview with Martin Koby, transcript 45, 47–48, 49.

29. Interview with Sara Spier of 27 June 1986, transcript 5–6.

30. Frieda Menco-Brommet, interview with author, 18 June 1986, transcript 8.

31. Interview with Sara Spier of 20 June 1984, 4.

32. Interview with Frieda Menco-Brommet, 7–8.

33. Interview with Bertje Bloch-van Rhijn, 20, 24.

34. Interview with Sara Spier of 20 June 1984, 5.

Members of the German order police publicly humiliate a Jew in Sosnowiec, Poland, who is forced to kneel in the grass while they cut his hair. 1939–1940. (Eva Better-Heitner Sak, courtesy of USHMM Photo Archives)

A German/Polish sign on a streetcar before the establishment of the Warsaw ghetto mandating segregated seating. The sign reads: "For Jews/For Non-Jews." 1940. (American Jewish Joint Distribution Committee, courtesy of USHMM Photo Archives)

The Westerbork camp orchestra, led by Heinz Neuberg. Westerbork was a transit camp in the Netherlands. November 1941–1942. (Nederlands Instituut voor Oorlogsdocumentatie, courtesy of USHMM Photo Archives)

Dutch Jews sort through clothing at a workshop established by the Jewish Council on Oude Schansstraat in the Jewish quarter of Amsterdam. May 1942 – 1943. (Nederlands Instituut voor Oorlogsdocumentatie, courtesy of USHMM Photo Archives)

The photograph is part of an album commissioned by the Jewish Council to document life and work in the Jewish quarter of Amsterdam during the German occupation. Most of the images show Jews at work in self-help agencies established to aid both those in Amsterdam and prisoners at the Westerbork and Vught transit camps.

Isaiah Trunk **The Jewish Councils**

Introduction: Some Basic Issues That Faced the Jewish Councils – Jacob Robinson

This volume by Isaiah Trunk is the first detailed analysis, in any language, of the "self-government" the Nazis imposed upon the Jews in Eastern Europe. Along with this central theme other aspects of internal Jewish life also come to light.

While the volume speaks for itself, it was felt that some interpretive remarks on the contents of the book might help the reader familiarize himself with its subject matter and the basic problems which are raised.

The first question to be discussed is the attitude of Jewish communal leaders toward joining the Councils. Two views are predominant in the sources and literature: one condemning the prewar communal leaders (and others) for accepting membership in the Councils, and the other finding no fault.

The proponents of the "noncooperation" view believe that under the circumstances and from the viewpoint of Jewish survival a "leaderless" Jewry would have been the lesser evil and that a larger percentage of Jews would have survived the Holocaust. This view proceeds on the following three assumptions: (1) having extirpated the Jews from the general administrative framework of, say, occupied Poland, the Nazis would have tolerated the existence in this territory of two million nomads while at the same time proceeding to the partial extermination of Gypsies as nomads (*umherziehende*); (2) in condition of rationing food these nomads would have been able to find shelter and survive for some thirty months (September 1939–March 1942) prior to the beginning of deportations; (3) the Jews would have resigned themselves to such a situation without opposition.

The opposite view refers to the spontaneous emergence after the German occupation of new "committees" and to the attempts to continue the activities of the prewar Jewish communal institutions prior to Nazi initiative (as e.g., in Warsaw and Lublin) as proof of the continuing if not reinforced sense of responsibility of Jews concerned with the fate of their coreligionists. The proponents of the positive attitude also emphasize the fact that neither the leadership nor the masses did have or could have had a clear idea of the Nazi plan for the future which, as we know now, was crystallized as the Final Solution decision only in the spring of 1941 in connection with the Barbarossa operation.

A more subtle view is taken by those who differentiate between the situation in (1) German-occupied Poland, (2) the Baltic states and eastern Poland, including Eastern Galicia, which for 23 months were under Soviet occupation or influence, (3) and in the occupied territories of the U.S.S.R. prior to September 1939. The first blow of the German occupation fell on Poland. In the two other areas, despite the silence of the Soviet-controlled press, the Jews might have had an inkling of what was in store for them. They learned the hard way, prior to the establishment of any form of Jewish organization: the *Einsatzgruppen* overran all these areas bringing within a short period of time death and destruction to some one and a half million Jews. In the formerly Soviet-occupied, now Nazi-occupied, territories, hesitations to join the Council manifested themselves, as exemplified in the case of Eishishkis (in wartime Lithuania). There, in July 1941, the rabbi had to draw lots to choose members of the Council from among the reluctant community because of lack of volunteers. But even in these areas persons of high reputation like Ephraim Barash (Bialystok), Dr. Elkhanan Elkes and Leon Garfunkel (Kaunas), assumed responsible positions in the respective Councils.

The situation was different in occupied portions of the U.S.S.R. In the first place there had been no Jewish communal organization in existence there for almost a quarter of a century. The reservoir of candidates for membership in Jewish Councils was thus limited. We have some information on only 15 ghettos in those territories and no general conclusion can be drawn concerning the attitude of local Jews toward joining the Councils.

The Councils started their activities in Poland as a continuation of the prewar *Gmina* ("community"). The official documents on the establishment of the Councils (the *Schnellbrief* of Reinhardt Heydrich of September 21, 1939; the ordinance of Hans Frank, governor general of the Government General, the mandates of the police chiefs of Warsaw and Łódź) charged them exclusively with matters of German concern. In fact, however, a large part of the activities of the Councils was extracurricular and traditionally Jewish (welfare, education, and religion).

It is interesting to note that the herding of Jews into ghettos did not meet with serious opposition on the part of the pre-Ghetto Councils and the Jews in general. One of the reasons for this attitude was the fear of Jews that they might be molested by the local population, either spontaneously or in outbursts instigated by the Nazis. The opposition that did exist was directed at two points: the area destined for the ghetto and the deadline for moving into the ghetto. A correspondence between Czerniakow and the Nazi authorities in Warsaw on these two aspects has been preserved.

Was it right not to oppose the establishment of the ghettos? The answer to this question by us now, using hindsight, depends on the evaluation of the probable alternative, which was concentration camps, a form of dwelling used in the case of the Soviet prisoners of war. The ghettos preserved the family, allowed for a minimum of privacy and partly – not everywhere – for some contacts with the outer world; all these advantages were missing in the camps.

Having assumed the dual responsibilities of office – traditional and Nazi-imposed – the Councils had early to face another dilemma arising from the exploitation of the labor of Jews aged twelve to sixty. Not all labor was of the same nature: there was menial work, skilled, technical work, manufacture of uniforms, construction work, precision work, and clerical work. Nor was there lack of variety as far as places of work are concerned: in and outside the ghettos, in ghetto workshops, in labor camps. The employers were municipal institutions, ghetto admin-

istration, the German army, SS business companies such as OSTI, and private German firms based in and around the ghettos. There was also a lack of complete uniformity in the question of wages, the length of working week and workday, food, housing conditions, and the type and character of guards. It should be mentioned that available manpower was everywhere (with the exception of Łódź) larger than the amount needed by the Germans.

The question is: Should the Councils have assumed responsibilities for the supply of labor or should they have left this domain to the Germans? The first reaction of members of Councils was: it is not for the representatives of the Jews to supply to the enemy labor needed for his own purposes. The Germans went about obtaining their necessary supply by organizing an indiscriminate hunt of ghetto dwellers in, for example, the Warsaw streets, complete with shooting and beating. The hunt, and the ensuing despair of the families, was witnessed by a member of the Council, leader of the Jewish-Socialist Bund, Shmuel (Artur) Zygelbojm (later, after emigration, a member of the Polish National Council in London, who committed suicide in 1943 as protest against the indifference of the world to the Holocaust). He told the Council: "We must tell the Germans that if they need labor they should turn to us and we will assign the necessary people." The dilemma was not resolved by this decision. On the contrary, the issue of forced labor became a paramount problem of equity and a test of the conscience of the Councils. The reservoir of manpower of the ghettos could provide all the labor required and more. Under these circumstances the first question raised was: Should the Council free people capable of paying ransom from the distasteful (to say the least) labor duty or not? It appears that in order to justify the emerging inequality created by the ransom policy, the majority of the Councils took the view that such discriminatory policy is morally justifiable if the ransom is used to help the laborers (whom the Germans paid niggardly or not at all), particularly if they worked in labor camps outside the ghettos. There were other factors which could and might have been taken into account in a policy of equitable supply of Jewish labor: a just turnover of labor candidates by labor days, the quality of labor required, the family relations of the laborers, chances of meeting Aryans outside and exchanging valuables for food. Whether these conditions were met in each and every ghetto is a matter of individual consideration, but the temper of the people, particularly in the larger ghettos, and the frequently heard charges of bribery in discharging the duty of labor supply does not make it seem that equitable conditions were met everywhere. Thus the solution of the question of principle only contributed to sharpening the problems of detailed implementation.

Charges concerning the ultimate ineffectiveness of the policy of "rescue through work" as a method of extending the life of the ghettos and its inmates have overshadowed the moral problem involved, a moral problem common to the Jews and to non-Jews in occupied Europe and in particular to the millions of foreign laborers in Germany employed mostly in the war effort of their enemy. The problem was a simple one: How could such service, offering considerable help to the Germans, be justified when the laborers' compatriots were engaged in a mortal fight with their employers as army regulars or *résistants*? With the Jews, the problem had a difference: the Jews had been extirpated from the economic life of the countries of their residence, and unable to create a self-sustained economy in the conditions of ghetto life; the only alternative to 100 percent unemployment lay in serving the enemy employer. West European non-Jews had still at their disposal one alternative: not to follow the call of the German authorities for work in Germany but, instead, go underground in their homeland under the protection of the sympathetic countrymen. Thus, out of 800,000 Dutchmen called up for work in Germany, 300,000 did not show up. No such possibility was at the disposal of the Jews. The lack of any articulate reflections on this moral issue either by the Jewish leadership or by the Jewish masses is the most striking proof of the hopelessness of dealing with moral problems while facing an amoral and cruel enemy.

That the "rescue-through-work" – perhaps a melancholic illustration of the folk saying "Respite of death is also life" (*Chaye shoo is oykh lebn*) – did not work in the long run does not by itself disqualify this policy. It is only by accident of military history that a

considerable part of Łódź Jews did not survive. By the end of July 1944 the Red army had reached the Vistula and established a bridgehead on its western shore, south of Warsaw. The Red army did not continue its advance, but stopped some 70 miles from Łódź. Less than a month later, in August 1944, the 68,000 Jews still alive in Łódź were "resettled."

The alternatives facing the Jews were work or resistance (either through rebellion or through flight to partisan groups). As a general phenomenon rebellion started in major ghettos in 1943, at a time when the majority of the Jewish population had already been destroyed, but also at a time when France did not yet have her *Maquis* and Tito's partisans had not yet become a serious factor, and when the Councils were no longer the only voice in Nazi-oppressed Jewry. The Warsaw Ghetto revolt of April 1943 was the first direct armed confrontation of local forces with the Nazis. The revolts in the ghettos were attempts "to save the Jewish honor." In view of the high price paid in human lives it proved to be no alternative to "rescue through work," however ineffective.

The possibility of rescue and resistance by flight from ghettos to nearby woods and marshes where partisans were active (or where new partisan groups could originate) raised moral issues among the candidates for such flights, and between them and the Councils. The would-be partisans had to take into consideration that chances for fighting the Germans and rescuing themselves were not good in view of the hostility of the majority of the partisan groups and the local population. The candidates for such flights also asked themselves whether it was right to go to the woods and leave their families in the ghettos, thus breaking family ties and depriving the populace of the protection of the young? The solutions to these questions were varied.

The Councils were faced in these cases by their own dilemma: Should they enforce the imposed isolation of the ghetto under their collective responsibility or overlook such daring and "illegal" acts allowing for some furtive contact between the partisans and the ghettos? The answer depended on the evaluation of the situation at a specific moment and the likely reaction of the local satraps. Here the moral solution was largely a result of the political acumen of a given

Council. Not all their previsions proved right, nor were all of their anxieties founded.

This is the place to discuss briefly the problem of the personal integrity of the members of the Councils. East European Councils (with numerous marked exceptions) are in this respect much worse off than, for example, the members of the *Joodse Raad* in Amsterdam or the *Reichsvereinigung* in Berlin. The latter two institutions came in for their share of criticism but it was always emphasized that the personal integrity of their members was never doubted. On the contrary, many Eastern European Council members were charged with various misdeeds from nepotism to the use of funds and property of the community for personal enrichment.

The critical test of the Council members' moral standards, political acumen, personal integrity, and sense of responsibility for the community came at a time when Councilmen, knowing the destination of deportees for "resettlement," did not resign their posts and frequently participated in the process of deportation to the death camps. Jewish communities had for centuries complied with demands of governments for deliveries of "replaceable goods" such as money, but they had never delivered "life itself." In this connection the following three questions arise: (1) Should the Council members have revealed to the people their knowledge of the impending disaster? (2) Should Jews have lent a hand, however reluctantly, to the selection of Jews for deportation which was equivalent to death? (3) Should Jews "voluntarily" have offered some victims for the Moloch at the price of rescuing others, which would mean nothing else than the assumption of the power to decide "Who shall live and who shall die" (*Mi le-hayim umi le-mavet*), a decision reserved in the tradition for God alone?

It is questionable whether Jews in Eastern Europe depended on the Councils for their information on impending disaster, although the appearance of a sizeable number of "volunteers" on the Umschlagplatz in Warsaw might have been proof that such was the case. In a different area, in Theresienstadt, Leo Baeck followed a policy of nonrevelation in view of his judgment that nothing could have been done to change the course of events. It was – in his view – advisable not to let victims know the truth and to spare them

the agony and ultimate desperation that comes from knowledge that the end is near and there is absolutely no way out. The analogy of the behavior of doctors in hopeless cases was invoked. Such a policy left, however, the distasteful impression that – whatever the motives – it was somehow identical with the Nazi policy of deception; and it provoked charges of "collaboration."

From the viewpoint of the traditional Jews (who constituted a minority in the Councils) the answer to the questions of Council participation in deportations was long ago given by the greatest codifier of Jewish law, Maimonides. Said Maimonides: ". . . if pagans should tell them [the Jews], 'Give us one of yours and we shall kill him, otherwise we shall kill all of you,' they all should be killed and not a single Jewish soul should be delivered."

The policy of rescuing some Jews by delivering others was a classical case of applicability of the Maimonides rule. But it appears that faced with such cases two equally authoritative rabbinates gave contradictory interpretations of Maimonides. The rabbi of Kaunas (Kovno), Abraham Duber Cahana Shapiro, ruled that "if a Jewish community . . . has been condemned to physical destruction, and there are means of rescuing part of it, the leaders of the community should have the courage to assume the responsibility, to act and rescue what is possible." By contrast the Vilna rabbinate, replying to the argument of the head of the ghetto that "by participating in the selection and delivering a small number of Jews, he is rescuing the rest from the death," took the strict view of Maimonides.

In other Councils two opposing views confronted each other in all sharpness: the contention that the selection of who shall die and who shall live should be left to the Germans, as against the contention that the Jews themselves should do it, not on a mechanically egalitarian basis but on a discriminatory qualitative basis.

The behavior of the individual members in the face of this tragic situation varied all the way from participation in the deportations to refusal, with the ensuing repression of nonparticipants and suicides.

Let us first have a look at those who did not refuse to execute the German orders even when it was clear to them that they were becoming what might have been loosely called "accomplices of the Nazis." Contemporary sources say that these Council members were motivated, among other things, by the hope for exemption from deportation for members and their families and friends. In addition the following objective considerations played a role:

1. Step by step the Nazi terror made the Councils more tractable. "In the beginning, relatively unimportant things were asked of them, replaceable things of material value like personal possessions, money, and apartments. Later, however, the personal freedom of the human being was demanded. Finally the Nazis asked for life itself" (Kasztner). This gradualism in demands, coupled with ever increasing terror, was an effective psychological device. Recalcitrant members of Councils and their families were exposed to reprisals against themselves and the community for their unwillingness to obey Nazi selection orders.

2. The demand for "life itself" came in Poland after some 30 months of attrition when the Nazi authorities had apparently changed the qualification for membership in the Council from "remaining influential personalities and rabbis" (Heydrich's *Schnellbrief*) to obedient implementors of Nazi orders. The fluctuation in the composition of the membership was to a large extent due to Nazi intervention and resulted in a worsening of the stature of the membership in the Council, both in their moral qualities and in their sense of communal responsibility. The remaining original Council members justified their lack of refusal to participate in the selection by the argument that they would be repressed and replaced by unscrupulous persons.

3. It was also claimed that in case of failure of the *Judenrat* fully to comply with Nazi demands the Germans would do the job themselves with much more efficiency and cruelty. This indeed happened, particularly in the larger ghettos, following the mostly "unsatisfactory" results of the Council "participation."

Are these explanations sufficient for a verdict of not guilty? This is a matter for consideration in each individual case and would largely depend on how accurately the Council members assessed the possible German reactions. Perhaps the fact that among the numerous accusations of misconduct brought against surviving Jews before Courts of Honor in the DP camps, national courts, and the courts of Israel there were only few members of Councils, may throw light on the inevitable fate of the Council members. During the war at least two heads of ghettos (Rumkowski and Gens) had pledged to appear before a Jewish court after the end of the war and plead their case; but they had not survived. A special case is that of the *Joodse Raad* in The Netherlands, where members of the Council survived, the chances for hiding were much better than in Eastern Europe, and the death camps far away and unbelievable; a Jewish Court of Honor condemned them on several counts, including participation in the selection and transportation of the Jews to the East, but not for shipping them knowingly to their death. The acts of vengeance meted out by the Resistance to traitors and informers did not embrace Council members.

So much for the apologetic explanations offered by Council members. But there was another group of Council members who, having realized that not all of the victims could be saved, considered it their *duty* to make the selections themselves in the belief that the best elements of the community must be preserved for its future rehabilitation. Perhaps the most outspoken and eloquent presentation of this viewpoint was made by Reszö Kasztner: "Once again we were confronted with the most serious dilemma, the dilemma which we had been faced with throughout our work: Should we leave the selection to blind fate or should we try to influence it? . . . We did, tried to do it. We convinced ourselves that – as sacred as every human being has always been to the Jews – we nevertheless had to strive to save at least those who all their lives had labored for the Community [*Osekim be-Tsorkhe Tsibur*] and, by the same token those women whose husbands were in the labor camps; we also had to see to it that children, especially orphans, would not be left to destruction. In brief: truly holy principles had to be employed to sustain and guide the frail human hand which, by writing down on paper the name of an unknown person, decided on his life or death. Was it grace of fate (*Gnade des Schicksals*) if, under these circumstances, we were not always able to prevail in these endeavors?"

History had given a precedent for qualitative vs. egalitarian selection in the case of the "cantonists" in the period of Czar Nicholas the First (1825–1856) when Jewish boys were forcibly inducted into the army for 25 years, and many of them were converted to the Russian-Orthodox Church. When the Community Councils (Kahals*) in Russia were charged with the duty to submit a certain number of youths under threat of cruel personal punishment they were not faced with a choice among rich, middle class, or poor. The Czarist government released the merchants from the heavy duty. Nor had the middle class any need to ask favors from the Kahal: by paying the license fee for merchants they freed the children from this duty. The choice consequently was between poor and poor. The Kahal gave preference in releasing from this duty to the learned and brilliant (gute kep) boys, the future religious leaders.

We have reached now the last problem to be considered: Was the Jewish Council a positive or a negative factor in the final outcome of the Holocaust? The problem refers to the broad outcome of the Holocaust, not to the isolated individual cases of casualties charged – rightly or wrongly – to the Councils or the individual cases of rescue attributed – rightly or wrongly – to them. Did their participation or nonparticipation influence the dreadful statistics? The following facts should help in formulating an enlightened answer:

1. In large areas of Eastern Europe at least two million victims were murdered without any participation at all on the part of Jews. This refers particularly to victims of the Einsatzgruppen in both the initial phase of the war and during the later stages.

2. In the larger ghettos in Poland and in the Baltic states where there was Jewish participation it was of importance in the initial, not in the final, stages of deportations; the later deportations, as has been indicated above, were carried out by German forces, while the Jewish police played only a secondary role.

3. With few exceptions the process of extermination was finished by early 1943, a year and a half prior to Himmler's autumn 1944 "stop extermination" order. Whatever survivors of the fatal year (spring 1942 – spring 1943) remained or could have

remained alive were destroyed (one may even say at a leisurely pace) during the following months.

4. Above all, the German will to destroy the Jewish people (Vernichtungswille) was directed with particular fury against Eastern European Jewry. The Nazi official statements are full of warnings of the dangers to Germany of East European Jewry, which is represented as the greatest source of Jewish power, a mighty stream from which Jews spread out to all corners of the world, as the reservoir for the existence and constant renewal of world Jewry. The Nazis claimed that without the addition of fresh East European Jewish blood, Jewry in the West would long ago have disappeared. It is difficult to believe that with this determination the Nazis would not have used every day and every device to implement the Final Solution to the letter.

It would appear, then, that when all factors are considered, Jewish participation or nonparticipation in the deportations had no substantial influence – one way or the other – on the final outcome of the Holocaust in Eastern Europe. . . .

THE ORGANIZATIONAL STRUCTURE OF THE JEWISH COUNCILS

THE COUNCILS WERE CONCEIVED by the Nazis not as an instrument for organizing life in the ghettos or for strengthening the structure of the ghetto, but the opposite; as an instrument which, in their hands, would help them to realize their plans concerning the Jewish population in the occupied territories and, in particular, their extermination plan. The Councils were permitted, at most, to take care of distributing the meager supplies and maintaining a certain standard (only too low) of sanitation (for the continuous epidemics would also threaten the Nazis themselves); they were permitted to preserve "peace and order" as understood by the authorities.

The ramified Jewish organization was originally created to carry out, precisely and efficiently, all the regulations and directives of the occupation authorities. This was the definition of its role in the very first document about the Council of Elders (the "urgent letter" of Heydrich of September 21, 1939), in the

---

*The word Kahal (Community Council) was used in Russia, the word Kehila elsewhere.

regulation concerning the establishment of the Jewish Councils of November 28 of the same year, issued by Hans Frank, and in official Nazi declarations dealing with Jewish self-rule in the occupied territories.

The councils had to serve only one purpose – to execute Nazi orders regarding the Jewish population.

Other activities undertaken by the Councils, with the consent of the authorities, in the sphere of internal ghetto life (social welfare, economic and cultural work) were performed, in fact, outside their prescribed tasks. Such other activities, which dealt with the internal requirements of the Jewish population, were sometimes accorded a certain degree of tolerance, and even of encouragement; they served the Nazi-propagated illusion that the continued existence of the ghettos was guaranteed, and also concealed the Final Solution (*Endziel*) from the Jews for as long as necessary.

The tasks of the Councils can be divided into three classes:

1. Tasks imposed by the authorities, such as conduct of the census of the Jewish population, the supply of forced labor, registration of candidates for the work camps, for deportation, etc.

2. Routine tasks in social welfare, medical care, and in the economic and cultural fields – tasks which were, in the main, a continuation of prewar communal activities.

3. New tasks made essential by the complete elimination of the Jewish population in the ghetto from governmental and municipal services, such as food supplies, the management of the ghetto dwellings, industry, health, police and judicial services, etc.

These varied duties of the Councils necessitated the growth of a ramified, administrative apparatus. The organizational structure of this apparatus expanded as the isolation of the Jewish population from the general, governmental, and municipal framework was completed.

The turning point in this development was the confinement of the Jewish population in the ghettos, an act which isolated it almost absolutely. The Nazis intended the "autonomy" of the ghettos to be absolute, to include every aspect of a self-reliant, organized, social unit.

The Nazi-created Jewish ghetto necessarily became a Jewish city *sui generis*, linked to the main city only by slender links which had to be maintained for purely technical reasons, e.g., lighting, water supply, sewage, and limited telephone connection (up to a certain period). Generally the ghettos were cut off from the normal postal services and, in some ghettos, special post offices were opened. Suitable administrative machinery had, therefore, to be created in the ghettos to serve the needs of the Jewish population in those matters normally dealt with by the government and the municipality. It was also necessary to set up special departments to carry out the orders and directives of the authorities with regard to forced labor, collection of taxes, delivery of various materials and merchandise, of forced-labor workers, transfers, evacuations, and the like.

From the start of the occupation, the Germans excluded Jews from the benefits of social services such as pensions for war invalids, sick benefits, etc.[1] Jewish bank accounts were withheld and Jewish property confiscated;[2] forced labor duty for the Jews was ordered.[3] In many places the Jews were also excluded from the general system of food supply. As a result of all these measures, even before the ghettos had been established, Jews were faced with most urgent tasks: to provide in short order some social and medical services, if only on a minimal scale; to take care of food supply and distribution; and to search for new sources of income for countless people eliminated from the national economies and from state and community frameworks.

A particularly urgent field of activities demanding immediate attention was the necessity to provide shelter for the overflow of homeless people who had lost all their possessions as a result of the war operations. Masses of desolated, penniless refugees surged from their ruined dwelling places into the larger communities, where some sort of lodgings had to be found for them. The ranks of these unfortunates were soon augmented by the thousands of Jews whom the Germans threw out of their homes. The Germans complemented this deluge of aimlessly wandering people without any tangible means of existence by systematic spoliation of Jewish property and by relentless, random arrests for forced labor. By such measures these people's economic existence was entirely broken down.

New departments had to be established, and old ones revitalized or reorganized by the Councils, to cope with this ever-increasing responsibility and with the overriding necessity to deal with the hostile authorities on a daily basis. The departments of welfare and medical care, food supply, and forced-labor duty were the earliest ones established. Later came the crucial moment when the Jews were enclosed in the ghettos, where, according to the plans of the Nazis, the "ghetto autonomy" was to be complete and self-sustaining in all sectors of community life. It then became particularly important to extend the existing administrative apparatus (which already took care of forced labor, imposed financial sanctions, and supervised deliveries of materials) to include policing of the ghetto area, management of real estate to organize the food distribution, etc. . . .

The departments of registration and vital statistics came into being quite early, in accordance with Heydrich's circular letter of September 21, 1939 (Part 2, Par. 3), which ordered the Councils to carry out a census of the Jewish population according to age. At the end of October 1939 a statistical bureau was established in Warsaw following the order to take a census of Jews residing in the Polish capital. The census took place on October 28.[4] In Lublin the registration department was established on February 22, 1940, and its first duty was to carry out the census there.[5] In Łódź a department for this purpose was established on May 9, 1940, soon after the Jews were closed up in the ghetto.[6] Prior orders during October 1939 had directed the forced labor department to carry out the registration of males eighteen to sixty years old and females twenty-two to fifty-five years old.

To take care of the deliveries of merchandise ordered by various authorities, there were established in some of the ghettos special offices, such as the acquisition office (*Beschaffungsamt*) at Lwów, the material deliveries office (*Sachleitungskommission*) at Żółkiew, etc.[7]

The "resettlement" of the Jews into the overcrowded ghettos – for the most part located in desolate, squalid, slum-ridden sections of the towns – suddenly forced upon the community leaders ex-

tremely heavy responsibilities: to move the worldly goods of thousands of dislodged families; to find the living space necessary to shelter them; to try to distribute this insufficient room among the people rendered homeless on short notice; to move dislodged institutions of public service into some new quarters; to speed up repairs of ruined buildings to create additional living space. These agonizing tasks all demanded simultaneous solution. Among the new departments that mushroomed in the ghettos, those that dealt with providing homes were necessarily among the first and most important to come into being. Initially called resettlement departments or commissions, they were renamed tenants' departments as time passed.

It was also necessary to serve in other fields. Isolated in the ghettos, robbed of personal property, forced to give up their businesses and positions of employment, and, as a rule, even compelled to surrender their homes, native Jews and refugees alike, businessmen and salaried workers, had been deprived of their livelihood and customary means of sustenance. All required immediate attention and assistance in their search for some means of support for themselves and their families. People had to start all over from scratch. Trade had to be organized, new sources of income created. Simultaneously, it was necessary to plan and bring to life a network for distribution of allotted food rations; to open schools; to make arrangements for distribution of mail (as a rule the Jews were excluded from general postal service); to establish management of real estate; and, in places like Łódź, for example, to take over servicing gas and electricity for the ghetto on behalf of the municipality. Last, but not least, when Passover approached, some of the ghettos created *ad hoc* commissions to take care of seasonal necessities, such as providing matzoth, etc.

The administrative structure of the Councils grew in stages, accretions depending on the realities of life in the ghetto, the necessity to take care of ever-growing tasks for the ghetto inmates, and the heavy duties imposed by the occupation authorities. The structure of the Councils also depended on the type of the ghetto: whether life was totally regimented by a forceful bureaucratic apparatus, or some opportunities for free enterprise were left to the inmates. Added to everything else, the enormous paperwork demanded by the supervisory authorities necessitated the establishment of new offices, if only to diminish the heavy work load of existing departments. . . .

Notes

1. VB1GG, No. 13 (Dec. 21, 1939), Par. 5; VB1GG, Vol. I, No. 18 (March 13, 1940), Par. 8.

2. VBIGG, Part II (1940), 23.
3. VBIGG, No. 1, 6–7; No. 13 (Dec. 21, 1939); No. 14 (Dec. 23, 1939).
4. *Bericht Warschau*, 7.
5. *Sprawozdanie*, 56.
6. ZC, Doc. 110.
7. Zaderecki, 445; testimony by Rabbi David Kahane, 15–16 (YIA); Gerszon Taffet, *Zagłada Żydów żołiewskich* (Łódź, 1946), 25–26.

CHAIM A. KAPLAN **Scroll of Agony**

October 16, 1939

LIFE MOVES ALONG BY ITSELF. There is no transportation, no water, no electricity. Everything creeps, and this has given foundation to flourishing rumors that the conquerors won't remain here. But there is one thing the conquerors do not ignore, that they return to incessantly, as though from the very outset they had come here for that purpose alone. A certain psychosis of hatred and loathing toward "the *Jude*" has infected them, and if they do anything with care and forethought, it is in the Jewish area.

Here are a few pearls in the course of one day: First, Mayor Starzynski, in the name of the local commissar appointed by the German military command, announced with special pleasure that the German-appointed courtyard commandants are required to furnish a list of the residents of each courtyard who require public assistance, and on the basis of this, everyone will receive a legal document entitling him to receive, free of charge, bread, meals, clothing, and linen which the city will furnish at its own expense – except for the Jews.

Second, in a conversation which lasted two minutes, and which assumed the character of an order through the addition of a threat that "otherwise, they alone are responsible for their lives," the Jewish Council* was ordered to furnish a list of the Jewish residents of Warsaw from sixteen to sixty years of age. For what purpose? Nobody knows. But it is certain that it's not for the benefit of the Jews. Our hearts tell us that a catastrophe for the Jewry of Poland is hidden in this demand.

Third, Rosensztat, a Jewish pharmacist from Grzybowska Street, came to the conquerors with a request for "spirits," without which no drugstore can function. They asked him if he was a Jew. When he said yes, they informed him that he wouldn't receive any until he fired his Jewish employees, and that the manager, who until now had been Rosensztat himself, must also be an Aryan. Henceforward it is forbidden for the Jewish owner to cross the threshold of his own pharmacy. The Aryan manager will send the monthly accounts to him at home.

Fourth, the price of merchandise has gone down unnaturally – because everyone is afraid of confiscation. Jews plead with their Christian acquaintances to accept certain sums for safekeeping, so that they won't have to deposit anything in excess of 2,000 zloty in the bank under the supervision of the conqueror. But the Christian "friends" refuse, because their merchants' association has forbidden its members to give assistance to Jews in any form whatsoever.

Fifth, today Moshe Indelman,[†] an editor of the newspaper *Hajnt*, was arrested. They told his wife that if her husband didn't return, she could find out about his fate at Third of May Street. M.I. is my friend and comrade.

Sixth, there is a widespread rumor that Vladimir Jabotinsky has founded a Jewish Legion of 200,000 men; that England has proclaimed a Jewish State in Palestine and an Arab State in Syria; that Chaim Weizmann has been made President, and so on. I don't believe any of these rumors. I record them only for remembrance.

October 18, 1939

Our lives grow gloomier from day to day. Racial laws have not yet been formally decreed, but actually our defeat is inevitable. The conqueror says bluntly that there is no hope for Jewish survival. There is room for the assumption that a beginning is being made now.

REPRINTED WITH THE PERMISSION OF SIMON & SCHUSTER, INC., FROM **SCROLL OF AGONY: THE WARSAW DIARY OF CHAIM A. KAPLAN**, TRANSLATED AND EDITED BY ABRAHAM I. KATSH, 52–54, 55–56, 144–45, 205–09, 222–26, 229–30, 262–63, 289–90, 383–89, 398–400. COPYRIGHT © 1963, 1973 BY ABRAHAM I. KATSH.

*The Jewish Community Council (Hebrew: *Kehillah*) had been replaced, at German orders, by the Jewish Council (German: *Judenrat*) on October 4, 1939. The last head of the *Kehillah*, Mauryc Majzel, was not elected but was appointed by the Polish Government. He fled Warsaw immediately after the outbreak of the war, and Adam Czerniakow was the appointed head of the *Judenrat*.
†Moshe Yinnon, now in the United States and the editor of *Hadoar*, a Hebrew weekly.

So far there has been free trade in the streets. This is a trade of pennies, whose practitioners are boys and girls, young men and women driven to this sort of business by poverty. It is destined to be forbidden. It too will be taken out of the hands of the Jews. Every public place shows hatred and loathing toward the Jews. Isolated incidents of blows and violence against Jews have grown too numerous to count. Eyewitnesses tell horrifying stories, and they are not exaggerations.

The future of the schools for Jewish children is not yet known. In general the conquerors have no dealings with Jewish representatives. We are like grains of sand. There is no prior consultation regarding our own lives. They make decrees by themselves and there is no changing them. Reasons are not required. There is only one reason – to destroy, to kill, to eradicate.

Let anyone who wishes to consider the depths of the tragedy of Polish Jewry come to the Joint* building (13 Leszno Street) and see the vale of tears. But even the Joint has no legal authority, and the conqueror knows nothing of its existence. It is our good fortune that the Joint's funds are in the hands of the American consulate and the enemy has no access to them. Otherwise he would confiscate them to the last cent. But the Joint's relief money is like a drop in the ocean. Great God! Are you making an end to Polish Jewry? "The populace" cannot understand: Why is the world silent?

October 19, 1939

There are no schools, elementary or high, Jewish or Polish. Many school buildings were burned, and a school that has been burned will never rise again, with so many people homeless. Even the schools that remain are in ruins. There isn't a building in Warsaw whose windows haven't been broken, particularly on the side facing the street – and when any glass is available, they raise the prices so exorbitantly that glass for a double window costs 200 zloty. There are school buildings in which the cost of glass would run to several thousand zloty. . . .

October 21, 1939

Some time ago I stated that our future is be-

clouded. I was wrong. Our future is becoming increasingly clear. Today the legal destruction began, with an order barring Jews from the two branches of the economy in which 50 percent of the Jewish community supported itself. It makes one's blood freeze, and a man is ready to commit suicide out of desperation. This isn't just a small economic deprivation that makes things difficult but will not endanger our survival. It is a savage slash that has no equal in the history of the oppression of the Jewish people. The cruel decree is short and decisive, comprising only seven paragraphs, but it suffices to topple our entire economic structure. The decree says: It is strictly forbidden for Jews to trade in textile goods (manufactures) and processed hides (leather) and any sort of manufacturing that involves these materials. With terrible savagery the ax has struck at the most active artery of the Jewish economy. All violators of this order will be severely punished, even by capital punishment.

After this it will be proper to say "blessed be the righteous judge"† for Jewish business in Poland. Besides the traders in hides and fabrics, thousands of Jews who were indirectly supported from this will be deprived of all livelihood.

But in the decree there is one detail that arouses various thoughts: it affects only the left bank of the Vistula, and excepts the right bank. This is hard to understand. For what reason was the left bank set apart from the right bank? Those who understand politics seek to prove by this that the right bank will belong to the Russians. Thus Warsaw for the Germans, Praga for the Russians. This is the comedy of life. . . .

May 2, 1940

In a spiritual state like the one in which I find myself at this time, it is difficult to hold a pen, to concentrate one's thoughts. But a strange idea has stuck in my head since the war broke out – that it is a duty I must perform. This idea is like a flame imprisoned in my bones, burning within me, screaming: Record! Perhaps I am the only one engaged in this work, and that strengthens and encourages me.

When the conqueror runs rampant, he makes no distinction between Jews and Poles, even though he knows the Jew has no thoughts of revolt. The Pole is

*American Jewish Joint Distribution Committee, *Ed.*
†The prayer said at funerals and upon hearing of a death.

beaten for whatever sin he commits; the Jew is beaten day and night at every opportunity, whether he has sinned or not. When the day of reckoning comes the tyrant lumps them both together, and there is no escaping his wrath.

The prison on Dzielna Street is filled with prisoners, and therefore the entire area around it has become a place ripe for depredations. Gendarmes visit the area frequently, and every one of their visits leaves an impression on the bodies of Jews. The Nazis pass like a storm through the Jewish streets, whose inhabitants know from experience that many of them will come out of it toothless and eyeless. It is an attack of beasts of prey, devoid of any human feeling, upon innocent people walking unaware through the street. And not only upon men – women too are included. Even a mother standing by her baby's cradle is not secure against sudden attack. Sometimes the Germans beat people about the shoulders with long whips while sitting in a car driven along close to the curb; sometimes they pour down their blows while they stand outside the car. Then you see before you animals on two legs: murderous faces; a terrible fury of wild men in destructive rage. Whoever falls into their hands is reduced to a heap of bones. As I say, the Nazis make no distinction between men and women, or, in the case of women, between a young girl and a mother beside a cradle. Today I saw with my own eyes how a Jewish baby's cradle was turned upside down after they had beaten the miserable mother until she fell under the weight of her suffering. Her hysterical screams echoed through the entire street, but the Nazi gendarme carefully finished his "job" before he returned to his car.

Jewish passersby are aware of every appearance of a car whose occupants are the servants of the Führer. When they first notice it from a distance, a flight begins, an escape into the doorways of the houses. In a single instant the street takes on the appearance of a graveyard. In every place they go there is silence, and you won't find a single living soul on the street. Thousands flee, but many are caught. Fear reigns in every corner.

This is the custom every day of the year, so that occurrences of this sort are a fleeting thing, an act of the moment. Whatever happens, happens – and then

the danger passes. Everyone returns to his work and his occupation. Life makes its own demands. . . .

October 8, 1940

Jewish Joke I:

The Germans are beating the Jews because England doesn't want to make peace; the Poles are beating them because the same England did not prepare herself properly for battle and is being defeated.

Jewish Joke II:

The Führer asks [Hans] Frank*, "What evils and misfortunes have you brought upon the Jews of Poland?"

"I took away their livelihood; I robbed them of their rights; I established labor camps and we are making them work at hard labor there; I have stolen all their wealth and property."

But the Führer is not satisfied with all these acts.

So Frank adds: "Besides that, I have established *Judenraten* and Jewish Self-Aid Societies."

The Führer is satisfied, and smiles at Frank. "You hit the target with the *Judenraten*, and Self-Aid will ruin them. They will disappear from the earth!"

Jewish Joke III:

Frank has ordered that on the Day of Atonement, 5701, the Jews of Cracow must open their stores for business.

One day out of the year he allows the Jews to do business.

Frank came to Warsaw to inaugurate the aid project for next winter. Notices written in German in huge letters joyfully announced his arrival. *Volksgenossen* [Germans] were ordered to hang out flags in honor of the guest. German Warsaw was jubilant.

And do not be surprised when I say "German Warsaw," even though its German population is only a negligible minority. Here quantity is not important, quality is the determinant. One German outweighs a thousand Poles and tens of thousands of Jews.

The Germans have the power now, and they are the real lords of the city. The war broke out for their benefit, and they were a main political cause of the conquest of Poland and its loss of sovereignty. The whole world was created just for them. Poland is no longer Polish even ethnographically. Don't ask where

*Governor General of occupied Poland, *Ed.*

twenty million Poles disappeared to! German science which serves Nazism has caused them to disappear – and not more than ten million Poles can be found. And those who remain are obviously not worthy to rule. As for the Jews, they don't count at all. They are cattle. When the conqueror's newspapers wrote about Lodz and its industrial development they didn't mention the Jews even obliquely. It was as if they had never existed.

Frank's coming made no special impression on the city. They didn't turn out to see him and his companions; in fact the population pretended not to notice him. Everyone ignored this tyrant whose wickedness and cruelty are even greater than that of the Führer. This is good. It is a sign that the Poles have a political sense. Even though great military and political changes bode ill for their future, they remain stubborn. You will not find one single public-spirited citizen among them who is willing to be the conquerors' representative, to talk to his people and make them realize that they cannot change reality and must accept the yoke of German rule – like Hacha in Czechoslovakia and Quisling in Norway. We could also add Pétain in France, that stupid old man who willingly said Kaddish* for his country.

October 10, 1940

Clouds are covering our skies. Racial segregation is becoming more apparent each day.

Yesterday an order was published that the Jews must make way before every German, both soldiers and civil servants in uniform. Making way means that the Jews must step aside until the Germans leave the sidewalk. You must always keep your eyes open and guard yourself against daydreaming and conversation lest you fail to do the proper honor to a Nazi you encounter. Today we have already had our first victims, who were beaten because of the order. You go out trembling, full of panic lest you meet a Nazi.

All people whose ancestors did not stand before Mount Sinai are allowed to walk in the streets until eleven at night. For Jews outside the walls, the curfew is seven; inside the walls, nine. In the morning, no Jew who lives outside the walls can be on the street before eight.

The Jewish trolley is a mockery of the poor. Trolley cars with white trim (for Aryans only) with two cars pass by empty, while dozens of passengers wait at the stop; no one dares to enter the empty cars because it is not a Jewish trolley. In the Jewish tram, the crowding and pushing make it almost impossible to breathe. No one standing can sit down, and no one sitting can get up. The passengers neither sit nor stand, but rather hang – it is like the plague of darkness in the land of Egypt. There is no filthier place, capable of spreading contagious diseases, than a Jewish trolley on a single ride, where everything is infected, when sick people sweat and slobber on you.

Yet with all this the Jews are "content with their lot," and say decisively that the maximal evil has not yet come, that there is some sort of psychological barrier preventing the conquerors from pouring their full wrath upon us. Here the Jews surmise: What will happen to us when a new war breaks out between the conqueror and Russia-America? Then we will simply be eradicated. The Bolshevik land will again be called a Jewish state, and the United States all the more so.

October 12, 1940
End of Yom Kippur, 5701

On the New Year we prayed illegally. The ban on communal worship was still in effect. In secret, in side rooms near the dark, closed synagogues we prayed to the God of Israel like Marranos in the fifteenth century.

But one day before the eve of the Day of Atonement the *Zyd* newspaper reached us from Cracow, bringing us permission for communal worship. This permission was not unconditional, however. It is still forbidden to pray publicly in the synagogues, and they remain locked. The law was relaxed only to permit communal worship in small groups in private homes, on condition that they don't make noise and that there is no crowding.

The Jewish community of Warsaw left nothing out in its prayers, but poured its supplications before its Father in Heaven in accordance with the ancient custom of Israel. To our great sorrow, as the day drew to a close, at a time when the gates of tears were still open, we learned that a new edict had been issued for us, a barbaric edict which by its weight and results is

*Traditional Jewish prayer for the dead, *Ed.*

greater than all the other edicts made against us up to now, to which we had become accustomed.

At last the ghetto edict has gone into effect. For the time being it will be an open ghetto, but there is no doubt that in short order it will be closed. In Lodz the ghetto edict was not carried out all at once, but rather step by step, and many signs indicate that it will be the same in Warsaw. After the ghetto plan was postponed two weeks ago, we were almost tranquil. But the enemy of Israel neither sleeps nor slumbers.

This new edict was issued in a somewhat humane form – perhaps for the sake of world opinion – but we know that in its new form it is still the last link of the chain of troubles and misfortunes.

Before the thirty-first of October the Jews who live in the streets outside the walls must move lock, stock, and barrel to the streets within the walls; and all the Aryans (read Poles) living in the streets within the walls must move to the Aryan quarter. To a certain extent the edict has hurt the Poles more than the Jews, for the Poles are ordered to move not only from the ghetto, but from the German quarter as well. Nazism wants to separate everyone – the lords by themselves, the underlings by themselves, the slaves by themselves. The blessed and the accursed must not mingle.

A hundred and twenty thousand people will be driven out of their homes and will have to find sanctuary and shelter within the walls. Where will we put this great mass of people? Most of them are wealthy, accustomed to beautiful apartments and lives of comfort, and they will be totally impoverished from now on. Their businesses and livelihoods were directly connected with the areas where they lived. In leaving their homes they are also leaving their incomes.

The Gentiles too are in mourning. Not one tradesman or storekeeper wants to move to a strange section, even if it be to an Aryan section. It is hard for any man, whether Jewish or Aryan, to start making his life over. And so the panic in captured Warsaw, occupied by harsh masters, is great. As I have said, for the time being we are in an open ghetto; but we will end by being in a real ghetto, within closed walls.

Hundreds of Germans are coming in, refugees from the English bombs, half-mad women with their children. They complain angrily to their fat, comfort-

able relatives who are enjoying the spoils of a strange land out of all danger. An eyewitness reports that a German soldier dared to write these words on the wall of one of the trolley cars: "*Wir fahren hin un her. Wir haben kein Heimat mehr!*"*

Maybe this is the beginning of the removal of the yoke which Churchill is trying so hard to accomplish. . . .

November 10, 1940

The conquerors' radio emphasized and reemphasized that this is not a ghetto, but rather a Jewish quarter, like the Polish quarter or the German quarter. In whispers the constant rumor was that Roosevelt had a hand in these concessions. The oppressed Jewish masses enjoy rumors of this sort. It is good in our terrible troubles to believe that some mighty hand is guiding us, that our sufferings are seen and our sighs are heard.

But we woke up, and our souls were empty.

In our favor there were flourishing, unfounded rumors; against us there were unalterable, hard facts. All the concessions were blown away like smoke. A time extension was given only once, and that was for the benefit of the Poles. We had hopes for Praga, that the edict would be softened in its favor, but it was a dream. By the fifteenth of November not a Jew will be left there. A city of fifty thousand Jews is going into exile.

Most significantly, in all the thoroughfares leading to the Aryan quarters high walls are being erected blocking the paths to the Aryan world before us. At present only the streets united with the Jewish ghetto by car tracks are still open. Wherever you turn the murderers have blocked the way. Moreover, the walls being erected now are higher and sturdier than the ones that were put up earlier. Before our eyes a dungeon is being built in which half a million men, women, and children will be imprisoned, no one knows for how long.

The *Judenrat* is building this great mass grave with its own funds. All of this is a clear proof, because if the conquerors wished to leave the ghetto open they would not need to build high, fortified walls to block the path of life before us.

The *Judenrat* is burdened with much other work

*"We ride back and forth. We have no more homeland!"

in preparing to organize life within a closed ghetto. Under its supervision a Jewish police force is being recruited which will have authority over the buried-alive Jews of the ghetto. Nine thousand young men have already registered as candidates for this force. By the way, each applicant included a five-zloty registration fee, which even the abject poor paid in the hope of being accepted for the ghetto police, although there will be salary for these policemen. Among the other preparations are negotiations with the Aryan owners of pharmacies in the Jewish quarter. In the area set aside for the ghetto there were formerly twenty-one pharmacies, seven of them Jewish, the rest Aryan. As soon as the conquerors came the Jewish druggists were pushed out of their businesses. Now, with the creation of the ghetto, the conquerors intend to leave in the area only eleven pharmacies, which will be under the supervision of the *Judenrat* and will once again have Jewish personnel. The same applies to the management of Jewish-owned apartment houses. From now on there will be no room for Aryan managers. The houses will be turned over to the control of the *Judenrat*, which will employ the agents removed from them by force and deprived of their livelihoods. All of these are bad signs.

The day is not distant when we will be penned in like cattle, forcibly removed from the outside world like a camp of unclean lepers. . . .

November 19, 1940

If it were said that the sun has darkened for us at noon it would not be merely a metaphor. We will molder and rot within the narrow streets and the crooked lanes in which tens of thousands of people wander idle and full of despair.

The matter of food supplies, in particular, has contributed to confusion. Since communications between us and the villages is cut off, our food will be given to us by the conquerors. This will amount to ninety-percent starvation. What good will ten decagrams of coarse bread a week do?

Anger at black marketeering has become tremendous. The wealthy, and even the ordinary well-to-do, had hoarded food. Only the poor are left with nothing, because they couldn't afford to stock up. It is they who are the victims of the black marketeers and it is

hard to see them in their distress. There is nowhere to earn a penny. Toil and poverty were their lot even in ordinary times, and now a ton of coal costs 800 zloty; a loaf of coarse bread, three zloty; a litre of milk, two zloty; a kilo of butter, 30 zloty. And so on. . . .

December 2, 1940

Life in the ghetto is becoming "normal." The chaos lasted no more than a week. When half a million people are locked in a small cage, faced with hunger, privation, epidemics, atrocities, naturally it causes a stir. Even the conquerors were confused. This is a unique political experiment. The intention was to starve and impoverish us in body and in spirit, to segregate us from the outside world; to undermine our very existence. A great project of this sort demands extraordinary exertions and cannot be brought into effect by words alone. But to our sorrow, it must be admitted that the tyrants succeeded.

Entry and exit permits are given only to Aryan officials who hold posts in one of the government institutions within the ghetto. Certain Jews too get permits of this sort, and these include the Jewish Gestapo agents, the destroyers from our midst, as well as an insignificant number of individuals who fill some important position of service for the government in an institution outside the ghetto boundaries. Aside from these, there are also Jewish boys under the age of ten, who, not being marked by the "badge of shame," sometimes manage to sneak across the border, because the border guards do not recognize that they are the children of the inferior race.

These children are clever, and they are sent by their parents to buy food cheaply. Usually they are successful in their mission, and bring home bargains. This week I got a bargain of this sort myself: a quarter-kilo of butter for six zloty, which our relative Emek brought in from the other side of the wall. God bless him!

While the rich were hoarding food the poor were going around mourning and desolate, their eyes expressing anger at those complacent people upon whom the famine had not made an impression. This jealousy, which was like a fire contained within their bones, prompted such talk as: "Let them hoard to their hearts' content. When we're starving we will take it by force. Justice does not require allowing the bourgeoisie to enjoy all good things at a time when the people are dying of starvation." . . .

April 3, 1941

Like the Egyptian Passover, the Passover of Germany will be celebrated for generations. The chaotic oppression of every day throughout this year of suffering will be reflected in the days of the coming holiday. Last year the Joint's project was functioning full force. It was not conducted properly and many people criticized it, but in the last analysis it fed the hungry and brought the holiday into every Jewish home. We lacked for nothing then.

This year everything is changed for the worse, and we are all faced with a Passover of hunger and poverty, without even the bread of poverty. First of all, the Joint has divested itself of all activity in connection with the holiday. In effect it has disappeared from the communal stage, and its voice is no longer heard. Self-Aid support is also a matter of leaning on a shattered reed; and the new taxes did not help to ease its burdens. We thought they would quiet our fears about the support of the soup kitchens, but we were wrong. We Jews are not afraid of a Jewish government. Many evade payment of the tax, and no threat of punishment does any good with the misers. If the Jews of Warsaw who are able to pay had obeyed Czerniakow's decree and turned over the tax of two zloty apiece each month willingly, the problem of feeding the hungry would not be so serious. The courtyard committees who were charged with the assessments had to fight the miserable creatures for every penny. A strong, healthy father of a family of five, who spends 30 zloty a day for the needs of his household and whose home is filled with good things, was ready to put out the eyes of the chairman of the courtyard committee because he would not give him a reduction on his assessment of two zloty per person. "A poor man like me pay ten zloty a month? God in heaven!"

And so there were arguments and quarrels in every courtyard. The members of the courtyard committees are the scapegoats.

The end result is that the collection of the tax goes on with the greatest difficulty. In theory the recalcitrants should be punished, and there is even a special office for this purpose. But this punishment-machine does not function at the necessary tempo. The courtyard committees overlook much, out of their unwillingness to make enemies, and the punishment office overlooks much for personal reasons. The result of all this is that the tax has not improved the situation and the soup kitchens are closed almost every other day.

As the holiday drew near, the Self-Aid made the customary Passover appeal for money for the poor. But this project was born in an unlucky hour and its results will be nil. At present – one week before the holiday – the project's treasury is empty.

What, then, will we eat during the eight days of the coming holiday? I am afraid we will turn our holiday into a weekday. For prayer there are no synagogues or houses of study. Their doors are closed and darkness reigns in the dwelling places of Israel. For eating and drinking there is neither matzoth nor wine. . . .

January 4, 1942

The words of the poet have come true in all their dreadful meaning: " 'Tis not a nation nor a sect but a herd." Gone is the spirit of Jewish brotherhood. The words "compassionate, modest, charitable" no longer apply to us. The ghetto beggars who stretch out their hands to us with the plea: "Jewish hearts, have pity!" realize that the once tender hearts have become like rocks. Our tragedy is the senselessness of it all. Our suffering is inflicted on us because we are Jews, while the real meaning of Jewishness has disappeared from our lives.

Our oppressors herded us into the ghetto, hoping to subdue us into obedient animals. Instead, however, we are splitting and crumbling into hostile, quarrelsome groups. It is painful to admit that ever since we were driven into the ghetto our collective moral standard has declined sharply. Instead of uniting and bringing us closer, our suffering has led to strife and contention between brothers. The Nazis, possibly with malice aforethought, put us in the hands of the *Judenrat* so that we might be disgraced in the sight of all. It is as if they were saying, "Look at them! Do you call them a people? Is this your social morality? Are these your leaders?"

It is not at all uncommon on a cold winter morning to see the bodies of those who have died on the sidewalks of cold and starvation during the night. Many God-fearing, pious souls who, if the day happens to be the Sabbath, are carrying the *tallith** under their arms, walk by the corpses and no one seems to be moved by the sight. Everyone hastens on his way praying silently that his will not be a similar fate. In the gutters, amidst the refuse, one can see almost naked and barefoot little children wailing pitifully. These are children who were orphaned when both parents died either in their wanderings or in the typhus epidemic. Yet there is no institution that will take them in and care for them and bring them up as human beings. Every morning you will see their little bodies frozen to death in the ghetto streets. It has become a customary sight. Self-preservation has hardened our hearts and made us indifferent to the suffering of others. Our moral standards are thoroughly corrupted. Disgraceful as it may sound, we must admit the bitter truth: Everyone steals! Petty thievery, such as picking pockets or stealing a hat or an umbrella, is common. Because kosher meat is terribly expensive, people have relaxed their observance of the laws regarding the eating of kosher food. Not only atheists and derelicts are guilty of this, but synagogue sextons and pious men as well.

It is Nazism that has forced Polish Jewry to degrade itself thus. Nazism has maimed the soul even more than the body! . . .

July 26, 1942

The terrible events have engulfed me; the horrible deeds committed in the ghetto have so frightened and stunned me that I have not the power, either physical or spiritual, to review these events and perpetuate them with the pen of a scribe. I have no words to express what has happened to us since the day the expulsion was ordered. Those people who have gotten some notion of historical expulsions from books know nothing. We, the inhabitants of the Warsaw ghetto, are now experiencing the reality. Our only good fortune is that our days are numbered — that we shall not have long to live under conditions like these, and that after our terrible sufferings and wanderings we shall come to eternal rest, which was

denied us in life. Among ourselves we fully admit that this death which lurks behind our walls will be our salvation; but there is one thorn. We shall not be privileged to witness the downfall of the Nazis, which in the end will surely come to pass.

Some of my friends and acquaintances who know the secret of my diary urge me, in their despair, to stop writing. "Why? For what purpose? Will you live to see it published? Will these words of yours reach the ears of future generations? How? If you are deported you won't be able to take it with you because the Nazis will watch your every move, and even if you succeed in hiding it when you leave Warsaw, you will undoubtedly die on the way, for your strength is ebbing. And if you don't die from lack of strength, you will die by the Nazi sword. For not a single deportee will be able to hold out to the end of the war."

And yet in spite of it all I refuse to listen to them. I feel that continuing this diary to the very end of my physical and spiritual strength is a historical mission which must not be abandoned. My mind is still clear, my need to record unstilled, though it is now five days since any real food has passed my lips. Therefore I will not silence my diary!

We have a Jewish tradition that an evil law is foredoomed to defeat. This historical experience has caused us much trouble since the day we fell into the mouth of the Nazi whose dearest wish is to swallow us. It came to us from habit, this minimizing of all edicts with the common maxim, "It won't succeed." In this lay our undoing, and we made a bitter mistake. An evil decree made by the Nazis does not weaken in effect, it grows stronger. The mitigating paragraphs are increasingly overlooked and the more severe paragraphs intensified. At the beginning, the time of the "negotiations," a directive was issued to the *Judenrat* to deport 6,000 a day; in point of fact they are now deporting close to 10,000. The Jewish police, whose cruelty is no less than that of the Nazis, deliver to the "transfer point" on Stawki Street more than the quota to which the *Judenrat* obligated itself. Sometimes there are several thousand people waiting a day or two to be transported because of a shortage of railroad cars. Word has gotten around that the Nazis are satisfied that the extermination of the Jews is being carried out with all requisite efficiency.

*Jewish prayer shawl, *Ed.*

This deed is being done by the Jewish slaughterers.

The first victim of the deportation decree was the President, Adam Czerniakow, who committed suicide by poison in the *Judenrat* building. He perpetuated his name by his death more than by his life. His end proves conclusively that he worked and strove for the good of his people; that he wanted its welfare and continuity even though not everything done in his name was praiseworthy. The expulsion proclamation posted in the city streets on the afternoon of July 22 was not signed in the usual manner of *Judenrat* notices, "Head of the *Judenrat*, Certified Engineer Adam Czerniakow," but merely "*Judenrat.*" This innovation astonished those circles who examine bureaucratic changes in notices. After the president's death, the reason became clear. Czerniakow had refused to sign the expulsion order. He followed the Talmudic law: If someone comes to kill me, using might and power, and turns a deaf ear to all my pleas, he can do to me whatever his heart desires, since he has the power, and strength always prevails. But to give my consent, to sign my own death warrant – this no power on earth can force me to do, not even the brutal force of the foul-souled Nazi.

A whole community with an ancient tradition, one that with all its faults was the very backbone of world Jewry, is going to destruction. First they took away its means of livelihood, then they stole its wares, then its houses and factories, and, above all, its human rights. It was left fair prey to every evildoer and sinner. It was locked into a ghetto. Food and drink was withheld from it; its fallen multiplied on every hand; and even after all this they were not content to let it dwell forever within its narrow, rotten ghetto, surrounded with its wall through which even bread could be brought in only by dangerous smuggling. Nor was this a ghetto of people who consume without producing, of speculators and profiteers. Most of its members were devoted to labor, so that it became a productive legion. All that it produced, it produced for the benefit of those same soldiers who multiplied its fallen.

Yet all this was to no avail. There was only one decree – death. They came and divided the Warsaw ghetto into two halves; one half was for sword, pestilence, and destruction; the other half for famine and slavery. The vigorous youth, the healthy and productive ones, were taken to work in the factories. The old people, the women, the children all were sent into exile.

The President, who had a spark of purity in his heart, found the only way out worthy of himself. Suicide! In the end the Nazis would have killed him anyhow, as is their custom in the areas from which they expel the Jewish population; nor would the President have been the last to be shot. From the moment of his refusal to sign the expulsion order he was a saboteur in the eyes of the Nazis and thus doomed to death. With a president one must be very exacting. In any event, he did well to anticipate the Nazis.

He did not have a good life, but he had a beautiful death. May his death atone for his wrongs against his people before becoming president. There are those who earn immortality in a single hour. The President, Adam Czerniakow, earned his immortality in a single instant.

July 27, 1942

Anyone who could see the expulsion from Warsaw with his own eyes would have his heart broken. The ghetto has turned into an inferno. Men have become beasts. Everyone is but a step away from deportation; people are being hunted down in the streets like animals in the forest. It is the Jewish police who are cruelest toward the condemned. Sometimes a blockade is made of a particular house, sometimes of a whole block of houses. In every building earmarked for destruction they begin to make the rounds of the apartments and to demand documents. Whoever has neither documents that entitle him to remain in the ghetto nor money for bribes is told to make a bundle weighing 15 kilos – and on to the transport which stands near the gate. Whenever a house is blockaded a panic arises that is beyond the imagination. Residents who have neither documents nor money hide in nooks and crannies, in the cellars and in the attics. When there is a means of passage between one courtyard and another the fugitives begin jumping over the roofs and fences at the risk of their lives; in time of panic, when the danger is imminent, people are not fussy about methods. But all these methods only delay the inevitable, and in the end the police take men, women, and children. The destitute and impoverished are the first to be deported. In an instant the truck becomes crowded. They are all alike: poverty makes them equal. Their cries and wails tear the heart out.

The children, in particular, rend the heavens with their cries. The old people and the middle-aged deportees accept the judgment in silent submission and stand with their small parcels under their arms. But there is no limit to the sorrow and tears of the young women; sometimes one of them makes an attempt to slip out of the grasp of her captors, and then a terrible battle begins. At such times the horrible scene reaches its peak. The two sides fight, wrestle. On one side a woman with wild hair and a torn blouse rages with the last of her strength at the Jewish thieves, trying to escape from their hands. Anger flows from her mouth and she is like a lioness ready for the kill. And on the other side are the two policemen, her "brothers in misfortune," who pull her back to her death. It is obvious that the police win. But during the fight the wailing of the captives increases sevenfold, and the whole street cries with them.

But isolated incidents don't hold up the operation. The police do what is incumbent upon them. After the completion of the arrests in one house, they move on to another. The *Judenrat* prepares a daily list of houses in which blockades will be made that day. And here a new source of income is opened up for the graft-chasing police. The wealthy and the middle class have yet to be brought to the transports. For those who have no documents, banknotes turn into documents. There is almost a fixed price for ransom, but for some it is cheaper, all according to the class of the ransomed one and the number of people in his household.

Two actual cases are known to me. One of the members of our family ransomed himself off with a substitute for money. In place of the ready cash which he didn't have at the time of the hunt, he gave a silk umbrella as a "gift" not to be returned. An acquaintance of mine, a Hebrew teacher, a downtrodden pauper with a crippled son, was forced to give 300 zloty — his last nest egg, since he has no expectation of new earnings from teaching Hebrew. In this instance the price was high, for expulsion of a cripple means expulsion to the gates of death. Sick people and cripples are killed by the Nazis while still en route.

But from the time they began to hunt down passersby on the street, the sorrow of the expulsion became even greater. For this barbarism the beloved *Judenrat* will find no atonement. One who is seized in his apartment supplies himself with some clothing and food for the journey. His loved ones take their leave of him, fall on his neck. Not so one who is seized on the street. He is taken to the transport as he is, without extra clothing, without food and sustenance, and usually without a penny. No entreaties avail him. He is led out to the transfer point like a lamb to the slaughter.

Life in the ghetto has been turned upside down. Panic is in its streets, fear on every face, wails and cries everywhere you turn. Trade has ceased; bargaining has been silenced; and most important, smuggling has stopped. When there is no smuggling, costs go up, so that the price of bread has reached 60 zloty. Prices have increased tenfold, all businesses have ceased to exist. Everyone's staff of bread has been broken. From whence cometh our help? We are lost! We are lost!

July 28, 1942

The situation grows graver by the hour. Through the window of my apartment near the scene of the "hunting," I beheld those trapped by the hunt, and was so stricken that I was close to madness. For the detainee, the thread of his life is cut in an instant, and the work of an entire lifetime in which his best efforts were invested becomes abandoned property.

Before my very eyes they capture an old woman who walks with a cane. Her steps are measured, and she makes her way with great exertions. She is unable to straighten up. On her face there are marks of nobility and signs of a family status now past. She too was arrested by a lawless Jewish scoundrel. He needs clients, and even this old lady counts, "as is," without clothes or linens, without even food. She will be sent "to the East." She will be fortunate if she doesn't live long.

A young mother of two little children from 19 Nowolipki Street was caught and sent off. The dear children were left orphans. There is no comfort for her husband and their father. And there are similar victims by the hundreds. Today about 10,000 people were taken. They are shoved into freight cars which have no places to sit and no sanitary facilities. If anyone survives that journey, it is nothing less than a miracle.

In truth we have reached extremity. Death is precious when it is quick and swift, when it takes your soul and you pass on into your eternity. But a death which comes by the agonies of starvation and the tortures of the oppressor, who prolongs the death agony and turns his victims into living skeletons – this is the cruelest of punishments. Have we truly sinned more than any nation; have we transgressed more than any generation?

Never in my life had I known the pangs of hunger. Even after I was pushed into the ghetto I ate. But now I too know hunger. I sustain myself for a whole day on a quarter-kilo of bread and unsweetened tea. My strength is diminishing from such meager fare. At times I can't even stand up. I fall on my bed, but rest eludes me. I am in a state of sleep and am not asleep, of wakefulness and yet am not awake. I am plagued by nightmares. Fear and worry preoccupy me – fear lest I be seized and deported; worry about where to find my bread. My income has stopped. The sums owed to me by others are lost. Besides what he needs for food, no one has a penny to his name, and payment of debts isn't taken into consideration at all.

But the main thing is fear of expulsion. The only ones partially insured against expulsion are workers in the factories that German firms have taken under their protection. Many factories accept workers skilled in their trades, and even those who are unskilled but have money. Thus a new economy has begun in the lives of the ghetto Jews who have not yet been expelled.

I am tired. The sequel will come tomorrow, if I'm not caught. . . .

August 4, 1942
In the evening hours

I have not yet been caught; I have not yet been evicted from my apartment; my building has not yet been confiscated. But only a step separates me from

all these misfortunes. All day my wife and I take turns standing watch, looking through the kitchen window which overlooks the courtyard, to see if the blockade has begun. People run from place to place like madmen.

On the very day that I packed my possessions to turn them over to the relative who is my protector, my friend M. from Nowolipki Street brought me some of his belongings because he had heard that his block was in danger of blockade. My friend M. is "kosher" by virtue of the fact that he has an administrative position at the *Judenrat*. His documents are valid and carry full privileges. But the size of the ghetto is being steadily decreased, and there is therefore a danger that the function of an administrator will cease to exist. What did he do? He looked for some kind of factory, and found one, but only upon payment of ransom. Because he had no cash, he gave its equivalent, a precious stone worth several thousand zloty. This was the last of his savings for the bad times to come. When he handed over the stone he was destitute.

My lot is even worse because I have neither money nor a factory job, and therefore am a candidate for expulsion if I am caught. My only salvation is in hiding. This is an outlaw's life, and a man cannot last very long living illegally. My heart trembles at every isolated word. I am unable to leave my house, for at every step the devil lies in wait for me.

There is the silence of death in the streets of the ghetto all through the day. The fear of death is in the eyes of the few people who pass by on the sidewalk opposite our window. Everyone presses himself against the wall and draws into himself so that they will not detect his existence or his presence.

Today my block was scheduled for a blockade with Nazi participation. Seventy Jewish policemen had already entered the courtyard. I thought, "The end has come." But a miracle happened, and the blockade was postponed. The destroyers passed on to the Nalewki-Zamenhof block.

When the danger was already past I hurried to escape. Panic can drive a man out of his mind and magnify the danger even when it no longer exists. But already there is a fear that my block will be blockaded tomorrow. I am therefore trying to lay plans to escape with the dawn. But where will I flee? No block is secure.

Thousands of people in the Nalewki-Zamenhof block were driven from their homes and taken to the transfer point. More than thirty people were slaughtered. In the afternoon, the furies subsided a bit. The number of passersby increased, for the danger of blockade was over. By four in the afternoon, the quota was filled: 13,000 people had been seized and sent off, among them 5,000 who came to the transfer of their own free will. They had had their fill of the ghetto life, which is a life of hunger and fear of death. They escaped from the trap. Would that I could allow myself to do as they did!

If my life ends – what will become of my diary?

Janina Bauman **Behind the Walls**

30 May 1942

I'm furious with Zula. Something has been going on recently in Renata's and Joanna's home night after night and we were both dying to know what it was. Renata wouldn't say. Apparently she's nothing to do with it, much too absorbed in her own romance. But we've heard gossip from people who have been to Joanna's night-time parties. Very vague, though. It would never occur to me to go and ask Joanna, or try to get invited by her – she's older, after all, and has never been my friend. Yesterday, without even consulting me, Zula went uninvited to the party and stayed there over night. This morning she's told me all about it. In the tiniest detail. Thirteen people were there, including Zula, boys and girls, all but her about eighteen. Renata wasn't in. It appears she hasn't been sleeping at home lately. Where does she sleep then, I wonder? The parents don't object. They don't object to Joanna's parties, either. They slept peacefully in their room all night, Zula says.

Joanna and her friends didn't mind Zula being there, they were rather pleased to have her with them. They were playing games when she went in. It involved sitting on each other's knees and kissing. From time to time, they would drink vodka straight from the bottle. Somebody passed Zula the bottle and she drank, too. When the bottle was empty one of the boys got another and they sent it round again. After a while Zula felt tipsy, but she can remember they danced, then switched the light off and lay down on the floor, all next to each other. She fell asleep straightaway, but woke up after a time and heard a couple making love next to her. She thought the other couples were doing the same in the dark, and felt so terribly uneasy that she began to sob. A boy came over to comfort her and wanted to make love to her. She was very frightened and refused. The boy didn't sound offended though. In a fatherly way he told Zula that with life as it is we shouldn't wait for our one true love before making love, because we might never live that long.

We've been thinking and talking about what he said all day. Perhaps he was right, perhaps we've been wasting the last bits of our lives not even trying to find out what love is? Yet, the very idea of doing it drunk and in the presence of other people makes me sick. I would rather die not knowing . . . Zula says I'm right. She seems deeply distressed after what she saw last night. Serves her right. She shouldn't have gone there in the first place.

Our school year was drawing to a close. In the middle of June we sat the unofficial exams, supervised by our own teachers only. Irena, my friend from before the war who had joined the boys' courses a year earlier, came to me with a message from her group. The boys wanted to meet the girls from my group and suggested a party to celebrate the end of our exams. I said I had to ask my friends first, so Irena went off without any definite answer, leaving me torn by ambivalent feelings. I had no doubt that throwing a party at a time like that was shameful. On the other hand, I longed to meet the boys, to dance, to laugh.

Next morning I told the girls about the invitation. Hanka and Renata said at once that they were not interested. The remaining five were only too pleased to accept. I had to give Irena the answer but still couldn't make up my own mind. I was just thinking about it and had almost decided not to go, when two boys turned up grinning on my doorstep. To my great surprise one of them was the stranger I had danced with in the café, three months earlier. No less surprised than myself, this time he introduced himself to me. His name was Roman. He and his friend Marian belonged to Irena's study group. They came as deputies of the group to hear my answer, and, if it was "yes," to ask me to lend my gramophone for the party. It was going to be given in Roman's house. I was so excited and confused that I said, "Yes, of course," forgetting all my doubts. For a while we stood awkwardly in the corridor discussing the details of the coming event, then talking about everything and nothing. I noticed Roman was a bright, witty fellow, not nearly as shy as I had thought when I had first met him. Slightly suntanned, his open-necked blue shirt matching his sparkling eyes, he seemed far more attractive now than he had in the winter. I was pleasantly aware of being suntanned too, and knew that my summery green blouse matched my eyes as well. I could see that Roman and Marian had both noticed this.

The following days and nights were all dreams and sweet expectations. I was longing to see Roman again. On the appointed day, however, Marian turned up alone to fetch me and the gramophone to the party. Roman was too busy sorting things out, he said. I tried hard not to show my disappointment. In the street Marian stopped a rickshaw, being too lazy to carry the gramophone to the "little ghetto." I had never travelled in a rickshaw before, I found it disgusting to be pulled by a poor cycling man. I sat stiffly in the cart next to Marian, looking away from people in the street and dying with shame.

The party itself was not a success, either. The room Roman shared with his parents was large enough, but it was the only one they had in the big apartment, so the parents stayed there all the time. My friends behaved like silly geese, the boys talked mainly to each other, and Roman was busy with the records most of the afternoon. I danced with him only once and enjoyed it less than I had expected. We ate some tiny little sandwiches washed down with erzatz lemonade and the party was over. When all the people had left, I stayed behind to help Roman and his parents with the tidying up. Then Roman came to help me carry the gramophone home.

He did not even think of calling a rickshaw. For the first time the two of us were alone, except for the noisy, swarming crowd. We walked, talked and laughed all the way, finding there were lots of things to tell each other. We stopped at the entrance to my house. Roman pressed my hand and asked whether I would like to meet him again. His bright eyes were serious this time.

On the following evening I heard him whistling "Rosamunda" in the street below my open window. I ran down and we went for a walk again. For the next three weeks we spent all our spare time together, day after day. I was working in the cemetery full-time by then; Roman, too, had his own commitments, earning money by giving maths lessons. So there were only the evenings left. Usually we walked in the streets, since there were no nice places to go to. Sometimes Roman would come upstairs and stay in my room till almost curfew time. Mother and Sophie were always with us and they both enjoyed Roman's visits as much as myself. His special gift for telling stories, his vivacity and his wonderful sense of humour made us think he would later become a writer or actor or both.

Once Roman invited me to the cabaret. It was called "Sztuka" ("Art") and had been opened at Leszno Street the previous winter. I had been longing to go there all those months, and sitting there with Roman made me feel infinitely happy. The programme was good. Apart from old hits sung by pre-war stars, it dealt with the daily life of the ghetto. Bitter and sharp, the sketches and couplets mercilessly lashed corruption and indifference, hinted at the hollowness of our "cosy stability," brought laughter to the audience as well as tears. We left profoundly moved.

It was easy to talk to Roman, it was easy to be with him. We liked the same things, read the same books. It was also good being quiet together. I wanted to be alone with him and longed for him at night when I imagined something awful might happen to him. I was in love.

21 July 1942

There is nowhere to go, there is no way to be alone. The streets moan and yell with a thousand voices, they reek of rotten fish and dying bodies. Wherever we turn, whatever we look at, all is ugliness. So we run away and hide from it all in the flat. Here at least we are safe from sounds and smells. Not from other people, though.

We've spent this afternoon sitting on Henryk's couch in the corridor. For a while there was no one around and Roman stroked my cheek, and I stroked his, and we moved close to each other. But then Jadwiga suddenly opened her door and went to the loo, then back; then Sophie went up and down; then Henryk came home from his afternoon walk and, winking at us, shut himself in the kitchen to let us feel undisturbed. I could hardly bear it, so I asked Roman to go. My eyes filled with tears as I said it.

As we were saying goodbye Roman whispered something strange in my ear. He said the only way we could be left alone is to go to a hotel. There is a secret hotel in the ghetto, he said, and he's got enough money to book a room for a single night. We could go there tomorrow if I wanted to. He didn't look at me as he said it and he ran away in a hurry.

Now I'm sitting at the window thinking about it all. Everybody else is sound asleep. I wouldn't talk to anyone about it, anyway. Not even to Mother. What shall I do? How shall I answer him tomorrow? A hotel room . . . Something seedy, degrading . . . judging from the French novels, at least. A picture of a fallen woman in rags comes to mind. On the other hand, this is the only way we can be on our own. For a while . . . for an hour . . . for a whole night . . . God! I want it, I long for it . . . Yes, I'll go with him tomorrow!

Come gentle night, come loving black-
    brow'd night,
Give me my Romeo . . .

The next day, 22 July 1942, the mass deportation of people from the Warsaw ghetto began.

The wedding of a Jewish couple in Belgium during the German occupation. May 1940 – September 1944. (Yad Vashem Photo Archives, courtesy of USHMM Photo Archives)

Lina Wachenheimer walks through the mud in the Gurs transit camp in France. 1940–1944. (Morris Troper file, Yaffa Eliach Collection, Center for Holocaust Studies, donated to the Museum of Jewish Heritage, New York)

Hungarian Jews in the Mako ghetto in May 1944. The Mako Jews were transferred en masse to the Szeged ghetto in June. By the end of that month, 381,661 Hungarian Jews were deported to Auschwitz-Birkenau where the great majority were killed in the gas chambers at Birkenau. 5,742 Jews from Szeged, including most of the Jews of Mako, were among the 20,782 Jews sent to the Strasshof concentration camp in Austria. The transfer to Strasshof was part of an agreement between the Relief and Rescue Committee of Budapest, a Jewish organization led by Rezso Kasztner, and Adolf Eichmann. This agreement involved the payment of 5 million Swiss Francs in exchange for 30,000 Jews "put on ice" in Austria while a larger deal was negotiated to exchange Jews for much needed war materials for the Germans. Allied objections to this ransom scheme stopped the larger deal. Some seventy-five percent of the Hungarian Jews sent to Strasshof, including all of the Jews pictured here, survived the war. Circa May 1944. (Yad Vashem Photo Archives, courtesy of USHMM Photo Archives)

A child at a machine in a ghetto workshop in Kovno, Lithuania. 1941–1943. (George Kadish, courtesy of USHMM Photo Archives)

Lodz ghetto inhabitants cross a pedestrian bridge. The Lodz ghetto (Poland) was divided into three sectors by two major thoroughfares which passed through but did not belong to the Jewish district. Wooden and barbed wire fences prevented ghetto residents from stepping into the streets; they traversed via two wooden pedestrian bridges accessed by steep staircases. 1941. (Zydowski Instytut Historyczny Instytut Naukowo-Badawczy, courtesy of USHMM Photo Archives)

YISRAEL GUTMAN **Days of Battle**

THE FIRST DAY OF THE UPRISING

ON ROSH HASHANAH, the Jewish New Year, 1940, the Jewish residential quarter of Warsaw was subjected to a massive aerial bombardment. From the standpoint of its inhabitants, this was the first encounter with the might and means of the German enemy. On the eve of Passover, the festival of freedom, 1943, the Germans opened the final stage of their campaign to annihilate all trace of the Jewish community of Warsaw. This time, however, the penetration of German troops into the ghetto did not come as a surprise, for throughout the month of April persistent rumors had brought "the last stirring of life in the ghetto" to a halt. "Every day," Tuvia Borzykowski wrote, "and even a number of times each day, all the Jews would stop whatever they were doing and dash for shelter."[1] The least suspicion of heightened activity among the enemy's forces was sufficient to alarm the entire population and engender a state of alert. Nonetheless, the Jews could not ignore the approach of the Passover holiday. With a determination that had characterized the Jews for centuries and a resourcefulness that had reached unprecedented proportions during the occupation, the surviving remnant of the Warsaw ghetto prepared to celebrate the Passover, taking care to acquire the ritual Passover foods (matzos and wine) and cleansing their eating and cooking utensils as prescribed by religious law.

On April 18, 1943, the ghetto received reports – including authoritative information from the "Aryan" side – that the massing of troops had been noted in Warsaw and the Germans were evidently about to initiate the decisive *Aktion* against the ghetto. The lookout posts that had been set up in buildings throughout the ghetto were now reinforced, and the night of April 18 was spent watching and waiting. At 1:00 or 2:00 A.M. came the first reports on the deployment of enemy forces along the ghetto wall – units of the German gendarmerie and the Polish Po-

lice, who surrounded the ghetto with a cordon of guards 25 meters apart. Ż.O.B.* runners dashed from house to house alerting the population that an *Aktion* was expected the next morning. In many cases their warning was superfluous, since the tenants had already received word from the regular lookouts on the rooftops. Many residents of the ghetto abandoned their festive tables and gathered together in large groups. "No Jew slept that night. Belongings, underwear, bedding, [and] provisions were packed and taken into the bunkers."

The Ż.O.B. was put in a state of high alert. "At one in the morning," Borzykowski wrote, "the command received the latest reports, on the basis of which all the groups were mobilized immediately."[2] [Marek] Edelman[†] noted that the news arrived at 2:00 A.M.: "All the combat groups were alerted immediately, and at 2:15 – that is, in about fifteen minutes – they had taken up their combat positions."[3] As the forces were mustered, each fighter received a steel combat helmet and a knapsack filled with "underwear, provisions, [and] first-aid materials. In addition to the standard weapons at his disposal, every fighter was now given bombs, Molotov cocktails, etc."[4] Chaim Frimmer described the preparations for battle at the Ż.O.B.'s principal position in the Central Ghetto:

> In the evening a state of alert was proclaimed and the passwords were changed. Now we knew that the Germans were readying themselves for an *Aktion* in the ghetto. A single password was established for the fighters in all the groups – "Jan – Warsaw" – [and] we began fortifying the positions. The approach to the gate of the courtyard was blocked by a wagon that we turned wheels-up. We removed closets and the rest of the heavy furniture from the apartments and stacked them

YISRAEL GUTMAN, **THE JEWS OF WARSAW, 1939–1943: GHETTO, UNDERGROUND, REVOLT**, 367–76, 386–92, 397–400, 461–64. COPYRIGHT © 1982 BY YISRAEL GUTMAN. 1982. REPRINTED BY PERMISSION OF INDIANA UNIVERSITY PRESS.

*Żydowska Organizacja Bojowa – Jewish Fighting Organization, *Ed.*
†One of the Ż.O.B. commanders, *Ed.*

in the gateway. The windows were fortified with sandbags. People were assigned to their various positions. . . . I received an order from Berl Braudo to check the weapons and pass out ammunition to the men. We filled baskets with Molotov cocktails and passed them on to the positions. . . . Mordecai Anielewicz arrived and went into Yisrael [Kanal's] room. After consultation they came out and walked through the rooms and apartments, selecting appropriate spots for positions. People from other groups came to receive provisions, battle rations – rusks, sugar, groats. "Cjank" [doses of cyanide] was passed out to certain people, especially those whose tasks required them to be mobile and heightened their chances of being caught by the Germans and tortured during interrogation.[5]

In his summarizing report on the fighting in the ghetto, General [Jürgen] Stroop mentioned the factors that moved the Germans to initiate the final *Aktion* on April 19:

> In January 1943, following his visit to Warsaw, the *Reichsführer-S.S.* [Himmler] ordered the *S.S.- und Polizeiführer* of the Warsaw District [von Sammern] to transfer the equipment and armament plants located in the ghetto, *including their workers and machinery*, to Lublin. The execution of this order became hopelessly bogged down, because both the management of the factories and the Jews resisted the transfer by every means imaginable. As a result, the *S.S.- und Polizeiführer* decided to carry out the transfer of the factories by force in a large operation that was scheduled to last for three days.[6]

In January 1946, Franz Konrad, the SS officer in charge of the *Werterfassung* in von Sammern's headquarters, gave testimony that related to the first day of the April *Aktion*:

> A week before Easter 1943 – it was a Sunday morning – *S.S.- und Polizeiführer* von Sammern convened a meeting of the heads of the Security Police, *Obersturmbannfüher-S.S.* Hahn, the com-

manders of the S.S. units in Warsaw, [the commanders] of the cavalry and infantry reserve units, the commanders of the "Sipo" [Security Police] and the "Orpo" [Regular Police], and the officers in his headquarters (myself among them). At this meeting we were notified that on Monday he intended to transfer out the Jews who still remained in the Warsaw ghetto. During the discussion about the appropriate time for sending the various S.S. and police units into action, *Brigadeführer* Jürgen (Josef) Stroop entered and announced that he had been appointed to the post of *S.S.- und Polizeiführer* by order of the *Reichsführer-S.S.*[7]

That same day, April 18, the Polish Police was put under alert (Polish policemen were slated to take part in the encirclement of the ghetto). The declaration of a state of alert was evidently passed on to circles in the Polish underground, who in turn warned the ghetto underground that an *Aktion* might commence the next day.

The question remains whether the Germans were aware of the activities and preparations going on in the ghetto – i.e., that an armed Jewish force was deploying for resistance. It is absolutely certain that the commanders of the SS and the police knew that a resistance force was being organized in the ghetto and that they could expect armed opposition to any forthcoming *Aktion*. After all, the Germans had already experienced combat skirmishes in January. Even though they had experimented with the strategy of a relatively long waiting period and attempted to dismantle the ghetto by means of persuasion – as if disregarding the fact that an underground force was preparing itself to give battle whenever the *Aktion* began – the way in which von Sammern approached the forthcoming *Aktion* – namely his mobilization of an impressive military force and convening of the heads of the commands in Warsaw – indicates that he knew the April *Aktion* would not resemble the previous "resettlement operations," because this time the Jews could resist. All the same, it appears that von Sammern did not appreciate the extent of the resistance or know of the widespread network of bunkers in the ghetto. We may assume that he expected the forthcoming resistance to resemble the street fighting during the January deportation, meaning that the insurgents would try to attack the German troops head on. Von Sammern therefore decided to send in a large force on the first day of the operation in order to break the resistance with a single mighty blow. He likewise accepted as fact [Walter] Többens's* claims that the Ż.O.B. had foiled the peaceful evacuation of the population by pressure and terror tactics and that once the hard core of insurgents had been eliminated, the deportation would go smoothly, since the remainder of the Jews did not support the fighting underground.

The unfolding of events in the ghetto after the mass deportation in the summer of 1942 had undermined von Sammern's credit with Himmler, who decided to place the final task of liquidating the ghetto in the hands of a man who was new to Warsaw but had a reputation as an experienced police commander. Before being posted to Warsaw, Jürgen Stroop had served in the SS and Police Command in eastern Galicia and was regarded as a vigorous man who had proven his abilities and determination in operations against the partisans. Stroop reached Warsaw before the initiation of the *Aktion*, on the evening of April 17. The next day he appeared at the meeting called by von Sammern but did not immediately assume command of the operation, evidently preferring to remain in the position of a supervisor who would be ready to enter into action whenever intervention proved necessary or when the time appeared ripe to assume command. In reply to questions addressed to him after the war, Stroop reported, *inter alia*:

> The German command, and particularly my predecessor as *S.S.- und Polizeiführer*, von Sammern, did not take even the mildest resistance into account. A number of trouble-free deportations had preceded the final *Aktion*, so that Dr. von Sammern assumed that the final deportation would also be executed smoothly. Only on the eve of the *Aktion* did he receive a report that armed resistance could be expected. Of course, he didn't believe it, but for the sake of discipline he passed on the full assessment to [Friedrich] Krieger† so that the latter could act accordingly.[8]

It is unreasonable to believe that von Sammern assumed the forthcoming evacuation would resemble the *Aktionen* of the past or that he was surprised to receive a report pointing out the possibility of resistance and personally did not believe it. It is entirely possible, however, that von Sammern did not wish to admit his concern to Stroop or even to brief his successor on the true situation. Confessing to the truth of the matter would not improve his position or personal situation. At the same time, it is imperative to emphasize that the Germans never even imagined the potency of the resistance. General Rowecki, the commander of the A.K.‡, noted in his report on the uprising to the London-based government that "the resistance of groups of Jewish fighters was far beyond all expectations and took the Germans by surprise," and a survey of the Polish underground appraising the situation from May 8 to 14 stated: "The Germans regarded the prolongation of resistance in the ghetto as a stain on their reputation. The oversight that allowed such a line of resistance to come into being cost the commander of the SS and the police in the Warsaw District, von Sammern, his post. Police general Stroop was appointed in his place."[9]

While imprisoned in Poland, Stroop wrote:

> The residents of the ghetto knew about all the moves of the German authorities. They were ready for anything and took appropriate countermeasures. Thus the building of shelters in cellars, which was done in accordance with orders, was exploited for the construction of bunkers to defend the ghetto, and this was kept from the German authorities. Col. von Sammern told me that despite the secrecy, as early as April 17th [the Jews] were informed by telephone of the hour when the operation would begin! In my opinion, this was the crucial reason for the failure of the operational units under [von Sammern's] command to penetrate [the ghetto] during the morning hours of April 19, 1943! [The Jews] were prepared and were not intimidated by the use of armor and half-tracks (they had incendiary bottles, powerful homemade bombs, revolvers, low-caliber rifles, and even German uniforms). But they underestimated the fighting power of the police stationed in Warsaw.[10]

---

*German industrialist employing thousands of Jews from the Warsaw ghetto, *Ed.*
†Commander of police forces and responsible for security affairs in occupied Poland, *Ed.*
‡*Armia Krajowa* (Home Army) – the underground military organization in Poland, *Ed.*

The irony at this stage was that the isolated and doomed Jews were preparing for the German attack and were forewarned of its imminence, while the omnipotent German regime, backed by secret police and a network of informers of all kinds and nationalities, knew essentially nothing of what was going on in the ghetto. This important achievement must be credited to the success of the fighting organizations in the ghetto, particularly the Ż.O.B., in purging the ghetto of destructive elements and preparing it for the impending trial.

According to Stroop's report for April 20, the "Grand *Aktion*" commanded by von Sammern began at 3:00 A.M. on April 19 with an encirclement of the ghetto by reinforced troops. (As we have noted, the Jewish sources report that the lookouts spotted these forces at 1:00 or 2:00 A.M.) At 6:00 A.M., Stroop's report continues, came "the deployment of *Waffen-S.S.* to the extent of 850/16" (i.e., 850 soldiers and 16 officers). Simha Ratajzer, a Ż.O.B. fighter, subsequently described how the German forces entering the ghetto appeared from a lookout post in the Brushmakers' Area:

> At 4:00 in the morning we saw a column of Hitlerites at the Nalewki passage moving toward the Central Ghetto. [The column] marched and marched without end, a few thousand strong. Behind it came a few tanks, armored cars, light cannon, and a few hundred SS troops on motorcycles. "They're marching like they're off to war," I commented to Zippora, my partner in the position, and suddenly I sensed how weak we were. What are we and our force against an armed and equipped army, against tanks and armored cars, while we have only revolvers and, at best, grenades in our hands . . . .[11]

The German force penetrated the ghetto in two columns. One marched along Nalewki Street while the second (which had entered the gate at the corner of Gęsia and Zamenhofa streets) intended to spread out along the other main artery in the Central Ghetto, Zamenhofa-Miła. The Jewish forces in the Central Ghetto were deployed at three points: (1) a force composed of three Ż.O.B. combat squads took up position on the upper floors of the buildings at the corner of Gęsia and Nalewki streets; (2) four Ż.O.B. squads, together with the area headquarters and the general headquarters of the organization, were located in positions at the intersection of Zamenhofa and Gęsia streets; (3) the Ż.Z.W.* force in the Central Ghetto, which comprised the union's principal contingent, fortified itself in the sector of Muranowska Square. For months the fighters had been preparing escape routes over the rooftops, so that it would be possible to get from house to house without going out into the streets.

The first armed clash occurred on Nalewki Street, at the corner of Gęsia, where two Ż.O.B. combat squads (under the command of Zecharia Artstein and Lolek Rotblat) came into contact with the Germans. A German column moving up the center of the road while singing boisterously was attacked at the corner by forces positioned in the building at 33 Nalewki Street. The surprise was total and the power of the fire – especially the bombs and hand grenades – inflicted injuries to the enemy and sowed havoc in its ranks, so much so that the Germans retreated and dispersed, leaving their casualties lying on the street. Then the German troops tried to organize a counterattack. This time they no longer exposed themselves in the center of the street but hugged the walls of the buildings and sought shelter in the entrances. The heavy German fire met with only sporadic response from the Jewish side, but the Jews enjoyed a clear advantage: the Germans could not operate without exposing themselves. As one fighter explained in his memoirs, "while we were concealed in our positions," the Germans were easy targets. This second battle likewise ended in a German retreat. There were no casualties to the Jewish side.

While this clash was taking place on the corner of Nalewki and Gęsia, the main battle of April 19 raged at the corner of Zamenhofa and Miła streets. Four squads of Ż.O.B. fighters (under the command of Berl Braudo, Aaron Bryskin, Mordecai Growas, and Leib Gruzalc) positioned themselves around the square that dominated the intersection. Nearby, the Germans had chosen a place to establish an improvised headquarters. The arrival of their equipment – including tables, benches, and communications in-

Żydowski Związek Wojskowy – Jewish Military Union, *Ed.*

struments – was followed by the end of the main German column. Jewish policemen were forced to march at the head of this column to serve as a human wall and protect the German units by absorbing any burst of fire from the Jewish insurgents.

Chaim Frimmer, a fighter in Braudo's squad who viewed the German deployment and subsequent battle from one of the lookout posts, described the events as follows:

> At five in the morning a loud rumble was heard. Suddenly I saw from my lookout on the balcony that cars had come through the ghetto gate. They reached the square, stopped, and soldiers got out and stood to the side. Then a truck arrived carrying tables and benches. The distance between me and the cars was about 200 meters, and since I had good binoculars I could see them clearly. The tables were set up in a D-shape, wires were laid, and telephones were placed on them. Other cars came with soldiers bearing machine guns. Then motorcycle riders arrived [and] some ambulances and light tanks could be seen stopping by the entrance. The Latvians*, who had been standing there through the night, were removed and sent *en masse* in the direction of the *Umschlagplatz*. At six a column of infantry entered. One section of the column turned into Wolynska Street and the other remained in place, as if awaiting orders. Before long the Jewish Police came through the gate. They were lined up on both sides of the street and, as ordered, began to advance toward us. I would report everything to a fighter lying down not far from me [who in turn passed word on] to the command room, where Mordecai [Anielewicz], Yisrael [Kanał], and others were seated. When the column of Jewish Police reached our building, I asked how to proceed: Attack or not? The reply was to wait; Germans would surely follow, and the privilege of taking our fire belongs to them. And that's exactly what happened: After the Jewish Police crossed the street, an armed, mobile German column began to move. [I was ordered to wait] until the middle of the column had reached the balcony and then throw a grenade at it, which would serve as a signal to start the action. . . . . A mighty blast within the column was the signal to act. Immediately thereafter grenades were thrown at the Germans from all sides, from all the positions on both sides of the street. Above the tumult of explosions and firing, we could hear the sputter of the German Schmeisser [a submachine gun used by the German army] operated by one of our men in the neighboring squad. I myself remained on the balcony and spewed forth fire from my Mauser onto the shocked and confused Germans. . . . The battle lasted for about half an hour. The Germans retreated leaving many dead and wounded in the street. . . . Again my eyes were peeled on the street, and then two tanks came in, followed by an infantry column. When the tank came up to our building, some Molotov cocktails and bombs put together from thick lead pipes were thrown at it. The big tank began to burn and, engulfed in flames, made its way toward the *Umschlagplatz*. The second tank remained in place as fire consumed it from every side.[12]

The first of Stroop's daily reports described the progress of the fighting during the early morning hours of April 19 from the German viewpoint:

> As soon as the units deployed, a premeditated attack by the Jews and the bandits; Molotov cocktails were thrown on the tank and on two armored cars. The tank was burning fiercely. At first this attack caused [our] forces to retreat. Our losses in the first action were 12 men (6 SS men, 6 Trawniki[†] men). At close to eight o'clock, the second attack under the command of the undersigned.

It was only after the war, during his trial in Poland, that Stroop added details on what had happened from the moment that the forces under von Sammern's command were repulsed until Stroop assumed command of the operation:

> At 6:00 A.M. on April 19, Col. von Sammern initiated the *Aktion*, and he remained in com-

*Latvian militia who collaborated with the Germans, *Ed.*
†Stroop referred to the German unit dispatched from the nearby Trawniki labor camp as the Trawniki unit or the Trawniki men. *Ed.*

mand of it – by mutual agreement – since he had made all the preparations and was familiar with the place. I consented to come to the ghetto, which I had never seen before, at about 9:00 A.M. on April 19. At around 7:30 von Sammern turned up at my lodgings and announced that all was lost, that the forces he had sent into the ghetto had retreated and there were already dead and wounded. I can't remember how many. Von Sammern said that he would call Cracow and request that "Stuka" planes bomb the ghetto to quash the rebellion that had broken out. I told him not to because I wanted to review the situation on the spot. . . . I asked for a map of the ghetto and entered through the gate, while bullets showered down on me incessantly. . . . I handled the forces according to the rules of street fighting, lining stormtroopers along both sides of the main street so that they would not go charging forward blindly, as had evidently happened before. I issued the appropriate orders to the commanders of the units. My intention was to gain control of at least the buildings on the main street.

According to [Tuvia] Borzykowski [one of the fighters], the battle resumed on Nalewki Street about three hours after the German retreat. The enemy troops removed mattresses from the *Werterfassung* warehouse near the Ż.O.B. positions and constructed a protective barricade as they continued to fire. They operated in groups and were careful not to expose themselves to the snipers firing from the positions. When the barricade was set on fire by Molotov cocktails, the Germans threw their own incendiary bottles into the building at 33 Nalewki Street, where the Ż.O.B. position was located, setting it aflame. The fighters, who were forced to abandon their position and seek cover, evaded the Germans waiting for them in the street by escaping over the rooftops. The positions on Zamenhofa also came under heavy fire, and the order to withdraw was given as a hail of bullets pierced the ceilings of the rooms where the fighters were stationed. Those fighters took shelter in the bunker that housed their headquarters on Zamenhofa Street.

Stroop also reported that at about 7:30 his forces came up against "very strong resistance from a block of buildings, accompanied by machine-gun fire."[13] This is a reference to the battle that broke out in Muranowska Square, where the main contingent of the Ż.Z.W. was located. In the course of the fighting, the Ż.Z.W. unfurled a blue-and-white flag and the national flag of Poland. One of its members reported that on the day of the first battle, a machine gun had reached the union through the tunnel that extended to the "Aryan" side.[14] It was stationed in a position that dominated the entire square and effectively blocked the German advance. Each of the German attacks met with stiff resistance. Edelman noted that during the battle a tank was hit and set aflame, "the second one that day."[15] According to Stroop, "a special combat unit silenced the enemy, penetrated the buildings, [but] did not catch the enemy itself. The Jews and the criminals were fighting everywhere, position by position, and at the last moment they escaped and fled over the rooftops or through underground passages."[16]

On the first day of battle, then, the Jewish fighters attacked from three focal points. In each case, it was the insurgents who opened fire and surprised the enemy. The Germans were forced to withdraw from the ghetto after the first clash, and von Sammern lost his lead when he realized the strength of the Jewish resistance. When Stroop assumed command of the operation, he proceeded cautiously, adopting the tactics of house-to-house fighting. Yet he too was forced into a difficult and drawn-out battle in Muranowska Square. The losses to the Jewish side that day were relatively light. One member of the Ż.O.B. fell (Yechiel from Growas's squad, who fired the submachine gun), while the Ż.Z.W. probably lost a larger number of people.[17] The casualties on the German side (according to Stroop's reports) were one dead and twenty-four wounded, including fourteen SS men, two German gendarmes, six men from the Trawniki unit, and two Polish policemen.[18]

As early as the first day of the uprising, the Germans also met with opposition from a totally unexpected source – i.e., the resistance of the ghetto's population at large, which the Germans dubbed "the battle of the bunkers." Stroop described the nature and significance of this line of resistance in his comprehensive survey: "The number of Jews trapped in and removed from the buildings was very small. It turned out that Jews were hiding in sewers and specially equipped bunkers. During the first few days, only a few bunkers were believed to exist; but as the major operation continued, it became clear that the entire ghetto was systematically equipped with cellars, bunkers, and passages." Stroop's report on the first day of the fighting concludes: "During the search only 200 Jews were caught. Afterward stormtroops were sent into action against the bunkers known to us with orders to bring out their inhabitants and demolish the bunkers themselves. About 380 Jews were caught in this operation. The presence of Jews in the sewers was discovered."[19]

Thus we learn from Stroop's report that as a result of a day of stubborn fighting, which cost the Germans heavy losses, 580 Jews were trapped – about 1 percent of the ghetto's population at the time. According to Stroop, this "accomplishment" was achieved because the Germans knew the location of some of the "shops," and most of the victims of April 19 were trapped in them. On the first day of the operation, then, in addition to the organized and determined armed resistance of the fighting organizations, the Germans came up against the phenomenon of tens of thousands of people fortified below ground. . . .

THE TURNING POINT IN THE UPRISING

AS WE HAVE SEEN, after the initial days of battle, the German command reached the conclusion that the way to overcome the insurgents was to burn down or demolish the ghetto's buildings, thereby forcing the Jews to come out into the open. On April 26 Stroop reported that "during today's operation many housing blocks were set aflame. This is the only and ultimate way to defeat the rabble and scum of the earth and bring them above ground." His April 22 report illustrated this form of warfare and its results:

The fire that raged all night drove the Jews who – despite all the search operations – were still hiding under roofs, in cellars, and in other hiding places out of the housing blocks in order to escape the flames in one way or another. Scores of burning Jews – whole families – jumped from windows or tried to slide down sheets that had been tied together, etc. We took pains to ensure that those Jews, as well as others, were wiped out immediately.

Initially the Germans allocated three days for the liquidation of the ghetto. Stroop was naturally interested in accelerating the pace of the operation and evidently thought that the fire and demolition would achieve his aim quickly. On the fifth day of the *Aktion*, April 23, he believed that the revolt had come to an end. He therefore divided the ghetto into twenty-four sectors and ordered his troops, likewise divided into units according to sector, to comb the area in a final search. In his report for April 23, Stroop noted that "the troops were notified that the *Aktion* will end today," but it soon became evident that his announcement was premature, for "the Jews and the hooligans are [still] to be found in a number of blocks."[20]

The principal difficulty confronting Stroop at this stage of the uprising was the "battle of the bunkers," which continued for close to a month and evidently did not end even on May 16, 1943 – the day on which he officially pronounced the close of the "Grand *Aktion*" in the ghetto. After the war, during his interrogation, Stroop repeatedly stressed that "We did not find out about all the bunkers and strongholds set up and equipped for the uprising until after the start of the battle!" In each of his daily reports, he spoke of dozens of bunkers being discovered, cleaned out, and blown up. On May 24, 1943, when he replied in writing to questions addressed to him by Krieger, Stroop testified that 631 bunkers were destroyed during the "Grand *Aktion*."

The Germans needed special facilities for their campaign against the bunkers, such as police dogs, special listening devices to detect sounds underground, and poisonous gas for the bunkers whose inhabitants refused to come out. A gas of the chlorine variety was also used to annihilate the inhabitants of the bunkers, since the Germans would not dare to infiltrate the labyrinth of hiding places. Stroop does not mention the use of gas in his reports and would not confess to it even after the war. In both cases, he insisted that only smoke bombs were used to clear out the bunkers, but the truth is that many were killed by the poisonous gases used against these hideouts. In fact, it was the gas, more than anything else, that forced the victims to come out. There were also many cases of delayed complications and respiratory diseases, and people so affected later died in "Revir," the special section for the sick in the Majdanek concentration camp.[21]

All of these measures did little to bring about the swift defeat of the bunkers. On the contrary, the "battle of the bunkers" turned into a drawn-out operation in which the Germans made slow progress. The condition of the bunkers' inhabitants – meaning the entire population of the Central Ghetto, including the fighters – steadily deteriorated until it turned into a state of unrelieved suffering and torture. At the beginning of the uprising, the Germans set fire to individual buildings or housing blocks, but in the course of time the fire spread until it engulfed the entire ghetto. Many bunkers collapsed as a result of the blaze and the consequent buckling of building walls. When only the skeletons of buildings remained, the cellars grew so hot that it was impossible to breathe in them. But the Germans did not content themselves with the results of the fire and went on to blow up what remained of the gutted structures. Bunkers became uninhabitable and were abandoned. Yet even under these circumstances, the population of the bunkers did not give up the struggle, and they began to wander from bunker to bunker or seek cover among the ruins. One memoir described the scene in a central bunker at 30 Franciszkańska Street, where a number of injured Ż.O.B. members found shelter:

> I can't think of anything but breathing air. The heat in the bunker is unbearable. [But] it's not only the heat. The steaming walls give off an odor as if the mildew absorbed during decades had suddenly been released by the catalyst of heat. And there's no air. I sit here open-mouthed, as do all those around me, deluding ourselves that we can gulp down some air. There is no talk in the bunker [because] it is more difficult to breathe when you talk. But from time to time

> shouting [and] scuffles break out; nerves are taut, and for the most part the shouts are over nothing. We haven't eaten for twenty-four hours. Only dry bread is left and the water is more or less fit for drinking. All the food has spoiled. The heat and the odor have tainted it, so that the ample reserves are inedible.[22]

In another memoir, a man who wandered from one hiding place to another described the situation in one of these shelters: "The new hideout was not the most pleasant of places. It was crowded; cold crept through your bones; we had to stand in water above our hips; and the water pipe – which was in contact with the electricity cable – was electrified. . . ."[23] Despite it all, however, the inhabitants of the bunkers refused to surrender. They continued to struggle under great stress and intolerable physical conditions, and every instance of successfully evading the Germans was regarded as deliverance.

In addition to the sophisticated devices for exposing the bunkers, the Germans also employed informers, who were promised their lives in return for revealing the whereabouts of the bunkers' entrances. The Germans hauled these informers along with them, and when the entrance to a bunker was breached, they were ordered to call out in Yiddish for everyone to come out, since the bunker had been exposed and only those who would come out willingly had a chance of saving themselves. The Germans also forced the informers to stand directly in front of the entrance, since the initial response to their call was often a round of gunfire.

The "battle of the bunkers" proved to the Germans that the Jews were determined not to surrender themselves. On April 24 Stroop reported: "From time to time it became clear that despite the terror of the raging fire, the Jews and the hooligans preferred to turn back into the flames rather than fall into our hands." And on May 4 he confessed in his daily battle report: "Uncovering the bunkers becomes more difficult. Often it would be impossible to find [them] were it not for the treachery of other Jews. The command to leave the bunkers voluntarily is almost never obeyed; only the use of smoke bombs forces the Jews to respond to it."

Many bunkers were the strongholds of recalcitrants who not only preferred death by fire or gassing to capture but even fought back. Often they were members of the fighting organizations who had found their way into the bunkers and resisted when the Germans arrived, though it must be added that the armed struggle of individuals and unaffiliated groups focused primarily on the defense of the bunkers. On April 26 Stroop detailed a number of incidents of this nature:

> The entire former Jewish residential quarter was again combed today by the same stormtroopers going over the same sectors. That way I hoped that the commanders would approach as far as the open lines of the housing blocks and courtyards familiar to them so that they could advance further and infiltrate the labyrinth of bunkers and underground passages. Almost all the stormtroopers reported some resistance, but it was broken by firing back or blowing up the bunkers.[24]

The fortified labyrinth of subterranean bunkers and tunnels made the ghetto into a unique partisan fighting ground. Since a substantial portion of the bunkers was not uncovered by the police dogs, listening devices, or informers, the network of shelters that protected the remains of Warsaw's Jewish community posed a serious challenge to the Germans. A clear-cut order demanded that every Jew be trapped and liquidated or sent to a camp. Yet in the heart of a large metropolis, clandestine Jewish life continued to go on below ground, and even after weeks of employing the most radical and brutal tactics, the Germans had difficulty snuffing it out. The "battle of the bunkers" held down German troops and, above all, took time. And that time – the days and weeks – was precisely what discomfited the Germans most. The *Aktion*, conceived as a three-day final purge of the Warsaw ghetto, had turned into a drawn-out and far from routine battle in which German military and police forces were pitted against Jewish civilians holed up in bunkers. In full view of the Polish public, under the curious and mocking gaze of the population of a city that was the focus of constant security problems, the "battle of the bunkers" was regarded as

a blot on the Germans' prestige and a serious security risk.

The full-scale battle fought by the members of the combat organizations lasted primarily for the first three days of the uprising. From then on the Germans generally succeeded in overcoming the pockets of resistance, driving the fighters out of their positions, and forcing them to retreat into the bunkers, which thereafter served as bases for the combat forces. Although the network of subterranean shelters had originally been regarded as refuges for the noncombatant population, it now assimilated the fighters as well, allowing them to continue their struggle. It was from these bunkers that bands of fighters went out on raids and attacked the enemy. If the hundreds of fighters had been forced to operate in an unpopulated ghetto, or were opposed by a hostile population, the Germans would probably have suppressed the rebellion during the first days of open combat. While it is true that not all of the bunkers willingly accepted the fighters, for their presence was regarded as an additional risk and provocation of the Germans, most of them welcomed the combatants with open arms and agreed to place the defense of the bunker in their hands. As a rule, therefore, the network of bunkers played an important role in the Warsaw ghetto uprising by considerably extending the life of the revolt. In point of fact, it took the Germans longer to quell the Warsaw ghetto uprising than it had taken them to defeat entire countries. Moreover, the stand of the population in the bunkers accorded the uprising the character of a popular revolt in which thousands of civilians took part. Thus it was to the credit of the bunkers that the outburst of the combat squads developed into a partisan struggle that went on for an extended period of time.

On April 23, Mordecai Anielewicz wrote to his comrade Yitzhak Zuckerman, who was stationed on the "Aryan" side of the city:

> I can't begin to describe the conditions under which the Jews are living. Only an elect few will hold out under them. All the others will perish, sooner or later. Our fate is sealed. In the bunkers where our comrades are hiding, it is not even possible to light a candle at night for lack of

air. . . . During the day they sit in the hideouts. Starting in the evening we go over to the partisan method of action. At night six of our companies go out with two tasks before them: armed reconnaissance and the acquisition of arms.[25]

Marek Edelman wrote in *A Fighting Ghetto:*

Because conditions had changed so much, the Ż.O.B. revised its tactics [and] attempted to defend larger concentrations of people hiding from the Germans in bunkers. Thus, for example, two Ż.O.B. squads (Hochberg's and Berek's) moved a few hundred people from a shelter that had been blocked on 37 Miła Street to 7 Miła Street in broad daylight. This [latter] position, which contained a few thousand people, was held for over a week. In the meantime, the burning of the ghetto was drawing to a close. Places of shelter are sorely lacking and – even worse – there is a shortage of water. The fighters are going down into the shelters together with the civilian population. There they will continue to fight as best they can. The battles and clashes take place mostly at night now. During the day the ghetto is like a city of the dead. Only on the totally darkened streets do Ż.O.B. squads meet up with German units. Whoever fires first has the advantage. Our units circulate through the entire ghetto, [and] every night many from both sides are killed. The Germans and Ukrainians go out only in large units and more often than not set up ambushes.[26]

Thus even after all hopes of remaining underground for a prolonged period – perhaps even until the end of the war – were dashed, the alliance between the fighters and the many civilians living in the bunkers held fast. Even the bunker housing the Ż.O.B. headquarters at 18 Miła Street, in which the organization's command and principal force found refuge, was not a Ż.O.B. bunker per se but had been set up by a group of hardened smugglers. The fighters, for their part, combined the continuation of the armed struggle with the defense of the bunkers. Yet both the fighters and civilians in the ghetto realized

that the situation generated by the resistance could only be temporary.

Stroop's reports reveal that the armed clashes continued, and the troops charged with wiping out the bunkers were forced to operate under combat conditions. On April 23 he reported that "the Jews and the thugs restrained themselves until the last moment in order to pour intense fire on the units." On April 24 he commented that "from time to time the Jews continued to shoot, almost until the end of the operation. . . ." The next day Stroop noted that "today, as well, there was occasional armed resistance, and three revolvers and explosives were captured in one of the bunkers." Three days later he made note of the fact that "the external appearance of the Jews being caught now implies that the turn of the . . . leaders of the rebellion has come. Swearing against Germany and the Führer and cursing the German soldiers, they hurled themselves out of windows and off balconies." His report for April 28 stated that "today, as well, armed resistance was exhibited and broken in a number of places." On May 2 Stroop recorded that "the SS patrols operating at night sometimes met up with armed resistance from the Jews." The next day he elaborated that "in most cases, the Jews fought with weapons before abandoning the bunkers," and "last night shots were aimed at some of the patrols operating in the ghetto." On May 4: "In order to catch the Jews totally off guard, the troops on patrol wrapped their shoes in rags and other materials at night. Thirty Jews were shot to death in clashes with the patrol units." On May 5: "Today, as well, Jews fought in a number of places before being captured." As late as May 13 he wrote:

While mopping up one of the bunkers, a real battle took place in which Jews not only opened fire with .08-caliber revolvers and Polish Wiss pistols but even tossed oval-shaped, Polish-manufactured hand grenades at the SS men. After a few of the bunker's [fighters] were brought out and stood waiting to be searched, one of the women slipped her hand under her dress in a flash and – as has often happened – pulled a hand grenade out of her underwear, released the cap, and hurled it at the men who were searching her, while she herself jumped back quickly and took cover.[27]

Descriptions of battles in the bunkers were also available from Jewish sources. Marek Edelman described one such battle in a bunker at 30 Franciszkańska Street, a building with a number of courtyards and sophisticated bunkers. One of them had taken in some fighters who had earlier retreated from the Brushmakers' Area:

> . . . The shelter on 30 Franciszkańska Street, which housed an operative base of fighters who had broken through from the Brushmakers' Area, was uncovered on May 3. The men fought one of the most outstanding battles from the technical point of view. It lasted for two days, and 50 percent of our men fell. Berek was killed by a grenade. . . . It is difficult to speak of victory when people are fighting for their lives and so many are lost, but one thing can be said of this battle: We did not allow the Germans to execute their plans.[28] . . .

Starting in the first week of May, Stroop repeatedly noted in his reports that the struggle with the hard core of insurgents had begun and that he was engaged in annihilating the focal points of the revolt. On May 15 he reported:

> Last night patrol units in the ghetto reported that they did not come up against Jews, except on rare occasions. . . . In the exchange of fire that took place during the afternoon hours – when the thugs again fought with Molotov cocktails, revolvers, and homemade hand grenades – after the gang was destroyed, one of the policemen (Orpo) was wounded by a bullet in his right thigh. The last block that remains intact . . . was searched a second time and then destroyed by a special commando unit. Toward evening the synagogue in the Jewish cemetery, the mortuary room, and all the surrounding buildings were blown up or set to the torch.

It was the destruction of the largest Jewish synagogue in Warsaw – a building of special architectural design located outside the boundaries of the ghetto – that symbolized the "victory" over Warsaw's Jewish community and the end of the fighting in the ghetto. On May 16 Stroop wrote: "One hundred and eighty Jews, thugs, and the scum of humanity were killed. The 'Grand *Aktion*' ended at 20:15 [8:15 P.M.] with the demolition of the Warsaw synagogue."

Yet it was clear to Stroop that concluding the operation was not equivalent to wiping out all the bunkers and Jews who had fortified themselves in the ghetto. Despite his firm resolve, Stroop did not succeed in completing the liquidation of the ghetto. On May 13 he reported that he intended to conclude the "Grand *Aktion*" on May 16 "and turn over the task of the forthcoming operations . . . to a police battalion. . . ." Indeed, on May 16 he noted that he would charge said police battalion with "continuing or concluding the actions that have yet to be carried out."[29]

Proof of the fact that the Jewish resistance was not suppressed during the four weeks of the "Grand *Aktion*" under Stroop's command can be found in the daily reports of the Polish "Blue Police" that describe the situation after May 16. The report for May 18 states: "Jewish units emerge from underground and attack the Germans by surprise. At night the SS men withdraw to the borders of the ghetto; there is not a single German in the ghetto. SS men claim that thousands of Jews are hiding out among the ruins and in the underground niches." On May 20 the "Blue Police" review noted: ". . . Shots in the ghetto night and day. Sometimes they are accompanied by loud blasts of explosives – the demolition of certain buildings and the tossing of grenades by both sides." On May 21 there was again mention of "shooting in the ghetto from light weapons and both sides throwing grenades." On May 22 and 23:

> . . . Gunfire from light and automatic weapons and the sound of explosions. According to an unconfirmed report, Himmler's visit has made it certain that the area of the ghetto will be attacked and the wall surrounding it will be raised higher because the German police and SS men involved in security work in the ghetto are suffering heavy losses and the number of German functionaries who have fallen is excessive.

The report of May 27–31 states:

> On the 27th, 28th, 29th, and 30th of this month, exchanges of fire day and night, especially during the night of May 30; and during the day of May 31, heavy fighting [raged] on Przejazd and Leszno streets. . . . Jews attempted to break through to the "Aryan" side. On the other hand, during the day the Germans continue to pull Jews out of the bunkers and from under burned-out buildings and shoot them on the spot.

Finally, the last report we have from this source, covering June 1–2, states:

> The situation in the ghetto appears to be deteriorating. . . . Today the borders of the ghetto were surrounded by strong SS units and armored cars penetrated [the area]. We can expect the Germans to take far-reaching steps against the Jews in hiding. According to information from the "G" [probably the Gestapo], the German casualties who have fallen in the course of liquidating the Jews have been very heavy.[30]

Information from reliable Jewish sources also testifies to the presence of people in the ghetto after May 16, the date proclaimed by Stroop as the conclusion of the "Grand *Aktion*." In his book *The Last Ones*, Arie Najberg described the situation in the ghetto between May 19 and May 26:

> The strategy of the operation constantly changed. Up to then they had used armed force aided by technical support – fire, dynamite, listening devices – and sometimes by dogs. But as the *Aktion* progressed, it became more difficult to uncover the remaining bunkers and more difficult still to capture people alive. They therefore turned to ruses. When they entered an area, the German companies would bring along Poles and a Jewish informer. The informer would walk around in the courtyards and call out various names or shout in Yiddish: "Jews come out! The war is over!" The Poles served as "bait": They were supposedly sent from the "Aryan" side to

bring help to the Jews. But we who were hiding in the gutted buildings could hear the orders exactly as they were given, and we were not fooled. We also warned all the [other] Jews in our area.

From our point of view, it is interesting to note that Najberg writes of the weeks before and after May 16 as one continuous period. He was totally unaware that Stroop had proclaimed the conclusion of the "Grand *Aktion*," and many other Jews like him – ignorant of how the situation appeared to the Germans or what forces were being used to suppress the uprising and expose the people in hiding – continued to hide and fight. Najberg wrote of meeting hundreds of Jews at night, of battles and skirmishes with Germans and Poles in the area of the ghetto, of the building at 4 Walowa Street, which contained 150 people on June 3, 1943 (the day on which it was destroyed), and was referred to by its inhabitants as a "hotel." He described the residents of the bunkers in June 1943: "Those living in the shelters became harrowingly thin and looked like skeletons. After six weeks in these graves, they looked like ghosts frightened of the living."

Despite everything, groups of the "last survivors" holding out among the ruins or in the bunkers succeeded in making contact with individual Poles who helped them get out of the ghetto and infiltrate the Polish side of the city. Of Najberg's group, which numbered forty-five people living among the ruins, four remained alive on September 26, 1943 – more than five months after the outbreak of the revolt – when, still armed, they stole across the border to the "Aryan" side.

According to a Polish source, small mutually isolated groups of totally exhausted Jews remained in the ghetto until October. Individual survivors of these groups, like Najberg's band, succeeded in crossing over to the Polish sector of the city in September and October 1943 via the sewers and other passages.[31] We also know of one bunker that remained populated until January 1944.[32] In September the Germans sent a battalion of Polish laborers into the ghetto and ordered them to demolish the infrastructures and walls that were still standing in the area. Those who still remained in hiding evidently met their deaths during these demolition activities, although a few individuals continued to live in dugouts, totally cut off from nature, light, and human company.

The ghetto was destroyed. Hitler's Third Reich had accomplished its mission. No Jews or Jewish dwellings remained in the Warsaw ghetto.

Notes

1. Borzykowski, *Bein Kirot Noflim*, 26.
2. Ibid., 29.
3. Edelman, *Getto walczy*, 52–53.
4. Borzykowski, *Bein Kirot Noflim*, 29.
5. Aharon Carmi and Chaim Frimmer, *Min ha-Deleka ha-Hi (From That Conflagration)* (Tel Aviv, 1961), 215 (the memoirs of Chaim Frimmer).
6. See Kermish, *Mered Getto Varsha*, 128.
7. See Konrad's statement in Blumental and Kermish, *Ha-M eri veha-Mered*, 370. In fact, it was not until June 29, 1943, that Stroop was nominated, by order of Himmler, to the post of "*S.S.- und Polizeiführer* in the District of Warsaw."
8. Kermish, *Mered Getto Varsha*, 189–90.
9. See Mark, *Powstanie w getcie warszawskim*, Document No. 102, 335, 337.
10. Kermish, *Mered Getto Varsha*, 206. In the above-mentioned material by Moczarski. Stroop's arrival in Warsaw is described as follows: "On April 15 Stroop, who was at the headquarters of the *S.S.- und Polizeiführer* of Galicia, Katzman, received a telephone call." According to Moczarski, Stroop related in the first person: "Suddenly the telephone rang . . . . I heard an officer ask for me. The next thing I heard was the voice of Heinrich Himmler himself. I sensed that it was something important. The *Reichsführer-S.S.* gave me a brief order, as soldiers are wont to do, to leave for Cracow the next day and consult with Commander Krieger before going on to Warsaw." In the conversation he held with Krieger, Stroop was told that von Sammern was soft-hearted and could not be relied upon. When Stroop reached Warsaw, it turned out that his liaison in his new post was Dr.

Ludwig Hahn, the commander of the Security Police in the city. It is pertinent to point out that Hahn has succeeded in evading trial for many years and lives prosperously in the Federal Republic of Germany.

11. See Blumental and Kermish, *Ha-Meri ve-ha-Mered*, 249.
12. Carmi and Frimmer, *Min ha-Deleka ha-Hi*, 216–17.
13. Kermish, *Mered Getto Varsha*, 138–39, 211.
14. See the selection from the memoirs of Dr. Walewski in Lazar, *Mezada shel Varsha*, 245–46.
15. Edelman, *Getto walczy*, 55.
16. Kermish, *Mered Getto Varsha*, 139.
17. According to Halperin, eight members of Betar fell that day, including a member of the command, Eliyahu Halberstein. See *Ha-Emet al ha-Mered be-Getto Varsha*, 21.
18. See Stroop's statistics on 393. A full list of the wounded and their names appears in Wulf, *Das Dritte Reich*, 65–66.
19. Kermish, *Mered Getto Varsha*, 139.
20. Kermish, *Mered Getto Varsha*, 149.
21. See Yisrael Gutman, *Anashim va-Efer: Sefer Auschwitz-Birkenau (People and Ashes: The Book of Auschwitz-Birkenau)* (Tel Aviv, 1957), 196–97.
22. Gutman, *Mered ha-Nezurim*, 362.
23. B. Goldman, "75 Yom be-Getto Varsha ha-Ole be-Lehavot" ("75 Days in the Burning Warsaw Ghetto") in Blumental and Kermish, *Ha-Meri ve-ha-Mered*, 281.
24. Kermish, *Mered Gretto Varsha*, 151–52, 156, 171.
25. See Zuckerman and Basok, *Sefer Milhamot*, 158.
26. Edelman, *Getto walczy*, 61.
27. Kermish, *Mered Getto Varsha*, 149, 152, 154, 159, 161, 170, 172–73, 186. In each case of a reference to Stroop's reports, I refer the reader to the Hebrew translation in Kermish. At the same time, I have checked each translation against the original German and sometimes believe it necessary to render certain corrections; hence the differences between Kermish's version and the English translations given here.
28. Edelman, *Getto walczy* 62.
29. Ibid., 187, 192.
30. See Blumental and Kermish, *Ha-Meri ve-ha-Mered*, 345.
31. Arie Najberg, *Ha-Abronim: Be-kez ha-Mered shel Getto Varsha (The Last Ones: At the End of the Warsaw Ghetto Uprising)* (Tel Aviv, 1958), 110–11, 133–34, 189–91.
32. Yad Vashem Archive, O-3/714 (testimony of Stefania Fiedelzeid, who lived in a bunker within the area of the ghetto until January 1944).

342

Inhabitants of the Warsaw ghetto gather to listen to announcements on the public address system. Radios previously had been banned and confiscated by the German authorities. June – August 1941. (Raphael Scharf, courtesy of USHMM Photo Archives)

A Jewish woman eats the ration of soup she received at the public kitchen in the Kielce ghetto in Poland. January 1, 1942. (Rafal Imbro, courtesy of USHMM Photo Archives)

Two children warm their hands in a room in the ghetto of Bitol, located in Bulgarian-occupied Macedonia. Bulgaria gained Macedonia in April 1941 in return for participating in the Axis attack on Yugoslavia. (Central Zionist Archives, courtesy of USHMM Photo Archives)

A destitute woman and children on a street in the Warsaw ghetto. 1941. (Bundesarchiv Bild 101 I/134/780/34 A)

Jews captured during the suppression of the Warsaw ghetto uprising are marched to the *Umschlagplatz* (transfer point) for deportation. April 19, 1943 – May 16, 1943. (National Archives, courtesy of USHMM Photo Archives)

JERZY RADWANEK

AUSCHWITZ, POLAND... 1940 – With the outbreak of war, Jerzy Radwanek, a Polish Air Force pilot prepared for a secret intelligence mission. But before his flight could depart, the Gestapo received information about the clandestine operation; Jerzy was arrested and deported to Auschwitz in the fall of 1940.

Jerzy, along with other Polish inmates, established a secret military organization inside the camp, planning escape routes and documenting Nazi atrocities. Given the job of camp electrician, Jerzy was able to move about Auschwitz more freely than most other inmates. On several occasions, the young Polish prisoner was sent to the Jewish barracks to repair wiring and install lights. He was greatly disturbed by the plight of the Jewish inmates, and offered to help them in any way possible.

Often Jerzy would secretly create short circuits in the Jewish compound's fuse box. When he was called in to "fix the light," Jerzy would smuggle food and medicine in his toolbox to distribute to the Jewish women and children. He befriended several of these women, visited them often, and promised, if he survived, to tell the world of Nazi brutality and Jewish suffering. As a result of his efforts, Jewish inmates referred to Jerzy as the "Jewish Uncle" of Auschwitz.

(JFR Photo Archives)

CHAPTER 7 **The Machinery of Death and the Murderers**

Eyeglasses, clothing, footwear, and other personal effects taken from prisoners were found after liberation in warehouses at Auschwitz-Birkenau. October 14, 1945. (Philip Vock, courtesy of USHMM Photo Archives)

DEBÓRAH DWORK **Introduction**

THROUGHOUT THE **1930s,** Jews were increasingly marginalized and terrorized in German society, but even the brutality and viciousness of the November 1938 Pogrom (often called *Kristallnacht*; see Chapter 3) did not mean that a Holocaust loomed in the future. The invasion in 1939 of Poland brought Germans into contact with the Orthodox Jews of eastern Europe, whom they called *Ostjuden*, eastern Jews. The *Ostjuden*, unlike German Jews who spoke German and wore the same style clothes as other Germans, spoke Yiddish and dressed distinctively. The Germans saw these Jews as alien: the "other," the outsider, the stranger. Nazi propagandists singled out the *Ostjuden* as the main culprits for what they perceived to be the "mess" Poland was in. The Jews were at fault. The Jews were responsible. And therefore the Jews were the chief obstacle to the Germans as they sought to fulfill their mission: to reclaim the lands they believed had been theirs centuries earlier, and to reconstruct what they called the German East.

The Germans accused the Polish Jews of being lice ridden, diseased, and degenerate. Their solution to what they perceived to be a problem was to concentrate the Jews into ghettos where they became as lice infested and disease ridden as the Germans had said they were at the beginning. The ultimate – and intended – result was, as the Nazi philosopher Alfred Rosenberg told the Reich press department after a visit to the Warsaw ghetto, that "the sights are so appalling and probably also so well known to the editorial staffs that a description is superfluous. If there are any people left who still somehow have sympathy with the Jews then they ought to be recommended to have a look at such a ghetto. Seeing this race en masse, which is decaying, decomposing, and rotten to the core will banish any sentimental humanitarianism."[1] For Germans like SS officer Rolf-Heinz Hoeppner, compassion meant death "by some quick-acting means," which would be a more "humane" solution than letting them starve.

A catalyst was all that was needed to change the rhetoric of killing into actual mass murder. The invasion of the Soviet Union, code-named Operation Barbarossa, proved sufficient. The National Socialists had justified the war against Poland as the way to set right the twenty-year-old injustice wrought by the Versailles Treaty. The attack on Russia, by contrast, could not be attributed to unfair treaty terms. There was no historical justification for Operation Barbarossa, and the assault was not just defended but championed in the name of ideology. The war against the Soviet Union was depicted as a battle between good and evil, between the Germans and those puppets of the Jews, the Soviet subhumans. This view is clearly expressed in the excerpt from Heinrich

A catalyst was all that was needed to change the rhetoric of killing into actual mass murder. The invasion of the Soviet Union, code-named Operation Barbarossa, proved sufficient.

Himmler's *Der Untermensch* (The Subhuman). Preparing his generals for the invasion, Hitler explained that the battle to come was a struggle between two opposing ideologies: Nazism and Bolshevism – and Jews were "the reservoir of Bolshevism." The victors would be those who annihilated the other.

In one of his directives in preparation for war, Hitler declared (March 1941) that "within the area of military operations, the *Reichsführer-SS* [Himmler] will be entrusted, on behalf of the Führer, with special tasks for the preparation of the political administration. These tasks derive from the decisive struggle that will have to be carried out between two opposing systems."[2] To carry out these "tasks," Himmler strengthened his *Einsatzgruppen*, that is, his Operational Groups.

The function of the *Einsatzgruppen* was to arrest and murder political opponents and Jews. They already had been in operation in conjunction with Germany's *Anschluss* (annexation) of Austria in March 1938 and the conquest of Czechoslovakia precisely a year later, but in 1938 and early 1939 the Germans had been interested in the forced emigration of Jews as the solution to their "Jewish Problem." Prior to the invasion of Poland in September 1939, six major units with several hundred members each were formed, with one unit attached to each of the five advancing armies, and one unit specially designated for the area around the city of Posen. After Poland had been conquered, the *Einsatzgruppen* terrorized Jews and Polish intellectuals and other prominent leaders of Polish society. Their victims ran into the tens of thousands, and the *Einsatzgruppen* were well on their way toward evolving into what they became after the invasion of the Soviet Union: the mobile arm of the German murder machinery.

The five million Jews of Russia had been an important consideration in Hitler's calculations in December 1940 to invade the Soviet Union the following year. In late February or early March 1941, he gave Himmler and his *Einsatzgruppen* a special role in Operation Barbarossa. According to instructions issued in March by Field Marshal Wilhelm Keitel, that special role and the extraordinary tasks it entailed "stem from the need to settle once and for all the conflict between two opposing political systems."[3] The harsh ideological rhetoric that accompanied the invasion of the Soviet Union, the destructive fury of the assault, and the initial unprecedented military successes that did not culminate in victory framed the increasing violence against the Jewish populations perpetrated by the *Einsatzgruppen*.

Himmler's *Einsatzgruppen* followed the army as it advanced through Russia during the summer of 1941. As the historian Philippe Burrin has pointed out, they did not engage in genocide immediately. But as the Germans conquered hundreds of miles of territory and still the Soviets remained undefeated, Hitler and his generals, increasingly frustrated and enraged, dropped the conventions that guide "civilized" warfare and gave the *Einsatzgruppen* a free hand to murder Jews in the army rear. Their activities were hardly a secret. The *Einsatzgruppen* sent statements from the field to the Reich Security Main Office (RSHA) in Berlin, where the information was summarized into reports. Copies of

After the invasion of the Soviet Union, the *Einsatzgruppen* became the mobile arm of the German murder machinery.

these reports were distributed to diplomats, members of the foreign office, high-ranking SS, police, and army officers, and if needed, to industrialists. (An excerpt from The *Einsatzgruppen Reports* describes the directives the men were given, and includes one such report dated July 13, 1941 from the Soviet city of Minsk.) The Army, the only authority that could have restrained the killing, had stepped aside.

Who were these murderers? Not surprisingly, the first wave of men to have joined the *Einsatzgruppen* were volunteers and committed Nazis. But more men were needed when the genocidal practices developed in the Soviet Union were soon thereafter applied in Poland. This meant that larger segments of the German population were involved, not all of whom were staunch party members. In the chapter on the Jozefow Massacre from his book *Ordinary Men*, Christopher Browning has described and analyzed how ordinary Germans became mass murderers.

With the genocide of Russian Jewry, Hitler and his followers had embarked on the atrocity we call the Holocaust and they called the "Final Solution to the Jewish Problem." All Jews were targeted for death: east European Jews and west European Jews; the *Ostjuden* the Germans saw as so different from themselves and their Jewish neighbors in Germany. On September 1, 1941 all German Jews over the age of six were ordered to wear a Jewish star; on September 18 they were forbidden to travel except by special police permission. They were marked and trapped as Himmler prepared for their deportation to the ghettos of the East.

German soldiers of the *Waffen-SS* and the Reich Labor Service look on as a member of *Einsatzgruppe* D shoots a Ukrainian Jew kneeling on the edge of a mass grave filled with corpses. 1942. (Library of Congress, courtesy of USHMM Photo Archives)

The first transport of German Jews arrived on October 16 in the Polish city of Lodz, which had been annexed to Greater Germany. During the following eighteen days a total of 20,000 Jewish people were forced into the already overcrowded ghetto. The local German administrator (called a *Gauleiter*) panicked and ordered his SS chief to do whatever was needed to be done to resolve the situation. Remembering the gas vans used to kill the mentally ill (see Chapter 3), the latter deployed them to the village of Chelmno. There they were used to kill some 150,000 Jews between December 8, 1941 and April 9, 1943.

Chelmno was but one of the six killing centers established by the Germans in Poland to murder millions of Jews quickly and efficiently on an assembly-line basis. As the historian Raul Hilberg has explained, these killing centers were unprecedented in history. Concentration camps had a history; the British had established concentration camps during the South African Boer War in 1899, and the National Socialists had developed a whole network of such camps since they came to power in 1933 (see Chapter 3). Stationary killing installations had existed before, as in the T-4 program (see Chapter 3). The Germans fused the two and created a lethal camp in which a slew of specialists played their parts. (See the excerpt from Hilberg's magisterial work, *The Destruction of the European Jews.*)

Former participants in the by-then officially defunct T-4 program set up extermination camps in Belzec (not far from the city of Lvov), Sobibor (near Lublin), and Treblinka (not far from Warsaw). All three were in the Government General, where large numbers of Jews had lived for centuries and where their co-religionists and others had been dumped by the Germans after the division of conquered Poland (see

A tin of "Zyklon," the murderous chemical used in the gas chambers at Birkenau and Auschwitz camps. The hydrogen cyanide arrived absorbed in a porous solid, which was packaged in tins. The body heat of the packed chambers released the gas quickly. (Courtesy of Photo Archives, The Ghetto Fighters' House Museum, Israel)

Chapter 5). A long report written by the head of the SS Department of Health Technology, Kurt Gerstein, described the operation of the Belzec extermination camp (see the excerpt from Saul Friedländer's book on Gerstein). Opposed to the regime, Gerstein had joined the SS in the hope of sabotaging its programs. In June 1942 he was sent to the Polish city of Lublin with 100 kilos of a powerful, extremely toxic disinfestation product called Zyklon-B to be used to delouse clothing, although he did not know to whom that clothing belonged. A visit to the local SS headquarters in Lublin revealed not only that Jews owned the clothing, but also the existence of annihilation facilities to murder those Jews. One such killing center was in Belzec and two similar sites, Sobibor and Treblinka, had just been brought into operation.

The Germans murdered 500,000 Jews in Belzec, 200,000 in Sobibor, and 750,000 in Treblinka. These centers were called Operation Reinhard camps, named in memory of Reinhard Heydrich, Himmler's right-hand man, the head of the Reich Security Main Office, who had been shot dead in May 1942 by agents of the Czech government-in-exile. The Operation Reinhard camps were closed and dismantled in late 1943 when all the Jews the Germans could easily get their hands on had been annihilated. Majdanek, a camp near Lublin, and the mammoth annihilation center at Auschwitz, in the previously Polish area of Upper Silesia that had been annexed to Greater Germany, remained in operation when Belzec, Sobibor, and Treblinka were shut down.

Unlike the Operation Reinhard camps, Auschwitz developed slowly into a death camp. Initially, Himmler was interested in the town of Auschwitz as a model for German settlement in conquered Poland; the concentration camp he established in its suburbs was designed to terrorize the local population. It soon acquired additional functions. To facilitate German agricultural development of the area, Himmler made the camp the center of a huge agricultural experiment estate or scientific farm in the fall of 1940. And in early 1941 Auschwitz became a pawn in Himmler's attempt to attract the giant German chemical corporation, I.G. Farben, to the area. The terms of the bargain were that the camp was to supply the labor to construct an I.G. Farben synthetic rubber (or "buna") factory as well as the labor required to improve the town of Auschwitz into a place worthy of such an I.G. Farben enterprise. The slave laborers would be Soviet POWs and an additional camp, Birkenau, was established to hold them. In return, I.G. Farben was to finance and supply with building materials (which were difficult to obtain in wartime) Himmler's Germanization project in the area. Both hoped to profit greatly from this deal. I.G. Farben's money stimulated the growth of the camp and its integration into Europe's industrial and transportation infrastructure.

When large-scale mass murder of Jews began in the summer and fall of 1941 in the wake of Operation Barbarossa, the SS in Auschwitz was still fully committed to Himmler's project to develop the town and the region. It was when Hermann Göring directed the Soviet POWs from Auschwitz to German armaments factories in January 1942 that Himmler began to consider the systematic use of the emerging Final Solution within the context of what he called the "Auschwitz Project." This did not mean that it was to be an annihilation camp; in early 1942 Himmler was still dedicated to transforming the town of Auschwitz and the surrounding region into the centerpiece of his racial utopia. Only now, Jewish slaves instead of Soviet POWs were to provide the requisite labor.

At a meeting held on January 20, 1942 in a villa in the Berlin suburb of Wannsee, Himmler's associate Reinhard Heydrich both established and ensured that Himmler would have the power he needed to negotiate with German and foreign civilian authorities for the transfer of Jews to his SS empire. Himmler needed slave laborers for his stone quarries, brickyards, factories, agricultural projects, and land-reclamation works. Once Göring scotched the idea of Soviet POWs for these purposes, Himmler's eye fell on the Jews. Many people believe that the Final Solution was decided at the Wannsee Conference, but this is not the case. It was a conference about power. This short meeting of under ninety minutes attended by upper-level (but not top-level) bureaucrats was chaired by Heydrich, and his goal was to assert Himmler's authority.

Heydrich succeeded. The first transports of Jews fit for labor started to leave Slovakia for Auschwitz-Birkenau soon thereafter. When the Slovak government suggested that Himmler also take Jews unfit for labor in exchange for a cash payment, Himmler dispatched SS construction chief Hans Kammler to Auschwitz. Kammler toured the site, identified a peasant cottage, and ordered its transformation into a gas chamber. (See the excerpt from Dwork and van Pelt's book, *Auschwitz*.) Two months later, on July 4, 1942, the first transports of

Many people believe that the Final Solution was decided at the Wannsee Conference, but this is not the case. It was a conference about power.

Jews from Slovakia were submitted to a "selection" to determine who was "fit" and who was not. It was a simple procedure and took but a few seconds: With one glance and perhaps a few words ("How old are you?" "Hold out your hands!") a life or death decision was made. Those who could work were admitted into the camp. Those who could not were killed in the peasant cottage now known as Bunker I.

The killing at Auschwitz of selected categories of Jews became an institutionalized practice. An infrastructure to murder them (the gas chamber) and to dispose of their bodies (a crematorium) had been created. But it had not yet become policy. The main purpose of Auschwitz at this time remained construction (of a factory, a city, and a region) and not destruction (of Jews). Around mid-July 1942, Himmler was awarded the responsibility for German settlement in Russia – an authority he had coveted for more than a year. His view of Auschwitz and his plans for Auschwitz changed rapidly and dramatically. The "Auschwitz Project" was no longer of interest to him. The camp could be used to serve the systematic killing of Jews. Practice became policy. The camp architects received orders to design crematoria equipped from the outset with homicidal gas chambers on August 20, 1942. And two crematoria under development were retroactively fitted with gas chambers.

Prisoners finish construction of the ovens for crematorium II in Birkenau. 1942–1943. (Yad Vashem Photo Archives, courtesy of USHMM Photo Archives)

As Dwork and van Pelt have explained, the four new crematoria came into operation in 1943, after the Holocaust itself had peaked. The Judeocide had begun in 1941, and the Germans killed some 1.1 million Jews that year. In 1942, they murdered another 2.7 million Jews, of whom approximately 200,000 died in Auschwitz. The year the crematoria of Auschwitz came into operation the number of victims dropped to 500,000, half of whom were killed in Auschwitz. All the Jews whom the Germans had been able to catch easily had been trapped. By the end of 1943, the Germans closed down the death camps built specifically to exterminate Jews: Chelmno, Sobibor, Belzec, and Treblinka. Auschwitz remained to mop up the remnants of the Jewish communities of Poland, Italy, France, the Netherlands, and the rest of occupied Europe, as well as other groups with regard to whom, like the Roma and Sinti (Gypsies), policy had become more brutal over time. (See Yehuda Bauer's article, *"Gypsies."*)

An Italian Jew, a young man named Primo Levi, was deported to Auschwitz in January 1944. It was the last year of the war, and another 600,000 Jews would be killed in Auschwitz. Levi passed the selection and, as he was a chemist, he was sent to work in the Buna factory. "We are the slaves of the slaves, whom all can give orders to, and our name is the number which we carry tattooed on our arm and sewn on our jacket," Levi wrote in his memoir, *Survival in Auschwitz*. Primo Levi was an astute observer of the concentration camp world around him, and he laid bare the evil that the industrial giant I.G. Farben and Heinrich Himmler and his SS had created. In the end, I.G. Farben was but one of many civilian companies to take advantage of the "economically useful" (to use Levi's term) Jewish slaves.

Jews fit to be slaves were worked to death; the economically useless were murdered immediately. With more than 1.1 million victims from every corner of Europe, Auschwitz became the most lethal death camp of all. And because it was the last in operation and some of the inmates – like Primo Levi – survived, it was also the camp remembered best. And thus "Auschwitz" became a synonym for the "Holocaust."

> And thus "Auschwitz" became a synonym for the "Holocaust."

Notes

1. Quoted in Jeremy Noakes and Geoffrey Pridham, eds., *Nazism, 1919–1945*, 3 vols. (Exeter: Exeter University Publications, 1983–1988), vol. 3, 1069.
2. Yitzhak Arad, Shmuel Krakowski, Shmuel Spector, eds., *The Einsatzgruppen Reports* (New York: Holocaust Library, 1989), iii.
3. Document 447 –PS, in Office of United States Chief Counsel for Prosecution of Axis Criminality, *Nazi Conspiracy and Aggression*, 8 vols. (Washington, D.C.: Government Printing Office, 1946), vol. 3, 410.

Jews move their belongings into the Krakow ghetto in horse-drawn wagons. Circa 1940. (Archiwum Panstwowe w Krakowie, courtesy of USHMM Photo Archives)

German Jews from the town of Coesfeld are assembled for deportation to Riga, Latvia. December 10, 1941. (Fred Hertz, courtesy of USHMM Photo Archives)

Reichsführer-SS, SS-Hauptamt **Der Untermensch**

History dictates that as long as there are people on earth humans will struggle with sub-humans. As far as we can look back Jews led this battle against the peoples to the natural unfolding of life on our planet. One can calmly reach the conviction that this struggle for life or death is as much a natural law as the battle of the bacillus that causes the plague against the healthy body. — REICHSFÜHRER-SS HEINRICH HIMMLER 1935.

AS THE NIGHT RISES against the day, and as light and darkness are eternal enemies — so is man himself the greatest enemy of earth-ruling man.

The Untermensch — that biologically seemingly totally similar creature with hands, feet and a kind of brain, with eyes, and a mouth, is however a totally different, frightening creature. A throw towards Man, with humanoid facial features, the Untermensch is both spiritually and psychologically inferior to any animal. Within this being a vile chaos of wild, uncontrolled passions: nameless desire for destruction, most primitive desires, naked vulgarity.

Sub-human — and nothing else!

Then not any being that carries a human likeness is the same.

Woe the person who forgets that!

What this earth possesses of great works, thoughts and arts — Man has conceived, created and completed them. He thought and invented, with only one goal: to work himself up into a higher state of being, to give form to the inadequate, to replace that which did not suffice with better things.

Thus culture arose,

Thus the plough, the tool, the house came into being.

Thus man became social, thus came the family, the nation, the state. Thus Man became good and great. Thus he ascended over all forms of life.

Thus he became closest to God!

But the Untermensch also lived. He hated the work of the other. He raged against it, hidden as a thief, publically as a slanderer — as murderer.

He joined his equal.

The beast called the biest.

Never maintained the Sub-human peace, never brought he tranquillity. Since he needed the penumbral, the chaos.

He dreads the light of cultural progress.

He needs for self-preservation the bog, the hell, but not the sun.

And this underworld of Untermenschen found its own Führer: the Eternal Jew!

He understood them, he knew what they desired. He poked their lowest lusts and cravings, he let terror come over humanity.

It began in historical times with the destruction of the Persians, the festival of Purim, the first celebration of organized mass murder. 75,000 Aryan Persians fell victim to Jewish hatred. Still today does Jewry celebrate this act of terror as its highest religious holiday.

Eternal is the hatred of the Sub-human against the bright people, the carriers of light. Eternally threatens from the deserts the destruction of the West.

Eternally amass in far away steppes the forces of destruction, gathers Attila and Genghis Khan their hordes of Huns and rages over Europe, leaving behind a living apocalypse, fire and death, rape, murder and terror, in order that the world of light and thousandfold knowledge, the powers of progress and human greatness sink back in the abyss of the primordial state!

Eternal is the Will of the Sub-human:

That it would turn into waste where now still the light of noble knowledge creatively illuminates the darkness, then were his final goal to be reached, chaos.

Thus unfolds already for millennia the battle between the two opposites, following terrible, unpredictable laws, so is there always another Attila, a Genghis Khan, who breaks open the gates of Europe, who knows only one thing: the total destruction of all that is beautiful!

Today the embodiment of this will to destroy is Bolshevism! But this Bolshevism is no modern phe-

FROM REICHSFÜHRER-SS, SS-HAUPTAMT, **DER UNTERMENSCH**. BERLIN: NORDLAND, 1942. TRANSLATED BY ROBERT JAN VAN PELT.

nomenon. It is not a product of our own days. It is also not a novelty in the context of human history. Instead it is as old as the Jew itself. And Lenin and Stalin are its trailblazers.

The leading minds in a nation are slaughtered, and then the people falls into political, economic, cultural, spiritual, psychological and physical slavery. The rest of the nation, robbed of its own sense of self by countless admixture of blood, degenerates – and in the historically short course of centuries one remembers at best that once such a people existed.

– REICHSFÜHRER-SS Heinrich Himmler 1935

Yitzhak Arad **The Einsatzgruppen Reports**

Directives

There were a number of briefings about the aims and activities of the *Einsatzgruppen* in the Nazi-occupied territories of the Soviet Union. The first took place in Pretsch, and it was conducted by Bruno Streckenbach, Chief of Department One of the RSHA*. Streckenbach acted as spokesman for Himmler and Heydrich in explaining the Führer's order concerning the murder of the Jews.

The meeting is described in Otto Ohlendorf's[†] testimony at the Einsatzgruppen Trial No. 9 at Nuremberg.[1] It is also mentioned in the affidavit by Dr. Walter Blume, who headed SK 7a[‡]. "During June, Heydrich, Chief of the Security Police and the SD, and Streckenbach, head of Office I of the Reich Security Main Office [RSHA], lectured on the duties of the *Einsatzgruppen* and *Einsatzkommandos*. At this time we were already being instructed about the tasks of exterminating the Jews. It was stated that Eastern Jewry was the intellectual reservoir of Bolshevism and, therefore, in the Führer's opinion, must be exterminated. This speech was given before a small, select audience. Although I cannot remember the individuals present, I assume that many of the *Einsatzgruppe* and *Sonderkommando* chiefs were present."[2]

Another briefing was given by Heydrich at a meeting of the leaders of the *Einsatzgruppen* and *Einsatzkommandos* which took place on June 17. There again the Führer's order concerning the murder of the Jews was discussed, as stated by Standartenführer Dr. Walter Blume: "I heard another speech by Heydrich in the Prinz Albrecht Palace in Berlin, in the course of which he again emphasized these points."[3] Ervin Schulz, head of EK-5[§], testified at the Nuremberg trials that "some time during the first ten days of June 1941, the chiefs of the *Einsatzgruppen* and leaders of the *Kommandos* were called to the RSHA in the Prinz

Albrecht Palace to hear a speech by Heydrich in which he outlined the policy to be adopted, giving us some guidelines concerning the fulfillments of the tasks imposed upon the *Einsatzgruppen*."[4]

At the third meeting, which probably took place shortly before June 22, high-level SS and Police chiefs met in the office of the Chief of Order Police, General Kurt Daluege. As Heydrich was unable to attend, he sent them a memorandum dated July 2, 1941 (dated after the invasion of the Soviet Union), specifying who was to be eliminated:

Executions
All the following are to be executed:

Officials of the Commintern (together with professional Communist politicians in general);

Top- and medium-level officials and radical lower-level officials of the Party. Central committee and district and subdistrict committees;

People's Commissars;
Jews in Party and State employment, and other radical elements (saboteurs, propagandists, snipers, assassins, inciters, etc.) insofar as they are, in any particular case, no longer required to supply information on political or economic matters which are of special importance for the further operations of the Security Police, or for the economic reconstruction of the Occupied Territories . . .[5]

More details are contained in Report No. 111 dated October 12, 1941: "The principle targets of execution by the *Einsatzkommandos* will be: political

Yitzhak Arad, Shmuel Krakowski, Shmuel Spector, eds., **The Einsatzgruppen Reports: Selections from the Dispatches of the Nazi Death Squads' Campaign Against the Jews in Occupied Territories of the Soviet Union July 1941 – January 1943**, vii–ix, 22–24. Copyright © 1989 Yad Vashem Martyrs' Remembrance Authority. Reprinted by permission of The United States Holocaust Memorial Museum.

*RSHA – Reich Security Main Office, *Ed.*
†Commander of *Einsatzgruppe* D, *Ed.*
‡In this context refers to "Special Commandos" who assisted the *Einsatzgruppen* in the occupied territories of the Soviet Union. They immediately followed the combat troops to which they were attached. *Ed.*
§Operational Commandos of the *Einsatzgruppen* that operated behind the combat lines, *Ed.*

functionaries, . . . Jews mistakenly released from POW camps, . . . Jewish sadists and avengers, . . . Jews in general . . ."

According to the testimony of Otto Ohlendorf, head of *Einsatzgruppe D*, dated April 24, 1947, the objective was the "murder of racially and politically undesirable elements." Later on in the *Einsatzgruppen* trial, he said (October 1948): "The goal was to liberate the army's rear areas by killing Jews, Gypsies and Communist activists . . ."[6]

Armed with detailed instructions, the *Einsatzgruppen* began their bloody march to the East. . . .

THE CHIEF OF THE SECURITY POLICE BERLIN, AND THE SD

JULY 13, 1941

OPERATIONAL SITUATION REPORT USSR No. 21

. . . .

Einsatzgruppe B:
Location: Minsk

A civilian prison camp was built in Minsk by the first troops passing through. Almost all the male inhabitants of the town were placed into it. The Einsatzgruppe was asked to screen the camp together with the Secret Field Police. Only persons were set free who were able to clear themselves beyond reproach and who were neither politically nor criminally implicated. The remainder, left behind in the camp, will be subjected to a careful investigation. Each case will be decided upon in accordance with the results of the investigation. 1,050 Jews were subsequently liquidated. Others are executed daily. With regard to the non-Jews left in the camp, liquidation of the criminals, the officials, the Asiatics, etc., was started. A Jewish committee was also formed, a ghetto was set up, and the identification of Jews on outer garments started. The Bolsheviks set free the inmates of the Minsk prison except the political ones. These were shot by the Bolsheviks before their retreat. A search has been started for the criminal prisoners who have been set free.

In Vilnius by July 8th the local Einsatzkommando liquidated 321 Jews. The Lithuanian Ordnungsdienst which was placed under the Einsatzkommando after the Lithuanian political police had been dissolved was instructed to take part in the liquidation of the Jews. 150 Lithuanian officials were assigned to this task. They arrested the Jews and put them into concentration camps where they were subjected the same day to Special Treatment. This work has now begun, and thus about 500 Jews, saboteurs amongst them, are liquidated daily. About 460,000 rubles in cash, as well as many valuables belonging to Jews who were subject to Special Treatment, were confiscated as property belonging to enemies of the Reich. The former Trade Union building in Vilnius was secured for the German Labor Front (DAF) at their request, as well as the money in trade union bank accounts, totaling 1.5 million rubles. The arrest of several repeatedly convicted armed robbers indicated that in the future we shall have to reckon with such bandits. The Einsatzkommando was informed by Lithuanians that the Poles residing in Vilnius at the time of Bolshevik rule had formed armed cadres with a total strength of 12,000 men who had amassed considerable ammunition supplies. A search for these hordes of ammunition has been started.

Einsatzkommando 2 in Vilnius has confiscated vast documentary materials in the local Jewish museum which was a branch of the central Moscow Institute for Jewish Culture.

Apart from 215 Jewish and Bolshevik officials, 15 more NKVD* agents were shot in Bialystok. The NKVD office had been completely burnt down. Only in the cellar vaults was it possible to secure various lists. The executions continue all the time at the same rate. The Polish section of the population has shown that it supports the executions by the Security Police by informing on Jewish, Russian, and also Polish Bolsheviks. The security of the city and of the surrounding districts is not, at present, sufficiently assured, owing to a lack of Byelorussian police forces. When the Soviets entered Bialystok in 1939, they sent all police and judicial officials to Siberia, and set up a new administration. This set-up was, however, completely dissolved by the Russians before the

*Soviet Secret Police from 1934–1946, *Ed.*

Wehrmacht occupation. All official files and documents were destroyed. An auxiliary police force was formed, subordinate to the Einsatz unit in Bialystok, by recruiting the White Russian forces and former Polish criminal-police officials.

Only 96 Jews were executed in Grodno and Lida during the first days. I gave orders to intensify these activities. The headquarters of the Grodno Communist party was seized and the materials found in it were confiscated. A card index with photographs was found in the NKVD building. Other photographs were also found which provided information on the killing activity of the GPU*. Notes of a Russian officer were also found, showing individual preparations for war by the Soviets.

The activity of all the Kommandos has progressed satisfactorily. The liquidations, in particular, are in full swing and usually take place daily. The carrying out of the necessary liquidations is assured in every instance under any circumstances.

It emerges more and more clearly that the main responsibility lies with the rear section of the army area for the seizure of resistance groups, partisans, Red functionaries, and Jews. This is due to the gradual surfacing of fugitives who had escaped into the forests and swamps. It is, therefore, not practical to pull the Einsatzkommandos out of the area of the security sectors.

Notes

1. Nuremburg Military Tribunal (Case 9, Einsatzgruppen), vol. IV, 244.
2. Nuremburg Military Tribunal, vol. IV, 140.
3. Nuremburg Military Tribunal, vol. IV, 140.
4. Nuremburg Military Tribunal, vol. IV, 136.
5. Documents of the Holocaust, 375.
6. Nuremburg Military Tribunal, vol. IV, 244.

---

*Soviet Intelligence Agency from 1922–1923 that later gave way to the NKVD and the KGB, *Ed.*

Jewish men in the Soviet Union forced by *Waffen*-SS troops and SD officers to dig their own graves before being executed. 1942.
(State Archives of the Russian Federation, courtesy of USHMM Photo Archives)

German police and Ukrainian collaborators in civilian clothes look on as Jewish women are forced to undress before their execution. May 11, 1943.
(Glowna Komisja Badania Zbrodni Przeciwko Narodowi Polskiemu, courtesy of USHMM Photo Archives)

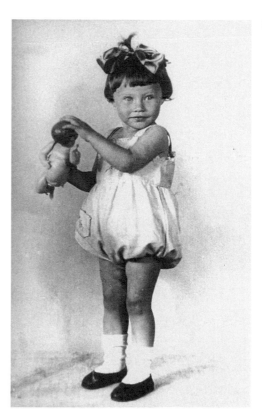

This map, entitled "Jewish Executions Carried Out by *Einsatzgruppe* A" and stamped "Secret Reich Matter," shows the number of Jews murdered (symbolized by coffins) in the Baltic states and Belorussia by late 1941. The legend near the bottom states that "the estimated number of Jews still on hand [was] 128,000."

This document accompanied a secret undated report on the mass murder of Jews by *Einsatzgruppe* A and was used as evidence by both the American and English prosecution teams during the International Military Tribunal trial of war criminals at Nuremburg. October 15, 1941 – January 31, 1942. (National Archives, courtesy of USHMM Photo Archives)

Portrait of two-year-old Mania Halef, a Jewish child from Kiev killed during the mass execution at Babi Yar.

On September 29 and 30, 1941, members of *Einsatzgruppe* C murdered 33,771 Kiev Jews at Babi Yar, a ravine in the northwest part of Kiev. In the following months tens of thousands of Jews, as well as Gypsies and Soviet prisoners of war, were murdered at Babi Yar, bringing the death toll to an estimated 100,000. 1936. (Yelena Brusilovsky, courtesy of USHMM Photo Archives)

Roma (Gypsy) couple sitting in the Belzec concentration camp in Poland. July 1940. (Jerzy Ficowski, courtesy of USHMM Photo Archives)

364

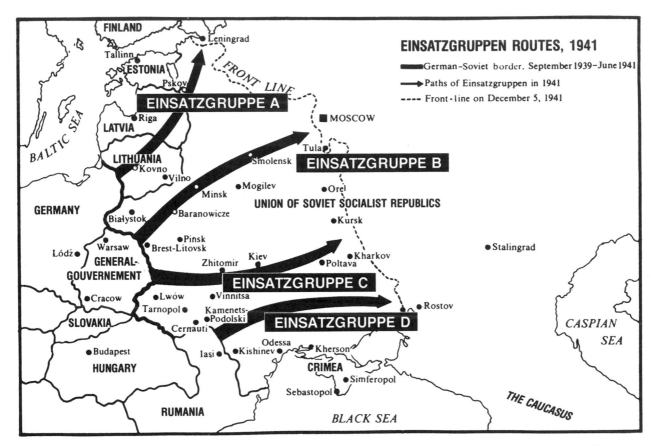

EINSATZGRUPPEN ROUTES, 1941

▬▬▬ German-Soviet border, September 1939–June 1941

→ Paths of Einsatzgruppen in 1941

---- Front-line on December 5, 1941

Yitzhak Arad, Shmuel Krakowski, Shmuel Spector, eds. **The Einsatz-gruppen Reports: Selections from the Dispatches of the Nazi Death Squads' Campaign Against the Jews in Occupied Territories of the Soviet Union July 1941 – January 1943**. Copyright © 1989 Yad Vashem Martyrs' Remembrance Authority. Reprinted by permission of The United States Holocaust Memorial Museum.

CHRISTOPHER R. BROWNING # Initiation to Mass Murder: The Józefów Massacre

It was probably on July 11 that [Odilo] Globocnik or someone on his staff contacted Major Wilhem Trapp and informed him that Reserve Police Battalion 101 had the task of rounding up the 1,800 Jews in Józefów, a village about thirty kilometers slightly south and east of Biłgoraj. This time, however, most of the Jews were not to be relocated. Only the male Jews of working age were to be sent to one of Globocnik's camps in Lublin. The women, children, and elderly were simply to be shot on the spot.

Trapp recalled the units that were stationed in nearby towns. The battalion reassembled in Biłgoraj on July 12, with two exceptions: the Third Platoon of Third Company, including Captain Wolfgang Hoffmann, stationed in Zakrzów, as well as a few men of First Company already stationed in Józefów. Trapp met with First and Second Company commanders, Captain Julius Wohlauf and Lieutenant Hartwig Gnade, and informed them of the next day's task.[1] Trapp's adjutant, First Lieutenant Hagen*, must have informed other officers of the battalion, for Lieutenant Heinz Buchmann* learned from him the precise details of the pending action that evening.

Buchmann, then thirty-eight years old, was the head of a family lumber business in Hamburg. He had joined the Nazi Party in May 1937. Drafted into the Order Police in 1939, he had served as a driver in Poland. In the summer of 1940 he applied for a discharge. Instead he was sent to officer training and commissioned as a reserve lieutenant in November 1941. He was given command of the First Platoon of First Company in 1942.

Upon learning of the imminent massacre, Buchmann made clear to Hagen that as a Hamburg businessman and reserve lieutenant, he "would in no case participate in such an action, in which defenseless women and children are shot." He asked for another assignment. Hagen arranged for Buchmann to be in charge of the escort for the male "work Jews" who were to be selected out and taken to Lublin.[2] His company captain, Wohlauf, was informed of Buchmann's assignment but not the reason for it.[3]

The men were not officially informed, other than that they would be awakened early in the morning for a major action involving the entire battalion. But some had at least a hint of what was to come. Captain Wohlauf told a group of his men that an "extremely interesting task" awaited them the next day.[4] Another man, who complained that he was being left behind to guard the barracks, was told by his company adjutant, "Be happy that you don't have to come. You'll see what happens."[5] Sergeant Heinrich Steinmetz* warned his men of Third Platoon, Second Company, that "he didn't want to see any cowards."[6] Additional ammunition was given out.[7] One policeman reported that his unit was given whips, which led to rumors of a *Judenaktion*.[8] No one else, however, remembered whips.

Departing from Biłgoraj around 2:00 a.m., the truck convoy arrived in Józefów just as the sky was beginning to lighten. Trapp assembled the men in a half-circle and addressed them. After explaining the battalion's murderous assignment, he made his extraordinary offer: any of the older men who did not feel

*One condition placed upon my access to the judicial interrogations must be made clear. Regulations and laws for the protection of privacy have become increasingly restrictive in Germany, especially in the past decade. . . . Before receiving permission to see the court records of Reserve Police Battalion 101, therefore, I had to promise not to use the men's real names. The names of the battalion commander, Major Wilhelm Trapp, and the three company commanders, Captain Wolfgang Hoffman, Captain Julius Wohlauf, and Lieutenant Hartwig Gnade, appear in other documentation in archives outside Germany. I have used their real names, for in their cases there is no confidentiality to breach. However, I have used pseudonyms (designated at first occurrence by an asterisk) for all other battalion members who appear in the text of this book. The notes refer to those giving testimony simply by the first name and last initial. While this promise of confidentiality and use of pseudonyms is, in my opinion, an unfortunate limitation on strict historical accuracy, I do not believe it undermines the integrity or primary usefulness of this study. (From the author's preface)

up to the task that lay before them could step out. Trapp paused, and after some moments one man from Third Company, Otto-Julius Schimke,* stepped forward. Captain Hoffmann, who had arrived in Józefów directly from Zakrzów with the Third Platoon of Third Company and had not been part of the officers' meetings in Biłgoraj the day before, was furious that one of his men had been the first to break ranks. Hoffmann began to berate Schimke, but Trapp cut him off. After he had taken Schimke under his protection, some ten or twelve other men stepped forward as well. They turned in their rifles and were told to await a further assignment from the major.[9]

Trapp then summoned the company commanders and gave them their respective assignments. The orders were relayed by the first sergeant, Arthur Kammer,* to First Company, and by Gnade and Hoffmann to Second and Third Companies. Two platoons of Third Company were to surround the village.[10] The men were explicitly ordered to shoot anyone trying to escape. The remaining men were to round up the Jews and take them to the marketplace. Those too sick or frail to walk to the marketplace, as well as infants and anyone offering resistance or attempting to hide, were to be shot on the spot. Thereafter, a few men of First Company were to escort the "work Jews" who had been selected at the marketplace, while the rest of First Company was to proceed to the forest to form the firing squads. The Jews were to be loaded onto the battalion trucks by Second Company and Third Platoon of Third Company and shuttled from the marketplace to the forest.[11]

After making the assignments, Trapp spent most of the day in town, either in a schoolroom converted into his headquarters, at the homes of the Polish mayor and the local priest, at the marketplace, or on the road to the forest.[12] But he did not go to the forest itself or witness the executions; his absence there was conspicuous. As one policeman bitterly commented, "Major Trapp was never there. Instead he remained in Józefów because he allegedly could not bear the sight. We men were upset about that and said we couldn't bear it either."[13]

Indeed, Trapp's distress was a secret to no one. At the marketplace one policeman remembered hearing Trapp say, "Oh, God, why did I have to be given these orders," as he put his hand on his heart.[14] Another policeman witnessed him at the schoolhouse. "Today I can still see exactly before my eyes Major Trapp there in the room pacing back and forth with his hands behind his back. He made a downcast impression and spoke to me. He said something like, 'Man, . . . such jobs don't suit me. But orders are orders.' "[15] Another man remembered vividly "how Trapp, finally alone in our room, sat on a stool and wept bitterly. The tears really flowed."[16] Another also witnessed Trapp at his headquarters. "Major Trapp ran around excitedly and then suddenly stopped dead in front of me, stared, and asked if I agreed with this. I looked him straight in the eye and said, 'No, Herr Major!' He then began to run around again and wept like a child."[17] The doctor's aide encountered Trapp weeping on the path from the marketplace to the forest and asked if he could help. "He answered me only to the effect that everything was very terrible."[18] Concerning Józefów, Trapp later confided to his driver, "If this Jewish business is ever avenged on earth, then have mercy on us Germans."[19]

While Trapp complained of his orders and wept, his men proceeded to carry out the battalion's task. The noncommissioned officers divided some of their men into search teams of two, three, or four, and sent them into the Jewish section of Józefów. Other men were assigned as guards along the streets leading to the marketplace or at the marketplace itself. As the Jews were driven out of their houses and the immobile were shot, the air was filled with screams and gunfire. As one policeman noted, it was a small town and they could hear everything.[20] Many policemen admitted seeing the corpses of those who had been shot during the search, but only two admitted having shot.[21] Again, several policemen admitted having heard that all the patients in the Jewish "hospital" or "old people's home" had been shot on the spot, though no one admitted having actually seen the shooting or taken part.[22]

The witnesses were least agreed on the question of how the men initially reacted to the problem of shooting infants. Some claimed that along with the elderly and sick, infants were among those shot and left lying in the houses, doorways, and streets of the town.[23] Others, however, stressed quite specifically that in this initial action the men still shied from shooting infants during the search and clearing operation. One policeman was emphatic "that among the Jews shot in our section of town there were no infants or small children. I would like to say that almost tacitly everyone refrained from shooting infants and small children." In Józefów as later, he observed, "Even in the face of death the Jewish mothers did not separate from their children. Thus we tolerated the mothers taking their small children to the marketplace in Józefów."[24] Another policeman likewise noted "that tacitly the shooting of infants and small children was avoided by almost all the men involved. During the entire morning I was able to observe that when being taken away many women carried infants in their arms and led small children by the hand."[25] According to both witnesses, none of the officers intervened when infants were brought to the marketplace. Another policeman, however, recalled that after the clearing operation his unit (Third Platoon, Third Company) was reproached by Captain Hoffmann. "We had not proceeded energetically enough."[26]

As the roundup neared completion, the men of First Company were withdrawn from the search and given a quick lesson in the gruesome task that awaited them. They were instructed by the battalion doctor and the company's first sergeant. One musically inclined policeman who frequently played the violin on social evenings along with the doctor, who played a "wonderful accordion," recalled:

> I believe that at this point all officers of the battalion were present, especially our battalion physician, Dr. Schoenfelder.* He now had to explain to us precisely how we had to shoot in order to induce the immediate death of the victim. I remember exactly that for this demonstration he drew or outlined the contour of a human body, at least from the shoulders upward, and then indicated precisely the point on which the fixed bayonet was to be placed as an aiming guide.[27]

After First Company had received instructions and departed for the woods, Trapp's adjutant, Hagen, presided over the selection of the "work Jews." The head of a nearby sawmill had already approached Trapp with a list of twenty-five Jews who worked for him, and Trapp had permitted their release.[28] Through an interpreter Hagen now called for craftsmen and able-bodied male workers. There was unrest as some 300 workers were separated from their families.[29] Before they had been marched out of Józefów on foot, the first shots from the woods were heard. "After the first salvos a grave unrest grew among these craftsmen, and some of the men threw themselves upon the ground weeping. . . . It had to have become clear to them at this point that the families they had left behind were being shot."[30]

Lieutenant Buchmann and the Luxembourgers in First Company marched the workers a few kilometers to a country loading station on the rail line. Several train cars, including a passenger car, were waiting. The work Jews and their guards were then taken by train to Lublin, where Buchmann delivered them to a camp. According to Buchmann, he did not put them in the notorious concentration camp at Majdanek but in another camp instead. The Jews were not expected, he said, but the camp administration was glad to take them. Buchmann and his men returned to Biłgoraj the same day.[31]

Meanwhile, First Sergeant Kammer had taken the initial contingent of shooters in First Company to a forest several kilometers from Józefów. The trucks halted on a dirt road that ran along the edge, at a point where a pathway led into the woods. The men climbed down from their trucks and waited.

When the first truckload of thirty-five to forty Jews arrived, an equal number of policemen came forward and, *face to face*, were paired off with their victims. Led by Kammer, the policemen and Jews marched down the forest path. They turned off into the woods at a point indicated by Captain Wohlauf, who busied himself throughout the day selecting the execution sites. Kammer then ordered the Jews to lie down in a row. The policemen stepped up behind them, placed their bayonets on the backbone above the shoulder blades as earlier instructed, and on Kammer's orders fired in unison.

In the meantime more policemen of First Company had arrived at the edge of the forest to fill out a second firing squad. As the first firing squad marched out of the woods to the unloading point, the second group took their victims along the same path into the woods. Wohlauf chose a site a few yards farther on so that the next batch of victims would not see the corpses from the earlier execution. These Jews were again forced to lie facedown in a row, and the shooting procedure was repeated.

Thereafter, the "pendulum traffic" of the two firing squads in and out of the woods continued throughout the day. Except for a midday break, the shooting proceeded without interruption until nightfall. At some point in the afternoon, someone "organized" a supply of alcohol for the shooters. By the end of a day of nearly continuous shooting, the men had completely lost track of how many Jews they had each killed. In the words of one policeman, it was in any case "a great number."[32]

When Trapp first made his offer early in the morning, the real nature of the action had just been announced and time to think and react had been very short. Only a dozen men had instinctively seized the moment to step out, turn in their rifles, and thus excuse themselves from the subsequent killing. For many the reality of what they were about to do, and particularly that they themselves might be chosen for the firing squad, had probably not sunk in. But when the men of First Company were summoned to the marketplace, instructed in giving a "neck shot," and sent to the woods to kill Jews, some of them tried to make up for the opportunity they had missed earlier. One policeman approached First Sergeant Kammer, whom he knew well. He confessed that the task was "repugnant" to him and asked for a different assignment. Kammer obliged, assigning him to guard duty on the edge of the forest, where he remained throughout the day.[33] Several other policemen who knew Kammer well were given guard duty along the truck route.[34] After shooting for some time, another group of policemen approached Kammer and said they could not continue. He released them from the firing squad and reassigned them to accompany the trucks.[35] Two policemen made the mistake of approaching Captain (and SS-Hauptsturmführer) Wohlauf instead of Kammer. They pleaded that they too were fathers with children and could not continue. Wohlauf curtly refused them, indicating that they could lie down alongside the victims. At the

midday pause, however, Kammer relieved not only these two men but a number of other older men as well. They were sent back to the marketplace, accompanied by a noncommissioned officer who reported to Trapp. Trapp dismissed them from further duty and permitted them to return early to the barracks in Biłgoraj.[36]

Some policemen who did not request to be released from the firing squads sought other ways to evade. Noncommissioned officers armed with submachine guns had to be assigned to give so-called mercy shots "because both from excitement *as well as intentionally* [italics mine]" individual policemen "shot past" their victims.[37] Others had taken evasive action earlier. During the clearing operation some men of First Company hid in the Catholic priest's garden until they grew afraid that their absence would be noticed. Returning to the marketplace, they jumped aboard a truck that was going to pick up Jews from a nearby village, in order to have an excuse for their absence.[38] Others hung around the marketplace because they did not want to round up Jews during the search.[39] Still others spent as much time as possible searching the houses so as not to be present at the marketplace, where they feared being assigned to a firing squad.[40] A driver assigned to take Jews to the forest made only one trip before he asked to be relieved. "Presumably his nerves were not strong enough to drive more Jews to the shooting site," commented the man who took over his truck and his duties of chauffeuring Jews to their death.[41]

After the men of First Company departed for the woods, Second Company was left to complete the roundup and load Jews onto the trucks. When the first salvo was heard from the woods, a terrible cry swept the marketplace as the collected Jews realized their fate.[42] Thereafter, however, a quiet composure – indeed, in the words of German witnesses, an "unbelievable" and "astonishing" composure – settled over the Jews.[43]

If the victims were composed, the German officers grew increasingly agitated as it became clear that the pace of the executions was much too slow if they were to finish the job in one day. "Comments were repeatedly made, such as, 'It's not getting anywhere!' and 'It's not going fast enough!' "[44] Trapp reached a decision and gave new orders. Third Company was called in from its outposts around the village to take over close guard of the marketplace. The men of Lieutenant Gnade's Second Company were informed that they too must now go to the woods to join the shooters. Sergeant Steinmetz of Third Platoon once again gave his men the opportunity to report if they did not feel up to it. No one took up his offer.[45]

Lieutenant Gnade divided his company into two groups assigned to different sections of the woods. He then visited Wohlauf's First Company to witness a demonstration of the executions.[46] Meanwhile, Lieutenant Hans Scheer* and Sergeant Ernst Hergert* took the First Platoon of Second Company, along with some men of Third Platoon, to a certain point in the woods. Scheer divided his men into four groups, assigned them each a shooting area, and sent them back to fetch the Jews they were to kill. Lieutenant Gnade arrived and heatedly argued with Scheer that the men were not being sent deep enough into the woods.[47] By the time each group had made two or three round trips to the collection point and carried out their executions, it was clear to Scheer that the process was too slow. He asked Hergert for advice. "I then made the proposal," Hergert recalled, "that it would suffice if the Jews were brought from the collection point to the place of execution by only two men of each group, while the other shooters of the execution commando would already have moved to the next shooting site. Furthermore, this shooting site was moved somewhat forward from execution to execution and thus always got closer to the collection point on the forest path. We then proceeded accordingly."[48] Hergert's suggestion speeded the killing process considerably.

In contrast to First Company, the men of Second Company received no instruction on how to carry out the shooting. Initially bayonets were not fixed as an aiming guide, and as Hergert noted, there was a "considerable number of missed shots" that "led to the unnecessary wounding of the victims." One of the policemen in Hergert's unit likewise noted the difficulty the men had in aiming properly. "At first we shot freehand. When one aimed too high, the entire skull exploded. As a consequence, brains and bones flew everywhere. Thus, we were instructed to place

the bayonet point on the neck."[49] According to Hergert, however, using fixed bayonets as an aiming guide was no solution. "Through the point-blank shot that was thus required, the bullet struck the head of the victim at such a trajectory that often the entire skull or at least the entire rear skullcap was torn off, and blood, bone splinters, and brains sprayed everywhere and besmirched the shooters."[50]

Hergert was emphatic that no one in First Platoon was given the option of withdrawing beforehand. But once the executions began and men approached either him or Scheer because they could not shoot women and children, they were given other duties.[51] This was confirmed by one of his men. "During the execution word spread that anyone who could not take it any longer could report." He went on to note, "I myself took part in some ten shootings, in which I had to shoot men and women. I simply could not shoot at people anymore, which became apparent to my sergeant, Hergert, because at the end I repeatedly shot past. For this reason he relieved me. Other comrades were also relieved sooner or later, because they simply could no longer continue."[52]

Lieutenant Kurt Drucker's* Second Platoon and the bulk of Sergeant Steinmetz's Third Platoon were assigned to yet another part of the forest. Like Scheer's men, they were divided into small groups of five to eight each rather than large groups of thirty-five to forty as in Wohlauf's First Company. The men were told to place the end of their carbines on the cervical vertebrae at the base of the neck, but here too the shooting was done initially without fixed bayonets as a guide.[53] The results were horrifying. "The shooters were gruesomely besmirched with blood, brains, and bone splinters. It hung on their clothing."[54]

When dividing his men into small groups of shooters, Drucker had kept about a third of them in reserve. Ultimately, everyone was to shoot, but the idea was to allow frequent relief and "cigarette breaks."[55] With the constant coming and going from the trucks, the wild terrain, and the frequent rotation, the men did not remain in fixed groups.[56] The confusion created the opportunity for work slowdown and evasion. Some men who hurried at their task shot far more Jews than others who delayed as much as they could.[57] After two rounds one policeman simply "slipped off" and stayed among the trucks on the edge of the forest.[58] Another managed to avoid taking his turn with the shooters altogether.

> It was in no way the case that those who did not want to or could not carry out the shooting of human beings with their own hands could not keep themselves out of this task. No strict control was being carried out here. I therefore remained by the arriving trucks and kept myself busy at the arrival point. In any case I gave my activity such an appearance. It could not be avoided that one or another of my comrades noticed that I was not going to the executions to fire away at the victims. They showered me with remarks such as "shithead" and "weakling" to express their disgust. But I suffered no consequences for my actions. I must mention here that I was not the only one who kept himself out of participating in the executions.[59]

By far the largest number of shooters at Józefów who were interrogated after the war came from the Third Platoon of Second Company. It is from them that we can perhaps get the best impression of the effect of the executions on the men and the dropout rate among them during the course of the action.

Hans Dettelmann,* a forty-year-old barber, was assigned by Drucker to a firing squad. "It was still not possible for me to shoot the first victim at the first execution, and I wandered off and asked . . . Lieutenant Drucker to be relieved." Dettelmann told his lieutenant that he had a "very weak nature," and Drucker let him go.[60]

Walter Niehaus,* a former Reemtsma cigarette sales representative, was paired with an elderly woman for the first round. "After I had shot the elderly woman, I went to Toni [Anton] Bentheim [his sergeant] and told him that I was not able to carry out further executions. I did not have to participate in the shooting anymore. . . . my nerves were totally finished from this one shooting."[61]

For his first victim August Zorn* was given a very old man. Zorn recalled that his elderly victim

could not or would not keep up with his countrymen, because he repeatedly fell and then simply lay there. I regularly had to lift him up and drag him forward. Thus, I only reached the execution site when my comrades had already shot their Jews. At the sight of his countrymen who had been shot, my Jew threw himself on the ground and remained lying there. I then cocked my carbine and shot him through the back of the head. Because I was already very upset from the cruel treatment of the Jews during the clearing of the town and was completely in turmoil, I shot too high. The entire back of the skull of my Jew was torn off and the brain exposed. Parts of the skull flew into Sergeant Steinmetz's face. This was grounds for me, after returning to the truck, to go to the first sergeant and ask for my release. I had become so sick that I simply couldn't anymore. I was then relieved by the first sergeant.[62]

Georg Kageler,* a thirty-seven-year-old tailor, made it through the first round before encountering difficulty. "After I had carried out the first shooting and at the unloading point was allotted a mother with daughter as victims for the next shooting, I began a conversation with them and learned that they were Germans from Kassel, and I took the decision not to participate further in the executions. The entire business was now so repugnant to me that I returned to my platoon leader and told him that I was still sick and asked for my release." Kageler was sent to guard the marketplace.[63] Neither his pre-execution conversation with his victim nor his discovery that there were German Jews in Józefów was unique. Schimke, the man who had first stepped out, encountered a Jew from Hamburg in the marketplace, as did a second policeman.[64] Yet another policeman remembered that the first Jew he shot was a decorated World War I veteran from Bremen who begged in vain for mercy.[65]

Franz Kastenbaum,* who during his official interrogation had denied remembering anything about the killing of Jews in Poland, suddenly appeared uninvited at the office of the Hamburg state prosecutor investigating Reserve Police Battalion 101. He told how he had been a member of a firing squad of seven or eight men that had taken its victims into the woods and shot them in the neck at point-blank range. This procedure had been repeated until the fourth victim.

> The shooting of the men was so repugnant to me that I missed the fourth man. It was simply no longer possible for me to aim accurately. I suddenly felt nauseous and ran away from the shooting site. I have expressed myself incorrectly just now. It was not that I could no longer aim accurately, rather that the fourth time I intentionally missed. I then ran into the woods, vomited, and sat down against a tree. To make sure that no one was nearby, I called loudly into the woods, because I wanted to be alone. Today I can say that my nerves were totally finished. I think that I remained alone in the woods for some two to three hours.

Kastenbaum then returned to the edge of the woods and rode an empty truck back to the marketplace. He suffered no consequences; his absence had gone unnoticed because the firing squads had been all mixed up and randomly assigned. He had come to make this statement, he explained to the investigating attorney, because he had had no peace since attempting to conceal the shooting action.[66]

Most of those who found the shooting impossible to bear quit very early.[67] But not always. The men in one squad had already shot ten to twenty Jews each when they finally asked to be relieved. As one of them explained, "I especially asked to be relieved because the man next to me shot so impossibly. Apparently he always aimed his gun too high, producing terrible wounds in his victims. In many cases the entire backs of victims' heads were torn off, so that the brains sprayed all over. I simply couldn't watch it any longer."[68] At the unloading point, Sergeant Bentheim watched men emerge from the woods covered with blood and brains, morale shaken and nerves finished. Those who asked to be relieved he advised to "slink away" to the marketplace.[69] As a result, the number of policemen gathered on the marketplace grew constantly.[70]

As with First Company, alcohol was made available to the policemen under Drucker and Steinmetz who stayed in the forest and continued shooting.[71] As darkness approached at the end of a long summer day and the murderous task was still not finished, the shooting became even less organized and more hectic.[72] The forest was so full of dead bodies that it was difficult to find places to make the Jews lie down.[73] When darkness finally fell about 9:00 p.m. – some seventeen hours after Reserve Police Battalion 101 had first arrived on the outskirts of Józefów – and the last Jews had been killed, the men returned to the marketplace and prepared to depart for Biłgoraj.[74] No plans had been made for the burial of the bodies, and the dead Jews were simply left lying in the woods. Neither clothing nor valuables had been officially collected, though at least some of the policemen had enriched themselves with watches, jewelry, and money taken from the victims.[75] The pile of luggage the Jews had been forced to leave at the marketplace was simply burned.[76] Before the policemen climbed into their trucks and left Józefów, a ten-year-old girl appeared, bleeding from the head. She was brought to Trapp, who took her in his arms and said, "You shall remain alive."[77]

When the men arrived at the barracks in Biłgoraj, they were depressed, angered, embittered, and shaken.[78] They ate little but drank heavily. Generous quantities of alcohol were provided, and many of the policemen got quite drunk. Major Trapp made the rounds, trying to console and reassure them, and again placing the responsibility on higher authorities.[79] But neither the drink nor Trapp's consolation could wash away the sense of shame and horror that pervaded the barracks. Trapp asked the men not to talk about it,[80] but they needed no encouragement in that direction. Those who had not been in the forest did not want to learn more.[81] Those who had been there likewise had no desire to speak, either then or later. By silent consensus within Reserve Police Battalion 101, the Józefów massacre was simply not discussed. "The entire matter was a taboo."[82] But repression during waking hours could not stop the nightmares. During the first night back from Józefów, one policeman awoke firing his gun into the ceiling of the barracks.[83]

Several days after Józefów the battalion, it would

seem, narrowly missed participation in yet another massacre. Units of First and Second Company, under Trapp and Wohlauf, entered Alekzandrów – a so-called street village composed of houses strung out along the road twelve kilometers west of Józefów. A small number of Jews was rounded up, and both the policemen and the Jews feared that another massacre was imminent. After some hesitation, however, the action was broken off, and Trapp permitted the Jews to return to their houses. One policeman remembered vividly "how individual Jews fell on their knees before Trapp and tried to kiss his hands and feet. Trapp, however, did not permit this and turned away." The policemen returned to Biłgoraj with no explanation for the strange turn of events.[84] Then, on July 20, precisely one month after its departure from Hamburg and one week after the Józefów massacre, Reserve Police Battalion 101 left Biłgoraj for redeployment in the northern sector of the Lublin district.

Notes

1. As neither Trapp, his adjutant Hagen, nor Lieutenant Gnade survived to be interrogated in the 1960s, the only direct witness to this meeting was Captain Wohlauf. His versions were so numerous and self-serving, and crucial aspects of the rest of his testimony so overwhelmingly contradicted by other witnesses, that he simply cannot be relied on.
2. Heinz B., HW 819–20, 2437, 3355, 4414.
3. Julius Wohlauf, HW 4329–30.
4. Friedrich Bm., HW 2091.
5. Hans S., G 328.
6. Bruno D., HW 1874
7. Alfred B., HW 440.
8. Rudolf B., HW 3692.
9. Otto-Julius S., 1953–54, 4576–79; August W., HW 2041–42, 3298, 4589. S. and W. were the only two witnesses who recalled Trapp's offer in precisely this way. Several others initially remembered a call for volunteers for the firing squad instead (Alfred B., HW 439–40; Franz G., HW 1189–90; Bruno G., HW 2020). Others, when questioned about the incident, either conceded the "possibility" that Trapp had made the offer (Anton B., HW 2693; Heinz B., HW 3356–57, 4415) or at least said they would not contest or deny it had happened. Trapp's stipulation about "older" men appears in S.'s testimony (HW 1953, 4578). W., who most explicitly confirmed S.'s testimony in other respects, did not mention this qualification and claimed that younger men stepped out as well. However, he does seem to have understood that Trapp made his offer to the older reservists. When asked to explain why he himself did not step out, he indicated that he was a relatively young volunteer, an "active" policeman – i.e., not a conscripted reservist (HW

2041–42, 4592). The greater precision and vivid detail of the S. and W. testimony and the subsequent behavior of the officers and noncoms of the battalion in accordance with Trapp's offer (i.e., those who belatedly asked out were released from firing squad duty – something the officers and noncoms could never have done so consistently without the prior sanction of the commanding officer) have persuaded me that a much greater probability rests with their version than with any other.
10. It may well be that First and Second Platoons of Third Company had already been stationed in a cordon surrounding the village *before* Trapp's speech. None of the men from these two platoons remembered the speech, and one witness (Bruno G., HW 2020) testified that the two platoons were not present.
11. Heinrich S., HW 1563; Martin D., HW 1596; Paul H., HW 1648; Ernst N., HW 1685; Wilhelm K., HW 1767, 2300; Bruno G., HW 2019; August W., HW 2039; Wilhelm Gb., HW 2147; Heinrich B., HW 2596; Walter Z., HW 2618; Anton B., HW 2656; Ernst Hr., HW 2716; Joseph P., HW 2742; Kurt D., HW 2888; Otto I., HW 3521; Wolfgang H., HW 3565; August Z., G 275; Eduard S., G 639; Hellmut S., G 646; Karl S., G 657.
12. Georg G., HW 2182.
13. Hellmut S., G 647.
14. Friedrich E., HW 1356.
15. Bruno R., HW 1852.
16. Harry L., G 223.
17. Ernst G., G 383.
18. Hans Kl., G 363.
19. Oskar P., HW 1743.
20. Erwin G., HW 2503.
21. Georg K., HW 2633; Karl S., G 657.
22. Wilhelm K., HW 1769; Friedrich Bm., HW 2091; Ernst Hn., G 506. For other accounts of the search, see Max D., HW 1345–46; Alfred L., HW 1351; Friedrick V., HW 1539; Friedrich B., HW 1579; Bruno D., HW 1875; Hermann W., HW 1947–48; Otto-Julius S., HW 1954; Bruno G., HW 2019; August W., HW 2040; Bruno R., HW 2084; Hans Kl., HW 2270; Walter Z., HW 2168–69; Anton B., HW 2687; Ernst Hr., HW 2716; Joseph P., HW 2742; August Z., G 275; Karl Z., G 318; Eduard S., G 640.
23. Friedrich B., HW 1579; Bruno G., HW 2019; August W., HW 2041.
24. Ernst Hr., HW 2716–17.
25. Walter Z., HW 2618. For confirming testimony, see Anton B., HW 2688; Joseph P., HW 2742.
26. Hermann W., HW 1948.
27. Ernst Hn., G 507, Two witnesses (Eduard S., G 642; Hellmut S., G 647) remembered the first sergeant but not the doctor.
28. August W., HW 2042.
29. Martin D., HW 1597.
30. Anton B., HW 2658–59.
31. Heinz B., HW 821–22. Not a single policeman interrogated in Hamburg had been part of the escort, so Buchmann's account is the only version of the fate of the work Jews. On the Luxembourgers making up the escort, see Heinrich E., HW 2167. For other accounts of the sorting of the workers and their being marched out of Józefów by Buchmann, see Wil-

helm K., HW 1768; Hermann W., HW 1948; Friedrich Bm., HW 2092–93; Ernst Hn., G 507.

32. For the testimony of First Company shooters, see especially Friedrich B., HW 1580–81l Friedrich Bm., HW 2091–93; Ernst Hn., G 507–8; Heinrich R., G 623; Hellmut S., G 646–47; Karl S., G 658–59.

33. Paul H., HW 1648–49.

34. Heinrich H., G 453.

35. Wilhelm I., HW 2237.

36. Friedrich Bm., HW 2092.

37. Hellmut S., G 647.

38. Heinrich Bl, HW 462.

39. Hermann W., HW 1948.

40. Alfred L., HW 1351.

41. Bruno R., HW 1852.

42. Erwin N., HW 1686.

43. Bruno D., HW 1870; Anton B., HW 4347; Wilhelm Gb., HW 4363; Paul M., G 202.

44. Ernst Hr., HW 2717.

45. Erwin G., HW 1640, 2505.

46. Friedrich Bm., HW 2092.

47. Wilhelm G., HW 2149.

48. Ernst Hr., HW 2718.

49. Wilhelm Gb., HW 2538.

50. Ernst Hr., HW 2719.

51. Ernst Hr., HW 2720.

52. Wilhelm Gb., HW 2539, 2149.

53. Erwin G., HW 1639–40, 2504; Alfred B., HW 2518.

54. Anton B., HW 4348. See also Max D., HW 2536.

55. Walter Z., HW 2619–20; Erwin G., HW 4345.

56. Heinrich S., HW 1567, 4364; Georg K., HW 2634.

57. Joseph P., HW 2743–45.

58. Paul M., G 206–7.

59. Gustav M., G 168.

60. Hans D., HW 1336, 3542.

61. Walter N., HW 3926, G 230.

62. August Z., G 277.

63. Georg K., HW 2634.

64. Otto-Julius S., HW 4579; Friederick V., HW 1540.

65. Rudolf B., HW 2434, 2951, 4357.

66. Franz K., HW 2483–86.

67. In addition to the above cases, another policeman who asked to be released when his nerves were finished after a few rounds was Bruno D., HW 1876, 2535, 4361.

68. Erwin G., HW 2505; confirmed by Rudolf K., HW 2646–47.

69. Anton B., HW 2691–93, 4348.

70. Willy R., HW 2085.

71. Alfred B., HW 440; Walter Z., HW 2621; Georg K., HW 2635; August Z., G 278.

72. Friedrich B., HW 1581.

73. Julius Wohlauf, HW 758.

74. Heinrich B., HW 2984.

75. Alfred B., HW 441.

76. August W., HW 2042.

77. Otto-Julius S., HW 1955.

78. Witness after witness used the terms *erschüttert, deprimiert, verbittert, niedergeschlagen, bedrückt, verstört, empört,* and *belastet* to describe the men's feelings that evening.

79. Friedrich Bm., HW 2093; Hellmut S., G 647.

80. Heinrich Br., HW 3050.

81. Wilhelm J., HW 1322.

82. Willy S., HW 2053. See also Wolfgang Hoffmann, HW 774–75; Johannes R., HW 1809; Bruno R., HW 2086.

83. Karl M., HW 2546, 2657.

84. Friedrich Bm., HW 2093–94. See also Karl G., HW 2194.

Two Jewish women drink tea at a railroad station in the Netherlands while they await transportation to the transit camp at Westerbork. May–June 1943. (Nederlands Instituut voor Oorlogsdocumentatie, courtesy of USHMM Photo Archives)

A transport of Dutch Jews marches under heavy guard to the Amersfoort concentration camp in the Netherlands. 1942. (Nederlands Instituut voor Oorlogsdocumentatie, courtesy of USHMM Photo Archives)

Two Jewish men wait beside a corpse-filled freight car for orders to remove the bodies. While the death train was halted at Mircesti, Romania, 327 bodies were removed and buried on the outskirts of the nearby town of Lugani. July 2, 1941. (American Jewish Joint Distribution Committee, courtesy of USHMM Photo Archives)

Deportation of Jews from the Drohobycz ghetto to a killing center. 1942. (Yad Vashem Photo Archives, courtesy of USHMM Photo Archives)

Jews from the Krakow ghetto who have been rounded-up for deportation to a killing center are crowded in the back of a truck. 1942. (Archiwum Panstwowe w Krakowie, courtesy of USHMM Photo Archives)

Greek Jews from the provinces with their belongings ride through German-occupied Salonika to the Baron de Hirsch ghetto. The Jewish inhabitants of the ghetto were later deported to Auschwitz during March and April 1943. Of the 48,000 Jews deported, 37,000 were gassed on arrival. November 1942 – March 1943. (Courtesy of the International Committee of the Red Cross)

Raul Hilberg **Origins of the Killing Centers**

The most secret operations of the destruction process were carried out in six camps located in Poland in an area stretching from the incorporated areas to the Bug. These camps were the collecting points for thousands of transports converging from all directions. In three years the incoming traffic reached a total of close to three million Jews. As the transports turned back empty, their passengers disappeared inside.

The killing centers worked quickly and efficiently. A man would step off a train in the morning, and in the evening his corpse was burned and his clothes were packed away for shipment to Germany. Such an operation was the product of a great deal of planning, for the death camp was an intricate mechanism in which a whole army of specialists played their parts. Viewed superficially, this smoothly functioning apparatus is deceptively simple, but upon closer examination the operations of the killing center resemble in several respects the complex mass production methods of a modern plant. It will therefore be necessary to explore, step by step, what made possible the final result.

The most striking fact about the killing center operations is that, unlike the earlier phases of the destruction process, they were unprecedented. Never before in history had people been killed on an assembly-line basis.[1] The killing center, as we shall observe it, has no prototype, no administrative ancestor. This is explained by the fact that it was a composite institution that consisted of two parts: the camp proper and the killing installations in the camp. Each of these two parts had its own administrative history. Neither was entirely novel. As separate establishments, both the concentration camp and the gas chamber had been in existence for some time. The great innovation was effected when the two devices were fused. We should therefore begin our examination of the death camp by learning something about its two basic components and how they were put together.

The German concentration camp was born and grew amid violent disputes and struggles between Nazi factions. Even in the earliest days of the Nazi regime, the importance of the concentration camp was fully recognized. Whoever gained possession of this weapon would wield a great deal of power.

In Prussia, Interior Minister (and later Prime Minister) Göring made his bid. He decided to round up the Communists. This was not an incarceration of convicted criminals but an arrest of a potentially dangerous group. "The prisons were not available for this purpose";[2] hence Göring established concentration camps, which he put under the control of his Gestapo (then, *Ministerialrat* [Rudolph] Diels).

Almost simultaneously, rival camps appeared on the scene. One was set up at Stettin by *Gauleiter* [Wilhelm] Karpenstein, another was established at Breslau by SA leader [Edmund] Heines, a third was erected near Berlin by SA leader [Karl] Ernst. Göring moved with all his might against these "unauthorized camps." Karpenstein lost his post, Ernst lost his life.

But a more powerful competitor emerged. In Munich the police president, Himmler, organized his own Gestapo, and near the town of Dachau he set up a concentration camp which he placed under the command of *SS-Oberführer* Eicke.[3] Soon Himmler's Gestapo covered the non-Prussian *Länder*, and in the spring of 1934 Himmler obtained through Hitler's graces the Prussian Gestapo (becoming its "deputy chief"). Along with Göring's Gestapo, Himmler captured the Prussian concentration camps. Henceforth all camps were under his control.[4]

Eicke, the first Dachau commander, now became the Inspector for Concentration Camps. His *Totenkopfverbände* (Death Head Units) became the guards. Thus the camps were severed from the Gestapo, which retained in the administration of each camp only one foothold: the political division, with jurisdiction over executions and releases. After the

outbreak of war, Eicke and most of his Totenkopfverbände moved into the field (he was killed in Russia),
and his deputy, the later Brigadeführer Glücks, took
over the inspectorate.

Eicke's departure marks the midpoint in the development of the concentration camps. Up to the
outbreak of war the camps held three types of prisoners:[5]

1. Political prisoners
   a. Communists (systematic roundup)
   b. Active Social Democrats
   c. Jehovah's Witnesses
   d. Clergymen who made undesirable speeches or
      otherwise manifested opposition
   e. People who made remarks against the regime
      and were sent to camps as an example to
      others
   f. Purged Nazis, especially SA men
2. So-called asocials, consisting primarily of habitual
   criminals and sex offenders
3. Jews sent to camps in *Einzelaktionen* [individual,
   random actions]

After 1939 the camps were flooded with millions of
people, including Jewish deportees, Poles, Soviet prisoners of war, members of the French resistance movements, and so on.

The inspectorate could not keep up with this influx. Therefore, from 1940 on the Higher SS and Police Leaders established camps of their own. We have
already noted in previous chapters the transit camps
in the west and the labor camps in Poland. During
the last stage of the destruction process, the Higher
SS and Police Leaders also put up killing centers.

At this point an office stepped in to centralize
and unify the concentration camp network: the SS
Economic-Administrative Main Office, the organization of *Obergruppenführer* Oswald Pohl. In a process
that took several years, Pohl finally emerged as the
dominant power in the camp apparatus. His organization incorporated the inspectorate and enveloped
almost completely the camps of the Higher SS and
Police Leaders.

Pohl entered the concentration camp picture
from an oblique angle. He was not a camp commander, nor was he a Higher SS and Police Leader. In

World War I he had been a naval paymaster, and in
the early days of the SS he had served in the *Verwaltungsamt* (Administrative Office) of the SS-Main Office. (The *Verwaltungsamt* dealt with financial and
administrative questions for the SS.) On February 1,
1934, Pohl took over the *Verwaltungsamt*, and by
1936 he had expanded its activities. It was now concerned also with construction matters, including the
construction of SS installations in concentration
camps. The *Verwaltungsamt* was therefore reorganized
to become the *Amt Haushalt und Bauten* (Budget and
Construction Office) – the first major step toward
overall control.

In 1940 Pohl broke loose from the SS-Main Office and established his own main office: the *Hauptamt Haushalt und Bauten*. At the same time he set up
a chain of SS enterprises in labor and concentration
camps. This business venture could not be placed under the *Hauptamt Haushalt und Bauten*, which was
nominally a state agency financed entirely with Reich
funds. Therefore, Pohl organized another main office,
the *Hauptamt Verwaltung und Wirtschaft* (VWHA) or
Main Office Administration and Economy. This was
Pohl's second step. The double organization, which
was analogous to Heydrich's apparatus before the
merger of the *Hauptamt Sicherheitspolizei* (Gestapo
and Kripo) and the *Sicherheitshauptamt* (SD) into the
RSHA*, is shown in Table 9-1.

On February 1, 1942, Pohl followed Heydrich's
example and combined his two main offices into a
single organization: the SS Economic-Administrative
Main Office, or *Wirtschafts-Verwaltungshauptamt*
(WVHA).

One month after this consolidation, Pohl took
his third major step. To ensure better labor utilization
in the camps and to make possible the unhampered
growth of his SS enterprises, he swallowed the inspectorate. The WVHA was now fully engaged in the
concentration camp business. From Table 9-2 it may
be seen that Hauptamt Haushalt und Bauten (I and
II) became *Amtsgruppen A, B*, and *C*, that the inspectorate was transformed into *Amtsgruppe D*, and that
the VWHA (III) emerged as *Amtsgruppe W*.[6]

With the inspectorate's incorporation into the
Pohl machine, the administration of the concentration camps acquired an economic accent. The ex-

*RSHA – Reich Security Main Office, *Ed.*

TABLE 9-1
ORGANIZATION OF THE HAUSHALT UND BAUTEN AND VWHA

HAUSHALT UND BAUTEN		VERWALTUNG UND WIRTSCHAFT
OFFICE I BUDGET OBF. LÖRNER	OFFICE II CONSTRUCTION GRUF. POHL	OFFICE III ADMIN. AND ECONOMY (SS ENTERPRISES) GRUF. POHL
I-1 SALARIES OSTUBAF. PRIETZEL	II-A WAFFEN-SS HSTUF. SESEMANN	III-A STAF. DR. SALPETER
		III-A/1 GERMAN EARTH AND STONE WORKS (*DEUTSCHE ERD- UND STEINWERKE* – DEST) STUBAF. MUMMENTHEY
I-2 LEGAL HSTUF. FRICKE	II-B SPECIAL TASKS USTUF. GEBER	III-B OBF. MÖCKEL
I-3 UNIFORMS AND CLOTHES STUBAF. WEGGEL	II-C CONCENTRATION CAMPS AND POLICE HSTUF. LIST	III-C OSTUBAF. MAURER
		III-C/3 GERMAN EQUIPMENT WORKS (*DEUTSCHE AUSRÜSTUNGSWERKE* – DAW) HSTUF. NIEMANN
I-4 LODGINGS OSTUBAF. KÖBERLEIN	II-D HSTUF. DR. FLIR	III-D STUBAF. VOGEL
I-5 ALLOCATION OF INMATE LABOR HSTUF. BURBÖCK	II-E PERSONNEL	III-S SPECIAL TASKS STUBAF. KLEIN
I-6 FOOD HSTUF. FICHTINGER		
I-H PERSONNEL USTUF. LANGE		
I-K TRANSPORTATION USTUF. LEITNER		

NOTE: Organization charts of Hauptamt Haushalt und Bauten and Hauptamt Verwaltung und Wirtschaft, 1941, in NO-620. The early history of the Pohl organization is based on his affidavit of March 18, 1947, NO-2574.

ploitation of the inmate labor supply, which had motivated Pohl to undertake this consolidation, now became the very reason for the existence of concentration camps. This factor brought into the killing center operations the same dilemma that we have already observed in the mobile killing operations and the deportations, namely the need for labor versus the "Final Solution." This time the quandary was entirely an

TABLE 9-2
ORGANIZATION OF THE WVHA

CHIEF, WVHA		OGRUF. POHL
DEPUTY		(BGF. FRANK) GRUF. GEORG LÖRNER
CHIEF, AMTSGRUPPE A	TROOP ADMINISTRATION	(FRANK) BGF. FANSLAU
AMT A-I	BUDGET	OBF. HANS LÖRNER
AMT A-II	FINANCE	(OSTUBAF. ECKERT) HSTUF. MELMER
AMT A-III	LAW	OBF. SALPETER
AMT A-IV	AUDITING	STAF. VOGT
AMT A-V	PERSONNEL	BGF. FANSLAU
CHIEF, AMTSGRUPPE B	TROOP ECONOMY	GRUF. GEORG LÖRNER
DEPUTY		(STAF. PRIETZEL) OBF. TSCHENTSCHER
FOOD INSPECTOR, WAFFEN-SS		STAF. PROF. SCHENK
AMT B-I	FOOD (NOT INCLUDING CONCENTRATION CAMPS)	OBF. TSCHENTSCHER
AMT B-II	CLOTHES (INCLUDING INMATES)	OSTUBAF. LECHLER
AMT B-III (AMT B-IV: TRANS- FERRED TO B-II, MARCH 3, 1942)	LODGINGS	STAF. KÖBERLEIN
	RAW MATERIALS	OSTUBAF. WEGGEL
AMT B-V	TRANSPORT AND WEAPONS	STAF. SCHEIDE
CHIEF, AMTSGRUPPE C	CONSTRUCTION	GRUF. DR. ING. KAMMLER
DEPUTY		(STUBAF. BASCHING) OSTUBAF. SCHLEIF
AMT C-I	GENERAL CONSTRUCTION MATTERS (INCLUDING CONCENTRATION CAMPS)	OSTUBAF. RALL
AMT C-II	SPECIAL CONSTRUCTION	OSTUBAF. KIEFER
AMT C-III	TECHNICAL	STUBAF. FLOTE
AMT C-IV	ARTISTIC	STUBAF. SCHNEIDER
AMT C-V	CENTRAL INSPECTION	(LENZER) OSTUBAF. NOELL
AMT C-VI	FINANCIAL	STAF. EIRENSCHMALZ
CHIEF, AMTSGRUPPE D	CONCENTRATION CAMPS	BGF. GLÜCKS
DEPUTY		OSTUBAF. LIEBEHENSCHEL
AMT D-1	CENTRAL OFFICE	(LIEBEHENSCHEL) OSTUBAF. HÖSS
AMT D-II	LABOR ALLOCATION	STAF. MAURER
AMT D-III	SANITATION	STAF. DR. LOLLING
AMT D-IV	ADMINISTRATION	(KAINDL) STUBAF. BERGER
CHIEF, AMTSGRUPPE W GERMAN ECONOMIC ENTERPRISES, INC.	ECONOMIC ENTERPRISES	OGRUF. POHL
FIRST MANAGER		OGRUF. POHL
SECOND MANAGER		GRUF. LÖRNER OBF. BAIER
CHIEF, W STAFF		
AMT W-I	GERMAN EARTH AND STONE WORKS (DEST) – REICH	OSTUBAF. MUMMENTHEY
AMT W-II	DEST – EAST	STUBAF. DR. BOBERMIN
AMT W-III	FOOD ENTERPRISES	HSTUF. RABENECK
AMT W-IV	WOOD PRODUCTS (INCLUDING DAW)	(HSTUF. MAY) HSTUF. OPPERBECK
AMT W-V	AGRICULTURAL	OSTUBAF. VOGEL
AMT W-VI	TEXTILES AND LEATHER	OSTUBAF. LECHLER
AMT W-VII	BOOKS AND PICTURES (INCLUDING NORDLAND PUBLISHING COMPANY AND DEUTSCHER BILDERDIENST)	STUBAF. MISCHKE
AMT W-VIII	SPECIAL TASKS (MONUMENTS, ETC.)	OBF. DR. SALPETER

internal SS affair. (The growth of the Pohl organization from 1929 to March 1942 is summarized in Table 9-3).

The consolidation process did not stop with the incorporation of the inspectorate, for Pohl also bit into the camps of the Higher SS and Police Leaders. He annexed some camps outright, controlled others by installing regional officials responsible to the WVHA (the SS economists [*SS-Wirtschafter*]),[7] and invaded the killing centers in the *Generalgouvernement* by acquiring control over the entire camp confiscation machinery in the territory. Concentration camps had become the principal factor in the power structure of Pohl. He in turn had emerged as the dominant figure in the sea of concentration camps.[8]

While Pohl tightened his hold over the camps, the camps absorbed ever larger numbers of inmates. The following figures indicate the growth of the increasingly important army of slaves in concentration camp enclosures:

September 1939: 21,400[9]
April 19, 1943: over 160,000[10]
August 1, 1944: 524,286[11]

The compilations do not include the camps of the Higher SS and Police Leaders, nor do they show the millions of deaths.

To keep up with the influx of victims, the camp network had to be extended. In 1939 there were six relatively small camps.[12] In 1944 Pohl sent Himmler a map that showed 20 full-fledged concentration camps (*Konzentrationslager* or KL) and 165 satellite labor camps grouped in clusters around the big KLs. (Again the camps of the Higher SS and Police Leaders were not included.)[13] Himmler received the report with great satisfaction, remarking that "just such examples show how our business has grown [*Gerade an solchen Beispielen kann man sehen, wie unsere Dinge gewachsen sind*]."[14] Pohl's empire was thus characterized by a threefold growth: the jurisdictional expansion, the increase in the number of camp slaves, and the extension of the camp network.

The six killing centers appeared in 1941–42, at a time of the greatest multiplication and expansion of concentration camp facilities. This is a fact of great importance, for it ensured that the construction

TABLE 9-3
POHL ORGANIZATION, 1929–42

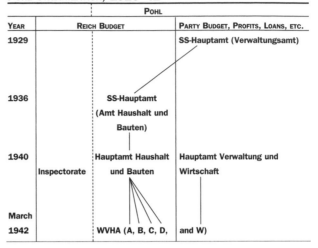

YEAR	REICH BUDGET		PARTY BUDGET, PROFITS, LOANS, ETC.
1929			SS-Hauptamt (Verwaltungsamt)
1936		SS-Hauptamt (Amt Haushalt und Bauten)	
1940	Inspectorate	Hauptamt Haushalt und Bauten	Hauptamt Verwaltung und Wirtschaft
March 1942		WVHA (A, B, C, D,	and W)

and operation of the killing centers could proceed smoothly and unobtrusively.

The death camps operated with gas. There were three types of gassing installations, for the administrative evolution of the gas method had proceeded in three different channels. One development took place in the Technical Referat of the RSHA. This office produced the gas van. We have already observed the use of the van in Russia and Serbia. In both of these territories the vans were auxiliary devices used for the killing of women and children only. But there was to be one more application. In 1941 Gauleiter Greiser of the Wartheland obtained Himmler's permission to kill 100,000 Jews in his Gau.[15] Three vans were thereupon brought into the woods of Kulmhof (Chełmno), the area was closed off, and the first killing center came into being.[16]

The construction of another type of gassing apparatus was pursued in the Führer Chancellery, Hitler's personal office. For some time, thought had been given in Germany to doctrines about the quality of life, from the simple idea that a dying person may be helped to die (*Sterbehilfe*) to the notion that life not worth living may be unworthy of life. This move from concern for the individual to a preoccupation with society was accomplished by representing retarded or malfunctioning persons, especially those with problems perceived to be congenital, as sick or harmful cells in the healthy corpus of the nation. The title of one monograph, published after the shock of World War I, could in fact be read as suggesting their destruction. It was called *The Release for Annihilation of Life without Value* [*Die Freigabe der Vernichtung lebensunwerten Lebens*].[17] The last three words of the German phrase were to grace official correspondence during the Nazi years.

Not until after the outbreak of World War II, however, did Hitler sign an order (predated September 1, 1939) empowering the chief of the Führer Chancellery, *Reichsleiter* Bouhler, and his own personal physician, Dr. [Karl] Brandt, "to widen the authority of individual doctors with a view to enabling them, after the most critical examination in the realm of human knowledge, to administer to incurably sick persons a mercy death."[18] The intention was to apply this directive only to Germans with mental afflictions,[19] but eventually the program encompassed the following three operations.[20]

1. Throughout the war, the killing, upon determination of physicians' panels, of about 5,000 severely handicapped children in hospital wards.
2. Until the late summer of 1941, the annihilation of about 70,000 adults in euthanasia stations equipped with gas chambers and bottled, chemically pure carbon monoxide gas. The victims, selected from lists screened by psychiatrists, were in the main institutionalized
   - senile persons, feebleminded persons, epileptics, sufferers from Huntington's chorea and some other neurological disorders,
   - individuals who had been treated at institutions for at least five years,
   - criminally insane persons, especially those involved in moral crimes.

   The euthanasia stations, which did not have resident patients, were
   - Grafeneck (after it was closed: Hadamar)
   - Brandenburg (after it was closed: Bernburg)
   - Sonnenstein
   - Hartheim
3. From the middle of 1941 to the winter of 1944–45, the pruning of concentration camp inmates too weak or bothersome to be kept alive and the killing of these people, upon superficial

psychiatric evaluation, in euthanasia stations under code 14 f 13.

The administrative implementation of this psychiatric holocaust was in the hands of Bouhler's Führer Chancellery. The man actually in charge of the program was a subordinate of Bouhler, *Reichsamtsleiter* Brack. For the technical aspects of the project, the Reichsamtsleiter obtained the services of *Kriminalkommissar* Wirth, chief of the Criminal Police office in Stuttgart and an expert in tracking down criminals.[21]

"Euthanasia" was a conceptual as well as technological and administrative prefiguration of the "Final Solution" in the death camps. In the summer of 1941, when the physical destruction of the Jews was in the offing for the whole of the European continent, Himmler consulted with the Chief Physician of the SS (*Reichsarzt-SS und Polizei*), *Gruppenführer* Dr. Grawitz, on the best way to undertake the mass-killing operation. Grawitz advised the use of gas chambers.[22]

On October 10, 1941, at a "final solution" conference of the RSHA, Heydrich alluded to Hitler's desire to free the Reich of Jews, if at all possible, by the end of the year. In that connection, the RSHA chief discussed the impending deportations to Łódź, and mentioned Riga and Minsk. He even considered the possibility of shipping Jews to concentration camps set up for Communists by *Einsatzgruppen* B and C in operational areas.[23] The Ostland, emerging as the center of gravity in this scheme, served to crystallize the idea of what was to be done to Reich deportees on their arrival.

By the end of the month the race expert (*Sonderdezernent für Rassenpolitik*) in Bräutigam's office in the East Ministry, *Amtsgerichtsrat* Wetzel, drafted a letter in which he stated that Brack was prepared to introduce his gassing apparatus in the east. Brack had offered to send his chemical expert, Dr. Kallmeyer, to Riga, and Eichmann had referred to Riga and Minsk in expressing agreement with the idea. "All things considered," wrote Wetzel, "one need have no reservation about doing away with those Jews who are unable to work, with the Brackian devices [*Nach Sachlage, bestehen keine Bedenken wenn diejenigen Ju-*

den, die nicht arbeitsfähig sind, mit den Brackschen Hilfsmittein beseitigt werden]."[24] There were, however, some second thoughts about directing a continuing flow of transports to the icy regions of the occupied USSR.[25] Dr. Kallmeyer, told to wait in Berlin because of the cold in the east, spent Christmas at home.[26] The scene of the action had already been shifted to the *Generalgouvernement.*

Under primitive conditions, three camps were built by *Amt Haushalt und Bauten* (after the reorganization of March 1942, the WVHA-C) and its regional machinery at Bełżec, Sobibór, and Treblinka. The sites were chosen with a view to seclusion and access to railroad lines. In the planning there was some improvization and much economizing; labor and material were procured locally at minimum cost.

Bełżec, in the district of Lublin, was the prototype. Its construction, according to Polish witnesses, was begun as early as November 1941. A locksmith who worked in the camp while it was being built provides the following chronology:[27]

October 1941	SS men approach Polish administration in town of Bełzec with demand for twenty workers. The Germans select the site.
November 1, 1941	Polish workers begin construction of three barracks: a waiting hall leading through a walkway to an ante-room, leading to a third building that had a corridor with three doors to three compartments, each of which had floor piping and an exit door. All six doors (entry and exit) in these three compartments were encased in thick rubber and opened to the outside.
November– December 1941	A contingent of about seventy black-uniformed eastern collaborators (Soviet prisoners of war released from captivity) lay narrow-
	gauge rail, dig pits, and erect a fence.
December 22, 1941	Polish workers are discharged.
January–February 1942	Watchtowers are built.

The Germans at the Bełżec site who had requisitioned the Polish work force were members of an SS construction Kommando.[28] The work was supervised by a "master from Katowice," an unidentified German with some knowledge of Polish who was in possession of building plans. When one of the Poles asked about the purpose of the project, the German only smiled.[29] Some time before Christmas, the construction chief (*Bauleiter*) showed the blueprints to an SS noncommissioned officer (Oberhauser) who was stationed in the area and who was going to be a functionary in the administration of the death camps. The drawings were plans of gassing installations (*Vergasungsanlagen*). By that time the construction of the buildings was substantially finished,[30] and shortly thereafter the chemist Dr. Kallmeyer arrived from Berlin.[31]

Sobibór, also in the Lublin district, was built, evidently more quickly, in March and April of 1942. Supervision of the construction was in the hands of Hauptsturmführer Thomalla, a master mason regularly assigned to the *Bauinspektion (Zentralbauleitung)* in Lublin.[32] Thomalla had some professional help from Baurat Moser, employed by the *Kreishauptmann* of Chełm (Ansel), in whose territory Sobibór was located.[33] To speed the work, Jewish labor from the surrounding region was employed extensively during the construction phase.[34]

At Treblinka (within the Warsaw district), where euthanasia physician Dr. Eberl was in charge, the *Zentralbauleitung* of the district, together with two contractors, the firm Schönbrunn of Liegnitz and the Warsaw concern Schmidt und Münstermann (builders of the Warsaw ghetto wall), were readying the camp.[35] Labor for construction was drawn from the Warsaw ghetto.[36] Dr. Eberl also availed himself of the resources of the ghetto for supplies, including switches, nails, cables, and wallpaper.[37] Again, the Jews were to be the unwitting contributors to their own destruction.

Even while the three camps were being erected, transports with Jewish deportees from the Kraków district, the Reich, and the Protektorat were arriving in the Hrubieszów-Zamość area. The director of the Population and Welfare Subdivision of the Interior Division in the Gouverneur's office of Lublin (Türk) was instructed by the *Generalgouvernement* Interior Main Division (Siebert) to assist Globocnik in making room for the Jews pouring into the district. Türk's deputy (Reuter) thereupon had a conversation with Globocnik's expert in Jewish "resettlement" affairs, *Hauptsturmführer* Höfle. The *Hauptsturmführer* made a few remarkable statements: A camp was being built at Bełżec, near the *Generalgouvernement* border in subdistrict (*Kreis*) Zamość. Where on the Dęblin-Trawniki line could 60,000 Jews be unloaded in the meantime? Höfle was ready to receive four or five transports daily at Bełżec. "These Jews would cross the border and would never return to the *Generalgouvernement* [*Diese Juden kämen über die Grenze und würden nie mehr ins Generalgouvernement zurückkommen*]."[38] The discussion, on the afternoon of March 16, 1942, was held a few days before the opening of Bełżec. During the following month Sobibór was finished, and in July, Treblinka.

The terrain of each camp was small – a few hundred yards in length and width. The layout was similar in all three camps. There were barracks for guard personnel, an area where the Jews were unloaded, an undressing station, and an S-shaped walkway, called *Schlauch* (hose), two or three yards wide that was bordered by high barbed-wire fences covered with ivy. The *Schlauch* was traversed by the naked victims on their way to the gassing facilities. The entire arrangement was designed to convince the Jews that they were in a transit camp, where they would be required to clean themselves on the way to the "east." The gas chambers, disguised as showers, were not larger than medium-sized rooms, but during gassings they were filled to capacity. At the beginning, no camp had more than three of these chambers. The gas first used at Bełżec was bottled, either the same preparation of carbon monoxide that had been shipped to the euthanasia stations or possibly hydrogen cyanide.[39] Later, all three camps (Sobibór and Treblinka from the start) were equipped with diesel motors. A German who briefly served at Sobibór recalls a 200-horsepower, eight-cylinder engine of a captured Soviet tank, which released a mixture of carbon monoxide and carbon dioxide into the gas chambers.[40] No crematoria were installed; the bodies were burned in mass graves.

The limited capacity of the camps troubled SS and Police Leader Globocnik; he did not wish to get "stuck."[41] During the summer of 1942 there was congestion of railway traffic in the *Generalgouvernement*, and the line to Sobibór was under repair. At Bełżec operations were reduced and interrupted, and at Sobibór the stoppage was prolonged. But Treblinka received transports to the point of overflow, and mounds of unburned bodies in various stages of decay confronted new arrivals of deportees.[42]

Between July and September an expansion was undertaken in the three camps. Massive structures, of stone in Bełżec and brick in Treblinka, containing at least six gas chambers in each camp, replaced the old facilities. In the new gas buildings the chambers were aligned on both sides of a corridor, and at Treblinka the engine room was situated at its far end. The front wall of the Treblinka gas house, underneath the gable, was decorated with a Star of David. At the entrance hung a heavy, dark curtain taken from a synagogue and still bearing the Hebrew words "This is the gate through which the righteous pass."[43]

The *Generalgouvernement* was the location also of a regular concentration camp of the WVHA, where Jewish transports were received from time to time. In German correspondence the camp was referred to as Lublin, whereas its common name after the war was Majdanek. Up to October 1942, the camp had facilities for men only. It had been built to hold prisoners of war (among them Jewish soldiers of the Polish army) under SS jurisdiction. Even during these early days, however, several thousand Jews, including men, women, and children, were brought into the camp from nearby localities. In September–October 1942, three small gas chambers, placed into a U-shaped building, were opened. Two of them were constructed for the interchangeable use of bottled carbon monoxide or hydrogen cyanide gas, the third for cyanide only. The area in front of the building was called *Rosengarten* and *Rosenfeld* (rose garden and rose field).

No roses adorned the camp – rather, the SS managers associated the facility with a typical name of Jewish victims. The gassing phase, which resulted in about 500 to 600 deaths per week over a period of a year, came to an end with the decision to wipe out the entire Jewish inmate population in one blow.[44] When the Lublin camp acquired administrative control of the Trawniki and Poniatowa labor camps, mass shootings took place at all three sites in the beginning of November 1943.[45]

Notes

1. The phrase was used by a camp doctor, Friedrich Entress, in his affidavit of April 14, 1947, NO-2368.
2. Testimony by Göring, *Trial of the Major War Criminals,* IX, 257.
3. See orders by Eicke, October 1, 1933, PS-778.
4. Camps for foreign laborers and prisoner-of-war camps were outside of Himmler's sphere. However, in October 1944 Himmler took over the PW camps in the rear.
5. By October 1943, 110,000 German prisoners, including 40,000 "political criminals" and 70,000 "asocials," had been sent to the concentration camps. Himmler speech before *Militärbefehlshaber* [military commanders], October 14, 1943, L-70.
6. See organization charts in documents NO-52 and NO-111.
7. Order by Pohl, July 23, 1942, NO-2128. Pohl to Himmler, July 27, 1942, NO-2128. SS economists were installed in Riga, Mogilev, Kiev, Kraków, Belgrade, and Oslo, later also in Hungary.
8. See the essay by Martin Broszat, "The Concentration Camps 1933–45," in Helmut Krausnick, Hans Buchheim, Martin Broszat, and Hans-Adolf Jacobsen, *The Anatomy of the SS State* (New York, 1968), 397–504.
9. Pohl to Himmler, April 30, 1942, R-129.
10. Pohl to OStubaf. Brandt, April 19, 1942, Himmler Files, Folder 67.
11. WVHA D-IV (signed Stubaf. Burger) to WVHA-B (Gruf. Lörner), August 15, 1944, NO-399.
12. Pohl to Himmler, April 30, 1942, R-129.
13. Pohl to Himmler, April 5, 1944, NO-20.
14. Himmler to Pohl, April 22, 1944, NO-20.
15. Greiser to Himmler, May 1, 1942, NO-246.
16. Judge Władyslaw Bednarz (Łódź), "Extermination Camp at Chełmno," Central Commission for Investigation of German Crimes in Poland, *German Crimes in Poland,* vol. 1, 107–17.
17. The authors were Karl Binding, a lawyer, and Alfred Hoche, a psychiatrist. (See 2d ed., Leipzig, 1922.) On further evolution of this thinking, see Stephen L. Chorover, *From Genesis to Genocide* (Cambridge, Mass., 1979), 78ff.
18. Order by Hitler, September 1, 1939, PS-630.
19. Affidavit by Dr. Konrad Morgen, July 19, 1946, SS(A)-67. Morgen was an SS officer whose assignment was the investigation of SS corruption. From this vantage point he gained insight into the killing phase of the destruction process.

20. For detailed descriptions, see Klaus Dorner, "Nationalsozialismus und Lebensvernichtung," *Vierteljahrshefte für Zeitgeschichte* 15 (1967): 121–52; Lothar Gruchmann, "Euthanasie und Justiz im Dritten Reich," *ibid.,* 20 (1972): 235–79; H. G. Adler, *Der verwaltete Mensch* (Tübingen, 1974), 234–39; and Florian Zehethofer, "Das Euthanasieproblem im Dritten Reich am Belspiel Schloss Hartheim 1938–1945," *Oberösterreichisches Helmatblatt* 32 (1978): 46–62.
21. Affidavit by Morgen, July 13, 1946, SS(A)-65. The chief psychiatric examiner for asylums was an SS physician, Prof. Werner Heyde. Each euthanasia station had its own medical director. The term "psychiatric holocaust" was coined by Peter Roger Breggin, "The Psychiatric Holocaust," *Penthouse,* January 1979, 81–84, 216. The stations were called "killing centers" by Leo Alexander, "Medical Science under Dictatorship," *New England Journal of Medicine* 24 (1949): 39–47. Alexander's designation is used here to describe the camps in which the gassings of the Jews took place.
22. Affidavit by Morgen, July 13, 1946, SS(A)-65.
23. Israel Police 1193.
24. Draft memorandum by Wetzel for Lohse and Rosenberg, October 25, 1941, NO-365. In Jerusalem, Eichmann declared that he had *not* discussed gas chambers with Wetzel. Eichmann trial transcript, June 23, 1961, sess. 78, R1; July 17, 1961, sess. 98, Bb1.
25. When Generalgouverneur Frank was in Berlin (middle of December 1941), he was told that "nothing could be done with the Jews in the Ostland." Frank in GG conference, December 16, 1941, Frank diary, PS-2233.
26. Helmut Kalimeyer (in Havana) to Dr. Stahmer (attorney), June 18, 1960, Oberhauser (Bełzec) case, 1 Js 278/60, vol. 5, 974–75.
27. Statement by Stanislaw Kozak, October 14, 1945, Bełzec case, vol. 6, 1129–33. The November 1, 1941, date is mentioned also by Eustachy Ukrainski (principal of grade school in the town of Bełzec), October 11, 1945, Bełzec, vol. 6, 1117–20. The presence of eastern collaborators at the end of 1941 is confirmed by Ludwig Obalek (mayor of Bełzec) in his statement of October 10, 1945, Bełzec case, vol. 6, 1112–14.
28. Statements by Josef Oberhauser, February 26 and September 15, 1960, Bełzec case, vol. 4, 656–60, and vol. 6, 1036–40.
29. Statement by Kozak, and statement by Edward Ferens (also a locksmith), March 20, 1946, Bełzec case, vol. 6, 1222–23.
30. Statement by Oberhauser, December 12, 1960, Bełzec case, vol. 9, 1678–93.
31. Kallmeyer to Stahmer, June 18, 1960, Bełzec case, vol. 5, 974–75. In the letter Kallmeyer asserts that he was not needed.
32. Statement by Georg Michalsen (Globocnik's *Aussiedlungsstab*), September 4, 1961, Sobibór case, 45 Js 27/61, vol. 4, 723–25. See also Richard Thomalla's personnel record in the Berlin Document Center.
33. Statement by *Landrat* Dr. Werner Ansel, June 15, 1960, Sobibór case, vol. 3, 416. Moser is mentioned also by Sobibór commander Franz Stangl, June 26, 1967, Treblinka case, 8 Js 10904/59, vol. 13, 3712–22.
34. Statement by Jan Stefaniuk (a non-Jewish worker at Sobibór), February 26, 1966, Sobibór case, vol. 13, 2694–95.

The gassing apparatus was tried out in the presence of an unnamed chemist. See Adalbert Rückerl, *NS-Vernichtungslager* (Munich, 1977), 165–66. Rückerl's book contains texts of German Federal Republic court judgments and selected testimony about all three of the Generalgouvernement camps as well as Kulmhof. For entries about the three camps, see encyclopedia by Główna Komisja Badania Zbrodni Hitlerowskich w Polsce, *Obozy hitlerowskie na ziemiach polskich 1939–1945* (Warsaw, 1979), 93–95, 459–61, 524–28. See also Ino Arndt and Wolfgang Scheffler, "Organisierter Massenmord an Juden in nationalsozialistischen Vernichtungslagern," *Vierteljahrshefte für Zeitgeschichte* 24 (1976): 105–35.

35. Indictment of Kurt Franz, enclosed by prosecutor Hühnerschulte to Landgericht in Düsseldorf, January 29, 1963, through the courtesy of the Israel police.

36. See entries by Czerniaków (chairman of Warsaw ghetto Jewish Council) in his diary (January 17; February 4 and 20; March 10, 27, and 29; April 9 and 18; May 23; and June 1, 1942), in Raul Hilberg, Stanislaw Staron, and Josef Kermisz, eds., *The Warsaw Diary of Adam Czerniakow* (New York, 1979), 316, 322, 328, 333, 338, 339, 341, 344, 358, 361. A labor camp (Treblinka I) was already in existence not far from the site. Jewish labor from the Warsaw ghetto was sent to Treblinka I, and its inmates, Poles as well as Jews, could be utilized for construction. Treblinka I, under *Hauptsturmführer* van Eupen, was not administratively joined to the death camp.

37. Eberl to Kommissar of Jewish district (Auerswald), June 26, 1942, facsimile in Jüdisches Historisches Institut Warschau, *Faschismus-Getto-Massenmord* (Berlin, 1961), 304. Eberl to Kommissar, July 7, 1942, facsimile in Alexander Donat, ed., *The Death Camp Treblinka* (New York, 1979), 255.

38. Memorandum by Reuter, March 17, 1942, in Jüdisches Historisches Institut, *Faschismus-Getto-Massenmord*, 269–70.

39. Bottled gas (*Flaschengas*) is mentioned by Oberhauser (*Obersturmführer* at Bełzec). See text of his statement in Rückerl, *NS-Vernichtungslager*, 136–37. The court judgment in the Oberhauser case identifies the gas as cyanide (Zyklon B). *Ibid.*, 133.

40. Testimony by "F" (Kurt Franz), *ibid.*, 165–66.

41. Brack to Himmler, June 23, 1942, NO-205.

42. Rückerl, *NS-Vernichtungslager*, 208–9.

43. *Ibid.*, 204. Information about the number and size of gas chambers in each camp rests not on documentation but on recollection of witnesses. There is agreement that the new chambers were larger than the old (the capacity for *simultaneous* gassing in Bełzec during the summer of 1942 was estimated at 1,500). Counts of gas chambers are given in the following ranges:

Bełzec	3, then 6
Sobibór	3, then 4, 5, or 6
Treblinka	3, then 6 or 10

It is likely that each facility was designed from the same basic plan; hence three is probably the initial capacity, and six the subsequent one. German defendants in Treblinka trial of 1965 (Franz et al.) indicated six chambers there after expansion. *Ibid.* A Jewish survivor, who was a carpenter at Treblinka, states that there were ten gas chambers. Jankiel Wiernik, "A Year in Treblinka," in Donat, *Treblinka*, 147–88, at 161. For a sketch drawn by Wiernik, see Filip Friedman, *This was Oswiecim* (London, 1946), 81–84; and Główna Komisja, *Obozy*, 526. See, however, two different sketches, in Donat, *Treblinka*, 318–19; and *Stern*, May 17, 1970, 170.

44. For a history of the Lublin camp, see Jozef Marszalek, *Majdanek* (Hamburg, 1982), particularly 24–44, 135–52; judgment of *Landgericht* Düsseldorf, April 27, 1979, in the matter of Ernst Schmidt, 8 Ks 1/75; affidavit by Friedrich Wilhelm Ruppert (Director, Technical Division, Lublin camp from September 1942), August 6, 1945, NO-1903; and Główna Komisja, *Obozy*, 302–12. On deliveries of Zyklon to the camp in 1943, see affidavit by Alfred Zaun (bookkeeper with Tesch und Stabenow, suppliers), October 18, 1947, NI-11937, and facsimiles of correspondence between Lublin camp and Tesch und Stabenow during June–July 1943; in Główna Komisja, *Obozy*, appendix, items 18, 140, and 141. The gas was routinely used in camps also for fumigation.

45. According to Ruppert, about 17,000 Jews were shot in Lublin in November 1943. Franz Pantli, an SS man in the camp, estimates 12,000. Affidavit by Franz Pantli, May 24, 1945, NO-1903. *Obersturmbannführer* Offermann cited 15,000 killed in Lublin, another 15,000 in Poniatowa, and 10,000 in Trawniki. Jüdisches Historisches Institut, *Faschismus-Getto-Massenmord*, 366–67n. See also Marszalek, *Majdanek*, 138.

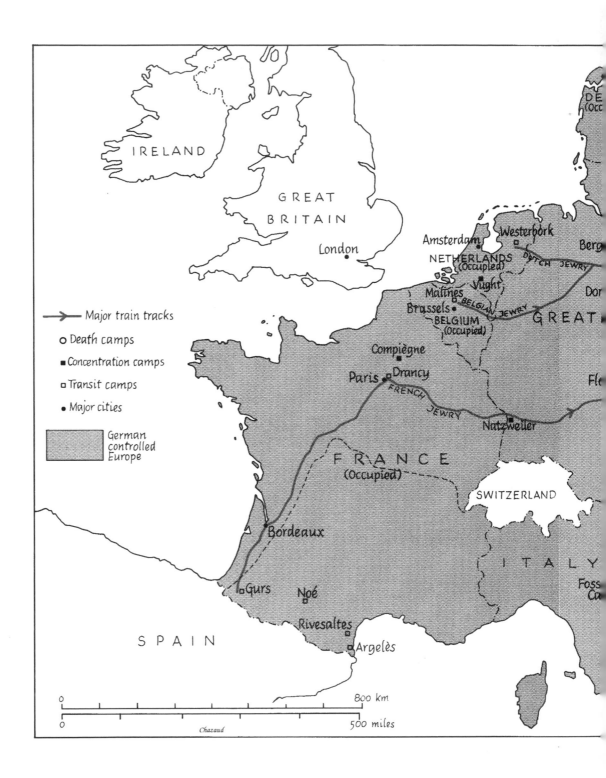

A square in a ghetto in Poland after an *Aktion* (roundup). The property of the deported Jews lies in piles in the square. (Courtesy of Photo Archives, The Ghetto Fighters' House Museum, Israel)

Property left behind by deported Jews is sold by townspeople in Bitol, Bulgarian-occupied Macedonia in March 1943. (YIVO Institute for Jewish Research, courtesy of USHMM Photo Archives)

SAUL FRIEDLÄNDER **Belzec and Treblinka**

TWO DAYS LATER, we left for Belzec. A small special station with two platforms was set up against a yellow sand hill, immediately to the north of the Lublin–Lvov railway. To the south, near the road, were some service buildings and a notice saying: "Waffen-S.S., Belzec Office." S.S. Group Leader Odilo Globocnik presented me to S.S.-*Hauptsturmführer* Obermeyer of Pirmasens, who showed great reserve when taking me over the installations. We saw no dead that day, but a pestilential odor blanketed the whole region. Alongside the station was a large hut marked "Cloak Room" with a wicket inside marked "Valuables." Further on, a hall, designated "Hairdresser," containing about a hundred chairs. Then came a passage about 150 yards long, open to the wind and flanked on both sides with barbed wire and notices saying: "To the Baths and Inhalation Rooms." In front of us was a building of the bathhouse type; left and right, large pots of geraniums and other flowers. On the roof, a copper Star of David. The building was labeled: "Heckenholt Foundation." That afternoon, I saw nothing else. Next morning, shortly after seven, I was told: "The first train will be arriving in ten minutes." A few minutes later a train did in fact arrive from Lemberg, with 45 wagons holding more than 6,000 people. Of these 1,450 were already dead on arrival. Behind the small barbed-wire windows, children, young ones, frightened to death, women and men. As the train drew in, 200 Ukrainians detailed for the task tore open the doors and, laying about them with their leather whips, drove the Jews out of the cars. Instructions boomed from a loudspeaker, ordering them to remove all clothing, artificial limbs, and spectacles. Using small pieces of string handed out by a little Jewish boy, they were to tie their shoes together. All valuables and money were to be handed in at the valuables counter, but no voucher or receipt was given. Women and young girls were to have their hair cut off in the hairdresser's hut

(an S.S.-*Unterführer* on duty told me: "That's to make something special for U-boat crews").

Then the march began. On either side of them, left and right, barbed wire; behind, two dozen Ukrainians, guns in hand.

They drew nearer to where [Christian] Wirth* and I were standing in front of the death chambers. Men, women, young girls, children, babies, cripples, all stark naked, filed by. At the corner stood a burly S.S. man, with a loud priestlike voice. "Nothing terrible is going to happen to you!" he told the poor wretches. "All you have to do is to breathe in deeply. That strengthens the lungs. Inhaling is a means of preventing infectious diseases. It's a good method of disinfection!" They asked what was going to happen to them. He told them: "The men will have to work building roads and houses. But the women won't be obliged to do so; they'll do housework or help in the kitchen." For some of these poor creatures, this was a last small ray of hope, enough to carry them, unresisting, as far as the chambers of death. Most of them knew the truth. The odor told them what their fate was to be. They walked up a small flight of steps and into the death chambers, most of them without a word, thrust forward by those behind them. One Jewess of about forty, her eyes flaming like torches, cursed her murderers. Urged on by some whiplashes from Captain Wirth in person, she disappeared into the gas chamber. Many were praying, while others asked: "Who will give us water to wash the dead?"†

I prayed with them. I pressed myself into a corner and cried out to my God and theirs. How glad I should have been to go into the gas chambers with them! How gladly I should have died the same death as theirs! Then an S.S. officer in uniform would have been found in the gas chambers. People would have believed it was an accident and the story would have been buried and forgotten. But I could not do this yet. I felt I must not succumb to the temptation

FROM **KURT GERSTEIN: THE AMBIGUITY OF GOOD** BY SAUL FRIEDLÄNDER, 106–13. COPYRIGHT © 1969 BY ALFRED A. KNOPF, INC. REPRINTED BY PERMISSION OF THE PUBLISHER.

*Commandant of Belzec, Sobibor, and Treblinka. *Ed.*
†Judaism requires that a dead body be cleansed before burial. *Ed.*

to die with these people. I now knew a great deal about these murders. Wirth had told me, "There are not ten people alive who have seen, or will see, as much as you." When the whole thing was over, all the foreign auxiliaries would be executed. I was one of the handful of people who had seen every corner of the establishment, and certainly the only one to have visited it as an enemy of this gang of murderers.

Inside the chambers, S.S. men were crushing the people together. "Fill them up well," Wirth had ordered, "700 to 800 of them to every 270 square feet." Now the doors were closed. Meanwhile, the rest of the people from the train stood waiting, naked. "Naked even in winter!" somebody said to me. "But they may catch their death!" "That's what they're here for!" was the reply. At that moment, I understood the reason for the inscription "Heckenholt." Heckenholt was the driver of the diesel truck whose exhaust gases were to be used to kill these unfortunates. S.S. sergeant Heckenholt was making great efforts to get the engine running, but it refused to start. Captain Wirth came up. He was obviously frightened because I was watching a disaster. Yes, I saw it all and I waited. Fifty minutes, seventy minutes ticked away on my stop watch, but the diesel would not work! Inside the gas chambers the people waited, waited in vain. They could be heard weeping, "as they do in the synagogue," said Professor Pfannenstiel, his eyes glued to a window in the wooden door.[1] Furious at the delay, Captain Wirth lashed out with his whip at the Ukrainian assisting Heckenholt. It was two hours and forty-nine minutes – all recorded by stop watch – before the diesel started. Right up to that moment, the people had been shut up alive in those four crowded chambers, four times 750 persons in four times 1,590 cubic feet of space! Another twenty-five minutes dragged by. Many of those inside were already dead. They could be seen through the small window when an electric lamp inside went on for a few moments and lit up the chamber. After twenty-eight minutes, few were left alive. Finally, at the end of thirty-two minutes, all were dead.

Some Jewish workers on the far side opened the wooden doors. In return for this terrible service, they had been promised their lives and a small percentage of the valuables and money collected. Inside, the peo-

ple were still standing erect, like pillars of basalt, since there had not been an inch of space for them to fall in or even lean. Families could still be seen holding hands, even in death. It was a tough job to separate them as the chambers were emptied to make way for the next batch. The bodies were tossed out, blue, wet with sweat and urine, the legs soiled with faeces and menstrual blood. A couple of dozen workers checked the mouths of the dead, which they tore open with iron hooks. "Gold to the left, other objects to the right!" Other workers inspected anus and genital organs in search of money, diamonds, gold, etc. Dentists moved around hammering out gold teeth, bridges and crowns. In the midst of them stood Captain Wirth, in his element. Showing me a large can full of teeth, he said: "See for yourself. Just look at the amount of gold there is! And we collected as much only yesterday and the day before. You can't imagine what we find every day – dollars, diamonds, gold! You'll see!" He took me to a jeweler who was responsible for all these valuables. Then they pointed out to me a man who had been one of the heads of Kaufhaus des Westens, a large Berlin department store, and another little man. These two were in charge of the Jewish work squads. The little man was being made to play the violin. "He was a captain in the Imperial Austrian Army," Wirth told me. "He holds the Knight's Cross of the German Iron Cross!"

Then the bodies were flung into large trenches, each about 100 yards by 20 by 12, which had been dug close to the gas chambers. After a few days the bodies would swell, raising the top of the mound as much as 6 to 10 feet as a result of gas formed inside the corpses. A few days later, once the swelling had subsided, the bodies would shake down again. Subsequently, I was told, the bodies were piled on train rails and burned to a cinder with diesel oil . . . At Belzec and Treblinka, they did not take the trouble to make anything like an accurate count of the number of people killed. The figures given on the radio by the British Broadcasting Co. are not correct; in actual fact, the total number of people involved was 25,000,000! Not Jews alone, but Poles as well and Czechs, who, so the Nazis said, were biologically valueless. Most of them died nameless. Commissions made up of pseudo doctors, ordinary young S.S. enlisted men in white coats, drove around the villages and towns of Poland and Czechoslovakia in limousines, checking off the aged, the consumptive, and the sick who were later to be executed in the gas chambers. These were "third class" Poles and Czechs who were judged unworthy to go on living because they were no longer able to work. Police Captain Wirth asked me not to propose any modifications in the gas chamber method when I returned to Berlin, but to leave it as it was. I lied, saying that if the prussic acid had deteriorated in transit and become very dangerous, I should be forced to bury it, which I at once did. The next day we drove in Captain Wirth's car to Treblinka, about 6 miles NNE of Warsaw. The equipment in that death camp was almost identical to the Belzec installations, but on an even larger scale: eight gas chambers and veritable mountains of clothing and underwear, 115 to 130 feet high. Then, in "honor" of our visit, a banquet was held for all those employed at the establishment. *Obersturmbannführer* Professor Doctor Pfannenstiel, Professor of Hygiene at the University of Marburg/Lahn, made a speech: "The work you are doing is great work and a duty so useful and so necessary." To me, he spoke of the establishment as "a blessing and a humanitarian arrangement." To all present, he said: "When one sees the bodies of these Jews, one understands the greatness of the work you are doing!"

The dinner itself was simple; but on Himmler's orders, those employed in the service were given whatever they wanted in the way of butter, meat, alcohol, etc. As we were leaving, we were offered several pounds of butter and a large number of bottles of liqueur. Not without difficulty I lied my way out of this by saying that I was kept adequately supplied from our farm. That being the case, Pfannenstiel took my share as well as his own, and we drove to Warsaw.[2]

Notes

1. Professor Pfannenstiel was later to deny having spoken these words, at least in the sarcastic sense imputed to him by Gerstein. He likewise denied the truth of details concerning him which follow later in the report. See 112.
2. Gerstein report.

DEBÓRAH DWORK AND ROBERT JAN VAN PELT **The Holocaust at Auschwitz**

IN THE AUTUMN OF 1941 it was clear to Himmler that Hitler was delighted with his policy to deport the German Jews to Russia. His public prophecy that, in the case of a war, the Jews would disappear from Europe was to be realized, Hitler told Himmler and Heydrich on 25 October. He had no qualms about it. "That race of criminals has on its conscience the two million dead of the First World War, and now already hundreds of thousands more. Let nobody tell me that all the same we can't park them in the marshy parts of Russia! Who's worrying about our troops?"[1] It also was obvious that the accompanying killing of Russian, Polish, and by then German Jews did not bother the Führer in the least. Even before the extermination camp at Kulmhof had come into operation, Hitler delighted his court with a saying of his old teacher Dietrich Eckart. "In all his life he had known just one good Jew," Hitler mused, "Otto Weininger, who killed himself on the day when he realized that the Jew lives upon the decay of peoples."[2]

By the end of November many individuals and agencies had taken the initiative to kill Jews [Wilhelm] Koppe had set up his own extermination installation in Kulmhof, and Erhard Wetzel and his colleagues in [Alfred] Rosenberg's Ministry for the Occupied Eastern Territories were negotiating with unemployed T4 specialists to bring their expertise to Riga and Minsk. It was time to establish once and for all that Himmler was in charge.

To that end, Heydrich invited top bureaucrats of the Reich Chancellery, the Ministries of Justice, Interior, Foreign Affairs, and the Eastern Territories, and from the Four-Year Plan, the Government General, the Chancellery of the National Socialist Party, and various SS agencies, such as the Race and Settlement Main Office and Greifelt's Staff Department of the Reich Commissioner of the Consolidation of the German Nation, to a meeting to be held on 9 December in the Berlin Interpol Office, at 56 Am grossen Wannsee. The object, he said, was to secure "a uniform view among the relevant central agencies of the further tasks concerned with the remaining work on this final solution." The meeting was especially urgent because "from 10 October onwards the Jews have been evacuated from Reich territory, including the Protectorate, to the East in a continuous series of transports."[3] Heydrich included a photocopy of Göring's authorization letter of 31 July with each invitation.

For five years Himmler had been unwilling to forgo the labor potential of concentration camp inmates, and if the scheduled meeting at Wannsee confirmed his authority over the Final Solution to the Jewish Question, there was no reason not to use the labor potential of the Jews as an integral part of that Solution. At Himmler's request the chief of SS construction, Hans Kammler, developed a provisional peace building program for the Waffen SS and the German police which required Jewish labor. Kammler believed that the only way the SS would get its share of the limited resources that were to be available for construction was to propose a bold plan that presupposed the allocation of money and materials to the SS, just as the armed services had such quotas. Kammler submitted a budget for a little over 13 billion marks, of which around 10 percent was to be spent in the annexed areas, and he ordered the design development of various projects to support the proposal.[4]

Himmler found Kammler's proposal insufficiently comprehensive, and suggested another 10 to 12 billion marks. Within two months he had come to the conclusion that this sum was laughable too. The SS building projects in the annexed territories alone would require 80 billion marks, which was sixty times the figure Kammler originally had budgeted. Himmler presumed that SS companies like DESt would supply him with stone, brick, chalk, and cement; he counted on a special arrangement with the Hermann-Göring-Werke for steel, and lumber was to be extracted from the Russian forests, but none of these materials could be produced without labor. Building construction, moreover, demanded skilled labor, which was going to be in very short supply. Himmler instructed Pohl to introduce vocational training for concentration camp inmates. "If we do not do this, then we will not get proper barracks, schools, offices, or houses for our SS men in Germany, and I, as Reich Commissioner for the Consolidation of the German Nation, will not be able to create the enormous settlements with which we will make the East German."[5]

Kammler proposed the creation of roving SS building brigades for the provisional peace program. Each brigade would consist of two regiments, and every regiment was to be divided into three battalions. The first battalion would prepare the building site, level the terrain, lay streets, and dig basements, drainage canals, and wells; the second would do the rough construction work; and the third would be responsible for painting, electrical installation, heating, and plumbing. Kammler calculated that, with all the resources of the concentration camps at his disposal, he could not muster even one brigade of 4,000 men. To cover the 1942 SS building program, he would need 175,000 workers – inmates, prisoners of war, Jews, etc."[6]

A paradoxical situation had developed in the SS empire. For Heydrich, chief of the Reich Main Security Office, the Jews were a nuisance to be deported, while for Kammler, chief of SS construction, Jews who could work were a valuable resource – and their value was rapidly rising as it became increasingly unlikely that Himmler would receive the other 90,000 Soviet prisoners of war the army had contracted to give him. Heydrich and Kammler articulated the conflict that, at the end of 1941, troubled Himmler. There was no place for Jews in the German utopia he had dedicated himself to creating, but he could not build it without them. These apparently mutually exclusive demands were resolved at the Wannsee conference rescheduled for 20 January 1942.

Heydrich chaired the meeting, opening with a reference to Göring's letter of July. He then proceeded to assert his central objective. "Primary responsibility

for the handling of the final solution of the Jewish question . . . is to lie centrally, regardless of geographic boundaries, with the *Reichsführer* SS and Chief of the German Police," he claimed flatly.[7] No one protested. He had prevailed, and he wrapped up the conference in ninety minutes. Too few Jews had emigrated between 1933 and 1939, and 11 million remained in Europe. "Under appropriate direction, in the course of the final solution, the Jews are now to be suitably assigned as labor in the East," he announced. "In big labor gangs, with the sexes separated, Jews capable of work will be brought to these areas, employed in roadbuilding, in which task a large part will undoubtedly disappear through natural diminution. The remnant that may eventually remain, being undoubtedly the part most capable of resistance, will have to be appropriately dealt with, since it represents a natural selection and in the event of release is to be regarded as the germ cell of a new Jewish renewal. (Witness the experience of history.)"[8] In view of the provisional peace program and discussions about the deployment of Jews in building brigades, apparently Heydrich meant what he said when he talked about labor gangs.

Himmler met Hitler three days after the Wannsee conference. There is no record of their conversation, but later that day Hitler hinted at the content of their talk. "If I withdraw 50,000 Germans from Volhynia, that's a hard decision to take, because of the suffering it entails," he complained. "The same is true of the evacuation of Southern Tyrol. If I think of shifting the Jew, our bourgeoisie becomes quite unhappy: 'What will happen to them?' Tell me whether this same bourgeoisie bothered about what happened to our own compatriots who were obliged to emigrate?" By 1942 this was pure fantasy, of course. If such a bourgeoisie ever had existed, it certainly had not raised its voice on behalf of the Jews for at least a decade. But such facts were of no concern to Hitler. "The Jew must clear out of Europe. Otherwise no understanding will be possible between Europeans. It's the Jew who prevents everything. When I think about it, I realise that I'm extraordinarily humane," he told his admirers. "I restrict myself to telling them they must go away. If they break their pipes on the journey, I can't do anything about it. But if they refuse to go voluntarily, I see no other solution but extermination." Jews were a danger and a threat. They were at the forefront of those who were ready to stab Germany in the back. "Why should I look at a Jew through other eyes than if he were a Russian prisoner-of-war? In the p.o.w. camps, many are dying. It's not my fault. I didn't want either the war or the p.o.w. camps. Why did the Jew provoke this war?"[9]

Three days after listening to his Führer, Himmler sent a telegram to Richard Glücks, the inspector of concentration camps. "As no Russian prisoners of war can be expected in the near future, I am sending to the camps a large number of Jews who have emigrated from Germany. Will you therefore make preparations to receive within the next four weeks 100,000 Jews and up to 50,000 Jewesses in the concentration camps."[10]

Having received full authority over the Final Solution, and with that over all of Europe's Jewry, Himmler was now free to dispatch Jews to take the place of the Soviet prisoners of war. Although he did not specify which camps would be affected, in only two were Soviets an essential part of the planned inmate population: Auschwitz and Majdanek. But while the idea to replace prisoners of war with Jews worked in principle, Himmler's initial plan to dispatch German Jews immediately for that purpose was not practicable. As it transpired, the immediate deportation of 150,000 Jews from the Reich and the protectorate of Bohemia and Moravia was difficult from an organizational point of view.[11] There were also delays due to the official procedures for the transfer of German Jewish property to the Reich. Himmler's telegram was premature. German Jews could not take the place of the Soviets. If a quick fix were to be found for Himmler's problem in Auschwitz, he would have to find another group of Jews who could be quickly assembled and moved and who did not warrant the attention of German bureaucrats.

The Jews of Hitler's client state of Slovakia, ruled by the Fascist cleric Monsignor Dr. Josef Tiso and the National Socialist professor Vojtech Tuka, fit the bill. As the Holocaust historian Yehuda Bauer has explained, in 1940 the German government had compelled Tuka to agree to send 120,000 Slovak workers

to the labor-strapped Reich. The Slovaks regretted this arrangement and dragged their feet. Finally, in the late summer of 1941 the Germans demanded the immediate transfer of 20,000 workers. Asked if they would take 20,000 Slovak Jews, the Germans declined. They were just beginning to deport all remaining Jews from the Reich.[12]

Tiso and Tuka continued to hold out. In the hope that the Germans would be prepared to take Jews instead of Christians, they concentrated thousands of young Slovak Jews into three labor camps. In January 1942 they again offered the German Labor Ministry 20,000 strong, young Jews for work in Germany. Within days a response came in the form of Dieter Wisliceny. Officially an attaché at the German embassy in Bratislava, Wisliceny was in fact Eichmann's local agent. He had learned from Eichmann that Himmler needed Jews to replace the Soviet prisoners of war in Auschwitz, and he was instructed to accept the Slovak offer of 20,000 able-bodied Jews on Germany's behalf: 10,000 would be sent to Auschwitz and 10,000 to Majdanek. The deal was made official on 16 February. "As part of the measures for the Final Solution of the European Jewish Question, the German Government is prepared to take over 20,000 young, strong Slovak Jews immediately and to transport them to the East, where there is need for labour," a senior official of the Foreign Office, Martin Luther, cabled the German legation in Bratislava.[13] Tiso and Tuka were delighted.

"The order came four weeks prior to the end of March," Helen Tichauer-Spitzer, one of the targeted 20,000 Jews, recalled. "End of February. They printed large placards which were pasted on kiosks. No written invitation. They announced that Jewish girls, unmarried, I think it was fifteen or sixteen through forty-five or fifty, were ordered to assemble on a certain date. It was the twenty-first of March, I remember, on a Monday."[14]

Helen understood that nothing good would come of this, but "the order said that if you don't report, your parents will be taken instead. So it was a little bit of a tricky business. Nobody wanted to sacrifice their parents. If I would have undertaken to escape to the neighboring countries, the parents would be taken instead."

Helen, however, seemed to have another option. She was a sign writer, and her "employer, who was German, decided to ask for an exemption because there was a shortage of manpower in the profession." The employer was successful; the exemption "was signed; it was ready." But "it was that bloody Monday which was the turning point in my life. I had to leave for the collection point early in the morning, before office time, so I could not go to my employer and collect the permission. I still had to leave because if I wouldn't have reported at the gathering point, they would have picked up my parents. It was a very tricky business. It was bad luck. One day difference and I could have stayed."[15]

Helen reported to "the gathering point, an empty ammunition factory near the railway station," where she was kept until Saturday morning. When another 999 people had been assembled, the Slovak Hlinka guards loaded them onto a train, squeezing them in to boxcars. "The journey took one day, one night, and late in the afternoon of the next day we arrived. We arrived on a Sunday." The train stopped "in an open field before the [Auschwitz] railway station. We had to leave everything behind. They marched us to the main gate. I went through the *Arbeit macht frei* gate."[16]

The Slovak women were destined for Birkenau, but there had been a delay in the Germans' building schedule. Birkenau officially had been in operation since the beginning of March, when the remaining Soviet prisoners of war, a group of German criminals, and 1,200 sick male inmates from the lazaret had been moved to BA I, the area designated for the women. The transfer of the women to Birkenau had to wait; in the meantime they were packed into ten specially walled-off barracks in the base camp at Auschwitz.

"They were not prepared for us," Helen Spitzer recalled. "They didn't know what to do with us. Everything went in such a hurry. They were so quick on the trigger. When we arrived, they just pushed us in to a barrack, and the next day they shaved us and put us into some old Russian uniforms."[17]

By the end of April ten Slovak transports had arrived and 9,655 Slovak Jews had been registered. None of the transports included old people or young children, and there were no selections on the train ramps.

While negotiations were carried on between the German Foreign Office and the Slovak government, Auschwitz already had become the destination for one particular group of Jews residing on Reich territory: those considered unfit for work in the so-called Schmelt program. A high-ranking SS officer and senior civil servant in the provincial administration, Albrecht Schmelt had established a special organization in 1941 to monopolize the forced labor of Jews left in Upper Silesia after the deportations to the Government General had been halted.[18] Schmelt employed some 50,000 Jews, and he felt that his program was burdened by too many mouths to feed. He knew about the Gestapo Summary Court executions in Auschwitz, and in mid-February he shipped some 400 older Jews to the camp.

The morgue of the crematorium in the main camp had been transformed in September 1941 into an effective gas chamber which could hold 900 people, so there was plenty of room to kill the elderly Jews with ease. Shortly before their arrival, the SS closed off the roads and emptied the offices that had a view of the crematorium. "A sad procession walked along the streets of the camp," Pery Broad remembered after the war. "All of them had large, yellow Jewish stars on their miserable clothes. Their worn faces showed that they had suffered many a hardship."[19]

It was not an ideal situation from the camp management perspective, Broad noted. Using the crematorium as a killing station for a transport of old people interrupted the life of the camp. Broad's superior, Maximilian Grabner, who had overseen the whole operation, had even had to run a truck engine to drown out the death cries of the victims. Whereas the Germans had felt no need to camouflage the execution of Polish hostages or resisters "duly" sentenced by a court of justice, the murder of elderly Jews was another matter. It was not a useful deterrent against resistance activities.

The Slovaks, in the meantime, realized that when the 20,000 young Jews they had got the Germans to take left home, many families would have no breadwinner and would become a burden on the Slovak economy. Eichmann initially refused even to discuss the matter but, after the successful "special treatment" of the elderly Upper Silesian Jews, concluded that the same solution could be applied to Slovak Jews unable to work.

The Germans had a few practical problems to work out. As the Slovak Jews were to be brought to Birkenau and not to Auschwitz, and as killing them in crematorium I would interrupt the life of the main camp, they considered building an extermination installation close to the new satellite camp. Hans Kammler* arrived in Auschwitz on Thursday, 27 February, to meet with [Rudolf] Höss† and [Karl] Bischoff‡. There are no minutes of this conference, but its content can be ascertained from a letter Bischoff wrote to Topf§ a week later. Kammler had decided to cancel their order for the backup incinerators included in the Birkenau plan of 6 January, Bischoff explained. The large crematorium with five triple-muffle incinerators that had been designated for the main camp was to go to Birkenau instead.[20] Obviously Kammler wanted construction to proceed quickly. Those furnaces had been ordered almost four months previously and he expected they would be available soon.[21] Furthermore, the designs for the crematorium that was to house these incinerators had been both completed and approved. On paper, at least, everything was ready for the crematorium they had agreed upon the previous October. A blueprint of the prisoner-of-war camp shows that Kammler decided to locate the new crematorium in the northwestern corner of Birkenau, adjacent to an abandoned cottage that had belonged to a Polish peasant named Wiechuja.[22] The interior of this cottage, known as "the little red house," was converted into two gas chambers within a few weeks, and on 20 March it was put into operation as "bunker 1."[23] The first group of victims was another transport of Schmelt Jews "unfit for work."[24]

There is no doubt that Kammler's visit led to the Germans' reversal of their decision about the mass deportation of Slovak Jewry. Once Kammler had organized the construction of the crematorium in Birkenau, the Reich Security Main Office permitted the German Foreign Office to negotiate seriously. On

3 March Tuka announced in the Slovak State Council that, pending certain financial arrangements, the Germans had agreed to take the remaining 70,000 Jews.[25] The Germans were doing them a favor and were to be compensated at the rate of 500 marks for every Jew deported. For this sum, however, the Slovak government was guaranteed that "the Jews accepted as part of the de-Judaization of Slovakia will remain permanently in the Eastern territories and will not be offered any possibility of re-immigrating into Slovakia."[26] The state was free to seize Jewish property left behind.

It took Eichmann another month to arrange the deportation of families. Several transports went to Lublin, where a selection took place just outside the station. Able-bodied men were marched to Majdanek; the "unfit for work" were forced back onto the train, which continued its journey to killing installations which Christian Wirth, the architect of the T4 gas chambers, had built at Belzec on Odilo Globocnik's instructions.

Throughout May and June, no Slovak Jews were killed in bunker 1 in Birkenau; all the victims were Upper Silesian Jews. With the destruction of these Jews, mass murder became a fixture of life in Auschwitz, but it was not yet the camp's primary purpose. The history of bunker 1 was rooted in the well-established function of the camp as an execution ground for people convicted by the Gestapo court in Kattowitz. The deportation of Schmelt Jews to Auschwitz was independent of the massive deportations overseen by Eichmann. It was, and remained, a local affair.

Bunker 1 also was used to kill sick inmates, and here too its murder function developed from earlier practices: the 14f13 program. Once bunker 1 was operational, it was unnecessary to transport victims hundreds of miles to gas them; a short truck ride to Birkenau sufficed. Regularly replenished with new arrivals from the main camp, the "isolation station" created on 13 March became a much used holding pen. Selections of inmates in the isolation station were introduced on 4 May, and an unknown number of sick prisoners were loaded onto trucks, brought to bunker 1, and killed. From that date on, periodic selections in the isolation station harvested up to

*Head of construction for the SS, *Ed.*
†Commandant of Auschwitz, *Ed.*
‡Chief architect at Auschwitz, *Ed.*
§The Topf and Sons boiler and furnace firm, *Ed.*

90 percent of its inmates for death in the gas chambers.[27]

Bunker 1 was not very efficient, and sometime in June Höss began to plan the transformation of a second cottage, the "little white house," into what was now known as a "bathing facility for special actions."[28] According to Jean-Claude Pressac, Bischoff attempted to improve the efficiency of this gas chamber by applying the advice given in the Degesch* pamphlet on how to design Zyklon B delousing chambers, but he could not obtain the necessary equipment. Following the architectural arrangement of the Degesch delousing chambers, Bischoff divided the cottage into four long, narrow, parallel rooms with doors on each side. This allowed for ample cross ventilation after the Zyklon B had done its work.[29]

Bunker 2 was operational by the end of June 1942. A Jewish *Sonderkommando*, or Special Squad, was formed on 4 July to service the killing installations.[30] That same day a first transport of 1,000 Jews was submitted to a selection on arrival. The Germans lined them up and chose 264 able-bodied men and 108 able-bodied women. The remaining 638 people were brought to the new gas chambers. André Lettich, a French Jewish doctor forced to work at bunker 2, described it as a "peaceful looking house."

> More than five hundred metres further on were two barracks: the men stood on one side, the women on the other. They were addressed in a very polite and friendly way: "You have been on a journey. You are dirty. You will take a bath. Get undressed quickly." Towels and soap were handed out, and then suddenly the brutes woke up and showed their true faces: this horde of people, these men and women were driven outside with hard blows and forced both summer and winter to go the few hundred metres to the "Shower Room." Above the entry door was the word "Shower." One could even see shower heads on the ceiling which were cemented in but never had water flowing through them.
>
> These poor innocents were crammed together, pressed against each other. Then panic broke out, for at last they realised the fate in store for them. But blows with rifle butts and revolver

shots soon restored order and finally they all entered the death chamber. The doors were shut and, ten minutes later, the temperature was high enough to facilitate the condensation of hydrogen cyanide, for the condemned were gassed with hydrogen cyanide. This was the so-called "Zyklon B," gravel pellets saturated with twenty per cent of hydrogen cyanide which was used by the German barbarians.

> Then, *SS Unterscharführer* Moll threw the gas in through the little vent. One could hear fearful screams, but a few moments later there was complete silence. Twenty to twenty-five minutes later, the doors and windows were opened to ventilate the rooms.[31]

The corpses of these 638 Slovak Jews, who had been promised an agricultural life in the Lublin area by their president, Monsignor Tiso, were buried in the adjacent meadow. . . .

The four new crematoria came into operation after the Holocaust itself had peaked. The Judeocide had begun in 1941, and the Germans killed some 1.1 million Jews that year. In 1942 they murdered another 2.7 million Jews, of whom approximately 200,000 died in Auschwitz. The year the crematoria of Auschwitz came into operation, the number of victims dropped to 500,000, half of whom were killed in Auschwitz.[32] All the Jews whom the Germans could catch easily had been trapped. By the end of 1943 the Germans closed down the death camps built specifically to exterminate Jews: Kulmhof (150,000 Jews), Sobibor (200,000 Jews), Belzec (550,000 Jews), and Treblinka (750,000 Jews). In these camps there was no selection process; nearly everyone who was shipped in was killed within hours of arrival. In terms of mortality, at the end of 1943 Auschwitz ranked behind Treblinka and Belzec. But it was the only camp that remained to mop up the remnants of the Jewish communities of Poland, Italy, France, the Netherlands, and the rest of occupied Europe.

As the killing wound down, Himmler talked about the task that since January had become his unique contribution to the future Europe. "One basic principle must be absolute for the SS man: we must

---

*German company for the extermination of vermin that oversaw the distribution of Zyklon B, *Ed.*

be honest, decent, loyal, and comradely to members of our own blood and to nobody else," Himmler declared at a meeting of SS leaders in Posen on 4 October 1943. It was now time to mention "a really grave matter" which hitherto had been surrounded by a "tactful" silence. "I am referring to the evacuation of the Jews, the annihilation of the Jewish people," he explained. "Most of you must know what it means to see a hundred corpses lie side by side, or five hundred, or a thousand. To have stuck this out and – excepting cases of human weakness – to have kept our integrity, that is what has made us hard. In our history, this is an unwritten and never-to-be-written page of glory." The liquidation of the Jews had eliminated the possibility of another stab in the back. If "we still had the Jews in every city as secret saboteurs, agitators, and demagogues . . . we probably would have reached the 1916–17 stage by now." It was difficult work, but they had managed. "We have carried out this heaviest of our tasks in a spirit of love for our people. And our inward being, our soul, our character has not suffered injury from it.[33]

With an average of 6,000 arrivals in Auschwitz during January through April 1944, the rate of murder was significantly reduced in comparison with monthly figures in 1943. The Hungarian Jews were the sole remaining major Jewish community in Europe, and the Germans occupied Hungary in March. The labor shortage had become so acute that in early April Hitler instructed Himmler to obtain 100,000 Jewish slave workers from Hungary immediately.[34] Auschwitz was now to acquire its last function which, remarkably, was identical to that which, three decades earlier, had led to the construction of the main camp. It once again was to become a gigantic labor exchange. Hungary's Jews were to be shipped in and slave workers were to be selected and shipped out again to the network of concentration camps in the Reich that served German industry. Those selected for work in Germany were to be kept in quarantine until transport to the west was available.

Jews found unfit for work were to be killed in the crematoria, and in the spring of 1944 the Germans expected that many, if not most, of the arrivals would be of no use to German industry. The crematoria

were overhauled. "Cracks in the brickwork of the ovens were filled with a special fireclay paste," Filip Müller, one of the very few survivors of the early Slovak transports and a *Sonderkommando* worker, recalled. "New grates were fitted in the generators, while the six chimneys underwent a thorough inspection and repair, as did the electric fans. The walls of the four changing rooms and the eight gas chambers were given a fresh coat of paint."[35] Crematoria II and III also got new elevators connecting the gas chamber with the incineration room, and the gas chambers of crematorium V were equipped with a new ventilation system to speed up the extermination process.

Not only were the existing killing and incinerating installations fully repaired; bunker 2, now renumbered bunker 5, was brought back from retirement too. Behind crematorium V the newly appointed manager of the crematoria, Otto Moll, put crews of inmates to work digging two huge cremation pits. "Accompanied by his henchmen, extermination expert Moll paced up and down the large site, giving instructions for the siting of pits, a fuel depot, the spot where the ashes were to be crushed, and all the rest of the devices which he had thought up for the extermination and obliteration of human beings."[36] Müller explained that Moll's most ingenious invention was a channel "to catch the fat exuding from the corpses as they were burning in the pit."[37] Finally, Moll created a store of conifer branches, waste wood, rags, barrels of alcohol, lubricating oil, and chlorinated lime to keep the fires going.[38]

To facilitate the system, the train lines were extended into the camp. "Day and night many hundreds of prisoners were busy laying railway tracks right up to crematoria 2 and 3. On the road between the building sites B1 and B2 the construction of a loading and unloading ramp complete with a three-track railway system was in progress in order to provide a direct link between the death factories, Auschwitz railway station and the outside world."[39]

The first transport of Hungarian Jews, 1,800 people, arrived in Auschwitz on 29 April and pulled over the new spur through the gate into Birkenau. A few weeks later Himmler boasted that "at the moment we are indeed bringing 100,000, and later another 100,000 male Jews from Hungary to concentration camps to build underground factories."[40] By the end of June, in just two months, half of Hungary's Jewry – 381,661 souls – had arrived in Auschwitz. With another 18,000 Jews brought in from other countries during the same period, Auschwitz received a record average of 200,000 deportees per month. One of them was the eighteen-year-old Alexander Ehrmann, who until the spring of 1944 had lived in the town of Kiralyhelmec. His transport pulled into Birkenau at night.

We arrived around one o'clock in the morning in an area with lights, floodlights, and stench. We saw flames, tall chimneys. We still did not want to accept that it was Auschwitz. We preferred to think we didn't know than to acknowledge, yes, we are there. The train stopped. Outside we heard all kinds of noises, stench, language, commands we didn't understand. It was in German but we didn't know what it meant. Dogs barked. The doors flung open, and we saw strange uniformed men in striped clothes. They started to yell at us in the Yiddish of Polish Jews: "*Schnell! Raus!*" We started to ask them, "Where are we?" They answered, "*Raus, raus, raus!*" Sentries and their dogs were there, and they yelled at us also. "*Macht schnell!*"

We got out and they told us to get in formations of five, and to leave all the luggage there. We asked one of the guys, "Tell me, tell me, where are we going?" "*Dort, geht,*" and he pointed towards the flames. We had to move on. So we formed up, true to family tradition, two parents, the oldest sister, and the next sister and the child on my sister's hand. My mother asked her, "Let me carry him," two and a half years old. She said, "No, I'll take care of my own son." So the three sisters and my two parents were walking and the two boys in the next row with three other people. We came up to [Josef] Mengele, we were standing there. He was pointing left, right. My sister was the first one, with a child, and he pointed to the right. Then my mother, who had a rupture, she had a big belly, she looked like she was pregnant, she wasn't. So I guess that made her go to that side. My father and the two sisters

were pointed to his left. He asked my father, "Old man, what do you do?" He said, "Farm work." And then came the next row and the two of us were told also to go after our father and two sisters; and he stopped and he called my father back. "Put out your hand!" So my father showed him his hand and Mengele smacked him across the face and pushed him to the other side. And he continued, "*Schnell!*" And the sentries were there, and the dogs and we have to move, and that's the last we saw of our parents and sister and nephew.

It started to get daylight, and we moved on to an area where there was barbed wire on both sides. We walked down an alley, a sentry so often spaced out. We kept on moving, we were prodded to move faster. We were told, "You will be coming to an area where you will be given a bath and change clothes and you'll be told what to do." We were walking, and beyond the barbed wire fences there were piles of rubble and branches, pine tree branches and rubble burning, slowly burning. We're walking by, and the sentries kept on screaming, "*Lauf! Lauf!*" and I heard a baby crying. The baby was crying somewhere in the distance and I couldn't stop and look. We moved, and it smelled, a horrible stench. I knew that things in the fire were moving, there were babies in the fire.[41]

At no other time in its history was Auschwitz less efficient as a labor exchange. Of the total 438,000 incoming Jews, between 10 and 30 percent were found fit to make their contribution to the German war effort. Most of them were dispatched to Bergen-Belsen, Buchenwald, Dachau, Gross-Rosen, Mauthausen, Neuengamme, Ravensbrück, Sachsenhausen, and 378 other camps in Himmler's empire. Alex Ehrmann and his sixteen-year-old brother were sent to Warsaw, where they were put to work in the ruins of the erstwhile ghetto "tearing down the walls" and "salvaging the bricks."[42]

At no other time was Auschwitz more efficient as a killing center. In May and June the number of people murdered exceeded the official incineration capacity of 132,000 corpses per month. Moll's pits were useful, too. The frenetic gassing and burning continued through July. In two months one-third of the total number of people murdered at Auschwitz were killed, and between one-half and two-thirds of all the 600,000 Jews the Germans killed in 1944. In the thirty-two months that Auschwitz operated as a designated extermination center, from March 1942 to November 1944, between 1 million and 1.1 million people were killed, or an average of 32,000 to 34,000 a month. During the Hungarian action the Germans, with dispatch and efficiency, increased that average five- to sixfold.

In August 1944, as the Hungarian action came to an end and the crematoria stood idle, Sara Grossman-Weil, her husband Menek, her mother- and father-in-law Feigele and Wolf, her brother-in-law Adek, his wife Esther, their adolescent daughter Regina, and their little girl Mirka were herded into a train of cattle cars in Lodz, the last of the hundreds of ghettos the Germans had established to cleanse the German East of Jews.

The ghetto of Lodz, which had been organized in early 1940 as a holding pen for the Nisko project, had survived at the expense of most of its inhabitants as a vast workshop. The German-appointed Eldest of the Jews, Chaim Rumkowski, had developed a policy to make the ghetto indispensible to the German war effort. If work would not set Jews free, it should at least guarantee survival. The Germans agreed, with a caveat: if the ghetto were an enormous workshop, only those who were capable to work could stay. Selections were instituted, and Sara put rouge on her gaunt cheeks to look healthy. "You would try to look straight, not to look sick. You would not bend, because this would suggest that you're not capable of doing the work you're doing. You would walk straight, or as well as you could, to show them that you are fit to remain."[43]

But there were those who could not be saved by all the rouge and posture in the world. In early September 1942 the Germans decreed that those who could not work – children under ten and old people over sixty-five – would have to leave. Forcing Rumkowski, his Jewish Council, and the Jewish ghetto police to share moral responsibility, the Ger-

mans demanded they execute the order. Their families would be exempt. When the decree was made known, it seemed that the nadir of perdition had been reached. "The sky above the ghetto . . . is unclouded," Josef Zelkowicz recorded. "Like yesterday and the day before, the early autumn sun shines. It shines and smiles at our Jewish grief and agony, as though someone were merely stepping on vermin, as though someone had written a death-sentence for bedbugs, a Day of Judgment for rats which must be exterminated and wiped off the face of the earth."[44] Like Josef Zelkowicz and everyone else, Sara witnessed dragnet operations to catch infants, toddlers, and elementary school children. "The children were taken away; thrown, literally thrown, onto the wagon. And when the mother objected, either she was taken with them or shot. Or they tore the child away from her and let her go. And all the children, small children, little ones, five-, six-, four-, seven-year-old ones were thrown, literally thrown, into this wagon. The cries were reaching the sky, but there was no help; there was no one to turn to, to plead your case, to beg."[45] Mirka Grossman was one of the few children to survive the selection.

With the action against the children and the elderly, the two-year death knell of the last Jewish community on Reich territory had begun. It ended on Wednesday, 2 August 1944, when the German mayor of Lodz informed Rumkowski that the ghetto would be resettled, workshop by workshop. "Factory workers will travel with their families," Rumkowski's final proclamation read. Sara Grossman-Weil left with her husband's family. They were herded to the train station and ordered onto the cattle cars. "You couldn't throw a pin in, one was sitting on top of the other, with the bundles. We were in this cattle car, this wagon, and we were riding, riding, riding. There was no end to it. And the little one asked, in Polish, 'Daddy, isn't it better that today it's a bad day, but tomorrow it will be better?' She was five years old. And her father said, 'Today doesn't matter, tomorrow will be much better.' "[46]

Tomorrow proved him wrong. The train with the survivors of the Lodz ghetto passed by Kattowitz and Myslowitz and crossed the Vistula at Neu-Berun. They arrived at the station of Auschwitz. The train turned into a spur and stopped. When the sun began to set, the train backed onto another spur, through a gate, and entered the enormous compound of Birkenau. It came to a halt. The bolted doors were opened. Sara Grossman, her relatives, and the rest of the people on the train were hauled out and told to form two columns, one of men, and one of women and children.

> I was standing there not knowing what's going on, overwhelmed with the amount of people around us, not believing that they threw us all out from these wagons in the manner they did. How they pushed and shoved and screamed. And these SS men with the dogs in front of us. I lost sight of what was going on. It's crazy. And I was standing with my mother-in-law and my sister-in-law with her little girl, when someone approached us, and said, "Give this child to the grandmother." And my sister-in-law gave the child to my mother-in-law. They went to the left, and we went to the right."[47]

Sara and the other women considered fit for work entered the camp. "As we were marching, I saw columns of women marching on the other side in the opposite direction who were half naked, shaven heads, stretching out their arms. 'Food, food. Give me your bread!' Screaming, shouting. I was overwhelmed. I thought that I found myself in an asylum, in a madhouse, in a place with only crazy people." This was the place she had heard about, always in whispers and always with dread. "They always called it Auschwitz, but we didn't know what it meant."[48]

They arrived at the delousing station, were registered, shaved and showered, and handed some rags and wooden shoes.

> From there they gathered us again in columns, in rags like the people whom I had seen an hour ago in the columns marching in the opposite direction. We had the same look, except we weren't shouting. We looked like crazy people, just like the rest of them. We were led to a lavatory, where we had to take care of our needs, and from there we went to a barrack, which was the house where

we would be staying. In this barrack we were given a bunk. The size of the bunk was approximately the size of not quite a twin bed, I would say considerably smaller. And on this bunk bed, five people had to find their sleeping quarters. And this was our new home.[49]

Sara remained in Birkenau for ten days, and then she was brought on another transport to a munitions factory at Unterlüss, eighteen miles northeast of Celle. Most of the inmates were Hungarian women. Sara recalled that sulfur was everywhere, "in the air, and in the bread that you were given as a ration at work, and in your mouth, eyes, hands, fingers; everything turned yellow. I was sick with the smell."[50]

Production at Unterlüss came to an end in March 1945. The satellite camp was closed, and the inmates were sent to Bergen-Belsen, where Sara was put in a barrack with hundreds of other women. "On the outside were hundreds of women dying of thirst, thirst, and thirst again."

> It was a sight that is beyond any description or understanding or imagination. You cannot, because when you see the pictures of the dead bodies, you just see pictures. You don't see the bodies, the eyes that talk to you and beg you for water. You don't see the mouths quietly trying to say something and not being able to utter a word. You see and you feel as I did, the agony of these people for whom death would be a blessing. They are just dying and can't die.[51]

All around the camp were mounds of bodies, and Sara was ordered to move corpses to a large pit.

> These mounds that you see on some of the pictures that are being shown about the Holocaust, they were real people. They were living, breathing, eating, feeling, thinking people, thousands upon thousands of them. Mothers and daughters and children. These pictures are real. And I saw it, I smelled it, I touched them. They were very, very real. This was Bergen-Belsen in March and the beginning of April in 1945.[52]

Sara survived, and was liberated on her birthday, the fifteenth of April.

There were no mounds of corpses in Auschwitz. The crematoria took care of that. "I was standing with my mother-in-law and my sister-in-law with her little girl, when someone approached us, and said, 'Give this child to the grandmother.' And my sister-in-law gave the child to my mother-in-law. They went to the left, and we went to the right. And I said, 'Why?' My mother-in-law took the little one and went to the left."[53] None of the new arrivals knew what "left" meant, and no one who went to the left survived to give testimony. It is from the accounts and reports of the slave or willing workers, and from documents and drawings, that we can follow the route that Feigele and Mirka took. They went to the left, crossed a train track, and came to a road parallel to the rails, running from the gate building at their left to two relatively large buildings at their right. An SS man directed them to the right, toward the two buildings. Another SS man 500 yards down the road told them to turn left, into a compound surrounding one of the two identical brick buildings with their square, squat chimneys. They were not led to the large entrance below the chimney, but walked past the building and then, beyond, along a 70-yard-long terrace. At the end of the paved asphalt they were told to take a sharp turn to the left, and descend a staircase ending at a door leading into a basement.

Today, in 1995, that underground space and a room connected to it at right angles are shallow pits overgrown with grass. In 1944 this place, originally designed as a mortuary, served as the penultimate stage in a process of destruction that had begun with the identification of Feigele and Mirka as Jews, and had continued with their incarceration in the Lodz ghetto, their deportation to Auschwitz, and their selection at the station. Robbed of their home and financial assets in 1939, of most of their other property during the four long years in the ghetto, and of their suitcases at the Auschwitz station, they now were to surrender the last things they owned: the clothes they wore. The basement they entered served as the undressing room.

Very few of the hundreds of thousands of people who entered that basement survived. One of them was Filip Müller. "At the entrance to the basement was a signboard, and written on it in several languages the direction: *To the baths and disinfecting rooms*. The ceiling of the changing room was supported by concrete pillars to which many more notices were fixed, once again with the aim of making the unsuspecting people believe that the imminent process of disinfection was of vital importance for their health. Slogans like *Cleanliness brings freedom* or *One louse may kill you* were intended to hoodwink, as were numbered clothes hooks fixed at a height of 1.50 meters."[54]

Feigele, Mirka, and the other Jews who had survived the Germans' abuse until that point were told to undress, and then herded into a small vestibule. Someone pointed to the right, to the doors of an oblong whitewashed room resembling the one they had just left. But, as Filip Müller knew, there were some important visible, and even more important invisible, differences between the two rooms. "Down the length of the room concrete pillars supported the ceiling. However, not all the pillars served this purpose: for there were others, too. The Zyclon B gas crystals were inserted through openings into hollow pillars made of sheet metal. They were perforated at regular intervals and inside them a spiral ran from top to bottom in order to ensure as even a distribution of the granular crystals as possible. Mounted on the ceiling was a large number of dummy showers made of metal. These were intended to delude the suspicious on entering the gas chamber into believing that they were in a shower-room."[55] Feigele, Mirka, and the others were crammed in, the doors closed, and the lights turned off.

While Feigele and Mirka were driven into the underground room, a van marked with a Red Cross sign parked along its side, which projected 1.5 feet above ground. Two "disinfecting operators" climbed onto the roof of the basement, carrying sealed tins manufactured by the Degesch company. They chatted leisurely, smoking a cigarette. Then, on signal, each of them walked to a one-foot-high concrete shaft, donned a gas mask, took off the lid, opened the tin, and poured the pea-sized contents into the shaft. They closed the lids, took off their masks, and drove off.

Müller witnessed everything from a short distance. "After a while I heard the sound of piercing screams, banging against the door and also moaning and wailing. People began to cough. Their coughing grew worse from minute to minute, a sign that the gas had started to act. Then the clamour began to subside and to change to a many-voiced dull rattle, drowned now and then by coughing."[56] Ten minutes later all was quiet.

An SS man ordered Müller and the rest of the death squad workers to take the elevator down into the basement. There they waited for the ventilating system to extract the gas from the room and, after some twenty minutes, unbolted the doors to the gas chambers. Contrary to Höss's assertion that he had adopted Zyklon B as a killing agent because it offered an easy death, the victims showed the marks of a terrible struggle.

This is where and how Germans killed Feigele, Mirka, and countless other human beings. Within hours of their arrival in Auschwitz nothing of the Jews remained but smoke, ashes, and our memory of them. Their bodies were brought to the ground floor with the same elevator that Müller had used to go down to the basement, and there they were cremated in one of the five incinerators with three muffles each in the center of the crematorium.

Today we know where Feigele and Mirka died: in a town the Germans always called Auschwitz. We know they built the town in 1270, and a Polish king bought it in 1457. We know the town declined under Polish rule. We know it had a modest existence along a major railway line in the nineteenth century. We know the region became the object of German rage in the 1920s. We know the National Socialists annexed the town to the Reich in 1939. We know they intended to repeat the initiatives of the Middle Ages.

Today we know that Feigele and Mirka died in a camp that was originally created as a labor exchange, that then served as a Polish army base, and that the Germans adapted into a concentration camp to terrorize a local population too useful to deport. We know that the camp acquired one function after another: it became a production site for sand and gravel, an execution site for the Gestapo in Kattowitz, the

center of a large agricultural estate to support ethnic German transplantees, a labor pool for constructing a synthetic rubber plant and a new town. We know that, throughout these transformations, Auschwitz remained the centerpiece of Himmler's ambitions in the recovery of German history in this onetime area of German settlement. We know that it became a center of extermination when he lost interest in the town and the region, and that it also served as the heart of a network of satellite camps to service various industries in the region, and that it finally became a labor exchange again, only this time the laborers were Jewish slaves.

Today we know who designed the building: Georg Werkmann, Karl Bischoff, and Walther Dejaco. We know who constructed the furnaces: the Topf & Sons company in Erfurt. We know the power of the forced-air system (over 4 million cubic feet per hour) to fan the flames. We know the official cremation capacity (thirty-two corpses) per muffle per day. We know that it was Bischoff who took the decision to change the larger morgue into an undressing room, and the smaller one into a gas chamber. We know that Dejaco drafted the plan that transformed a mortuary into a death chamber. We know the specifications of the ventilation system that made the room operable as a site for mass extermination: seven horsepower is required to extract the Zyklon B from the gas chamber in twenty minutes. We know that the building was brought into operation on 13 March 1943, when 1,492 women, children, and old people were gassed. We know about the difficulties the Germans had getting everything just the way they wanted. We know who paid the bills and how much was paid.

We know all of that. But we understand very little about many issues central to this machinery of death. Research into the history of the region, the intended future of the town, the development of the camp, and the changing design of the crematoria has been useful, but it is not the whole story about the Holocaust at Auschwitz. It is the questions of the victims and the survivors which loom large.

When Sara Grossmann faced selection upon arrival at Auschwitz in August 1944,

I lost sight of what was going on. It's crazy. And I was standing with my mother-in-law and my sister-in-law with her little girl, when someone approached us, and said, "Give this child to the grandmother." And my sister-in-law gave the child to my mother-in-law. They went to the left, and we went to the right. *And I said, "Why?"* My mother-in-law took the little one and went to the left. Regina, Esther, and I went to the right. To the left were all the people who were led to the gas chambers, crematorium, however you call it.

"Gas chambers, crematorium, however you call it." Half a century later, Sara Grossman was not precise. What mattered was that the men were separated from the women, and that the grandmother Feigele and the little girl Mirka went to the left, and the adolescent Regina, and the two sisters-in-law Esther and Sara to the right. And she is correct. That process of selection is the core and moral nadir of the horror of the Holocaust – the selection, and not the gas chambers and crematoria. The Germans and their allies had arrogated to themselves the power to decide who would live and who would die. "As though," Hannah Arendt accused Eichmann, "you and your superiors had any right to determine who should and who should not inhabit the world."[57]

Mirka, Sara, and hundreds of thousands of other deportees lined up for selection by a physician. Had he worked alone, he could have done little harm. But he did not. His work was but a small part of a system envisioned by ideologues, organized by bureaucrats, financed by industrialists, serviced by technocrats, operated by ordinary men, and supported by millions of Germans whose daily lives were improved by the goods shipped home to the Reich for their use.

And Sara's question remains: "And I said, 'Why?' "

Notes

1. Hitler, *Table Talk*, 87.
2. Ibid., 141.
3. As quoted in Noakes and Pridham, eds., *Nazism, 1919–1945*, 3:1125f.
4. Letter of Pohl to Himmler, December 1941, BAK, coll. NS 19, file 2065; also "Vorschlag für die Aufstellung von SS-Baubrigaden für die Ausführung von Bauaufgaben des Reichsführers-SS im Kriege und Frieden," ibid.
5. Letter of Himmler to Pohl, 31 January 1942, BAK, coll. NS 19, file 2065.
6. Kammler, "Vorschlag für die Aufstellung von SS-Baubrigaden für die Ausführung von Bauaufgaben des Reichsführers-SS im Kriege und Frieden," BAK, coll. NS 19, file 2065, 7ff.
7. Minutes of the Wannsee Conference, as quoted in Lucy S. Dawidowicz, ed., *A Holocaust Reader* (New York: Behrman House, 1976), 74.
8. Ibid., 78.
9. Hitler, *Table Talk*, 235f.
10. As quoted in Martin Broszat, "The Concentration Camps, 1933–45," in Helmut Krausnick, Hans Buchheim, Martin Broszat, and Hans-Adolf Jacobsen, *Anatomy of the SS State*, trans. Richard Barry, Marian Jackson, and Dorothy Long (New York: Walker, 1968), 483.
11. State of Israel, Ministry of Justice, *The Trial of Adolf Eichmann: Record of Proceedings in the District Court of Jerusalem*, 5 vols. (Jerusalem: Trust for the Publication of the Proceedings of the Eichmann Trial, 1993), 4:1424, 1431.
12. Yehuda Bauer, *Jews for Sale? Nazi-Jewish Negotiations, 1933–1945* (New Haven and London: Yale University Press, 1994), 65.
13. As quoted in State of Israel, *The Trial of Adolf Eichmann*, 4:1508.
14. Helen Tichauer-Spitzer, interview with Debórah Dwork and Robert Jan van Pelt, New York, N.Y., 20 April 1995, transcript, 24f.
15. Ibid., 25.
16. Ibid., 26ff.
17. Ibid., 28.
18. See Alfred Konieczny, "Die Zwangsarbeit der Juden in Schlesien im Rahmen der 'Organisation Schmelt,' " in Götz Aly et al., *Sozialpolitik und Judenvernichtung: Gibt es eine Ökonomie der Endlösung?*, Beiträge zur Nationalsozialistischen Gesundheits-und Sozialpolitik, 5 (Berlin: Rotbuch, 1987), 91ff.
19. Pery Broad, "Reminiscences," in Rudolf Höss, Pery Broad, and Johann Paul Kremer, *KL Auschwitz Seen by the SS*, trans. Krystyna Michalik (Warsaw: Interpress Publishers, 1991), 128f.
20. Letter of Bischoff to Topf, 5 March 1942, PMOB, box BW 30/25, 1; see also letter of Bischoff to Wirtz, 30 March 1942, PMOB box BW (B) 30/34, 37. These letters are published in Pressac, *Auschwitz*, 191, 193.
21. Letter of Bischoff to Topf, 22 October 1941, OAM, coll. 502/1, file 313 (USHRI, microfilm RG 11.001M.03, reel 41).
22. Reworked version of plan of Birkenau of 6 January 1942 (no date, but probably produced just after 27 February 1942), OAM, coll. 502/2, file 95. (USHRI, microfilm RG 11.001M.03, reel 63).
23. Czech, *Kalendarium*, 186.
24. Höss, *Death Dealer*, 31.
25. Bauer, *Jews for Sale?*, 66.
26. As quoted in State of Israel, *The Trial of Adolf Eichmann*, 4:1509.
27. Czech, *Kalendarium*, 206.
28. "Aktenvermerk Betr.: Anwesenheit von Obering. Prüfer

der Fa. Topf u. Söhne Erfurt, bezüglich Ausbau der Einäscherungsanlagen im K.G.L. Auschwitz," 21 August 1942, OAM, coll. 502/1, file 313 (USHRI, microfilm RG 11.001M.03, reel 41).

29. Pressac, with van Pelt, "The Machinery of Mass Murder at Auschwitz," 213.

30. Czech, *Kalendarium*, 241ff.

31. As quoted in Noakes and Pridham, eds., *Nazism, 1919–1945*, 3:1180.

32. Hilberg, *Die Vernichtung der europäischen Juden*, 3:1300; Piper, *Die Zahl der Opfer von Auschwitz*, table D (between 144 and 145).

33. Lucy S. Dawidowicz, ed., *A Holocaust Reader* (New York: Behrman House, 1976), 131ff.

34. Speer, *Infiltration*, 289.

35. Filip Müller, *Auschwitz Inferno: The Testimony of a Sonderkommando*, with Helmut Freitag, trans. Susanne Flatauer (London and Henley: Routledge & Kegan Paul, 1979), 124.

36. Ibid., 126.

37. Ibid., 130.

38. Ibid., 132.

39. Ibid., 123f.

40. As quoted in Speer, *Infiltration*, 289.

41. Alexander Ehrmann, interview with Debórah Dwork, West Bloomfield, Mich., 15 November and 13 December 1986 and 24 January 1987, transcript, 34f.

42. Ibid., 37f.

43. Sara Grossman-Weil, interview with Debórah Dwork, Malverne, N.Y., 29 and 30 April 1987, transcript, 22.

44. Josef Zelkowicz, "Days of Nightmare," in Dawidowicz, ed. *A Holocaust Reader*, 301f.

45. Grossman-Weil, transcript, 21; also Dwork, *Children with a Star*, 195f.

46. Grossman-Weil, transcript, 27; also Dwork, *Children with a Star*, 205.

47. Grossman-Weil transcript, 28; Dwork, *Children with a Star*, xixf.

48. Grossman-Weil transcript, 29.

49. Ibid.

50. Ibid., 30.

51. Ibid., 34.

52. Ibid.

53. Ibid., 28; Dwork, *Children with a Star*, xixf.

54. Müller, *Auschwitz Inferno*, 61.

55. Ibid., 60f.

56. Ibid., 115f.

57. Hannah Arendt, *Eichmann in Jerusalem: A Report on the Banality of Evil* (New York: Viking, 1963), 255f.

A group of Hungarian Jews upon their arrival in Birkenau. May 1944. (Yad Vashem Photo Archives, courtesy of USHMM Photo Archives)

Jews in Slovakia boarding enormously long trains to the death camps in Poland. March – October 1942. (Courtesy of Yad Vashem Photo Archives)

A warehouse full of shoes and clothing confiscated from prisoners and deportees gassed upon their arrival at Auschwitz-Birkenau. The Germans shipped these goods to Germany. After January 1945. (Lydia Chagoll, courtesy of USHMM Photo Archives)

Jewish women at forced labor on "Industry Street" in the Plaszow concentration camp in Poland. 1943–1944. (Leopold Page Photographic Collection, courtesy of USHMM Photo Archives)

Yehuda Bauer **Gypsies**

FOR THE NAZIS, Gypsies posed first a social and subsequently an ideological problem. If ever there was an Aryan population, surely it was the Gypsies. Their Indo-European history can be traced to the fifth century, when their clans headed westward from northwest India. According to some researchers, one stop on their migratory journey, a settlement at Gype near Modon in what is now Greece, may have been the source of the term *Gypsy*.[1] European Gypsies now call themselves Roma (humans).

By the fourteenth century, Gypsies had arrived in Western Europe. They did not settle on land, an impossibility for newcomers to feudal Europe, but became itinerant craftsmen and petty traders: tinkers, iron-, silver-, and goldsmiths, horse traders, and so on. As landless wanderers, they were soon marginalized and persecuted in the most brutal fashion. The Central and West European Gypsy tribes who called themselves the Sinti (from the Sindh River, in India) or the Manush (men, humans), were occasional targets of attempts to eliminate them or to kidnap their children to be raised as Christians. Gypsies were frequently subjected to eviction, criminalization, whipping, and forced labor. After the Diet of Freiburg in Germany in 1498, their lives were officially declared to be forfeit.

Over the centuries, anti-Gypsy prejudice in Central Europe and Germany resulted in both legal and illegal discrimination and persecution, partly forcing the Gypsies into a semicriminal existence. Large numbers must have perished in these persecutions between the fifteenth and nineteenth centuries, but others fled in search of relative security.

With the rise of the Third Reich, harassment of Gypsies continued. Gypsies were classified as "asocials." Being asocial was a serious crime in a Nazified society that insisted on regimentation based on settled existences. More important, the Nazis saw their "asocial" behavior as a genetically induced, unchange-able characteristic. They were defined as "parasites" or as "a peculiar form of the human species who are incapable of development and came about by mutation."[2]

These ideological quirks may have reflected practical problems as well. The Gypsy population was small; a report to SS chief Heinrich Himmler in 1941 indicated that there were 28,000 Sinti in Germany and 11,000 in Austria (predominantly of the Lalleri tribe).[3] But they formed, from a bureaucratic point of view, an inefficiently used labor potential; local authorities had to pay for social help, educational facilities, and so forth for the wanderers. Gypsies were accused of petty crimes, reflecting the hostility of the settled German population. An administrative decree of the Prussian Ministry of the Interior in 1936 spoke of the Gypsy "plague" and of the Gypsies as thieves, beggars, and swindlers.[4] A number of racist Nazi authors wrote learned books and articles about the Gypsies and their unassimilability to the German *Volk*.

The solution Nazi ideology found for all these problems was to argue that the Gypsies were no longer "pure" Gypsy Aryans but *Mischlinge*, or mixed-bloods. The definition of who was a Gypsy often ran parallel to the definition of Jews.

In 1936, in the course of a roundup of so-called asocials, about 400 Gypsies were sent to Dachau concentration camp. Until 1938, however, Gypsies could follow their traditional occupations in Germany more or less unhindered, though after 1937 every effort was made to deport Gypsies who were not German subjects or to prevent such people from entering Germany.

A racist ideologue with medical background, Dr. Robert Ritter, was empowered to set up the Research Office for the Science of Inheritance, later the Research Office for Race Hygiene and Population Biology.[5] Ritter was to examine the whole German Gypsy population for its racial characteristics; his findings were to determine Nazi policy. Ritter examined some 20,000 Roma and determined that about 90 percent were Mischlinge. He proposed to separate the Gypsies from the German population, separate the Mischlinge from the "pure" Gypsies, and send the Mischlinge to forced-labor camps, where they would be sterilized. Still, both types of Gypsies were considered "asocial." These ideas were by no means kept secret. Ritter presented them in 1937 at an international population congress in Paris.

A decree by Himmler on December 14, 1937, provided for preventive arrest of people who had not committed any illegal act but were endangering the community by their asocial behavior. The list for administrative enforcement published April 4, 1938, included "vagabonds (Gypsies)" along with beggars and prostitutes. A further Himmler decree (issued later but predated to December 8, 1938) promised to solve the Gypsy question "in accordance with the essence of their race." On March 15, 1939, Himmler declared that while Germany respected other races, a strict separation should be enforced between the "Gypsy plague" and Germans and between half-breeds and "pure" Gypsies. The police would deal with the problem. These measures appear to have been related to the tendency of the SS to put a maximum of new asocial prisoners in its camps, which were being converted to economic enterprises employing slave labor.

Probably 8,000 of the 11,000 Gypsies in Austria were members of the so-called Ungrika (Lalleri) tribe in the Burgenland, the eastern Austrian province bordering on Hungary. They had been living there since the eighteenth century as a settled village proletariat, some of whom were musicians, helpers in hunts, etc. Relations with the Austrian peasants were generally good, because the Gypsies fulfilled an important social function. After the "Anschluss," Gypsy children were forbidden to go to school, and the Gypsies were disenfranchised. In November 1940, the Nazis established a family concentration camp for Gypsies at Lackenbach in the Burgenland. By October 1941, 2,335 people were interned there. In November 1941, two transports of 1,000 Gypsies each arrived in Lodz, where they met the fate of other Gypsies who were deported there. It is likely that most of the 8,000 Burgenland Gypsies were murdered during the war, but we do not have exact figures. Many were deported to Auschwitz in 1943.[6]

On September 21, 1939, in the course of the conquest of Poland, Reinhard Heydrich, chief of the RSHA (Reich Main Security Office), issued orders regarding Jews which also included the provision that 30,000 German Gypsies (along with Poles and Jews from the newly acquired west Polish territories) should be deported to Poland, an edict that would have included most of the Reich's Gypsies. Over time, the policy toward the Roma became more brutal. In the autumn of 1941, 5,007 Austrian Gypsies, largely of the Lalleri tribe, were deported to the Lodz ghetto, then gassed at Chelmno in early 1942.

In April 1941, Ritter and his race hygiene office released their findings on Gypsies. Of the 18,922 Gypsies classified by Ritter, 1,079 were defined as "pure" Gypsies, 6,992 as "more Gypsy than German," 2,976 as half-breeds, 2,992 as more German than Gypsy, 2,231 as uncertain, and 2,652 as "Germans who behaved like Gypsies."[7] Ritter's definitions paralleled those applied to Jews: "A Gypsy is a person who, as a descendant of Gypsies, has at least three purely Gypsy grandparents. Moreover, a Gypsy half-breed is a person who has less than three Gypsies among his grandparents. In addition, a Gypsy half-breed is also a person who has two Gypsy half-breeds among his grandparents." Ritter defined these "half-breeds" as "highly unbalanced, characterless, unpredictable, unreliable, as well as lazy or disturbed and irritable, or in other words disinclined to work and asocial," especially if they carried within themselves "also from the local (i.e., German) side low-grade hereditary qualities."[8]

A year later, in May 1942, Gypsies were put under the same labor and social laws as the Jews.[9] Himmler issued a clarification on October 13, 1942, relating to Gypsy chiefs who would supervise the pure Sinti, for whom a certain freedom of movement would be allowed. According to a document of January 11, 1943, 13,000 Sinti and 1,017 Lalleri would be thus considered.[10]

As for all the other Gypsies, Himmler issued a decree on December 16, 1942, providing for their deportation to Auschwitz, with the exception of socially adapted former Wehrmacht soldiers (all Gypsies were supposed to have been discharged from the army after 1940, but practical implementation did not come on a large scale until 1942–43) and war industry workers in important positions. The RSHA issued an administrative order to implement this decree on January 29, 1943.

Orders regarding Gypsies, especially orders to be executed by organizations such as the Wehrmacht, were not always followed. There is evidence that some Gypsies, or part-Gypsies, were let alone. Others managed to hide their identity, which was easier for Gypsies than for Jews. In addition, the definitions contained in the decree were rather confusing. The order was to apply to "Gypsy Mischlinge, Roma Gypsies, and members of clans of Balkan origins who are not of German blood." This apparently meant that all non-Sinti Gypsies and all Mischlinge in Germany should be deported. Whether the order was to apply to Gypsies outside the official Reich boundaries – in Western Europe, Poland, Yugoslavia, Russia, etc. – was unclear.

Treatment of Gypsies in the various European countries differed considerably. In Bohemia and Moravia, which were part of the Reich, Gypsies shared the fate of the German Gypsies: discrimination, concentration, and annihilation. The number of Gypsies who were not caught in this process remains undetermined.

In Slovakia, which was half-independent, only desultory attempts were made to concentrate some of the wandering Gypsies in forced labor camps. As far as one can tell, Slovakian Gypsies were not deported. Hundreds were brutally murdered in a number of villages during the occupation of Slovakia by German troops after the failure of the Slovak national uprising in October 1944.[11]

For France, there is testimony that some 30,000 were interned under the supervision of the Secretariat for Jewish Affairs of the Vichy government. Many or most of them were later sent to camps, including Dachau, Ravensbrück, and Buchenwald. One estimate claims that 15,150 of them died, while 40,000 appear to have survived in French camps. Five hundred of the 600 Gypsies in Belgium are reported to have died in Polish camps.[12]

The situation in Holland is instructive. After the failure of the local Nazi police to concentrate the Gypsies in late March 1943 as they had been ordered, they received new orders in May to concentrate all "wandering" Gypsies. Because of exceptions, only 1,150 out of 2,700–3,000 wandering Gypsies were affected. Many of them fled in time or sold their wagons and thus were no longer considered wanderers. On May 16, 1944, 565 persons were arrested in their wagons, of whom 245 were deported to Birkenau via the Jewish camp of Westerbork.[13]

Some figures for Croatia, where the local Ustasha movement targeted Gypsies along with Serbs and Jews, report 90,000 Roma victims in local Ustasha murder camps, but another source puts the number at 26,000 (out of 27,000). In Serbia, there is no doubt that Gypsies, along with Jews, were murdered in retaliation for the Serb uprising against the Nazis.[14]

Some Italian Roma were sent to camps in Germany after the German occupation of the country in September 1943, but most escaped. For Hungary, one source claims that 30,000 were sent to German death camps, and only 3,000 returned.[15] While no evidence exists to substantiate that figure, there is evidence that in the last stages of the war, the fascist government of Ferenc Szalasi did try to concentrate and deport Gypsies in some provinces, without much success. The large Gypsy contingent in Romania (at least 280,000) was not attacked en masse, but about 25,000 of them were dumped in Transnistria, according to one source.[16]

In the Baltic States and the Soviet Union, Roma were murdered by some of the Einsatzgruppen, according to their reports. The Wehrmacht Field Police, in a communication of August 25, 1942, stressed the need to ruthlessly "exterminate" bands of wandering Gypsies.[17] In May 1943, Alfred Rosenberg, in charge of the Eastern Territories, suggested that Roma should be concentrated in camps and settlements but not treated the same as Jews. But Himmler would not permit the intrusion of another authority in what he considered to be his own area of competence. His order of November 15, 1943, determined that "sedentary Gypsies and part-Gypsies are to be treated as citizens of the country. Nomadic Gypsies and part-Gypsies are to be placed on the same level as Jews and placed in concentration camps. The police commanders will decide in cases of doubt who is a Gypsy."[18]

While the order applied only to the occupied Soviet areas, it seems to indicate a trend of thinking among top-level Nazi officials. Some sedentary Roma were drafted into labor brigades or sent to concentration camps, but the same fate befell other Soviet citizens as well [Donald] Kenrick estimates the number of Roma murdered in the USSR at about 35,000. That excludes Gypsies who were murdered by the Einsatzgruppen, especially in the south (Einsatzgruppe D under Otto Ohlendorf, who stated in his postwar trial that his group murdered tens of thousands of Gypsies). As far as we know, only a few Soviet Gypsies were sent to Auschwitz.[19]

There is information about Roma being sent to Jewish ghettos but kept separate from the Jews. We do not know whether they were sedentary or not, nor what their numbers were; nor do we know anything about their lives while in the ghettos. In most cases, we also have no information about their ultimate fate. They apparently constituted a small percentage of Polish Gypsies. It is possible that they were the wandering Gypsies Himmler referred to in the case of the USSR.[20]

Himmler's order regarding the USSR and the possibility that a similar policy might have been followed elsewhere contradict the other Himmler policy of allowing the "pure" Gypsies a wandering existence of sorts within the Reich confines. This latter policy, however, was challenged by Martin Bormann, Hitler's secretary, who was appalled at the possibility that wandering Gypsies would continue to be part of the German landscape. It seems that the problem was not discussed further and that the whole Gypsy "problem" was for Himmler and most other Nazis only a minor irritant. Since Nazis often solved minor social irritants by murder, this is apparently what happened to many of the Gypsies.

If this analysis is correct, a picture emerges of the Nazi policy toward the Gypsies. An originally Aryan population, so the policy went, had been spoiled by admixture of non-Gypsy blood and had therefore acquired hereditary asocial characteristics. In the Reich, their asocial behavior constituted a problem to be solved by police means, sterilization, and murder, primarily of those defined as half-breeds. What would happen to the "pure" minority was a matter for further discussion. In the territories controlled by the Reich, wandering Gypsies constituted an irritant that would be often removed by murder. Sedentary Gypsies, by and large, were not important enough to bother about. Gypsies caught by police would be shipped to concentration camps.

As German power declined, there was a tendency to utilize Gypsy manpower for military means, and some Gypsies interned in camps were used for this purpose, just as Nazi policy dictated the same use for German criminals interned in camps. How was this policy implemented in Auschwitz?

There is no evidence that Roma were sent to the Auschwitz concentration camp complex (or the gassing establishment at Auschwitz-Birkenau) before 1943. In the agreement signed on September 18, 1942, between Himmler and Nazi Justice Minister Otto Thierack, Gypsies were included among those groups whose members, if sentenced by regular German courts, were to be handed over to the SS for "annihilation through labor"; they appeared in third place, after security cases and Jews.[21] But during the remainder of 1942, this agreement apparently did not lead to any large-scale deportations to Auschwitz.

The Auschwitz *Kalendarium*[22] contains a notation for July 1942 that the total of those who had been killed in the camp was 4,124, of whom one was a Gypsy. On December 7, 1942, two Czech Gypsies escaped; one, Ignatz Mrnka of Banova, was recaptured on January 12, 1943, and the other, Franz Denhel, apparently managed to hide. Both had arrived at Auschwitz in a transport of 59 males from Bohemia, and it is unclear whether the others were Gypsies. The two escapees apparently had been marked as "asocials" by the SS because they were Gypsies. On April 7, a Polish woman, Stefania Ciuron, a Gypsy who had been sent to Auschwitz on February 12, fled from the camp and was apparently never caught.[23]

On January 29, 1943, an RSHA decree ordered the deportation of German Gypsies to Auschwitz. It is unclear whether this decree abolished the former provision by Himmler to preserve the racially "pure" Sinti and Roma of Germany. The general impression remains of a lack of clarity in Nazi thinking regarding the Gypsy "problem."

On February 26, 1943, the first transport of German Gypsies arrived in Auschwitz, containing a few families. They were placed in Birkenau IIe, a section of the Birkenau extension of Auschwitz that was to become the Gypsy family camp but which at that stage had not been completed. A second transport arrived on March 1. These two were followed by transports on March 3 and 5 (two transports). In these four transports, 828 Sinti and Roma from Germany were included, 391 males and 437 females.[24]

The major transports of Gypsies arrived in Auschwitz between March and May 1943, but smaller groups and a couple of larger ones were sent intermittently in the autumn of 1943 and until May 1944. Smaller groups and individuals were sent to Auschwitz in between these dates. One last group (18 persons from Vitebsk in Russia) arrived on June 17, 1944.

According to the *Kalendarium*, the larger groups consisted of 32 transports from Germany, four from what the *Kalendarium* calls Czechoslovakia, three from Poland (among them, on May 12, 1943, a transport with 971 persons), one from Germany and Hungary, one from Yugoslavia (on December 2, with 77 persons), and three mixed transports (on March 7 from Germany, Yugoslavia, Poland, and Czechoslovakia; on March 17 from Germany, Czechoslovakia, and Poland; and on January 17, 1944, from France, Belgium, Holland, Germany, and Norway). With no evidence that any Roma were deported from Slovakia to Auschwitz, it would seem that when Czechoslovakia is mentioned, Bohemia and Moravia are meant. These areas were under a German protectorate and were considered by the Nazis as part of the Reich.[25]

The great majority of the Roma sent to Auschwitz – 13,080, according to one source[26] – were Sinti from Germany and Lalleri and others from Austria and the Protectorate. Numbers from each of the other countries were small, with the exception of one large transport from Poland. There is no indication how or why these Gypsies were arrested or whether there was a policy of seeking them out, and if so, why this policy did not succeed or was not executed energetically. While a large proportion of the Gypsy pop-

ulation of the extended Reich was sent to Auschwitz, only very small numbers of Gypsies from the rest of Europe were affected. On the other hand, that these small numbers were included seems to indicate a trend toward an emerging policy on all Gypsies.

Almost all the Roma were interned in the BIIe Gypsy family camp at Birkenau. Writings on the subject do not explain why the Nazis treated the Gypsies differently from other arrestees, who were not housed in family camps, with the exception of the Theresienstadt Jewish family camp. As to the Theresienstadt Jews, there is sufficient documentary evidence that Nazis considered a possible Red Cross visit to Auschwitz in their decisionmaking. As far as the Roma are concerned, such considerations played no part. No documentary evidence is available to help solve the question.

But it would be a mistake to assume that the Gypsy family camp was unaffected by "normal" procedures at Auschwitz. On March 22, 1943, 1,700 Roma men, women, and children who had arrived in transports in the previous few weeks but had not been registered because of illness (mainly typhoid) were murdered by gassing. A second mass gassing of Roma occurred on May 25, 1943, when 1,035 persons were murdered; they were ill, mostly with typhoid.

Others continued to be kept in the family camp. Perhaps this policy was adopted due to a lack of clarity among Nazi bureaucrats about the Roma. They were obviously viewed as hereditary asocials, yet hesitation about them continued. By the end of 1943, 18,736 Roma had been interned in the BIIe camp, of whom at least 2,735 were later murdered by gassing.

Danuta Czech argues in the *Kalendarium*[27] that Himmler decided on the liquidation of the Gypsy family camp during his visit to Auschwitz in the summer of 1943, a visit that ended with the removal of Rudolf Höss as camp commandant. However, the first major attempt at liquidating the family camp did not occur until May 1944, or about nine months later. If Himmler said something about the Gypsies in the summer of 1943, it was not followed through on.

A number of Roma were among the individuals held at Auschwitz who tried, usually unsuccessfully, to escape. No known attempt has been made to find and interview individuals who did manage to escape.

In the spring of 1944, a number of Roma in Auschwitz were sent elsewhere. Thus on April 15, 1,357 men and women were sent to Buchenwald and Ravensbrück (the women's camp). Others were transferred to the main labor camps.

Accommodations in the Gypsy camp were in long, primitive wooden barracks, each of which had a smokestack at either end. Between the smokestacks, running the whole length of the barrack, was a thick pipe, which also served as a kind of table. On both sides of the pipe stood three-tiered wooden beds, on each of which a Gypsy family was accommodated. The inmates separated the beds with blankets which they had brought with them.

We know little about the internal organization of the Gypsy camp, but apparently the inmates organized in accordance with Roma custom in clans and families, trying to keep their culture intact as much as possible. SS attempts to make the Gypsies adjust to German order met with little success, and the Germans desisted from trying to turn the families into ordinary Auschwitz camp "material." The Gypsies played music and had circuslike performances, despite the hunger, disease, and deprivation. Under the deplorable unhygienic conditions, a rare sickness prevailed – noma – whose symptoms are somewhat akin to leprosy. The main sufferers were children and the aged.

On May 15, 1944, for unknown reasons, the camp command decided to murder the remaining 6,000 Roma in BIIe. The German commander of the family camp, Georg Bonigut, apparently disagreed with the decision and informed some of his Roma acquaintances of the fate that was awaiting them. On May 16, the SS surrounded the camp, intending to lead the inmates to the gas chambers. They were met by Roma armed with knives, iron pipes, and the like, and it was clear that there would be a fight. The Germans retreated, and the liquidation was temporarily postponed. On other occasions, when they met with organized resistance, the SS never hesitated to use brute force. Clearly, the weapons in the hands of the inmates did not pose any major threat to the well-armed Germans. Yet they desisted, perhaps owing to the general uncertainty and hesitancy surrounding the whole Gypsy "problem."[28]

On May 25, the SS separated out 1,500 Roma for work, and removed them from the family camp. On August 2, 1,408 more men and women were selected for work, and most of the remaining Gypsy men, women, and children were gassed.

Only a few Roma were housed in Auschwitz after that. Camp records show that on September 9, 1944, one Roma was sent from Auschwitz to Buchenwald. On October 5, 1,188 Gypsy inmates were transferred to Auschwitz from Buchenwald, apparently persons who were physically exhausted and destined to be killed. Most likely, all were gassed.

It appears that 2,735 Gypsies were murdered at Auschwitz in March and May 1943; 2,897 on August 2, 1944; and 800 probably on October 5, for a total of 6,432, out of 20,946 Gypsies registered in the two main books (Hauptbücher) covering the Gypsies that were found in Auschwitz after liberation. Subtracting the number gassed and those transferred elsewhere (probably at least 4,000) from the total registered, some 10,000 Gypsies remain unaccounted for. The most likely explanation is that illness, deprivation, and individual or small-scale acts of murder caused their demise. This supposition appears to be borne out by the few Gypsy postwar testimonies. The number of survivors, those transferred out of Auschwitz and alive at the war's end, is unknown.

An additional question arises: What happened to the German and Austrian Gypsies who were not deported to Auschwitz? According to Ritter's figures, there were 25,955 German Sinti Gypsies (not including 2,652 Germans "behaving like Gypsies"), and the number of Austrian Gypsies was estimated at 11,000, for a total of some 37,000. With 2,500 of these Gypsies deported to Poland in 1938–40 and 3,000 interned in Austrian camps (most all of whom were eventually killed), 5,000 sent to Lodz and gassed at Chelmno, and 13,000 deported to Auschwitz and killed there, we derive a total of up to 23,500 German and Austrian Gypsies killed. That would leave 13,500 unaccounted for. They may be the 14,017 Sinti and Lallcri defined by Himmler as pure or nearly pure Gypsies who would be spared.

As the war drew to its close and the German military situation became more and more desperate, the Nazis used some of the concentration camp inmates, as well as German criminal prisoners and Gypsies, as cannon fodder. According to one testimony, some 4,000 Gypsies were recruited into the Wehrmacht in these last stages. Only 700 survived.[29] One must regard this testimony with great caution until more documentary evidence emerges.

The murder of Gypsies in Auschwitz must be viewed from two perspectives: the fate that the Nazis prepared for the Gypsies generally and the fate of the Gypsies in the framework of Auschwitz.

While clear parallels existed with the plight of the Jews, it is precisely these parallels that also point to the major differences between the fate of the two groups. The Gypsies were defined in much the same way as the Jews were, but for opposite purposes, at least in theory. The "pure" Gypsies were, initially, to be spared as a separate, originally Aryan group, while the Mischlinge were destined for extermination. In the case of the Jews, all were to be murdered, except some grades of Mischlinge, who were to be sterilized or even let alone. There was logic in this, from a National Socialist ideological point of view, as the Jewish "race" had to be completely eliminated but not the "pure" Aryan Gypsies.

But Nazi thinking about the Gypsy problem was hopelessly muddled. "Pure" as well as Mischlinge Gypsies in Germany were considered genetically "asocial." Ritter and others argued in favor of their sterilization. The Nazis' Gypsy "problem" thus had both racial and social aspects. In the case of the wandering Gypsies, there was the additional irritant of old prejudices and practical considerations of administrators and soldiers who did not like groups of wanderers threatening their communications. To them, differentiations between racially pure and less pure wanderers must have been unimportant. In a social-psychological environment such as that, irritations were solved by murder. When wanderers were encountered, they were often annihilated; settled Gypsies were not disturbed. Nazis also differentiated between Gypsies in Germany and those elsewhere, because Gypsies in the occupied countries, especially in the East, did not pose a "racial" danger to Germans.

The second perspective is that of the fate of the Gypsies in Auschwitz. Only a minority of German,

Austrian, and Czech Gypsies and a tiny minority of non-German Gypsies were sent to Auschwitz, but their fate became a symbol for the general fate of the Gypsies. That the Germans kept the Gypsies alive in family groups for almost a year and a half without separating men from women indicates that no decision as to their fate had been made when they were sent to the camp. If there had been a plan to murder them, it would not have taken the SS that long to do so.

Yet, while the fate of the Gypsies at camp BIIe hung in the balance, they were treated just as badly as the other prisoners, and in some ways worse. There were very few privileged Gypsies. Most suffered from the terrible deprivation, hunger, disease, and humiliation. Evidence shows that in camps such as Ravensbrück, Gypsies were also subjects of medical experiments. An unknown number of men and women were sterilized. In Auschwitz, Dr. Josef Mengele conducted his notorious experiments on Gypsies as well as Jews. All or most of the Gypsy twins used in his experiments were killed, whereas at least some Jewish twins survived. Dr. Carl Clauberg's medical experiments at Auschwitz involved Gypsy women.

While Jews were the lowest group in Auschwitz, Gypsies were a very close second. Relations between the two groups varied. Jewish prisoner doctors and nurses in the Gypsy camp made some personal contacts. On the whole, however, the Gypsies were mainly separated in their camps and regarded every Gadja (non-Gypsy) with suspicion and hostility, and there were occasional clashes, induced by the horrible camp conditions.

One of the few Gypsy testimonies may provide insight into the psychology of the Gypsies at Auschwitz. The published interview, with an unnamed Sintitsa (a Sinti woman), was unedited, and so it retains the German slang used by the woman.[30]

"So, we were then living up there at Lehnerz with my parents," the woman said. "I was married, my sister was married, my brother, he was 15, not quite 16 and Mrs. Wagner's little one was 13 and they worked [in a factory]." The two boys were arrested but escaped from prison, and the police came and rearrested the brother, beating him up in front of his weeping mother. Then "they" came and arrested the mother and the witness's sister, with her eight month-old baby. The witness hid but was found and arrested for resistance to authority, "because I prevented them from beating up the boy. I did not resist. It was forbidden to move, in those days. We were forbidden to move, only to the workplace and back home, not to the left, not to the right, no pub, we could not enter anywhere, we had to sign our names to that."

The witness was deported to Auschwitz in the early spring of 1943 and received the number Z-3890. She was put into the women's camp, along with her mother and sister. She had blood in her lungs and was put into the hospital, "which was worse than a stable. The lice crawled all over our faces; I have never seen so many lice. In the blankets with which we had to cover ourselves they were as thick as nuts. I suddenly saw that my mother had come; they brought my mother, too. She wasn't there long; she died. She cried for water. I couldn't give her any; I was forbidden to get near the water. My mother then lay in my bed with me; they brought her to me, [she had] high fever, and then my mother died."

Her brothers, her father, her husband, and her three children – aged ten, eight, and six – were in the family camp. Another Gypsy woman suggested to her that she should volunteer to be a nurse in the family camp, where the woman prisoner-doctor was a Gypsy, too. Though she could hardly stand on her feet, the witness asked the other woman to help her get the job. She managed somehow to pass the examination by an SS doctor and became a nurse. When she was taken to the family camp, she saw her father.

> So I asked where the children were. So he said, they are in block 30. I can't forget that. And he asked about my mother, and so I said she was dead. And I asked for the children, for my brothers and so on, and he didn't know, they were not with him. And the SS came and tore me away from my father and brought me to the block . . . and so I worked with the camp doctors, they were prisoners, too, Jews. And they were good to us, yes, they helped us a lot.

> And so I was in there for a day, not quite, I went out again and went to the block where my chil-

dren were. They were only skin and bone, unrecognizable. They lay there, one can say, already dying. And so I said to my father, bring the children to the sick bay, bring the children in, I said, I will see what I can do. Had they come in there earlier, it might have made a difference. And so my father brought in the eldest the next day, she was ten. And when I saw her, she could not speak a word anymore. She only lay there, her eyes open, and not a word. Could only lie there, was more dead than . . . only breathed. So I spoke to her, [she did not speak] a word, then she died. They simply threw her there, with the other corpses. My own child.

And so one after the other. The one, she was six, was already dead when I came there. I did not see her anymore. Not long after, the other one died too. They were only skin and bones. Skin and bones, nothing else, one could count the ribs. The eyes so deep in the head. The children were dead, all three.

My father came into the sick bay, also died. Two uncles were in there, a cousin; and one of the uncles with all his family, and Mrs. Wagner, she had nine children, seven of them died in there. Seven, they came to me, I saw it myself. One of them was my sister-in-law, she was married to my brother. And then my father was dead, and I was just skin and bones, I could hardly stand. I only prayed that I should die, I could hardly live anymore. And if I had not had my strong religion, I would have killed myself. I am being honest. But I couldn't. Well, so I recovered a bit through the other women who spoke to me, "you have still siblings who need you," and so on.

In reading testimonies, it becomes clear that the fate of individual Roma deported to Auschwitz paralleled that of the Jews. However, it was not the same. There were no young Jewish children in the camp, with a few exceptions, as they and a large proportion of the women and the elderly were murdered upon arrival. The Gypsies saw their helpless family members die in the family camp one by one, from hunger and disease. Others were mutilated by sterilization or tortured in medical experiments.

The fate of the Gypsies in Auschwitz and elsewhere has been little reported, and the reports have often been stereotyped. Most researchers note that lack of information can be attributed to the suspicion and distrust with which the Gypsies, based on their collective experience, view the Gadja. Gypsies also would have had difficulty discussing aspects of their experience, since some of the basic taboos in Gypsy culture were violated at Auschwitz and elsewhere regarding standards of cleanliness and sexual contact. The sterilizations performed on many Gypsies were part of this violation. Most Gypsies could not relate their stories involving these tortures; as a result, most kept silent and thus increased the effects of the massive trauma they had undergone. In addition, very few Gypsies became members of the intellectual community, in Germany or elsewhere, so that too few from among their own number sought information about what happened to them. Even today, most of the research done on the fate of Gypsies is the work of non-Gypsies, especially Jews.

Notes

1. Rüdiger Vossen, ed., *Zigeuner* (Frankfurt am Main, 1983), 22–23.
2. Dr. Robert Ritter, quoted in Joachim Hohmann, "Der Völkermord an Zigeunern," lecture delivered at the Paris conference "La Politique Nazis d'Extermination," 3.
3. Statistics here closely follow my article "Jews, Gypsies and Slavs," in *UNESCO Yearbook on Peace and Conflict Studies* (Paris, 1985), esp. 81–86, and the literature cited therein.
4. Ibid., 5.
5. "Rassenhygienische und bevölkerungsbiologische Forschungssstätte," *Gesellschaft für bedrohte Völker* (Göttingen-Vienna, 1981).
6. Claudia Mayerhofer, *Dorfzigeuner* (Vienna, 1987); Erika Thurner, *Nationalsozialismus und Zigeuner in Österreich* (Vienna-Salzburg, 1983).
7. Cf. Tilman Zülch, ed., *In Auschwitz vergast, bis heute verfolgt* (Hamburg, 1979), 67.
8. Hohmann lecture, 17, quoting the Informationsdienst des Rassenpolitischen Amtes der NSDAP, April 20, 1941.
9. Ibid., 23. quoting the Informationsdienst des Rassenpolitischen Amtes der NSDAP, May 20, 1942.
10. Ibid., 85–86.
11. Ctibor Necas, *Nad osudem céskych a slovenskych Cikánu v letech 1939–1945* (Brno, 1981).
12. Donald Kenrick and Grattan Puxon, *The Destiny of Europe's Gypsies* (London, 1972), 103–7; Vossen, 85; Sybil Milton,

"Occupation Policy in Belgium and France," in Michael Berenbaum, ed., *A Mosaic of Victims: Non-Jews Persecuted and Murdered by the Nazis* (New York, 1990), 80–87.
13. Michael Zimmermann, *Verfolgt, vertrieben, vernichtet* (Essen, 1989), 62–63.
14. Menachem Shelah, "Genocide in Satellite Croatia during the Second World War," in Berenbaum, 20–36; Christopher R. Browning, "Germans and Serbs: The Emergence of Nazi Antipartisan Policies in 1941," in ibid., 64–73.
15. Kenrick and Puxon, 125–27; Joachim S. Hohmann, *Geschichte der Zigeunerverfolgung in Deutschland* (Frankfurt, 1988), 171–72. Hohmann states that there were 275,000 Gypsies in Hungary and Hungarian Transylvania and that there was a sterilization program in place in Hungary starting in 1942. The evidence is not convincing.
16. Kenrick and Puxon, 128–30; Hohmann, *Geschichte*, 171.
17. Kenrick and Puxon, 146–50.
18. Ibid., 150. Hohmann. *Geschichte*, 172, claims that East European Gypsies were included in the genocide wholesale, with the deportation eastward of the German Gypsies. I can find no proof of this.
19. Kenrick and Puxon, 149.
20. Jerzy Ficowski, a Polish writer who has tried to trace the fate of the Polish Gypsies, tells us that most of them fell victim to mass murders outside the concentration camps, committed by the Feldgendarmerie, the Gestapo, the SS, and Ukrainian fascists (Ficowski, "Die Vernichtung," in Zülch, 91–112). This is a rather inexact description. Gypsies brought into the Warsaw ghetto were murdered at Treblinka, but we have no list of ghettos in which Gypsies lived alongside Jews (with the exception of Lodz). Interestingly, Ficowski says (93) that in Volhynia, formerly in eastern Poland, where there was a Ukrainian majority, "only" Polish Gypsies were murdered (some 3,000–4,000); Ukrainian Gypsies were left alone. Small groups of Gypsies were brought to Majdanek and to the extermination camp of Belzec (a group of 20 persons is mentioned). The upshot is, according to Ficowski, that of the 18,000–20,000 Gypsies living in prewar Poland, only 5,000–6,000 survived. Ficowski's claim is, it seems, not conclusive, as there are many more Gypsies in Poland today than there would be if only 5,000–6,000 had survived the war. Cf. Jerzy Ficowski, "The Fate of the Polish Gypsies," in Jack N. Porter, ed., *Genocide and Human Rights* (Washington, D.C., 1982,) 166–77.
21. PS-654, Nuremberg Trial Documents. In the future, Gypsies and others who had transgressed would be handed over not to the courts but to the SS directly.
22. Danuta Czech, ed., *Kalendarium der Ereignisse im Konzentrationslager Auschwitz Birkenau 1939–1945* (Hamburg, 1989), 263. The material on which the *Kalendarium* was based includes lists prepared at the behest of the Nazis, lists and reports illegally copied by inmate clerks and preserved, documents abandoned when the Nazis retreated from Auschwitz in January 1945, and other materials, including testimonies of survivors. See the editor's introduction, 7–14.
23. Ibid., 354.
24. Ibid., 423, 426, 429, 432, 433.
25. Ibid., passim. On May 12, 1944, 39 children arrived from the Catholic children's institution of St. Josefspflege at Mulfingen, despite efforts of the sisters there to prevent the

tragedy. The children had been examined by Eva Justin, Ritter's aide, who first gained the children's trust, then registered and checked them, then caused them to be deported to Auschwitz. Justin died a respected German academic. Cf., Johannes Meister, "Die Zigeunerkinder von der St. Josefspflege in Mulfingen," in *Zeitschrift für Sozialgeschichte des 20 und 21 Jahrhunderts* 2, no. 2 (April 1987).

26. Zulch, 315.
27. Czech, 374–75.

28. Ibid., 774–75.
29. Testimony of Julius Hadosi, in Anita Geigges and Bernhard W. Witte, *Zigeuner Heute* (Bernheim, 1979), 276; see also Kenrick and Puxon, 162–65.
30. The testimony was published by Roland Schopf in Joachim S. Hohmann and Ronald Schopf *Zigeunerleben* (Darmstadt, 1980), 125–41. The interviewer was Eva Maria Parusel, and the testimony was included in a paper written in Fulda in 1976.

Women in the barracks of the newly liberated Auschwitz-Birkenau concentration camp. After January 27, 1945. (National Archives, courtesy of USHMM Photo Archives)

American soldiers walk past rows of corpses removed from the barracks in the Nordhausen concentration camp in Germany. April 11–15, 1945. (Donald S. Robinson, courtesy of USHMM Photo Archives)

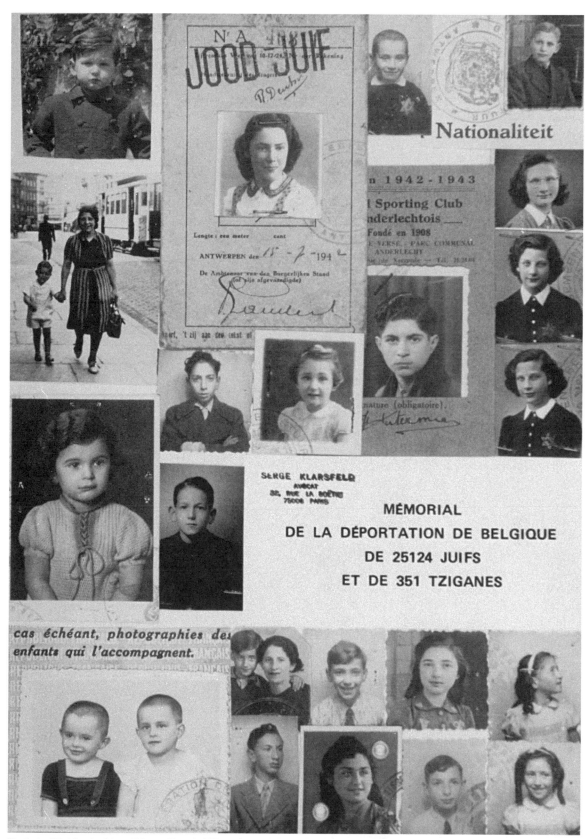

Montage of Belgian Jewish and Roma (Gypsy) children who were deported and killed. 1940–1943. (Serge Klarsfeld, courtesy of USHMM Photo Archives)

Primo Levi **On the Bottom**

THE JOURNEY DID NOT LAST more than twenty minutes. Then the lorry stopped, and we saw a large door, and above it a sign, brightly illuminated (its memory still strikes me in my dreams): *Arbeit Macht Frei*, work gives freedom.

We climb down, they make us enter an enormous empty room that is poorly heated. We have a terrible thirst. The weak gurgle of the water in the radiators makes us ferocious; we have had nothing to drink for four days. But there is also a tap – and above it a card which says that it is forbidden to drink as the water is dirty. Nonsense. It seems obvious that the card is a joke, 'they' know that we are dying of thirst and they put us in a room, and there is a tap, and *Wassertrinken Verboten*. I drink and I incite my companions to do likewise, but I have to spit it out, the water is tepid and sweetish, with the smell of a swamp.

This is hell. Today, in our times, hell must be like this. A huge, empty room: we are tired, standing on our feet, with a tap which drips while we cannot drink the water, and we wait for something which will certainly be terrible, and nothing happens and nothing continues to happen. What can one think about? One cannot think any more, it is like being already dead. Someone sits down on the ground. The time passes drop by drop.

We are not dead. The door is opened and an SS man enters, smoking. He looks at us slowly and asks, "*Wer kann Deutsch?*" One of us whom I have never seen, named Flesch, moves forward; he will be our interpreter. The SS man makes a long calm speech; the interpreter translates. We have to form rows of five, with intervals of two yards between man and man; then we have to undress and make a bundle of the clothes in a special manner, the woollen garments on one side, all the rest on the other; we must take off our shoes but pay great attention that they are not stolen.

Stolen by whom? Why should our shoes be stolen? And what about our documents, the few things we have in our pockets, our watches? We all look at the interpreter, and the interpreter asks the German, and the German smokes and looks him through and through as if he were transparent, as if no one had spoken.

I had never seen old men naked. Mr Bergmann wore a truss and asked the interpreter if he should take it off, and the interpreter hesitated. But the German understood and spoke seriously to the interpreter pointing to someone. We saw the interpreter swallow and then he said: "The officer says, take off the truss, and you will be given that of Mr Coen." One could see the words coming bitterly out of Flesch's mouth; this was the German manner of laughing.

Now another German comes and tells us to put the shoes in a certain corner, and we put them there, because now it is all over and we feel outside this world and the only thing is to obey. Someone comes with a broom and sweeps away all the shoes, outside the door in a heap. He is crazy, he is mixing them all together, ninety-six pairs, they will be all unmatched. The outside door opens, a freezing wind enters and we are naked and cover ourselves up with our arms. The wind blows and slams the door; the German re-opens it and stands watching with interest how we writhe to hide from the wind, one behind the other. Then he leaves and closes it.

Now the second act begins. Four men with razors, soap-brushes and clippers burst in; they have trousers and jackets with stripes, with a number sewn on the front; perhaps they are the same sort as those others of this evening (this evening or yesterday evening?); but these are robust and flourishing. We ask many questions but they catch hold of us and in a moment we find ourselves shaved and sheared. What comic faces we have without hair! The four speak a language which does not seem of this world. It is certainly not German, for I understand a little German.

Finally another door is opened: here we are, locked in, naked, sheared and standing, with our feet in water – it is a shower-room. We are alone. Slowly the astonishment dissolves, and we speak, and everyone asks questions and no one answers. If we are naked in a shower-room, it means that we will have a shower. If we have a shower it is because they are not going to kill us yet. But why then do they keep us standing, and give us nothing to drink, while nobody explains anything, and we have no shoes or clothes, but we are all naked with our feet in the water, and we have been traveling five days and cannot even sit down.

And our women?

Mr. Levi asks me if I think that our women are like us at this moment, and where they are, and if we will be able to see them again. I say yes, because he is married and has a daughter; certainly we will see them again. But by now my belief is that all this is a game to mock and sneer at us. Clearly they will kill us, whoever thinks he is going to live is mad, it means that he has swallowed the bait, but I have not; I have understood that it will soon all be over, perhaps in this same room, when they get bored of seeing us naked, dancing from foot to foot and trying every now and again to sit down on the floor. But there are two inches of cold water and we cannot sit down.

We walk up and down without sense, and we talk, everybody talks to everybody else, we make a great noise. The door opens, and a German enters; it is the officer of before. He speaks briefly, the interpreter translates. "The officer says you must be quiet, because this is not a rabbinical school." One sees the words which are not his, the bad words, twist his mouth as they come out, as if he was spitting out a foul taste. We beg him to ask what we are waiting for, how long we will stay here, about our women, everything; but he says no, that he does not want to ask. This Flesch, who is most unwilling to translate into Italian the hard cold German phrases and refuses to turn into German our questions because he knows that it is useless, is a German Jew of about fifty, who has a large scar on his face from a wound received fighting the Italians on the Piave. He is a closed, taciturn man, for whom I feel an instinctive respect as I feel that he has begun to suffer before us.

The German goes and we remain silent, although we are a little ashamed of our silence. It is still night and we wonder if the day will ever come. The door opens again, and someone else dressed in stripes comes in. He is different from the others, older, with glasses, a more civilized face, and much less robust. He speaks to us in Italian.

By now we are tired of being amazed. We seem to be watching some mad play, one of those plays in which the witches, the Holy Spirit and the devil appear. He speaks Italian badly, with a strong foreign accent. He makes a long speech, is very polite, and tries to reply to all our questions.

We are at Monowitz, near Auschwitz, in Upper Silesia, a region inhabited by both Poles and Germans. This camp is a work-camp, in German one says *Arbeitslager*; all the prisoners (there are about ten thousand) work in a factory which produces a type of rubber called Buna, so that the camp itself is called Buna.

We will be given shoes and clothes – no, not our own – other shoes, other clothes, like his. We are naked now because we are waiting for the shower and the disinfection, which will take place immediately after the reveille, because one cannot enter the camp without being disinfected.

Certainly there will be work to do, everyone must work here. But there is work and work: he, for example, acts as doctor. He is a Hungarian doctor who studied in Italy and he is the dentist of the Lager. He has been in the Lager for four and a half years (not in this one: Buna has only been open for a year and a half), but we can see that he is still quite well, not very thin. Why is he in the Lager? Is he Jewish like us? "No," he says simply, "I am a criminal."

We ask him many questions. He laughs, replies to some and not to others, and it is clear that he avoids certain subjects. He does not speak of the women: he says they are well, that we will see them again soon, but he does not say how or where. Instead he tells us other things, strange and crazy things, perhaps he too is playing with us. Perhaps he is mad – one goes mad in the Lager. He says that every Sunday there are concerts and football matches. He says that whoever boxes well can become cook. He says that whoever works well receives prize coupons with which to buy tobacco and soap. He says that the water is really not drinkable, and that instead a coffee substitute is distributed every day, but generally nobody drinks it as the soup itself is sufficiently watery to quench thirst. We beg him to find us something to drink, but he says he cannot, that he has come to see us secretly, against SS orders, as we still have to be disinfected, and that he must leave at once; he has come because he has a liking for Italians, and because, he says, he "has a little heart." We ask him if there are other Italians in the camp and he says there are some, a few, he does not know how many; and he at once changes the subject. Meanwhile a bell rang and he immediately hurried off and left us stunned and disconcerted. Some feel refreshed but I do not. I still think that even this dentist, this incomprehensible person, wanted to amuse himself at our expense, and I do not want to believe a word of what he said.

At the sound of the bell, we can hear the still dark camp waking up. Unexpectedly the water gushes out boiling from the showers – five minutes of bliss; but immediately after, four men (perhaps they are the barbers) burst in yelling and shoving and drive us out, wet and steaming, into the adjoining room which is freezing; here other shouting people throw at us unrecognizable rags and thrust into our hands a pair of broken-down boots with wooden soles; we have no time to understand and we already find ourselves in the open, in the blue and icy snow of dawn, barefoot and naked, with all our clothing in our hands, with a hundred yards to run to the next hut. There we are finally allowed to get dressed.

When we finish, everyone remains in his own corner and we do not dare lift our eyes to look at one another. There is nowhere to look in a mirror, but our appearance stands in front of us, reflected in a hundred livid faces, in a hundred miserable and sordid puppets. We are transformed into the phantoms glimpsed yesterday evening.

Then for the first time we became aware that our language lacks words to express this offence, the demolition of a man. In a moment, with almost prophetic intuition, the reality was revealed to us: we had reached the bottom. It is not possible to sink lower than this; no human condition is more miserable than this, nor could it conceivably be so. Nothing belongs to us any more; they have taken away our clothes, our shoes, even our hair; if we speak, they will not listen to us, and if they listen, they will not understand. They will even take away our name: and if we want to keep it, we will have to find ourselves the strength to do so, to manage somehow so that behind the name something of us, of us as we were, still remains.

We know that we will have difficulty in being understood, and this is as it should be. But consider what value, what meaning is enclosed even in the smallest of our daily habits, in the hundred possessions which even the poorest beggar owns: a handkerchief, an old letter, the photo of a cherished person. These things are part of us, almost like limbs of our body; nor is it conceivable that we can be deprived of them in our world, for we immediately find others to substitute the old ones, other objects which are ours in their personification and evocation of our memories.

Imagine now a man who is deprived of everyone he loves, and at the same time of his house, his habits, his clothes, in short, of everything he possesses: he will be a hollow man, reduced to suffering and needs, forgetful of dignity and restraint, for he who loses all often easily loses himself. He will be a man whose life or death can be lightly decided with no sense of human affinity, in the most fortunate of cases, on the basis of a pure judgment of utility. It is in this way that one can understand the double sense of the term "extermination camp," and it is now clear what we seek to express with the phrase: "to lie on the bottom."

*Häftling**: I have learnt that I am Häftling. My number is 174517; we have been baptized, we will carry the tattoo on our left arm until we die.

The operation was slightly painful and extraordinarily rapid: they placed us all in a row, and one by one, according to the alphabetical order of our names, we filed past a skillful official, armed with a sort of pointed tool with a very short needle. It seems that this is the real, true initiation: only by "showing one's number" can one get bread and soup. Several

---

*Prisoner.

days passed, and not a few cuffs and punches, before we became used to showing our number promptly enough not to disorder the daily operation of food-distribution; weeks and months were needed to learn its sound in the German language. And for many days, while the habits of freedom still led me to look for the time on my wristwatch, my new name ironically appeared instead, a number tattooed in bluish characters under the skin.

Only much later, and slowly, a few of us learnt something of the funereal science of the numbers of Auschwitz, which epitomize the stages of destruction of European Judaism. To the old hands of the camp, the numbers told everything: the period of entry into the camp, the convoy of which one formed a part, and consequently the nationality. Everyone will treat with respect the numbers from 30,000 to 80,000: there are only a few hundred left and they represented the few survivals from the Polish ghettos. It is as well to watch out in commercial dealings with a 116,000 or a 117,000: they now number only about forty, but they represent the Greeks of Salonica, so take care they do not pull the wool over your eyes. As for the high numbers they carry an essentially comic air about them, like the words "freshman" or "conscript" in ordinary life. The typical high number is a corpulent, docile and stupid fellow: he can be convinced that leather shoes are distributed at the infirmary to all those with delicate feet, and can be persuaded to run there and leave his bowl of soup "in your custody"; you can sell him a spoon for three rations of bread; you can send him to the most ferocious of the Kapos to ask him (as happened to me!) if it is true that his is the *Kartoffelschalenkommando*, the "Potato Peeling Command," and if one can be enrolled in it.

In fact, the whole process of introduction to what was for us a new order took place in a grotesque and sarcastic manner. When the tattooing operation was finished, they shut us in a vacant hut. The bunks are made, but we are severely forbidden to touch or sit on them: so we wander around aimlessly for half the day in the limited space available, still tormented by the parching thirst of the journey. Then the door opens and a boy in a striped suit comes in, with a fairly civilized air, small, thin and blond. He speaks French

and we throng around him with a flood of questions which till now we had asked each other in vain.

But he does not speak willingly; no one here speaks willingly. We are new, we have nothing and we know nothing; why waste time on us? He reluctantly explains to us that all the others are out at work and will come back in the evening. He has come out of the infirmary this morning and is exempt from work for today. I asked him (with an ingenuousness that only a few days later already seemed incredible to me) if at least they would give us back our toothbrushes. He did not laugh, but with his face animated by fierce contempt, he threw at me "*Vous n'êtes pas à la maison.*" And it is this refrain that we hear repeated by everyone: you are not at home, this is not a sanatorium, the only exit is by way of the Chimney. (What did it mean? Soon we were all to learn what it meant.)

And it was in fact so. Driven by thirst, I eyed a fine icicle outside the window, within hand's reach. I opened the window and broke off the icicle but at once a large, heavy guard prowling outside brutally snatched it away from me. "*Warum?*" I asked him in my poor German. "*Hier ist kein warum*" (there is no why here), he replied, pushing me inside with a shove.

The explanation is repugnant but simple: in this place everything is forbidden, not for hidden reasons, but because the camp has been created for that purpose. If one wants to live one must learn this quickly and well:

No Sacred Face will help thee here! It's not
A Serchio bathing-party . . .

Hour after hour, this first long day of limbo draws to its end. While the sun sets in a tumult of fierce, blood-red clouds, they finally make us come out of the hut. Will they give us something to drink? No, they place us in line again, they lead us to a huge square which takes up the center of the camp and they arrange us meticulously in squads. Then nothing happens for another hour: it seems that we are waiting for someone.

A band begins to play, next to the entrance of the camp: it plays *Rosamunda*, the well-known sentimental song, and this seems so strange to us that we look sniggering at each other; we feel a shadow of relief, perhaps all these ceremonies are nothing but a colossal farce in Teutonic taste. But the band, on finishing *Rosamunda*, continues to play other marches, one after the other, and suddenly the squads of our comrades appear, returning from work. They walk in columns of five with a strange, unnatural hard gait, like stiff puppets made of jointless bones; but they walk scrupulously in time to the band.

They also arrange themselves like us in the huge square, according to a precise order; when the last squad has returned, they count and recount us for over an hour. Long checks are made which all seem to go to a man dressed in stripes, who accounts for them to a group of SS men in full battle dress.

Finally (it is dark by now, but the camp is brightly lit by headlamps and reflectors) one hears the shout *"Absperre!"* at which all the squads break up in a confused and turbulent movement. They no longer walk stiffly and erectly as before: each one drags himself along with obvious effort. I see that all of them carry in their hand or attached to their belt a steel bowl as large as a basin.

We new arrivals also wander among the crowd, searching for a voice, a friendly face or a guide. Against the wooden wall of a hut two boys are seated on the ground: they seem very young, sixteen years old at the outside, both with their face and hands dirty with soot. One of the two, as we are passing by, calls me and asks me in German some questions which I do not understand; then he asks where we come from, *"Italien,"* I reply; I want to ask him many things, but my German vocabulary is very limited.

"Are you a Jew?" I asked him.

"Yes, a Polish Jew."

"How long have you been in the Lager?"

"Three years," and he lifts up three fingers. He must have been a child when he entered, I think with horror; on the other hand this means that at least some manage to live here.

"What is your work?"

"Schlosser," he replies. I do not understand. *"Eisen, Feuer"* (iron, fire), he insists, and makes a play with his hands of someone beating with a hammer on an anvil. So he is an ironsmith.

"Ich Chemiker," I state; and he nods earnestly with his head, *"Chemiker gut."* But all this has to do with the distant future: what torments me at the moment is my thirst.

"Drink, water. We no water," I tell him.

He looks at me with a serious face, almost severe, and states clearly: "Do not drink water, comrade," and then other words that I do not understand.

"Warum?"

"Geschwollen," he replies cryptically. I shake my head, I have not understood. *"Swollen,"* he makes me understand, blowing out his cheeks and sketching with his hands a monstrous tumefaction of the face and belly. *"Warten bis heute Abend."* "Wait until this evening," I translate word by word.

Then he says: *"Ich Schlome. Du?"* I tell him my name and he asks me: "Where your mother?"

"In Italy." Schlome is amazed: a Jew in Italy? "Yes," I explain as best I can, "hidden, no one knows, run away, does not speak, no one sees her." He has understood; he now gets up, approaches me and timidly embraces me. The adventure is over, and I feel filled with a serene sadness that is almost joy. I have never seen Schlome since, but I have not forgotten his serious and gentle face of a child, which welcomed me on the threshold of the house of the dead.

We have a great number of things to learn, but we have learnt many already. We already have a certain idea of the topography of the Lager; our Lager is a square of about six hundred yards in length, surrounded by two fences of barbed wire, the inner one carrying a high tension current. It consists of sixty wooden huts, which are called Blocks, ten of which are in construction. In addition, there is the body of the kitchens, which are in brick; an experimental farm, run by a detachment of privileged Häftlinge; the huts with the showers and the latrines, one for each group of six or eight Blocks. Besides these, certain Blocks are reserved for specific purposes. First of all, a group of eight, at the extreme eastern end of the camp, forms the infirmary and clinic; then there is Block 24 which is the *Krätzeblock*, reserved for infectious skin-diseases; Block 7, which no ordinary Häftling has ever entered, reserved for the *"Prominenz,"* that is, the aristocracy, the internees holding the highest posts; Block 47, reserved for the *Reichsdeutsche* (the Aryan Germans, "politicals" or criminals); Block 49, for the Kapos alone; Block 12, half of which, for use of the *Reichsdeutsche* and the Kapos, serves as canteen, that is, a distribution center for tobacco, insect powder and occasionally other articles; Block 37, which formed the Quartermaster's office and the Office for Work; and finally, Block 29, which always has its windows closed as it is the *Frauenblock*, the camp brothel, served by Polish Häftling girls, and reserved for the *Reichsdeutsche*.

The ordinary living Blocks are divided into two parts. In one *Tagesraum* lives the head of the hut with his friends. There is a long table, seats, benches, and on all sides a heap of strange objects in bright colors, photographs, cuttings from magazines, sketches, imitation flowers, ornaments; on the walls, great sayings, proverbs and rhymes in praise of order, discipline and hygiene; in one corner, a shelf with the tools of the *Blockfrisör* (official barber), the ladles to distribute the soup, and two rubber truncheons, one solid and one hollow, to enforce discipline should the proverbs prove insufficient. The other part is the dormitory: there are only one hundred and forty-eight bunks on three levels, fitted close to each other like the cells of a beehive, and divided by three corridors so as to utilize without wastage all the space in the room up to the roof. Here all the ordinary Häftlinge live, about two hundred to two hundred and fifty per hut. Consequently there are two men in most of the bunks, which are portable planks of wood, each covered by a thin straw sack and two blankets.

The corridors are so narrow that two people can barely pass together; the total area of the floor is so small that the inhabitants of the same Block cannot all stay there at the same time unless at least half are lying on their bunks. Hence the prohibition to enter a Block to which one does not belong.

In the middle of the Lager is the roll-call square, enormous, where we collect in the morning to form the work-squads and in the evening to be counted. Facing the roll-call square there is a bed of grass, carefully mown, where the gallows are erected when necessary.

We had soon learned that the guests of the Lager are divided into three categories: the criminals, the politicals and the Jews. All are clothed in stripes, all are Häftlinge, but the criminals wear a green triangle next to the number sewn on the jacket; the politicals wear a red triangle; and the Jews, who form the large majority, wear the Jewish star, red and yellow. SS men exist but are few and outside the camp, and are seen relatively infrequently. Our effective masters in practice are the green triangles, who have a free hand over us, as well as those of the other two categories who are ready to help them – and they are not few.

And we have learnt other things, more or less quickly, according to our intelligence: to reply "*Jawohl*," never to ask questions, always to pretend to understand. We have learnt the value of food; now we also diligently scrape the bottom of the bowl after the ration and we hold it under our chins when we eat bread so as not to lose the crumbs. We, too, know that it is not the same thing to be given a ladleful of soup from the top or from the bottom of the vat, and we are already able to judge, according to the capacity of the various vats, what is the most suitable place to try and reach in the queue when we line up.

We have learnt that everything is useful: the wire to tie up our shoes, the rags to wrap around our feet, waste paper to (illegally) pad out our jacket against the cold. We have learnt, on the other hand, that everything can be stolen, in fact is automatically stolen as soon as attention is relaxed; and to avoid this, we had to learn the art of sleeping with our head on a bundle made up of our jacket and containing all our belongings, from the bowl to the shoes.

We already know in good part the rules of the camp, which are incredibly complicated. The prohibitions are innumerable: to approach nearer to the barbed wire than two yards; to sleep with one's jacket, or without one's pants, or with one's cap on one's head; to use certain washrooms or latrines which are "*nur für Kapos*" or "*nur für Reichsdeutsche*"; not to go for the shower on the prescribed day, or to go there on a day not prescribed; to leave the hut with one's jacket unbuttoned, or with the collar raised; to carry paper or straw under one's clothes against the cold; to wash except stripped to the waist.

The rites to be carried out were infinite and senseless: every morning one had to make the "bed" perfectly flat and smooth; smear one's muddy and re-pellent wooden shoes with the appropriate machine grease; scrape the mudstains off one's clothes (paint, grease and rust-stains were, however, permitted); in the evening one had to undergo the control for lice and the control of washing one's feet; on Saturday, have one's beard and hair shaved, mend or have mended one's rags; on Sunday, undergo the general control for skin diseases and the control of buttons on one's jacket, which had to be five.

In addition, there are innumerable circumstances, normally irrelevant, which here become prob-lems. When one's nails grow long, they have to be shortened, which can only be done with one's teeth (for the toenails, the friction of the shoes is suffi-cient); if a button comes off, one has to tie it on with a piece of wire; if one goes to the latrine or the wash-room, everything has to be carried along, always and everywhere, and while one washes one's face, the bun-dle of clothes has to be held tightly between one's knees: in any other manner it will be stolen in that second. If a shoe hurts, one has to go in the evening to the ceremony of the changing of the shoes: this tests the skill of the individual who, in the middle of the incredible crowd, has to be able to choose at an eye's glance one (not a pair, one) shoe, which fits. Be-cause once the choice is made, there can be no second change.

And do not think that shoes form a factor of sec-ondary importance in the life of the Lager. Death begins with the shoes; for most of us, they show themselves to be instruments of torture, which after a few hours of marching cause painful sores which be-come fatally infected. Whoever has them is forced to walk as if he was dragging a convict's chain (this ex-plains the strange gait of the army which returns every evening on parade); he arrives last everywhere, and everywhere he receives blows. He cannot escape if they run after him; his feet swell and the more they swell, the more the friction with the wood and the cloth of the shoes becomes insupportable. Then only the hospital is left: but to enter the hospital with a diagnosis of "*dicke Füsse*" (swollen feet) is extremely dangerous, because it is well known to all, and espe-cially to the SS, that here there is no cure for that complaint.

And in all this we have not yet mentioned the work, which in its turn is a Gordian knot of laws, taboos and problems.

We all work, except those who are ill (to be rec-ognized as ill implies in itself an important equip-ment of knowledge and experience). Every morning we leave the camp in squads for the Buna; every evening, in squads, we return. As regards the work, we are divided into about two hundred *Kommandos*, each of which consists of between fifteen and one hundred and fifty men and is commanded by a Kapo. There are good and bad Kommandos; for the most part they are used as transport and the work is quite hard, especially in the winter, if for no other reason merely because it always takes place in the open. There are also skilled Kommandos (electricians, smiths, brick-layers, welders, mechanics, concrete-layers, etc.), each attached to a certain workshop or department of the Buna, and depending more di-rectly on civilian foremen, mostly German and Pol-ish. This naturally only applies to the hours of work; for the rest of the day the skilled workers (there are no more than three or four hundred in all) receive no different treatment from the ordinary workers. The detailing of individuals to the various Kommandos is organized by a special office of the Lager, the *Arbeits-dienst*, which is in continual touch with the civilian direction of the Buna. The *Arbeitsdienst* decides on the basis of unknown criteria, often openly on the ba-sis of protection or corruption, so that if anyone man-ages to find enough to eat, he is practically certain to get a good post at Buna.

The hours of work vary with the season. All hours of light are working hours: so that from a minimum winter working day (8–12 a.m. and 12.30–4 p.m.) one rises to a maximum summer one (6.30–12 a.m. and 1–6 p.m.). Under no excuse are the Häftlinge allowed to be at work during the hours of darkness or when there is a thick fog, but they work regularly even if it rains or snows or (as occurs quite frequently) if the fierce wind of the Carpathians blows; the reason being that the darkness or fog might provide opportunities to escape.

One Sunday in every two is a regular working day; on the so-called holiday Sundays, instead of working at Buna, one works normally on the upkeep of the Lager, so that days of real rest are extremely rare.

Such will be our life. Every day, according to the established rhythm, *Ausrücken* and *Einrücken,* go out and come in; work, sleep and eat; fall ill, get better or die.

. . . And for how long? But the old ones laugh at this question: they recognize the new arrivals by this question. They laugh and they do not reply. For months and years, the problem of the remote future has grown pale to them and has lost all intensity in the face of the far more urgent and concrete problems of the near future: how much one will eat today, if it will snow, if there will be coal to unload.

If we were logical, we would resign ourselves to the evidence that our fate is beyond knowledge, that every conjecture is arbitrary and demonstrably devoid of foundation. But men are rarely logical when their own fate is at stake; on every occasion, they prefer the extreme positions. According to our character, some of us are immediately convinced that all is lost, that one cannot live here, that the end is near and sure; others are convinced that however hard the present life may be, salvation is probable and not far off, and if we have faith and strength, we will see our houses and our dear ones again. The two classes of pessimists and optimists are not so clearly defined, however, not because there are many agnostics, but because the majority, without memory or coherence, drift between the two extremes, according to the moment and the mood of the person they happen to meet.

Here I am, then, on the bottom. One learns quickly enough to wipe out the past and the future when one is forced to. A fortnight after my arrival I already had the prescribed hunger, that chronic hunger unknown to free men, which makes one dream at night, and settles in all the limbs of one's body. I have already learnt not to let myself be robbed, and in fact if I find a spoon lying around, a piece of string, a button which I can acquire without danger of punishment, I pocket them and consider them mine by full right. On the back of my feet I already have those numb sores that will not heal. I push wagons, I work with a shovel, I turn rotten in the rain, I shiver in the wind; already my own body is no longer mine: my belly is swollen, my limbs emaciated, my face is thick in the morning, hollow in the evening; some of us have yellow skin, others grey. When we do not meet for a few days we hardly recognize each other.

We Italians had decided to meet every Sunday evening in a corner of the Lager, but we stopped it at once, because it was too sad to count our numbers and find fewer each time, and to see each other ever more deformed and more squalid. And it was so tiring to walk those few steps and then, meeting each other, to remember and to think. It was better not to think.

IRENA SENDLER

WARSAW, POLAND ... 1942 – During the Holocaust, Irena Sendler (also known as Irena Sendlerowa) worked for Zegota, a unit within the Polish underground established specifically to help Jews in hiding. As a health worker, she had access to the Warsaw ghetto, and between 1942 and 1943 she led hundreds of Jewish children out of the ghetto to safe hiding places.

Some children, after being sedated, were carried out in potato sacks; others were placed in coffins. Still others entered a church in the ghetto that had two entrances. One entrance opened into the ghetto, the other opened into the "Aryan" side of Warsaw. They entered the church as Jews and exited as Christians.

In time, the Germans became aware of Irena's activities, and on October 20, 1943, she was arrested and imprisoned by the Gestapo. But no one could break her spirit. She withstood torture, refusing to betray either her associates or any of the Jewish children in hiding. Sentenced to death, Irena was saved at the last minute when Zegota members bribed one of the Germans to halt the execution. She escaped from prison and for the rest of the war was pursued by the Gestapo.

Irena Sendler does not think of herself as a hero. "I want the Jewish community to know that there was resistance and a spirit among the Jews in the ghetto."

(JFR Photo Archives)

CHAPTER 8 **Rescue**

A group of Jewish youth hiding from the Germans in the French village of Le Chambon-sur-Lignon pose for a picture in the snow. The people of this small village of just five thousand, led by their Protestant ministers André Trocmé and Edouard Theis, opened their homes and rescued several thousand Jews. Circa 1941. (Elizabeth Kauffman Koenig, courtesy of USHMM Photo Archives)

DEBÓRAH DWORK **Introduction**

IN 1944, the German government realized that its ally Hungary had become an increasingly uneasy military partner. The worse the situation got for the Germans on the eastern front, the more the Hungarians' support wavered. Fearing that the Hungarian government would conclude a separate peace with the Allies, the German army swept into the country to take control in March.

At that time, there were 750,000 Jews in Hungary; they were the last great Jewish community still in existence in Europe. As Raul Hilberg has pointed out in his book, *The Destruction of the European Jews*, by March 1944 "we have seen all the deportations in Europe; we have seen how, one by one, all the Jewish communities were crushed." And he asked, "What, then, was so unusual in the fate of Hungarian Jewry?" His answer: "There is but one factor that distinguishes the Hungarian case from all others: in Hungary the Jews *had* survived until the middle of 1944. They were killed in Hitler's final year of power, in an Axis world that was already going down in defeat ... The success of these operations, in the twilight of the Axis, should tell us much about the Germans, who began the venture, about the Hungarians, who were drawn into it, about the Jews, who suffered it, and about the outside powers, who stood by and watched it come to pass."

Not everyone stood by and watched. The purpose of this chapter is to examine individual actions, rescue networks, and negotiation efforts to save Jews. To help, hide, or transport Jews was sometimes complicated and always dangerous. Yet as a chapter from Debórah Dwork's *Children With A Star* makes clear, both gentiles and Jews from all walks of life helped individually, and they worked collectively to establish rescue organizations. The words "organizations" and "networks" are misleading, however. These initiatives were hardly planned, streamlined, coordinated operations with a central office and a flow chart. On the contrary: networks grew haphazardly and by chance; one step led to the next, one contact yielded another.

Jews in Budapest congregate in front of the Swedish embassy in 1944 to receive "protective passports." (Courtesy of Photo Archives, The Ghetto Fighters' House Museum, Israel)

The way rescue initiatives developed is clearly illustrated by the efforts of the Swedish Legation in the Hungarian capital city of

Budapest. The legation was besieged by requests for help from desperate Jews. Sweden was a neutral nation; perhaps its representatives could offer protection or asylum. From a strictly legal point of view, the legation was supposed to help only Swedish citizens and the citizens of other countries whose interests were represented by the legation because of the war. But as one of the legation members, Per Anger, explained years later, "Something had to be done, and quickly. Every day the situation of the Jews worsened."[1]

The legation members went to work. First, they issued provisional passports. This was nothing more than a travel document that legitimately could be given to people with relatives or business connections in Sweden. As it did not provide legal protection, the legation negotiated with the new, Nazi-sympathizing Hungarian authorities to strengthen its status. They were successful: Jews with provisional passports would be treated as if they were Swedish citizens, and were exempt from wearing the Star of David.

Useful as the provisional passport was as a rescue stratagem, it could not be issued for masses of people. Therefore, an entirely new document was created, certifying that Swedish relatives had applied for Swedish citizenship on behalf of the Jewish person in question. Validated with the minister's signature, stamps, and seal, it was respected by the Hungarians and Germans whose job it was to round up Jews. Rescue strategies were rarely secure for long, however. A decree was issued invalidating foreign citizenship obtained after March 1944. Recognition as an applicant for Swedish citizenship no longer protected anyone from anything – let alone saved a Jew from deportation.

It was just about this time that the thirty-two year-old Raoul Wallenberg, a businessman and a member of a prominent family of financiers, was appointed Secretary of the Swedish Legation in Budapest. (See Per Anger's discussion of Raoul Wallenberg's unique achievement in his memoir, *With Raoul Wallenberg in Budapest*.) In the following months, he proved to be courageous, clever, passionately committed, and indefatigable, and he inspired hundreds of people to work together to create a rescue organization. In the first instance, he took the ideas that had been tried before and pushed them one significant step farther, creating "protective passports": identification papers in the Swedish national colors of blue

A protection document (*Schutzpass*) issued by the Swedish legation in Budapest to the Hungarian Jew, Lili Katz. The pass bears the initials of Raoul Wallenberg in the bottom left corner. August 25, 1944. (Lena Kurtz Deutsch, courtesy of USHMM Photo Archives)

and yellow, carrying the Swedish three-crown symbol, and signed by the minister. Explaining that the holder was under the protection of the Swedish Legation until emigration could be arranged, the passport claimed security for the bearer.

Wallenberg established a special department to fabricate these documents. His staff quickly grew to some four hundred people, primarily Jews, who were themselves exempt from wearing the star and, in theory at least, protected against deportation. It is estimated that some fifteen thousand to twenty thousand passports were issued. In some cases, the documents did not deter the Germans and their allies. Wallenberg organized checkpoints on the major roads out of Budapest and at the border station to demand the release of Jews who had been picked up even though they held these papers. It is said, too, that Wallenberg's staff at these checkpoints, people brave enough to confront the German authorities directly, dared to hand out passports hurriedly, secretly, right there on the spot.

The Swedish Legation was but one of the foreign legations in Budapest that undertook methods to save Jews. The Swiss, Spanish, and Portuguese also were heavily involved in these activities, as was the Papal Nuncio, Angelo Rotta. It is important to note, however, that these activities were organized in 1944, when the Swiss, Spanish, Portuguese, and Swedes knew that Germany had lost the war. This did not mean that Hungarian Jews were less at risk. Not at all. They were slaughtered as mercilessly as their co-religionists elsewhere. Nor did it mean that rescuers were less at risk. Again, not at all. Their efforts were just as fraught with danger as were rescue actions everywhere else in Nazi-occupied Europe. But the neutral nations knew that the defeat of Germany was in sight. And certainly this gave their governments an impetus to support rescue endeavors.

The situation faced by Irena Sendlerowa in Warsaw, Poland in September 1939 was completely different. Poland was the first country invaded by Germany (see Chapter 5), and the Germans immediately established a harsh occupation regime that was ruthless to the Poles and deadly for the Jews. When the Germans marched into Poland, Irena Sendlerowa was working in the Social Welfare Department of the Municipal Administration of Warsaw. From the beginning, she created a network to provide financial and material assistance to needy Jews. As Debórah Dwork has explained in an excerpt from *Children With A Star*, Sendlerowa continued these activities even after the Warsaw ghetto was created. Working with a close colleague, Irena Schultz, and Eva Rechtman, a Jewish woman on the other side of the ghetto wall, Irena Sendlerowa organized a network that helped some three thousand Jews.

The creation of a Council for the Aid to Jews, or Zegota, was a great help to Irena Sendlerowa and Irena Schultz. It provided them with a more secure financial base, and it expanded the number of contacts it was safe for them to approach for help. Zegota was started by people who, horrified by the Germans' persecution of the Jews, were determined

Motivated by humanitarian beliefs and religious principles, people of very different political ideologies formed an alliance to aid and assist Jews during the Nazi years.

to do all they could to thwart the enemy's goal. Motivated by humanitarian beliefs and religious principles, people of very different political ideologies formed an alliance to aid and assist Jews during the Nazi years. Representatives of Polish political parties ranging from right to left and from two Jewish underground organizations active in "Aryan" Warsaw participated in the work of the council. Operating in Warsaw, Krakow, Lwow, Lublin, Radom, Kielce, and other places, Zegota helped Jews by securing hiding places and providing financial assistance and false documents.

Saving children was a central focus of Zegota's efforts and a separate Children's Bureau was established in July 1943, directed by Irena Sendlerowa. Mass deportations of the Jews from Warsaw to the Treblinka death camp had begun in 1942, and she and her colleagues were determined to smuggle the children out of the ghetto to hide them on the Aryan side. By the end of 1943, the Children's Bureau had found places for more than 600 children. In total some 2,500 children were registered by the Warsaw branch alone. In the face of danger and despite arrests, discoveries, and constant fear, the council persevered and, according to one estimate, 40,000 to 50,000 Jews benefited in some way from its activities.

Individuals like Raoul Wallenberg, Per Anger, Irena Sendlerowa, Irena Schultz, and Eva Rechtman worked on their own initiative and used whatever bureaucratic machinery was available to them. Sometimes – rarely, but sometimes – a bureaucracy itself was used for rescue purposes. In Italian-occupied Croatia, more than 80 percent of the Jews were saved by officials of the Italian Foreign Ministry and officers of the Italian army. Faced with a directive from the Germans and their Croatian allies to extradite the Jews from the Italian zone, and with an order from the Italian fascist dictator, Benito Mussolini, to comply with the request, the officials and officers chose not to do so. As Daniel Carpi has explained in his article, "The Rescue of Jews in the Italian Zone of Occupied Croatia," the Italians did not want to be – or to be seen to be – submissive to the Germans. And they did not want to send the Jews to certain death. It was a question of both professional pride and moral principle.

While the Italian army and the Foreign Ministry stood firm against, resisted, the murderous antisemitism of the Germans in Croatia on principle, the Catholic Church, from which moral principle might have been expected, did not resist at all. The great majority of Protestant mainline theologians were

A Jewish child in hiding (fifth from left) stands among a group of Polish children dressed for their First Communion. Eve Nisencwajg (b. 1936) was placed in the home of Wiktoria Szumielewicz in 1941. For the duration of the war, Eve posed as their orphaned niece. Circa 1943. (Eve Nisencwajg Bergstein, courtesy of USHMM Photo Archives)

no more stalwart. In the chapter on "The Jewish Question" in his book, *The Catholic Church and Nazi Germany*, the historian Guenter Lewy has described and analyzed the failure of the Church to insist on one of its own fundamental tenets: the unity of the human race. The excerpt from Saul Friedländer's book, *Nazi Germany and the Jews*, shows that the Protestant churches in Germany did no better.

Yet individual Catholic priests and Protestant ministers, as well as nuns, monks, bishops, and prelates, were courageously and selflessly engaged in all kinds of rescue efforts. Official directives and doctrine notwithstanding, these dedicated religious people followed the dictates of their own conscience. Just one such example is the archbishop of Toulouse, Monsignor Jules-Gérard Saliège, who publicly decried antisemitism, condemned racism, and denounced the deportation of the Jews in a pastoral letter read in all the parishes of his diocese. Through his good offices, many doors were opened to rescue workers. Similarly, the Protestant ministers of the French village Le Chambon-sur-Lignon, André Trocmé and Edouard Theis, were such ardent advocates for rescue work that their message and their actions encouraged a similar stance among their parishioners. Other ministers in neighboring villages were of like mind, and their congregations too participated in resistance work. At a time when the German domination of Europe seemed as if it would go on forever, the people of the Plateau Vivarais-Lignon opened their homes to the persecuted Jews. No one was turned away. Two chapters of Philip Hallie's book, *Lest Innocent Blood Be Shed: The Story of the Village of Le Chambon and How Goodness Happened There*, illuminate how André and his wife Magda Trocmé inspired others, but they also show the great importance of everyone's involvement on the Plateau. In time, Le Chambon became a center for many different types of rescue as well as a hub of armed resistance.

Pastor André Trocmé and his wife Magda inspired their fellow villagers in Le Chambon-sur-Lignon to provide refuge to thousands of Jews. (Courtesy of Nelly Trocmé Hewett)

In this chapter we discuss at such great length the initiatives, networks, and negotiations to preserve and maintain Jewish life that a word of caution may be helpful. First, however numerous these heroic endeavors were, there were far too few of them. And not enough of the actions attempted were, in the end, successful.

Rescue was a rare activity, but it was undertaken and it is a part of the historical legacy of the Holocaust. Indeed, just because it was rare does not mean we cannot or should not learn from it. On the contrary: efforts to save Jews, whether by an individual, a group, or through negotiation, offer us – and our students – models of what was possible under German occupation. The excerpted selections for Chapters 5, 6, and 7 have explained how difficult life was for both gentiles and Jews throughout Nazi Europe, and how very efficiently the machinery of death and the murderers operated. What we now can understand is that, under those circumstances, it is astonishing rescue activities were undertaken at all. These endeavors teach us that people could transcend the hardships they endured each day and organize help for others. Through them we learn that it was possible to circumvent difficulties and negotiate obstacles. Not everyone stood by silently. Not everyone participated in genocide. Other forms of behavior were practicable and feasible.

The next chapter will focus on the rescuers themselves. The aim of this chapter is to investigate precisely what these women and men of valor and courage did. By studying their actions, we learn not only that despite the terror of the German occupation such initiatives were conceivable and viable; we also learn how rescue was achieved, what was done. Many people during the war did not do more to help simply because they did not know what to do or how to do it. Certainly there were those who were too fearful to help, but sometimes people failed to act because they lacked imagination, resourcefulness, enterprise, or just plain common sense. They were unprepared; they had no models. With the help of the example of the rescuers, we are now a little better prepared to give aid to those in danger, wherever and whenever that might be.

With the example of the rescuers, we are now a little better prepared to give aid to those in danger, wherever and whenever that might be.

Note

1. Per Anger, *With Raoul Wallenberg in Budapest* (New York: Holocaust Library, 1981), 46.

Debórah Dwork **Into Hiding**

Ivan Buchwald was five years old, separated from his parents, and about to be deported to Auschwitz from his home town of Novi Sad in Yugoslavia. "We marched in a long line, row upon row of people, going to the station. We were walking along right next to a wood and an aunt, Etel Sheer, who lived in Vrbas, twenty miles from Novi Sad, and who was quite a character, suddenly ran out of the wood and picked me up in her arms, and ran into the wood again. . . . I went with my aunt to live with her for the rest of the war. Her house was in the country. I was hidden for the rest of the war, and I survived. Well, I wasn't *hidden*. They kept me at home as much as they could and it was drummed into me that on no account must I say that I was Jewish, although even at the age of five I knew I was Jewish. My parents must have been somewhat observant. Luckily her home was in the middle of the country, and all the neighbors who knew kept quiet."[1]

Ivan Buchwald's rescue was extremely dramatic and, a hastily devised maneuver, very different from the planned and orderly departure of Anne Frank and her family (who have come to be seen as paradigmatic of Jews in hiding during the war) from their home to their hiding place. Anne Frank's parents, Otto and Edith, made financial and practical arrangements for the hiding period well in advance of the actual move. Ivan Buchwald's parents were deported before they could formulate such plans. The Frank family hid as a unit. Buchwald was alone. The Franks remained in the city totally obscured from the world's vision (in hiding and hidden). Buchwald was taken into the country where he was in hiding but visible. The Franks lived in the attic for twenty-five months and ultimately were betrayed. Buchwald's clandestine existence lasted less than a year, and he survived. In other particulars also the two children could not have differed more: one was female, the other male; Anne was an adolescent, Ivan a young child; she was a relatively sophisticated urbanite who had some sense of national, cultural, and religious identity, while he was still unformed – he knew he was Jewish in the same way as he knew his own name. In short, in terms of culture, class, age, gender, degree of religious identification, and experience they shared little. Yet both were marked as Jews, as the other, the stranger, and at the behest of their elders both went into hiding for some period of the war in an effort to survive the German machinery of death.[2] . . .

Arrangements for hiding were made in one of two ways: informally through a family and friend network, or with the help of some type of organization. In other words, the problem of an individual child was resolved through a personalized solution, while those who were concerned with the plight of all Jewish children tried to devise a generalized, or universally applicable solution. There was also a rare third pattern. Sometimes no arrangements were made, but the child, operating independently, nevertheless went into hiding. All of these plans were precarious at best – there were no guarantees – but to hide oneself, to function alone, was in many ways the most insecure of all. To do so meant that the young person spent the war years on the run, moving from place to place constantly maintaining an existence outside the law or, alternatively, by obtaining false papers and simply living and working illegally, "passing" as a gentile. In either case the child had to be of an age to be able to care for himself, and the majority of those who undertook to hide themselves in this way were older than the young people who are the subject of our study. There were children who did do so, however, and Jerzy Kosinski and Jack Kuper were amongst them. Kosinski's poetic memoir, *The Painted Bird*, and Kuper's fictionalized *Child of the Holocaust* depict their extraordinary ordeals. Kosinski was six and Kuper eight years old when they were left on their own to wander from village to village in rural Poland, hiding their Jewish identity and past history, and scrambling to survive by doing odd jobs for peasant farmers in exchange for food and a place to sleep.[3]

By their very nature children were too young to operate independently, and arrangements were made for them. The most common situation was that of informal contacts. Thus, for example, Margaret Ascher-Frydman, who came from a prominent and assimilated family, was helped through her parents' acquaintanceships. In the summer of 1942 she, her mother, and her younger sister were living in the Warsaw ghetto. Frydman's mother sought a refuge for her daughters, then aged twelve and six. "My mother learned that there were some children in [The Family of Mary] convent, and asked a woman, a friend, a wife of a lawyer whom my father knew and who was very religious, whether she could ask the sisters to take me. And they took us [the two girls] on the ninth of September. . . . We came to the convent, the sisters were there, and the Sister Superior said yes; she accepted us."[4] In Rome, the eighteen-year-old Roberto Milano and his friends were helped in very much the same way; that is, through his father's gentile business associates. On 8 September 1943 the Italian government asked the allies for an armistice and it became clear that Germany would occupy Italy. The situation for Italy's Jews who, until then, had been spared the worst, became urgent. A few of Milano's friends' fathers met in his parents' home to discuss the current state of affairs, and they decided that the boys had to hide. The following day Milano and three of his companions went into the Abruzzi mountains. "We went to this area because it was the birthplace of a delivery man for my father's stores. He was a trustworthy person who had worked for my father for thirty years, and he himself suggested that we be sent to that tiny village where there were not even streets, and which could be reached only by climbing through the woods and up the mountains."[5] The physical circumstances of Milano and Frydman could not have been farther removed, but both were menaced by the threat of deportation, and in both cases arrangements for their flight to safety were made informally, through the family's own network of contacts.

"Informal" contacts meant that the parents would ask a friend, or a friend of a friend, or the relative of a gentile relative-by-marriage whether she would hide, or help to hide, their family. Families usually separated when they went into hiding (unlike the well-known example of Anne Frank's household). Some did so to reduce the risk of total annihilation. Most, however, found that for purely logistical reasons it was impossible to remain together as a single unit. To hide one person was an enormous undertaking; it required space and food as well as constant vigilance and luck. The more people hidden in one place, the greater the risk and the more onerous the task. Furthermore, families separated because there were more opportunities for children to be hidden than for their parents. It was easier to hide a child; if they were young enough they did not need papers, and even older children simply were not the subject of official curiosity. Often they could be passed off as relatives come to stay or war orphans from a bombed city or evacuated area. The net result of these practical and sensible considerations was that the child found herself alone, separated from her family. Eline Veldhuyzen-Heimans, for instance, was just under three years old when she went from Amsterdam, where she lived with her parents, to Zuilen, where she was hidden from 1942 to 1944. According to Heimans, extensive arrangements had not been made. The family with whom she was hidden were relatives of neighbors who lived around the corner from her parents. From what she was told after the war, she understood that the whole matter was settled very simply. "In a conversation [between her parents and their neighbors] it was once mentioned that they had family who lived in such and such a place, and were prepared to take a child." Heimans called her foster parents "aunt" and "uncle," and they introduced her as their niece to their neighbors and friends.[6]

Georges Waysand, who at fourteen months of age was even younger than Eline Heimans, was explained to neighbors as an evacuee. Waysand's parents were communists and Jews, and deeply involved in the Resistance. As they both were very active "there was naturally the question of who will take care of me." According to Waysand, it was through the communist network that his parents located a family to look after him. He was not well treated there "so [my parents] took me back. And they asked friends whether they didn't know of another place. Finally they selected the village where I was going to be, [and] they brought me to a house where I was just supposed to stay for a few days, because it was a house used by the Resistance movement." In the end, Waysand remained with this family in La Bassée, in the north of France. "In the street they said that I was a 'child of the coast,' which means that when there was the bombing of Dunkirk, all the children were taken out of that zone, which was not so far away, and were housed with families all over the country. They said, 'He's one.' The only problem was that I was also a little bit dark, and I didn't look like the children of Dunkirk! But they managed to say that to the people in the street, and apparently everybody made believe that. They didn't ask any questions."[7]

Waysand's parents' contacts were, as we have seen, through an organization (the communist apparatus), but as they themselves were members, the people with whom the arrangements were made were simply their friends or comrades; the actual contact was an informal one. In other instances, however, such networks operated as an organization to hide children. The term "organization" may be misleading. Within the context of the war and the resistance work of hiding children, all that it is meant to imply is the creation of a network or system to save children, rather than individual, informal family and friend arrangements. Such an "organization" could have been started by just one person, or a family like the Boogaards which developed their own network and hid hundreds of Jews (as well as others) on their and their neighbors' farms in the Haarlemmermeer area of Holland.[8] It could have been a group formed by a number of disparate people whose common cause was their concern about the Jews, like Żegota (the Council for Aid to Jews) in Warsaw, or the Naamloze Venootschap (or NV, the Dutch equivalent to Ltd, i.e. limited company) in the Netherlands. And finally, extant institutions, such as the Protestant and Catholic churches, self-help associations like the Oeuvre de Secours aux Enfants (OSE), youth groups from the scouts to university student clubs, or as in the case of Georges Waysand, the apparatus of political par-

ties, undertook to hide children as part of their resistance work.

For all three genres of organizational arrangement the pertinent questions are the same: how was contact made between those who needed help and those willing to offer it, and how did the system function? Antoinette Sara Spier, a fifteen-year-old girl living in Arnhem in 1942, remembered that "a brother of my mother was living quite near the Haarlemmermeer, and it was his idea that we had to hide there. He thought it would be safe and he had the address of the farmer Boogaard, that famous farmer who always came to save the Jewish people." Sara Spier and her cousin Joop Mogendorff were the first of the family in Arnhem to be hidden. "We were very fond of each other, and our parents decided to send us together so it wouldn't be too bad for us. It was a good idea, I think. We went together with Johannis Boogaard. And when we arrived the brother of my mother was already there with his wife and two children. They were very cheerful when we came, they made jokes, so it made it a bit easy for us and well, we sulked just for a few minutes. Still, I found it very difficult to leave home. Yes, it was difficult – with that strange looking man. He was wearing a frock coat and it was very strange. But I felt safe because my cousin was with me, and when I came there I saw family."[9]

Joop's younger brother, Paul Mogendorff, was almost ten years old in late August 1942 when Johannis Boogaard returned to Arnhem to bring the boy to his farm in the Haarlemmermeer. His memories of that day express his sense of the normality and inevitability of his transition from family life in the morning to a clandestine existence in the afternoon. "A man came to our house. He was Oom [uncle] Hannis, Hannis Boogaard. He was helping Jewish people because he was convinced that Jewish people should be saved. He was a very religious man . . . and he helped many people," Mogendorff explained. "He collected me that day; he was wearing a tuxedo with long tails. Yes, he was wearing tails which was very funny, of course. That was his best suit; he was a farmer." Paul Mogendorff had been to school that morning. "I just came home at lunch time, and I went off two hours later to my hide-out. . . . I remember that I didn't wear a star when I went off, of course not. [My parents] told me to be quiet in the train. Actually, I don't remember many extraordinary things. Nothing special. I just went with this man and he told me he would be good to me, so I accepted this. And I understood why. I really understood why. I was then almost ten years old, so I was old enough to understand what was happening."[10]

The Boogaard family had come to hide Jewish children more or less by happenstance. The elderly farmer, Johannis Boogaard, his adult daughter Aagje and four sons, Antheunis, Willem, Hannis, and Piet, their cousin Metje and their families were known anti-Nazis in Nieuw Vennep. During the first two years of the German occupation the Boogaards manifested their political sentiments through individual acts of economic sabotage. Then, early in 1942, they took in Jan de Beer, a young gentile man who had been called up for forced labor service in Germany and had refused to go. Among the labor conscripts who subsequently took refuge on the Boogaards' farm was a Jewish fellow. When he asked if his parents also could hide on the farm as they too were in danger, the Boogaards saw a need to be met and a responsibility to accept. From then on, Hannis Boogaard traveled throughout the country to find Jews, especially children, and bring them to the Haarlemmermeer. As in the case of Sara Spier and her Mogendorff cousins, contact usually was made through family connections between the Boogaards and those who wished to hide.[11]

The Boogaards also found a way to help children who did not have the advantage of familial networks to make either informal or organizational arrangements. Aided by two women collaborators in Amsterdam, Truus de Swaan-Willems and Lies de Jong, Hannis Boogaard had children abducted from the Jewish orphanage in Amsterdam and brought to his farm. Lies de Jong had been a resident of the orphanage in her youth; she knew the habits of the institution and its personnel. It was her task to pick up children as they walked in a queue to school and on outings. She passed them on to de Swaan-Willems who, in turn, handed them over to Hannis Boogaard. It was in this way that Maurits Cohen came to the Boogaard family. In 1942 Cohen was eight years old

and living in a Jewish children's home in Amsterdam. "On a certain day, we small children walked along the streets in Amsterdam. The underground came and took me out of the line of children into a urinal and they cut off the star – back on the street – and I was sent to [the] farmer [Boogaard]. I was not told in advance; it just happened."[12] Maurits Cohen, Sara Spier, and Paul Mogendorff did not remain on the Boogaard farm long. It was their point of depature for the next three years of hiding; their access to the network which evolved out of the Boogaards' initial efforts.

The Boogaard family took on the work of hiding Jews and other people who had to disappear out of a deep religious conviction and strong anti-German sentiment. Their network began with a familial nucleus. As their operations became increasingly complex, other people joined them in their efforts. Other groups did not begin with such an organic core. People who were unrelated to each other, and indeed shared nothing except their common cause, came together to establish organizations to accomplish the same ends. Their motivations varied. Animated by political ideology, humanitarian beliefs, and religious principles, they formed alliances to aid and assist Jews through the Nazi years.[13] Thus, for example, in Poland late in September of 1942 people as different as Zofia Kossak-Szczucka, a well-known novelist and one of the founders as well as President of the conservative Catholic social organization, the Front for Reborn Poland, and the democrat Wanda Krahelska-Filipowiczowa worked together to found the (clandestine) Temporary Committee to Help Jews. The Committee's activities were centered in Warsaw, but branches were opened and contacts maintained in Cracow and Lwów also. In the first two months of operation the Committee aided 180 Jews, primarily children. At the same time, the Committee submitted a proposal to establish a permanent and national version of itself to the Delegatura (the representative body on Polish soil of the Government in Exile in London). The Delegatura accepted the proposal in November and early the next month they established the Council for Aid to Jews (Rada Pomocy Żydom, or RPZ), which was known by the cryptonym Żegota. Representatives of the political parties of the Delegatura participated in the work of the Council, including the Front for Reborn Poland, Democratic Party, Polish Socialist Party "Liberty-Equality-Independence," Bund, Jewish National Committee, Union of Polish Syndicalists, and Peasants' Party; in other words, the entire political spectrum was committed to this endeavor.

The purpose of Żegota was to help Jews by securing hiding places for them, and by providing financial assistance and false documents to those leading a clandestine existence. Like its predecessor, Żegota's activities were concentrated in Warsaw, but it too functioned to some degree in a number of areas in Poland (Cracow, Lwów, Radom, Kielce, and Piotrków, among others). Furthermore, saving and caring for children remained a central focus of the Council's efforts: in July 1943 a Children's Bureau was established under the direction of Irena Sendlerowa. She was well chosen for the task. When the Germans invaded Poland in 1939, Sendlerowa was working in the Social Welfare Department of the Municipal Administration of Warsaw. From the beginning, she created a network to provide financial and material assistance. "I decided to take advantage of my job to assist the Jews," she explained. "The Social Welfare Department of the Municipal Administration had a wide network of centres in various districts at that time. I managed to recruit trustworthy people to cooperate with me, at least one in each of ten centres. We were compelled to issue hundreds of false documents and to forge signatures. Jewish names could not figure among those of people getting assistance." She continued these activities even after the ghetto was instituted. By that time, Sendlerowa and her collaborators "had about 3,000 people in our care, of which 90 percent found themselves behind the ghetto walls from the very first day. With the setting up of the ghetto our whole system of assistance, built up with such great effort, was destroyed. The situation became even more complicated when the gates of the ghetto were closed. We then had to solve the problem of how to legally get into the ghetto." Sendlerowa obtained documents for herself and her close colleague Irena Schultz which allowed them to enter the ghetto legally, and she established contact with Eva Rechtman who, on the other side of the wall, organized a secret network of women employed by the Jewish charitable organization CENTOS. In this way, Sendlerowa and Schultz were able to bring money, food, medicine, and clothing (which they obtained by presenting false documentation to the Social Welfare Department) into the ghetto, where it was distributed by Rechtman and her associates.[14]

The creation of Żegota provided an additional impetus to this undertaking. Sendlerowa and Schultz began to work under its aegis; their activities gained a more secure financial basis and their network of contacts expanded. It was none too soon. Mass expulsions of the Jews from Warsaw had begun in 1942, and Sendlerowa and Schultz were determined to smuggle children out of the ghetto to hide them on the "Aryan" side. They had addresses of families in the city who were willing to take the children; their problem was to spirit them out of the ghetto. According to Irena Sendlerowa, Schultz specialized in this. In her account of their activities she explained that "the children were usually brought out of the ghetto through the underground corridors of the public courts building and through the tram depot in Muranów district." The children were placed with families or in orphanages and convents; the former received a maximum of 500 zlotys a month from the Council, in addition to clothing, food parcels, and milk coupons as needed. By the end of 1943, in addition to those in private homes the Children's Bureau had found berths for 600 youngsters in public and ecclesiastical (over 550 children), and relief organization (at least 22 young people), institutions. In total, some 2,500 children were registered by the Warsaw branch of the Council.[15]

The Council for Aid to Jews was one branch of Poland's official underground work; as we have seen, it was formed with the consent of the Delegatura, and representatives of the political parties of which that organization was composed participated in the Council's efforts. Other underground groups equally devoted to saving Jews – and Jewish children in particular – were organized far less formally. Unaffiliated with any established association or political party, they were formed by people who, very simply, felt the need to act. It is important to note that many of these groups, which were organized specifically to protect human lives, did not receive either honor or attention after the war. Indeed, while much is known about the armed resistance, the history of the organizations which helped children has only recently become part of the legitimate public past. There are a number of reasons for this: practical, political, and social. First, as the majority of these underground networks (like the NV or Piet Meerburg Group) did not apply for or receive financial assistance from their respective national central councils of resistance organizations, their work was never on public record. But there were also ideological reasons for the marginalization of underground activity dedicated to the rescue and relief of children. For many years after the war, each country's "Resistance Movement" was defined in terms of those groups which undertook activities of a more public nature: armed defiance, underground newspapers, lightning attacks to destroy records or steal documents, tactical maneuvers, sabotage. These more "heroic" operations were clearly patriotic and nationalistic, and they became part of the history of the honor of each country. Saving children was, by contrast, neither a public deed at the time nor the stuff of glory afterwards. In short, celebrating or commemorating such work did little to foster the ideology of the suffering of the nation under Nazism, and of the illustrious deeds which were undertaken to throw off the yoke of oppression. Less obviously nationalistic and manifestly humanitarian, the business of saving lives during the war was not politically useful in reconstructing a national consciousness and patriotic pride when the hostilities ended.

Finally, the majority of the resistance workers who undertook to save and sustain life were women, and the people for whom they cared were children – Jewish children. In other words, the disparity between this and other resistance work is the difference between the nursery and the battlefield; one is private the other public, the former is seen as personal, family history, while the latter is national in scope and character; the realm of women and children in contrast to the domain of men. These divisions were enhanced by the fact that the rescuers' perception of the work they had done, their view of their achievements, was rather different from that of the militant resisters. After the war these women underground workers dis-

appeared from public life. They did not seek publicity and they had left few records. Unlike the men who had joined the official resistance and who assemble each year at the national monuments of remembrance to mourn their fallen comrades, these women to this day speak unceremoniously of their activities as just another job that had to be done, and they insist that they are not remarkable for having undertaken it. As Rebecca van Delft, one of the couriers of the Dutch NV group put it, the question was "would I be ready to accompany Jewish children by train from Amsterdam to Heerlen (in the province of Limburg, in the south of Holland) where better could be found homes for them to hide, in order to save them out of the hands of the Germans. Of course I was willing to do such a thing: it was just a natural thing to do." Van Delft was eighteen or nineteen years old at the time, and living at home with her family in Amstelveen, just south of Amsterdam. She did not discuss her decision with her parents; "I don't remember [asking them] for their permission: it was evident that I should do such a thing, being asked for." In fact, van Delft explained, the work only could have been done by women. "For young men it was very dangerous to do such a thing by train, because the German soldiers always asked young men to show their identification cards: young men should be working in factories in Germany. But young women they would not so easily suspect – and indeed, during the time I did the job I was never stopped by a German soldier."[16] Jooske Koppen-de Neve, who was brought into the NV network both by Rebecca van Delft and through her friendship with the first people the group hid, the Braun family, echoed van Delft's assessment of her role in the operation. "To praise [me] would be the worst thing that ever could be for me. Everything I did during those days was just normal. Any other person in my place would have taken that on, I'm sure of that. . . . When it comes so real to you in person, in a living person then, yes, you get involved. You can't get on with your ordinary things."[17] As another woman who was central to the passage of children out of Amsterdam to hiding places in the provinces commented, "Yes, we did it, of course we did it. It's nothing special that we did it. We were in the circumstances to do that. The circumstances were that I was there. . . . We met Christian people who wanted to help Jewish children, and therefore we did it. I always say it was nothing special."[18] . . .

Let us return to the question of how informally established underground groups which were organized to save Jewish child life functioned. Unlike, for example, the Council for Aid to Jews, these networks were not officially established or recognized by a national central council of resistance organizations. How were they created, how did they operate, and how were contacts made between them and those they wished to help? The history of the NV group is essentially typical of the development and operation of the marvelous, but tragically too few, underground networks which sprang up spontaneously throughout Europe to rescue Jewish children from Nazi persecution. The organization which became the NV began with an encounter between two young men, Gerard and Jacob Musch, who refused to accept the German invaders' deprivation of human liberty, and Marianne Marco-Braun and her family, who were in danger. The Brauns had come to Amsterdam from Vienna in 1938. Marianne was then fifteen years old. In Amsterdam, the family took the unusual step of conversion to the Dutch Reformed Church; "there we made new friends," Braun explained. "So when things, after the invasion, got worse as they did slowly and gradually, there was a lot of concern for us in the church where every Sunday we used to go for service." In May 1942 "we had to wear the star," she recalled. "And with the star, of course, on Sundays we went to church. So then [the situation] was even more obvious, and people used to come and commiserate and think how terrible it was." Soon thereafter, Marianne and her brother Leo "were called up to go to Germany for work. That's when really all people, all the friends, were very concerned. . . . This is when the brothers Jacob and Gerard Musch came to us. We knew them, but not all that well. They came up one day and they said to us, 'Are you going? What's happening?' I said, 'Well, what can we do?' They said, 'We could possibly find you some addresses to hide.' " This was "a totally new idea" for Braun and her family, and initially her parents opposed it. "I remember my father said, 'This won't be possible; they can hide you, but for how long? They [the Germans]

will find you in the end. It's not possible to be hidden; the Germans are far too clever and sophisticated. And where can you be hidden? Eventually, they'll find you.' "

So we sat and we didn't know what to do; we didn't know what to do. [Gerard and Jacob] came back the next day and they said they had an address for us, for my brother and for me. I said, "But we can't go without our parents. What about our parents?" They felt it was more important to take us, being young. I couldn't take that. I said, "No, we can't go unless you find something also for my parents." So they went away again and a couple of days later they came back and said they had found an address for my parents, too.

By that time it was near the date when we were called up . . . and we had to decide. One moment we said, yes, we'll go, and the next moment we said (as a family it was), we can't do it. We'd better go to the labor camps. [We] finally decided, yes, we must go. But then it had to be very quick. I remember some school friends of mine came and arranged everything. You see, it was already quite dangerous. . . .

Gerard and Jaap came and said everything is arranged. There was a curfew already at night when people were not allowed to walk the streets after a certain hour. So we quickly had to go with them. We said goodbye to our parents and of course one didn't know if one would see them again or when. They would come back for the parents a few days later. . . . We spent the night at the Musch house. The next morning they took us up to Friesland where they had found addresses for us. I stayed with a schoolteacher, my brother with a farmer.[19]

[It is important to note that Jacob (or Jaap) and Gerard Musch, the original two central figures of the organization that eventually was known as the NV, came to create an underground network to save Jewish children's lives more or less by happenstance. In the spring of 1942 they had no such formed concept. Like so many others who became involved in this work, they did not have numerous Jewish friends. But when they realized that the Brauns were in danger and needed help, they were ready to organize that assistance.] Gerard Musch co-opted his friend Dick Groenewegen van Wyck and, after resolving the immediate problem of placing the Braun family, the three young men began to plan a way to rescue Jewish children from the Germans. They concentrated their energies on children because they themselves were young and they felt they would not be able to deal so effectively or authoritatively with older people, and also because they believed they would have greater success in hiding children. They faced two major practical problems: finding homes for the children, and establishing contacts with those who needed to be hidden. They did not have an easy start. They went to the northern province of Friesland in the hope of securing addresses but, perhaps because they did not have sufficient connections or the right introductions, they were unsuccessful. Undaunted by their failure, they decided to try the southern province of Limburg. There, in the fairly large mining town of Heerlen, they made contact with a Protestant minister named Gerard Pontier. As the population of Limburg was overwhelmingly Catholic, the Protestant community was tightly knit. Dominee Pontier knew his congregants personally, and the church members were well acquainted with each other, and each other's business. It was through this chain of contact that the Musches and Groenewegen came to the Vermeer family in nearby Brunssum, which became the secure core of the network in the area. Truus Grootendorst-Vermeer still remembers when Jaap Musch came to the door to speak with her parents. And suddenly half her family was involved – her mother and father, her brother Piet, and very soon Truus herself, who gave up her job to do this work full time. "My parents couldn't afford to do without my salary then. (I gave them everything and got pocket money!) So for them and for me it was a big step. . . . I thought, here these bloody Germans are doing something against innocent people, and that put my back up. They were so arrogant. I can still see them coming in. We first heard the planes going over, that was for Rotterdam. But then, not an hour later, the German soldiers came through the streets. We were all hanging out of the windows. If looks could have killed, they all would have been dead! . . . I'll never forget that hate feeling. Yes, I liked my office job, but I liked the people more."[20]

At that time, Truus Vermeer had a friend (whom she married after the war), Cor Grootendorst, and she sent a message to him telling him to come to Limburg. There was work to do. "And that's how I became number six!" Cor recalled.

> *CG*: Our work was in the first place finding addresses. Going to families (and you almost felt like a salesman), knocking on doors through introductions. We didn't go blindly from house to house. We had to know that the people were safe, and there was a reasonable chance that they might be willing to help. [The introductions came] mostly through the clergy.
>
> *TV*: My mother, because of her big family, was very well known to and had a good name with a Catholic priest. So we also went to a priest and we got addresses from him as well.
>
> *CG*: It worked like a snowball virtually. You get one address and even if it's a yes or no, there always would be a person against the Germans. Whether the answer was, "I don't dare to," or for some reason "I can't," the stock question was, "Do you know anyone else who might be willing?" And they gave you two or three addresses. It's like a chain. So it was not too difficult to find potential addresses of people who might help you.[21]

Leaving the local people (the Vermeer family and Truus's friend Cor) to identify potential hiding addresses, Jaap and Gerard Musch and Dick Groenewegen returned to Amsterdam to get children. By this time (the summer of 1942) the situation for the Jews in the Netherlands had become desperate. During the first half of 1942 the Germans had forced the Jewish population to leave their homes throughout the Netherlands and relocate in Amsterdam. As they were permitted to lodge only in Jewish quarters or to live with Jewish families, a ghetto without walls was created. This physical concentration of the Jews facilitated the process of wholesale deportation, which began in July 1942. Initially, Jews (like Marianne Braun and her family) were sent letters commanding them to report for "labor service," but by the late summer the Germans decided that too few were complying with these written orders. The *razzias* began. Arrested Jews were marched or driven to a central deportation point, first the Central Office for Jewish Emigration, and then from mid-October, to a theater, the Hollandsche Schouwburg. There the Germans processed the captive Jews for removal from Amsterdam to the transit camp of Westerbork.

The Germans interned enormous crowds in the theater; often more than 1,500 people plus their allowed luggage were packed into the building. People were held there for days, sometimes for weeks. There was no room to sleep, the hygienic conditions were abominable, and the noise was unbearable – even for the jailers. To reduce their own discomfort, the Germans decided to send children under the age of twelve across the street to a child-care center. This crèche had been a well-established neighborhood institution used by working-class families. In 1942 it was taken over as an annex to the Schouwburg. The director, Henriette Rodriguez-Pimentel, and the young Jewish women who assisted her, had no illusions as to the fate awaiting the children. They were determined to smuggle the children out of the crèche and pass them on to others who would take them to safe addresses. As every person, adult or child, who entered the Schouwburg was registered by an employee of the Jewish Council (which was controlled by the Germans of course), Pimentel needed help from an insider to destroy the children's records. This task was undertaken by Walter Süskind and Felix Halverstad. Their positions with the Council did not give them access to the registration cards, but they too were resolute and concocted all sorts of ruses to rifle the records. Thus a number of children disappeared from the files of the bureaucracy, and this meant that neither their parents nor the crèche personnel would be held responsible for them. Officially they did not exist. It was now up to Pimentel and her assistants to get the children out of the crèche and to pass them to resistance workers to be hidden.[22]

Jaap and Gerard Musch and Dick Groenewegen knew about the crèche but not about its underground traffic, and they had no connections with Jews who had not yet been arrested. Probably through Piet Meerburg, a leader of an Amsterdam student operation devoted to the same cause,[23] they were given the name of Joop Woortman, alias Theo de Bruin. De Bruin was the sort of person who knew almost everybody in the city ("a real Amsterdammer"), and he was a serious and dedicated resister. Because of his huge social network, which included many Amsterdam Jews, de Bruin had been approached early in the occupation for help in obtaining false identity cards, ration coupons, and, finally, hiding places. This work became increasingly consuming, and by the time he met the Musch brothers he and his wife, Semmy, were constantly involved with it.

Semmy Woortman-Glasoog's recollection of the initial meeting was that "the boys came to our house. We had a meeting, we talked, but the boys didn't know too much because they were very young. But Jaap was a serious man and Theo was, on this point, also very serious. And we talked about what we could do and how it would take shape. I listened and I told them, 'You have to realize that if you are going to do what you are talking about, then your life after this is a gift. If you don't want that, you shouldn't go on.' And they all said, yes, they wanted to do it. I think the younger boys didn't realize exactly what they did. But Jaap, he knew what he did, he knew; and Theo knew very well, and I knew."[24]

In the plan they evolved, each small group of people was responsible for one link of the network. To delimit danger in case of arrest they did not tell each other how they proceeded or with whom they had contact. Theo de Bruin (and to some extent Semmy also) made the connections with the crèche and with the Jewish families who had not yet been taken to the Schouwburg. According to Rebecca van Delft, who had worked with him, de Bruin was a man of "almost improbable courage and boldness" who did things others considered impossible, including "simply picking up [children] during a *razzia* in the street."[25] Sometimes he sent one of the younger men to collect crèche children from the agreed delivery point, or he gave them the address of a Jewish family with a child to be hidden. But in general it was he who undertook that part of the rescue work. Gerard, Jaap, and Dick got the children from Theo and Semmy and, with a few young women who had joined the organization, brought them to Limburg.

Marianne Braun had been the connecting link between the original women couriers, Rebecca van Delft and Jooske Koppen-de Neve, and the Musch brothers. Van Delft, de Neve, and Braun had been good friends at school, and remained close after Braun was forced to leave the Amsterdam Lyceum to attend a Jewish school. When Braun and her family went into hiding, Marianne told the Musches about her friends. It was Gerard who went to visit Rebecca to ask her if she would accompany Jewish children from Amsterdam to Heerlen. "One day in summertime (as I remember, July 1942) at our door came Gerard Musch – an unknown young person, who told me that he came as a friend of Marianne Braun, and if he could have a personal talk with me. It all seemed mysterious to me."[26] Van Delft agreed and soon thereafter told her friend Jooske de Neve about the underground network and put her in touch with Gerard and Jaap. De Neve was more than happy to become involved. She had been vexed by the Germans' abuse of the Jews since the first measures had been instituted, and especially so when she experienced the ostracism of her friend Marianne. After Braun had been barred from the Amsterdam Lyceum, de Neve went to visit her in her home in the Jewish quarter. "I don't remember exactly where or how that looked. I only remember that I entered that ghetto and then things hit me. I was very confused. It was so horrible that I was very determined to do something about that, as far as for me it could be possible. I was completely *bouleversée*, absolutely turned around. It made me sick, physically sick: the realization of driving together human beings, like cattle; the humiliating facet of it, and being oneself human as well. To be, yes, to be witness of such a thing – that I couldn't digest."[27]

The introduction of the star made it impossible for de Neve to remain inactive. When she saw Braun with a star the nature of her feelings metamorphosed. It was not simply that the situation made her sick, "from that moment on I felt *responsible* for her. . . . Things changed that horrible day when I saw Marianne and her brother Leo with a star on their clothes.

That was a *horrible* experience. . . . We had heard of it by then, of course. But then you saw, suddenly, the dividing of people; how malicious it was. Yes, I can still feel that now – the fury that such things are possible."[28]

By midsummer 1942, Theo de Bruin found children who were then passed to Gerard, Jaap, Dick, Rebecca, and Jooske. The women traveled alone with the children, or in the company of one of the men, passing as a married couple. The children were brought to foster homes in Heerlen which had been arranged for them by the Vermeer family and Cor Grootendorst. In the autumn, de Bruin began to get children from the crèche as well. With the permission of the parents, Süskind and Halverstad destroyed the children's registration records, and Pimentel and her assistants smuggled the youths out of the child-care center. There were two nearly impossible aspects of this system. The first was practical: how to get the children out of the crèche? After all, they may not have existed on paper, but they were real children and the crèche was guarded by the Germans. Many stratagems were devised to elude their control. For instance, as the young women who worked in the crèche were not under arrest, they were free to go in and out of the building. They took advantage of this mobility and, in their backpacks, carried out infants with pacifiers or bottles in their mouths, praying that the babies would not start to cry. Articles commonly in use in the crèche and therefore not likely to arouse suspicion were used for the same purpose: potato sacks, food crates, valises. Older children had to be smuggled out in other ways. Accompanied by one or two of the staff, toddlers and older children were allowed to go on walks. Sometimes on such occasions a few of the unregistered children were included in the outing and, at a previously specified point, whisked away from the rest of the group by an underground worker. Finally, Pimentel obtained the cooperation of a neighboring institution. At one side of the crèche was a small teachers' training college, the Hervormde Kweekschool. Seen from the street the two buildings were not connected, as there was an alley between them. Contrary to appearances, however, their back gardens adjoined. "The head of the school, Professor van Hulst, saw in the garden that there were a lot of

Jewish children and, well, he was good (we call it good or not good) so he tried to help. . . . We could bring the children from the garden of the crèche to the garden of the Kweekschool and the students and other 'illegal' people came to the Kweekschool and took them out [by the two side streets,] the Plantage Parklaan and the Plantage Kerklaan."[29] As the entrances to the college were not guarded, the controls could be avoided completely.

The first of the two almost insuperable problems – smuggling the children out of the crèche – was practical. The second was emotional: to obtain the parents' permission to hide their child. Who would be willing to give up a child? Who could imagine that life in the "labor camps" was not life but death? The parents did not know the young men and women who asked to hide their children; they were total strangers. They had no reason to trust them. Surely it was better to remain together as a family than to give up one's child to an unknown young person. Ida Groenewegen-van Wyck-Roose, who came into the NV through her friendship with Dick (they married later) related one such tragic encounter. "Dick had a very sad experience with a Jewish couple who lived in Amsterdam with a very small boy. They didn't know Dick, but Dick had their address, and he said, 'We have a good address for your child in Limburg, so please give me your child.' And they said, 'No, we cannot. We must think it over.' Dick sat there for hours to talk and talk and, well, they couldn't make up their minds. It was very difficult for them. Finally, they said, 'Leave him here one last night and come back tomorrow morning.'" There was a *razzia* that night and when Dick returned the following day "they were all gone."[30]

This conscious act of separation of parents and children was so painful that many of the resistance workers who were involved with rescuing children came to believe as they grew older that they were able to do this work precisely because they themselves did not have children. At that time they simply did not understand or comprehend the intensity of the parent-child relationship. "We were still very young," Cor Grootendorst reflected. "We were all aged between twenty and twenty-five. Now as parents and grandparents you start thinking. What would your reaction be if a youngster, twenty years old, comes and knocks on your door? Would you so willingly trust them enough to give your child away?"[31] Piet Meerburg, another Dutch student devoted to saving Jewish children during the Nazi occupation, has given this problem some thought over the past near half-century.

There must be a reason why most of the people working with the children were so young. My explanation is that we were not fathers ourselves, we were not mothers ourselves. You don't realize if you're twenty or twenty-one. Of course it makes an impression on you if you see it – if you go to the parents and they give their child away, and they don't know if they'll ever see the child again. But as a boy of twenty-one you don't realize what it means. You think it's very unpleasant; you can cry about it, but you don't realize. And I think that's good; that's why we could do it. And that's the reason so many young people did it and not older people. For older people I think it was very difficult to do that; they realized much more clearly what it did to the parents. . . .

I now realize I understood only half of it. It's a very difficult decision the parents had to make. I think only the very intelligent and wise people came to the conclusion that they had to get rid of the children, because it's so unnatural to give your child to a complete stranger whom you've never seen before, knowing, well, the chances that you will see your child again is what percent – I don't know. The parents cried tremendously most of the time, which was very depressing. But I think the people who did it had a lot of courage. It took very much courage – and you know how Jewish mothers are. For a Jewish mother to give away her son or her daughter to a strange *goy*, that's something. It took a lot of courage in my opinion, and foresight.[32]

Nevertheless, parents driven to desperation by the situation were willing to give away their children to a "strange goy [gentile]"; the NV had 252 young people under its care and Piet Meerburg's group between 300 and 400.[33]

The development of Piet Meerburg's network was remarkably similar to that of the NV. Early in 1942 Meerburg was at the University of Amsterdam.

> One day I was sitting at the students' club and I was studying with a friend, a Jewish boy. We were sitting together in the club and he was called to the telephone. He came back, and he said to me, "I have to go home, there's something wrong with my family – the Germans." I said to be careful. I never saw him again. . . . Well, if you experience something like that you say, "Why am I studying? . . . Then (that was about mid '42) things got really bad. You live within the city, you see what happens, you see the *razzias*. You see the Jewish people picked up, the whole blocks of houses. . . . At that time I said, "I stop my studies." There was only one thing: that you resist these absolutely inhuman and impossible actions of the Germans.[34]

Meerburg began to set up a network to save Jewish children from deportation by the Germans because, he said, "it presented itself. . . . Children were completely helpless. You had to take care of them from the beginning to the end. . . . And if something went wrong, you had to take them away. If a grown-up is in trouble, he can go on the street, but a child is much more dependent on your help."[35]

Like the Musch brothers, Piet Meerburg went to Friesland to obtain hiding addresses, and he also approached ministers and priests: "people that you could trust a little bit more." Meerburg was successful in his attempts and, through the religious leaders, set up small bases of operation. The other center for Meerburg's organization, like that of the NV, was in the south where Nico Dohmen, a student hiding from the Germans' compulsory labor service, and Hanna van der Voort, the daughter of the family with whom Dohmen was staying, organized an extensive network in the small North Limburg town of Tienray. Van der Voort was a maternity nurse; she knew everyone in the area and was trusted by them. It was not difficult for her to find hiding addresses. Tienray was a farming community and overwhelmingly Catholic. Families were large and they took in an-

other child without much fuss. According to Dohmen, a typical response was, "Well, okay, we have five [children] at the table, six at the table is also possible." In this way 132 children were hidden.[36]

The basic operating procedures of the Meerburg group and the NV were very much the same. Both got children from the crèche as well as from families that had not yet been arrested.[37] In both networks women couriers and local workers were not only an essential component of the operation, they constituted a majority of the members. Meerburg estimated that 90 percent of his co-workers were women, and he cited the same reason for this overwhelmingly female involvement as did Rebecca van Delft. "It was much more suspicious for a boy of twenty to travel with a child than for a girl. It was absolutely a big difference. We went to fetch the children from the crèche together, but then the woman student accompanied them on the train to Friesland and Limburg."[38] In many other respects the two networks had similar experiences. One of the interesting and unexpected problems the underground workers from both groups faced was that the foster parents had preferences as to the age and gender of the child they wished to have, and that the vast majority of requests was for "a girl of four years old. For a girl of four or five years old you could get as many places as you wanted."[39] This prejudice in favor of girls may have been due to the fact that Jewish boys were circumcised while the rest of the Dutch male population was not,[40] but both Iet Groenewegen and Nico Dohmen believed it had more to do with the foster parents' ideas about boys and girls. Groenewegen thought it was because "a lot of mothers loved little girls. They could make nice little dresses and play with them like a doll." Dohmen's feeling was that it had more to do with the behavioral concomitants of being "a little doll" rather than the dressing up itself. The foster parents, he explained, felt "more confident to have a girl; boys were a bit more strange for them. . . . Boys are more naughty and not as easy to handle as girls."[41] In any case, this was not a fundamental problem for the foster parents; preferences were largely irrelevant; they took whatever child the organizations could smuggle out of Amsterdam. For example, of the 132 children for whom van der Voort and Dohmen took responsibility, only about 30 were girls.[42]

Monetary considerations were not a factor in the decision to take a child. Despite the financial strain supporting an extra person put on their family budgets, few of the foster families would accept money from the resistance organizations. (According to Nico Dohmen, "no more than 70 guilders [a month] were paid for 132 children.") Indeed both networks were run on very little money. Train travel cards for the workers and ration coupons for the children were supplied by other underground groups. Clothes were pooled and handed around. Shoes were the biggest problem – as they were for everyone in the Netherlands – and many children learned to wear wooden clogs.[43]

The great majority of children did not remain with one family for the entire period of the war. Some lived with as few as two or three families, while others were at as many as thirty addresses. These changes were made for practical and emotional reasons. Foster parents began to suspect that their neighbors guessed the child was Jewish, and not a Rotterdam evacuee, which was the standard explanation. The children themselves sometimes betrayed their identity by singing Jewish songs, or talking about their past lives. Then too, resistance workers found that the children were enormously adaptable but not infinitely so, and sometimes it happened that the cultural difference between the foster parents and children was too great, or the family interaction patterns too different. The relationship simply did not work and the child had to move on.

This meant that the local workers were constantly preoccupied with visiting the children and foster families, and with finding new addresses. The NV was centered in a mining district and the van der Voorst-Dohmen branch of the Meerburg group in a farming community. In addition to the (working-class) miners and farmers, the two communities also had their share of middle-class people. The resistance workers were not selective with regard to income or education level as to whom they approached. Those who were recommended, who were considered safe, were asked if they would be willing to take in a child. Both networks found that "people with more money and better positions felt more exposed. They were more afraid, more attached to their possessions and

status." In other words, they felt "they had more to lose."[44] The miners and small farmers were, by contrast, far more willing to open their homes. The underground workers had a number of explanations for this disparity. Their experience was that the poorer people were "closer to needs and suffering; . . . they were used to helping each other more than perhaps the wealthier people [did]."[45] Thus, those who agreed to be foster parents focused on the fact that "the child had no parents" and they were concerned with "the difficulties of getting food in the big cities in Holland." They were not so interested in the Jewish identity of the children. Living so far from the major cities, and especially from Amsterdam, they did not "one hundred percent realize the danger they had in hiding such a child."[46] Many had never known a Jew before, none of their neighbors was radically afflicted by the German regime, they did not see the *razzias*. Just 200 kilometers away from the street scenes of Nazi violence and murder, people could not imagine it; it was so totally foreign to their daily lives, so removed from the social order they knew. Their self-help systems, community structures, and strict adherence to religious tenets were not destroyed by the German invasion.[47] In other words, their very isolation made them less fearful and, less blinded by fear, they were better able to see the child in need as a human being to be helped.

We have considered how children came to be hidden through informal family and friend contacts, and with the help of two types of organizational network: family groups like that begun by the Boogaards in the Haarlemmermeer, and groups that were run by a disparate group of people who came together because of a common dedication to saving children. Some of these were formally structured, like Żegota; others like the NV and Piet Meerburg networks far less so. The third genre of organizational arrangement involved the transformation of an extant structure from legal to illegal work.

The charitable preventive health care organization, OSE (Obsczestvo Sdravochraneniya Eryeyev, or Society for the Health of the Jewish Population), was founded by Jewish physicians in Russia in 1912. After the revolution its headquarters were moved to Berlin and, following the election of Hitler in 1933, to Paris. It was there that the society took the name "Oeuvre de Secours aux Enfants et de Protection de la Santé des Populations Juives." Like the Russian and German branches, the French division of OSE focused on medical prophylaxis in general and child welfare in particular. The OSE leadership in France was responsive to the deteriorating situation in Europe, and in 1937 began to concentrate on the protection of Jewish children. This work was done legally at first; later, when France was occupied and the Jews were besieged, the organization and its operations went underground.[48]

When the war began in 1939, OSE was supporting 300 refugee children, primarily from Germany and Austria, in special homes created for the purpose (*maisons d'enfants*). The organization also provided extra-institutional help, and subsidized many young people who lived in poverty with their parents. The fall of France in June 1940 and the subsequent division of the country into the northern "occupied" zone and the southern "free" zone under the collaborationist government of Marshal Pétain in Vichy forced OSE to move quickly. In the midst of the occupation of Paris and the mass exodus to the south, OSE emptied its *maisons d'enfants* in the Parisian suburbs. The children and most of the OSE staff fled to the southern zone, and for purely practical reasons the organizational apparatus split along the geographic lines. "OSE-Sud" became responsible for the activities carried out in the unoccupied zone and two officers, Falk Walk and Eugène Minkovski, continued with their work in Paris. Due to their efforts the OSE office on the Champs-Elysées remained open throughout the war.[49]

As it became increasingly clear that, at least initially, foreign Jews were at greater risk than their French-born co-religionists, the first task of OSE-Nord was to smuggle central and eastern European children across the demarcation line into the free zone. OSE-Sud, in its turn, immediately began to develop its network of services. Medical and social assistance were made available to the great number of refugees arriving in Vichy France, and more homes were opened to accommodate children sent to the south by their parents, as well as those who were or-

phaned and abandoned. The most important centers for these activities were in Marseille, Lyon, Grenoble, Montpellier, Périgueux, Toulouse, Limoges, Nice, and Chambéry, but services were also provided in a more modest way in other cities and towns.

In addition to the medical and social aid offered to adults and children living more or less normally and the support of the children in the *maisons d'enfants*, OSE refused to abandon the Jews enclosed in internment camps.[50] The French internment or concentration camps (*camps d'internement*, or *camps de concentration*) had been built in the spring of 1939 at the insistence of the ultra-conservative right to minimize the perceived security problem posed by the flood of refugees from the Spanish Civil War. By the time war was declared in September many of these refugees had returned to Spain. The camps were ready for the incarceration of all enemy aliens but specifically for foreign Jews. Stateless, impoverished, decontextualized, and unable to speak French well, foreign-born Jews were particularly vulnerable to administrative harassment and maltreatment. A year later (after the fall of France in 1940) there were thirty-one camps in the southern zone and perhaps half as many in the occupied north.[51]

The antisemitic decrees in the north and the passage of similarly oppressive legislation in Vichy ensured that all Jews, but especially those who were neither French nor financially well off, were at special risk of imprisonment, and when the round-ups began in 1941 it was to those camps that the Jews were sent. The most urgent task of OSE was to find ways to liberate the internees and to provide emotional and material support to those who remained. Like a number of other philanthropic organizations,[52] OSE sent social workers to live in the camps as voluntary interns (*internes volontaires*) "to share the daily life of the internees, to know their real needs, to provide whatever assistance was possible, and to defend their meager rights," as OSE workers reflecting in 1946 on their experiences explained.[53] Or, as Vivette Samuel-Hermann, who, during what should have been her student years, was an OSE *internée volontaire* in Rivesaltes put it, her role was quite simply "to be present." Just to be there was significant. In the camps at that time "to be present" could still mean something. That was why there were representatives of international philanthropic foundations. If someone was there, the guards and the people who represented Vichy could not give full vent to their evil side."[54] It was a job that required commitment and engendered despair. "I do not really know how to depict or to make you understand, uncle, what goes on and the entirely exceptional nature of the events we live," an anonymous social worker wrote on 17 November 1941. "My only hope is that the people who come from here and have seen with their own eyes the walking cadavers of Drancy will find, perhaps, the words and expressions needed to make you feel the depth of the tragedy and the moral importance of our work."[55]

The Oeuvre specialized in health care. To combat disease and alleviate malnutrition and its concomitants, OSE started medical services and opened clinics, infirmaries, pharmacies, and food distribution centers. OSE concentrated specifically on child welfare and instituted a crèche and children's program in a number of the larger camps. The primary concern of the organization, however, and its most essential business was not to ameliorate life in the camps but to extricate those sequestered in them. In a September 1941 report on their activities, especially on behalf of young people, they stressed "the liberation of children. As always that question is the essence of our main preoccupation. . . . The prolonged stay in a camp constitutes a permanent danger for a child and we must strive to free as many as possible."[56] While OSE pressed the interests of individual adults who had reason to be administratively exempt according to the particulars of each case, it presented the problem of child internees to the government as an issue of general principle. Following prolonged and intensive negotiations, Vichy for a short time allowed young people under the age of fifteen to leave the camps on the condition that they were placed in OSE homes and that they were granted a residence certificate by the prefect of the department to which they were to go. Montpellier, which is the Hérault departmental seat, quickly became the center for efforts to liberate the children through legal channels. The préfect of Hérault (Benedetti) and his associates (Ernest, the general secretary of the Préfecture de l'Hérault

and Frédérici, the chef de service) were willing to provide the necessary permits. A number of OSE vacation camps were set up in the area and the children were passed from them to other departments as at their age no other legal formalities were required. In this way more than a thousand children were freed from the Vichy concentration camps.[57]

While OSE-Sud worked to protect children by legal means, OSE-Nord, operating under the conditions of occupation, engaged in clandestine activities from the moment the Germans marched into Paris. Initially OSE-Nord concentrated on the secret transfer to the south of refugee children. After the ferocious manhunt in Paris of 16–17 July 1942 (the round-up of the Vélodrome d'Hiver, or Vél d'Hiv, as it was known), OSE-Nord engaged in a plethora of underground activities. Named for the indoor sports arena in which the arrested Jews were incarcerated, the *rafle* [or round-up] of the Vél d'Hiv was the result of the so-called Spring Wind operation to arrest 28,000 foreign and stateless Jews in the Greater Paris region. Ordered by the Germans but conducted entirely by French police and their auxiliaries, the *razzia* trapped 12,884 people in two days. A total of 6,900 people, of whom 4,051 were children, were forced into the Vél d'Hiv. Single men and women, and families without children (5,984 souls), were sent to Drancy. There the deportation trains were filled and began to roll.[58] For OSE-Nord there could be no more delusions about the ultimate fate of Jews caught in the occupied zone, and their main objective was to hide as many people as possible. In January 1943 one of the two OSE-Nord directors, Falk Walk, was arrested, sent to Drancy and deported. The other, Eugène Minkovski, remained in Paris and, together with five women collaborators (Hélène Matorine, Simone Kahn, Jeanine Lévy, Céline Vallée, and Madame Averbouh), organized a child camouflage service. Using a youth club as a cover for their activities, they passed Jewish children to gentile families, who hid them. The OSE workers maintained contact with the foster families throughout the war to ensure that the children were well treated and to provide maintenance funds, ration coupons, and false identity papers as needed. This network helped 700 children to survive the German occupation in the north.[59]

Clandestine activities to save Jewish children were undertaken later in the south than in the north. Until the wave of *razzias* that began in the occupied zone swept over the demarcation line, washing away pretense and stripping bare the antisemitic collusion of Vichy, the OSE staff in the "free" zone (like everyone else) operated under the illusion that a French government would deal more kindly with its Jewish citizens and refugees than would the German invaders. In the wake of the August 1942 dragnets which ravaged several cities in the south, OSE decided more or less officially to begin underground operations. The legal structure of children's homes and health care centers remained intact, but they also served as a screen for the organization of secret border crossings, for laboratories to produce false identity papers, and to hide those in imminent danger of arrest. The German occupation of the free zone in November 1942 meant that fewer resources could be wasted on legal work; more energy had to be channeled toward clandestine activities. At a meeting in Lyon on 16 January 1943 the OSE directorate decided on "the systematic camouflage of children sheltered in the various children's homes." The young people in the OSE residences had become too obvious and too vulnerable a target. They had to be hidden.[60]

An extensive network was developed to move, screen, and save the children in OSE's care. The architect of *le réseau Garel* or Garel network, as it came to be called, was a young man named Georges Garel, who had gained the great respect of the OSE leadership through his devoted efforts to liberate the children caught in the brutal *rafle* in Lyon and subsequently incarcerated in the concentration camp of Vénissieux.[61] "Some months later," Garel recalled, "Dr Joseph Weill (of the central governing board of l'Union OSE) proposed to me that I organize a clandestine network in the southern zone of France for children of trapped Jewish families."[62] Garel was well chosen for the job. He was not an official leader of any Jewish organization so was unknown to the authorities, he was involved in resistance activities and thus had useful contacts, and he was dedicated.

With an introduction from his contemporary (and later brother-in-law) Charles Lederman (a member of OSE whom Garel knew through other resis-

tance activities and with whom he had worked in Vénissieux), Garel met with Monsignor Jules-Gérard Saliège, the elderly, partly paralyzed, and very popular archbishop of Toulouse. From the beginning of the occupation Saliège had publicly decried antisemitism and condemned racism and racial programs. He had also been among the first Catholic prelates in France to denounce the deportation of the Jews in a pastoral letter read in all the parishes of his diocese on 23 August 1942.[63] And he was ready to help Georges Garel. "Monsignor Saliège advised me not to create a new philanthropic organization but to work within the framework of the Catholic or other charitable organizations which already existed. He had the great kindness to give me a short note of recommendation worded thus: 'I enjoin your good will for the bearer and his plans.' " Furnished with this reference, Garel made contact with public, private, religious, and nonsectarian organizations. The network grew rapidly until it covered nearly the entire southern zone. In each department or diocese a philanthropic society or institution took in children. Among many others these included Catholic (such as the Conférences de St Vincent de Paul) and Protestant (Comité Inter-Mouvements auprès des Evacués or the Conseil Protestant de la Jeunesse) charities, and official (le Secours National, for instance) and private (Mouvement Populaire des Familles) groups.[64]

Garel and his associates divided the children into two groups: those who could "pass" as gentiles, and those who for cultural, religious, or linguistic reasons could not do so. The former, with false identity cards or birth certificates and doctored food and clothing ration cards, were dispersed in "Aryan" milieus where they were not known. This group remained under the direct surveillance of Georges Garel. The other children, more than a thousand young people, were cared for by a *réseau* [network] run by a young woman named Andrée Salomon (the "Circuit B"); they lived at home with their own families or, using their own names, with other families. Andrée Salomon's Circuit B looked after these children openly until OSE went underground in February 1944. When OSE was forced into an entirely clandestine existence the children were smuggled over the French border, primarily into Switzerland but occasionally also into Spain.[65]

The children of the *réseau* Garel remained in France. His system was extensive but uncomplicated. He and his OSE collaborators found organizations and institutions willing to help save the children, and they prepared the young people for their new lives, teaching them their new names and family histories and providing them with the appropriate (false) documentation and ration coupons. The children were then passed to the receiver agencies which, in turn, either kept them under their own aegis (in group homes, orphanages, convents, or boarding schools) or matched them with foster families. Thus, two circles were created. The first, composed of Jews, was responsible for running the *réseau* and maintained contact with the parents if they were in France. The second, made up of individual gentile organizations, was directly responsible for the children in their new surroundings. These receiver institutions remained independent of each other throughout the war. They did not communicate amongst themselves about the OSE children; all contact was through Garel alone. This structure ensured a greater degree of safety. If a child were betrayed, only one atomized part of the network would be uncovered. Then too, if the children were in an entirely gentile environment the camouflage was more secure and it was less likely that they would reveal their true identity inadvertently. Finally, the two-circle division also helped to avoid direct communication between parents remaining in France and their hidden children. Such contact was fraught with difficulties and could lead to disclosure all too easily. (Letters, for example, were passed through Garel from the personnel of one circle to that of the other.) However excellent the idea of separate Jewish and gentile circles may have been in theory, Garel found that in practice "often the non-Jews were incapable of resolving questions [that arose] because the environment was strange and things escaped them." Jewish *résistants* with false identity cards were put on the personnel lists of the institutions and organizations which had taken Jewish children into their care. As members of the staff they were able to have contact with the hidden young people and to ease some of their difficulties.

With more than 1,500 children to look after by the summer of 1943, the network had become so extensive that Garel divided it into four separate geographic sections. Garel was the central coordinator, and a regional director with an assistant or two ran each area. The *réseau* had become comprehensive too; it was supported by an infrastructure of services. The clothing department saw to outfitting the children either by purchasing ready-made items or by finding the material and having garments made. The documents staff dealt with identity and ration cards, birth and baptismal certificates. They obtained false papers in a number of ways. Initially they altered authentic, used papers. Later on they cajoled legitimate forms out of sympathetic mayors' offices or bought them on the black market. As the need for such papers increased, counterfeit documents were printed on the underground presses. Finally, a transport division was responsible for moving children quickly and at short notice when it was necessary to do so.[66]

The *réseau* Garel and Salomon's Circuit-B differed from the networks run by Żegota, the Boogaards, or the NV in that the former were developed within an already extant organization (OSE), depended on preexisting institutions, and were run by Jews for the benefit of their co-religionists.[67] In other respects, however, the OSE rescue and protection operations had much in common with the underground groups. It is obvious, but bears repeating, that all were dedicated to maintaining Jewish child life in the face of ruthless persecution and despite the risks such work posed. These networks were run by young people who refused to be daunted. Unlike so many others, they were not incapacitated by intimidation. Then too, a great majority of OSE couriers, like their counterparts in the clandestine organizations, were women. Women assistants worked in the OSE *maisons d'enfants*, and when these were closed and the children dispersed, the women carried on with the responsibility of safeguarding the children's lives. At times they, like Irena Sendlerowa and Andrée Salomon, were the architects of the systems. But they were always integral, intrinsic, and essential to their operation. They worked on the ground, finding homes for the children, escorting them from endangered locations to hiding places, obtaining false papers, food, shoes, clothes. What they undertook was perilous and terribly exhausting. Finally, the OSE *réseau* in practice functioned very much like the other networks. It too depended on courageous and sympathetic gentiles to shelter children for the duration of the war. Like the foster families who collaborated with formally founded organizations such as Żegota, family-based operatives such as the Boogaard network, or spontaneous almost fortuitous enterprises such as the NV, the gentiles who joined effort with OSE were, by and large, unsophisticated and far from wealthy. They, like their cohorts elsewhere, were paid minimal sums (a maximum of 500 francs a month) to defray the costs of caring for the children, who came equipped with ration cards, a set of clothes, and little else. Like those who cooperated in similar aid and rescue operations, the OSE foster families preferred to "adopt" children who spoke without a foreign accent and who could blend in physically and culturally with the rest of the population. They too requested young girls rather than older boys. The same cover stories of bombardment or city famine were told. And, as the *résistante* Madeleine Dreyfus recalled, in the end the OSE foster families retracted their requests and dismissed the adduced pretexts. They took in the children simply and solely because they were youngsters in need.

Dreyfus was officially the chief OSE administrator in Lyon and, unofficially, the *assistante-chef* for the Lyon-based section of the Garel network. Arrested for her underground work on 27 November 1943, she was deported to Bergen-Belsen via Le Fort Montluc and Drancy, and was one of the few to return after the war, in May 1945. Prior to her arrest Dreyfus and another *résistante*, Marthe Sternheim, were in charge of finding places for children to hide and they scoured the countryside in search of sympathetic homes. In her account of her clandestine activities Dreyfus emphasized the part played by these foster families.

> I was specially responsible for the area of Chambon-sur-Lignon. The first contact obviously was with the Pastor Trocmé and his wife who received us as they know how to do and gave us advice and valuable information. It was in this way that I came to make the acquaintance of

Madame Deléage (she was widowed) and her daughter Eva (now Eva Phillit who lives in St Étienne). They lived in the hamlet of Tavas and they immediately devoted themselves to our cause. [Mme Deléage] was our devoted friend, she herself contacted those families most likely to help us, to help us hide those little Jewish children hunted by the Gestapo, very aware of what she risked, she herself hiding numerous children at her place and insisting that the small farmers with whom she took contact accepted those children "from Lyon and St Étienne so poorly fed and who needed to build themselves up in the fresh air of the Haute Loire." Those people knew very well what sort of children these were, but everyone pretended "as if" one believed that tale. . . .

> Here is how things were organized: Many times each month I would take the train to Lyon with about ten children. Sometimes these children were entrusted to us by their parents, sometimes they were children who managed to escape from the hands of the Nazis at the moment of their parents' arrest. We would go to St Étienne to take the small local rail line from Tence that brought us to Chambon.

Often, Dreyfus was met at the station by Eva Deléage. They deposited the children at the Hotel May and then made the rounds of farmers who might consider taking one child, or even two children if they were siblings who did not want to be separated.

> In general these small farmers "prepared" by their pastor and Madame Deléage responded to our demands rather quickly. If it was a question of boys over twelve years old it was rather difficult, however. "They talk back," we were told. I remember one day when a "case" of two fourteen-year-old boys remained – a difficult task. I went from farm to farm throughout the whole area surrounding Chambon . . . no one wanted my two boys. Finally I arrived at the house of an older couple, the Courtials, and I recited my tale to them: these were children from the city who were hungry, of course they had their ration

coupons, and the air of Chambon, etc. . . . etc. . . . The Courtials answered amiably but firmly that it really was not possible for them to take the two. Then I played all to win all and I told them the truth: "These were two Jewish boys whose parents had been arrested and whom the Germans pursued so as to imprison them along with their parents." Not a single hesitation remained: "But you should have said so sooner, certainly you must bring your two boys to us."[68]

Notes

1. Ivan Shaw, interview with author, London, England, 7 May 1987, transcript 4.
2. Anne Frank, *The Diary of Anne Frank: The Critical Edition*, edited by David Barnouw and Gerrold van der Stroom (New York: Doubleday, 1989) [*De Dagboeken van Anne Frank* (The Hague: Staatsvitgeverij, 1986)]; idem, *Tales from the Secret Annex* (New York: Washington Square Press, 1983); Miep Gies, *Anne Frank Remembered* (New York: Simon and Schuster, 1987).
3. Jerzy Kosinski, *The Painted Bird* (New York: Bantam, 1978); Jack Kuper, *Child of the Holocaust* (New York: New American Library, 1980).
4. Margaret Ascher-Frydman, interview with author, Paris, France, 5 June 1987, transcript 2. The Congregation of Franciscan Sisters of the Family of Mary was specially committed to helping Jewish children. According to Władysław Bartoszewski, the Family of Mary "concealed several hundred Jewish children in their homes throughout the country [Poland]." Bartoszewski, "On Both Sides of the Wall," in Bartoszewski and Levin (eds) *Righteous Among Nations: How the Poles Helped the Jews, 1939–1945* (London, Earlscourt, 1969), lxxxii–iii. See also the testimonies of Irena Sendler and Władysław Smolski, *ibid.*, 51 and 347–52. Philip Friedman mentions the Sisters in *Their Brothers' Keepers* (New York: Holocaust Library, 1978), 124. In Ewa Kurek-Lesik's study of "The Conditions of Admittance and the Social Background of Jewish Children Saved by Women's Religious Orders in Poland from 1939–1945" (*Polin*, 3 (1988): 244–75), she found that "two-thirds of the 74 female religious communities in Poland took part in helping Jewish children and adults" (246) the Family of Mary amongst them. Kurek-Lesik has estimated that at least 1,500 children were saved in this way. According to Kurek-Lesik, the sisters of the Family of Mary and the sisters of the Grey Ursulines were encouraged to participate in such rescue activities by their superiors. In other orders, the decision to help was taken on a local basis by each individual convent. Kurek-Lesik's research on the social background of the children who came to the convent and the means by which the contact was made coincides with my own. She has found that although the children who were taken in were, by and large, from professional and educated families, finances were by no means the determining factor: "a decided majority of Jewish children were taken in with no provision for their keep" (268). Rather, it was a question of contacts with the gentile world, access to the community outside the ghetto, fluency in the national language, and chance. "The condition governing the admission of the Jewish child into the house of a female religious community in Poland during 1939–1945 was its fortuitous arrival at the convent gates," Kurek-Lesik has concluded (272).
5. Roberto Milano, interview with author, Rome, Italy, 6 June 1985, transcript 3.
6. Eline Veldhuyzen-Heimans, interview with author and Robert Jan van Pelt, Culemborg, The Netherlands, 13 June 1986, transcript 2–4.
7. Georges Waysand, interview with author, Paris, France, 30 May 1987, transcript 1–3, 5–6.
8. Maurits Cohen, interview with author, The Hague, The Netherlands, 9 June 1986, transcript 3. Cohen claims the Boogaard family organization helped to save 324 people.
9. Antoinette Sara Spier, interview with author, Amsterdam, The Netherlands, 27 June 1986, transcript 1–2. Also interview of 20 June 1984, transcript 3–5.
10. Paul Mogendorff, interview with author, Zevenaar, The Netherlands, 20 June 1986, transcript 2, 5.
11. There is very little published literature on the Boogaard family. See: Cor van Stam, *Wacht Binnen de Dijken* (Haarlem: Uitgeverij de Toorts, 1986) 67–95, and the article by the investigative reporters Anita van Ommeren and Ageeth Scherphuis, "De Onderduikers in de Haarlemmermeer," *Vrij Nederland*, 16 March 1985, 1–25 and a follow-up in the letters section of *Vrij Nederland*, 30 March 1985.
12. Interview with Maurits Cohen, transcript 1–2.
13. The issue of the motivation to help is a fascinating topic and there is a developing psychological and sociological literature which focuses on this question. See, for example, Eva Fogelman and V.L. Wiener, "The Few, the Brave, and the Noble," *Psychology Today* 19 no. 8 (August 1985): 60–65; Samuel P. and Pearl M. Oliner, *The Altruistic Personality* (New York: The Free Press, 1988); Nechama Tec, *When Light Pierced the Darkness* (New York: Oxford University Press, 1986).
14. Irena Sendler, "People Who Helped Jews," in Bartoszewski and Lewin (eds.), *Righteous Among Nations*, 41–2.
15. Władysław Bartoszewski, "On Both Sides of the Wall," and Sendler, "People who Helped Jews," in Bartoszewski and Lewin, eds., Righteous Among Nations, xliv–lii and 41–62 (see also the section, "Under the Wings of 'Żegota,'" 41–108); Friedman, Their Brothers' Keepers, 118–21; Yisrael Gutman and Shmuel Krakowski, Unequal Victims: Poles and Jews During World War II (New York: Holocaust Library, 1986), 252–99; Yisrael Gutman, "The Attitude of the Poles to the Mass Deportations of Jews from the Warsaw Ghetto in the Summer of 1942," and Joseph Kermish, "The Activities of the Council for the Aid to Jews ('Żegota') in Occupied Poland," in Yisrael Gutman and Efraim Zuroff, eds., Rescue Attempts During the Holocaust, Proceedings of the Second Yad Vashem International Historical Conference (Jerusalem: Yad Vashem, 1977), 413–4, 367–98 (see also the debate, 451–63); Kazimierz Iranek-Osmecki, He Who

Saves One Life (New York: Crown Publishers, 1971), 139–51, 224–6, 234–7, 315–6; Teresa Prekerowa, "The Relief Council for Jews in Poland, 1942–1945," in Chimen Abramsky, Maciej Jachimczyk, and Antony Polonsky, eds., *The Jews in Poland* (London: Basil Blackwell, 1986), 161–76; *Saving Jews in War-Torn Poland* (Melbourne: Polish Weekly, 1969), 22–3, 40–1.

16. Written testimony of Rebecca van Delft to author, Graft-de Rijp, The Netherlands, 16 June 1986, 5–6.

17. Jooske Koppen-de Neve, interview with author, Amerongen, The Netherlands, 7 August 1987, transcript 24, 4.

18. Anon., interview with author, Amsterdam, The Netherlands, 19 June 1986, transcript 22.

19. Marianne Marco-Braun, interview with author, London, England, 9 May 1987, transcript 8, 10–2.

20. Ida Groenewegen van Wyck-Roose, Cor Grootendorst, and Truus Grootendorst-Vermeer, interview with author, Nieuw Vennep, The Netherlands, 1 July 1986, transcript 3.

21. Ibid., 4.

22. Interview with anon., transcript 1–2; Anita van Ommeren and Ageeth Scherphuis, "De Crèche, 1942–1943," *Vrij Nederland*, 18 January 1986, 2–21; Jacob Presser, *The Destruction of the Dutch Jews* (New York: Dutton, 1969) [*Ondergang* (The Hague: Staatsuitgeverij, 1965)], 281–82.

23. Interview with Groenewegen, Grootendorst, and Grootendorst, transcript 8; Semmy Riekerk-Glasoog, interview with author, Amsterdam, The Netherlands, 4 July 1986, transcript 19.

24. Interview with Semmy Riekerk-Glasoog, transcript 20. Of the five people at that original meeting, only Semmy Riekerk-Glasoog is still living. Jaap Musch was caught by the Germans on 7 September 1944 and shot on the spot for his underground activities. Theo Woortman was arrested on 19 July 1944 in Amsterdam and sent to Amersfoort. On 4 September he was deported to Bergen-Belsen where he died on 12 March 1945. Gerard Musch and Dick Groenewegen were arrested in Amsterdam's central railway station on 9 May 1944. Both were deported, Dick to Burscheid (via Amersfoort) and Gerard to Sachsenhausen (via Vught). Both survived and died of natural causes much later (Musch in 1979 and Groenewegen in 1985). For a history of the NV, see the journalist Max Arian's personal and historical account, "Het grote kinderspel," in *De Groene Amsterdammer*, 4 May 1983, 5–7, 9; and his interview with Semmy Riekerk in the same issue, 10–12. See also the master's thesis of Bert-Jan Flim at Groningen University, *De NV en Haar Kinderen, 1942–1945*, May 1987; and a series of articles by Jan van Lieshout in the *Limburgs Dagblad*: "Joop Woortman: 'Breng ze maar naar Limburg' " (25 May 1977); "De ongehuwde vaders en moeders van Brunssum" (26 May 1977); "Elke dreumes was een drama" (27 May 1977); "De vliegende non van het pompstation" (28 May 1977).

25. Statement by van Delft, 7.

26. Ibid., 4.

27. Interview with Jooske Koppen-de Neve, transcript 9.

28. Ibid., 3–4.

29. Interview with anon., transcript 2–3.

30. Interview with Groenewegen, Grootendorst, and Grootendorst, transcript 9.

31. Ibid., 9.

32. Piet Meerburg, interview with author, Amsterdam, The Netherlands, 27 June 1986, transcript 5, 13.

33. Interviews with Groenewegen, Grootendorst, and Grootendorst, transcript 12; and Meerburg transcript 12.

34. Interview with Meerburg, transcript 3–4.

35. Ibid., 5.

36. Ibid., 6; see also Nico Dohmen, interview with author, Baarn, The Netherlands, 30 June 1986, transcript 23. There is, if anything, even less printed material on the Meerburg group than on the NV. See the series of short articles by Jan van Lieshout in the *Limburgs Dagblad*: "Het grote gezin van 'Tante Hanna' en 'Oom Nico' " (4 May 1977); "Het verraad van Tienray" (5 May 1977); "Duitser verleid: Hanna bevrijd" (6 May 1977); "Rietje het vergeet – mij – nietje," (10 May 1977); and the master's thesis of Paul J.M. Dolfsma, *Uit de illegaliteit naar de studie. De ontstaansgeschiedenis van de stichting Onderlinge Studenten Steun en haar bioscoop Kriterion*, Amsterdam, 1985, chapter 3: "Verzet van studenten," 50–84.

37. It is not clear whether the figures adduced by Meerburg and Dohmen are incompatible. According to Meerburg, one-third of the 3–400 children hidden by his network came from the crèche. (11.) Nico Dohmen estimated that 80 percent of the 132 children hidden in the Tienray area were rescued from the crèche. Perhaps the majority of the children smuggled out of the crèche and passed to the Meerburg group were sent to Nico Dohmen and Hanna van der Voort.

38. Meerburg, transcript 10–1.

39. Interviews with Meerburg, transcript 17; also Dohmen, transcript 8, and Groenewegen, Grootendorst, and Grootendorst, transcript 4–5.

40. Interview with Groenewegen, Grootendorst, and Grootendorst, transcript 5.

41. Ibid., 5, and interview with Dohmen, transcript 8.

42. Interview with Dohmen, transcript 15.

43. Ibid., 15; also interviews with Meerburg, transcript 4, 6, and Marco-Braun, transcript 18.

44. Interview with Groenewegen, Grootendorst, and Grootendorst, transcript 15.

45. Ibid., 15; also interview with Meerburg, transcript 16. The comparative willingness of poorer people to open their homes to Jews in contrast to the hesitancy of those who were financially better off was well recognized at the time. It is not clear whether this was a popular (and perhaps populist) myth, but a common saying was: "The poor offer you shelter, the rich someone else's address." My own research tends to support this contention.

46. Interview with Dohmen, transcript 7, 23–4.

47. Interview with Meerburg, transcript 10, 25–6.

48. There is a fair amount of published literature on OSE and a wealth of archival documentation. See first, inter alia: *The American OSE Review*; Centre de Documentation Juive Contemporaine (CDJC), *L'activité des organisations juives en France sous l'Occupation* (Paris: Centre de Documentation Juive Contemporaine, 1983 reissue of 1947 text), 117–79; Hillel J. Kieval, "Legality and Resistance in Vichy France: The Rescue of Jewish Children," *Proceedings of the American Philosophical Society*, 124, no. 5 (October 1980): 339–66; Serge Klarsfeld, *The Children of Izieu* (New York: Abrams, Inc., 1985) [*Les enfants d'Izieu: Une tragedie juive* (Paris:

Publiée par Serge Klarsfeld, 1984)]; Anny Latour, *The Jewish Resistance in France* (New York: Holocaust Library, 1981) [*La résistance juive en France* (Paris: Stock, 1970)]; Lucien Lazare, *La résistance juive en France* (Paris: Stock, 1987); Ernst Papanek and Edward Linn, *Out of the Fire* (New York: William Morrow, 1975), especially 34–5; Zosa Szakowski, *Analytical Franco-Jewish Gazetteer, 1939–1945* (New York: Frydman, 1966), 73–5 and *passim*. See also Jacques Adler, *The Jews of Paris and the Final Solution* (New York: Oxford University Press, 1987), 167, 226–27 [*Face à la persécution: les organisations juives à Paris de 1940 à 1944* (Paris: Calmann-Lévy, 1985)]; Yehuda Bauer, *A History of the Holocaust* (New York: Franklin Watts, 1982), 291–3; David Diamant, *Les juifs dans la Résistance française, 1940–44* (Paris: Le Pavillon, 1971), 56–9; Dorothy Macardle, *The Children of Europe* (London: Victor Gollancz, 1949), 184–8; Sabine Zeitoun, *Ces enfants qu'il fallait sauver* (Paris: Albin Michel, 1989), 145–70. The major archival collections are in the Centre de Documentation Juive Contemporaine and the OSE institution itself in Paris and in the YIVO in New York.

49. CDJC, *L'activité des organisations juives*, 118–22.

50. There is a plethora of documents in the archives which describe the activities undertaken by OSE. See, for example, CDJC doc.CCCLXVI–11 "Rapport sur l'activité de l'Union OSE pour les mois Juin, Juillet, et Août 1941." OSE was engaged in a number of concerns, but the children commanded their primary interest. The report noted that 1,201 children were under their sole care, which was about 100 more than in the previous trimester. "The series of tragic cases encountered during the last trimester continues and often we are obliged to admit immediately to our homes children who, in the majority of cases, have nearly been picked up [by the police]; they remain alone in the world without support and it is impossible for us not to take them." (4.)

51. Michael Marrus and Robert Paxton, *Vichy France and the Jews* (New York: Schocken, 1983), 64–5, 165–6; Joseph Weill, *Contribution à l'histoire des camps d'internement dans l'Anti-France* (Paris: Éditions du Centre, 1946) 9–15, 21–2.

52. The Unitarian Service Committee, YMCA, Caritas, American Friends' Service Committee, Secours Suisse aux Enfants, Service Social d'Aide aux Emigrants, and CIMADE were very active.

53. CDJC, *L'activité des organisations juives*, 129.

54. Vivette Samuel-Hermann, interview with author, Paris, France, transcript 8.

55. CDJC doc. CCXIII–86, "Rapport sur les conditions de vie à Drancy."

56. CDJC doc. CCCLXVI–11, 9.

57. Klarsfeld, *The Children of Izieu*, 18–9; CDJC doc. CCLXVI 13 "OSE."

58. Diamant, *Les juifs dans la Résistance française*, 119–20; Claude Levy and Paul Tillard, *Betrayal at the Vél d'Hiv* (New York: Hill and Wang, 1969 [*La Grande Rafle du Vél d'Hiv* (Paris: Laffont, 1967)]; Marrus and Paxton, *Vichy France and the Jews*, 250–2; Georges Wellers, *L'étoile jaune à l'heure de Vichy* (Paris: Fayard, 1973), 83–5; CDJC doc. CCXIV–74, "Situation au 25 Août 1942," 1–3.

59. CDJC, *L'activité des organisations juives*, 141–2; CDJC docs. CCXVI–12a, "Exposé sur le circuit Garel," 2;

CCXVIII–104, "Travail clandestin de l'OSE. Témoignage de M. Georges Garel," 8–9; CCLXVI–13; CCLXVI–16, "La situation actuelle du judaisme en France," July 1941, 25. According to this report, 1,000 to 1,200 children were evacuated by OSE-Nord from the Occupied Zone to the south.

60. CDJC doc. CCXVII–12a, 1.

61. Late in August 1942, some 1,200 Jews were arrested in a sudden dragnet operation in Lyon and sent to the Vénissieux internment camp. Shortly thereafter Garel, who was a resister but not a member of OSE, managed to enter Vénissieux in an official capacity to help liberate the children who were legally entitled to their freedom, as well as a number who were decreed prey: 108 in all. Garel, Charles Lederman, Elisabeth Hirsch, and Hélène Lévy from OSE, the director of the interconfessional philanthropic group Les Amitiés Chrétiennes, l'Abbé Glasberg, Madeleine Barot, the general secretary of the Protestant Comité Inter-Mouvements auprès des Evacués (CIMADE), the Jesuit priest Pierre Chaillet, and others worked furiously to free children under sixteen years of age who were not technically under arrest. Within a few days the policy with regard to the children had been changed, but by that time they had "disappeared." See, inter alia, Bauer, *A History of the Holocaust*, 292; Diamant, *Les juifs dans la Résistance française*, 58; Lazare, *La résistance juive*, 208–11; René Nodot, *Les enfants ne partiront pas!* (Lyon: Nouvelle Lyonnaise, 1970); Weill, *Camps d'internement dans l'Anti-France*, 206–9; CDJC doc. CCXVIII–104, 1–3. Lily Garel-Taget, interview with author, Paris, France, 19 June 1987, transcript 4–6; and Elisabeth Hirsch, interview with author, Neuilly-sur-Seine, France, transcript 22, 24.

62. CDJC doc. CCXVIII–104, 3.

63. Diamant, *Les juifs dans la Résistance française*, 132; Lazare, *La résistance juive*, 179–81; Marrus and Paxton, *Vichy France*, 206, 271.

64. CDJC, *L'activité des organisations juives en France*, 157–60; CDJC doc. CCXVIII–104, 3–5.

65. CDJC doc. CCXVII–12a, 1–2. According to a statement by the American Joint Distribution Committee, OSE was responsible for smuggling 2,000 children into Switzerland. CDJC doc. CCCLXVI–14, "American Joint Distribution Committee," 5. Bruno-Georges Loinger, interview with author, Paris, France, 25 June 1987, transcript 1–10.

66. CDJC docs. CCXVII–12a, 1–2; CCXVIII–104, 3–8.

67. OSE was merely one already extant institution to develop networks to protect and save Jewish children. In France alone such work was undertaken by a spectrum of organizations: public, private, Catholic, Protestant, communist, and socialist. Indeed, within just the Jewish community a plethora of associations formed special child welfare services. The Young Zionists (Jeunesses Sionistes), Jewish Scouts (Éclaireurs Israélites de France), Committee for Refugee Assistance (Comité d'Assistance aux Réfugiés), Rehabilitation and Training Organization (ORT), and Zionist socialist groups like Hashomer Hatzair, Dror, and Gordonia were committed to the protection of young people. There were also numerous newly created groups, of course.

68. Unpublished statement of Madeleine Dreyfus, in possession of author, 2–3.

WLADYSLAW BARTOSZEWSKI, WARSAW, POLAND... 1939 – Wladyslaw Bartoszewski was 17 in 1939 when the Germans invaded Poland. He participated in the defense of Warsaw, was arrested in 1940, and was sent to Auschwitz. Released in 1941, he joined the Polish underground and continued to be active in other organizations such as Zegota, the Council for the Aid to Jews. Bartoszewski worked for the freedom of both the Jews and the Poles. After the war, Wladyslaw was imprisoned by the Polish government for eight years. He has since served as Poland's ambassador to Austria and as Minister of Foreign Affairs. (Zydowski Instytut Historyczny Instytut Naukowo-Badawczy, courtesy of USHMM Photo Archives)

WALTER UKALO, BRODY, POLAND... 1942 – Walter and his family provided food and shelter for their neighbor Dorothy and her infant daughter Sabina for several months. Dorothy's husband had already been killed by the Germans. When Walter's father was killed by the Germans in 1942 for hiding Jews, Walter found another hiding place for Dorothy, Sabina, and Dorothy's two sisters. In 1943, Walter joined Zegota, the Council for the Aid to Jews, where he distributed false papers, money and clothing to Jews in hiding. After liberation, Walter married Dorothy, adopted Sabina, and moved to the United States. (JFR Photo Archives)

JOZSEF KOVACS, DEBRECEN, HUNGARY... OCTOBER 1942 – Lieutenant Jozsef Kovacs commanded a slave labor company of 150 Jewish men. He treated these Jewish slave laborers humanely and decently – he did not abuse them and even disobeyed orders from his commandant by smuggling care packages that were sent to the men from their families.

In the fall of 1942, the entire battalion was ordered to the Russian front. The reassignment meant certain death. Lieutenant Kovacs persuaded his superiors that the "seasoned soldiers" in his company were needed to give basic training to new recruits. By switching their assignment, Lieutenant Kovacs saved the lives of these 150 Jewish men. They were not sent to the Russian front where many men in their battalion died within a few months.

Lieutenant Kovacs was punished for being a "Jew-lover" and sent to the Russian front. He sustained wounds and survived the war. (JFR Photo Archives)

ALICE SCHIFFER, ANZEGEN, BELGIUM... 1942 – Alice cared for two young girls, Inge and Lydia Kollmann, for six months during the war. She adopted the children, had them baptized, and placed them in a convent where they remained until liberation. Alice continued to look after the girls while they were in the convent. In the photograph with Alice is Inge. (JFR Photo Archives)

BARBARA MAKUCH, SANDOMIERZ, POLAND... 1942 – Barbara hid ten-year-old Malka Hymans in her home for more than a year. When it became too dangerous, she took Malka to a convent in Lvov. Barbara was arrested by the Gestapo for helping Jews and was sent to Ravensbrück, a German concentration camp, where she remained until liberation two years later. (JFR Photo Archives)

Per Anger Wallenberg's Last Acts, His Unique Achievement

Wallenberg's words, the last time we saw each other, were typical of him and of the seriousness with which he took his assignment. "I'd never be able to go back to Stockholm without knowing inside myself I'd done all a man could do to save as many Jews as possible." And he did all that a man could, to the very last. He was tireless in his efforts to save Jews from deportation. Many are the stories of how he could pop up on the most unexpected occasions and succeed in preventing the removal of Jews with protective passports, or stop the Arrow Crossmen from forcing their way into the Swedish houses. He swamped the Arrow Cross* authorities with written petitions for relief for his charges. It was often he who was the prime mover in the neutral legations' protests, through joint memoranda, to the Arrow Cross regime, against the inhuman treatment of the Jews.

Even if the mass deportations to Auschwitz by rail had stopped, the Germans made sporadic attempts to ship groups of Jews off by train.

Wallenberg always had people on watch who could warn him in time to get to the station before the train's departure. On one occasion, he arrived with several long lists of the holders of protective passports and demanded in an authoritative tone to check whether any such persons had by mistake been taken aboard. The Germans were taken by surprise and, right under their noses, Wallenberg pulled out a large number of Jews. Many of them had no passport at all, only various papers in the Hungarian language – drivers licenses, vaccination records or tax receipts – that the Germans did not understand. The bluff succeeded.

Another time, when I was there, the Germans tried to stop us with guns. But we stood our ground, showed our Swedish diplomatic passports, and were able to leave with our charges.

One day when Wallenberg was elsewhere, I rushed out to a station from which a trainload of Jews was about to depart. There was no time to debate with the Germans. I explained that a terrible mistake had been made, since apparently they were about to deport Jews who had Swedish protective passports. Should they not be released immediately, I would make sure that [Edmund] Veesenmayer† was informed. The reaction to this proved to be the same as on the tenth of October, when we were sending home the group of Swedish women and children. The German train commander did not dare to risk being reported to the dreaded Veesenmayer. I went into the cars to call the roll, but found only two Jews with protective passports. However, with the help of the Hungarian police officer there, Batizfalvy (who secretly cooperated with Raoul Wallenberg and me), I succeeded, despite the SS commandant's orders, in freeing 150 Jews from the station even though 148 had no protective passports.

Wallenberg sometimes arranged for special expeditions in which Jews who looked Aryan, dressed in Arrow Cross uniforms, raided camps and prisons and on several occasions succeeded in freeing a large number of Jews on the pretext that they were being taken away to deportation.

How many persons did Wallenberg save? To that question, a clear-cut answer can hardly be given.

I witnessed his stopping the deportation of a total of several thousand Jews at train stations, from the Swedish houses, and during the death march to the Austrian border.

It was through these acts that the rumor was spread of his almost superhuman ability, in seemingly hopeless situations, to snatch victims from the Nazi executioners. He became hated but feared by the Arrow Crossmen. He became the Budapest Jews' hope of rescue from the final liquidation.

Yet it was not through the kind of personal inter-

Per Anger, **With Raoul Wallenberg in Budapest,** 89–93. Copyright © 1981, 1996 by Per Anger. Washington, D.C.: Holocaust Library, 1981. Reprinted by permission of the United States Holocaust Memorial Museum.

*Hungarian fascist party, *Ed.*
†German ambassador to Hungary, *Ed.*

vention just described that he made his greatest contribution. It was as a negotiator that he achieved his greatest results. He was the driving force behind the agreements entered into with the Arrow Cross regime concerning their respecting not only the 5,000 Swedish protective passports but also corresponding documents of the other neutral legations.

Wallenberg was always conscious of the fact that saving as *many* persons as possible was what mattered. "You know yourself," he remarked on one occasion, "how we're besieged every day by people who plead for a job at the legation, for asylum or for a protective passport for themselves and their relations. When they can't come themselves, they send their Aryan friends to ask help for them. All of them want to meet me personally. I've got to be firm. Time doesn't allow me to devote myself to single cases when it's a question of life or death for Budapest's entire Jewish population."

Wallenberg held to this line rigorously.

To accomplish his ends, he applied every means. He bribed Arrow Cross officials. Sometimes he threatened execution. Other times he promised pardon after the arrival of the Russians. He used Foreign Minister Kemény's wife (who was of Jewish descent and greatly admired him) to influence her husband to approve the protective passports and so on.

As I mentioned earlier, after the war had ended, it was established that 50,000 Jews who lived in the foreign houses, the international ghetto, had survived. They were generally equipped with protective passports or similar documents issued by the neutral legations and the International Red Cross. Of these, Wallenberg had protected nearly half, around 20 to 25,000.

But Wallenberg's contribution extended even fur-ther. Besides his efforts for the international ghetto, toward the end he also worked to protect the inhabitants of Budapest's general or so-called sealed ghetto, where around 70,000 had been forced together. He could sometimes arrange for food deliveries to the starving, and he managed on several occasions to forestall the Arrow Crossmen's rampages in the ghetto.

But the Arrow Crossmen had, in their fanatical hatred of the Jews, decided to commit mass murder in the ghetto at the last minute. When Wallenberg got wind of this, he demanded that the German commander, General Schmidthuber, prevent the killing. Otherwise, Wallenberg would make sure that Schmidthuber would swing on the gallows when the Russians came.

Schmidthuber was shaken by Wallenberg's words and stopped the planned operation against the ghetto.

Thus Wallenberg contributed to saving still another 70,000 lives.

Jenö Lévai, in his book, *Raoul Wallenberg – Hero of Budapest*, praises Wallenberg's efforts for the Jews in the sealed ghetto. He adds: "It is of the utmost importance that the Nazis and the Arrow Crossmen were not able to ravage unhindered – they were compelled to see that every step they took was being watched and followed by the young Swedish diplomat. From Wallenberg they could keep no secrets. The Arrow Crossmen could not trick him. They could not operate freely, they were held responsible for the lives of the persecuted and the condemned. Wallenberg was the 'world's observing eye,' the one who continually called the criminals to account.

"That is the great importance of Wallenberg's struggle in Budapest."

Daniel Carpi **The Rescue of Jews in the Italian Zone of Occupied Croatia**

FOLLOWING ITS DEFEAT in the *Blitzkrieg* of April 1941, Yugoslavia was occupied by the Axis powers, and divided into various sectors. Several districts were annexed to the neighbouring countries – Hungary, Bulgaria, and the Axis states – while two separate states, which were supposed to eventually become independent – Serbia and Croatia – were created from the remaining parts of Yugoslavia. Serbia never gained independence, even ostensibly, and throughout the war was under German military rule. Croatia, on the other hand, was declared an "independent state" (*Nezavisna Država Hrvatska*). The Italians helped establish the Croatian state in the hope that it would be an Italian satellite and a base for expanding Italian political and cultural influence in the Balkans. Ante Pavelić, the leader of the *Ustaša*, the Croatian fascist party, was appointed head of state. He had spent many years in Italy as a political exile, and had established close ties with the Fascist Party and its leaders. Indeed, a few days after the establishment of the new Croatian state, Pavelić came to Rome, and on May 18, 1941, signed a series of agreements with Mussolini, which were designed to serve as a basis for the friendly relations between the two states. They agreed that a monarchy ruled by a descendant of the Italian royal family would be established in Croatia and the Duke of Spoleto was chosen for this post. They also agreed upon the boundaries between the two countries, and Croatia ceded part of the Dalmatian coast – between the cities of Zadar and Split – as well as most of the islands off the coast to the Italians.

It soon became clear, however, that these initial successes of Italian diplomacy were meaningless. From the very beginning, the Italians were prevented from extending their influence over all the territory of the Croatian state because of the opposition of the Germans, who considered this state a vital base for maintaining their influence in the Danube Basin even after the end of the war. This conflict of interests be-

tween the two Axis powers led to a compromise, a sort of "partition agreement," which was signed by Ciano and Ribbentrop in Vienna on April 21 and 22, 1941. According to the agreement, "independent" Croatia was to be divided into two – the northeastern section was to be controlled by the German Army and the southwestern section by the Italian Army. Moreover, the agreement was supposedly signed only due to the current security situation and merely for the duration of the war.

Thus even prior to the summer of 1941, three distinct regions were created in the territory which was to be included in the "Independent State of Croatia" – a region which was annexed to Italy (commonly referred to as Sector A); a region occupied by the Italian Army (Sector B); and a third region which was controlled by the German Army. In the latter two areas, the civil administration was handed over to the Croatian authorities. As early as August 1941, however, the Italian Army was forced to take over administrative duties in parts of Sector B – in effect throughout a strip about 50 kilometers wide along the coast – in order to stop the atrocities committed by bands of the *Ustaša* against the Serbian minority. Thus sector B was divided into two: an area in which all civilian and military authority was in the hands of the Italian Army, and an area in which the Italian Army controlled only the major strategic points. The former was usually referred to as Sector C.

This complex breakdown into sectors, with borders which were never completely delineated, set the stage for the great tragedy which befell the Jews of Croatia. It was also the framework within which the conditions, which in several respects were exceptional, were created for the rescue of some of these Jews.

The persecution of the Jews of Croatia began shortly after the establishment of the Croatian state, and information regarding their plight reached the

Daniel Carpi, "The Rescue of Jews in the Italian Zone of Occupied Croatia," Yisrael Gutman and Efraim Zuroff, eds., **Rescue Attempts During the Holocaust**, 468–506. Copyright © 1977 Yad Vashem. Reprinted by permission of Yad Vashem Martyrs' Remembrance Authority.

Italian Foreign Ministry early in the summer of 1941. The reports included descriptions of the brutal behavior of the *Ustaša* and of Croatian government officials toward Jews and Serbs, and these documents also express deep revulsion at these inhuman acts. One gets the impression, however, that the reports were still fairly routine. Even the two long and detailed memoranda sent by Jews to the Italian Foreign Ministry – one by a group of refugees from Sarajevo[1] and the other by the Chairman of the Union of Jewish Communities of Italy – did not make an impact. In any event, we have no evidence of any changes which took place as a result. According to the documents of the Foreign Ministry, a change took place in the spring of 1942, when the first reports on "masses" of Jewish refugees who were fleeing Croatia, and even Serbia and Bosnia, in order to seek refuge in the sectors under the control of the Italian Army, began reaching the Italian Foreign Ministry. The first report was sent on May 15 by Giuseppe Bastianini, the civilian governor of Dalmatia, who was particularly concerned over this development because, in his words, thousands of Jewish refugees had already settled in Dalmatia. He asked the Foreign Ministry and the Command of the Italian Army in Croatia to act quickly to find an immediate solution to this problem.

Thus, within a short time, most of the elements destined to play a role in this episode and in the rescue activities were activated: the Foreign Ministry in Rome and its liaison office attached to Italian Army Headquarters in Croatia and Dalmatia; the Italian Legation in Zagreb; the Italian civilian governor of Dalmatia, and the headquarters of the Second Army in Croatia and Dalmatia.

Bastianini initially believed that due to considerations of logistics, internal security, and politics, thousands of refugees should not be allowed to remain in Dalmatia. He therefore ordered the army to block the entry of additional refugees and to expel those who had already arrived. This step, which at first was apparently taken on his own initiative, was quickly confirmed by an "order by higher authorities," which he received from Rome (apparently from the Ministry of the Interior), and which directed him to carry out the expulsion immediately. Nevertheless, this directive

was not implemented – with the exception of a few isolated cases – because all those involved in the matter quickly realized that under no circumstances could the refugees be given over to the Croatians, a step tantamount to condemning them to persecution, torture, and even death.

While there was general agreement on this principle, there was, however, no unanimity as to what the best solution would be. Bastianini insisted that the refugees not remain in Dalmatia. He suggested concentrating them in an area in Croatia, which would be selected in consultation with the Croatian Government, on the condition that the Italian Foreign Ministry obtain "guarantees" from the Croatians in advance that these Jews would be treated humanely and given decent living conditions. If this condition were not guaranteed in advance, Bastianini wrote, that it would "be impossible for me to carry out the instructions I mentioned above" regarding the extradition of the refugees.

The Foreign Ministry was not at all enthusiastic about Bastianini's suggestion and it in turn proposed – in a document signed by Ciano, even though the initiative came from the Italian Legation in Zagreb – that the refugees be concentrated in Sector B, i.e., in the area of Croatia occupied by the Italian Army. In this way, the problems of the Governor of Dalmatia would be solved, and no one would have to depend upon the good will – if indeed it could be thus labelled! – of the Croatian authorities. The Italian Army was in charge of Sector B and it would guarantee the welfare and safety of the refugees.

Even this solution, which at first glance seemed exceedingly simple and practical, was fraught, however, with serious and almost insurmountable difficulties. By the middle of 1942, the control exercised by the Italian Army over most of Sector B had weakened – either because of the pressure of the *Ustaša* or because of the activities of the Communist partisans – to such an extent that it became highly doubtful whether the Italians would be able to take on the additional and unconventional task of guarding the Jewish refugees. For this reason, General Mario Roatta, the Commander of the Second Army, rejected the suggestion. He noted that in Sector B (Crkvenica-Cirquenizza) there was already a small concentration of approximately 300 Jews whom the Italian Army had undertaken to protect. Moreover, they were barely succeeding in this task due to the pressure of the Croatians who incessantly demanded that these Jews be turned over to them. Roatta added, however, that the refugees then in Dalmatia should not be abandoned, because if they were to fall into the hands of the Croatians, they would be transported to the Jasenovac concentration camp, and "the consequences are well-known to everyone." He suggested therefore that the refugees be interned on one of the islands off the coast of Dalmatia, i.e. in Sector A, since in his opinion they could easily be protected there without causing unnecessary difficulties for the Italian civil administration.

This first round of correspondence had no practical consequences, for Bastianini rejected Roatta's suggestion out of hand, claiming that it could not be implemented. The fact that no decision was reached, however, had very positive consequences. All those involved in the issue understood that if their desire was to ensure the safety of the refugees, they should not reach a hasty decision. As a result, they continued to correspond with one another at a leisurely pace, raising various possible solutions. In the meantime, certain facts were created which no one questioned. The refugees who succeeded in reaching safety were not expelled, and here and there they even began to rebuild their lives, with the help of DELASEM* or upon their own initiative.

Hardly more than a month had elapsed since the beginning of this correspondence, when a dramatic turnabout occurred. Soon this peripheral matter concerning the fate of several thousand refugees became an issue of principle, morality, and policy, which involved the political and military policymakers of the two Axis powers, and in several respects strained the friendly relations between Italy and Germany.

The beginning of this turnabout was purely coincidental. One day in June 1942 – apparently around the 20th of the month – a group of German officers and engineers serving in a unit of the Todt Organization which was in charge of bauxite mining in Mostar, the capital of Herzegovina, passed through that city. They were accommodated at the staff headquarters of the Italian "Murge" division, which was

stationed there, and one of the German engineers commented about some sort of "agreement between the governments of Germany and Croatia to deport all the Croatian Jews, including those of Herzegovina, to the Russian areas occupied by the Germans." These remarks – made in the course of a friendly conversation among comrades at arms – aroused the ire of the Italian hosts, either because they considered the agreement a blow to the status and authority of the Italian Army – the district of Herzegovina was included in Sector B – or due to humanitarian principles. As a result, they appealed to the headquarters of the Second Army, which in turn contacted the Foreign Ministry in Rome, and expressed the opinion that this agreement should not be carried out with regard to the Jews of Sector B, at least as long as the Italian Army was still stationed there.

This time, the various levels of Italian officialdom did not delay. On June 23, 1942, the first cable concerning the issue was sent to Rome, four days later a memorandum was sent, and on June 28, Ciano's personal secretary, the Marquis Blasco Lanza d'Ajeta replied that, "Also for reasons of a general nature this Ministry agrees that the said agreement between the governments of Germany and Croatia should not be carried out in the areas under our occupation."

The policy adopted by the Italians, and the various steps which led to it, are fully clarified and confirmed in one of the documents of the German Foreign Ministry published by Sabille.[2] A memorandum submitted to Ribbentrop on July 24, 1942 stated that an agreement had been reached between the Germans and the Croatians on the deportation of all the Jews of Croatia; that the agreement had already been formulated in writing; and that the Croatians favored the deportation, but insisted that it encompass all the Jews, including those in Sector B, whose number they estimated at about 4,000-5,000 persons. The author of the memorandum added that in his opinion the Croatians would need forceful German support to carry out the plan, since stubborn opposition by the Italians was anticipated, and in fact there were already many indications of such opposition. Thus, for example, the Italian Chief of Staff in Mostar had only recently announced that he would not agree to the deportation of Jews from the city,

---

Delegazione Assistenza Emigranti – organization established by the Union of Jewish Communities of Italy to assist refugees, *Ed.*

since it was against the declared policy of the Italians, who granted full equality to all residents. Even more caustic comments were made in the presence of the German commander of the Todt unit which was supervising the bauxite mining in the area. The same memorandum also states that Siegfried Kasche, the German Ambassador in Zagreb, expressed his opinion that the deportation could begin immediately, but that he also believed that "for reasons of principle" it must be implemented throughout the country. The memorandum seems to indicate even though it does not say so explicitly, that the German Foreign Ministry was requested to assist in the operation by asking the top political officials in Rome to order the army commanders in Croatia to change their position.

Even before this memorandum was written, the Germans had, in fact, turned on several occasions to the Italian Legation in Zagreb and pointed out the extreme security danger posed by the presence of numerous Jewish refugees in Sector B. They evaded the Croatian "racial laws," engaged in espionage, and cooperated with the enemy. As early as July 7, Casertano, the Italian envoy in Zagreb, had reported regarding these repeated protests, noting that "This German concern, which already smells of interference, could be a prelude to some official step" in the future. Apparently the Italian authorities were not particularly impressed by this warning. Thus throughout the month of July and the first half of August 1942, they continued to leisurely correspond and discuss the placement of the refugees, despite the fact that during this entire period more and more information was received from the Italian Legation in Zagreb about the intensification of the persecution of the Jews in Croatia, including the news of the concentration of thousands of Jews and their deportation to the "territories of the East." According to this same source, this news seemed to indicate that "the Jewish problem in this country, which had already been dealt with in a most drastic manner in the past, was now approaching the stage which would perhaps constitute its final solution."[3]

Finally, on August 17 (according to one of the sources, August 18), 1942, an official intervention was made. Early in the morning, as was the custom of

German diplomats, Prince Otto von Bismarck, the counsellor in the German Embassy in Rome, brought a telegram from Von Ribbentrop requesting his Italian counterpart "to see that instructions be given to the Italian military authorities in Croatia so that the operation planned by the Germans and the Croatians for a massive transfer of the Jews of Croatia to the territories of the East will be able to be carried out in the Italian-occupied zone as well." Verax, who apparently was among those who received the German counsellor, knew Bismarck personally and he described him as an average man, obsessed by feelings of inferiority vis-à-vis the Anglo-Saxon world, a man who at times allowed himself to whisper criticism of the Nazi policies in a confidant's ear, yet was always ready to carry out orders, even of the most humiliating nature.[4] On that morning as well, after he had fulfilled his mission, Bismarck whispered in the ears of the Italian officials that "the matter concerned several thousand people" and that "the purpose of the planned operation was in fact their physical dispersal and elimination." In response, he was told that his request would be considered and that it would be brought to [Foreign Minister, Count Galeazzo] Ciano and Mussolini for a decision.

Ciano's response is not known, and it appears that he refrained from taking an unequivocal position in this matter. This was not the case as far as Mussolini was concerned. The memorandum presented to him by officials of the Foreign Ministry contained three short paragraphs: the substance of Ribbentrop's appeal, the whispered warning of Bismarck, and a summary of the abovementioned report sent by the Italian Legation in Zagreb on August 6, 1942. On the basis of this information, Mussolini was asked to decide whether to accept or reject Ribbentrop's appeal. Mussolini's answer was anything but ambiguous. On the page which he was given (and which has been preserved), he wrote in the upper right hand corner "*nulla osta*" – ("there is no opposition"), and signed next to it with the famous "M."

Thus, with one stroke of the pen, and on the basis of two words written by Mussolini on a piece of paper with a coarse pencil, the fate of 3,000 individuals had been sealed. "There is no opposition," he wrote, and the meaning of these words was that the

Jewish refugees should be handed over to the Germans, even though it was clear beyond a shadow of a doubt that this meant their death.

Several days later, on August 29, Ciano's office informed Army Headquarters of the contents of the German Embassy's appeal and of the decision of "the Royal Government" that there should be "no opposition" to handing over the Jewish refugees who had found shelter in Sector B. (Of course no mention was made of Sector A, which had been annexed to Italy.) This communication, which was transmitted in the name of "the Government" was tantamount to an explicit command to the General Staff to see to it that the decision be implemented. It should be noted, however, that no date was set for the beginning of the operation and no timetable of any sort was included in the communication – an omission which perhaps was not accidental.

In theory, the die had been cast. In fact, at the very moment that this decision was made, the real rescue efforts, planned from above and coordinated with the various branches, began in earnest. Among those who took part in this activity were several commanders of the Italian Army stationed in Croatia, among them General Mario Roatta and Giuseppe Pièche, the general of the Carabinieri forces, (who after the war was awarded a special citation by the Union of Jewish Communities of Italy for his bold efforts on behalf of the Jews), and Vittorio Castellani, the head of the liaison bureau between the Foreign Ministry and Army Staff Headquarters in Yugoslavia (*Ufficio collegamento con il Comando Superiore delle FF.AA. Slovenia Dalmazia – Supersloda*). In Rome, several high-ranking officials of the Foreign Ministry initiated and participated in the plan, particularly Ambassador Luca Pietromarchi, who was the head of the department which dealt with the problems of territories occupied by the Italian Army (*Gabinetto, Affari Politici, Ufficio Slovenia, Croazia, Dalmazia, Montenegro, Grecia e Isole Ionie*), Signor Roberto Ducci, head of the "Croatian Office" (*Gabinetto, Affari Politici, Ufficio Croazia*), and the Marquis d'Ajeta, head of the Minister's Secretariat.

During the initial consultations which took place in the Foreign Ministry after Mussolini's response was received, these officials – and perhaps others as well

about whom we have no information – decided that on principle they would not accede to the decisions of the Ministry regarding the extradition of the Jewish refugees from Croatia. They considered the issue to be one of humanitarian concern, a matter of principle in which they simply could not give in – on a practical level – under any circumstances. They decided to adopt delaying tactics, in the hope that the longer they could put off the implementation of the plan, the more likely it was that it would eventually be abandoned.

This decision was further reinforced upon receipt of a new report from the Italian Legation in Zagreb on August 22, 1942. The report, which was the most detailed and accurate hereto received on the subject, stated that the deportation to Poland (it is noteworthy that until then the indefinite term "territories of the East" had been used) of the remnants of the Jews of Croatia had recently begun; that the deportations were being carried out in special railway cars provided by the Croatian authorities; and that the Croatians even obligated themselves to pay the Germans 30 marks for each Jew who was taken out of the country. The report further stated that the representative of the Vatican in Zagreb, Monsignor Ramiro Marcone, had intervened via diplomatic channels to stop the deportations but his intervention had been futile. It seemed, however, that "Aryans" married to Jews would not be deported. Besides describing the events, the author of the report also noted that the German Ambassador in Zagreb had once again approached him and demanded that the Jews of Croatia who had fled to Sector B be included in the deportations, stating that the German Government would soon take formal steps in this matter. (The German Ambassador in Zagreb also reported on this step.)[5]

The picture was thus very clear to the officials of the Italian Foreign Ministry. They also had already made their own decision and had chosen the tactics which were to be used. Nothing remained to be done except to begin to implement the plan which, of course, required careful coordination between the diplomatic and military elements, and this type of coordination, by its nature, required oral communication, rather than the use of the regular channels. This is what occurred, although clear evidence was also left in writing, which enables us to trace several of the major steps which were taken. It seems that the participants did not insist upon preserving the "conspiratorial" nature of their activities – apparently they did not deem it necessary. This fact is indicative of the extent to which they depended on the widespread support of various military and government circles in this operation.

The first stages of the delaying process are very clearly outlined in a confidential summary composed by the staff of "Supersloda," a copy of which was attached to a letter written by Castellani, the liaison officer between the Foreign Ministry and "Supersloda" staff headquarters, to his superiors in Rome. Written on September 11, 1942, Castellani's letter relates that immediately upon his return to Second Army headquarters following his visit to Rome, he met with General Roatta. They discussed the "well-known problem of the Jews," and Castellani learned that "he [Roatta] agrees completely with our point of view." "Supersloda" will therefore reply to General Staff Headquarters in the spirit of the points raised in the summary which was attached, and it would do so "without any undue haste." The summary stated that while "Supersloda" was, naturally, ready to carry out the orders of the General Staff regarding the extradition of the Jewish refugees, the staff nonetheless considered it its duty to point out the practical difficulties hindering the execution of this program as well as the political considerations which in their opinion made it necessary to refrain from actually carrying it out. The refugees were very few in number, since most of Croatian Jewry "had been slaughtered by the *Ustaša* during the previous summer, particularly in the Gospic and Pago camps." The refugees were scattered throughout both parts of Sector B (areas B and C), where the control of the Italian Army was limited to several places. Moreover, even in those locations, the refugees were mixed together with local Jews and Jews from Sector A (who, of course, were not candidates for expulsion). Thus in order to carry out the instructions, it would first be necessary to determine where the refugees were located, their exact number, and who should be handed over. In addition to the great effort involved, which would be totally out of proportion to the number of refugees involved, the extradi-

tion of the refugees would cause inestimable damage to the good name and prestige of the Italian Army in Croatia and throughout the Balkans. It would be interpreted as a disavowal of the express obligation assumed by the Italians to ensure that no one would be discriminated against because of their religion or race in the areas under their occupation. Moreover, such a move was also likely to arouse the suspicions of the Serbian population that once the Jews had been extradited they too would be handed over to the "wild men of the *Ustaša*," a suspicion which might undermine the peace in this area which in any event was far from stable. Finally, the report noted that even though the behavior of the refugees had not aroused any security worries until then, a plan to transfer them to special camps on one of the islands off the coast of Dalmatia had recently been discussed. From the tone of the report, it is obvious that the writer considered this to be the most practical and desirable solution.

This document sums up the major points which the Foreign Ministry officials and the officers of "Supersloda" agreed would serve as the basis of their attempts to prevent the extradition of the Jews. Indeed, "Supersloda's" response, sent on September 22, 1942 to the General Staff, repeated these same points, albeit more briefly and in a somewhat laconic style. Castellani, who two days later sent a copy of this response to the Foreign Ministry, bemoaned the style and the abbreviations, and found it necessary to explain that "the formulation of this response was also very difficult, and the final version was not arrived at until after a series of six drafts" because "General Roatta's position is extremely difficult, and he is constantly preoccupied (and perhaps not unjustly) that his friends in Rome might be given an excuse to depict him as rebelling against the instructions of his superiors." These clear-cut comments are evidence of their fear that there were officers in the General Staff whose opinions were contrary to those which had hereto been voiced. (It is possible that this comment also, or mainly, referred to Marshal Ugo Cavallero, the Chief of Staff, who was considered to be decidedly pro-German. In his diary, Ciano labelled him a "servant of the Germans." According to the documents of the Foreign Ministry, however, one gets the impression that as far as the Jews of Croatia were concerned, Cavallero's position was no different than that of Roatta or his other colleagues.)

In late September 1942, the situation was therefore fairly clear. The Italian staff officers in Croatia continued, "without any undue haste," their discussions about plans to concentrate the Jewish refugees in special camps – at that time the inclination was to intern them on one of the islands off the coast of Dalmatia – and they also began taking a census of the refugees. At General Staff Headquarters in Rome, there was no response to "Supersloda's" remarks and suggestions, either because they too considered this the wisest way of dealing with the matter, or because they believed that at that time there were more crucial military problems that required their attention. The Foreign Ministry, on the other hand, followed the development of the events with interest, tensely and fearfully awaiting the German response.

They did not have to wait long. At the end of September, Pavelić met with Hitler at German Staff Headquarters and in the course of one of their discussions, the question of the Jews of Croatia was raised. Hitler emphasized that "the Jews are the underground communication channels and the junction points of all the resistance movements" and he demanded that their activities be stopped once and for all. [German Foreign Minister, Joachim von] Ribbentrop, who was also present at that discussion, recalled Mussolini's decision concerning the extradition of the Jews of Croatia, and added that, "evidently this decision has not yet been transmitted to the local Army headquarters."[6] They finally decided that the German Embassy in Rome should ask the Italian Foreign Ministry what had been done to transmit Mussolini's instructions to the army personnel involved.[7] Thus, on October 3, Johann Von Plessen, a counsellor in the German Embassy in Rome, contacted the Italian Foreign Ministry, and reminded them of the previous decision to hand over the Croatian Jews living in the "area under the control" of the Italian Army. He also declared that according to the information which had reached the Germans, the competent military authorities had not yet received the proper instructions in the matter. He added orally – according to the testimony of Verax[8] – that "certain German elements had opined that the

Italian Foreign Ministry was somehow involved in this delay."

This diplomatic maneuver led to an Italian reaction on several fronts. On October 7, Ciano sent an urgent cable to the General Staff, in which he informed them of the Germans' complaint, reminded them of the prior agreement of "His Majesty's Government" and asked that he be informed immediately what instructions had been issued and what steps had been taken. Either intentionally, or merely due to a slip of the pen, Ciano wrote about the extradition of the Jews "to the German authorities," even though until then they had always spoken of handing the Jews over to the Croatians. Ciano also added that the Germans had complained that, according to the information which they had, the Italian officers in Croatia had stated that they had received no instructions whatsoever regarding this matter.

This last item aroused a certain uneasiness among the officers of the Italian General Staff. In a cable sent on October 12, they informed "Supersloda" of the Foreign Minister's appeal, emphasized the seriousness of the German complaint, and demanded that the matter be clarified. They also asked that a report on the results of the census and the steps which had been taken to implement the orders concerning the extradition of the Jewish refugees to "the German authorities," be sent immediately.

This time "Supersloda" did not delay. One day later, on October 13, it sent a strongly-worded response that no one had ever discussed the handing over of the Jews to "the German authorities," thus it was only natural that no Italian officer had issued any "statement" on this matter, neither to the Germans nor to anyone else. It was the Croatians – and not the Germans – who had time and again asked them to hand over the Jews; and it was to them that "Supersloda" had responded that it had to receive explicit instructions from Rome. The Germans' complaint was thus unfounded. As for the census, it had been ascertained that the total number of Jews in Sector B was 2,025. (In his letter of October 15, 1942, to the Foreign Ministry, however, Castellani noted that this figure did not include 1,626 additional refugees who at the time were "in the midst of being transferred from Spalato to Ragusa" – i.e. from Split to Dubrovnik –

and for this reason they were not included in the census in either place). What presently had to be determined was how to divide the Jews who had been counted in the census into the various groups – those who were to be handed over to the Croatians and those who were to continue to benefit from the protection of the Italians. In order to do so, "Supersloda" added, it required further instructions from the Foreign Ministry, which would list the exact criteria which were to be used to classify the Jews. At the end, the cable stated that "Supersloda" had not changed its position as outlined in the report of September 22 – that the interests of Italy demanded that the Jews not be handed over. It had also not received any new instructions, since according to the oral instructions given by the Chief of the General Staff Marshal Cavallero to General Roatta, "Supersloda" was to refrain from taking any additional action until further notice. In any event, the opinion of "Supersloda" was that the members of the Italian armed forces should not under any circumstances be given the task of extraditing the Jews. If this shameful act had to be carried out, the Croatians should come and collect the Jews themselves.

In the course of the ensuing developments, it became clear that of all the arguments used by "Supersloda" – all of which were of great moral weight – the one which led to the most practical results was "Supersloda's" request that the Foreign Ministry establish the criteria which were to be used in deciding "who was a Croatian Jew." It soon became clear that this question, which at first glance had seemed so simple, was fairly complicated, since it had to be formulated as follows: "Who was a Jewish refugee residing in Sector B, who was originally from one of the Croatian districts which had not initially been included in the area of the Italian occupation?" This formulation enabled anyone interested to ask many other questions such as: What was the definition of "refugee"? What was the cutoff date, after which a Jew who had come to Sector B was considered a refugee? What should be done with a Jew who was in fact a refugee, but whose family had originally lived in one of the cities of Sector B? What should be the fate of those Jews who had in fact fled from Croatia but who had originally lived elsewhere, for example Poland, Hungary, Slovakia, or even Spain or Portugal (from whence their ancestors had emigrated at the end of the 15th century)? Questions of this sort could be asked *ad infinitum*.

It soon became clear that this matter of "criteria" could serve as very useful ammunition. One could easily find exceptions in the family origins of most of the Jews, and thus it was easy to claim that every case had to be investigated carefully and that the matter could not therefore be completed within a short time, particularly under the difficult wartime conditions.

The correspondence concerning these questions went on for a long time, and we need not review the details. It is sufficient to note that immediately after Von Plessen's visit to the Foreign Ministry, the legal advisor of the Ministry was asked to give his opinion as to who could be considered a "resident" – as opposed to a "refugee" – of the areas under the control of the Italian Army, and who could claim Italian citizenship. On the basis of this initial legal opinion, which was dated October 13, 1942, the officials of the Foreign Ministry established a number of guidelines, which were intentionally broad and vague, and which later, with minor revisions in their formulation, became the basis for all subsequent directives. According to these guidelines, a "resident" was generally an individual who had been officially registered in the local population register. As far as being granted Italian citizenship was concerned, however, the following people would also be taken into consideration: individuals born in the area, those who had resided there "for a fairly long time," a person whose relatives (until the third degree) lived there, those who had real estate in that area, as well as individuals who had rendered outstanding service to the Italian occupation authorities – even if they did not fulfill any of the above criteria.

These guidelines were sent to "Supersloda" on October 16, and the Foreign Ministry repeated them verbatim in a cable sent to the General Staff on November 3. Since they were so broad, it is not surprising that the Italian Army authorities in Croatia claimed from time to time that not only was the clarification of the family origin of the Jews a complicated matter that would take a very long time, but that the number of those who in the end would be extradited would, according to all estimates, be very small indeed. Why then all the unnecessary anxiety concerning the matter? The problem is known and is being dealt with, and in the meantime no security problems are envisaged as a result.

Parallel to this approach, which combined both delaying and diversionary tactics, the officials of the Foreign Ministry also attempted other steps which were more suited to their talents as professional diplomats. They began to conduct discussions with the Croatian authorities in Rome and Zagreb, and attempted to convince them to forego their demand for the extradition of the Jews.

Verax, who apparently was personally involved in this activity, mentions a conversation with Stj. Perić, the Croatian Ambassador in Rome, which took place on October 20, 1942. At this time, the ambassador said that his government would be willing to forgo its extradition request if the Italian Government were to undertake to transfer these Jews to Italy (to the "old Italian districts," as he defined it, even excluding Sector A, which had been annexed to Italy) and hand over all their property to the Croatians. According to Verax's testimony, Perić added that he personally hoped that the Italian Government would accept this condition "because he is well aware of the fate awaiting those Jews who are deported by the Germans to the territories of the East."[9]

Verax was encouraged by the ambassador's comments, by his formal suggestion, as well as his personal remarks. He did not know, however, that on the same day that Perić had presented his government's proposal to the officials of the Foreign Ministry, the Croatian Foreign Minister, Mladen Lorkovic, had contacted Siegfried Kasche, the German Ambassador in Zagreb, had informed him of the Italian proposals, and told him that his government did not intend to accept them unless the Germans gave their explicit approval and unless regardless of what happened all the Jews' property would be handed over to the Croatians. That very day, Kasche sent a report to the German Foreign Ministry protesting the Italian diplomatic maneuvers – in which he saw signs of the influence of the Vatican – and expressed his opinion that these proposals be rejected outright because "to hand over the Jews to Italy would be tantamount to reversing our entire European policy vis-à-vis the Jews."[10]

As could be expected, the response of the German Foreign Minister was shortly forthcoming. The next day, October 21, (according to another document – on October 22), Prince Von Bismarck came to the Italian Foreign Ministry and demanded that the Croatian Jews be handed over immediately "not to the German armed forces, but to the Croatian authorities who were working in close cooperation with special units of the German police."

This appeal, and similar appeals which were subsequently submitted to the Italians almost every day, confused the Italian officials. They sensed that they were about to be "caught in the act" and that their maneuvers had brought them to a dead-end from which they had to extricate themselves as quickly as possible lest all their efforts came to naught. They therefore set up a small committee which was to come up with a new plan of action that could be endorsed by both Ciano and Mussolini and which, at the same time, would enable those involved to resist pressure from the Germans.

The committee worked very diligently and in the course of a few days prepared five drafts (in effect five different formulations of two alternative proposals), at least two of which were seen by the Foreign Ministry. The fifth draft, which was accepted by all involved on October 23, was presented to Mussolini for his endorsement. This time, Mussolini's signature was not preserved on the paper, but there is no doubt that he personally endorsed the plan, since it is referred to on many occasions as the "instructions of the Duce." It appears that Mussolini saw no contradiction between this endorsement and his earlier decision of August 21, 1942. In fact, at first glance there appears to be no contradiction between the two.

According to the plan, the General Staff would instruct "Supersloda" "to coordinate the handing over of the Croatian Jews found in the area of the Italian occupation with the Croatian authorities." However, since these Jews had become mixed up with the rest of the Jews, some of whom were eligible for Italian citizenship, the General Staff should direct "Supersloda" to first of all clarify the origin of every Jew, for it was inconceivable that Jews who were eligible for Italian citizenship and were residing in the area of the Italian occupation would be negatively discriminated against in comparison with Jews who possessed Italian citizenship and were residing in one of the countries occupied by the Germans. (In these countries the Italians ensured that the civil rights of their citizens, including the Jews, were protected.) In the meantime, in order to carry out this investigation properly, the General Staff should *immediately* issue instructions that *all* the Jews living in the area of the Italian occupation, regardless of their origin should be concentrated in special camps. The fact that the words "immediately" and "all" were emphasized in the original, is an indication of the importance which was attached to the directive to concentrate the Jews, which was the only important innovation in this plan.

The purpose of this directive was clear. The Italians feared that under the political and military circumstances which had developed, they would find it difficult to continue protecting the Jews who were scattered throughout a very wide area over which they were increasingly losing control. Similarly, it would be difficult for them to continue putting off the Germans' request, without having some new and convincing excuse. The concentration of all the Jews in a few places would tend to facilitate the problem of protecting them and, at the same time, make things a little easier for the Italian diplomats, who could now point to the fact that "practical steps" had already been taken towards carrying out the plan to extradite the Jews. Moreover, thus the current claim of the Germans, that the refugee problem had to be solved immediately, because as long as they were free the refugees constituted a serious security risk, could be absolutely refuted. Now the Jews would be held as prisoners in camps, where they could certainly not engage in hostile activities.

Once the plan had been accepted and endorsed by Mussolini, all the Italians had to do was to inform their German and Croatian allies and begin carrying it out. This time, the Croatians unwittingly helped in the matter. On October 26, 1942, the *Poglavnik* himself, Ante Pavelić, intervened in the matter, and instructed his ambassador in Rome to propose again to the Italian Foreign Ministry the suggestions previously put forth by the Croatian Government concerning the transfer of the Jews to one of the "old districts" of Italy. It is difficult to ascertain what Pavelić's rationale was in making this additional appeal after his foreign minister had brought these suggestions to the attention of the Germans and in so doing had brought about the failure of the whole matter. Perhaps he did not know about Lorkovic's initiative; perhaps he knew about it and opposed it. At any rate, it was now easy for Ciano's secretary, the Marquis d'Ajeta, to reply to Perić in a cold and somewhat discourteous fashion that the Italian Government rejected these proposals outright. It would adhere to the original plan concerning the handing over of the Jewish refugees to the Croatians, and the Duce had already given orders to concentrate all the Jews in camps as the first step in the process of identification and extradition. The Italians were not interested in discussing the issue any further at this time. Perić, who a week earlier had admitted that he hoped for a different solution to the problem, apparently did not understand the meaning of the change in the Italian position. He announced that he had taken note of the message and expressed the satisfaction of his government at the decision.[11]

The following day, October 28, d'Ajeta met with the German Ambassador, Von Mackensen. He informed him of the "Croatian initiative" and of Italy's outright refusal to accept it, because in d'Ajeta's words, as reported by Von Mackensen, "Italy is not Palestine." D'Ajeta also expressed his displeasure that the suggestion was raised at all, claiming that it was an attempt on the part of the Croatian Government to transfer the responsibility for a problem which belonged solely to them and which they alone had to solve, to the Italians. Finally, d'Ajeta informed him of the new steps which *Il Duce* had ordered, whose clearcut aim was to begin the implementation of the extradition program.

Von Mackensen listened to these words with great satisfaction, and in this spirit he reported the conversation to Berlin.[12] When the German Foreign Ministry relayed this report to its ambassador in Zagreb, however, Kasche responded in a completely different manner. He had discussed the matter with Lorkovic and had expressed his doubts as to the true intentions of the Italians. Lorkovic, in turn, became furious, and on the spot sent a long cable to Perić instructing him to once again clarify his government's position to the officials of the Italian Foreign Ministry.[13] In the meantime, this move allowed the Italians to again raise the idea of a "trade agreement" with the Croatians, the major points of which were that the refugees would hand over their property to the Croatians if the latter would forgo their demand for the refugees' extradition. (On this matter see below, regarding the discussion between Roatta and Mussolini in late November.) In essence, however, these contacts and discussions were merely a matter of tactics, and few people believed that they would actually lead to any practical developments.

In the meantime, new facts were being created at a dizzying pace. On October 28, the day on which the conversation between d'Ajeta and Von Mackensen took place, Marshal Cavallero, the Italian Chief of Staff, personally instructed the army staff stationed in Croatia to immediately carry out the following three activities: 1) to intern all the Jews located in the area of the Italian occupation in special concentration camps; 2) to divide these Jews into two groups, one consisting of Croatian Jews and the other of Jews eligible for Italian citizenship; 3) to send a list of all the Jews in each of the two groups to General Staff Headquarters. According to the cable, additional instructions would eventually be sent concerning the methods to be used in carrying out the extradition.

This time, the instructions of the General Staff could not be considered ambiguous, and they were carried out without delay. In the course of a few days, all the Jews – approximately 3,000 in number – were rounded up and concentrated in a number of buildings requisitioned for this purpose in the area of Dubrovnik and Split as well as on the island of Lopud and in the Porto Re (Kraljevica) camp, to which 1,161 Jews, most of whom had formerly been in Cirquenizza (Crkvenica), were transferred.

These instructions, which were issued so suddenly, and were put into effect without prior warning and without any explanation as to their true purpose, aroused different responses among the Jews, Italian officers, and Croatian population – reactions which ranged from extreme anger and great fear, to mockery and visible pleasure.

The terrible fear that their fate had been sealed and that they were about to be given over to their Croatian and German torturers, was aroused among the Jews. There were outbursts of despair and even a few cases of suicide.[14] In fact, the situation became so bad that General Roatta himself deemed it necessary to visit the Porto Re camp to meet Jewish representatives and reassure them regarding the future.[15]

During the first days after receipt of the order to round up the Jews, the officers of "Supersloda,"[16] the commander of the *Carabinieri* unit of the Fifth Corps,[17] and General Roatta himself[18] responded furiously. Apparently, none perceived the true intentions of the new orders which they had received, and they all expressed their anxiety as to what would happen to the Jews after they had been rounded up and all the investigations had been completed. They feared that the next step would be the extradition of the refugees – that was the most logical move and this was expressly stated in the instructions issued by the General Staff. They therefore unequivocally and energetically opposed these moves, both on political-practical grounds and owing to moral and humanitarian considerations.

The commander of the *Carabinieri* of the Fifth Corps, Lieutenant-Colonel Pietro Esposito Amodio, wrote at length about these reasons, such as the damage that would be done to the image and prestige of the Italian Army in the eyes of the other minorities in Croatia and the Balkans. He also presented a lengthy and exhaustive summary of the reactions of the local population – the vast majority of whom were Croatians – to the rounding up of the Jews and their deportation from the area. (The *Carabinieri* unit involved was also assigned to supervise Cirquenizza. Most of the Jews who had previously been there were transferred to the Porto Re camp.) From his description, it seems that the initial reaction of the local population was surprise mixed with satisfaction and joy at the calamity. This was followed by an element of scorn for the Italians, which was rooted in rumors circulated by the Croatian authorities that the Germans had forced the Italian Government to take these steps. According to these rumor-mongers, this episode revealed that "it is not true at all that Italy is a great power as her press and propaganda attempt to prove. In fact, she is a small country that has been reduced to the status of a vassal of greater Germany, and she will no longer be able to oppose any demand made by Germany, or perhaps even by the Croatian Government, if it receives appropriate German support." These and similar rumors, the report continued, have made a deep impression upon the native population and have caused inestimable damage to Italian interests. Many people now believe that the day is approaching when the Italian Army will be forced to evacuate so that the German Army can take over, and "many Croatians no longer fear to ask the Italian soldiers and sergeants, simply and openly, *when* the Italian troops will be leaving the area."

According to the report, these charges were widespread among the general population and especially in circles unfriendly to the Italians, and that was probably true. At times, however, it is difficult to distinguish in the language of the report between the comments of the anti-Semitic and anti-Italian Croatians, which were presented to give an indication of the current atmosphere, and the musings of the author himself.

While the Jews were already being rounded up – but it is unlikely as a direct reaction to this step – the Foreign Ministry in Rome received a brief message from General Giuseppe Pièche, the commander of the *Carabinieri* in Northern Croatia and Slovenia, who reported that according to the information at his disposal, "the Croatian Jews who had been deported from the area of the German occupation to the territories of the East had been 'liquidated' by poison gas which had been introduced into the train carriages into which they had been sealed." The message was dated November 4, 1942.

Perhaps it is difficult today to accurately assess the impact which this news made at that time and to what extent it was astounding and shocking. Although certain circles in the Foreign Ministry were already aware of the fact that expulsion to the "territories of the East" meant physical destruction, this brief statement of General Pièche's nonetheless aroused deep astonishment. On the spot it was decided that the message had to be brought to Mussolini's attention, and it is conceivable that he was influenced by it, as we shall see later on. What is certain is that this news had a profound effect upon the officials of the Foreign Ministry and it reinforced their conviction to continue working to prevent the deportation of the Jews at all costs.

Several days later, the Foreign Ministry received a letter sent on November 5 by Raffaele Guariglia, the Italian Ambassador to the Vatican, who reported that it had become known to the "Secretariat of State" that the Germans were demanding that "2,000-3,000 Jews, most of them elderly, women and children" who were presently in the Italian occupied zone of Croatia, be handed over to them. The "Secretariat of State" asked the ambassador to intervene in the matter with the Foreign Minister "in order to possibly prevent the extradition of these people."

We do not know what provoked this step by the Vatican. We have already mentioned that in the documents of the Foreign Ministry there are indications that an appeal was made by Monsignor Marcone, the Vatican representative in Zagreb, to the *Poglavnik*, in the wake of which it seems that the situation of "Aryans" married to Jews was ameliorated.[19] Similarly, we found that the Germans suspected that the Vatican was somehow connected with the position adopted by the Italian officials regarding the deportation of the Croatian Jews.[20] This suspicion, however, was unfounded. Today it is clear that the "Secretariat of State" – through Ambassador Guariglia – formally intervened to save the refugees, although we still do not know the full background to this activity, its immediate cause, and who initiated it. The proximity of the dates of the roundup of the Jews of Croatia (the beginning of November) and Ambassador Guariglia's letter (November 5), seems to indicate that the two are somehow connected.

The rounding up of the Jews and their internment in several localities was carried out in less than a week, and was completed during the first week of November. The Italians now hoped that they would be given a reasonable amount of time in order to make the necessary – and even unnecessary – investigations concerning the origin of these Jews. This time, however, the Germans were suspicious. They were not content to receive generalized explanations and requested that they be given complete copies of the instructions issued to "Supersloda" regarding this matter, and a copy was indeed given to Von Bismarck on November 11, 1942.

The text which was delivered to Von Bismarck was not exactly identical with the one sent earlier to "Supersloda."[21] Yet it is not the difference in the details, but rather the difference in tone which is noteworthy. The document given to the Germans stressed the fact that *all* the Jews, regardless of their origin, had been interned and therefore there was no reason to fear that they might engage in hostile activities in the future. In the letter that was sent to "Supersloda" on November 17, on the other hand, the Marquis d'Ajeta emphasized the fact that because *all* the Jews had been rounded up without any prior screening, the Italian authorities now had to undertake exhaustive investigations in order to ensure that the Jewish "residents" would not be denied their rights, while remaining fully conscious of "the consequences which these clarifications are likely to bring about." Indeed, the extensive correspondence on this issue indicates that the officers of "Supersloda" took this remark very seriously, and whenever they thought that there was any room for doubt, they contacted the Foreign Ministry and requested appropriate instructions.[22]

In late November or early December, General Roatta visited Rome and met with Mussolini. At that time, crucial events were occurring which were to affect the outcome of the war. In Russia, the Red Army celebrated its first great victories, and the defensive alignment of the Axis powers in North Africa began to crumble in the wake of the landing of the American Army in Algeria. Despite all this, the two leaders found time to discuss the fate of the Jewish refugees in Croatia. Roatta expounded at length on the political and military reasons which, in his opinion, made it imperative for the Italians not to hand over the refugees to the Croatians under any circumstances. He even mentioned the severe damage which had been caused to the prestige of the Italian Army because of the roundups which had been carried out in early November. Roatta was of the opinion that all the refugees should be transferred to camps located in Italy proper, and that a compromise should be worked out with the Croatians on the basis of their "proposal" – as he called it – that the Croatians renounce their demand for the extradition of the Jews and the Jews relinquish their property and their Croatian citizenship.

Apparently Mussolini tended now, more than in the past, to accept such a solution and he himself summarized the conversation with two clear and un-

ambiguous directives: "1) all the Jews would continue to be kept in concentration camps; 2) in addition to the investigations which would continue to be conducted regarding the origin of each internee, the collection would commence of applications of Jews willing to relinquish – in accordance with the above-mentioned proposal of the Croatian Government – their Croatian citizenship and the property they owned in Croatia."[23]

These two directives, besides confirming the earlier policies, also contained two important innovations – first and foremost, that at least in the forseeable future, none of those rounded up would be extradited, not even those who would be classified as "refugees"; the second was that for the first time the possibility was raised – to be more exact, the possibility was not *ab initio* denied – that some day in the future the problem of the refugees would be solved by transferring them to Italy. This possibility was, in fact, never realized, and fortunately so, for it is very doubtful whether most of the refugees would have eventually been saved (as they were in Yugoslavia) had they been sent to Italy.

A few days later, on December 9, Von Bismarck once again visited the Foreign Ministry to ask his by-now standard question concerning the extradition of the Jewish refugees in Croatia. This time, however, he also offered a new suggestion. His government understood, he said, the severe difficulties involved in transferring thousands of Jewish refugees through territory in which "bands of rebels" were active. He therefore proposed that these Jews be transferred by sea to Trieste and from there straight to Germany.

It was clear that in this manner the Germans intended to forcefully present their demand. The Italian officials were startled by this suggestion and were not able to offer any response on the spot, except to mutter that technical difficulties, such as the lack of boats, would prevent the implementation of this proposal.

Apparently Von Bismarck accepted this response and did not react.[24] Nevertheless, the officials of the Foreign Ministry were worried by the tone of the new German proposal and a few days later, upon their own initiative, they contacted the German Embassy in Rome and reported once again that the staff of the Italian Army in Croatia had been ordered some time ago to round up all the Jews "in a small number of concentration camps," and that they were presently under the strictest possible surveillance.[25]

For several weeks after this answer, there is little information on the diplomatic activity regarding the fate of the Jewish refugees from Croatia. Perhaps it is only coincidental that few documents from the months January-February 1943 have survived. Perhaps the decisive events which occurred at the time, both on the Eastern front and in North Africa, caused the leaders of the Axis to forget this "worry." In the January 22, 1943 entry in his diary, Ciano described the situation of the Axis powers on the two fronts in the bleakest possible terms. According to the Italian Foreign Minister, Mussolini himself considered the German bulletin of that day as the most grave report received since the beginning of the war. The following day, Tripoli fell to the British Army, and thus the last remnant of the "Italian Empire" in Africa, which had always been the great dream of the Fascist leadership, was lost. Several days later, on January 31, 1943, Stalingrad fell to the Red Army and a large German force surrendered. With astounding suddenness, the great turnabout in the balance of power between the two fighting blocs became apparent, and for the first time since the start of the war it became conceivable that the Axis powers might be defeated, and perhaps in the not too distant future.

Public opinion in Italy was deeply affected by these events, and in their wake – for reasons which cannot be elaborated upon here – opposition to the regime began to gain ground among wide sections of the Italian population. Mussolini sensed this, although he apparently did not realize just how strong the opposition was. In order to undercut his opponents, he decided to make large-scale changes in the leadership of the party, government, and the high command of the army. Some of these changes were to have an influence – in certain cases which was positive – on the fate of the Jewish refugees in Croatia.

On January 31, 1943, a week after the fall of Tripoli, Marshal Cavallero, the Chief of Staff, was replaced by General Vittorio Ambrosio. In 1941, Ambrosio had been the commander of the Italian forces in Croatia – he was General Roatta's predecessor – and thus the general background of the Jewish

refugee problem was well known to him. Five days later, on February 5, the Foreign Minister was replaced. Ciano was appointed Ambassador to the Vatican in place of Guariglia, while Mussolini himself assumed the post of Foreign Minister. In addition, he appointed Bastianini, who until then had been Governor of Dalmatia and was one of the first people to deal with the question of the Jewish refugees in Croatia, as Deputy Minister, the man actually responsible for running the ministry. Finally, in mid-February, General Ambrosio recalled Roatta from Croatia and gave him a command in Italy proper. (Both Ambrosio and Roatta later played a crucial role in determining the army's policy after Mussolini had been deposed and arrested.) Ambrosio appointed General Mario Robotti the commander of the Italian Army in Yugoslavia in Roatta's place. Robotti had formerly been one of the leading officers of the Italian occupation forces in Croatia and was deeply involved in all the activities that had hereto been undertaken in order to save the Jewish refugees.

In this atmosphere of uncertainty regarding the future, which pervaded the ranks of the Italian leadership in early 1943, the Germans renewed their pressure for the extradition of the Jewish refugees, and this time they did so at the highest diplomatic level. Toward the end of February, the German Foreign Minister, Von Ribbentrop, visited Rome, and spent three days conferring with Mussolini. According to detailed testimony which has been preserved in the documents of the Italian Foreign Ministry, Von Ribbentrop raised the issue of the fate of the Jews living in Southern France in the course of these talks,[26] but he undoubtedly also dealt extensively with the fate of the Jewish refugees from Croatia. Evidence to this effect exists in the testimony of Colonel Vincenzo Carlà which was given on March 6, 1945, about two years after the event.[27] Carlà, who at that time was one of the leading officers of "Supersloda," relates that he accompanied General Robotti when the latter traveled to Rome "early in 1943." In fact, the General had an audience with Mussolini at the beginning of March. Carlà also accompanied his commander on this visit, although he was not present during the actual meeting. Together with other officers, he waited in a room next to Mussolini's office. Upon leaving,

General Robbotti told him that Mussolini had said: "Minister Von Ribbentrop was in Rome for three days and employed all kinds of pressure to ensure that the Yugoslavian Jews will be extradited. I tried to put him off with excuses, but he persisted, so in order to rid myself of him I was forced to agree. The Jews should be transferred to Trieste and given over to the Germans." General Robotti expressed his adamant opposition to Mussolini, repeating the reasons that had been put forth previously – the extradition was inhuman and it went against the interests of the Italian Army in that area. Mussolini was not insistent, and summarized the discussion by saying: "O.K., O.K., I was forced to give my consent to the extradition, but you can produce all the excuses that you want so that not even one Jew will be extradited. Say that we simply have no boats available to transport them by sea and that by land there is no possibility of doing so."[28]

Thus the conversation ended – according to the testimony of Colonel Carlà, who heard the details from General Robotti. Even if we assume that here and there the two witnesses embellished the description, the basic content of the testimony is undoubtedly accurate. It is confirmed by Verax,[29] and various details concerning General Robotti's trip to Rome, such as the date and its general purpose, are confirmed by a cable sent to him by General Ambrosio inviting him to the meeting.[30]

The German pressure, therefore, bore no fruit, even when applied at the highest level. As spring approached, however, a new danger, potentially more severe than all the others, became evident. Everyone realized that the Allies would resume their offensive in the Mediterranean area in full force in the spring, and many thought that following the surrender of the Axis forces in Tunisia, Italy would be the Allies' next target. This opinion also gained currency among Italian statesmen and military men. They began to argue that in view of this bleak prospect, it was imperative to bring at least part of the armed forces still stationed in the occupied areas of France and Croatia back to Italy as soon as possible, and to hand over the responsibility for the areas which would be evacuated to the Germans or their allies. As is known, however, these proposals were not accepted because of the stubborn opposition of Mussolini and his inner circle, who

were captivated by their delusions of grandeur and thus neglected the defense of their own country. The proposals themselves, however, represented a severe threat to the safety of the Jews interned in Sector B, and officials of the Foreign Ministry, as well as the Italian Army officers in Croatia, were forced to consider how to deal with this danger.

It should be noted that at that time, the Italian authorities already possessed full and detailed information on the refugees – their number, origin, and citizenship. After the Jews had been concentrated in the camps, and especially during the long winter months, the census had been completed, as were the relevant "investigations." It was determined that 2,661 Jews were interned in the various camps, 893 of whom claimed Italian citizenship in accordance with the guidelines of the Foreign Ministry listed above; 283 possessed foreign citizenship (German, Hungarian, Polish, Portuguese, and Albanian – the Albanians were at that time considered to be subjects of the Italian crown!); and 1,485 were Croatian Jews who could not prove any "right" to any other citizenship. All these refugees lived in areas under the jurisdiction of three corps of the Second Army: 1,172 under the jurisdiction of the Fifth Corps, in the Cirquenizza (Crkvenica) camp; 615 under the jurisdiction of the Eighteenth Corps, on the islands of Lesina and Brazza (Hvar, Brac): and 874 under the jurisdiction of the Sixth Corps in Cupari, Mlini, Gravosa, Isola di Mezzo.[31]

These figures, which appear to be reliable and exact, do not match the number of Jews who were eventually liberated. Their number, according to a Jewish source which seems to be reliable, was approximately 3,500.[32] Perhaps the officers of "Supersloda" purposely minimized the number of the internees, especially the number of Croatians among them, or perhaps during the months between March and September, additional Jews, who at first had not been rounded up and were therefore not included in the census, later entered the camps. In any event, the documents of the Foreign Ministry from then on deal with the fate of the 2,661 Jews counted in the census of the internees and who, it was feared, would fall into the hands of the Croatians as a result of border changes which might be made in the future.

By this time, there were few options left for solving the problem and, in effect, the choice was between two possible solutions: either to transfer the refugees to Italy itself, or to concentrate them all in one camp in the annexed area (Sector A), as close as possible to the old Italian border, in order to make it easier for the Italian Army to guard them and, in an emergency, to transport them across the border.

As expected, the General Staff and the Foreign Ministry differed on this question. The former supported the first option, since it would have freed them from any further responsibility in the matter. Moreover, under the conditions which existed at that time, it really would have been difficult to set up a camp which could accommodate thousands of refugees. The Foreign Ministry, on the other hand, pressed for the adoption of the second option since, among other reasons, it feared that the Ministry of the Interior – which from the very beginning had not been particularly well disposed toward the measures taken on behalf of the Jews of Croatia – would object to, or at the least hinder, the transfer of refugees to camps in Italy. Moreover, without the consent of the Ministry of the Interior, under whose jurisdiction these camps would be, no such solution could be effected.

Throughout March and the beginning of April, the issue was debated at length in the correspondence between the various bodies until a compromise of sorts was finally reached, whereby the Jews would be concentrated on the island of Arbe (Rab) in Sector A, but their transfer to this site would be carried out in two stages. During the first stage, 1,489 Jews under the jurisdiction of the Sixth and Eighteenth Corps would be transferred. They were further away and were scattered in various places, so the fear that they might fall into the hands of the Croatians was more real. Meanwhile, the Jews under the jurisdiction of the Fifth Corps, who were already concentrated in the Porto Re camp located several tens of kilometers from the Italian border, would remain there a few months longer, until the necessary arrangements could be made on the island of Arbe for their absorption.[33]

In fact, however, almost no time at all passed between the transfer of the two groups. The transfer of the first group was delayed time and again and began close to the end of May – whereas the transfer of the

Porto Re group began on July 5, 1943. By the latter half of July, all the Jews were already concentrated on the island of Arbe, several kilometers off the Italian mainland.

The Arbe camp (officially entitled "*Campo di concentramento per internati civili di guerra* – Arbe") was a large camp, in which approximately 20,000 individuals were incarcerated (according to some sources – 15,000), mainly Croatian and Slovene citizens. A separate wing of the camp was set aside for the Jews in which the conditions were fairly satisfactory although not comfortable. They were housed by families or groups of individuals. Dr. Jaša Romano, who was a prisoner in the camp, wrote about the life of the Jewish inmates, the internal organization, welfare and cultural activities, as well as about the contacts between the Jews and leaders of the underground in the non-Jewish section of the camp, and I see no reason to repeat what he has written.[34] There is room, however, to dwell upon the significant changes which occurred in the condition and the status of the Jewish refugees during the short period they were in Arbe, as a result of the political developments that occurred in Italy at the time.

The transfer of the Jews to Arbe was completed around July 20, 1943. Several days later, on the night of July 24–25, Mussolini's regime was overthrown. Literally overnight, twenty years of government by the Italian Fascist Party were ended, and a government of "technocrats," headed by Marshal Pietro Badoglio, was established. It negotiated with the Allies regarding the conditions for a cease-fire for 45 days, and finally, on September 8, surrendered unconditionally.

During these forty-five days, the general political framework in Italy was radically altered and simultaneously, the condition and status of the Jews in Italy and in the Italian-occupied areas, and especially that of the Croatian Jews interned in the Arbe camp, also changed. The question which now confronted the new Italian Foreign Minister Guariglia, the officials of the Foreign Ministry, and the officers of "Supersloda" was no longer how to evade the pressure of the Germans to hand over the refugees, but rather how to free these Jews from the camp without endangering their lives, at a time when releasing them might very well constitute a death trap for them, especially if in the future the Italian Army would be forced to retreat from the areas it had hereto occupied in Croatia.

The subject was discussed at length by the military and political authorities both in Rome and in Croatia. The officers of "Supersloda" again proposed that the refugees, or at least part of them, such as the women and children and men with professions that might benefit the Italian economy, be transferred to Italy.[35] The Foreign Ministry, on the other hand, thought that due to the political and logistical circumstances, there was no chance that this solution would be acceptable to the various responsible bodies, and it demanded that first and foremost the physical survival of the refugees be guaranteed. Finally, on August 19, the newly-appointed Secretary-General of the Foreign Ministry, Augusto Rosso, sent a detailed cable to "Supersloda," which was undoubtedly composed in accordance with the wishes of the Foreign Minister, in which he summarized the basic position of the latter vis-à-vis the Jewish problem in general and the question of the Jewish refugees from Croatia in particular.

The Foreign Ministry attributed particular importance to this document as is evident from the fact that on the very day it sent the cable to "Supersloda," it also sent a copy to the branch of the Ministry of the Interior which dealt with matters of demography and race (*Direzione Generale Demografia e Razza*), and which had been in charge of implementing the racial laws against the Jews since 1938. Needless to say, the Foreign Ministry had hereto not kept this branch informed of the steps taken in the matter of the Jewish refugees of Croatia, and one may assume that it often had to make special efforts to ensure that the information would *not* reach them. Now, however, times had changed. The project to save the Jews no longer had to be kept secret, and the officials of the Foreign Ministry found it useful to keep their "colleagues" in the Ministry of the Interior informed of this new situation, "no matter what happens" as they explicitly stated in the accompanying letter, and in order to warn them in clear and unambiguous terms that they should not intervene in the matter.

The cable of the Foreign Ministry instructed the Italian General Staff in Croatia that "Croatian Jews should not be released [from the camps] and are not to be abandoned in the hands of strangers without some sort of protection [thus being] exposed to potential acts of retaliation, unless they themselves prefer to be released and to be sent out of our area of occupation." At the same time, the Italians should prevent these refugees from coming "en masse" to Italy, in the wake of the Italian Army, if it would be forced to retreat, and therefore they must see to it that even in such a situation the Jewish refugees should be able to stay on the island of Arbe, where they would have "adequate protection." In the meantime, the army authorities could begin dealing with each case individually, in a friendly manner, in order to find individual solutions – all, of course, in accordance with the limitations imposed by the difficult conditions of the time.

As for the policy adopted by the Foreign Ministry in regard to the Jewish problem, the author of the cable asserts that "the racial policy which was adopted in Italy never prevented us from preserving those humanitarian principles which are an indelible part of our spiritual patrimony. Today more than ever we are commanded to preserve them. It is nonetheless desirable, from a political point of view as well, that this position be properly presented and made known."

Two elements which complemented each another thus influenced the establishment of the Ministry's policy – the humanitarian principle which the author of the cable and his colleagues certainly believed in sincerely and wholeheartedly, and political interests, which they were aware of and were anxious to fulfill. How fortunate that an elevated moral principle and an important national interest should coincide in this case.

In reality, however, it soon became clear that the matter was much more complex than it had originally been considered. The "Supersloda" officers did not contest the moral principles which were the basis of the Foreign Ministry's directives, and they certainly were willing to serve the interests of their country. As individuals who were in close proximity to the events, however, they fully realized that no guarantee or promise would be of value to the Jewish refugees if they were left alone in the midst of a hostile population, at the mercy of the Croatian authorities. They also did not take into account that Tito's partisans could play a central role in saving Jews, as they eventually did. For these reasons, they maintained their position that, no matter what had occurred during the previous months, the only solution to the problem of the Jewish refugees was their original proposal to transfer them to Italy. The officers of "Supersloda" emphasized this point in a detailed letter sent to Castellani on August 29, 1943, in which they suggested – in response to the directives of the Foreign Ministry – to immediately begin transferring the first groups of refugees to Italy – elderly and sick refugees as well as those whose families were situated on the other side of the border.

This impassioned plea met with no response. In a desperate attempt to bring about action and prevent the tragedy which they believed was imminent, the officers of "Supersloda" decided on September 7, 1943, to send Major Prolo, one of their officers, to Rome in order to speed up the handling of their proposal and convince the Ministry of the Interior to agree to its implementation. This step was taken too late, however. On the evening of September 8, 1943, the Allied Command suddenly announced the surrender of the Badoglio government. The Italian Army laid down its arms and, in most places, the German Army immediately took over. Shortly thereafter, the island of Arbe also fell to the Germans and their Croatian allies.

Thus, for the Jewish internees in the Arbe camp, the day of liberation was one of great danger. It was, however, the day on which, for the first time since the beginning of the war, they were given an opportunity to cease being powerless and persecuted refugees and to become the masters of their own fate. For the first time, they were free to organize, to make their way to the areas which had already been liberated by the partisans, and to participate in the struggle against the common enemy.

Of the Jews who were in the Arbe camp at that time – 2,661 according to the Italian sources and approximately 3,500 according to Dr. Romano's testimony – only 204 individuals, mainly elderly and sick people, decided to remain where they were. They were captured by the Germans, transferred by sea to Trieste and from there were deported to Auschwitz.[36]

The rest set out to join the partisans. Some were organized in a special Jewish unit, the Fifth Battalion, which operated jointly with four battalions of Slovenes, in the framework of the partisan brigade formed in Arbe. Many doctors, engineers, and nurses joined the regular partisan units. The Jews who could not bear arms – in Arbe there were some 500 children under the age of 16[37] – found refuge among the civilian population in the liberated area. From among the Jews who joined the partisans, 277 did not live to see the day of liberation – 136 fell in battle and 141 were killed in the course of the war.

Two and one-half years passed from the invasion of Yugoslavia to the surrender of the Italian Army, and an additional year and a half elapsed before the end of the war. Throughout this entire period, the Jews of Croatia were mercilessly oppressed and the majority did not survive. Some were the victims of the terror unleashed by the "wild men of the *Ustaša*"; others were killed by German soldiers; some died as a result of the torture, hunger, and disease in the concentration camps of Croatia, while others were killed with their brethren in the German death camps. Only a few succeeded in joining the partisans and fighting in the struggle for their freedom and the liberation of the other peoples of Yugoslavia. Very few indeed lived to witness the final day of victory.

The percentage of Jewish survivors among those who escaped to the Italian zone of occupation, however, was relatively high – about 2,200 out of a total of 2,661 according to the Italian figures and approximately 3,000 out of 3,500 according to the figures of Dr. Romano. In addition, thousands of Jewish refugees managed to reach Italy, whether with the consent of the Italian authorities and the aid of DELASEM – such as the group of Jewish children who were housed in the village of Nonantola near Modena[38] – or by traversing circuitous routes and illicitly crossing the border, activities which the local army commanders were generally well aware of.

These small-scale rescue activities were the product of the efforts of several groups, a few of which were composed of refugees or Italian Jews, while others consisted of officials of the Foreign Ministry and officers of the Italian Army. In this lecture I only dealt with the work of the non-Jewish groups, which indeed were not the only factor, but whose role was undoubtedly of great, and perhaps from a practical point of view of decisive, significance.

Having reached the end of my lecture, I must pose the almost traditional question: What motivated these men to do what they did?

I have been asked this question many times in relation to this episode, as well as to other events, and the query always pains me because in my opinion it is an indication of a profound distortion in our thinking regarding the period of the Holocaust. The logical and natural question is not, "Why did so and so refuse to participate in cold-blooded murder or even try somehow to stop it?" but rather "How was it that so many people, and even entire nations, directly or indirectly sanctioned such deeds?" It is true that one cannot understand the history of a period without comprehending its internal logic and specific nature, but the criteria by which one measures human behavior cannot be arbitrarily changed to suit the character of this or that period, and it certainly cannot be made to suit the value system which governed the actions of the Nazis. Basic and universal moral norms are always binding, even in times of crisis, even when the majority of mankind ignores them, and the devotion to these norms requires no explanation.

Nevertheless, since I have answered questions of this sort in the past, I shall attempt to do so this time as well.

First of all, it should be noted that the initial activities of the Italian Army officers to save the Jews of Croatia were not in any way exceptional or unusual in relation to their operations in the area. When the "Independent State of Croatia" was established, and particularly during the spring and summer months of 1941, the members of the *Ustaša* brutally slaughtered many of the Serbian minority left in their state, including those living in Sector B, which was occupied by the Italians. At the time, the Italian Army was ordered to end this slaughter, and several times the forceful actions of the Italians led to clashes with their allies the *Ustaša*. The Italians finally decided to take away the authority for the civilian administration in Sector B from the Croatians, and from then on, order was maintained in that region. In the spring of 1942, when the *Ustaša* intensified the persecution of the

Jews throughout the area of the Croatian state, the officers and soldiers of the Italian Army who were stationed there understood that it was their obligation to protect the residents, and first and foremost the persecuted minorities; quite naturally, the Jews – both the local ones and the refugees – were also included.

Thus the initial steps taken to save the Jews were part of the general responsibility of the Italian Army in the region and a continuation of its activities to save the Serbian population. There is no doubt, however, that the Italians eventually devoted special attention to the rescue of the Jews, and for them it assumed political and moral significance far beyond their general interest in maintaining order in the region.

The Italians realized the political aspects of the problem in the spring of 1942, when the Croatian-German agreement to deport all the Jews in Croatia became known. The fact that the agreement had been signed without their knowledge, by a state which, it had been previously agreed, would be under their exclusive sphere of influence, was a severe blow to the status and prestige of the Italian Army. Moreover, according to the terms of the agreement, it was to include the Jews living in the area of the Italian occupation as well. From that time on, the opinion became widespread among various Italian political and military officials that the extradition of the Jews to the Croatians would be tantamount to a surrender to German orders and, would for the peoples of the region, constitute a public admission of the weakness of the Italian Army.

All the arguments which the officers of "Supersloda" used so frequently in their appeals to the General Staff to justify their opposition to the extradition of the Jews, were basically true. Perhaps they at times embellished them a bit, or even a lot, but they certainly believed that they were true. Beyond the subjective sensitivity of the Italians, who regarded themselves as the weak and deprived partner of the Axis who had been shunted aside due to the Nazis' tremendous power, there were legitimate political interests which dictated that the Italians not accede to the demands of the Germans and the Croatians to extradite the Jews, and the officers of "Supersloda" understood this very well.

At the same time, whoever thinks that the episode of the rescue of the Jewish refugees of Croatia can be explained solely on the basis of diplomatic interests errs. Soldiers and civilians on all levels participated in the rescue work and almost everyone regarded the issue first and foremost as a humanitarian problem, which had to be solved for reasons of conscience, which were beyond political considerations.

In view of the enormity of the tragedy which befell the Jews of Yugoslavia, this episode naturally seems quite insignificant. It was, however, a small episode in which a great deal of humanitarianism was revealed, and it is in this light that it should be evaluated, within the broader context of the rescue activities undertaken during the period of the Holocaust.

Notes

1. Daniel Carpi, "Le Toledot ha-Yehudim be-Split u-be-Sarayevo (Te'udot Hadashot min ha-Shanim 1941–1942)," *Yalkut Moreshet,* No. 10, 1969, 109–121.
2. Poliakov-Sabille, *op. cit.,* 164–165 (English edition).
3. Report of the Italian Legation in Zagreb, August 6, 1942, Archives of the Italian Foreign Ministry (hereafter – AIFM).
4. Verax, *op. cit.,* 23.
5. Poliakov-Sabille, *op. cit.,* 166.
6. Part of the protocol of this meeting is quoted in a memorandum of the Italian Foreign Ministry, dated October 20, AIFM.
7. Poliakov-Sabille, *op. cit.,* 167.
8. Verax, *op. cit.,* 25.
9. *Ibid.*
10. Poliakov-Sabille, *op. cit.,* 171–172.
11. A report on the conversation which had taken place on October 27 was included in the cable sent by the Foreign Ministry to "Supersloda" and to the Italian Legation in Zagreb on October 31, 1942, AIFM.
12. Poliakov-Sabille, *op. cit.,* 174–175.
13. *Ibid.,* 176–177.
14. Report by Castellani, November 18, 1942, AIFM.
15. The Jewish representatives sent a letter of thanks for the visit which took place on November 27, 1942. It was attached to Castellani's report of December 6, 1942 to the Foreign Office, AIFM.
16. Memorandum to Ciano, November 3, 1942, AIFM.
17. Report to "Supersloda," November 8, 1942, AIFM.
18. Letter to the Foreign Ministry, November 4, 1942, AIFM.
19. Report of the Italian Consulate in Zagreb, August 22, 1942, AIFM.
20. Poliakov-Sabille, *op. cit.,* 171–172.

21. Letter of the Foreign Ministry to "Supersloda", November 3, 1942, AIFM.
22. Letters of "Supersloda" to the Italian Foreign Ministry, November 3, 5, and 20; December 13, 14, and 16, 1942, AIFM.
23. Report of Castellani to the Foreign Ministry, December 3, 1942, AIFM.
24. Minutes of the meeting of November 9, 1942, AIFM.
25. Report of the Foreign Office to the General Staff, December 15, 1942, AIFM.
26. Memorandum of March 14, 1943, to which a report of February 25, 1943, by the German Embassy in Rome and the reply by the Foreign Ministry dated March 9, 1943 are attached, AIFM.
27. Poliakov-Sabille, *op. cit.,* 152–153.
28. Copy of the testimony of Col. Carlà, which was given in the Italian War Office on March 6, 1945, is preserved in the *Centre de Documentation Juive Contemporaine* in Paris and I am indebted to that institute for making a copy of the document available to me.
29. Verax, *op. cit.,* 27.
30. A photostat of the document was published in the pamphlet, Državna Komisija za Utvrdivanje Ziocina Okupatora i Njihovih Pomagaća, *Saopćenje o Talijanskim Zločinima Protiv Jugoslavije i Njenih Naroda* (The Atrocities Committed by the Italians Against Yugoslavia and her Peoples), Belgrade 1946, 165.
31. Reports of February 27, March 9 and 20, 1943, AIFM.
32. Jaša Romano, "Jevreji U Logoru Na Rabu I Njihovo Uključivanje U Narodnooslobodilački Rat" (Jews in The Rab Camp and Their Participation in the Liberation War), *Zbornik* No. 2, 1973, (hereafter–Romano), 70.
33. Correspondence between "Supersloda" and the Foreign Ministry, March 20, 25, and 31; April 5 and 16, 1943, AIFM.
34. Romano, *op. cit.,* 70.
35. Letters of "Supersloda" to the Foreign Ministry, July 28 and August 29, 1943, AIFM.
36. Romano, *op. cit.,* 70–72; Zdenko Löwenthal (ed.), *Zločini fašističkih okupatora i njihovih pomagača protiv Jevreja u Jugoslaviji* (The Crimes of the Fascist Occupants and their Collaborators against Jews in Yugoslavia), Belgrade, 1957, 23.
37. These children were the subject of lengthy negotiations between the leaders of the Jews interned in Arbe and the Italian authorities. The former sought to transfer the children to Turkey (and from there to Palestine). Permission was not granted, due to the opposition of the Mufti of Jerusalem. I plan to deal with this episode, which lies outside the purview of this lecture, in an article entitled "The Negotiations Regarding the Transfer of Jewish Children from Croatia to Turkey and Eretz Israel in the Year 1943," which will appear in the forthcoming volume (XII) of *Yad Vashem Studies.*
38. Ilva Vaccari, *Villa Emma,* Modena, 1960.

REFIK VESELI, KRUJA, ALBANIA... NOVEMBER 1943 – Mosa and Gabriela Mandil were professional photographers who lived in Novi Sad, Yugoslavia, where Mosa operated a photo studio until the German invasion in April 1941. The Mandil family of four fled south to the Italian-controlled province of Kosovo where they were imprisoned along with other Jewish families in the city of Pristina. They remained in Pristina from October 1941 until May 1942. While in prison, Mosa volunteered to take photographs of Italian soldiers who, in turn, made it possible for the Mandils to escape to Italian-occupied Albania.

Once in Albania, the family settled in Kavaja where they remained until the summer of 1943. Learning of the impending German occupation of Albania, the Mandils moved to the capital, Tirana, where they sought safety in numbers. Mosa found work in the photography studio of an Albanian who had worked for his father in Belgrade. Also employed in this studio was a sixteen-year-old Albanian apprentice, Refik Veseli. When the Germans occupied Albania in September 1943, Refik obtained his parents' permission to hide the Mandil family in their home in the mountain village of Kruja. From November 1943 until liberation in October 1944, the Mandils were sheltered by the Veseli family. Seven-year-old Gavra and his five-year-old sister Irena lived openly as Muslim villagers, but their parents remained hidden in the Veselis' barn. After the war the Mandils returned to Novi Sad, where they re-opened their photo studio. In 1946, Refik Veseli joined the family in Novi Sad and completed his training with Mosa.

In the photograph are Refik Veseli with Gavra Mandil. (Gavra Mandil, courtesy of USHMM Photo Archives)

GAVRA AND IRENA MANDIL, NOVI SAD, YUGOSLAVIA... SEPTEMBER 1940 – Gavra and Irena Mandil pose next to a Christmas tree. The photograph was taken by their father Mosa Mandil, who often used his children as models to advertise his photo studio. This photograph, which was taken in the fall of 1940 to promote the upcoming Christmas season, later saved the lives of the family. During their escape from Yugoslavia by train in April 1941, the Mandils were stopped by the Germans, who demanded to see papers. When the Germans accused them of being Jews, Mosa showed them this photo and the family was left alone. (Gavra Mandil, courtesy of USHMM Photo Archives)

GUENTER LEWY **The Jewish Question**

1. THE SETTING

DESPITE SIMILARITIES between many anti-Jewish measures of the medieval Church and those enacted by the Nazi regime, the differences between Hitler's racial anti-Semitism and Christian anti-Judaism were many. Nazi anti-Semitism was rooted in a perverted social Darwinism, a view of the world that differentiated between superior and inferior people according to their racial stock, and demanded the elimination of those considered an impediment to racial purity and national greatness. Christian hostility to the Jews was built on certain theological conceptions developed in the first three centuries of Christianity. Except for a limited period in Spain, when "pure" – that is Christian – blood (*limpieza de sangre*) was demanded as a condition of belonging to the community of the redeemed in Christ, the Christian churches have always accepted Jewish converts and disregarded racial ancestry and national origin. All those baptized could be Christians.

And yet, significant as these distinctions between modern anti-Semitism and Christian anti-Judaism are, it is also true that the Nazis' ferocious assault upon European Jewry took place in a climate of opinion conditioned for such an outrage by centuries of Christian hostility to the Jewish religion and people. Numerous Christian theologians throughout the history of Christianity had painted the Jews as a people who had betrayed God and had called upon themselves a permanent curse by crucifying Jesus the Christ. The historical accuracy of the cry "His blood be upon us and upon our children" and the orthodoxy of a theological interpretation that saw in these words an acknowledgment of the guilt of all Jews for the death of Jesus have been successfully challenged by recent scholarship.[1] But for many centuries Christian preaching and religious instruction derived their intensely anti-Jewish character from just such conceptions.[2] In medieval times the recital of the Passion of Christ in Good Friday sermons was frequently followed by acts of violence against the Jews, for whom this holy day became a day of dread. Hitler's racial anti-Semitism and its logical outgrowth, Auschwitz, a French Jewish scholar has concluded, appeared on ground which previous centuries had prepared. "Without centuries of Christian catechism, preaching and vituperation, the Hitlerian teachings, propaganda and vituperation would not have been possible."[3]

By the nineteenth century the Jews of western and central Europe had largely been emancipated. Most of the restrictive measures imposed by the Church and secular rulers had been eliminated; superstitious beliefs, like those in Jewish ritual murder, had been condemned by both Pope and philosopher. But the Enlightenment and the growth of secular thinking had not eliminated the antagonism between Christian and Jew; the old hatreds reappeared clothed in a different garb. The new anti-Semitism found political, economic and social arguments to buttress its hostility toward the Jews. Yet the old notions of the Jews as killers of Christ and murderers of innocent Christian children continued to fester in the popular mind and provided nourishment for the more recent brand of anti-Jewish sentiment.[4]

Some elements of German Catholicism during the nineteenth century, as Catholic Nazis later proudly noted, shared in the growth of this new anti-Semitism. Publicists like Karl von Vogelsang (1818–1890) and Joseph Edmund Jörg (1819–1901) argued for breaking the yoke of economic exploitation under which the Christian nations were suffering. "The people," warned Jörg in the *Historisch-Politische Blätter* of 1860, "have their irrepressible instinct and woe unto the Jewish outrages when once it flares up."[5]

Two Catholic bishops were also to be found preaching this gospel. Bishop Martin of Paderborn (1812–1879) exposed Jewish wickedness in the Talmud and concluded that the stories of Jewish ritual murder of Christian children at Eastertime were true.[6] Bishop Keppler of Rottenburg (1852–1926) returned from a visit to the Holy Land amazed at the poverty of the Jews of Jerusalem. "It is hard to believe," he wrote, "that these are tribal brothers of that perverted part of the Jewish people which outside of Palestine constitutes a thorn in the side of Christian peoples, reduces them to servitude with the golden chains of millions and with pens saturated with poison, contaminates the public wells of education and morality by throwing into them sickening and purulent substances."[7]

Goaded by the fact that many prominent Jews participated in the anti-Catholic drive of the 1870s, the press of the Catholic Center party in the summer of 1875 began a vigorous anti-Semitic campaign. The party expected political benefit from its onslaught against "Jews and Liberals," but, as one well-informed student of the period correctly notes, the sheer vehemence of the attack revealed the existence of deeper roots.[8] The campaign soon ended as abruptly as it had started, but Catholic hostility toward "Jewish liberalism" remained strong for many years and was to experience a full revival in the Third Reich. Even a progressive Catholic like Matthias Erzberger was not entirely free of anti-Semitic sentiment. The charge of the Socialists that the Christian trade unions included Catholic priests, an alien element in the working-class movement, Erzberger met by describing the excessive Jewish influence in the Social Democratic party, using the pejorative phrase *stark verjudet*.[9]

Beginnings of racial anti-Semitism, too, were to be found. Christianity, observed one writer later to attain prominence as a Center party politician, forbids the hatred of other races. "But Christianity does not prohibit defense against the harmful influences caused by the peculiarities of a certain race."[10] German Catholicism, unlike its Austrian counterpart, never brought forth a prominent anti-Semite such as Karl Lueger in Vienna. But the undercurrents were there just the same.

During the Weimar republic organized German Catholicism came into repeated conflicts with the growing National Socialist movement, but anti-Semitism was not one of the primary bones of contention. On the contrary, many Catholic publicists –

like the Franciscan father Erhard Schlund – agreed with the Nazis on the importance of fighting the Jews' "hegemony in finance, the destructive influence of the Jews in religion, morality, literature and art, and political and social life." The nationalist movement, the same author observed, had a healthy core, "the endeavor to maintain the purity of the German blood and German race." Around this good core there lay merely a bad shell of extremism.[11]

This plea for a moderate anti-Semitism was a fairly typical and perfectly respectable view inside the Church. The Jesuit Gustav Gundlach, for example, writing in a reference work edited by Bishop Buchberger of Regensburg, argued that a political anti-Semitism, fighting the Jews' "exaggerated and harmful influence," was permitted as long as it utilized morally admissible means.[12] Bishop Buchberger himself concluded in 1931 that it was "justified self-defense" to ward off the rule of "an overly powerful Jewish capital." It was unjust and un-Christian merely to blame all Jews for these failings or to convert this economic struggle into one of race or religion.[13] Vicar General Mayer of Mainz found that Hitler in *Mein Kampf* had "appropriately described" the bad influence of the Jews in press, theater and literature. Still, it was un-Christian to hate other races and to subject the Jews and foreigners to disabilities through discriminatory legislation that would merely bring about reprisals from other countries.[14]

The charge of excessive Jewish influence in German public life was factually false and morally indefensible. In the press of the Left, for example, which was attacked as totally *verjudet*, less than 20 of 400 editors were Jews.[15] But even if the figures had yielded a different picture, such a disproportionate representation should not have given rise to concern unless the critics had already been convinced beforehand that Jews were dangerous and harmful. A finding that 90 per cent of all editors were blondes, for example, would not have provoked an anti-blonde movement. But reasoned argument was, of course, notably absent from the anti-Semitic agitation, especially in that emanating from the more extreme camp. There, also, one could find a number of Catholic clergymen. In the eyes of Curate Roth, an early supporter of the Hitler movement, the Jews were a morally inferior race who would have to be eliminated from public life. "If in the course of proceeding against the Jews as a race some good and harmless Jews, with whom immorality because of inheritance is latent, will have to suffer together with the guilty ones, this is not a violation of Christian love of one's neighbor as long as the Church recognizes also the moral justification of war, for example, where many more 'innocents' than 'guilty' have to suffer."[16] Roth, who later became an official in the Nazi Ministry of Ecclesiastical Affairs, was allowed to wield his poisonous pen without ever being formally disciplined by the Church.

Similar views were propounded by Dr. Haeuser, whose book appeared in 1923 with the *Imprimatur* of the diocese of Regensburg. Haeuser called the Jews Germany's cross, a people disowned by God and under their own curse. They carried much of the blame for Germany having lost the war and they had taken a dominant role in the revolution of 1918. The time had come to put them in their place, though Haeuser stressed that the Jews should be allowed to live as guests in Germany.[17] Father [Wilhelm Mavia] Senn called even German Catholicism *verjudet* and termed the Hitler movement, despite certain exaggerations, "the last big opportunity to throw off the Jewish yoke."[18]

Catholic anti-Semitism manifested itself in still another form. The people of Deggendorf in Bavaria for many years had been commemorating the miraculous emergence of "a lovely little child" from a consecrated wafer which allegedly had been stolen and "tortured" by the Jews of the town on September 30, 1337. On the same day, the chroniclers reported, the pious citizens of Deggendorf, acting "out of legitimate zeal pleasing to God," killed off all the Jews. "God grant," the inscription under a picture depicting the massacre and exhibited in one of the town's churches said, "that our fatherland be forever free from this hellish scum." In a play composed by a Benedictine monk and performed every year during the week-long celebrations, the Jews were called names such as "brood of Judas," "hordes of the devil," "poison mixers," etc. The historical accuracy of this tale of blasphemy and miraculous recovery had never been certified, but in view of the 10,000 guests that every year attended the commemoration exercises and

the wholesome religious atmosphere created by them, the Church authorities saw little reason to be sticklers for historical truth. The effects of this perpetuation of the worst medieval anti-Jewish prejudices upon contemporary attitudes toward the Jews are not difficult to guess.[19]

Concentrating her fire upon liberals and freethinkers, many of whom were of Jewish descent, the Church during the Weimar republic did practically nothing to stem the inroads anti-Semitism was making on German life. The number of individual Catholics, both clerics and laymen, who fought the hostility to their Jewish fellow citizens was also very small. The *Verein für die Abwehr des Antisemitismus*, an organization of Christians and Jews struggling against the rising anti-Semitic agitation, had two Catholic priests on its board of sponsors – the curate Franz Rödel being the only active priest-participant in the work of the group. Only a few Catholic voices were raised against the anti-Semitic tirades of the Nazis and their allies. Franz Steffen, a Catholic journalist, rejected the slanderous attack upon the Jews as false, and called anti-Semitism un-Christian and in conflict with Catholic doctrine. After disposing of the Jews, Steffen prophesied, the Nazis would next turn against the Catholics. "No believing Catholic may join the ranks of these people, no Catholic may support them in any way or help them into power through his vote, for he would thereby forge chains for our religious freedom."[20] A Catholic editor objected to the publication of one of the more notoriously inflammatory anti-Semitic books by a Catholic publisher in Paderborn and asked the Catholics to remember that anti-Semitism and anti-Catholicism usually grew on the same soil.[21] Father Muckermann, in January 1932, protested the immoral and criminal designs of the Nazis, who were marching through the streets calling for death to the Jews. Muckermann mentioned the recently committed 109 defacements of Jewish cemeteries and synagogues and added that to expose these outrages is "our Christian, human and German duty."[22]

The German bishops during these years spoke up against the Nazis' glorification of race and blood, but they had practically nothing to say specifically about the widespread anti-Semitic propaganda and acts of violence. Cardinal Faulhaber in a sermon delivered in 1923 declared that every human life was precious, including that of a Jew.[23] In 1932 Cardinal [Karl Joseph] Schulte, in reply to a letter from a Jewish organization seeking help, expressed his sympathies in the face of the numerous acts of vandalism, especially the desecration of Jewish graves, that had occurred in Cologne.[24] But a Church that justified moderate anti-Semitism and merely objected to extreme and immoral acts was ill-prepared to provide an effective antidote to the Nazis' gospel of hate. The roots of the Church's failure to protest or act against the later National Socialist policy of extermination lie right here, in the highly ambivalent attitude of the Church toward the Jews which we can trace from the early days of Christianity up to Hitler's accession to power and beyond.

2. REHEARSAL FOR DESTRUCTION

HITLER, UPON ENGAGING in his first measures against the Jews, was well aware of the Church's long anti-Jewish record. In his talk with Bishop Berning and Monsignor Steinmann on April 26, 1933, he reminded his visitors that the Church for 1,500 years had regarded the Jews as parasites, had banished them into ghettos, and had forbidden Christians to work for them. "He saw in the Jews nothing but pernicious enemies of the State and Church, and therefore he wanted to drive the Jews out more and more, especially from academic life and the public professions."[25] He, Hitler said, merely intended to do more effectively what the Church had attempted to accomplish for so long. This service to a common cause, and not the elevation of race above religion, motivated his hostility toward the Jews.[26]

The reaction of the two Church dignitaries to Hitler's attempt to identify his brand of anti-Semitism with the age-old anti-Judaism of the Church is not known. What we do know, however, is that from the time Hitler came to power all the German bishops began declaring their appreciation of the important natural values of race and racial purity, and they limited their dissent to insisting that this goal be achieved without resort to immoral means. The article on "Race" in the authoritative handbook on topical religious problems, edited by Archbishop Gröber, expressed this position in the following words:

> Every people bears itself the responsibility for its successful existence, and the intake of entirely foreign blood will always represent a risk for a nationality that has proven its historical worth. Hence, no people may be denied the right to maintain undisturbed their previous racial stock and to enact safeguards for this purpose. The Christian religion merely demands that the means used do not offend against the moral law and natural justice.[27]

In his celebrated Advent sermons of 1933 Cardinal Faulhaber observed that the Church did not have "any objection to the endeavor to keep the national characteristics of a people as far as possible pure and unadulterated, and to foster their national spirit by emphasis upon the common ties of blood which unite them." The defense and love of one's own race should not lead, however, to the hatred of other nations, and the loyalty to one's race did not supersede the obligations to the Church.[28] For these qualifications Faulhaber was severely criticized by the Nazis and his palace was fired on – needlessly so, as it turned out, for few German Catholics paid attention to Faulhaber's reservations. When Hitler started to pursue the purity of the German blood in his own ruthless way, the overwhelming majority of the German Catholics, as we shall see later, dutifully obeyed his orders and promptly forgot the warnings against using extreme and immoral means in the defense of one's race given out by their bishops.

The Church's reluctance to antagonize the Nazis unnecessarily can be seen in the way she defended the Old Testament. [Alfred] Rosenberg's attacks upon the "Jewish Bible," an alleged affront to every true German, hit the Church in a cardinal point of doctrine, where no yielding was possible. All members of the episcopate, therefore, resolutely and repeatedly reaffirmed their fidelity to the Old Testament. In several instances, Catholic teachers of religion who refused to teach the Old Testament were deprived of the *missio canonica* (ecclesiastical teaching license). Cardinal Faulhaber's Advent sermons in 1933, in particular, are remembered for their eloquent vindication of the sacred character of the scriptures of the Old Testament. But Faulhaber went out of his way to make clear that he was not concerned with defending his Jewish contemporaries. We must distinguish, he told the faithful, between the people of Israel before the death of Christ, who were vehicles of divine revelation, and the Jews after the death of Christ, who have become restless wanderers over the earth. But even the Jewish people of ancient times could not justly claim credit for the wisdom of the Old Testament. So unique were these laws that one was bound to say: "People of Israel, this did not grow in your own garden of your own planting. This condemnation of usurious land-grabbing, this war against the oppression of the farmer by debt, this prohibition of usury, is not the product of your spirit."[29] It, therefore, is little short of falsification of history when Faulhaber's sermons in 1933 are hailed by one recent Catholic writer as a "condemnation of the persecution of the Jews."[30]

Whatever ambiguity may still have attached to his position after these pronouncements, Faulhaber soon acted to dispel. In the summer of 1934 a Social Democratic paper in Prague published a sermon against race hatred which Faulhaber had allegedly preached. The Basel *National-Zeitung* in Switzerland reprinted excerpts from this sermon, and the World Jewish Congress at a meeting in Geneva praised the Cardinal's courageous stand. But the sermon turned out to be a fabrication, and Faulhaber had his secretary write a widely publicized letter to the Jewish organization protesting against "the use of his name by a conference that demands the commercial boycott of Germany, that is, economic war." The Cardinal, the letter continued, "in his Advent sermons of the previous year has defended the Old Testament of the Children of Israel but not taken a position with regard to the Jewish question of today."[31]

Lesser Church dignitaries quite naturally took the cue from their Archbishop. An article written by a canon of the cathedral chapter of Regensburg, and published in *Klerusblatt*, the organ of the Bavarian Priests' Association, advised Catholic teachers to point out to pupils that the sacred books of the Old Testament were not only beyond the Jewish mentality, but in direct conflict with it. "The greatest mira-

cle of the Bible is that the true religion could hold its own and maintain itself against the voice of the Semitic blood."[32]

The embarrassing fact that Jesus had been a Jew was handled in a similar manner. In a pastoral letter of 1939 Archbishop Gröber conceded that Jesus Christ could not be made into an Aryan, but the Son of God had been fundamentally different from the Jews of his time – so much so that they had hated him and demanded his crucifixion, and "their murderous hatred has continued in later centuries."[33] Jesus had been a Jew, admitted Bishop Hilfrich of Limburg in his pastoral letter for Lent 1939, but "the Christian religion has not grown out of the nature of this people, that is, is not influenced by their racial characteristics. Rather it has had to make its way against this people." The Jewish people, the Bishop added, were guilty of the murder of God and had been under a curse since the day of the crucifixion. Christianity, the Bishop of Limburg concluded, was therefore not to be regarded as a product of the Jews; it was not a foreign doctrine or un-German. "Once accepted by our ancestors, it finds itself in the most intimate union with the Germanic spirit."[34]

The attempt to swim with the anti-Semitic tide was even more pronounced in the previously cited *Handbuch* of Archbishop Gröber. Marxism here was defined as "the materialistic socialism founded primarily by the Jew Karl Marx,"[35] and Bolshevism was characterized as "an Asiatic state despotism, in point of fact in the service of a group of terrorists led by Jews."[36] The Führer, the same article found, had correctly described the struggle against this evil force as a defense of European civilization against Asiatic barbarism. "No people can avoid this clash between its national tradition and Marxism, which is opposed to national ties and led mostly by Jewish agitators and revolutionaries."[37] The article on "Art" pointed out that most of the unhealthy and un-German manifestations in art since the nineteenth century had been the work of Jews or those under Jewish influence. The politicizing of art was also in good part due to "the uprooted and atheistically perverted Jew."[38]

When convenient and useful, the Church used the concept "Jew" after the manner of the Nazis, that is, as a term of racial classification. Early in their rule, the Nazis had begun to make extensive propagandistic use of a nineteenth century rabble-rousing anti-clerical book, *Der Pfaffenspiegel*. Soon the sorry spectacle developed of the Church trying to undermine the effectiveness of this piece by arguing that the Protestant author, Otto von Corvin, had been a half-Jew, while the Nazis retorted that he was fully "Aryan."

In pronouncements read from the pulpit, pastoral letters and articles in church newspapers the Church supported this charge by invoking the authority of the notorious anti-Semitic *Handbuch der Judenfrage* by Theodor Fritsch – a work which, according to Waldemar Gurian, should never be quoted by respectable writers and scholars[39] – where Corvin had been listed as the son of a Jewess. Even Provost Lichtenberg, a man who later paid with his life for trying to help the Jews, found it necessary in 1935 to address a personal letter to Hitler in which he protested the use of the book and pointed out that Corvin, "according to the latest research, was not of Aryan descent."[40] A few days later the Catholic press all over Germany reported newly revealed evidence according to which Corvin "had been not only a Jew, but also a convict."[41]

When the Nazis challenged the non-Aryan ancestry of Corvin, one of their favorite church-baiting authors, the Catholic polemicists fell back upon the fact that Corvin's book had originally been published by a Jewish firm, that he had been a friend of Jews and that Corvin had exhibited traits such as lack of compassion, cold sarcasm, a presumptuous self-confidence, "in short, all that which today again we regard as especially opposed to the Aryan mentality." In view of these characteristics, one Catholic writer concluded, Corvin could well have been of Jewish descent, even if, as now shown, he in fact was not.[42] Corvin, another author wrote, had all his life been under the pronounced influence of "liberal-freethinking-Freemason Judaism." No wonder his contemporaries regarded this unGerman personality as a Jew.[43]

Some bishops, despite all evidence to the contrary, were unwilling to forgo the disparaging argument of Corvin's Jewish ancestry. Bishop Buchberger in a pastoral letter in February 1937, called Corvin a

"half-Jew and Freemason," and as late as January 1942 Archbishop Gröber spoke of the author of the *Pfaffenspiegel* as a "half-Jewish writer."[44]

If such language could be endorsed and used by members of the episcopate, it is no wonder that lower-ranking figures in the Church felt free to express their anti-Semitic sentiments still more openly. Thus the theologian Karl Adam defended the preservation of the German people's pure blood as a justified act of self-defense, for blood was the physiological basis of all thinking and feeling, and "the myth of the German, his culture and his history are decisively shaped by blood." The repulsion of the Jewish mentality in press, literature, science and art now undertaken by the state was a necessary measure, though "the Christian conscience must insist that these legal ordinances be implemented in a spirit of justice and love."[45] Thus also an article on the revolution of 1918 in the paper of the Bavarian priests exposed the role of the Jews in this stab in the back of the undefeated German army. "While the front made superhuman sacrifices and fought with admirable bravery against a world of enemies, the Jew Emil Barth equipped his *Untermenschen* [subhumans] with hand grenades and automatic pistols in order to attack the national defense from the rear. . . ." These acts of treason, the article suggested, actually began in 1914, when the Jew Karl Liebknecht refused to vote for the war appropriations.[46]

And so it went. The Jews had had a "demoralizing influence on religiosity and national character."[47] The Jews, as a spiritual community, had brought the German people "more damage than benefit."[48] The Jews had displayed a mortal hatred for Jesus, while the Aryan Pontius Pilate would gladly have let him go free. The Jews had been "the first and most cruel persecutors of the young Church."[49] The Jews had killed Jesus and in their boundless hatred of Christianity were still in the forefront of those seeking to destroy the Church.[50] These are some relevant examples of Catholic writing during the years 1933–1939, all published in journals edited by priests or in books bearing the *Imprimatur*. From this ruthless intellectual onslaught upon the Jews it was but a small step to the position of the veteran National Socialist priest, Father Senn, who in 1934 hailed Hitler as "the tool of God, called upon to overcome Judaism. . . ."[51]

If we take into account this climate of opinion within the Church, we will find it easier to understand why the Church retreated in the face of the Nazis' anti-Semitic legislation, even where these ordinances touched upon vital domains of ecclesiastical jurisdiction such as the sacrament of matrimony. According to canon law, the Church has exclusive jurisdiction over the marriage of Catholics. In practice, however, the Church in many countries had recognized the right of the state to impose certain conditions on marriage, so long as these did not conflict with natural law. For example, the state could insist on fulfillment of certain medical prerequisites, require the consent of parents to the marriage of minors, etc; in Germany the Church had agreed that normally a civil marriage ceremony had to precede the ceremony conducted by the priest, though Article 26 of the Concordat of 1933 had somewhat broadened the kinds of instances in which a priest could disregard this legal requirement.[52] How should the Church respond, however, if the state imposed requirements such as the prohibition of marriage between baptized persons belonging to different races?

As early as 1934 the Church had made clear to the Nazi government that the enactment of a law forbidding racially mixed marriages would create a very difficult situation. In the eyes of the Church, the German bishops pointed out in a memorandum, every Catholic, whether born to a pure German or to a racially mixed marriage, whether baptized as a child or as an adult, was equally entitled to the sacraments. Hence, if two baptized persons of racially mixed stock insisted on being married by a priest, the latter would have to comply, even if the state were to have prohibited such a union.[53]

This, however, is precisely what the state soon did, for one of the practical results of the so-called Nuremberg laws of September 15, 1935, was to make it illegal for two Catholics to marry when one was considered racially "non-Aryan" under the standards set up by the law. (Since the persecution of the Jews had led to many new conversions to the Catholic religion, the number of such marriages was undoubtedly rising at the time.) The central office of information of the German episcopate in Berlin reported in Sep-

tember 1935 that earlier Catholic couples of racially mixed descent had been traveling to England to get married there, but now even those marriages had become illegal, and the Church had a very serious problem on its hands.[54] What did she do? In some instances priests circumvented the law by using a provision of the Concordat of 1933 which, in cases of "great moral emergency," permitted a church marriage without a preceding civil ceremony;[55] but by and large the Church conformed to the law, bowing to what earlier she had termed an inadmissible infringement of her spiritual jurisdiction.

For some elements in the Church, to be sure, bowing was unnecessary, for they actually welcomed the Nuremberg laws. While a distinguished German Catholic in exile, Waldemar Gurian, was denouncing the Nuremberg ordinances as violations of natural law and of the moral teachings of the Church, and declaring that they were "only a stage on the way toward the complete physical destruction of the Jews,"[56] an article in the *Klerusblatt* of January 1936 was justifying the new anti-Jewish statutes as indispensable safeguards for the qualitative makeup of the German people.[57] So, too, Bishop Hudal, the head of the German Church in Rome, said that the Nuremberg laws were a necessary measure of self-defense against the influx of foreign elements. The Church in her own legislation, the Bishop contended, had held a radical position on the Jewish question "until the walls of the Ghetto had been torn down in the nineteenth century by the liberal state first and not by the Church." Consequently, from the point of view of the Church there could be no objection to laws containing discriminatory provisions for Jews. "The principles of the modern state [based on the rule of equal treatment before the law] have been created by the French Revolution and are not the best from the standpoint of Christianity and nationality."[58]

The Church surrendered in a similar fashion when the so-called Aryan clause was applied to clerical teachers of religion. This ordinance, enacted in 1938, meant that priests teaching religion in the public schools had to submit proof of their Aryan descent before they could continue in their posts. However, the policy in question affected very few clerics and had no further ramifications. Such was not the case when the Church agreed to supply data from her own records on the religious origin of those under her care. A decree of April 7, 1933, which resulted in the discharge of numerous Catholic civil servants, had also provided for the dismissal of all Jews (except front-line veterans of the first World War, those in government service since 1914, and close relatives of fallen soldiers) from the civil service. Henceforth, anyone applying for government employment – and soon for various other positions as well – had to submit proof that he was not a Jew. Since prior to 1874–1876 births had been registered only by the churches, the latter were asked to help in determining who was or was not fully Aryan, for under Nazi law this depended on the racial (i.e., religious) status of parents and grandparents. The Church co-operated as a matter of course, complaining only that priests already overburdened with work were not receiving compensation for this special service to the state.[59] The very question of whether the Church should lend its help to the Nazi state in sorting out people of Jewish descent was never debated. On the contrary. "We have always unselfishly worked for the people without regard to gratitude or ingratitude," a priest wrote in the *Klerusblatt* in September of 1934. "We shall also do our best to help in this service to the people."[60] And the co-operation of the Church in this matter continued right through the war years, when the price of being Jewish was no longer dismissal from a government job and loss of livelihood, but deportation and outright physical destruction.[61]

The bishops sometimes sought to protect the non-Aryan Catholics, for whom the Church felt a special responsibility. The Ministry of Ecclesiastical Affairs in 1936 asked for statistics about the number of Jews converted to the Catholic Church in the years 1900–1935. Cardinal Bertram suggested that this request be complied with.[62] But when the Ministry later sought permission to consult the diocesan files on conversions and mixed marriages, the Church withheld her consent "on grounds of pastoral secrecy."[63] For the same reason Cardinal Bertram in 1938 refused to open the diocesan archives to researchers working for a new state institute for the study of the Jewish question.[64]

The Church's concern for Catholic non-Aryans expressed itself in other ways as well. In September 1933 Archbishop Bertram had inquired from the Papal Secretary of State whether the Holy See could not put in a good word with the German government for the Jewish converts to the Catholic religion who were being made destitute on account of their "non-Aryan descent."[65] Soon the *St. Raphaelsverein*, a Catholic organization founded in 1871 for the protection of German émigrés and presided over by Bishop Berning, began to take care of these Catholics. In a notice published in all the diocesan gazettes in November 1933 the *St. Raphaelsverein* acknowledged that these non-Aryans were not fully German and gave them the advice "for the time being to feel themselves as guests [*Gastvolk*]."[66] But despite this concession to Nazi ways of thinking, the organization tried its best to retrain or otherwise facilitate the emigration of Catholic non-Aryans. This help was extended to practicing Catholics provided they were not in trouble with the Nazi state on political grounds.[67] Similarly, an organization of "Christian-German Citizens of Non-Aryan or not Pure Aryan Descent," established in 1933 with the encouragement of the Church and later renamed *Paulus Bund*, insisted in its bylaws that membership was open only to Christians "who take their stand alongside the new Germany."[68] In the years 1936–1937 the *St. Raphaelsverein* helped 516 Catholic non-Aryans; in 1938 it facilitated the emigration of 1,850 such persons.[69] Occasionally Jews married to Catholics were also aided. But the recent claim of a German Catholic paper[70] that the *St. Raphaelsverein* helped 1,950 Jews to emigrate and supported 25,000 Jews has no foundation in fact unless one still wants to use the concept Jew as a term of racial classification.

During these years prior to the adoption of the "Final Solution of the Jewish Question," the Church extended neither aid nor sympathy to other than Catholic non-Aryans. A few instances are on record where individual churchmen spoke up in defense of the Jews. In March 1933 a priest in the Rhineland in a sermon characterized the vilification of the Jews as unjust and was fined 500 marks for abuse of the pulpit.[71] Another priest, in Bavaria in 1936, declared that the stories being told in Germany about the Jews were a pack of lies.[72] There probably were other such occurrences, and here and there acts of Good Samaritanism may have taken place that have remained unrecorded. But the Church as such, speaking through the voice of her bishops, remained silent.

In 1934 a German Catholic priest, who for reasons of safety chose to remain anonymous, took his Church to task for this quiescence in the face of injustice. The Church, he argued, had a special duty to oppose the growing hatred of the Jews that was spreading even among believing Christians, and her failure to preach brotherly love toward the Jews jeopardized not only the Christian religion, but civilization itself. The Nazis' treatment of the Jews, the priest argued, violated justice, truth and love – yet the Church did not feel called upon to respond. She was, he said, too preoccupied with her own confessional interests. "What a good opportunity would the Jewish question have afforded for a truly 'Catholic Action'!"[73]

The hands-off policy of the Church stood out especially in the fateful days of November 1938. The Nazis, in the wake of the assassination of a German embassy official in Paris by a seventeen-year-old Jewish boy, unloosed a pogrom that has entered history under the name *"Kristallnacht"* (the night of glass). During the night of November 9–10 the display windows of Jewish shops all over Germany were shattered, about 20,000 male Jews were arrested and herded into concentration camps, 191 synagogues were set on fire and 76 others completely destroyed.[74] Thirty-six Jews were killed during this well-organized action; a much larger number succumbed to the sadistic treatment meted out to them in Buchenwald and other concentration camps where they were imprisoned. Cardinal Faulhaber is said to have provided a truck for the Chief Rabbi of Munich so that he could save some of the religious objects from his synagogue before it was completely demolished.[75] Provost Lichtenberg in Berlin, on the morning after the pogrom, prayed for the persecuted non-Aryan Christians and Jews, and added, "What took place yesterday, we know; what will be tomorrow, we do not know; but what happens today that we have witnessed; outside [this church] the synagogue is burning, and that also is a house of God."[76] Lichtenberg's protest remained a solitary act of witness. His bishops remained silent in the face of the burning temples and the first round-up of the Jews.

3. THE FINAL SOLUTION

IN A SPEECH DELIVERED on January 30, 1939, the Führer served public notice of his intentions: "If international Jewry should succeed, in Europe or elsewhere, in precipitating nations into a world war, the result will not be the Bolshevization of Europe and a victory for Judaism, but the extermination of the Jewish race."[77] A few months later Hitler attacked Poland and World War II began. On July 31, 1941, Heydrich was charged "with making all necessary preparation . . . for bringing about a complete solution of the Jewish question in the German sphere of influence in Europe."[78] The machinery of destruction went into action.

It began with a decree, dated September 1, 1941, which provided that all Jews six years of age or over could appear in public only when marked with a Jewish star; they were not to leave their place of domicile without special permission. The marking of the Jews had first been applied in Poland, and now the system of identification was extended to the entire Reich. The decree covered so-called Mosaic Jews as well as baptized Jews; only those who had converted before September 15, 1935, the date of the Nuremberg laws, and non-Aryans married to an Aryan partner were exempt from this order.

The wearing of the Jewish star had a paralyzing effect upon those who were forced to do so. Even more than before, the Jews now felt themselves a separate group marked for a fate about which some were beginning to have forebodings. Many were afraid to leave their houses, and this fear created a special problem for the affected Catholics. In a number of towns these Catholic non-Aryans applied to the police for permission not to have to wear the Jewish star when going to and attending church services, and they asked their bishops to support their applications.[79] The bishops were sympathetic to this request, as they were upset over the prospect of "Jews" attending services, which could only aggravate the hostility of the Nazis toward the Church. Also they were not sure how their parishioners would react to these Jewish Catholics.

On September 17 Cardinal Bertram addressed a letter to the episcopate in which he took up this new problem. His counsel was to avoid "rash measures that could hurt the feelings of the Jewish Catholics, as the introduction of special Jewish benches, separation when administering the sacraments, introduction of special services in specific churches or private houses." The segregation of the Catholic non-Aryans would violate Christian principles and, therefore, should be avoided as long as possible. The priests, Bertram suggested, might however advise the Jewish Catholics to attend the early mass whenever possible. An admonishment to the faithful to exercise brotherly love toward the non-Aryans similarly should be postponed until disturbances resulted. "Only when substantial difficulties result from attendance at church by the non-Aryan Catholics," the Archbishop of Breslau continued "(like staying away of officials, party members and others, demonstrative leaving of divine services), should the Catholic non-Aryans be consulted about the holding of special services." In case a reminder to the faithful to treat the Jewish Catholics with love should become necessary, Bertram suggested a statement that included St. Paul's admonishments to the Romans and Galatians not to forget that among those believing in Christ there is neither Jew nor Greek, for all are one in Jesus Christ (Romans 10:12, Galatians 3:28).[80]

In Berlin, meanwhile, Bishops Wienken and Berning were trying to obtain permission from the Gestapo for the Jewish Catholics not to wear the Star of David while in Church, but their efforts failed. On October 27 Berning wrote Bertram that the Gestapo had refused any concessions in this matter. On the other hand, Berning reported, almost nowhere had difficulties resulted from the attendance of the non-Aryan Catholics at divine services. A certain number had merely refrained from coming to church.[81] The Catholic Church thus had been spared the adoption of racial segregation.

Mass deportations of German Jews toward the east began on October 15, 1941. Bishop Berning, in the letter just referred to, informed Bertram that while discussing the question of the Jewish star with the Gestapo he had also pointed out the harshness ac-

companying "the evacuation of the non-Aryans" and had requested some ameliorations. He had been told that Christian non-Aryans would be evacuated only in exceptional cases, such as when earlier conflicts with the Gestapo had occurred. For the time being non-Aryans in mixed marriages would not be affected by these measures. The Church authorities, Berning continued, could obtain from the local Gestapo offices the dates scheduled for the deportations from their town, they could find out whether Christian non-Aryans were among those to be deported and in such cases exercise pastoral care before deportation. Those deported, he had been told, would go into the eastern territories, where they could participate in the divine services of the Poles.[82]

The promises made by the Gestapo to Bishop Berning were not honored. On October 27 the Bishop of Limburg informed Bishop Wienken, the episcopate's troubleshooter in Berlin, that the transport of Jews from Frankfurt earlier in the month had included Catholic non-Aryans to whom no preferred treatment had been granted. Their fate was especially sad since they were being regarded by their *Rassengenossen* (racial partners) as apostates. Hilfrich inquired whether for this reason it might not be possible to achieve their exemption. If that were impossible they should at least be put into special settlements, where they could be given religious care more easily.[83] Wienken replied a few days later that negotiations about the deportation of Catholic non-Aryans had been started at the highest level.[84] The bishops of the Cologne and Paderborn church provinces, meeting in November 1941, also suggested that the government be petitioned in matters of the deportations. They furthermore recommended that non-Aryan or half-Aryan priests and nuns volunteer to accompany the deportees in order to hold services for them and provide religious instruction for the children.[85]

While the bishops were preoccupied with the Catholic non-Aryans' pastoral care before deportation and during their resettlement, rumors were spreading about the fate of the Jews in the east. These rumors had been making the rounds ever since the attack upon Russia on June 22, 1941, which had brought in its wake the employment of special detachments (*Einsatzgruppen*) assigned to the job of murdering Jews. Soldiers returning from the Eastern Front were telling horrible stories, how in occupied Russia Jewish civilians – men, women and children – were being lined up and machine-gunned by the thousands. Their military superiors had issued orders forbidding such talebearing, as well as the taking of snapshots at mass executions, but the gruesome reports persisted. By the end of 1941 the first news had also trickled back about the fate of the deported German Jews who had been shot by mobile killing detachments near Riga and Minsk.[86] In the spring of 1942 the leaflets of the "White Rose," composed by a group of students and a professor of philosophy at the University of Munich, told of the murder of 300,000 Jews in Poland and asked why the German people remained so apathetic in the face of these revolting crimes.[87]

In December 1941 the first death camp began operations near Lodz. Sobibor, Treblinka and Auschwitz went into operation in the course of the year 1942. By the end of 1942 more than 100,000 German Jews had been sent to their death in the east, and the vague rumors about their fate had been replaced now by hard and persistent reports that included details of the mass gassings. In August 1942 Colonel Kurt Gerstein, who had joined the S.S. to investigate the stories of extermination for himself, tried to tell the Papal Nuncio in Berlin about a gassing he had witnessed near Lublin. When Monsignor Orsenigo refused to receive him, he told his story to Dr. Winter, the legal advisor of Bishop Preysing of Berlin, and to numbers of other persons. He also requested that the report be forwarded to the Holy See.[88] During the same period other reports about the extermination of the Jews reached the bishops through Catholic officers serving in Poland and Russia.[89] For a long time Dr. Joseph Müller, an officer in [Wilhelm] Canaris's Military Intelligence Service and also a confidant of Cardinal Faulhaber, had kept the episcopate well informed about the systematic atrocities committed in Poland.[90] Another source of information was Dr. Hans Globke, a Catholic and a high official in the Ministry of the Interior entrusted with handling racial matters. It is, then, clear that by the end of the year 1942 at the latest, the German episcopate was possessed of quite accurate knowledge of the horrible events unfolding in the east.

Until 1942 half-Jews and quarter-Jews, the so-called *Mischlinge*, as well as non-Aryans married to Aryans, had been exempt both from wearing the yellow star and from deportation. The number of such persons in the Reich-Protektorat area was estimated at above 150,000.[91] Though the Nuremberg laws had forbidden marriages between Jews and Aryans, they had not annulled existing mixed marriages. With the progress of the Final Solution, however, this loophole was now to be closed. A conference of experts in March 1942 decided upon the compulsory dissolution of racially mixed marriages, to be followed by the deportation of the Jewish partner. If the Aryan partner failed to apply for a divorce within a certain period of time, the public prosecutor was to file a petition for divorce, which the courts would have to grant.

The bishops heard of the contemplated measure through Dr. Globke in the Ministry of the Interior, and they reacted promptly. On November 11, 1942, Archbishop Bertram, in the name of the episcopate, addressed a letter of protest against the planned compulsory divorce legislation to the Ministers of Justice, Interior and Ecclesiastical Affairs. The intervention of the bishops, he insisted, was not due "to lack of love for the German nationality, lack of a feeling of national dignity, and also not to underestimation of the harmful Jewish influences upon German culture and national interests." The bishops merely felt called upon to emphasize that the duty of humane treatment also existed toward the members of other races. Among the persons affected by the contemplated measure, Bertram went on, were many thousands of Catholics whose marriages, according to Catholic doctrine, were indissoluble. Respect for the religious rights of the Catholic Christians was an indispensable condition for the peaceful co-operation of Church and State, which had never been as necessary as in the present situation. The bishops therefore hoped, the letter ended, that the government would withdraw the planned divorce ordinance.[92]

Despite the fact that the ordinance was still tied up in bureaucratic difficulties, the Gestapo in February 1943, in the course of deporting the last German Jews, seized several thousand Christian non-Aryans in mixed marriages. In Berlin alone about 6,000 such men were arrested on February 27. But then something unexpected and unparalleled happened: their Aryan wives followed them to the place of temporary dentention and there they stood for several hours screaming and howling for their men. With the secrecy of the whole machinery of destruction threatened, the Gestapo yielded and the non-Aryan husbands were released.[93] Here was an example of what an outraged conscience could achieve, even against Hitler's terror apparatus.

The German episcopate, after the downfall of the Nazi regime, has taken credit for preventing the compulsory divorce of mixed marriages.[94] There is strong reason to assume that the lion's share of the credit belongs to the courageous women of Berlin who, in the last days of February 1943, dared to defy the seemingly all-powerful Gestapo and caused the Nazis to fear similar outbursts in the future if they moved to break up these marriages by divorce or deportation.

A few days after this unique event Bertram composed another letter. This time he also sent copies to the chief of the Reich Chancellery, Lammers, and to the *Reichssicherheitshauptamt* (RSHA), Himmler's headquarters. About 8,000 Christian non-Aryans, Bertram complained, had been seized and deported. The episcopate could not silently accept these measures. He then repeated what in November 1942 he had said about the illegitimacy of compulsory divorce.[95] On April 16 Bishop Preysing informed his fellow bishops that the contemplated divorce decree was soon to be made public. He urged, for the time being, that the matter be treated as strictly confidential, but in the event that the order should be issued, a statement drawn up by Bertram was to be read from the pulpits. This statement, in a manner similar to the earlier letters of protest, reaffirmed the indissolubility of Christian marriage and the validity of this principle even in the case of racially mixed marriages. It asked for prayer for the unfortunates affected by the decree.[96]

About two months later Preysing sent word to his colleagues through a messenger that the threatened decree had been postponed. The bishops were asked to write letters to all the ministries; they should inquire in strong language as to the whereabouts of the deportees, demanding pastoral care for the Christians and threatening a public protest. The point of departure should be concern for the Christian Jews, "but beyond this one should speak clearly about the out-

rages inflicted upon the Jews generally."[97] We do not know how many bishops acted upon Preysing's request.

In November 1943 Bertram sent out another appeal in the name of the entire episcopate to the Minister of the Interior and the RSHA. The episcopate, he wrote, had received information according to which the non-Aryans evacuated from Germany were living in camps under conditions that would have to be called inhuman. A large number of the sufferers had already succumbed. "In view of the reputation of the German name at home and abroad," and in view of the commands of the Christian moral law concerning the duties owed fellow men even of foreign races, the bishops considered it necessary to plead for an amelioration of conditions in these camps. In particular, Bertram continued, the bishops wished to demand the benefit of pastoral care for the imprisoned Catholics. The episcopate would gladly designate priests for divine services and the administration of the sacraments in the camps.[98]

Bertram's letter neither employed strong language nor did it say anything very definite about the outrages against the Jews, as Bishop Preysing had suggested. This conciliatory tone, his failure to call a spade a spade, was not owing to the lack of information about the extermination machinery, now operating at peak capacity. Additional proof, if such were indeed needed, can be found in Bertram's next and last letter to the government in this matter, dispatched in January 1944. Reports had been received, the Cardinal wrote, that the ordinances enacted for the Jews were now to be applied also to the *Mischlinge*. These Christians had already been declared unworthy of military service, could not attend institutions of higher learning, etc. Now one heard that they were to be conscripted into special formations for labor service. "All these measures," Bertram continued, "aim clearly at segregation at the end of which threatens extermination." In the name of the episcopate he felt obligated to point out that any change in the meaning of the term "Jew" now – that is, after the Nuremberg laws had been accepted as the final word in this matter for almost ten years – would seriously undermine confidence in the law. The legislation of 1935 had not regarded the *Mischlinge* as a danger to people and Reich. Since 1935 only the Jews had been involved in "certain special regulations." The *Mischlinge* were Germans and Christians, and had always been rejected by the Jews. "The German Catholics, indeed numerous Christians in Germany," Bertram warned, "would be deeply hurt if these fellow Christians now would have to meet a fate similar to that of the Jews." Ordinances segregating the *Mischlinge* would seriously threaten the unity of the inner front, a danger to be avoided at all cost. The bishops would not be able to reconcile it with their conscience to remain silent in the face of such measures.[99]

The bishops did make a few public pronouncements that criticized unjust treatment of foreign races, but these were couched in very general language, did not mention the Jews by name and might be considered equally directed at the Nazis' harsh policy toward the Slavic *Untermenschen* (subhumans). A pastoral letter of the new Archbishop of Cologne, Dr. Joseph Frings, read in his archdiocese on December 20, 1942, insisted that all men had the right to life, liberty, property and marriage, and that these rights might not be denied even to those "who are not of our blood or do not speak our language."[100] The joint pastoral letter of the German episcopate of August 1943 reminded the faithful that the killing of innocents was wrong even if done by the authorities and allegedly for the common good, as in the case of "men of foreign races and descent." The bishops called for love of "those innocent humans who are not of our people and blood" and of "the resettled." The pastoral letter stressed that the holiness of the bond of matrimony included so-called racially mixed marriages.[101] In his Christmas sermon of 1943 and in March 1944 Archbishop Frings again emphasized that it was wrong to kill innocents just because they belonged to another race.[102]

Ever since the defeat of the Third Reich these pronouncements have been cited as proof that the bishops did publicly protest the extermination of the Jews. Possibly some Catholics did indeed think of the Jews when their spiritual leaders castigated the murder of those not of German blood. But neither the word "Jew" nor "non-Aryan" ever crossed the lips of the bishops. The provincial administrator of the Re-

gensburg area in Bavaria reported in October 1943 that the joint pastoral letter castigating the killing of innocents had not had any lasting effect: "The population pays scant attention to such involved pronouncements burdened with stipulations."[103]

Unlike the case of the extermination of Germans in the euthanasia program, where the episcopate did not mince words and succeeded in putting a stop to the killings, the bishops here played it safe. The effect of their public protests on the Final Solution consequently was nil. These very general statements neither changed the policies of the government nor inspired any change in the behavior of German Catholics. The trains shipping Jews to their doom continued to roll; the factories where Jewish slave laborers were worked to death kept on consuming their victims; the guards maintained their stations and saw to it that none escaped. Close to half the population of the Greater German Reich (43.1 per cent in 1939) was Catholic, and even among the S.S., despite all pressures to leave the Church, almost a fourth (22.7 per cent on December 31, 1938)[104] belonged to the Catholic faith. Yet their bishops might just as well not have said a word on the killing of innocents. The machinery of extermination continued to function smoothly, with everyone conscientiously doing his assigned job. The episcopate had repeatedly issued orders to exclude from the sacraments Catholics who engaged in dueling or who agreed to have their bodies cremated. The word that would have forbidden the faithful, on pain of excommunication, to go on participating in the massacre of the Jews was never spoken. And so Catholics went on participating conscientiously, along with other Germans.

There was, however, at least one Catholic churchman in Germany for whom the Christian duty to love one's neighbor amounted to more than a pious formula – the sixty-six-year-old Provost Lichtenberg of Berlin, who, right through the stepped-up anti-Semitic agitation, continued to say a daily prayer for the Jews. He was finally arrested on October 23, 1941, a week after the first of the mass deportation of Jews had begun. During questioning by Himmler's henchmen, the Provost asserted that the deportation of the Jews was irreconcilable with the Christian moral law, and asked to be allowed to accompany the deportees as their spiritual adviser. Sentenced to two years imprisonment for abuse of the pulpit, Lichtenberg was seized by the Gestapo upon his release in October 1943 and shipped off to the concentration camp at Dachau. He died during the transport on November 5, 1943.[105]

The passivity of the German episcopate in the face of the Jewish tragedy stands in marked contrast to the conduct of the French, Belgian and Dutch bishops. In Holland, where the Church as early as 1934 had prohibited the participation of Catholics in the Dutch Nazi movement, the bishops in 1942 immediately and publicly protested the first deportations of Dutch Jews,[106] and in May 1943 they forbade the collaboration of Catholic policemen in the hunting down of Jews, even at the cost of losing their jobs.[107] In Belgium members of the episcopate actively supported the rescue efforts of their clergy, who hid many hundreds of Jewish children.[108] And in France the highest dignitaries of the Church repeatedly used their pulpits to denounce the deportations and to condemn the barbarous treatment of the Jews.[109]

Throughout western Europe untold numbers of priests and members of the monastic clergy organized the rescue of Jews, hid them in monasteries, parish houses and private homes. Many lay Catholics in France, Holland and Belgium acted in a similar fashion, thus saving thousands of Jewish lives. The concern of the Gentile populations of these countries for their Jewish fellow citizens was undoubtedly one of the key factors behind the bold public protests of the French, Dutch and Belgian bishops – just as the absence of such solicitude in Germany goes a long way toward explaining the apathy of their German counterparts.

To be sure, the episcopate of the occupied countries was acting against a foreign oppressor, whereas the German bishops would have had to oppose their own government, which they regarded as the legitimate authority. But the German episcopate had demonstrated their willingness to risk such a clash and exhibited their power to mold public opinion and achieve results in the euthanasia program. If they failed to speak up for the Jews facing the same gas chambers, one of the main reasons was the widespread indifference of the German population. In France, Belgium and Holland declarations of solidarity and help for the Jews were almost universally regarded as signs of patriotism. In Germany, on the other hand, the bishops in so acting would have incurred new charges of being un-German and in league with Germany's mortal enemies. Their own followers would probably have failed to understand and approve such sympathy for the Jews, whom the Church for many long years had branded as a harmful factor in German life.

As late as March 1941 Archbishop Gröber, in a pastoral letter abounding in anti-Jewish utterances, had blamed the Jews for the death of Christ and added that "the self-imposed curse of the Jews, 'His blood be upon us and upon our children,' has come true terribly until the present time, until today."[110] Now, when the bishops perhaps might have wanted to protest the inhuman treatment of the Jews, they found themselves prisoners of their own anti-Semitic teachings. As in Poland, where the clergy similarly conformed to the indifference of their surroundings, an important reason why the German episcopate did not act against the "Final Solution of the Jewish Question" was their fear that in such an endeavor they could not count on the support of their faithful. That the Church had done her share in inculcating the very sentiments which now stood in the way of a more Christian conduct adds a tragic element to this sad story.

Once again, then, the failure of the episcopate mirrored the failures of the Catholic *milieu*. In sharp contrast to the countries of western Europe, in Germany only a handful of Jews were hidden by the clergy or otherwise helped by them in their hour of distress.[111] A few cases are recorded where individual Catholics hid and saved Jews,[112] but only in Berlin did a significant number of Jews find refuge with friends and neighbors; according to Provost Grüber, most of these courageous men and women were workers, often not connected with any church.[113] In Freiburg, Dr. Gertrud Luckner, an official of the *Caritas* (the large Catholic philanthropic organization) helped Jews to get across the Swiss border, sent packages to deportees and distributed money from a special fund established by the episcopate for non-

Aryans. She was arrested in November 1943 while trying to bring a sum of money to the few remaining Jews in Berlin, and spent the rest of the war in a concentration camp.[114]

There were, then, exceptions but the over-all picture was one of indifference and apathy. "Among the Christians," a group of German Protestant and Catholic theologians concluded in 1950, "a few courageously helped the persecuted, but the large majority failed disgracefully in the face of this unheard-of provocation of the merciful God."[115] Well over 100,000 German Jews were sent to an unknown fate in the east about which few Germans initially had any precise knowledge, but about which few, on the other hand, could have had any great illusions. Yet, these deportations went off without causing a ripple. The reports of the *Regierungspräsidenten* (provincial administrators), generally known for their candidness, noted that the deportation of the Jews had caused no adverse public reactions. The report from Ansbach in Bavaria was one of the shortest: "Except for some suicides and attempted suicides no trouble whatsoever was encountered."[116] The Church, custodian of Christian love and charity, stood by silently.

4. THE ROLE OF THE PAPACY

IN APRIL 1933 a communication reached Pope Pius XI from Germany expressing grave concern about the Nazis' anti-Semitic aims and requesting the Supreme Pontiff to issue an encyclical on the Jewish question. The letter was written by the philosopher Dr. Edith Stein, a Jewish convert to Catholicism and later known as Sister Teresia Benedicta a Cruce of the Order of the Carmelites.[117] Edith Stein's request was not granted. Nine years later, in August 1942, the Gestapo removed her from a Dutch monastery, where she had sought refuge, and sent her to Auschwitz to be gassed. The debate whether or not the Papacy could have prevented or should at least have vigorously protested the massacre of the Jews of Europe, of which Edith Stein was one of the victims, has been going on ever since and has acquired new vigor as a result of [Rolf] Hochhuth's play *Der Stellvertreter**.

In 1928 Pius XI had accompanied the dissolu-

tion of the missionary society "The Friends of Israel" with a condemnation of anti-Semitism.[118] But once the Nazis were established in power, the Pontiff, like the German episcopate, seems to have limited his concern to Catholic non-Aryans. At the request of Cardinal Bertram the Papal Secretary of State in September 1933 put in "a word on behalf of those German Catholics" who were of Jewish descent and for this reason suffering "social and economic difficulties."[119] In the following years the Holy See repeatedly took issue with the Nazis' glorification of race, but the Jewish question specifically was never discussed. In 1934 the influential Jesuit magazine *Civiltà Cattolica*, published in Rome and traditionally close to Vatican thinking, noted with regret that the anti-Semitism of the Nazis "did not stem from the religious convictions nor the Christian conscience . . . but from their desire to upset the order of religion and society." The *Civiltà Cattolica* added that "we could understand them, or even praise them, if their policy were restricted within acceptable bounds of defense against the Jewish organizations and institutions. . . ."[120] In 1936 the same journal published another article on the subject, emphasizing that opposition to Nazi racialism should not be interpreted as a rejection of anti-Semitism, and arguing – as the magazine had done since 1890 – that the Christian world (though without un-Christian hatred) must defend itself against the Jewish threat by suspending the civic rights of Jews and returning them to the ghettos.[121]

Pius XI's encyclical *Mit brennender Sorge* of March 1937 rejected the myths of race and blood as contrary to revealed Christian truth, but it neither mentioned nor criticized anti-Semitism *per se*. Nor was anti-Semitism mentioned in the statement of the Roman Congregation of Seminaries and Universities, issued on April 13, 1938, and attacking as erroneous eight theses taken from the arsenal of Nazi doctrine.[122] On September 7, 1938, during a reception for Catholic pilgrims from Belgium, Pius XI is said to have condemned the participation of Catholics in anti-Semitic movements and to have added that Christians, the spiritual descendants of the Patriarch Abraham, were "spiritually Semites." But this statement was omitted by all the Italian papers, including

---

*The Deputy, written in 1963, attacks the role of the Catholic Church and Pope Pius XII during the Holocaust. *Ed.*

L'Osservatore Romano, from their account of the Pope's address.[123]

The Vatican's criticisms of the new Italian racial legislation introduced in 1938 centered upon those parts which conflicted with the canon law's provisions concerning marriage. When Italian theaters and other public facilities in December 1938 began to exclude Jews, *L'Osservatore Romano* complained that these measures no longer merely aimed at the segregation of the Jews, but smacked of un-Christian persecution.[124] The *Civiltà Cattolica* similarly objected to being claimed as an ally by the Fascist press extolling racial anti-Semitism. "As always," writes a well-informed recent student of the period, "the views of *Civiltà Cattolica* were in accord with those of the Pontiff, though it was clear that the Jesuit fathers had nothing against a moderate anti-Jewish policy in Italy."[125]

The elevation of Cardinal Pacelli to the Papacy in the spring of 1939 brought to the chair of St. Peter a man noted for his pro-German sentiments and diplomatic skill. Hochhuth's Pope possessed of "aristocratic coldness" and eyes having an "icy glow" is perhaps a bit stylized, but all biographers agree that Pius XII, in contrast to his predecessor, was unemotional and dispassionate, as well as a master in the language of diplomatic ambiguity. "Pius XII," recalls Cardinal Tardini, "was by nature meek and almost timid. He was not born with the temperament of a fighter. In this he was different from his great predecessor."[126] Whether Pius XI would have reacted to the massacre of the Jews during World War II differently from Pacelli is a question on which it is tempting to speculate, but to which no definite answer is possible.

That the Holy See had no intrinsic objection to a policy of subjecting the Jews to discriminatory legislation became again clear when in June 1941 Marshal Pétain's Vichy government introduced a series of "Jewish statutes." The cardinals and archbishops of France made known their strong disapproval of these measures. But Léon Bérard, the Vichy Ambassador at the Holy See, was able to report to Pétain, after lengthy consultations with high Church officials, that the Vatican did not consider such laws in conflict with Catholic teaching. The Holy See merely counseled that no provisions on marriage be added to the

statutes and "that the precepts of justice and charity be considered in the application of the law."[127] In August 1941 the consequences of this discriminatory policy could not yet be clearly seen, but the episode illustrates anew the Vatican's willingness to go along with anti-Semitic measures, administered with "justice and charity." When mass deportations from France got under way in 1942 the Papal Nuncio, without invoking the authority of the Holy See, requested Laval to mitigate the severity of the measures taken against the Jews of Vichy France,[128] but such pleas by that time could no longer halt the machinery of destruction.

Meanwhile, there was growing criticism of the Pope's failure to protest publicly against Nazi atrocities and especially against the murder of the Jews in the Polish death factories. Harold H. Tittmann, the assistant to Roosevelt's personal representative at the Holy See, Myron C. Taylor, in July 1942 pointed out to the Vatican that its silence was "endangering its moral prestige and is undermining faith both in the Church and in the Holy Father himself."[129] After authorization by Secretary of State Hull, Tittmann and several other diplomatic representatives at the Vatican in September 1942 formally requested that the Pope condemn the "incredible horrors" perpetrated by the Nazis. A few days later Taylor forwarded to the Papal Secretary of State, Luigi Maglione, a memorandum of the Jewish Agency for Palestine that reported mass executions of Jews in Poland and occupied Russia, and told of deportations to death camps from Germany, Belgium, Holland, France, Slovakia, etc. Taylor inquired whether the Vatican could confirm these reports, and, if so, "whether the Holy Father has any suggestions as to any practical manner in which the forces of civilized public opinion could be utilized in order to prevent a continuation of these barbarities."[130]

On October 10 the Holy See replied to Taylor's note that up to the present time it had not been possible to verify the accuracy of the severe measures reportedly taken against the Jews. The statement added, "It is well known that the Holy See is taking advantage of every opportunity offered in order to mitigate the suffering of non-Aryans."[131] In conversation with high-placed officials of the Curia, Tittmann was told that the Pope's silence was due to the following reasons: the desire of the Holy See to maintain its absolute neutrality in the world-wide conflict, the importance of Papal pronouncements standing the test of time (which quality was difficult to achieve in the heat of the passions of war and the errors resulting therefrom) and the fear that any clearly pointed protest would worsen the situation of Catholics in the Nazi-occupied countries. The Pope hesitated to condemn German atrocities, Tittmann also learned, because he did not want to incur later the reproach of the German people that the Catholic Church had contributed to their defeat.[132] After the Western Allies in December 1942 had vigorously denounced the cold-blooded extermination of the Jews, Tittmann again inquired from the Papal Secretary of State whether the Holy See could not issue a similar pronouncement. Maglione answered that the Holy See, in line with its policy of neutrality, could not protest particular atrocities and had to limit itself to condemning immoral actions in general. He assured Tittmann that everything possible was being done behind the scenes to help the Jews.[133]

Two days later, in the course of a lengthy Christmas message broadcast over the Vatican radio, Pope Pius made another of his many calls for a more humane conduct of hostilities. All men of good will, the Pope demanded, should bring the life of the nations again into conformity with the divine law. Humanity owed the resolution to build a better world to "the hundreds of thousands who, without personal guilt, sometimes for no other reason but on account of their nationality or descent, were doomed to death or exposed to a progressive deterioration of their condition."[134] Addressing the Sacred College of Cardinals in June 1943 the Pontiff spoke of his twofold duty to be impartial and to point up moral errors. He had given special attention, he recalled, to the plight of those who were still being harassed because of their nationality or descent, and who, without personal guilt, were subjected to measures that spelled destruction. Much had been done for the unfortunates that could not be described yet. Every public statement had had to be carefully weighed "in the interest of those suffering so that their situation would not inadvertently be made still more difficult and unbear-

able." Unfortunately, Pius XII added, the Church's pleas for compassion and the observance of the elementary norms of humanity had encountered doors "which no key was able to open."[135]

The precise nature of these interventions prior to June 1943 has not been revealed to this day. We do know that Nuncio Orsenigo in Berlin made inquiries several times about mass shootings and the fate of deported Jews. Ernst Woermann, the director of the political department of the German Foreign Ministry, on October 15, 1942, recorded that the Nuncio had made his representation with "some embarrassment and without emphasis."[136] State Secretary Weizsäcker told Monsignor Orsenigo on another such occasion that the Vatican had so far conducted itself "very cleverly" in these matters and that he would hope for a continuation of this policy. The Nuncio took the hint and "pointed out that he had not really touched this topic and that he had no desire to touch it."[137] Himmler, when received by Count Ciano on his visit to Rome in October 1942, praised the "discretion" of the Vatican.[138]

There were other diplomatic representations. That of the Nuncio in Vichy France has already been mentioned. In Slovakia, where 52,000 Jews had been deported in the spring of 1942, the Vatican in the summer of that year pointed out to the Quisling government, at whose head stood a Catholic priest, Dr. Josef Tiso, that the deported Jews had been sent away not for labor service, but for annihilation. The deportations ground to a halt, for Eichmann's emissary had instructions to avoid "political complications." Thereafter, the Slovakian Jews lived in relative security until September 1944.[139] However, the case of Catholic Slovakia was a special one, and in the over-all balance one has to agree with the Pope's own finding that the Holy See was unsuccessful in opening the doors that barred relief for the hapless victims. But did the Holy See try all the keys in its possession?

The Pope's policy of neutrality encountered its most crucial test when the Nazis began rounding up the 8,000 Jews of Rome in the fall of 1943. Prior to the start of the arrests, the Jewish community was told by the Nazis that unless it raised 50 kilograms of gold (the equivalent of $56,000) within thirty-six hours, 300 hostages would be taken. When it seemed that the Jews themselves could only raise part of this ransom, a representative of the community asked for and received an offer of a loan from the Vatican treasury. The Pope approved of this offer of help, which, as it later turned out, did not have to be invoked.[140] But the big question in everyone's mind was how the Supreme Pontiff would react when the deportation of the Jews from the Eternal City began.

The test came on the night of October 15–16. While the roundup was still going on a letter was delivered to General Stahel, the German military commander of Rome. Bearing the signature of Bishop Hudal, the head of the German Church in Rome, it said:

> I have just been informed by a high Vatican office in the immediate circle of the Holy Father that the arrests of Jews of Italian nationality have begun this morning. In the interest of the good relations which have existed until now between the Vatican and the high German military command . . . I would be very grateful if you would give an order to stop these arrests in Rome and its vicinity right away; I fear that otherwise the Pope will have to make an open stand which will serve the anti-German propaganda as a weapon against us.[141]

A day later, Ernst von Weizsäcker, the new German Ambassador at the Holy See, reported to Berlin that the Vatican was upset, especially since the deportations had taken place, as it were, right under the Pope's window:

> The people hostile to us in Rome are taking advantage of this affair to force the Vatican from its reserve. People say that the bishops of French cities, where similar incidents occurred, have taken a firm stand. The Pope, as supreme head of the Church and Bishop of Rome, cannot be more reticent than they. They are also drawing a parallel between the stronger character of Pius XI and that of the present Pope.[142]

Contrary to Hudal's and Weizsäcker's apprehensions, however, the man in the Vatican palace remained silent. On October 18, over 1,000 Roman Jews – more than two-thirds of them women and children – were shipped off to the killing center of Auschwitz. Fourteen men and one woman returned alive. About 7,000 Roman Jews – that is, seven out of eight – were able to elude their hunters by going into hiding. More than 4,000, with the knowledge and approval of the Pope, found refuge in the numerous monasteries and houses of religious orders in Rome,[143] and a few dozen were sheltered in the Vatican itself. The rest were hidden by their Italian neighbors, among whom the anti-Jewish policy of the Fascists had never been popular. But for the Germans, overwhelmingly relieved at having averted a public protest by the Pope, the fact that a few thousand Jews had escaped the net was of minor significance. On October 28 Ambassador Weizsäcker was able to report:

> Although under pressure from all sides, the Pope has not let himself be drawn into any demonstrative censure of the deportation of Jews from Rome. Although he must expect that his attitude will be criticized by our enemies and exploited by the Protestant and Anglo-Saxon countries in their propaganda against Catholicism, he has done everything he could in this delicate matter not to strain relations with the German government and German circles in Rome. As there is probably no reason to expect other German actions against the Jews of Rome, we can consider that a question so disturbing to German-Vatican relations has been liquidated.
>
> In any case, an indication for this state of affairs can be seen in the Vatican's attitude. *L'Osservatore Romano* has in fact prominently published in its issue of October 25–26 an official communiqué on the Pope's charitable activities. The communiqué, in the Vatican's distinctive style, that is, very vague and complicated, declares that all men, without distinction of nationality, race or religion, benefit from the Pope's paternal solicitude. The continual and varied activities of Pius XII have probably increased lately because of the greater sufferings of so many unfortunates.
>
> There is less reason to object to the terms of

this message . . . as only a very small number of people will recognize in it a special allusion to the Jewish question.[144]

When an Italian law of December 1, 1943, provided for the internment of all Jews in concentration camps and for the confiscation of their property, *L'Osservatore Romano* criticized these measures as too harsh. But Weizsäcker reassured Berlin that these "commentaries are not official. They have not been broadcast by the Vatican radio."[145] During the following months searches for Jews took place periodically. The Pope, continuing acts of charity, maintained his silence.

The criticism leveled against Pius XII for his failure to protest the massacre of the Jews of Europe, including those in his own diocese of Rome, is composed of two main parts. It has been argued first, most recently by Hochhuth, that the Pope could have saved numerous lives, if not halted the machinery of destruction, had he chosen to take a public stand and had he confronted the Germans with the threats of an interdict or the excommunication of Hitler, Goebbels and other leading Nazis belonging to the Catholic faith. As examples of the effectiveness of public protests it is possible to cite the resolute reaction of the German episcopate to the euthanasia program. In a number of other instances, notably in Slovakia, Hungary and Rumania, the forceful intervention of the Papal Nuncios, who threatened the Quisling governments with a public condemnation by the Pope, was able, albeit temporarily, to stop the deportations.[146] At the very least, it has been suggested, a public denunciation of the mass murders by Pius XII, broadcast widely over the Vatican radio and read from the pulpits by his bishops, would have revealed to Jews and Christians alike what deportation to the east entailed. The Pope would have been believed, whereas the broadcasts of the Allies were often shrugged off as war propaganda. Many of the deportees, who accepted the assurances of the Germans that they were merely being resettled, might thus have been warned and given an impetus to escape. Many more Christians might have helped and sheltered Jews, and many more lives might have been saved.

There exists, of course, no way of definitively proving or disproving these arguments. Whether a Papal decree of excommunication against Hitler would have dissuaded the Führer from carrying out his plan to destroy the Jews is very doubtful. A revocation of the Concordat by the Holy See would have bothered Hitler still less. However, a flaming protest against the massacre of the Jews, coupled with the imposition of the interdict upon all of Germany or the excommunication of all Catholics in any way involved with the apparatus of the Final Solution, would have been a far more formidable and effective weapon. It certainly would have warned many who were deceived by the Germans' promises of good treatment. Yet this was precisely the kind of action which the Pope could not take without risking the allegiance of the German Catholics. Given the indifference of the German population toward the fate of the Jews, and the highly ambivalent attitude of the German hierarchy toward Nazi anti-Semitism, a forceful stand by the Supreme Pontiff on the Jewish question might well have led to a large-scale desertion from the Church. When Dr. Edoardo Senatro, the correspondent of *L'Osservatore Romano* in Berlin, asked Pius XII whether he would not protest the extermination of the Jews, the Pope is reported to have answered, "Dear friend, do not forget that millions of Catholics serve in the German armies. Shall I bring them into conflicts of conscience?"[147] The Pope knew that the German Catholics were not prepared to suffer martyrdom for their Church; still less were they willing to incur the wrath of their Nazi rulers for the sake of the Jews whom their own bishops for years had castigated as a harmful influence in German life. In the final analysis, then, as [Léon] Poliakov has also concluded, "the Vatican's silence only reflected the deep feeling of the Catholic masses of Europe"[148] – those of Germany and eastern Europe in particular. The failure of the Pope was a measure of the Church's failure to convert her gospel of brotherly love and human dignity into living reality.

Some writers have suggested that a public protest by the Pope would not only have been unsuccessful in helping the Jews, but might have caused additional damage – to the Jews, to the *Mischlinge*, the Church, the territorial integrity of the Vatican and the

Catholics in all of Nazi-occupied Europe. It is tempting to dismiss this argument by asking what worse fate could have befallen European Jewry than the disaster that did overtake it. Since the condition of the Jews could hardly have become worse, and might have changed for the better, as a result of a Papal denunciation, one could ask why the Church did not risk the well-being and safety of the Catholics and of the Vatican. Why did she not at least attempt to help the Jews?

The Catholic bishops of Holland tried this gamble. In July 1942, together with the Protestant Church, they sent a telegram of protest against the deportation of the Dutch Jews to the German *Reichskommissar* and threatened to make their protest public unless the deportations were halted. The Germans responded by offering to exempt from deportation non-Aryans converted to Christianity before 1941 if the churches would remain silent. The Dutch Reformed Church agreed to the bargain, but the Catholic Archbishop of Utrecht refused, and issued a pastoral letter in which he denounced the wrong done to the Jews. The Germans retaliated by seizing and deporting all the Catholic non-Aryans they could find, among them the noted philosopher Edith Stein.[149] Once the inability of the Pope to move the masses of the faithful into a decisive struggle against the Nazis is accepted as a fact, there is thus some basis for the contention that a public protest, along with any good that would have come of it, might have made some things worse, if not for the Jews, at least for the *Mischlinge* and the Catholics themselves.

The silence of the Pope had other, perhaps still weightier, reasons. As Mr. Tittmann was told by highly placed officials of the Curia, the Holy See did not want to jeopardize its neutrality by condemning German atrocities. The Vatican wanted to preserve its good name with the Germans, as well as with the Western Allies, and the Pope was unwilling to risk later charges that he had been partial and had contributed to a German defeat. Moreover, as already discussed in an earlier context, the Vatican did not wish to undermine and weaken Germany's struggle against Russia. In the late summer of 1943 the Papal Secretary of State, Luigi Maglione, termed the fate of Europe dependent upon a victorious resistance of

Germany at the Eastern Front,[150] and Father Leiber, one of the secretaries of Pius XII, recalls that the late Pope always looked upon Russian Bolshevism as more dangerous than German National Socialism.[151] Hitler, therefore, had to be treated with some forebearance.

Finally, one is inclined to conclude that the Pope and his advisors – influenced by the long tradition of moderate anti-Semitism so widely accepted in Vatican circles – did not view the plight of the Jews with a real sense of urgency and moral outrage. For this assertion no documentation is possible, but it is a conclusion difficult to avoid. Pius XII broke his policy of strict neutrality during World War II to express concern over the German violation of the neutrality of Holland, Belgium and Luxembourg in May 1940. When some German Catholics criticized him for this action, the Pope wrote the German bishops that neutrality was not synonymous "with indifference and apathy where moral and humane considerations demanded a candid word."[152] All things told, did not the murder of several million Jews demand a similarly "candid word"?

The discussion whether a Papal denunciation would have helped or harmed the Jews leaves untouched the one question that perhaps is the most compelling. It concerns the moral integrity of the Church, the performance of the Church as a guardian of the moral law. This second point at issue involves the Pope, the Bishop of Rome and Head of the Church, as much as all the other bishops called upon to provide moral leadership for their flock. In his first encyclical to the world, issued in October 1939, Pius XII described his duties as the Deputy of Christ in these words:

> As vicar of Him who in a decisive hour pronounced before the highest earthly authority of that day the great words: "For this I was born, and for this I came into the world: that I should give testimony to the truth. Every one that is of the truth heareth my voice" (St. John xviii, 37), we feel we owe no greater debt to our office and to our time than to testify to the truth with Apostolic firmness: "To give testimony to the truth." This duty necessarily entails the exposition and

confutation of errors and human faults; for these must be made known before it is possible to tend and to heal them. "You shall know the truth and the truth shall make you free" (St. John viii, 32). In the fulfillment of this our duty we shall not let ourselves be influenced by earthly considerations nor be held back by mistrust or opposition, by rebuffs or lack of appreciation of our words, nor yet by fear of misconceptions and misinterpretations.[153]

Similarly the German bishops repeatedly affirmed their duty boldly to preach the word of God and fearlessly to condemn injustice. "The bishop," stressed Cardinal Faulhaber in 1936, "no longer would be the servant of God if he were to speak to please men or remain silent out of fear of men."[154] "I am aware," declared Bishop Galen in a sermon delivered in July 1941, "that as bishop, as harbinger and defender of the legal and moral order desired by God, which grants everyone basic rights and liberties not to be invaded by human demands, I am called upon . . . courageously to represent the authority of the law and to brand as an injustice crying to heaven the condemnation of defenseless innocents."[155] But these noble sentiments remained an empty formula in the face of the Jewish tragedy.

There were those within the Church cognizant of this failure. Writing under the impact of German atrocities in Poland and the defeat of France in June 1940, Cardinal Eugène Tisserant, a high official of the Vatican library, complained to Cardinal Suhard, Archbishop of Paris, that "our superiors do not want to understand the real nature of this conflict." He had pleaded with Pius XII, Tisserant said, to issue an encyclical on the duty of the individual to follow the dictates of his conscience rather than blindly execute all orders, no matter how criminal.

> I fear that history will reproach the Holy See with having practiced a policy of selfish convenience and not much else. This is extremely sad, especially for those [of us] who have lived under Pius XI. Everyone [here] is confident that, after Rome has been declared an open city, members of the Curia will not have to suffer any harm; that is a disgrace.[156]

Criticism of the Church's failure to offer unequivocal moral guidance could be heard also in Germany. The Jesuit Alfred Delp, a member of the German resistance, addressed a conference of priests at Fulda in 1943 and decried the fact that the Church had neglected to stand up for human dignity, the precondition of any Christian existence. "Has the Church," he asked, "forgotten to say 'Thou shalt not,' has the Church lost sight of the commandments, or is she silent because she is convinced of the hopelessness of her clear and firm preaching? Has the 'imprudence' of John the Baptist died out or has the Church forgotten man and his fundamental rights?"[157] The decisive question, Delp asserted on another occasion, is whether the Christians will be able and willing to stand up, not only for the Church and the Christian, but for man himself. The preoccupation with the question of the success or failure of bearing moral witness was in itself already a sign of moral corruption.[158] The silence of the Church on what was being done to the Poles and Jews and on the horrors committed in the concentration camps, Delp told a gathering of Bavarian churchmen in October 1943, threatened the acceptance of the Church by the new Germany that would arise after the downfall of the Nazi regime.[159] But Father Delp was an exceptional figure, whose vision transcended the institutional concerns of the Church. His counsel was not heeded.

Catholic theologians have long debated the dividing line between "Christian prudence" and "unChristian cowardice." This line is often hard to locate, and no amount of casuistry about silence in the face of crime that is permissible in order to prevent worse will alleviate the arduous task of searching for it. Situations exist where moral guilt is incurred by omission. Silence has its limits, and that also holds true, as another German Jesuit had reminded his Church as early as 1935, for the silence "to prevent worse." "For ultimately," wrote Father Pribilla, "the worst that could really happen is that truth and justice would no longer find spokesmen and martyrs on earth."[160] When Hitler set out on his murderous campaign against the Jews of Europe truth and justice found few defenders. The Deputy of Christ and the German episcopate were not among them. Their role gives a special relevance to the question the young girl in Max Frisch's *Andorra* asks her priest: "Where were you, Father Benedict, when they took away our brother like a beast to the slaughter, like a beast to the slaughter, where were you?"[161] This question still waits for an answer.

Notes

1. The literature on the subject is too voluminous to be listed here. See, most recently, Ludwig von Hertling, S.J., "Die Schuld des jüdischen Volkes am Tode Christi," *Stimmen der Zeit*, CLXXI (1962), 16–25.
2. For an empirical study of this problem see Bernhard E. Olson, *Faith and Prejudice* (New Haven, 1963) and the earlier work of Paul Déman, N.D.S., "La Catéchèse chrétienne et le peuple de la Bible," *Cahiers Sioniens*, VI (1952), special number 3–4.
3. Jules Isaac, *Jésus et Israël* (Paris, 1948), 508.
4. Cf. Eleonore Sterling, *Er ist wie du: Aus der Frühgeschichte des Antisemitismus in Deutschland (1815–1850)* (Munich, 1956).
5. *Historisch-Politische Blätter*, I (1860), 593, quoted in Emil Ritter, ed., *Katholisch-konservatives Erbgut: Eine Auslese für die Gegenwart* (Freiburg, Br., 1934), 239.
6. Konrad Martin, *Blicke ins talmudische Judentum*, abridged ed. by Josef Rebbert (Paderborn, 1876), 44.
7. Paul Wilhelm von Keppler, *Wanderfahrten and Wallfahrten im Orient*, 7th ed. (Freiburg, Br., 1912), 313.
8. Paul W. Massing, *Rehearsal for Destruction: A Study of Political Anti-Semitism in Imperial Germany* (New York, 1949), 17.
9. Matthias Erzberger, *Christliche oder sozialdemokratische Gewerkschaften?* (Stuttgart, 1898), 29–30, quoted in Klaus Epstein, *Matthias Erzberger and the Dilemma of German Democracy* (Princeton, 1959), 402.
10. Hans Rost, *Gedanken and Wahrheiten zur Judenfrage* (Trier, 1907), 89.
11. Erhard Schlund, O.F.M., *Katholizismus und Vaterland* (Munich, 1923), 32–33.
12. Gustav Gundlach, S.J., "Antisemitismus," *Lexikon für Theologie und Kirche*, 2nd rev. ed. (Frieburg, Br., 1930), I, 504. The new edition of this work, published after the downfall of Nazism, has replaced this article by one that condemns all types of anti-Semitism.
13. Michael Buchberger, *Gibt es noch eine Rettung?* (Regensburg, n.d. [1931]), 97–98.
14. Dr. Mayer, "Kann ein Katholik Nationalsozialist sein?" in Wild, *op. cit.*, 12.
15. Harry Pross, ed., *Die Zerstörung der Deutschen Politik* (Frankfurt a.M., 1959), 242.
16. Josef Roth, *Katholizismus und Judenfrage* (Munich, 1923), 5.
17. Philipp Haeuser, *Jud und Christ oder Wem gebührt die Weltherrschaft?* (Regensburg, 1923).
18. Wilhelm Maria Senn, *Katholizismus und Nationalsozialismus* (Münster, 1931), 80.
19. In 1960 Dr. Franz Rödel, a retired Catholic priest and the organizer of the *Katholisch-Judaeologischen Institut* in Jetzendorf/Ilm, unsuccessfully appealed to the Bavarian Bishops' Conference to abolish the commemoration exercises of Deggendorf and to remove the offensive pictures and inscriptions in the church erected for the miraculous event in question. In a detailed memorandum he exposed the historical falsehoods involved, but nothing came of his plea until a mass circulation magazine, *Der Spiegel*, picked up the incredible story. Only then did the Church authorities move into action and the affair has now been converted into an annual call for forgiveness for the wrongs done to the Jews.
20. Franz Steffen, *Antisemitische und deutschvölkische Bewegung im Lichte des Katholizismus* (Berlin, 1925), 88.
21. Felix Langer, *Der "Judenspiegel" des Dr. Justus kritisch beleuchtet* (Leipzig, 1921), 30.
22. Muckerman, *Der Gral*, XXVI (1932), 273.
23. Sermon on December 31, 1923, in Faulhaber, *Deutsches Ehrgefühl*, 19.
24. "Der Erzbischof von Köln für den inneren Frieden," *Münchener Katholische Kirchenzeitung*, no. 15, April 10, 1932, 170.
25. Memorandum of unknown authorship, *Documents on German Foreign Policy*, C, I, doc. 188, 347.
26. Report of Bishop Berning, Müller, *Kirche und NS*, 118.
27. Article "Rasse" in Gröber, *Handbuch der religiösen Gegenwartsfragen*, 536.
28. Sermon of December 31, 1933, in Faulhaber, *Judaism, Christianity and Germany*, 107.
29. Sermon of December 17, 1933, *ibid.*, 68–69.
30. Yves M.-J. Congar, O. P., *Die katholische Kirche und die Rassenfrage*, trans. W. Armbruster (Recklinghausen, 1961), 68.
31. *AB Munich*, November 15, 1934, supplement.
32. J. Scherm, "Der alttestamentliche Bibelunterricht: Planungen und Wegweisungen," *Klerusblatt*, XX (1989), 225.
33. Pastoral letter of January 30, 1939, *AB Freiburg*, no. 3, February 8, 1939, 15.
34. Pastoral letter for Lent 1939, *AB Limburg*, no. 1, February 6, 1939, 1–8.
35. Article "Marxismus," Gröber, *Handbuch der religiösen Gegenwartsfragen*, 404.
36. Article "Bolschewismus," *ibid.*, 86.
37. *Ibid.*, 87.
38. Article "Kunst," *ibid.*, 372.
39. Waldemar Gurian, "Anti-Semitism in Modern Germany" in Koppel S. Pinson, ed., *Essays on Anti-Semitism* (New York, 1946), 235.
40. Lichtenberg to Hitler, December 10, 1935, BA Koblenz, R 43 II/175.
41. *Klerusblatt*, XVI (1935), 817; *Münchener Katholische Kirchenzeitung*, no. 50, December 15, 1935, 795. The new evidence was first reported by the *Münsterer Kirchenblatt* of December 1, 1935.
42. Clemens Gahlen, *Der zerbrochene Pfaffenspiegel* (Bocholt, 1938), 19.
43. Joseph Schneider, *Wider den Pfaffenspiegel* (Aschaffenburg, 1937), 21 and 65.
44. *AB Regensburg*, no. 2, February 5, 1937, 22; Konrad Hofmann, ed., *Hirtenbriefe des Erzbischofs Gröber* (Freiburg, Br., 1947), 145.
45. Adam, *Theologische Quartalschrift*, CXIV (1933), 60–62.

46. "Vor 17 Jahren: Marxismus über Deutschland," *Klerusblatt*, XVI (1935), 785–88.

47. F. Schühlein, "Geschichte der Juden," *Lexikon für Theologie und Kirche*, 2nd rev. ed. (Freiburg, Br., 1933), V, 687.

48. Gustav Lehmacher, S.J., "Rassenwerte," *Stimmen der Zeit*, CXXVI (1933), 81.

49. "Verdient die katholische Kirche den Namen 'Judenkirche'?," *Klerusblatt*, XVIII (1937), 542.

50. Theodor Bogler, O.S.B., *Der Glaube von gestern und heute* (Cologne, 1939), 150.

51. AKD *Mitteilungsblatt*, no. 6, May 15, 1934, [8].

52. Erwin Roderich Kienitz, *Christliche Ehe: Eine Darstellung des Eherechts und der Ehemoral der katholischen Kirche für Seelsorger und Laien* (Munich, 1938), 47–54.

53. *Denkschrift über die Reform des Deutschen Strafrechtes*, mimeographed, 39, copy in DA Passau.

54. Circular letter of the "Kirchliche Informationsstelle der Bischöflichen Behörden Deutschlands," no. 341, September 16, 1935, DA Eichstätt.

55. This was the complaint of Alfred Richter, "Parteiprogramm der NSDAP und Reichskonkordat: Zum dritten Jahrestag der Unterzeichnung des Reichskonkordats (20. Juli 1933)," *Deutschlands Erneuerung*, XX (1936), 468. The occurrence of such marriages was confirmed to me by the former Vicar General of Hildesheim, Dr. Wilhelm Offenstein, in an interview on February 5, 1962. The German Federal Republic subsequently legalized these illegal marriages.

56. *Deutsche Briefe*, no. 52, September 27, 1935, 6–7.

57. Regierungsrat Münsterer, "Die Regelung des Rassenproblems durch die Nürnberger Gesetze," *Klerusblatt*, XVII (1936), 47.

58. Hudal, *op. cit.*, 75 and 88.

59. Cf. *Niederschrift der Konferenz der bayerischen Bischöfe in München am 21. März 1934*, 3.

60. J. Demleitner, "Volksgenealogie," *Klerusblatt*, XV (1934), 503.

61. All of the diocesan archives preserved contain voluminous files of correspondence in connection with the certification of Aryan descent.

62. Bertram to the German bishops, October 14, 1936, DA Eichstätt.

63. Vicar General Buchwieser of Munich to Kerrl, November 18, 1937, copy in DA Eichstätt.

64. Bertram to the "Forschungsabteilung Judenfrage des Reichsinstituts für die Geschichte des neueren Deutschland" in Munich, January 20, 1938, copy in DA Mainz, J XXIII.

65. Bertram to Pacelli, September 2, 1933, copy in DA Passau; printed in Müller, *Kirche und NS*, doc. 87, 190.

66. Corsten, *Kölner Aktenstücke*, doc. 17, 16.

67. Cf. Report of the "Sonderhilfswerk des St. Raphaelsvereins für Persönlichkeiten die infolge Abstammung oder aus anderen Gründen ihre Existenz verloren haben," May 31, 1935, DA Mainz, file "St. Raphaelsverein."

68. Neuhäusler, *op. cit.*, II, 389; DA Mainz, V/xvi.

69. *Protokoll der Verwaltungsratssitzung und der Hauptversammlung des St. Raphaelsvereins in Dortmund am Freitag, den 27. August 1937*, mimeo, 12 pp., DA Mainz, file "St. Raphaelsverein"; minutes of the Fulda Bishops' Conference of August 1939, BA Koblenz, R 43 II/177a.

70. *Petrusblatt* (Berlin), no. 16, April 16, 1961, 3.

71. BA Koblenz, R 43 II/174.

72. Report of the Gestapo Munich, January 1, 1937, BGS Munich, MA 1946/019.

73. Von einem deutschen, römisch-katholischen Priester, "Die katholische Kirche und die Judenfrage," *Eine heilige Kirche*, XVI (1934), 177.

74. From a report of Heydrich to Göring, November 11, 1938, quoted in Poliakov, *op. cit.*, 17.

75. Hugh Martin *et al.*, *Christian Counter-Attack* (New York, 1944), 24.

76. Quoted in Erb, *op. cit.*, 43.

77. Quoted in Poliakov, *op. cit.*, 30.

78. Quoted in Raul Hilberg, *The Destruction of the European Jews* (Chicago, 1961), 262.

79. Several such letters can be found in DA Limburg, file "Nichtarier."

80. Bertram to the German bishops, September 17, 1941, DA Limburg, file "Nichtarier."

81. Berning to Bertram, October 27, 1941, copy in DA Limburg, file "Nichtarier."

82. *Ibid.*

83. Hilfrich to Wienken, October 27, 1941, DA Limburg, file "Nichtarier."

84. Wienken to Hilfrich, October 30, 1941, DA Limburg, file "Nichtarier."

85. *Niederschrift über die Konferenz der Bischöfe der Kölner- und Paderborner Kirchenprovinz am 24. und 25. November 1941 in Paderborn*, mimeo, 5.

86. Herman, *op. cit.*, 234; Bernhard Lösener, "Das Reichsministerium des Inneren und die Judengesetzgebung: Aufzeichnungen," *Vierteljahrshefte für Zeitgeschichte* IX (1961), 310.

87. Inge Scholl, *Die weisse Rose* (Frankfurt a.M., 1961), 126–28.

88. "Augenzeugenbericht zu den Massenvergasungen," *Vierteljahrshefte für Zeitgeschichte*, I (1953), 193. The opening scene of Hochhuth's play *Der Stellvertreter* is based on Gerstein's account, which is considered fully reliable by all students of the subject.

89. Interview with Dr. Gertrud Luckner, March 9, 1962. One such officer, Dr. Alfons Hildenbrand, took special leave from his unit stationed near Minsk in order to report about the massacres he had witnessed to Cardinal Faulhaber, Cf. Thomas Dehler, "Sie zuckten mit der Achsel," Fritz J. Raddatz, ed., *Summa inuria oder Durfte der Papst schweigen?* (Reinbek bei Hamburg, 1963), 231.

90. Interview with Dr. Joseph Müller, March 26, 1962.

91. Hilberg, *op. cit.*, 267.

92. Bertram to Thierack, November 11, 1942, Archives of the Ministry of Justice, Bonn, R 22 Gr. 5/XXII-2; copy in DA Aachen.

93. Ruth Andreas-Friedrich, *Berlin Underground 1938–1945*, trans. Barrows Mussey (New York, 1947), 92; Philip Friedman, *Their Brothers' Keepers* (New York, 1957), 93.

94. Cf. the affidavit of Bishop Preysing for Globke, January 18, 1946, printed in *Petrusblatt*, no. 32, August 7, 1960, 3.

95. Bertram to Thierack, March 2, 1943, Archives of the Ministry of Justice, R 22 Gr. 5/XXII-2; copy in DA Mainz, 1/1.

96. Preysing to the German bishops, April 16, 1943, DA Limburg, file "Nichtarier."

97. Memo on oral information from Preysing relayed to the Bishop of Limburg etc. on June 26, 1943, by Father Odilo

Braun, O.P., DA Limburg, file "Nichtarier." Father Braun, a friend of Alfred Delp, was arrested by the Gestapo in 1944, but escaped with his life.

98. Bertram to the Minister of the Interior and the RSHA, November 17, 1943, copy in DA Limburg, file "Nichtarier."

99. Bertram to Thierack, January 29, 1944, BA Koblenz, R 22 Gr. 5/XXI, la.

100. Pastoral letter of December 12, 1942, Corsten, *Kölner Aktenstücke*, doc. 218, 269.

101. Joint pastoral letter of August 19, 1943, *ibid.*, doc. 227, 301–3.

102. Sermons of December 25, 1943, and March 12, 1944, *ibid.*, docs. 232–233, 310.

103. Report of October 10, 1943, BGS Munich, MA 1946/C38.

104. From an internal S.S. report, NA Washington, T-580, roll 42, file 245.

105. Erb, *op. cit.*, 46–65. According to the *Freiburger Rundbrief*, I (1948), 16, Bishop Kaller of Ermland asked the permission of the Papal Nuncio to go as a priest to Theresienstadt, a Ghetto city for old people, decorated veterans and other Jews of prominence. This request does not seem to have reached the hands of the Gestapo.

106. For the text of the protests see W. W. Visser't Hooft, ed., *Holländische Kirchendokumente* (Zollikon-Zürich, 1944), 58–60.

107. Werner Warmbrunn, *The Dutch under German Occupation 1940–1945* (Stanford, Cal., 1963), 161.

108. Friedman, *op. cit.*, 70–71; C. Leclef, ed., *Le Cardinal van Roey et l'Occupation Allemande en Belgique: Actes et Documents* (Brussels, 1945), ch. 8.

109. Emile Maurice Guerry, *L'Eglise Catholique en France sous l'Occupation* (Paris, 1947), 33–65; Jules Géraud Saliège, *Fürchtet euchnnicht: Hirtenbriefe und Ansprachen* (Offenburg, 1949), 150–51; Friedman, *op. cit.*, 49–51.

110. Pastoral letter of March 25, 1941, *AB Freiburg*, no. 9, March 27, 1941, 388.

111. The case of a Jewish mother and her son, who were hidden in a monastery near Berlin, is described by Kurt R. Grossmann, *Die unbesungenen Helden* (Berlin, 1957), 153.

112. Cf. Gertrud Ehrle, ed., *Licht über dem Abgrund* (Freiburg, Br., 1951), 118–124.

113. Heinrich Grüber, "Zu Rolf Hochhuth's 'Stellvertreter,' " Raddatz, *op. cit.*, 202.

114. Grossmann, *op. cit.*, 113; Ernst Schnydrig, "Hilfe für die verfolgten Juden," Zentralvorstand des Deutschen Caritasverbandes, *An der Aufgabe gewachsen* [60th anniversary Festschrift] (Freiburg, Br., 1957), 74–77; interview with Dr. Gertrud Luckner, March 9, 1962.

115. "Thesen christlicher Lehrverkündigung im Hinblick auf umlaufende Irrtümer über das Gottesvolk des Alten Bundes" (Schwalbacher Thesen), *Freiburger Rundbrief*, II (1949–50), no. 8/9, 9.

116. BGS Munich, MA 1946/C35.

117. Cf. Hilda Graef, *Leben unter dem Kreuz: Eine Studie über Edith Stein* (Frankfurt a.M., 1954), 130.

118. *Acta Apostolica Sedis*, XX (1928), 104, quoted in Luigi Sturzo, *Nationalism and Internationalism* (New York, 1946), 46. On the dissolution of the society "Amici Israel" see Franz Rödel, "Der Papst und das 'Erkorene Volk Gottes'," *Abwehrblätter*, XXXVIII (1928), 88–89.

119. Note of the Papal Secretariat of State to the German government, September 9, 1933, *Documents on German Foreign Policy*, C, I, doc. 425, 794.

120. *Civiltà Cattolica*, no. 2024, quoted in Daniel Carpi, "The Catholic Church and Italian Jewry under the Fascists (to the Death of Pius XI)," *Yad Vashem Studies*, IV (1960), 51.

121. *Ibid.*, 51–52.

122. Cf. Congar, *op. cit.*, 69.

123. The statement was first reported by *La Croix*, no. 17060, September 17, 1938. It is accepted as accurate by Sturzo, *op. cit.*, 47.

124. No. 288 of December 13, 1938, reported by Bergen, December 13, 1938, PA Bonn, Pol. III, 22.

125. Richard A. Webster, *The Cross and the Fasces: Christian Democracy and Fascism in Italy* (Stanford, Cal., 1960), 126.

126. Tardini, *op. cit.*, 59.

127. Quoted in Poliakov, *op. cit.*, 300.

128. Abetz to the Foreign Ministry, August 28, 1942, PA Bonn, Staatssekretär, Vatikan, Bd. 4.

129. Tittmann to the Secretary of State, July 30, 1942, *U. S. Diplomatic Papers 1942*, III, 772.

130. Taylor to Maglione, September 26, 1942, *ibid.*, 776.

131. Tittmann's summary of Holy See statement of October 10, 1942, *ibid.*, 777.

132. Tittmann to the Department of State, October 6, 1942, *ibid.*; Tittmann dispatch of September 8, 1942, Department of State Papers, 740.00116 European War 1939/573, 1/2.

133. Tittmann to the Department of State, December 22, 1942, Department of State Papers, 740.0016 European War 1939/689.

134. Corsten, *Kölner Aktenstücke*, doc. 220, 280. The message was mimeographed and distributed in Germany by the diocesan chanceries. I have seen a copy in DA Eichstätt.

135. Pius XII to the Cardinals, June 2, 1943, excerpts in *AB Munich*, August 12, 1943.

136. Memo of Woermann, PA Bonn, Staatssekretär, Vatikan, Bd. 4.

137. Weizsäcker to Woermann etc., December 5, 1941, quoted in Hilberg, *op. cit.*, 441.

138. *The Ciano Diaries: 1939–1943*, ed. by Hugh Gibson (New York, 1946), 530.

139. Poliakov, *op. cit.*, 159–60; Hilberg, *op. cit.*, 469–70.

140. Hilberg, *op. cit.*, 427

141. Gumbert (of the German Embassay at the Quirinal) to the Foreign Ministry, October 16, 1943, PA Bonn, Inland IIg, 192. Bishop Hudal had signed this letter at the urging of several anti-Nazi officials in the German legations at the Quirinal and Holy See who had composed it. I have used the English translation of Hilberg, *op. cit.*, 429.

142. Weizsäcker to the Foreign Ministry, October 17, 1943, PA Bonn, Inland IIg, 192. The translation is that of Poliakov, *op. cit.*, 297, n. 16.

143. Cf. Robert Leiber, S.J., "Pius XII und die Juden in Rom 1943–1944," *Stimmen der Zeit*, CLXVII (1960–61), 429–30.

144. Weizsäcker to the Foreign Ministry, October 28, 1943, PA Bonn, Inland IIg, 192. The English translation is that of Poliakov, *op. cit.*, 297–98, n. 16.

145. Weizsäcker to the Foreign Ministry, December 3, 1943, PA Bonn, Pol. III, 22.

146. Cf. Hilberg, *op. cit.*, 539; Gerald Reitlinger, *The Final Solution* (New York, 1953), 431–32. The successful interven-

tion of the Papal Nuncio in Rumania was attested to by the former Chief Rabbi of Rumania at the Eichmann trial (cf. *New York Times*, May 24, 1961, 12).

147. Statement of Dr. Senatro on March 11, 1963, at a public discussion in Berlin (Raddatz, *op. cit.*, 223).

148. Poliakov, *op. cit.*, 302.

149. Louis de Jong, "Jews and non-Jews in Nazi-Occupied Holland," Max Beloff, ed., *On the Track of Tyranny* (London, 1960), 148–49.

150. Reported by Weizsäcker, September 23, 1943, PA Bonn, Staatssekretär, Vatikan, Bd. 4.

151. Robert Leiber, S.J., "Der Papst und die Verfolgung der Juden," Raddatz, *op. cit.*, 104.

152. Pius XII to the German bishops, August 6, 1940, copy in DA Regensburg.

153. Encyclical letter *Summi Pontificatus*, October 20, 1939, *International Conciliation*, no. 355 (December 1939), 556.

154. Sermon on February 6, 1936, Faulhaber, *Münchener Kardinalspredigten*, 1st series, 17.

155. Sermon on July 13, 1941, Heinrich Portmann, ed., *Bischof Galen spricht* (Freiburg, Br., 1946), 49.

156. Tisserant to Suhard, June 11, 1940, published from the files of the German Reich Chancellery (BA Koblenz, R 43 II/1440a) by Eberhard Jäckel, "Zur Politik des Heiligen Stuhls im Zweiten Weltkrieg: Ein ergänzendes Dokument," *Geschichte in Wissenschaft und Unterricht*, XV (1964), 45. The letter was found and confiscated by the Germans during a search of the official residence of Cardinal Suhard in Paris.

157. Alfred Delp, S.J., *Zwischen Welt und Gott* (Frankfurt a.M., 1957), 97.

158. *Ibid.*, 293 and 233.

159. Report on a talk by Delp at an "Informationskonferenz der bayerischen Ordinariate" in Munich on October 25, 1943, DA Passau.

160. Pribilla, *Stimmen der Zeit*, CXXVIII (1935), 305.

161. Max Frisch, *Andorra* in *Three Plays*, trans. Michael Bulloch (London, 1962), 254.

510

THE DIKI FAMILY, KALYGA LITINSKOHO, UKRAINE... 1941 – The Diki and Nachlis families were friends before the war. In 1941, all the Jews, including the Nachlis family, which consisted of two brothers and their families, were forced to move into the ghetto. Months later, the Nachlis family managed to escape from the ghetto and fled to the Diki home where they were hidden behind a fake wall for almost two years. In November 1943 the Nachlis family left the Diki farm and went to a village occupied by the Romanian Army. Soon after they left, the Germans raided the Diki home. Nikolai Diki escaped, but his father Vasilyi was arrested.

This portrait, created by the Diki family, is a tribute to the two families who survived through those terrible times together. The top row is the Diki family, the bottom row the seven members of the Nachlis family they saved. (JFR Photo Archives)

HELENA RUTKOWSKA, GAJOWKA, POLAND... 1943 – Helena and her family hid a young Jewish woman, her sister, and her niece in their one-room home for a year. Although they were already a family of twelve, the Rutkowskis gave food and shelter to these women. The Rutkowski family obtained Polish passports for the women. Despite great danger and continuous threats from neighbors who accused them of hiding Jews, both families survived. Pictured in the photograph are Helena (left) and her friend Miriam (right). (JFR Photo Archives)

SWEDEN... OCTOBER 1943 – Jewish refugees are ferried out of Denmark aboard Danish fishing boats bound for Sweden. (Frihedsmuseet, courtesy of USHMM Photo Archives)

VIRA VERTEPNA, ROMANIVKA, UKRAINE... 1942 – When the Germans occupied Tarnopol, Poland (now Ukraine) in 1941, Bronia Felberbaum and her parents Sophie and Jacob were taken to the ghetto in Velyki Birky. Jacob knew many Christian families in Velyki Birky and through one of them contacted Helen Balyk. Helen promised to hide the family on her parents' farm, if they were able to get there.

One day, the Gestapo officer for whom Sophie worked as a maid told her the ghetto would be liquidated that night. He allowed the entire family to spend the evening at his home; in the early hours of the morning, they fled to the woods. The Germans burned the ghetto to the ground that day, killing everyone inside. Those who tried to escape were shot.

The Felberbaums hid for days in different barns and in the woods. Finally, they reached the farm of Helen's parents, Franciska and Josef Balyk. The Balyk family hid and cared for the Felberbaums. Josef built a hiding place next to the stable. Franciska, her daughter Lucia and granddaughter Vira brought food to the Felberbaum family each day. It was not easy to obtain, but they never let the Felberbaums go hungry.

After liberation, Bronia's family returned to Tarnopol, which became part of Ukraine. The borders were open then, but Jacob refused to leave the Balyks. They had become family. Following Jacob's death in 1958, Bronia and her mother left the Ukraine as part of the repatriation agreement with Poland. They emigrated to the United States in 1960.

As Bronia wrote to Yad Vashem, "I am forever grateful to these kind, noble people, who risked everything they had to take in three Jewish strangers, when no one else would."

Photo of Vira Vertepna and her husband Panas Stochansky (JFR Photo Archives)

SAUL FRIEDLÄNDER **Consenting Elites, Threatened Elites**

I

ABOUT THIRTY SA MEN from Heilbronn arrived in Niederstetten, a small town in southwest Germany, on Saturday, March 25, 1933. Breaking into the few Jewish homes in the area, they took the men to the town hall and savagely beat them while local policemen kept watch at the building entrance. The scene was repeated that morning in neighboring Creglingen, where the eighteen male Jews found in the synagogue were also herded into the town hall. There the beatings led to the deaths of sixty-seven-year-old Hermann Stern and, a few days later, fifty-three-year-old Arnold Rosenfeld.

At the Sunday service the next day, Hermann Umfried, pastor of Niederstetten's Lutheran church, spoke up. His sermon was carefully phrased: It began with standard expressions of faith in the new regime and some negative remarks about Jews. But Umfried then turned to what had happened the previous day: "Only authorities are allowed to punish, and all authorities lie under divine authority. Punishment can be meted out only against those who are evil and only when a just sentence has been handed down. What happened yesterday in this town was unjust. I call on all of you to help see to it that the German people's shield of honor may remain unsullied!" When the attacks against Pastor Umfried started, no local, regional, or national church institution dared to come to his support or to express even the mildest opposition to violence against Jews. In January 1934 the local district party leader (*Kreisleiter*) ordered Umfried to resign. Increasingly anguished by the possibility that not only he but also his wife and their four daughters would be shipped off to a concentration camp, the pastor committed suicide.

Eight years and eight months later, at 2:04 P.M. on November 28, 1941, the first transport of Jews left the Niederstetten railroad station. A second batch boarded the train in April 1942, and the third and last in August of that year. Of the forty-

two Jews deported from Niederstetten, only three survived.[1]

The boycott of Jewish businesses was the first major test on a national scale of the attitude of the Christian churches toward the situation of the Jews under the new government. In historian Klaus Scholder's words, "during the decisive days around the first of April, no bishop, no church dignitaries, no synod made any open declaration against the persecution of the Jews in Germany."[2] In a radio address broadcast to the United States on April 4, 1933, the most prominent German Protestant clergyman, Bishop Otto Dibelius, justified the new regime's actions, denying that there was any brutality even in the concentration camps and asserting that the boycott – which he called a reasonable defensive measure – took its course amid "calm and order."[3] His broadcast was no momentary aberration. A few days later Dibelius sent a confidential Easter message to all the pastors of his province: "My dear Brethren! We all not only understand but are fully sympathetic to the recent motivations out of which the *völkisch* movement has emerged. Notwithstanding the evil sound that the term has frequently acquired, I have always considered myself an anti-Semite. One cannot ignore that Jewry has played a leading role in all the destructive manifestations of modern civilization."[4]

The Catholic Church's reaction to the boycott was not fundamentally different. On March 31, at the suggestion of the Berlin cleric Bernhard Lichtenberg, the director of the Deutsche Bank in Berlin and president of the Committee for Inter-Confessional Peace, Oskar Wassermann, asked Adolf Johannes Cardinal Bertram, chairman of the German Conference of Bishops, to intervene against the boycott. Himself reticent about intervening, Bertram set about asking other senior German prelates for their opinions by stressing that the boycott was part of an eco-

FROM **NAZI GERMANY AND THE JEWS: VOLUME I: THE YEARS OF PERSECUTION, 1933–1939**, 41–49, 343–45. COPYRIGHT © 1997 BY SAUL FRIEDLÄNDER. REPRINTED BY PERMISSION OF HARPERCOLLINS PUBLISHERS, INC.

nomic battle that had nothing to do with immediate church interests. From Munich, Michael Cardinal Faulhaber wired Bertram: HOPELESS, WOULD MAKE THINGS WORSE. IN ANY CASE ALREADY DYING DOWN. For Archbishop Conrad Gröber of Freiburg, the problem was merely that converted Jews among the boycotted merchants were also being damaged.[5] Nothing was done.

In a letter addressed at approximately the same time to the Vatican's secretary of state, Eugenio Cardinal Pacelli, the future Pope Pius XII, Faulhaber wrote: "We bishops are being asked why the Catholic Church, as often in its history, does not intervene on behalf of the Jews. This is not possible at this time because the struggle against the Jews would then, at the same time, become a struggle against the Catholics, and because the Jews can help themselves, as the sudden end of the boycott shows. It is especially unjust and painful that by this action the Jews, even those who have been baptized for ten and twenty years and are good Catholics, indeed even those whose parents were already Catholics, are legally still considered Jews, and as doctors or lawyers are to lose their positions."[6]

To the clergyman Alois Wurm, founder and editor of the periodical *Seele* (Soul), who asked why the church did not state openly that people could not be persecuted because of their race, the Munich cardinal answered in less guarded terms: "For the higher ecclesiastical authorities, there are immediate issues of much greater importance; schools, the maintaining of Catholic associations, sterilization are more important for Christianity in our homeland. One must assume that the Jews are capable of helping themselves." There is no reason "to give a pretext to the government to turn the incitement against the Jews into incitement against the Jesuits."[7]

Archbishop Gröber was no more forthcoming when he stated to Robert Leiber, a Jesuit who was to become the confessor of Pius XII: "I immediately intervened on behalf of the converted Jews, but so far have had no response to my action. . . . I am afraid that the campaign against Judah will prove costly to us."[8]

The main issue for the churches was one of dogma, particularly with regard to the status of converted Jews and to the links between Judaism and Christianity. The debate had become particularly acute within Protestantism, when, in 1932, the pro-Nazi German Christian Faith Movement published its "Guidelines." "The relevant theme was a sort of race conscious belief in Christ; race, people and nation as part of a God-given ordering of life."[9] Point 9 of "Guidelines," for example, reads: "In the mission to the Jews we see a serious threat to our people [*Volkstum*]. That mission is the entry way for foreign blood into the body of our *Volk*. . . . We reject missions to the Jews in Germany as long as Jews possess the right of citizenship and hence the danger of racial fraud and bastardization exists. . . . Marriage between Germans and Jews particularly is to be forbidden."[10]

The German Christian Movement had grown in nurturing soil, and it was not by chance that, in the 1932 church elections, it received a third of the vote. The traditional alliance between German Protestantism and German nationalist authoritarianism went too deep to allow a decisive and immediately countervailing force to arise against the zealots intent on purifying Christianity of its Jewish heritage. Even those Protestant theologians who, in the 1920s, had been ready to engage in dialogue with Jews – participating, for example, in meetings organized under the aegis of Martin Buber's periodical, *Der Jude* – now expressed, more virulently than before, the standard accusations of "Pharisaic" and "legalistic" manifestations of the Jewish spirit. As Buber wrote in response to a particularly offensive article by Oskar A. H. Schmitz published in *Der Jude* in 1925 under the title "Desirable and Undesirable Jews": "I have once again . . . noted that there is a boundary beyond which the possibility of encounter ceases and only the reporting of factual information remains. I cannot fight against an opponent who is thoroughly opposed to me, nor can I fight against an opponent who stands on a different plane than I."[11] As the years went by, such encounters became less frequent, and German Protestantism increasingly opened itself to the promise of national renewal and positive Christianity heralded by National Socialism.

The German Christian Movement's ideological campaign seemed strongly bolstered by the election, on September 27, 1933, of Ludwig Müller, a fervent Nazi, as Reich bishop – that is, as some sort of Führer's coordinator for all major issues pertaining to the Protestant churches. But precisely this election and a growing controversy regarding pastors and church members of Jewish origin caused a widening rift within the Evangelical Church.

In an implementation of the Civil Service Law, the synod governing the Prussian Evangelical Church demanded the forced retirement of pastors of Jewish origin or married to Jews. This initiative was quickly followed by the synods of Saxony, Schleswig-Holstein, Braunschweig, Lübeck, Hesse-Nassau, Tübingen, and Württemberg.[12] By the early fall of 1933, general adoption of the so-called Aryan paragraph throughout the Reich appeared to be a foregone conclusion. A contrary trend, however, simultaneously made its appearance, with a group of leading theologians issuing a statement on "The New Testament and the Race Question," which clearly rejected any theological justification for adoption of the paragraph[13] and, on Christmas 1933, Pastors Dietrich Bonhoeffer and Martin Niemöller (a widely admired World War I hero), founded an oppositional organization, the Pastors' Emergency League (*Pfarrernotbund*), whose initial thirteen hundred adherents grew within a few months to six thousand. One of the league's first initiatives was to issue a protest against the Aryan paragraph: "As a matter of duty, I bear witness that with the use of 'Aryan laws' within the Church of Christ an injury is done to our common confession of faith."[14] The Confessing Church was born.

But the steadfastness of the Confessing Church regarding the Jewish issue was limited to support of the rights of non-Aryan Christians. And even on this point Martin Niemöller made it abundantly clear, for example in his "Propositions on the Aryan Question" ("*Sätze zur Arierfrage*"), published in November 1933, that only theological considerations prompted him to take his position. As he was to state at his 1937 trial for criticism of the regime, defending converted Jews "was uncongenial to him."[15] "This perception [that the community of all Christians is a matter to be taken with utter seriousness]," wrote Niemöller in the "Propositions," "requires of us, who as a people have had to carry a heavy burden as a result of the influence of the Jewish people, a high degree of self-denial, so that the desire to be freed from this demand [to maintain one single community with

the converted Jews] is understandable. . . . The issue can only be dealt with . . . if we may expect from the officials [of the Church] who are of Jewish origin . . . that they impose upon themselves the restraint necessary in order to avoid any scandal. It would not be helpful if today a pastor of non-Aryan origin was to fill a position in the government of the church or had a conspicuous function in the mission to the people."[16]

Dietrich Bonhoeffer's attitude changed over the years, but even in him a deep ambivalence about the Jews as such would remain. "The state's measures against the Jewish people are connected . . . in a very special way with the Church," he declared with regard to the April boycott. "In the Church of Christ, we have never lost sight of the idea that the 'Chosen People,' who nailed the Saviour of the world to the cross, must bear the curse of the action through a long history of suffering."[17] Thus it is precisely a theological view of the Jews that seems to have molded some of Bonhoeffer's pronouncements. Even his friend and biographer Eberhard Bethge could not escape the conclusion that in Bonhoeffer's writings "a theological anti-Judaism is present."[18] Theological anti-Judaism" was not uncommon within the Confessing Church, and some of its most respected personalities, such as Walter Künneth, did not hesitate to equate Nazi and Jewish interpretations of the "Jewish election," as based on race, blood, and *Volk*, in opposition to the Christian view of election by God's grace.[19] Such comparisons were to reappear in Christian anti-Nazi polemics in the mid-thirties and later.

The "Aryan paragraph" applied to only twenty-nine pastors out of eighteen thousand; among these, eleven were excluded from the list because they had fought in World War I. The paragraph was never centrally enforced; its application depended on local church authorities and local Gestapo officials.[20] From the churches' viewpoint, the real debate was about principle and dogma, which excluded unconverted Jews. When, in May 1934, the first national meeting of the Confessing Church took place in Barmen, not a word was uttered about the persecutions: This time not even the converted Jews were mentioned.[21]

On the face of it the Catholic Church's attitude toward the new regime should have been firmer than that of the Protestants. The Catholic hierarchy had expressed a measure of hostility to Hitler's movement during the last years of the republic, but this stance was uniquely determined by church interests and by the varying political fortunes of the Catholic Center Party. The position of many German Catholics toward Nazism before 1933 was fundamentally ambiguous: "Many Catholic publicists . . . pointed to the anti-Christian elements in the Nazi program and declared these incompatible with Catholic teaching. But they went on to speak of the healthy core of Nazism which ought to be appreciated – its reassertion of the values of religion and love of fatherland, its standing as a strong bulwark against atheistic Bolshevism."[22] The general attitude of the Catholic Church regarding the Jewish issue in Germany and elsewhere can be defined as a "moderate anti-Semitism" that supported the struggle against "undue Jewish influence" in the economy and in cultural life. As Vicar-General Mayer of Mainz expressed it, "Hitler in *Mein Kampf* had 'appropriately described' the bad influence of the Jews in press, theater and literature. Still, it was un-Christian to hate other races and to subject the Jews and foreigners to disabilities through discriminatory legislation that would merely bring about reprisals from other countries."[23]

Soon after he took power, and intent on signing a Concordat with the Vatican, Hitler tried to blunt possible Catholic criticism of his anti-Jewish policies and to shift the burden of the arguments onto the church itself. On April 26 he received Bishop Wilhelm Berning of Osnabrück as delegate from the Conference of Bishops, which was meeting at the time. The Jewish issue did not figure on Berning's agenda, but Hitler made sure to raise it on his own. According to a protocol drafted by the bishop's assistant, Hitler spoke warmly and quietly, now and then emotionally, without a word against the church and with recognition of the bishops: "I have been attacked because of my handling of the Jewish question. The Catholic Church considered the Jews pestilent for fifteen hundred years, put them in ghettos, etc., because it recognized the Jews for what they were. In the epoch of liberalism the danger was no longer recognized. I am moving back toward the time in which a fifteen-hundred-year-long tradition was implemented. I do not set race over religion, but

I recognize the representatives of this race as pestilent for the state and for the church and perhaps I am thereby doing Christianity a great service by pushing them out of schools and public functions."[24] The protocol does not record any response by Bishop Berning.

On the occasion of the ratification of the Concordat, in September 1933, Cardinal Secretary of State Pacelli sent a note to the German chargé d'affaires defining the church's position of principle: "The Holy See takes this occasion to add a word on behalf of those German Catholics who themselves have gone over from Judaism to the Christian religion or who are descended in the first generation, or more remotely, from Jews who adopted the Catholic faith, and who for reasons known to the Reich government are likewise suffering from social and economic difficulties."[25] In principle this was to be the consistent position of the Catholic and the Protestant churches, although in practice both submitted to the Nazi measures against converted Jews when they were racially defined as Jews.

The dogmatic confrontation the Catholic hierarchy took up was mainly related to the religious link between Judaism and Christianity. This position found an early expression in five sermons preached by Cardinal Faulhaber during Advent of 1933. Faulhaber rose above the division between Catholics and Protestants when he declared: "We extend our hand to our separated brethren, to defend together with them the holy books of the Old Testament." In Scholder's words: "Faulhaber's sermons were not directed against the practical, political anti-Semitism of the time, but against its principle, the racial anti-Semitism that was attempting to enter the Church."[26] Undoubtedly this was the intention of the sermons and the main thrust of Faulhaber's argumentation, but the careful distinctions established by the cardinal could mislead his audience about his and the church's attitude toward the Jews living among them.

"So that I may be perfectly clear and preclude any possible misunderstanding," Faulhaber declared, "let me begin by making three distinctions. We must first distinguish between the people of Israel before and after the death of Christ. Before the death of Christ, during the period between the calling of

Abraham and the fullness of time, the people of Israel were the vehicle of Divine Redemption. . . . It is only with this Israel and the early biblical period that I shall deal in my Advent sermons." The cardinal then described God's dismissal of Israel after Israel had not recognized Christ, adding words that may have sounded hostile to the Jews who did not recognize Christ's revelation: "The daughters of Zion received their bill of divorce and from that time forth, Ahasuerus wanders, forever restless, over the face of the earth." Faulhaber's second theme now followed:

"We must distinguish between the Scriptures of the Old Testament on the one hand and the Talmudic writings of post-Christian Judaism on the other. . . . The Talmudic writings are the work of man; they were not prompted by the spirit of God. It is only the sacred writings of pre-Christian Judaism, not the Talmud, that the Church of the New Testament has accepted as her inheritance.

"Thirdly, we must distinguish in the Old Testament Bible itself between what had only transitory value and what had permanent value. . . . For the purpose of our subject, we are concerned only with those religious, ethical and social values of the Old Testament which remain as values also for Christianity."[27]

Cardinal Faulhaber himself later stressed that, in his Advent sermons, he had wished only to defend the Old Testament and not to comment on contemporary aspects of the Jewish issue.[28] In fact, in the sermons he was using some of the most common clichés of traditional religious anti-Semitism. Ironically enough, a report of the security service of the SS interpreted the sermons as an intervention in favor of the Jews, quoting both foreign newspaper comments and the Jewish Central Association's newspaper, in which Rabbi Leo Baerwald of Munich had written: "We take modest pride that it is through us that revelation was given to the world."[29]

Discussion of the Concordat with the Vatican was item 17 on the agenda of the July 14 cabinet meeting. According to the minutes, the Reich chancellor dismissed any debate about the details of the agreement. "He expressed the opinion that one should only consider it as a great achievement. The Concordat gave Germany an opportunity and created an area of trust which was particularly significant in

the developing struggle against international Jewry."[30]

This remark can hardly be interpreted as merely a political ploy aimed at convincing the other members of the government of the necessity of accepting the Concordat without debate, as the fight against world Jewry was certainly not a priority on the conservative ministers' agenda. Thus a chance remark opens an unusual vista on Hitler's thoughts, again pointing toward the trail of his obsession: the "developing struggle" against a global danger – world Jewry. Hitler, moreover, did indeed consider the alliance with the Vatican as being of special significance in this battle. Is it not possible that the Nazi leader believed that the traditional anti-Jewish stance of the Christian churches would also allow for a tacit alliance against the common enemy, or at least offer Nazism the advantage of an "area of trust" in the "developing struggle"? Did Hitler not in fact say as much to Bishop Berning? For a brief instant there appears to be an ominous linkage between the standard procedures of politics and the compulsions of myth.

Notes

1. Eberhard Röhm and Jörg Thierfelder, *Juden-Christen-Deutsche*, vol. 1, *1933–1935* (Stuttgart, 1990), 120ff.
2. Klaus Scholder, *Die Kirchen und das Dritte Reich*, vol. 1, *Vorgeschichte und Zeit der Illusionen 1918–1934* (Frankfurt am Main, 1977), 338ff.
3. Ibid.
4. Wolfgang Gerlach, *Als die Zeugen schwiegen: Bekennende Kirche und die Juden* (Berlin, 1987), 42.
5. *Akten deutscher Bischöfe über die Lage der Kirche 1933–45*, vol. 1: *1933–1934*, ed. Bernhard Stasiewski (Mainz, 1968), 42n, 43n.
6. Ernst Christian Helmreich, *The German Churches Under Hitler: Background, Struggle and Epilogue* (Detroit, 1979), 276–77. For the German original see *Akten deutscher Bischöfe*, vol. 2, 54n.
7. Ernst Klee, *"Die SA Jesu Christi": Die Kirche im Banne Hitlers* (Frankfurt am Main, 1989), 30.
8. For the quotations see Helmreich, *The German Churches*, 276–77.
9. Klaus Scholder, "Judaism and Christianity in the Ideology and Politics of National Socialism," in Otto Dov Kulka and Paul Mendes-Flohr, eds., *Judaism and Christianity Under the Impact of National Socialism 1919–1945* (Jerusalem, 1987), 191ff.
10. Quoted in Doris L. Bergen, *Twisted Cross: The German Christian Movement in the Third Reich* (Chapel Hill, N.C., 1996), 23. On November 13, 1933, the leader of the Berlin district of German Christians, one Dr. Krause, declared at a

meeting of the movement at the Sportpalast: "What belongs to it [the new Christianity] is the liberation from all that is un-German in the ritual and faith, the liberation from the Old Testament with its Jewish retribution morals and its stories of cattle dealers and pimps. . . . In the German Volk Church there is no place for people of foreign blood, either at the pulpit or below the pulpit. All expressions of a foreign spirit which have penetrated it . . . must be expelled from the German Volk Church." Ulrich Thürauf, ed., *Schulthess Europäischer Geschichtskalender* 74 (1933), 244.

11. Quoted in Paul R. Mendes-Flohr, "Ambivalent Dialogue: Jewish-Christian Theological Encounter in the Weimar Republic," in Kulka and Mendes-Flohr, *Judaism and Christianity*, 121.

12. Uriel Tal, "Law and Theology: on the Status of German Jewry at the outset of the Third Reich," in *Political Theology and the Third Reich* (Tel Aviv, 1989), 16. The English version of this text appeared as a brochure published by Tel Aviv University, 1982.

13. For the intense theological debates raised by the introduction of the "Aryan paragraph," see ibid.

14. Scholder, *Die Kirchen und das Dritte Reich*, 612ff.

15. Robert Michael, "Theological Myth, German Anti-Semitism and the Holocaust: The Case of Martin Niemöller," *Holocaust and Genocide Studies* 2 (1987): 112. (The title "Propositions on the Aryan Question" should be considered a euphemism, in the same way as "Aryan paragraph" in fact meant "Jewish paragraph.")

16. Gerlach, *Als die Zeugen schwiegen*, 87.

17. Michael, "Theological Myth," 113.

18. Ibid.

19. Quoted in Uriel Tal, "On Structures of Political Theology and Myth in Germany prior to the Holocaust," in Yehuda Bauer and Nathan Rotenstreich, eds., *The Holocaust as Historical Experience* (New York, 1981), 55.

20. Richard Gutteridge, *Open Thy Mouth for the Dumb! The German Evangelical Church and the Jews 1879–1950* (Oxford, 1976), 122.

21. Günther van Norden, "Die Barmen Theologische Erklärung und die 'Judenfrage'," in Ursula Büttner et al., eds., *Das Unrechtsregime*, vol. 1, *Ideologie – Herrschaftssystem – Wirkung in Europa* (Hamburg, 1986), 315ff.

22. Guenter Lewy, *The Catholic Church and Nazi Germany* (New York, 1964), 17.

23. Ibid., 271.

24. *Akten deutscher Bischöfe*, vol. 1, 100–102.

25. Klee to Foreign Ministry, September 12, 1933, *Documents on German Foreign Policy, Series C*, 793–94.

26. Scholder, *Die Kirchen und das Dritte Reich*, 660.

27. His Eminence Cardinal Faulhaber, *Judaism, Christianity and Germany: Advent Sermons Preached in St. Michael's, Munich, in 1933* (London, 1934), 5–6. Faulhaber's argument reflects a long-standing Christian polemic tradition regarding the Talmud. See in particular Amos Funkenstein, "Changes in Christian Anti-Jewish Polemics in the Twelfth Century," in *Perceptions of Jewish History* (Berkeley, Calif., 1993), 172–201 and particularly 189–96.

28. Helmreich, *The German Churches Under Hitler*, 262.

29. Heinz Boberach, ed., *Berichte des SD und der Gestapo über Kirchen und Kirchenvolk in Deutschland 1934–1944* (Mainz, 1971), 7. Although as a rule church dignitaries avoided comments regarding the contemporary aspects of the Jewish issue, some local Catholic newpapers drew the attention of their readers to the brutal treatment of the Jews. For example, on May 23, 1933, the Catholic *Bamberger Volksblatt* explicitly mentioned the death in Dachau of the young local court clerk, Willy Aron, who was Jewish. For the significance of the case, see Norbert Frei, *Nationalsozialistische Eroberung der Provinzpresse: Gleichschaltung, Selbstanpassung und Resistenz in Bayern* (Stuttgart, 1980), 273–75.

30. Quoted in Walter Hofer, ed., *Der Nationalsozialismus: Dokumente 1933–1945* (Frankfurt am Main, 1957), 130.

**LOUISA (LEFT) AND BEATRIX (RIGHT) STEENSTRA, GRONINGEN, THE NETHERLANDS...
1940** – Louisa and her husband Albert hid four Jewish men on the second floor of their home. In January 1945, three months before liberation, the Germans raided the home, killing the four Jews and Albert. Louisa and her daughter Beatrix managed to escape and were protected by the resistance until the end of the war. (JFR Photo Archives)

ARISTIDES DE SOUSA MENDES, BORDEAUX, FRANCE... 1940 –
The Portuguese Consul General in Bordeaux, France, Aristides de Sousa Mendes, illegally issued entry visas to thousands of Jews who sought asylum in Portugal. He was recalled by the Portuguese government for his actions, dismissed from the foreign service, and denied his retirement and severance benefits. He died in poverty in 1954, leaving a wife and 13 children. (JFR Photo Archives)

RHEIMS, FRANCE... 1940–1945 – Jewish man (right) dressed as a woman to evade capture by the Nazis. At left is the female friend who protected him. (YIVO Institute for Jewish Research, courtesy of USHMM Photo Archives)

ONA URBONAS, KOVNO, LITHUANIA... 1941 – Maria and Andrius Urbonas and their two children, Ona and Juozas, hid Yerachmiel Siniuk, a disabled escapee from the Kovno ghetto, for several months in their home. Yerachmiel then smuggled seven more Jews out of the ghetto and hid them in the Urbonas barn. The Urbonases provided shelter, food, and clothing to these eight men and women for the duration of the war. Pictured in the photograph are Ona and her husband. (JFR Photo Archives)

MARIA FARKAS, BUDAPEST, HUNGARY... 1944 – The Farkas family helped many Jews during the war. They provided food and shelter to the Jacobs family; a father, mother and daughter Susanne who lived secretly in their apartment in Budapest until liberation. The family also hid nine-year-old Marika Fuchs in their weekend home in Isaszeg. (JFR Photo Archives)

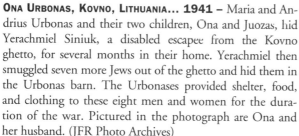

MARIA PAUEROVA, DRAZOVCE PRI NITRE, CZECHOSLOVAKIA... **1944** – Martin Zapletal was separated from his family and sent to the Sered concentration camp in Slovakia. Upon his escape, he asked Maria Pauerova for help. Maria and her mother Anna sheltered Martin in their one-room apartment. At the end of the war, Maria helped Martin arrange for his wife and child to return to Czechoslovakia. (JFR Photo Archives)

Philip P. Hallie Help — 1940–1944

BURNED SHOES AND THE QUAKERS

1

The winter following the conquest of France – the winter of 1940–1941 – was one of the most ferocious in the history of modern France. In Le Chambon the snow was piled high against the gray walls and buildings, and *la burle** seemed never to stop its whirling. In the granite presbytery Magda Trocmé was putting small pieces of wood and dried genêts into the kitchen stove to keep the heat as high as possible without wasting fuel. The big black stove stood against the wall facing the Rue de la Grande Fontaine, the crooked street along which her husband would later walk on his way to an internment camp.

Concentrating – as she always did – upon the details of what she was doing, the calculation of just the right number of bits of fuel to put in the stove, she was slightly startled to hear a knock at the outer door of the presbytery[†]. Someone had come through the "poetic gate" that opened onto the Rue de la Grande Fontaine, and was standing in the shallow doorway of the presbytery itself, standing in the wind and snow blowing off the Lignon River. She closed the stove, went through the dark little hallway, and opened the outer door.

There before her, only the front of her body protected from the cold, stood a woman shawled in pure snow. Under her shawl her clothes, though once thick, had been whipped thin by the wind and the snow of that terrible winter. But her face had been whipped even thinner by events; she was visibly frightened, and was half-ready to step back, trembling with fright and cold. The first thing that Magda Trocmé recalls seeing was the hunger in that face and in those dark eyes.

Here was the first refugee from the Nazis to come to the presbytery door[‡]. This is the way Magda Trocmé started her description of the incident in a conversation with me thirty-six years later:

"A German woman knocked at my door. It was in the evening, and she said she was a German Jew, coming from northern France, that she was in danger, and that she had heard that in Le Chambon somebody could help her. Could she come into my house? I said, 'Naturally, come in, and come in.' Lots of snow. She had a little pair of shoes, nothing. . . ."

There was a big wooden table in the middle of the kitchen, and, after asking her to take off her shawl and coat, Magda had the woman sit at the side of the table facing the stove, where she gave her something to eat. They started to talk. The pastor's wife spoke German, and she soon learned a story that was to become familiar. The woman had run away from Hitler's Germany because of the increasingly vicious racial laws, and had found herself in the Occupied Zone, where the lives of foreign Jews were in constant danger; and so she had kept running until she crossed the demarcation line and entered the Free Zone, where there were fewer German troops and less danger.

Magda Trocmé is not given to long, ruminative chats. When she talks, she does so swiftly, with a breathless, heavy voice whose pace and tone seem to be saying, "Come, now, let's get this talking over with and *do* what we're supposed to be doing." She has powerful arms that are frequently being used to move things and to push herself away from tables and up from chairs so that she can cope with human physical needs instead of the "nonsense" she often finds in conversations between idle people. Accordingly, her first reaction, after seeing that the woman was fed and comfortable, was to get up and go for help. Idle compassion was as alien to Magda Trocmé as idle talk.

EXCERPTS FROM CHAPTERS 5 AND 7 FROM **LEST INNOCENT BLOOD BE SHED: THE STORY OF THE VILLAGE OF LE CHAMBON AND HOW GOODNESS HAPPENED THERE** BY PHILIP P. HALLIE, 119–31, 166–70, 175–77, 195–200. COPYRIGHT © 1979 BY PHILIP P. HALLIE. REPRINTED BY PERMISSION OF HARPERCOLLINS PUBLISHERS, INC.

*The winter wind on the plateau on which Le Chambon is located, *Ed.*
[†]The presbytery was not a center of placement of refugees. Those who happened to come there were helped. *Ed.*
[‡]No one knows when the first refugee arrived in Le Chambon. Here Magda Trocmé speaks of the first refugee she helped. *Ed.*

Standing, she calmed the woman with a few words, urged her to warm herself at length near the stove, and to put her soaking-wet shoes, for a little while, in the oven attached to the stove. Then she put on her own shawl, pushed open the kitchen door, went through the little hallway, out into the bitterly cold courtyard, through the "poetic gate," and into the streets of Le Chambon. She walked west toward the square and the town hall.

The snow and wind were incidental to her; mainly she was thinking that the woman had to have *papers*, especially identification papers. There were frequent surprise checks for papers and frequent roundups, even this early in the Occupation. Without papers, the woman was in danger of deportation back to Germany and Hitler.

She walked up the few steps of the village hall and into the mayor's office. She remembers that she was confident that the papers would be forthcoming; after all, there were Frenchmen in this village, not Nazi racists. Almost as a matter of course, she told the mayor about her German refugee, expecting him to sit down with her and help her make plans for the welfare of the refugee.

And so the mayor's response surprised her. "What?" he said. "Do you dare to endanger this whole village for the sake of one foreigner? Will you save one woman and destroy us all? How dare you suggest such a thing to me? I am responsible for the welfare of this French village. Get her out of Le Chambon tomorrow morning, no later."

She did not argue; she simply arose and went back into the snow. As she went down the hill toward the presbytery, she analyzed the situation. She had gone to the authorities and revealed to them the presence of an illegal, unregistered refugee in her home. The fact that the refugee was in the home of the Protestant minister of a Protestant village not only exposed the refugee to action by those authorities; it seemed to invite such action, since the presbytery was the single most conspicuous home in the village, and the duties of the authorities were clear. The mayor, Frenchman though he was, was still under the command, ultimately, of Hitler. The mayor could justify his action not only by pointing to the photograph of the handsome, eighty-four-year-old Marshal Pétain, who had ordered the "surrender on demand" of for-

eign refugees, but also he could and did justify it by pointing to his own role as leader and protector of the village of Le Chambon-sur-Lignon. For him, moral obligations held only in the realm of "one of us": native Frenchmen; they did not apply to "one of them": foreigners, German Jews. For him, it was "our people, our lives"; it was the trust laid upon us by our leaders that determined what was good and what was evil.

All of this had something to do with the mental fog in southern France, the incapacity to resist a French leader above whom the French saw only vaguely, in a cloud of doubts, the Nazi Führer. But the mayor had emphasized the other source of paralysis in France: fear of reprisals, fear that a whole village might become an object of suspicion, and, because of the Nazi conquerors in great numbers above the demarcation line, even a target for destruction.

But Magda Trocmé did not dwell upon these matters during that walk down from the town hall. Her main thought was that the refugee was now in great danger because she was known to the mayor. For her to stay in Le Chambon against the orders of the official leader of the village, *and with his full knowledge of her presence and location,* was absurd. If Magda allowed her to stay in the presbytery, she would, in effect, be dooming her to capture.

And so Magda Trocmé had to get her out of Le Chambon. Like others in the Unoccupied Zone, she had a "line" to other people who opposed Pétain's measures. Even in those early days of the Occupation, many resisters knew of others who could be trusted in an emergency; and Magda Trocmé knew of a certain Catholic family who were enemies of the National Revolution and who were courageous and compassionate persons. She would send the refugee to them.

Probably because of the separation of Catholics from Protestants in France (I have met some French Catholic families who have never knowingly met a French Protestant), she did not know that there was growing near Lyons, not more than a hundred miles from Le Chambon, a powerful Catholic network whose main task was to save Jewish refugees: the *Témoignage Chrétien* (Christian Witness), the organization of the courageous Father Chaillet. In any case, at this early stage in the Resistance, people had only the names of scattered individuals on their "lines."

When she came back into the kitchen, she saw

the woman still sitting before the stove, shoeless. Swiftly Magda ran to the oven beside the stove and opened the oven door. The shoes were still in the oven, burned black. The two women gasped.

For the refugee to leave by the next morning, she had to have shoes. But Le Chambon was a poor village, especially in the winter months when there were no tourists. And Le Chambon was poorer than ever now, what with this extremely severe weather and the difficulty of finding supplies after the supply lines to the cities had been smashed in the sudden, overwhelming defeat of France. It was especially difficult to find shoes, since the adults in the village could not buy shoes legally and could not afford to buy them on the black market; only children could buy them, one pair a year, on their birthdays and with a coupon. This was one of the reasons why the awkward wooden shoes of old were being used more and more of late; there was wood enough in the forests in and around Le Chambon, and there were still some woodworkers. But shoes for long walks were almost an impossibility to find for adults of modest means. André Trocmé – who had agreed completely with every move she had made on behalf of the refugee – once got a pair of leather shoes for his big feet only because somebody about his size had died in the not-too-distant city of Saint-Étienne, and a friend had arranged for him to receive them.

Magda Trocmé is not one to work hard before a crowd of idle onlookers; she is like *la burle* – busy, but also making everything around her busy as well. That night there was a network of shoe-seekers in the village, and she was pushing through the snow in the middle of the network. Even in that harsh winter she brought back the shoes before the night was far gone.

The next morning, the woman left. Later Magda was to reflect, "She was a Jew. What did she think of a Christian community, walking in the snow without knowing where she was going?"

It is true that Magda Trocmé had sent her to another family, but who was to help the woman get there? And exactly what would she find there? For the rest of the Occupation, Magda Trocmé and all the other people of Le Chambon would know that from the point of view of the refugee, turning somebody away from one's door is not simply a refusal to help; it is an *act of harmdoing*. Whatever one's excuses for not taking a refugee in, from the point of view of that refugee, your closed door is an instrument of harmdoing, and your closing it does harm.

A while later – while her husband was away – another Jewish refugee appeared at the presbytery door. Magda Trocmé had a fresh idea. Vichy is Vichy. Understood. But what about Jews helping their fellow Jews? At this time, the French wife of an influential French rabbi was staying in Le Chambon to escape the rigors of the Occupied Zone where she and her family were permanent residents. Magda went to visit her and asked her to help with this German Jew. The answer she received struck the iron of egotistic human reality even more deeply into her soul than had the answer of the mayor: "A German Jew? But it is because of the foreign Jews that our French Jews are persecuted. They are responsible for our worries and difficulties." Again that hard line between "one of us" and "others"; again the idea that moral obligation has to do only with "one of us," not "one of them."

These two events were important in the history of the presbytery and of the refugees in Le Chambon. They were important not only because these two refugees were the first of hundreds who would come to the presbytery door, and not only because these two events showed how narrow the domain of love was to some people, but also because they helped the Trocmés realize the concrete meaning of the "city of refuge" passage in Deuteronomy 19:10: "lest innocent blood be shed in your land . . . and so the guilt of bloodshed be upon you."

And there was another lesson, a very practical one, that the Trocmés and Le Chambon learned from these events: they must *conceal* from the authorities and from unsympathetic citizens any help they were giving refugees. To reveal that help would be to betray the refugees, to put them in harm's way. Either conceal them or harm them – those were the alternatives.

But in Le Chambon in the beginning of the 1940s, concealment meant lying – lying both by omission and by commission. It meant not conveying to the authorities any of the legally required information about new foreigners in Le Chambon, and it meant making false identity and ration cards for the refugees so that they could survive in Vichy France. It meant, for example, changing the name Kohn to the good old French name Colin so that the refugee could have the life-giving identity and ration cards to protect against roundups, when identity cards were usually checked, and to protect against hunger, since the basic foods were rationed. Such cards made it unnecessary to report a new foreign refugee to the mayor – only a Frenchman with, perhaps, an accent had come to town.

But for Magda and the other Chambonnais, the making of counterfeit cards was not simply a matter of practicality. It raised profound moral problems. To this day, Magda remembers her reaction to hearing about the making of the first counterfeit card. During that first winter of the Occupation, [Édouard] Theis* came into the presbytery and said to her, "I have just made a false card for Monsieur Lévy. It is the only way to save his life." She remembers the horror she felt at that moment: duplicity, for any purpose, was simply wrong. She and the other leaders knew that ration cards were as important as identity cards – the Chambonnais were so poor that they could not share their food with refugees and hope to survive themselves. Nonetheless, none of those leaders became reconciled to making counterfeit cards, though they made many of them in the course of the Occupation. Even now, Magda finds her integrity diminished when she thinks of those cards. She is still sad over what she calls "our lost candor."

How, then, could they lie and violate one of the commandments given to Moses? Theis and Trocmé saw that deep in Christianity is the belief that man is never ethically pure – in this world he finds himself sinning no matter what his intentions are. The best he can do is acknowledge and lessen his sins. Such a view is part of Judaism, too. In 1972, Magda Trocmé went to Israel to participate in the ceremony awarding her husband – posthumously – the Medal of Righteousness. Part of the ceremony involved planting a tree in memory of André Trocmé (there is a tree in Israel for every person who has received the Medal of Righteousness). During the ceremony, one of the speakers said, "The righteous are not exempt from evil." Magda remembers the sentence word for word. The righteous must often pay a price for their righteousness: their own ethical purity.

She is aware of these depths, but they do not comfort her. She still feels anguish for the children of Le Chambon who had to unlearn lying after the war, and who could, perhaps, never again be able to understand the importance of simply telling the truth. But usually when she says this, she suddenly straightens up her body, with typical abruptness and vigor, and adds, "Ah! Never mind! Jews were running all over the place after a while, and we had to help them quickly. We had no time to engage in deep debates. We had to help them – or let them die, perhaps – and in order to help them, unfortunately we had to lie."

But her daughter, Nelly, points out that the children, as far as Nelly could see, never had the problem of unlearning lying. She remembers the children, among them herself, seeing the situation with the clear eyes of youth. She remembers their seeing that people were being helped in a desperate situation by these lies. And the children were convinced that what was happening in the homes of Le Chambon was right, simply right.

What the children saw was what the rest of the Chambonnais saw: the *necessity* to help that shivering Jew standing there in your door, and the necessity not to betray him or her to harmdoers. In this way of life the children were raised, and – at least according to Nelly – they did not feel their parents to be guilty of any wrongdoing.

There were many women in Le Chambon whose homes were the scenes of events like those in Magda Trocmé's kitchen. There was, for instance, round-faced, sparkling-eyed Madame Eyraud, whose husband was *très chic* in the violent Maquis, despite her own nonviolence. When I asked her why she found it necessary to let those refugees into her house, dragging after them all those dangers and problems, including the necessity of lying to the authorities, she could never fully understand what I was getting at. Her big, round eyes stopped sparkling in that happy face, and she said, "Look. Look. Who else would have taken care of them if we didn't? They needed our help, and they needed it *then*." For her, and for me under the joyous spell she casts over anybody she smiles upon, the spade was turned by hitting against a deep rock: there are no deeper issues than the issue of *people needing help then*.

The fact is that the Chambonnais were as candid, as truthful with the authorities as they could have

*Assistant pastor and headmaster of the new private secondary school "École Nouvelle Cévenole", *Ed.*

been without betraying the refugees. Trocmé was perfectly willing, as were the other Chambonnais, to tell the authorities that there were refugees in Le Chambon. As a matter of fact, they felt that it was their duty to do so, and the letter to [Georges] Lamirand* says this outright: "We feel obliged to tell you that there are among us a certain number of Jews." The spirit of Le Chambon in those years was a strange combination of candor and concealment, of a yearning for truth and of a commitment to secrecy. They were as open as love permits in a terrible time.

2

Magda's words to her first refugee, "Naturally, come in, and come in," were part of an ethical action. Ethics, especially the ethics of crisis, of life and death, deals with the lives and deaths of particular human beings. In the context of a life-and-death ethic, refusals like the refusal to ring the bell of the temple are ethical only insofar as Amélie† and André Trocmé were ethical, only insofar as particular human beings were involved in their deeds. Such refusals made the difference between life and death for a given individual only indirectly – they helped Le Chambon to resist Vichy and the Nazis, and so helped develop the spirit that would save particular human lives. But it is one thing to resist a government and its National Revolution; it is another to face a shivering, terrified Jew on your doorstep. Life-and-death ethics has to do with hurting and helping individual human beings. It has to do with betraying, torturing, humiliating, killing them, and with helping them.

When that first German Jew appeared in the doorway of the presbytery, ethics became incarnate in Le Chambon for Magda Trocmé. Only then were two individual human beings involved: one in danger, and one being asked to help. This was what Magda Trocmé meant when she said to me, "Helping Jews was more important than resisting Vichy and the Nazis."

But how did Le Chambon become a place where so much help was being given that the police had to come with their automobiles and buses in order to try to stop it? How did Le Chambon become a village of refuge? This much is certain: in the course of the first two years of the Occupation, Le Chambon became the safest place for Jews in Europe. How did a life-and-death ethic become incarnate across the whole commune of Le Chambon?

3

Even in normal winters, the mistral rushes down the Rhone River valley from the icy Alps at speeds between thirty and fifty miles an hour, especially from December through March. But the winter of 1940–1941 was an especially bitter one, and the "masterly wind" (the literal meaning of the old Provençal word *maestral*) struck the great port city of Marseilles with damp, cold, unremitting force. There was much rain, and there was even snow in that southern city. The mistral cut through the thin, wet clothing of the many refugees wandering through the streets, and it penetrated the windows and doors of many houses. Influenza was common, not only among the refugees who were going from door to door looking for help in obtaining the life-giving papers that would permit them to leave France; it was common even among those who had lived through many Marseilles mistrals.

Later in the winter of Magda Trocmé's encounter with the refugee, André Trocmé walked out of the Gare Saint-Charles, the main railroad station of Marseilles, stiffly, as was his manner with that painful back. He lumbered down the many steps just outside the main entrance to the station, and stepped onto the Boulevard d'Athènes. Not far away was the beige-and-black four-story building at 29 Boulevard d'Athènes. The two middle stories of this building were the offices of the American Friends Service Committee. Trocmé went in.

He had just obtained permission to make this visit from the presbyterial council of his church. At a recent meeting he had told his parishioners that he felt the need to help the many refugees who were pouring into southern France from Central and Eastern Europe. Many of them had been put into the terrible internment camps that had sprung up across southern France. The camps were practically destitute of clothing, food, and medical supplies, and the filth was maddening. All his life he had kept close to Jesus

*Vichy government's General Secretary to Youth, *Ed*.
†Concierge of the church and a Darbyste, which meant that she was one of the most radical Protestants in France, *Ed*.

Christ by helping those who were suffering. He had urged his parish to let him continue this work in the part of France that needed him most, and they had consented. Moreover, they were ready to give him supplies and money for the refugees.

He had come to the Quakers because he was convinced that he could best show his love for Jesus and for his fellowmen by working with the Friends, who were already bringing desperately needed supplies and consolation to people in internment camps like the ones at Gurs and Argelès. With this in mind, he walked into one of the stark little offices and introduced himself to Burns Chalmers, who was responsible for many of the Quakers' activities on behalf of the inmates of the camps in southern France.

Trocmé knew that the Quakers had long ago grown proficient at carving out for themselves an ethical space within which they could move with comparative freedom. He knew that what they did in that space was turn all their psychological and financial resources toward diminishing suffering and death. I do not know how much André Trocmé knew about the Quakers' activities in the nineteenth century on behalf of the slaves and freedmen of the United States, but he knew a great deal about what they had done in Germany after World War I. He knew that from 1918 on they had fed about a million and a half German children with what the Germans still called *Quaker Speise* (Quaker food). The Germans remembered even as late as 1940 that the Quakers were no nation's enemies and no nation's friends. The Germans – and André Trocmé – knew that their only enemies were suffering and killing, and each human being was their friend.

Trocmé knew also that the Friends had carved out another ethical space in France. They had been trusted enough by the Vichy government to be allowed to care for the many kinds of sufferers in southern France: victims of war, starving children in schools, and prisoners in the camps.

The two had never met, but Chalmers had heard of Trocmé as a nonviolent leader whose prestige and influence in southern France were very great. It is important to see that for Chalmers, as for other Quakers, the power to lead people was of central importance. Though the Quakers did not take sides in

any national or political struggles, they had to be sure that the nations in which they worked would not hinder their efforts. Freedom to act within their ethical space was essential to their efficacy; without it, they could not be of service to those in need; without it, they would have in their hands only the worthless coin of simple compassion. And so they had to be protected by powerful leaders native to the country in which they worked. Trocmé, after only a half-dozen years in the south of France, was widely recognized not only in his own department of Haute-Loire, but in other departments, including neighboring Ardèche, as an important religious leader. . . .

THE INSPIRED AMATEURS

1

There is a French word that applies to the Trocmés and to the spirit they created in the presbytery: the word is *accueillant*. English words like "welcoming" and "receptive" convey some of its meaning. It was because the Trocmés were by temperament and by conviction *accueillants* that the idea of a place of refuge could become a reality in Le Chambon. If their abundant energies had been confined to preserving the peace of mind and the comfort of themselves and of the parish that was in their charge, the idea Trocmé brought back from the Nimes conversations with Chalmers would have remained only an idea. But in the openness of the presbytery, the idea found a fructifying atmosphere and flourished.

When in the terrible winter of 1941 Trocmé returned from the last of the Nimes conversations with Chalmers, he found a wife as ready as he was to make Le Chambon a city of refuge. But without a presbyterial council that was itself *accueillant*, and without a parish that supported that council, the story of Le Chambon would not be the story of a city of refuge. As soon as he returned from his last conversation with Chalmers, Trocmé convened the council and presented to them the idea of opening their village and their own houses to strangers who would bring danger with them. Without going into details, he tells us in his autobiographical notes that he "won an easy victory" and the council committed the parish to the task in one meeting.

One of the reasons for the swiftness of their action was the personality of Trocmé, and another was the solidity and power of the ideas he and Chalmers had discussed in Nimes. But there is a deeper reason for their speedy decision. The history of the Protestants in France, and specifically the history of the Protestants in The Mountain, in the two adjoining villages of Le Mazet and Le Chambon, had prepared them for a certain kind of resistance to governmental authorities. Farther south in France, the revocation of the tolerant Edict of Nantes in 1685 had produced, in time, the bloody battles between the government and the Camisards, the Huguenots deep in the south of France. But during these battles, which took place during the first decade of the eighteenth century, Le Chambon with its sister village Le Mazet engaged in a different kind of resistance. They fought no bloody battles with dragoons, but instead used the devices peculiar to mountain people: silence, cunning, and secrecy. They resisted the authority of the government as firmly as did the Camisards, but they resisted by quietly refusing to abjure their faith, and by quietly conducting their services in meadows within the pine forests, and with a portable *chaire* (pulpit). This was the kind of resistance peculiar to The Mountain: the resistance of exile.

Such a tradition fit beautifully with the ideas Trocmé and Chalmers had formed in Nimes. The Quaker and the Huguenot agreed that, to use Chalmer's words uttered long after the conversation, "there was no limit to what might be possible in terms of the reclamation of persons." They did not want to kill any follower of Pétain or Hitler for any reason, because that human being *could* be "reclaimed." And they believed that the victims of Vichy and the Nazis were also reclaimable, could also be "saved." Trocmé himself, being a Huguenot, was more ready for clandestine activities than were the Quakers, who chose always to "speak truth to power," but now the differences between the two groups were unimportant; both were bent on resisting the violation of their own consciences and of other human lives not by killing but by saving.

After he won his "easy victory" with the presbyterial council, the first major step Trocmé took was to choose a head for the first house of refuge in Le Chambon. According to the agreement with Chalmers, this "monitor" would be in charge of feeding, clothing, protecting, and educating young children whose parents had been deported. He chose his second cousin Daniel Trocmé, a young teacher of languages, history, and geography, who was now in southwest France.

Daniel Trocmé would die for that conscience before the Occupation was over, but this was, of course, unknown to the pastor, and so he made Daniel the head of the first house, the Crickets, which was a dilapidated old boardinghouse for children situated about two miles away from the center of the village. When in the course of the Occupation the Quakers left southern France, they kept sending money faithfully to Daniel and the Crickets by way of Geneva. Sometimes the couriers who brought this money were arrested, and some were shot by the Germans, but the money kept coming.

2

The development of Le Chambon as a place of refuge proceeded more and more swiftly as more and more Chambonnais and more and more organizations and governments outside France became aware of the need for such a refuge and of the capacity of the village to satisfy that need. A mid-Occupation letter gives a summary of the situation in Le Chambon shortly after the Germans moved down to occupy southern France: "3,300 parishioners, of whom 2,000 are peasants, 700 are villagers, and from 500 to 600 people from outside Le Chambon: 160 refugees from central Europe, adults, students, children in six [seven, including the Farm School] different houses; 300 students at Cévenol School; plus 30 teachers and 15 heads of [school] residences . . ." But there is another way of understanding the anatomy of the rescue activities of Le Chambon. Imagine a marksman's target with its concentric rings around a bull's-eye. Put the groups of Le Chambon that inspired and led the rescue of the refugees closest to the bull's-eye, and put the groups peripherally involved with those efforts farther from the center of the target. Outside the target, put the enemies of the refugees, Vichy and the Nazis.

Those who were most directly involved in the rescue effort were those who started and guided it, and so the presbytery should be at the bull's-eye of the target. Not only did André Trocmé bring the idea of a city of refuge to Le Chambon; he also set an example by keeping refugees in the presbytery throughout the Occupation. Moreover, many of the refugees who came to Le Chambon passed through the doors of the presbytery. After the arrival of the one o'clock train (or some other means of transportation), many would come to the presbytery, and would receive some food until a temporary house in the village itself could be found for them; then, if they were not staying at the presbytery, they would go to this temporary shelter. While they were there, false cards of identification and false ration cards would be made by Darcissac and others. Then, after a few days, equipped with their cards, they would usually move to a more permanent shelter, or, later in the Occupation when Le Chambon was overcrowded with refugees, they would be made part of a team to be conducted across the mountains to neutral Switzerland. . . .

3

It is tempting to make the Trocmés all-important in the story of Le Chambon, but it is wrong to do so. Though the ideas and some of the energy behind a place of refuge came from them, very little would have been accomplished in Le Chambon without what we may broadly call "the houses" of the village. The presbytery and the temple could not have moved an inert mass of coolly self-centered people into doing what was done in Le Chambon. It was the houses, the homes in Le Chambon that made a village of refuge work. A family of refugees might come to town in winter, and the morning after their arrival they might find a wreath of holly leaning against their front door, with no hint of the identity of the giver. A little boy would come to Miss Maber's door, screaming in a high-pitched voice, so that the whole neighborhood could hear, that the English teacher had better hide Henri because the police were after him.

Miss Maber would calm the boy, glance around to be sure that no strangers had heard him, and then go straight to the house of a mousy little Chambon naise who was known to have an empty room. She would ask the tiny woman if she would hide Henri, and the woman would answer immediately, "Yes. There is a room downstairs, and the door opens into the woods. If the police come, he could have time to get away."

Though in my target diagram of the rescue activities of Le Chambon I put "the houses" outside of the bull's-eye and outside of the innermost ring of the target, this does not mean that the houses are less important to the rescue activities than the presbytery and the temple; it means only that the original idea and impulse for creating a village of refuge came from those places, and that those places guided the activities. *For the refugees themselves*, the houses were *the* scene and the source of those activities. What I have called the "kitchen struggle" of Le Chambon did occur in kitchens, in homes all over the village.

But there were different kinds of houses, and therefore somewhat different kinds of rescue activities occurring there. There were the funded houses, the places, like Daniel Trocmé's the Crickets, financed by great organizations in the outside world. The Quakers, American Congregationalists, even national governments like those of Sweden and Switzerland, helped finance those houses. By the middle of the Occupation there were seven of them.

One of these houses was the Farm School, funded by Switzerland. It was located far out in the countryside. Though its original purpose was to teach efficient farming methods to the students of the Cévenol School and to the farmers in the area of Le Chambon, early in its history it became a principal place of refuge, one of the safest homes in the area, not only because it had a clear view of all the roads from the nearby villages, but because the barking dogs of the surrounding farmers gave refugees plenty of time to disappear into the pine forests nearby.

Another funded house outside the village was the Flowery Hill. It was perhaps the most effective "underground railroad station" (to use the language of nineteenth-century American history) in the area. Just as American slaves in the nineteenth century stayed for a while in a place that protected them from capture and helped get them closer and closer to the North Star and freedom, so the Flowery Hill sheltered people who would soon be going to Switzerland. Besides certain Catholic groups, the World Council of Churches, and Sweden, the Flowery Hill was financed by one of the most remarkable rescue machines in the history of Europe, the redoubtable Cimade.

The Cimade was originated and led by women alone. In 1939, when they began, they helped care for displaced Alsatians who had been evacuated by the French from their homes on the border between France and Germany. But in 1940, after the defeat of France, they turned their attention to the most endangered human beings in Europe: Jews fleeing from Central and Eastern Europe. At first they tried to relieve some of the suffering in the terrible, disease-ridden internment camps of southern France, and they made careful records of the horrors there in order to mobilize world opinion against them. But these activities did not satisfy their need to help, and so they developed a web of *équipes* (teams) in the summer of 1942, when the intentions of the Nazis toward the Jews were plain, and with these teams they took through the mountains of France to neutral Switzerland the refugees who were most dangerous to their hosts and most endangered themselves, the Jews.

In the last year of the Occupation, one of the members of such a team was Pastor Édouard Theis, who was then fleeing from the Gestapo. He joined them in leading groups of refugees through dangerous mountain terrain and through even more dangerous German troops to the Swiss border.

The Flowery Hill of Le Chambon was one of the houses in their complex network. With the thick woods to its north and a wide command of all approaching roads to its south, east, and west, its main function was to house the old, the sick, and women with small children only until the Cimade could make arrangements with Swiss authorities for their reception in Switzerland and could put together a team to take them to the border.

Aside from the funded houses, there were the *pensions*, the boardinghouses toward the center of the village. There was, for instance, the boardinghouse of Madame Eyraud, she of the round, pink face and the ready wit and even readier maternal affection. Her *pension* stood where two busy roads, the Street of the Soul's Song and the Street of Lambert, crossed. She kept only boys, usually fourteen of them, and they were usually not all Jews. Sometimes an adolescent would appear at her door with no baggage, because in Lyons or Saint-Étienne, where he came from, he had returned home from the factory and found the police surrounding his house waiting to take him to Germany for forced labor. . . .

7

Once, in conversation with me, Magda Trocmé found herself comparing what happened in Le Chambon during the war with what the Cimade was then doing all over southern France. The Cimade, she said, was an organization with one clear goal and a definite organizational structure that reached down from international organizations into the teams for spiriting refugees across the natural and human obstacles between Le Chambon and neutral Switzerland. Madeleine Barot and other women had created and led it. But who had created Le Chambon? Magda Trocmé's husband had led it in his innovative way, but he had not created this little Huguenot community. It used its own deep resources to help the refugees. He had inspired it, but he had not made it what it was, the way Barot and the others had made the Cimade.

And saving refugees was *the* function of the Cimade; it was the only reason for its existence. But what was *the* function of Le Chambon, even during the war? Living, maybe; but to say this is to say something too vague to allow one to compare the two groups meaningfully. And Magda Trocmé went on, in her own breathless way: "You know? Saving refugees was a *hobby* for the people of Le Chambon! Oh, yes!" she called out in her slightly raucous, Italian-accented voice. "It was a hobby in Le Chambon."

Of course she did not mean a hobby in the sense of a pastime or a source of fun. No one knew better than she what sacrifices and what dangers the Chambonnais had taken upon themselves when they accepted refugees into their houses while they were all "under the German cup." She meant a hobby in the sense of something done by an untrained amateur, a lover of the thing done, not a professional, skillful practitioner of an art or science. She meant that the people of Le Chambon saved refugees on the side, so to speak, as an avocation, not as part of their vocation, as a way of saving lives, not as a way of making a living.

When a refugee comes to your door and you say, as Magda Trocmé did, "Naturally, come in, and come in," you are not inventing an institution, nor are you participating in one that has already been invented. And when the refugees start arriving in larger and larger numbers (like a drop of oil, spreading, with no stages in their increase) and the one o'clock afternoon train that brings them is more and more full, you are still only a person, not a rescuer, only a person accepting people from the outside into the very center of your home. Your vocation is perhaps that of a carpenter, a painter, a housewife, or a farmer; it is certainly not that of a rescuer.

Trocmé's decision to make a place of refuge in the funded houses was only a part of what happened in Le Chambon. Before that decision, refugees were sheltered in the village, and after it, many different kinds of ways were devised for helping the refugees: the *pensions*, the farmhouses, private homes in the village proper, and the residences of the Cévenol School. Le Chambon became a village of refuge not by fiat, not by virtue of the decision Trocmé or any other person made, but by virtue of the fact that, after Magda Trocmé's first encounters with refugees, no Chambonnais ever turned away a refugee, and no Chambonnais ever denounced or betrayed a refugee. In addition to the burdens of their harsh life during the Occupation, they found themselves taking on the burdens of the constantly increasing danger and the constantly increasing hunger. There was no one decision that made Le Chambon a place of refuge, the safest in Europe, but an attitude expressed in French as being *toujours prêt, toujours prêt à rendre service* (always ready, always ready to help).

For this reason, the target diagram we have been using to summarize the rescue activities in Le Chambon is somewhat misleading. Inspiration and guidance did emanate from the presbytery and the temple, but the village became a place of refuge more by accretion

than by planning. The rings of our diagram were far from being as closely and neatly related to each other in Le Chambon as they are in the diagram itself. In the end, each private home, each *pension*, even each funded house simply coped on its own.

We cannot understand the rescue activities of Le Chambon if we do not realize that the village was far from being an organization with neatly meshing parts. We can understand them only if we see how discreet those rescue activities were. They were *discrete* in the sense of being separate from each other, distinct, and they were *discreet* in the sense that they were silent, even cautious with each other. Miraculously, there were no chatterboxes or gossips or boasters or frightened complainers – at least none that I have been able to discover – among those who housed the refugees. Magda Trocmé, with her immense powers of speedy speech and extensive knowledge of what was happening in the houses of Le Chambon (the most extensive, perhaps, of anybody in the village except her husband), was, during the Occupation, utterly silent about those activities. A Chambonnais once told me, "You cannot make a place of refuge with a bunch of talkative people." The Chambonnais practiced their avocation in secrecy.

For example, Madame Marion, who had a boardinghouse for girls, might see a light in the house next door in a room that had been vacant for months. Ah, she would think, I shall have a little joke with Madame Russier [or some other common Chambonnais name]; I shall ask her who is there. The next time she encountered her, she would ask Madame Russier whether a relative had come to visit her. Madame Russier would look at her half-humorously and say, "Well, Madame Marion, I thought I should clean up the room, you know, air it out a bit in the cool evening air. . . ." And both would know, though neither would say so, that another refugee or another family of refugees had come to Le Chambon.

Now the French, especially in the villages, are a very private people, as the windows tightly shuttered at night suggest, and as Laurence Wylie has shown so memorably in his *Village in the Vaucluse*. But discretion during the Occupation was not simply a result of custom; it was a felt necessity. As few people as possible had to know the whereabouts of a refugee or a refugee family because the greater the number of people who knew, the greater the probability that an idle word or gesture would trigger an arrest and deportation, and the greater the probability that severe questioning by the authorities would cause somebody to give damning information about another.

If you possess a dangerous bit of information, there is usually a limit to the amount of resistance, the amount of secrecy you can maintain, especially under the influence of a very powerful adversary. For most human beings, there is a point beyond which silence is impossible when they are subjected to torture or even trickery. But if people are ignorant of certain dangerous facts, facts dangerous when they are revealed to an adversary possessing great power, then as far as those facts are concerned, there are no limits to the resistance those people can exert. There is nothing for them to reveal, and so there is no danger of their revealing anything. Those who do not know a secret are the best guardians of that secret. An awareness of these considerations led various leaders of the French Resistance who knew many dangerous facts to commit suicide before they reached that point when they could no longer resist divulging the knowledge they had. If they had been ignorant of those facts, their silence concerning them, their silent resistance, would have been endless. And so the Chambonnais wished to know or divulge to each other as few facts as possible concerning the refugees.

Though they were discreet, as silent and as separate as possible regarding the refugees, the amateurs of Le Chambon had a sense of fellowship with each other in the face of the suffering they were helping to alleviate. Many of them attended the temple sermons of Theis and Trocmé and participated in the weekly discussions with the *responsables* of the parish. Because of such sessions, and because of a feeling that they were, in the words of Madame Eyraud, "doing something of consequence" *(quelque chose pleine de conséquences)*, there was a sense of fellowship not entirely dissimilar to the feeling of fellowship at the camp at Saint-Paul d'Eyjeaux when Theis, Darcissac, and Trocmé were imprisoned there. It was this feeling of fellowship in doing, again to quote Madame Eyraud, "something good" *(quelque chose de bien)*, that made the Chambonnais come so swiftly to the presbytery on the night that the leaders were arrested,

and that made them sing to Trocmé as he walked to the police cars.

On the surface in ordinary times during the Occupation, when there was no visible crisis, the lives of the people of Le Chambon showed few signs of such solidarity. Magda Trocmé once said: "If it had been an organization, it could not have worked. How can you have a big organization deciding on people who were streaming through houses? When the refugees were there, on your doorstep, in danger, there were decisions that had to be made then and there. Red tape would have kept us from saving many of them. Everybody was free to decide swiftly on his own." Again the important element of time – only independent individuals could act swiftly and surely in those circumstances. Le Chambon in the first four years of the 1940s was a world in which delay in letting somebody come into your house amounted to a decision *not* to help in that all-important *now*.

What unified and divided the Chambonnais then was what we might grasp by way of the metaphor of "atmosphere." People shared a dangerous and helpful atmosphere the way people share physical air; it was all around them, and yet each drew it into his or her own life, the way we share and divide the air we breathe.

This intermingling of separateness and communion is nowhere more clearly exhibited than in the important activity of making identity and ration cards for foreign refugees. The cards could be made only from fresh blanks; old cards with former impressions of a governmental seal could not be converted. Somehow these blanks turned up in the houses of the people of Le Chambon when new refugees arrived. Everybody I have asked – and I have asked heads of *pensions*, heads of private homes, and even leaders like Roger Darcissac and Magda Trocmé – gives me a different account of where they came from. One suggested the Cimade; another was fairly certain that a secretary to a mayor in some town hall – either the town hall of Le Chambon itself or the town hall of Le Mazet, or perhaps the city hall of Le Puy, the principal city of the region – supplied them; still another suggested that a Jew living in the nearby town of Tence secured the cards and somehow had them sent to the right Chambonnais for distribution. And still another suggested that they came from nearby

Yssingeaux. Magda Trocmé, among others, did not claim to know who supplied them, and she, like the others, never asked. For her, the blanks turned up in her kitchen near the entrance from the little hallway that opens to both the kitchen and the dining room, or they appeared deeper in the house, sometimes in her husband's office. Since the doors to the presbytery were not locked, it would have been easy for any one of many people to place the cards in the house without being noticed.

She, like the others who never asked, felt that knowing where they came from was both unnecessary – they almost invariably arrived in time – and dangerous for all concerned. Despite this ignorance, the cards continued to come throughout the Occupation. Somebody knew and somebody cared about each new refugee and about each new group of refugees that came to Le Chambon, though for most of the Chambonnais there was only silence on the subject. This efficacious silence is a symbol and an example of the intermingling of privacy and communion that pervaded Le Chambon during the rescue activities.

VLADIMIR CHERNOVOL

VODIANA, UKRAINE... 1942 – Gregory Lantsman was a Jewish pilot in the Soviet Army when his plane was shot down over Ukraine. Surviving the crash, Gregory wandered the countryside seeking shelter. The Germans had already killed his family and wiped out his regiment.

By chance, Gregory met Vladimir Chernovol, a Ukrainian teacher, who was out for a walk. Gregory told Vladimir that he was Jewish. Vladimir understood that without assistance, Gregory would surely be caught and killed. He offered to take him in.

With great difficulty Vladimir was able to obtain Ukrainian identity papers for Gregory. But soon the Germans were forcibly taking young Ukrainian men for hard labor. Gregory was one of those selected. He managed to escape from the train and returned to the safety of Vladimir's home. Though there were many close calls, Vladimir was able to hide Gregory until liberation in May 1944.

(JFR Photo Archives)

CHAPTER 9 **The Rescuers**

Olga Kukovic holding her medal and certificate from Yad Vashem, Israel's Holocaust Martyrs' and Heroes' Remembrance Authority, recognizing her as a Righteous Among the Nations. In October 1941, the *Ustasi*, Hitler's Croatian collaborators, began to round up the Jews of Sarajevo, Yugoslavia. Olga Kukovic saved the lives of Isidor Baruh and his sister Hannah by disguising them as Muslims and helping them flee to Mostar, then under Italian occupation. (JFR Photo Archives)

DEBÓRAH DWORK **Introduction**

A YOUNG JEWISH MAN NAMED ISIDOR BARUH was walking down a street in Sarajevo, Yugoslavia in October 1941 when someone, an anonymous kind soul, told him to go into hiding immediately. The Ustasi, Croatian fascist collaborators with the Germans, were rounding up all the remaining Jews in the city. Fortunately, Isidor was near the home of his sister's friend, Olga Kukovic. Isidor ran to Olga's home. She took him in and, without losing a minute, phoned Isidor's sister, Hanna, and told her to join them immediately. All of them understood both the urgency of the situation and the danger involved: Hanna's husband already had been killed.

Isidor's wife and child, as well as another sister, Berta, had escaped some time earlier to the city of Mostar, which was under Italian occupation. (See Chapter 8.) Safe for the moment in Olga's home, Hanna and Isidor decided to attempt the same route: they too would try to make their way to Mostar. Olga went to work to disguise her friends as Moslems. It was a creative but also quite plausible solution: Sarajevo was then, as now, an ethnically diverse city with a population almost equally divided among Serbs, Croats, and Moslems. Olga darkened Isidor's red hair, put a fez on his head, gave him Moslem garb to wear, and took his photograph. Bribing a man who worked for the police, Olga obtained a forged passport for the brother and sister, identifying them as Moslem. Dressed in Moslem robes, Hanna with a veil over her face and Isidor with a fez, they traveled to Mostar. All five members of the family – Isidor and his wife and child, Hanna, and Berta – survived the war and returned to Sarajevo. In 1949 they moved to the new state of Israel, where Olga visited them fifteen years later. Today (2000), Olga is in her eighties, and lives in Belgrade, Serbia.

There are no written or pictorial records of this event, no letters or diary, no photograph of Hanna and Isidor dressed as Moslems making their way to safety. No one would know of this event if the Baruh family had not given testimony to Yad Vashem, the Israeli Holocaust Martyrs' and Heroes' Remembrance Authority. It is an incident in the history of private life, of the everyday relations between ordinary people, not of public policy, of the orders, rules, and regulations by the authorities.

The aim of this chapter is to understand the profound significance of just such an incident: a young Moslem woman harboring and helping her Jewish friends in the midst of the Holocaust. This was the very heart, the stuff and substance of resistance. Olga Kukovic is considered a "lamed-vov," one of the righteous souls of Jewish tradition for whose

> No one would know of this event. It is an incident in the history of private life, of the everyday relations between ordinary people, not of public policy, of the orders, rules, and regulations by the authorities.

sake God permits the world to continue to exist. According to this time-honored myth, their number was limited to thirty-six ("lamed-vov," in Hebrew), and when one died another came into the world at the same instant. During the Holocaust another legend was born: Because human torment was so great, thousands of lamed-vovs sprang up spontaneously throughout Europe to combat the evil they witnessed. These outwardly unremarkable, seemingly normal people became rescuers. They held fast to an earlier ethic and morality.

Olga Kukovic was such a rescuer. She did the improbable and unimaginable and it was, she maintained, the most ordinary thing in the world to have done. But this was a time when what had been unthinkable – the mass murder of one's Jewish neighbors – now occurred every day, and so what had been ordinary – neighborliness between gentiles and Jews – was now extraordinary. To invite one's Jewish friends into one's home, to help them when they were in need, in short, to do "the most ordinary" things, was now a tremendous undertaking. It required courage and determination.

Passport photograph of Raoul Wallenberg (1912–?). Wallenberg was a Swedish businessman and diplomat who saved the lives of tens of thousands of Jews in Budapest in the second half of 1944. With the support of the World Jewish Congress and the American War Refugee Board, the Swedish Foreign Ministry sent Wallenberg to Budapest in July 1944 to help protect the 200,000 Jews who remained in the capital after the deportations of the provincial Jewish communities in the spring. During the critical three-month period between the seizure of power by the Arrow Cross on October 15 and the liberation of the capital, Wallenberg saved Jews by issuing thousands of protective documents, by securing the release of Jews from deportation trains, death march convoys, and labor service brigades, and by establishing the International Ghetto, a network of thirty-one protected houses in the capital. Wallenberg was detained by Soviet agents on January 17, 1945 and was never heard from again. June 1944. (Hagstromer & Qviberg Fondkommission AB, courtesy of USHMM Photo Archives)

It is in our understanding of Olga Kukovic, Irena Sendlerowa, Per Anger, Raoul Wallenberg, the people of the Plateau Vivarais-Lignon (See Chapter 8), and thousands of others, that we realize the significance of personal resistance to the Germans and their allies, and that we recognize the importance of the private realm in history. The history of private relations is of singular importance to our understanding of the Nazi era. In the Nazi state, there were no walls, no boundaries, no limits to the public realm. The German bureaucracy and terror apparatus penetrated the private realm in an unprecedented manner. We need only think of the way in which the Nuremburg Laws codified the personal as well as professional relations between Jews and gentiles, or the use of children as informants against their own parents, or the indoctrination of young women to encourage them to bear children for the Fatherland, to understand that the personal was under attack, was besieged, by this regime.

In this chapter we focus on the women and men, gentile and Jewish, who stood firm against and actively defied the evil surrounding them. These rescuers resisted the assault on their personal morality and their own way of thinking. And they went further: to help, aid, and save Jews.

Who were these brave souls? They were in every corner of Europe and beyond. An excerpt from Yehuda Bauer's book, *Jewish Reactions to the Holocaust*, presents a Japanese consul in Kovno, Lithuania, whose name was Sempo Sugihara and a Portuguese consul in Bordeaux, France, by the name of Aristedes de Sousa Mendes. There were Jews amongst them, as Nechama Tec's book, *Defiance* and Debórah Dwork's *Children With A Star* (see the excerpt in Chapter 8), establish. And if Nechama Tec has described and analyzed the largest armed rescue of Jews by Jews in *Defiance*, she has investigated Christian rescue of Jews in Nazi-occupied Poland in her book *When Light Pierced the Darkness*. Rescuers, in short, were of all ages, social classes, education levels, economic spheres, religions, and nationalities.

Why they acted to save lives when so many others, indeed the vast majority of the rest of the world (and Europeans in particular) did not, is not totally clear. But the process by which the rescuers came to help Jews, and the social, psychological, and physical barriers they had to overcome are rather well delineated by these scholars. (See the excerpt from Professor Tec's book, *When Light Pierced the Darkness*.) Rescuers, like perpetrators, were not born to a particular role or function. They became rescuers step by step. In his book, *Perpetrators, Victims, Bystanders*, Raul Hilberg has noted that rescuers were the "exact opposite" of perpetrators, and he is correct. One worked to save Jews, the other to murder them. But prior to the war, the people who became rescuers were not yet saints or even necessarily saintly, and the people who became killers were not yet villains or even necessarily villainous.

This is the power and the heart of the example of the rescuers. It is precisely because those who helped Jews during the war were ordinary people, people like our students and like us, that we can learn from them. If they had been paragons of virtue we could not have followed their development and imagined ourselves taking the steps they did. But they were not and, despite their protestations, they are forceful models for us.

The women and men who saved Jews did what they believed to be correct at the time. As the excerpt from Miep Gies's memoir, *Anne Frank Remembered*, and the interview with Magda Trocmé in Carol Rittner and Sondra Myers's collection, *Courage to Care*, clearly illustrate, now, more than half a century later, rescuers still do not feel that their behavior was extraordinary, or that they should be specially honored for their actions. Miep Gies was one of the four gentile people centrally involved in helping Anne Frank and her family when they went into hiding in Amsterdam. Magda Trocmé was very involved in rescue activities in the village of Le Chambon (discussed in Chapter 8). In fact, of course, the moral stance – and the practical help – of people such as

> Why those who acted to save lives when so many others, indeed the vast majority of the rest of the world (and Europeans in particular) did not, is not totally clear.

Their legacy to us is in the
example they set.

Miep Gies, Magda Trocmé, Sempo Sugihara, and Olga Kukovic was exceptional. Their wonderful deeds and their remarkable feats should be admired, and their moral integrity and rectitude are to be esteemed. It would be a mistake to admire and esteem the rescuer from afar, for their legacy to us is in the example they set.

YEHUDA BAUER **Rescue Attempts Out of Lithuania**

RESCUE ATTEMPTS OUT OF LITHUANIA

AT THE BEGINNING OF THE WAR, at the end of 1939 and the beginning of 1940, about 14,000 Jewish refugees from Poland, including more than 2,000 yeshivah students and their teachers and over 2,000 members of youth movements, especially of the left-wing Zionist movements, reached neutral Lithuania. The members of Betar, the Revisionist youth movement, had been directed to go to Vilno (Vilnius) before the outbreak of the war, and were already there. The left-wing Zionist pioneer movements reached Lithuania, complete with their leaderships. Yitzhak Zuckermann, Mordechai Anielewicz and Yosef Kaplan – people who later became famous in the ghetto uprisings – had all reached Vilno, which was then neutral, crossing the border under the most harsh of conditions.

Those leaders of Zionist movements in Poland who had escaped earlier to the Soviet-occupied eastern part of Poland felt there was danger in remaining where they were, and they thus made their way to Vilno. These included such men as Moshe Sneh, then leader of the General Zionists in Poland, and later head of the high command of the Haganah in Palestine, and Zerah Warhaftig, later the representative in the Knesset of the National Religious Party. Also there were Abraham Bielopolski, leader of the Right Poalei Zion, and some of the leaders of the anti-Zionist Bund. One could say that a large part of the national leadership of Polish Jewry was now concentrated in Vilno.

The problem facing them was how to get out. A small group managed to leave, with the assistance and the initiative of a man now named Zvi Barak, who was then head of the Palestine Office in Kovno, Lithuania. He organized around himself a group of those people, and they did their utmost for the immigration of Jews into Palestine. Thus, a few hundred of them who were in possession of entry permits left Lithuania for Sweden, some of them by air from

Latvia, through the services of the same airline which had earlier included among its pilots one of the leaders of the Nazis, Hermann Goering. In 1940, these Jews were flown through Sweden to Holland and France, and from there they made their tortuous way to Palestine.

But in June 1940 the Soviets occupied Lithuania, and the gates of emigration were locked. Most of these Jews had Polish passports, and they had nowhere to go. The Soviet belt was tightening around these refugees, and they faced expulsion to Siberia. How was one to escape? It appears that a certain yeshivah student came to the office of the Dutch consul in Riga, Latvia, and asked him if there was any place to which one could escape. The consul replied that there was one place where one needed no entry visa – it is true, one would not be allowed in, but an entry visa was not required. This place was Curacao in the West Indies. The young man asked for a written document. The consul had no objection, and stamped his passport with a rubber stamp which said that there was no need for an entry visa into Curacao – which was the plain truth. Following this incident, many Jews came and received such stamps or pieces of paper.

Here, then, was a place one could not enter, but which required no entry visa. But how was one to reach Curacao? Through the Soviet Union, of course: but the Russians were not issuing any transit visas. Later on, it transpired that one could obtain a transit visa, provided the destination was Japan. The visa to Japan could also only be used as a transit visa, since the Japanese were obviously not willing to take in Jewish refugees as permanent residents. They searched for a Japanese consul, and, strangely enough, a Japanese consul was found in Kovno. His name was Sempo Sugihara. There was also a German employee in the Japanese consulate, a local German resident, and the consul's task was to spy on behalf of the

Japanese government. The Jews addressed themselves to Sempo Sugihara, explained their situation to him and asked for visas to aid in their rescue. The consul cabled Tokyo, asking whether he was authorized to issue transit visas, since the passports had a stamp in them confirming that no entry visa was required for Curacao. The answer was delayed, presumably since the Japanese Foreign Office in Tokyo had more urgent preoccupations. Such was the situation in early August 1940, and everyone knew that by the end of the month Mr. Sugihara was to close his consulate and leave Kovno, as he was ordered to do by the Soviets.

It was clear to the Japanese consul that issuing these visas meant rescuing these people. He began to issue transit visas without waiting for instructions from his superiors. Meanwhile, on August 20, he received an urgent message from Tokyo, forbidding him to issue visas. But Sempo Sugihara continued to issue them, and it appears that he issued no fewer than 3,000. With these visas, 2,400 Jews reached Japan. After the war, Sempo Sugihara was put on trial by the democratic Japanese government, and was required to pay the penalty for refusing to obey the orders of the wartime Japanese authorities. He was dismissed from the diplomatic service. Today, there is a tree in his name on the Avenue of Righteous Gentiles in Yad Vashem in Jerusalem. It seems that he deserves 2,400 trees, since that is the number of people saved by this single individual, who knew nothing whatsoever about Jews. He saw before him suffering human beings, and he decided to sacrifice his career for their sake.

An additional 1,100 Jews were also saved and arrived in Palestine. These included Dr. Israel Scheib-Eldad, Nathan Mor, future leaders of the Stern Group (LHY), some of the leaders of the youth movements, and some private individuals. Some of them had entry permits into Palestine – that is, promises that immigration visas had been issued. The British consul in Kovno, Thomas Preston, whose attitude to Zionism was hostile, was supposed to issue their permits. Until the very last moment – he was to leave Kovno on September 4, 1940 – he delayed and postponed the issuing of the permits. At the last moment he announced that he was willing to issue the

permits but had no paper, secretary or typewriter. Zvi Barak and his friends brought him the materials, and they began to print the permits which bore the consul's signature. He soon left, but many Jews wanted to be rescued. Permits were forged, but one could hardly do this on a large scale, since detection of the forgery would annul all the permits. Despite this, about 400 additional permits were forged, complete with "British" stamps and signatures. But whereas on the genuine British stamp one had a lion and a unicorn, as on British passports, on the stamps forged in Kovno there appeared two cats! With the help of these "cats," 400 Jews were rescued, and they came by boat from Odessa to Constantinople. In Constantinople, the British authorities detected the forgery. Some of these people had to suffer in a Turkish transit camp, but eventually they reached Palestine.

Altogether – whether by means of Jewish self-help or with the assistance of the Japanese consul and his German assistant – 3,500 Jews were rescued; 2,400 of them reached Japan and 1,100 reached Palestine – this out of 14,000 Jewish refugees in Lithuania, quite apart from 250,000 indigenous Lithuanian Jews, out of millions of Jews in Eastern Europe. In practice, there was no way out; but by means of combined ingenuity, Jewish and non-Jewish, a few managed to escape. The vast majority remained.

The Palestinian contribution to this issue was support from afar. Palestinian Jews were not positioned in Lithuania or in Moscow, and there was nothing they could do on the spot. They dispatched cables and wrote letters, and they knocked on the doors of the Foreign Office in London, asking for help through the British ambassador in Moscow. They demanded of the immigration department of the British Administration in Palestine the issuing of immigration permits – and this was the sum total of the possibilities open to them. Initiative could not come from Palestine, but from the other end.

That was the Lithuanian story. Another story, almost parallel to the story of Sempo Sugihara, occurred in Bordeaux, France. In June 1940 the Germans occupied France, and numerous Jewish refugees assembled in the harbor city of Bordeaux, since there existed in it, both before and after the surrender, the

French government in transit. Bordeaux became tantamount to the capital once Paris had fallen. It was there that the representatives of the American Joint in France, who had previously been stationed in Paris, came, as did about 30,000 Jews.

The United States was very far away, and it did not issue entry visas. No one knew where to escape. Those who could, jumped on the British ships evacuating British troops from France in June 1940, and some Jews were successful. The large majority, however, remained there with nowhere to go.

These Jews felt that they had to leave in a hurry, since the Germans were approaching. The nearest place was Spain, but the Spaniards would only issue transit visas to those who possessed entry visas to Portugal, and the Portuguese would only issue transit visas to those who had an entry visa to a further destination. The Lithuanian story repeated itself in Bordeaux. In Bordeaux there was a Portuguese consul general, Aristide de Susa Mendes. He had very clear instructions from Lisbon: he was to issue no visas at all, least of all to Jews, since Portugal would be unable to rid itself of them. Portugal was locked and sealed.

What happened now is not entirely clear, but we have the testimony of a Belgian rabbi of Polish origin, who was himself a refugee in Bordeaux. He mentions in his testimony that he spent a night in the house of the consul, de Susa Mendes. His family included five children, and they had nowhere to sleep. He came to the Portuguese consulate and asked for a visa. The answer was negative. He then said to the consul: If you cannot give me a visa, let me at least sleep on your floor with my family. De Susa Mendes agreed. During the night, the testimony continued, they talked. We are not absolutely certain that the story is accurate, but it makes sense. It is a fact that de Susa Mendes was a descendant of Marranos*, although he was a believing and practicing Catholic. From his brother, who was the Portuguese ambassador in Warsaw, he had learned about the Jewish problem. By the morning, he had come to the conclusion that if one Catholic could inflict all that injustice on the Jews (and he meant Hitler, who was officially a Catholic), it was permissible for another Catholic to sacrifice himself for the sake of the Jews.

He threw open the gates of the Portuguese con-

sulate general in Bordeaux and began to sign visas. He had ten children, and the older ones sat with him and his wife and stamped Portuguese visas in the passports of Jews who were seeking an escape route from France. This is an incredible story, but it happens to be true. We do not know quite how many thousand visas he stamped, but it is clear that the number was extremely large. Some days later, the consul received urgent telegrams from Portugal, in which he was required to explain his action, which was contrary to all regulations. In another day or two, a representative of the Portuguese Foreign Office who outranked de Susa Mendes arrived in Bordeaux. It appears that the people in Lisbon had come to the conclusion that he had gone out of his mind, and he was ordered to return to Lisbon immediately.

On his way to Portugal, he passed through the small town of Hendaye, near the Pyrenean border, where there was a Portuguese deputy consul. For several hours, Mendes sat in that consulate and put more stamps in passports before crossing the border. When he arrived at the Spanish border, he came across a large crowd of refugees. The Spaniards did not understand what was going on, since all these refugees had Portuguese transit visas, and this looked suspicious to them. De Susa Mendes came to the rescue once again. He presented himself as the Portuguese consul general in Bordeaux who had issued these visas, and demanded that the refugees be allowed to cross.

Thanks to the intervention of de Susa Mendes, whole convoys crossed the border. It is difficult today to reconstruct the exact figures and dates. Mendes returned to Lisbon, was dismissed from the diplomatic service, and worked for a period in the small Jewish community in Lisbon. No one recognized him or looked after him, and he died in abject poverty. His daughter, who later emigrated to the United States, sent a letter to the Israeli government, in which she related the whole story. At first, she was not believed, and was asked to produce witnesses. But a large number of witnesses came forward, and the story was authenticated in all its details. There is now a tree in the Avenue of the Righteous Gentiles bearing the name of Aristide de Susa Mendes. It appears that he, too, deserves a whole forest.

If we take an overall view of this issue, it is very

*Jews who converted to Catholicism, but who secretly continued Jewish practices, *Ed.*

disturbing. The two largest operations for the rescuing of Jews, both in quantity and in impressive quality, were those conducted in Lithuania and in Bordeaux. Among the two, the larger one, as far as the number of people rescued is concerned, was the one carried out by a single individual, Aristide de Susa Mendes. He did it for religious and humanitarian reasons, as a Catholic who wanted to save human beings and was prepared to sacrifice himself in the process. Had there been many like him in the international political leadership circles of the time, among those people who wielded far greater influence than that of the insignificant consul general, it is likely that many more people might have been res-

cued. Jews have been nurtured on a civilization which maintains that he who has saved one soul is like unto him who has saved a whole world. Here there were so many worlds which could have been saved. It cannot, of course, be claimed that all the Jews who perished in the Holocaust could have been rescued, but numerous individuals could have been saved; very few of them were saved, and Aristide de Susa Mendes, singlehanded, saved a few thousand of them.

No aid in these two affairs by the Western governments was to be seen. The initiative was taken *in spite of* the Western and neutral governments involved. It was the initiative of individual persons, and no more than that.

NECHAMA TEC **From Self-Preservation to Rescue**

PREFACE

MY RESEARCH about the Nazi annihilation of European Jews alerted me to a serious omission and an equally serious distortion. The omission is the conspicuous silence about Jews who, while themselves threatened by death, were saving others. The distortion is the common description of European Jews as victims who went passively to their death.

This book is based on evidence that corrects both. It shows that under conditions of human degradation and suffering, Jews were determined to survive – they refused to become passive victims. Propelled by the desire for freedom, risking death, many escaped from the ghettos to the countryside and forests of wartime Western Belorussia. There some of them created a Jewish partisan unit, the Bielski partisan detachment, that gave protection to all Jewish fugitives.

Assuming the dual role of rebels and rescuers, this group grew into a forest community of more than 1,200 that distinguished itself as the most massive rescue operation of Jews by Jews.

The history of this community – composed of fighters, rescuers, children, older men, and women – fits into my past research about personal courage, resistance, refusal to accept evil, and mutual help.

It is also tied to my personal history, that of a hidden child. I belong to a small minority of Polish Jews who survived World War II by staying illegally in the forbidden Christian world. For three years, protected by Christian Poles, I lived under an assumed name, pretending to be Catholic. At the end of the war I resumed my former identity, determined to put this past behind me, and shied away from all wartime memories.

For some unexplained reason, by 1975 these childhood experiences began to demand attention. When these demands turned into a compelling force, I decided to revisit my past by writing an autobiography.

As I was recapturing my wartime life, the same few questions kept recurring. What was it like for other Jews who tried to pass as Christians? What made some Poles defy all the dangers and risk their lives for Jews, who traditionally were regarded as "Christ killers" and who for many still unexplained reasons were blamed for every conceivable ill? Who were these rescuers? Who were the Jews who benefited from this protection?

Later, with my autobiography behind me, eager to find answers to these questions, I embarked on research that examined two groups: the rescuers and the rescued. I had assumed that each group, the Polish rescuers and the Jewish survivors, would react in different ways to their respective circumstances.

This study took me to several archival collections. At one, the Jewish Historical Institute in Warsaw, I came upon the story of Oswald Rufeisen. A Jewish youth of seventeen when World War II began, he survived by pretending to be half German and half Polish. He became an interpreter and a secretary in a German gendarmerie in Western Belorussia, wore a Nazi uniform, and in this capacity, while risking his life, saved hundreds of Christians and Jews.

I was intrigued by Oswald Rufeisen, not only because of his unusual life, but also because I was not sure how to classify him. His case presented me with a dilemma – was he a rescuer or a survivor? In the end, I classified him as a survivor, and concentrated on the help he received while passing as a non-Jew.

After I finished writing about Polish rescuers and Jewish survivors, I made Oswald Rufeisen's story the focus of my next book. Only after I concentrated on writing about him did I become aware that some Jewish survivors I had written about, although in less dramatic ways, had also helped others. Why had I overlooked their acts of altruism? Was my insensitivity to Jews as rescuers based on the assumption that one could not simultaneously be a victim and a rescuer? Did I think that as the main targets of Nazi persecution Jews would focus only on their own survival?

While I was considering these questions, in 1986, representatives of the organization of Partisans, Underground Fighters and Ghetto Rebels of Israel asked me to write a factual account of the Bielski partisan unit. Those representatives had survived World War II by fighting and hiding in the forests of Western Belorussia. They offered to help me find materials, take care of translations, and locate people for interviews, in Israel and the United States.

Prior to this request, and quite independently, I had been interested in the Bielski partisan group and its charismatic leader Tuvia Bielski. Both the unit's opposition to the Germans and its protection of Jews piqued my interest and seemed a logical extension of my previous projects. Intrigued by this special connection between fighting and rescue, I embarked on this study. I wanted to begin my research with an interview with Tuvia Bielski, the group's commander. Although I spoke to Tuvia on the phone, my efforts at meeting him were frustrated.

Each time I called for an appointment, his wife, Lilka, offered a different reason for not setting up a meeting. The first few refusals had to do with trips to Florida, later with Tuvia's failing health. I persisted and eventually was given a date.

But when I arrived at the Bielski home in Brooklyn in May, 1987, I was greeted by a distraught Lilka who told me that Tuvia had had a bad night and was not in a position to see me. Because I was leaving for Israel the next day, I was determined to get at least some kind of a personal impression of the man. Politely, but firmly, I explained that it had taken me two hours to reach their home, and that I would be very disappointed if I could not see him. I continued by promising that I would be brief.

It worked. Soon I was moving into a dining room dominated by a massive table surrounded by equally massive chairs. The hand-embroidered tablecloths reminded me of some faraway European place. The walls were covered with photographs and with what seemed like framed diplomas. These wall hangings contributed to the room's crowded feeling. Tuvia appeared in each picture, alone or in the company of others. What looked like diplomas turned out to be expressions of gratitude for his wartime achievements. The entire place had a somber, old-fashioned flavor.

My contemplation of the surroundings was interrupted by Tuvia's noiseless appearance. He was closely followed by his wife who, without actually touching him, gave the impression of holding him up. Towering over us, erect, yet with an obvious effort, the man I had waited for moved toward me. His face was covered by a tentative, sad smile. He knew why I had come and told me, in a feeble voice, how glad he was that I wanted to write about him.

Trying to sound friendly, not to offend, I explained to Lilka that I had to conduct the interview alone, without observers. Reluctantly, she consented to leave. Before she did, she pointed to one of the framed photos, taken at a recent Waldorf-Astoria dinner, in honor of her husband's eightieth birthday. She explained that this was sponsored by the Bielski partisans. She must have wanted me to say something pleasing. I did. Perhaps accustomed to this ritual, perhaps gratified, Tuvia looked on in silence, as a smile played around his mouth.

When we sat down for the interview, I told him that he could speak Yiddish or one of the other languages he knew. He settled on Yiddish and began to whisper. I had difficulties hearing and kept hoping my tape recorder had a better ear than I. But then, slowly, as Tuvia became absorbed in his past, his voice began to change. Soon the muffled sound was replaced by a vigorous voice. With this transformation came a sense of humor. And then, chuckling, Tuvia described how some of his men would shudder and hide their heads as soon as they fired a shot. Here and there, his mind would wander into some unexpected path, but would return with a minimum of prodding. Before my very eyes this weary giant became an animated and witty storyteller. When after a little over two hours I told him that the meeting was coming to an end, he objected, assuring me that he was not tired at all. I knew, however, that Lilka, who occasionally would peek into the room, was of a different opinion. Remembering my promise to her, I took leave, saying that this was only one of many more future meetings. I told him that I was going to Israel and that I would call soon after my return. With a resigned smile, he said, "By then I may not be around any more."

In Israel, the news reached me that Tuvia Bielski had died. He was buried in Jerusalem in a ceremony reserved for the country's national heroes.

Although I could not interview Tuvia again, the

partisans I met with provided me with glimpses into the many facets that made up this extraordinary man. This book is about them, their courage, and their experiences.

Westport, Conn.   N.T.
January 1993

FROM SELF-PRESERVATION TO RESCUE

PEOPLE WHO ARE EXPOSED to extreme dangers may be paralyzed into inaction. Whether this occurs is in part contingent on the extent to which they define a situation as hopeless. As a rule, fighting requires hope, yet hope tends to fade with grave dangers. Those who have been sentenced to death tend to give up hope. Yet hope dies reluctantly. For some individuals condemned to death even a slim chance of survival turns the wish to live into an all-consuming passion. During the Nazi occupation, among the Jews in Western Belorussia, a clinging to hope and life was expressed in a variety of ways.

In the summer of 1941, when the Germans occupied Western Belorussia they were already experienced in the murder of Jews and seemed less concerned with keeping their crimes secret. And since in this part of Poland most mass shootings happened close to home, Jews who had eluded the killings had a hard time denying the grim reality.

As special targets, faced with overpowering destructive forces, many Jews obeyed German orders. Their compliance was based on a host of arguments. Some reasoned that opposition to the Germans, although personally gratifying, would only hasten the destruction of all Jews. Others claimed that by conforming to the German demands they would gain time. They had hoped that in the meantime the war would end and thus interfere with the Nazi plan to murder them. Others, especially older people, rejected the idea that the Germans intended to annihilate all Jews. They pointed out that it was to the Germans' advantage to keep some of them alive, as part of the labor force. Still others argued that in view of the Nazi superior power all Jewish opposition would be a suicidal gesture resulting in immediate death rather than the possibility of survival.

Some Jews had hoped to avoid death through compliance. In the end practically all of them perished as did most Jews who opposed the enemy. Those who refused to submit to German terror were the rebels; they were more independent and often endowed with leadership qualities. United in their refusal to become victims, they were preoccupied with opposition to the enemy through self-preservation. As these rebels continued to elude the Germans, they began to feel more self-assured. While they came to feel personally less threatened, the leaders among them were ready to consider other issues.

Some of these rebels switched their attention from self-preservation to revenge. Although they knew that death was a real possibility, they opted for revenge through armed resistance. The more successful they were, the more absorbed they became in this nearly impossible struggle.

Indeed, many Jewish partisans preoccupied with revenge had perished. Among them were such heroic leaders as Atlas, Kaplinski, and Dworecki.[1] If given the opportunity, these fallen heroes and others like them would have argued that their deaths had been different from the deaths of defenseless ghetto inmates. Indeed, they were. And yet, by fighting the Germans, these Jewish partisans speeded up their own deaths and the deaths of their followers.

Tuvia Bielski's opposition to the Germans was different. Whatever feelings of revenge he had, these took a back seat to his determination to save lives. Refusing to become a victim, rejecting the role of avenger, Tuvia Bielski concentrated on gathering Jewish fugitives and protecting their lives.

Tuvia's opposition to the Germans had the support of his entire family. The Germans, however, succeeded in murdering many of them. Defiance did not work for some of the Bielski family any better than it worked for the majority of Jews.

Clearly, survival in a hostile and devastated setting was unlikely. Moreover, German terror led to the destruction of Jewish traditions, making Jewish prewar leaders ineffective. But a strong and able leader could help improve the chances for survival. Tuvia Bielski was such a leader. His skills developed gradually, keeping pace with the community he headed.

A one-time peasant, a resident of a small provincial town, Tuvia Bielski was an unlikely leader, an unlikely hero. He was both different from and more independent than most of his fellow Jews. Social upheavals propelled him into a position of prominence. Extraordinary times require extraordinary leaders, unbound by old traditions.

And so, independent, set apart from traditional leaders, Tuvia's reactions to the German onslaught were unusual. With his two brothers, Asael and Zus, Tuvia became a part of the small minority of Jews who, from the very start, vowed never to be ghetto inmates. Their refusal to become victims was linked to a determination to stay alive. The three brothers joined forces, enlarged their group to include more relatives and friends, and elected Tuvia their commander. From the outset Tuvia was concerned with saving lives and argued that the survival of their group depended directly on its enlargement and hence on bringing more Jews into their camp.

Time and survival of the expanding group led to feelings of confidence. With some initial success came greater freedom to consider the welfare of others – at first, family and friends. The group grew. The group's growth and survival made Tuvia even more sensitive to the needs of other Jews, those who were not necessarily relatives or friends.

Tuvia's concerns about the Jewish plight were further strengthened when the Germans stepped up their persecutions of Jews in 1942. That summer witnessed the liquidation of many ghettos and the resultant murder of most Jews.

The longer the Bielski otriad* continued to oppose the Germans, the more involved it became with the rescue of Jews. While saving many lives, the Bielski partisans also participated in military moves against the Germans. But rather than inflicting damage on the enemy, preservation of life remained their major, all-absorbing mission.

As an independent charismatic leader, untouched by political ideology, Tuvia made no distinction among different kinds of Jews: the old and the young, the weak and the strong. Quite naturally, the rescue efforts of the Bielski otriad came to include all Jews, no matter who they were.

As an effective leader, Tuvia was able to persuade others to listen to him and to obey. With time, he converted more and more people to his open-door

policy of taking in every Jew. The growing support for Tuvia's policies and the success of these policies were intricately connected.

But Tuvia's achievements were sprinkled with criticism. Some of his partisans had argued that, after all, without the cooperation of his brothers, of Lazar Malbin, of the young fighters who followed his orders, he could not have made it. True. Still, Tuvia's leadership and vision brought these people together in the first place. Moreover, it was his ability to control, to organize, and to protect that made the people follow his orders.

A general needs an army and an army needs a general. Tuvia was a superb general and he led his people to victory. Most prominent among Tuvia's victories was the rescue of more than 1,200 Jews, all condemned to death. But Tuvia's achievements went beyond such rescues. The Bielski partisans stood for justice, attacking and killing local collaborators. By punishing informers they helped reduce the Jewish death toll and at the same time intimidated other potential collaborators. This resulted in safer roads which, in turn, encouraged more ghetto escapes.

Eventually the local population realized that the Bielski otriad would punish all those who mistreated Jews. Such knowledge prevented some peasants from dismissing or denouncing their Jewish charges. It also prevented some from refusing help.

Moreover, whenever Jewish partisans in Soviet detachments felt threatened by Russian partisans they could count on finding protection in the Bielski otriad. Indeed, on the eve of the manhunt of 1943, twenty-two Jewish fighters from the Orlanski detachment found refuge in the Bielski camp. They came because they had been exposed to anti-Semitic threats.

In a different way the Bielski otriad saved the lives of the Kesler group. They had come to the Bielski detachment reluctantly, but if they had refused to join they would have been killed by the Victor Panchenko group.[2] These examples represent only a fraction of the Jews who were protected from Russian partisan threats.

The Bielski otriad initiated other forms of rescue. Special guides were sent into ghettos to help people escape, and scouts searched the roads for Jewish fugitives in need of protection. While most of those col-

*A partisan detachment group, Ed.

lected by the guides and scouts ended up in the Bielski otriad, some did not. A few joined Soviet detachments, while others found refuge among the local population. Still the activities of these guides and scouts added to the number of Jews saved by the Bielski otriad.

The degree of rescue was also affected by the losses of life. It is not easy to determine exact casualties of an expanding community like the Bielski otriad. Nor is it easy to compare the attrition rates of different partisan groups. Precise estimates are hard to find, yet those available for the Bielski otriad list specific names of places and names of the dead. Most other estimates seem to lack such supporting facts.

Under conditions in which attrition occurred it was extremely difficult for people fighting for survival to make precise records. In an environment so hostile, devastated, and devastating, people with limited hope for survival and with minimal resources are not likely to make systematic tabulations.

Attrition had many components. The major part of attrition was probably death from enemy attacks. But death also resulted from disease, suicide, unintended injuries, punishment mandated by the group's authorities, and from incidents among the armed group members. Desertions, expulsions, and accidental separation also occurred.

Thus, in the absence of systematic records, one cannot know either exact numbers or causes of the attrition that led to a reduction in the number of partisans who survived the war. Of course, merely to compare the survivors with the initial recruits is inadequate, since there usually was a continuing and poorly recorded influx of new partisans.

It might also be inaccurate to make simple direct comparisons of the losses of the Bielski otriad and those of other partisan groups. However, by reviewing the most reliable estimates and taking into account the many sources of uncertainty and the nature of the estimates, we can learn much about the relative attrition of these groups.

Independently, two former Bielski partisans estimated that fifty people had died in their otriad.[3] One of the partisans, Chaja Bielski, followed up her statement with a thorough search. The end results are very similar to the initial estimate.

Listing specific names, places, and dates, the number of people who died in the Bielski otriad came to fifty-five. Included in this group are four people whose death was ordered by the otriad's authorities, one suicide, and one person who drowned. When these special individuals are excluded from the fifty-five, this leaves forty-nine people who died because of enemy attacks.

Based on the conservative figure of the total number of Bielski group members of 1,200, the forty-nine deaths represent an attrition rate of less than five percent. When offering these estimates, Chaja cautions that her figures are approximate.[4]

In contrast to figures from the Bielski otriad, one frequently quoted source says that the size of the entire Russian partisan movement rose "from 30,000 in January 1942 to 175,000 by June 1944. The personnel turnover resulting from casualties, sickness and desertions over a three-year period brought the total of men who at one time or another participated in the partisan movement to about 400,000 or 500,000. . . . These figures represent the number of partisans present in regular, permanently, organized combat units."[5]

One can make a rough estimate of the attrition rate for the Russian partisan movement by assuming that the participation was uniformly spread out over the three-year period (thirty-six months) for an average number of participants of about 14,000 per month. Thus the estimated total number of incoming participants over the eighteen-month period from January 1942 to June 1944 was 250,000. This adds to the starting value of 30,000 in January 1942 and gives an intake of 280,000, of which only 175,000 were left in June 1944. This gives a conservative estimated attrition rate of forty percent.[6]

Other estimates for partisan deaths in different Soviet otriads vary. For example, one partisan from the Ponomarenko detachment tells that they lost one-third; out of one hundred fifty partisans, fifty died. This is an attrition rate of thirty-three percent. For most detachments such information is not available.[7] An article in the *Encyclopedia Judaica* states that one-third of the Jewish partisans who served in Russian otriads perished.[8] Another study of Jewish partisans in Lithuania estimates that fifty-three percent of them died.[9]

More vulnerable than guerilla units were small, unprotected family groups. Indeed, of the single individuals who reached the Bielski otriad, many were sole survivors of small family camps. Also, in some forests, family groups were abandoned by fighting partisans before a raid. Unprotected, such camps were easily destroyed.[10] But even "properly" protected family camps suffered heavy losses. For example, in the Parczow forest in Poland, of the 4,000 Jewish ghetto runaways who found their way into this forest only two hundred survived the war. This shows an attrition rate of ninety-five percent.[11] In contrast, the Bielski otriad lost only five percent of its people.

Indeed, no matter what group the Bielski detachment is compared to, it seems to have had by far the smallest losses. Much of the credit for this successful protection of lives belongs to the group's commander, Tuvia Bielski.

Perhaps the Bielski otriad and its charismatic leader can serve as a model showing the link between self-preservation and the selfless protection of others.

In times of upheaval among the ruins of established society, those who are independent and removed from the mainstream of tradition are likely to see hope where there is none.[12] Threatened by overpowering forces of destruction, those with hope will concentrate more vigorously than others on overcoming death. When this struggle yields a semblance of success, self-preservation makes room for concern about the welfare of others. While at first these others are an extension of self, such as close family members, with time and with further success, they come to include friends. Feeding on their own achievement and gaining more support, the protectors and the protected soon come to include anyone threatened by destruction and death. Each becomes transformed from a prospective victim to a rescuer, blurring the distinctions between the rescuer and the rescued. What had begun as an unrealistic glimmer of hope turned into a chance to survive, a cooperative effort. Armed with a trust in a better future, those who are independent and free from social constraints can more easily transfer their hopes, their possibilities, and their successes to the less hopeful and less resourceful. This transfer creates its own reality, a reality that opposes the life-threatening environment and death.

And so, in times of crisis, when old, established leaders fail, the uninitiated, the independent who are free from traditional constraints have the opportunity to develop their leadership skills and their strategies of survival. At first equipped only with hope and a feeling of self-worth, they soon translate these hopes into actual gains. Success may carry them into the position of leadership and power. Hope, independence, ability to organize, and the resultant success lead to more opportunities and greater achievements.

When the upheavals show signs of receding to previous societal realities, the skills of the independent charismatic leader become obsolete. In part by changing conditions, in part by their own inability to fit into these conditions, such leaders are pushed aside. Although the leaders retreat, the fruits of their achievement remain.

As commander of a forest community dedicated to the preservation of life, Tuvia Bielski gave to the Jewish people many precious gifts: hopes, dreams, and their very lives.

Notes

1. *Sefer Hapartisanim Hajehudim* (*The Jewish Partisan Book*) (Merchavia: Sifriat Poalim, Hashomer Hatzair, 1958), Vol. 1, 337, 346.

2. I describe the move of the Kesler group to the Bielski otriad in Chapter 6. The literature contains several accounts of Jewish partisans who were disarmed by Soviet partisans. For one example see Dov Levin, *Fighting Back: Lithuanian Jewry's Armed Resistance to the Nazis, 1941–1945* (New York: Holmes & Meier, Publishers, Inc., 1985), 184–186.

3. The two Bielski partisans who offered the estimate of fifty dead were Chaja Bielski, Personal Interview, Haifa, Israel, 1987–1991, and Baruch Kopold, Personal Interview, Haifa, Israel, 1990.

4. When I asked Chaja to be more specific she sent me the following letter.

   "Dear Nechama: You asked me to complete a very emotional and difficult task. This is why it took me such a long time to fulfill it. I found it extremely difficult to remember all the names of all the people who died in our partisan camp. 48 years went by trying to do justice is hard on my memory, as I said before. But I appreciate them very much because they gave their lives to bring a piece of bread for an old man, child and woman. They fought against the Nazis making ambushes on the roads and put explosives under the railway lines. They remain in my memory as holy men.

   1/5/43 *Chrapiniewo*: Sonia Bielski; Regina Titkin; Grisha Meitis; Izchak Leibovicz; Elijahu Bakshit; Herzl Efroimski; Bernstein; Lova Wolkin; one more, I don't remember his name.

11/4/43 *Zabeitowo*: Lansman.
The end of January: Aba Wolfowicz.
3/43 (by an ambush): Motl Dworzecki; Josef Zelikowicz; Szumanski, the son; David Sztein.
4/43 in a hutor, near the village Dobre-Pole: Alter Titkin; Abraham Polonski; Rubin Polonski; Joshua Ostaszynski; Jehuda Kowalski; Leibel Gimpiłowski; Leizer Chaitowicz; Szumanski (the second son); Israel, from Delatitz; one more.
Jasinowo: Miriam Cipilewicz; Mrs. Białabroda; Haim Bloch; a baby; and two guards.
Abraham Kalmonowicz (he hanged himself).
8/43 *Nalibocka Forest*: Kaplan; Gwenofelski, drowned.
9/43 *Żurawielnik*: Ida Bielski; Jacob Slucki; Abraham Mowszowicz; Otminova *Nalibocka Forest*: Israel Kesler; Mr Bialobroda; Josef Szmulowicz.
7/12/44 Nalibocka Forest: Elijachu Ostaszynski; Pacowski; Mark Epsztein; Zvi Leibowicz; Gordon; Sara Gierszonowski; Szumanski (the father); Luk; one more.
Elijahu Jewnowicz (was killed by the Nazis in a hutor).
Chana (from Nowojelnie).
Hirsh Feldman; Shmuel Lisman.
Polonecki.

Nechama, please look if the list is O.K. Maybe you'll have to ask other witnesses too." Note that this attack had happened on July 9, 1944. See Note 50 in chapter 14.
5. John A. Armstrong (ed.), *Soviet Partisans In World War II* (Madison: The University of Wisconsin Press, 1964), 151.
6. Professor Herbert Spirer, a statistician and friend, helped me with these calculations.
7. Jacov Greenstein, Personal Interview, Tel Aviv, Israel, 1984–1990.
8. "Russia," *Encyclopedia Judaica* (Jerusalem: Keter Publishing House Ltd., 1971), Vol. 15, 478.
9. Dov Levin, "Baltic Jewry's Armed Resistance to the Nazis," in Isaac Kowalski (ed.), *Anthology of Armed Resistance to the Nazis, 1939–1945*, 3 volumes (New York: Jewish Combatants Publishing House, 1986), Vol. 3, 42–48.
10. Yitzhak Arad, *The Partisan from the Valley of Death to Mount Zion* (New York: Holocaust Library, 1979), 115–134; for additional descriptions of the plight of different family camps in different areas see Yehuda Merin and Jack Nusan Porter, "Three Jewish Family-Camps in the Forests of Volyn, Ukraine During the Holocaust," *Jewish Social Science*, Vol. 156, No. 1 (1984), 83–92.
11. Shmuel Krakowski, *The War of the Doomed: Jewish Armed Resistance in Poland, 1942–1944* (New York: Holmes & Meier Publishers, Inc., 1984), 59. This study, 80–100, shows that south of Lublin the survival rate of Jews in the forest was much lower, in some cases nonexistent. The precarious situation of Jewish partisans is also described by Harold Werner, *Fighting Back: A Memoir of Jewish Resistance* (New York: Columbia University Press, 1992), 104, 141, 155–56.
12. Nechama Tec, *When Light Pierced the Darkness: Christian Rescue of Jews in Nazi-Occupied Poland* (New York: Oxford University Press, 1986), 150–183. Only after I finished writing this book did I read the recently published book by Raul Hilberg, *Perpetrators, Victims, Bystanders: The Jewish Catastrophe, 1933–1945* (New York: HarperCollins, 1992). Particularly relevant are Hilberg's discussions of Survival and the determination of people to live. See 186–191.

SEMPO SUGIHARA, KOVNO, LITHUANIA... JULY 1940 – Sempo Sugihara was an intelligence officer assigned by Japan's ambassador in Berlin to open a consulate in Kovno, Lithuania to gather information about tensions between Germany and the Soviet Union. However, from the time of his arrival in Kovno in August 1939, and the Soviet invasion of the Baltic States on June 15, 1940, Sugihara learned of the atrocities committed against Jews in Poland. Towards the end of July 1940, three weeks before the Soviets intended to close all foreign consular offices in Lithuania, Sugihara was approached by Dr. Zorah Warhaftig of the Jewish Agency Palestine Office, to provide Japanese transit visas to Polish-Jewish refugees in Lithuania for travel across the USSR. Warhaftig had arranged for the refugees to be allowed transit across Russia if they were issued visas by the Japanese government. These visas would then be used by refugees to travel on to the Dutch colonies of Curacao. The Japanese government denied Sugihara permission to issue these visas, but at great personal risk, he ignored the order and worked feverishly in the three short weeks left to him to hand-write visas, regardless of whether these refugees had the necessary supporting documents.

It is estimated that Sugihara issued at least 1,600 visas. Since entire families were included on a single visa, he helped thousands of people to escape. None of the refugees reached Curacao. From Japan, most went to Shanghai, others to the United States, Canada, or Palestine. On September 1, 1940, after his office was closed by Soviet authorities, Sugihara and his family left Kovno for his new post in Germany. Sugihara was dismissed from the Japanese Foreign Service after the war. (Hiroki Sugihara, courtesy of USHMM Photo Archives)

OSKAR SCHINDLER, KRAKOW, POLAND... 1941 – Oskar Schindler, a German businessman, went to Poland in 1941 to take advantage of the Jewish labor source. All of his laborers came from the Krakow ghetto. When the ghetto was liquidated in 1943, the remaining Jews were sent to the Plaszow labor camp. With his business and political connections, Schindler was able to convert his factory into a sub-camp of Plaszow. Months later the factory was closed and its employees were ordered to Auschwitz. In defiance of the order, Schindler compiled a list, "Schindler's List," of over 1,000 names of "indispensable" Jewish workers. He succeeded in having these men and women transferred to a new factory in Brünnlitz, thus saving over 1,000 people from the death camp. (Yad Vashem Photo Archives, courtesy of USHMM Photo Archives)

ALEXANDER ROSLAN, WARSAW, POLAND... MARCH, 1943 –
In the months just prior to the liquidation of the Warsaw ghetto, fewer than 50,000 Jews remained, including three little boys: Jacob, Shalom, and David Gutgeld. Their mother had died; their father was in Russia. The boys' Aunt Hanna escaped the ghetto to seek help from the family's pre-war chauffeur. She arrived at his apartment only to find that he had been killed by the Germans. The owner of the chauffeur's flat, Alexander Roslan, volunteered to help Hanna and offered to hide the three boys. In spite of the risk to himself and his family, which included two children, he helped Hanna smuggle the boys out of the ghetto and hid them in his small apartment. Alexander also offered to hide Aunt Hanna. She thanked him, but said she would join them after Passover. The final Nazi *aktion* against the Warsaw ghetto was launched on the first day of Passover. Hanna was deported to Auschwitz and never heard from again.

When Shalom and Jacob became ill with scarlet fever, Alexander smuggled the sick boys into a hospital. Shalom died; Jacob survived. Jacob and David remained with Alexander and his family until liberation. After the war, the boys went to Palestine to be reunited with their father. With Alexander Roslan in the photograph are Jacob (left) and David (right) Gutgeld. (JFR Photo Archives)

Becoming a Rescuer: Overcoming Social, Psychological, and Physical Barriers

NECHAMA TEC

AFTER GERMANY'S 1939 TAKEOVER of Poland the German administration was in full control of the country. Its subjugation of the population was by no means limited to Jews. Personal and political liberties were abolished for everyone immediately. In one of their first suppressive moves, the Germans turned to the Polish elites (i.e., intellectuals and professionals, clergy and army officers), and many of them were murdered. Others were sent to German concentration camps. Most early inmates of the just-completed Auschwitz were in fact members of the Polish elite.

However, persecution was not limited to the society's upper echelons. Following the annexation of parts of western Poland to the Reich, the Nazis began to Germanize the region. This involved removal of large segments of the native population. Such transfers were performed forcibly and without regard to human cost. As a result many Poles lost their lives.

In addition, guided by their own economic needs throughout the war the Germans continued to deport Poles for work to the Reich. Of an estimated 2.5 million who were thus used, many were worked to death, while others returned in wretched condition.[1]

Finally, too, throughout the long years of German occupation, any signs of political opposition brought a swift and brutal response. Reprisals for illegal acts led to mass killings. As Polish hostility and opposition to the occupying forces grew, so did the frequency and brutality of these reprisals. Most of those caught were executed on the spot. More often than not, these victims were uninvolved in any underground activities. The more "fortunate," those who were caught but not immediately executed, were sent to concentration camps or to forced-labor camps in Germany.[2]

Nazi abuses created an atmosphere of terror and caused many deaths. It has been claimed that the Nazis succeeded in virtually eliminating the Polish intelligentsia.[3] Other estimates put the toll in numbers of civilian victims at somewhere from 1[4] to more than 2 million[5] of a total of more than 30 million. More precise figures are elusive.

To save Jews, while their own lives were threatened, required Polish rescuers to cope with a formidable combination of physical, psychological, and social pressures and barriers. What were they?

Individual experiences of each rescuer varied in most unusual ways, but in combination they point to two broad impediments: Polish anti-Semitism and the Nazi implementation of the Final Solution.

For a concrete illustration of the rescuers' predicaments I turn first to the factory worker Stefa Dworek. At first she apologetically told me that she had not done much; she saved only one Jewish woman. Besides, it had all happened by chance.

My questions revealed that this simple but refined woman, from a poor working class background, had only an elementary school education. Mother of two sons, and practically a mother to her younger brother, Stefa Dworek had been married twice, but each husband had left her.

In the summer of 1942 Stefa's first husband, Jerzy, brought home a young Jewish woman named Irena. Ryszard Laminski, a Polish policeman who was also working for the Polish underground, had introduced Jerzy to the Jewish woman and had promised to move Irena to a more permanent shelter within the week.

Irena, who had Polish documents but could not use them, looked very Jewish, so there was simply no way she could have passed for a Christian. It was agreed that during her brief stay she would not leave the apartment. To protect her against unexpected visitors in the one-room apartment, the Dworeks pushed a free-standing wardrobe away from the wall. The space between the wardrobe and the wall became Irena's temporary hiding place. For more serious encounters they prepared a hiding place in the attic.

They were able to do this because their apartment was at the very top of the stairs.

Stefa soon discovered that Laminski, a married man, was not only Irena's protector but her lover. After a week, distressed, he came to tell them that he had been unable to find a new place for his mistress. Another week passed, and then another. Laminski continued to come, each time apologizing for his failure to find Irena shelter, each time leaving food or money. But Laminski's limited funds barely covered Irena's expenses. Yet, Stefa did not mind. Although she herself was poor, she had no intention of making a business out of saving a life. They all shared what they had.

As for the awaited transfer to another haven, Laminski's efforts continued to be fruitless. After a few months, danger came from an unexpected source. Jerzy Dworek demanded that Irena leave. He insisted that his life was in danger and that he had no intention of dying for a Jewess. When Stefa pointed out that he was the one who had taken her in in the first place, Jerzy became abusive, shouting that unless Irena left he would stop coming home. In the heat of their argument, Stefa accused her husband of sexual indiscretions, while he threatened to denounce all of them. The quarrel ended with Jerzy storming out of the apartment, swearing to destroy them.

What did Stefa do? *I called Laminski . . . [and] he went to talk to my husband. He told him, "Here is my pistol; if you will denounce them you will not live more than five minutes longer. The first bullet will go into your head." After that my husband stopped coming. To Laminski he said that he could not live with a wife who has a Gestapo lover (meaning Laminski). This ended my marriage. But Ryszard Laminski continued to come, helping us, warning us about danger. He never abandoned us.*

How did Stefa feel about this development? After all, this stranger had come for one week and ended by staying for nineteen months. Was Stefa aware of the danger? *Sure I knew. Everybody knew what could happen to someone who kept Jews. I knew, but who knows, maybe I was not so fully aware. Besides, for a week I thought that it would be all right. Then it continued. . . . Sometimes when it got dangerous, Irena herself would say, "I am such a burden to you, I will leave." But*

I said, "Listen, until now you were here and we succeeded, so maybe now all will succeed. How can you give yourself up?" I knew that I could not let her go. The longer she was here the closer we became.

My husband hated Jews. Maybe . . . because he did not know them. . . . Anti-Semitism was ingrained in him. Not only was he willing to burn every Jew but even the earth on which they stood. Many Poles feel the way he did. I had to be careful of the Poles.[6]

What kind of life did the two women lead? Irena never went out, and none of the neighbors knew about her. Stefa's thirteen-year-old brother was fond of Irena and helped to protect her. The fewer people knew, the safer it was. Stefa recalled: *An aunt came to me, slept here, and she did not know. Years later when she found out my aunt was angry. But I explained that she might have told someone, then that someone tell another person, and this would start a whole chain. After all, I had to be careful. It was a question of my child's and brother's life, the life of the Jewish woman and my own.*

In time the two women became good friends. Stefa recognized that conditions around them were partly responsible for their closeness. *We had to cooperate. We slept together. We ate from the same plate. I was afraid to have one extra plate on the table. If someone would come in they would see an extra plate. There was no time to hide it.*

Sometimes Stefa and her brother found themselves in strange situations. Once, for example, when Stefa was about to go to the ghetto to find out about Irena's relatives, Irena developed nervous hiccups: *A neighbor came in. My brother and I began to talk fast, sneeze, shout. We did not want her to hear the hiccups. The neighbor looked at us surprised, and left. . . . I tried to arrange it so that the neighbors would not visit me. No one suspected us. They were only suspicious when Laminski came. But they might have thought that he was my lover.*

In 1944, during the Polish uprising in Warsaw, it was too dangerous to stay in the apartment. To avoid recognition, Irena bandaged her face. In the cellar, Stefa introduced her to the neighbors as a cousin who had just arrived.

Eventually the Poles lost the battle, incurring terrible losses, and the victorious Germans began to evacuate the civilian population.[7]

Stefa and Irena heard that mothers with young children would be allowed to stay. In Irena's case evacuation would have meant exposure to many people, danger, and possible death. After all, she could not keep her face bandaged forever, and the bandage in itself could arouse suspicion. Recognizing the danger, Stefa had no intention of abandoning her friend.

When we were about to be evacuated I told Irena to take my baby. I told her: "I will try to stay with you, in case I get lost take care of him, like of your own child." . . . . When the German saw her with the child he told her to return to the apartment. Somehow I too was allowed to go with her.

Stefa cried as she spoke, but I began to doubt her story. I could not imagine giving my child away! I asked for an explanation: How could Stefa risk losing her baby? Surprised, she shrugged and then answered: *Irena would not have harmed him. She would have taken good care of him. Besides no one knew what might have become of me. I could have died too.*

Stefa continued to cry and I continued to doubt. My doubts lingered until I came across Irena's testimony before a historical commission in Warsaw. In this official document Irena praised Stefa for her many sacrifices and exceptional behavior toward her.[8] The testimony also contains Irena's version of the incident with the baby: *Before the end of the war there was a tragic moment. . . . We learned that the Germans were about to evacuate all civilians. My appearance on the streets even with my bandaged face could end tragically. Stefa decided to take a bold step which I will remember as long as I live. She gave me her baby to protect me. As she was leaving me with her child she told me that the child would save me and that after the war I would give him back to her. But in case of her death she was convinced that I would take good care of him. . . . Eventually we both stayed.*[9]

The reaction of Stefa's husband as well as the constant fear of denouncements by neighbors and relatives were related to Polish anti-Semitism – indeed, all Poles who saved Jews had to cope with obstacles that were related in some degree to the traditionally strong Polish anti-Semitism.

The cultural climate of Poland was antagonistic toward Jews. The very presence of Polish anti-Semitism implied an opposition and hostility to Jewish rescue. Those eager to save Jews were aware that by following their inclinations they would be inviting the censure of their fellow citizens.

As I have pointed out earlier, in prewar Poland in particular, anti-Jewish measures and ideologies had penetrated into religious, educational, economic, and political spheres of life. Although an integral part of the Polish culture, not all forms of anti-Semitism were explicit. The form I call diffuse cultural anti-Semitism remained vague and free-floating. In contrast to the direct and explicit anti-Jewish measures, this vague and yet all-encompassing sort of anti-Semitism has been taken for granted. It attributes to the Jew any and all negative traits, but it calls for no special action. Still, because of its pervasiveness: *Even the objectively most accomplished Jew will not be evaluated without these negative associations. One sees the Jew only through such negative glasses. One cannot free oneself of these deeply ingrained negative images. They are so common that only an exceptionally independent person can perceive a Jew as an individual to be judged dispassionately on the same basis as anyone else.*[10]

People tended to accept this form of anti-Semitism without much thought or awareness. It was expressed in such generally accepted and widely used utterances as "Be a good boy or the Jew will get you." "You are dirty like a Jew." "Don't be a calculating Jew!" and many, many others.

In the Polish language the very term Jew (*Żyd*) is something polite people are reluctant to use. Yet, it is the only correct term; others such as "a person of Mosaic faith" or "an Israelite" sound archaic, pompous, and downright phony. Still one can easily insult a person by simply calling him a Jew (*Żyd*). The term evokes strong negative images.

To this day as a Polish Jew I feel a strange sensation when I use the term *Żyd*. The Christians I spoke to also conveyed a certain uneasiness and embarrassment when they used the term. Thus, for example, the rescuer Eva Anielska began a story: *I had a dear, dear friend . . .* I interrupted to make sure, *Was she a Jewess?* Embarrassed, she answered: *Yes, but I resent applying this term to her.* Her friend meant much to her, and she was reluctant to refer to her as a Jew. In a similar situation when talking about his best friend, the rescuer Stach Kaminski noted: *He was my friend.*

I did not refer to him as a Jew. I did not see a Jew in him.

Unobtrusive and latent though it is, this diffuse cultural form of anti-Semitism acts as an insidious foundation for all other forms. Many Poles, and particularly the rescuers, find objectionable other more explicit forms of anti-Semitism, but this almost subconscious type they tend to shrug off as insignificant. Expressions that reflect this form of anti-Semitism are dismissed as mere jokes.

Many rescuers were nevertheless conscious of their early, ever-present exposure to this diffuse cultural anti-Semitism.

Stop being a bad boy or the Jew will get you! This kind of warning was a guarantee of good behavior. *I was afraid of the Jew. I grew up with the idea that the Jew was a serious menace, a threat, to be avoided at any cost.* The speaker, Stach Kaminski, is a Pole, a highly sophisticated man, a man who has held a number of high diplomatic posts. During the war he played an important role in the Council for Aid to Jews, part of the Polish underground, devoted exclusively to helping Jews. His name appears in many historical sources of that period as one who had rescued many Jews. During the war he risked his life for the very people whom, as a child, he saw as a danger and threat. Did he come from what could commonly be described as an anti-Semitic family? Not at all. A prominent doctor, his father not only had many Jewish patients, but was proud to display his knowledge of the Yiddish language. During his childhood and adolescence Stach knew many Jews, some of whom became his friends. Yet he saw nothing wrong with ridiculing Jews and telling jokes about them, emphasizing that: *Ridicule was only an innocent pastime. It never developed into any hostile action.*

One of my closest friends was a Jew. To celebrate our high school graduation we both got drunk. It was then that my friend cried and insisted that I swear to him that I was not an anti-Semite. I remember being bewildered, not quite sure of what it was all about. . . . I knew that Jews were strange and different and that we objected to them on many grounds. But he was a friend of mine, I did not see him as a Jew. I was confused. Stach's relation to Jews, while complicated and involved, is by no means unique.

Bolesław Twardy, a known journalist-writer who spent most of his life actively fighting anti-Semitism and protecting Jews, bears a resemblance to Stach Kaminski. During the war he too was a central figure in the Council for Aid to Jews. His courageous deeds are also recorded in the history of those days. Bolesław remembers: *They tried to bring me up as an anti-Semite. As a little boy I used to run after Jews calling them names. I did this as a matter of fact, quite naturally. Once the older children made me pursue a rabbi. They taught me to call him "goy" [a term applied by Jews to Christians]. I can still see the rabbi stop, look at me with very intelligent, penetrating eyes, and then burst into free, good-natured merry laughter. His reaction made me uneasy. I felt ashamed. Later on I was less eager to run after Jews.*

Exposure to and acceptance of such general anti-Jewish views is said to have been more automatic and pervasive among the simple and uneducated. Consider the teenage daughter of a poor blacksmith who, during the war and after a major action against Jews, passed near the ghetto and noticed someone lying behind the fenced ditch. Coming closer, she realized that it was a Jewish woman, alive and in need of help. She ran for wire cutters, cut the wire, and then brought the woman to her parents, who welcomed her with open arms.

In time, a close and warm relationship developed between the family and their charge. The young girl in particular doted over the newcomer, referring to her lovingly as "my foundling." Eventually the villagers became suspicious. Danger loomed. If denounced they could all perish. But they were not about to abandon the Jewish woman. Instead, they decided that the young girl should leave with her and protect her with her typically Polish looks. As the two were forced to move from place to place, their attachment and love grew stronger. At one point the Jewish woman asked how her friend felt about Jews. The unhesitating answer was: *Oh, I hate them! The Jews are horrible. They are dirty thieves. They cheat everybody. Jews are a real menace. For Passover they catch Christian children, murder them, and use their blood for matzo.* In vain her Jewish friend tried to point out the absurdity of such accusations. The girl was only willing to concede that her friend did not commit these acts. As for the rest of the Jews, she was convinced that they did.

Frustrated and exhausted, the woman burst into tears. The young girl put her arms around her, saying: *Please don't cry, it breaks my heart to see you so unhappy. You know that you are dearer to me than a sister! But you must understand that I sucked these stories with my mother's milk. Can you expect me to give them up?* Despite her convictions about Jews, however, the blacksmith's daughter also extended help to other Jewish strangers, whom she presumably considered to be guilty of murdering Christian children.[11]

The environment in which Polish rescuers lived was hostile to the Jews and unfavorable to their protection. Poles were reminded at every turn that Jews were unworthy, low creatures and that helping them was not only dangerous but also reprehensible. Not only did rescuers know that their protection of Jews would meet with Polish disapproval, but many feared that this Polish disapproval would come with actual reprisals.

Speaking to the Jews he had been hiding, a simple peasant expressed his apprehension about Poles: *I don't want anyone to know. I don't want you to leave in daylight, who knows what people might do? I am just a peasant and don't understand things, but there are bad people. You will leave at night. You will go down the trail the same way you came.*[12]

The experience of the kind peasant rescuer, Jan Rybak, also illustrates the point. Well-to-do, hardworking, and ever eager to help anyone, Jan was respected and loved by the rest of the villagers. However, when at the end of the war it became known that he had saved Jews, the other peasants underwent an abrupt change of heart and began treating their former favorite with hostility and contempt. Eventually someone denounced Jan to a Polish anti-Semitic underground group (a remnant of the wartime Polish underground that after the war refused to disband but continued to engage in terrorist activities against the Russians, the Jews, and Poles who saved Jews). Members of this group caught Jan Rybak and took him to a nearby forest to be shot. At the last moment defying his captors, Jan escaped, but after this episode death threats forced the entire Rybak family to relocate to another area where no one knew about their past.

Many rescuers, however, were not as fortunate. Wacek, for example, was a young Pole who was always cheerful and carefree, never turning away anyone who asked for help. His inexhaustible efforts on behalf of the persecuted and the needy often involved Jews. His courage and kindness in such matters earned him a reputation that eventually cost him his life. Right after the liberation Wacek was murdered by members of an illegal Polish underground group only because he had been so eager to save Jews.[13]

Polish anti-Semitism was also expressed in less severe ways. After the war when her fellow Poles became aware that Stefa Dworek had saved a Jewish woman, they considered her stupid. Similarly, Janka Polanska, young and defiant, refused to keep her help to Jews a secret. On realizing that to most Poles her protection of Jews was unacceptable, Janka began to feel like an outsider in the country she loved so well. A patriot who also participated in the Polish underground, Janka fought an inner battle. Eventually she tried to resolve the conflict by marrying a Jew and emigrating to Israel.

Janka remembered one particularly unpleasant incident that happened soon after the war. A Polish janitor who in the past had treated her with special consideration became hostile on learning that Janka had saved Jews. The furious and disappointed janitor accused her of deceiving him, because he had wrongly believed her to be a decent person. To underscore his disapproval, he returned a jar of jam that Janka had given him for his little daughter, asserting that his conscience did not allow him to accept gifts from those who saved Jews.

What about the rescuers themselves? How did they personally relate to Jews? Did they manage to escape from the pervasive anti-Semitism? Whereas most of the Polish protectors I spoke to tried to play down anti-Semitism, none fully denied its existence. Ironically, the more imbued they were with anti-Jewish images and values, the more inclined they were to say that Polish anti-Semitism was insignificant. When asked directly about their personal attitudes, all deplored anti-Semitism and condemned prewar anti-Jewish practices that dominated Poland's religious, economic, educational, and political life. In fact, some of the rescuers had defended Jews even before the war. Bolesław Twardy did it by attacking anti-Semitism in the press, a position that earned him the reputation of a "Jewish lackey." Stach Kaminski explained: *I could joke and make fun of Jews, but I opposed hurting them. When the Endeks [National Democrats] were physically attacking Jews at the university, my friends and I defended them. As a human being and as a Socialist I could not tolerate these anti-Semitic excesses.*

Eva Anielska's opposition to Jewish discrimination took another form. *I was brought up in such a way that I saw no difference between Jews and Poles. I tried to stand up for the Jews and I paid for it. Because I crossed out the word Christian on my student identification card, I was expelled from the university . . . three times. There were those who defended me and that is why I was reinstated. But later on when I completed my studies I could find no employment.*

Most rescuers consciously tried to dissociate themselves from the prevailing anti-Semitic climate and succeeded in dissociating themselves from anti-Jewish actions and ideologies. However, only a few helpers managed to steer clear of the influence of the diffuse cultural anti-Semitism. Most were caught in its clutches in different ways and in varying degrees.

Rescuers often explained that anti-Semitism existed because not only were the Jews different and strange, they were also unwilling to assimilate. In a sense, then, the Jews themselves were blamed for anti-Semitism.

The most negative view of the Jews was expressed by the Catholic writer Marek Dunski, whose writings and political affiliation clearly identify him as an anti-Semite. At first Dunski tried to evade questions related to anti-Semitism. Only after considerable prodding did he say that he was never a "philo-Semite" – a polite way of admitting to being an anti-Semite. Eventually he said that Jewish propaganda from abroad was responsible for Polish anti-Semitism. Asked whether he thought that the Jews themselves create anti-Semitism, he answered: *There are certainly Jewish groups who do this. . . . There were tremendous differences between Jews and Poles, and these differences created resentment. It was the Jews who refused to assimilate. Maybe they thought that it was better for them to be separate from the rest of the Poles. In large measure*

acceptance depended on the Jews themselves. Poles accepted those who wanted to assimilate.

Pointing to the inevitability of anti-Semitism, Roman Sadowski, a writer and rescuer, explained: *Wherever there are Jews there is anti-Semitism. People resent those who differ from them. The Jews did not blend into their environment and it was their strangeness that created anti-Semitism. In this respect, people are not different from animals. Take for example a group of ordinary mice; if you place a white one among them they will devour it. It is the same with Jews.*

While Bolesław Twardy agrees that the cultural strangeness of the Jews is responsible for anti-Semitism, he does not feel that this is inevitable. *The Jews were very different. . . . Their orthodox way of dressing in itself created a great deal of resentment. After all, their caftan was an insignificant thing, why did the Jew have to continue wearing it? It was an unnecessary source of irritation which could easily have been given up. One could dress as everyone else without giving up one's Jewishness. . . . Jews . . . are too aggressive, they do not know moderation. This has happened in Spain, in Germany, in the Middle Ages. It has always been the case if you look at their behavior historically. It is a trait which the Jews have and which has to do with their kind of upbringing . . . if aggressiveness, striving, and this pushiness to the limits would not occur, they would be looked upon positively, they would be accepted.*

Because he saw these deplorable traits as a part of the Jewish upbringing, he did not consider them inevitable.

Eva Anielska believes that the special position of the Jew in society fostered the emergence of these traits. Hers is a sympathetic view: *It is the tragedy of the Jews that they were deprived of a country. Without a homeland there is no security. The characteristics of greediness, aggressiveness, and pushiness develop in those who are deprived of a country and who because of it find themselves in an insecure and precarious position. Such traits are necessary for sheer survival. And so, I am convinced that it is the history of the Jews which is responsible for their distasteful traits. The traits for which the Jews have been hated. . . . A similar transformation took place after the 1944 Polish Warsaw uprising, when all Poles were evacuated. Without homes and without means of support, the Poles found themselves in a very insecure position. In their new surroundings, they be-came aggressive, pushy, and greedy. They too, like the Jews, were disliked by the Poles to whose places they came uninvited.*

Tomasz Jurski, a courageous protector of Jews, tried to justify and understand their alleged cowardli-ness: *In general, people who are constantly discrimi-nated against take on certain characteristics which are objectionable. Among the objectionable Jewish traits is the idea of the Jew as a coward. But it is hard to be fear-less under the conditions in which Jews lived. The Jews were pariahs.*

As a rule the rescuers held contradictory images about Jews. For example, taking first the position that Jewish refusal to assimilate creates anti-Semitism, the rescuer Roman Sadowski then added: *While the priest welcomed a convert, the same was not true for the people in general. To them the Jew was a Jew, different and therefore to be despised.* Similarly, insisting that Jewish unwillingness to assimilate was the cause of anti-Semitism, Stach Kaminski later said: *As far as the as-similated Jews were concerned, we always laughed at their written and spoken Polish. Their use of the lan-guage was faultless, too perfect, and therefore we ridi-culed and made fun of it.*

Apart from inconsistencies in the same individ-ual, different rescuers tended to ascribe to the Jews di-verse and contradictory traits. As a group the Jews were seen as lacking in unity, but they were also seen as too clannish. When applied to the Jews, both of these conditions were interpreted negatively.

Stefa Krakowska, who selflessly protected Jews, felt that . . . *Jews are too clannish. . . . A Jew would not buy from a Pole. But this was not true for Poles, they bought from all.* Others support her position. Emil Jablonski, whose testimony I read at the Jewish Historical Institute in Warsaw, was asked by the archivist, Jan Krupka, to meet me at the institute. I knew beforehand that for two years he had hidden his penniless Jewish friend in a one-room apartment and under trying circumstances. From the start Emil impressed me as a cultured, well-informed man, and I was eager to hear his story. When he com-mented about anti-Semitism he turned to postwar Poland, asking: *When you consider 1968 and the purge against the Jews, the Jews themselves are partly to blame.*

You know of course about their meeting in Zakopane?

No, I knew nothing about such a meeting, and urged him to tell me. *In Poland in 1968 it was clear that the Jews had been singled out for special treatment and that they were about to lose their power. It was then that all the Polish Jews who held the most prominent po-sitions called for a meeting in Zakopane. The aim of this meeting was to devise a unified Jewish strategy, to coun-teract the measures the Polish government was about to take against them. At least 2000 Jews participated in that meeting, all of whom filled the highest posts in Poland. Naturally coming together for the purpose of op-posing the existing system did not make a good impres-sion. Understandably such a move was interpreted as a Jewish conspiracy. Don't you think that this show of Jew-ish solidarity was unwise?*

Unfamiliar with the postwar era in Poland, I asked a number of Polish historians about this meet-ing. They all laughed, saying that it must be a figment of someone's imagination. Not easily dissuaded, I also asked a friend of mine, a publisher of one of the most influential Polish newspapers in Warsaw. He too claimed that such a meeting never took place. After a few more attempts, I had to accept their unanimous verdict.

Perhaps it is no coincidence that Emil, so con-vinced about a Jewish conspiracy, was also convinced that in prewar Poland all property was owned by Jews. He insisted that this was a well-established fact, reflected in a common Jewish saying: "Yours are the streets and ours are the houses."

Contrasting with the accusation of excessive Jew-ish solidarity was the accusation of their excessive di-visiveness. The rescuer Hela Horska, for example, asserted that *the Jews are their own worst enemy. They make terrible distinctions among themselves; the Polish and Lithuanian Jews see themselves as better than the others; German Jews see themselves as superior to the rest, and so forth. There is no end to this. Every synagogue caters to different groups. It is appalling how they differ-entiate and argue among themselves. . . . There is no unity and no solidarity. This is a Jewish tragedy.*

Referring to his wartime experiences, Bolesław Twardy commented: *After I became a member of the Council for Aid to Jews, one of my tasks was to distribute funds and keep contact with the few remaining ghettoes.*

The Jews in these ghettoes were on the verge of death from starvation. Through our help we were hoping to keep them alive a little longer.

It was then that I was again faced with this glaring divisiveness. The Jewish members of the council wanted me to report to them about the political affiliation of the Jews whom I supplied with funds. They felt that this money should be allocated only to certain political groups. To me this seemed outrageous. To ask someone who is dying of hunger what political party he belongs to was almost indecent. In good conscience, therefore, I falsified their political affiliation.

Further complicating the picture is the fact that most Christian helpers attributed to the Jews not only the negative images but also many valued and positive traits. Most admired in the Jew superior intelligence, self-discipline, hard work, and close family ties. Surprisingly, it was not unusual for the same person to see the Jew both in negative and positive terms.

Marek Dunski, who tends to blame the Jews for the existence of anti-Semitism, and who emphasizes their many negative traits, had no difficulty seeing them positively. As a writer who valued literacy, he noted that *Poles have to reach a certain level in order to read, whereas all Jews are literate. Maybe this is related to the Jewish religion. Maybe it is related to the Jewish brains. They seem more intelligent than Poles. The Jew, in difficult situations, more so than a Pole, knows how to overcome the difficulties.*

In general, a common Jew, a poor one, is more educated, more intelligent than his Polish counterpart. The Jews work hard. They like to work. They do not mind exerting themselves. Poles, instead of working hard, systematically improvise. They lack the perseverance of the Jew. They are impatient, and want to succeed fast.

Surprisingly enough, even some Polish Jews were affected by this diffuse cultural anti-Semitism. To illustrate, Szymon Rubin, a prominent scientist and the first survivor I interviewed, was four when his parents decided to move to a small village and pass for Christians. Because of Szymon's age they felt it best not to tell him that he was a Jew. In general, he had an exceptional capacity for reconstructing the past, but flatly denied having been exposed to anti-Semitism while passing: *I heard nothing negative about Jews. After all, at that time, and in the village I*

lived, there were no Jews. No one talked about them. There was simply no reason to bring up the subject. . . . When the war ended two people came to visit us, two Jewish partisans. I remember wondering why my parents had dealings with Jews. They gave them food and let them stay with us. Surprised, I asked why they did it. It was then that my parents explained to me that I too was Jewish. I remember being terribly hurt. For me it was a serious blow. I was upset by this discovery. When I pointed out that he must have been exposed to anti-Jewish views, otherwise he would not have reacted this way, he smiled in disbelief. He was totally unaware of this possibility.

Although clearly Szymon and many of the Polish rescuers were influenced by the diffuse cultural anti-Semitism, I would not label him or them as anti-Semites. Indeed, perhaps the category of anti-Semite should be reserved for a certain strength and level of adherence to anti-Semitic views rather than simple adherence per se. I do not know what that certain strength or level ought to be. What I do know, however, is that if in Poland it was so hard for some Jews to escape from these anti-Semitic influences, how can one expect non-Jews to have succeeded in doing so? Still, to the extent that Polish rescuers were at all imbued with the diffuse cultural anti-Semitism, they had to cope and overcome their own anti-Jewish images and values.

Even though Polish anti-Semitism could and did function as a collective and personal impediment to Jewish rescue, without the Nazi policies of destruction such rescue would not have been necessary in the first place. That is, while Polish anti-Semitism facilitated and contributed to Jewish annihilation, it was not responsible for it. The ultimate responsibility for the creation and implementation of the Final Solution lies with the Nazis. Moreover, their policies and actions functioned as the most powerful obstacles and barriers to Jewish protection.[14]

Foremost among these obstacles and barriers was the Nazi prohibition that carried with it the ever-present possibility of death. I have noted earlier that on October 15, 1941 the Nazis passed a law demanding the death penalty for all Jews who without permission left their residential quarters. This law also specified that "the same punishment applied to persons who knowingly provide hiding places for Jews," and that "accomplices will be punished in the same way as the perpetrator, and an attempted act in the same way as an accomplished one."[15] Any Christian who learned that a Jew was breaking this law had an obligation to report the crime or be subject to the same punishment. Determined to make both the Jews and Poles fully aware of this law, the Nazis publicized it widely; even in the most remote villages people soon knew of it. The Nazis were also determined that this law should be obeyed.[16] Transgressions were promptly followed by executions,[17] which were also widely publicized.

All Poles knew that to help Jews was to risk one's life. Frequently, however, more than their own lives were at stake. The Nazis adhered to the principle of collective responsibility. This meant that punishment applied not only to the "transgressors" but also to their families. In fact, children of all ages, including infants, were subjected to the same fate as the "guilty" adults. Nazi interpretations of collective responsibility often came to include neighborhoods, communities, and Poles in general. Equally chilling was the practice of public executions. The Germans understood that official notices of those punished were not as effective as eye-witness accounts. They were right.

One official announcement, for example, reports that on March 15, 1943, in the village of Siedlisko, not far from Cracow, the farmer Baranek and his family were executed for harboring Jews. Each name was followed by the age: forty-four, thirty-five, ten, nine, and fifty-eight. The notice ends with a statement that the four Jews sheltered by Baranek were shot as well.[18]

Years later what did the eyewitnesses remember? What did they tell about the victims and the events?

Wincenty Baranek, aged forty-four, was a prosperous and highly respected farmer. Deeply religious, he had a reputation as a generous man, eager to help others. All who knew him agreed that he was very special. Only in retrospect did some of his neighbors realize that by 1942 fear had changed him. He became quiet, less outgoing, and engrossed in his thoughts. Once, for example, this pious man went into church and stood in front of the altar without removing his hat. Only after a vigorous nudge did he

remember where he was. Red-faced and confused, he apologetically reached for his hat.

His wife, Lucja, seemed to have suffered as well. She too was remembered warmly, with affection. The entire village liked and respected her. This was quite an accomplishment, almost a miracle, because Lucja was a great beauty and women ought to have been envious of her. But she never gave them any reason for gossip. Lucja was an excellent housekeeper and a wonderful mother. Her two sons, ten and nine, were model children, well mannered, and also very gifted. She was special and in a class by herself; whatever she did was exceptional. She was the only one in the entire village who borrowed books from the town's library. Every free moment she had she read.

A neighbor's glimpse of Lucja shortly before the tragedy points to the strain she must have been under. *One evening as I was passing the Baranek's house my ears caught the sound of suppressed yet desperate weeping. When I came closer I saw Lucja framed in an unlit window holding a handkerchief over her mouth. Her sobs were filled with pain as if at any moment they would break her heart. Amazed, I asked: "Lusia, what in the name of God happened to you my dear?" Immediately she stopped. In a casual but strange voice she said: "Oh nothing! Nothing at all. It just came over me, for no reason at all." She vanished into the darkness of the room.*

When the Germans drove up to the farm at dawn, Baranek had time to ask a neighbor if they had visited others as well. Upon hearing that they came only to his place, he said: *I am lost, all is lost, the children!* In the initial confusion, caused by the arrival of the Nazis and neighbors, Baranek succeeded in telling the children to hide. They did. But as soon as the Germans realized that the boys were missing, they stopped searching for the Jews and began to look for them. After they found the boys, they shut them up in a room and ordered one of the neighbors to watch them.

Later on, people said that the children were about to jump out of the window. They might have succeeded in saving themselves, because the Germans were busy in another part of the house. But the neighbor who was standing guard forced them back into the room: *How his conscience allowed him to do this I don't know. Still, now when we think about this terrible past, we feel that we ought to have behaved differently. But then it was something else. In those days, at the Baranek's farm, we were terrorized and paralyzed into inaction. One wrong move could have meant death. Passively we watched as the Germans led out the husband and wife.*

The couple moved toward the barn, erect and stiff, as if they were to be wed. Only their faces were already dead. The atmosphere was churchlike, eerie. The silence was total, oppressive. When the two reached the barn a German soldier gave a key to the man, directing him to unlock the door. This done, the two were led inside. Then husband and wife kneeled.

Still in silence, the Germans brought out the boys. The children held hands. They, too, were made to walk toward the barn. Their bodies refused to remain calm and shook vigorously. At the sight of the children the crowd burst into loud sobs and groans. But the guards reacted swiftly. Shouting *"Ruhe, Ruhe"* (quiet, quiet), they followed up by indiscriminately hitting whomever was close to them with the butts of their guns. The crowd obeyed; the noise stopped. In silence they watched as the children were made to kneel in front of their parents. Shots and more shots exploded into the heavy air. The kneeling figures tumbled in quick succession, then scattered in different directions as if taking leave. Stunned, the crowd looked on. But the executioners had not finished. They brought out four men, the Jews who had been sheltered by the dead farmer. In full view of those present, the soldiers shot each of them several times. They continued to shoot into their dead bodies, as if trying to kill them over and over again.[19]

Instead of bullets, the Germans used fire in the village of Stary Cieplow. Here, too, they came at dawn, surrounding four farms at once. Because two of the farms were next to each other, the Germans moved one of the families – husband, wife, and five children – out of their own and into the neighbor's hut, a fragile old structure in need of repairs. In each place the victims were closely watched as their most valuable possessions were loaded onto special wagons. This done, they set fire to the three houses. That day thirty-three Poles and an unknown number of Jews were burned alive. In a nearby house a niece of one of

the families stood at her window. Let me reconstruct her story:

The guards led them in the direction of the neighbor's hut. The man, Adam Kowalski, at the head of the group, held the hand of each son: Henryk, six, and Stefan, five. It was like when he would go with the children for a walk, except now his head was bent down low, his legs were dragging as if refusing to move. The man was followed by his wife. In her arms she held a baby not yet seven months old. Two girls (Janka, sixteen and Zosia, twelve) walked behind their mother. Janka had her new boots on, a cherished gift from her father. The seven, surrounded by the German soldiers who kept prodding them on with the butts of their guns, moved on. When the mother reached the open door she took the baby from her chest, turned toward the soldier, and made a gesture, as if offering him the child. Perhaps she was begging for mercy? Perhaps she was trying to save the little one? The German pushed her violently. Still clinging to the child, she fell somewhere beyond the threshold. Mother and baby disappeared from view. . . . The guards shut the door securely and then encircled the hut. Against the white snow they looked like black columns. Immobile, they waited.

Soon, above the gray sky, from two different directions, came a pale pink patch. Fire! This must have been the signal the Germans were waiting for. Two of them moved closer to the hut. An explosion, a broken window were followed by desperate cries. Were these voices real, or was it an illusion? Eagerly the fire spread into all directions, up and around, and around again. With it came black thick clouds.

Suddenly the door fell. Someone ran through it. It was a girl. She ran ahead with her arms moving widely trying to push away the fumes. Her new shiny black boots contrasted sharply with the white snow. A long, thick golden pigtail, half undone, bounced against her back. Janka had escaped from the burning grave! The Germans lifted their machine guns but did not aim. Was it a miracle? Would they let fate decide and spare the girl? No; they were teasing! Only for a moment did they give hope. Hope that made what followed even more horrible. They fired several shots. The girl staggered, lost her balance. With out-stretched arms, like a wounded bird, she fell facing toward heaven. In no time two Germans were at the victim's side. Like hyenas, they came to inspect their prey. Were they still searching for signs of life? No. They were tempted by something else. Roughly, one of them pulled the boots off the dead body. Another grabbed the girl's golden pigtail and dragged her over the snowy ground. When he came close to the burning hut he lifted her up like a useless discarded sack and tossed her into the flames.

Making sure that all went according to plan, the Germans continued to stand guard. They left only when faced with a heap of half-burned ashes.[20]

Occasionally, the authorities would spare the very young. This, for example, happened to Henryk Kryszewicz Wołosymowicz. Too young to remember, he knows the family's history. During the war Henryk's parents had sheltered Jews. One night the Germans came to their farm, shot his father and the Jews. They took the mother to prison, but she never came back. Two years old, Henryk and his four young siblings were spared.[21]

At times the Nazis would show leniency even toward the guilty. The Polish socialist Płuskowski was among these few fortunate cases. A clerk in the city administration of Warsaw, he was assigned during the war to the Warsaw ghetto. There Płuskowski established contact with the Jewish underground and provided them with forged documents and ammunition. After the liquidation of the Warsaw ghetto he continued to shelter Jews. Eventually, the Nazis caught up with him and sent him to a concentration camp in Germany. He was liberated by the Americans in 1945.[22]

In sharp contrast was the fate of the young Pole, Nowak. In the spring of 1944 in Skarzysko at the age of twenty-five, he was publicly hanged in the town's square. His crime was the smuggling of food to starving Jews who lived and worked in a local ammunition factory.[23]

The wide range of punishments is further illustrated by the burning of entire villages. In the winter of 1944 the Germans learned that the village of Huta Pienacka offered food and occasional shelter to about 100 Jews from the surrounding forests. As a reprisal, the Nazis, together with the Ukrainian police, surrounded the village and set fire to it allowing no one to leave. All day long the assailants kept watch, making sure that no one left. In this case even the an-imals were made to share the fate of the villagers.[24]

Despite occasional and partial lapses, the principle of collective responsibility remained an awesome reality, as a rule including the rescuer's entire family. Did this principle prevent Poles with families from participating in Jewish rescue? Not likely. Most Polish helpers were married, and many had children.[25] Moreover, a majority said that in their efforts to save Jews they had the support of their families.[26]

Yet some Poles preferred to conceal their help to Jews even from those with whom they shared a home. Some rescuers were not sure they could trust their relatives; others wanted to shield their families from anxiety and possibly from death.

Staszek, a carriage maker, was among the rescuers who kept his aid activities secret from the relatives in his household. A young unmarried man, he lived with his mother and sister, who he felt would have objected to his protection of Jews. Initially, Staszek offered shelter to one close friend, who then asked that this privilege be extended to his relatives and friends. Requests for shelter from new people continued to grow but Staszek was unable to refuse, rationalizing that saving one Jew could lead to the same death penalty as saving many. Eventually, he was keeping thirty-two fugitives in a bunker he had built underneath his house.

At one point the Nazis caught him in a raid and were about to send him to Germany for labor. Knowing that the lives of thirty-two people depended on his freedom, disregarding caution, he escaped. This was only one of many close calls, but no matter what happened he was determined, and he continued to take care of his group for almost two years. Until the very end neither his mother nor his sister knew that anyone else besides Staszek shared their home. All survived. For his valor Staszek was awarded a gold medal by the Israeli government.[27]

When helping Jews, then, Poles had to overcome several layers of obstacles. The outer and strongest layer was the Nazi prohibition that made helping Jews a crime punishable by death. Next came the explicit anti-Jewish ideologies and the pervasive anti-Semitism that made help to Jews both a highly dangerous and disapproved of activity. Last, these Poles had to overcome their own diffuse cultural anti-

Semitism. While struggling with these layers of impediments, what kind of aid did these Poles offer? What was involved in offering this aid?

Notes

1. Lucy S. Dawidowicz, *The War against the Jews, 1933–1945* (New York: Holt, Rinehart and Winston, 1975), 395.

2. Here are a few of the many sources that describe what life was like for the Poles under the Nazi occupation: Władysław Bartoszewski, *1859 Dni Warszawy* [1859 Warsaw days] (Kraków: Wydawnictwo Znak, 1974); Władysław Bartoszewski, *Straceni Na Ulicach Miasta* [Perished in the streets of the city] (Warszawa: Książka I Wiedza, 1970); Ludwik Landau, *Kronika Lat Wojny I Okupacji* [War chronicle], 3 vols. (Warszawa: Państwowe Wydawnictwo Naukowe, 1962); Landau perished while trying to survive by passing. Stefan Korboński, *The Polish Underground State: A Guide to the Underground* (Boulder, Colo.: East European Quarterly, 1978); Stanisław Wroński and Maria Zwolakowa, *Polacy I Żydzi, 1939–1945* [Poles and Jews] (Warszawa: Książka I Wiedza, 1971).

3. Nora Levin, *The Holocaust* (New York: Schocken Books, 1973), 163.

4. Władysław Bartoszewski, *The Blood Shed Unites Us* (Warsaw: Interpress Publishers, 1970), 229.

5. Levin, *Holocaust,* 163; Wroński and Zwolakowa, *Poles and Jews,* 450.

6. Stefa thought that initially her husband might have been paid by Laminski for accepting his mistress. Money she felt was her husband's reason for accepting Irena.

7. For an excellent account and study of the Polish Warsaw uprising, see Janusz Z. Zawodny, *Nothing but Honor: The Story of the Warsaw Uprising, 1944* (Stanford, Calif.: Hoover Institution Press, 1979).

8. After coming across Irena's testimony, I asked Stefa Dworek's permission to use it. By using it I am revealing the real name of Mrs. Dworek which is Stanisława Davidžiuk. She answered me promptly, allowing me to use her name whenever I choose. Even though the real name of this rescuer and the rescued can be easily traced through the reference below, in the text in line with my established procedure I prefer to use a fictitious name.

9. Władysław Bartoszewski and Zofia Lewinówna, *Ten Jest Z Ojczyzny Mojej* [This one is from my country] (Kraków: Wydawnictwo Znak, 1969), 582–584.

10. Ludwik Hirszfeld, *Historia Jednego Życia* [The story of one life] (Warszawa: Pax, 1957), 424.

11. Izabella Stachowicz Czajka, *Ocalił Mnie Kowal* [I was saved by a blacksmith] (Warszawa: Czytelnik, 1956).

12. Oskar Pinkus, *The House of Ashes* (New York: The World Publishing House Co., 1964), 198.

13. Ibid., 223.

14. I am reiterating what I have already said in the introductory chapter. For a comprehensive treatment of this issue, see Helen Fein, *Accounting for Genocide* (New York: The Free Press, 1979).

15. Lucy S. Dawidowicz, ed., *A Holocaust Reader* (New York: Behrman House Inc., 1976), 67.

16. In some Polish sources it has been asserted that Poland was the only European country where an official law demanded the death sentence for saving Jews. See Bartoszewski, *Blood Shed Unites Us,* 227; Tatiana Berenstein and Adam Rutkowski, "O Ratowaniu Żydow Przez Polaków W Okresie Okupacji Hitlerowskiej" [Saving Jews by Poles during Hitler's occupation], *Biuletyn Zydowskiego Instytutu Historycznego,* no. 35 (1960): 3–46; Wroński and Zwolakowa, *Poles and Jews,* 402. The document in the text was excerpted from Wroński and Zwolakowa, *Poles and Jews,* 436. Note that not all executions had to do with the rescuing of Jews.

17. In the protectorate of Bohemia and Morawia, in the wake of the Heydrich assassination in 1942, Kurt Daluege, the new reich protector, "issued an ordinance establishing the death penalty for anyone aiding or failing to report persons engaged in activities hostile to the Reich, including sheltering Jews." See Livia Rothkirchen, "Czech Attitudes towards the Jews during Nazi Regime," *Yad Vashem Studies* 13 (1979): 314. This information is especially important, since the Czechs generally had a positive record of Jewish toleration. Still, 90 percent of the Czech Jews died and, according to Rothkirchen, only 424 survived in hiding (315). I am grateful to Lawrence Baron for bringing these facts to my attention.

  I also found a reference to Norway stating that "the Germans made public announcements in Norwegian that anyone extending aid to Jews in the way either of clothing, food or shelter would be liable to execution together with his family. Perhaps the phrase "would be liable" suggests that execution was only a possibility because the statement continues: ". . . several hundred patriots were interned in the Grini concentration camp." Arieh L. Bauminger, *Roll of Honor* (Jerusalem: Yad Vashem, 1970), 64.

18. Wroński and Zwolakowa, *Poles and Jews,* 417.

19. I have translated freely from the Polish. See Bartoszewski and Lewinówna, *This One Is from My Country,* 855–859.

20. I have translated freely from the Polish. Ibid., 862–865.

21. Ibid., 868.

22. Philip Friedman, *Their Brothers' Keepers* (New York: Holocaust Library, 1978), 127.

23. Wroński and Zwolakowa, *Poles and Jews,* 435.

24. Ibid., 433.

25. Of the 189 rescuers in my sample, 60 percent were married, 7 percent widowed, and 33 percent single. Also, 43 percent of them had children and 57 percent were childless.

26. Considered in terms of family support for rescue, the information is as follows:

Family situation	Percent
Family supports efforts to save Jews	60
Family opposes, disapproves of efforts to save Jews	12
Live alone	28
	n = 144

27. Staszek's case is described in Ruth M. Gruber, "The Pole Who Saved 32 Jews," *Hadassah Magazine,* December 1968, 21, 36.

TATYANA KONTSEVICH, BEREZHANY, UKRAINE... 1944 – Tatyana and her family hid Shimon Redlich, his mother, and his aunt and uncle in their attic for several months during the war. German soldiers often tried to search the attic, but Tatyana succeeded in diverting the soldiers from the secret hiding place. In the photograph are Tatyana with her daughter and son. (JFR Photo Archives)

GÉZÁNÉ HERCZEGH, BUDAPEST, HUNGARY... 1944 – While her husband was away on a forced labor detail, Gézáné and her family hid and fed eighteen Jews in the cellar of their office building. (JFR Photo Archives)

PANAYOTIS AND LEONIDAS GIORTSAS, CALOTHRONION, GREECE... 1941 – Aron Yerushalmi, Moshe Weinbaum and Asher Schwarz, three Jews from Palestine, volunteered to serve in the British army. They were captured by the Germans in Greece but managed to escape from the train bound for Germany. The men fled from village to village in search of food and shelter. They received little help until they met Panayotis and his father, Leonidas, who fed, clothed and sheltered the men. Leonidas procured false identity cards for Aron, Moshe and Asher, and father and son accompanied the soldiers to Athens where they were given shelter by relatives. When Aron and Asher were captured, Panayotis returned to Athens for Moshe and took him back to the village. In August 1942, Moshe was arrested by the Italians and sent to a prison camp. Panayotis managed to bring him food. In 1946, Leonidas was killed by the Communists and his home was burned. Taken in 1942, the photograph shows Asher Schwarz and Moshe Weinbaum (top row, left to right) and Aron Yerushalmi, Leonidas Giortsas, and a friend (bottom row, left to right). (JFR Photo Archives)

Raul Hilberg **Helpers, Gainers, and Onlookers**

IN THE COURSE OF THE ONSLAUGHT on European Jewry, some people in the non-Jewish population helped their Jewish neighbors, many more did or obtained something at the expense of the Jews, and countless others watched what had come to pass.

Help was by and large scarce and it was rendered most often at the last moment, after the start of roundups or deportations. Even then, the helpers seldom took the initiative. Sometimes the Jews were warned of danger, as in the French city of Clermont-Ferrand, where telephone calls or personal messages, some of them from gendarmes or secretaries, reached prospective deportees.[1] In Denmark there was an actual search for people in need, but in the usual case throughout Europe, the potential rescuer was approached by a victim or by someone already engaged in assisting stranded people. In short, most of the helpers were initially passive and most recipients of their kindness had already taken the critical step of leaving an apartment, ghetto, or camp.

There were two kinds of help. One was occasional, transitory, and relatively risk-free, such as alerting an unsuspecting victim of planned arrests, giving directions to fleeing Jews, diverting pursuers, or providing destitute individuals with small amounts of food, clothing, or money. The second was the more durable help, particularly shelter over time. Often enough payment was tendered for such protection, but that is not to say that the helper acted solely for profit or even that, all things considered, there was a business deal. For Poles or Ukrainians, a German discovery of their acts could be lethal.

What kind of persons were helpers? Basically, one may distinguish between people who wanted to save specific individuals or categories of individuals and those who willingly assisted almost any Jews, including total strangers. The selective helpers included first of all friends, relatives by intermarriage, and former business associates, employers, or employees. In all these situations a relationship or bond had been formed before the war, and there might have been some expectation of assistance in times of trouble. Sometimes, a gentile household was prepared to harbor a Jewish child. This kind of decision was considered when Jewish parents were in dire circumstances. There were also occasions when a non-Jewish man was attracted to a Jewish woman or when a gentile woman was drawn to a Jewish man. Probably, most of these encounters were brief or even casual. When relationships developed, they were obviously complicated, especially for a Jewish woman, even if no compulsion was exercised by the man. Of this, little is said in memoirs.[2]

The less discriminating helpers were motivated either by opposition to the German regime or by feelings of pure sympathy or humanitarian obligation. The oppositionists were sometimes political, like Oskar Schindler, who filled a plant with Jewish workers in order to save them, or Polish sanitation workers who helped Jews hiding in the sewers of Lvov, or several left-wing or Communist German civilians in the Bialystok area who actually supplied Jewish resisters in the ghetto with weapons.[3] The humanitarians have been the subject of an extensive literature.[4] They have been called altruists, righteous gentiles, and good samaritans, but there is little that they outwardly had in common. They were men or women, older or younger, richer or poorer. Like the perpetrators, whose exact opposites they were, they could not explain their motivations. They would characterize their actions as ordinary or natural, and after the war some of them were embarrassed by praise. Often they were members of a community, like the Protestants of Le Chambon in France, who sheltered many Jews in a small area, or they were at least in touch with like-minded people in a loose network of helpers. Many of them had to make their decisions instantaneously. In this sense, they shared a personality characteristic with the Jewish fugitive who also acted rapidly. Finally, they had to have the inner flexibility to alter or abandon personal routines, particularly if a promise of three days of safety had to be extended to three weeks or three months.[5] They might indeed have been reluctant to make concession after concession, and there might have been tension between them and their lodgers, but they were still in a special category by virtue of the choice they had made.

Gainers outnumbered givers in the Jewish catastrophe. In many instances, little or nothing had to be done by the beneficiaries to enjoy the largesse. When Jewish enterprises were liquidated, the non-Jewish manufacturers and distributors automatically gained market shares. Jewish emigration, followed by ghettoization and deportation, freed well over 1 million apartments, although sometimes, as in Minsk, ghetto dwellings were rejected by dissatisfied ethnic Germans.[6] Levies imposed on Jewish communities were occasionally distributed to local inhabitants, as in Tunisia, and so on.

Active profiting was not eschewed either. Already in 1933 German medical students persecuted their fellow Jewish students to rid themselves of the competition.[7] German enterprises and their agents in banks, coveting a Jewish business, would take over their prey in unequal negotiations, assisted by regulations of the state. In black market trading in occupied Poland, the Polish suppliers were in a position to siphon off cash and valuables from the victims. Some individuals turned in escaping Jews for monetary rewards, and some extorted money or possessions from victims trying to live in hiding or disguise. When the Jews were already dead, the looters became busy. In the Radom District they rummaged in emptied ghettos tearing out everything they could. In Riga, they broke into piled-up suitcases, and on the site of Belzec, where the Germans had shut down a death camp, they searched for gold in the ashes.[8] Non-German takers making use of their various opportunities, as in Slovakia, were heard to say: "Better we than the Germans."[9]

During the stages of concentration, deportations, and killings, the perpetrators tried to isolate the victims from public view. The administrators of destruction did not want untoward publicity about their work. They wanted to avoid criticism of their methods by passers-by. Their psychic balance was jeopardized enough, especially in the field, and any sympathy extended to the victim was bound to result in additional psychological as well as operational complications. Voyeurs were not welcomed either. Such watching, especially by Germans, was considered an indecency. But regardless of whether the spectacle repelled or attracted the viewer, any rumors and stories carried from the scene were an irritant and a threat to the perpetrator.

Precautions were consequently plentiful. In Germany, Jews were sometimes moved out in the early morning hours before there was traffic in the streets. Furniture vans without windows were used to take Jews to trains. Loading might be planned for a siding where human waste was collected. In Poland, the local German administrators would order the Polish population to stay indoors and keep the windows closed with blinds drawn during roundups of Jews, even though such a directive was notice of an impending action. Shooting sites, as in Babi Yar in Kiev, were selected to be at least beyond hearing distance of local residents.

Not all of these measures were totally successful. To begin with, the actuality could not be hidden in any case. The non-Jewish population did not have to view the proceedings to realize that the Jews were disappearing. In the small railroad station at Sobibor, a Polish switchman just outside the camp became aware of the silence. "Forty cars had arrived and then – nothing."[10] Beyond inference, there were glimpses of the action itself. Some of these discoveries were made by people who stumbled upon the occurrence. Thus in occupied Poland, a German army inspector complained that soldiers had become inadvertent witnesses of an operation in which blows with rifle butts were delivered to the bodies of Jewish women in advanced stages of pregnancy.[11] Often enough the onlookers could not be barred. In 1943 on the island of Corfu they gathered to watch from street corners and balconies.[12] In the Hungarian city of Szeged, where Jews were marched, flanked by Hungarian gendarmes, to the train one morning in 1944, people stood in the street and laughed.[13] The hanging of two Jews in Zhitomir during 1941 was watched by a crowd of soldiers from rooftops.[14]

In Munich an SS lieutenant was on trial before the highest SS and Police court for photographing shootings he had ordered. He had the film developed in two private shops in southern Germany and then showed the photographs to his wife and various acquaintances, risking the spread of their contents across the border into neutral Switzerland. The SS court could not condone such behavior.[15]

The observers had gained access to a secret. Some of them indicated to the victims that they knew something, but without sharing their insight with clarity. Once, unsuspecting Jewish deportees on their way to Sobibor heard Polish voices utter the incomprehensible words: "Jews, you are going to burn!"[16] Another time, Polish peasants gestured to Jews on their way to Treblinka that their throats would be cut.[17] And that is where they left it, between a warning and a taunt.

Notes

1. John F. Sweets, *Choices in Vichy France* (Oxford and New York, 1986), 132.
2. In the Galician area of Poland, German private company managers kept Jewish women as sexual slaves. Report by the Security Service in Galicia (Kommandeur of Security Police/III-A-4) to Obersturmbannführer (Lieutenant Colonel) Karl Gengenbach and Obersturmbannführer Willi Seibert in Berlin and to Standartenführer (Colonel) Heim in Krakow, July 2, 1943, National Archives of the United States Record Group 242, T 175, Roll 575. See also the novel about a Pole and a Jewish woman by Hermann Field and Stanislaw Mierzenski, *Angry Harvest* (New York, 1958).
3. On Schindler, see Thomas Keneally, *Schindler's List* (New York, 1982). On Lvov, see Philip Friedman, *Their Brothers' Keepers* (New York, 1957), 207. On Bialystok, see the statement by Liza Czapnik in Jüdisches Historisches Institut Warschau, *Faschismus – Getto – Massenmord* (Berlin, 1961), 500–502.
4. See in particular Nechama Tec, *When Light Pierced the Darkness* (New York and Oxford, 1986); Samuel P. Oliner and Pearl M. Oliner, *The Altruistic Personality* (New York, 1988); and the earlier work by Friedman, *Their Brothers' Keepers*.
5. See Jacob Presser, *The Destruction of the Dutch Jews* (New York, 1969), 381–405.
6. Stadkommissar Wilhelm Janetzke to Generalkommissar Wilhelm Kube, November 17, 1942, enclosing report by city inspector Herbert Löbel and city employee Werner Plenske, November 16, 1942, and Kube's reply expressing annoyance, November 20, 1942, U.S. Holocaust Memorial Museum Archives, Record Group 22.03 (Belarus Central State Archives), Roll 11, Fond 370, Opis 1, Folder 486.
7. Michael Kater, *Doctors under Hitler* (Chapel Hill, N.C., 1989), 169–72.
8. War Diary, Armament Command Radom, August 24, 1943, Wi/ID 1.37, folder once located in the Federal Records Center in Alexandria, Virginia. Neuendorff in Generalbezirk Latvia to Reichskommissar Ostland/IIh (Finance), December 4, 1941, National Archives Record Group 242, T 459, Roll 21. Large excerpt from the report of a Polish court in Zamosz, October 10, 1945, investigating Belzec, in Adalbert Rückerl, *NS-Vernichtungslager* (Munich, 1977), 143–45.
9. Thirteenth Situation Report of the German Security Service in Žilina, Slovakia, covering events of May 1942 in the Žilina transit camp, National Archives Record Group 242, T 175, Roll 584. The culprits, according to the report, were members of the Slovak Hlinka Guard who mistreated the captive Jews and took from them valuables, clothes, underwear, and shoes.
10. Statement by Jan Piwonski in Claude Lanzmann, *Shoah* (New York, 1986), 67.
11. Report by an army inspector in the Generalgouvernement of Poland for July 6–August 21, 1942 (signed Neuling), Yad Vashem Microfilm JM 3499.
12. Statement by Armando Aaron in Lanzmann, *Shoah,* 129.
13. Statement by Tibor Vago in Lea Rosh and Eberhard Jäckel, *Der Tod ist ein Meister aus Deutschland* (Hamburg, 1990), 289.
14. See the photographs and related German testimony in Ernst Klee, Willi Dressen, and Volker Riess, eds., *"Schöne Zeiten"* (Frankfurt am Main, 1988), 106–8.
15. Judgment of the SS and Police court in Munich against Max Täubner, May 25, 1943, reprinted in large excerpt in *ibid.*, 184–90.
16. Statement by Itzhak Lichtman in Miriam Novitch, *Sobibor* (New York, 1980), 80–85.
17. Statements by the Treblinka survivor Richard Glazar and by several Polish witnesses in Lanzmann, *Shoah*, 34–45, 37.

Dit is een foto, zoals ik me zou wensen, altijd zo te zijn. Dan had ik nog wel een kans om naar Holywood te komen. Maar tegenwoordig zie ik er jammergenoeg meestal anders uit.

Annefrank.
18 Oct. 1946
Zondag.

ANNE FRANK A page from Anne Frank's diary, which reads: "This is a photograph of me as I wish I looked all the time. Then I might still have a chance of getting to Hollywood. But at present, I'm afraid, I usually look quite different. Anne Frank, 10 October 1942, Sunday." (© AFF/AFS Amsterdam, The Netherlands)

MARGOT FRANK Margot Frank on roller-skates in Amsterdam. (© AFF/AFS Amsterdam, The Netherlands)

MIEP GIES, AMSTERDAM, THE NETHERLANDS... JULY 1942 – Miep Gies and her husband Henk were friends with Anne Frank's parents. In 1941, Otto Frank began to make plans for his family to go into hiding and he asked Miep if she would help. She said yes without hesitation. In 1942 when Margot Frank, Otto's oldest daughter, received orders for deportation, the family went into hiding. A total of eight Jews hid in a concealed annex to Otto Frank's factory.

Miep and three other helpers had to find food for the eight Jews in hiding. This was an enormous and dangerous job, as food was scarce and one could not buy it without German-issued ration coupons. Anne wrote in her diary on Sunday, July 11, 1943, "Miep has so much to carry, she looks like a pack mule. She goes forth every day to scrounge up vegetables, and then bicycles back with her purchases in large shopping bags. She is also the one who brings five library books with her every Saturday. We long for Saturdays because that means books ... Ordinary people don't know how much books can mean to someone cooped up. Our only diversions are reading, studying and listening to the radio."

On August 4, 1944, Miep was working quietly at her desk when a man in plain clothes burst through the door and pointed a gun straight at her. The eight Jews in hiding were betrayed for a bounty of 60 guilders. They were arrested and deported to concentration camps. Later that day, Miep climbed to the empty attic hiding space. Lying on the floor were Anne's diary and papers. Miep resolved that she would keep them for Anne's return. When friends found out about the arrest, they gave Miep money to see if she could bribe German officials to have them released. But her brave bid failed. She kept the diary and waited for Anne to return. Miep never read the diary.

Otto Frank was the only one of the eight to survive. When he returned from Auschwitz, he lived with the Gies family. Miep did not give Anne's diary to him, still hoping that she might return. Finally Otto Frank received a letter informing him that Anne and Margot died at Bergen-Belsen, just one month before the camp was liberated. It was then that Miep gave Otto the diary. In the photograph are Miep and Henk Gies on their wedding day. (© AFF/AFS Amsterdam, The Netherlands)

Miep Gies **Refugees**

It was the first Sunday in July, a warm summer night. Henk and I, Mrs. Samson, and the others had eaten our evening meal and were all engaged in our various activities. For me, Sunday evening meant doing small things to get ready for a new workweek.

These days anything unusual was immediately upsetting, and when there came an insistent ringing of our bell, tension rose in the apartment at the sound. Our eyes darted from one to another. Quickly, Henk went to the door and I followed him. There stood Herman van Daan in quite an agitated condition. Henk and I spoke quietly to him, not wanting to upset Mrs. Samson and her family.

"Come right away," Van Daan entreated in a hushed but urgent voice. "Margot Frank has received a postcard ordering her to appear for forced-labor shipment to Germany. She's been ordered to bring a suitcase with winter things. The Franks have decided to go immediately into hiding. Can you come right now to take a few things that they'll need in hiding? Their preparations aren't complete, you see."

"We will come," Henk told him. We put on our raincoats. To be seen carrying bags and packages would be too dangerous; we could hide much under our baggy old raincoats. It might appear odd to be wearing raincoats on a warm, dry summer night, but it was better than having bags full of possessions in our arms.

Henk made some explanation to Mrs. Samson so as not to alarm her and the others, and we left with Mr. van Daan. When Mr. Frank had confided in me about the hiding plan, I had that very night told Henk about our conversation. Without discussion, Henk had affirmed his unconditional assistance to the Franks and agreed that the plan was a sound one. But neither of us had expected the Franks to go into hiding this soon. Walking quickly but not hurrying, in order not to attract attention, we went toward the Merwedeplein. On the way, Van Daan told us that

Mr. Frank had just told his girls about the hiding plan but not where the hiding place was.

"You can imagine," he explained, "they're in a state of great confusion. There's so much to do and so little time, and their damned lodger seems to be hanging about, making it all quite difficult."

Walking to the Franks', I suddenly felt a great sense of urgency for my friends. Conscripting a sixteen-year-old girl for forced labor was a new abomination the Germans were inflicting on the Jews. Yes, I thought, the sooner our friends got safely out of sight, the better. And how many more young girls like Margot have they conscripted? Girls with no father like Mr. Frank and no hiding plan? Girls who must be horribly frightened tonight. With these thoughts, I had to force myself not to run the rest of the way to the Merwedeplein.

When we arrived at the Frank apartment, few words were exchanged. I could feel their urgency, an undercurrent of near-panic. But I could see that much needed to be organized and prepared. It was all too terrible. Mrs. Frank handed us piles of what felt like children's clothes and shoes.

I was in such a state myself that I didn't look. I just took and took as much as I could, hiding the bunches of things the best way I could under my coat, in my pockets, under Henk's coat, in his pockets. The plan was that I'd bring these things to the hiding place at some later date when our friends were safely inside.

With our coats bursting, Henk and I made our way back to our rooms and quickly unloaded what we'd had under our coats. We put it all under our bed. Then, our coats empty again, we hurried back to the Merwedeplein to get another load.

Because of the Franks' lodger, the atmosphere at the Frank apartment was muted and disguised. Everyone was making an effort to seem normal, not to run, not to raise a voice. More things were handed to us.

Reprinted with the permission of Simon & Schuster from **Anne Frank Remembered: The Story of the Woman Who Helped to Hide the Frank Family** by Miep Gies and Alison Leslie Gold, 93–98. Copyright © 1987 by Miep Gies and Alison Leslie Gold.

Mrs. Frank bundled, and sorted quickly, and gave to us as we again took and took. Her hair was escaping from her tight bun into her eyes. Anne came in, bringing too many things; Mrs. Frank told her to take them back. Anne's eyes were like saucers, a mixture of excitement and terrible fright.

Henk and I took as much as we could, and quickly left.

Early the next day, Monday, I woke to the sound of rain.

Before seven thirty, as we had arranged the night before, I had ridden my bicycle to the Merwedeplein. No sooner had I reached the front stoop than the door of the Franks' apartment opened and Margot emerged. Her bike was standing outside. Margot had not handed her bicycle in as ordered. Mr. and Mrs. Frank were inside, and Anne, wide-eyed in a nightgown, hung back inside the doorway.

I could tell that Margot was wearing layers of clothing. Mr. and Mrs. Frank looked at me. Their eyes pierced mine.

I made an effort to be assuring. "Don't worry. The rain is very heavy. Even the Green Police won't want to go out in it. The rain will provide a shelter."

"Go," Mr. Frank instructed us, taking a look up and down the square. "Anne and Edith and I will come later in the morning. Go now."

Without a backward glance, Margot and I pushed our bicycles onto the street. Quickly, we pedaled away from the Merwedeplein, going north at the first turning. We pedaled evenly, not too fast, in order to appear like two everyday working girls on their way to work on a Monday morning.

Not one Green Policeman was out in the downpour. I took the big crowded streets, from the Merwedeplein to Waalstraat, then to the left to Noorder Amstellaan to Ferdinand Bolstraat, Vijzelstraat to Rokin, Dam Square, Raadhuisstraat, finally turning onto the Prinsengracht, never so glad before to see our cobbled street and murky canal.

All the way we had not said one word. We both knew that from the moment we'd mounted our bicycles we'd become criminals. There we were, a Christian and a Jew without the yellow star, riding on an illegal bicycle. And at a time when the Jew was ordered to report for a forced-labor brigade about to

leave for parts unknown in Hitler's Germany. Margot's face showed no intimidation. She betrayed nothing of what she was feeling inside. Suddenly we'd become two allies against the might of the German beast among us.

Not a soul was about on the Prinsengracht. After opening the door, we carried our bicycles into the storeroom, then we left the room and shut the door. I opened the next door to the office and shut the door against the rain. We were soaked through to the skin. I could see that Margot was suddenly on the verge of crumbling.

I took her arm and led her past Mr. Frank's office and up the stairway to the landing that led to the hiding place. It was approaching the time that the others would be coming to work. I was now afraid that someone would come, but I kept silent.

Margot was now like someone stunned, in shock. I could feel her shock now that we were inside. As she opened the door, I gripped her arm to give her courage. Still, we said nothing. She disappeared behind the door and I took my place in the front office.

My heart too was thumping. I sat at my desk wondering how I could get my mind onto my work. The pouring summer rain had been our shelter. Now one person was safe inside the hiding place. Three more had to be protected by the rain.

Mr. Koophuis arrived at work and took Margot's bicycle somewhere that I didn't know. Soon after he left I could hear the warehouseman arriving, stamping the water off his shoes.

Late in the morning I heard Mr. and Mrs. Frank and Anne coming through the front office door. I had been waiting for that moment and quickly joined them and hurried them along past Mr. Kraler's office up the stairway to the door of the hiding place. All three of them were quite wet. They were carrying a few things, and all had yellow stars sewn onto their clothes. I opened the door for them and shut it when they had vanished inside.

In the afternoon when no one was around and all was quiet, I went upstairs to that door myself and disappeared into the hiding place, closing the door tight behind me.

Entering the rooms for the first time, I was surprised by what I saw. In total disorder were sacks and boxes and furnishings, piles of things. I could not imagine how all these things had been brought up to the hiding place. I had not once noticed anything being brought in. Perhaps it had been brought at night, or on Sundays when the office was closed.

On this floor there were two quite small rooms. One was rectangular with a window, and the other long and thin, also with a window. The rooms were wood-paneled, the wood painted a dark green, the wallpaper old and yellowish and peeling in places. The windows were covered by thick, white, makeshift curtains. There was a toilet in a large room, with a dressing area off to the side.

Up a steep flight of old wooden steps was a large room with sink and stove and cabinets. Here too the windows were covered with curtains. Off this large room was another rickety stairway to an attic and storage area. The steps to the attic cut through a tiny garret-type room, again filled with piles and sacks of things.

Mrs. Frank and Margot were like lost people, drained of blood, in conditions of complete lethargy. They appeared as though they couldn't move. Anne and her father were making efforts to create some order out of the multitude of objects, pushing, carrying, clearing. I asked Mrs. Frank, "What can I do?"

She shook her head. I suggested, "Let me bring some food?"

She acquiesced. "A few things only, Miep — maybe some bread, a little butter; maybe milk?"

The situation was very upsetting. I wanted to leave the family alone together. I couldn't begin to imagine what they must be feeling to have walked away from everything they owned in the world — their home; a lifetime of gathered possessions; Anne's little cat, Moortje. Keepsakes from the past. And friends.

They had simply closed the door of their lives and had vanished from Amsterdam. Mrs. Frank's face said it all. Quickly, I left them.

MALWINA SAWKO, PODHAJCE, POLAND... JUNE 1943 – Israel Friedman bribed a German officer to give him and his daughter Berta a four-day pass from the ghetto to buy food in the countryside. The ghetto was liquidated while they were away. Their entire family had been murdered. Israel and Berta found shelter on the farm of Malwina Sawko and her parents, Jozef and Antonia. Israel and Berta lived in an earthen hole under the cowshed for almost two years. When the Russian Army liberated the area in February 1944, they fled from their hiding place in the middle of the night so no one would know that the Sawko family had sheltered them. Pictured in the photograph are Malwina and her husband. (JFR Photo Archives)

GONCHAR FAMILY, IOCIPENOK, UKRAINE... SUMMER 1942 – When the Germans began to liquidate the ghetto, Rachelle and her daughter Valentina escaped and went to the Gonchar family for help. Denis, Fedora, and their two teenage sons Stepan and Ivan did not turn away their friends. In the winter Rachelle and Valentina lived in a small hole behind the oven and in the summer they lived in the shed. The brothers brought them food and water every day. The Gonchars obtained forged papers that enabled Valentina to get a job while her mother remained hidden. The village was liberated by the Russians in March 1944 and Rachelle and her daughter returned to their home. With Denis and Fedora Gonchar in the photograph are their sons Stepan and Ivan. (JFR Photo Archives)

Carol Rittner, R.S.M. and Sondra Myers **Magda Trocmé**

My husband, André Trocmé, was a Protestant minister. During the war, we lived with our four children in the small village of Le Chambon-sur-Lignon in central France. People were content to be there, and we were happy to be able to take care of them, although it was the first time that we lived among peasants. Previously, we had lived in a city, but we appreciated this change, because it is always interesting to get to know different people.

The village of Le Chambon was a Protestant one, with a big church. On Sundays the sermon was something very important, because at that time there were no movies, no special lectures. The sermon was something that everyone wanted to hear. My husband's preaching was different because he was a conscientious objector. The Protestant Church was not happy about it, because at that time conscientious objectors were not admitted as ministers. But the parish wanted a man like my husband, not only because of his ideas about war and peace but on account of his general ideas about truth and justice.

My husband was a very impressive man. He was interesting and genuine, original. He always thought that he had to preach for peace, for better love and understanding. The parish asked for him because the people wanted him. So later, when the danger came, how could they not back him?

My husband's mother was German and his father French. My father was Italian and my mother was Russian; we were a good combination. We tried to encourage the parish to be more broad-minded than they perhaps would have been if they had not been living with international people.

We had the opportunity to go to see our families, sometimes in Italy, sometimes in Germany, and we saw what was going on there, especially in Germany. Even before the war, we already knew the truth about what was happening to Jews and others. It was not that we were more clever than the others, but we had more experience and could guess what would happen

if the Germans invaded France. Little by little, André tried to prepare the population, preaching to them, preparing them to stand fast. When the dangers came, we were not surprised.

The people in our village knew already what persecutions were because their ancestors were the old Huguenots who, when they accepted the Reformation, were persecuted by the Catholic kings of France. They talked often about their ancestors. Many years went by and they forgot, but when the Germans came, they remembered and were able to understand the persecution of the Jews better perhaps than people in other villages, for they had already had a kind of preparation.

When *la drôle guerre*, the "funny war," was declared in 1939, nothing happened. We knew, of course, that the Germans were coming always nearer to us. We also realized that our government was changing, that Marshal Pétain, who was a very old man, had become the head of the government and that many people believed in him and thought he was like the flag – a symbol – because he was a national hero from World War I. But what many people did not realize was that World War I was very different from World War II.

After the fall of France, André went on preaching as he always did. He spoke against the war. Little by little the Germans, having crossed the border and being in Paris, arrived in our region. The danger was there. They started to persecute the Jews, but we never imagined what would happen to the Jews in France.

Even before the Germans crossed the Vichy line, some Jews managed to get into our part of France, and they tried to come to where we were. It started with the French Jews who often came to our village for the summer. Our peasants were so poor that they took paying guests in the summer. Some of the French Jews were in Le Chambon before the real danger came because they were afraid to stay in the city.

They were afraid of the Germans because they knew something about what was happening in Germany. Then the German Jews came. At first, they were paying guests in the hotels and at the farms. Later they became refugees.

Why did they come to us? Because we were in the mountains, because it was a Protestant place, because someone had spoken, perhaps, of a minister who at that time had funny ideas, who was a conscientious objector. You could not know how people knew that they might have a good place in our town. I can tell you what happened in our house, but I cannot tell you what happened in other houses, although I know that little by little there were Jews all over the place.

When the "funny war" started to be a real one, a poor woman came to my house one night, and she asked to come in. She said immediately that she was a German Jew, that she was running away, that she was hiding, that she wanted to have shelter. She thought that at the minister's house she would perhaps find someone who could understand her. And I said, "Come in." And so it started. I did not know that it would be dangerous. Nobody thought of that.

But all at once, many people were in the village. When you hear that there are nice people who will receive you in their homes in a certain place, and you think you are in danger — and later when you really are in danger — you will do anything to get there. But there was no advertisement. They just came.

Those of us who received the first Jews did what we thought had to be done — nothing more complicated. It was not decided from one day to the next what we would have to do. There were many people in the village who needed help. How could we refuse them? A person doesn't sit down and say I'm going to do this and this and that. We had no time to think. When a problem came, we had to solve it immediately. Sometimes people ask me, "How did you make a decision?" There was no decision to make. The issue was: Do you think we are all brothers or not? Do you think it is unjust to turn in the Jews or not? Then let us try to help!"

It was not something extraordinary. Now that the years have gone by, perhaps we exaggerate things a little, although I can tell you that things did get complicated later. But in the beginning, when the first Jew came to my house, I just opened the door and took her in without knowing what would happen later. It was even simpler than one might suppose.

In the beginning, we did not realize the danger was so big. Later, we became accustomed to it, but you must remember that the danger was all over. The people who were in the cities had bombs coming down and houses coming in on their heads, and they were killed. Others were dying in the war, in battles. Other people were being persecuted, like those in Germany. It was a general danger, and we did not feel we were in much more danger than the others. And, you see, the danger was not what you might imagine.

You might imagine that the people were fighting with weapons in the middle of the square, that you would have had to run away, that you would have had to go into a little street and hide. The danger was not that kind at all. The danger was in having a government that, little by little, came into the hands of the Germans, with their laws, and the French people were supposed to obey those laws.

The police were no longer "French" police; they were police that acted for the Vichy government that was under the Germans. At that time, we were more afraid of the police and the Vichy government than we were of the Germans, who were not yet really in our country.

We started to disobey in very little ways. For example, in our school it was suggested that we put a picture of Marshal Pétain on the wall. We decided not to do it. It was a small disobedience, but then we started to be more disobedient. In the mornings, to give another example, the flag had to be put up in front of the school and the children were supposed to salute it. We decided not to do it. Ours was a private school, a school founded by the Protestants, not the school of the state. The state school did as the marshal said, but we disobeyed.

Because the director of the public school was one of our friends, he said, "You don't want a flag. I understand. If they want to salute the flag, they can come to my school." At that time, we were just across the street. For a while, some teachers and students went to the flag at the public school. Little by little, it was forgotten and it stopped.

It is true that we had Jewish children in our village. Once when my husband was in Marseilles, he spoke to Burns Chalmers, who was responsible for many of the Quakers' activities on behalf of the inmates of the concentration camps in the south of France. André told him that he wanted to volunteer to go to one of the French camps where there were Jewish children and help take care of them. Chalmers said to him, "But Monsieur Trocmé, we have volunteers for the camps. We have lots of volunteers for the camps. What we do not have is a place, a village, a house, a place to put people who are hiding, people that we can save. We get people out of the camps, but nobody wants them. It is dangerous to take them. Is your village prepared to do such a thing?"

My husband came back to the village and he spoke to the council of the church, and they said, "OK, go ahead." Within minutes, they were willing to help. They did not always agree one hundred percent with all that my husband said, but they agreed in general with him, and so they helped.

Yes, there were dangers, but up until then, nothing had happened. More and more we would disobey. We had a habit of doing it. One day, finally, the governor – the prefect of the Department of the Haute-Loire – Monsieur Bach, came and said to my husband, "Now you must give the names of all the Jews that are here." It was at the time that the Jews had to put on the sign, the yellow star.

My husband said, "No, I cannot. First, I do not know their names" – they often changed their names – "and I don't know who they are. And second, these Jews, they are my brothers."

"No," Monsieur Bach said, "they are not your brothers. They are not of your religion. They are not of your country."

"No, you are wrong," André responded. "Here, they are under my protection."

"You must give me their names," said the prefect, "or who knows? Maybe you will be taken to prison, if you don't tell me who they are."

Immediately I prepared a suitcase. I put into it everything that I thought would be necessary in prison, something warm, a change, and so on. We called that suitcase "the prison suitcase." Then the prefect left, and it was put aside.

Some months later, it was February 13, 1943, around seven o'clock in the evening, two *gendarmes* knocked at the door of the old parsonage in Le Chambon-sur-Lignon. I was cooking and my husband was not home. They asked to see Pastor Trocmé, and I told them that he was at a meeting, and that he was coming back later, but that I could answer all their questions because I knew all about my husband's work. They said that it was something very personal and that they wanted to wait. So I put them in his office, and I went on cooking, doing whatever I had to do, and I forgot about them. When my husband came back, it was about eight o'clock or eight-thirty, he rushed into the house, with his Bible under his arm, with his papers, and went into his office. After awhile he came out and said, "I've been arrested." Why arrested? At that time, nobody even dared to ask why such things happened.

And I said, "Oh my goodness, what about the suitcase?" It was now February and the suitcase was empty, because it had been put together the past August.

And then the *gendarme* said, "What is this suitcase business?" So I told him and he said I could have all the time I needed to prepare André's things, but that no friends or neighbors could be aware of what was happening. These *gendarmes*, you know, were French people, and they were very much worried about doing what they were doing. It was a dirty job, but what could they do? If you are a *gendarme*, you arrest people. There we were, and it was time to eat, so I said to the *gendarmes*, "Sit down and eat."

People now, when they write a book, or when they write a newspaper article, or a magazine article, or when they speak of these things, they say, "Oh, what a wonderful woman. The *gendarmes* came to arrest her husband, and she invited them to sit down and eat with them." It was nothing at all. We always said, "Sit down," when somebody came. Why not say it to the *gendarmes*? And besides, I had to hunt around for the suitcase so that I could pack it. They could just as well sit down and get out of the way.

Before my husband left, you cannot imagine what happened. A young girl, Suzanne Gibert, rang the doorbell. Her father was a church counsellor, and we had been invited to their home because it was her father's birthday. Of course, we had forgotten because of all the excitement. She came, saw the police, ran away, told everyone what was happening in the parsonage, and a few minutes later, the people of the village started a sort of "procession" coming to say good-bye and to bring presents – queer presents, things that we had not seen in years began to appear. A box of sardines, which is nothing now, but at that time a box of sardines was put aside for the worst time, for the future. A candle. We had no candles for light. At the end, we discovered that matches were missing, and the *gendarme* captain gave his own. Someone else brought a piece of soap – we had soap but it was like stone – but somebody brought my husband real soap. And someone brought toilet paper – not a roll, but loose, flat papers. There it was, wonderful toilet paper.

It was only later, when I was able to visit my husband in the camp – it was not a concentration camp, but a Vichy detention camp – that he said to me, "Do you know what was on that paper? With a pencil, very carefully, the person who gave this toilet paper had written on it verses of the Bible, of encouragement, of love and understanding. I had a message, but I don't know from whom."

My husband was a prisoner, and yet someone took the time to write him messages of love and understanding. It was a compensation. People would forget that there was some danger, because they were involved in the work.

I remember once toward the end of June 1943, my husband was not home, and I was called by a girl, Suzanne Heim, early in the morning. She told me that the Gestapo was taking away young people from the student home, "La Maison des Roches." Most of the students there were of military age and foreigners. The Gestapo had gone to the children's home where Daniel Trocmé, my cousin, lived, and had taken him with them to the student home. I went there immediately from my kitchen. I had an apron on, so when I arrived the Gestapo thought I was a maid of the house. They let me in, and I sat in the kitchen. I tried to go into the dining room where all the Jewish students were in a line. My cousin Daniel who was responsible for the students was with them. The Gestapo screamed at me and kicked me out, but they let me go into the kitchen, which meant that they

thought I was a maid, that I was someone belonging to the house. After a while I had to go to the village.

When I returned, my young son Jean-Pierre, who was 13, came to be with me for the moment when the students were taken, because he did not want me to be alone. I saw all those boys passing to go into a little room where there was a man with a booklet with many names. He was interrogating them, interviewing them one by one. Most of those who went through had a little bit of paper and said to me, "Send this to my mother. Here's the address of my father. This is for my fiancée. I have some money in my room." They did not know that all the rooms had already been searched and that there was no longer any money, no jewels in the rooms. But it did not matter. We would help them anyhow if possible. My son was so upset when he saw those Gestapo beating those Jews as they were in line coming down the stairs, going into the trucks. They were beating some of those young boys and screaming, "*Schweine Juden! Schweine Juden!*"

We saw all those young people get into the trucks, and my cousin Daniel said to me, "Do not worry. Tell my parents that I was very happy here. It was the best time of my life. Tell them that I like traveling, that I go with my friends."

When they left, my son was green, I would say, like a sick boy. And he said, "Mother, I am going to get revenge later. Such things cannot happen again. I am going to do something when I am grown up." And I said to him, "But you know what your father says: 'If you do such a thing, someone else is going to take revenge against you. And that is why we are never finished. We go on and on and on. We must forgive, we must forget, we must do better.'" He was silent, and we left. And Daniel never came back.

During the war things were very difficult. When my husband after a few weeks did return safely from the Vichy camp, we continued our work taking care of people. After the war, I traveled in America for the Fellowship of Reconciliation. I spoke English at that time much better. I was asked lots of times to speak about these things, to say what the lesson was that we must learn from all this.

The lesson is very simple, I think. The first thing is that we must not think that we were the only ones who helped during those times. Little by little, now that we speak of these things, we realize that other people did lots of things too. Also, we must not be afraid to be discussed in books or in articles and reviews, because it may help people in the future to try to do something, even if it is dangerous. Perhaps there is also a message for young people and for children, a message of hope, of love, of understanding, a message that could give them the courage to go against all that they believe is wrong, all that they believe is unjust.

Maybe later on in their lives, young people will be able to go through experiences of this kind – seeing people murdered, killed, or accused improperly; racial problems; the problem of the elimination of people, of destroying perhaps not their bodies but their energy, their existence. They will be able to think that there always have been some people in the world who tried – who will try – to give hope, to give love, to give help to those who are in need, whatever the need is.

It is important, too, to know that we were a bunch of people together. This is not a handicap, but a help. If you have to fight it alone, it is more difficult. But we had the support of people we knew, of people who understood without knowing precisely all that they were doing or would be called to do. None of us thought that we were heroes. We were just people trying to do our best.

When people read this story, I want them to know that I tried to open my door. I tried to tell people, "Come in, come in." In the end, I would like to say to people, "Remember that in your life there will be lots of circumstances that will need a kind of courage, a kind of decision of your own, not about other people but about yourself." I would not say more.

Magda Trocmé and her daughter Nelly Trocmé Hewett are in the movie "The Courage to Care". Magda Trocmé died near Paris in 1995. During the German occupation of France, she and her husband, Pastor André Trocmé, helped Jews hide in and around the village of Le Chambon. André Trocmé died in 1971 in Geneva, Switzerland. Madame Trocmé and her husband have been honored by Yad Vashem. *Ed.*

YAD VASHEM – DEPARTMENT FOR THE RIGHTEOUS AMONG THE NATIONS
Righteous Among the Nations – per Country and Ethnic Origin*
January 1, 2002

POLAND	5,632
NETHERLANDS	4,464
FRANCE	2,171
UKRAINE	1,755
BELGIUM	1,322
HUNGARY	587
LITHUANIA	504
BELARUS	497
SLOVAKIA	412
GERMANY	358
ITALY	295
GREECE	243
YUGOSLAVIA (SERBIA)	113
CZECH REPUBLIC	103
LATVIA	93
CROATIA	91
AUSTRIA	83
RUSSIA	79
ALBANIA	60
MOLDOVA	52
ROMANIA	48
SWITZERLAND	38
BOSNIA	34
NORWAY	20
DENMARK**	17
BULGARIA	15
GREAT BRITAIN (INCLUDING SCOTLAND)	13
SWEDEN	10
MACEDONIA	9
ARMENIA	6
SLOVENIA	4
SPAIN	3
ESTONIA	2
CHINA	2
BRAZIL	1
JAPAN	1
LUXEMBOURG	1
PORTUGAL	1
TURKEY	1
USA	1
TOTAL PERSONS	**19,141**

* These figures are not an indication of the number of Jews saved in each country.

** The Danish Underground requested that all its members who participated in the rescue of the Jewish community not be listed individually but as one group.

Reprinted by permission of Yad Vashem, The Holocaust Martyrs' and Heroes' Remembrance Authority, Jerusalem, Israel.

VARIAN FRY

MARSEILLES, FRANCE ... AUGUST 1940 – Shortly after Germany's defeat of France in June 1940, Varian Fry, an American journalist, traveled from New York to Marseilles as a representative of a newly formed refugee organization, the Emergency Rescue Committee. Fry was sent to help facilitate the emigration of political leaders, artists, writers, scientists and journalists who were suddenly at risk under the terms of the Franco-German Armistice which called for the "surrender on demand" of the most vocal and visible enemies of the Third Reich. From his very first hours in Marseilles, Fry was shocked to learn that standing between safe flight for thousands of refugees was a near-impossible series of governmental hurdles. Refugees were caught in a seemingly endless web of bureaucratic red tape.

In direct opposition to French authorities and to the American consulate, Fry quickly set up a loosely organized relief bureau and began to supply refugees with the means for escape.

Varian Fry turned his three-week mission into a stay of thirteen months, until French authorities eventually expelled him for engaging in illegal activities. However, as a result of his unorthodox actions, more than 1,200 persons were ushered to safety in the West. Among them were the artists Marc Chagall and Jacques Lipshitz; the writers Lion Feuchtwanger, Heinrich Mann and Franz Werfel; and political philosopher Hannah Arendt.

Varian Fry is the only American recognized by Yad Vashem as a "Righteous Among the Nations."

(Annette Fry, courtesy of USHMM Photo Archives)

CHAPTER 10 **After the Holocaust**

Young mothers take their babies for a stroll in the Landsberg DP (Displaced Persons) camp. Dorit Mandelbaum is in the baby carriage on the left. Her mother Anka is pushing the carriage. Circa 1948. (Dorit Mandelbaum, courtesy of USHMM Photo Archives)

Dorit was born on June 2, 1946, in the Landsberg-am-Lech DP camp in Germany. Anka and her family were forced into the Warsaw ghetto in 1940. Jakub Mandelbaum went to the ghetto to persuade his future wife Anka to flee. In 1941 Anka escaped, only to be arrested and imprisoned. She managed to jump out of a bathroom window and fled. On the last leg of the long walk to Jakub's hometown of Kozienice, Anka met an elderly Pole who pretended to be her father and helped her to board a boat crossing the Vistula River to Kozienice. Soon after her arrival, Anka and Jakub married. From 1942 until the end of 1944, Jakub was transferred from one forced labor camp to another. Finally in January 1945, he was transferred to the Mauthausen concentration camp where he was in a *Straffkommando* (Punishment Commando). On May 5, 1945, the American army liberated the camp, and Jakub Mandelbaum rushed back to Kozienice to search for his family. Anka Mandelbaum was deported from the Kozienice ghetto to Auschwitz-Birkenau, which she survived until liberation in January 1945. After the war, Jakub and Anka Mandelbaum left Poland for Germany. They spent five years in the Landsberg-am-Lech DP camp, where their only daughter Dorit was born in 1946.

DEBÓRAH DWORK **Introduction**

IN MAY 1945, the last remnants of the Third Reich were overrun, and the Holocaust came to a close. According to the first published estimates, some six million Jews had died, 67 percent of the Jews who had come under Nazi rule.* In some countries, such as Nazi-annexed and occupied Poland, the mortality had been enormous. In other places, like Denmark, which had enjoyed relative autonomy under Nazi rule for a long time (see Chapter 5), the percentage of Jews who had been killed was less.

Throughout the vast reaches of what had been Nazi-occupied Europe, Jewish survivors faced the task of reestablishing themselves and their communities. Many found they could not re-create their lives and their homes in the villages, cities, and towns from which they had been deported. Uprooted, they joined millions of gentiles who were on the road as well. These were the displaced persons of postwar Europe: hundreds of thousands of surviving Jews, refugees of all stripes, Germans deported from the east of Europe, former prisoners of war, and civilians who had been incarcerated in the thousands of camps Nazi Germany had established in the countries they conquered. New camps, Displaced Persons Camps, were organized by UNRRA, the United Nations Relief and Rehabilitation Administration, both to provide shelter for and to control the masses of escapees, evacuees, émigrés, refugees, and displaced persons.

Despite the extraordinary assaults the Jews had endured, initially they were not categorized separately or treated differently from the other inmates. Furthermore, unlike many of the gentiles in the DP camps, the Jews had nowhere to go, no country to which to return. The way the Allies saw it, the remaining remnant of European Jewry was to sit in those camps until they got visas to go to British-controlled Palestine, the United States, Australia, Canada, or elsewhere. Former concentration camp inmates found themselves inmates of displaced persons camps, without the right to work or the right to leave and, as Mark Wyman noted in an excerpt from his book *DP: Europe's Displaced Persons, 1945–1951*, sometimes even guarded by ex-Nazis.

Newspaper reports of these conditions prompted President Harry Truman to ask Earl Harrison, Dean of the University of Pennsylvania Law School and the American representative on the Inter-Governmental Committee on Refugees, to investigate this situation. Harrison turned out to be a sensitive and sensible analyst. "As matters now stand," he reported to Truman in August 1945, "we appear to be treating the Jews as the Nazis treated them, except that we do not exterminate them."[1] Harrison urged the Allies in general, and Truman in particular, to recognize the special needs of the Jewish DPs, to organize separate camps for them, and to help them leave Europe as quickly as possible.

> Surviving Jews had nowhere to go after the war, no country to which to return.

---

* That figure was recalculated on the basis of more complete statistics. The current estimate is between 5,100,000 and 6,000,000.

By early 1946, ten DP camps for Jews had been established in Germany and Austria, and they became the new centers of European Jewry. Violent antisemitic incidents in postwar Eastern Europe brought waves of Jewish refugees into the camps. The new inmates had found that not only was there nothing to which to return, it was in fact dangerous to return to their former homes. And so they left, and the DP camp population swelled. There were 18,361 Jews in UNRRA camps in Germany and Austria at the end of 1945, and 97,333 a year later; by September 1947 the number had climbed to 167,529. At that time, Jews comprised 25 percent of all DPs, despite their ardent wish to leave the camps and their unceasing efforts to emigrate.

While survivors faced the task of creating new lives for themselves, finding countries in which to do so, and reconstituting a Jewish community, the gentile populations faced the question of their responsibility for what had happened to their Jewish fellow citizens. The aim of this chapter is to delineate some of these problems, and to explore how successive generations have come to understand the Holocaust during the past half century. The Italian Jewish survivor Primo Levi tried for fifty years to fathom what had happened to him and his generation. In the end, he focused on the fragility of memory and history. (The preface and first chapter of his book, *The Drowned and the Saved*, are excerpted here.) The Holocaust was one of the greatest atrocities western civilization both permitted and endured, and the question is: How did both those who were alive at the time as well as those born after the war comprehend, or come to terms with, this horror? What is remembered and what is, if not forgotten, at least relegated to the background?

The enormity of the crimes committed by many Germans shocked the Allies into the unprecedented action of assembling an International Military Tribunal immediately after the war to bring those accused to justice. Deliberately held in the city of Nuremburg because it was the site of the annual mass Nazi party rallies, as well as to show the precedence of democracy over the Nuremburg Laws passed a decade earlier by the Nazi state, the trials came to carry the name of the city: the Nuremburg Trials. The mandate of the International Military Tribunal was to try war crimes, crimes against peace, and crimes against humanity.

The Holocaust was seen as a crime against humanity, which was defined as the "murder, extermination, enslavement, deportation, and other inhumane acts committed against any civilian population, before

Defendants in the dock at the Nuremberg Trials. Seated in the front row are: (left to right) Hermann Göring (Field Marshal and Commander-in-Chief of the German Air Force), Rudolf Hess (deputy to the Führer), Joachim von Ribbentrop (Foreign Minister), and Wilhelm Keitel (Chief, High Command of the Armed Forces). Göring, von Ribbentrop, and Keitel were sentenced to death. Hess was given a life sentence. Circa 1945–1946. (Courtesy of National Archives)

or during the war, or persecutions on political, racial, or religious grounds." For the American and British prosecutors in particular, the Holocaust was the core Nazi evil. "The Nazi Movement will be of evil memory in history because of its persecution of the Jews, the most far-flung and terrible racial persecution of all time," the American prosecutor Robert H. Jackson declared in his summary statement.[2] His British colleague Sir Hartley Shawcross agreed. "If there were no other crime against [the accused], this one alone, in which all of them are implicated, would suffice. History holds no parallel to these horrors."[3]

Notwithstanding these sentiments, or perhaps this rhetoric, most of the crimes tried by the tribunal at Nuremburg were crimes against the peace, which did not focus on the Holocaust of the Jews. A pattern seemed to have emerged: few gentiles were prepared to confront the Holocaust, let alone come to a conclusion about it. To the extent that the Nuremburg Trials investigated the genocide of the Jews at all, it was seen as a pan-European atrocity. As was appropriate for an International tribunal, the whole sweep of Europe was considered. And as the tribunal did not probe too deeply into the particulars of specific communities, the public was satisfied that justice had been done. Once the defendants at Nuremburg were convicted, the Holocaust receded from the public arena. Too close an examination into what had happened to the Jews in each individual country generated more troubling questions than people or their governments were willing to face.

Mourners and local residents watch as men shovel dirt into the mass grave of the victims of the Kielce (Poland) pogrom. The Kielce pogrom erupted on July 4, 1946 after local residents accused a group of Jewish survivors of kidnapping a Polish child to use his blood for making matzah (a revival of the medieval, anti-Jewish blood libel). The Primate of Poland, Cardinal August Hlond, blamed the pogrom on Jewish support of communism and the suffering of the Polish people.

Three days after the pogrom the victims were buried in a mass grave in the Jewish cemetery. The government ordered Polish military units and local residents to attend the funeral. July 1946. (Leah Lahav, courtesy of USHMM Photo Archives)

In Poland, the country that had become the graveyard of Europe's Jews, not only were few people able to grasp what had happened but, as the waves of new inmates in the DP camps proved, anti-Jewish violence was all too common. It has been estimated that as many as two thousand Jews were murdered in the period between the liberation of Poland in 1944 and 1947.[4] Most were killed when they returned to their hometowns to look for other family members, to reclaim their personal belongings, their businesses, their property. But there were also organized pogroms in some dozen cities and towns. The most vicious episode was the Kielce Pogrom of July 4, 1946, in which forty-two Jews were killed and over fifty injured by local townspeople who attacked the Jewish Center at Planty Street, a group home for Holocaust survivors. Another thirty Jews were killed on trains or in train stations in the Kielce area that day. At the time, only about 250 Jews were living in the district capital town; the prewar community had numbered about 25,000, a third of the total population. For Holocaust survivors, the message was clear: Jews were not wanted in postwar Poland. There was no place for survivors individually and there was no future for a Jewish community.

On the state level, if the communist government was initially sympathetic to the Jews, it also embraced an ideology of internationalism that ignored the Jews as a people who had suffered both specially and disproportionately. Thus the concentration camp at Auschwitz became a monument to commemorate the "resistance and martyrdom" of "Poles and citizens of other nationalities."[5] Jews were included among the "other nationalities." In the Soviet Union, the murder of the Jews was seen as a part of the general murder of civilians by racist fascism (in itself the ultimate expression of monopoly-capitalism), and had no special place in history. According to this ideology, there was nothing unique in the treatment of the Jews during the war.

Unlike the communist regimes that erased the unique nature of the persecution of the Jews as a matter of principle, the postwar French government ignored the fate of the Jews for pragmatic reasons. The wartime Vichy government (see Chapter 5) had followed a policy of collaboration, and to raise the issue of the Jews would have raised the question of the complicity of thousands of French citizens. The Vichy leadership was prosecuted, but their role in the genocide of the Jews was not explicitly acknowledged as one of their crimes.

The newly established and fiercely fought for State of Israel certainly recognized that the Jews of Europe had been persecuted as had no other group or nation, but that government faced another problem: coping with the trauma of the survivors. The official rhetoric emphasized a causal relation between the Holocaust and Jewish resistance to the Germans, and the establishment of the Israeli state. In everyday life, however, survivors were told to forget the past and to engage with the future. This was a different genre of amnesia. This was an amnesia imposed on the victims. The new emigrants from the death camps, forests, and hiding places of Europe were encouraged to adopt new names and to begin a new life with their immigration to Israel.

It was not until the 1960s, after the Eichmann Trial and the Six Day War, that the Holocaust acquired a public profile in Israel.

Defendant Adolf Eichmann listens as an Israeli court declares him guilty on all counts. December 15, 1961. Eichmann was executed by hanging on the night of May 31, 1962. (Central Zionist Archives, courtesy of USHMM Photo Archives)

Adolf Eichmann had been the Chief of the Department of Jewish Affairs in the Gestapo, and was one of the most notorious Nazi war criminals. He had escaped to Argentina after the war, where he was hiding under the astonishingly inappropriate name of Richard Klementz. (*Klementz* means "mercy" in German.) Discovered by Israeli agents in 1960, Eichmann was abducted by them from Argentina and brought to Israel to stand trial. Many people outside Israel condemned the abduction, questioned the legality of the trial, and criticized the Israeli government. The government remained adamant. It was their task to defend the interests of the survivors in particular, and the Jewish people in general. Seen in this light, Israelis began to identify with, and to perceive themselves as heirs of, the Jewish victims of the Holocaust. This was a major turning point in Israeli society: The State of Israel and the Holocaust were united in a tragic bond.

Holocaust survivors took the witness stand and, for the first time, claimed the public ear as they spoke. Most of the witnesses had immigrated to Israel after the war; they came from all walks of life and represented many different Jewish communities of Europe. Describing their personal experiences, they explained what daily life was like under the Germans and their allies, and successfully challenged the stereotype that Jews "had gone like sheep to the slaughter" during the Holocaust.

If the Eichmann Trial was the first major step in the integration of survivors as survivors into the body politic of Israel, and the first major step in public recognition of the central importance of the Holocaust, the Six Day War of 1967 between Israel and the Arab states of Egypt, Jordan, and Syria completed those processes. In the weeks before the war, the Arabs had threatened to wipe Israel off the map. For the Jews of Israel, the historical parallel was clear: Now Israel stood alone, just as the Jews of Europe had stood alone during the Holocaust. The memory of the past and the experience of the present intersected. Broadcast after broadcast from the Arab world predicted the annihilation of Israel, and in the Israeli press the precedent of the Holocaust was invoked and reiterated. The amnesia of the postwar period in Israel had come to an end.

A similar pattern can be discerned in the United States, where hundreds of thousands of survivors had found a home after the war. They too had been enjoined to forget about the past and to get on with their new lives in a new land. The Six Day War and the 1973 Yom Kippur War between Israel and the Arab states of Egypt and Syria brought the Holocaust out of obscurity and into focus. For a brief but searing moment, many Americans feared that they were about to witness a repetition of the past. Would Israel be wiped off the map? Was the Holocaust about to be repeated – or completed?

Every country has its own history of political and social reaction to the Holocaust after the war, but they all have certain elements in common. For the first two to three decades after the war there was not much

Describing their personal experiences in public for the first time at the Eichmann trial, Holocaust survivors explained what daily life was like under the Germans and their allies, and successfully challenged the stereotype that Jews "had gone like sheep to the slaughter" during the Holocaust.

interest in the particular persecution and suffering of the Jews in Nazi Europe. Some time between the 1960s and 1980s a new consciousness about, or recognition of, the unique nature of this persecution and that suffering emerged, sometimes triggered by international events, sometimes by purely local circumstances. The situation in the Netherlands, described by Debórah Dwork and Robert Jan van Pelt in their essay, "The Netherlands," is in that sense paradigmatic.

The paradigm holds true even for West Germany. After the war, nearly everyone in Germany wanted nothing better than to repress and forget the past. With the establishment of the Federal Republic of Germany (as West Germany was called), the government initiated an officially sanctioned effort to come to terms with the past: through reparations and restitutions (*Wiedergutmachung*) the German state sought to monetarize German culpability and guilt. There was no public discussion about that culpability and guilt. On the contrary: While the German Chancellor, Konrad Adenauer, accepted responsibility for the crimes of the Third Reich and expressed his government's readiness to pay reparations, he insisted that Germany was under no legal obligation to do so.

Claims were advanced by the State of Israel on behalf of the half million survivors who had become Israeli citizens and by the Conference on Jewish Material Claims Against Germany on behalf of survivors who had settled outside of Israel, as well as on behalf of the entire Jewish people who were entitled to financial compensation for Jewish property seized or stolen by the Nazis and their allies, and that had remained heirless after the war. Both Israel and the Claims Conference made it very clear that they advanced claims only for material compensation, for lost property, and for the rehabilitation of the survivors. No amount of money, however, could atone for the destruction of human life. And the payment by Germany of the claims in no way implied that the crimes against individual Jews or the Jewish people of Europe were either forgiven or forgotten.

Painful discussions ensued. The first agreements were reached in September 1951. These were followed by successive alterations and emendations that will continue into the first years of the twenty-first century. The central revisited questions focus on who is entitled to compensation, what is to be restituted, and which of the many atrocities that were perpetrated are to be compensated.

Notwithstanding the ongoing discussions, the landmark agreement in 1951 was seen as a great achievement by the State of Israel on behalf of the Jewish people. David Ben-Gurion, then prime minister of Israel, described the negotiations in historic terms in a letter to one of the central participants, Dr. Nahum Goldmann. "For the first time in the history of relations between people, a precedent has been created by which a great state [the Federal Republic of Germany], as a result of

---

No amount of money, however, could atone for the destruction of human life.

moral pressure alone, takes it upon itself to pay compensation to the victims of the government [Nazi Germany] that preceded it." This certainly would not have happened had Israel not existed as an independent state, as Ben-Gurion well understood. "This is beyond question the outcome of the rebirth of the State of Israel. There has arisen a protector and defender of its rights."[6]

The payments also had practical consequences. Israel was then in its infancy, with few financial resources and a lot of new immigrants. For the most part, survivors of the Holocaust, many of these immigrants, arrived impoverished and debilitated. The *Wiedergutmachung* funds helped to rehabilitate these immigrants and to absorb them into the community. These were crucial tasks, both for the survivors and for the early development of the state.

However important the compensation agreements were in "the history of relations between people" and however necessary for the rehabilitation of the survivors, the restitution payments effectively silenced other attempts in Germany to deal with the Holocaust. Adenauer had made the *Wiedergutmachung* program an important part of his agenda for the Federal Republic of Germany, and he had made it clear to the West Germans that if they wanted to make a new beginning, to dispel the cloud of Nazi Germany, they had to pay these reparations to the Jewish victims of the Nazi state. The subtext was clear: Once the program was in place, no more need be said about the Holocaust. Nazism was discussed and decried, but the Holocaust did not loom large in those lessons about history and politics.

It was only in the 1960s that German historians began to consider the Final Solution as an integral part of National Socialism. By the end of that decade, two opposing schools of thought had formed. The intentionalists believed that the National Socialist leadership had intended to carry out a Holocaust from the beginning. The functionalists, by contrast, held that a major cause of the Holocaust was the fierce competition in the violent bureaucratic jungle of the Third Reich, which pitted various institutions and agencies against one another in a struggle for power and Hitler's approval. The intentionalists concentrated on the leaders and ideologues, while the functionalists focused on the bureaucrats and functionaries. The sharp division in German scholarship never crossed the ocean. American scholars largely occupied a position somewhere between the two extremes.

By the 1980s, an emerging focus of Israeli and American historians and sociologists was to try to understand the Holocaust from a comparative perspective. Contemporary genocides prompted scholars to investigate closely the genocide of the American Indians, Armenians, and Romani, and genocides in Cambodia, China, East Timor, Kurdistan, and Stalinist Russia, in the hope that if these atrocities could be understood, perhaps such mass murders could be prevented in

> Restitution payments effectively silenced other attempts in Germany to deal with the Holocaust.

"Events happen because they are possible. If they are possible once, they are possible again. In that sense the Holocaust is not unprecedented, but a warning for the future."

– Yehuda Bauer

the future. This, in turn, encouraged consideration of the place of the Holocaust within the context of mass murder and genocide. Was the Holocaust an unprecedented event? And if so, how is it relevant to what passed before and, even more important, to what may happen in the future? Let us give the last word to Yehuda Bauer, whose article "On the Place of the Holocaust in History" is reprinted here. "Events happen because they are possible. If they are possible once, they are possible again. In that sense the Holocaust is not unprecedented, but a warning for the future."

Notes

1. Mark Wyman, *DP: Europe's Displaced Persons, 1945–1951* (London: Associated University Presses, 1989), 135.
2. International Military Tribunal, *Trial of the Major War Criminals,* 41 vols. (Nuremburg: Secretariat of the Tribunal, 1947–1949), vol. 19, 404.
3. Ibid., 501.
4. Michael C. Steinlauf, "Poland," in David S. Wyman, ed., *The World Reacts to the Holocaust* (Baltimore: Johns Hopkins Univesity Press, 1996), 112.
5. This language is used in the 1947 law passed by the Polish parliament, establishing the State Museum at Auschwitz-Birkenau.
6. Nana Sagi, *German Reparations: A History of the Negotiations* (Jerusalem: Magnes, 1980), 4.

MARK WYMAN **Jews of the Surviving Remnant**

> I felt free, without fear – freed from Poland, and from the concentration camp.
> That was the first time I felt like a free person without fear.
>   – Polish Jew Remembering Feldafing DP Camp

TRAINS WERE PASSING in the night across Eastern Europe in the spring and summer of 1946, carrying human cargoes with vastly different expectations. Rolling eastward from the zones of Germany were thousands of repatriated Poles, their trains decorated with leafy branches and Polish flags, their patriotic songs rising above the rumble of the cars as they moved toward repatriation.

But other trains were going toward the West. These carried Polish Jews, traveling across the continent to Germany and Austria in both legal and illegal journeys. These passengers sang, too, but instead of the Polish national hymn and Polish marching airs they chorused a joyful "Pioneers Prepare Themselves for Palestine." Their train cars were not decorated with Polish flags. An American journalist, I. F. Stone, rode with one Jewish group across Czechoslovakia and noted that sometimes an eastbound and a westbound train were stopped at the same time in a station, and Polish Jews and Polish Catholics got out on opposite sides of the platform to stretch their legs. There was no mixing, Stone reported, "no one shouted across the platform from one train to the other. Their mutual misery created no common bond between peoples who regarded each other as oppressors and oppressed. The hate and fear that flowed between us was almost tangible, like a thick current in the hot summer night."[1]

There was a momentous story in this. Groups were choosing their futures: thousands thought, pondered, discussed, and made decisions that would direct the flow of their people for generations.

For many Jews, that decision came easily. Europe had become the graveyard of their people, its major monuments not the Eiffel Tower and Saint Peter's but the Nazi death camps where humans were turned into objects and plundered for their labor, gold fillings, hair. A newly arrived American serving with the UNRRA landed in Munich in July 1945 and made

his way to nearby Dachau, one of the most infamous of the concentration camps. It had not yet been made presentable for tourists, and he could still see human ashes before the crematorium, fingernail scratches running down the gas chamber walls. The very silence shrieked.[2] Auschwitz in Poland was the leader in this macabre competition, its gas chambers killing from 12,000 to 15,000 each day in May and June of 1944, part of the camp's estimated 2 million victims, mainly Jews. Hitler's *Einsatzgruppen* (mobile death squads) operated at will over Poland and other conquered areas from 1941 on, as talk of a "final solution" of the Jewish question spread among the German leadership.[3]

Stories began to filter out. But the stories came into a disbelieving world, its credulity put on guard by the falsified Belgian atrocity tales of the First World War. The new stories told of the creation of *Judenrein* (Jew-free areas) in what were formerly Jewish population centers. They told of Nazi doctors experimenting with Jewish children, of mass murders. One story later passed on by an architect concerned his trip with a German Sixth Army Officer near Kiev one day in March 1942. As they drove by a ravine called Babi Yar, the architect suddenly saw the moist earth bubbling with small explosions. He was told that it was the thaw releasing gases from the 35,000 bodies covered there, the result of a two-day massacre of Jews. "Here my Jews are buried," the German officer explained. But some European Jews managed to elude the Nazis, hiding with gentile friends or in forests or melting unnoticed into the population; the earliest postwar surveys found 20,000 Jews left in Germany and 7,000 in Austria, with 80,000 surviving inside Poland (over 130,000 others had fled into Russia), 90,000 in Hungary, 100,000 in Rumania.

The war's death toll of Jews was finally estimated at almost 6 million, 72 percent of European Jewry.[4]

The impact of this Holocaust, as it eventually

MARK WYMAN, DPS: EUROPE'S DISPLACED PERSONS, 1945–1951, 131–55, 224–28. COPYRIGHT © 1989 BY ASSOCIATED UNIVERSITY PRESSES, INC. COPYRIGHT © 1998 BY CORNELL UNIVERSITY. USED BY PERMISSION OF THE PUBLISHER, CORNELL UNIVERSITY PRESS.

came to be known, was felt and continues to be felt in many areas of the world, on many activities and institutions. But in 1945 its impact was felt most severely by the *She'erit Ha-pletah* – the spared, or surviving, remnant of European Jews.

Like the tattoos that large numbers of Jews carried on their arms as permanent physical reminders of the concentration camps ("I saw few Jewish arms in Europe without a tattooed number," I. F. Stone reported), many of the psychological scars could also be observed readily. The *katzetler* or *katzetnik* (concentration camp veterans) broke into tears easily, fell apart at a knock at the door, froze when a black limousine stopped nearby. Some refused to enter ambulances being used to transfer ailing Belsen inmates to the ship for Sweden, because they remembered that the Nazis had used such vehicles, complete with Red Cross emblems, to carry Jews away to the gas chambers. And some would cry out in nightmares, shrieking "Deutschen!" They dwelt on the past, reliving it in their conversations again and again. Having seen small incidents of hatred in the 1930s lead to catastrophe in the Third Reich, they now became extremely sensitive to any hint of anti-semitism, generalizing from and exaggerating any such report.[5]

Many Jewish DPs lacked the capacity for anything sustained, as evidenced in their early responses in the DP camps. "They become fatigued after a few hours' work," one American worker reported. A newspaper correspondent in Austria encountered Jews resisting efforts by the American Jewish Joint Distribution Committee (the "Joint") to begin work projects. Some of the camp's DP tailors said they could make more money on their own, while "the rest of the people are too tired and indifferent to bother," the correspondent observed.[6]

One of the continuing effects of the war on Jewish DPs centered on their loss of close relatives. Receiving a tiny bit of evidence that a family member was still alive, they would travel hundreds of miles to track it down, usually returning only with additional details on the final hours of their loved one. Some fantasized against all evidence that one of the family had somehow survived, was still alive, waiting perhaps in another country overseas; they would meet someday. Continually frustrated in their search, they

developed a fear of loving anyone, afraid they would lose that person and suffer again. Many developed guilt over having survived. An American traveling with a mixed group of Jewish and Christian DP children found that the Jews put "great importance on kinship; they valued a family tie, however distant."[7]

Outsiders had problems dealing with such people, for cynicism and suspicion were everywhere. Jewish DPs were often hostile, forcing some psychiatrists to give up their efforts in the camps because of a lack of rapport. A British DP official was flabbergasted at the refusal of a group of Jews to move into more commodious huts, but a Jewish writer later saw in the incident the problem of the "concentration camp psychology, which was ridden with inferiority complexes and resulting aggressiveness." Many Jewish DPs simply rejected the right of non-Jews to tell them what to do any longer.[8]

Placing the Jews of the *She'erit Ha-pletah* in the decrepit conditions of the first improvised DP camps created a volatile mixture. One problem lay with the victorious armies. Having just fought a war against an enemy who persecuted individuals according to their religion, the Allies were not willing to resort to such classifications in dealing with the refugees. A British official cautioned in 1944 that just because Jews could be "identified by certain characteristics," and because Nazi policies had inserted the Jewish question into world politics, there were still "not sufficient reasons for treating 'Jews' as a separate national category." As a result, Jews who struggled out of the concentration camps initially found themselves classified as "enemy nationals" if they originated in Germany, Austria, or other Axis nations; in some DP camps they were placed among their former Nazi guards and tormentors. General Eisenhower asserted in early August 1945 that his headquarters "makes no differentiation in treatment of displaced persons."[9]

Differentiation, however, became the goal of Jewish agency workers and DP spokesmen. The basis of their claim was that Jews had been singled out *as Jews* by the Nazis. "The fact was that we had not faced the Auschwitz crematoriums as Poles, Lithuanians, or Germans," one Auschwitz survivor stressed. "It was as Jews that we had become victims of the greatest catastrophe of our people." Although gypsies were killed, even slaughtered, by the Germans, not all Gypsies were ferreted out across Europe, and some were even protected; the anti-Gypsy policy was not the same as the anti-Jewish policy.

The refugee president of the Landsberg DP camp, Samuel Gringauz, noted that the Nazis' targeting of Jews had produced a sort of Jewish universalism not present before, under which Jews who formerly felt distinct from other Jews now felt one with them. He drew on his own concentration camp experiences:

> A Jewish tailor from Rhodes who could find no one in the camp to understand him, and a Hungarian druggist baptized thirty years before, lay in the same wooden bunk with me, shared their experience as Jews with me, and died only because they were Jewish. That is why the *She'erit Hapletah* feels itself to be the embodiment of the unity of Jewish experience.[10]

Conditions of Jews in the camps soon caught the eyes of journalists, Western officials, and Jewish spokesmen. As early as 21 July 1945, the World Jewish Congress appealed to the Allied leaders meeting at Potsdam to release the former concentration camp inmates from "conditions of the most abject misery." The WJC charged that Jews at the Lingen DP camp were housed in "indescribably filthy" structures, with inadequate medical and other supplies and personnel. Worse, the congress found that in some cases ex-Nazis had been placed in charge of their former victims and were "treating them with neglect and contempt."

The *Jewish Chronicle*, a London newspaper, compared American troops with Hitler's SS in reporting an incident in which Jewish DPs were driven from their huts by General Patton's Third Army. DP protests against this rough handling drew the response from the soldiers that " 'this was the only way to deal with Jews.' "[11]

These stories reached Washington. President Harry S. Truman, only recently installed in office, soon wrote to the dean of the University of Pennsylvania Law School and asked him to investigate conditions in Europe, especially the situation of the Jewish displaced persons. The dean was Earl G. Harrison, who had been serving as American representative on the Inter-Governmental Committee on Refugees. After making contact with Jewish representatives in Europe, Harrison left the itinerary laid out by the army and probed into situations that, it seems likely, the military would have avoided. An inhabitant at the Belsen DP camp remembered Harrison visiting them, chain-smoking as tears streamed down his face. "He was so shaken he could not speak," the Belsen man recalled. "Finally, he whispered weakly: 'But how did you survive, and where do you take your strength from now?' "[12]

Harrison's report to Truman in early August 1945 was devastating. "As matters now stand, we appear to be treating the Jews as the Nazis treated them except that we do not exterminate them," he wrote. Harrison referred to the DP camps holding Jews as "concentration camps," where they wore the "rather hideous striped pajama" they had worn earlier when controlled by the Nazis (some were forced to wear leftover German SS uniforms), and existed on rations composed principally of bread and coffee, all the while guarded closely by American soldiers. Meanwhile, they could look not far off and see German civilians, "to all appearances living normal lives in their own homes."

Harrison's report, as might be expected, called for a vast improvement in food, clothing, and housing for the Jewish DPs. But he went beyond this to urge two sharp shifts in policy:

> The first and plainest need of these people is a recognition of their actual status and by this I mean their status of Jews. . . . While admittedly it is not normally desirable to set aside particular racial or religious groups from their nationality categories, the plain truth is that this was done for so long by the Nazis that a group has been created which has special needs. Jews as Jews (not as members of their nationality groups) have been more severely victimized than the non-Jewish members of the same or other nationalities.

This meant segregated DP camps for Jews, he stressed, with their own representatives to deal with the military authorities.

Harrison's second major proposal was for immediate help for Jews to leave Germany and Austria – through emigration to the United States and other countries if possible, but mainly through opening the doors into British-controlled Palestine. The Palestine issue "must be faced," he wrote. "For some of the European Jews, there is no acceptable or even decent solution for their future other than Palestine." The main solution lay, he stressed, "in the quick evacuation of all nonrepatriable Jews in Germany and Austria, who wish it, to Palestine."[13]

President Truman responded quickly to Harrison's report. He pressured General Eisenhower to improve conditions in the DP camps and sent a copy of the Harrison document to British prime minister Clement Atlee with the recommendation that British-controlled Palestine be opened for Jewish settlement. Truman commented later that year that the issue had stimulated the greatest volume of mail in the history of the White House.[14]

Eisenhower was stung by Harrison's findings. The general made his own inspection, then responded somewhat defensively and emphasized the army's enormous problems in Europe in the aftermath of the war. But he went on to authorize the creation of special Jewish DP centers, the selection of camp guards from among the DPs themselves, and an increase in the daily minimum caloric level to twenty-five hundred for "racial, religious and political persecutees." He also appointed a Jewish adviser and a Jewish liaison officer. In mid-November the British Zone finally permitted segregation of Jews within DP camps, although the new policy stated that "special camps exclusively for Jews will not be established."[15]

As a result of these changes, by early January 1946 the British Zone of Germany had one major heavily Jewish camp at Höhne (near the site of Belsen concentration camp) with 9,000 Jews, while the American Zone had twelve camps that were entirely Jewish, led by Landsberg and Wolfratshausen with more than 5,000 each, and Feldafing with 3,700. In the French Zone more than three-fourths of the Jews lived in households taken from the Germans; no segregation was authorized. The Jewish camps soon were electing their own spokesmen, aided by the formation in July 1945 of the Central Committee of Liberated Jews, an umbrella leadership group for Jews in the western zones.[16]

These new Jewish spokesmen found the occupation authorities in Germany and Austria generally cooperative from late 1945 on. General Mark Clark, head of the U.S. occupation forces in Austria, instructed his assistants in October 1945 that Truman's orders were to be carried out "not only because they were orders" but because Clark believed the Jews' treatment during the war made them "entitled to first consideration." Jewish writers later referred to the months from late 1945 to mid-1947 as the "humanitarian period" of Occupation-Jewish relations. And in the meantime the Jewish DP camps emerged as the new centers of European Jewry, speaking for Jews, settling disputes, offering practical help and spiritual guidance. Remnants of the traditional Jewish centers in Hamburg, Lübeck, Bremen, and Düsseldorf now turned to the camps for leadership.[17]

The environment of the Jewish DPs began to change in other ways as well. The new political environment – perhaps *philosophical* environment is more accurate – flowed from two major developments, only slightly evident in the summer of 1945 but more apparent with each passing day: (1) a sharp upsurge in support for Zionism, the movement to re-establish Judaism's base in its ancient home of Palestine (Israel), and (2) the continuance and even the increase of virulent anti-Semitism in Poland and other areas of Eastern Europe.

These two changes in turn affected each other, and were essential ingredients in the growing international debate over the Palestine question. The DP issue, already frustrating to occupying powers and host nations, now took on new complexity.

Zionism's growth came from several factors. It was paradoxical that rising support for a Jewish homeland was accompanied by little or no increase in religiosity among the Jewish remnant – in fact, some argued that religious practice had declined from the thirties, because Orthodox Jews had been more noticeable and for that reason were more readily eliminated by the Nazis. But this new Zionism was not a religious movement: it drew strength from traditional Jewish beliefs, but only because they were given new relevance by events of the Hitler era. Koppel Pinson of [the] "Joint," after working for a year among Jewish DPs, argued that Zionists "were the only ones that had a program that seemed to make sense after this catastrophe." The Palestine return became so identified with salvation for Europe's Jews, he emphasized, that "emotionally and psychologically as well as in a real physical sense it became dangerous to think outside this complex."[18]

This was because each week after V-E Day seemed to bring forth new evidence of the degradation and extermination of Europe's Jews during the war. And already whispers were heard of the probability of another war, between Americans and Russians, or even between Americans and the rumored underground Nazi movement. What would be the fate of the Jews then?

The head of the Landsberg DP camp's Jews, Dr. Samuel Gringauz, presented the argument for Jewish pessimism in the camp newspaper:

> We do not believe in progress, we do not believe in the 2,000-year-old Christian culture of the West, the culture that, *for them*, created the Statue of Liberty in New York and Westminster Abbey on the Thames, the wonder gardens of Versailles and the Uffizi and Pitti palaces in Florence, the Strassbourg *Münster* and the Cologne cathedral; but *for us*, the slaughters of the Crusades, the Spanish Inquisition, the blood bath of Khmielnicki, the pogroms of Russia, the gas chambers of Auschwitz and the massacres of entire Europe.

I. F. Stone encountered older Jews who put it more simply, as they told of their desire to go to Palestine despite not considering themselves Zionists: "I'm a Jew. That's enough. We have wandered enough. We have worked and struggled too long on the lands of other peoples. We must build a land of our own."[19]

In the recorded comments and letters of such people, and in reminiscences of Jews moving through the postwar period, the idea appears repeatedly that Palestine represented *home*. Virtually none had ever been there, but a return – *Aliyah* – to the land of Israel was a foundation block of their faith, repeated

each year during Passover Seder prayers: "Next year in Jerusalem." Perhaps this image meant little in earlier years; it is not unusual for ritual to lose significance. But now, with all that had once meant home mixed with the dust, eliminated, destroyed, the thought came forward again. They still had a home. Children traveling on a cold train en route to a French port, to board a Haifa-bound ship, explained to concerned UNRRA* workers, "Hardships? It is worth them all. We are going home."[20]

The symbol of Palestine the home also became a positive affirmation of Jewish existence. It was a way to finally show the world the Nazis had failed. Everything – even personal comfort – had to be sacrificed for Palestine. Plans to remove Jewish orphans to better conditions in Jewish homes in England were blocked by the Jewish Central Committee of the British Zone, which resolved that the children "who were with us in the Ghettos and concentration camps . . . must stay where they are until their Aliyah." The committee demanded that the first allocations for Palestine go to the children. At the same time in late 1945, delegates broke into tears as a Rome conference of Polish Jews voted for a ringing declaration to proceed "by all ways and means" to Palestine, despite British opposition. It was their last hope for survival, the delegates asserted, and they would go "because they owed such action to the 5,000,000 or more Jews of Europe exterminated by Nazism." UNRRA staff workers, trying to compile statistics on this phenomenon, distributed a questionnaire among 19,000 Jewish DPs and found that 18,700 listed "Palestine" as their first choice for emigration, but then 98 percent also wrote "Palestine" as their second choice. At the Fürth DP camp near Nürnberg, however, alert staff members told the DPs not to repeat "Palestine" for second choice, but to write another preference for emigration. One-fourth then wrote in "crematorium."[21]

An important difference in this new Zionism was that it temporarily overwhelmed divisions that had been rife among European Jews, divisions that earlier had left them almost incompetent to meet the challenges of the Hitler era. Earlier generations of Jews had debated extensively over Zionism – whether Jews should dream of resettlement at all, and even where

*United Nations Relief and Rehabilitation Administration, *Ed.*

their Land of Zion should be. At various times, Texas, Uganda, and the Argentine had been proposed, as well as Palestine. Britain's Balfour Declaration in 1917, supporting a Jewish national home in Palestine, stimulated the Zionists, although some sought only a federal arrangement with Arabs. Even in wartime, in the face of Nazi attacks, the different groups within Judaism had trouble working together; the antagonists included socialist bundists versus Zionists, Zionists versus assimilationists, the Orthodox versus the nonobservant, radicals versus capitalists, and socialists versus Communists. These and other divisions made a farce of the Third Reich's assertion that Jews represented a powerful conspiratorial group controlling vast areas of European life. In fact, no overall organization existed among the Jews of Europe, not even an information chain that might have kept them abreast of dangers.

That long-sought unity would appear only in 1945, and even then some outsiders might have missed it because of the multiplicity of political parties and organizations visible in the camps. The Belsen DP camp soon had elections fought out by General Zionists and Revisionists, as well as members of Hashomer Hatzair, Mapai, Mizrachi, Aguda, and Poale Zion. Several groups within the camp ran their own schools; most had their own newspapers. One participant called the Belsen DP camp not only a Jewish community but "an intense Zionist community. . . . I felt there as if I was back in my Lithuanian home town." But despite their differences these groups cooperated, he stressed. "It was based on a genuine compromise and an appreciation that, in the first place, they were all Zionists."[22]

The second major change in the Jewish DPs' environment arose out of events in the newly liberated areas of Eastern Europe. Release from concentration camps or forced labor was usually followed by a frantic search for family members, but for those Jews who returned to their homes in Eastern Europe the search was usually doubly numbing: not only were they unable to locate their kin, but former neighbors often turned upon them with a bitter anti-Semitism that recalled the recent days of Hitler's reign.

David Lubetkin's story will perhaps speak for thousands.[23]

David Lubetkin (not his real name) was liberated in Buchenwald near the end of the war, and a few weeks later, while scanning the names posted on a military bulletin board, he saw his two sisters listed as survivors in the concentration camp at Bergen-Belsen. Soon David and a friend headed off on bicycles to link up with their kin.

The next step was to return to Poland, to learn whether others of the family had survived. If three Lubetkins had made it through the war, why not more? David had high hopes for reuniting the entire family – parents and six children – who had been seized and sent away on 13 September 1939 after Germans overran their village.

The Russians also wanted David to go home. After taking over the Buchenwald area in midsummer of 1945, when zonal boundaries were re-drawn, Soviet officials encouraged all Poles to go back to rebuild their homeland. "Trains are prepared," they announced in the Buchenwald area. "Those who will not go on train, will have to go on foot." There was no other option.

And so David and his sisters boarded an eastward-bound train, heavily loaded with Buchenwald veterans who traveled with both expectation and apprehension. "It was not a joyful, singing trip," he said. Soon he joined with others, forming a group of eleven Jews from the same Polish town. At the German-Polish border they had to leave the train and wait a day for another to carry them into Poland. While the eleven prepared their night's shelter, however, a Polish border guard – Jewish, it turned out – talked privately with them. He showed some surprise at their return: "Why did you come back to hell? I'm looking to get away from hell."

That set them thinking. But they continued on, and two days later David and his friends received another jolt as they disembarked onto the railway platform in their hometown in central Poland. A local policeman, whom they had known before the war as the son of the village ice cream vendor, greeted them: "So many of you lived through the war? Why didn't they get you all?"

It was an ominous welcome. In one respect it should not have been surprising, however, for their village had been torn in the 1930s with anti-Semitic agitation. Warnings had been stenciled repeatedly on

Jewish-owned shops: "Swoj do Swego" (Stay with your own) and "Zyd twoj wrog" (Jews are your enemies), among other slogans.

Despite this history of anti-Jewish activity the returning Jews were taken aback. "I expected they would have learned something from the war," David said. "I expected them to have changed in their thinking and ideas by then, due to the suffering they themselves had experienced." But such was not the case.

And so the few Jews making their way back to the village clustered together, sharing food and shelter and fears, welcoming the Jews starting to trickle in from the Soviet Union as well as the continuing arrivals from liberated Germany. Meanwhile, local anti-Semitism worsened as Polish nationalism flowered.

By November 1945, David, at his sisters' urging, decided it was time to get out. He and a cousin – the only surviving kinsman they had found – realized they had an advantage in their escape: they looked Polish. On the first leg of their train trip they sat next to a pretty gentile girl and listened respectfully to her diatribes against Jews.

It was a fortunate deception. On that day-long ride to Poznan they saw four Jewish passengers thrown out of windows while the train lumbered on, victims of roving bands of ultranationalistic *Armia Krajowa*.

The two cousins had chosen Poznan as their first destination because they knew trains left from there for Berlin. As luck would have it, a Soviet train carrying goods from Moscow to Berlin was then in the station, and by pooling their cash they bought two bottles of whiskey and several sausages, adequate to bribe a Russian soldier to allow them on board. Better than merely boarding, they were hidden in a baggage car filled with office furniture, which was not opened until the train entered Berlin.

At Berlin they made their way to the Zehlendorf transit camp in the United States sector, producing concentration camp release documents to prove they were Jewish. Later they were taken into western Germany, ending up at the Feldafing DP camp in early December 1945. Their next task was to plot the escape of David's sisters.

The experiences of David Lubetkin were repeated over and over across Eastern Europe in the first months after the war. Thousands of Jews returned home, including some 130,000 who had spent the war years in the Soviet Union. But they discovered that the defeat of the Third Reich was not the defeat of anti-Jewish feeling. Reborn anti-Semitism became so widespread that the new Polish regime finally ordered that attacks on Jews were to be punishable by death or life imprisonment.[24]

This anti-Semitism had both an ancient and a modern history. It had been woven into European tradition long before the modern era, but took on a viciously nationalistic character after the First World War and the rebirth of the Polish nation. Anything not identified as completely Polish was opposed vigorously in those years, which meant that Lithuanians, Jews, and non-Catholics could be depicted as enemies of the new Polish nation. One account stated that anti-Jewish disorders were "daily occurrences" in Poland by the mid-1930s. The Nazis later built on this hatred, encouraging divisions among the peoples they conquered. The invaders recruited warders among Poles and Ukrainians for Jewish labor camps, and in turn they used Jews to compile lists of Polish Catholics for deportation. The Germans also put a renewed emphasis on anti-Semitism in occupied Poland and added some new twists, such as a traveling exhibit called "The Jewish Contagion," which made its way from town to town. Small wonder, then, that some Polish Resistance groups opposed Jews, disarming them, driving them away. One ex-partisan admitted he hid his Jewish identity from his fellow partisans throughout the war; to do otherwise was to invite being shot while on patrol – by his comrades.[25]

The result was that anti-Semitism, so much identified in the outside world with Hitler, did not collapse when the Nazis retreated from Poland, and the first words heard by returning Jews were often such as these: "The one bad thing about Hitler is that he didn't kill all the Jews."[26]

Only two factors in 1945 were new amid this anti-Semitism. Many Poles had acquired property (buildings, jewelry, clothing) that Nazis had seized from Jews in 1939–40; now they feared it would be taken away and returned to the prewar Jewish owners. In fact, such returns were being authorized by the new Communist regime. Also, stories were circulating that Jews had helped the Soviet Union in its ultimately successful efforts to take over eastern Poland, and were now helping the Soviet-imposed regime.[27]

The latter argument appears to have been widely believed. General Wladyslaw Anders stated in his memoir of the war that when the Russians invaded in 1939, "a number of Polish Jews, especially the young ones, who had made no secret of their joy at the entry of Soviet troops, began to cooperate" with Soviet officials. A book on Poland published in London after the war, *The Dark Side of the Moon*, noted the Soviets' inability to enlist Polish minorities in their cause. This was especially surprising in the case of the Jews, the anonymous author stated, for "nobody in Poland, they say, welcomed the Red Army in the same way as the Jews." (Thirty-five years and thousands of miles away, a Polish ex-DP thought back on those years and remembered that he had been told in the DP camps that when the Russians invaded in 1939, the Jews sided with them. "People resented that," he said.) In addition, several Jews were leading officials in the postwar Communist regime in Warsaw.[28]

There was no time to investigate and refute such charges amid the heated nationalism of 1945 and 1946. Attacks on Jews began even before the Germans were defeated. In the spring of 1945 a right-wing Polish group proclaimed it a sign of patriotism to kill Jews. A Polish government report stated that 351 Jews were murdered in Poland between November 1944 and October 1945, with anti-Jewish riots occurring during 1945 at Cracow on 20 August, in Sosnowiec on 25 October, and in Lublin on 19 November. But none held the terror of the incident at Kielce.[29]

It occurred in July 1946, when a Christian boy in the city some 120 miles south of Warsaw returned after a three-day absence with tales of a blood ritual. Jews had kidnapped him, he said, and took him into a cellar where he watched as fifteen other Christian children were murdered. As the story spread some five thousand protestors gathered around the Jewish community building. Men in Polish army uniforms brought the Jews out, then released them to the mob. Local militia, a Socialist factory director, even some members of the clergy took part in what rapidly turned into a melee. Forty-one Jews were killed at Kielce, and soon Jews were building stockade-like

structures in various areas of Poland. The Catholic church's reaction surprised many: Poland's August Cardinal Hlond criticized Jews for increasing anti-Semitism by taking leading appointments in a government "that the majority of Poles do not want." When a Cracow priest denounced the riot, he was forbidden to continue ecclesiastical duties.

The Kielce boy's story was eventually revealed as a fabrication.[30]

In nearby countries anti-Semitism also became violent, as nationalism flared up in the aftermath of the German retreat and surrender. Anti-Hungarian demonstrations in Kosice, Czechoslovakia, were soon combined with anti-Jewish demonstrations, while in Presov five Jews were killed in what appeared to be a pogrom. German Jews in Prague, meanwhile, were attacked as Germans. Bucharest crowds screaming their support of king and country "fell to beating up all the Jews they could lay hands on," often with the thick staffs used to carry their Rumanian flags.[31]

The piling of murder upon murder, the shouts in the street and the rumors in the marketplace, all helped drive thousands of returned Jews out of Poland and neighboring countries from late 1945 on.

The impact of the Kielce killings in 1946 was immediate: some 16,000 Polish Jews fled the country that month; 23,000 more left in August (including almost 4,000 who crossed into Czechoslovakia one night), and another 23,000 left in September. A UNRRA official was on hand as fleeing Polish Jews arrived at the Zeilsheim DP camp near Frankfurt; he gazed out on

> what appeared to be an endless queue of refugees, packs and bundles on their backs, plodding up the path toward the camp. Never had I seen such a bedraggled lot of people. Mothers held infants to their breasts, clutching the hands of tiny youngsters who stumbled alongside them. As I watched, a group halted and, throwing their bundles to the ground, literally fell in their tracks from exhaustion, unable to make the last few yards to the camp. . . . They had arrived in the last few days from Cracow and Polish Silesia, more than seven hundred miles distant. Fathers, mothers and children alike, hitch-hiked, rode

trucks, jumped freight trains, slept in the forests at night and somehow managed to reach here.[32]

Was this organized or unorganized?

Lt. Gen. Sir Frederick E. Morgan, briefly UNRRA's chief of operations in Germany, believed it was organized. This outflow from Poland, he charged, was "nothing short of a skillful campaign of anti-British aggression on the part of Zion aided and abetted by Russia." Although it was presented to the world by "Zionist propaganda" as being the "spontaneous surge of a tortured and persecuted people," Morgan held that it was really a well-organized drive by the American Joint Distribution Committee and related Jewish groups to pack the Jewish DPs into Germany. Their ultimate aim was to force the opening of Palestine for emigration – meaning "death to the British," Morgan charged.

The UNRRA officer was called on the carpet for such charges, restored to his post, then fired later by a new UNRRA chief for similar remarks.[33]

Other accounts challenged Morgan's claim that the movement was organized, for journalists found "infiltrees," as they were called, who had fled on their own and linked up with others as they headed west. In fact, soon after Morgan made his comments at a press conference in early 1946, a UNRRA investigator stated that "all the infiltrees with whom we spoke said that there was no organized program." Others noted that many people, not just Jews, wanted to leave their homes in Europe; a Netherlands survey estimated that even 20 percent of the Dutch population wished to emigrate.[34]

But organization was present; that became increasingly obvious. A probe by the U.S. Third Army in January 1946 discovered that a group of 250 Jewish refugees heading for Munich had been detoured at one point, then sent in another direction where better facilities would be available. Within two weeks of the opening of a new camp for Jews, the report stated, a new group of 200 infiltrees arrived there, without having passed through any other camp en route. The report said that Zionist committees along the way gave advice and assistance, and many trying to reach Italy were found in possession of forged passes. When the UNRRA ran an investigation in

June and July 1946, interrogation of infiltrees at three major collection points confirmed that "the movements are fairly well organized, but . . . the fear of persecution is still the predominant motive." And that was before Kielce.[35]

Some evidence was also found for Morgan's charge that the movement aimed at pressuring the British. The western zones were obvious goals for anyone on the loose in Europe then, for few other spots were prepared to care for large numbers of refugees. But it is also on record that David Ben Gurion told the Jewish Agency in October 1945, "If we succeed in concentrating a quarter million Jews in the American zone, it will increase the American pressure [on the British]." This pressure would arise not through financial burdens, Ben Gurion added, "but because they see no future for these people outside *Eretz-Yisrael* [the Land of Israel]." A January 1946 probe by the UNRRA found a "strong impression" that one motive behind the organized flow of Jews was to "bring the questions of the future of the Jews and of Zionism to a head."[36]

The escape of one Polish Jew illustrates the mixed pattern of organized and unorganized flight that became common in late 1945 and much of 1946. Returning to her Polish hometown in April 1945, Chana Wilewska (not her real name) was met by the same apartment building janitor who had thrown out her family in 1939. Then, he had worn a large swastika badge; now he pleaded, "I didn't know what I was doing!" Gaining entry, she struggled in the ensuing weeks to regain family furniture and heirlooms, all the while overhearing anti-Jewish comments in the streets and rumors of attacks on Jews in nearby towns.[37]

Then came a letter from her uncle, who was serving with General Anders's Polish army in Italy. He told her to join him and sent forged papers with a fellow soldier who was returning to Poland for a visit. The papers were inadequate, however; two attempts to cross the border using them resulted only in two rebuffs.

Chana decided to work out her own plan. Since her mother had been born in Czechoslovakia, she went to the city hall and obtained a permit to visit her relatives in that country. The permit got her across the border in April 1946. Upon arrival at her mother's native city, she went immediately to the Jewish community center, where she met a visiting member of the Jewish Brigade who took her to Prague. It was in Prague that she was delivered to the headquarters of the *Bricha*, the organized exodus. (*Bricha* means "flight" in Hebrew.)

After several days' wait, persons running the Bricha center in Prague took her with a group of fifty fleeing Jews by train to the German border. All were given forged papers attesting to the legality of their trip in case they were caught. They were taken at night to a house, where they waited until 2:00 A.M. Three guides came for them, leading them in a two-hour trek over the mountains into Germany. (Chana believes that the border guards had been bribed, for the group of fifty traveled with no fear of capture.)

Early the next morning the group walked into a German train station, waited while their Bricha guides purchased their tickets, then boarded a train that eventually crossed into the American Zone. Most entered DP camps, as suggested by their Bricha guides. Chana, meanwhile, elected not to enter a camp and instead registered as a German, which was easy to do since she had grown up in Polish Silesia.

Organized. Unorganized. At times disorganized. All three describe the massive exodus of Jews out of Eastern Europe beginning in late 1945. Undoubtedly many would have fled even without help, for a tenuous string of escape routes had existed sporadically in wartime. It is just as certain, however, that many were encouraged to leave by the knowledge that they would receive assistance along the way.

Yehuda Bauer, an Israeli scholar and expert on the Bricha, argues that despite what some Israelis would later claim, the postwar exodus from Poland received its early organizational drive from resident Polish and Lithuanian Jews – not from the special agents sent from Palestine, known as *shlichim* (emissaries). Ex-partisans first helped Polish Jews find the best border crossings, then forged Red Cross documents for them. Large numbers were assisted in traveling by train into Berlin, or down through Rumania into Yugoslavia or toward Italy.[38]

The most famous ruse employed in the early

months of the Bricha was known as the "Greek bluff." Polish Jews who crossed into Czechoslovakia were given documents showing them to be Greeks who had been imprisoned by the Nazis and now were finally returning to Athens or Salonika. They were forbidden by their Bricha guides to speak Polish, Russian, or Yiddish, since the guards might recognize those as being something other than Greek, but they could talk in Hebrew because the men at the border would not know that. Since no Greek consulates were located in border towns, the travelers' papers could not be checked, and border guards were happy to speed the supposed Greek victims of Hitler on their way to a Hellenic homecoming. (The ultimate compliment for this ruse came when a group of authentic Greeks was arrested crossing into Czechoslovakia. Their documents were so different from those the guards were accustomed to view that they were charged with having forged papers.)[39]

Finally, in October 1945, the first emissaries arrived from Palestine, ten months after the initial groups of Polish Jews had escaped south into Romania and others had fled through Czechoslovakia and Germany. Now the Bricha became an established organization across much of the Continent, although local Jews continued to run most of the day-to-day operations in Poland. Members of the Jewish Brigade, a British military unit from Palestine that saw action near the end of the war in Italy, began to show up anywhere the Bricha needed them, helping Jews steal across frontiers, transporting them in disguised military trucks, carrying supplies, foiling occupation forces repeatedly. The Joint Distribution Committee provided food and clothing for many of the travelers.[40]

But six months after Lieutenant General Morgan charged that a well-organized, fully financed operation was moving thousands of Jews out of Eastern Europe, the reality was that the escape routes were being blocked, largely through British pressure and Soviet reluctance to go along with the exodus. And the truth was that the organizers were unable to cope with the mounting flow of refugee traffic.[41]

At that point a major shift occurred: the Czechoslovaks changed their minds. On 25 July 1946, the Czechoslovak cabinet officially recognized the Bricha, granting it permission to transport Jews across Czechoslovakia. The only proviso was that travelers were not to remain on Czechoslovak soil. (When I. F. Stone traveled with such a group, he found that a Czechoslovak policeman accompanied it to ensure that no one fled the train; in fact, his presence seems to have assured that none of the Jews would be harmed.) Poland then opened its borders also, so by late 1946 there was no legal barrier between any Polish Jew and the DP camps of Austria and Germany. The routes uncovered earlier that year by a UNRRA investigation were still in use, only now they were bulging with refugees:

> The movement into Berlin, for instance, has come almost exclusively on the rail route between Stettin and Berlin; the movement into Bavaria has been, first, on a rail route from Poland to Prague to Pilsen and to Hof in Germany, and second, along the rail route from Budapest to Vienna to Linz to Salzburg and to Munich.[42]

As this influx started to crowd western zone reception centers, Allied policymakers began to understand that they faced a new situation. The realization frequently came in a sudden confrontation, as experienced by Alexander Squadrilli, at that time displaced persons executive with the U.S. Army in Frankfurt. Squadrilli began to receive desperate pleas from officials in Austria, calling for trains to transport the infiltrees out of the vastly overcrowded centers there. Squadrilli dispatched empty train cars to Austria and later went to the camp sidings when they were due to return. "I was out there when the first train arrived," he said. "Some Jews were getting off with bundles and children on their backs. I would look into these people's eyes: it was as if they were seeing right through me – they had a hard glitter in their eyes, that told me they had reached the end of their tolerance – they would cut my throat if I did anything against them."[43]

Some authorities tried to block entry into their zones. But higher-ups intervened, ordering the infiltrees placed in Jewish camps and provided with regular DP food, shelter, and care; these officials also reversed an order that forbade organized groups from

entering the U.S. Zone. In Austria the occupation forces quickly gave up efforts to block these "infiltrees"; they did an about-face and assisted them in moving through. "I could put a division up there on the line but it wouldn't stop the Jews," a high-ranking American officer told one correspondent. And the chief of British DP operations for Austria added, "I find it good policy to play along with the chaps who can turn the tap on and off. They buzz me and announce they have a thousand for my zone and I usually manage to settle for about 500." This became known as the "Green Plan," and it would be tolerated as long as the Jews were just passing through.[44]

In April 1947, however, the United States finally clamped down on the continuing influx. Nothing would be done to stop the infiltrees from coming into the American zones, the new order stated, but they could no longer enter DP camps. Private groups, such as the American Joint Distribution Committee and other Jewish agencies, would have to care for them.[45]

This loosening of occupation policy from 1945 to 1947 opened the doors to the West for thousands of east European Jews. Entering the American zones at rates of 2,000 or more a week, the Jewish population under UNRRA care in Germany and Austria jumped from 18,361 in December 1945 to 97,333 in December 1946; 167,529 were receiving IRO [International Relief Organization] care on 30 September 1947. Thousands of others were not under UNRRA or IRO care. The influx into the U.S. Zone of Germany was so great that the expected decline in camp population from repatriation did not take place. More than 107,000 DPs were repatriated in the last half of 1946, and 16,000 other DPs were removed from the camps as ineligible – but total camp population rose by 8,000.[46]

The 1947 statistics on Jews receiving UNRRA care were dominated by the 122,313 Jews from Poland; there were also 18,593 from Romania, 8,445 from Hungary, 6,602 from Czechoslovakia, and 6,167 from Germany. By then, Jews accounted for 25 percent of displaced persons in Germany and Austria, a sharp rise from the 3.7 percent reported at the end of September 1945 (when many Jews were still classified by nationality).[47]

New camps for infiltrees were opened, a few of

them luxurious – as at Bad Gastein in Austria – but most at the other end of the comfort spectrum. A visitor to the Zeilsheim DP camp near Frankfurt found four families crammed into a room measuring twelve by eighteen feet; he learned that a baby had been born that morning on the stoop outside the main office, and that there was no fresh milk for the camp's sixty new-born babies – while nearby German farmers pastured herds of milk cows. Visitors were appalled at the impermanence and squalor of these overcrowded infiltree centers. Various reasons for these conditions were advanced. One observer concluded that the refugees had a "burning desire to get out, and to shut out any implication that they may have to remain where they are for any serious length of time."[48]

As had happened with other DPs, it was this contrast of wretched overcrowding in the camps with well-housed Germans nearby that put bitterness into the hearts of many, and led some in the UNRRA and IRO to urge major shifts in priorities. This was behind the publicized resignation of the Landsberg camp's welfare director in December 1945 and the resulting army investigation.

The Landsberg director, Dr. Leo Srole, a sociologist, protested the overcrowding, underfeeding, and lack of adequate housing (some of which had been declared "unfit for German prisoners of war"), while expressing fear of impending epidemics, since outbreaks of cholera had been reported in Eastern Europe, source of most of the infiltrees. (In a recent interview, Srole, now of Columbia University, said the overcrowding in late 1945 held the potential for a serious crisis, based on a stalemate between the army and the powerless DPs. "In that setting, I tried to arouse action through that letter of protest, to break the deadlock." It worked. Reporters attending the nearby Nürnberg trials were largely responsible for the extensive publicity given to Srole's resignation.) The military made a quick investigation, and additional camp installations for the incoming Jews were ordered. In February 1946 the army ordered that infiltrees were to be housed and cared for according to the same standards applied to earlier arrivals.[49]

This chaos helped diffuse power in some camps. Much of the power was gathered by sophisticated DPs who organized quickly to protect themselves, to

block unwanted actions by authorities, or simply to seek more supplies from the UNRRA or voluntary agencies. Sometimes the disorder was used by agency workers to gain influence, for many of them had access to great quantities of supplies. The situation at the Neustadt camp in March 1946 angered a UNRRA welfare officer in the British Zone:

> There is no control of supplies distributed by the Jewish agencies. . . . They distribute it to whom they will and how they like, taking double ration for themselves. Occasionally food is given to Polish hospital patients, but only those who are friendly with the committee.
>
> There is no satisfactory control of the DP population in the camp, consequently the food from Belsen is drawn on the strength of about 650, although the actual number of Jews in Neustadt is only around 400. There is constant movement of displaced persons in and out of the camp without any permit, which makes it possible for the same displaced person to be registered and collect food at Belsen and Neustadt at the same time.
>
> The morale among the Jewish displaced persons is unsatisfactory. There is resistance toward any rehabilitative project and tendency toward isolation from the rest of the camp. The Jewish displaced persons, for instance, have not drawn any knitting wool because they would not accept the general scheme of control.
>
> The present staff cannot cope with the situation.[50]

Less than four months later another UNRRA official complained of political infighting between Jewish groups – at Schwebda they were "fighting for the souls" of 150 unaccompanied children – and admitted that competent UNRRA personnel refused to leave jobs in stable Polish and Baltic camps "for the immense difficulties which confront personnel in infiltree centers."[51]

But this intense feeling, this anger at the outside world, also led to a burning desire to celebrate everything that was Jewish. The Joint Distribution Committee's supply network strained to provide enough kosher food for the Orthodox, although a donation of ten million pounds of kosher beef from the Irish Republic helped through a difficult period in early 1947.

A major need for special foods came during Jewish festivals, the succession of events that mark the seasons of the Jewish year. These were days when Jewish feeling was most concentrated, and they took on special meaning, special poignance, after liberation. For years Jews had met only secretly on those days, had passed messages, exchanged looks. Now they celebrated publicly and, as one escaped Polish Jew explained, "Jewish life began to exist again!"[52]

Several of the holidays were contemplative, sad events, bringing happiness after the war only in that they could now be commemorated openly again. But one holiday was sheer joy – Purim, the annual festival of the deliverance of Jews from a massacre planned by Haman as related in the Book of Esther. Traditionally at that springtime event an effigy of Haman is ridiculed and attacked in a joking manner, to the accompaniment of noisemakers, hooting, and singing.

Purim 1946 became very special – perhaps the most special Purim for generations. It was the occasion when Europe's Jews finally threw off the worry and fear under which they had lived since the early 1930s and danced and laughed in the warm sunlight of freedom again. The DPs at Landsberg, one of the largest Jewish camps, turned the event into an exhilarating rebuke to Nazism – in the very city where Hitler wrote *Mein Kampf*. A recent study by Toby Blum-Dobkin dramatically presents the festival's importance in Landsberg in 1946.[53]

Camp leaders saw an opportunity to turn Purim week at Landsberg into rehabilitative activity that would spruce up the camp, help its Jewish residents shake off their despair and celebrate their joy at having survived. Streets were cleaned and buildings scrubbed all week long, while the DPs secretly planned costumes and floats, all to focus on a carnival on 24 March.

Haman's defeat was marked as Hitler's defeat: on the day of the carnival the grounds were filled with tombstones for Hitler, walls were decorated and ornamented, slogans and caricatures appeared everywhere. The camp newspaper reported:

Hitler hangs in many variants and in many poses: A big Hitler, a fat Hitler, a small "Hitler," with medals, and without medals. Jews hung him by his head, by his feet, or by his belly. Or: a painter's ladder with a pail and brush, near a tombstone with the inscription: "P.N." (*po nikbar*) here lies Hitler, may his name be blotted out.

Groups from the camp paraded – the orchestra, sports clubs, unions, and kibbutzim – along with members of the trade schools, police and hospital staff.

But the day meant more than merriment. It also included the reading of a chapter from the *Megillah*, part of the traditional Purim service. And the speeches to the crowd also stressed the broader significance of Purim, 1946, in the DP camps across Europe:

Hitler Germany was the embodiment of the bestial jungle. The Beast is conquered, not only for us, but for all of humanity. This is the meaning of the festival that we celebrate today. A year ago today, in the concentration camps, we did not imagine that the prophecy of the Prophet Ezekiel would be fulfilled: "dry bones" again become a living people. We must rebuild our lives from the ground up and build our own home.

That night at the Landsberg camp they burned a copy of *Mein Kampf* – the chief testament of Adolph Hitler, who had warned in 1944 that unless Germany was victorious, "Jewry could then celebrate the destruction of Europe by a second triumphant Purim festival."

Europe had been nearly destroyed, because of Hitler, but some Jews he had tried to destroy lived on – and now commemorated their escape from both Haman's and Hitler's massacres. Europe was saved. And for the Jews of the *She'erit Ha-pletah*, Purim 1946 was a time of redeeming significance.

Thoughts of Palestine were quickened by these celebrations. The *Mossad le Aliyah Bet*, the underground group aiding emigration, sought to oblige, sending twelve ships illegally to Palestine with forty-four hundred European Jews between May and December 1945. Larger ships left in 1946, with elaborate strategies devised to outwit the British in European ports. The British were increasingly able to catch these ships en route, however. As in the famous case of the *Exodus* in 1947, many ships were forced to return to Europe or deposit their passengers in detention camps on Cyprus.[54]

But some Jews made it into Palestine despite British capture. One was Carl Friedman, who journeyed from a Nazi labor camp to liberated Bucharest and traveled from there into Austria using forged papers provided by the Bricha. He then gave up his wristwatch to purchase passage for his group of six Czechoslovak Jews over the Alps into Italy. Their next stop was a Jewish Brigade camp at Padua, from which they went to a new Kibbutz at Nonontola, where five hundred east European Jews gathered to undergo training for Palestine. Friedman recalled that the training even included methods to travel from the ship to the nearby shore.

> They told us all of the things that can happen, what the circumstances are, the chance to arrive or not to arrive. They had been building with barrels, empty barrels and they put wood around them to let us down in the middle of the water, because the ship cannot reach, to let us reach the port . . . 20 or 30 people can fit in it. To let them come ashore.

It was almost to no avail. Leaving with 950 others on the *Enzo Sereni* in December 1945, Friedman ultimately saw the ship intercepted by the British off Haifa; the passengers were forced into the British camp at Atlit but then released, apparently included in the shifting British legal admission totals. For Carl Friedman, Palestine – home – had been reached.[55]

World events soon changed the Palestine situation. In April 1946 the Anglo-American Committee of Inquiry called for admission of 100,000 Jews into Palestine immediately, and under mounting pressure the British turned the issue over to the United Nations. On 1 September 1947, the United Nations Special Committee on Palestine unanimously recommended that Britain give up its mandate on Palestine

and partition it into separate Arab and Jewish states. This was approved by the UN General Assembly on 29 November 1947, and when word of the UN vote was flashed to Europe around midnight, the lights came on in the Jewish camps, DPs rushed out and the dancing and singing went on for hours. The British mandate would end on 15 May 1948. The state of Israel was born.[56]

By that time some 69,000 European Jews had made it into Palestine since the end of the war, or into detention on Cyprus. They were part of the estimated 250,000 east European Jews who had escaped into Western Europe through the Bricha. After the state of Israel was established, 331,594 European Jews emigrated there through 1951. Others, however, began looking elsewhere as doors began to open; 165,000 European Jews ultimately emigrated to other countries from 1946 to 1950.[57]

Why did they turn away from Israel? Many had relatives in America or other countries, but it should also be stated that opportunities for emigration began to appear by late 1947 that had not been present in 1945. At war's end only Palestine had seemed possible – that was the only "home." Malcolm Proudfoot, an early student of postwar refugee movements, speculated that the state of Israel might not have come into being if other countries had welcomed Europe's Jews earlier.[58]

The Bricha and the Jewish DPs' suffering in overcrowded camps must be counted as major factors in the rise of modern Israel. Armed struggle by the Haganah* in Palestine was important, but, as Yehuda Bauer argued, the presence of Jewish DPs in Europe kept pressure on American opinion makers, while winning the world's sympathy, and ultimately helped swing the United Nations behind the partition of Palestine.

It all signified that DPs were increasingly being drawn into international politics, and their desire for better conditions, as well as their hope for emigration, would put them into more conflicts with their Western protectors as the cold war took on new intensity.

Notes

1. I. F. Stone, *Underground to Palestine* (New York: Boni and Gaer, 1946), 43, 60–62.

*Underground Jewish military organization dedicated to the establishment of the State of Israel, *Ed.*

2. Leo Srole, autobiographical article in *Harvard Class of 1933: Fiftieth Anniversary Report* (Cambridge, Mass.: Harvard Class of 1933, 1983), 523.

3. Nora Levin, *The Holocaust: The Destruction of European Jewry, 1933–1945* (New York: Schocken Books, 1973), 5–6, 315–16.

4. Levin, *Holocaust*, 20, 254–55. Malcolm J. Proudfoot, *European Refugees: 1939–1952 – A Study in Forced Population Movement* (Evanston, Ill.: Northwestern University Press, 1956), 334–42. Henry L. Feingold, "Who Shall Bear Guilt for the Holocaust: The Human Dilemma," *American Jewish History* 68, no. 3 (March 1979): 278.

5. Stone, *Underground*, 46. Josef Rosensaft, "Our Belsen," in *Belsen* (Israel: Irgun Sheerit Hapleita Me'haezor Habriti, 1957), 29. Helen Epstein, *Children of the Holocaust: Conversations with Sons and Daughters of Survivors* (New York: Putnam's, 1979), 105–107, 115. Samuel Gringauz, "Jewish Destiny as the DP's See It," *Commentary* 4, no. 6 (December 1947): 504.

6. Koppel S. Pinson, "Jewish Life in Liberated Germany – A Study of the Jewish DP's," *Jewish Social Studies* 9 (April 1947): 110. Hal Lehrman, "Austria: Way-Station of Exodus – Pages from a Correspondent's Notebook," *Commentary* 2, no. 6 (December 1946): 571.

7. Pinson, "Jewish Life," 110. Epstein, *Children*, 105–107, 213. Tadeusz Grygier, *Oppression: A Study in Social and Criminal Psychology* (Westport, Conn.: Greenwood Press, 1954, 1973), 200–201. Cornelia Goodhue, "We Gain New Candidates for Citizenship," *The Child*, July 1946, 6–7.

8. Grygier, *Oppression*, 41–44. Yehuda Bauer, *Flight and Rescue: BRICHAH* (New York: Random House, 1970), 266, 272.

9. British official quoted in Bauer, *Flight and Rescue*, 51–52. Leonard Dinnerstein, "The U.S. Army and the Jews: Policies toward the Displaced Persons After World War II," *American Jewish History* 68, no. 3 (March 1979): 355–56; Dinnerstein, *America and the Survivors of the Holocaust* (New York: Columbia University Press, 1982), 13, 28.

10. Norbert Wollheim, "Belsen's Place in the Process of 'Death-and-Rebirth' of the Jewish People," in *Belsen*, 55. Bauer, *Flight and Rescue*, 35–36. Gringauz, "Jewish Destiny," 503.

11. *Times* (London), 21 July 1945, 4. *Jewish Chronicle*, quoted in Dinnerstein, *America*, 17.

12. Bauer, *Flight and Rescue*, 76. Paul Trepman, "On Being Reborn," *Belsen*, 134.

13. "Report of Earl G. Harrison," *Department of State Bulletin*, 30 September 1945, no. 13, 456–63 (reprinted in Dinnerstein, *America*, app. B, 291–305). Earl G. Harrison, "The Last Hundred Thousand," *Survey Graphic*, December 1945, 469–73.

14. Joseph B. Schechtman, *The United States and the Jewish State Movement – The Crucial Decade: 1939–1949* (New York: Herzl, 1966), 137–38, 142.

15. Gen. Dwight D. Eisenhower to President Harry S. Truman, 8 October 1945, in *The Papers of Dwight David Eisenhower* (Baltimore: Johns Hopkins University Press, 1978), 6:414–17. Dinnerstein, *America*, chap. 2, passim. Order from R. B. Longe, lt. col., for brigadier, chief, PW & DP Div. Hq., PW & DP Div. Main Hq., Control Commission for G (BE), Bunde, BAOR, 19 November 1945, UNRRA Archives, Germany Mission, British Zone (Lemgo) Central Registry, Repatriation.

16. Proudfoot, *European Refugees*, 342n. Bauer, *Flight and Rescue*, 69, 73. Levin, *Holocaust*, 710–11.

17. Bauer, *Flight and Rescue*, 84–87. Samuel Gringauz, "Our New German Policy and the DP's," *Commentary* 5, no. 6 (June 1948): 510–11. Ephraim Londner, "Religious Life in Belsen," in *Belsen*, 184.

18. Pinson, "Jewish Life," 117.

19. Yehuda Bauer, *The Jewish Emergence From Powerlessness* (Toronto: University of Toronto Press, 1979), 63. Gringauz quote from *Landsberger Lager Cajtung*, reprinted in Pinson, "Jewish Life," 114n. Stone, *Underground*, 52.

20. Marion E. Hutton, "UNRRA Shelters Unattended Children," *The Child*, July 1946, 29.

21. S. Adler-Rudel, "The Surviving Children," in *Belsen*, 125. Pinson, "Jewish Life," 116–17. *New York Times*, 27 November 1945, 5. Gringauz, "Jewish Destiny," 501–509. Bauer, *Flight and Rescue*, 59–60. Gerold Frank, "The Tragedy of the DP's," *New Republic* 114, no. 13 (1 April 1946): 437–38.

22. Bauer, *Jewish Emergence*, 47, 52–53. M. Lubliner, "Jewish Education in Belsen," 160–61; Josef Fraenkel, "The Cultural Liberation of Belsen," 166; and Z. Zamarion (Halpern), "A Shaliach in Belsen," 179, in *Belsen*. Levin, *Holocaust*, 19–20, 61–62, chap. 17. Bauer, *Flight and Rescue*, 29–30, 36. Jon Kimche and David Kimche, *The Secret Roads: The 'Illegal' Migration of a People—1938–1948* (New York: Farrar, Straus and Cudahy, 1955), 171–72.

23. Polish Jew (anonymous), interview with author.

24. Levin, *Holocaust*, 279. "The Infiltrees," *Commentary* 1, no. 2 (February 1946): 43.

25. Levin, *Holocaust*, 165–68. Tatiana Berenstein and Adam Rutkowski, *Assistance to the Jews in Poland – 1939–1945* (Warsaw: Polonia, 1963), 18–19. Bauer, *Jewish Emergence*, 62–64. Polish Jew (anonymous), interview with author.

26. Stone, *Underground*, 51.

27. Inter-Governmental Committee on Refugees, *Memorandum: From the American Resident Representative*, no. 4, 30 April 1946, 3–4. Bauer, *Jewish Emergence*, 64. Yitzhak Arad, *The Partisan: From the Valley of Death to Mount Zion* (New York: Holocaust Library, 1979), 176–77.

28. Wladyslaw Anders, *An Army in Exile: The Story of the Second Polish Corps* (London: Macmillan, 1949), 19. *The Dark Side of the Moon* (London: Faber and Faber, 1946), 210. Arad, *Partisan*, 27, 160–61, 186. Pole (anonymous), interview with author.

29. Bauer, *Flight and Rescue*, 115. Bauer, *Jewish Emergence*, 65. *Commentary*, November 1945, 33–34. Arad, *Partisan*, 186.

30. Dinnerstein, *America*, 107–109. *New York Times*, 13 July 1946, 1, 5. *Commentary*, 2, no. 2 (August 1946): 140. Bauer, *Jewish Emergence*, 65.

31. *Commentary*, 1, no. 1 (November 1945): 33; 2, no. 4 (October 1946): 327–35.

32. Proudfoot, *European Refugees*, 340–42. Dinnerstein, *America*, 112. Bauer, *Flight and Rescue*, chap. 7 passim. Ira A. Hirschmann, *The Embers Still Burn* (New York: Simon and Schuster, 1949), 75–76.

33. Lt.-Gen. Sir Frederick Morgan, *Peace and War – A Soldier's Life* (London: Hodder and Stoughton, 1961), 236–37,

246–51, 256. *Commentary* 1, no. 4 (February 1946): 44–46; March 1946, 66.

34. Frank, "The Tragedy," 437. Genêt, "Letter From Wurzburg," *New Yorker*, 6 November 1948, 116–17. Jay B. Krane, "Observations on the Problem of Jewish Infiltrees" (confidential) 18 January 1946, UNRRA Archives, Germany Mission, Infiltrees. David Bernstein, "Europe's Jews: Summer, 1947," *Commentary* 4, no. 2 (August 1947): 104.

35. *New York Times*, 27 January 1946, 1, 27. Jay B. Krane, "Report on Infiltrees in the U.S. Zone" (confidential) 10 July 1946; "Observations," 18 January 1946, UNRRA Archives, Germany Mission, Infiltrees.

36. Bauer, *Jewish Emergence*, 66–67. Krane, "Observations," 18 January 1946.

37. Polish Jew (anonymous), interview with author.

38. Bauer, *Flight and Rescue*, vii–viii, 118–19. Bauer, *Jewish Emergence*, 62–63, 65–67. Kimche and Kimche, *Secret Roads*, 83–84.

39. Kimche and Kimche, *Secret Roads*, 85–86. Bauer, *Flight and Rescue*, 28–29.

40. Bauer, *Flight and Rescue*, 45, 66–67, 118–19, 121. Bauer, *Jewish Emergence*, 63, 67.

41. Kimche and Kimche, *Secret Roads*, 87–89.

42. Ibid., 87–92. Stone, *Underground*, 43. Krane, "Observations," 18 January 1946, 6.

43. Alexander E. Squadrilli, interview with author.

44. Bauer, *Flight and Rescue*, 81–82, 87–89, 190–91, 248–49. Dinnerstein, *America*, 105. Krane, "Observations," 18 January 1946, 4. Lehrman, "Austria: Way-Station," 565–72.

45. *New York Times*, 17 April 1947, 6. Lucius D. Clay, *Decision in Germany* (Garden City, N.J.: Doubleday, 1950), 232.

46. U.S. Office of Military Government for Germany, *Weekly Information Bulletin*, no. 78, 3 February 1947, 24.

47. Proudfoot, *European Refugees*, 238–39. Preparatory Commission for the IRO, *PCIRO News Bulletin*, no. 6, 8 December 1947, 1–3; no. 11, 24 March 1948, 1–2. *New York Times*, 26 October 1946, 7.

48. Stone, *Underground*, 112–13. Hirschmann, *Embers Still Burn*, 74ff. Bernstein, "Europe's Jews," 107.

49. Leo Srole, interview with author. See accounts of Srole's acts in *New York Times*, 6 December 1945, 7; 7 December 1945, 5. U.S. Army, *Displaced Persons*, Occupation Forces in Europe Series, 1945–46, Training Packet 53 (Frankfurt am Main, Germany: U.S. Army, n.d.), 105.

50. H. Hrachovska, dist. welfare officer, Hq. 8 Corps District, to Col. C. J. Wood, UNRRA dist. dir. Hq. 8 Corps Dist. British Zone, 29 March 1946, UNRRA Archives, Germany Mission, British Zone (Lemgo) Central Registry, Repatriation. This is another Neustadt than the camp discussed at the beginning of chap. 2.

51. Krane, "Report on Infiltrees," 10 July 1946, 2.

52. *New York Times*, 6 February 1947, 3. Polish Jew and former Jewish agency worker (anonymous), interviews with author.

53. Information on the Landsberg carnival is from Toby Blum-Dobkin, "The Landsberg Carnival: Purim in a Displaced Persons Center," Yeshiva University Museum, 1979 Catalogue, *Purim: The Face and the Mask* (New York: Yeshiva University, 1979), 52–58. For information on the Landsberg DP camp, see Leo Srole, "Why the DPs Can't Wait," *Commentary* 3, no. 1 (January 1947): 13–21.

54. Kimche and Kimche, *Secret Roads*, 84, 98, 100–106. *New York Times*, 8 September 1947, 6.

55. Carl Friedman oral history interview, William E. Wiener Oral History Library of the American Jewish Committee, 1 December 1974, 20–23.

56. Schechtman, *United States*, 153. Bauer, *Jewish Emergence*, 74–75. Bauer, *Flight and Rescue*, 320–21. Arad, *Partisan*, 207. *New York Times*, 1 December 1947, 5.

57. Proudfoot, *European Refugees*, 358–61. Bauer, *Flight and Rescue*, 319–21. Bauer, *Jewish Emergence*, 73.

58. Proudfoot, *European Refugees*, 361.

Inmates waving a camp-made American flag greet U.S. Seventh Army troops upon their arrival at the Allach concentration camp in Germany. April 30, 1945. (National Archives, courtesy of USHMM Photo Archives)

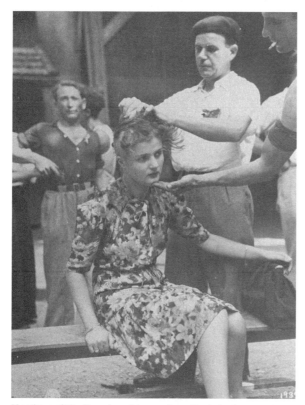

Members of the French resistance shear the hair of a young woman who consorted with the Germans during the occupation. August 29, 1944. (National Archives, courtesy of USHMM Photo Archives)

General Dwight D. Eisenhower, Supreme Allied Commander in the West, accompanied by General Omar Bradley (left), and Lt. General George S. Patton, inspect stolen art treasures hidden in the Merkers salt mine in Germany. April 12, 1945. (National Archives, courtesy of USHMM Photo Archives)

Primo Levi **The Drowned and the Saved**

PREFACE

THE FIRST NEWS about the Nazi annihilation camps began to spread in the crucial year of 1942. They were vague pieces of information, yet in agreement with each other: they delineated a massacre of such vast proportions, of such extreme cruelty and such intricate motivation that the public was inclined to reject them because of their very enormity. It is significant that the culprits themselves foresaw this rejection well in advance: many survivors (among others, Simon Weisenthal in the last pages of *The Murderers Are Among Us*) remember that the SS militiamen enjoyed cynically admonishing the prisoners:

> However this war may end, we have won the war against you; none of you will be left to bear witness, but even if someone were to survive, the world will not believe him. There will perhaps be suspicions, discussions, research by historians, but there will be no certainties, because we will destroy the evidence together with you. And even if some proof should remain and some of you survive, people will say that the events you describe are too monstrous to be believed: they will say that they are the exaggerations of Allied propaganda and will believe us, who will deny everything, and not you. We will be the ones to dictate the history of the Lagers.*

Strangely enough, this same thought ("even if we were to tell it, we would not be believed") arose in the form of nocturnal dreams produced by the prisoners' despair. Almost all the survivors, orally or in their written memoirs remember a dream which frequently recurred during the nights of imprisonment, varied in its detail but uniform in its substance: they had returned home and with passion and relief were describing their past sufferings, addressing themselves to a loved one, and were not believed, indeed were not even listened to. In the most typical (and cruelest) form, the interlocutor turned and left in silence. This is a theme to which we shall return, but at this point it is important to emphasize how both parties, victims and oppressors, had a keen awareness of the enormity and therefore the noncredibility of what took place in the Lagers – and, we may add here, not only in the Lagers, but in the ghettos, in the rear areas of the Eastern front, in the police stations, and in the asylums for the mentally handicapped.

Fortunately, things did not go as the victims feared and the Nazis hoped. Even the most perfect of organizations has its flaws, and Hitler's Germany, especially during the last months before the collapse, was far from being a perfect machine. Much material evidence of the mass exterminations was suppressed, or a more or less dextrous attempt was made to suppress it: in the autumn of 1944 the Nazis blew up the gas chambers and crematoria at Auschwitz, but the ruins are still there, and despite the contortions of epigones it is difficult to justify their function by having recourse to fanciful hypotheses. The Warsaw ghetto, after the famous insurrection in the spring of 1943, was razed to the ground, but thanks to the superhuman concern of a number of fighter-historians (historians of themselves!), in the rubble, often many meters deep, or smuggled beyond the wall, other historians would later rediscover the testimony of how the ghetto lived and died day by day. All the archives in the Lagers were burned during the final days of the war, truly an irremediable loss, so that even today there is discussion as to whether the victims were four, six, or eight million – although one still talks of millions. Before the Nazis had recourse to the gigantic multiple crematoria, the innumerable corpses of the victims, deliberately killed or worn down by hardship and illness, could have constituted evidence and somehow had to be made to disappear. The first solution, macabre to the point of making one hesitate to speak of it, had been simply to pile up the bodies,

*German word meaning "camps," *Ed.*

hundreds of thousands of bodies, in huge common graves, and this was done, in particular at Treblinka and other minor Lagers, and in the wake of the German army in Russia. This was a temporary solution decided upon with bestial insouciance when the German armies were winning on all fronts and final victory appeared certain; they would decide afterward what should be done, and in any case the victor is the master even of truth, can manipulate it as he pleases. Somehow the common graves would be justified, or made to disappear, or attributed to the Soviets (who, for that matter, proved at Katyn not to be lagging too far behind). But after Stalingrad there were second thoughts: best to erase everything immediately. The prisoners themselves were forced to exhume those pitiful remains and burn them on pyres in the open, as if so unusual an operation of such proportions could go completely unnoticed.

The SS command posts and the security services then took the greatest care to ensure that no witness survived. This is the meaning (it would be difficult to excogitate another) of the murderous and apparently insane transfers with which the history of the Nazi camps came to an end during the first months of 1945: the survivors of Maidanek to Auschwitz, those of Auschwitz to Buchenwald and Mauthausen, those of Buchenwald to Bergen-Belsen, the women of Ravensbrück to Schwerin. In short, everyone had to be snatched away from liberation, deported again to the heart of a Germany that was being invaded from the west and east. It did not matter that they might die along the way; what really mattered was that they should not tell their story. In fact, after having functioned as centers of political terror, then as death factories, and subsequently (or simultaneously) as immense, ever renewed reservoirs of slave labor, the Lagers had become dangerous for a moribund Germany because they contained the secret of the Lagers themselves, the greatest crime in the history of humanity. The army of ghosts that still vegetated in them was composed of *Geheimnisträger*, the bearers of secrets who must be disposed of; the extermination plants, also very eloquent, having been destroyed, had to be moved to the interior, it was decided, in the absurd hope of still being able to lock those ghosts up in Lagers less threatened by the advancing fronts and to

exploit their final ability to work, and in the other, less absurd hope that the torment of those Biblical marches would reduce their number. And in fact their number was appallingly reduced, yet some nevertheless had the luck or the strength to survive and remained to bear witness.

Less well known and less studied is the fact that many bearers of secrets were also on the other side, although many knew little and few knew everything. No one will ever be able to establish with precision how many, in the Nazi apparatus, could *not not know* about the frightful atrocities being committed, how many knew something but were in a position to pretend that they did not know, and, further, how many had the possibility of knowing everything but chose the more prudent path of keeping their eyes and ears (and above all their mouths) well shut. Whatever the case, since one cannot suppose that the majority of Germans lightheartedly accepted the slaughter, it is certain that the failure to divulge the truth about the Lagers represents one of the major collective crimes of the German people and the most obvious demonstration of the cowardice to which Hitlerian terror had reduced them: a cowardice which became an integral part of mores and so profound as to prevent husbands from telling their wives, parents their children. Without this cowardice the greatest excesses would not have been carried out, and Europe and the world would be different today.

Without a doubt those who knew the horrible truth because they were (or had been) responsible had compelling reasons to remain silent; but inasmuch as they were depositories of the secret, even by keeping silent they could not always be sure of remaining alive, witness the case of Stangl and the other Treblinka butchers, who after the insurrection there and the dismantling of that Lager were transferred to one of the most dangerous Partisan areas.

Willed ignorance and fear also led many potential "civilian" witnesses of the infamies of the Lagers to remain silent. Especially during the last years of the war, the Lagers constituted an extensive and complex system which profoundly compentrated the daily life of the country; one has with good reason spoken of the *univers concentrationnaire*, but it was not a closed universe. Small and large industrial companies, agricultural combines, agencies, and arms factories drew profits from the practically free labor supplied by the camps. Some exploited the prisoners pitilessly, accepting the inhuman (and also stupid) principle of the SS according to which one prisoner was worth another, and if the work killed him he could immediately be replaced; others, a few, cautiously tried to alleviate their sufferings. Still other industries – or perhaps the same ones – made money by supplying the Lagers themselves: lumber, building materials, cloth for the prisoners' striped uniforms, dehydrated vegetables for the soup, etc. The crematoria ovens themselves were designed, built, assembled, and tested by a German company, Topf of Wiesbaden (it was still in operation in 1975, building crematoria for civilian use, and had not considered the advisability of changing its name). It is hard to believe that the personnel of these companies did not realize the significance of the quality or quantity of the merchandise and installations being commissioned by the SS command units. The same can be, and has been, said with regard to the supplies of the poison employed in the gas chambers at Auschwitz: the product, substantially hydrocyanic acid, had already been used for many years for pest control in the holds of boats, but the abrupt increase in orders beginning with 1942 could scarcely go unnoticed. It must have aroused doubts, and certainly did, but they were stifled by fear, the desire for profit, the blindness and willed stupidity that we have mentioned, and in some cases (probably few) by fanatical Nazi obedience.

It is natural and obvious that the most substantial material for the reconstruction of truth about the camps is the memories of the survivors. Beyond the pity and indignation these recollections provoke, they should also be read with a critical eye. For knowledge of the Lagers, the Lagers themselves were not always a good observation post: in the inhuman conditions to which they were subjected, the prisoners could barely acquire an overall vision of their universe. The prisoners, above all those who did not understand German, might not even know where in Europe their Lager was situated, having arrived after a slaughterous and tortuous journey in sealed boxcars. They did not know about the existence of other Lagers, even those only a few kilometers away. They did not know for whom they worked. They did not understand the significance of certain sudden changes in conditions, or of the mass transfers. Surrounded by death, the deportee was often in no position to evaluate the extent of the slaughter unfolding before his eyes. The companion who worked beside him today was gone by the morrow: he might be in the hut next door, or erased from the world; there was no way to know. In short, the prisoner felt overwhelmed by a massive edifice of violence and menace but could not form for himself a representation of it because his eyes were fixed to the ground by every single minute's needs.

This deficiency conditioned the oral or written testimonies of the "normal" prisoners, those not privileged, who represented the core of the camps and who escaped death only by a combination of improbable events. They were the majority in the Lager, but an exiguous minority among the survivors: among them, those who during their imprisonment enjoyed some sort of privilege are much more numerous. At a distance of years one can today definitely affirm that the history of the Lagers has been written almost exclusively by those who, like myself, never fathomed them to the bottom. Those who did so did not return, or their capacity for observation was paralyzed by suffering and incomprehension.

On the other hand, the "privileged" witnesses could avail themselves of a certainly better observatory, if only because it was higher up and hence took in a more extensive horizon; but it was to a greater or lesser degree also falsified by the privilege itself. The discussion concerning privilege (not only in the Lager) is delicate, and I shall try to go into it later with the greatest possible objectivity. Here I will only mention the fact that the privileged par excellence, that is, those who acquired privilege for themselves by becoming subservient to the camp authority, did not bear witness at all, for obvious reasons, or left incomplete or distorted or totally false testimony. Therefore the best historians of the Lagers emerged from among the very few who had the ability and luck to attain a privileged observatory without bowing to compromises, and the skill to tell what they saw, suffered, and did with the humility of a good chronicler, that is, taking into account the complexity of the Lager phenomenon and the variety of human destinies being played out in it. It was in the logic of things that these historians should almost all be political prisoners: because the Lagers were a political phenomenon; because the political prisoners, much more than the Jews and the criminals (as we know, the three principal categories of prisoners), disposed of a cultural background which allowed them to interpret the events they saw; and because, precisely inasmuch as they were ex-combatants or antifascist combatants even now, they realized that testimony was an act of war against fascism; because they had easier access to statistical data; and lastly, because often, besides holding important positions in the Lager, they were members of the secret defense organization. At least during the final years, their living conditions were tolerable, which permitted them, for example, to write and preserve notes, an unthinkable luxury for the Jews and a possibility of no interest to the criminals.

For all the reasons touched on here, the truth about the Lagers has come to light down a long road and through a narrow door, and many aspects of the *univers concentrationnaire* have yet to be explored in depth. By now more than forty years have passed since the liberation of the Nazi Lagers; this considerable interval has, for the purposes of clarification, led to conflicting results, which I will try to enumerate.

In the first place, there has been the decanting, a desirable and normal process, thanks to which historical events acquire their chiaroscuro and perspective only some decades after their conclusion. At the end of World War II, quantitative data on the Nazi deportations and massacres, in the Lagers and elsewhere, had not been acquired, nor was it easy to understand their import and specificity. For only a few years now has one begun to understand that the Nazi slaughter was dreadfully "exemplary" and that, if nothing worse happens in the coming years, it will be remembered as the central event, the scourge, of this century.

By contrast, the passage of time has as a consequence other historically negative results. The greater part of the witnesses, for the defense and the prosecution, have by now disappeared, and those who remain, and who (overcoming their remorse or, alternately, their wounds) still agree to testify, have ever more blurred and stylized memories, often, un-

beknownst to them, influenced by information gained from later readings or the stories of others. In some cases, naturally, the lack of memory is simulated, but the many years that have gone by make it credible. Also, the "I don't know" or "I did not know" spoken today by many Germans no longer shocks us, as it did or should have when events were recent.

Of another or further stylization we are ourselves responsible, we survivors, or, more precisely, those among us who have decided to live our condition as survivors in the simplest and least critical way. This does not mean that ceremonies and celebrations, monuments and flags are always and everywhere to be deplored. A certain dose of rhetoric is perhaps indispensable for the memory to persist. That sepulchres, "the urns of the strong," kindle souls to perform lofty deeds, or at least preserve the memory of accomplished deeds, was true in Foscolo's time and is still true today; but one must beware of oversimplifications. Every victim is to be mourned, and every survivor is to be helped and pitied, but not all their acts should be set forth as examples. The inside of the Lager was an intricate and stratified microcosm; the "gray zone" of which I shall speak later, that of the prisoners who in some measure, perhaps with good intentions, collaborated with the authority, was not negligible. Indeed, it constituted a phenomenon of fundamental importance for the historian, the psychologist, and the sociologist. There is not a prisoner who does not remember this and who does not remember his amazement at the time: the first threats, the first insults, the first blows came not from the SS but from other prisoners, from "colleagues," from those mysterious personages who nevertheless wore the same striped tunic that they, the new arrivals, had just put on. This book means to contribute to the clarification of some aspects of the Lager phenomenon which still appear obscure. It also sets itself a more ambitious goal, to try to answer the most urgent question, the question which torments all those who have happened to read our accounts: How much of the concentration camp world is dead and will not return, like slavery and the dueling code? How much is back or is coming back? What can each of us do so that in this world pregnant with threats at least this threat will be nullified?

I did not intend, nor would I have been able, to do a historian's work, that is, exhaustively examine the sources. I have almost exclusively confined myself to the National Socialist Lagers because I had direct experience only of these; I also have had copious indirect experience of them, through books read, stories listened to, and encounters with the readers of my first two books. Besides, up to the moment of this writing, and notwithstanding the horror of Hiroshima and Nagasaki, the shame of the Gulags, the useless and bloody Vietnam War, the Cambodian self-genocide, the *desaparecidos* of Argentina, and the many atrocious and stupid wars we have seen since, the Nazi concentration camp system still remains a *unicum*, both in its extent and its quality. At no other place or time has one seen a phenomenon so unexpected and so complex: never have so many human lives been extinguished in so short a time, and with so lucid a combination of technological ingenuity, fanaticism, and cruelty. No one wants to absolve the Spanish conquistadors of the massacres perpetrated in the Americas throughout the sixteenth century. It seems they brought about the death of at least sixty million Indios; but they acted on their own, without or against the directives of their government, and they diluted their misdeeds – not very "planned" to tell the truth – over an arc of more than one hundred years, and they were also helped by the epidemics that they inadvertently brought with them. And, finally, have we not tried to dispose of them by declaring that they were "things of another time"?

THE MEMORY OF THE OFFENSE

HUMAN MEMORY IS A MARVELOUS but fallacious instrument. This is a threadbare truth known not only to psychologists but also to anyone who has paid attention to the behavior of those who surround him, or even to his own behavior. The memories which lie within us are not carved in stone; not only do they tend to become erased as the years go by, but often they change, or even grow, by incorporating extraneous features. Judges know this very well: almost never do two eyewitnesses of the same event describe it in the same way and with the same words, even if the event is recent and if neither of them has a personal interest in distorting it. This scant reliability of our memories will be satisfactorily explained only when we know in what language, in what alphabet they are written, on what surface, and with what pen: to this day we are still far from this goal. Some mechanisms are known which falsify memory under particular conditions: traumas, not only cerebral ones; interference from other "competitive" memories; abnormal conditions of consciousness; repressions; blockages. Nevertheless, even under normal conditions a slow degradation is at work, an obfuscation of outlines, a so to speak physiological oblivion, which few memories resist. Doubtless one may discern here one of the great powers of nature, the same that degrades order into disorder, youth into old age, and extinguishes life in death. Certainly practice (in this case, frequent reevocation) keeps memories fresh and alive in the same manner in which a muscle often used remains efficient, but it is also true that a memory evoked too often, and expressed in the form of a story, tends to become fixed in a stereotype, in a form tested by experience, crystallized, perfected, adorned, installing itself in the place of the raw memory and growing at its expense.

I intend to examine here the memories of extreme experiences, of injuries suffered or inflicted. In this case, all or almost all the factors that can obliterate or deform the mnemonic record are at work: the memory of a trauma suffered or inflicted is itself traumatic because recalling it is painful or at least disturbing. A person who has been wounded tends to block out the memory so as not to renew the pain; the person who has inflicted the wound pushes the memory deep down, to be rid of it, to alleviate the feeling of guilt.

Here, as with other phenomena, we are dealing with a paradoxical analogy between victim and oppressor, and we are anxious to be clear: both are in the same trap, but it is the oppressor, and he alone, who has prepared it and activated it, and if he suffers from this, it is right that he should suffer; and it is iniquitous that the victim should suffer from it, as he does indeed suffer from it, even at a distance of decades. Once again it must be observed, mournfully, that the injury cannot be healed: it extends through time, and the Furies, in whose existence we are forced to believe, not only rack the tormentor (if they do rack him, assisted or not by human punishment), but perpetuate the tormentor's work by denying peace to the tormented. It is not without horror that we read the words left us by Jean Améry, the Austrian philosopher tortured by the Gestapo because he was active in the Belgian resistance and then deported to Auschwitz because he was Jewish:

> Anyone who has been tortured remains tortured. . . . Anyone who has suffered torture never again will be able to be at ease in the world, the abomination of the annihilation is never extinguished. Faith in humanity, already cracked by the first slap in the face, then demolished by torture, is never acquired again.

Torture was for him an interminable death: Améry killed himself in 1978.

We do not wish to abet confusions, small-change Freudianism, morbidities, or indulgences. The oppressor remains what he is, and so does the victim. They are not interchangeable. The former is to be punished and execrated (but, if possible, understood), the latter is to be pitied and helped; but both, faced by the indecency of the irrevocable act, need refuge and protection, and instinctively search for them. Not all, but most – and often for their entire lives.

By now we are in possession of numerous confessions, depositions, and admissions on the part of the oppressors (I speak not only of the German National Socialists but of all those who commit horrendous and multiple crimes in obedience to a discipline): some given in court, others during interviews, others still contained in books or memoirs. In my opinion, these are documents of the utmost importance. In general, the descriptions of the things seen and the acts committed are of little interest: they amply coincide with what victims have recounted; very rarely are they contested; judgments have been handed down and they are by now part of history. Often they are regarded as well known. Much more important are the motivations and justifications: Why did you do this? Were you aware that you were committing a crime?

The answers to these two questions, or to others which are analogous, are very similar to each other, independently of the personality of the interrogated person, be he an ambitious and intelligent professional like Speer or a gelid fanatic like Eichmann, a short-sighted functionary like [Franz] Stangl in Treblinka or Höss in Auschwitz, or an obtuse brute like Boger and Kaduk, the inventors of torture. Expressed in different formulations and with greater or lesser arrogance, depending on the speaker's mental and cultural level, in the end they substantially all say the same things: I did it because I was ordered to; others (my superiors) have committed acts worse than mine; in view of the upbringing I received, and the environment in which I lived, I could not have acted differently; had I not done it, another would have done it even more harshly in my place. For anyone who reads these justifications the first reaction is revulsion: they lie, they cannot believe they will be believed, they cannot not see the imbalance between their excuses and the enormity of pain and death they have caused. They lie knowing that they are lying: they are in bad faith.

Now, anyone who has sufficient experience of human affairs knows that the distinction (the opposition, a linguist would say) good faith/bad faith is optimistic and smacks of the Enlightenment, and is all the more so, and for much greater reason, when applied to men such as those just mentioned. It presupposes a mental clarity which few have and which even these few immediately lose when, for whatever reason, past or present reality arouses anxiety or discomfort in them. Under such conditions there are, it is true, those who lie consciously, coldly falsifying reality itself, but more numerous are those who weigh anchor, move off, momentarily or forever, from genuine memories, and fabricate for themselves a convenient reality. The past is a burden to them; they feel repugnance for things done or suffered and tend to replace them with others. The substitution may begin in full awareness, with an invented scenario, mendacious, restored, but less painful than the real one; they repeat the description to others but also to themselves, and the distinction between true and false progressively loses its contours, and man ends by fully believing the story he has told so many times and continues to tell, polishing and retouching here and there the details which are least credible or incongruous or incompatible with the acquired picture of historically accepted events: initial bad faith has become good faith. The silent transition from falsehood to self-deception is useful: anyone who lies in good faith is better off. He recites his part better, is more easily believed by the judge, the historian, the reader, his wife, and his children.

The further events fade into the past, the more the construction of convenient truth grows and is perfected. I believe that only by this mental mechanism is it possible to interpret, for instance, the statements made in 1978 to *L'Express* by Louis Darquier de Pellepoix, former commissioner of Jewish affairs in the Vichy government around 1942, and as such personally responsible for the deportation of seventy thousand Jews. Darquier denies everything: the photographs of piles of corpses are montages; the statistics of millions of dead were fabricated by the Jews, always greedy for publicity, commiseration, and indemnities: there may perhaps have been deportations (he would have found it difficult to dispute them: his signature appears at the foot of too many letters giving orders for these very deportations, even of children), but he did not know where to or with what results; there were, it is true, gas chambers in Auschwitz, but only to kill lice, and anyway (note the coherence!) they were built for propaganda purposes after the end of the war. It is not my intention to justify this cowardly and foolish man, and it offends me to know that he lived for a long time undisturbed in Spain, but I think I can recognize in him the typical case of someone who, accustomed to lying in public, ends by lying in private, too, to himself as well, and building for himself a comforting truth which allows him to live in peace. To keep good and bad faith distinct costs a lot: it requires a decent sincerity or truthfulness with oneself; it demands a continuous intellectual and moral effort. How can such an effort be expected from men like Darquier?

Reading the statements made by Eichmann during the Jerusalem trial, and those of Rudolph Höss (the penultimate commander of Auschwitz, the inventor of the hydrocyanic acid chambers) in his autobiography, one can see in them a process of re-elaboration of the past, more subtle than Darquier's. In substance, these two defended themselves

in the classical manner of the Nazi militia, or, better yet, of all militiamen: we have been educated in absolute obedience, hierarchy, nationalism; we have been imbued with slogans, intoxicated with ceremonies and demonstrations; we have been taught that the only justice was that which was to the advantage of our people and that the only truth was the words of the Leader. What do you want from us? How can you even think to expect from us, after the fact, a behavior different from ours and that of all those who were like us. We were the diligent executors, and for our diligence we were praised and promoted. The decisions were not ours because the regime in which we grew up did not permit autonomous decisions: others have decided for us, and that was the only way it could have happened because our ability to decide had been amputated. Therefore we are not responsible and cannot be punished.

Even projected against the background of the Birkenau smokestacks, this reasoning cannot be considered purely the fruit of impudence. The pressure that a modern totalitarian state can exercise over the individual is frightful. Its weapons are substantially three: direct propaganda or propaganda camouflaged as upbringing, instruction, and popular culture; the barrier erected against pluralism of information; and terror. Nevertheless, it is not permissible to admit that this pressure is irresistible, especially in the brief twelve-year term of the Third Reich. In the affirmations and exculpations of men responsible for such serious crimes as were Höss and Eichmann, the exaggeration and, to an even greater degree, the manipulation of memory is obvious. Both were born and raised long before the Reich became truly "totalitarian," and their joining the Nazi party was a choice dictated more by opportunism than enthusiasm. The re-elaboration of their past was a later work, slow and (probably) not methodical. To ask oneself whether it was done in good or bad faith is naive. They too, so strong in the face of others' suffering, when fate put them before judges, before the death they deserved, built a convenient past for themselves and ended by believing in it, especially Höss, who was not a subtle man. As he appears in his writings, he was in fact a person so little inclined to self-control and introspection that he does not realize he is confirming his coarse anti-Semitism by the very act in which he abjures and denies it, nor does he realize how slimy his self-portrait as a good functionary, father, and husband actually is.

As a comment on these reconstructions of the past (but not only on these: it is an observation that holds for all memories) one must note that the distortion of fact is often limited by the objectivity of the facts themselves, around which there exists the testimonies of third parties, documents, *corpora delicti*, historically accepted contexts. It is generally difficult to deny having committed a given act, or that such an act was committed; it is, on the contrary, very easy to alter the motivations which led us to an act and the passions within us which accompanied the act itself. This is an extremely fluid matter, subject to distortion even under very weak pressure; to the questions Why did you do this? or What were you thinking as you did it? no reliable answers exist, because states of mind are by nature labile and even more labile is the memory of them.

An extreme case of the distortion of the memory of a committed guilty act is found in its suppression. Here, too, the borderline between good and bad faith can be vague; behind the "I don't know" and the "I do not remember" that one hears in courtrooms there is sometimes the precise intent to lie, but at other times it is a fossilized lie, rigidified in a formula. The rememberer has decided not to remember and has succeeded: by dint of denying its existence, he has expelled the harmful memory as one expels an excretion or a parasite. Lawyers for the defense know very well that the memory gap, or the putative truth, which they suggest to their clients, tends to become forgetfulness and the actual truth. It is not necessary to trespass in the field of mental pathology to find human examples whose declarations perplex us: they are most certainly false, but we are unable to detect whether the subject does or does not know he is lying. Supposing, absurdly, that the liar should for one instant become truthful, he himself would not know how to answer the dilemma; in the act of lying he is an actor totally fused with his part, no longer distinguishable from it. A glaring example of this during the days in which I am writing is the behavior in court of the Turk Ali Agca, the would-be assassin of Pope John-Paul II.

The best way to defend oneself against the invasion of burdensome memories is to impede their entry, to extend a *cordon sanitaire*. It is easier to deny entry to a memory than to free oneself from it after it has been recorded. This, in substance, was the purpose of many of the artifices thought up by the Nazi commanders in order to protect the consciences of those assigned to do the dirty work and to ensure their services, disagreeable even for the most hardened cutthroats. The *Einsatzkommandos*, who behind the front lines in Russia machine-gunned civilians beside common graves which the victims themselves had been forced to dig, were given all the liquor they wanted so that the massacre would be blurred by drunkenness. The well-known euphemisms ("final solution," "special treatment," the very term *Einsatzkommando*, literally, "prompt-employment unit," disguised a frightful reality) were not only used to deceive the victims and prevent defensive reactions on their part: they were also meant, within the limits of the possible, to prevent public opinion, and those sections of the army not directly involved, from finding out what was happening in all the territories occupied by the Third Reich.

At any rate, the entire history of the brief "millennial Reich" can be reread as a war against memory, an Orwellian falsification of memory, falsification of reality, negation of reality. All of Hitler's biographies, while disagreeing on the interpretation to be given to the life of this man so difficult to classify, agree on the flight from reality which marked his last years, especially beginning with the first Russian winter. He had forbidden and denied his subjects any access to truth, contaminating their morality and their memory; but, to a degree which gradually increased and attained complete paranoia in the Bunker, he barred the path of truth to himself as well. Like all gamblers, he erected around himself a stage set woven of superstitious lies and in which he ended by believing with the same fanatical faith that he demanded from every German. His collapse was not only a salvation for mankind but also a demonstration of the price to be paid when one dismembers the truth.

Also in the certainly much vaster field of the victim one observes a drifting of memory, but here, evidently, fraud is not involved. Anyone who suffers an injustice or an injury does not need to elaborate lies to exculpate himself of a guilt he does not have (even though, due to a paradoxical mechanism of which we shall speak, he may well feel ashamed of it); but this does not exclude the fact that his memories may also be altered. It has been noticed, for instance, that many survivors of wars or other complex and traumatic experiences tend unconsciously to filter their memory: summoning them up among themselves, or telling them to third persons, they prefer to dwell on moments of respite, on grotesque, strange, or relaxed intermezzos, and to skim over the most painful episodes, which are not called up willingly from the reservoir of memory and therefore with time tend to mist over, to lose their contours. The behavior of Count Ugolino is psychologically credible when he becomes reticent about telling Dante of his terrible death; he agrees to do so not out of acquiescence but only out of a feeling of posthumous revenge against his eternal enemy. When we say, "I will never forget that," referring to some event which has profoundly wounded us but has not left in us or around us a material trace or a permanent void, we are foolhardy: in "civilian" life we gladly forget the details of a serious illness from which we have recovered, or those of a successful surgical operation.

For purposes of defense, reality can be distorted not only in memory but in the very act of taking place. Throughout the year of my imprisonment in Auschwitz I had Alberto D. as a fraternal friend: he was a robust, courageous young man, more clear-sighted than the average and therefore very critical of the many who fabricated for themselves, and reciprocally administered to each other, consolatory illusions ("The war will be over in two weeks," "There will be no more selections," "The English have landed in Greece," "The Polish Partisans are about to liberate the camp," and so on, rumors heard nearly every day and punctually given the lie by reality). Alberto had been deported together with his forty-five-year-old father. In the imminence of the great selection of October 1944, Alberto and I had commented on this event with fright, impotent rage, rebellion, resignation, but without seeking refuge in comforting truths. The selection came, Alberto's "old" father was chosen for the gas, and in the space of a few hours Alberto changed. He had heard rumors that seemed to him worthy of belief: the Russians are close by, the Germans would no longer dare persist in the slaughter, that was not a selection like the others, it was not for the gas chamber, but had been made to choose the weakened but salvageable prisoners, in fact like his father, who was very tired but not ill; indeed, he even knew where they would be sent, to Jaworzno, not far away, to a special camp for convalescents fit only for light labor.

Naturally his father was never seen again and Alberto himself vanished during the evacuation march from the camp, in January 1945. Strangely, without knowing about Alberto's behavior, his relatives who had remained hidden in Italy, escaping capture, behaved in the same way, rejecting an unendurable truth, constructing a different one for themselves. As soon as I was repatriated, I considered it my duty to go immediately to Alberto's hometown to tell his mother and his brother what I knew. I was welcomed with courteous affection, but as soon as I began my story the mother begged me to stop: she already knew everything, at least as far as Alberto was concerned, and there was no point in my repeating the usual horror stories to her. She *knew* that her son, he alone, had been able to slip away from the column without being shot by the SS. He had hidden in the forest and was safe in Russian hands; he had not yet been able to send any word, but he would do so soon, she was certain of it; and now, would I please change the subject and tell her how I myself had survived. A year later I was by chance passing through that same town, and I again visited the family. The truth was slightly changed: Alberto was in a Soviet clinic, he was fine; but he had lost his memory, he no longer even remembered his name; he was improving though and would soon return – she had this from a reliable source.

Alberto never returned. More than forty years have passed. I did not have the courage to show up again and to counterpose my painful truth to the consolatory "truth" that, one helping the other, Alberto's relatives had fashioned for themselves.

An apology is in order. This very book is drenched in memory; what's more, a distant memory. Thus it draws from a suspect source and must be protected against itself. So here then: it contains more considerations than memories, lingers more willingly on the state of affairs such as it is now than on the retroactive chronicle. Furthermore, the data it contains are strongly substantiated by the imposing literature that has been formed around the theme of the man submerged (or "saved"), also through the collaboration, voluntary or not, of the culprits of that time; and in this corpus the concordances are abundant, the discordances negligible. As for my personal memories, and the few unpublished anecdotes I have mentioned and will mention, I have diligently examined all of them: time has somewhat faded them, but they are in good consonance with their background and seem to me unaffected by the drifting I have described.

The main cell block in the Nuremburg prison, where defendants standing trial before the International Tribunal were incarcerated. One guard was posted at the entrance of each defendant's cell in order to prevent suicide attempts. November 24, 1945. (National Archives, courtesy of USHMM Photo Archives)

Thousands of spectators surround the gallows in the Smolensk (Russia) city square to witness the execution by hanging of seven convicted German war criminals. 1945. (Central State Archive of Documentary Film and Photography, courtesy of USHMM Photo Archives)

Displaced Persons in the Bergen-Belsen DP camp carry banners and flags to a demonstration protesting the forced return to Europe of the Exodus, a ship carrying 4,500 Jewish refugees to Palestine. The Exodus became a symbol of the "illegal" Jewish immigration to Palestine after the Holocaust. 1947. (Gedenkstatte Bergen-Belsen, courtesy of USHMM Photo Archives)

The "illegal" immigrant ship Josiah Wedgewood sailed from Vado (Italy) in June 1946 and was intercepted by the H.M.S. Venus while attempting to run the British blockade of Palestine. The ship, carrying 1,300 European Jewish refugees, was taken to Haifa, and her passengers transferred to the nearby Athlit detention camp. The sign reads: "We survived Hitler. Death is no stranger to us. Nothing can keep us from our Jewish Homeland. Our blood will be on your head if you fire on an unarmed ship." July 27, 1946. (Courtesy of Yad Vashem Photo Archives)

Debórah Dwork and Robert Jan van Pelt **The Netherlands**

The Jonas Daniel Meijerplein, once the heart of Jewish Amsterdam and later the hub of the ghetto without walls instituted by the Germans during the Occupation, is framed by the Portuguese Synagogue, the four shuls that form the Ashkenazi Synagogue complex, and the statue of the dockworker on strike in February 1941 against the first German-imposed anti-Jewish measures. In a very real sense, the three structures that now make the square famous constitute an architectural exhibition of the history of the Jews in the Netherlands. The Portuguese Synagogue remains as it was in the seventeenth century, untouched by the war in general or the Germans in particular. Gorgeous and empty, it is owned by the Portuguese-Israelite community, but there are few Sephardic Jews in the city to use it. The fate of the Ashkenazi shuls was very different. The complex, dating from the seventeenth and eighteenth centuries, was plundered by the Germans during their five-year rule. The synagogues survived as a deserted hulk. Purchased by Amsterdam's city council in 1955, the Ashkenazi complex ceased to have any connection with the Jewish community. For more than thirty years the building was abandoned; finally, in 1987 it was restored to provide a new home for the city-run Jewish Historical Museum. No longer a living Jewish communal building, it is now a municipal museum to preserve the memory of the Jews in the Netherlands. The dockworker – the quintessential symbol of Dutch resistance – faces the museum, his back to the splendid relic of the Jewish community, the Portuguese Synagogue. It is the victims and not the survivors who command his attention; his loyalty lies with the dead.

The statue of the dockworker was erected in 1952, seven years after the liberation of the Netherlands. Standing in the center of the Dutch capital, it expresses the immediate postwar belief that the Dutch nation as a whole had gallantly, if unsuccessfully, defended its Jewish citizens. By 1970 the self-perception of the Dutch had changed, and another monument was erected far from Amsterdam, in a forest clearing near the village of Westerbork. In the 1930s a camp had been built in that bleak and desolate spot. First a compound for German refugees, it then became the transit center on the train route from homeland and haven to destruction and death. More than one hundred thousand Jews were deported to the East from Westerbork.

The creation of the monument in Westerbork marked a watershed in the history of the Dutch response to the Holocaust. Dutch self-satisfaction, expressed in the heroic pose of the dockworker, had given way to a genuinely felt empathy with the victims. This metamorphosis began in 1945 with the conclusion of 350 years of Dutch Jewish history. Starting in the Jonas Daniel Meijerplein in the late sixteenth century, the history of Dutch Jewry was, in a fundamental sense, terminated in Westerbork on September 13, 1944, with a last transport of 279 persons to Bergen-Belsen.

Before the Holocaust

Arriving in Amsterdam at the end of the sixteenth century, the so-called Portuguese Jews settled in an area adjacent to what is now the Jonas Daniel Meijerplein. They were the first generation of the Jewish community that was to endure until the German Occupation. Expelled from Spain in 1492, these Jews traveled to Portugal, where they made a home for themselves as crypto-Jews. When Spain annexed Portugal a century later, they were driven out of the Iberian Peninsula and fled to the Netherlands. In the Dutch Republic, which was at war with the country that had persecuted them, the Sephardic refugees found a tolerant haven where they were entitled to

Debórah Dwork and Robert Jan van Pelt, "The Netherlands" in David S. Wyman, ed., **The World Reacts to the Holocaust,** 45–77. Baltimore: The Johns Hopkins University Press, 1996. "The Netherlands" Copyright © 1996 by Debórah Dwork and Robert Jan van Pelt. Used by permission of the authors.

practice their own religion and participate in economic life. They flourished as a community (with a population of about four hundred in 1610 and three thousand in 1780), they engaged in business and education, and there was always a core of respected scholars and wealthy merchants.[1] The Sephardic community took an active role in the life of the city of Amsterdam and in the affairs of the republic. They were a visible, confident, and accepted minority. It was their privilege to obtain permission to construct a Jewish communal building (the Portuguese Synagogue), which in size competed with and in decoration exceeded major Protestant churches, just inside the most important city gate.[2] It was the site that later became the Jonas Daniel Meijerplein. The community had become an integral and integrated part of the city landscape.

In the 1620s a second group of Jews immigrated to the Netherlands. The new arrivals from Germany formed a semi-autonomous Ashkenazi "nation." The German Jews were joined three decades later by their Polish coreligionists fleeing from pogroms in Ukraine. The two groups together were known as the *Hoogduitse* (High German) nation. With a population of five thousand in 1680 and thirty thousand a century later, theirs was a far larger community than that of their Sephardic cousins. It was also much poorer.

The Christian community was, in general, tolerant of Jewish customs, which were practiced publicly, and of the participation of Jews in Dutch life – in education, publishing, business, trade, colonial enterprises, and so on. In the seventeenth and eighteenth centuries anti-Semitism, such as it was, was directed mainly against the High German nation, perhaps because the Portuguese Jews were seen as an exotic, stable community with a glorious past. The Sephardic Jews' very reason for being in the Netherlands fit the Dutch conception of their own struggle against Spain. They were in essence, fellow sufferers. All Jews were granted full citizenship in 1796, and the two nations' special legal status of semi-autonomy was revoked. Jews were part of the general community, and the anti-Semitism they experienced was moderate in tone and certainly nonaggressive. It was an anti-Semitism that was not perceived as dangerous, but as a slightly unpleasant element in an otherwise safe, if impoverished, existence.

Dutch Jews on the whole were not well-off financially. Indeed, by the end of the eighteenth century both the Sephardic community and the *Hoogduitse* community were poverty-stricken. In Amsterdam, which was the center of Dutch Jewry, 54 percent of Portuguese Jews and 87 percent of High German Jews were supported in 1799 by richer members of their respective communities. A half-century later, in 1849, the fortunes of the former had declined, while those of the latter had improved; yet the welfare of both was completely out of proportion to that of the general population. Thus, 63 percent of Portuguese Jews and 55 percent of the *Hoogduitse* but only 17 percent of the gentile population of Amsterdam received aid. It was not until the end of the nineteenth century that the situation improved, and even then it was still not very good, with 11.2 percent of the Sephardic and 11.6 percent of the Ashkenazi Jews but only 2 percent of the gentiles requiring assistance.

Unemployment, underemployment, and poorly paid employment were constant. Even those who had work were relatively destitute. The two-fifths of all working Jews who were in trade, most of them peddlers, managed to make a living but were rarely economically comfortable. The diamond industry absorbed two-thirds of all Jews in industrial occupations but was highly fluctuating. Thus, although there was a Jewish bourgeoisie, there was also a real *Lumpenproletariat* that warmly supported socialism and was disaffected from Jewish communal authority. The two main religious bodies, or "churches" *(kerkgenootschappen)*, the Portuguese-Israelite and the Dutch-Israelite (successor to the *Hoogduitse* community), were controlled by the rich, which alienated most working-class Jews. The community was divided and fragmented: Ashkenazi and Sephardic, bourgeois and proletariat, economically conservative and socialist.

The economic crisis of the 1930s exacerbated the divisions within the Jewish community, which at the time had 110,000 members, of whom 90,000 lived in Amsterdam. The contrast between rich and poor was sharper than in Dutch society generally. The average income of those Jews who paid taxes was 20 percent higher than that of the general population, while the percentage of Jews whose income was below the line where tax began to apply was at least equal to or greater than the percentage of poor in the Dutch population at large. The poorer and the richer Jews lived in distinct neighborhoods, and they voted differently (the poor voting "red," the rich for one of the liberal parties). Most important, there was no Jewish ideology connecting the two groups. The synagogue had lost its attraction, and the small Zionist movement, which had 3,000 members, was a middle-class affair. It was, in short, a fragmented community without leadership. As one historian put it, seen from a Jewish perspective, Dutch Jewry had already ceased to exist before the Germans arrived.[3]

The disaffection within the Jewish community was not due to, or in reaction to, anti-Semitism. By the 1930s most Jews felt themselves to be very well integrated in Dutch society, even though they had only limited access to the highest government posts and to the officer corps in the armed forces and even though there was not one Jewish mayor and only thirteen of the twenty thousand policemen and gendarmes were Jews. These manifestations of the limitations of acceptance were not experienced as a problem, and in general Jews believed that social advancement was possible. Nevertheless, it was commonly understood that admission came at a price. As the unsentimental, pragmatic Dutch Zionist leader Fritz Bernstein observed wryly in 1935: "The Jew is only admitted to non-Jewish circles when he can bring something with him that compensates for his disadvantage of being a Jew; he must bring a surplus of talent or significance or position or education, or wealth in comparison to the circle in which he desires admittance. . . . *In the best of circumstances the Jew faces a kind-hearted tolerance on the part of truly well-bred gentiles, who consider it their duty not to let it appear to the Jew that his Jewishness makes a difference,* just as a civilized person tries to hide from the invalid that his handicap is noticed."[4]

The essentially mild genre of anti-Semitism that prevailed in the Netherlands must be understood within the unique context of Dutch society. Unlike in other European countries, in Holland there was no clear differentiation between a dominant and relatively homogeneous culture and the "foreign" culture of the Jews. The Dutch nation was itself fragmented into a number of virtually independent societies, none of which could claim a majority. These societies were perceived as columns, or *zuilen*, on which the state rested. In addition to the Catholic *zuil* (which, with 30 percent of the population, was the largest), there were three Protestant *zuilen* and two secular *zuilen*, one social-democratic and the other liberal. Each *zuil* had its own political party, newspaper, trade union, schools, university, sports societies, broadcasting system, and so on. The various *zuilen* considered each other at best with indifference and more usually with suspicion. Thus the Catholic *zuil's* attitude toward the Jews was not very different from their attitude toward members of the other *zuilen*. In only one way did the situation of the Jews differ from that of members of other religious denominations: while the specific character of their group would have justified a Jewish *zuil*, there was none. This was because of both the size and the fragmentation of the Jewish community. Any group that made up at least 10 percent of the population could, if it so wished, form a *zuil*, and at no more than 2 percent the Jews did not qualify. Then too, the Jewish bourgeoisie belonged to the liberal *zuil*, and the Jewish working class to the social-democratic *zuil*.

What united these different societies was the House of Orange, not as the embodiment of the ideology of monarchy, but as the representation of the glorious history of the Netherlands. All groups, including the Jews, shared the history of the Dutch Republic in the late sixteenth and seventeenth centuries. This national-historical consciousness ultimately rested on the notion of what it meant to be a *Nederlander*, a Dutchman. Jews perceived themselves to be, and were recognized by their Christian countrymen to be, *Nederlanders* whose earliest ancestors had lived in Palestine but whose later forebears had participated in writing the most illustrious page in Dutch history, a page of glory and tolerance. Gentile Dutchmen shared the sentiments that Abraham Asscher (owner of a large diamond factory, liberal member of the Provincial Estates of North Holland, chairman of numerous Jewish organizations, and the leader of the Dutch-Israelite community) expressed in 1935 at the official third centennial of the establishment of the *Hoogduitse/Nederlands-Israelitische* community. "As Dutchmen and as people who belong to the Jewish community, we consider it the greatest happiness for our country to have been ruled for centuries by a royal house such as that of Orange, which from generation to generation has maintained the life goal of its brilliant founder, William the Taciturn: the high principles of freedom of conscience and religious tolerance," Asscher declared. "It is well known that Her Majesty our Queen has carried on this tradition for the sake of the happiness of our country. We know that she acts in total accordance with the spirit of the Dutch people."[5]

There were no functional implications or actual manifestations of this concept of the *Nederlander*, however. To be Dutch meant, as the historian Hans Blom has put it, to have "a well-considered contentment about the unique and exemplary nature of Dutch society,"[6] but it did not signify a commitment to an inclusive Dutch nation incorporating all the *zuilen* or all the disparate groups living in the country – Catholics, liberals, Jews, socialists, Protestants, communists, and so on. There was no mutual loyalty among them, only a shared self-satisfaction. In practical terms, the sole unifying element was the extremely efficient bureaucracy of the civil service, which spread its web across the nation. The different *zuilen* of which Dutch society was composed did not drift apart, because each individual was connected to the apparatus of the state through this net. Everyone and everything was registered; everyone and everything had a place and was in place.

The heterogeneous character of the Dutch state had several implications, the most important of which was that each of the participating societies considered itself a minority. The Catholics, for instance, saw themselves as a minority in a generally Protestant country. Thus the Jewish minority had no special function as a scapegoat, and anti-Semitism was of little value as a theme to gain votes. The agenda of the Dutch fascist party, the Nationaal Socialistische Beweging (National Socialist Movement), or NSB, was to transmute the pluralism in which the nation was grounded into unity; their ideal was a single *volk*, or people. Their aim was to destroy the *zuilen* structure

of Dutch society and to reconstruct the nation on an ideology of homogeneity. The concept of the *Nederlander* was to be given substance.

Initially, Jews were not excluded from this process. By the mid-thirties, however, the NSB had discovered the political potential of anti-Semitism. According to the Dutch National Socialists, the divisions in Dutch society were not only unnecessary but harmful, and the Jews were to blame for these fissures. Indeed, perhaps it was a ploy of the Jews to divide what was, and ought to have been, one united gentile *Nederlandse* society, thus rendering it powerless. The NSB pointed to the decline of Dutch commercial and cultural preeminence in the second half of the seventeenth century, the adoption of French, and the loss of specifically Dutch characteristics in society, art, and architecture and attributed these trends to the establishment of the *Hoogduitse* Jewish community in the Netherlands. Clearly, the Jews were responsible for the ills of the nation. (The Portuguese Jews, by contrast, were considered with greater benevolence, since their arrival had preceded the period of Dutch glory and thus they were perceived to have participated in it.)

The NSB move toward anti-Semitism was influenced by events in Germany, and the *zuilen* too were susceptible to Nazi ideology and propaganda. They slowly became aware of a Jewish Problem. The Nazi postulate that Europe had suffered a moral degeneration since the beginning of the Industrial Revolution as a direct result of Jewish emancipation began to be accepted in Catholic and Protestant circles. Much of the new philosophy coming out of Germany was interpreted by these elements of Dutch society as staunchly Christian, and they found it attractive. By the end of the 1930s many people believed that a Jewish Problem or a Jewish Question indeed existed and that a solution was needed. Even a relatively mild and not altogether unsympathetic review of the issue, J. van der Ploeg's *Het Joodsche Vraagstuk: Een Maatschappelijk Probleem* (The Jewish Question: A Social Problem), published shortly before the German occupation, argued that it "is important, both for the Jew and the non-Jew, to come to an arrangement before it is too late. If one allows anti-Semitism and the hatred for Jews to run its course, outbursts will occur in which the Jew will become the victim and the persecutors of Jews will be dishonored. A just and speedy arrangement can prevent this, and is therefore of self-evident interest to both parties."[7] The "arrangement," which van der Ploeg suggested but did not specify, was to be based on the recognition that the Jews were an alien element within Dutch society and should be treated accordingly.

While a more virulent strain of anti-Semitism was articulated in the Netherlands throughout the mid- to late 1930s, the Dutch were rather reserved with regard to Nazism as such, and many rejected it completely. As elsewhere in Europe, however, Nazism was perceived as a preferable alternative to communism, which was greatly feared. This led to a certain relativism vis-à-vis German anti-Semitism. "In Russia the persecution of Christians is worse than the persecution of the Jews in Germany," one paper declared. "We lament what is done east of us against the Jews, but in our own country Christians suffer worse at the hands of revolutionary elements," another proclaimed.[8] In general, however, the Dutch tradition of neutrality prevailed. Christian Holland kept its distance from the events in Germany. The secular liberal and socialist *zuilen* and the Communist Party responded more energetically to anti-Semitism, although there were great differences of opinion concerning how to proceed, and as a result there were no collective actions.

The Dutch Jewish community also kept its distance from the developments in Germany. There were no collective actions against the Nazi government's persecution of the Jews, nor was there an appreciable solidarity between Dutch and German Jews. Dutch Jews considered themselves to be first and foremost *Nederlanders*, while German Jews remained *Duitsers*. The differences between them were more important than the bonds they shared; Judaism, as we have seen, did not greatly signify in prewar Holland. Dutch Jews feared that the arrival of their German coreligionists (whose presence was the result of their Jewishness and who claimed a connection with the Dutch Jews on that basis) would upset the carefully preserved ideology that the Dutch Jew, like the Dutch Catholic or the Dutch Protestant, was an ordinary *Nederlander* like all other *Nederlanders*. And to some extent their

fear was rational: it was undoubtedly as a result of the arrival between early 1933 and April 1938 of some twenty-five thousand Jewish refugees, of whom around twelve thousand came to depend on public assistance, that many Dutchmen started to reconsider the position of the Jewish community in relation to other Dutch communities (or Dutch society as a whole, as the NSB claimed).[9]

The Dutch government exploited this tension both to limit immigration and to profit financially. In 1938 the borders effectively were closed to Jewish refugees, and new arrivals were returned to Germany. The sole exception to this policy occurred after Kristallnacht, when the regulations were relaxed for a short time and another seven thousand refugees were allowed into the country. By the time the war began in 1939, there were some thirty thousand Jewish refugees in the Netherlands, as about two thousand of the more than thirty-two thousand who had entered the country had found other havens. The government justified the immigration restrictions by claiming that they would prevent the rise of anti-Semitism at home. Furthermore, The Hague required the Dutch Jewish community to care for the refugees. Thus, Westerbork, the internment camp for German Jewish refugees, was built by the Dutch government, but it was the Dutch Jewish community that paid for its construction and operating costs. It went without saying that "their own community would pay for those of the same race and faith."[10]

The leadership of the Jewish community, insofar as one could speak of a community, allowed this to happen. No one dared to criticize the Dutch government's policy. To the contrary: during a protest meeting against Kristallnacht in November 1938, Asscher thanked the government both

> for the way in which it has demonstrated its recognition of the seriousness of the situation [in Germany] and also for the great amount of work which has been done by a number of its prominent members and civil servants. . . . Indeed we mention with praise the fact that the Dutch government has been the first to express publicly the need to help those unfortunates, the first to try to find other countries to help. We are well aware of

the many difficulties the government encounters in its sincere desire to help solve this problem. It is absolutely certain that the Dutch government is not able to realize what really was necessary for the German Jews: safety and hope for the future of all.[11]

In short, the leader of the Dutch Jewish community excused a Dutch government that turned back refugees at the Dutch-German border! The Jewish press agreed. Only a small minority within the Dutch Jewish community expressed disgust with its own leadership and indignation with the government. The Dutch Jewish leadership "did not demand anything," the *Centraal Blad voor Israelieten* (Central Journal for Israelites) wrote in December 1939. "God forbid – not even the application of existing legislation: that could give rise to anti-Semitism. [Our representative] requests in a submissive fashion and trembles at a frown on the forehead of a minister. He fights only when other Jews attempt to normalize the legal situation of the refugees. . . . Then he battles against those Jews. Yes, he thanks the government publicly for the creation of camps, where Jews are imprisoned, instead of simply keeping silent because we must accept these camps."[12] Two years later that same representative, Abraham Asscher, was to head the German-imposed Jewish Council.

The unwillingness of the Dutch Jewish leadership to criticize the refugee policy reveals the extent of their insecurity. The Jewish community had begun to drift into a realm characterized by "instability, uncertainty, anxiety – no concrete fear, but a vague, far echo, as it were, of the persecutions which had victimized their ancestors for centuries."[13]

THE HOLOCAUST ERA

ON THE EVE OF WORLD WAR II the Dutch Jewish community of 140,000 people was vulnerable. This figure included approximately 118,000 people who had been born in the Netherlands or who had acquired Dutch nationality through naturalization, about 14,500 Jews who still carried German passports, and some 7,500 Jews who had obtained passports from other countries, mainly in Latin America. All of them, regardless of their citizenship status or the nationality of their passports, were imperiled. Just how great their jeopardy was became clear six years later, in 1945. Nearly annihilated, with 75 percent of its members murdered, Dutch Jewry suffered even greater losses than did Jews in neighboring Belgium (40 percent) and France (25 percent) or across the North Sea in Norway (40 percent) and Denmark (1.6 percent). A number of factors contributed to this staggeringly high mortality rate.[14] In the Netherlands the SS had a free hand, whereas in Belgium and France there were tensions between the dominant Wehrmacht and the SS and Heydrich's security service, the SD, and in Denmark the government ran the country without direct German interference until the late summer of 1943; after that date the population did not cooperate with the Germans. The Netherlands, moreover, was policed by a greater force (five thousand men) than, for example, was its larger neighbor, France, to which the Germans sent only three thousand men. The specific situation of the Jews within Dutch society was an equally important factor, however. Jews in the Netherlands had never suffered at the behest of the government or the civil service. During their centuries of citizenship they had learned to expect protection from "above," and they were not suspicious of national authority or their own leaders. The system had worked well for nearly three hundred years, and the trust it had engendered blinded the Jews and prevented them from realizing that that very system could be a tool for their destruction. In short, the Jews were like other Dutchmen and reacted to the Germans like other Dutchmen: they were, for the most part, cooperative, administratively efficient, and loyal to the authority, and they assumed that their leaders had the best intentions.

These perceptions and beliefs resulted in a general passivity among the Dutch population in general and among the Jews in particular. For the first three years of the Occupation the general attitude in the Netherlands (shared by gentiles and Jews) was one of accommodation, and the Germans could do as they wished. Deeply divided by the *zuilen* structure of their society, the Dutch did not develop a general spirit of resistance in the sense of Dutchman against

German. Indeed, for a time the NSB successfully appropriated the label "true Dutchman" for its own vision of a national regeneration on racial-historical foundations. The various *zuilen* felt no loyalty to each other, and no Jews belonged to the *zuilen* in which the spirit of resistance was strongest, the Christian fundamentalists. Furthermore, the lack of cohesiveness among the Dutch Jews and the ill will between them and the German Jewish refugees crippled the community. Paralyzed by passivity, fragmentation, trust in authority, and suspicion of each other, the Dutch offered little resistance to the German occupation for three years. It was not difficult for the Nazis to achieve most of their goals during that time. Step by step, the move from Holland to Poland was secured on Dutch soil.[15]

The road to Auschwitz was opened with the registration of Jewish enterprises in October 1940. A month later, Jewish public servants, including teachers and professors, were dismissed from their jobs. Registration of Jews followed in January 1941: the official tally was 140,552 Jews, 14,549 half-Jews, and 5,719 quarter-Jews. Within weeks, in early February 1941, the Germans allowed NSB storm troopers to wreak havoc in the Jewish quarter of Amsterdam. To everyone's surprise, however, they were beaten off by the inhabitants of the neighborhood, and one of the storm troopers was mortally wounded. On February 12 the Germans sealed off the Jewish quarter and established a Jewish Council headed by Abraham Asscher and David Cohen, a professor of ancient history at the University of Amsterdam.

Tension and violence mounted quickly. On February 19 a German patrol entered a popular ice cream parlor (the Koco) located outside the Jewish quarter but run by two German Jewish refugees. As it had been a Nazi target, some of the regular clients had installed a primitive self-defense system using ammonia. Sprayed with the fluid as they came through the door, the patrol opened fire and arrested the owners and everyone else on the premises. One of the proprietors, Ernst Cahn, was the first Jew to be killed by the Germans in the Netherlands; he was executed in March. The Germans used the battle in the Jewish quarter and the Koco incident as a pretext to arrest four hundred Jewish men on February 22 and 23;

they were sent to Buchenwald and then on to Mauthausen, where they died. The incarceration of these men sparked off a general strike that began on the Amsterdam docks on February 25 and quickly spread to the rest of the city. This act of Dutch gentile solidarity with their Jewish neighbors was ruthlessly suppressed. The Germans immediately informed the Jewish Council that they would continue to arrest, deport, and even shoot large contingents of Jews on a daily basis until the strike ended. Asscher contacted forty industrial leaders and convinced them to bring the strike to an end; by February 27 everyone was back at work.

Throughout 1941 and early 1942 the noose tightened. In July 1941 special identity cards for Jews were issued, and in September the Zentralstelle fuer Juedische Auswanderung (Central Office for Jewish Emigration), headed by Ferdinand aus der Fuenten, began operation. With the start of the new academic year, Jewish children were thrown out of schools; now segregated from their gentile friends, they began to attend schools newly established by the Jewish community. Travel restrictions were imposed that autumn, and by the end of the year the Jews were concentrated in a few designated areas of the country. By that time the Germans had already sequestered most of the Jewish wealth and possessions, allowing Jews to keep only a few personal possessions and no precious metals except a wedding ring, a silver (but not gold) watch, four pieces of table silver per person, and gold and platinum teeth. (These the Germans later retrieved in the undressing rooms of the gas chambers or in little rooms next to them marked "Goldarbeiten.") Finally, in May 1942 the Germans introduced the yellow Jewish star marking.

The first deportations to Poland began two months later. The "resettlements," as they were termed, were announced formally in the newspapers. The evening papers of Monday, June 29, 1942, announced that all Jews were to leave Holland as poor as they had been when they came. Three days earlier the Jewish Council had been informed that the Germans would send "police-controlled labor contingents" of Jewish men and women between sixteen and forty years old to Germany. In a meeting held on June 27, the members of the council had considered resigning in protest, but in the end they decided to cooperate with the Germans in order to save what they could. A week of haggling began in which the Jewish Council tried to obtain exemptions for themselves, their aides, and their families; to improve the transit conditions for those who had to leave; and to reduce the daily quota of deportees.

Aus der Fuenten's Central Office for Jewish Emigration began with the German Jewish refugees. Aus der Fuenten had been notified by Eichmann that the shuttle between Westerbork and Auschwitz was to begin on July 15, and the Central Office for Jewish Emigration marked the fourteenth as the date to load the trains in preparation for the deportation from Westerbork to Auschwitz. Six trains were to take 4,200 Jews from Amsterdam to the transit camp in Drente, whence they were to leave for Poland. Four thousand Jews were called up to register for these transports; most did not respond. A massive dragnet on July 14 caught 500 Jews, who were held as hostages, and the Jewish community was informed that if those who had not responded to the summons for deportation remained obstinate, the 500 would share the fate of the February 1941 hostages. This moral blackmail convinced a number of people: when the first two trains left that night, 962 Jews of the 1,400 who had been called up were on board. The next two trains were not so full: despite the pressure, fewer than half of those summoned presented themselves. Yet registration had risen, and the hostages were released.

During the next twelve months, as transports carried Jews from Amsterdam to Westerbork, and from Westerbork to an "unknown destination" in the East, the Jewish Council concerned itself very little with the fate of those who had left, a bit more with the future of those who, for the moment, remained, and primarily with its own fate. The council's aim was to preserve "the best" for rebuilding the community after the war; it translated into a policy of cooperation. Indeed, the members of the Jewish Council were so convinced of the value to the community of cooperation with the Germans that they beseeched their coreligionists to comply with their directives and enjoined them not to go into hiding. In the end, between twenty thousand and twenty-five thousand Jews hid during the war; of these, fewer than half were caught.

Some twenty-one hundred Jews managed to escape to Switzerland despite the extreme difficulties of traversing Belgium and France to get there. And another ten thousand Jews, married to gentiles, survived in Holland.

Between July 1942 and July 1943, when the Jewish community was dismantled, few people resisted the Germans. By the time the spirit of resistance finally spread, it was too late for the Jews. It was not until the end of the summer of 1943 that the resistance movement and the underground press began to expand rapidly. By then 82,000 Jews had been deported, and most of the rest of the 115,000 Jews who were ultimately to be shipped east were already detained in concentration camps such as Vught or the central transit camp at Westerbork.[16]

THE POST-HOLOCAUST ERA

ONLY 5,450 JEWS RETURNED from the camps in 1945; an estimated 2,000 who had survived the war outside the Netherlands were repatriated also. They returned to a country in chaos. Several hundred thousand forced laborers, voluntary workers, prisoners of war, merchant seamen, and other Dutchmen were streaming back into the country. They joined the one million civilians who had been evacuated during the war and were now in search of their homes.[17] Among them were some 10,000 Jews who had survived the war in hiding. With a severe housing shortage, a shattered economy, and serious civil disturbance as tens of thousands of Nazi collaborators were rounded up, the government paid little attention to the Jews. The latter, who numbered approximately 30,000 by 1946 (including those who were partners in mixed marriages and 5,000 surviving German Jews who had arrived as refugees before the war), were not granted special assistance or privileges. To recognize the plight of the Jews as unique was, according to the official position, to continue the German distinction between gentile and Jew. As the minister of interior of the Dutch government-in-exile declared in October 1944, it was the aim of the government to eradicate "as soon as possible, the discriminated position in which the Jews have been put by the occupier."[18]

The problem with this ideology was that it led to another genre of humiliation. The oppression of the Jews by the Germans and their Dutch allies had been different from the abuse others had suffered, and the postwar passion to create parity between gentiles and Jews obscured their special plight. The popular postwar perception of the nation's immediate past was that history had caught up with them; the struggle of their ancestors had been realized in their own time. Holland had faced a supreme test, just as she had three and a half centuries earlier. Many citizens had failed, but the resistance had saved the honor of the Netherlands and had created a new concept of the *Nederlander*. The Jews, however, were found wanting as a group. The common belief was that the Jews had been singled out in the trial but had not resisted. One expression of this view appeared in the 1949 book *De Tyrannie Verdrijven* (Tyranny Expelled). The author, Klaas Norel, a resistance fighter and an editor of the underground newspaper *Trouw* (Loyalty), described the deportation of the Jews. "The Jews did not offer resistance against the pogroms," he maintained. "This absence of resistance is no surprise. It was not expected that the Jews, who do not exert themselves when there is no chance of success would fight. . . . The Jews may not be heroes, but they are certainly cunning. . . . Only when the Nazis reached out their claws towards their capital and goods did the Jews awaken. And then very good: with great craftiness they were able to snatch away uncounted millions from the enemy."[19]

The Jews were not part of this new idea of *Nederlanderschap*. They now were perceived as the Other. Their history was now seen as different from the history of "the Dutch people." In the first years after the war there was a real effort to demolish the *zuilen* structure, which had characterized Dutch society. The experience of common suffering and common resistance had brought Catholics and Protestants, liberals and socialists, together. But the Jews did not share this common bond, and they, the outsiders, were accused of having a sense of exclusive community. As one observer complained, "The Jews have a very strong mutual bond – which is laudable, by the way – which brings them to use their energy and influence to help them achieve positions they want; the result of this is the disproportionate representation of the Jewish element." The Jews' behavior, the critic argued, should be countered with a *numerus clausus*, restricting the participation of Jews in the economy and public institutions to their representative percentage in the population. "It is possible that there will be Jews who will consider themselves hurt by this, but such feelings are not justified. It is up to them to prove that we have worried ourselves without any real reason."[20]

In his 1946 book, *Onze Joden en Duitschland's Greep naar de Wereldmacht* (Our Jews and Germany's Bid for World Power), H. W. J. Sannes described the generally prevalent feeling very well. Most people realized intellectually that the Nazis' racial theories were nonsense and that the Jews were not the great antagonists of the Aryans, as the Germans had claimed. Yet reason was not enough because, as he confessed, "I have my personal experiences with cunning, immodest, impertinent, greedy and fraudulent Jews and this experience cannot be gainsaid. Even if I am not able to describe exactly what I have against them, they are in any case repugnant to me. What happened during the Occupation is revolting, but it is still good that we have got rid of them. This is what one hears in Holland."[21]

Sannes had sympathy for the Jews, and at the end of his book he welcomed them back, emphasizing that he hoped they would be able to rebuild their lives – as Dutchmen. "I feel myself a friend of the Jews. Not because they are Jews, *but because they are Dutchmen* and because they have shown themselves in the past to be good patriots. Their faith is of no interest to me. Their race is as little significant to me as that of an Aryan. Among the good things that I wish for our Jews who have returned, is first: *that they will feel themselves to be Dutch*."[22]

The only way Jews could participate in the popular postwar conception of Dutch society was to demonstrate their gratitude to the resistance. Blind to the Jews' own resistance to the German murder machinery, gentile Dutchmen demanded grateful acknowledgment from the surviving Jews. In an article that expressed a common sentiment, the resistance newspaper *De Patriot* observed (July 2, 1945) that "all the Jews who were in hiding who emerge again have the noble, principled and consistently Christian feeling of the Dutch population to thank for their lives." Risking everything, Christians had protected Jews on humanitarian grounds. "The emerging Jews may thank God for that help, and must feel themselves to be very small indeed. Perhaps much better people [than they] were killed on their behalf. And those who now come out of hiding should consider also that there is much to repay. Many people encountered difficulties because of the help given to Jews." In conclusion *De Patriot* claimed, "There is no doubt that the Jews, because of the German persecution, enjoyed great sympathy from the Dutch population. Now the Jews must refrain from excessive behavior, they must think constantly how grateful they ought to be, and they must express that gratitude first of all to make good what must be made good to those who have become victims because of the Jews."[23]

Given homecoming messages of this sort, it is not surprising that the first major monument relating to the Holocaust was erected by the survivors to honor those who had helped them. It was the first major war monument erected in Amsterdam. Designed by Job Wertheim, who had survived the war in Theresienstadt, the monument is a wall with five reliefs moving from the Jewish periphery ("Resignation") to a Christian center ("Defense," "Protection," "Resistance") and back to the Jewish periphery ("Mourning"). The texts below the allegorical figures read: "Resigned in God's Will," "United with you in Defense," "Protected by your Love," "Strengthened by your Resistance," and "Mourning with you."[24] The dedication speech of the monument committee chairman, on February 22, 1950, reflected the prevailing ideology. We must not forget, he said, "what non-Jews, at risk to their own lives, have done for us. . . . The remaining 20,000 Jews have that to thank for their salvation. With fervent compassion we remember the more than 100,000 Jews who could find no help. With even more gratitude have we, the survivors, dedicated this monument, to which also the smallest and the poorest have contributed."[25] In his acceptance speech the mayor of Amsterdam proudly expatiated on the activities of the Dutch citizenry on behalf of the Jews. The fact that not everyone had re-

sisted the German's orders warranted but a single remark. The monument was not meant to be a reminder of that shame; rather, it was intended to encourage future generations to choose justice over injustice, resistance against suppression. It was, in other words, a command to remain faithful to one's *Nederlanderschap*: to face the oppressor and to act against him. It was a question of choice, and neither the monument committee chairman nor the mayor recognized that Jews also had faced an extreme challenge and that they also had made courageous and righteous choices. The victims had no place in the ideology of the monuments, which invoked Calvinist imagery and depended on Christian phraseology.

As Jews, the survivors had no place at all. It was their task to re-create a material and moral universe in which they could live once again. Among the first of the very practical problems they faced were the administrative struggles and legal battles to regain their possessions. The financial loss to the Dutch Jewish community was 650–700 million guilders, and the survivors attempted to recover their share of this sum. The entire German-imposed structure, which had legitimized every aspect of their material ruin (real estate, stocks and bonds, inheritances, bank account holdings, insurance policies, etc.), had to be dismantled, and the survivors struggled through this web to reclaim what had been theirs. It pitted them against their fellow countrymen; for years they fought with the stock exchange officials, the insurance companies, and the bank presidents. It took a very long time; most of the claims were settled in the early 1950s, but some cases still had not come to closure more than twenty years after the war ended.[26]

The survivors' loss was overwhelming. They had, of course, lost their property, their businesses, their resources, and their security. They had also lost their families. And so there was a succession of legal battles to obtain guardianship of the approximately 1,450 Jewish children who had survived the war in hiding with Christian families and had no relatives left when the war was over.[27]

Finally, the survivors confronted the moral dilemmas posed by the behavior of the Jewish community leaders during the Occupation. It was a complicated issue. Many felt that the destruction of the

Dutch Jews was solely the responsibility of the Germans, and they did not want to judge those Jews who, as members or employees of the Jewish Council or as members of the staff at Westerbork, had collaborated with the Germans. Others believed that no one had the moral right to judge, especially as virtually all the survivors had, for a time, accepted the Jewish Council and its policies. Still others feared that an investigation of Jews by Jews would be a gift to anti-Semites. The overwhelming sentiment, however, was the sense of complete desolation and despair: the proceedings would not bring back the dead, and those who survived needed to focus their attention and concentrate their energy on rebuilding their lives.[28]

Despite these deep reservations, a Jewish Council of Honor was established. The first meeting, on December 15, 1946, initiated a very painful period for the Jewish community. The council was to judge only those whom the Nazis had defined as Jews, including half-Jews and quarter-Jews who were born to gentile mothers. It was decided that neither the establishment of the Jewish Council nor membership on it was in itself problematic, so long as one had not participated for personal gain. Similarly, simply to have carried out German orders gave no cause for criticism. But those who had retained their positions after August 15, 1942, when it was obvious that the Jewish Council had become a tool to liquidate the Dutch Jewish community, were to explain their actions. After a year of excruciating hearings, the Council of Honor ruled to exclude Abraham Asscher and David Cohen from any public office in the Jewish community for the rest of their lives. This had no practical significance, as Asscher already had given up his membership in the very community he had tried to serve and Cohen voluntarily had renounced all future positions. As Hans Knoop observed in his study of the Jewish Council, the Council of Honor had not addressed the central weakness of Asscher and Cohen. The tragedy was that they had adapted and adjusted rather than reacted and resisted. They had been philanthropists before the war, and they had carried out their business on the council as if they still had no greater responsibility than to continue to be philanthropists. But philanthropy was not what was needed from the leaders of a community destined for death.

They issued the deportation notices and urged the Jews in *Het Joodsche Weekblad* [The Jewish Weekly] to obey these summons to the letter. But they found another task to do – or did they consider it to be their primary one? – to ensure that those who left for Auschwitz traveled with at least one extra pair of socks. Cohen declared after the war that "thanks to our efforts no Jew suffered from hunger in occupied Holland." That is the case. But thanks to Asscher and Cohen the deportation of the Jews in the Netherlands achieved a greater measure of perfection and efficiency than anywhere else in occupied Europe.[29]

The attempts of the survivors to reconstruct their individual and communal lives occurred within a radically changed demographic situation. The Portuguese community had been reduced to a few families, who continued to worship in the enormous Portuguese Synagogue in Amsterdam. In Amsterdam there were enough surviving members of the *Nederlandse Israelietische* community to reestablish a shul, although the proud historic center at the Jonas Daniel Meijerplein had to be abandoned, as the Germans had reduced it to a ruin. In a few of the other large cities communities reestablished themselves, albeit on a very modest scale. In the provinces there simply were not enough survivors for viable communities. In many towns only a few Jewish families had returned, and there were neither the financial nor the human resources to maintain a synagogue. The only two groups that increased significantly were the Liberal community, which had been introduced just before the war by Jewish refugees from Germany, and the Zionists. Under the charismatic leadership of Rabbi Jacob Soetendorp, the previously marginal Liberal community grew to equal the Orthodox, building a large new synagogue in Amsterdam and restoring for its own use the gorgeous baroque Portuguese synagogue in The Hague. The Zionists also enjoyed a new popularity. The experience of the war in Europe, the very different War of Independence in Palestine, and the subsequent establishment of the state of Israel and the continued anti-Semitism at home invigorated the movement.

By the end of the 1940s the anti-Semitism of the

immediate postwar period had disappeared and the Netherlands had established excellent relations with Israel; in 1948 it was the first country to establish an embassy in Jerusalem. The economic condition of the Jewish community stabilized, and from a financial point of view the relative situation of the average Jewish family improved significantly. Largely proletariat before the war, the Jewish community that emerged in the early 1950s was largely middle and upper middle class. This was due, in part, to reparation settlements, but it was also due to the fact that the survival rate of professional and wealthier Jews had been higher than that of the proletariat. (This had little to do with the Jewish Council's policy to preserve "the best" and much more to do with the ability of those who had not been ruined completely by 1942 to contribute financially to their own salvation.) Surviving Jews began to be increasingly visible in society, but it was clear that they were not part of an energetic or dynamic community. In fact, the number of Jews had declined from around 30,000 in 1946 to roughly 26,500 a decade later. Emigration to the United States (1,399), Israel (1,209), Canada (440), and Australia (286), and the combined effect of a very low birth rate and a high death rate accounted for this decrease. The population has remained stable since then, and in some of the smaller cities synagogues have begun to function once again, but the Jewish community of the 1990s, much smaller and at least as fragmented as it was before the war, has a limited future.

That the Jews were marginal after the war was manifested in the social life of the nation and in the Dutch self-image, especially with regard to the years under occupation. We have seen how the ideology of the first monument to commemorate the destruction of the Dutch Jews honored the resisters and ignored the victims. It was the former who deserved the monuments, who deserved their place in history. Throughout the 1950s and early 1960s the history of the war was seen as a battle between German suppression and Dutch resistance.[30] This perception of the past was expressed again and again, in print as well as in stone.

The first important scholarship about the war years was a four-volume work published between 1949 and 1954. The title, *Onderdrukking en Verzet* (Suppression and Resistance), brackets the popular paradigm and is the central theme of all the articles. In the foreword the editors wrote that the two words "suppression" and "resistance" signified a duality. "Yes, because from the moment that the best of our people were awakened and readied themselves for this task, one could not think of the one without the other. Tyranny and terror were pitted against the imprisoned spirit of Liberty, a magnificent struggle, which in the end brought to the ever-growing legion the 'V' of Victory."[31] Collaborators did not figure in this text. As the editors made clear, those who had placed themselves outside the community had also placed themselves outside the history as understood in *Onderdrukking en Verzet*.

The third volume of the series, published in 1950, included Abel J. Herzberg's "Kroniek der Jodenvervolging, 1940–1945," the first systematic chronicle of the destruction of the Jews. This work, which was to be republished in 1955, 1978, and 1985, applied the dominant perspective to the Holocaust. "The persecution of the Jews in the Netherlands, even if it happened on Dutch soil, is not properly Dutch history," Herzberg maintained. "It did not arise from Dutch circumstances. One can even say with certainty that it could not have arisen from it. The *resistance* against the persecution of the Jews has been a Dutch affair."[32]

The statue of the dockworker (1952) and the official Dutch memorial to the war years, the National Monument (1956), were merely official expressions of this interpretation of the war years. Collaboration had not occurred; the tragedy the Jews had endured was not recognized. For the chairman of the National Monument Committee, Dr. M. L. van Holthe tot Echten, "war dead" meant those of the resistance who had fallen in battle. "All the dead from that time of terror, whose names are engraved in our hearts, considered their lives less than their yearning for freedom," he declared in his dedication speech.[33] "Resistance" signified male combatants, not the women of the underground networks, and certainly not Jewish resistance.[34]

Despite the films and photographs of the slave labor and death camps, the tangible aide-mémoire of returning Jews as well as the intangible reminder of the memory of Jewish life in the Netherlands, the publication of Anne Frank's diary in 1947, and the establishment of the foundation named after her in 1957, the fate of the Dutch Jews remained of marginal interest. Indeed, Anne Frank, who has come to be seen as paradigmatic of the Jews in the Netherlands, was almost forgotten by the early 1950s; she became of interest again only as her fame grew abroad. Her hiding address, 263 Prinsengracht, was of little importance within the historic geography of Amsterdam until the 1960s, after the first monument to honor Jews was erected in 1962. That memorial was constructed in the Hollandsche Schouwburg, a theater in the former Jewish quarter of Amsterdam, which had served as a collection point for the deportation of the Jews between July 1942 and the late summer of 1943. The monument was dedicated in the ruins of the theater's stage, from which the names of those who were to be transported had been called during the war. The auditorium, where the waiting, incarcerated Jews lived in extremely crowded conditions, has been pulled down and replaced by a memorial garden. Yet the facade still stands, symbolic of the fate of the Jewish community after the war. It is a haunted, painful place, a place of doom that, unlike the Anne Frank House, so full of hope and life, never became an important site in Amsterdam. Even its dedication was attended by only a small gathering.[35]

History, however, was closing in on the Netherlands. The received version of the past that had worked so well for a decade and a half began to fall apart. Time, the opportunity for reflection, the advent of prosperity, the well-reported Eichmann trial in Jerusalem, and the debates about what to do with the war criminals imprisoned in the Netherlands led to a reinterpretation of history. In Louis de Jong's television series *Bezetting* (Occupation) the issue of the Jews finally was raised, albeit in a limited context. The twenty-one episodes, aired between 1960 and 1965, became a national event. People who did not have a television went to those who did. The streets were empty.

Like its predecessors, *Bezetting* was a black-and-white vision, with occupiers and resisters, villains and heroes. The great mass of people who accommodated were left out, and everyone could identify with the heroes. But de Jong specifically included the persecution of the Jews. He did not bridge the question of responsibility. According to him, the mass murder of the Jews could not be stopped because no one could imagine it; but for the first time the cataclysm of the Holocaust was addressed. "I feel a great need to speak some words to you as an introduction to what follows," de Jong said in the episode chronicling the early stages of the Shoah in Holland.

> As the result of the persecution of the Jews more than 100,000 of our fellow citizens were killed – men, women and children. I do not only want merely to mention these human losses – I want especially to point out that these losses occurred not as the result of a sudden explosion of a bomb, not as the result of death in military battle, but because all these struggling people were caught in the wheels of a merciless machine of destruction that, especially in the years 1942 and 1943, operated right through our own society. Young people who did not live through this period of fathomless horror ask us older people questions, often questions of conscience, which always converge on this one: How could this happen? It is a question with many answers. One of the answers is – and that I want to mention specifically first – that the imagination of most people (Jews and non-Jews) was unable to grasp in time that the National Socialists literally meant what they said when they spoke about the destruction of the Jews.[36]

Nearly twenty years after the end of the war, the murder of the Dutch Jews had become a central event in Dutch history. If Willy Lages, head of the SD in Amsterdam; Ferdinand aus der Fuenten, head of the Central Office for Jewish Emigration and as such responsible for the roundups of Jews; Franz Fischer, nicknamed "Juden-fischer" (Jewfisher), who worked for the SD in The Hague and who was responsible for the deportation of thirteen thousand Jews from that city; and Joseph Kotaella, a guard from the concentration camp in Amersfoort, were not released in the early 1960s from prison in the Netherlands, they have de Jong to thank.

De Jong had written the Jews into the history of

the Netherlands during the war. In his work these citizens who had been specially identified, segregated, isolated, and murdered were members of Dutch society. The disaster that had befallen them was part of the occupation of the nation. It was the historian Jacob Presser, however, who questioned the paradigm of suppression versus resistance, shaped the problem of responsibility, and, as we shall see, precipitated the recognition of the dull gray of everyday collusion. In 1950 Presser was commissioned by the Rijksinstituut voor Oorlogsdocumentatie (State War Documentation Institute), or RIOD, headed by Louis de Jong, to write the history of the Jews during the Occupation. "We hesitated for a long time before we invited him to write *Ondergang* [Destruction]," de Jong explained later. "I knew what it would unlock. And that happened. He suffered when he wrote the book. But we allowed him to work at his own pace, for ten years. When it was finished [my colleague] Sijes and I had great objections. We objected to the whole work, to the scholarly approach, the method, and the division." One of the main problems was that as Presser began his narrative with the invasion of the Netherlands on May 10, 1940, he failed to include a historical background. Furthermore, Presser did not distinguish between the different phases of the persecution, and he treated the persecutors as a homogeneous group. In short, for him the five-year oppression was a storm that had beaten the Jews senselessly, and the book was written from the victims' perspective alone. According to de Jong, "Long conversations followed. At the end Presser said that he shared our criticism, and that he wanted to think it over again. He took the manuscript with him, but after a week he returned with the statement, 'I'm sorry, you are right, but I have no energy left to change it. This is the way it must be published.' "[37]

Whatever de Jong's criticisms, Presser's *Ondergang* swept the country. His was the voice of lost neighbors, brothers, sisters, parents. "As I became more involved with the subject," Presser explained in the introduction,

> an understanding grew slowly of a special moral obligation, which I prefer to describe, carefully circumventing great words, as the calling to be the voice of those who, fated to an eternal silence,

would be heard only here and now, only for this one time. One time more on earth will their lamentation, their accusation, resound. Nothing was left of their most pitiful possessions in their last hours; their ashes were scattered in the winds. They had no one in the world other than the historian who could hand down their message. I believe that I should not hesitate to call this a holy duty, a duty that I tried to fulfil as far as my powers allowed me to do so.[38]

His story was of their death.

> This book concerns the history of a murder. A murder, indeed a mass murder, on a scale never known before, with malice aforethought and committed in cold blood. The murderers were Germans; the murdered, Jews – in the Netherlands roughly a hundred thousand, fewer than 2 percent of the total number of victims the Germans made with their *Endloesung der Judenfrage*. In a process in which they were put outside the law and isolated, the Jews who lived in this country were robbed of all their possessions, deported, and killed in a scientifically systematic, technically almost flawless style. Town dwellers and country folk, the pious and the freethinkers, the healthy and the sick, the old and the young, families and single people, Dutchmen and foreigners: men, women, and children. Without haste, well thought out, registered, and following the proper formalities. Often the murderers were thugs and illiterates, but often, too, educated men and intellectuals with an ineradicable love of literature, the visual arts, and music; many were caring fathers, not without *Gemuet* (feeling); almost all of them celebrated Christmas, after which they continued their job: the murder of countless men, women, and children, defenseless people, fellow people.[39]

From the very beginning *Ondergang* was seen as a monument, or testament. "The war is over, the liberation remembered, and there will be much joy, even perhaps at our war memorials. Only one thing is still missing: a memorial for the Jews who succumbed almost defenseless,"[40] the influential *Algemeen Handelsblad* (General Business Journal) observed. The politician Han Lammers urged that the book be subsidized so that anyone could afford to buy it; only thus would it be possible to "make the monument that Presser's book is into a National Monument."[41]

There was no doubt that Presser's work was – and was accepted as – a monument. But was it a monument to the Dutch Jews or to Dutch failure? *Ondergang* was a tremendous achievement, but its great value and its unique genius was that in reaction to it people, ordinary citizens, began to question their own role and perhaps even their own culpability. An editorial in the newspaper *Trouw* began to question the attitude of the Dutch gentiles during the war. It noted that many had felt pity but few had resisted; that all had signed statements that they were not Jews. The civil servants had remained at their posts, and a part of the Dutch police had aided and abetted the Germans at the roundups of Jews; at least one of the Germans responsible for the implementation of the Final Solution in the Netherlands (Lages) had praised the Dutch for the way they had supported him and helped him reach his goal.[42]

So strong was the Dutch identification with *Ondergang* that a debate followed over whether Presser had been the right person to write the book. The argument was that this calamity was part of Dutch history and should not be relegated to the victims alone. A long letter in the authoritative *Nieuwe Rotterdamse Courant* (New Rotterdam Courant) by a certain J. S. Wijne asserted that Presser should not have written the book, since he was emotionally too close to the events he described: someone who had some distance from the subject should have written the history. "This is especially important as it concerns Jewish Dutchmen," the writer continued. "It happens that those who were persecuted and destroyed were not Dutch Jews but Jewish Dutchmen. And this concerns every Dutchman. That is the reason why the task of writing the history of the destruction of the Jewish Dutchmen should not have been given to a Jewish Dutchman. The danger is that many, especially non-Jewish Dutchmen, will consider *Ondergang* a work of Jewish history and will use that as an excuse to feel that it does not concern them."[43] Many people responded to this letter; the vast majority were of the opinion that only a Jew could have written the book.

As one woman, B. Buitenrust Hettema, put it, "A person who did not belong to the victims psychologically could never have written this sober and simultaneously deeply touching, complete indictment. An indictment? A judgment? A requisitory? More honest than Professor Presser, more merciful than this talented historian, with more justice?" And she concluded her letter with an insight shared by many in those days in 1965. "We live. Many of those whom we are about to remember would also live today if we had had a little bit more courage, a little bit more sense of responsibility, a little less cowardice, a little less love of ease."[44]

While the general response to *Ondergang* was shame and guilt, there was also a certain sense of self-satisfaction. The book was the result of a government commission, after all. It was the government that had taken the initiative for a description of its own failure and the failure of its people. This was unique indeed. The Jewish community, by contrast, was far less constricted by guilt and considerably less self-satisfied. *Ondergang* was enormously important to the Dutch Jews, but they could afford sharper criticism. The day the book was published the Jewish weekly *Nieuw Israelietisch Weekblad* (New Israelite Weekly) ran a selection of some seven pages, accompanied by a long editorial. In the following weeks the journal traced the responses to the book, quoting long excerpts from various reviews. Avid as interest was, the book's focus on the victims alone raised serious questions for the survivors about their own place in history. In a radio broadcast the Jewish historian Jaap Meijer criticized the title, *Ondergang*, because it implied the total destruction of Dutch Jewry. Where were the survivors? Presser's silence about postwar Jewish history was, Meijer remarked, a symptom of his failure to situate his argument within the context of Dutch Jewish history as a whole.[45]

While the Dutch gentiles were busy with guilt and pride, and the surviving Jews wondered about their historical role, the scholarly community was caught between a concept of professional detachment and a prevailing standard of political correctness. The historian Herman von der Dunk, for example, wrote a fair and sober assessment of Presser's achievement and failure for a prominent Dutch historical journal.

Von der Dunk criticized the emotional element in the book, which had so touched the nation. "It is a writing of history that not only emerges from emotion but also cultivates that emotion, and it is not appropriate today. It is as if Presser himself still cannot believe what has happened and assumes that his readers also must share that disbelief." Presser had not tried to write history, but to commemorate. Yet, as von der Dunk concluded, "to commemorate, to commemorate personally, and to write history are two different things."[46] Reasonable as this review was, the editors of the journal rejected it because it lacked the desired reverence for *Ondergang*.

The political consequences of *Ondergang* were immediate and practical as well as long-term and ideological. When war erupted in the Middle East on June 5, 1967, the government and the general population championed the Israelis. The leader of the Social Democratic Party, Joop den Uyl, declared in Parliament that "Holland is party to the conflict, Holland ought to be party and ought to manifest that."[47] As a result, the Dutch state organized a program of financial support of Israel, and it invited all civil servants to donate 0.5 percent of their income to the beleaguered nation for three months. It was the Dutch form of war reparations, or *Wiedergutmachung*.[48]

The Dutch had come to a new understanding of their society and their history.[49] And it was with the realization that Holland had emerged from the war essentially unchanged – that the great revolution had not occurred – that the old order began to crack. In the mid-1960s a generation came of age that had been born during or just after the war. They had been raised with stories of the Occupation in which resistance was considered the norm. But current scholarship showed that very few had been active in the resistance. In the eyes of many young people, the older generation had failed and their structures were obsolete. It was up to them, the younger generation felt, to take up the tradition of resistance, but it now became a resistance against the society they had inherited. They identified government authority with the oppression of the Occupation, and the resistance with the so-called New Left movement or with the more radical, anarchistic "provos" (provocateurs). It

was no accident that one of the leaders of the New Left movement was among the first to review Presser's book. Han Lammers summarized its significance: "The fairy tale is finished, the fable of the small Holland that acted so well towards its Jews. . . . To preserve the myth that Holland 'did so well' is in fact to aid a falsification of history."[50]

The role of Presser's book in this political development was explicated by Evert Werkman in the newspaper *Het Parool* (The Password), a former underground publication: "*Ondergang* is a book that no one can finish without getting the feeling that he has lived, and perhaps still lives, in a crazy world, because it is in *this, our society* that this could happen."[51] The essence of this insanity, Werkman argued, was to be found in the small chapter on the Jewish children, the contemporaries of the provo generation. Presser summarized their history in a few sentences. "They wore the star and went into the gas chamber. Many, many thousands of children, in one long night of Herod. A number survived in hiding and a few even came back from elsewhere, where some of them had seen everything, including cannibalism. And as a matter of fact, those children went back to the school benches, just as before. That is, more or less, more or less."[52] The children had been powerless; no one had spoken up for them. They were symbolic of others without power: the poor, the working class.

One of the reasons that Presser's book made such an impact on the reform movement was its explicit thesis that the intellectuals and the rich, who had controlled the Jewish Council, had sacrificed the "little people" in order "to prevent worse." In *Ondergang* Presser reported a joke he had heard during the war. "When Asscher and Cohen [the two co-chairmen of the Jewish Council] were the only Jews left, and the Germans demanded the deportation of one of them, then Cohen would say to his fellow-chairman: 'Go now, Bram, to prevent worse – in the interest of the Jewish community.'" As Presser explained, the principle of the joke guided the Jewish Council until the end. "Even in May 1943, when the Jewish Council was ordered to select 7,000 people for deportation, the cup was not yet full, and the Council tried to preserve 'the best.' The best meant the intelligentsia and the well-to-do, . . . for the salvation of this dwindling group they sacrificed an ever larger group of lesser people and those who were not the best. The orange sellers for the sake of the caste of the rich and the scholars, for the sake of those like the chairmen themselves."[53]

For the New Left, the Jewish Council became a symbol of Dutch society and everything wrong with it. Presser's book also provided a hero, however, who served as an example to the provo movement. Friedrich Weinreb was a shadowy person whose cause the radicals championed in the complicated Weinreb Affair, as it came to be called, which held the public's attention throughout the late 1960s.[54] Weinreb was a Dutch Jew of Galician origin. He was just one of the many victims of Nazism, and he was especially badly treated by the SD. He became famous because of a kind of game he appears to have played with the Germans that allowed him and perhaps a few others to survive the war. At the command of a nonexistent "General von Schumann," Weinreb created a list of Jews who were to be allowed to emigrate. Hundreds of people desperately sought to be registered. In September 1942 the SD heard of the list and arrested Weinreb. Although they knew that the list was nonsense, they believed that it was the product of some Army officers who had duped Weinreb to gain access to Jewish property. The SD released Weinreb as bait and allowed him to continue his work, now under surveillance. In January 1943 the SD realized that there were no German officers behind it, that it had been Weinreb's invention all along, and they arrested him and sent him to Westerbork. All the Jews on the list were deported to the East. The game was over, or so it seemed at the time. In June 1943 Weinreb, who had not yet been deported, was brought back to The Hague. One of the SD officers had decided to revive the list to do precisely what they had suspected the Army officers of doing: to gain access to hidden Jewish property. Weinreb became bait once again, this time to catch not German officers but Jewish property and Jewish people in hiding. A number of Jews in Westerbork profited from this second game because they got a stay of deportation while, unbeknownst to them, the Germans searched for property they were believed to own. When the SD tired of this in February 1944, Weinreb and his family went into hiding. They survived the war.

After the war some Jews believed that they owed their survival to Weinreb, while others believed that they had been duped by him. There were accusations that he had used the money that people paid to get on his list for his own profit and that, to keep his list alive and his game going, he had betrayed people who helped Jews in hiding because he had to satisfy the SD's desire for action. He was tried in 1947 and 1948 and convicted for having committed espionage in prison and for embezzlement of the money entrusted to him by the people on his list. On November 27, 1947, he was sentenced to three and a half years of imprisonment. A year later, on October 25, 1948, a special council increased the sentence to six years, but on December 11 he was freed in an amnesty in honor of the fifty-year jubilee of Queen Wilhelmina's reign.

Herzberg had discussed the Weinreb case in his *Kroniek der Jodenvervolging*. He believed that Weinreb had practiced deceit but that he nevertheless had saved some people. In his analysis of the judgment against Weinreb he remarked, "If I have understood everything well, then the accused Weinreb was reproached not for his poker game and not for his reckless ante and not for the committed deceit but for his flight from the consequences, when it touched his own life, a flight to which he has not admitted. It is as if the judge wants to say: 'He who wants to play poker in history, must bring his own life as his stake. He who does not dare to do that, must remain at home.' A judge can hardly give another judgment. But the unanswered question is, what is more courageous: to play poker or to stay at home? To escape the consequences which may arise in certain situations, or to escape the situations, because one may have to face consequences?"[55]

Presser did not agree with Herzberg's measured judgment. For him Weinreb was an ingenious helper, a savior of many Jews, a kind of counterproof to the accusation that the Jews had allowed themselves to be slaughtered by the Germans without any resistance.[56] As so often happens in history, the Jewish hero had been turned into a villain by the gentiles. According to Presser, Weinreb's conviction had been an attempt by Dutch society (or, better, the Dutch establishment) to elude its own passivity. "The Jew Weinreb has become the scapegoat; he has paid for the failure of countless non-Jews. He must have failed, as they had failed, *because* they had failed. Just as they had not done their duty, neither had he. If there were no Jewish traitors, it was necessary to invent them. The few who came to trial after the war were insignificant. Now here was one of a stature that sufficed."[57] Based on Weinreb's own stories and a rather careless investigation of the trials of 1947 and 1948, Presser's judgment was precipitous, and he did not include his discussion of the Weinreb case in the English edition of *Ondergang*. But that did not matter in 1965. Two prominent journalists linked to the New Left movement, Renate Rubinstein and Aad Nuis, began a campaign to rehabilitate Weinreb. They found him in Switzerland and persuaded him to write his memoirs, which appeared under the title *Collaboratie en Verzet, 1940–1945: Een poging tot ontmythologisering* (Collaboration and Resistance, 1940–1945: An attempt at demystification) in three fat volumes in 1969.[58] Describing himself as a combatant against the establishment who had challenged the bureaucracy and the rules of society, Weinreb depicted himself as the sole precursor of the provo movement. It was a pleasing portrait, and many people were convinced that if everyone had been like Weinreb, no Jews would have been deported. Weinreb, in short, became the patron saint of a new kind of Holland. By the end of the 1960s the old resistance fighters, whose organizations were firmly entrenched in the center right of the political spectrum, were identified with the establishment. An alternative vision of resistance was required, and Weinreb provided it. He came to be seen as a new incarnation of that old Dutch hero Tijl Uilenspiegel, a "point of light of imaginative intelligence . . . in a country of burghers and barbarians."[59]

The whole country began to discuss the case. Champions of both sides wrote articles and pamphlets. There were public meetings and forums to discuss the issue. Weinreb's book was selected to receive the prestigious prose award of the city of Amsterdam in 1970, but the city unprecedentedly rejected the jury's decision and the award was withheld. A television program about Weinreb's theological vision (he had acquired a reputation as a cabalist) was scheduled, withdrawn at the last moment in response to many protests by members of the anti-Weinreb faction, and rescheduled after protests by members of the pro-Weinreb faction. Many people considered it

the Dutch Dreyfus case. One of the most prominent Dutch authors, Willem Frederik Hermans, attacked Weinreb and his supporters fiercely in his sarcastic but masterfully written *Van Wittgenstein tot Weinreb* (From Wittgenstein to Weinreb [1970]).[60]

Although Weinreb was at the center of the dispute, the Holocaust was the context of the debate. It was the genocide of the Jews that framed this singularly important attempt by the Dutch to define what a good *Nederlander* ought to be. The answer to which they had come, the new public awareness of the dull gray of everyday collusion, informed the next affair to seize Dutch interest. As the Weinreb case waned, the next episode in the affair of the Four of Breda, the German war criminals in Breda prison in the Netherlands, began to unfold. Willy Lages was released in 1966 because he was said to be dying; he lived comfortably for another five years. This left the Three of Breda, and in 1969 the New Left pressed for their release, which the Right opposed. By 1969, however, the Jews had a voice, and they participated in the public debate. "Soon you will organize a hearing, but 120,000 Dutch Jews cannot be heard anymore," the author Meijer Sluyser reminded the minister of justice. "Invisible, they will be present in the room where you seek counsel and will have to take your decision – witnesses, Jews, like you and me, flesh of our flesh, blood of our blood, mind of our mind."[61] Ironically, the urge to release them was a result of the close reading of *Ondergang*. Presser had forced the Dutch to rethink their behavior during the war, and they were left with the question whether they were so different from the Three of Breda. The left-wing *Vrij Nederland* (which had supported Weinreb) argued for their release. The director of the Catholic Discharged Prisoners' Aid Society neatly framed the dilemma the Dutch faced. "At the same time as we obstinately insist on the imprisonment of the three war criminals in Breda, we repress our own guilt. We also have been guilty of the deportation of the Jews. I myself was a bit involved in the resistance, but I did not actually help Jews. I blame myself for that, that is no secret. The Germans were not the only ones who committed war crimes. Dutchmen helped to find Jews, to transport them; without the help of Dutchmen it would not have been possible."[62] Despite this equation, the three were not released. "Mercy for the victims," as the *Haarlems Dagblad* (Haarlem Daily) called it, prevailed.[63]

The primary victims of the German occupation had become central in the nation's history and memory of the war years. A quarter of a century after Liberation, in the Twenty-Five-Year Jubilee commemorations (1970), the fate of the Jews was the focus of remembrance. It was Presser who had forced the nation to recognize what they formerly had relegated to obscurity, and he was invited to give the keynote speech in the May 5 ceremony in the Lawrence Church in Rotterdam (which had been destroyed in 1940 and only recently rebuilt) in the presence of the Royal House, the government, and other dignitaries. His address was to be aired on national television and radio. A month before the event, however, Presser was hospitalized with stomach cancer. He died on April 30 of complications pursuant to a major operation. His last words were reported to have been "5 May." On the eve of Liberation Day, the national day of commemoration of the war dead (May 4), his body was cremated. A few months later he himself was commemorated in a special session of the Dutch Academy, to which he had been elected as the result of *Ondergang*. De Jong delivered the eulogy. "In *Ondergang*," he said, "[Presser] drowned himself in waves of bewilderment, confronted as he was with a process of massive destruction that he perceived to be completely irrational, absolutely meaningless, and, in essence, beyond comprehension. Whoever dares to speak here about a failure ought to keep in mind that Presser's inability to transcend this most personal grief and his failure to represent that which cannot be represented reveal the sensitive and vulnerable human being Presser was."[64]

Presser's work had fundamentally affected the Dutch memory and remembrance of the war. Shortly after his death the long-overdue monument in Westerbork was unveiled.[65] More than a hundred thousand Jews had been deported to the East from Westerbork, and there had not been a single attempt to blow up the railroad tracks. But gentiles often stood along the crossings and waved to the passing trains. It was a gesture, Louis de Jong wrote, that touched the deportees deeply.

By 1970 Westerbork had become the site of a row of enormous radiotelescopes, for the same reason that it had been a convenient spot for a transit camp: it is the most remote spot in the Netherlands, far away from radio interference and removed from society. The monument is the last bit of track. On one side is the buffer stop, and on the other the ends of the track are turned to the heavens, imitating the gesture of the telescopes. The poet Wim Ramaker visited Westerbork and wrote about the experience.

Who dares to raise his voice here?
Departure point of a whole people:
with known destination left for Auschwitz,
Sobibor, Theresienstadt, Bergen-Belsen, Kosel . . .

And nobody saved them
To be sure there was much waving when they passed by
A gesture that always touched the deported deeply
but nobody shifted the point to life,
or changed the track

Scores of trains have left from here,
according to schedule
often Tuesdays,
exactly on time,
because no one was allowed to die too late

Stand for a moment . . .
now the point of departure and arrival have almost caught
up with each other
Here left a whole people:
more than one hundred and two thousand Jewish fellow
citizens,
children, mothers, fathers,
fathers, mothers, children
and also babies and those old of days
were gassed, shot, burned alive,
beaten to death, hanged
while we waved

At last the rails are shifted
of sadness twisted
and at the place where they were readied for their journey
stand telescopes
to amplify their silent whispering in the universe
and to wave again
when they wave.[66]

That the war years were a period of exceptional importance to the Dutch and in their history is reflected in their monuments, the context of the numerous public "affairs" that gripped their attention, and their reception first of de Jong's televised series, then of Presser's *Ondergang*, and then, from 1969 through 1988, of de Jong's twelve-part *Het Koninkrijk der Nederlanden in de Tweede Wereldoorlog* (The Kingdom of the Netherlands in the Second World War). Nearly all the parts consist of two six-hundred-page volumes. Printed on special paper reserved for the production of Bibles, it has become something of a bible. There is a scholarly edition with footnotes as well as a popular version without footnotes but otherwise complete.

The enormous size of the work, which is dedicated to a mere five years of Dutch history, and the astonishing sales it commands suggest that this period is of normative significance. It is a caesura in Dutch history, a decisive period that can be neither forgotten nor ignored. The Occupation years were a period of conflict between suppression and resistance, wrong and right, evil and good, and the destruction of the Jews is an important part of that strife.

A fundamental and deeply troubling paradox emerged from this position, however. Although the Occupation years had been an era of struggle between suppression and resistance, wrong and right, evil and good, most people who lived through that time had simply carried on with daily life as usual. Ordinary people followed their ordinary routine as they ordinarily did. Rationing, bombing, and closed borders had inconvenienced them, but the war had not changed them. There was a fundamental continuity between Dutch society before, during, and after the war. It had been a period of normative significance, but few had noticed. The details of this continuity were the focus of a long television production aired on October 15, 1974, that traced the history of the Netherlands between 1938 and 1948, *Vastberaden, maar soepel en met mate* (Resolute, to a Certain Extent, but Flexible). The purpose of this film, inspired by Marcel Ophuls's *Le Chagrin et la Pitié* (The Sorrow and the Pity), which follows the history of Clermont-Ferrand during the Occupation, was to trace, not the highways of Dutch history, but the side

streets, that is, the streets where people actually lived.[67] It was not history from above, but the story of those below – of ordinary people.

Vastberaden, maar soepel en met mate differed from *Le Chagrin et la Pitié* in one important aspect. Ophuls's aim had been to demolish the myth that all Frenchmen had been in the resistance. This was no longer necessary in the Netherlands: the idea had been discredited in the mid-1960s. "The myth of the absolutely heroic fatherland that refused to bow under the boot of the tyrant does not live here anymore," one of the filmmakers, H. J. A. Hofland, explained. "This myth is sometimes revived at solemn ceremonies, but on normal days most people are quite able to face the largest part of the truth: that the number of people in the resistance was relatively small, that the Amsterdam streetcar company helped with the deportation of the Jews, that the Dutch train personnel went on strike only in September 1944 and before that had provided many services to the Germans for four long years, that most people did not want to give shelter to the persecuted, that countless people paid for the administrative precision of the state and individual communities with their freedom and their lives, etc." And he concluded, "That people were not so courageous as it appears in our national histories is a fact which crops up again and again automatically. It is more difficult to reveal the continuity within the society."[68]

The prevalent concern to maintain the status quo resulted in daily accommodation and even individual and national collaboration. A striking example revealed in the film was the cooperation of the Dutch authorities with the Germans beginning in September 1944 to ensure that after the German collapse no revolution would occur that would change the structure of society. The most important thing was to maintain order and tranquillity in the period of change. Shown without judgment, "without the interference of a professional moralist, a professional patriot, or a professional historian,"[69] this elucidation of the continuity within Dutch society and of the importance of the ordinary changed Dutch historiography and reeducated the Dutch population.[70]

By the mid-1970s the Dutch had come to an understanding of their individual and national (often silent) collusion and therefore (tacit) collaboration. As a society, they accepted responsibility for their implicit participation in the murder of their fellow Jewish citizens. They understood the Holocaust to be a catastrophe for gentile *Nederlanders* as well as Jewish Dutchmen. In subsequent years the significance of the war, and the lessons Dutch citizens should learn from it and should teach their children, remained part of public discourse. Expressed in films, monuments, books, articles, television productions, and school textbooks, the message that personal behavior was (and is) political action was reiterated again and again.

Jan Wolkers's 1977 monument is an expression of this acceptance of the political significance of private acts. An urn containing ashes of those who had died in Auschwitz had been placed in the Oosterbegraafplaats (East Cemetery) in Amsterdam soon after the war, and it became a custom for mourners to lay flowers there. In January 1977, the thirty-second anniversary of the liberation of Auschwitz, a memorial designed by the Netherlands's most popular author and sculptor was dedicated on that spot. "To make a monument at the site where an urn with the ashes of victims from Auschwitz rests on Dutch soil seems an impossible task," Wolkers explained to the crowd that had gathered for the unveiling. "How can you find a form to commemorate a crime which you feel will not be effaced even when our planet will be dissolved into the universe in two or three thousand centuries? You can beat your brains until they burst to imagine an image which can just begin to represent roughly that shame and that suffering. You look up at the sky and you do not understand how the blue expanse rested over that horror, as untouched and peaceful as over a meadow with flowers. And in a vision of justice you see the blue sky over you crack, as if the horror which happened here on earth below her has violated eternity forever."[71] Wolkers's monument was a two-hundred-square-foot surface of cracked mirrors reflecting the sky. His design — and his address — took the nation one step further: while the annihilation of the Dutch Jews was represented in the Schouwburg monument as a Jewish tragedy and in the Westerbork memorial as a national disaster, in the Oosterbegraafplaats it was seen as a universal cataclysm.

Just how far the popular perception of the war had evolved was clearly seen in the Dutch reaction to the American television series *Holocaust*. Broadcast in Germany in 1978, *Holocaust* had a massive impact. The influential German magazine *Der Spiegel*, which had mocked the series as "gas chambers a la Hollywood" before it was aired, respectfully referred to it as "Holocaust: The Past Returns" a few days later. Learning from the German experience, the Dutch decided to prepare the public, and a whole program was set up to counsel and help people during and after the broadcasts. Schools received information packages, and roundtable discussions by experts and special documentaries to place the series in its historical context were aired. When the series finally was broadcast in 1979, it was an anticlimax, not because the preparation had been so intense (as it transpired, it was unnecessary), but because the questions *Holocaust* engendered had been asked and answered in the Netherlands years earlier.[72]

In Germany the discussion of *Holocaust* centered on the conundrum, How could it have happened? The series marked a moment of revelation. For all the academic study of the "unresolved past" (as the Germans call the Nazi era), it had taken an American television series to affect the public consciousness. It was a very difficult moment for the Germans. The dramatization, which concentrated on the German Jewish family Weiss and the German gentile family Dorf, allowed each German to identify with the Weiss family while simultaneously recognizing themselves in the Dorfs. This paradox gave the series its specific power in the German context. The war, which had been seen in terms of a military-political conflict, was suddenly discovered as a moral issue. The question of culpability, especially that of the responsibility of each individual vis-à-vis his or her neighbors, had not been raised. In the Netherlands that moment had occurred more than a decade earlier; with Presser's *Ondergang* the paradigm of "suppression and resistance" had been transformed into one of "collective failure." Furthermore, while in Germany the film initiated a debate over the statute of limitations for war crimes, in Holland the affair of the Three of Breda had already raised the problem. The only aspect of the program that excited interest was the one element that had been a secondary Dutch concern throughout their dialogue with the Holocaust since De Jong's *De Bezetting*: Was it in good taste? In an article in the liberal weekly magazine *De Haagse Post* (The Hague Post), the filmmaker H. J. A. Hofland maintained that "it was clear what the answer would be. Anyone who measures with aesthetic norms must consider 'Holocaust' a melodrama with the signature of an American soap opera. In the same way as actors address a hall here as if they actually want to reach a hall beyond, so the Americans have learned to look regularly to a point beyond the horizon, whatever the situation in which they find themselves. That is the hallmark of their tragedy and their pain. You used to see it in Peyton Place . . . and it was also present in *Holocaust*."[73] Thus the issue at stake was not so much the relationship of the Dutch to their past as it was their relationship to the dominant culture of 1979, that of the United States. The film *Holocaust* was first and foremost American.

Holocaust underscored another lesson, however: it had reinforced and emphasized that the Holocaust becomes meaningful when we can identify with its victims, and with the choices people had to make. The real issue of the 1980s was not the confession of guilt but a genuine attempt to integrate the Holocaust into daily life, as an issue that informs the day-to-day ethics of human life. An obvious example was the application of its lessons to the daily reality of racism. A few days after the last part was broadcast, Rafael Shibboleth, a curator at the Jewish Historical Museum in Amsterdam, remarked that "if people think about what we can do vis-à-vis minorities, then we more or less have reached our goal with the airing of *Holocaust*." "Each country has its own Jews," Rabbi Sonny Herman added. "Holocaust means that every minority can be persecuted."[74]

This understanding of the Holocaust as an issue that concerns the solidarity of a majority with a persecuted or discriminated-against minority defines the approach to the education about the genocide of the Jews in Dutch schools. The school textbook *Grenzen aan solidariteit* (Limits to solidarity),[75] published in 1990 and adopted for use throughout the Netherlands, pursues the dilemmas of this social ethic. The book is neatly divided into eighteen chapters, half

focusing on historical issues and half on ethical questions. In the first part, a short introduction to Judaism, the history of the Jews, and the history of the Jews in the Netherlands are followed by two lessons on anti-Semitism and one on Hitler and the Thousand Year Reich. The last three chapters of the historical section are entitled "From Isolation to Murder," and they delineate the process by which the Jews were segregated and deported to their death. The text then moves to the difficult moral and ethical conundrums raised by the Holocaust. Two chapters focus on the attitude of Dutch gentiles, and two on the attitude of Dutch Jews. Questions about the Jews in the death camps, the perpetrators, whether there are limits to solidarity, whether the Holocaust is unique or one of many genocides, and whether not choosing is also a choice are explored. In *Grenzen aan solidariteit* the issue of the Holocaust begins with the decisions ordinary people make in everyday situations. Treason, suppression, heroism, and resistance are rooted in the problems we must face all the time, even in our own – especially in our own – neighborhoods.

Half a century after the persecution of the Jews began in the Netherlands, how and what the next generation will be taught about the Occupation has emerged as the central issue.[76] No longer looking back with Calvinist, smug self-righteousness or equally Calvinist self-flagellating guilt, the Dutch now identify their responsibility constructively. Their task is to educate. It is this that makes the Dutch response to the Holocaust unique. Like the other European nations, Holland too failed in its responsibility to its Jewish citizens during the Occupation. And after the war was over the Dutch, like other European peoples, reveled in the delusion of a national resistance. What makes the Dutch exceptional is that the same generation that lived through the war caring only about their ordinary concerns came to recognize and accept responsibility for their accommodation, complicity, and collusion.

History and memory frame a commonly accepted social ethic in the increasingly multicultural society of the Netherlands. The primary place of children in this national agenda has led to the juxtaposition of the task the Dutch now face and their treatment of Jewish youngsters fifty years ago. On

November 1, 1941, Jewish children were thrown out of all the playgrounds in Amsterdam-Zuid, a neighborhood where some seventeen thousand Jews lived. At the order of the authorities, one of these playgrounds became a Jewish market; the rest were reserved for use by gentile children alone. Just four years later, thirteen thousand of the seventeen thousand Jewish inhabitants had been murdered. In 1986 the people of Amsterdam-Zuid and the local society of market stall owners collected sixty-five thousand guilders to create a monument to that incident. "Remember, so that our children, irrespective of their ancestry, will be able to play together. If we can play with each other as children, we must be able to live together as adults," the text reads.[77] The four-figure statue depicts two gentile children at play and two Jewish children locked out of the playground. It is the counterpart to the dockworker monument. The memorial to those who participated in the February strike against the Germans commemorates a certain form of heroism and resistance. The children's monument, by contrast, illustrates the first step of an oppression that, unstopped, led to mass murder. Acceptance of the German-imposed regulations, accommodation to the Occupation authority, began at home, in the neighborhoods, with children. There is no better place, the Dutch feel, to start anew than with the education of children at home and in the local neighborhood schools.

Notes

The authors would like to thank Dr. van Galen Last and Dr. Barnouw of the Rijksinstituut voor Oorlogsdocumentatie in Amsterdam for their advice and help. Please note that the authors have used the term "Holocaust" instead of "Judeocide" for consistency of usage in this volume.

1. Statistical information about the situation of the Jews before World War II is largely from Louis de Jong's monumental standard work on the history of World War II in Holland, *Het Koninkrijk der Nederlanden in de Tweede Wereldoorlog*, 12 vols. ('s-Gravenhage, 1969–88), 5, pt. 1:481ff. See also Joseph Michman, Hartog Beem, and Dan Michman, *Pinkas: Geschiedenis van de Joodsche Gemeenschap in Nederland*, trans. Ruben Verhasselt, ed. Joop Sanders and Edward van Voolen (Amsterdam, 1992).
2. The Calvinist city authorities did not grant a similar privilege to other Protestant denominations or to Roman Catholics. The Lutherans did not obtain permission to build a major church building until twenty years after the completion of the Portuguese Synagogue; the Catholics were obliged to worship in *schuilkerken* (hidden churches) until the end of the eighteenth century.
3. Jaap Meijer, *Hoge Hoeden Lage Standaarden: De Nederlandse Joden Tussen 1933 en 1940* (Baarn, 1969), 35.
4. Fritz Bernstein, *Over Joodsche problematick* (1935), quoted in Meijer, *Hoge Hoeden Lage Standaarden*, 93–94.
5. Abraham Asscher, quoted in Hans Knoop, *De Joodsche Raad: Het Drama van Abraham Asscher en David Cohen* (Amsterdam, 1983), 22.
6. J. C. H. Blom, *De Muiterij op de Zeven Provincien* (Utrecht, 1975), 27.
7. J. van der Ploeg, *Het Joodsche Vraagstuk: Een Maatschappelijk Probleem* (1940), quoted in Meijer, *Hoge Hoeden Lage Standaarden*, 187.
8. *De Spiegel*, April 8, 1933, quoted in Dienke Hondius, *Terugkeer: Antisemitisme in Nederland rond de bevrijding* (The Hague, 1990), 17.
9. Bob Moore, *Refugees from Nazi Germany in the Netherlands, 1933–1940* (Dordrecht, 1986), 81ff.
10. Dick Houwaart, *Westerbork: Het begon in 1933* (The Hague, 1983), 51.
11. Asscher, quoted in Knoop, *De Joodsche Raad*, 26–27.
12. *Centraal Blad voor Israelieten*, December 28, 1939, quoted in Knoop, *De Joodsche Raad*, 28–29.
13. De Jong, *Het Koninkrijk der Nederlanden*, 5, pt. 1:506.
14. J. C. H. Blom, "De Vervolging van de Joden in Nederland in Internationaal Vergelijkend Perspectief," in *Crisis, Bezetting en Herstel: Tien studies over Nederland, 1930–1950* (The Hague, 1989), 134–50. See also Johannes Houwink ten Care, "Heydrich's Security Police Forces and Jewish Policy: The Case of Occupied France and Occupied Holland" (paper delivered at RIOD/PONTEG [State War Documentation Institute/National Program in Nineteenth and Twentieth Century History] Congress, "Deportation and Resistance in [Western] Europe, 1941–1944," Amsterdam, November 23–24, 1992; publication forthcoming).
15. The account of the persecution and deportation of the Dutch Jews is based on de Jong, *Het Koninkrijk der Nederlanden*, and Jacob Presser, *Ondergang: De Vervolging en Verdelging van het Nederlandse Jodendom, 1940–1945*, 2 vols. (The Hague, 1965), published in English as *Ashes in the Wind: The Destruction of Dutch Jewry*, trans. Arnold Pomerans (Detroit, 1988).
16. Guus Meershoek, "The Amsterdam Police and the Deportations," and Peter Romijn, "The Dutch Local Government and the Persecution of the Jews" (papers delivered at RIOD/PONTEG Congress, "Deportation and Resistance in [Western] Europe, 1941–1944," Amsterdam, November 23–24, 1992; publication forthcoming).
17. There were some 430,000 Dutchmen outside the borders who had to be reintegrated in the society, the largest groups among them being 90,000 men pressed into work in Germany in 1944, 250,000 more or less voluntary workers, 10,000 prisoners in concentration camps, 12,000 prisoners of war, 2,000 forced laborers in Norway, and 60,000 men who had served in the Dutch units of the Allied forces or in the Dutch merchant navy or who had been behind Allied lines in Belgium and France. In addition, there were 350,000 Dutchmen who had been in hiding in Holland to escape forced labor in Germany or to escape being picked up by the Gestapo for being known resisters.

18. Quoted in Hondius, *Terugkeer*, 53.
19. Klaas Norel, *De Tyrannie Verdrijven*, quoted in ibid., 92.
20. W. J. Koenig-Soeters, "Ethiek en jodenvraagstuk," *Vrij Nederland*, August 4, 1945, quoted in ibid., 90.
21. H. W. J. Sannes, *Onze Joden en Duitschland's Greep naar de Wereldmacht* (Amsterdam, 1946), 7. Dienke Hondius discusses the problem at length in her study of Dutch anti-Semitism after the war (see *Terugkeer*, 87–104) and confirms earlier discussions of the phenomenon by de Jong (*Het Koninkrijk der Nederlanden*, 12, pt. 1:121ff.) and Presser (*Ondergang*, 2:501, 515f.). Even so cautious a writer as Daniel Schorr, who reported on the postwar situation of the Dutch Jewish community in the *American Jewish Year Book* in 1947, noted that two years after liberation the identity cards carried by Jews were still marked with a *J*, and he acknowledged that Jewish leaders in the Netherlands were troubled by public anti-Semitism ("The Netherlands," *American Jewish Year Book, 1947–1948* [Philadelphia, 1947], 339–40). Indeed, the problem was so public and so acute that a number of intellectuals in Amsterdam convened a work group to describe and analyze current anti-Semitism. According to Hondius, the group found that the root of the problem was an overblown perception by many Dutchmen of their own role as resisters, while the perceived accommodation of the Jewish Council was considered to be characteristic of Jews (*Terugkeer*, 116–22).
22. Sannes, *Onze Joden*, 299. This message was internalized. For a general discussion of the postwar adaptation of Jewish child survivors, see Debórah Dwork, "My War Began in 1945," *Children With a Star: Jewish Youth in Nazi Europe* (New Haven, Conn., 1991), 253–70.
23. *De Patriot*, July 2, 1945, quoted in Hondius, *Terugkeer*, 96.
24. "Wij spraken met: Joh. Wertheim, beeldhouwer," *Nieuw Israelitisch Weekblad*, February 17, 1950.
25. "Monument van Joodse dankbaarheid te Amsterdam onthuld," *Algemeen Handelsblad*, February 23, 1950.
26. For a comprehensive discussion, see de Jong, *Het Koninkrijk der Nederlanden*, 12, pt. 2:680–708.
27. Elma Verhey, *Om het Joodse Kind* (Amsterdam, 1991); Debórah Dwork, "Custody and Care of Jewish Children after the War: The Case of Netherlands" (1996, forthcoming). See also Joel Fishman, "The Anneke Beekman Affair and the Dutch News Media," *Jewish Social Studies* 40 (1978), 42–54; idem, "The Ecumenical Challenge of Jewish Survival: Pastor Kalma and Postwar Dutch Society, 1946," *Journal of Ecumenical Studies* 15 (1978), 461–76; idem, "The Jewish Community in Post-War Netherlands, 1944–1975," *Midstream* 22 (1976), 42–54; idem, "Jewish War Orphans in the Netherlands: The Guardianship Issue, 1945–1950," *Wiener Library Bulletin*, n.s. 27, nos. 30–31 (1973–74), 31–36; idem, "The War Orphan Controversy in the Netherlands: Majority-Minority Relations," in *Dutch Jewish History: Proceedings of the Symposium on the History of the Jews in the Netherlands, 1982*, ed. Jozeph Michman (Jerusalem, 1984), 421–32; Jozeph Michman, "The Problem of the Jewish War Orphans in Holland," in *She'erit Hapletah, 1944–1948: Rehabilitation and Political Struggle*, Proceedings of the Fifth Yad Vashem International Conference, 1985 (Jerusalem, 1990), 187–209.
28. See Knoop, *De Joodsche Raad*, 182–220; and de Jong, *Het Koninkrijk der Nederlanden*, 12, pt. 1:469–75.
29. Knoop, *De Joodsche Raad*, 219f.
30. The changing view of the war in postwar historiography has been the subject of a number of recent works. In 1983 two important studies were published: Jan Bank, *Oorlogsverleden in Nederland* (inaugural lecture, Erasmus University in Rotterdam, October 27, 1983) (Baarn, 1983); and J. C. H. Blom, *In de ban van goed en fout? Wetenschappelijke geschiedschrijving over de bezettingstijd in Nederland* (inaugural lecture, University of Amsterdam, December 12, 1983) (Bergen, 1983). See also Ernst H. Kossmann, "Continuiteit en Discontinuiteit in de Naoorlogse Geschiedenis van Nederland," *Ons Erfdeel* 28 (November–December 1985), 659–68; and the proceedings of a conference on postwar Dutch historiography of the war years, held at the Free University in Amsterdam on May 10–11, 1990 (the fiftieth anniversary of the German invasion in 1940): J. P. B. Jonker, A. E. Kerstens, and G. N. van der Plaat, eds., *Vijftig Jaar na de Inval: Geschiedschrijving en Tweede Wereldoorlog* (The Hague, 1990).
31. J. J. van Bolhuis et al., eds. *Onderdrukking en Verzet: Nederland in oorlogstijd*, 4 vols. (Amsterdam, 1949–54), 1:5.
32. Abel J. Herzberg, *Kroniek der Jodenvervolging, 1940–1945* (Amsterdam, 1985), 9.
33. "National monument op de Dam door koningin Juliana onthult," *De Nieuwe Rotterdamse Courant*, May 4, 1956.
34. For a discussion of gendered resistance, see Dwork, *Children With A Star*, chap. 2, esp. 40f.
35. "Eeuwige Vlam in Schouwburg," *De Volkskrant*, May 5, 1962.
36. L. de Jong, *De Bezetting: Tekst en beeldmateriaal van de uitzendingen over de Nederlandse Televisie-Stichting over het Koninkrijk der Nederlanden in de Tweede Wereldoorlog, 1940–1945* (Amsterdam, 1966), 353.
37. Louis de Jong, quoted in Max Pam, *De Onderzoekers van de Oorlog: Het Rijksinstituut voor Oorlogsdocumentatie en het Werk van Dr. L. de Jong* (The Hague, 1979), 61.
38. Presser, *Ondergang*, I:viii. We chose to translate directly from the Dutch edition and not to use the English version of the book, *The Destruction of the Dutch Jews*, trans. Arnold Pomerans (New York, 1969), republished in 1988 as *Ashes in the Wind: The Destruction of Dutch Jewry*. Pomerans's translation is imprecise at best, and more often it is simply wrong. It does not pick up the subtle sarcasm and irony of the Dutch original.
39. Presser, *Ondergang*, 1:3.
40. "Monument," *Algemeen Handelsblad*, April 24, 1965.
41. Han Lammers, quoted in *De Groene Amsterdammer*, April 24, 1965.
42. "Zij droegen een ster," *Trouw*, April 24, 1965.
43. J. S. Wijne, "Waarom prof. Presser?" *Nieuwe Rotterdamse Courant*, April 27, 1965.
44. B. Buitenrust Hettema, "Waarom Presser niet?" ibid., May 4, 1965.
45. Jaap Meijer, "Uit de Boekerij," Nederlandse Christelijke Radio Vereniging, May 31, 1965.
46. Herman von der Dunk, "Het boek van Presser," in *Kleio heeft duizend ogen: Over historie en historici* (Assen, 1974), 52.
47. Joop den Uyl, quoted in R. B. Soetendorp, *Pragmatisch of principieel: Het Nederlandse beleid ten aanzien van het Arabisch-Israelisch conflict* (Doctoral diss., Leiden University, 1983), 98.

48. Soetendorp, *Pragmatisch of principieel*, 99.
49. For a concise description of the social context of the Dutch attitude toward World War II in the 1960s, see Kossmann, "In de naoorlogse geschiedenis van Nederland," *Ons Erfdeel* 28 (November–December 1985), 659–68.
50. Han Lammers, quoted in *De Groene Amsterdammer*, April 24, 1965.
51. Evert Werkman, "Ondergang der Joden, boek met aanklacht," *Het Parool*, April 22, 1965.
52. Presser, *Ondergang*, 2:122.
53. Ibid., 1:525.
54. For a succinct description of the Weinreb case, see I. Schoeffer, "Weinreb, een affaire van lange duur," *Tijdschrift voor Geschiedenis* 95 (1982), 196–224.
55. Abel J. Herzberg, quoted in Dick Houwaart, *Weinreb: Een Witboek* (Amsterdam, 1975), 21–22.
56. Schoeffer, "Weinreb," 202.
57. Presser, *Ondergang*, 2:110.
58. Friedrich Weinreb, *Collaboratie en Verzet, 1940–1945: Een poging tot ontmythologisering*, 3 vols. (Amsterdam, 1969).
59. Renate Rubinstein, "Korte Verantwoording," in ibid., I:vii.
60. Willem Frederik Hermans, *Van Wittgenstein tot Weinreb: Het sadistische universum 2* (Amsterdam, 1970).
61. Meijer Sluyser, "Excellentie Polak op uw hearing kunnen 120,000 joden niet meer worden gehoord," *Nieuw Israelitisch Weekblad*, September 5, 1969.
62. Y. Postma, quoted in J. van den Berg, "Het onmogelijke verhaal van de Drie van Breda," *Vrij Nederland*, September 20, 1969.
63. "Twee soorten barmhartigheid," *Haarlems Dagblad*, October 23, 1969.
64. Louis de Jong, "Jacques Presser" (eulogy delivered before the Literary Section of the Royal Academy of Science, Amsterdam, November 9, 1970; ms., RIOD), 16.

65. Wim Ramaker, *Sta een ogenblick stil . . .: Monumentenboek, 1940/45*, with photos by Ben van Bohemen (Kampen, 1980), 90–91.
66. Ibid., 11.
67. H. J. A. Hofland, Hans Keller, and Hans Verhagen, *Vastberaden, maar soepel en met mate: Herinneringen aan Nederland, 1938–1948* (Amsterdam, 1976), 7ff.
68. Ibid., 32–33.
69. Ibid., 35.
70. See Bank, *Oorlogsverleden in Nederland;* Blom, *Crisis, Bezetting en Herstel;* Kossmann, "Continuiteit en Discontinuiteit"; Jonker, Kerstens, and van der Plaat, *Vijftig Jaar na de Inval*; and Gerhard Hirschfeld, *Fremdherrschaft und Kollaboration: Die Niederlande unter deutscher Besatzung, 1940–1945* (Stuttgatt, 1984).
71. Jan Wolkers, quoted in Ramaker, *Sta een ogenblik stil . . .*, 128.
72. *Rondom Holocaust: Een onderzoek naar de effecten van een omstreden televisie-serie op jongeren* (Hilversum, 1980), 204–5.
73. H. J. A. Hofland, "Het wonder van Hollywood," *De Haagse Post*, May 12, 1979.
74. Riet Diemer, "Holocaust in Nederland leverde geen 'explosie' op," *Trouw*, May 8, 1979.
75. Paul Vigeveno and Ton van der Meer, *Grenzen aan solidariteit: een lessenserie over de Holocaust* (Malmberg, 1990).
76. For a short discussion on the significance of the jubilee for the remembrance of the Holocaust, see Robert-Jan van Pelt, "After the Walls Have Fallen Down," *Queens Quarterly* 96 (autumn 1989), 641f.
77. "In Amsterdam herdenkingsbeeld voor Joodse kinderen," *Het Vrije Volk*, September 2, 1986.

Natan Rolnik holds a name card to help any surviving family members locate him at the Kloster Indersdorf DP camp in Germany. This photograph was published in newspapers in the hope of reuniting the family. After May 7, 1945. (Gift of Robert Marx, Yaffa Eliach Collection, Center for Holocaust Studies, donated to the Museum of Jewish Heritage, New York)

Group portrait of the wedding parties at a double ceremony in the Feldafing DP camp in Germany. 1945. (Alexander Ferson, courtesy of USHMM Photo Archives)

Children play in the kindergarten in the Bergen-Belsen DP camp. 1946–1948. (Nederlands Instituut voor Oorlogsdocumentatie, courtesy of USHMM Photo Archives)

Yehuda Bauer **On the Place of the Holocaust in History**

Abstract – The Holocaust was a human event, perpetrated for human reasons which can be historically explained. As an event within history, it is unprecedented in terms of the murderers' motivation: a mission to rescue Germany, Europe and the world from their supreme enemy, the Jews. Other events, such as that which seems to most closely parallel the Holocaust, the Armenian massacres by the Turks in World War I, bear certain similarities to the Holocaust. Yet, in its attempt at total physical annihilation of all Jews everywhere, the Holocaust is unprecedented. It stands at the extreme end of a continuum of human brutality, extending from mass murder, which has become commonplace, to genocide, and to Holocaust.

LET ME BEGIN THIS ESSAY with a perhaps somewhat theoretical statement about history as I see it and practise it in my writing, because I believe that with a topic such as the Holocaust, the historian's biases should be stated unequivocally. I shall then go on to discuss the Holocaust within a set of concepts rooted, I hope, in the historiography of our century, and I shall then try to make some comparisons with other genocidal events.

The first problem is that of the objectivity of the historian. Following upon some ideas recently put forward by Karlheinz Deschner,[1] I would start by denying the possibility of an "objective" stance. We are the result of our environment, tradition, education, and so on – that is, in the best of cases, when we try to be as objective as we possibly can. The influence of that environment can be disastrous, as we may be crucially and negatively influenced by a consensus of fellow-historians, or even of a regime, and write what is acceptable to a certain public rather than what we feel should be said. Even worse – we sometimes really believe that what we say is ours, whereas in fact it is nothing but a reflection of the views of a majority, or a group, or a charismatic individual, or some outside influence. We need to be aware of our bias, our subjective approach, in order to formulate an interpretation of the facts that will be legitimately rooted in the atmosphere and the context of whatever period we describe. We must be aware of a situation which we discuss with our students, but which we sometimes tend to forget ourselves, namely that the very decision to deal with some facts rather than others is itself subjective, for, as Goethe said,

"Every fact is already a theory." "Only the mindless person is objective," said Droysen, and indeed, objectivism is basically uninteresting, because it reflects the basic chaos of an infinite chain of events, in itself meaningless.[2]

Do we then conform to a subjectivism that dictates the rewriting of history in every generation? It is, after all, a fact that every period looks at past events from a different perspective from the one which preceded it: the historians of 1987 look at the French Revolution differently from the way it was looked at in 1887. Yet the knowledge and self-perception that accompany an approach which is conscious of its biases can neutralize such biases to a certain degree – never completely, to be sure, but sufficiently to enable the historian to draw what may be termed "legitimate" conclusions from his study. A legitimate conclusion would be one that not only avoids identification with known outside interference, but one that reflects a certain insight into the period and the atmosphere of that period. It is then obvious that another age will reinterpret the same event differently from ours, taking its departure from a set of insights that will, in their turn, reflect the atmosphere and the context of the period which we study. We can, after all, generalize, if we stick to what is essential and central in the events we discuss, while we openly state what our bias may be, and try to overcome it to the best of our ability.

My biases are obvious. I think that the planned total murder of a people was an unheard-of catastrophe in human civilization, because once it has happened, it can be repeated. Any historical event is a

YEHUDA BAUER, "ON THE PLACE OF THE HOLOCAUST IN HISTORY," HOLOCAUST AND GENOCIDE STUDIES, 1987, VOL. 2, NO. 2, 209–20, BY PERMISSION OF YEHUDA BAUER AND OXFORD UNIVERSITY PRESS.

possibility before it becomes a fact, but when it becomes a fact it also serves as a possible precedent. And while no event will ever be repeated precisely as it first happened, it will, if it is followed by similar events, become the first of a line of analogous happenings. The Holocaust can be a precedent, or it can become a warning. That is my first bias.

My second bias is that I believe, on the strength of the historical evidence, that the Nazi regime was just about the worst regime that ever disfigured the face of this earth. Worst from what point of view? Worst from the point of view of a basically liberal approach that values, in line perhaps with Jewish tradition, human life above everything else. From these points of view, then, I am not objective, but then an objectivity that would not accept these starting points would be totally unacceptable, because it would run counter to what I assume is our common understanding of morality. Morality, in this context, is based on the idea that acts or intentions that run counter to the right of individuals and groups to exist, to live, run counter also to the idea of the continued existence of human life altogether; hence their unacceptability. In this sense, morality as here presented is an absolute value – that is, absolute as long as one posits the existence of the human race as a desired condition.

These are my first points, or my basic assumptions. My second theme relates to the problem of definitions. Is the Holocaust definable? Is it desirable to define it? To start with, definitions are in themselves abstractions from reality. Any historiographical definition is designed to help us understand the event or events which is being defined. As life is infinitely more complex than any definition, and definitions are only crutches to enable us to walk more easily, no definition can be fully adequate to the event it describes. We can but hope to approximate to a description of reality. The reality itself is beyond us, our description of it is selective, and the understanding we expect of our public of that description may perhaps be better if our definition is so carefully defined that it is as close as possible to an adequate description. The immediate pitfall lies of course in the propensity of people to say that because something happened, it had to happen. This scourge of determination is very prevalent and we must say quite clearly

that the Holocaust did happen, but it did not have to happen. It was one of the possibilities inherent in the situation, but not the only one. True, from a certain point onward, mass murder, given the context of Nazi ideology and policy and military superiority in Europe, became inevitable; or, perhaps, it became inevitable that it should have been attempted. But this inevitability was already close to the murder itself. If you retreat in time from, say, early 1941, mass murder was not inevitable, even if you say, with Eberhard Jäckel for instance, that the idea of physical elimination of the Jews was with Hitler from 1924 or 1925. Thus, for instance, a coalition of the Powers in 1938, coupled with the disaffection of the Beck group among the German military, might well have prevented the war. This is not speculation, but a statement based on the real interests of the Powers at the time.

The intentionalist historians, of whom Jäckel is one, as well as Helmut Krausnick or Gerald Fleming or Lucy Dawidowicz, say that Hitler's intentions, and therefore his role, in the process leading up to the murder are central; the role of the others was much less so, and the entourage of Hitler, according to Jäckel, was actually rather unhappy about the decision.[3] Certainly before 1941 they did not envisage mass murder, as Himmler's memorandum on the treatment of alien nationals of 25 May 1940, for instance, shows, because this says that the idea of a physical destruction of a nation is a Bolshevik concept unacceptable to Germans.

So the murder of the Jews was not inevitable, as nothing is that ultimately happens. The next question then is whether the murder is explicable. This may seem an odd question – is not all history explicable? Well, there are many who would argue that an event of such magnitude – a "tremendum," as some term it – cannot ultimately be explained, the depravity of the perpetrators and the horror of the events are too much. This retreat into mysticism is usually reserved for the Holocaust. I am afraid I cannot accept it. The murder was committed by humans, for irrational reasons that can be rationally analysed. Of course, as I have already stated, the reality of any series of events can never be re-experienced but only described, and even that can never be done fully. We cannot re-live;

we can only empathize. If your child hurts his finger, even though you identify totally with him, you still cannot feel his pain; you can only know vicariously what he may feel. How much more so, when one is dealing with historical events of the past. The murder of the Jews is, from this point of view, not very different from other horrors of which history knows so many. What about the mass murder of the Cathars in France? The tortures inflicted by the Mongols in Iran or Russia? The gassing of soldiers in World War I? The mass murder of the Saxons by Charlemagne? And so on. Moreover, if the Holocaust defies explanation, then it is extra-historical or meta-historical, and it is therefore irrelevant. The mystifiers, with the best of intentions, achieve the opposite of what presumably is their aim, namely, the possibility of identification and empathy with the victims. You cannot identify with what is inexplicable. There is, it is true, a dimension of pain and suffering which it is difficult to describe, and writers, poets, dramatists and philosophers will forever grapple with the problem of presenting it. But surely this does not mean that the events are in any real sense beyond the possibility of explanation? In principle, then, the Holocaust is a human event, perpetrated for reasons that are, unfortunately, human and which can be explained, despite great difficulty in doing so, for emotional, or practical, or whatever reasons.

If we have established both the lack of inevitability and the explicability of these events, let us then proceed to look at the murder of the Jews in relation to roughly similar murders. The accepted twentieth-century term for these horrendous events is 'genocide', coined, as we know, by Raphael Lemkin in late 1942 or early 1943. As I have pointed out elsewhere,[4] Lemkin's definition is contradictory. On the one hand, he clearly defined genocide as the "destruction of a nation or of an ethnic group . . . . Generally speaking, genocide does not necessarily mean the immediate destruction of a nation, except when accomplished by mass killings of all members of a nation. It is intended rather to signify a coordinated plan of different actions aiming at the destruction of essential foundations of the life of national groups, with the aim of annihilating the groups themselves" (what he means here really is to say "the groups as such").[5] Yet

in the preface to the work in which this definition is offered, he clearly states that "the practice of extermination of nations and ethnic groups . . . is called by the author 'genocide'." The destruction of the essential foundations of national life includes, according to Lemkin, the destruction of the economic foundations of national life, its religious institutions, its moral fibre, its education system, and also includes selective mass killings of targeted parts of the conquered people.[6]

But surely there is a contradiction here? On the one hand, if genocide means the extermination of a nation or a people, then the destruction of their religious life is not possible, because the people themselves are dead. On the other hand, as Lemkin points out, a denationalization programme does not necessarily have to lead to the total killing of everyone. It has been argued that I am wrong in my analysis, because what Lemkin meant was a process whereby the destruction of the foundations of national life leads to total extermination. As we have seen in the brief quote above, this is not what Lemkin says. In other words, we have two distinct processes, both of which are termed genocide by Lemkin – one, a radical and murderous denationalization process which destroys the nation but leaves most of the individuals composing it alive, and the other a programme of total murder.

This is not an academic discussion. Lemkin's definitions were adopted, more or less, by the United Nations, and in the Genocide Convention, approved on 9 December 1948, genocide is defined as "any of the following acts committed with intent to destroy, in whole or in part, a national, ethnical or religious group, as such." Again, both meanings are included, and the phrase "in whole *or* in part" would indicate that what is meant is not the development of partial destruction into total murder, but two variations that do not necessarily follow one upon the other.

The real historical context in early 1943 consisted of the information that Lemkin possessed at the time. What was happening to Poles, Czechs, Slovenes, Serbs and Russians was known to Lemkin, a Jewish refugee from Poland living in the United States. Disturbing information had also been received concerning the fate of the Jews, but there was an understandable reluctance on the part of decent human beings to believe that these accounts were literally or completely true. What was happening to Slavic peoples fitted Lemkin's description of denationalization, accompanied by selective mass murder; or, rather, Lemkin's definition was made to fit the real historical developments. The vagueness with which he contemplates the possibility of total murder of all Jews reflects the state of consciousness in America of the Jewish fate at the time.

The United Nations are not a symposium of scholars – far from it. Documents emerging from there are less than perfect, because they reflect political pressures and horse-trading between states. Thus, pressure was brought in 1948 to include, for instance, the destruction of political groups within the definition of genocide. The inclusion of religious groups was accepted after a prolonged struggle. Of course, religious groups are not usually regarded as ethnic units – though in both Christianity and Islam in pre-modern eras the general community of the faithful was regarded as a "nation" or a "people." The rise of modern nationalism has made such definitions impossible, but these groups were included in the 1948 document, as part of a compromise, despite the lack of logic. To regard the UN document as the final word on the issue would therefore also be illogical. The lack of consistency in the UN Convention is apparent the moment we continue the quote. It says that genocide means any of the following acts: '(a) Killing members of the group; (b) Causing serious bodily or mental harm to members of the group; (c) Deliberately inflicting on the group conditions of life calculated to bring about its physical destruction in whole or in part; (d) Imposing measures intended to prevent births within the group; (e) Forcibly transferring children of the group to another group."[7] Again, we see the confusion between partial and total destruction, which are presented as alternatives. And again, if one creates conditions of life that produce total loss of life, there is little point in creating other conditions designed to bring about partial destruction. Also, one can of course create conditions of starvation designed to kill everyone, and then the phrase "conditions of life" may be marginally acceptable. But to lead people into gas chambers is hardly covered by the term "conditions of life."

Let us now turn from definitions to reality. What made the murder of the Jews an event that many of us would define, despite some obvious difficulties, as unprecedented? First of all, it was neither the number of the victims nor even their proportion in relation to the total number of the Jews in Europe at the time. Many more non-Jews than Jews were killed in World War II, whichever calculation you take. And in World War I you can argue that the proportion of Armenians murdered by the Ottoman regime, as compared to the total number of Armenians in Turkey, was higher than or at least equal to that of the Jews in World War II. We know too little about the numbers of Romanies (Gypsies) killed to be able to tell, but there, too, the proportion was high. The method of murder of many Jews, by gassing, again is not unprecedented. Quite apart from the mutual murder of soldiers in World War I, the so-called euthanasia killings in Germany were done by gassing; and while millions of Jews were killed by gassing, thousands of Romanies, and some Soviet soldiers and Polish political prisoners suffered a similar fate.

What made the Holocaust unprecedented is, I think, *the motivation of the murderers*. One is inclined to say "ideology", but that is not quite accurate, because we know today that many of the actual murderers had no significant antisemitic background, and did not undergo any training that would have instilled antisemitism in them. The problem of the motivation is indeed crucial for an understanding of what occurred. Extreme antisemitism was, at the end of the last century, coterminous with a racialist interpretation of society, whereas among most European peoples, a social, political and economic antisemitism prevailed which was really a secular translation of traditional Christian Judeophobia. This kind of, let us call it moderate, antisemitism was current among the aristocracy and the *haute bourgeoisie* as well as among the middle classes. The workers' movements were also strongly infected by an antisemitism which stemmed from the early French and Russian utopian socialists, from the anarchist movement, and from the young Marx and Engels. However, these movements largely freed themselves from this infection, and towards the end of the nineteenth century became the opponents of antisemitic movements. The major social crises of the early twentieth century brought about the rise of seemingly marginal political groups that saw in the Jews the embodiment of evil. While one can see their influence in several countries, Germany proved to be a fertile ground for these groups because of the political and economic upheavals that came after the loss of the war in 1918.

The National-Socialist movement did not come to power *because* of antisemitic propaganda. Of course, anyone who voted for the Nazis knew he was voting for an antisemitic movement; but the Nazi Party's programme had no clear proposals about what to do with the Jews, and the "moderate" antisemitic mood so prevalent in Europe neutralized any distaste for the antisemitism of the Nazi Party. While, however, even amongst most Nazi Party members, as Peter Merkl[8] has found, antisemitism was not the prime ideological or political attraction, it certainly was a basic ideological tenet for the Nazi leadership. This leadership was a group of intellectuals, difficult as that may be for us to swallow today. Disaffected intellectuals, to be sure, or, if you like, a kind of "*lumpenintelligentsia.*" Their ideology consisted of a secularized Christian anti-Judaism combined with the racialist ideas of the *fin de siècle*. The Jew was a satanic element introduced into history by evil forces – see for instance Dietrich Eckardt's "Gespräche mit Adolf Hitler," Munich 1923 – and in order for humanity to survive, it had to be cleansed of his influence. Jewish influence was corrosive and corrupting, and its aim was the control of the world and, in essence, its destruction. Hence the pseudo-medical terminology used by the Nazis to describe the way the Jews had to be dealt with: the imagery was that of a sick body which had to be cured of a cancerous growth, or of bacillae, or viruses, and so on. The satanic imagery and the myth of the Jewish desire to control the world can be found in Christianity in a religious form in the preachings of John Chrysostomos as early as the fourth century. The language of antisemitism was that of the positivist science of the late nineteenth century, and the ideology was attractive because it gave seemingly total answers to difficult questions. It was combined with racialism as a complete explanation of social phenomena. But this so-called Social

Darwinism, the idea that races are in constant struggle with each other, and that the more beautiful is the stronger, the stronger is the better, and the better has a moral right to rule over and, if necessary, destroy the others, was not in Nazi ideology, I think, the general principle of which antisemitism was a special case. On the contrary, looking closely at Nazi writings and speeches, it appears that racism was adopted because it supported the basic antisemitic approach. In other words, the explanation of social and political phenomena was based on antisemitism, and the racist element was derived from antisemitism, not the other way round.

Thus, the division of peoples in Nazi literature is never very clear. The Aryan race, for instance, included Slavs, but the argument was presented that the Poles and Russians had been contaminated with Mongol influences. Hence one could argue that the Slavs were subhuman, but still human in a way; the proof of their humanity in Nazi eyes lies in the fact that the Nazis kidnapped Polish children to bring them up as Germans, which they could not have done if they had not been Aryans. But what was to be done with Magyars, Finns and Turks, not to speak of the Japanese, with whom there was a close alliance? Were they not Mongols, or of yellow racial extraction, too? The Japanese were nominated, *mirabile dictu*, to be honorary Aryans, as were the Arabs, the cousins of the Jews themselves. The Magyars were considered to be better even than the Italians, whom the German Nazis despised. The Aryan principle went by the board, despite all the valiant attempts to keep it up. But, on the other hand, it was abundantly clear who the non-Aryans were: the only non-Aryans were the Jews, and they were not really human, they only looked human.

The upshot is that the Nazis believed that it was their mission to free Germany, and then Europe, and if possible the world, of the Jews. The motivation of the murderer was indeed unprecedented: a global ideology, not just a Germanic one, intended for German consumption.

In his seminal article "Die 'Endlösung' und das deutsche Ostimperium," published in the *Vierteljahreshefte für Zeitgeschichte* in 1972,[9] Andreas Hillgruber put forward a thesis which is now generally accepted, namely that Nazism rested on two ideological pillars: the idea of conquest for *Lebensraum*, and the idea of the necessary elimination of the Jews. The latter was to be achieved at first by emigration, and then gradually mass murder evolved. The war itself, I would argue, was linked, before it began, with these two central notions. Both could be postponed for tactical reasons, as the Ribbentrop–Molotov Pact, or before that the Polish–German neutrality Pact of 1934, or indeed the relative moderation of Hitler himself *vis-à-vis* the antisemitic radicals in the Nazi Party in the 1930s show. Yet the constant aim of the Nazi movement – and I would go along with Jäckel, Krausnick and Hillgruber on this – was to expand territorially, and get rid of the Jews. One was dependent on the other, because of course the Jews controlled Soviet Russia *and* plutocratic America, and you could not achieve a breakthrough for the German *Lebensraum* unless you eliminated the Jewish influence. Hence the Jews were the real enemy, lurking behind all the political and military foes of the Nazi empire. In a very real sense, World War II *was* a war against the Jews.

This kind of motivation is different from that of any other known form of genocide. In the Armenian case, which offers the closest parallels to the Holocaust, the motivation was political. The Jemiyet of Talaat and Enver and their clique desired a Pan-Turkic empire stretching from Edirne and Istanbul to Uzbekistan and Tadzhikistan, and the Armenians, an alien nation, were an obstacle that they wanted to remove. The massacres are more the result of a wild chauvinism than an ideologically motivated murder, and chauvinism has at least *some* realistic background in national movements. The Turks never planned the murder of Armenians outside of Turkey.

I would therefore offer the following corrective to the Lemkin definitions. I would argue that genocide is the proper name for the brutal denationalization process accompanied by selective mass murder described by Lemkin and the UN Convention. A plan for the total physical annihilation of a people, everywhere one finds them, I would, for the lack of a better term, call Holocaust. That of course means that I

am using the term Holocaust in two ways: first, as a description of what actually happened and what was planned as far as the Jews were concerned, by the Nazis; and second, any parallel event that may occur in the future, after a precedent has been created. I am therefore using the term both specifically, and generically. The specificity of the Holocaust, which was caused by the motivation described above, found its expression in the simple policy executed by the Nazis: anyone born of three Jewish grandparents was sentenced to death for the crime of having been born. This indeed is unprecedented: it never happened before, but it is not unprecedented in the sense that once it has happened, it could happen again.

What is the relationship between the Nazi policy towards the Jews and their policy towards Poles, Romanies, Czechs, and others? As far as the Slavic peoples were concerned, there were no plans for total physical annihilation. A first draft of the so-called *Generalplan Ost* which was submitted to Himmler at the end of 1941 by Dr. Konrad Meyer-Hetling, foresaw the expulsion of 31 million people in the Polish and Soviet areas and the Germanization of the rest of them, presumably by methods that would include liquidation of the intelligentsia and any potential leaders. But the plan did not go into any details; these were later to be considered by Dr. Erhard Wetzel, an important SS official and racial expert. The Baltic peoples were to be eliminated as such, the Germanizable elements were to be absorbed, and those who were not Germanizable were to be invited to become the ruling class of the Slavic expellees in the east. As far as the Poles were concerned, Wetzel thought that "it is obvious that the Polish question cannot be solved in such a way that one would liquidate the Poles in the same manner as the Jews. Such a solution . . . would be a standing accusation against the German people into the far distant future.[10] Therefore, he proposed to Germanize some, and deport the rest to Western Siberia, where their antagonism to the Russians would ensure that no united anti-German front would ever be formed. The anti-German elements would of course be annihilated, that went without saying. Ukrainians who could not be Germanized would also be used against the Russians, and the Byelorussians would form a helot population reserve, to be used for labour.

As with the Poles, Wetzel opposed the total mass murder of the Russians, which had been proposed by Prof. Dr. Phil. Wolfgang Abel of the Kaiser Wilhelm Institute, the same august scientific institution, by the way, which also supported that other famous double Ph.D., Josef Mengele. Russians were needed for labour, but had to be kept on a very short leash. Himmler's reaction to Wetzel's proposals was positive. These plans might well have been tried out in practice had Stalingrad not put an end to them. So slavery, deportation, destruction of nationalities, or in other words, genocide; but not Holocaust.

A similar conclusion can be provisionally reached as far as the Gypsies are concerned. We still have no clear idea of German policies regarding the Romanies in an all-European context. In Slovakia, for instance, they were concentrated in camps, but then left alone. In the Soviet areas, they were mass-murdered in the South, but left alone in the North and Centre. In Poland, wandering groups of Romanies were murdered, others were put into ghettos with the Jews and then killed, others again, especially the settled ones, were left alone. With the German Gypsies a clear policy was followed. According to a Himmler order of December 1942, all Romanies considered to be of mixed race, including Germans who behaved as Gypsies, were to be sent to camps – in effect, to Auschwitz, where they were for the most part killed. However, about 14,000 Romanies who were supposedly racially pure were to be left under the supervision of nine Gypsy chiefs, and were to be allowed to roam Germany under Nazi supervision. In other words, racially pure Gypsies were to be preserved, the others killed.[11] What is abundantly clear is that none of these policies are parallel to the Final Solution, but they all form a background without which the murder of the Jews is hardly imaginable. In other words, genocide and Holocaust do have a connection: it was within the context of generally genocidal policies, of the rearrangement of the European map of settlement of nationalities, that the Holocaust became what we know it was. And yet, there is a clear distinction between the genocidal policies towards the Aryan peoples and the annihilation policies towards the Jews.

This, however, does not end the matter by a long way. If Holocaust seems possible against the background of genocide, genocide itself has a modern background of some importance. George L. Mosse in his writings makes the statement, with which I agree, that it was the brutalization of warfare and its mass character in World War I, that forms the backdrop to subsequent genocidal policies.[12] The fact that World War I is not characterized by the mass murder of civilians should not mislead us. Mass killing of people in funny clothes called uniforms is still mass murder, even if we call it warfare. It was the collapse of norms supposedly accepted in the nineteenth century, though they were often observed in the breach, that burst the dams that had contained the Thanatos, as Freud called it, the death instinct. We therefore should postulate a continuum of human brutality, which is one of the marks that distinguish humans from animals, because animals never engage in mass murder of their own species. In this I am speaking only of our own times, because we do not have sufficient knowledge to enable us to determine to what extent such events are paralleled in past periods of history. Mass murder in modern times, then, has become a common phenomenon, and whether you talk of the terrible slaughter of Chinese people by the Japanese in the 1930s, or the murder of Chinese communists in Indonesia, or the mass dying of the kulaks, or the mutual killings on the Indo-Pakistani border, you are talking of things that arouse curiosity, but no longer arouse the kind of reaction that says that these things are impossible. The continuum extends to genocide and to Holocaust, as I have tried to point out.

We are then left with the question of how to evaluate events that fit somewhere between any nicely balanced definitions. Let us take as an example the case of the murder of vast numbers of Kampuchean citizens by their own government in the wake of the turnover of Kampuchea by the Pol Pot regime. Is this genocide, or Holocaust, or what? I think we can take our own definitions only as general indications, not as absolute guides, and in this spirit I would venture to say that when a government murders its own citizens this can perhaps be termed auto-genocide.[13] The threat of the murder of the Ibo people at the hand of the Nigerian government in the 1960s was averted at the last moment, and the millions of victims were largely from starvation as a result of a civil war. This was no genocide – the Ibo people were promised, and in part given, opportunities of participation in the Nigerian government, their language and culture were not destroyed, and after the end of the civil war no mass killings of Ibo occurred. We have here, as in a number of other cases, incidents of mass murder.

There are, however, some marginal cases where our definitions are clearly inadequate, if taken too rigidly. An obvious case in point is that of the Armenian massacres, already referred to. The parallels with the Holocaust are very impressive: a political decision to murder all Armenians in Turkey was taken and transmitted to provincial governors in February 1915. The murder of young men, soldiers in the Turkish Army, was followed by mass killings and then, mainly, by deportations in the form of death marches into the Syrian desert, utilizing the help both of released criminals and of Kurdish tribesmen. As we know, murder by death marches was perpetrated by the Nazis, especially in early 1945, on a large scale. The use of non-Turkish helpers parallels that of the notorious *Hiwis*[14] by the Nazis. And the fact that Turkish doctors had a centrally important part in both the decision-making and the execution reminds us of the role of the German doctors, as described recently by Robert Jay Lifton in his book *The Nazi Doctors.*[15]

Clearly, this is more than genocide, and yet, there are important differences between the Armenian massacres and the Holocaust of the Jews, as I have already tried to point out. We have to refer back, I think, to the limitations of any post-factum definition of live historical processes, and use the concept I have called "continuum." On this continuum of murderous behaviour, the Armenian massacres would figure nearest to the Holocaust or, if you will, they belong to Holocaust-related events. One could use similar language regarding the fate of the Ache Indians in Paraguay, or of the Pierce-Nez Indians in the American North-West at the end of the last century, or of

the Hutu people in Rwanda and Burundi, and there are other examples.

I have already alluded to the social pathology that lies behind all these events. We have no really satisfactory social psychology that would tell us under what circumstances such events will be likely to occur. If science is the capability to predict, given similar circumstances, then clearly neither history nor social psychology are sciences nor, in my humble estimation, are they ever going to be. But we can perhaps have approximations, and here I think the use of Freudian methods, using his concept of Thanatos, already mentioned above, may turn out to be useful. If it is true that we have within us, as one of our basic instincts, the capacity for murderous behaviour, but that this Thanatos instinct can be sublimated and turned around, then what we may need is a kind of "early warning system" that will tell us when a society is in danger of creating conditions under which the Thanatos drive may express itself. Here the importance of the Holocaust lies in its being an extreme example from which one can draw conclusions about the lesser stages of a possible pathology.

Lastly, perhaps, the question arises of why we should bother to differentiate between different kinds of murder. What is the difference, after all, between a resistance fighter executed by the Nazis and a Jewish child thrown into a burning pit? They are both dead, killed by the servants of the same regime. I am putting it in this extreme form, because it makes the answer much clearer: true, both are dead, and our making distinctions decades afterwards will not make any difference to them, but *we* are alive, and for us these distinctions are important. If you make no distinction between one disease and another, between a stomach-ache and an ulcer and a cancer, and give aspirin to all three patients, the results will be disastrous. We do, after all, make differentiations between different kinds of good or evil. To help an old lady to cross a street and to save her from a burning building are both good deeds, but we do not put them in the same category. A thief is not a robber, though both are evildoers, and they will be punished differently. Manslaughter was distinguished from wilful murder as long ago as in the Second Book of Moses, and different punishment was provided. You will, I think, have to analyse different causes and therefore different kinds of social prophylactic and clinical treatment for different kinds of murderous behaviour. To walk out into the streets with large banners saying "we are against all murder" will hardly be helpful. In order to work against the repetition of the Holocaust we must distinguish it from the other types of murderous behaviour; just as our struggle against the repetition of genocide must be informed by the specific symptoms of what genocide was or is. I would therefore suggest that what we are engaged in is not what is known as a purely academic exercise, but that this particular academic exercise may, and I believe should, have practical application.

The fate of Hungarian Jewry in the Holocaust may serve as an example of the kind of social behaviour that is attendant upon processes of destruction.

To start with, the behaviour of the victims requires a great deal of explanation. The suddenness of the death threat produced a widespread paralysis and a denial of the danger. It has been argued, in Israel as well as elsewhere, that Hungarian Jews did not know what was in store for them. This however is confusing information with knowledge, a subject I have written about rather extensively.[16] There is no doubt in my mind that people had information – perhaps not everyone, but very many. Thousands of Hungarians came back from the Ukrainian front and told their stories, which in many cases included the massacring of Jews. In the summer of 1943, several thousands of Jewish labour battalion members were permitted to return from the Ukraine to Hungary; they dispersed among the different communities, and told their stories. The BBC broadcast in Hungarian, and told its story from December 1942, onwards. Some 2,500 Polish Jews escaped to Hungary via Subcarpathian Russia, dispersed among the larger communities and told their stories. Even the official press carried indications of the fate of the Jews in Poland. Slovak refugees streamed in from early 1942 on, and from about July–August of that year they had reasonably accurate information about their relatives being murdered, though they may not have known the details or the name of Auschwitz.

This does not of course mean that this informa-

tion was internalized and translated into knowledge. For the most part, as I have just said, people rejected it, because the knowledge that imminent death was a strong possibility for them would have been life-threatening. From the Budapest Judenrat, members of the Zionist youth movements were sent to the provincial ghettos to warn the Jews there of the impending deportations and their meaning. In every known instance they were chased out from the ghettos, as rumour-mongers and *agents provocateurs*.

But objective circumstances, too, helped to make the victims into passive sufferers. The suddenness of the process has already been mentioned, and produced a shock. The discovery that, by and large, the Hungarian population did not object to the deportation of the Jews, and that in fact many hoped to derive material benefit from it, was another factor in a sense of helplessness and of being abandoned, which produced paralysis. The Nazis, as we know, were very few, and they used Hungarian security forces just as they used Ukrainian, Latvian, Byelorussian or Lithuanian helpers in the occupied Soviet regions. The behaviour of these forces was sadistic and brutal – a clear parallel for instance to the Armenian massacres. The abandonment of personal responsibility, personal conscience, and their transfer to another superego – the fascist regime, or the *Führer*, or the Hungarian ruler, Horthy, and so on – enabled individuals who normally would not dream of acting in this way to cease all repression of their destructive instincts and instead to act out what apparently all of us possess in our subconscious. The behavior of the victims helped in this, because in most cases they behaved just like victims do who invite sadistic behaviour – with passivity and resignation. Where there was resistance, against the background of compliance in other places, such aggression made it easy for the gendarmes to act out a sadistic and brutal repression policy. It is interesting that the SS, for instance, opposed, in theory at least, sadism and what they called "needless" brutality, in order to maintain a self-image of superior Nordic man. The slogan was *"Eiskalt,"* cold-blooded murder with no investment of emotive factors. We still lack a proper analysis of this phenomenon, its use in real life and its meaning. In Hungary, the German Nazis had little contact with their Jewish victims – they left it to their Hungarian underlings and were satisfied with their superior position as the initiators and controllers.

The snowballing effect of a murderous policy can be seen throughout the few months of direct German control of Hungary. The murders, executed everywhere without appreciable opposition, except for a few outstanding cases, meant that you do not have to have an ideological identification with a murderous policy, it is quite enough that you do not oppose it, for it to take place. Hungarian antisemitism was not, by and large, of the murderous kind. But had all Hungarian Lutherans been deported to Auschwitz, I would assume that the reaction of the population would have been quite different.

However, the snowballing effect can be seen in a converse fashion as well: once the big Powers, especially the United States, in a declaration by Roosevelt in March 1944, warned Hungary against the maltreatment of Jews, neutral representatives in Budapest began intervening against the policies executed by the Nazis and the Horthy regime. Starting with Vice-Consul Charles Lutz of the Swiss legation, this was taken up by the Papal Nuncio, the Swedes (even before the arrival of Raul Wallenberg in July 1944) the Spaniards, the Portuguese, even the Turks.[17] There was a rush of rescue actions, some of which were more successful and some less. One can document this contradictory behaviour among the Hungarian neighbours of Jews in Budapest as well – on the one hand, a radicalization of the Nyilas (the Hungarian fascists) and their brutal and sadistic behaviour, on the other hand a growing willingness to help and support.

This leads me to my last observation, and it is this: generally speaking, in the Holocaust one can see extremes of human behaviour. That means that while it is, unfortunately, a laboratory of mass murder, it is also an area where the most heroic and sublime acts took place, in response to the extreme situation. Extreme danger aroused extreme response – not always and not everywhere, but sometimes. In fact, the best example of this is in the concentration camp world, *l'univers concentrationnaire*. There, the Nazis tried to exercise complete control and change all the norms of behaviour that are current in the civilizations we

know. But this attempt at total control also means that if even one person succeeded in opposing the system, the whole system, *ipso facto*, broke down. Successful opposition meant the maintenance of human dignity, of mutual help, of moral norms. But this is true not just of one person, but of thousands, maybe tens of thousands, we will never know; so many of them succumbed physically, though they were victorious spiritually. This is true of both Jews and non-Jews in many of the camps, and appears to provide us with some encouragement – the most terribly murderous and repressive system ultimately failed, though it managed to murder millions.

The Holocaust, then, is the extreme point on a continuum of mass murders and genocides that disfigure our century. Beyond the Holocaust stands the threat of orbicide, the threat of self-destruction of the human species, the ultimate victory of Thanatos. It belongs to a similar category, yet it cannot be identified with Holocaust.

Notes

1. Karlheinz Deschner, "Was ist Geschichtsschreibung, und was könnte sie sein?," in *Über Karlheinz Deschner*, ed. Hermann Gieselbusch (Reinbek: Rowahlt, 1986), 15–38.
2. *Ibid.*, 22.
3. Eberhard Jäckel, *Hitlers Herrschaft* (Stuttgart: DVA, 1986), 105–22.
4. Yehuda Bauer, "The Holocaust in Contemporary History," in *Studies in Contemporary Jewry* 1 (1984), 201–24.
5. Raphael Lemkin, *Axis Rule in Occupied Europe* (Washington: Carnegie Endowment for International Peace, 1944), 78ff.
6. *Ibid.*, xi.
7. Bauer, "The Holocaust," 204.
8. Peter Merkl, *The Making of a Stormtrooper* (Princeton: Princeton University Press, 1980), *passim*. Peter Merkl, *Political Violence Under the Swastika* (Princeton: Princeton University Press, 1975), *passim*.
9. Andreas Hillgruber, "Die 'Endlösung' und das deutsche Ostimperium als Kernstück des rassenideologischen Programms des Nationalsozialismus," *Vierteljahreshefte für Zeitgeschichte* (1972), No. 2, 133–53.
10. Helmut Heiger, "Der Generalpian Ost," *Vierteljahreshefte für Zeitgeschichte* (1958), No. 2, 281–325.
11. Tilman Zulch, ed., *In Auschwitz vergast, bis heute verfolgt* (Hamburg: 1979), *passim*.
12. George L. Mosse, *Toward the Final Solution* (New York: H. Fertig, 1978), 174. George L. Mosse, *Nazism* (New Brunswick: Rutgers University Press, 1978), 54ff., and elsewhere.
13. I am grateful to Christopher Browning for having convinced me that this indeed is so. The Pol Pot massacres were based on genetic criteria: the personal convictions of targeted indi-

viduals did not matter, as long as the individuals belonged to families of intellectuals, French speakers, etc.

14. *"Hilfswillige,"* or those willing to help. This was the Nazi term for Byelorussian, Ukrainian, Baltic and other local militias recruited by the Germans.

15. Robert Jay Lifton, *The Nazi Doctors* (New York: Basic Books, 1986). On the role of Turkish doctors in the Armen-

ian massacres, see Vahakn N. Dadrian, "The Role of Turkish Physicians in the World War I Genocide of Ottoman Armenians," *Holocaust and Genocide Studies* 1 (1986), 169–92.

16. Yehuda Bauer, *The Holocaust in Historical Perspective* (Seattle: University of Washington Press, 1978), 94–155.

17. Yehuda Bauer, *American Jewry and the Holocaust* (Detroit: Wayne State University Press, 1981), 380–447.

Jewish Population Change 1939–1945

	1939	1945	Decrease[†]	% Decrease[†]
Austria	60,000	7,000	53,000	88%
Belgium	90,000	40,000	50,000	56%
Bulgaria	50,000	47,000	3,000	6%
Czechoslovakia	315,000	44,000	271,000	86%
Denmark	6,500	5,500	1,000	15%
France	270,000	200,000	70,000	26%
Germany*	565,000	80,000	485,000	89%
Greece	74,000	12,000	62,000	84%
Hungary	400,000	200,000	200,000	50%
Italy	50,000	33,000	17,000	34%
Luxembourg	3,000	1,000	2,000	67%
Netherlands	140,000	20,000	120,000	86%
Norway	2,000	1,000	1,000	50%
Poland	3,350,000	50,000	3,300,000	99%
Romania	800,000	430,000	370,000	46%
USSR	3,020,000	2,500,000	520,000	17%
Estonia	4,500			
Latvia	95,000			
Lithuania	145,000			
Yugoslavia	75,000	12,000	63,000	84%

Note: The statistics for 1939 refer to prewar borders, and postwar frontiers have been used for 1945. The figure of 80,000 for Germany includes 60,000 displaced persons. The estimate of 2,600,000 for the USSR comprises about 300,000 refugees, deportees, and survivors from newly acquired territories.

* The Jewish population figure for Germany is for 1933, not 1939. (Source: *Historical Atlas of the Holocaust*, United States Holocaust Memorial Museum)

Raul Hilberg, *The Destruction of the European Jews*, Revised and Definitive Edition, 1048. Yale University Press. Copyright © 1985 by Raul Hilberg. Reproduced with the permission of the publisher.

[†] Column has been added to the original chart, *Ed.*

Contributors

PER ANGER was a member of the Swedish diplomatic service for forty years. He wrote his memoir entitled *With Raoul Wallenberg in Budapest: Memories of the War Years in Hungary.*

YEHUDA BAUER is Professor Emeritus of Holocaust Studies at The Hebrew University of Jerusalem and former director of the International Institute for Holocaust Research at Yad Vashem. He is also Academic Advisor to the Intergovernmental Task Force on Holocaust Education, Remembrance and Research. He is the author of several works including: *Rethinking the Holocaust; Jewish Reactions to the Holocaust; Jews for Sale?: Nazi-Jewish Negotiations, 1933-1945;* and *A History of the Holocaust;* and he is co-editor with Nathan Rotenstreich of *The Holocaust as Historical Experience: Essays and a Discussion.*

CHRISTOPHER R. BROWNING is Professor of History at the University of North Carolina. He is the author of *Ordinary Men: Police Battalion 101 and the Final Solution in Poland; Nazi Policy, Jewish Workers, German Killers;* and *The Path to Genocide: Essays on Launching the Final Solution.*

DANIEL CARPI is Professor of Jewish History at Tel Aviv University. He has also served as Chair for the History and Culture of the Jews of Salonika and Greece at the Diaspora Research Institute of Tel Aviv University. His published works include *Between Mussolini and Hitler: The Jews and the Italian Authorities in France and Tunisia.*

WILLIAM CARR was Professor Emeritus of German History at the University of Sheffield in the United Kingdom. He is the author of *A History of Germany: 1815-1945; The Origins of the Wars of German Unification; Hitler: A Study in Personality and Politics;* and *Hitler's War Machine.*

EUGEN DIESEL is the author of *Germany and the Germans.*

DEBÓRAH DWORK is the Rose Professor of Holocaust History at Clark University. She is the author of *Children With A Star: Jewish Youth in Nazi Europe* and co-author with Robert Jan van Pelt of *Auschwitz: 1270 to the Present* and *Holocaust: A History.*

662

HENRY L. FEINGOLD is Professor Emeritus of History at Baruch College and the Graduate Center of the City University of New York. He is the author of *Bearing Witness: How America and Its Jews Responded to the Holocaust; The Politics of Rescue: The Roosevelt Administration and the Holocaust, 1938-1945;* and editor of the five-volume series, *The Jewish People in America.*

KLAUS P. FISCHER is Instructor of Philosophy and History at Allan Hancock College in Santa Maria, California. His published works include *Nazi Germany: A New History* and *The History of an Obsession: German Judeophobia and the Holocaust.*

SAUL FRIEDLÄNDER has held the Maxwell Cummings Chair of European History at Tel Aviv University since 1975. He is also Professor of Holocaust History at the University of California, Los Angeles. His most recent book is *Nazi Germany and the Jews: The Years of Persecution 1933-1939,* which is the first volume of a two-volume work. His other books include *Kurt Gerstein: The Ambiguity of Good* and his memoir, *When Memory Comes.*

MIEP GIES is recognized by Yad Vashem as "A Righteous Among the Nations." Gies wrote her memoir, *Anne Frank Remembered: The Story of the Woman Who Helped to Hide the Frank Family.*

YISRAEL GUTMAN is Professor Emeritus of Jewish History at The Hebrew University of Jerusalem and former Director of the International Institute for Holocaust Research at Yad Vashem. He is the author of *The Jews of Warsaw, 1939-1943: Ghetto, Underground, Revolt* and co-editor with Efraim Zuroff of *Rescue Attempts During the Holocaust.* He is also co-editor with Jehuda Reinharz, Ezra Mendelsohn, and Chone Shmeruk of *The Jews of Poland Between Two World Wars* and co-editor with Michael Berenbaum of *Anatomy of the Auschwitz Death Camp.*

PHILIP P. HALLIE was Professor of Philosophy at Wesleyan University. His books include *Lest Innocent Blood Be Shed: The Story of the Village of Le Chambon and How Goodness Happened There; Rescue & Goodness: Reflections on the Holocaust;* and *Tales of Good and Evil, Help and Harm.*

RAUL HILBERG is Professor Emeritus of Political Science at the University of Vermont. He is the author of the three-volume work, *The Destruction of the European Jews.* He has also written *Perpetrators, Victims, Bystanders: The Jewish Catastrophe 1933-1945* and *The Politics of Memory: The Journey of a Holocaust Historian.*

MARION A. KAPLAN is Professor of History at Queens College and at the Graduate Center of the City University of New York. She is the author of *Between Dignity and Despair: Jewish Life in Nazi Germany* and *The Making of the Jewish Middle Class: Women, Family, and Identity in Imperial Germany*. She is also co-editor with Renate Bridenthal and Atina Grossman of *When Biology Became Destiny: Women in Weimar and Nazi Germany*.

TRACY H. KOON was Assistant Professor of History at the University of Virginia when she wrote *Believe, Obey, Fight: Political Socialization of Youth in Fascist Italy, 1922-1943*.

PRIMO LEVI was a survivor of Auschwitz. He wrote three memoirs, *Survival in Auschwitz: The Nazi Assault on Humanity; The Reawakening;* and *Moments of Reprieve*. In addition, he is the author of many books including *If Not Now, When?; The Drowned and the Saved;* and *The Periodic Table*.

GUENTER LEWY is Professor Emeritus of Political Science at the University of Massachusetts, Amherst. His published works include *The Catholic Church and Nazi Germany* and *The Nazi Persecution of the Gypsies*.

MICHAEL R. MARRUS is Dean of Graduate Studies and Professor of History at the University of Toronto. He is the author of *The Unwanted: European Refugees in the Twentieth Century; The Holocaust in History; The End of the Holocaust; Victims of the Holocaust; The Politics of Assimilation: A Study of the French Jewish Community at the Time of the Dreyfus Affair;* and co-author with Robert O. Paxton of *Vichy France and the Jews*.

EZRA MENDELSOHN is Professor of Jewish History at the Institute of Contemporary Jewry at The Hebrew University of Jerusalem. He is the author of *The Jews of East Central Europe Between the World Wars; On Modern Jewish Politics;* and *Zionism in Poland: The Formative Years, 1915-1926*.

SONDRA MYERS is executive co-producer with Carol Rittner of the film, *The Courage to Care* as well as co-editor with Carol Rittner of the book, *The Courage to Care: Rescuers of Jews During the Holocaust*.

WILLIAM NICHOLLS is Professor Emeritus of Religious Studies at the University of British Columbia, Vancouver, Canada. He is the author of *Christian Antisemitism: A History of Hate*.

CAROL RITTNER, R.S.M. is Professor of Holocaust Studies at The Richard Stockton College of New Jersey. She is executive co-producer with Sondra Myers of the film *The Courage to Care* as well as co-editor with Sondra Myers of the book, *The Courage to Care: Rescuers of Jews During the Holocaust*. She is also the editor of *Anne Frank in the World: Essays and Reflections* and of *Elie Wiesel: Between Memory and Hope;* and co-editor with John K. Roth of *Different Voices: Women and the Holocaust*.

WOLFGANG SOFSKY is Associate Professor of Sociology at the University of Göttingen in Germany. He is the author of *The Order of Terror: The Concentration Camp*.

NECHAMA TEC is Professor of Sociology at the University of Connecticut. She is the author of several books including *Defiance: The Bielski Partisans; When Light Pierced the Darkness: Christian Rescue of Jews in Nazi-Occupied Poland;* and her memoir, *Dry Tears: The Story of a Lost Childhood*.

ISAIAH TRUNK was a historian at the YIVO Institute for Jewish Research in New York. His books include *Judenrat: The Jewish Councils in Eastern Europe Under Nazi Occupation* and *Jewish Responses to Nazi Persecution*.

ROBERT JAN VAN PELT is Professor of Cultural History in the School of Architecture at the University of Waterloo in Ontario, Canada. He is the author of *Architectural Principles in the Age of Historicism* and *The Case for Auschwitz* and co-author with Debórah Dwork of *Auschwitz: 1270 to the Present* and *Holocaust: A History*.

BERNARD WASSERSTEIN is Professor of Modern History at the University of Glasgow and former President of the Oxford Center for Hebrew and Jewish Studies in the United Kingdom. He is the author of several books including *Britain and the Jews of Europe, 1939-1945* and *Secret War in Shanghai*.

EUGEN WEBER is Professor Emeritus of Modern European History at the University of California, Los Angeles. He is the author of *The Hollow Years: France in the 1930s*.

MARGARET COLLINS WEITZ is Professor of Humanities and Modern Languages at Suffolk University in Massachusetts. She is the author of *Sisters in the Resistance: How Women Fought to Free France, 1940-1945* and *Femmes: Recent Writings on French Women*.

665

ROBERT S. WISTRICH is Professor of History and Hebrew Studies at The Hebrew University of Jerusalem. He is the author of *Antisemitism: The Longest Hatred; The Jews of Vienna in the Age of Franz Joseph; Hitler's Apocalypse: Jews and the Nazi Legacy;* and *Who's Who in Nazi Germany*.

DAVID S. WYMAN is Professor Emeritus of History and Judaic Studies at the University of Massachusetts, Amherst. His books include *The Abandonment of the Jews: America and the Holocaust, 1941-1945* and *Paper Walls: America and the Refugee Crisis, 1938-1941*. He is also editor of *The World Reacts to the Holocaust* and of the thirteen-volume series, *America and the Holocaust*.

MARK WYMAN is Professor of History at Illinois State University. His published works include *DPs: Europe's Displaced Persons, 1945-1951* and *Round-Trip to America: The Immigrants Return to Europe, 1880-1930*.

LENI YAHIL is Professor Emeritus at Haifa University. She is the author of several books including *The Rescue of Danish Jewry: Test of a Democracy* and *The Holocaust: The Fate of European Jewry, 1932-1945*.

Index

The texts included in this book have been excerpted from the original works and the citations have been renumbered to be consecutive here. Please refer to the source to obtain the original citation.

Please note that various figures have been adduced regarding the number of Jewish men arrested on 9–10 November 1938 and sent to concentration camps. We believe that circa 26,000 is the most accurate.

Please note, too, that various figures have been adduced with regard both to the number of Jews killed and the number who survived. Our research shows that between 5.1 and 6 million Jews, some two-thirds of European Jewry, died during the Holocaust.